# Autodesk® Revit Architecture Fundamentals

## ASCENT – Center for Technical Knowledge®

**SDC Publications**
P.O. Box 1334
Mission KS 66222
913-262-2664
www.SDCpublications.com
Publisher: Stephen Schroff

**Copyright © 2022** ASCENT – Center for Technical Knowledge®, a division of Rand Worldwide™

All rights reserved. No part of this manual may be reproduced in any form by any photographic, electronic, mechanical or other means, or used in any information storage and retrieval system, without prior written permission of the publisher, SDC Publications.

**Examination Copies**
Books received as examination copies are for review purposes only and may not be made available for student use. Resale of examination copies is prohibited.

**Electronic Files**
Any electronic files associated with this book are licensed to the original user only. These files may not be transferred to any other party.

**Trademarks**
The following are registered trademarks or trademarks of Autodesk, Inc., and/or its subsidiaries and/or affiliates in the USA and other countries: 123D, 3ds Max, Algor, Alias, AliasStudio, ATC, AutoCAD LT, AutoCAD, Autodesk, the Autodesk logo, Autodesk 123D, Autodesk Homestyler, Autodesk Inventor, Autodesk MapGuide, Autodesk Streamline, AutoLISP, AutoSketch, AutoSnap, AutoTrack, Backburner, Backdraft, Beast, BIM 360, Burn, Buzzsaw, CADmep, CAiCE, CAMduct, CFdesign, Civil 3D, Cleaner, Combustion, Communication Specification, Constructware, Content Explorer, Creative Bridge, Dancing Baby (image), DesignCenter, DesignKids, DesignStudio, Discreet, DWF, DWG, DWG (design/logo), DWG Extreme, DWG TrueConvert, DWG TrueView, DWGX, DXF, Ecotect, ESTmep, Evolver, FABmep, Face Robot, FBX, Fempro, Fire, Flame, Flare, Flint, FMDesktop, ForceEffect, FormIt, Freewheel, Fusion 360, Glue, Green Building Studio, Heidi, Homestyler, HumanIK, i-drop, ImageModeler, Incinerator, Inferno, InfraWorks, Instructables, Instructables (stylized robot design/logo), Inventor LT, Inventor, Kynapse, Kynogon, LandXplorer, Lustre, MatchMover, Maya, Maya LT, Mechanical Desktop, MIMI, Mockup 360, Moldflow Plastics Advisers, Moldflow Plastics Insight, Moldflow, Moondust, MotionBuilder, Movimento, MPA (design/logo), MPA, MPI (design/logo), MPX (design/logo), MPX, Mudbox, Navisworks, ObjectARX, ObjectDBX, Opticore, Pipeplus, Pixlr, Pixlr-o-matic, Productstream, RasterDWG, RealDWG, ReCap, Remote, Revit LT, Revit, RiverCAD, Robot, Scaleform, Showcase, ShowMotion, Sim 360, SketchBook, Smoke, Socialcam, Softimage, Sparks, SteeringWheels, Stitcher, Stone, StormNET, TinkerBox, ToolClip, Topobase, Toxik, TrustedDWG, T-Splines, ViewCube, Visual LISP, Visual, VRED, Wire, Wiretap, WiretapCentral, XSI.
All other brand names, product names, or trademarks belong to their respective holders.

ISBN-13: 978-1-63057-514-4
ISBN-10: 1-63057-514-3

Printed and bound in the United States of America.

# Contents

Preface ..................................................................................................... xi

In This Guide ........................................................................................... xiii

Practice Files .......................................................................................... xv

## Revit Tools and Project Setup

### Chapter 1: Introduction to Revit ........................................................ 1-1

**1.1 BIM and Revit** ............................................................................ 1-2
    Workflow and BIM ..................................................................... 1-3
    Revit Terms ............................................................................... 1-4
    Revit and Construction Documents ........................................... 1-5

**1.2 Overview of the Interface** ......................................................... 1-7

**1.3 Opening and Saving Projects** ................................................. 1-27
    Opening Projects ..................................................................... 1-28
    Saving Projects ....................................................................... 1-29

**1.4 Viewing Commands** ................................................................ 1-31
    Zooming and Panning ............................................................. 1-31
    Viewing in 3D .......................................................................... 1-33
    ViewCube ................................................................................ 1-37
    Visual Styles ........................................................................... 1-39

**Practice 1a Open and Review a Project** ........................................ 1-40

**Chapter Review Questions** ............................................................ 1-49

**Command Summary** ....................................................................... 1-51

### Chapter 2: Starting a Project ........................................................... 2-1

**2.1 Selecting a Project Template** ................................................... 2-2

**2.2 Linking and Importing Files** ..................................................... 2-4
    Linking and Importing CAD Files .............................................. 2-4
    Linking and Importing Raster Image Files ................................ 2-8
    Linking and Importing PDF Files ............................................. 2-10

|     | 2.3 | Linking in Revit Models | 2-12 |
| --- | --- | --- | --- |
|     | 2.4 | Modifying Imported/Linked Files | 2-14 |
|     |     | Managing Links | 2-17 |
|     |     | Modifying the Visibility of Imported/Linked Files | 2-19 |

Practice 2a Start a Project and Link Files ........................................ 2-22

|     | 2.5 | Setting Up Levels | 2-26 |
| --- | --- | --- | --- |
|     |     | Modifying Levels | 2-28 |
|     |     | Creating Plan Views | 2-30 |

Practice 2b Set Up Levels ................................................................. 2-33

|     | 2.6 | Creating Grids | 2-38 |
| --- | --- | --- | --- |
|     |     | Modifying Grid Lines | 2-41 |

Practice 2c Add Grids ........................................................................ 2-44

Chapter Review Questions ............................................................... 2-47

Command Summary ......................................................................... 2-49

## Chapter 3: Working with Views .......................................................... 3-1

|     | 3.1 | Modify How the Project Browser Displays | 3-2 |
| --- | --- | --- | --- |
|     | 3.2 | Duplicating Views | 3-5 |
|     | 3.3 | Modify How the View Displays | 3-8 |
|     |     | View Control Bar | 3-8 |
|     |     | View Properties | 3-9 |
|     |     | Hiding and Overriding Graphics | 3-12 |
|     |     | Visibility/Graphic Overrides | 3-15 |
|     |     | View Templates | 3-17 |

Practice 3a Duplicate Views and Set the View Display ................... 3-19

|     | 3.4 | Adding Callout Views | 3-22 |
| --- | --- | --- | --- |
|     |     | Working with Crop Regions | 3-25 |
|     |     | Plan Regions | 3-26 |

Practice 3b Add Callout Views ......................................................... 3-29

|     | 3.5 | Creating Elevations and Sections | 3-34 |
| --- | --- | --- | --- |
|     |     | Elevations | 3-35 |
|     |     | Sections | 3-36 |
|     |     | Modifying Elevations and Sections | 3-37 |
|     |     | 3D Section Views | 3-41 |

Practice 3c Create Elevations and Sections .................................... 3-44

Chapter Review Questions ............................................................... 3-52

Command Summary ......................................................................... 3-55

## Chapter 4: Revit Families ............................................................................ 4-1

### 4.1 About Revit Families ............................................................................ 4-2
The Different Kinds of Families ........................................................ 4-3
Working with Component Families ................................................... 4-6
Loading Components ....................................................................... 4-7
Placing Components ........................................................................ 4-9

### 4.2 Modifying Components ....................................................................... 4-12

### 4.3 Creating Additional Family Types in a Project ............................... 4-14
Families with Connectors ............................................................... 4-15

### Practice 4a Load Components ................................................................. 4-16

### Chapter Review Questions ....................................................................... 4-21

### Command Summary ................................................................................. 4-23

## Chapter 5: Basic Sketching and Modify Tools ................................... 5-1

### 5.1 Adding General Building Elements ................................................... 5-2
Draw Tools ....................................................................................... 5-3
Drawing Aids .................................................................................... 5-6
Reference Planes ............................................................................. 5-9
Editing Building Elements .............................................................. 5-12
Selecting Multiple Elements .......................................................... 5-15
Measuring Tool ............................................................................... 5-17
Filtering Selection of Multiple Elements ........................................ 5-18

### Practice 5a Sketch and Edit Elements .................................................... 5-20

### 5.2 Working with Basic Modify Tools .................................................... 5-25
Moving and Copying Elements ...................................................... 5-25
Rotating Elements .......................................................................... 5-27
Mirroring Elements ......................................................................... 5-29
Creating Linear and Radial Arrays ................................................ 5-30

### Practice 5b Work with Basic Modify Tools ............................................. 5-33

### 5.3 Working with Additional Modify Tools ............................................ 5-41
Aligning Elements .......................................................................... 5-41
Splitting Linear Elements ............................................................... 5-43
Trimming and Extending ................................................................ 5-44
Offsetting Elements ........................................................................ 5-45

### Practice 5c Work with Additional Modify Tools ..................................... 5-47

### Chapter Review Questions ....................................................................... 5-51

### Command Summary ................................................................................. 5-55

# Design Development

## Chapter 6: Adding Columns .................................................................. 6-1
### 6.1 Adding Columns .................................................................. 6-2
Modifying Columns .................................................................. 6-5
### 6.2 Adding Isolated Footings .................................................................. 6-7
### Practice 6a Add Columns .................................................................. 6-9
### Chapter Review Questions .................................................................. 6-15
### Command Summary .................................................................. 6-16

## Chapter 7: Modeling Walls .................................................................. 7-1
### 7.1 Modeling Walls .................................................................. 7-2
### 7.2 Modifying Walls .................................................................. 7-10
Wall Joins .................................................................. 7-13
Editing Wall Profiles .................................................................. 7-15
Wall Openings .................................................................. 7-17
### 7.3 Adding Wall Footings .................................................................. 7-19
Wall Profiles and Footings .................................................................. 7-21
### Practice 7a Model the Exterior Shell .................................................................. 7-24
### Practice 7b Add Interior Walls .................................................................. 7-28
### Practice 7c Model Additional Walls .................................................................. 7-42
### 7.4 Adding Room Elements .................................................................. 7-50
### Practice 7d Add Room Elements .................................................................. 7-54
### Chapter Review Questions .................................................................. 7-63
### Command Summary .................................................................. 7-66

## Chapter 8: Working with Doors and Windows .................................................................. 8-1
### 8.1 About Doors and Windows .................................................................. 8-2
### 8.2 Creating Additional Door and Window Sizes .................................................................. 8-8
### Practice 8a Adding Doors and Windows .................................................................. 8-9
### Chapter Review Questions .................................................................. 8-20
### Command Summary .................................................................. 8-22

## Chapter 9: Working with Curtain Walls .................................................................. 9-1
### 9.1 Creating Curtain Walls .................................................................. 9-2
### 9.2 Adding Curtain Wall Grids .................................................................. 9-6
Modifying Curtain Wall Grids .................................................................. 9-7
### Practice 9a Work with Curtain Walls .................................................................. 9-11

## Contents

    **9.3 Working with Curtain Wall Panels** .................................................. **9-17**
        Creating a Curtain Wall Panel ............................................................. 9-19

    **9.4 Attaching Mullions to Curtain Wall Grids** ...................................... **9-21**
        Modifying Mullions ............................................................................... 9-22

    **Practice 9b Add Mullions and Panels to Curtain Walls** ..................... **9-24**

    **Chapter Review Questions** .................................................................. **9-33**

    **Command Summary** ............................................................................. **9-35**

### Chapter 10: Modeling Floors ........................................................... 10-1

    **10.1 Modeling Floors** ............................................................................. **10-2**
        Modifying Floors .................................................................................. 10-5
        Joining Geometry ................................................................................. 10-6

    **Practice 10a Model Floors** .................................................................... **10-8**

    **10.2 Creating Shaft Openings** ............................................................. **10-16**

    **10.3 Creating Sloped Floors** ............................................................... **10-17**
        Creating Multiple Slopes for Drainage .............................................. 10-18

    **Practice 10b Create Shaft Openings and Sloped Floors** ................ **10-21**

    **Chapter Review Questions** ................................................................ **10-26**

    **Command Summary** ........................................................................... **10-27**

### Chapter 11: Modeling Ceilings ......................................................... 11-1

    **11.1 Modeling Ceilings** ........................................................................... **11-2**
        Sketching Ceilings .............................................................................. 11-4
        Modifying Ceiling Grids ....................................................................... 11-5

    **11.2 Adding Ceiling Fixtures** .................................................................. **11-7**

    **Practice 11a Model Ceilings and Add Ceiling Fixtures** ................... **11-10**

    **11.3 Creating Ceiling Soffits** ................................................................ **11-16**

    **Practice 11b Create Ceiling Soffits** ................................................... **11-18**

    **Chapter Review Questions** ................................................................ **11-23**

    **Command Summary** ........................................................................... **11-25**

### Chapter 12: Modeling Roofs ............................................................. 12-1

    **12.1 Modeling Roofs** .............................................................................. **12-2**
        Modify the Footprint of a Roof ............................................................ 12-6

    **Practice 12a Create Roofs by Footprint** ............................................. **12-8**

    **12.2 Creating Roofs by Extrusion** ....................................................... **12-16**
        Modify Extruded Roof ....................................................................... 12-21
        Joining Roofs .................................................................................... 12-22
        Attaching Walls to Roofs .................................................................. 12-23

**Practice 12b Create Roofs by Extrusion** .......................................................... 12-25

**Chapter Review Questions** .................................................................................. 12-28

**Command Summary** .............................................................................................. 12-30

## Chapter 13: Modeling Stairs, Railings, and Ramps ........................................ 13-1

### 13.1 Creating Component Stairs ........................................................................ 13-2
Creating Runs ........................................................................................................ 13-3
Creating Other Types of Runs ............................................................................. 13-6
Creating Landings ................................................................................................. 13-9
Adding Supports .................................................................................................. 13-10

**Practice 13a Create Component Stairs** ............................................................. 13-11

### 13.2 Modifying Component Stairs ..................................................................... 13-21
Multistory Stairs ................................................................................................... 13-24

**Practice 13b Modify Component Stairs** ............................................................ 13-26

### 13.3 Working with Railings .................................................................................. 13-34
Modifying Railings .............................................................................................. 13-36

**Practice 13c Work with Railings** ......................................................................... 13-38

### 13.4 Creating Ramps ............................................................................................. 13-47

**Practice 13d Create Ramps** .................................................................................. 13-50

**Chapter Review Questions** .................................................................................. 13-53

**Command Summary** .............................................................................................. 13-55

# Construction Documentation

## Chapter 14: Creating Construction Documents ............................................... 14-1

### 14.1 Setting Up Sheets ......................................................................................... 14-2
Sheet (Title Block) Properties ........................................................................... 14-4

### 14.2 Placing and Modifying Views on Sheets .................................................. 14-6

### 14.3 Duplicating Sheets and Swapping Views ................................................. 14-8

### 14.4 Modifying Views and View Titles ............................................................. 14-11

**Practice 14a Set Up Sheets** .................................................................................. 14-15

### 14.5 Printing Sheets ............................................................................................. 14-22
Printing Options .................................................................................................. 14-22
Export Views and Sheets to PDF ..................................................................... 14-28

**Chapter Review Questions** .................................................................................. 14-29

**Command Summary** .............................................................................................. 14-32

# Contents

## Chapter 15: Working with Annotations ... 15-1

### 15.1 Working with Dimensions ... 15-2
Modifying Dimensions ... 15-5
Setting Constraints ... 15-10

### Practice 15a Work with Dimensions ... 15-16

### 15.2 Working with Text ... 15-23
Editing Text ... 15-26
Spell Checking ... 15-30
Creating Text Types ... 15-31

### Practice 15b Work with Text ... 15-33

### 15.3 Adding Detail Lines and Symbols ... 15-39
Using Symbols ... 15-40

### Practice 15c Add Detail Lines and Symbols ... 15-41

### 15.4 Creating Legends ... 15-45

### Practice 15d Create Legends ... 15-48

### Chapter Review Questions ... 15-51

### Command Summary ... 15-53

## Chapter 16: Adding Tags and Schedules ... 16-1

### 16.1 Adding Tags ... 16-2
Tagging in 3D Views ... 16-12

### Practice 16a Add Tags ... 16-14

### 16.2 Working with Schedules ... 16-20
Schedule View Properties ... 16-29
Filtering Elements from Schedules ... 16-31
Modifying Schedules ... 16-33
Modifying a Schedule on a Sheet ... 16-35
Split a Schedule Across Multiple Sheets ... 16-35
Filter by Sheet ... 16-37

### Practice 16b Work with Schedules ... 16-39

### Chapter Review Questions ... 16-47

### Command Summary ... 16-48

## Chapter 17: Creating Details ... 17-1

### 17.1 Setting Up Detail Views ... 17-2
Referencing a Drafting View ... 17-5
Saving Drafting Views ... 17-6

### 17.2 Adding Detail Components ... 17-9
Detail Components ... 17-9
Repeating Details ... 17-11

**17.3 Annotating Details** ............................................................................... 17-13
    Creating Filled Regions ............................................................... 17-13
    Adding Detail Tags ..................................................................... 17-16

**Practice 17a Create a Detail Based on a Section Callout** ................ 17-17

**Practice 17b Create a Detail in a Drafting View** .............................. 17-26

**Chapter Review Questions** ........................................................... 17-30

**Command Summary** ..................................................................... 17-32

## Appendix A: Additional Tools for Design Development ........................... A-1

  A.1  Selection Sets ................................................................... A-2

  A.2  Purging Unused Elements ................................................. A-5

  A.3  Editing Wall Joins ............................................................. A-6

  A.4  Wall Sweeps and Reveals ................................................ A-8

  A.5  Creating Curtain Wall Types with Automatic Grids .......... A-11

  A.6  Creating Fascias, Soffits, and Gutters ............................. A-14
    Fascias ........................................................................ A-14
    Soffits .......................................................................... A-15
    Gutters ........................................................................ A-16

  A.7  Creating Dormers ............................................................ A-17

  A.8  Enhancing Views ............................................................ A-20
    Splitting Faces ............................................................. A-21
    Applying Materials ....................................................... A-22
    Editing Plan and Section Profiles ................................ A-25

  A.9  Introduction to Revit Worksharing ................................... A-27
    Worksharing Definitions .............................................. A-28
    Saving a Workshared Project ..................................... A-32

**Command Summary** ..................................................................... A-34

## Appendix B: Additional Tools for Construction Documents ...................... B-1

  B.1  Working with Guide Grids on Sheets ................................ B-2

  B.2  Revision Tracking ............................................................. B-4
    Issuing Revisions ........................................................ B-9

  B.3  Path of Travel and Route Analysis ................................. B-10

  B.4  Annotating Dependent Views ......................................... B-13
    Annotating Views ........................................................ B-14

  B.5  Creating Building Component Schedules ...................... B-17

  B.6  Importing and Exporting Schedules ............................... B-20

  B.7  Creating a Repeating Detail ........................................... B-22

| | |
|---|---|
| **B.8 Keynoting and Keynote Legends** | **B-24** |
| Keynote Legends | B-27 |
| **Command Summary** | **B-29** |
| **Index** | **Index-1** |

# Preface

The Autodesk® Revit® software is a powerful Building Information Modeling (BIM) program that works the way architects think. The program streamlines the design process through the use of a central 3D model, where changes made in one view update across all views and on the printable sheets.

The objective of the *Autodesk® Revit® 2023: Fundamentals for Architecture* guide is to enable you to create a full 3D architectural project model, including walls, doors, windows, components, floors, ceilings, roofs, and stairs, using the basic tools that the majority of architectural users need. This includes how to navigate the user interface and use the basic drawing, editing, and viewing tools. The final part of the course focuses on creating construction documents.

**Topics Covered**

- Understanding the purpose of BIM and how it is applied in the Autodesk Revit software.
- Navigating the Revit workspace and interface.
- Selecting a template and linking CAD and Revit files as the basis of a project.
- Creating levels and grids as datum elements for the model.
- Understanding the Project Browser and working with views.
- Understanding Revit families and components.
- Working with the basic sketching and modifying tools.
- Creating a 3D building model with columns, walls, curtain walls, windows, and doors.
- Adding floors, ceilings, and roofs to the building model.
- Modeling stairs, railings, and ramps.
- Setting up sheets for plotting with text, dimensions, details, tags, and schedules.
- Creating details.

### Prerequisites

- Access to the 2023.0 version of the software, to ensure compatibility with this guide. Future software updates that are released by Autodesk may include changes that are not reflected in this guide. The practices and files included with this guide might not be compatible with prior versions (e.g., 2022).
- An understanding of architectural terminology is an asset.

### Note on Learning Guide Content

ASCENT's learning guides are intended to teach the technical aspects of using the software and do not focus on professional design principles and standards. The exercises aim to demonstrate the capabilities and flexibility of the software, rather than following specific design codes or standards, which can vary between regions.

### Note on Software Setup

This guide assumes a standard installation of the software using the default preferences during installation. Lectures and practices use the standard software templates and default options for the Content Libraries.

### Lead Contributor: Cherisse Biddulph

Cherisse is an Autodesk Certified Professional for Revit as well as an Autodesk Certified Instructor. She brings over 19 years of industry, teaching, and technical support experience to her role as a Learning Content Developer with ASCENT. With a passion for design and architecture, she has worked in the industry assisting firms with their Building Information Modeling (BIM) management and software implementation needs as they modernize to a BIM design environment. Although her main devotion is the Revit design product, she is also proficient in AutoCAD, Autodesk BIM 360, and Autodesk Navisworks. Today, Cherisse continues to expand her knowledge in the ever-evolving AEC industry and the software used to support it.

Cherisse Biddulph has been the Lead Contributor for *Autodesk Revit: Fundamentals for Architecture* since 2020.

# In This Guide

The following highlights the key features of this guide.

| Feature | Description |
|---|---|
| **Practice Files** | The Practice Files page includes a link to the practice files and instructions on how to download and install them. The practice files are required to complete the practices in this guide. |
| **Chapters** | A chapter consists of the following: Learning Objectives, Instructional Content, Practices, Chapter Review Questions, and Command Summary.<br>• **Learning Objectives** define the skills you can acquire by learning the content provided in the chapter.<br>• **Instructional Content**, which begins right after Learning Objectives, refers to the descriptive and procedural information related to various topics. Each main topic introduces a product feature, discusses various aspects of that feature, and provides step-by-step procedures on how to use that feature. Where relevant, examples, figures, helpful hints, and notes are provided.<br>• **Practice** for a topic follows the instructional content. Practices enable you to use the software to perform a hands-on review of a topic. It is required that you download the practice files (using the link found on the Practice Files page) prior to starting the first practice.<br>• **Chapter Review Questions**, located close to the end of a chapter, enable you to test your knowledge of the key concepts discussed in the chapter.<br>• **Command Summary** concludes a chapter. It contains a list of the software commands that are used throughout the chapter and provides information on where the command can be found in the software. |
| **Appendices** | Appendices provide additional information to the main course content. It could be in the form of instructional content, practices, tables, projects, or skills assessment. |

# Practice Files

To download the practice files for this guide, use the following steps:

1. Type the URL **exactly as shown below** into the address bar of your Internet browser to access the Course File Download page.

   **www.SDCpublications.com/downloads/978-1-63057-514-4**

2. On the Course File Download page, click the **DOWNLOAD File** button, to download the .ZIP file that contains the practice files.

3. Once the download is complete, unzip the file and extract its contents.

   **The recommended practice files folder location is:**
   *C:\Revit 2023 Fundamentals for Architecture Practice Files*

   *Note: It is recommended that you do not change the location of the practice files folder. Doing so may cause errors when completing the practices.*

# Revit Tools and Project Setup

This guide is divided into three sections: Revit Tools and Project Setup, Design Development, and Construction Documentation.

The first section provides an introduction to the Autodesk® Revit® software, including working with the software interface, setting up a drawing, incorporating datum elements, adding families, and using the basic drawing and modify tools.

This section includes the following chapters:

- Chapter 1: Introduction to Revit
- Chapter 2: Starting a Project
- Chapter 3: Working with Views
- Chapter 4: Revit Families
- Chapter 5: Basic Sketching and Modify Tools

# Chapter 1

# Introduction to Revit

Building Information Modeling (BIM) and Revit® work hand in hand to help you create smart, 3D models that are useful at all stages in the building process. Understanding the software interface and terminology enhances your ability to create and navigate around in the various views of the model.

## Learning Objectives in This Chapter

- Describe the concept of Building Information Modeling in conjunction with applying Revit.
- Navigate the graphic user interface, including the ribbon (where most of the tools are found), Properties (where you make modifications to element information), and the Project Browser (where you can open various views of the model).
- Open existing projects and save projects.
- Use viewing commands to navigate around the model in 2D and 3D views.

## 1.1 BIM and Revit

Building Information Modeling (BIM) is an approach to the entire building life cycle, including design, construction, and facilities management. The BIM process supports the ability to coordinate, update, and share design data with team members across disciplines.

Revit is a model authoring software. It enables you to create complete 3D building models (as shown on the left in Figure 1–1) that provide considerable information reported through construction documents, and enables you to share these models with other programs for more extensive analysis.

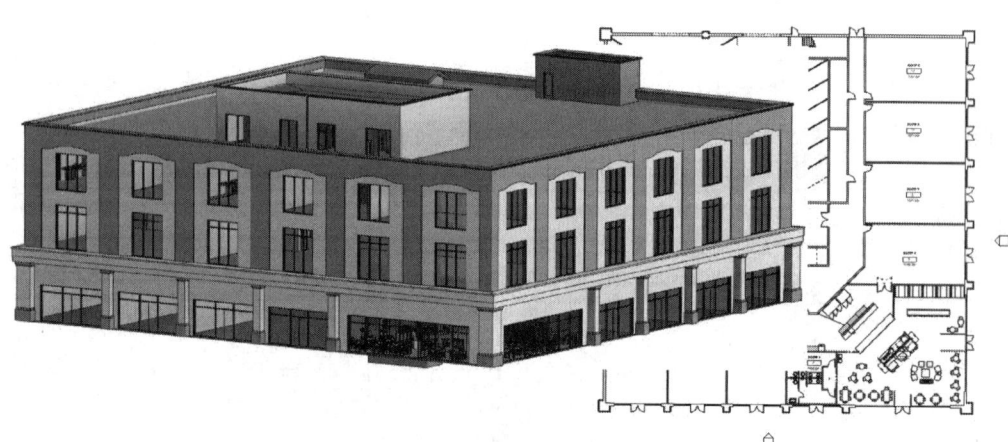

Figure 1–1

Revit is a Parametric Building Modeler software:

- *Parametric:* A relationship is established between building elements: when one element changes, all other related elements and/or geometry is modified as well. For example, when you place a door in a wall, the door removes part of the wall and stays inside that wall if it moves.

- *Building:* The software is designed for working with buildings and the surrounding landscape, as opposed to gears or highways.

- *Modeler:* A project is built in a single file based on the 3D building model, as shown on the left in Figure 1–1. All views, such as plans (as shown on the right in Figure 1–1), elevations, sections, details, construction documents, and reports are generated based on the model.

- It is important that everyone who is collaborating on a project works in the same version and build of the software.

## Workflow and BIM

BIM has changed the process of how a building is planned, budgeted, designed, constructed, and (in some cases) operated and maintained.

In the traditional design process, construction documents are created independently, typically including plans, sections, elevations, details, and notes. Sometimes, a separate 3D model is created in addition to these documents. Changes made in one document, such as the addition of a light fixture in a plan, have to be coordinated with the rest of the documents and schedules in the set, as shown in Figure 1–2.

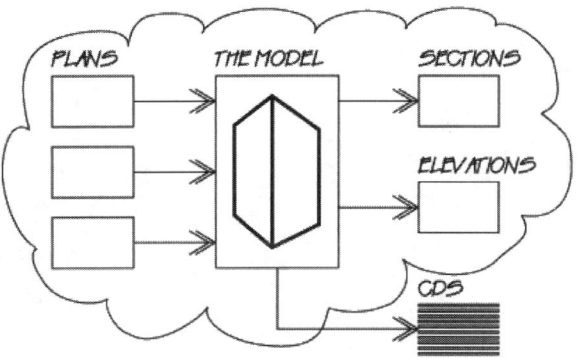

Figure 1–2

In BIM, the design process revolves around the model, as shown in Figure 1–3. Plans, elevations, and sections are simply 2D versions of the 3D model, while schedules are a report of the information stored in the model. Changes made in one view automatically update in all views and related schedules. Even construction documents update automatically with callout tags in sync with the sheet numbers. This is called bidirectional associativity.

By creating complete models and associated views of those models, Revit takes much of the tediousness out of producing a building design.

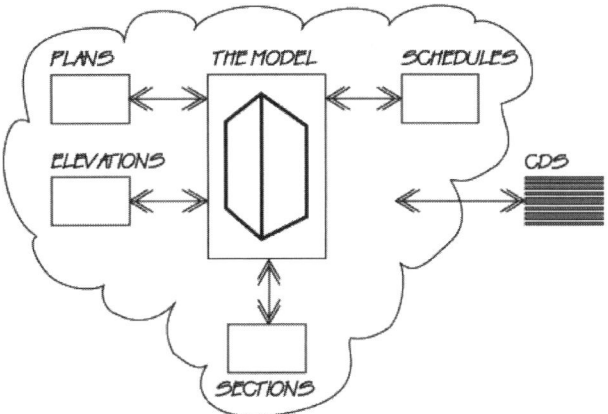

Figure 1–3

## Revit Terms

When working in Revit, it is important to know the typical terms used to describe items. Views and reports display information about the elements that form a project. There are three types of elements: Model, Datum, and View-specific, as shown in Figure 1–4 and described below:

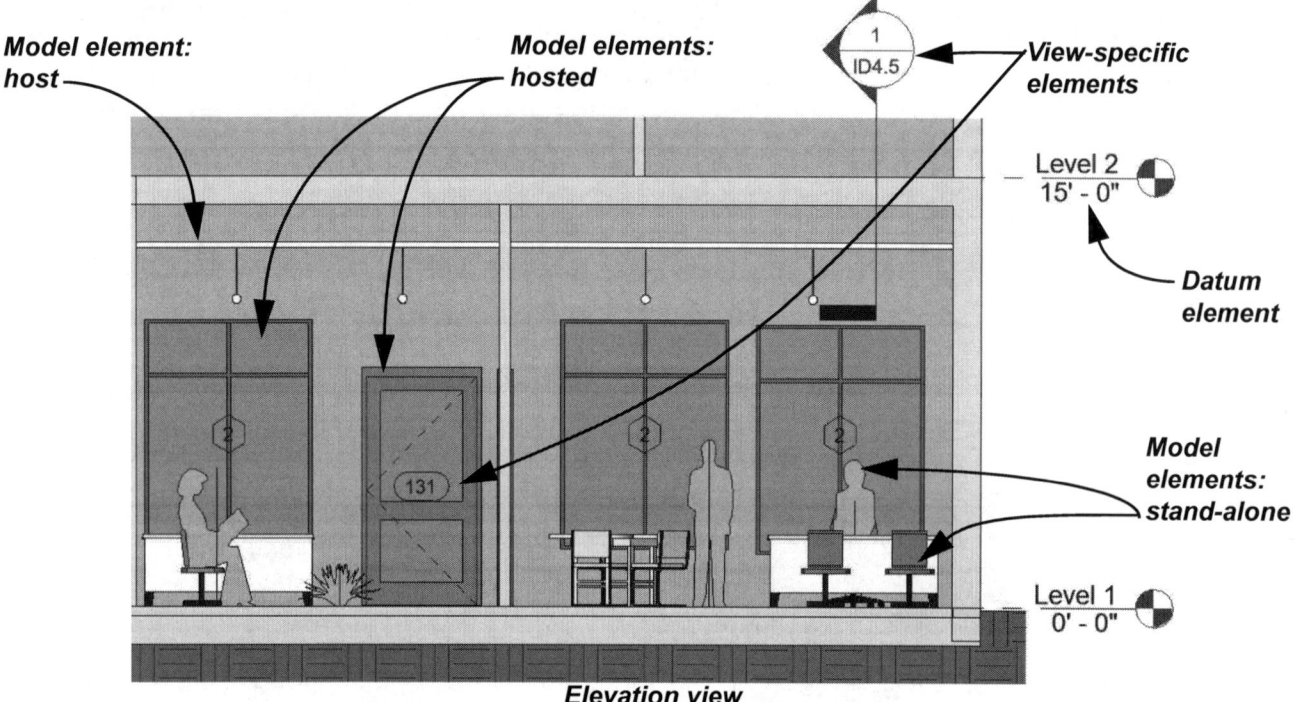

Figure 1–4

| Views | Views enable you to display and manipulate the model. For example, you can view and work in floor plans, ceiling plans, elevations, sections, schedules, and 3D views. You can change a design from any view. All views are stored in the project. |
|---|---|
| Reports | Reports, including schedules, gather information from the building model element that can be presented in the construction documents or used for analysis. |
| Model Elements | Model elements include all parts of a building, such as walls, floors, ceilings, and roofs. |
| Component Elements | Component elements are placed from inserted families, such as plumbing fixtures, lighting fixtures, mechanical equipment, columns, beams, furniture, and plants.<br>• Host elements, such as walls, support other categories of components like doors, windows, and casework.<br>• Hosted elements must be attached to a host element, such as doors must be placed on a (host) wall.<br>• Stand-alone elements do not require hosts. |

# Introduction to Revit

| **Datum Elements** | Datum elements define the project context, such as the levels for the floors, grids, and reference planes. |
|---|---|
| **View-specific Elements** | View-specific elements only display in the view in which they are placed. The view scale controls their size. These include annotation elements such as dimensions, text, tags, and symbols as well as detail elements such as detail lines, filled regions, and 2D detail components. |

*The software includes tools for architectural, mechanical, electrical, plumbing, and structural design.*

- Revit elements are "smart": the software recognizes them as walls, columns, plants, ducts, or lighting fixtures, etc. This means that the information stored in their properties automatically updates in schedules, which ensures that views and reports are coordinated across an entire project, and are generated from a single model.

## Revit and Construction Documents

In the traditional workflow, the most time-consuming part of the project is the construction documents. With BIM, the base views of those documents (i.e., plans, elevations, sections, and schedules) are produced automatically and update as the model is updated, saving hours of work. The views are then placed on sheets that form the construction document set.

For example, a floor plan is duplicated. Then, in the new view, all but the required categories of elements are hidden or set to halftone and annotations are added. The plan is then placed on a sheet, as shown in Figure 1–5.

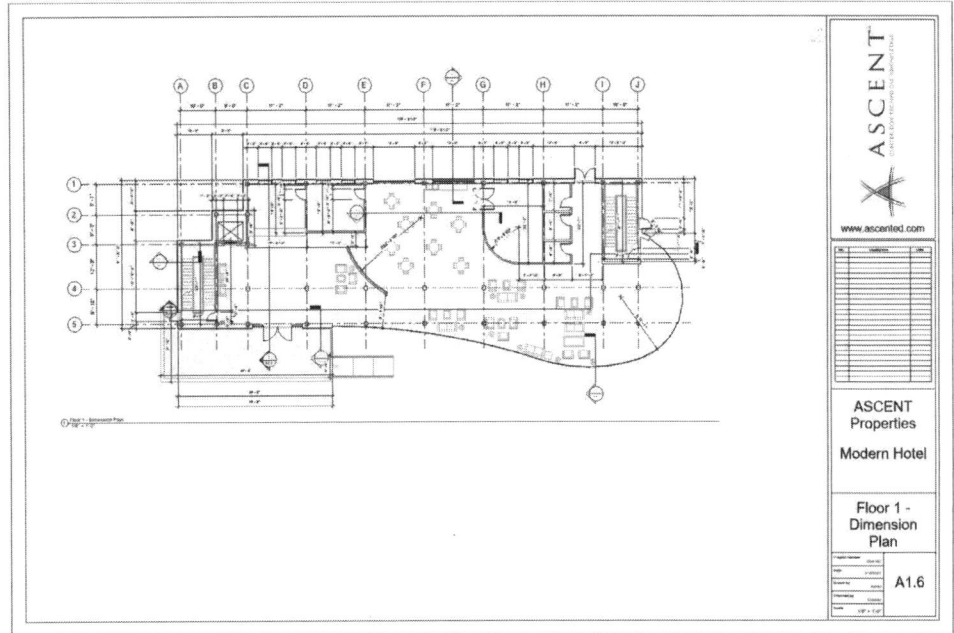

Figure 1–5

© 2022, ASCENT - Center for Technical Knowledge®

- Work can continue on a view and is automatically updated on the sheet.

- Annotating views in the preliminary design phase is often not required. You might be able to wait until you are further along in the project.

# 1.2 Overview of the Interface

The Revit interface is designed for intuitive and efficient access to commands and views. It includes the ribbon, Quick Access Toolbar, Navigation Bar, and Status Bar, which are common to most of the Autodesk software. It also includes tools that are specific to Revit, including Properties, the Project Browser, and the View Control Bar. Revit includes access to tools for architectural, mechanical, electrical, plumbing, and structural design but can be altered by setting up a customized workspace that is more tailored to your specific discipline. A breakdown of the Revit interface is shown in Figure 1–6.

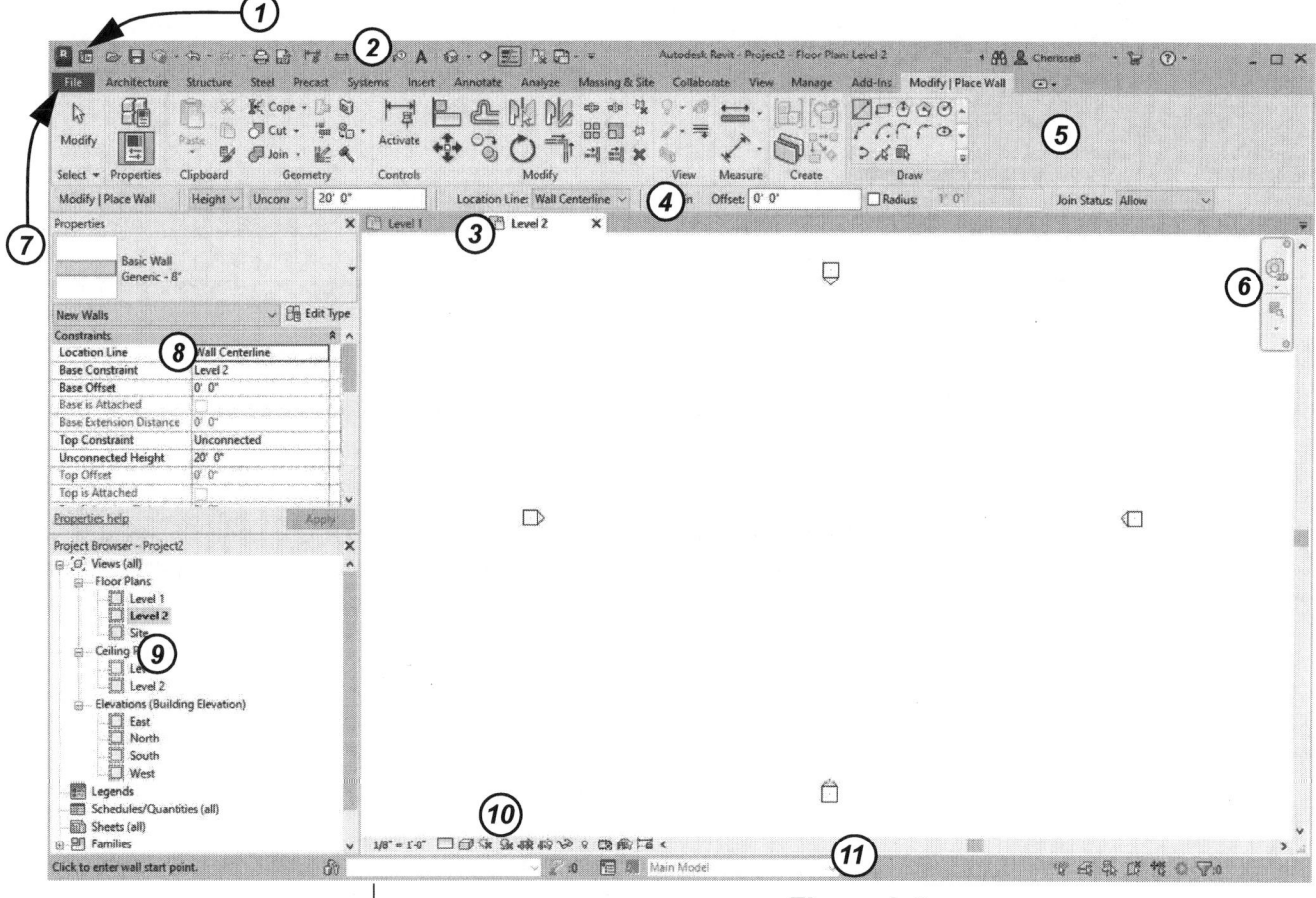

Figure 1–6

| 1. Home Screen | 7. File Tab |
| --- | --- |
| 2. Quick Access Toolbar | 8. Properties |
| 3. View Tabs | 9. Project Browser |
| 4. Options Bar | 10. View Control Bar |
| 5. Ribbon | 11. Status Bar |
| 6. Navigation Bar | |

## 1. The Home Screen

When you first open Revit, the **Home** screen displays with recently used projects and families, as shown in Figure 1–7.

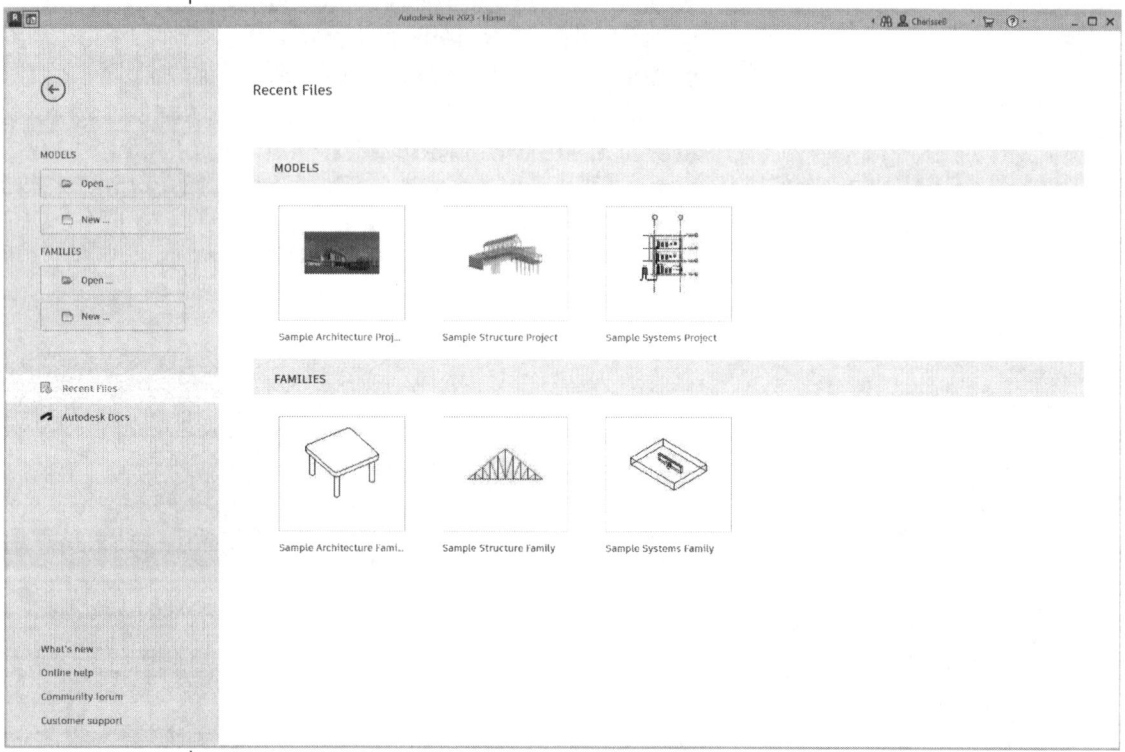

Figure 1–7

- From the Home screen, you can select the picture of a recently opened project or use one of the options on the left to open or start a new project using the default templates.

- In the Quick Access Toolbar, click (Home) to return to the screen.

- In the Home screen, click (Back) to return to the active model.

- Press <Ctrl>+<D> to toggle between the Home screen and the active model.

## 2. Quick Access Toolbar

The Quick Access Toolbar (shown in Figure 1–8) includes commonly used commands, such as **Home, Open**, **Save**, **Undo**, **Redo, Print**, and **PDF**. It also includes **Activate Controls and Dimensions** to reduce clutter when selecting multiple elements in a view, and frequently used annotation tools, including Measuring tools, **Aligned Dimension**, **Tag by Category**, and **Text**. Viewing tools, including several different 3D Views and **Sections**, are also easily accessed here.

Figure 1–8

The top toolbar also hosts the InfoCenter (as shown in Figure 1–9), which includes the Autodesk sign-in, access to the Autodesk App Store, and Help options. A search field, as shown in Figure 1–10, is also available to find help on the web.

Figure 1–9

Figure 1–10

### Hint: Customizing the Quick Access Toolbar

Right-click on the Quick Access Toolbar, as shown in Figure 1–11, to change the docking location of the toolbar to be above or below the ribbon, or to add, relocate, or remove tools on the toolbar.

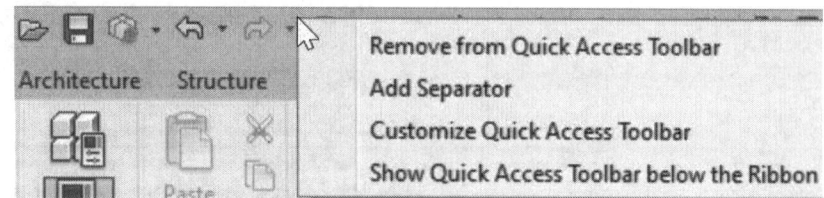

Figure 1–11

You can also right-click on a tool in the ribbon (e.g., the **Move** command) and select **Add to Quick Access Toolbar**, as shown in Figure 1–12.

Figure 1–12

If you have added a lot of icons to the Quick Access Toolbar, ▸▸ (Expand) will display at the end of the toolbar. Click ▸▸ to show the additional tool icons you have added, as shown in Figure 1–13.

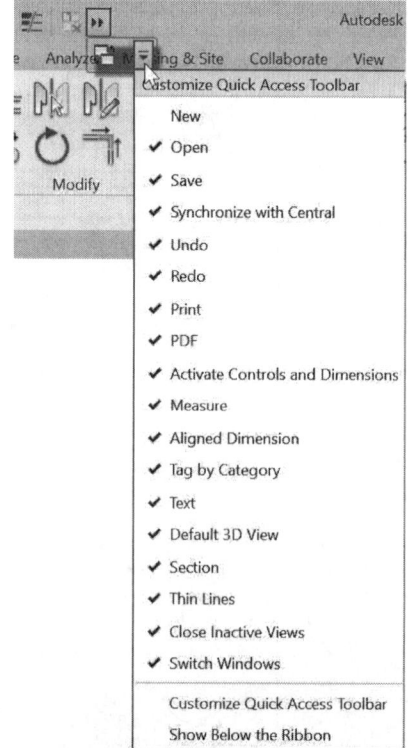

Figure 1–13

## 3. View Tabs

*In 3D views, you can also use the ViewCube to orbit the view.*

Each view of a project opens in its own tab and can be pulled out of the application window and moved to another monitor. Each view displays a Navigation Bar (for quick access to viewing tools), the View Control Bar, and elevation markers, as shown in Figure 1–14.

- To close a tab, press the **X** that displays when you hover over the tab or the name in the list, as shown in Figure 1–14.

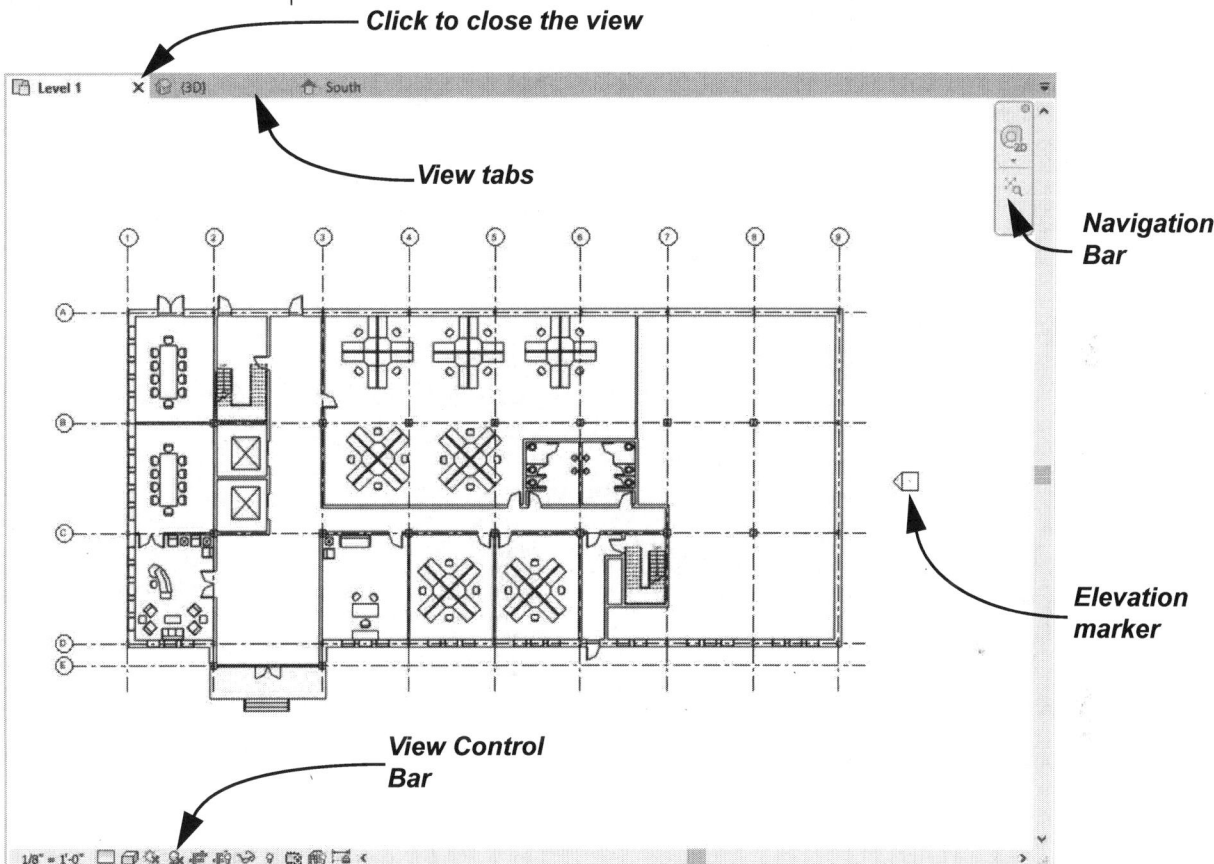

Figure 1–14

> **Hint: Elevation Markers**
>
> You can hover your cursor over a marker's arrowhead to see what the view name is, as shown in Figure 1–15. You can also double-click on the arrowhead to open the view.
>
>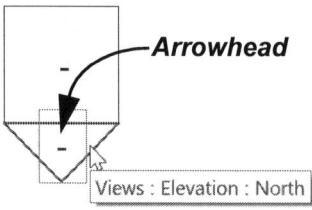
>
> Figure 1–15

- Click on the tab along the top of the drawing area to switch between views. You can also:

  - Press <Ctrl>+<Tab>.
  - Select the view in the Project Browser.
  - In the Quick Access Toolbar (shown on the left in Figure 1–16) or *View* tab>Windows panel (shown on the right in Figure 1–16), expand (Switch Windows) and select the view from the list.

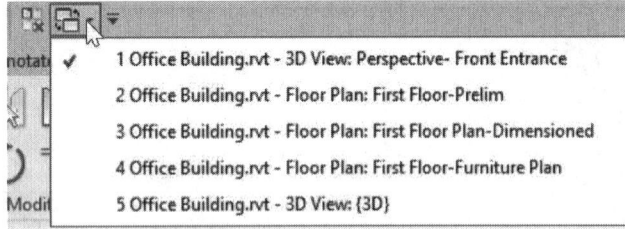
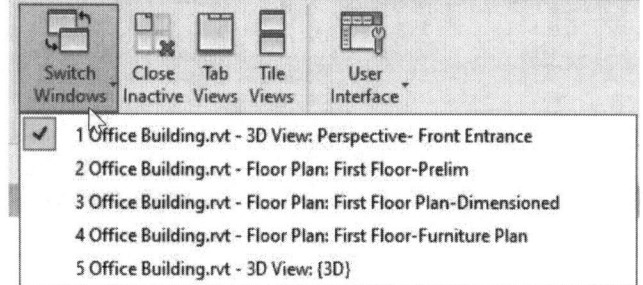

Figure 1–16

- Expand the drop-down list at the far end of the tabs, as shown in Figure 1–17 to select a view from the list.

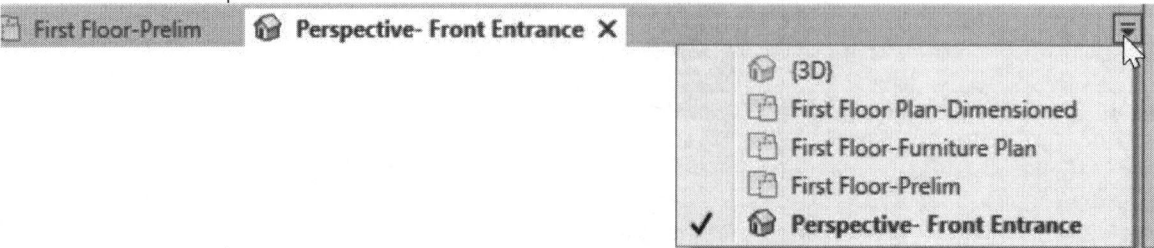

Figure 1–17

- To close all open views except the current view, in the Quick Access Toolbar or *View* tab>Windows panel, click (Close Inactive Views). If you have multiple projects open, one view of each project remains open. If you have dragged a view to another monitor, that view will need to be manually closed by clicking the **X** in the upper-right corner.

- You can switch between tabbed and tiled views from the *View* tab>Windows panel or by typing shortcuts. For tabbed views (as shown on the left in Figure 1–18), click (Tab Views) or type **TW**. For tiled views (as shown on the right in Figure 1–18), click (Tile Views) or type **WT**.

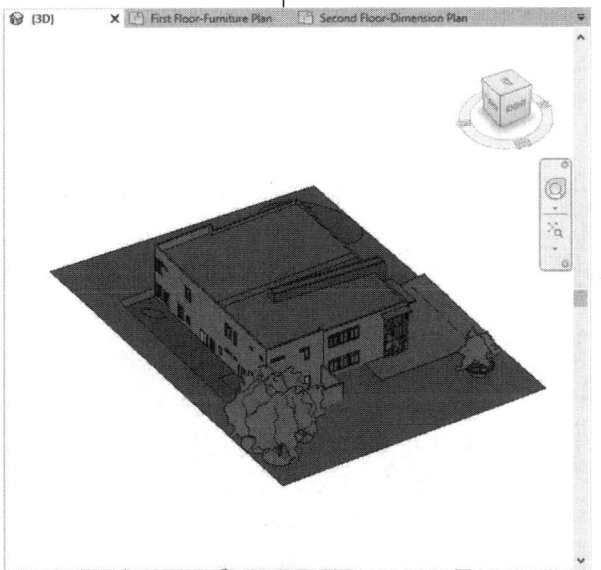 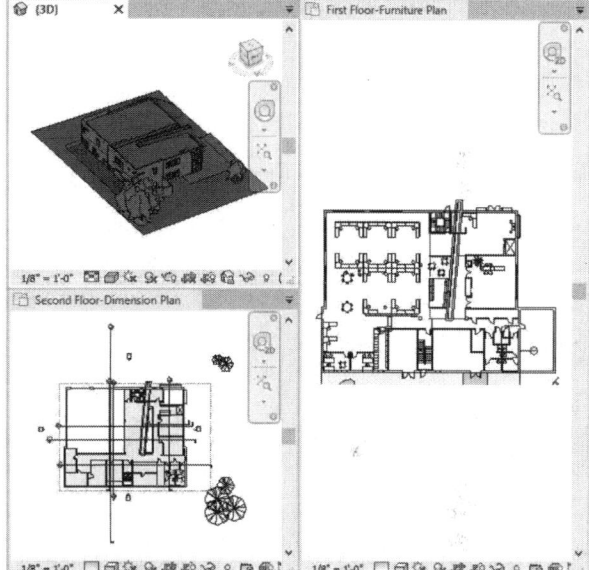

**Figure 1–18**

- When you are working with tiled views, you can type **ZA** (Zoom All to Fit) to zoom to fit the full model in each of the different views.

- Drag the edge of tiled views to resize them as needed.

### 4. Options Bar

The Options Bar displays options that are related to the selected command or element. For example, when the **Rotate** command is active it displays options for rotating the selected elements, as shown at the top in Figure 1–19. When the **Place Dimensions** command is active it displays dimension related options, as shown at the bottom in Figure 1–19.

*Options Bar for Rotate command*

*Options Bar for Dimension command*

**Figure 1–19**

### 5. Ribbon

The ribbon contains tools in a series of tabs and panels, as shown in Figure 1–20. Selecting a tab displays a group of related panels. The panels contain a variety of tools, grouped by task.

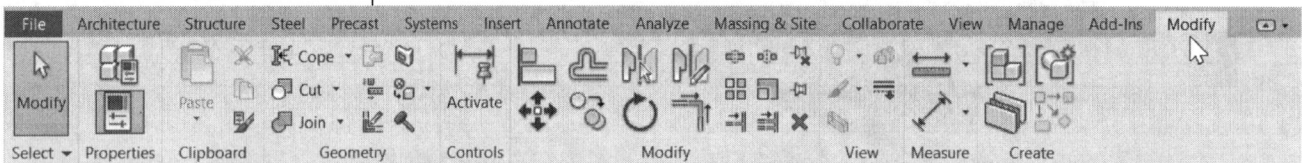

**Figure 1–20**

When you start a command that creates new elements or you select an element, the ribbon displays the *Modify* contextual tab. This contains general editing commands and command-specific tools, as shown in Figure 1–21.

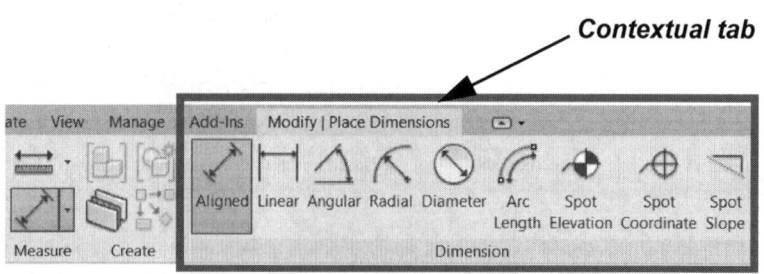

**Figure 1–21**

- When a command is toggled on, the icon will be highlighted in blue. When it is toggled off, the icon is gray (not highlighted), as shown in Figure 1–22.

# Introduction to Revit

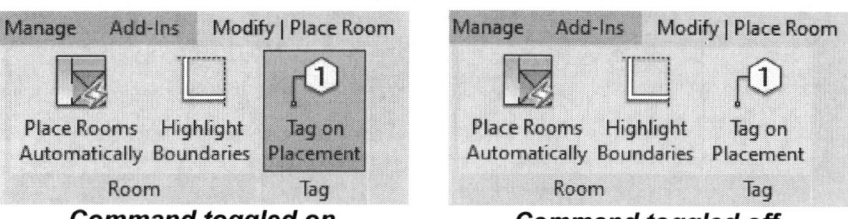

Command toggled on      Command toggled off

**Figure 1–22**

- When you hover over a tool on the ribbon, tooltips display the tool's name and a short description. If you continue hovering over the tool, a graphic displays (and sometimes a video), as shown in Figure 1–23.

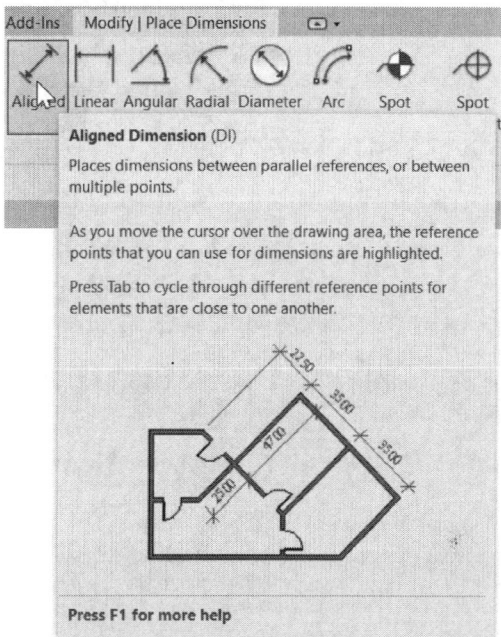

**Figure 1–23**

- Many commands have shortcut keys. For example, type **AL** for **Align** or **MV** for **Move**. They are listed next to the name of the command in the tooltips. Do not press <Enter> when typing shortcuts. A list of shortcuts can be found in the Autodesk Revit Help, which can be accessed by clicking (Help) in the upper-right corner of the interface or pressing <F1>.

    - For convenience, both the RVTKeyboardShortcuts.xlsx and RVTKeyboardShortcuts.pdf files have been downloaded for you and can be found in the practice files *Reference* folder.

- To arrange the order in which the ribbon tabs are displayed, select the tab, hold <Ctrl>, and drag it to a new location. The location is remembered when you restart the software.

- Any panel can be dragged by its title into the view window to become a floating panel. Click the **Return Panels to Ribbon** button (as shown in Figure 1–24) to reposition the panel in the ribbon.

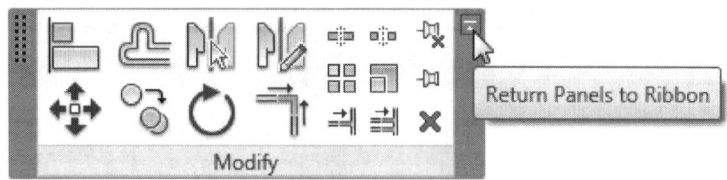

Figure 1–24

> **Hint: Ending a Command**
>
> When you are finished working with a tool, you typically default back to the **Modify** command. To end a command, use one of the following methods:
>
> - In any tab on the ribbon, click (Modify).
> - Type the shortcut **MD**.
> - Press <Esc> once or twice to revert to **Modify**.
> - Right-click and select **Cancel...** once or twice.
> - Start another command.

## 6. Navigation Bar

The Navigation Bar enables you to access the 2D and Full Navigation (3D views) Wheel to navigate the view, as well as the Zoom in Region viewing commands, as shown in Figure 1–25.

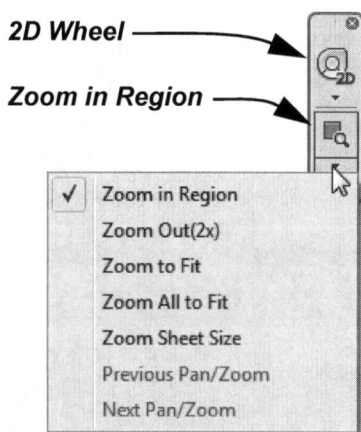

Figure 1–25

# Introduction to Revit

## 7. File Tab

The *File* tab of the ribbon provides access to file commands, Options settings, and documents, as shown in Figure 1–26. Hover the cursor over a command to display a list of additional tools.

*If you click the primary icon, rather than the arrow, it starts the default command (excluding Save as and Export, which require an option to be selected).*

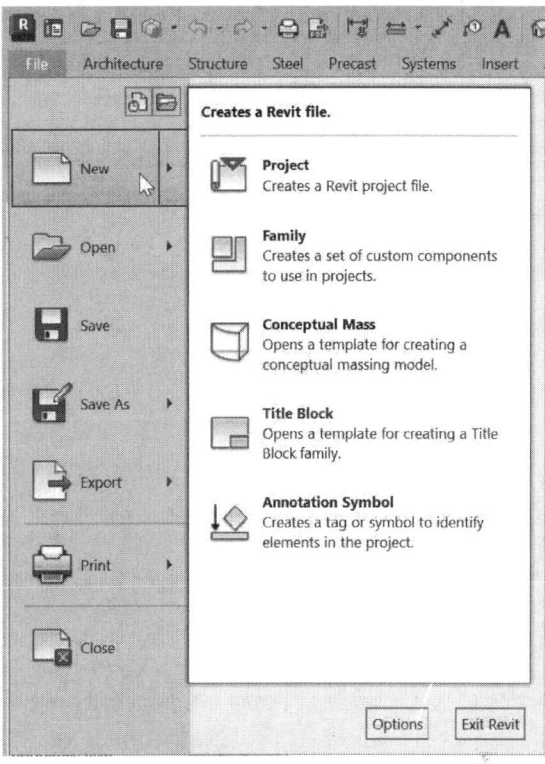

Figure 1–26

- To display a list of recently used documents, click  (Recent Documents). The documents can be reordered as shown in Figure 1–27.

*Click  (Pin) next to a document name to keep it available.*

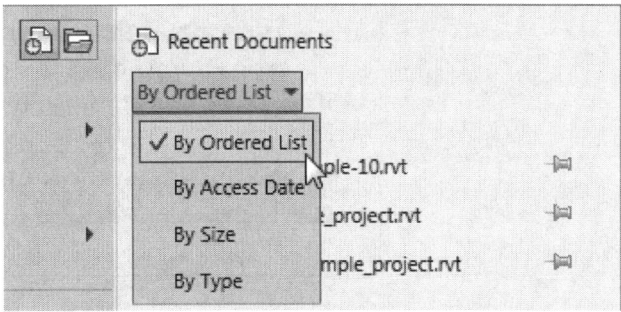

Figure 1–27

*You can use the Open Documents list to change between views.*

- To display a list of open documents and views, click ▭ (Open Documents). The list displays the documents and views that are open, as shown in Figure 1–28.

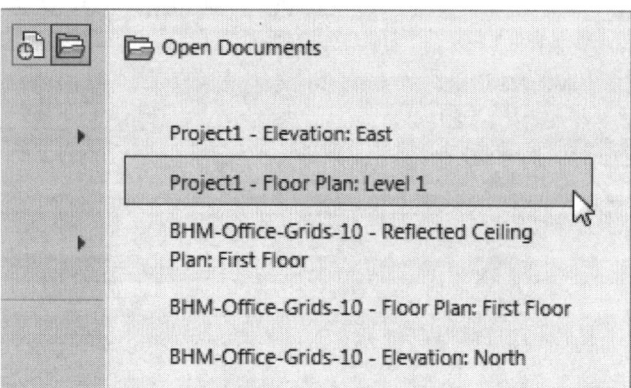

Figure 1–28

- Click ▭ (Close) to close the current project.

- At the bottom of the menu, click **Options** to open the Options dialog box or click **Exit Revit** to exit the software.

### 8. Properties

Properties contains several parts, as shown in Figure 1–29. The Type Selector can be found at the top, which enables you to choose the size or style of the element you are adding or modifying. The options available in Properties enable you to make changes to information (parameters). There are two types of properties:

- **Instance properties** are set for the individual element(s) you are creating or modifying.

- **Type properties** control options for all elements of the same type. If you modify these parameter values, all elements of the selected type change.

Properties is usually kept open while working on a project to easily permit changes at any time. If it does not display, in the *Modify* tab>Properties panel, click ▭ (Properties), or type **PP**. Alternatively, you can right-click in the view and select **Properties**.

*Some parameters are only available when you are editing an element. They are grayed out when unavailable.*

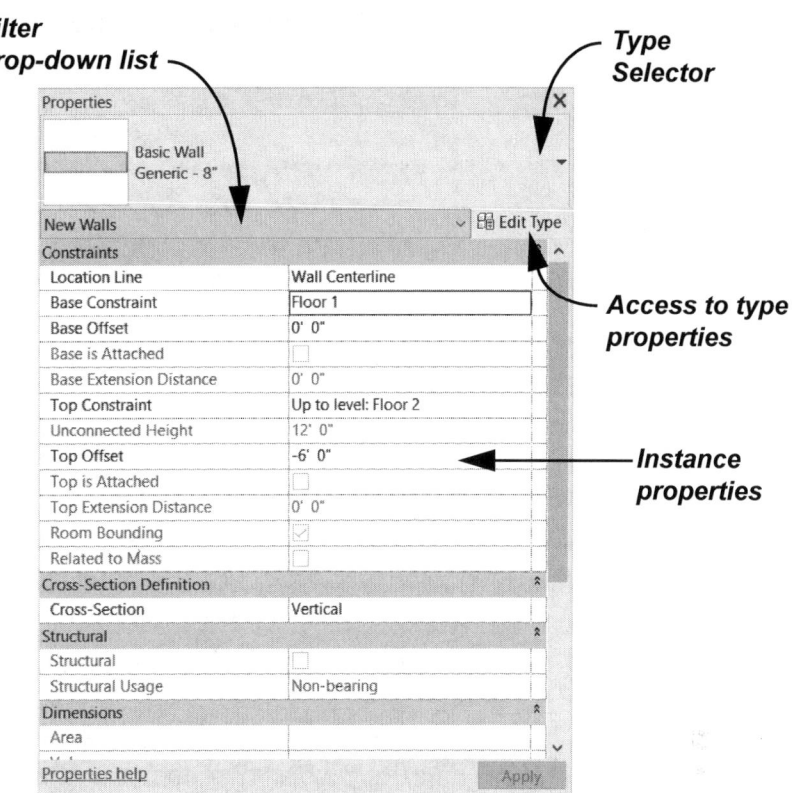

Figure 1–29

- Options for the current view display if the **Modify** command is active, but you have not selected an element.

- If a command or element is selected, the options for the associated element display.

- You can save the changes either by moving the cursor off of Properties, by pressing <Enter>, or by clicking **Apply**.

- When you start a command or select an element, you can set the element type in the Type Selector, as shown in Figure 1–30.

*You can limit what shows in the drop-down list by typing in the search box.*

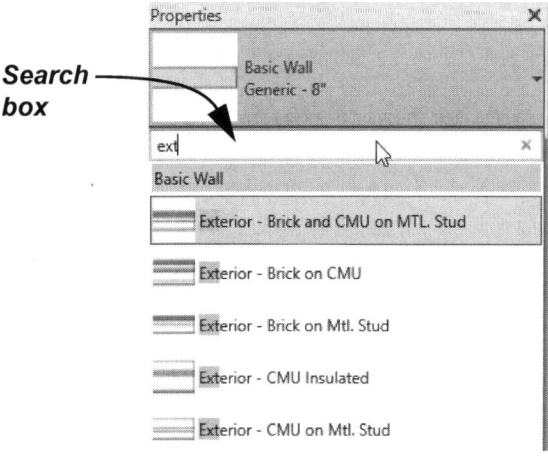

Figure 1–30

- When multiple elements are selected, you can filter the type of elements that display using the drop-down list, as shown in Figure 1–31.

- Properties can be placed on a second monitor, or floated, resized, and docked on top of the Project Browser, as shown in Figure 1–32. Click a tab to display its associated information.

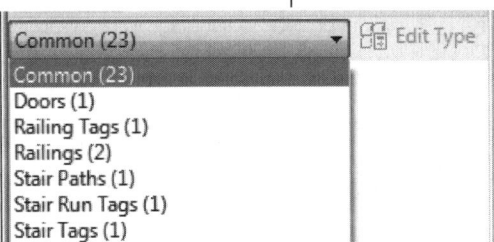

Figure 1–31

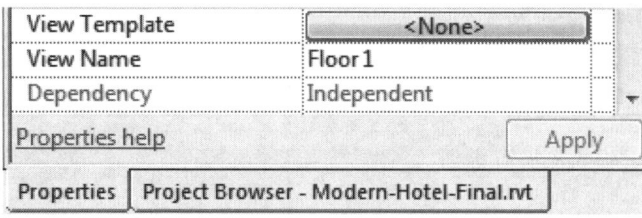

Figure 1–32

## 9. Project Browser

The Project Browser (shown in Figure 1–33) lists all the views of the model in which you can work and any additional views that you create, such as floor plans, ceiling plans, 3D views, elevations, sections, etc. It also includes schedules, legends, sheets (for plotting), lists of families by category, groups, and Revit links. The name of the active view is bold, and views that are placed on sheets will have a status icon next to the level's name.

*The name of the active project is displayed at the top of the Project Browser.*

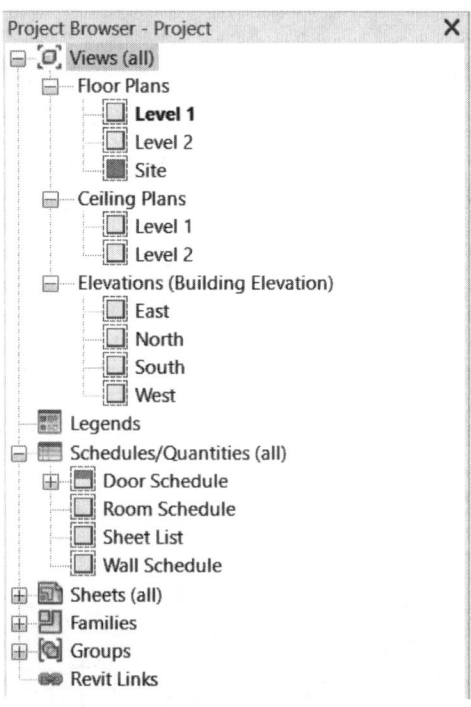

Figure 1–33

Introduction to Revit

- To display the views associated with a view type (e.g., floor plans, ceiling plans, etc.), click ⊞ (Expand) next to the section name. To hide the views in the section, click ⊟ (Collapse). You can also expand and collapse sets using the shortcut menu, as shown in Figure 1–34.

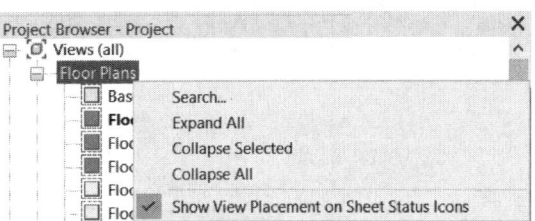

Figure 1–34

- To open a view, double-click on the view name or right-click and select **Open**.

- To rename a view, slowly click twice on the view name and the text will highlight so it can be changed, as shown in Figure 1–35. You can also right-click on a view name and select **Rename...**, or press <F2>.

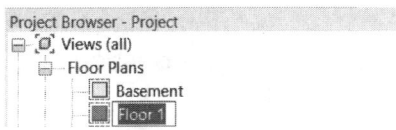

Figure 1–35

- If you no longer require a view, you can delete it. Right-click on its name in the Project Browser and select **Delete**.

- The Project Browser can be customized by changing the Browser Organization or its location within the application. The Project Browser can be floated, resized, or docked on top of Properties.

## How To: Search the Project Browser

1. In the Project Browser, right-click on the top level view and select **Search...**.
2. In the Search in Project Browser dialog box, type the words that you want to find (as shown in Figure 1–36) and click **Next**.

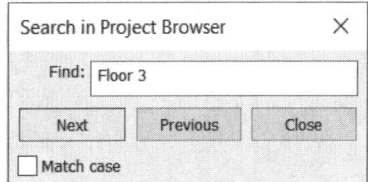

Figure 1–36

3. In the Project Browser, the first instance of that search highlights, as shown in Figure 1–37.

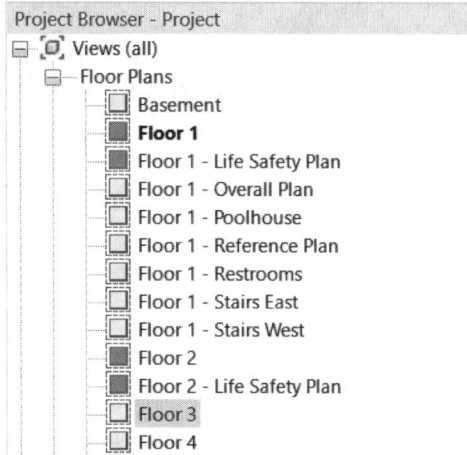

Figure 1–37

4. Continue using **Next** and **Previous** to move through the list.
5. Click **Close** when you are done.

**View Placement on Sheet Status Icon**

The box to the left of the view name indicates if that view has been placed on a sheet.

- A box that's filled in indicates the view is on a sheet.

- A white (empty) box indicates the view is not on a sheet.

- A half-filled box indicates the view is partially placed on a sheet (e.g., in the case where a schedule has multiple views because of the schedule's length).

**Find in Project Browser**

When working in a view, you can quickly locate it in the Project Browser by right-clicking in an empty space in the view (with nothing selected) and selecting **Find in Project Browser**. The view will highlight in the Project Browser.

You can also locate an element in the Project Browser by selecting the element in a view, right-clicking, and selecting **Find in Project Browser**.

## 10. View Control Bar

The View Control Bar (shown in Figure 1–38) displays at the bottom of each view window. It controls aspects of that view, such as the scale and detail level. It also includes tools that display parts of the view and hide or isolate elements in the view.

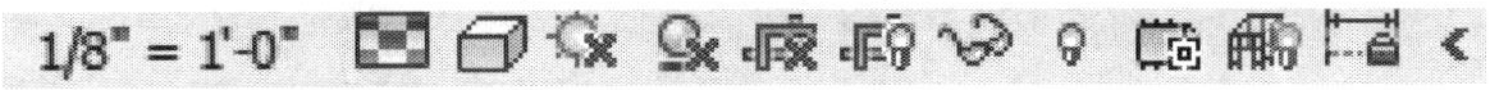

Figure 1–38

- The number of options in the View Control Bar change when you are in a 3D view, as shown in Figure 1–39.

Figure 1–39

| Tool | Tooltip | Description |
|---|---|---|
| 1/8" = 1'-0" | View Scale | Set the scale of individual views. |
| | Detail Level | Set the detail level of a view. |
| | Visual Style | Various graphic style representations. |
| | Sun Path On/Off | Controls the visibility of the sun's path. |
| | Shadows On/Off | Controls elements' shadow visibility in a view. |
| | Show/Hide Rendering Dialog | Available in 3D only. Shows or hides the rendering dialog box. |
| | Crop View | Define the crop boundaries for a view. |
| | Show/Hide Crop Region | Display the crop region in a view. |
| | Unlocked/Locked 3D Views | Lock a 3D view's orientation. |
| | Temporary Hide/Isolate | Temporarily isolate/hide by category or element (view specific). |
| | Reveal Hidden Elements | View hidden elements or unhide them in the active view. |
| | Worksharing Display | Available when worksharing is enabled. Controls display settings. |

| | | |
|---|---|---|
| ⬚ | **Temporary View Properties** | Enable, apply or restore view properties and display recent templates and apply them. |
| 🏠 | **Show or Hide the Analytical Model** | Only used for Structural and MEP to display the analytical information. |
| 🗄 | **Highlight Displacement Sets** | Also known as exploded views. |
| ⊢ | **Reveal Constraints** | Temporarily view the dimension and alignment constraints in the active view. |
| 🖼 | **Preview Visibility** | Available in the Family Editor only. Controls the visibility of the preview. |

## 11. Status Bar

The left-hand side of the Status Bar provides information about the current process, such as the next step for a command, as shown in Figure 1–40.

Click to enter wall start point.

Enter wall end point. (SZ) to close loop. Space flips orientation.

**Figure 1–40**

The right-hand side of the Status Bar provides selection options that enable you to control how the software selects specific elements in a project by toggling selection options on and off, as shown in Figure 1–41.

**Figure 1–41**

- 🔗 **Select links:** When this option is toggled on, you can select linked CAD drawings or Revit models. When it is toggled off, you cannot select them when using **Modify** or **Move**.

- 📎 **Select underlay elements:** When this option is toggled on, you can select underlay elements. When it is toggled off, you cannot select them when using **Modify** or **Move**.

- 📌 **Select pinned elements:** When this option is toggled on, you can select pinned elements. When it is toggled off, you cannot select them when using **Modify** or **Move**.

- **Select elements by face:** When this option is toggled on, you can select elements (such as the floors or walls in an elevation) by selecting the interior face or selecting an edge. When it is toggled off, you can only select elements by selecting an edge.

- **Drag elements on selection:** When this option is toggled on, you can hover over an element, select it, and drag it to a new location. When it is toggled off, the Crossing or Box select mode starts when you press and drag, even if you are on top of an element. Once elements have been selected, they can still be dragged to a new location.

When a selection option is toggled off, the icon will have a red X on it ( ).

You can also set the selection option from the ribbon. Expand the Select panel's title and select the option(s), as shown in Figure 1–42.

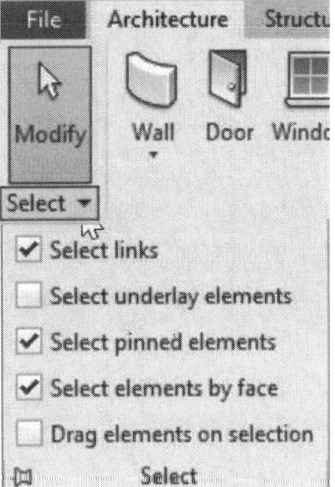

Figure 1–42

Other options in the Status Bar are related to worksets and design options (advanced tools).

**Hint: Shortcut Menus**

Shortcut menus help you to work smoothly and efficiently by enabling you to quickly access required commands. These menus provide access to basic viewing commands, recently used commands, and the available browsers, as shown in Figure 1–43. Additional options vary depending on the element or command that you are using.

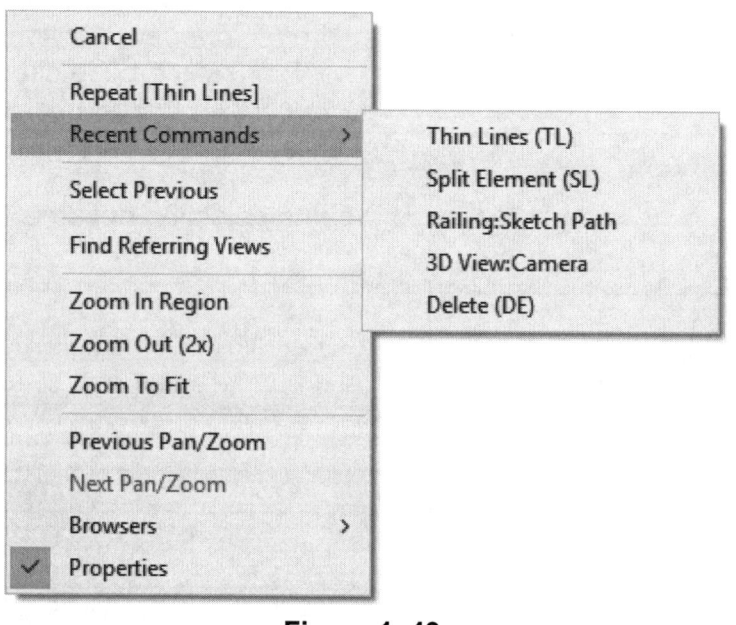

Figure 1–43

# 1.3 Opening and Saving Projects

File operations to open existing files, create new files from a template, and save files in Revit are found in the *File* tab, as shown in Figure 1–44.

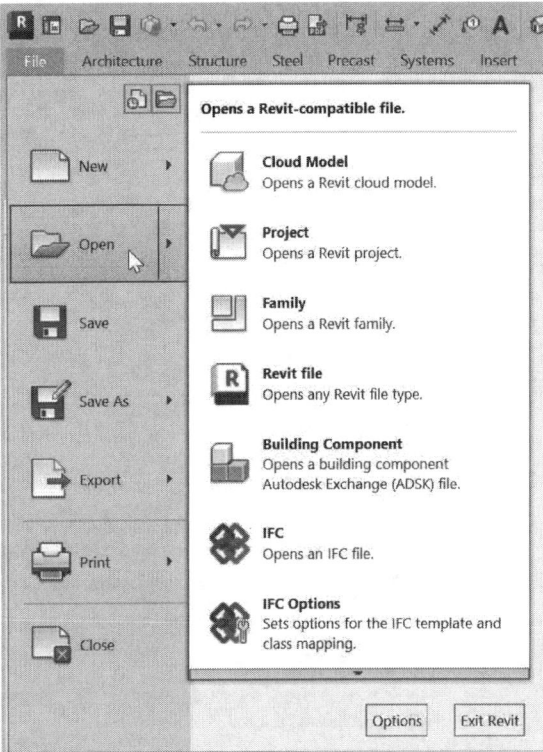

**Figure 1–44**

There are three main file formats:

- **Project files (.rvt):** These are where you do the majority of your work in the building model by adding elements, creating views, annotating views, and setting up printable sheets. They are initially based on template files.

- **Family files (.rfa):** These are separate components that can be inserted in a project. They include elements that can stand alone (e.g., a table or piece of mechanical equipment) or are items that are hosted in other elements (e.g., a door in a wall or a lighting fixture in a ceiling). Title block and annotation symbol files are special types of family files.

- **Template files (.rte and .rft):** These are the base files for any new project or family. Project templates (**.rte**) hold standard information and settings for creating new project files. The software includes several templates for various types of projects. You can also create custom templates. Family templates (**.rft**) include base information for creating families. Template files are usually saved as a new file.

## Opening Projects

To open an existing project, in the Quick Access Toolbar or *File* tab, click (Open), or press <Ctrl>+<O>. The Open dialog box opens, and you can navigate to the required folder and select a project file. An example of the Open dialog box is shown in Figure 1–45.

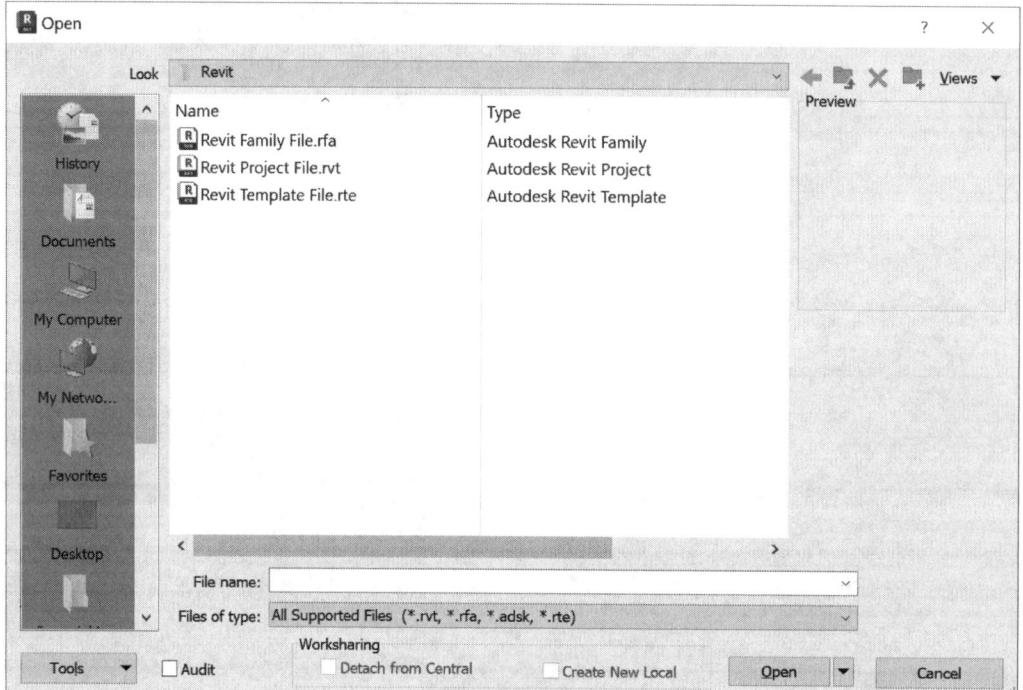

Figure 1–45

- The software release version of the currently selected project displays below the preview. Do not open a drawing that should remain in an earlier version, as you cannot save back to previous versions.

  Note: It is important that everyone working on a project uses the same software version (e.g., 2022) and is on the same updated version (e.g., 2022.1). While your software may be able to open files created in its earlier versions, it will not be able to open files created in versions newer than the one you are using currently. For example, if you are working in Revit 2022, you cannot open a model created in Revit 2023.

- When you open a file created in an earlier version, the Model Upgrade dialog box (shown in Figure 1–46) indicates the release of a file and the release to which it will be upgraded. If needed, you can cancel the upgrade before it completes.

# Introduction to Revit

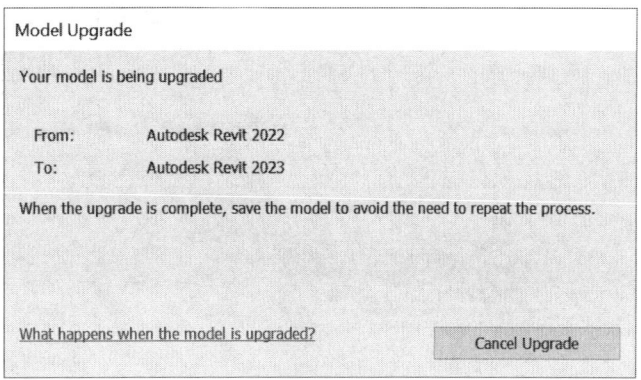

Figure 1–46

## Saving Projects

It is important to save your projects frequently. In the Quick Access Toolbar or *File* tab, click (Save), or press <Ctrl>+<S> to save your project. If the project has not yet been saved, the Save As dialog box opens, where you can specify a file location and name.

- To save an existing project with a new name, in the *File* tab, expand (Save As) and click (Project).

- If you have not saved in a certain amount of time, the software will notify you with the Project Not Saved Recently alert box, as shown in Figure 1–47. Select **Save the project**. If you want to set reminder intervals or not save at this time, select one of the other two options shown in Figure 1–47.

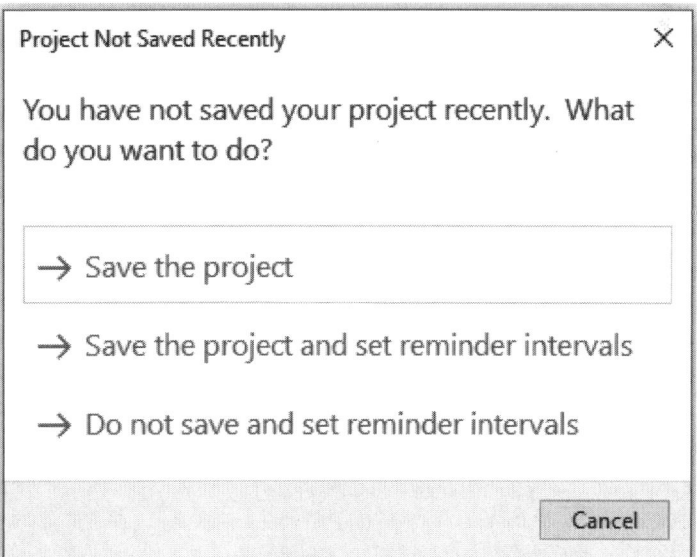

Figure 1–47

- You can set the *Save Reminder interval* to **15** or **30 minutes**, **One**, **Two**, or **Four hours**, or to have **No reminders** display. In the *File* tab, click **Options** to open the Options dialog box. Select **General** and set the interval, as shown in Figure 1–48.

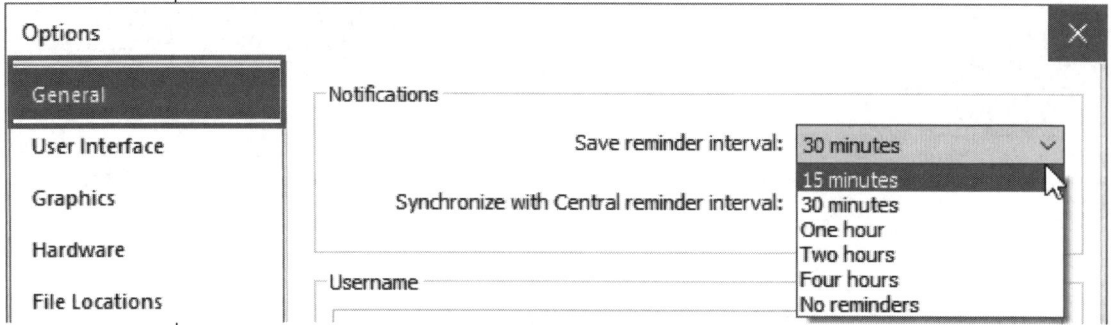

Figure 1–48

## Saving Backup Copies

By default, the software saves a backup copy of a project file when you save the project. Backup copies are numbered incrementally (e.g., **My Project.0001.rvt**, **My Project.0002.rvt**, etc.) and are saved in the same folder as the original file. In the Save As dialog box, click **Options...** to control how many backup copies are saved. The default number is three backups. If you exceed this number, the software deletes the oldest backup file.

## 1.4 Viewing Commands

Viewing commands are crucial to working efficiently in most drawing and modeling programs and Revit is no exception. Once in a view, you can use the Zoom controls to navigate in it. You can zoom in and out and pan in any view. There are also special tools for viewing in 3D.

**Zooming and Panning**

### Using the Mouse to Zoom and Pan

Use the mouse wheel (shown in Figure 1–49) as the main method of moving around the models.

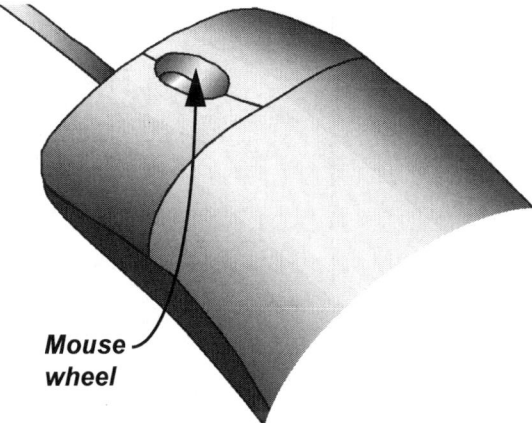

Figure 1–49

- Scroll the wheel on the mouse up to zoom in and down to zoom out.
- Hold the wheel and move the mouse to pan.
- Double-click on the wheel to zoom to the extents of the view.
- In a 3D view, hold <Shift> and the mouse wheel and move the mouse to orbit around the model.
- When you save a model and exit the software, the pan and zoom location of each view is remembered. This is especially important for complex models.

## Zoom Controls

A number of additional zoom methods enable you to control the screen display. **Zoom** and **Pan** can be performed at any time while using other commands.

- You can access the **Zoom** commands in the Navigation Bar in the upper right corner of the view (as shown in Figure 1–50). You can also access them from most shortcut menus and by typing the shortcut commands.

*(2D Wheel) provides cursor-specific access to **Zoom** and **Pan**.*

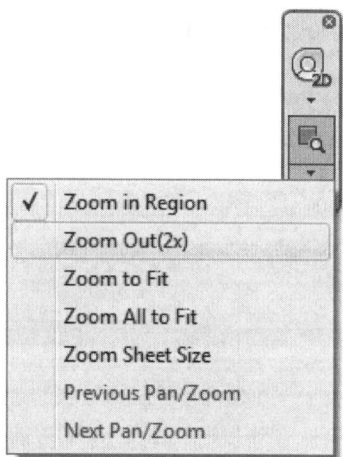

Figure 1–50

## Zoom Commands

| | Command | Description |
|---|---|---|
| | **Zoom In Region (ZR)** | Zooms in to a region that you define. Drag the cursor or select two points to define the rectangular area you want to zoom in to. This is the default command. |
| | **Zoom Out(2x) (ZO)** | Zooms out to half the current magnification around the center of the elements. |
| | **Zoom to Fit (ZF or ZE)** | Zooms out so that the entire contents of the project only display on the screen in the current view. |
| | **Zoom All to Fit (ZA)** | Zooms out so that the entire contents of the project display on the screen in all open views. |
| | **Zoom Sheet Size (ZS)** | Zooms in or out in relation to the sheet size. |
| N/A | **Previous Pan/Zoom (ZP)** | Steps back one **Zoom** command. |
| N/A | **Next Pan/Zoom** | Steps forward one **Zoom** command if you have done a **Previous Pan/Zoom**. |

# Viewing in 3D

Even if you started a project entirely in plan views, you can quickly create 3D views of the model, as shown in Figure 1–51. There are two types of 3D views: isometric views created by the **Default 3D View** command and perspective and orthographic 3D views created by the **Camera** command.

**Figure 1–51**

Working in 3D views helps you visualize the project and position some of the elements correctly. You can create and modify elements in both isometric and perspective 3D views, just as you can in plan views.

- Once you have created a 3D view, you can save it and easily return to it.

- Perspective 3D views are visual representations of what the model would look like if you were standing in the model.

- Orthographic 3D views can have a scale applied to them so that the entire model's components are at the same size no matter where the camera is positioned or its distance from the model.

## How To: Create and Save a 3D Isometric View

1. In the Quick Access Toolbar or *View* tab>Create panel, click (Default 3D View). The default 3D southeast isometric view opens, as shown in Figure 1–52.

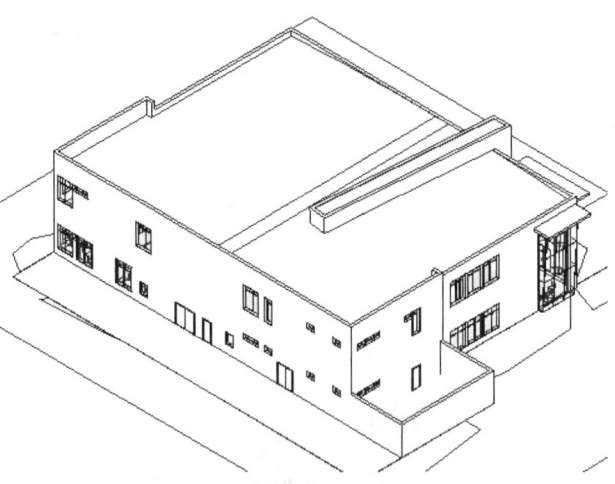

Figure 1–52

*You can spin the view to a different angle using the mouse wheel or the middle button of a three-button mouse. Hold <Shift> as you press the wheel or middle button and drag the cursor.*

2. Modify the view to display the building from other directions.
3. In the Project Browser, slowly click twice on the {3D} view or right-click on the {3D} view and select **Rename...**.
4. The name is placed in a text box with the original name highlighted, as shown in Figure 1–53. Type a new name in the text box, as shown in Figure 1–54.

Figure 1–53    Figure 1–54

*All types of views can be renamed.*

- When changes to the default 3D view are saved and you start another default 3D view, it displays the southeast isometric view once again. If you modified the default 3D view but did not save it to a new name, the **Default 3D View** command opens the view in the last orientation you specified.

## How To: Create a Perspective 3D View

1. Switch to a Floor Plan view.
2. In the Quick Access Toolbar or *View* tab>Create panel, expand (Default 3D View) and click (Camera).
3. Place the camera on the view.
4. Point the camera in the direction in which you want it to shoot by placing the target on the view, as shown in Figure 1–55.

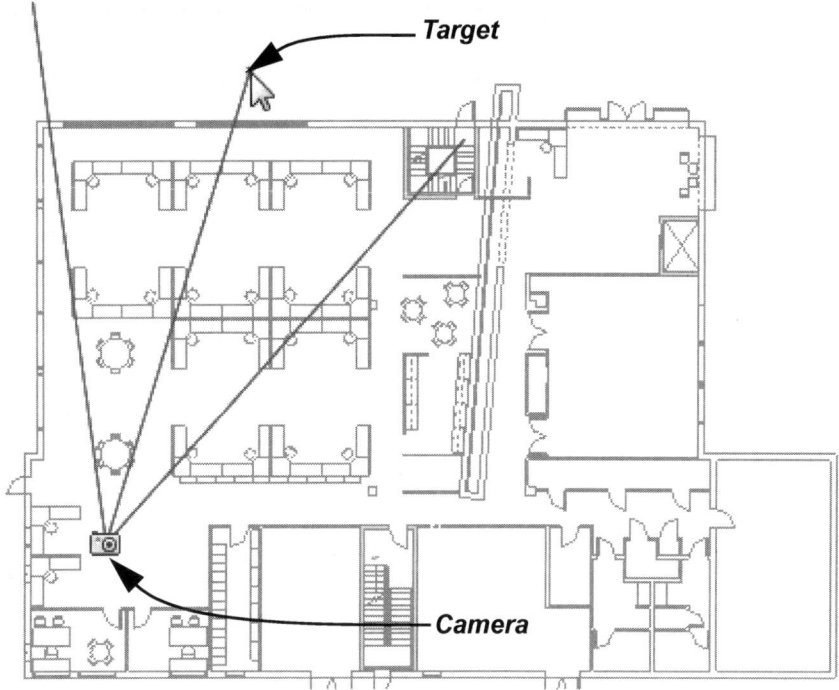

Figure 1–55

A new view is displayed, as shown in Figure 1–56.

Figure 1–56

## How To: Create an Orthographic 3D View

1. Switch to a floor plan view.
2. In the Quick Access Toolbar or *View* tab>Create panel, expand  (Default 3D View) and click  (Camera).
3. In the Options Bar, uncheck **Perspective** and set the *Scale*, *Offset*, and *From* which level, as shown in Figure 1–57.

Figure 1–57

*Use the round controls to modify the display size of the view and press <Shift> + the mouse wheel to change the view.*

4. Place the camera on the view.
5. Point the camera in the direction in which you want it to shoot by placing the target on the view, as shown in Figure 1–58.

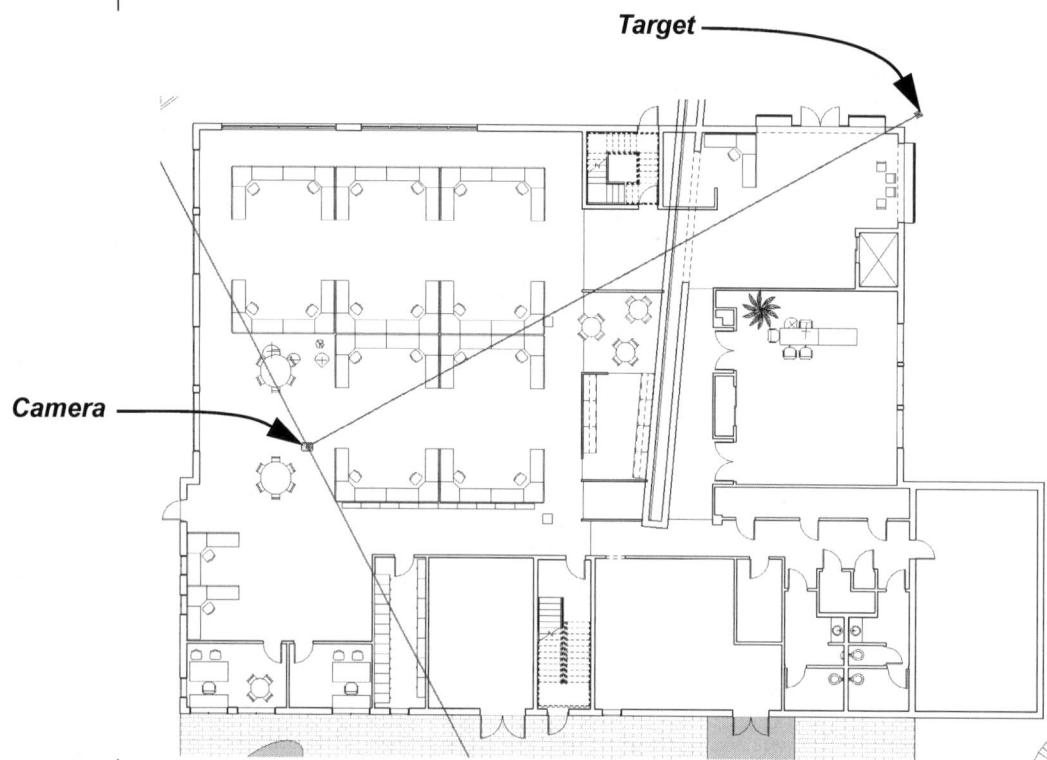

Figure 1–58

- A new view is displayed, as shown in Figure 1–59. If needed, the *Eye Elevation* and *Target Elevation* can be adjusted in Properties.

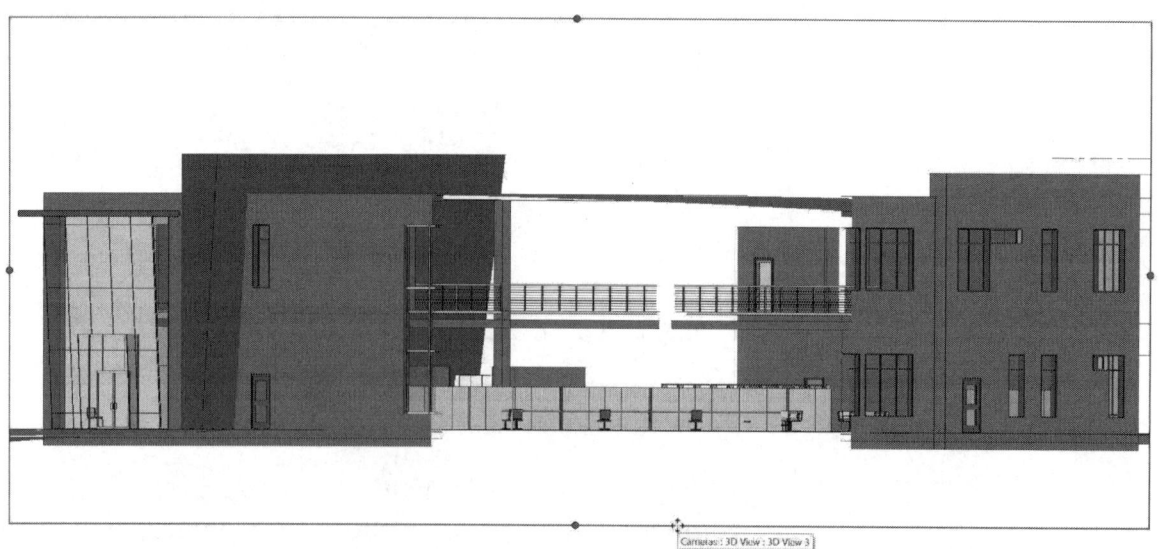

Figure 1–59

6. In Properties, scroll down and adjust the *Eye Elevation* and *Target Elevation* as needed.

### How To: Modify Camera 3D Views

1. In a plan view, select the camera or target icon and drag it within the view to reposition the placement.
2. In Properties, scroll down and adjust the *Eye Elevation* and *Target Elevation* as needed.

- To display the camera and camera controls in a plan view, select the camera's crop boundary in the perspective view, then switch back to the plan view.

  - Alternatively, while in a plan view, you can right-click on the perspective 3D view in the Project Browser and select **Show Camera**, as shown in Figure 1–60. The camera and camera crop boundaries will display.

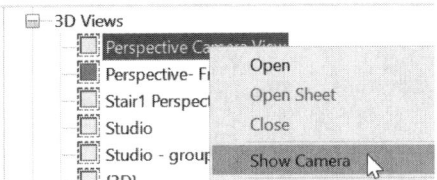

Figure 1–60

- For perspective 3D views, if the view becomes distorted, reset the target so that it is centered in the boundary of the view (called the crop region). In the *Modify | Cameras* tab> Camera panel, click (Reset Target).

## ViewCube

The ViewCube provides visual clues as to where you are in a 3D view. It helps you move around the model with quick access to specific views (such as top, front, and right), as well as corner and directional views, as shown in Figure 1–61.

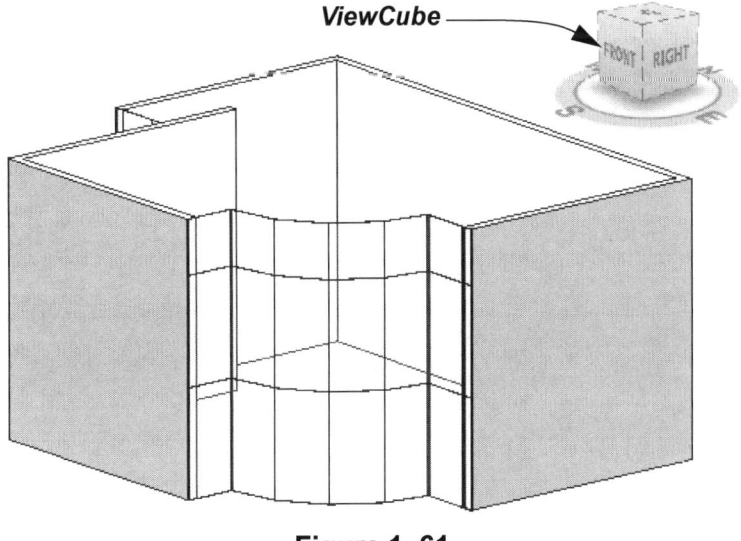

Figure 1–61

Move the cursor over any face of the ViewCube to highlight it. Once a face is highlighted, you can select it to reorient the model. You can also click and drag on the ViewCube to orbit the box, which rotates the model.

- (Home) displays when you roll the cursor over the ViewCube. Click it to return to the view defined as **Home**. To change the Home view, set the view as you want it, right-click on the ViewCube, and select **Set Current View as Home**.

- The ViewCube is available in isometric and perspective views.

You can switch between Perspective and Isometric mode by right-clicking on the ViewCube (as shown on the left in Figure 1–62) or clicking on (ViewCube contextual menu) to the lower right of the ViewCube (as shown on the right in Figure 1–62) and selecting **Perspective** or **Orthographic**.

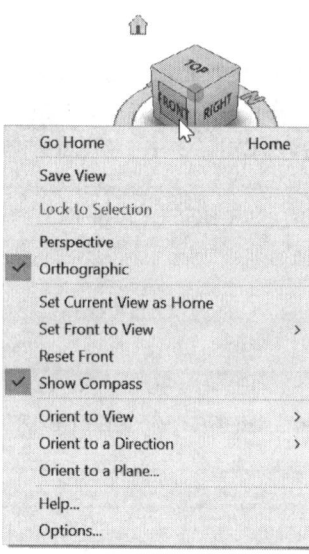  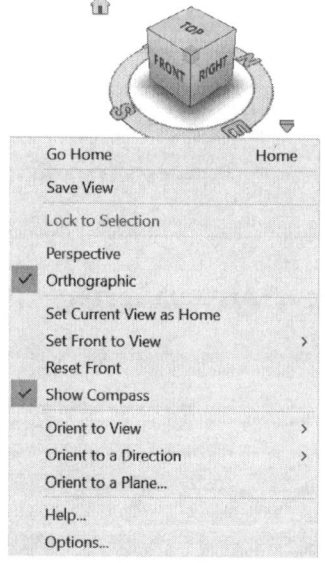

**Right-click on ViewCube**   **Context menu on ViewCube**

**Figure 1–62**

You can create 3D views that are oriented to a specific view. for more information, refer to *Chapter 3: Working with Views*.

## Visual Styles

Any view can have a visual style applied. The **Visual Style** options found in the View Control Bar (as shown in Figure 1–63), specify the shading of the building model. These options apply to plan, elevation, section, and 3D views.

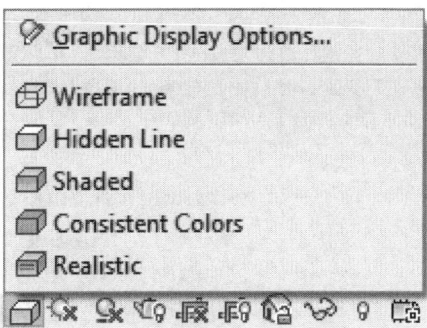

Figure 1–63

- (Wireframe) displays the lines and edges that make up elements, but hides the surfaces. This can be useful when you are dealing with complex intersections.

- (Hidden Line) displays the lines, edges, and surfaces of the elements, but it does not display any colors. This is the most common visual style to use while working on a design.

- (Shaded) and (Consistent Colors) give you a sense of the materials, including transparent glass. An example showing an exterior and interior view using Consistent Colors is shown in Figure 1–64. Landscape components will display as gray outlines of the objects until the Realistic visual style is used.

Figure 1–64

- (Realistic) displays what is shown when you render the view, including Rich Photorealistic Content (RPC) components and artificial lights. It takes a lot of computer power to execute this visual style. Therefore, it is better to use the other visual styles most of the time as you are working.

# Practice 1a

# Open and Review a Project

## Practice Objectives

- Navigate the graphic user interface.
- Manipulate 2D and 3D views by zooming and panning.
- Create 3D isometric and perspective views.
- Set the visual style of a view.

In this practice, you will open a project file and view each of the various areas in the interface. You will investigate elements, commands, and their options. You will also open views through the Project Browser and view the model in 3D, as shown in Figure 1–65.

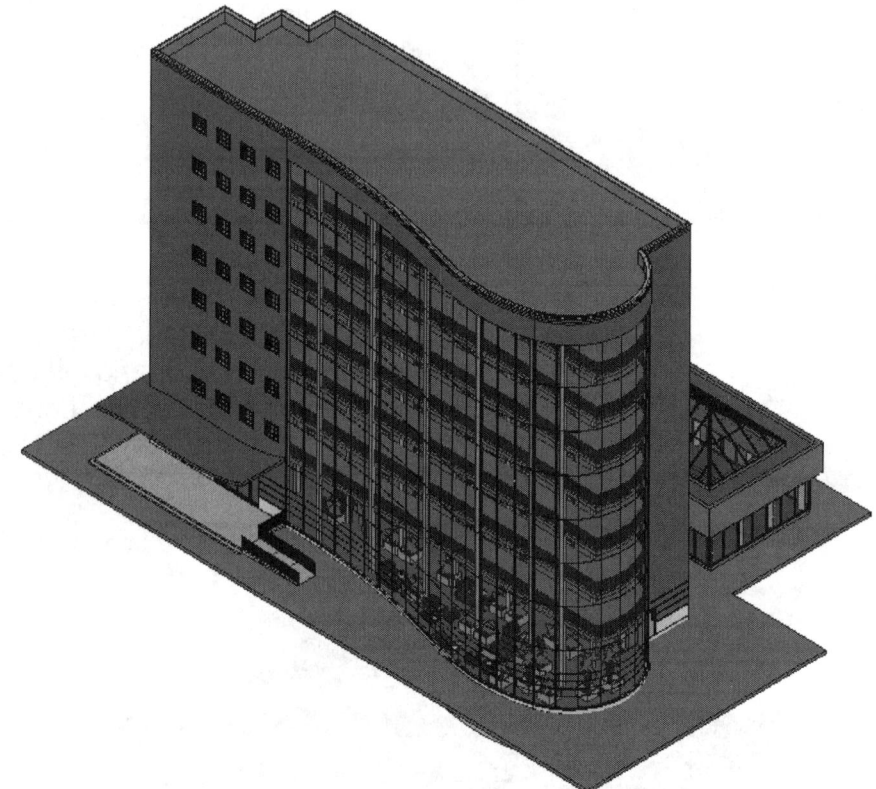

**Figure 1–65**

- This is a version of the main project you will work on throughout this guide.

Introduction to Revit

## Task 1 - Explore the interface.

1. In the *File* tab, expand (Open) and click (Project).

    - If you are on the Home screen, in the *MODELS* section, click **Open....**

2. In the Open dialog box, navigate to the practice files folder and select **Hotel-Final.rvt**.

3. Click **Open**. The 3D view of the modern hotel building opens in the view window.

4. In the Project Browser, expand the *Floor Plans* node. Double-click on **Floor 1** to open it. This view is referred to as **Floor Plans: Floor 1**.

*If the Project Browser and Properties are docked over each other, use the Project Browser tab at the bottom to display it.*

5. Take time to review the floor plan to get acquainted with it.

6. Review the various parts of the screen.

7. In the view, hover the cursor over one of the doors. A tooltip displays describing the element, as shown in Figure 1–66.

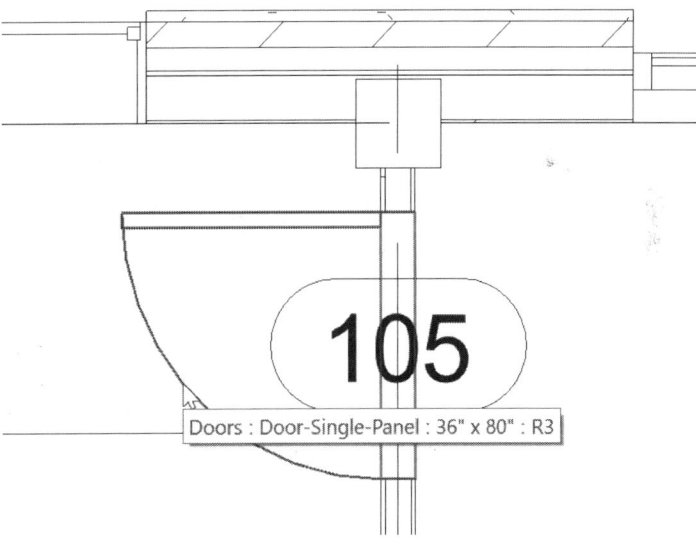

Figure 1–66

8. Hover the cursor over another element to display its description.

9. Select a door. The ribbon changes to the *Modify | Doors* tab.

10. Click in an empty space in the view to release the selection.

11. Hold <Ctrl> and select several elements of different types. The ribbon changes to the *Modify | Multi-Select* tab.

12. Press <Esc> to clear the selection.

13. In the *Architecture* tab>Build panel, click  (Wall), or type the shortcut **WA**. The ribbon changes to the *Modify | Place Wall* tab and at the end of the ribbon, the Draw panel is displayed. It contains tools that enable you to create walls. The rest of the ribbon displays the same tools that are found on the *Modify* tab.

14. In the Select panel, click  (Modify) to return to the main ribbon.

15. In the *Architecture* tab>Build panel, click  (Door), or type the shortcut **DR**. The ribbon changes to the *Modify | Place Door* tab and displays the options and tools you can use to create doors.

16. In the Select panel, click  (Modify) to return to the main ribbon.

17. Save the project.

### Task 2 - Look at views.

*You might need to widen the Project Browser to display the full names of the views.*

1. In the Project Browser, verify that the *Floor Plans* node is open. Note that some views have a blue icon next to them, which indicates that they have been placed on a sheet.

2. Right-click on **Floor 1** and select **Open Sheet**, as shown in Figure 1–67. Sheet A1.1 opens.

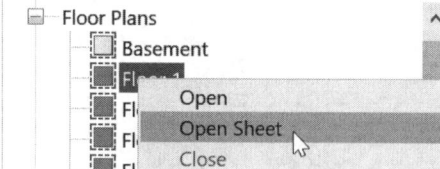

**Figure 1–67**

3. On the **A1.1 - Ground Floor Plan** tab, click on the X to close the view, as shown in Figure 1–68.

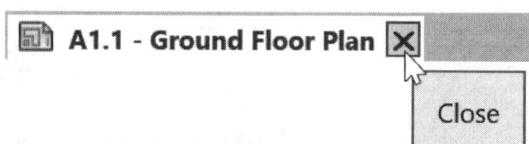

**Figure 1–68**

4. In the Project Browser, double-click on the **Floor 1 - Furniture Plan** view.

5. This floor plan displays with the furniture, but without the annotations that were displayed in the **Floor 1** view.

6. Open the **Floor 1 - Life Safety Plan** view by double-clicking on it.

7. The walls and furniture display, but the furniture is grayed out and red lines describing important life safety information display.

8. At the top of the views, click each tab to switch between the open views.

9. In the *View* tab>Windows panel, click ⊟ (Tile Views) or type **WT**. All of the open views are tiled. Type **ZA** (for Zoom All) to zoom out to the extents of each view, as shown in Figure 1–69.

    • Depending on which is the active view when you tile the views, the order they tile in may differ from what is shown in the image.

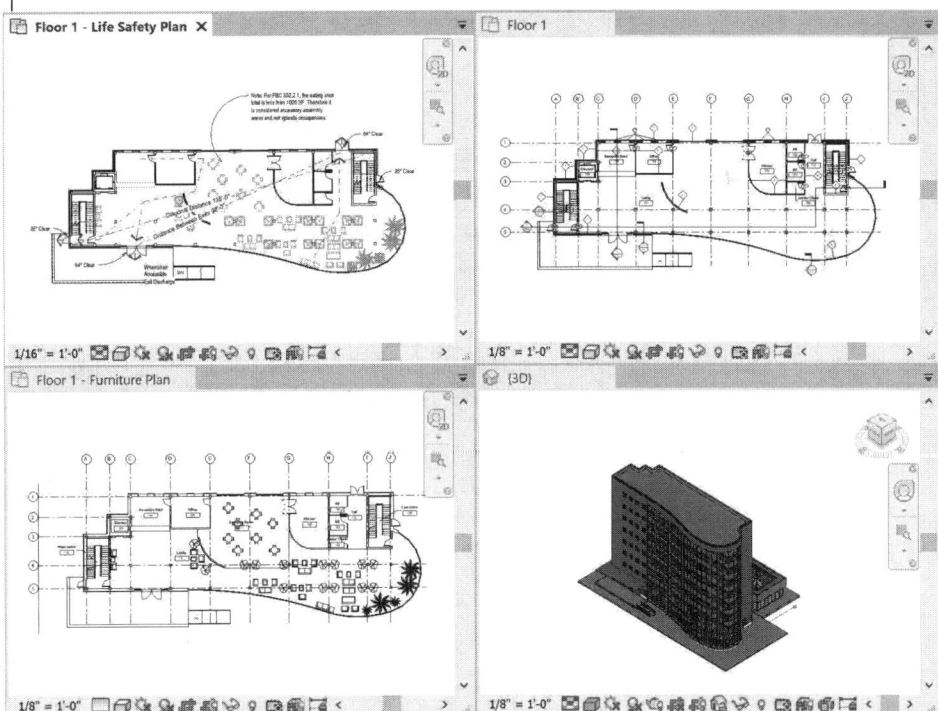

Figure 1–69

10. Click inside the Floor 1 view to make it active.

11. In the *View* tab>Windows panel, click ▢ (Tab Views), or type **TW**. The views return to the tabs and the Floor 1 view is first in the group of view tabs.

12. Type **ZA** to zoom all in the view.

13. Using your mouse wheel, zoom in to the left side of the view so that you can clearly see the east elevation marker, as shown in Figure 1–70.

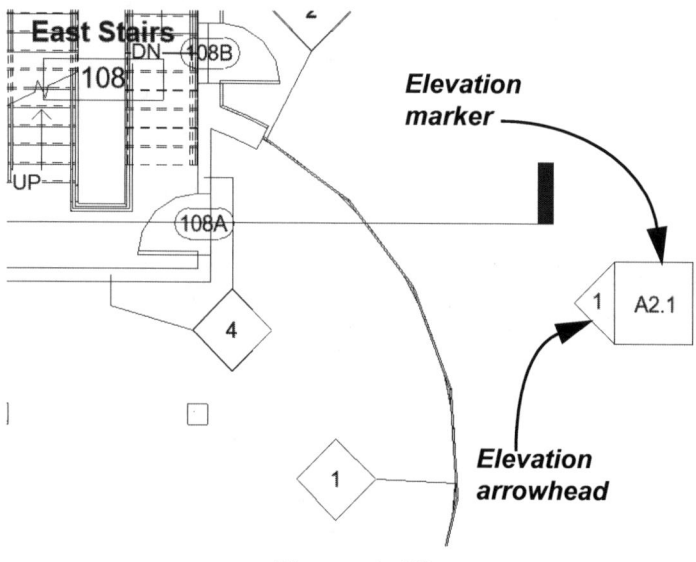

Figure 1–70

14. Double-click on the elevation arrowhead to open the view. The **East** elevation view opens.

15. Switch back to the Floor 1 view and type **ZA** to zoom all.

16. Using your mouse wheel, zoom in to the west side of the building and double-click on the **1/A2.2** section marker arrowhead, as shown in Figure 1–71.

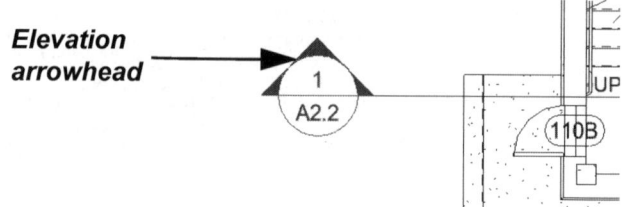

Figure 1–71

17. The **E/W Building Section** view opens.

18. In the Project Browser, expand *Sections (Building Section)* node and note that the **E/W Building Section** view is bold, meaning it is the active view.

19. At the bottom of the view window, in the View Control Bar, click ▢ (Visual Style) and select **Shaded**. The elements in the view are now easier to read.

20. In the Project Browser, scroll down to the *Sheets (all)* node and expand the node.

21. View several of the sheets. Some have views already applied (e.g., **A1.5 - Floor 2 - Floor Plan View**, as shown in Figure 1–72).

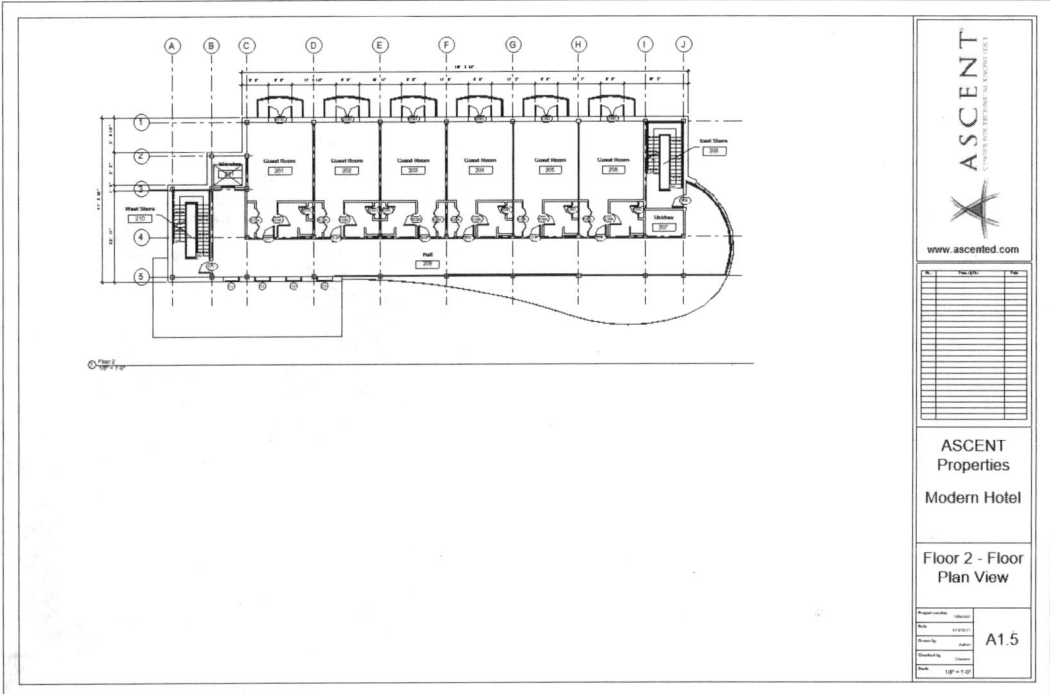

Figure 1–72

22. Save the project.

## Task 3 - Practice viewing tools.

1. At the far right of the view tabs, expand Switch Windows and select **Floor 1**, as shown in Figure 1–73.

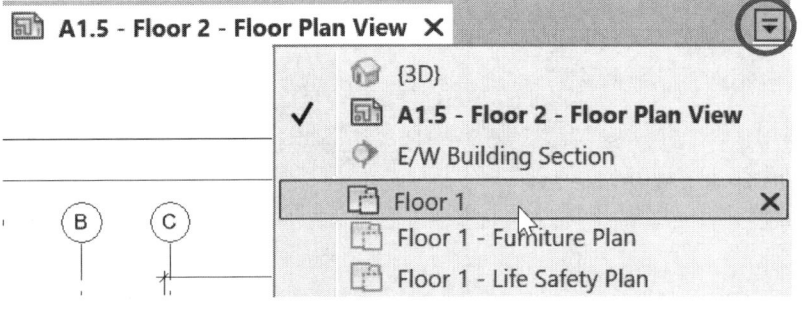

Figure 1–73

2. In the Navigation Bar, click and select **Zoom In Region** or type **ZR**. Zoom in on the stairs.

3. Pan to another part of the building by holding and dragging the middle mouse button or wheel. Alternatively, you can use the 2D Wheel in the Navigation Bar.

4. Double-click on the mouse wheel to zoom out to fit the extents of the view.

5. In the Quick Access Toolbar, click (Default 3D View) to open the default 3D view, as shown in Figure 1–74.

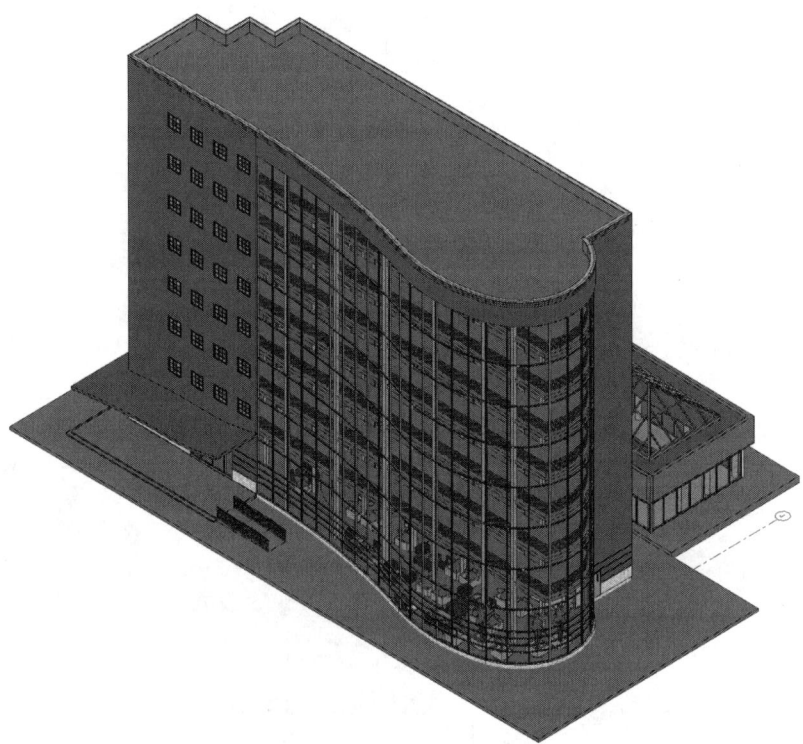

**Figure 1–74**

6. Hold <Shift> and use the middle mouse button or wheel to orbit the model in the 3D view.

7. In the View Control Bar, change the *Visual Style* to (Shaded). Then, try (Consistent Colors). Which one works best when you view the back of the building?

8. Use the ViewCube to find a view that you want to use.

*The ViewCube is located in the upper right corner of the view.*

# Introduction to Revit

9. In the Project Browser, expand *3D Views* and right-click on the {3D} view and select **Rename....** and type in a new name for the view as **3D Model**. Alternatively, you can slowly click twice on the view name to rename the view.

10. Review the other 3D views that have already been created.

11. In the Quick Access Toolbar, click (Default 3D View). A new **{3D}** view is created and appears in the Project Browser within the *3D Views* section.

12. Press <Ctrl>+<Tab> to cycle through the open views.

13. In the Quick Access Toolbar, expand (Switch Windows) and select the **Hotel-Final.rvt - Floor Plan: Floor 1** view, as shown in Figure 1–75.

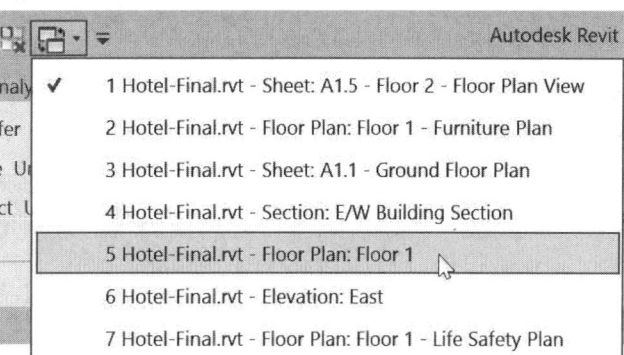

Figure 1–75

14. In the Quick Access Toolbar, click (Close Inactive Views). This closes all of the other windows except the one in which you are working.

15. In the Quick Access Toolbar, expand (Default 3D View) and click (Camera), as shown in Figure 1–76.

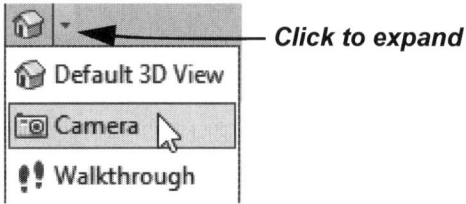

Figure 1–76

16. Click the first point near the Lobby room name and click the second point (target) outside the building, as shown in Figure 1–77.

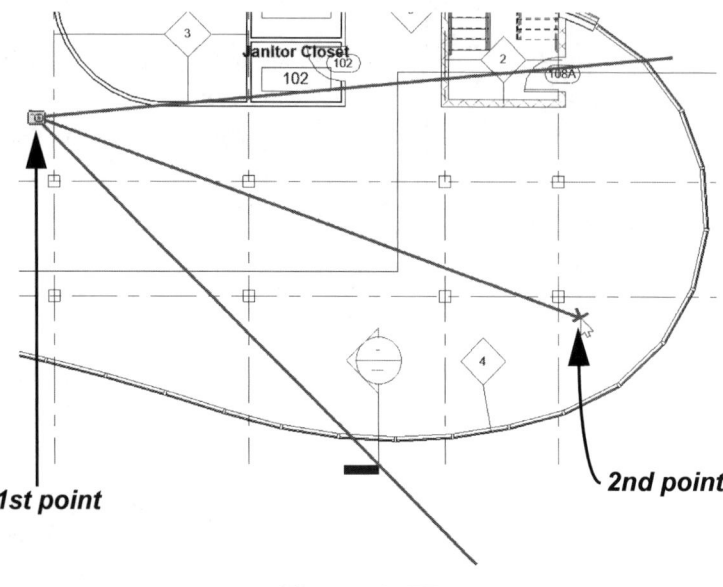

**Figure 1–77**

17. The furniture and planters display even though they did not display in the floor plan view.

18. In the View Control Bar, set the *Visual Style* to (Realistic).

19. In the Project Browser, right-click on the new camera view and select **Rename...**. Type **CAM - Lobby Seating Area**.

20. In the Quick Access Toolbar, click (Save) to save the project.

21. In the *File* tab, click (Close). This closes the entire project.

# Chapter Review Questions

1. When you create a project in Revit, do you work in 3D or 2D?

    a. You work in 2D in plan views and in 3D in non-plan views.

    b. You work in 3D almost all of the time, even when you are using what looks like a flat view.

    c. You work in 2D or 3D depending on how you toggle the 2D/3D control.

    d. You work in 2D in plan and section views and in 3D in isometric views.

2. What is the purpose of the Project Browser?

    a. It enables you to browse through the building project, similar to a walk through.

    b. It is the interface for managing all of the files that are required to create the complete architectural model of the building.

    c. It manages multiple Revit projects as an alternative to using Windows Explorer.

    d. It is used to access and manage the views of the project.

3. Where do you change the Visual Style?

    a. Ribbon

    b. View Control Bar

    c. Options Bar

    d. Properties

4. What is the difference between Type Properties and Properties?

    a. Properties stores parameters that apply to the selected individual element(s). Type Properties stores parameters that impact every element of the same type in the project.

    b. Properties stores the location parameters of an element. Type Properties stores the size and identity parameters of an element.

    c. Properties only stores parameters of the view. Type Properties stores parameters of model components.

5. When you start a new project, how do you specify the base information in the new file?

   a. Transfer the base information from an existing project.

   b. Select the right template for the task.

   c. Revit automatically extracts the base information from imported or linked file(s).

6. What is the main difference between a view made using (Default 3D View) and a view made using (Camera)?

   a. Use Default **3D View** for exterior views and **Camera** for interiors.

   b. **Default 3D View** creates a static image and a **Camera** view is live and always updated.

   c. **Default 3D View** is isometric and a **Camera** view is perspective.

   d. **Default 3D View** is used for the overall building and a **Camera** view is used for looking in tight spaces.

Introduction to Revit

# Command Summary

| Button | Command | Location |
|---|---|---|
| **General Tools** | | |
| | Home | • **Quick Access Toolbar**<br>• **Shortcut:** <Ctrl>+<D> |
| | Modify | • **Ribbon:** All tabs>Select panel<br>• **Shortcut:** MD |
| | New | • *File* tab<br>• **Shortcut:** <Ctrl>+<N> |
| | Open | • **Quick Access Toolbar**<br>• *File* tab<br>• **Shortcut:** <Ctrl>+<O> |
| | Open Documents | • *File* tab |
| | Properties | • **Ribbon:** *Modify* tab>Properties panel<br>• **Shortcut:** PP |
| | Recent Documents | • *File* tab |
| | Save | • **Quick Access Toolbar**<br>• *File* tab<br>• **Shortcut:** <Ctrl>+<S> |
| | Synchronize and Modify Settings | • **Quick Access Toolbar** |
| | Synchronize Now | • **Quick Access Toolbar**>expand Synchronize and Modify Settings |
| | Type Properties | • **Ribbon:** *Modify* tab>Properties panel<br>• **Properties**>Edit Type |
| **Select Tools** | | |
| | Drag elements on selection | • **Ribbon:** All tabs>expanded Select panel<br>• **Status Bar** |
| | Filter | • **Ribbon:** *Modify | Multi-Select* tab> Filter panel<br>• **Status Bar** |
| | Select Elements By Face | • **Ribbon:** All tabs>expanded Select panel<br>• **Status Bar** |
| | Select Links | • **Ribbon:** All tabs>expanded Select panel<br>• **Status Bar** |
| | Select Pinned Elements | • **Ribbon:** All tabs>expanded Select panel<br>• **Status Bar** |

|  | Select Underlay Elements | • **Ribbon:** All tabs>expanded Select panel<br>• **Status Bar** |
|---|---|---|
| **Viewing Tools** | | |
|  | Camera | • **Quick Access Toolbar**>expand Default 3D View<br>• **Ribbon:** *View* tab>Create panel> expand Default 3D View |
|  | Close Inactive Views | • **Quick Access Toolbar**<br>• **Ribbon:** *View* tab>Windows panel |
|  | Default 3D View | • **Quick Access Toolbar**<br>• **Ribbon:** *View* tab>Create panel |
|  | Home | • **ViewCube** |
| N/A | Next Pan/Zoom | • **Navigation Bar**<br>• **Shortcut Menu** |
| N/A | Previous Pan/Zoom | • **Navigation Bar**<br>• **Shortcut Menu**<br>• **Shortcut:** ZP |
|  | Shadows On/Off | • **View Control Bar** |
|  | Show Rendering Dialog/ Render | • **View Control Bar**<br>• **Ribbon:** *View* tab>Graphics panel<br>• **Shortcut:** RR |
|  | Switch Windows | • **Quick Access Toolbar**<br>• **Ribbon:** *View* tab>Windows panel |
|  | Tab Views | • **Ribbon:** *View* tab>Windows panel<br>• **Shortcut:** TW |
|  | Tile Views | • **Ribbon:** *View* tab> Windows panel<br>• **Shortcut:** WT |
|  | Zoom All to Fit | • **Navigation Bar**<br>• **Shortcut:** ZA |
|  | Zoom in Region | • **Navigation Bar**<br>• **Shortcut Menu**<br>• **Shortcut:** ZR |
|  | Zoom Out (2x) | • **Navigation Bar**<br>• **Shortcut Menu**<br>• **Shortcut:** ZO |
|  | Zoom Sheet Size | • **Navigation Bar**<br>• **Shortcut:** ZS |
|  | Zoom to Fit | • **Navigation Bar**<br>• **Shortcut Menu**<br>• **Shortcut:** ZF, ZE |

| Visual Styles | | | |
|---|---|---|---|
| | 🔲 | **Consistent Colors** | • **View Control Bar**: |
| | 🔲 | **Hidden Line** | • **View Control Bar**<br>• **Shortcut:** HL |
| | 🔲 | **Realistic** | • **View Control Bar** |
| | 🔲 | **Shaded** | • **View Control Bar**<br>• **Shortcut:** SD |
| | 🔲 | **Wireframe** | • **View Control Bar**<br>• **Shortcut:** WF |

# Chapter 2

# Starting a Project

Starting a project in Revit begins by using a template. You can then link in a CAD file or an existing Revit model, if these are available. From there, you can add the framework for a building, including levels to define vertical heights and grids to define the structural layout for architectural and structural columns.

## Learning Objectives in This Chapter

- Link and import CAD files to be used as a basis for developing a design.
- Link and import raster image and PDF files.
- Link existing Revit models to develop and coordinate with other disciplines.
- Add and modify levels to define floor-to-floor heights and other vertical references.
- Add and modify grids to provide locations for model elements.

# 2.1 Selecting a Project Template

New projects are based on a project template file. The template file includes preset levels, views, and some families, such as wall styles and text styles. When using templates, most of the views are set to display only the elements specific to the template, so it is best practice to select a template that reflects your company's discipline.

- Check with your BIM manager about which template you need to use for your projects. Your company might have more than one based on the type of project you are designing.

### How To: Start a New Project

1. In the *File* tab, expand (New) and click (Project), as shown in Figure 2–1, or press <Ctrl>+<N>.

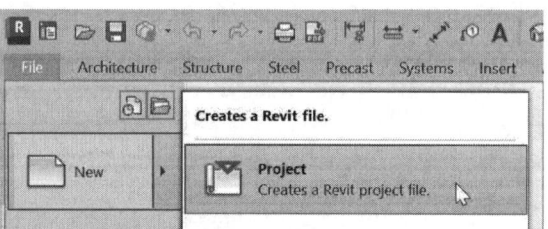

Figure 2–1

2. In the New Project dialog box (shown in Figure 2–2), select the template that you want to use and click **OK**.

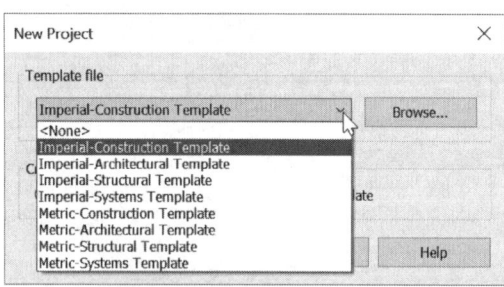

Figure 2–2

*The list of template files is set in the Options dialog box in the File Locations tab. It might vary depending on the installed product and company standards.*

> **Hint: Revit Worksharing**
>
> If established by your company that worksharing is needed, you would typically want to start a worksharing project on your local network once a project has been created.
>
> - For more information on worksharing, see *A.9 Introduction to Revit Worksharing*.
>
> - For more information about establishing and using worksets, refer to the ASCENT guide *Autodesk Revit: Collaboration Tools*.

## 2.2 Linking and Importing Files

### Linking and Importing CAD Files

CAD files can be imported or linked into a Revit project. As an example, a designer might lay out a floor plan using the standard 2D AutoCAD software, and you then need to incorporate that information into your structural model. In addition, many renovation projects start with existing 2D drawings. Instead of redrawing from scratch, link or import the CAD file (as shown in Figure 2–3) and trace over it in Revit. You can also print a hybrid drawing that is part Revit project and part imported/linked drawing.

*When you select an imported or linked CAD file, you can see in the tooltip that it is called an Import Symbol.*

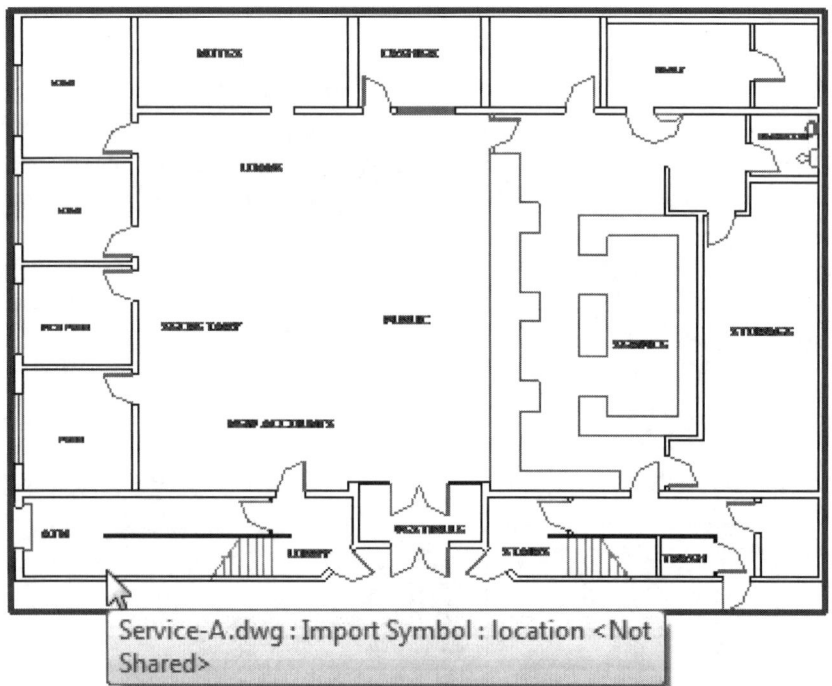

Figure 2–3

- When you hover your cursor over an imported or linked CAD file, a tooltip displays indicating that it is an import file.

- CAD file formats that can be imported or linked include AutoCAD® (DWG and DXF), MicroStation (DGN), 3D ACIS modeling kernel (SAT), Trimble SketchUp (SKP), FormIt (AXM), 3D Shape (OBJ and STL), and Rhino (3dm).

- When linking or importing a CAD file, you can specify a level or a named horizontal reference plane in the project to position the CAD file at.

# Starting a Project

## Linking vs. Importing

- **Link:** A connection is maintained with the original file and the link updates if the original file is updated.

- **Import:** No connection is maintained with the original file. It becomes a separate element in the Revit model.

## How To: Link or Import a CAD File

1. Open the view into which you want to link or import the file.
   - For a 2D file, this should be a 2D view. For a 3D file, open a 3D view.

2. In the *Insert* tab>Link panel, click (Link CAD), or in the *Insert* tab>Import panel, click (Import CAD).

3. In the Link CAD Formats (shown in Figure 2–4) or Import CAD Formats dialog box, select the file that you want to import.
   - Select a file format in the **Files of type** drop-down list to limit the files that are displayed.

*The dialog boxes for Link CAD Formats and Import CAD Formats are the same.*

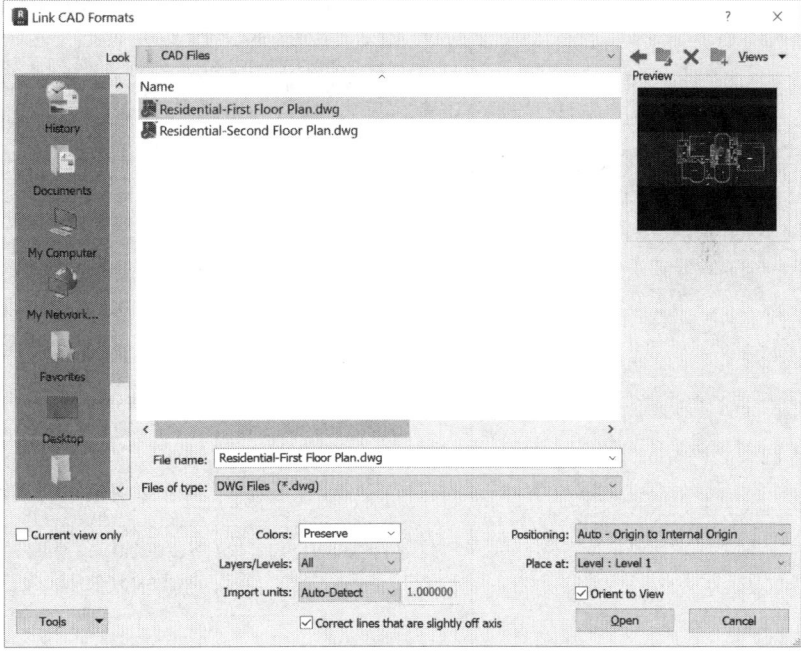

Figure 2–4

4. If **Current view only** is selected, as shown in Figure 2–5, you can set all options except the *Place at* and the *Orient to View* options. The view will only display in the current view.

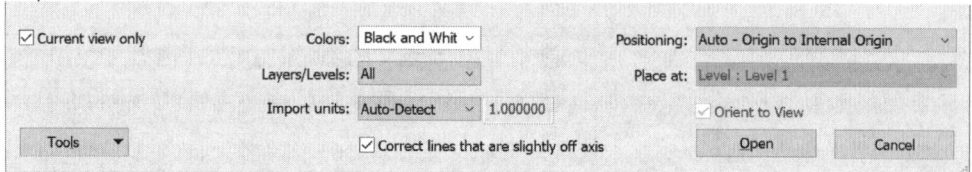

Figure 2–5

5. If you would like to place the CAD file at a level or reference plane, verify **Current view only** is unchecked and set the *Place at* option, as shown in Figure 2–6.

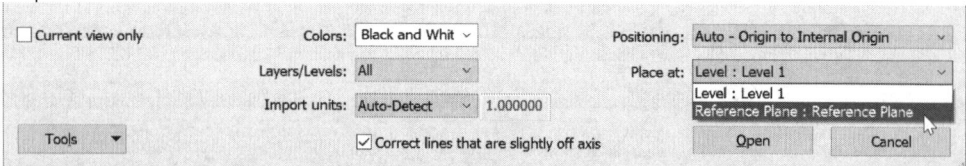

Figure 2–6

6. Click **Open**.

## Link and Import Options

| | |
|---|---|
| **Current view only** | Determine whether the CAD file is placed in every view, or only in the current view. This is especially useful if you are working with a 2D floor plan that you only need to have in one view. |
| **Colors** | Specify the color settings. Typical Revit projects are mainly black and white. However, other software frequently uses color. You can **Invert** the original colors, **Preserve** them, or change everything to **Black and White**. |
| **Layers/Levels** | Indicates which CAD layers are going to be brought into the model. Select how you want layers to be imported: **All**, **Visible**, or **Specify**.... |
| **Import units** | Select the units of the original file, as required. **Auto-Detect** works in most cases. |
| **Correct lines...** | If lines in a CAD file are off axis by less than 0.1 degree, selecting this option straightens them. It is selected by default. |

# Starting a Project

| Positioning | Specify how you want the imported file to be positioned in the current project:<br><br>Auto - Center to Center    Auto - Center to Center<br>Auto - Origin to Internal Origin    Auto - Origin to Internal Origin<br>Manual - Origin    Auto - By Shared Coordinates<br>Manual - Center    Manual - Origin<br>    Manual - Center<br><br>    *Import option*        *Linking option*<br><br>The default position is **Auto - Origin to Internal Origin**. |
|---|---|
| **Place at** | Select a level or named reference plane at which to place the imported file. If you selected **Current view only**, this option is grayed out. |
| **Orient to View** | Used to orient the CAD file on import/link. |

- When a file is positioned **Auto - Origin to Internal Origin**, it is pinned in place and cannot be moved. To move the file, click on the pin to unpin it, as shown in Figure 2–7.

*For more information on importing and linking CAD files, see the ASCENT guide Autodesk Revit: Collaboration Tools.*

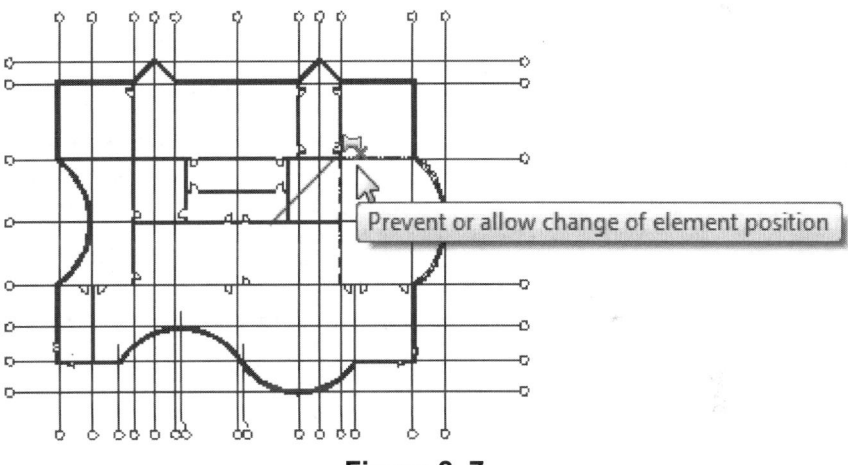

Figure 2–7

## Linking and Importing Raster Image Files

Raster images are made up of pixels or dots in a file that create a picture. For example, a raster file is created when you scan a blueprint and then import or link it into Revit to reference or trace. You can add raster images to any 2D view, including sheet views (as shown in Figure 2–8). They can be used as background views or as part of the final drawing. Imported or linked images can be placed behind model objects and annotations.

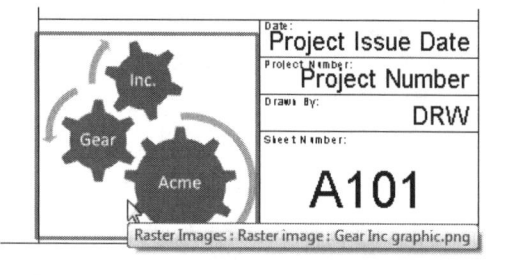

Figure 2–8

- Link a PDF or raster image into a 2D view if you need to reference a file that will be updated throughout the project cycle and to keep the project's file size from increasing when importing files.

- Linked PDFs or raster images can be scaled, rotated, and moved just like an imported PDF or raster image. Any changes made to the PDF or raster image will update in the project it is linked into when you open the project.

- A PDF can be imported into Revit as a raster image. If the PDF contains vector data, you can snap to the elements in the PDF.

*For more information about the different types of files and how to import them, refer to the ASCENT guide Autodesk Revit: Collaboration Tools.*

### How To: Import and Link an Image

| To... | Then... |
| --- | --- |
| Import an image file | In the *Insert* tab>Import panel, click (Import Image). |
| Link an image file | In the *Insert* tab>Link panel, click (Link Image). |

1. In the Import Image or Link Image dialog box, select the image you want to insert. You can insert .BMP, .JPG, .JPEG, .PNG, and .TIF files.

# Starting a Project

2. Click **Open**. Four blue dots and an "x" illustrate the default size of the image file, as shown on the left in Figure 2–9. Click on the screen to place the image. It displays with the shape handles still visible, as shown on the right in Figure 2–9.

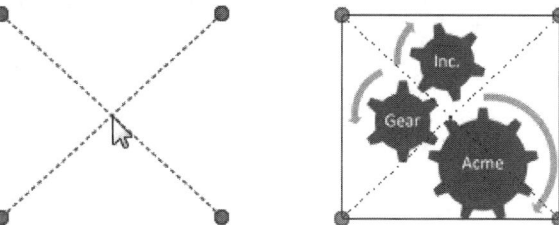

Figure 2–9

- In Properties, you can adjust the height and width and also set the *Draw Layer* to either **Background** or **Foreground**, as shown in Figure 2–10.

| Dimensions | |
|---|---|
| Width | 1' 5 185/256" |
| Height | 1' 1 41/64" |
| Horizontal Scale | 1.000000 |
| Vertical Scale | 1.000000 |
| Lock Proportions | ✓ |
| Other | |
| Draw Layer | Background |

Figure 2–10

- You can select more than one image at a time and move them as a group to the background or foreground.

- In the *Modify | Raster Images* tab (shown in Figure 2–11), you can access the Arrange options and **Manage Images**.

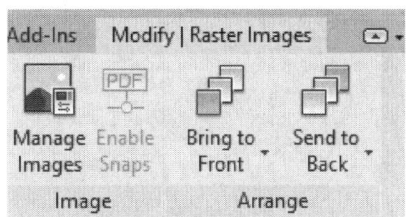

Figure 2–11

## Linking and Importing PDF Files

PDF files are often created for sharing information with people that do not have the original program and when you do not want anyone to change the original information. They can also be used as underlays when the original information includes vector data.

### How To: Import and Link a PDF File

| To... | Then... |
| --- | --- |
| Import a PDF file | In the *Insert* tab>Import panel, click (Import PDF). |
| Link a PDF file | In the *Insert* tab>Link panel, click (Link PDF). |

1. In the Import PDF or Link PDF dialog box, navigate to the location where the PDF file is stored, select it, and click **Open**.
2. In the Import PDF or Link PDF dialog box (Figure 2–12 shows the Import PDF dialog box), select the page you want to import/link and click **OK**.

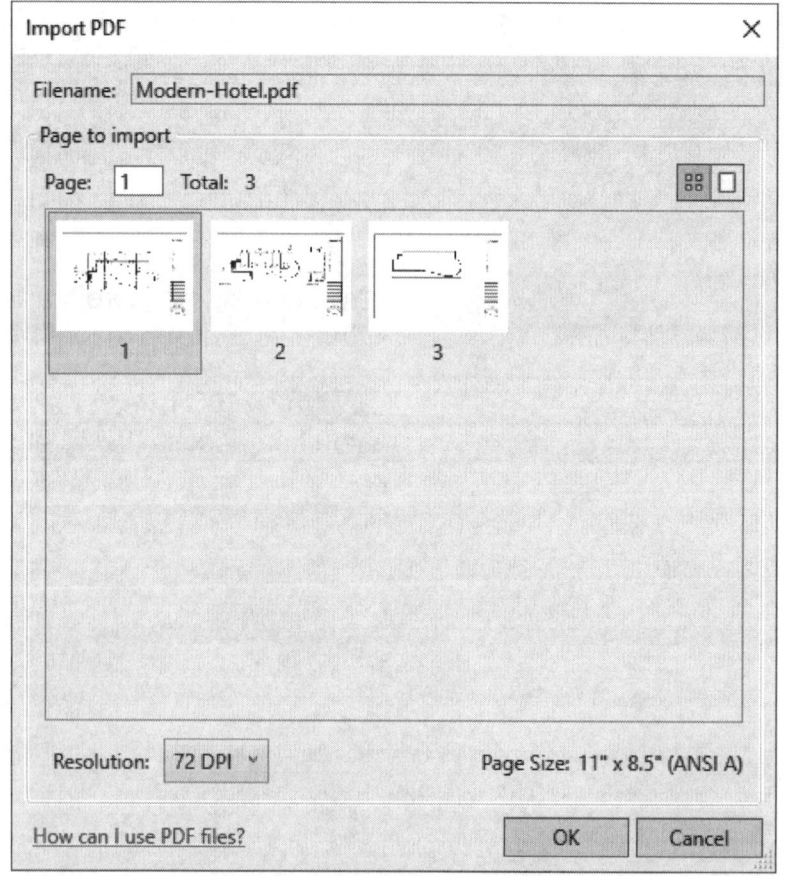

Figure 2–12

- Only one page can be imported/linked at a time, but you can import/link additional pages by repeating the process.

3. In Properties, you can specify the size and scale of the image, as shown in Figure 2–13.
    - If the PDF comes from a vector source, you can also choose to enable snaps and trace over the elements in the PDF.
    - The Foreground/Background status can also be set in the Options Bar and in Properties.

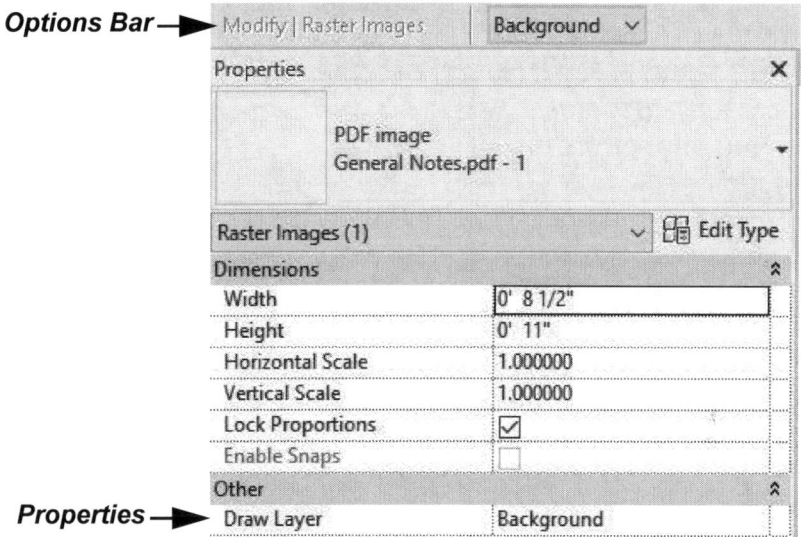

Figure 2–13

## 2.3 Linking in Revit Models

You can link Revit models directly into a project. These models can be an existing building that you are creating an addition to, as shown in Figure 2–14, or engineering models that you are checking to ensure that they line up with your model. They are also used for campus-like projects where the same building is repeated multiple times. They are full 3D models.

*A linked model automatically updates when the original file is changed.*

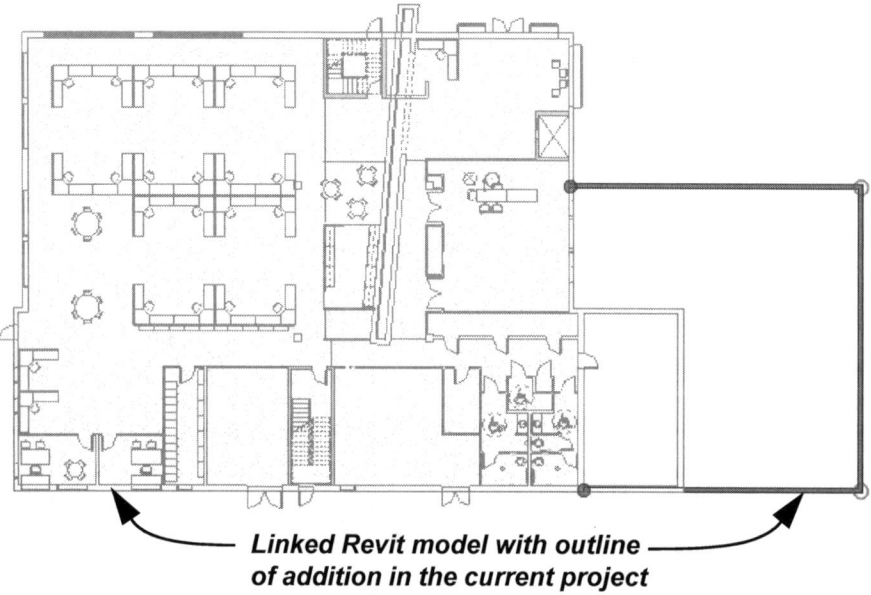

**Linked Revit model with outline of addition in the current project**

Figure 2–14

- Architectural, structural, and MEP models created in Revit can be linked to each other as long as they are from the same release cycle.

- When you use linked models, clashes between disciplines can be detected and information can be passed between disciplines.

- Revit models are always linked. They cannot be imported.

# Starting a Project

## How To: Add a Linked Model to a Host Project

1. In the *Insert* tab>Link panel, click ![Link Revit icon] (Link Revit).
2. In the Import/Link RVT dialog box, select the file that you want to link. Before opening the file, set the *Positioning*, as shown in Figure 2–15.

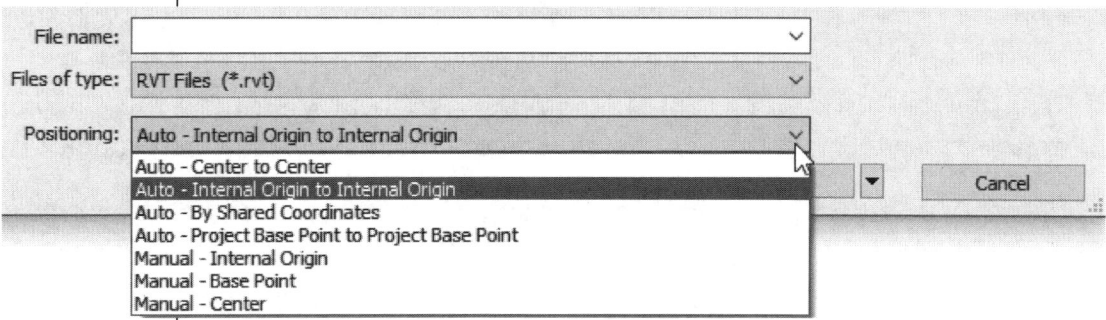

Figure 2–15

3. Click **Open**.
4. Depending on how you decide to position the file, it is automatically placed in the project or you can manually place it with the cursor.

As the links are loading, do not click on the screen or click any buttons. The more links present in a project, the longer it takes to load.

## 2.4 Modifying Imported/Linked Files

When you select an imported/linked file, you can modify it by arranging the Foreground/Background status, modifying its Type Properties, querying information about elements in the file, and deleting layers. You can also modify the Visibility/Graphic Overrides of each imported/linked instance.

- An imported/linked file is called an *import symbol* once it is inserted into a project, as shown in Figure 2–16.

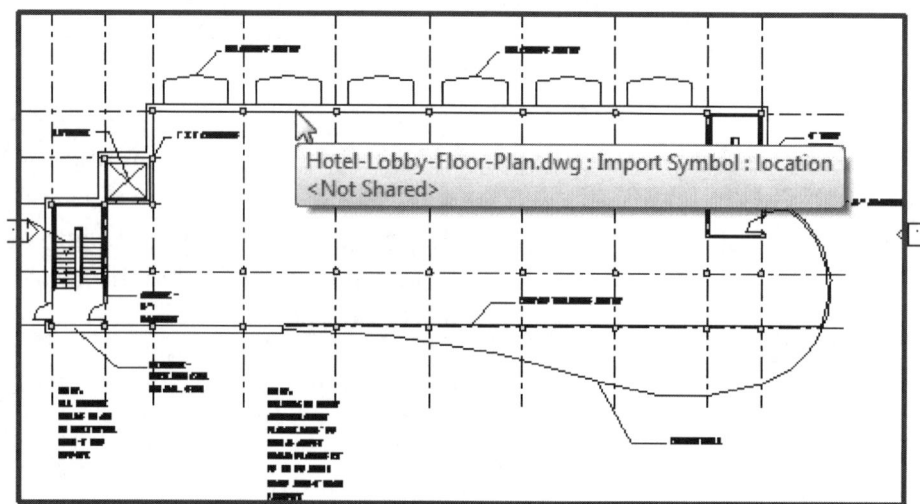

Figure 2–16

### Setting an Imported or Linked File to Halftone

To see the difference between the host model elements and the linked or imported file, you can set the linked/imported file to halftone, as shown in Figure 2–17.

Starting a Project

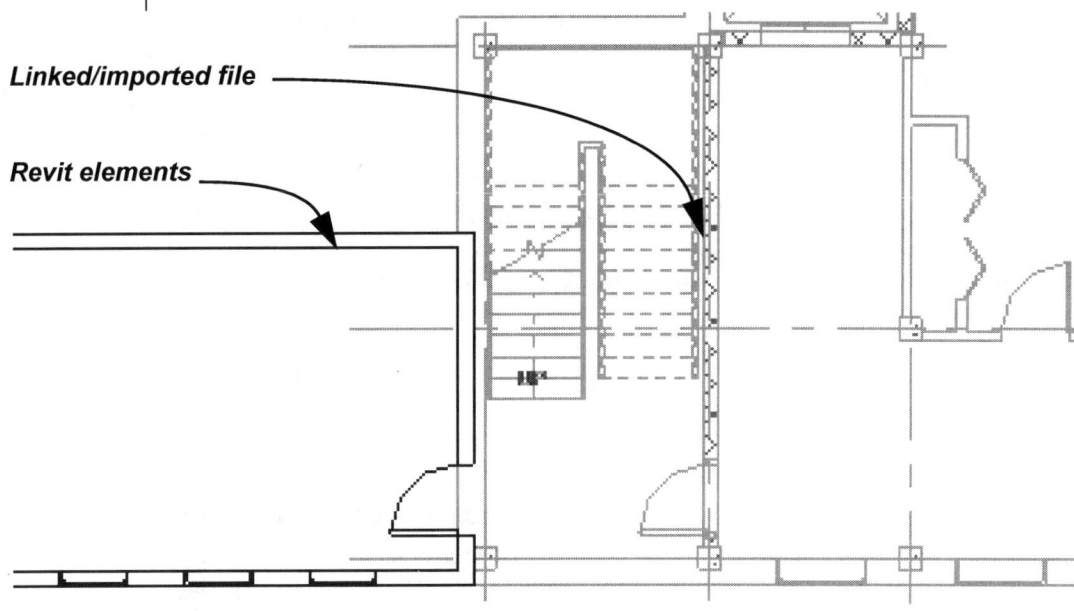

Figure 2–17

## How To: Set an Element Halftone

1. Select the imported file.
2. Right-click and select **Override Graphics in View>By Element...**.
3. In the View Specific Element Graphics dialog box, select **Halftone**, as shown in Figure 2–18.

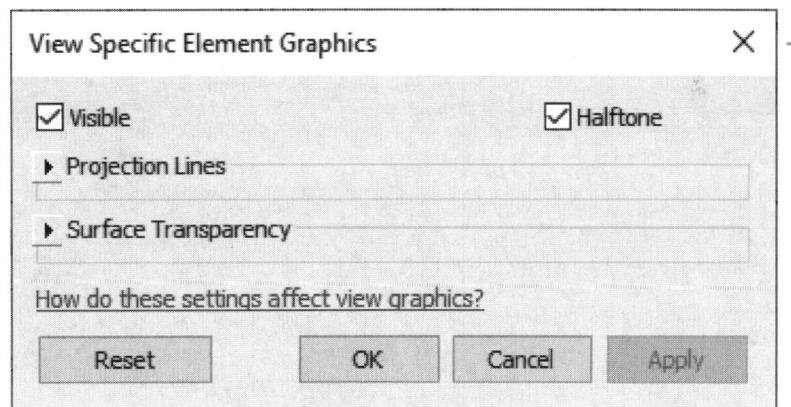

Figure 2–18

4. Click **OK**.

- You can use this method to set any element or category to halftone.

## Draw Layer

Linked CAD files are typically in the background of a view. To change this, select the CAD file in the view and in the Options Bar or in Properties, in the *Other* section, change the *Draw Layer* to **Foreground**.

## Editing Raster Files

Select an imported/linked image to make changes. Once it is selected, you can resize the image as you did when you first inserted it or specify the *Width* and *Height* values in Properties.

- Select **Lock Proportions** in the Options Bar to ensure that the length and width resize proportionally to each other when you adjust the size of an image.

- Use the standard modification tools to **Move**, **Copy**, **Rotate**, **Mirror**, **Array**, and **Scale** images. Images can also be grouped together into detail groups.

- The Foreground/Background status can also be set in the Options Bar and in Properties, as shown in Figure 2–19.

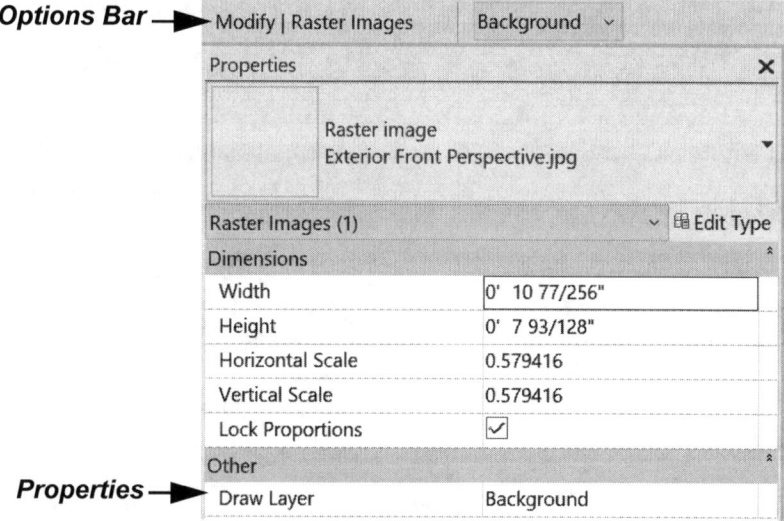

Figure 2–19

- In the *Modify | Raster Images* tab>Arrange panel (shown in Figure 2–20), use the Arrange tools to move images to the front or back of other images or objects.

# Starting a Project

- You can snap to edges of images, as shown in Figure 2–21.

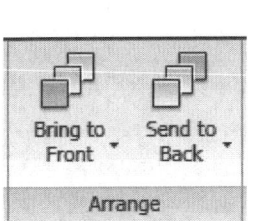

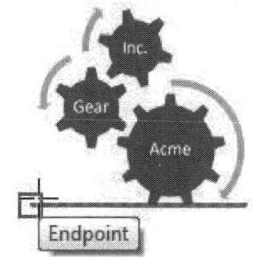

Figure 2–20

Figure 2–21

## Managing Links

The Manage Links dialog box (shown in Figure 2–22) enables you to reload, unload, add, and remove links, and it also provides access for you to set other options. To open the Manage Links dialog box, in the *Insert* tab>Link panel, click (Manage Links). Alternatively, you can go to the *Manage* tab>Manage Projects panel and click (Manage Links).

- You can also select the link and click (Manage Links) in the *Modify | RVT Links* tab>Link panel.

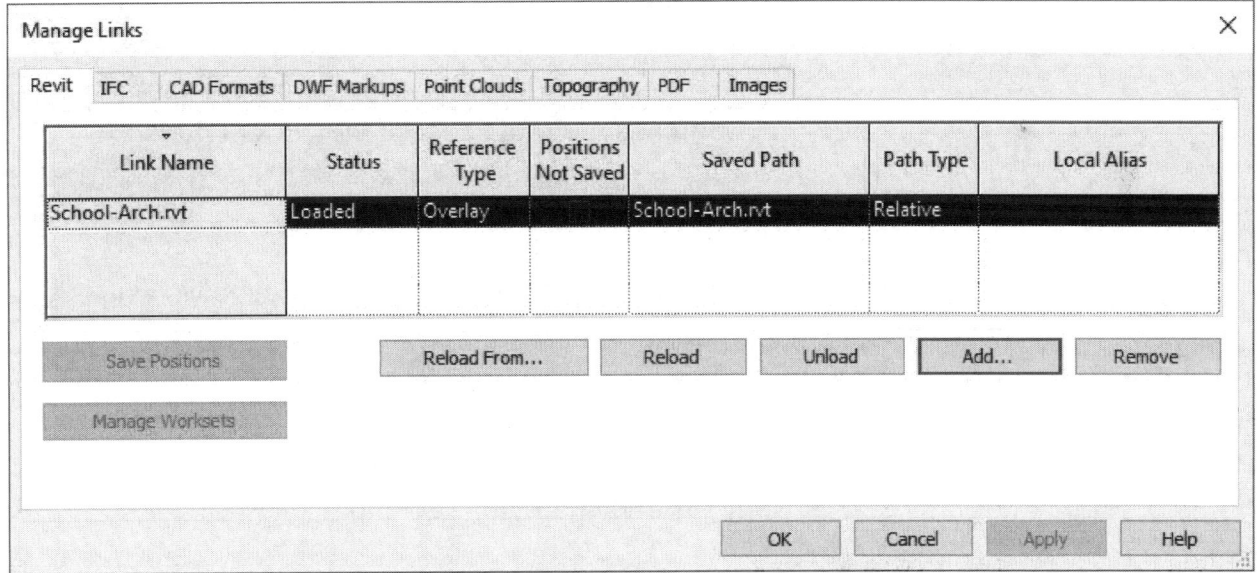

Figure 2–22

- The Manage Links dialog box does not show imported CAD files.

- You can manage both imported and linked images and PDFs.

*Some of these options are also available in the Project Browser. Expand the Revit Links node, then right-click on the Revit Link and select **Reload**, **Unload**, or **Reload From**….*

The following options are available:

- **Reload From:** Opens the Add Link dialog box, which enables you to select the file you want to reload. Use this if the linked file location or name has changed.
- **Reload:** Reloads the file without additional prompts.
- **Unload:** Unloads the file so that the link is kept, but the file is not displayed or calculated in the project. Use **Reload** to restore it.
- **Add:** Opens the Import/Link RVT dialog box, which enables you to link additional models into the host project.
- **Remove:** Deletes the link from the file.

Links can be nested into one another. How a link responds when the host project is linked into another project depends on the option in the *Reference Type* column.

- **Overlay:** The nested linked model is not referenced in the new host project.
- **Attach:** The nested linked model displays in the new host project.

The option in the *Path Type* column controls how the location of the link is remembered.

- **Relative**
  - Searches the root folder of the current project.
  - If the file is moved, the software still searches for it.
- **Absolute**
  - Searches the entire file path where the file was originally saved.
  - If the original file is moved, the software is not able to find it.
- Other options control how the linked file interfaces with worksets and shared positioning.

# Modifying the Visibility of Imported/Linked Files

If you have used the imported/linked file as a guideline for tracing, you can toggle off the visibility of the entire image using the Visibility/Graphic Overrides dialog box, without removing it from the project in case you need it later. You can also toggle off individual layers or levels.

## How To: Hide individual Layers

1. In the *View* tab>Graphics panel, click  (Visibility/Graphics), or type **VG** or **VV** to open the Visibility/Graphic Overrides dialog box.
2. Switch to the *Imported Categories* tab. It displays a list for each imported instance and their layers/levels, as shown in Figure 2–23.
3. To have the linked/imported file display in halftone, check the box in the *Halftone* column.

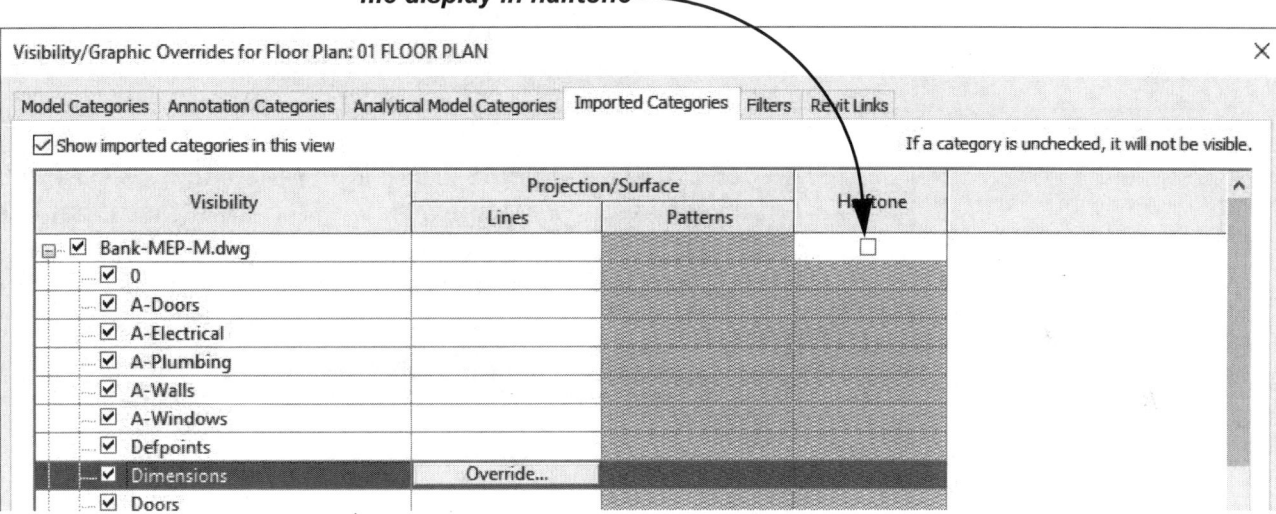

Figure 2–23

4. Click the plus sign beside the file name to expand a list of the layers or levels in that file.
5. Clear the check mark from the individual layers that you do not want to display.
   - Typically, these layers contain similar information, such as all windows or all notes in a drawing. However, it is not as definite as using Revit elements. An item might have been misplaced on a different layer and, if so, it does not toggle off.
6. Close the dialog box.

- To toggle off the entire file, clear the checkmark next to the file name.

## Temporarily Hide/Isolate

You might want to temporarily remove linked or imported files from a view, modify the project, and then restore the elements. Instead of completely toggling the elements off, you can temporarily hide them.

Select the elements you want to hide (make invisible) or isolate (keep displayed while all other elements are hidden) and click (Temporary Hide/Isolate). Select the method you want to use, as shown in Figure 2–24.

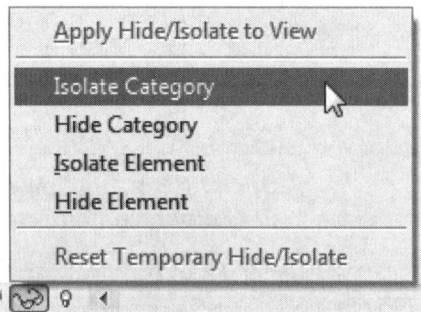

Figure 2–24

- The category or elements are hidden or isolated. A cyan border displays around the view with a note in the upper left corner, as shown in Figure 2–25. It indicates that the view contains temporarily hidden or isolated elements.

Figure 2–25

- Click (Temporary Hide/Isolate) again and select **Reset Temporary Hide/Isolate** to restore the elements to the view.

- If you want to permanently hide the elements in the view, select **Apply Hide/Isolate to View**.

- Elements that are temporarily hidden in a view are not hidden when the view is printed.

## Hide Elements in a View

When working in views, you can quickly hide linked or imported files. To hide the imported or linked file, select it and right-click to display the shortcut menu, then select **Hide in View** and select either **Elements** or **Category**, as shown in Figure 2–26.

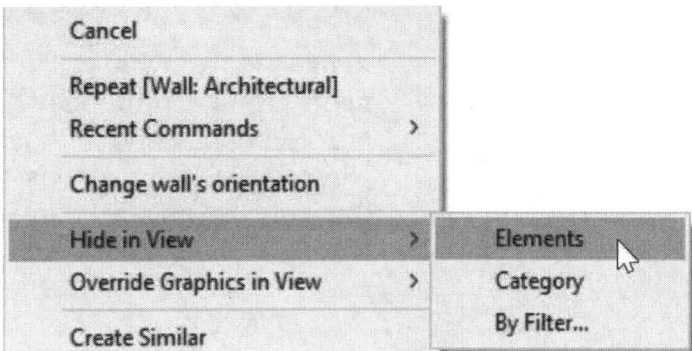

**Figure 2–26**

# Practice 2a  Start a Project and Link Files

## Practice Objectives

- Start a Revit project.
- Link a CAD file.
- Link a Revit file.

In this practice, you will start a Revit project, then import floor plans created in AutoCAD and use them as a base layout for the first floor lobby and for a typical guest floor. You will then link in a Revit model that includes a standard poolhouse and platform for the building, as shown in Figure 2–27.

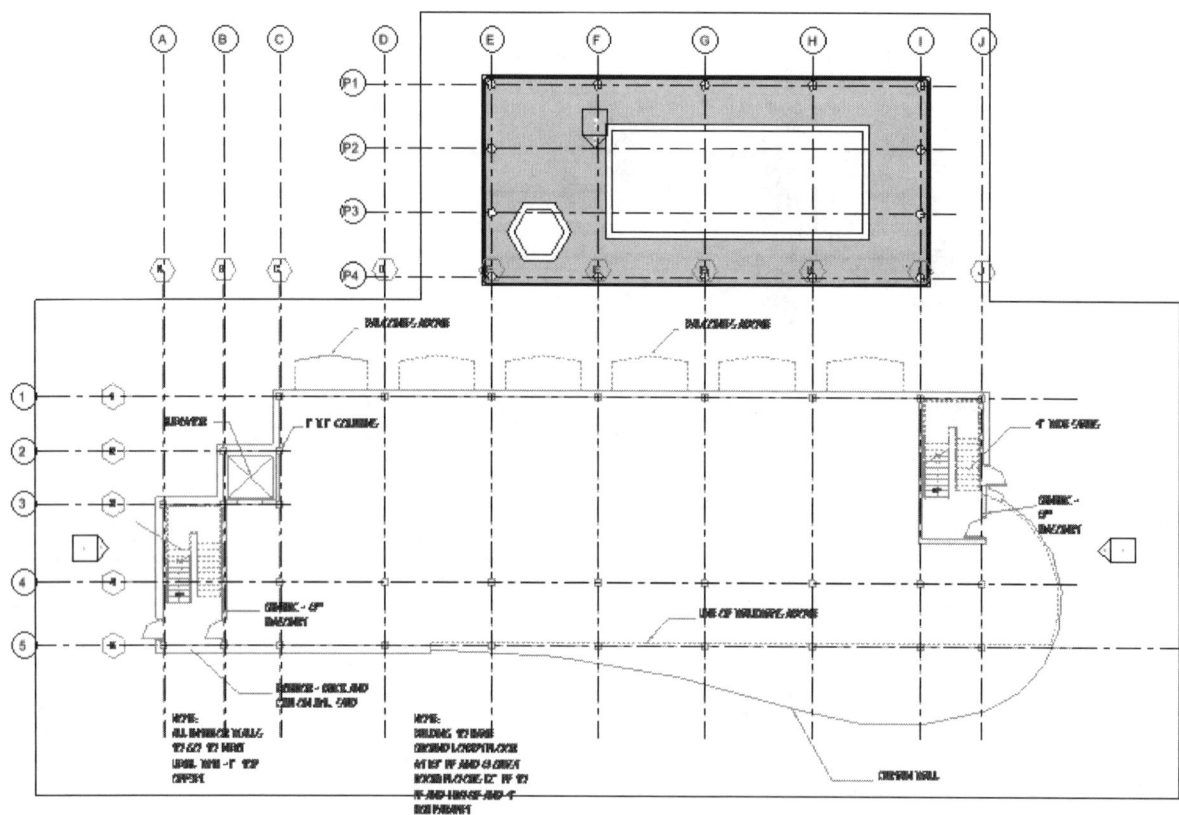

Figure 2–27

### Task 1 - Start a project.

1. In the *File* tab, expand  (New) and click  (Project).

    - Alternatively, if you are on the Home screen, click the **New** button under the *MODEL* section.

# Starting a Project

2. In the New Project dialog box, expand the *Template file* list, select the default **Imperial-Architectural Template**, and click **OK**. (There are no elements in this file, only datums and basic views.)

3. Save the project as **Hotel-Start.rvt**.

4. Review the Project Browser and note that the project has default floor plan, ceiling plan, and elevation views. By default, the **Floor Plans: Level 1** view is open and displays in bold in the Project Browser, as shown in Figure 2–28.

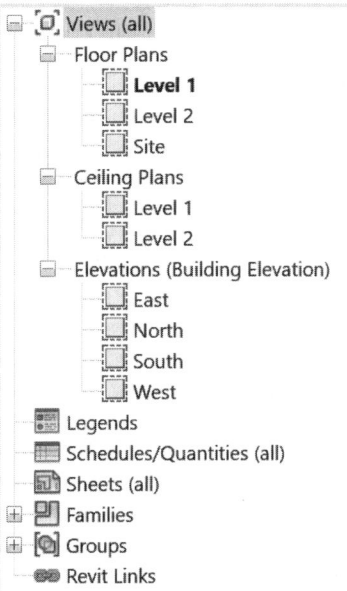

**Figure 2–28**

## Task 2 - Link a CAD file.

1. In the *Insert* tab>Link panel, click (Link CAD).

2. In the Link CAD Formats dialog box, navigate to the practice files *CAD Files* folder and select the file **Hotel-Level-1.dwg**, then set the following options:

    - Select **Current view only**
    - *Colors:* **Black and White**
    - *Layers/Levels:* **All**
    - *Import Units:* **Auto-Detect**
    - *Positioning:* **Auto - Origin to Internal Origin**

3. Click **Open**. The linked CAD file is placed in the project on the **Floor Plans: Level 1** view.

4. Select the linked CAD file. It is a single imported symbol and pinned in place because it was imported origin to internal origin.

5. In the Options Bar, change *Background* to **Foreground**.

6. With the CAD file still selected, right-click and select **Override Graphics in View>By Element...**.

7. In the View-Specific Element Graphics dialog box, select **Halftone** and click **OK**.

8. Click in an empty space in the view to release the selection. The linked file displays in halftone, as shown in Figure 2–29.

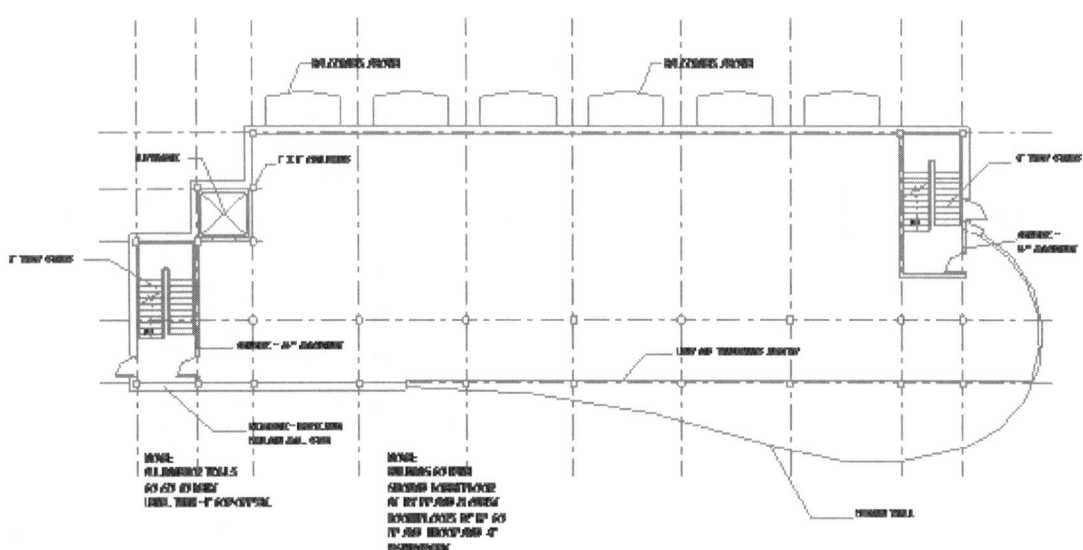

Figure 2–29

9. Open the **Floor Plans: Level 2** view. The CAD file linked in Level 1 does not display because you specified to link the CAD file with **Current view only** selected.

10. Link the CAD file **Hotel-Level-2.dwg** using the options that were used for Level 1.

11. Override the graphics and set the linked file to **Halftone**.

12. Save the project.

### Task 3 - Link in a Revit file.

1. In the Quick Access Toolbar, click (Default 3D View). Neither of the linked CAD files display in this view.

2. In the *Insert* tab>Link panel, click (Link Revit).

Starting a Project

3. Navigate to the practice files *Revit Link Files* folder and select **Hotel-Pool.rvt**. Verify that the *Positioning* is set to **Auto - Internal Origin to Internal Origin** and click **Open**.

4. In the View Control Bar, change the *Visual Style* to (Shaded).

5. Select one of the levels and type **VH** to hide in view.

6. Type **ZF** to fit all the model to the view or **ZA** to zoom all, as shown in Figure 2–30.

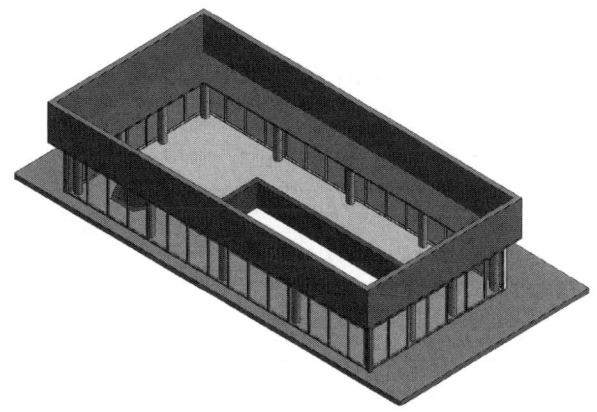

Figure 2–30

7. Along the top of the view window, select the *Level 1* tab to switch back to this view. Both the linked CAD file and linked Revit file display in this view.

8. Open the Visibility/Graphic Overrides dialog box by typing **VV**.

9. Click on the *Revit Links* tab. Next to **Hotel Pool.rvt**, check the checkbox for **Halftone**, as shown in Figure 2–31.

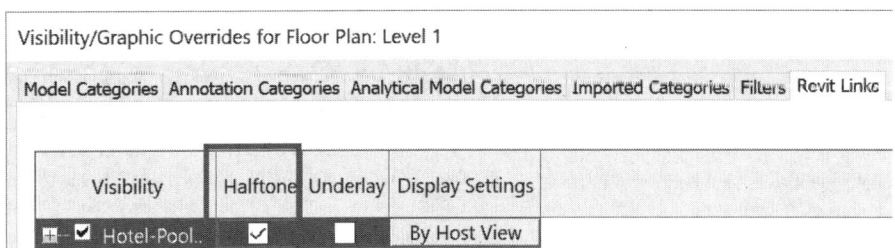

Figure 2–31

10. Click **OK**.

11. Select the text that is part of the CAD file below the platform and in Properties, in the *Other* section, change the *Draw Layer* to **Foreground**.

12. Save and close the project.

# 2.5 Setting Up Levels

Levels define stories and other vertical heights, such as the parapet and other reference heights shown in Figure 2–32. The default template includes two levels, but you can define as many levels in a project as required. They can go below 0'-0" or in the negative (for basements) as well.

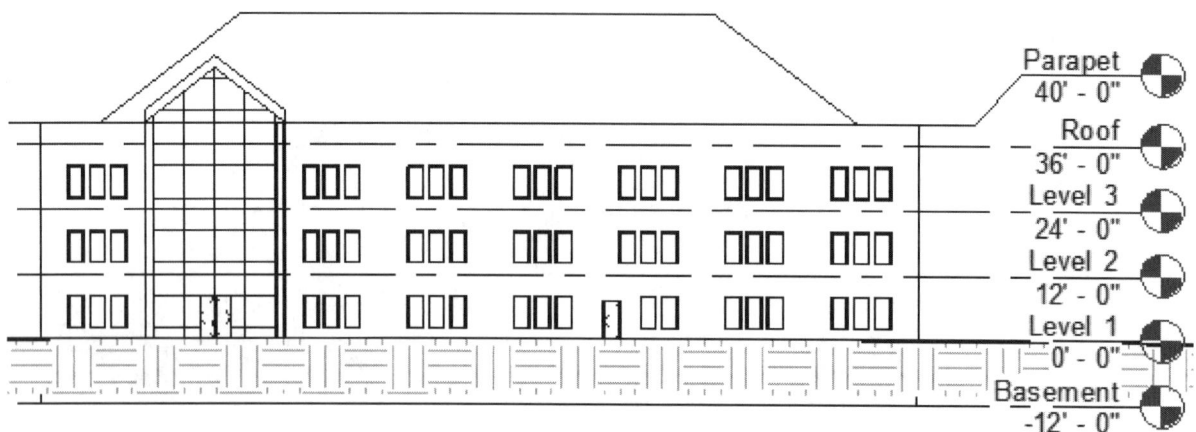

Figure 2–32

- You must be in an elevation or section view to define levels.

- Once you constrain an element to a level, it moves with the level when the level is changed.

## How To: Create Levels

1. Open an elevation or section view.
2. In the *Architecture* tab>Datum panel, click (Level), or type **LL**.
3. In the Type Selector, set the level head type, if needed.
4. In the Options Bar, select or clear **Make Plan View** as needed. You can also click **Plan View Types...** to select the types of views to create when you place the level.
5. In the *Modify | Place Level* tab>Draw panel, click either (Pick Lines) to select an element or (Line) to sketch a level.
6. Continue adding levels as needed.

- Level names are automatically incremented as you place them. This automatic numbering is most effective when you use names such as Floor 1, Floor 2, etc. (as opposed to First Floor, Second Floor, etc.). In addition, this makes it easier to find the view in the Project Browser.

# Starting a Project

- A fast way to create multiple levels is to use the (Pick Lines) option. In the Options Bar, specify an *Offset,* select an existing level, and then pick above or below to place the new level, as shown in Figure 2–33.

*You specify above or below the offset by hovering the cursor on the needed side.*

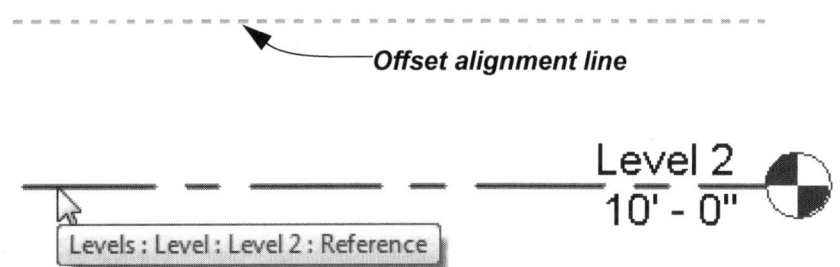

Figure 2–33

- When using the (Line) option, alignments and temporary dimensions help you place the line correctly, as shown in Figure 2–34.

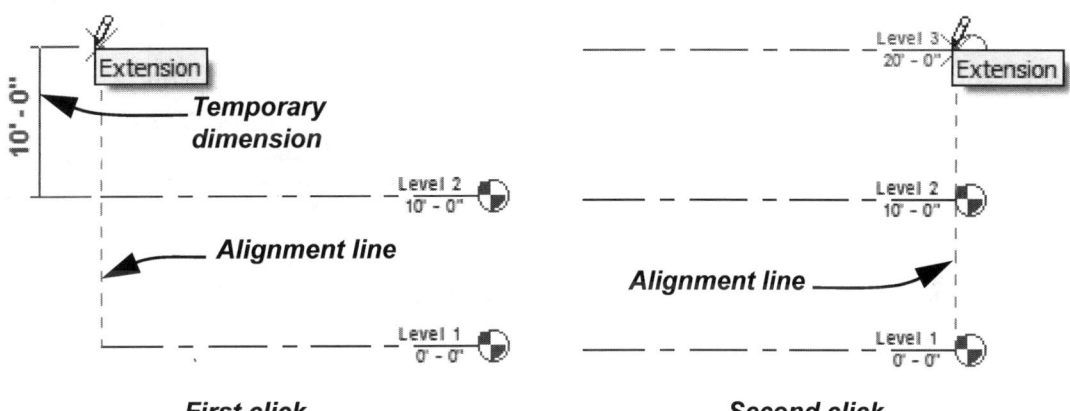

Figure 2–34

- Sketch the level lines from left to right or right to left to keep consistent.

- You can also use (Copy) to duplicate level lines. The level names are incremented but a plan view is not created. These are called **reference levels**.

- Levels display in the default 3D view. They can be modified and copied, but cannot be created in this view.

- Levels can be hidden in any view.

## Modifying Levels

You can change levels using standard controls and temporary dimensions, as shown in Figure 2–35 to the levels' appearance. You can also make changes to the name and height of the level by selecting on the individual items in the view as well as change these in Properties. You can change just the name of the level in the Project Browser but not the height.

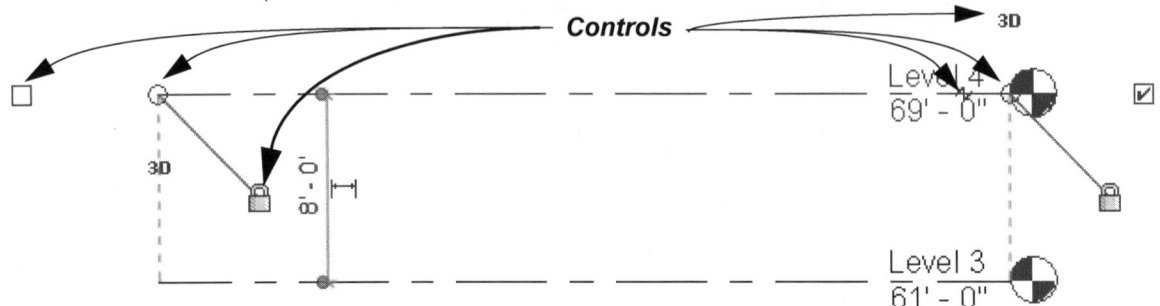

Figure 2–35

- ☑ ☐ (Hide / Show Bubble) displays on either end of the level line and toggles the level head symbol and level information on or off.

- 2D 3D (Switch to 3d / 2d extents) controls whether any movement or adjustment to the level line is reflected in other views (3D) or only affects the current view (2D).

- ⊕ (Modify the level by dragging its model end) at each end of the line enables you to drag the level head to a new location.

- 🔒 🔓 (Create or remove a length or alignment constraint) controls whether the level is locked in alignment with the other levels. If it is locked and the level line is stretched, all of the other level lines stretch as well. If it is unlocked, the level line stretches independent of the other levels.

- Click ↯ (Add Elbow) to add a jog to the level line, as shown in Figure 2–36. Drag the shape handles to new locations as needed. This is a view-specific change.

# Starting a Project

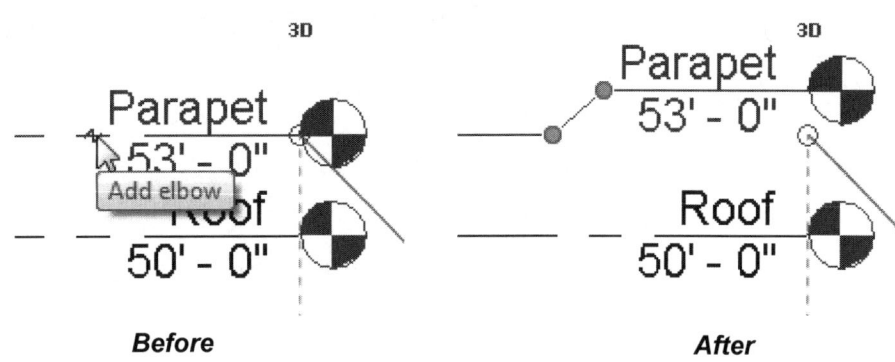

**Figure 2–36**

- To change the level name or elevation, double-click on the information next to the level head, or select the level and modify the *Name* or *Elevation* fields in Properties, as shown in Figure 2–37.

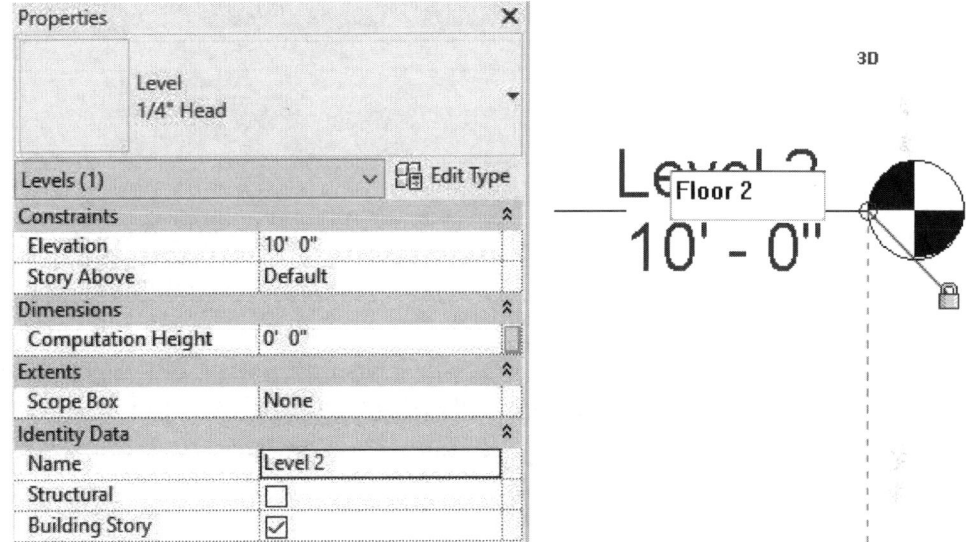

**Figure 2–37**

- When you rename a level, an alert box opens, prompting you to rename the corresponding views, as shown in Figure 2–38.

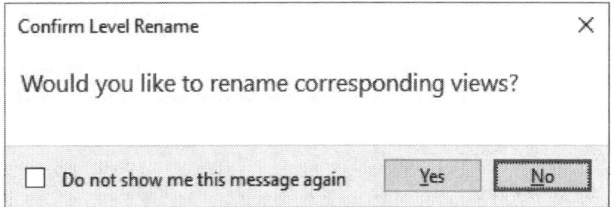

**Figure 2–38**

- The view is also renamed in the Project Browser.

> **Hint: Copying Levels and Grids from Other Projects**
>
> Levels and grid lines can be added by drawing over existing levels or grids in an imported or linked CAD file. It can also be copied and monitored from a linked Revit file. Some projects might require both methods.
>
> - For more information on using the Copy/Monitor tools, see the ASCENT guide *Autodesk Revit: Collaboration Tools*.

- If you delete a level, the views related to that level are also deleted. A warning displays, as shown in Figure 2–39.

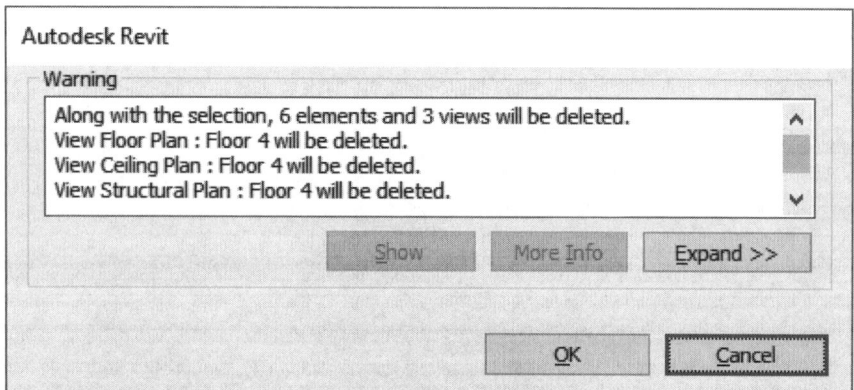

Figure 2–39

## Creating Plan Views

By default, when you place a level, plan views for that level are automatically created. If **Make Plan View** was toggled off when adding the level, or if the level was copied, you can create plan views to match the levels.

- Level heads with views are blue and level heads without views are black, as shown in Figure 2–40.

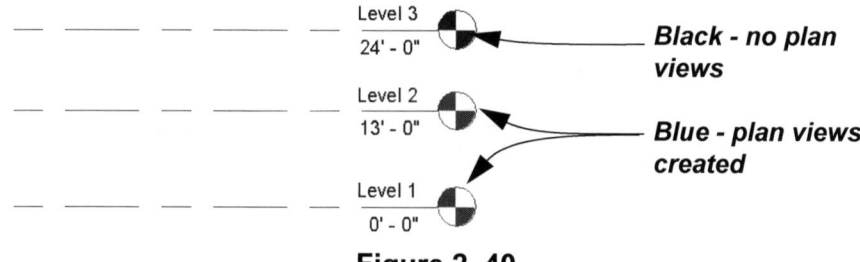

Figure 2–40

*Typically, you do not need to create plan views for levels that specify data, such as the top of a storefront window or the top of a parapet.*

# Starting a Project

## How To: Create Plan Views

1. In the *View* tab>Create panel, expand (Plan Views) and select the type of plan view you want to create, as shown in Figure 2–41.
2. In the New Plan dialog box (shown in Figure 2–42), select the levels for which you want to create plan views. Hold <Ctrl> to select more than one level.

- Clear **Do no duplicate existing views** to create a copy of an existing view.

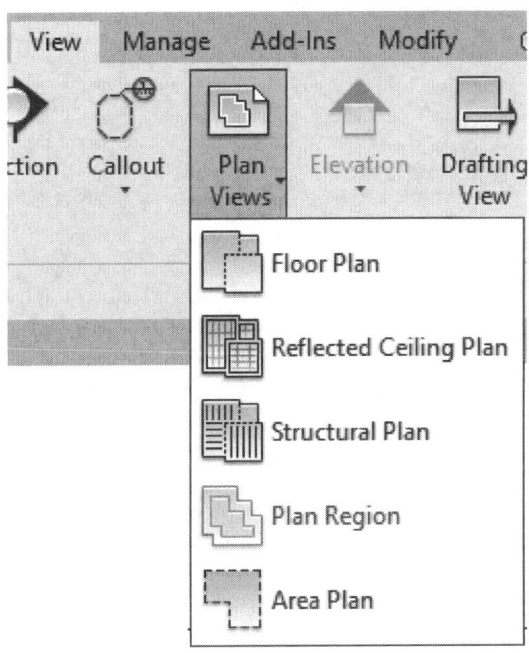

**Figure 2–41**

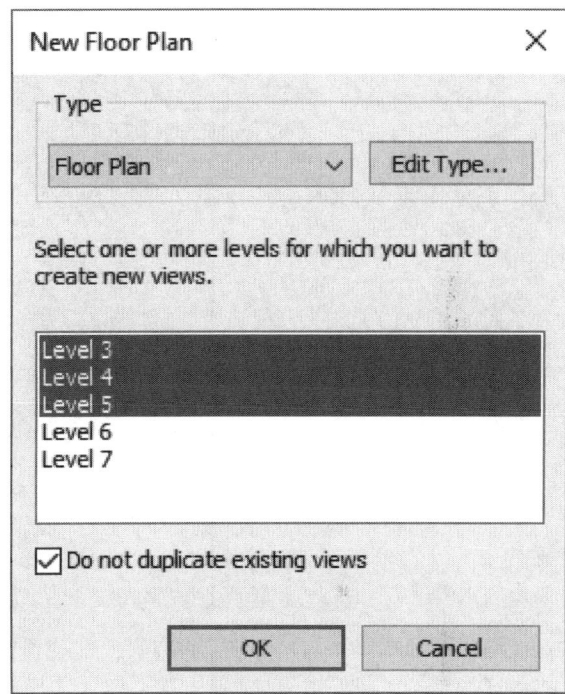

**Figure 2–42**

3. Click **OK**.

- Once a plan view is made from a level, you can double-click on the level head to open the related floor plan view. You create other plan views similar to creating a floor plan. Ceiling plans are typically created by default when you add a level with a view. If you do not want a level to have a ceiling plan, you can right-click on its name in the Project Browser and select **Delete**, as shown in Figure 2–43.

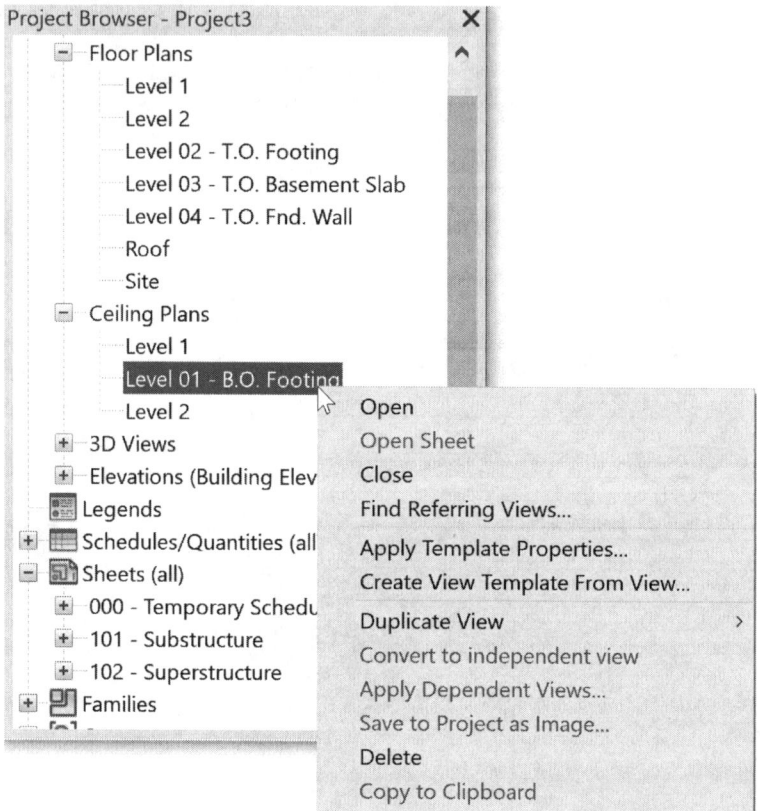

Figure 2–43

# Practice 2b

# Set Up Levels

## Practice Objective

- Add and modify levels.

In this practice, you will set up the levels required in the Modern Hotel project, including the floors, the top of the footing, and the parapet, as shown in Figure 2–44. You should see the linked Revit model on your screen. (The RVT link has been hidden in the figure below for clarity.)

**Figure 2–44**

1. Open the project **Hotel-Levels.rvt** from the practice files folder.

2. Open the **Elevations (Building Elevation): North** view. You will see your project's **Level 1** and **Level 2** levels, as well as the levels and grid lines that are part of the linked Revit file.

3. Select the linked Revit file.

4. In the View Control Bar, expand (Temporary Hide/Isolate) and select **Hide Element**. This toggles off the linked Revit file.

5. Zoom in on the level names.

6. Slowly click twice on the name *Level 1* and rename it to **Floor 1**, as shown in Figure 2–45. Press <Enter>.

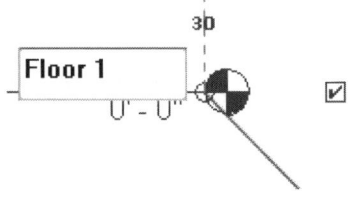

Figure 2–45

7. Click **Yes** or press <Y> when prompted to rename the corresponding views.

8. Repeat the process and rename *Level 2* as **Floor 2**. Click on the height of Floor 2 and change it from **10'-0"** to **18'-0"**.

9. In the *Architecture* tab>Datum panel, click (Level).

10. In the Options Bar, verify that **Make Plan View** is selected. Click **Plan View Types...**.

11. In the Plan View Types dialog box, click **Structural Plan** to deselect it (so that only **Ceiling Plan** and **Floor Plan** are selected), as shown in Figure 2–46. Click **OK**.

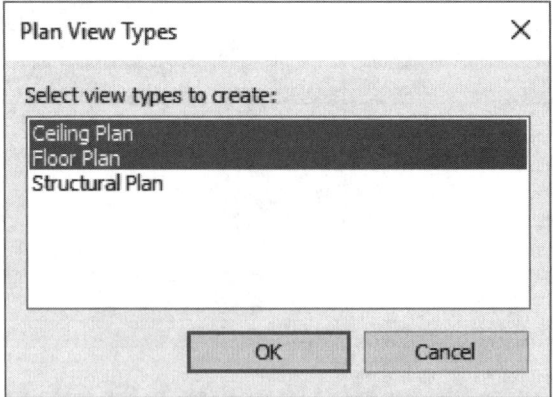

Figure 2–46

12. In the *Modify | Place Level* tab>Draw panel, click (Pick Lines). In the Options Bar, set the *Offset* to **12'-0"**.

# Starting a Project

13. Hover the cursor over the level line of **Floor 2** and move the cursor slightly upward until you see the dashed alignment line display above the **Floor 2** level. Click to create the new level **Floor 3**.

14. Create additional levels until there are a total of nine levels, all with the *Offset* of **12'-0"**.

15. Click ▷ (Modify) and select the **Floor 9** level.

16. Rename *Floor 9* as **Roof**. (Rename the corresponding views.)

17. Click ▷ (Modify).

18. Start the **Level** command again.

19. In the *Modify | Place Level* tab>Draw panel, click ⚆ (Pick Lines).

20. In the Options Bar, clear the **Make Plan View** option and set the *Offset* to **5'-0"**. Create one additional level above the **Roof** level. This level does not need a plan view.

21. Rename the top level as **Parapet**, as shown in Figure 2–47.

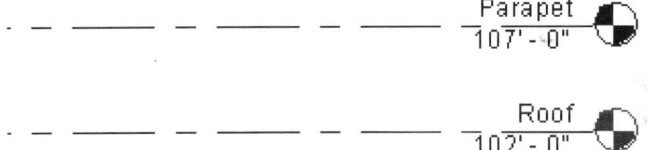

Figure 2–47

22. Zoom and pan to the Floor 1 level. Select the Floor 1 level line.

23. In the *Modify | Levels* tab>Modify panel, click ⌁ (Copy).

24. In the Options Bar, select **Multiple**.

25. In the view, click Floor 1's level line for the copy start point. For the second point, click below Floor 1 (the distance does not matter right now as you will set this in the next few steps).

26. Click again below the level you just placed to make two new levels below Floor 1.

27. Click (Modify) to end the command.

28. Rename the level below Floor 1 to **Basement** and set the height to (negative) **-10'-0"**.

29. Rename the level below Basement to **T.O. Footing** and set the height to (negative) **-12'-0"**, as shown in Figure 2–48. You can modify the levels for clarity by selecting the level and clicking the (Add Elbow) control between the level name and height.

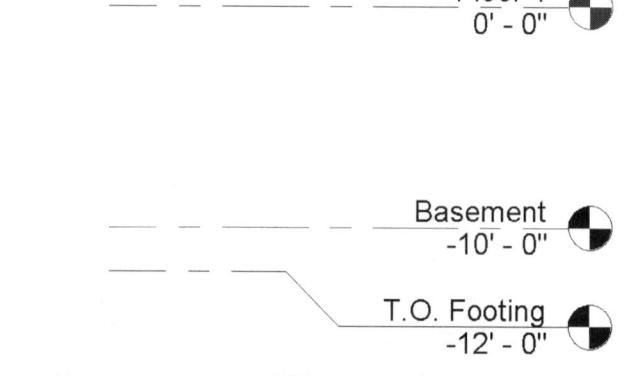

Figure 2–48

30. In the View Control Bar, select (Temporary Hide/ Isolate) and select **Reset Temporary Hide/Isolate**.

31. Select the Floor 1 level line. Select (Drag the extents of the level in the model) and drag the level over until it is far enough away from the linked model. The other levels will follow because of the alignment constraint.

32. Zoom out to display the entire project.

- Because the Basement and T.O. Footing were copies of Floor 1, you need to create a floor plan view.

33. In the *View* tab>Create panel, expand (Plan Views) and select (Floor Plan).

34. In the New Floor Plan dialog box, select **Basement** and **T.O. Footing**. (Hint: Use <Ctrl> to select the two levels.)

35. Click **OK**. The floor plan views now show in the Project Browser and the T.O. Footing view (or the last view to be created) becomes the active view.

36. Create a new ceiling plan view. In the *View* tab>Create panel, expand  (Plan Views) and select  (Reflective Ceiling Plan).

37. In the New RCP dialog box, select **Basement** and click **OK**.

38. Select the *Floor 1* tab above the view window to make it the active view.

39. Close any open views by going to the Quick Access Toolbar and clicking  (Close Inactive Views).

40. Open the **Default 3D** view.

41. Because you hid the levels when linking in the models, you need to unhide them. In the View Control Bar, click  (Reveal Hidden Elements).

42. Select one level and in the *Modify | Levels* tab>Reveal Hidden Elements panel, click  (Unhide Category).

43. In the View Control Bar, click  (Close Reveal Hidden Elements).

44. In the Project Browser, select both the **Parapet** and **Roof** views in the *Ceiling Plans* section. Right-click and select **Delete** to delete the views.

45. Save and close the project.

## 2.6 Creating Grids

Grids are annotation elements that display in most views, including plan, ceiling, section, and elevation views. They help organize your design when developing a layout and describe the pattern and location for columns, as shown in Figure 2–49. Grids can be multi-segmented, arcs, or straight lines, and they can be hidden in the view if needed.

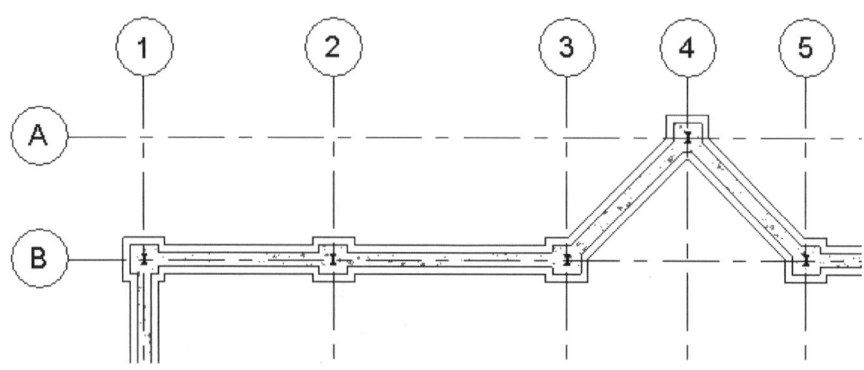

Figure 2–49

Each line or arc in a grid is a separate entity and can be placed, moved, and modified individually.

Grids cannot be drawn in a 3D view but grids can be displayed in a 3D view, perspective view, or in a 3D view with a selection box. and when you click on a grid, the surface contour displays.

### How To: Create a Grid

1. In the *Architecture* tab>Datum panel, click (Grid), or type **GR**.
2. In the Properties Type Selector, select the grid type, which will control the size of the bubble and the linestyle.
3. In the *Modify | Place Grid* tab>Draw panel, shown in Figure 2–50, select the draw method you want to use.

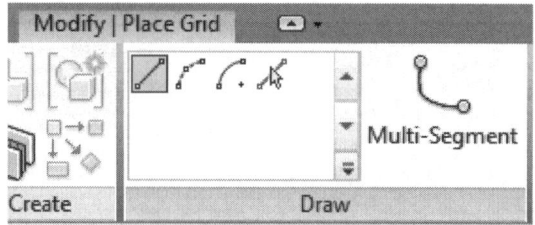

Figure 2–50

4. In the Options Bar, set the *Offset* if needed.
5. Start drawing grid lines.

*If you are upgrading a model to the 2023 version, you will need to turn on the grids.*

# Starting a Project

- Grids can be sketched at any angle, but you should ensure that all parallel grids are sketched in the same direction (e.g., from left to right or from bottom to top).

- When using the Multi-Segment tool, shown in Figure 2–51, sketch the line and click ✓ (Finish Edit Mode) to complete the command.

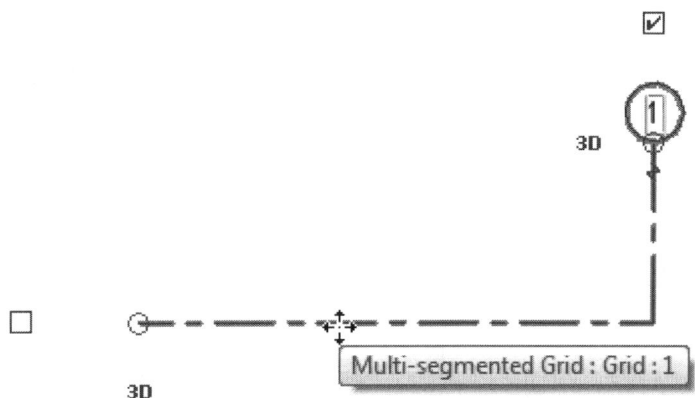

Figure 2–51

## How To: Show Grids in 3D

1. Open a 3D or perspective view and press <Esc> twice to verify nothing is selected.
2. In Properties, click **Edit...** next to *Show Grids*, as shown in Figure 2–52.

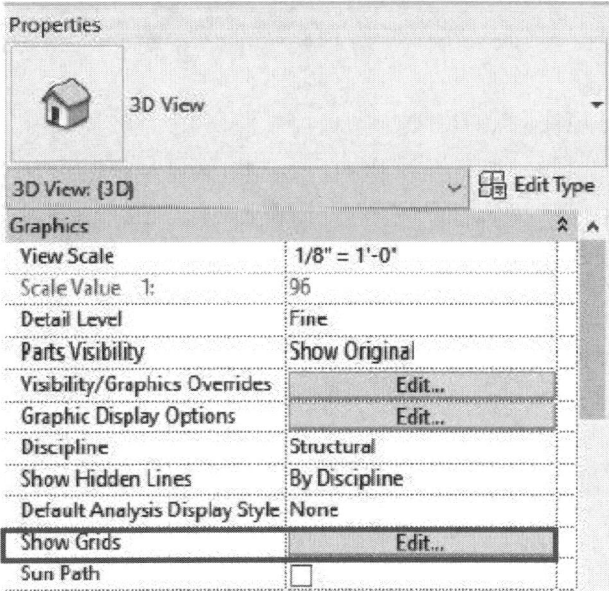

Figure 2–52

3. In the Show Grids dialog box, select the level(s) that you want the grids to display at in the 3D view, as shown in Figure 2–53.

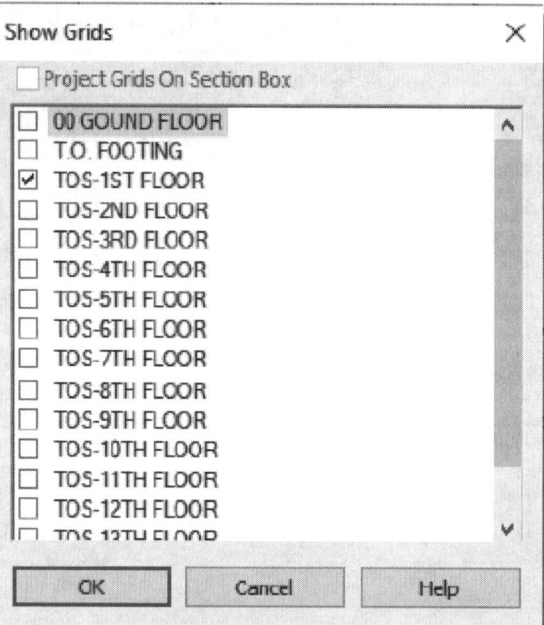

Figure 2–53

4. Click **OK**.
5. (Optional) To display the grids on the bottom of a section box, in Properties, verify that **Section Box** is selected, and click **Edit...** next to *Show Grids*.
6. In the Show Grids dialog box, select only the **Project Grids On Section Box** option, as shown in Figure 2–54, and click **OK**.

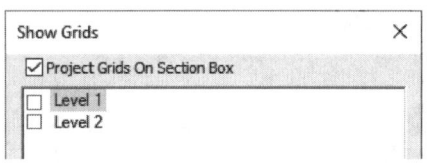

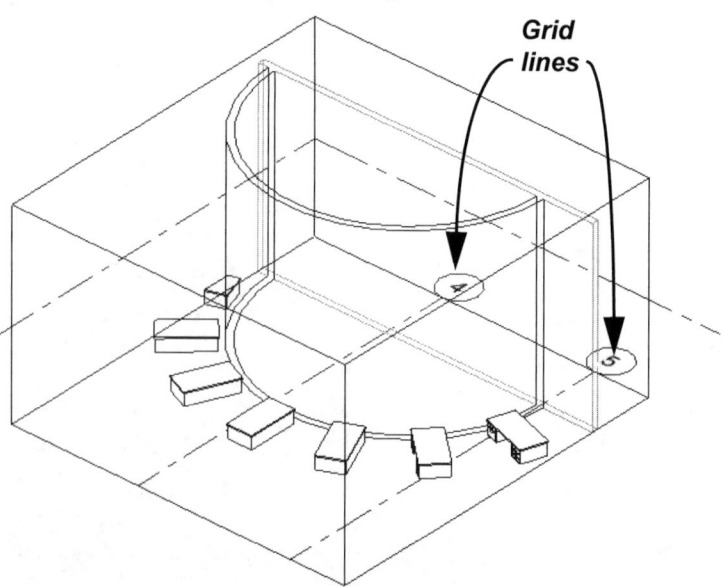

Figure 2–54

Starting a Project

## Modifying Grid Lines

Grid lines are very similar to level lines. You can modify grid lines using controls, alignments, and temporary dimensions in the view (as shown in Figure 2–55). You can change the bubble type using the Type Selector.

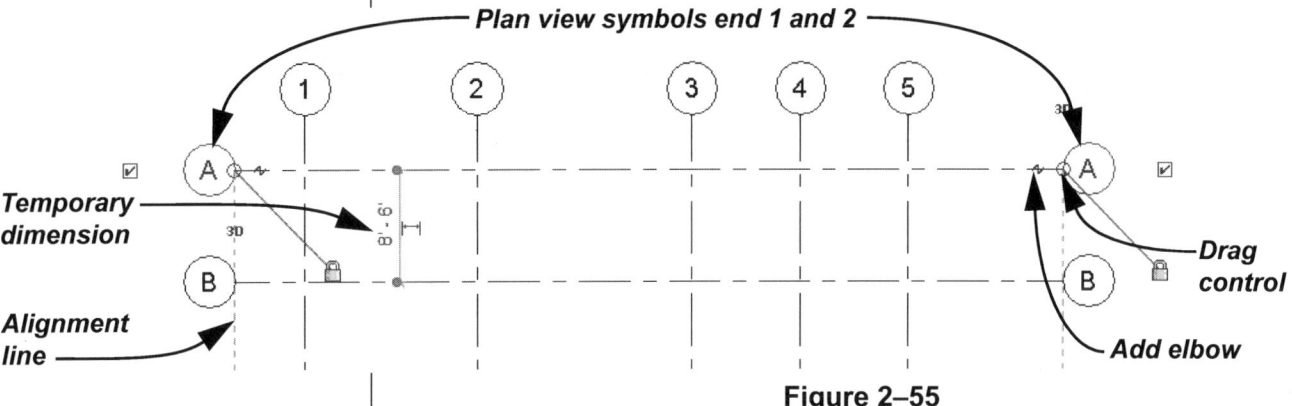

Figure 2–55

- Grid numbers can be numbers, letters, or a combination of the two. To modify a grid number, double-click on the number in the bubble and type the new letter/number. You can also change the grid number by entering a new *Name* in Properties.

- Grid numbers increment automatically.

- In a 3D view, you can modify the grid line name and adjust the grid line and grid distance.

  - Click the ⌖ (Drag the extents of the grid in the model) control to lengthen the grid line.
  - Modify the temporary dimension (as shown in Figure 2–56) to change the grid line's distance from another grid line.

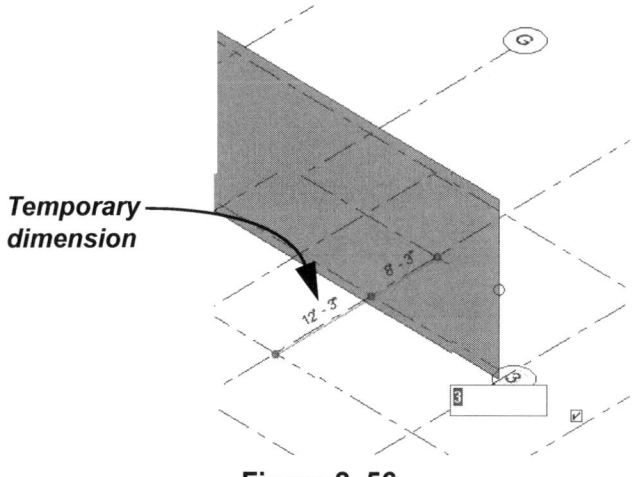

Figure 2–56

- Change the grid line name by selecting the bubble and typing in a new name; alternatively, the name can be changed in Properties.
- In Type Properties, change the way the grid **Plan View Symbols Ends** display, as shown in Figure 2–57. The first pick point is plan view symbol end 1 and the second pick point is plan view symbol end 2.

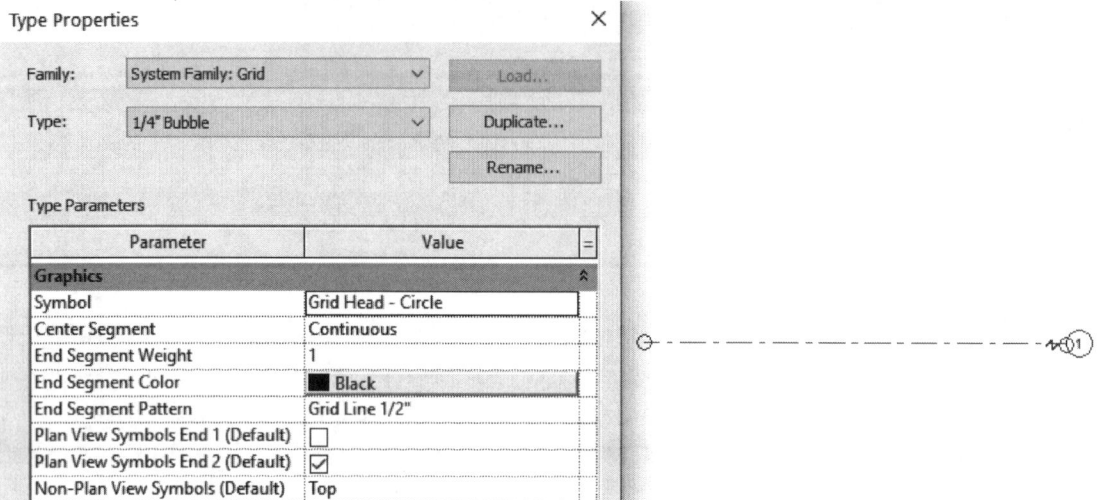

Figure 2–57

# Starting a Project

## Hint: Propagating Datum Extents

If column grids do not display in a view, this might be due to adding a level after the grid lines were added. To display the grid lines in plan views, select the grid lines in a view in which they are displayed. In the *Modify | Grids* tab>Datum panel, click (Propagate Extents). In the Propagate datum extents dialog box (shown in Figure 2–58), select the views to project the grid lines to.

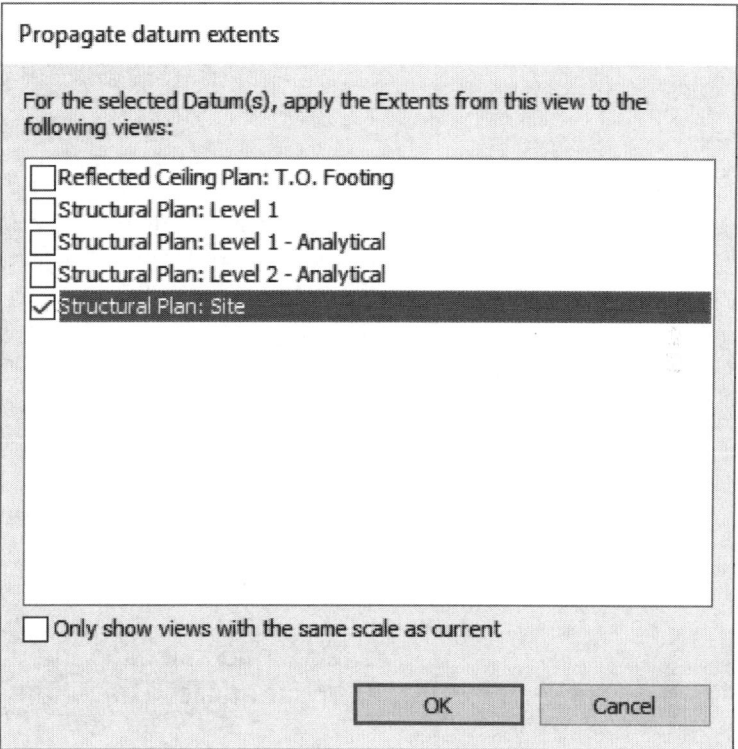

Figure 2–58

- This also works for levels.

- (Propagate Extents) is particularly useful to make grid lines display the same in all views.

# Practice 2c

# Add Grids

**Practice Objective**

- Add and modify grid lines.

In this practice, you will add grid lines using information in the imported file.

1. Open the project **Hotel-Grids.rvt** from the practice files folder.

2. From the Project Browser, open the **Floor Plans: Floor 1** view.

3. Select the linked Revit file with the pool (**Hotel-Pool.rvt**). In the View Control Bar, expand  (Temporary Hide/Isolate) and select **Hide Element**.

4. In the *Architecture* tab>Datum panel, click  (Grid).

5. In the *Modify | Place Grid* tab>Draw panel, click  (Pick Lines).

6. Select the first vertical grid line on the left of the linked file. Zoom into the grid and click inside the bubble, type **A**, and press <Enter>.

7. Continue selecting the vertical grid lines displayed in the imported file. The letters automatically increment.

8. Click the first horizontal grid line and change the letter in the bubble to **1**.

9. Continue selecting the horizontal grid lines. The numbers automatically increment.

10. Click  (Modify) to end the command.

11. Select the CAD file (**Hotel-Level-1.dwg**). In the View Control Bar, expand  (Temporary Hide/Isolate) and select **Hide Element**.

12. Only the grids should now display, as shown in Figure 2–59. Check the lengths of all grid lines. Modify the length by dragging the ends if needed.

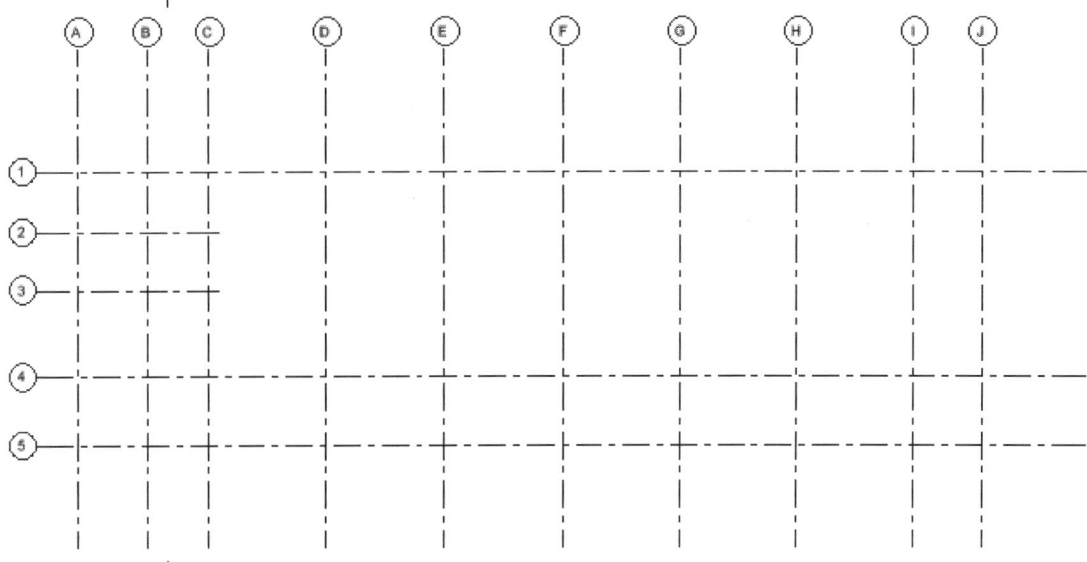

**Figure 2–59**

13. In the View Control Bar, select (Temporary Hide/ Isolate) and select **Reset Temporary Hide/Isolate**.

14. Open the default 3D view by selecting the tab at the top of the view. Note that you do not see the grids.

15. Click (Modify).

16. In Properties, in the *Graphics* section, click **Edit...** next to *Show Grids*.

17. In the Show Grids dialog box, select **Floor 1** and click **OK**.

18. The grids now display. Select the linked Revit file with the pool (**Hotel-Pool.rvt**).

19. In the View Control Bar, expand (Temporary Hide/Isolate) and select **Hide Element** to see the grids unobstructed as shown in Figure 2–60.

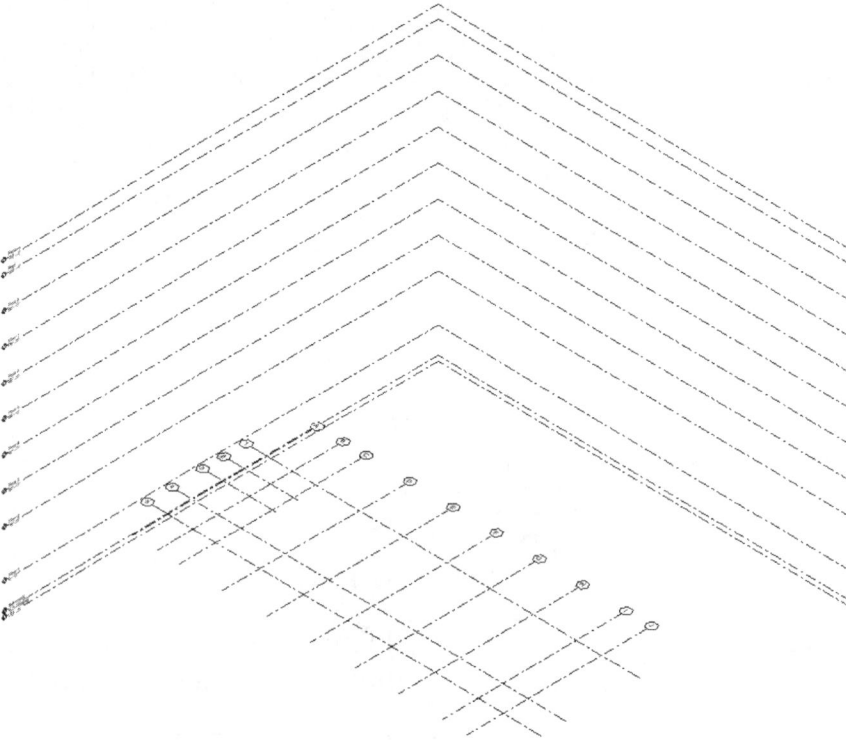

Figure 2–60

20. In the View Control Bar, select (Temporary Hide/ Isolate) and select **Reset Temporary Hide/Isolate**.

21. Save and close the project.

# Chapter Review Questions

1. What type of view do you need to be in to add a level to your project?

    a. Any non-plan view.

    b. As this is done using a dialog box, the view does not matter.

    c. Any view except for 3D.

    d. Any section or elevation view.

2. How do you line up grid lines that might be different lengths, as shown in Figure 2–61?

    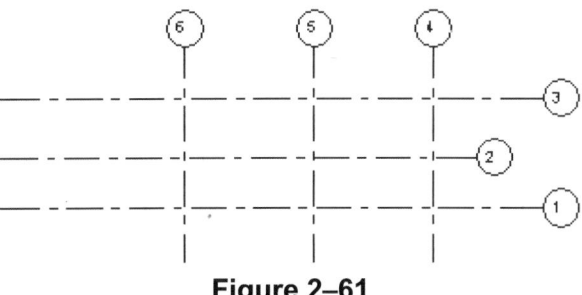

    **Figure 2–61**

    a. Use ⬚ (Trim/Extend Multiple Elements) to line them up with a common reference line.

    b. Select the grid line and use the drag control to line up with the other grid lines.

    c. Select the grid line, right-click and select **Auto-Align**.

    d. In Properties, change the *Length* and then use ✥ (Move) to get them into position.

3. Grids can be displayed in a 3D view.

    a. True

    b. False

4. In order for architectural columns to move with grids, what needs to be selected when placing the column?

    a. In the ribbon, select **At Grids**.

    b. Set the *Top Constraint* to grids.

    c. Columns always move with grids no matter what type.

    d. In Properties, select **Moves With Grids**.

5. Which of the following types of CAD formats can you import into Revit? (Select all that apply.)

    a. .DWG

    b. .XLS

    c. .SAT

    d. .DGN

6. Imported CAD files cannot be reloaded in the Manage Links dialog box.

    a. True

    b. False

7. To modify linked CAD files, you need to open what dialog box?

    a. Type Properties

    b. Link CAD

    c. Manage Links

    d. Insert from File

# Command Summary

| Button | Command | Location |
|---|---|---|
| | **Grid** | • **Ribbon:** *Architecture* tab>Datum panel<br>• **Shortcut:** GR |
| | **Import CAD** | • **Ribbon:** *Insert* tab>Import panel |
| | **Level** | • **Ribbon:** *Architecture* tab>Datum panel<br>• **Shortcut:** LL |
| | **Link CAD** | • **Ribbon:** *Insert* tab>Link panel |
| | **Link PDF** | • **Ribbon:** *Insert* tab>Link panel |
| | **Link Revit** | • **Ribbon:** *Insert* tab>Link panel |
| | **Multi-Segment (Grid)** | • **Ribbon:** *Modify | Place Grid* tab>Draw panel |
| | **Import PDF** | • **Ribbon:** *Insert* tab>Import panel |
| | **Propagate Extents** | • **Ribbon:** *Modify | Grids* or *Modify | Levels* tab>Datum panel |
| | **Temporary Hide/Isolate** | • **View Control Bar** |

# Chapter 3

# Working with Views

Views are the cornerstone of working with Revit® models as they enable you to see the model in both 2D and 3D. As you are progressing through your project, you can duplicate and change views to display different information based on the same view of the model. Callouts, elevations, and sections are especially important views for construction documents.

## Learning Objectives in This Chapter

- Modify the organization and display of the project browser.
- Duplicate views so that you can modify the display as you are creating the model and for construction documents.
- Change the way elements display in different views to show required information and set views for construction documents.
- Create callout views of parts of plans, sections, or elevations for detailing.
- Add building and interior elevations that can be used to demonstrate how a building will be built.
- Create building and wall sections to help you create the model and to include in construction documents.
- Create 3D section views using selection boxes and Orient to View.

# 3.1 Modify How the Project Browser Displays

When starting a project using the supplied Revit templates, the Project Browser displays the default organization for the tabs as **all** (as shown in Figure 3–1). You also see a status icon next to the view that indicates if the view has been added to a sheet: a white box indicates the view is not on a sheet while a colored box indicates the view is on a sheet.

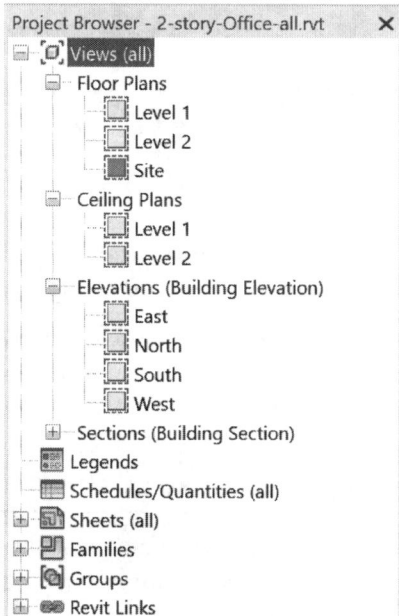

Figure 3–1

You can customize how the views are displayed in the Project Browser by changing the Browser Organization for each of the tabs: *Views*, *Sheets* or *Schedules*, as shown in Figure 3–2.

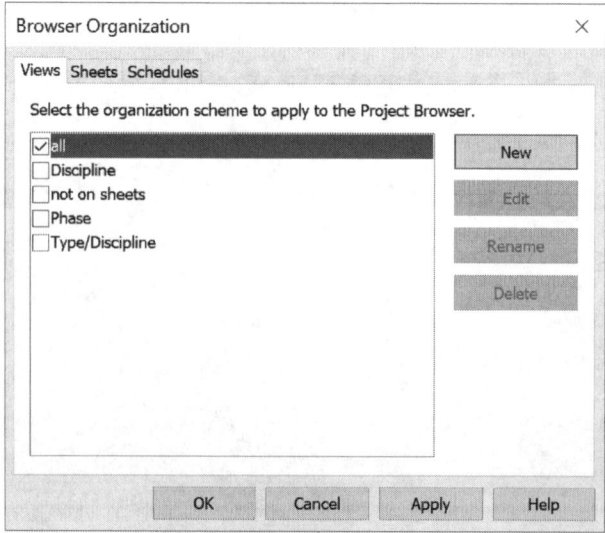

Figure 3–2

# Working with Views

## How To: Turn Off the Sheet Status Icon

1. In the Project Browser, right-click on any of the view names or on the *Views (all)* node at the top.

2. Select **Show View Placement on Sheet Status Icons**, as shown in Figure 3–3.

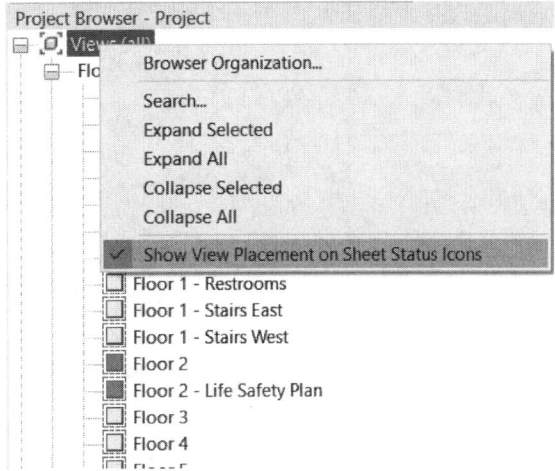

Figure 3–3

## How To: Change How the Project Browser Displays Views

1. In the Project Browser, right-click on **Views (all)** and select **Browser Organization...**, as shown in Figure 3–4.

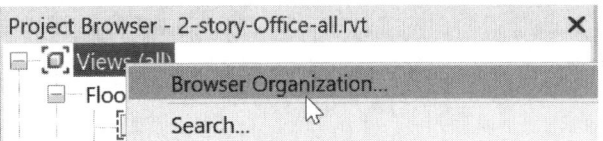

Figure 3–4

2. In the Browser Organization dialog box, select **Type/Discipline**, as shown in Figure 3–5.

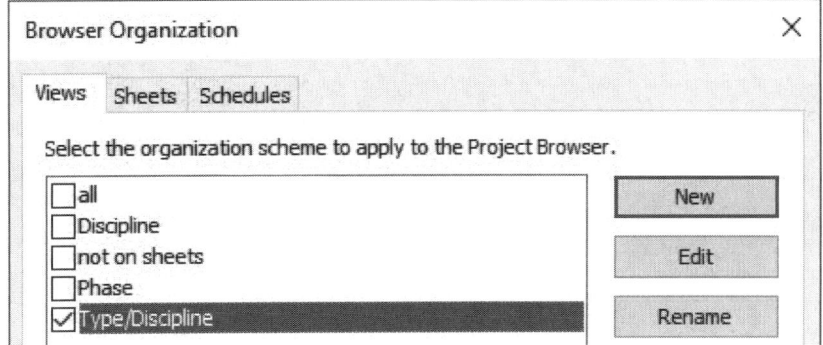

Figure 3–5

3. The Project Browser updates to sort by view type (e.g., Floor Plans, Ceiling Plans, etc.), then by discipline. Figure 3–6 shows the difference between the two browser organization types.

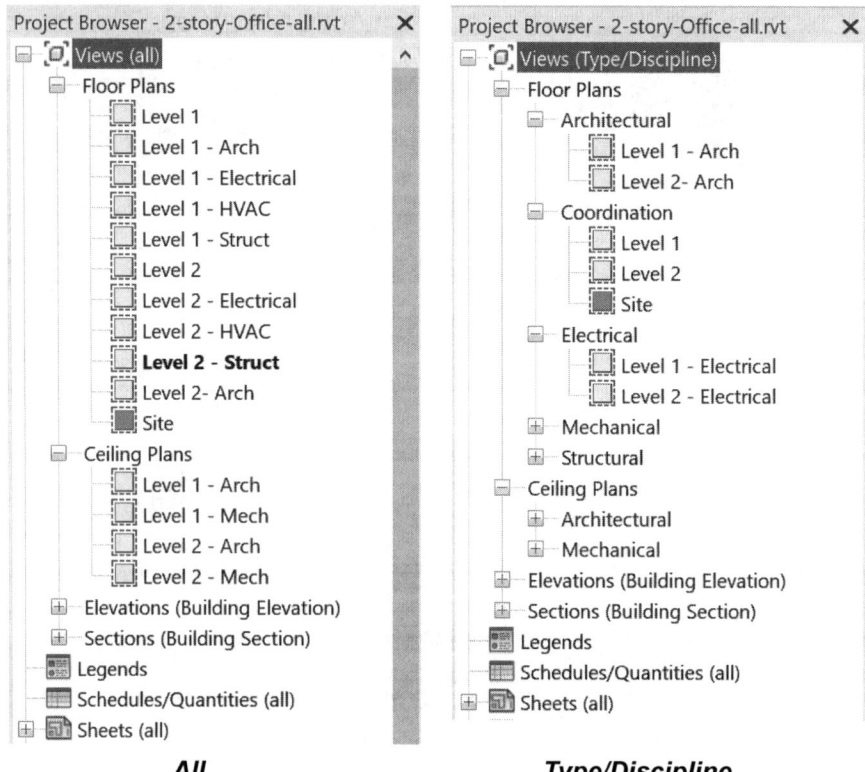

Figure 3–6

# 3.2 Duplicating Views

Once you have created a model, you do not have to recreate the elements at different scales or copy them so that they can be used on more than one sheet. Instead, you can duplicate the required views and modify the view to suit your needs.

## Duplication Types

**Duplicate** creates a copy of the view that only includes the building elements and view properties, as shown in Figure 3–7. Annotation and detailing are not copied into the new view. Building model elements automatically change in all views, but view-specific changes made to the new view are not reflected in the original view.

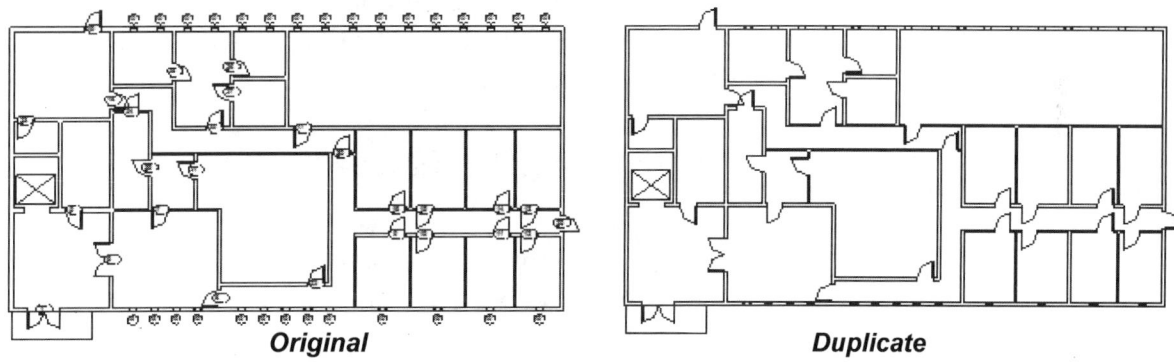

*Original*  *Duplicate*

**Figure 3–7**

**Duplicate with Detailing** creates a copy of the view and includes all annotation and detail elements (such as tags), as shown in Figure 3–8. Any annotation or view-specific elements created in the new view are not reflected in the original view.

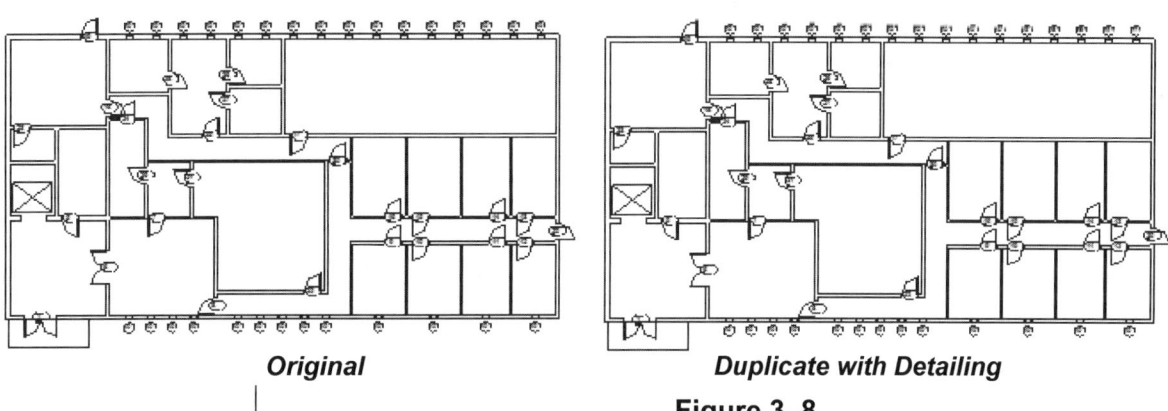

*Original*  *Duplicate with Detailing*

**Figure 3–8**

**Duplicate as a Dependent** creates a copy of the view and links it to the original (parent) view, as shown in the Project Browser in Figure 3–9 (Show View Placement on Sheet Status Icons is turned off). View-specific changes made to the overall view, such as changing the *Scale*, are also reflected in the dependent (child) views and vice-versa.

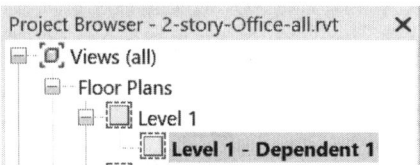

Figure 3–9

- Use dependent views when the building model is so large that you need to split the building onto separate sheets, while ensuring that the views are all at the same scale.

- If you want to separate a dependent view from the original view, right-click on the dependent view and select **Convert to independent view**.

### How To: Create Duplicate Views

1. Open the view you want to duplicate.
2. In the *View* tab>Create panel, expand **Duplicate View** and select the type of duplicate view you want to create, as shown in Figure 3–10.

*Most types of views can be duplicated.*

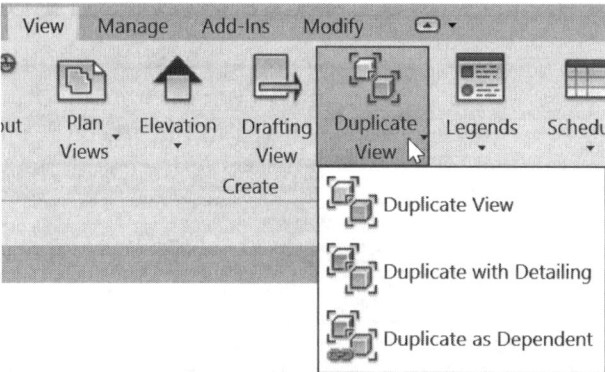

Figure 3–10

- Alternatively, you can right-click on a view in the Project Browser and select the duplicate type you want to use, as shown in Figure 3–11.

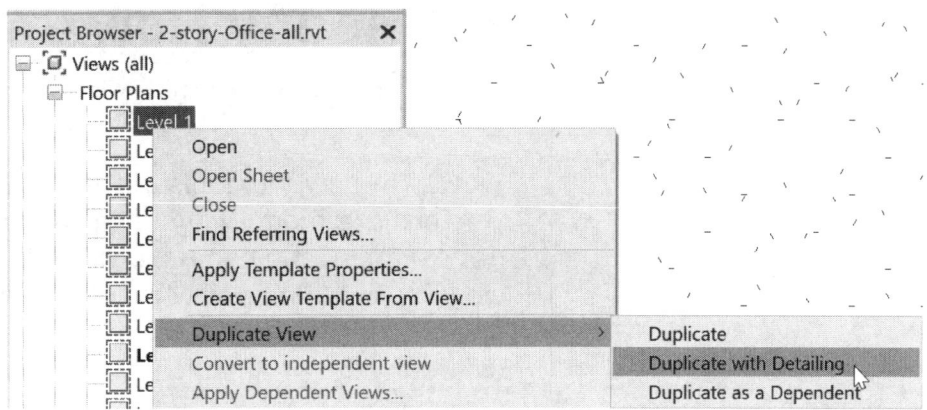

Figure 3–11

- To rename a view, slowly click twice on the view name and the text highlights so you can change it, as shown in Figure 3–12. You can also right-click on a view name and select **Rename...**, or press <F2>.

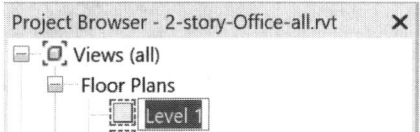

Figure 3–12

- Ceiling plans are typically created by default when you add a level with a view. If you do not want a level to have a ceiling plan, you can right-click on its name in the Project Browser and select **Delete**, as shown in Figure 3–13.

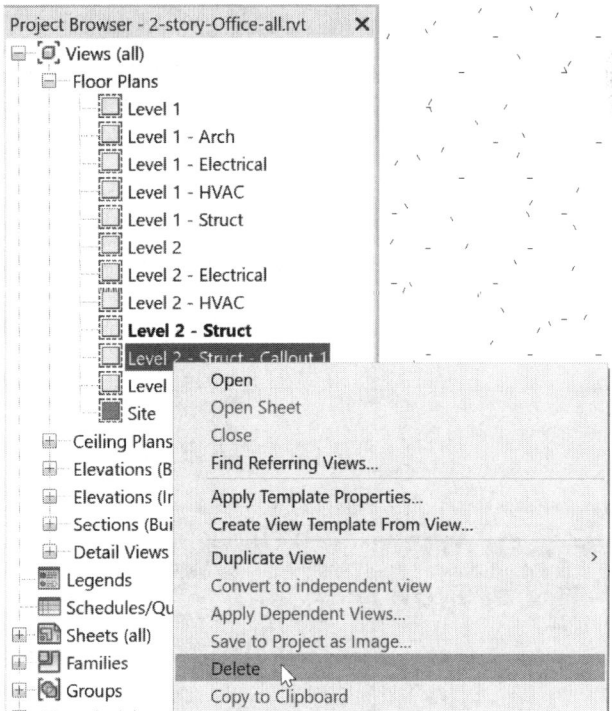

Figure 3–13

## 3.3 Modify How the View Displays

Views are powerful tools that enable you to create multiple versions of a model without having to recreate building elements. For example, you can have views that are specifically used for working on the model, while other views are annotated and used for construction documents. Different disciplines can have different views that show only the features they require, as shown in Figure 3–14. Properties of one view can be independent of the properties in other views.Once you have modified how a view needs to display, you can create a view template and apply that template to other views.

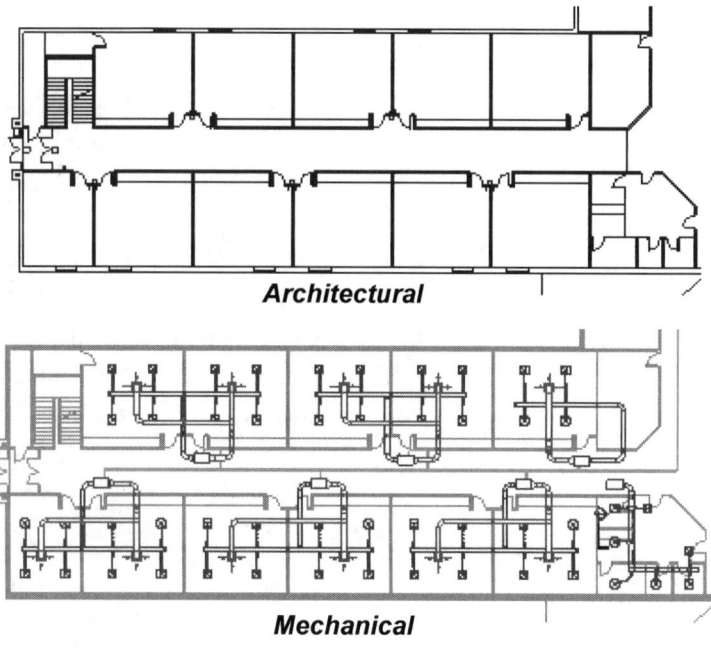

*Architectural*

*Mechanical*

**Figure 3–14**

The view display can be modified in the following locations:

- View Control Bar
- Properties
- Shortcut menu
- Visibility/Graphic Overrides dialog box

## View Control Bar

The most basic properties of a view are accessed using the View Control Bar, shown in Figure 3–15. These include the *Scale*, *Detail Level*, and *Visual Style* options. Additional options include temporary overrides and other advanced settings.

**Figure 3–15**

# Working with Views

- The **Detail Level** controls whether you see compound structure of elements (Coarse or Medium Detail) or full scale elements (Fine Detail), as shown in Figure 3–16.

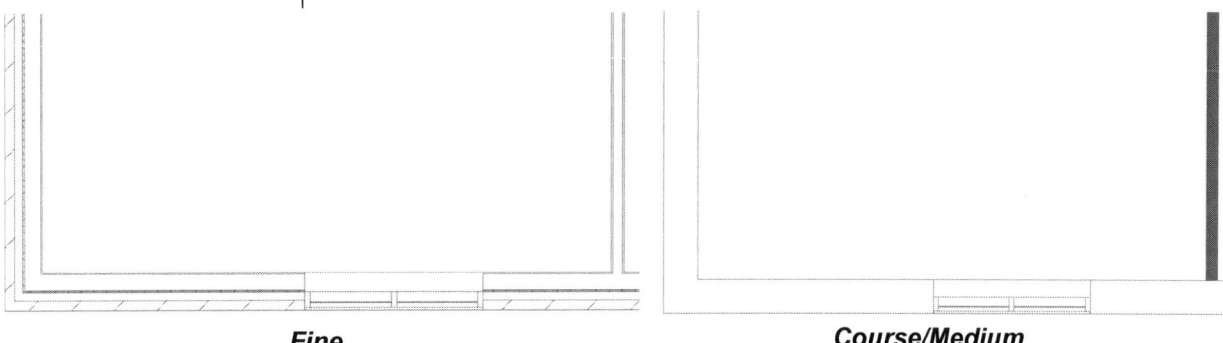

*Fine*      *Course/Medium*

**Figure 3–16**

## View Properties

You can modify how a view displays by modifying the views properties, as shown in Figure 3–17. These properties include *Underlays* and *View Range* as well as many others. The *Discipline* of a view can also be set here.

*The options in Properties vary according to the type of view. A plan view has different properties than a 3D view.*

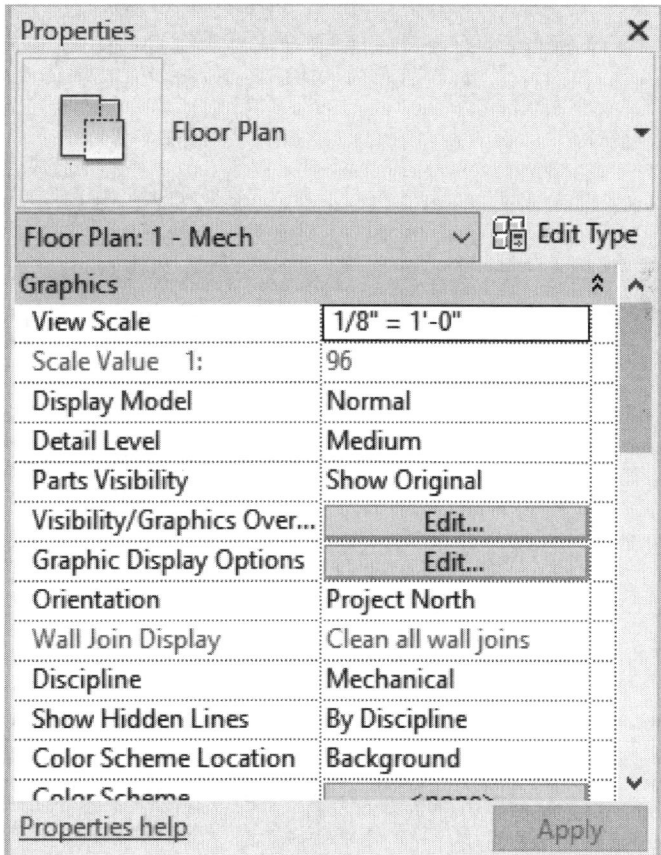

**Figure 3–17**

## Setting an Underlay

Setting an *Underlay* is helpful if you need to display elements on a different level, such as the basement plan shown with an underlay of the first floor plan in Figure 3–18. You can then use the elements to trace over or even copy to the current level of the view.

*Underlays are only available in Floor Plan and Ceiling Plan views.*

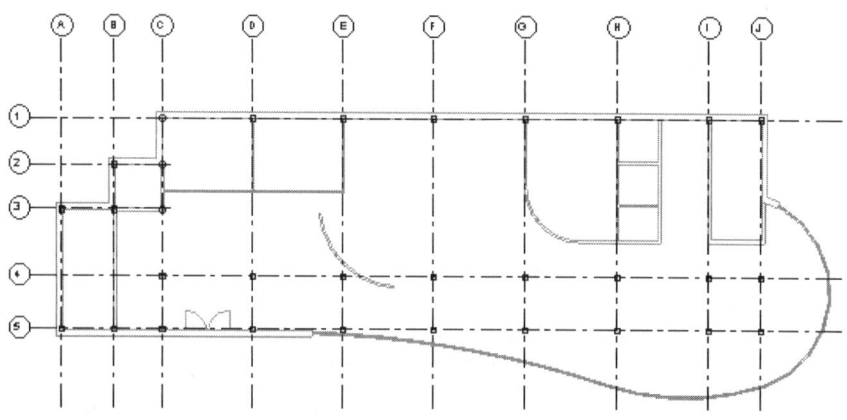

Figure 3–18

In Properties, in the *Underlay* section, specify the *Range: Base Level* and the *Range: Top Level*. You can also specify the *Underlay Orientation* to **Look down** or **Look up**, as shown in Figure 3–19.

| Underlay | |
|---|---|
| Range: Base Level | Floor 2 |
| Range: Top Level | Floor 3 |
| Underlay Orientation | Look down |

Figure 3–19

- To prevent moving elements in the underlay by mistake, in the Select panel, expand the panel title, and clear **Select underlay elements**. You can also toggle this on/off using  (Select Underlay Elements) in the Status Bar.

## Setting the View Range

The View Range controls the cut planes that control the visibility of plan views, as shown in the Sample View Range key in Figure 3–20. Elements outside the cut planes do not display unless you include an underlay.

# Working with Views

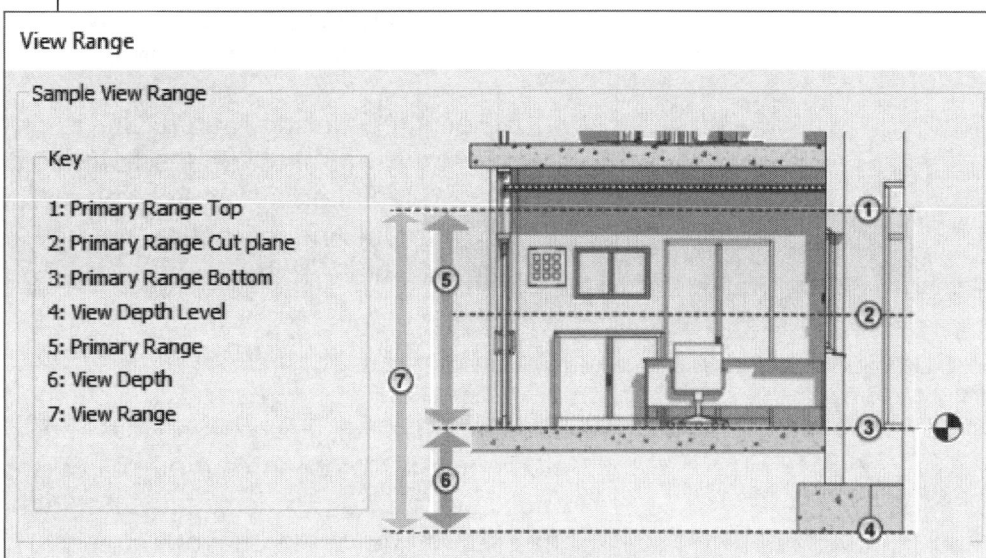

Figure 3–20

## How To: Set the View Range

1. In Properties, in the *Extents* section beside *View Range*, select **Edit...**, or type **VR**.
2. In the View Range dialog box, as shown in Figure 3–21, modify the Levels and Offsets for the *Primary Range* and *View Depth*.
   - Click **<<Show** to display the Sample View Range key.
3. Click **OK**.

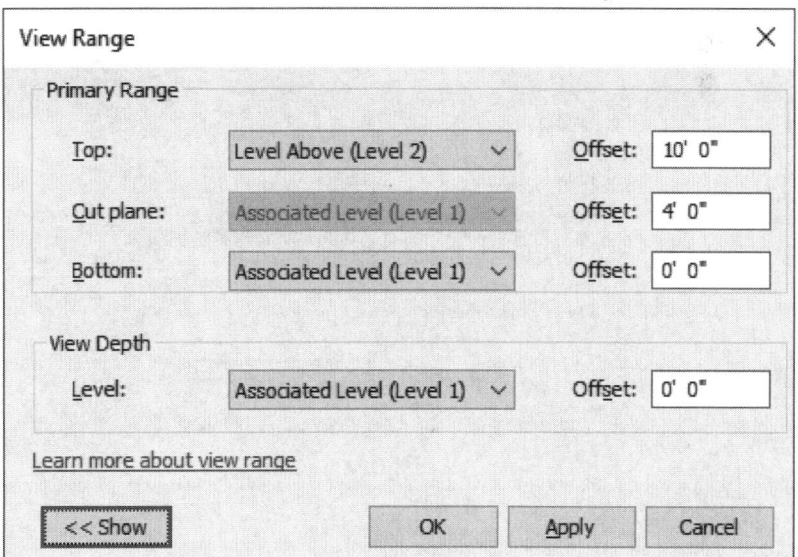

Figure 3–21

- If the settings used cannot be represented graphically, a warning displays, stating the inconsistency.

- A Reflected Ceiling Plan (RCP) is created, as if the ceiling is reflected by a mirror on the floor, so that the ceiling is the same orientation as the floor plan. The cutline is placed just below the ceiling to ensure that any windows and doors below do not display.

### Setting the Discipline of a View

You can utilize discipline in a view to display discipline-specific elements and to organize the Project Browser. When you duplicate or create a view, if it is not in the expected grouping in the Project Browser, you would need to set the *Discipline* in Properties. The view properties of *Discipline* (shown in Figure 3–22) control the visibility of some elements and applies grouping in the Project Browser. For example, you can separate the coordination plans from the architectural plans, as shown in Figure 3–23.

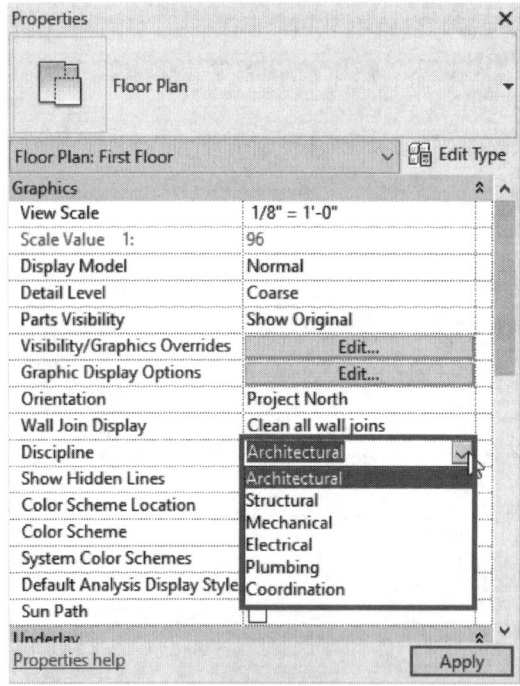

Figure 3–22

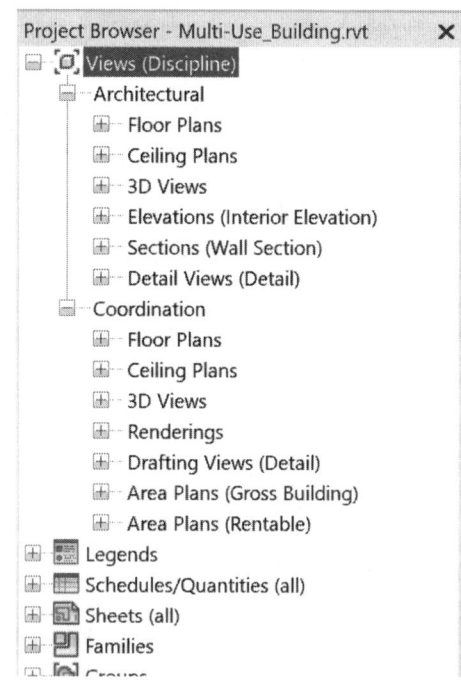

Figure 3–23

## Hiding and Overriding Graphics

Two common ways to customize a view are by hiding individual elements or a category in a view and by modifying how elements display graphically in a view by element or category (e.g., altering lineweight, color, or pattern).

# Working with Views

An element is an individual object such as one wall or a piece of furniture in a view, while a category includes all instances of a selected element, such as all walls or furniture in a view.

In the example shown in Figure 3–24, a furniture plan has been created by toggling off the structural grids category and then graying out all of the walls and columns.

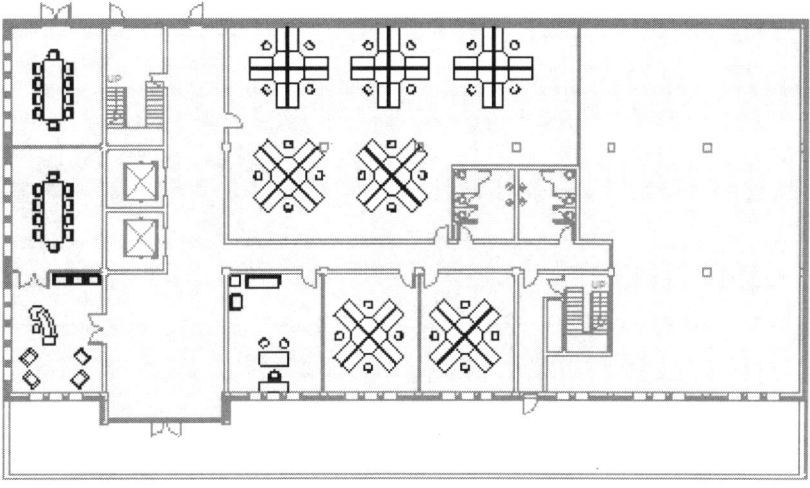

**Figure 3–24**

## How To: Hide Elements or Categories in a View

1. Select the elements or categories you want to hide.
2. Right-click and select **Hide in View>Elements** or **Hide in View>Category**, as shown in Figure 3–25.
   - A quick way to hide entire categories is to select an element(s) and type **VH**.

*The elements or categories are hidden in the current view only.*

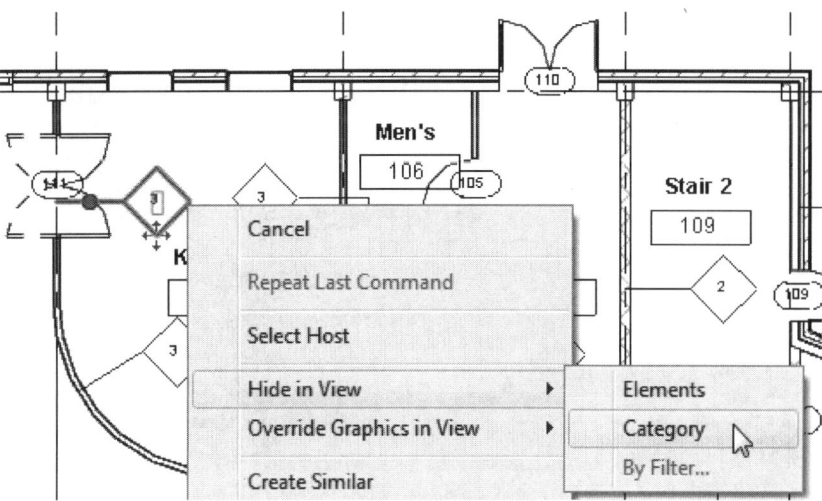

**Figure 3–25**

## How To: Override Graphics of Elements or Categories in a View

1. Select the element(s) you want to modify.
2. Right-click and select **Override Graphics in View>By Element** or **By Category**. The View-Specific Element (or Category) Graphics dialog box opens, as shown in Figure 3–26.

*The exact options in the dialog box vary depending on the type of elements selected.*

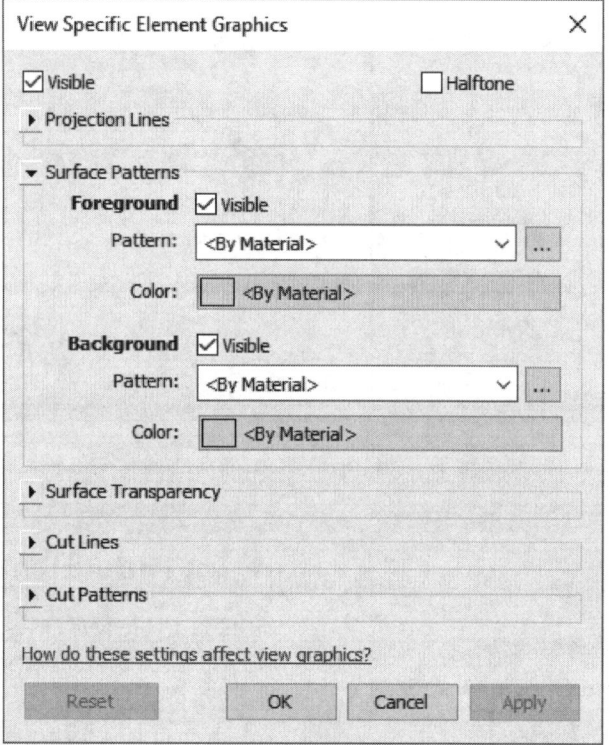

**Figure 3–26**

3. Select the changes you want to make and click **OK**.

### View-Specific Options

- Clearing the **Visible** option is the same as hiding the elements or categories.

- Selecting the **Halftone** option grays out the elements or categories.

- The options for *Projection Lines* and *Cut Lines* include **Weight**, **Color**, and **Pattern**. The options for *Surface Patterns* and *Cut Patterns* include **Visibility**, **Pattern**, and **Color** for the Foreground and Background, as shown above in Figure 3–26.

- **Surface Transparency** can be set by moving the slider bar, as shown in Figure 3–27.

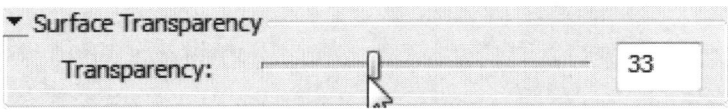

Figure 3–27

- The View-Specific Category Graphics dialog box includes **Open the Visibility Graphics dialog...**, which opens the full dialog box of options.

## Visibility/ Graphic Overrides

The options in the Visibility/Graphic Overrides dialog box (shown in Figure 3–28) control how every category and sub-category of elements is displayed per view. You can toggle categories on and off, override the *Projection/Surface* and *Cut* information, set categories to *Halftone*, and change the *Detail Level*.

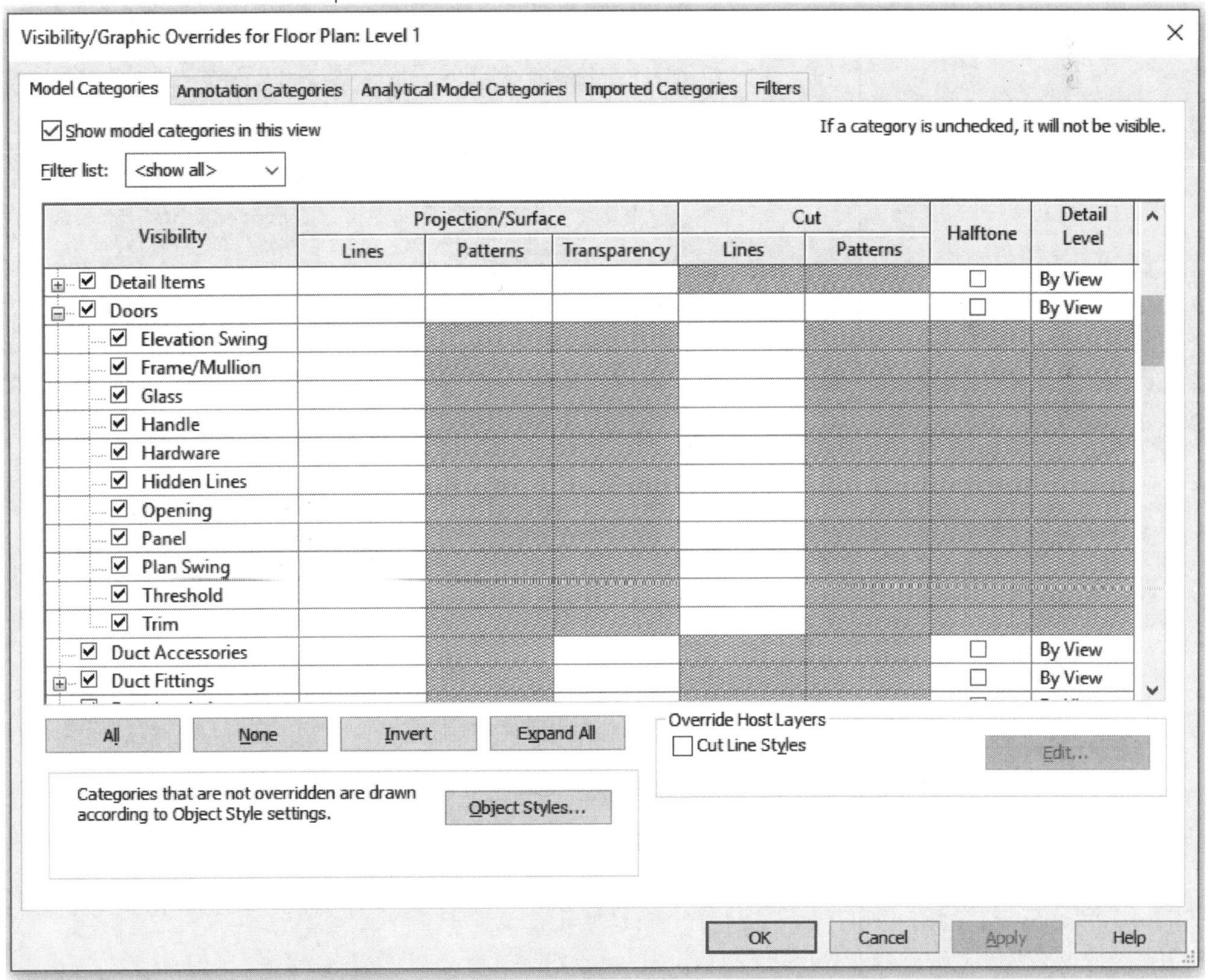

Figure 3–28

To open the Visibility/Graphic Overrides dialog box, type **VV** or **VG**. It is also available in Properties: in the *Graphics* section, beside *Visibility/Graphic Overrides*, click **Edit...**.

- The Visibility/Graphic Overrides are divided into *Model*, *Annotation*, *Analytical Model*, *Imported,* and *Filters* categories.

- Other categories might be available if specific data has been included in the project, including *Design Options*, *Linked Files*, and *Worksets*.

- To limit the number of categories showing in the dialog box select a discipline from the *Filter list*, as shown in Figure 3–29.

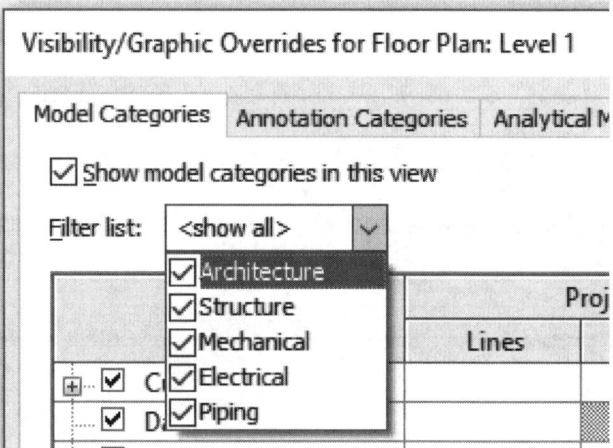

Figure 3–29

- To help you select categories, use the **All**, **None**, and **Invert** buttons. The **Expand All** button displays all of the sub-categories.

# Working with Views

> **Hint: Restoring Hidden Elements or Categories**
>
> If you have hidden categories, you can display them using the Visibility/Graphic Overrides dialog box. To display hidden elements, however, you must temporarily reveal the elements first.
>
> 1. In the View Control Bar, click 💡 (Reveal Hidden Elements). The border and all hidden elements are displayed in magenta, while visible elements in the view are grayed out, as shown in Figure 3–30.
>
>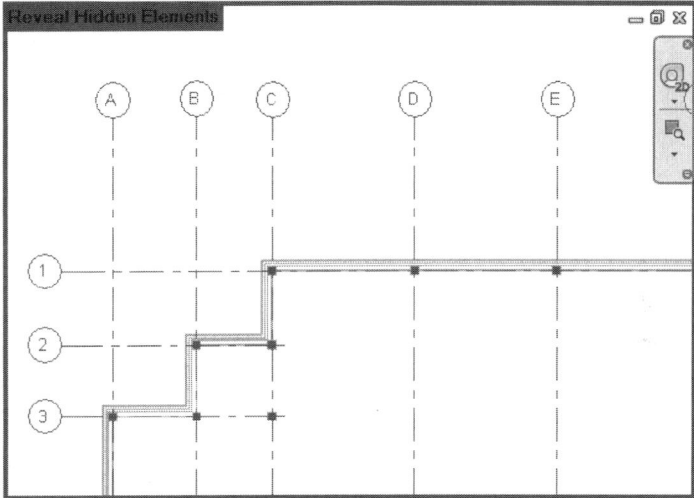
>
> Figure 3–30
>
> 2. Select the hidden elements you want to restore, right-click, and select **Unhide in View>Elements** or **Unhide in View>Category**. Alternatively, in the *Modify* contextual tab> Reveal Hidden Elements panel, click (Unhide Element) or (Unhide Category).
> 3. When you are finished, in the View Control Bar, click (Close Reveal Hidden Elements) or, in the *Modify* contextual tab>Reveal Hidden Elements panel, click (Toggle Reveal Hidden Elements Mode).

## View Templates

A powerful way to use views effectively is to set up a view and then save it as a view template. You can apply view templates to views individually or through Properties. Setting the view template using Properties helps to ensure that you do not accidentally modify the view while interacting with it.

### How To: Create a View Template from a View

1. Set up a view, as needed.
2. In the Project Browser, right-click on the view and select **Create View Template from View**.
3. In the New View Template dialog box, type in a name and click **OK**.
4. The new view template is listed in the View Templates dialog box. Make any modifications needed in the *View properties* section.
5. Click **OK**.

### How To: Specify a View Template for a View

1. In the Project Browser, select the view or views to which you want to apply a view template.
2. In Properties, scroll down to the *Identity Data* section and click the button beside *View Template*.
3. In the Apply View Template dialog box, select the view template from the list, as shown in Figure 3–31.

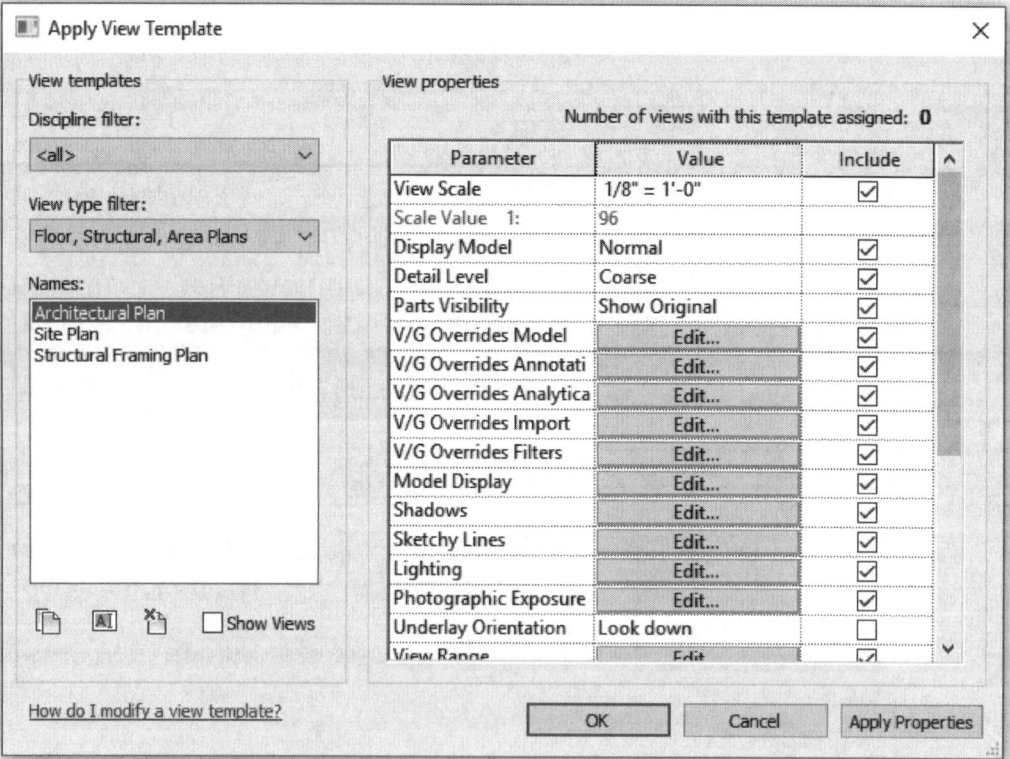

Figure 3–31

4. Click **OK**.

- In the View Control Bar, use  (Temporary View Properties) to temporarily apply a view template to a view.

# Practice 3a

# Duplicate Views and Set the View Display

### Practice Objectives

- Duplicate and rename views.
- Hide elements in views.
- Modify the graphic display of elements in views.

In this practice, you will duplicate views and then modify them by changing the scale, hiding elements, and changing other elements to halftone to prepare them to be used in construction documents. The finished views of the second floor are shown in Figure 3–32.

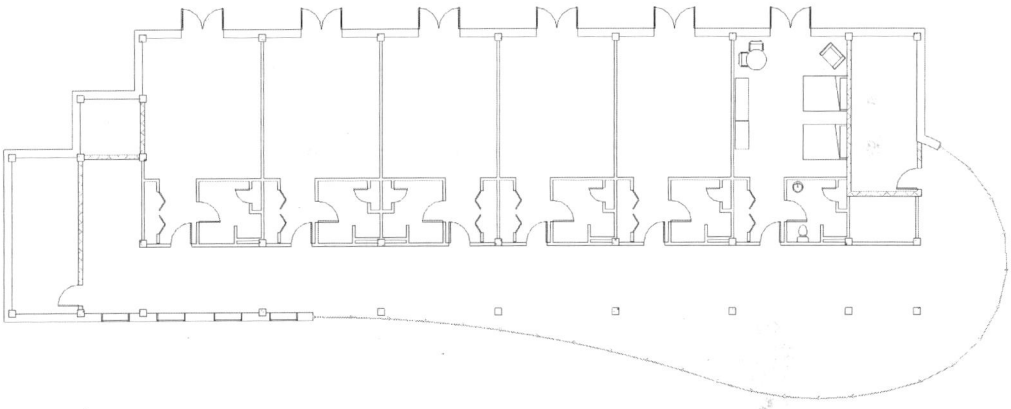

Figure 3–32

- Elements have been added to this model to demonstrate what happens when working with views.

### Task 1 - Duplicate and modify the Floor 1 floor plan view.

1. Open the project **Hotel-Display.rvt** from the practice files folder.

2. Close any other projects you may have open.

3. Open the **Floor Plans: Floor 1** view. This view shows the room and door tags.

4. In the Project Browser, right-click on the **Floor Plans: Floor 1** view and select **Duplicate View>Duplicate with Detailing**. This creates a view with all the tags, grids, and elevation markers.

5. In the Project Browser, slowly click twice on the duplicated view name. Rename it **Floor 1 - Reference Plan**. You will use this view later to place callouts and sections.

6. In the Project Browser, right-click on the **Floor Plans: Floor 1** view and select **Duplicate View>Duplicate**. This creates a view without all of the tags, but includes the grids and elevation markers.

7. Rename it to **Floor 1 - Overall Plan**.

8. With the Floor 1 - Overall Plan view active, in the View Control Bar, change the *Scale* to **1/16"=1'-0"**.

    - All of the annotations become larger, as they need to plot correctly at this scale.

9. Activate the 3D view by selecting on its tab along the top of the view.

10. Type **WT** to tile the four open windows and then type **ZA** to zoom out to fit all the view in their new windows. Compare the various floor plans.

11. Save the project.

### Task 2 - Duplicate and modify the Floor 2 floor plan view.

1. Type **TW** to return to the tab views.

2. Click on the X, as shown in Figure 3–33, to close the **Floor 1 - Reference Plan** and **Floor 1 - Overall Plan** views.

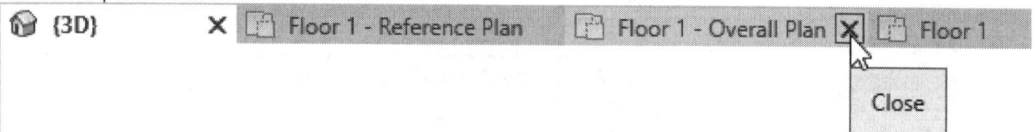

Figure 3–33

3. Open the **Floor Plans: Floor 2** view. Note that the view displays door and room tags, as well as the CAD and Revit linked files.

4. In the Project Browser, right-click on the same view and select **Duplicate View>Duplicate**. This creates a new view without any annotations or the CAD file.

5. Rename this view to **Typical Guest Room Plan**.

# Working with Views

6. Type **VV** to open the Visibility/Graphic Overrides dialog box. Click on the *Revit Link* tab and clear the **Modern-Hotel-Pool.rvt** option in the *Visibility* column.

7. Click **OK**.

8. Select one of the grids and one of the elevation markers and type **VH** (Hide in View Category).

9. Select everything in the view with a crossing window. In the *Modify | Multi-Select* tab>Selection plane, click ▼ (Filter).

10. In the Filter dialog box, click **Check None**, then only check the check boxes for **Curtain Panels**, **Curtain Wall Grids**, and **Curtain Wall Mullions**.

11. Click **OK**.

12. With all the curtain walls selected, right-click and select **Override Graphics in View>By Element...**.

13. In the View Specific Element Graphics dialog box, select **Halftone** and click **OK**. The curtain walls are now halftone.

14. Click in an empty space in the view to release the selection.

15. Type **WT** to tile the four windows and then type **ZA** so that the model displays fully in the view and you can see the differences in the views.

16. Save and close the project.

## 3.4 Adding Callout Views

Callouts are details of plan, elevation, or section views. When you place a callout in a view, as shown in Figure 3–34, it automatically creates a new view clipped to the boundary of the callout, as shown in Figure 3–35. You can create rectangular or sketched callout boundaries.

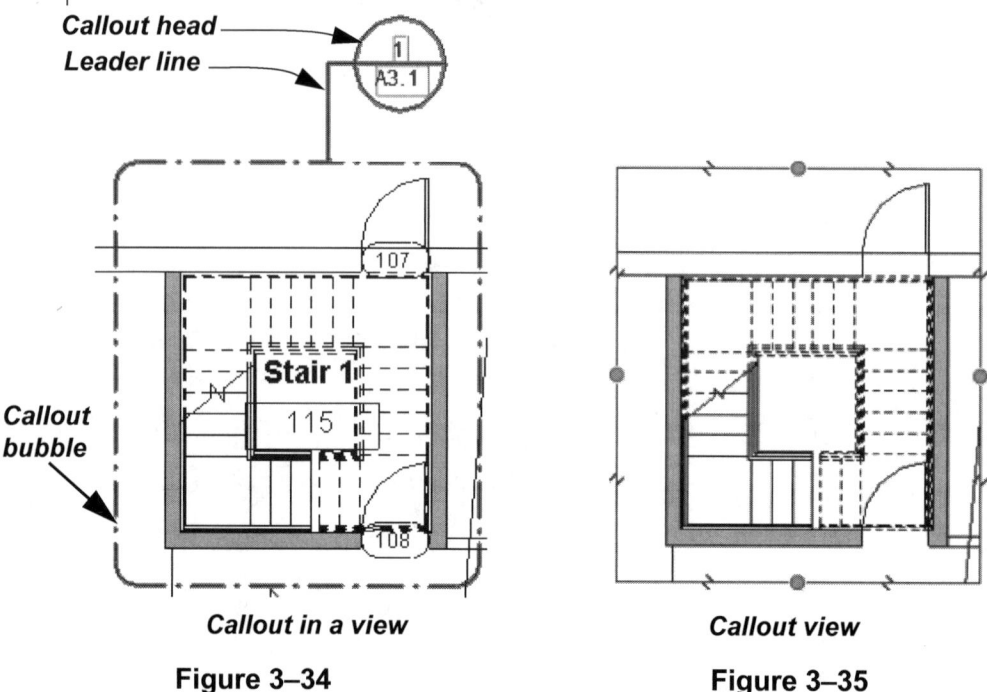

Figure 3–34 — Callout in a view

Figure 3–35 — Callout view

- Callout views are saved in the same node in the Project Browser as the original view. For example, the callout view of a floor plan is placed within the Floor Plans node.

- To open the callout view, double-click on its name in the Project Browser or on the callout head (verify that the callout bubble is not selected before you double-click on it).

### How To: Create a Rectangular Callout

1. In the *View* tab>Create panel, click (Callout).
2. Select points for two opposite corners to define the callout bubble around the area you want to detail.
3. Select the callout bubble and use the shape handles to modify the location of the bubble and any other edges that might need changing.
4. In the Project Browser, you can rename the callout view.

## How To: Create a Sketched Callout

1. In the *View* tab>Create panel, expand (Callout) and click (Sketch).
2. Sketch the shape of the callout bubble using the tools in the *Modify | Edit Profile* tab>Draw panel, as shown in Figure 3–36.

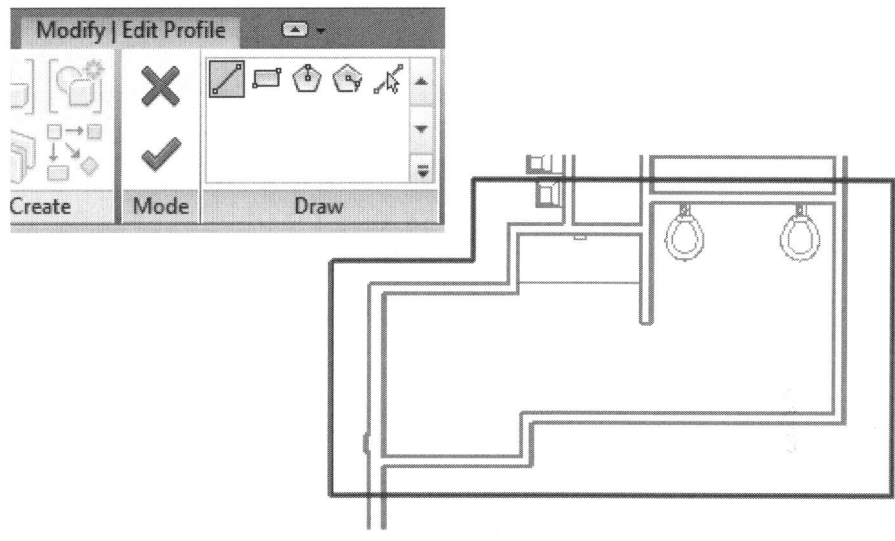

Figure 3–36

3. Click (Finish) to complete the boundary.
4. Select the callout bubble and use the shape handles to modify the location of the bubble and any other edges that might need to be changed.
5. In the Project Browser, rename the callout.

## Modifying Callouts

Callouts are cropped versions of the original view. When you modify them you are changing the crop region of the view.

- You can select the Drag Head grip of the callout bubble (as shown in Figure 3–37) to move the callout head to a different location. You can modify the leader landing by dragging the grip at the landing.

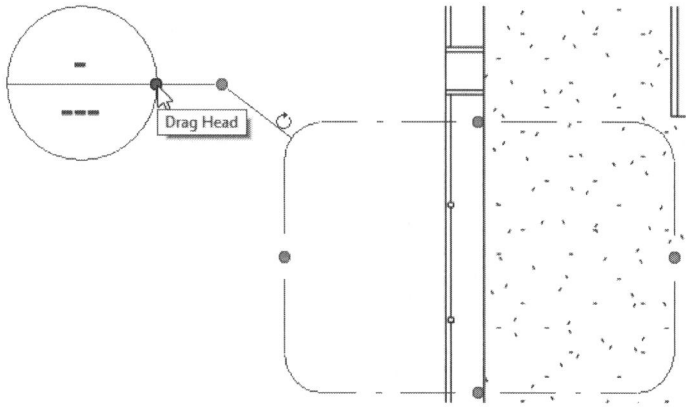

**Figure 3–37**

- If you change the size of the callout bubble in the original view, it automatically updates the callout view and vice-versa.

- Callouts can be reshaped. Select the callout bubble or crop region and, in the *Modify | Floor Plan* tab>Mode panel, click (Edit Crop) and use the Draw tools to modify the sketch.

- If you want to return a sketched or modified callout or crop region to a rectangular configuration, click (Reset Crop).

# Working with Crop Regions

Plans, sections, elevations, and 3D views can all be modified by changing how much of the model is displayed in a view. One way to do this is to set the Model crop region. If there are dimensions, tags, or text near the crop region, you can also use the Annotation crop region to include these, as shown in Figure 3–38.

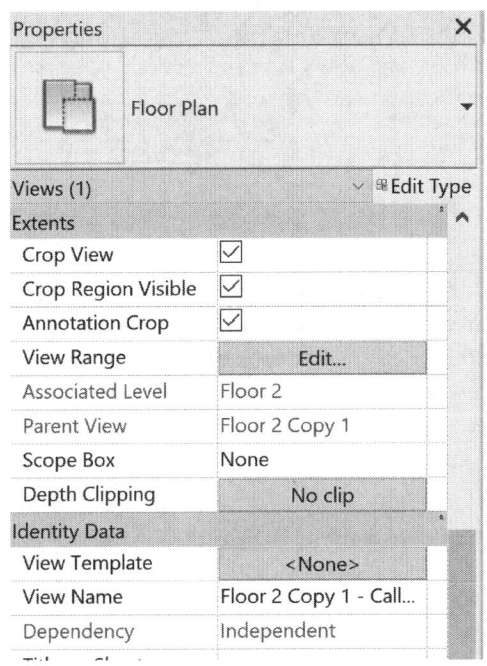 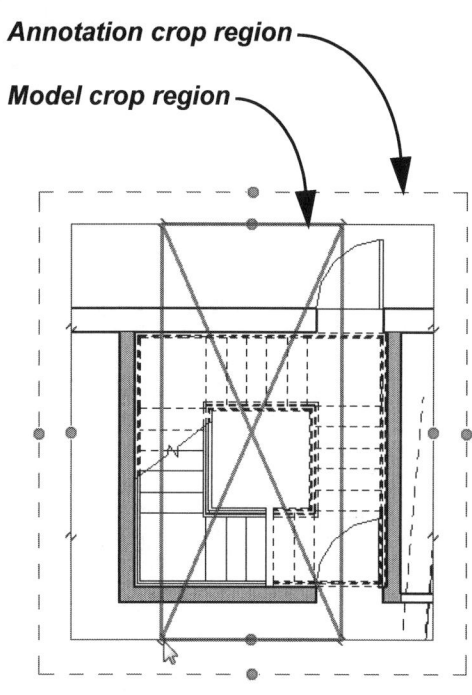

**Figure 3–38**

*Zoom out if you do not see the crop region when you set it to be displayed.*

- To display the crop region, in the View Control Bar, click ◧ (Show Crop Region). Alternatively, in Properties, in the *Extents* section, select **Crop Region Visible**. **Annotation Crop** is also available in this area.

- It is best practice to hide a crop region before placing a view on a sheet. In the View Control Bar, click ◧ (Hide Crop Region).

- Resize the crop region using the ● control on each side of the region.

*Breaking the crop region is typically used with sections or details.*

- Click ⌇ (Break Line) control to split the view into two regions, horizontally or vertically. Each part of the view can then be modified in size to display what is needed and be moved independently.

- The annotation crop region crops any annotation outside of the crop region and any annotations that it touches. If the model crop region crops an element that is tagged, the tag or annotation will automatically be cropped as well. You can turn on Annotation Crop and resize the crop region closer to the model crop region using the grip controls or by using the Crop Region Size dialog box, as shown in Figure 3–39. In the *Modify | Floor Plan* tab>Crop panel, click (Size Crop) to open the dialog box.

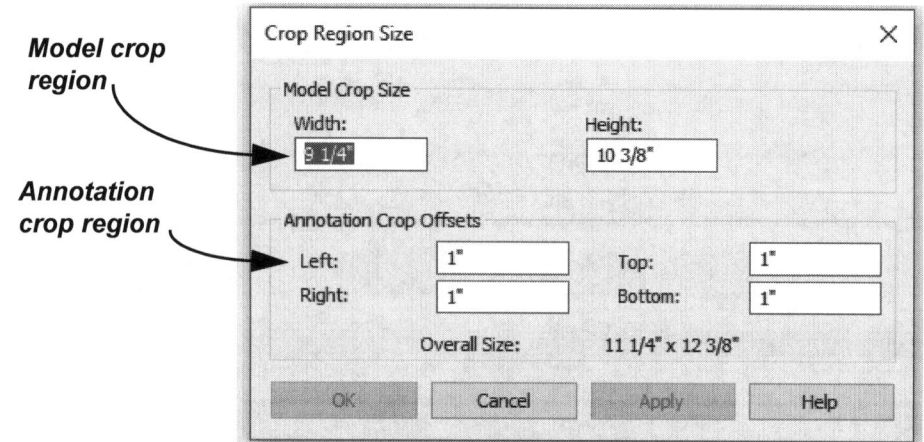

Figure 3–39

## Plan Regions

When you have a plan view with multiple levels of floors or ceilings, you can create plan regions that enable you to set a different view range for part of a view (as shown in Figure 3–40) for a set of clerestory windows.

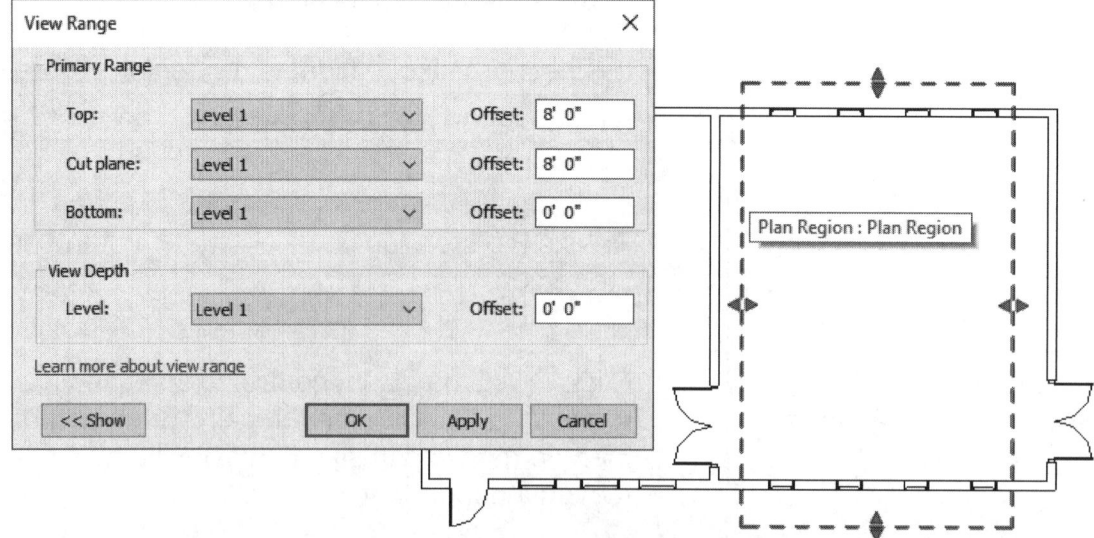

Figure 3–40

# Working with Views

## How To: Create Plan Regions

1. In a plan view, in the *View* tab>Create panel, expand  (Plan Views) and select  (Plan Region).
2. In the *Modify | Create Plan Region Boundary* tab>Draw panel, select a draw tool and create the boundary for the plan region.
    - The boundary must be closed and cannot overlap other plan region boundaries, but the boundaries can be side by side.
3. Click  (Finish Edit Mode).
4. In the *Modify | Plan Region* tab>Region panel, click  (View Range).
5. In the View Range dialog box, specify the offsets for the plan region and click **OK**. The plan region is applied to the selected area.

- Plan regions can be copied to the clipboard and then pasted into other plan views.

- You can use shape handles to resize plan region boundaries without having to edit the boundary.

- If a plan region is above a door, the door swing displays, but the door opening does not display, as shown in Figure 3–41.

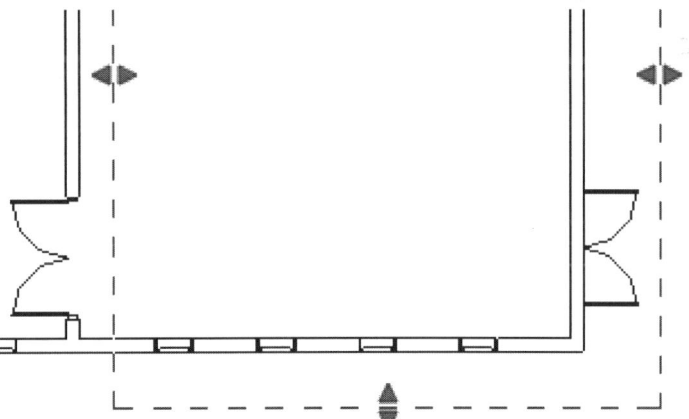

**Figure 3–41**

- Plan regions can be toggled on and off in the Visibility/Graphic Overrides dialog box on the *Annotation Categories* tab. If they are displayed, the plan regions are not included when printing and exporting.

**Hint: Depth Clipping and Far Clipping**

**Depth Clipping**, shown in Figure 3–42, is a viewing option that sets how sloped walls are displayed if the *View Range* of a plan is set to a limited view.

**Far Clipping** (shown in Figure 3–43) is available for section and elevation views.

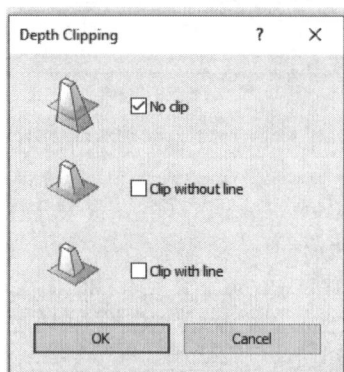
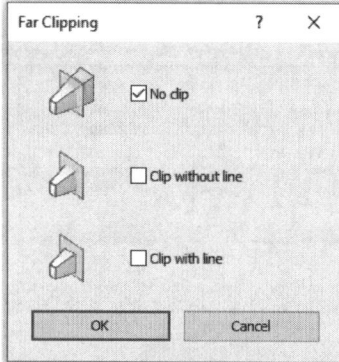

Figure 3–42  Figure 3–43

- An additional Graphic Display Option enables you to specify *Depth Cueing*, so that items that are in the distance will be made lighter.

# Practice 3b | Add Callout Views

## Practice Objectives

- Modify crop regions.
- Create callouts.
- Override visibility and graphic styles in views.
- Create view templates.

In this practice, you will create callout views of a guest room and make modifications to the visibility graphics so that one displays the furniture and the other does not, as shown in Figure 3–44, then create view templates from the view to use in other practices. You will also add callout views for other areas that need enlarged plans.

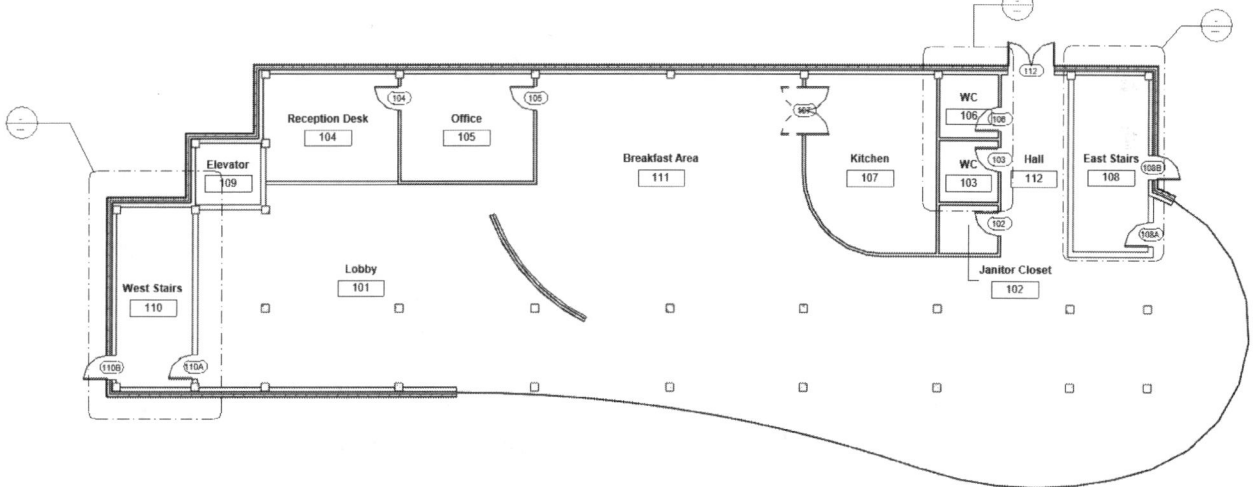

Figure 3–44

- Furniture and dimensions have been added to this model to demonstrate what happens when working with views.

### Task 1 - Add callout views.

1. Open the project **Hotel-Callouts.rvt** from the practice files folder.

2. Open the **Floor Plans: Typical Guest Room Plan** view. (Dimensions, furniture, and plumbing fixtures have been added to this room.)

3. Note that the *Scale* is set to **1/8"=1'-0"**.

4. In the *View* tab>Create panel, expand (Callout) and select (Rectangle).

5. In the Type Selector, verify that **Floor Plan** is selected.

6. Place a callout around the guest room with furniture, as shown in Figure 3–45. Move the callout bubble, callout head, and leader line, as needed.

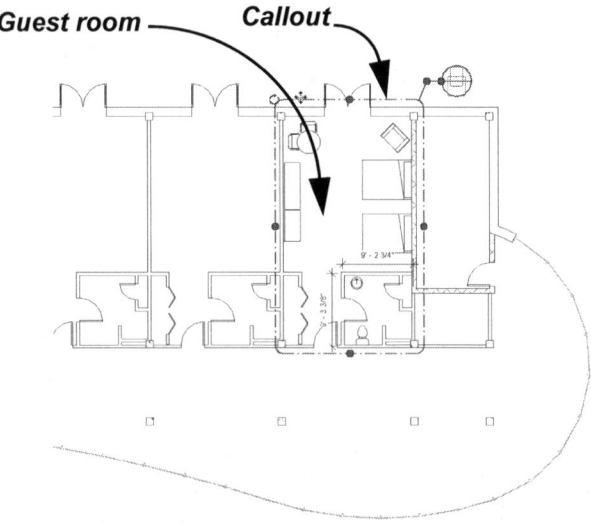

Figure 3–45

7. Click in an empty space in the view to release the selection.

8. Double-click on the callout head to display the view. Note that the *Scale* is automatically set to **1/4"=1'-0"**, as it is a partial plan view.

9. In the Project Browser within the Floor Plans node, rename the Typical Guest Room Plan - Callout 1 view to **Typical Guest Room - Furniture Plan**. Note that the dimensions do not display because callouts will not copy from the original view.

10. Save the project.

## Task 2 - Override graphics in views.

1. Click on the **Floor Plans: Typical Guest Room Plan** view tab to make it the active view.

2. Open the Visibility/Graphic Overrides dialog box by typing **VV**.

# Working with Views

3. In the dialog box, set the *Filter list* to **Architecture** (by clearing the checkmarks for the other options). In the *Visibility* column, clear **Casework** (as shown in Figure 3–46), **Furniture**, **Furniture Systems**, and **Plumbing Fixtures** (not shown).

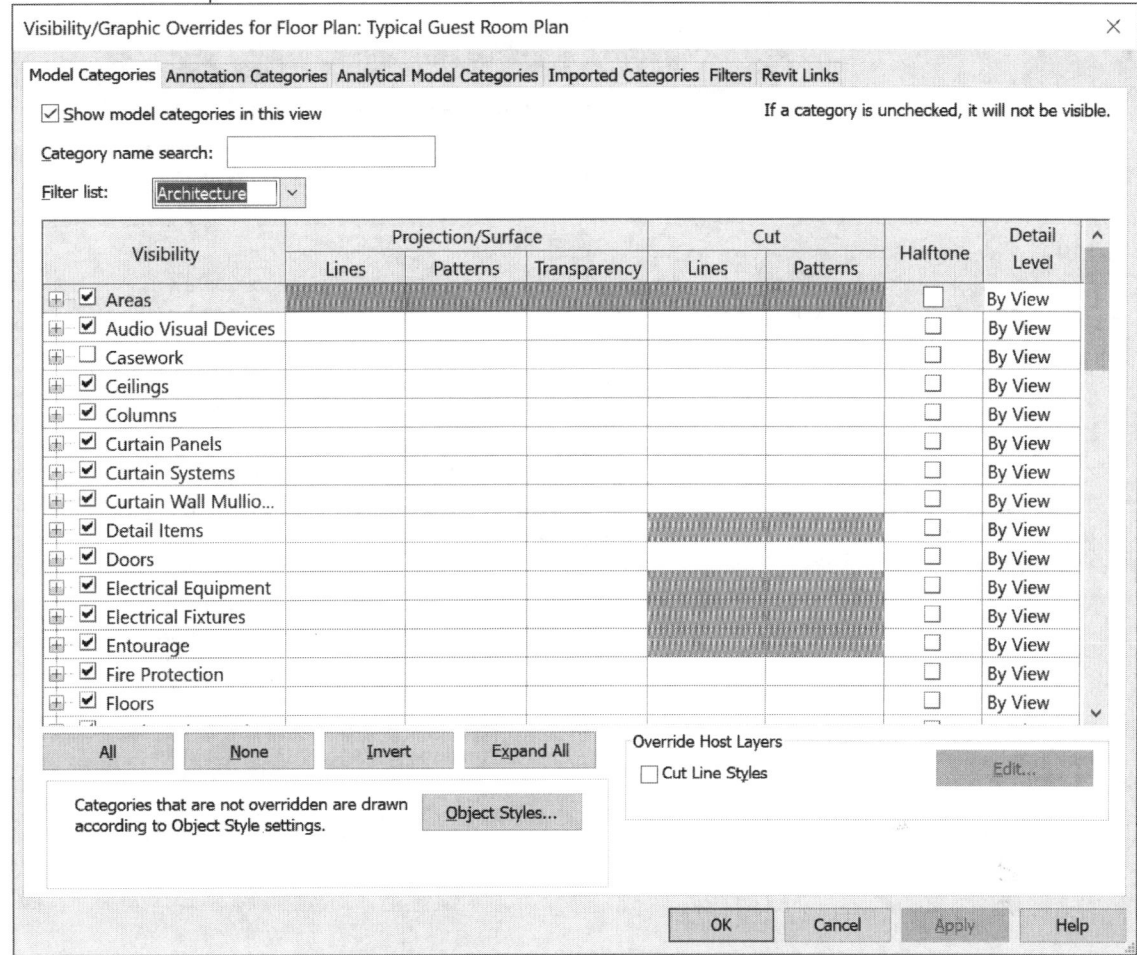

Figure 3–46

4. Click **OK**. The furniture and plumbing fixtures are removed from the view, but the dimensions still display.

5. Click on the **Floor Plans: Typical Guest Room - Furniture Plan** view tab to make it the active view. Note that the furniture and plumbing fixtures show in this view.

6. Reopen the Visibility/Graphic Overrides dialog box. On the *Model Categories* tab, at the bottom of the table, click **All** and place a checkmark in one of the *Halftone* columns. Click **Apply**. All of the elements are set to halftone.

7. Click **None** to clear all categories.

8. In the *Halftone* column, clear the **Casework**, **Furniture**, **Furniture Systems**, and **Plumbing Fixtures** categories.

9. Click **Apply** to set the changes without exiting the dialog box.

10. In the *Annotation Categories* tab, clear **Show annotation categories in this view**, as shown in Figure 3–47. No annotation elements will display in this view even if they are added in other views of this part of the model.

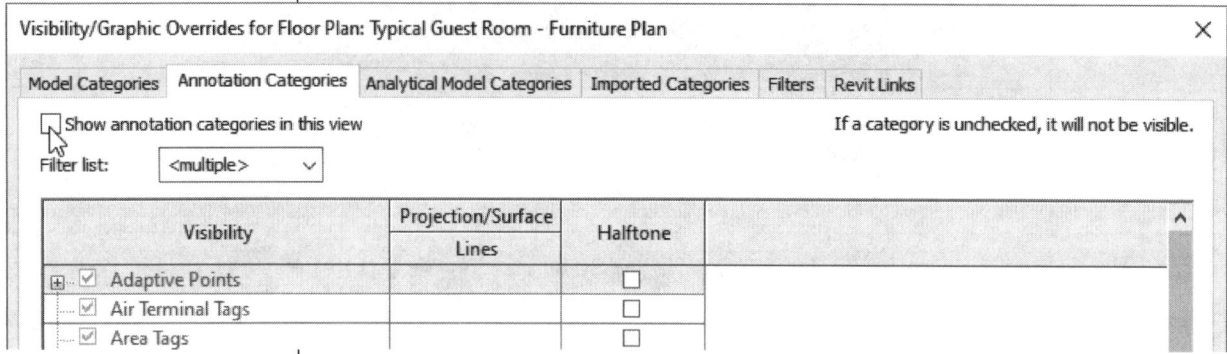

Figure 3–47

11. Click **OK** to close the dialog box. The view should display with all existing elements in halftone, as shown in Figure 3–48.

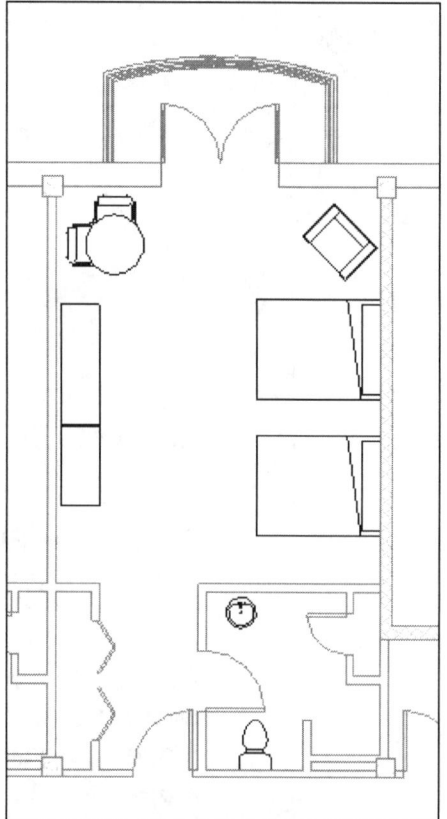

Figure 3–48

12. Save the project.

# Working with Views

## Task 3 - Create a view template.

1. In the Project Browser, right-click on the **Typical Guest Room Plan** view and select **Create View Template From View...**.

2. In the New View Template dialog box, type **Dimension Plan** and click **OK**.

3. In the View Templates dialog box, click **OK**.

4. Repeat creating a view template but using the **Typical Guest Room - Furniture Plan** view. Name the new view template **Furniture Plan**.

    - Creating a view template from a view can be used on other plan views as needed.

5. Save the project.

## Task 4 - Additional callouts.

1. Open the **Floor Plans: Floor 1 - Reference Plan** view.

2. In the *View* tab>Create panel, click (Callout) and add floor plan callouts to the stairs and restrooms.

3. In the Project Browser, rename the created callout views as shown in Figure 3–49 (grids have been hidden in the figure for clarity).

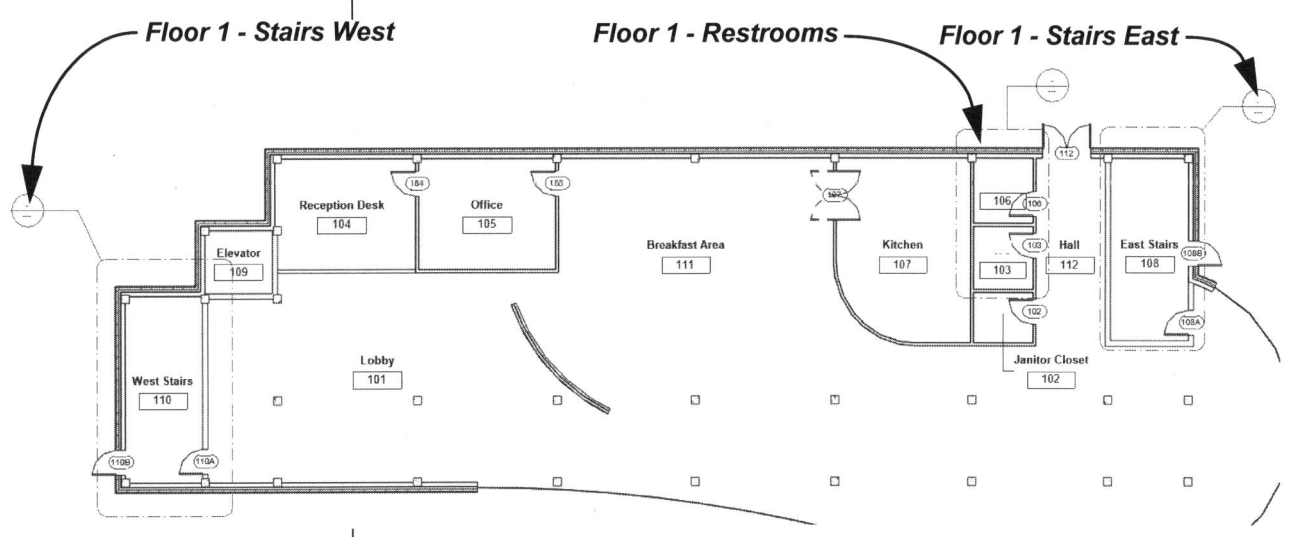

**Figure 3–49**

4. Save and close the project.

## 3.5 Creating Elevations and Sections

Elevations and sections are critical elements of construction documents and can assist you as you are working on a model. Any changes made in one of these views (such as the section in Figure 3–50), changes the entire model and any changes made to the project model are also displayed in the elevations and sections.

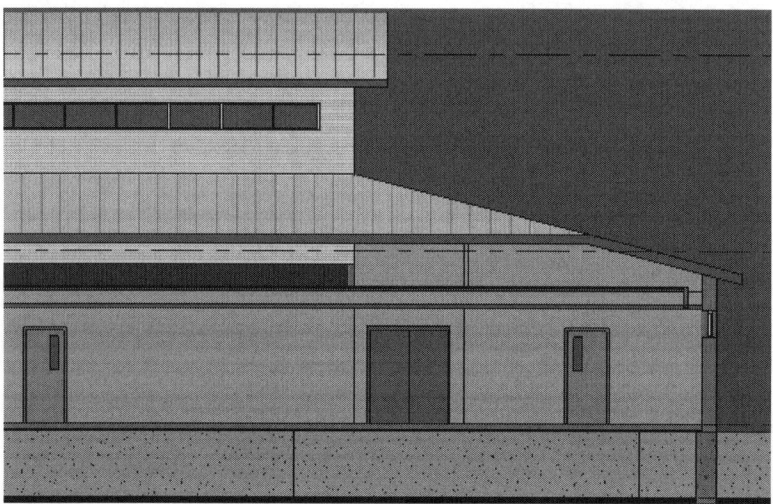

**Figure 3–50**

- In the Project Browser, elevations are separated by elevation type and sections are separated by section type, as shown in Figure 3–51.

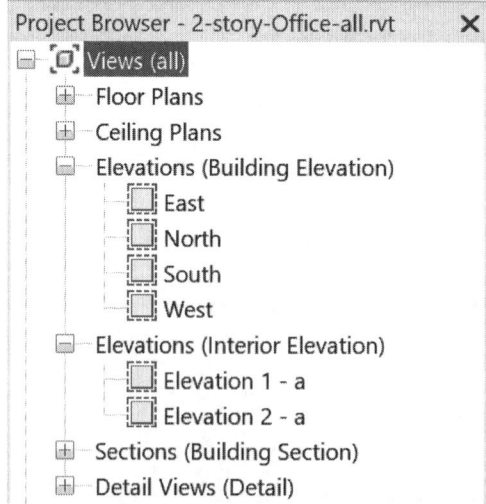

**Figure 3–51**

- To open an elevation or section view, double-click on the marker arrow or on its name in the Project Browser.

## Elevations

- To give the elevation or section a new name, in the Project Browser, slowly click twice on the name or right-click on it and select **Rename...**.

Elevations are *face-on* views of the interiors and exteriors of a building. Four exterior elevation views are defined in the default template: **North**, **South**, **East**, and **West**. You can create additional building elevation views at other angles or interior elevation views, as shown in Figure 3–52.

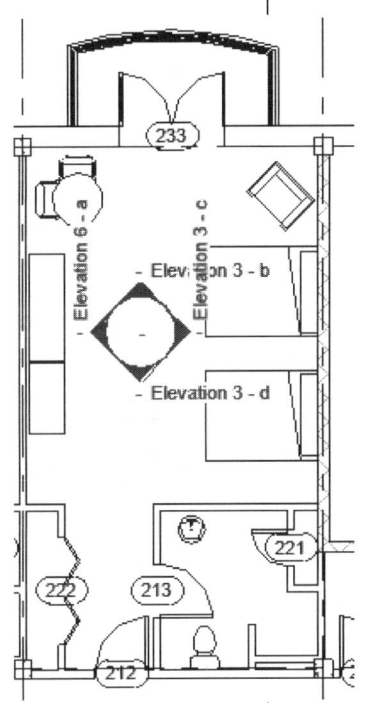
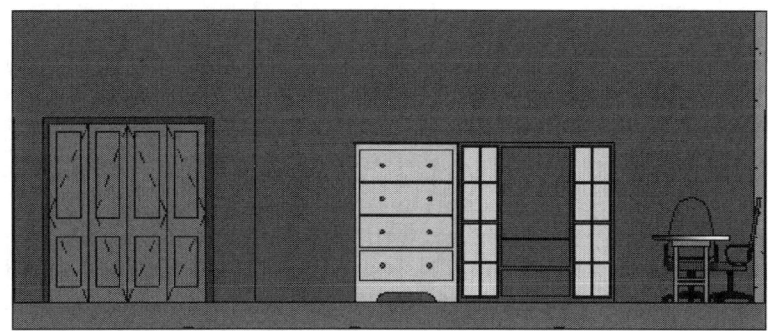

**Figure 3–52**

- Elevations markers must be placed in plan views.

- When you add an elevation or section to a sheet, the detail and sheet number are automatically added to the view title and elevation/section marker.

### How To: Create an Elevation

1. In the *View* tab>Create panel, expand (Elevation) and click (Elevation).
2. In the Type Selector, select the elevation type. Two types come with the templates: **Building Elevation** and **Interior Elevation**.
3. Move the cursor near one of the walls that defines the elevation. The marker follows the angle of the wall.
4. Click to place the marker.

*The software remembers the last elevation type used, so you can click the top button if you want to use the same elevation command.*

- The length, width, and height of an elevation are defined by the walls and ceiling/floor at which the elevation marker is pointing.

- When creating interior elevations, ensure that the floor or ceiling above is in place before creating the elevation or you will need to modify the elevation crop region so that the elevation markers do not show on all floors.

## Sections

Sections are slices through a model. You can create a section through an entire building or through one wall for a detail. Sections can be created in plan, elevation, and other section views. You can flip, resize, or split a section. Figure 3–53 shows all the components of a section marker.

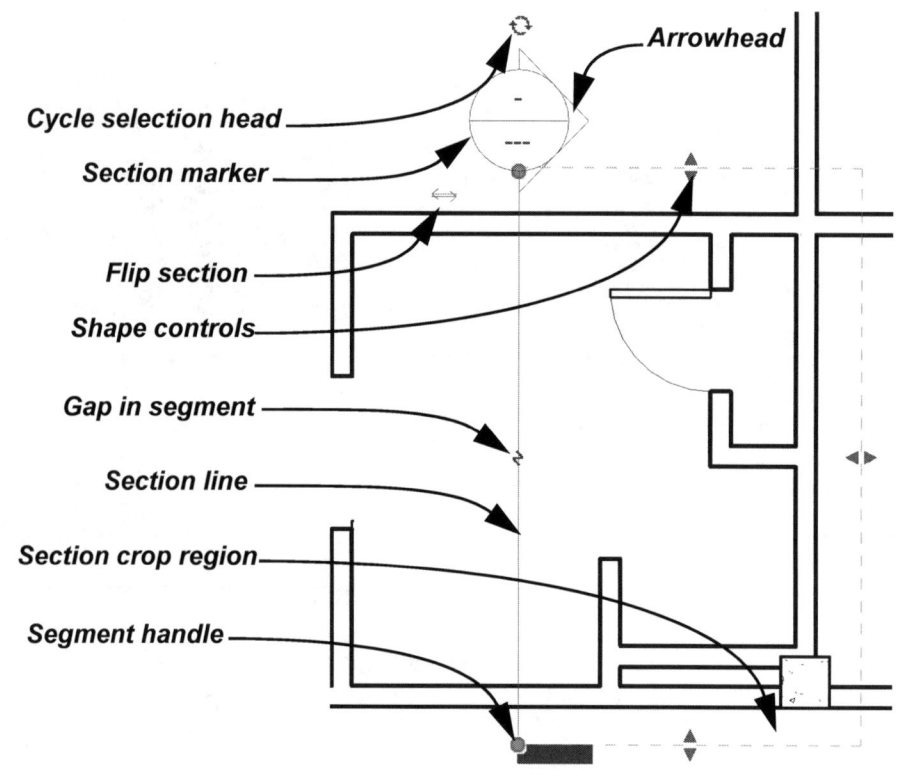

Figure 3–53

### How To: Create a Section

1. In the *View* tab>Create panel or in the Quick Access Toolbar, click (Section).

2. In the Type Selector, select **Section: Building Section** or **Section: Wall Section.** If you want a section in a Drafting view select **Detail View: Detail.**

3. In the view, select a point where you want to locate the crop region and section marker.
4. Select the second or end point that defines the section.
5. The shape controls display. You can flip the arrow and change the size of the cutting plane, as well as the location of the bubble and flag.

- When placing a section you can snap to other elements in the model as the start and end points of the section line. You can also use the **Align** command to reorient a section line to an element such as an angled wall.

- Section lines can also be used as an alignment object and can be snapped to when placing other geometry.

## Modifying Elevations and Sections

There are two parts to modifying elevations and sections:

- To modify the markers (as shown in Figure 3–54), select the arrowhead (triangle) part of the section marker and use the controls to change the length and depth of elevations and sections. There are other specific type options as well.

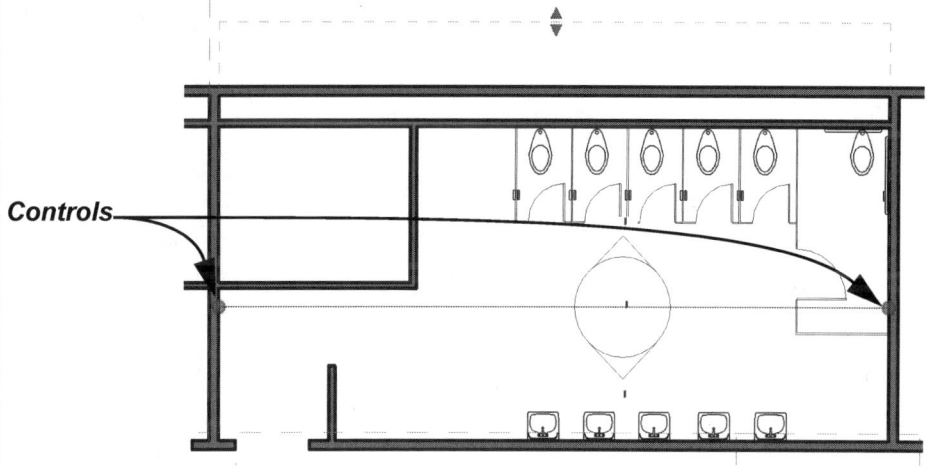

Figure 3–54

- To modify the view (as shown in Figure 3–55), select the crop region and use the controls to modify the size or create view breaks.

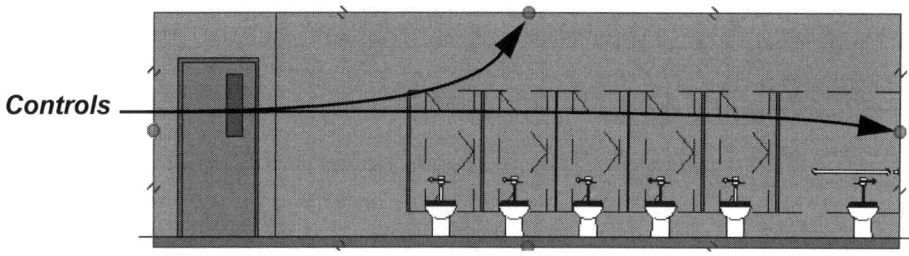

Figure 3–55

## Modifying Elevation Markers

When you modify elevation markers, you can specify the length and depth of the clip plane, as shown in Figure 3–56.

- Select the arrowhead of the elevation marker (not the circle portion) to display the clip plane.

- Drag the round shape handles to lengthen or shorten the elevation.

- Adjust the ▲▼ (Drag) controls to modify the depth of the elevation.

To display additional interior elevations from one marker, select the circle portion (not the arrowhead) and place a checkmark in the Show Arrow box in the directions that you want to display, as shown in Figure 3–56.

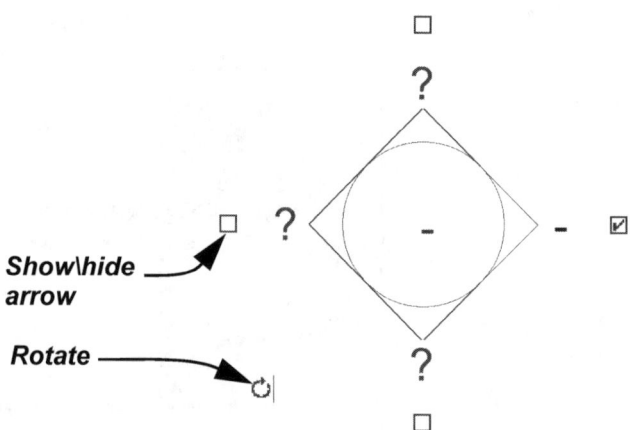

Figure 3–56

- Use the ↻ (Rotate) control to angle the marker (e.g., for a room with angled walls).

# Working with Views

## Modifying Section Markers

When you modify section markers, various shape handles and controls enable you to modify a section, as shown in Figure 3–57.

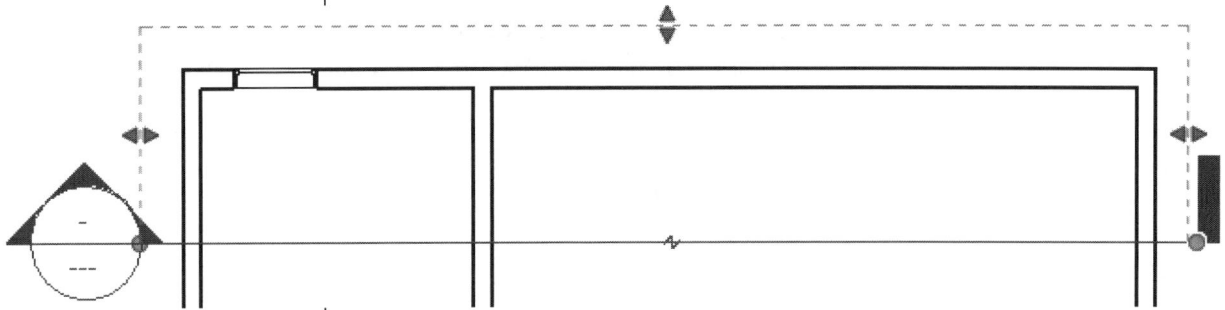

Figure 3–57

- Adjust the ▲▼ (Drag) controls to change the length and depth of the cut plane.

- Drag the segment handle controls at either end of the section line to change the location of the arrow or flag without changing the cut boundary.

- Click ⇆ (Flip Section) to change the direction of the arrowhead, which also flips the entire section.

- Click ↻ (Cycle Section Head/Tail) to switch between an arrowhead, flag, or nothing on each end of the section.

- Click ⤲ (Gaps in Segments) to create an opening in section lines, as shown in Figure 3–58. Select it again to restore the full section cut.

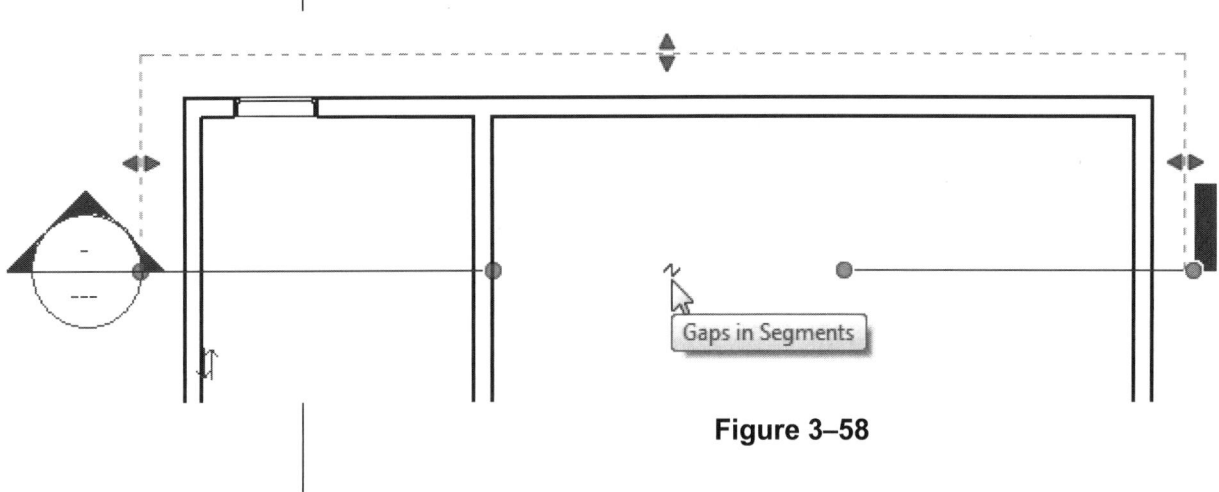

Figure 3–58

## How To: Add a Jog to a Section Line

1. Select the section line you want to modify.
2. In the *Modify | Views* tab>Section panel, click (Split Segment).
3. Select the point along the section line where you want to create the split, as shown in Figure 3–59.
4. Specify the location of the split line, as shown in Figure 3–60.

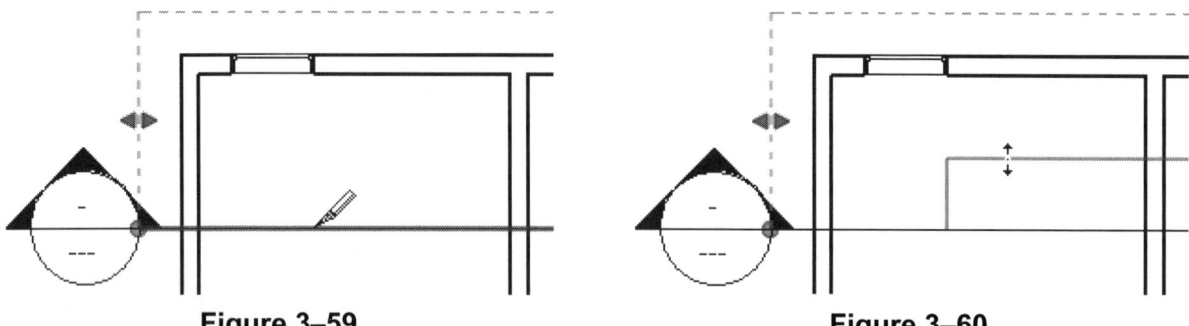

**Figure 3–59**  **Figure 3–60**

- If you need to adjust the location of any segment on the section line, modify it and drag the shape handles along each segment of the line, as shown in Figure 3–61.

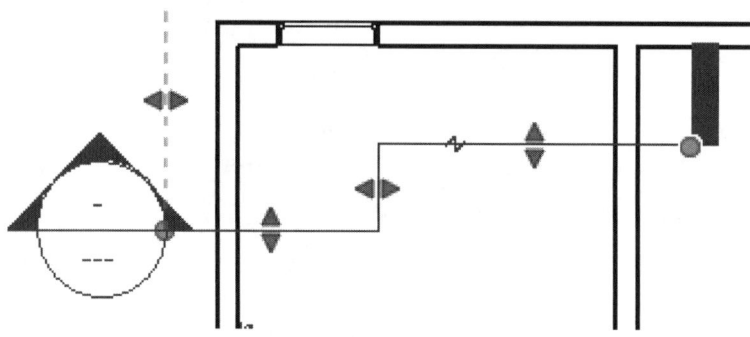

**Figure 3–61**

To bring a split section line back into place, use the shape handle to drag the jogged line until it is at the same level with the rest of the line.

- For more information on enhancing views such as sections and elevation, see *A.8 Enhancing Views*.

# 3D Section Views

There are two ways you can create section views of your 3D model: creating a selection box, as shown in Figure 3–62, and orienting to a view. Both of these are very helpful as you are working and also can be used in construction documents and presentations.

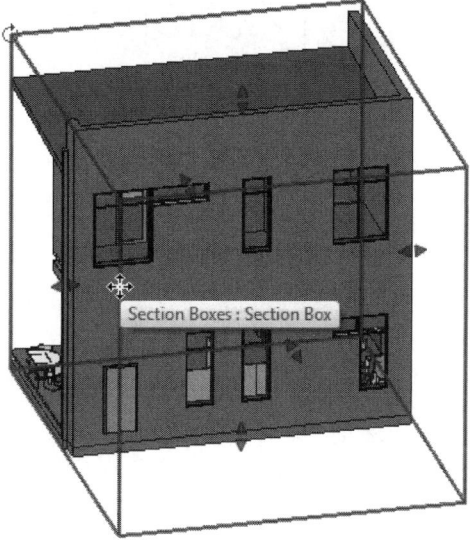

Figure 3–62

## How To: Create a Selection Box

1. In a 3D view, select the elements you want to isolate. In the example shown in Figure 3–62, the front wall was selected.
2. In the *Modify* tab>View panel, click (Selection Box), or type **BX**.
3. The view is limited to a box around the selected item(s).
4. Use the controls of the Section Box to modify the size of the box to show exactly what you want.

- To toggle off a section box and restore the full model, in the view's Properties, in the *Extents* area, clear the check from **Section Box**.

## How To: Orient a 3D View to a View

1. Open a 3D view.
2. Right-click on the ViewCube and select **Orient to View>Floor Plans, Elevations, Sections,** or **3D Views**, as shown in Figure 3–63, and select the view from the list.

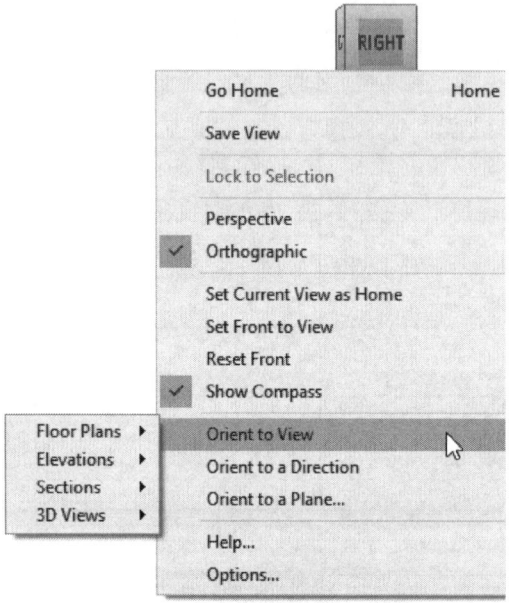

Figure 3–63

3. The view displays as shown, in the partial floor plan view of a stair, in Figure 3–64. Use the 3D view rotation tools to navigate around the 3D model, as shown in Figure 3–65.

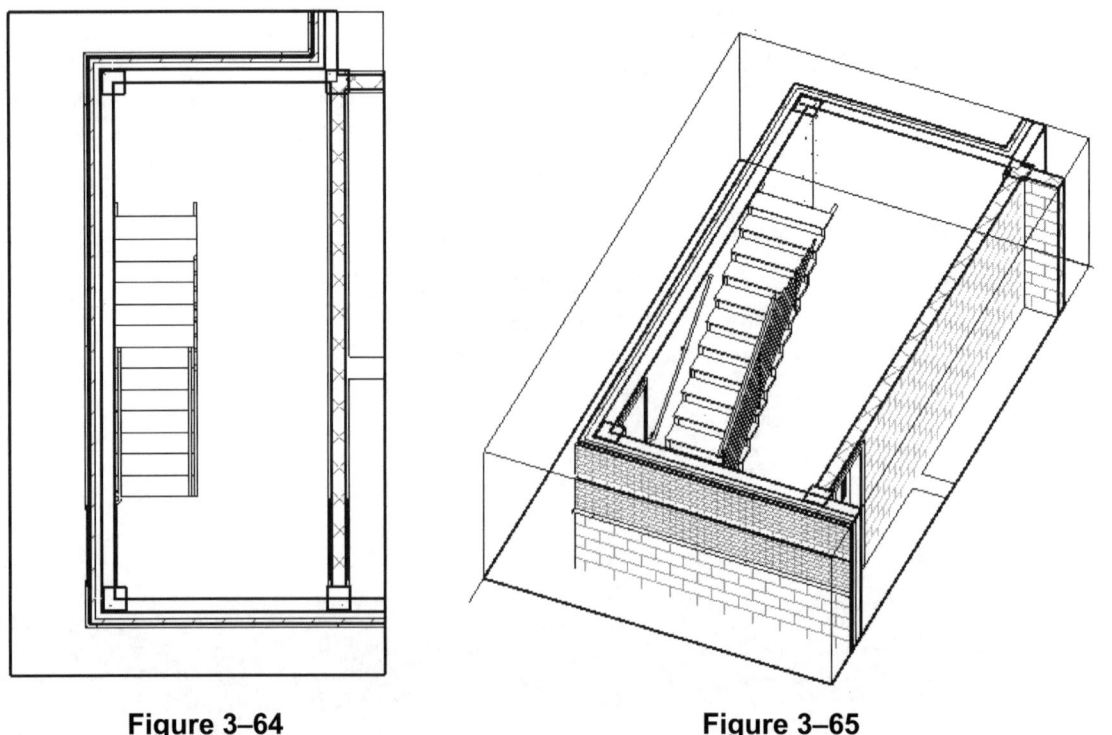

Figure 3–64      Figure 3–65

# Working with Views

- **Orient to a Direction** enables you to position the view in a specific direction, as shown in Figure 3–66. This is similar to using the orientation planes of the ViewCube.

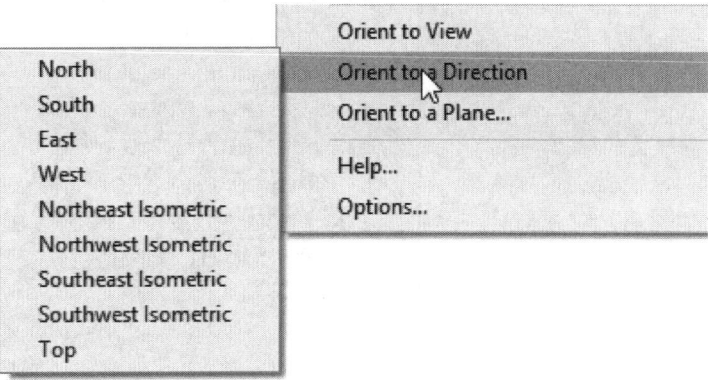

Figure 3–66

- **Orient to a Plane** opens the Select Orientation Plane dialog box and enables you to specify a level, grid, or named reference plane, or pick a plane or a line, as shown in Figure 3–67. The view is not cut at the plane but oriented in that direction.

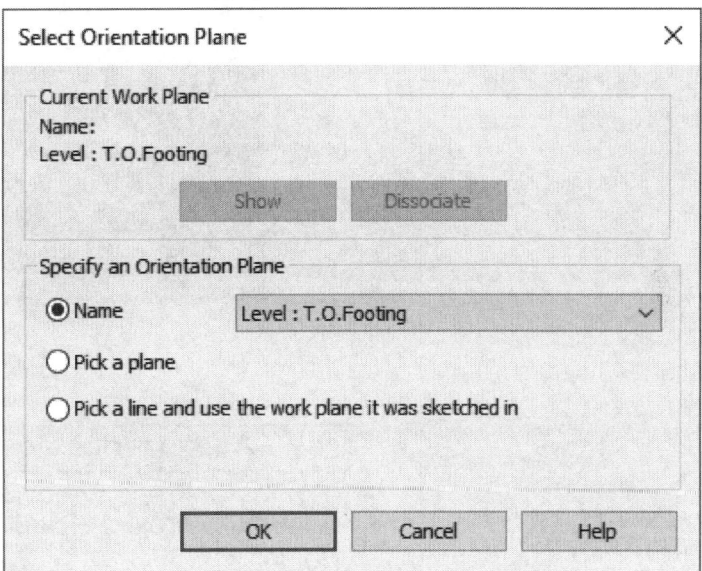

Figure 3–67

# Practice 3c

# Create Elevations and Sections

## Practice Objectives

- Create exterior and interior elevations.
- Add building sections and wall sections.

In this practice, you will create exterior elevations of the poolhouse and interior elevations of the restrooms. You will also add building sections, as shown in Figure 3–68, and several wall sections to the project.

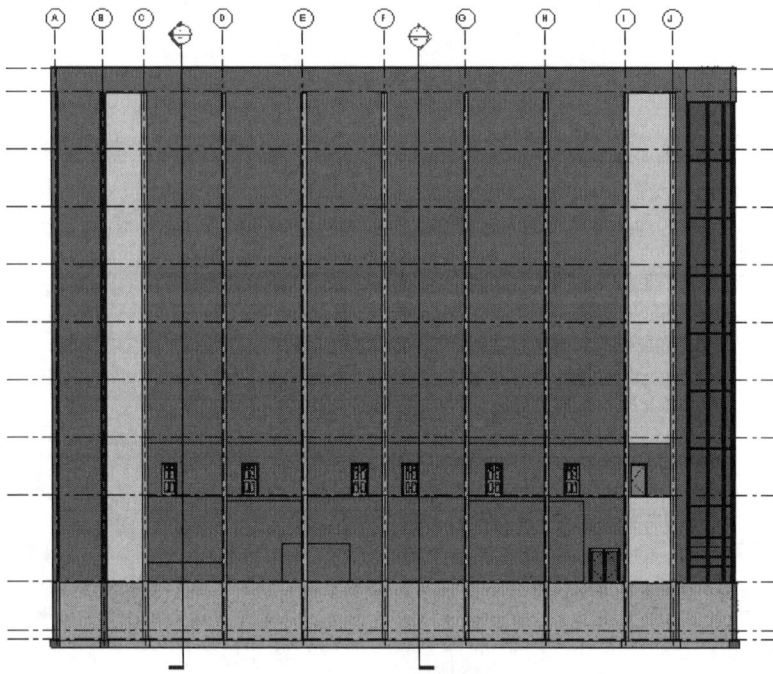

Figure 3–68

### Task 1 - Add exterior elevations.

1. Open the project **Hotel-Elevations.rvt** from the practice files folder.

2. Verify you are in the **Floor Plans - Floor 1** view. Find and note the two restrooms in the hotel labeled **RR**.

3. Open the **Floor Plans: Floor 1 - Reference Plan** view.

4. Move the **North** elevation marker between grids C and D, as shown in Figure 3–69.

5. In the View Control Bar, click (Show Crop Region).

# Working with Views

6. Ensure that there is enough space above the poolhouse to add an elevation mark at this scale. If not, move the crop region up.

7. In the *View* tab>Create panel, expand (Elevation) and click (Elevation). In the Type Selector, select **Elevation: Building Elevation**.

8. Place an elevation marker outside of the pool building, as shown in Figure 3–69. (Callouts are not shown in the image for clarity.)

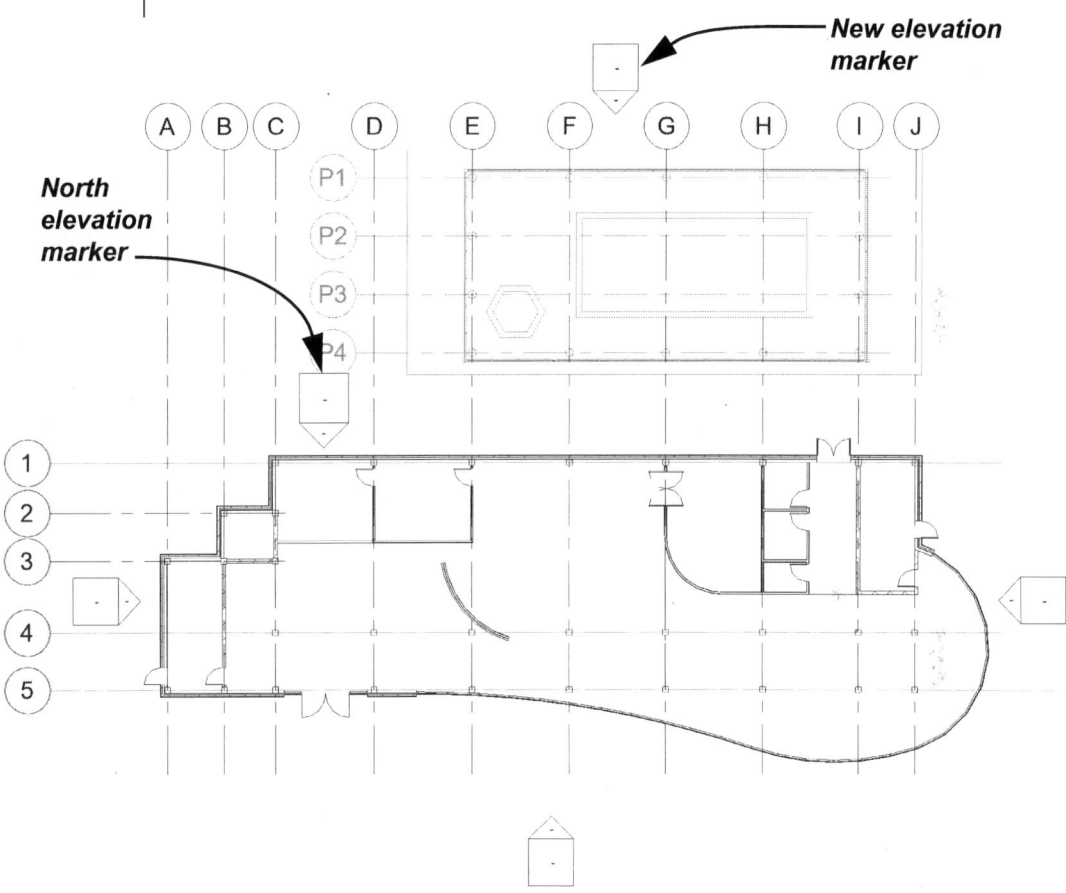

**Figure 3–69**

9. Because the poolhouse is a linked file, the elevation marker does not know in which direction to point the elevation's arrowhead. If needed, select the elevation marker and uncheck/check the appropriate direction, as shown in Figure 3–70.

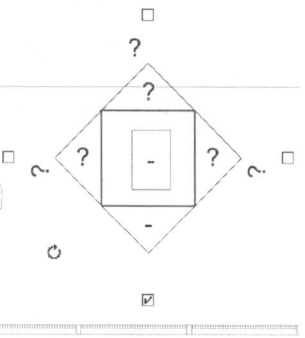

Figure 3–70

10. Click  (Modify) and select the arrowhead on the new elevation marker.

11. Change the length and depth of the elevation crop region to just be around the poolhouse, as shown in Figure 3–71. (Note: Grids are hidden in the image to clarify the view.)

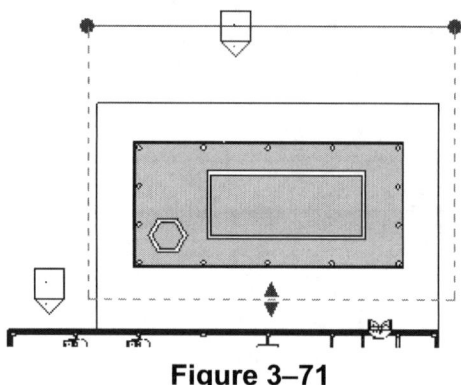

Figure 3–71

12. Double-click on the arrowhead to open the elevation view.

13. In the elevation view, use the crop region segment handles to change the crop region so that the height is up to **Floor 3** and the bottom is just below the floor line. Bring the sides in close to the pool building.

14. Hide the grids and levels so that the elevation is similar to that shown in Figure 3–72.

# Working with Views

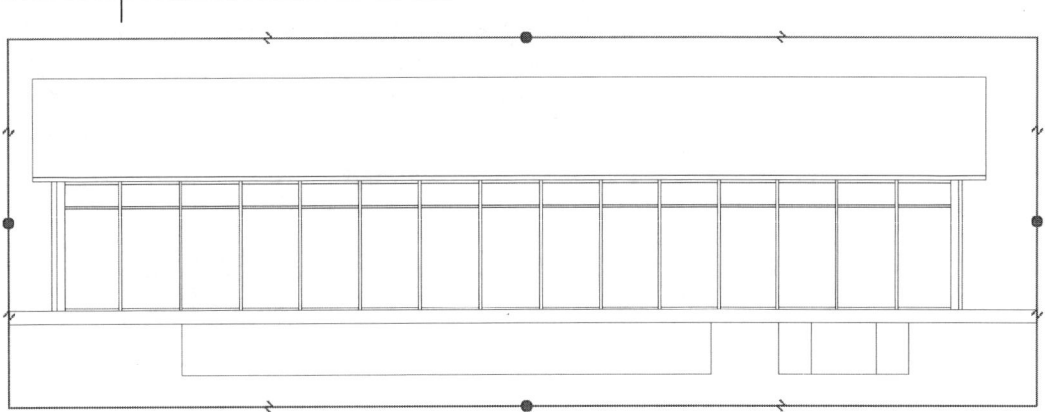

Figure 3–72

15. Click (Hide Crop Region).

16. In the Project Browser, in the *Elevations (Building Elevation)* area), rename the elevation (Elevation 1 - a if you selected this direction first) as **Pool-North**.

*In this project, North is considered the top of the project.*

17. Return to the **Floor Plans: Floor 1 - Reference Plan** view.

18. Add elevation markers to the other sides of the poolhouse.

19. Open the new elevations. Resize and rename them accordingly.

20. If needed, hover over the elevation marker and the tooltip will display the name of the view, as shown in Figure 3–73.

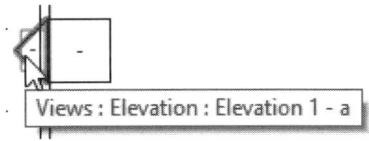

Figure 3–73

21. Save the project.

## Task 2 - Add interior elevations.

1. Open the **Floor Plans: Floor 1 - Restrooms** view.

2. In the *View* tab>Create panel, click (Elevation).

3. In the Type Selector, select **Elevation: Interior Elevation**.

4. Place an elevation in the top restroom.

5. Click (Modify).

6. Select the circle part of the interior elevation marker and check the box opposite the current checkbox, as shown in Figure 3–74. This places an elevation in each direction.

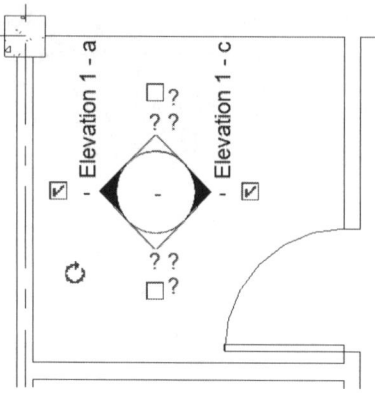

Figure 3–74

7. Repeat for the other restroom.

8. In the topmost restroom, select the elevation marker arrow that is pointing west. In Properties, change the view's name in the *Identity Data* section (as shown in Figure 3–75) according to the room number and which direction the arrow is facing, so this elevation marker will be named **RR106-West**.

*Project north is straight up in the model.*

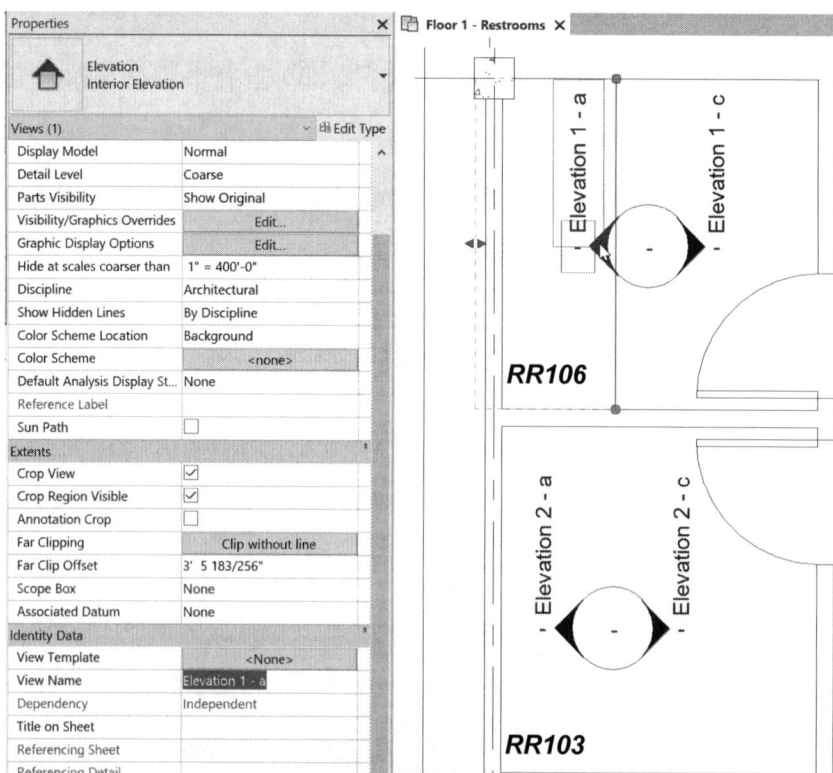

Figure 3–75

# Working with Views

*Doing this keeps these markers from showing up in other plans at larger scales.*

9. Repeat with the remaining elevation markers. The topmost restroom will be named RR106-East, and the restrooms below that will be named RR103-West and RR103-East.

10. Select all of the elevation marker arrows (not the squares) and, in Properties, set the *Hide at scales coarser than* to **1/4"=1'-0"**, as shown in Figure 3–76.

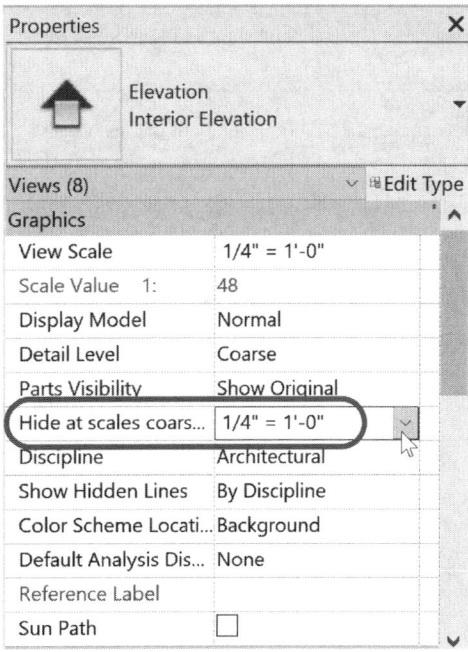

Figure 3–76

11. Open the elevation **RR103-East**. The interior elevation should automatically stop at the boundaries of the walls and ceiling.

12. Save the project.

**Task 3 - Clean up a view and add building sections.**

1. Open the **Floor Plans: Floor 1 - Reference Plan** view.

2. Type **ZA** (Zoom All To Fit) to zoom out to the extents of the view.

3. In the *View* tab>Create panel, click (Section).

4. In the Type Selector, select **Section: Building Section**.

5. Draw a horizontal section and a vertical section through the building, as shown in Figure 3–77.

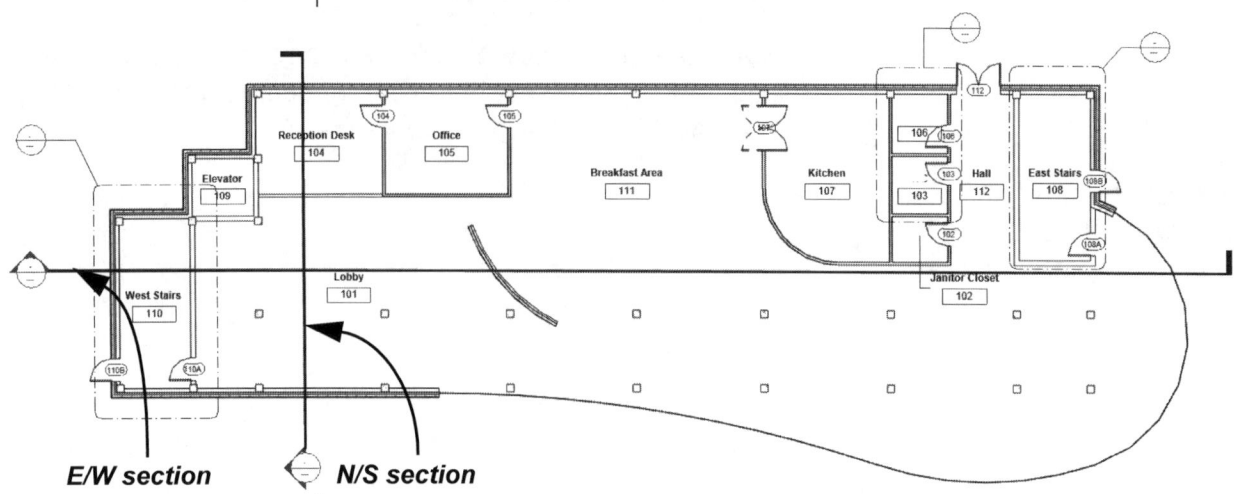

Figure 3–77

6. In the Project Browser, under *Sections (Building Section)*, rename them to **E/W Building Section** and **N/S Building Section**.

7. Select the E/W Building Section line and drag the section down so it goes through the stairwell doors, as shown in Figure 3–78.

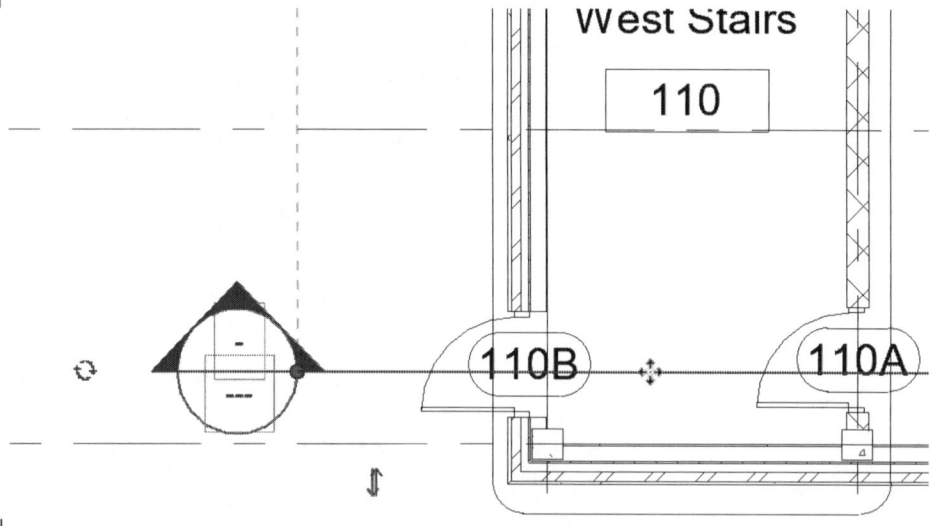

Figure 3–78

8. View each of the building sections.

9. Save the project.

*You are using the **Floor 2** view to place the wall sections, as you want to ensure that they go through certain features, such as doors and windows.*

## Task 4 - Add wall sections.

1. Open the **Floor Plans: Floor 2** view.

2. Turn on the crop region and adjust it to be tighter around the hotel.

3. Turn off the crop region.

4. Select a grid line and the DWG and type **VH** to hide them in this view.

5. Type **ZA** (Zoom All To Fit) to zoom out to the extents of the view.

6. In the *View* tab>Create panel, click (Section). In the Type Selector, select **Section: Wall Section**.

7. Draw four wall sections, as shown in Figure 3–79 (tags and elevations are turned off for clarity in the figure). Ensure that the front wall section passes through a window and the back wall section passes through a door.

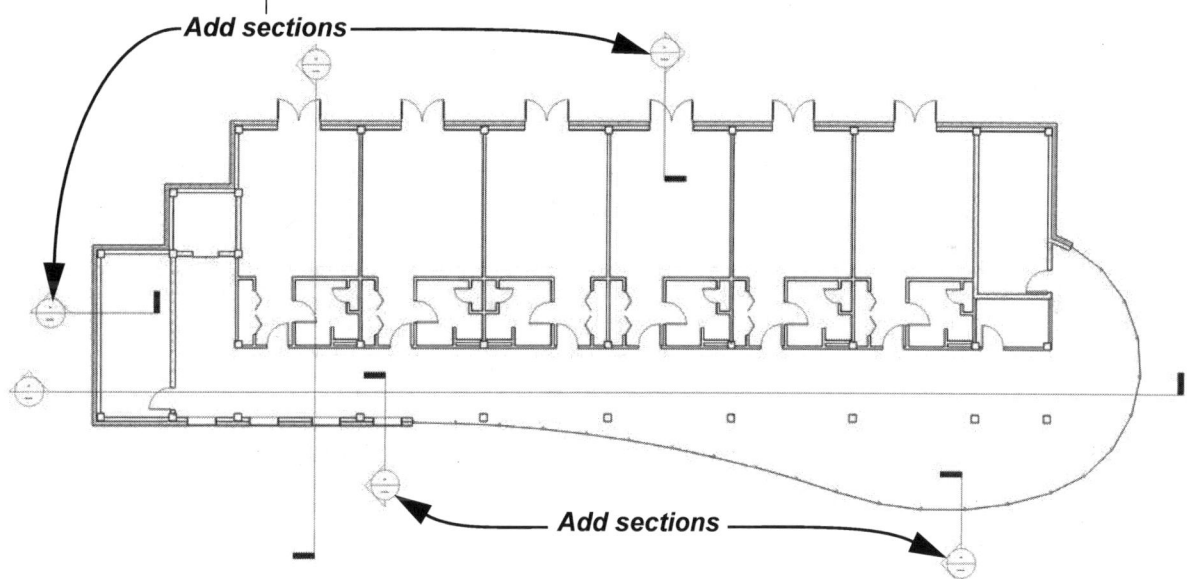

**Figure 3–79**

8. Move any annotation elements so they do not interfere with the section cut.

9. View each of the wall sections.

10. Save and close the project.

# Chapter Review Questions

1. Which of the following commands creates a view that results in an independent view displaying the same model geometry and containing a copy of the annotation?

    a. Duplicate

    b. Duplicate with Detailing

    c. Duplicate as a Dependent

2. Which of the following is true about the Visibility/Graphic Overrides dialog box?

    a. Changes made in the dialog box only affect the current view.

    b. It can only be used to toggle categories on and off.

    c. It can be used to toggle individual elements on and off.

    d. It can be used to change the color of individual elements.

3. If you want to hide just one of the elevation markers in a view, what do you have to do?

    a. Select the elevation marker, then right-click and select **Hide in View>By Filter**.

    b. Select the elevation marker, then right-click and select **Hide in View>Category**.

    c. Select the elevation marker, then right-click and select **Hide in View>Elements**.

    d. In the Visibility/Graphic Overrides dialog box, uncheck **Elevations**.

4. What is the purpose of creating a callout?

    a. To create a boundary around part of the model that needs revising, similar to a revision cloud.

    b. To create a view of part of the model to export to the AutoCAD® software for further detailing.

    c. To create a view of part of the model that is linked to the main view from which it is taken.

    d. To create a 2D view of part of the model.

5. You placed dimensions in a view but only some of them display, as shown on the left in Figure 3–80. You were expecting the view to display as shown on the right in Figure 3–80. What do you need to modify to see the missing dimensions?

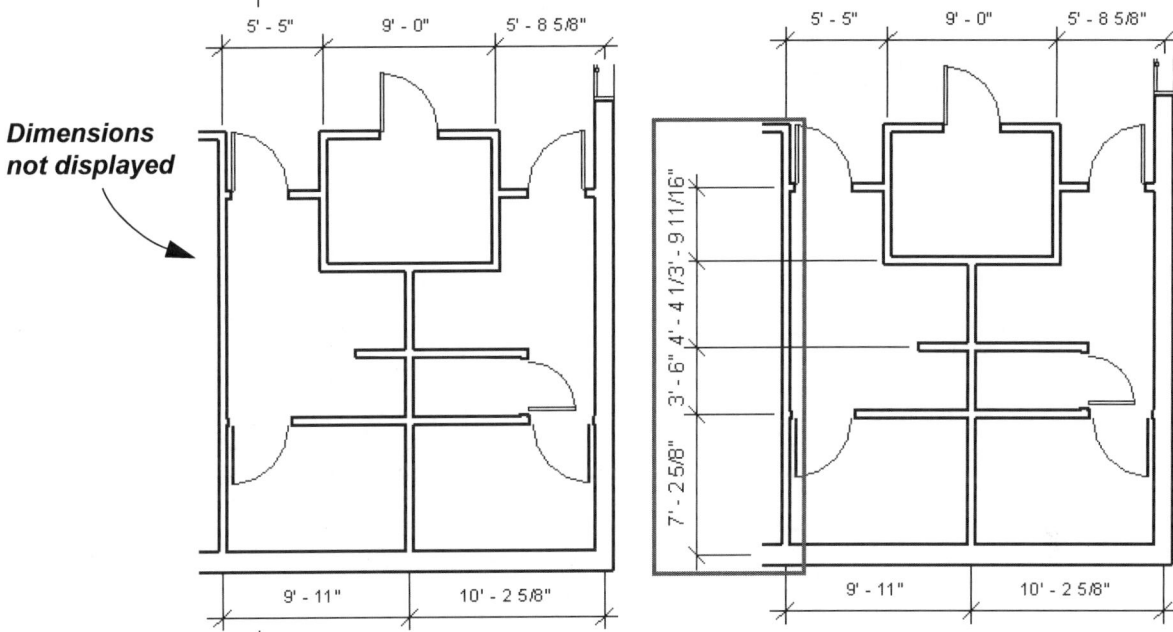

Figure 3–80

   a. Dimension Settings
   b. Dimension Type
   c. Visibility/Graphic Overrides
   d. Annotation Crop Region

6. How do you create multiple interior elevations in one room?

   a. Using the **Interior Elevation** command, place the elevation marker.

   b. Using the **Elevation** command from the Properties Type Selector, change to **Interior Elevation** and place the first marker, select it and select the appropriate Show Arrow boxes.

   c. Using the **Interior Elevation** command, place an elevation marker for each wall of the room you want to display.

   d. Using the **Elevation** command, select a Multiple Elevation marker type, and place the elevation marker.

7. How do you create a jog in a building section, such as that shown in Figure 3–81?

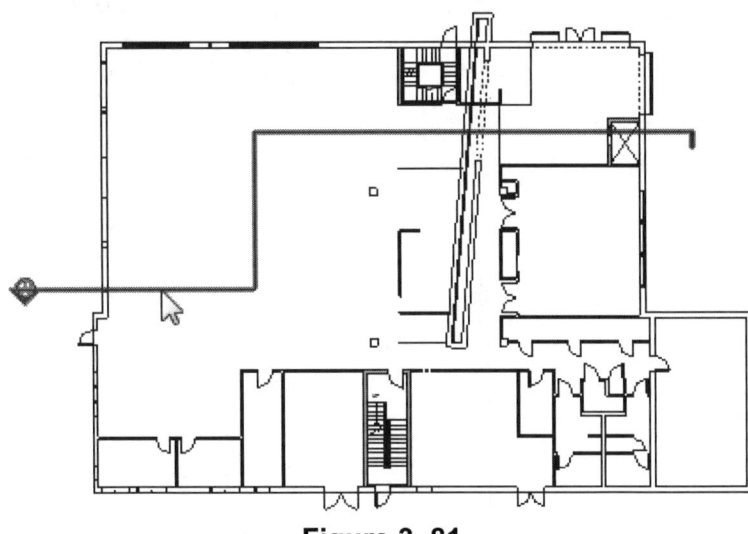

Figure 3–81

a. Use the **Split Element** tool in the *Modify* tab>Modify panel.

b. Select the building section and then click **Split Segment** in the contextual tab.

c. Select the building section and click the blue control in the middle of the section line.

d. Draw two separate sections and use the **Section Jog** tool to combine them into a jogged section.

# Command Summary

| Button | Command | Location |
|---|---|---|
| **Views** | | |
| | Elevation | • **Ribbon:** *View* tab>Create panel> expand Elevation |
| | Callout: Rectangle | • **Ribbon:** *View* tab>Create panel> expand Callout |
| | Callout: Sketch | • **Ribbon:** *View* tab>Create panel> expand Callout |
| | Duplicate | • **Ribbon:** *View* tab>Create panel> expand Duplicate View<br>• **Right-click:** (*on a view in the Project Browser*) expand Duplicate View |
| | Duplicate as Dependent | • **Ribbon:** *View* tab>Create panel> expand Duplicate View<br>• **Right-click:** (*on a view in the Project Browser*) expand Duplicate View |
| | Duplicate with Detailing | • **Ribbon:** *View* tab>Create panel> expand Duplicate View<br>• **Right-click:** (*on a view in the Project Browser*) Duplicate View |
| | Plan Region | • **Ribbon:** *View* tab>Create panel> expand Plan Views |
| | Section | • **Ribbon:** *View* tab>Create panel<br>• **Quick Access Toolbar** |
| | Split Segment | • **Ribbon:** (*when the elevation or section marker is selected*) Modify | *Views* tab> Section panel |
| **Crop Views** | | |
| | Crop View | • **View Control Bar**<br>• **View Properties:** Crop View (*check*) |
| | Do Not Crop View | • **View Control Bar**<br>• **View Properties:** Crop View (*clear*) |
| | Edit Crop | • **Ribbon:** (*when the crop region of a callout, elevation, or section view is selected*) Modify | *Views* tab>Mode panel |
| | Hide Crop Region | • **View Control Bar**<br>• **View Properties:** Crop Region Visible (*clear*) |
| | Reset Crop | • **Ribbon:** (*when the crop region of a callout, elevation or section view is selected*) Modify | *Views* tab>Mode panel |

| | | Show Crop Region | • **View Control Bar**<br>• **View Properties:** Crop Region Visible (*check*) |
|---|---|---|---|
| | | Size Crop | • **Ribbon:** (*when the crop region of a callout, elevation or section view is selected*) *Modify | Views* tab>Mode panel |
| **View Display** | | | |
| | | Hide in View | • **Ribbon:** *Modify* tab>View Graphics panel>Hide>Elements *or* By Category<br>• **Right-click:** (*when an element is selected*) Hide in View>Elements *or* Category |
| | | Override Graphics in View | • **Ribbon:** *Modify* tab>View Graphics panel>Hide>Elements *or* By Category<br>• **Right-click:** (*when an element is selected*) Override Graphics in View>By Element *or* By Category<br>• **Shortcut:** (*category only*) VV or VG |
| | | Plan Region | • **Ribbon:** *View* tab>Create panel expand Plan Views |
| | | Selection Box | • **Ribbon:** *Modify* tab>View panel<br>• **Shortcut:** BX |
| | | Reveal Hidden Elements | • **View Control Bar** |
| | | Temporary Hide/Isolate | • **View Control Bar** |
| | | Temporary View Properties | • **View Control Bar** |

# Chapter 4

# Revit Families

To develop your 3D model, you will need to add various Revit® family elements, such as furniture, lighting fixtures, mechanical equipment, and structural framing elements. These components can be loaded from your company's template, the Revit Library, or a custom library. If the family elements are parametric, you can modify the components to have different sizes to control the visibility of items as needed to relay design intent for various aspects of the project.

## Learning Objectives in This Chapter

- Place components in a project to further develop the design.
- Load components from the Revit Library.
- Change component types and locations.

# 4.1 About Revit Families

*Family creation is covered in the ASCENT guide Autodesk Revit BIM Management: Template and Family Creation.*

All elements added to your projects are created with families. A family contains different elements, materials, and properties (called parameters). Within the family, you can have multiple family types with different parameters. For example, you can have a desk family that contain various family types for different sizes of that desk.

Components are elements that can be loaded externally. These can include freestanding components, such as the table and chairs shown in Figure 4–1. They can also include wall-, ceiling-, floor-, roof-, face-, and line-hosted components. These hosted components must be placed on the referenced element, such as the upper wall cabinets shown in Figure 4–1.

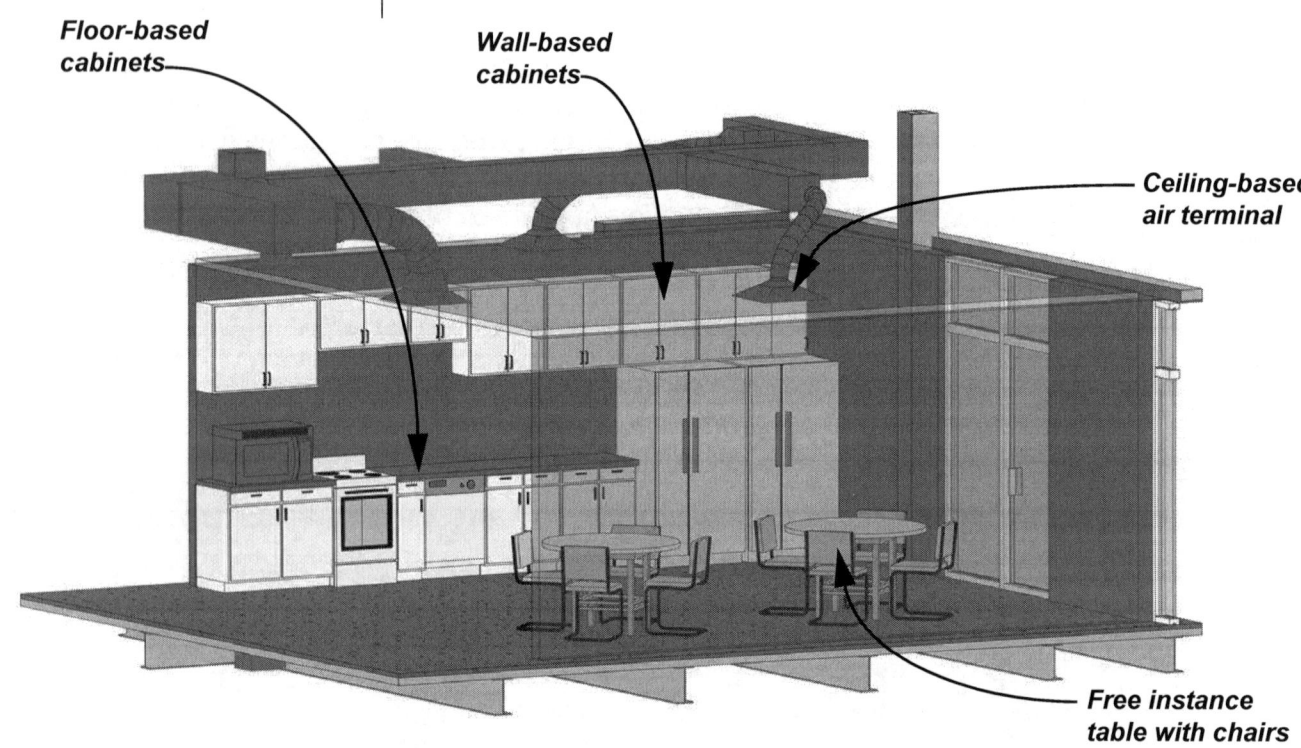

**Figure 4–1**

## Host-based vs. Free-instance Families

*Host-based* families are dependent on a host. Examples include a pendant light fixture (which requires a ceiling) and a clock or mirror (which requires a wall), as shown in Figure 4–2.

*Free-instance* families do not need a host. Examples include the sideboard and candle holder shown in Figure 4–2.

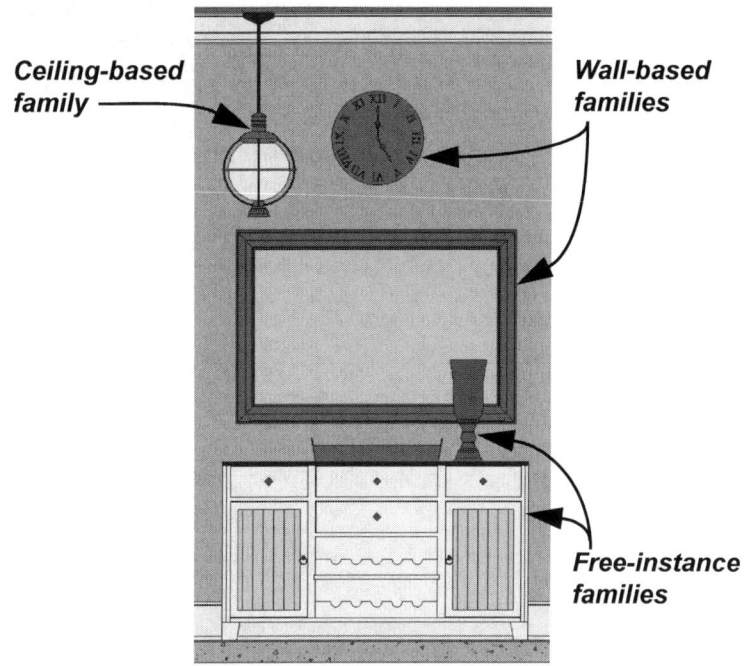

Figure 4–2

## The Different Kinds of Families

There are three kinds of families: system families, loadable families, and in-place families. Loadable and system families are what are typically used in a project, whereas in-place families are reserved for custom objects that are unique to the project.

**System families** are families that are predefined in Revit projects and templates. System families include walls, wall foundations, floors, structural slabs, ceilings, stairs, railings, and roofs, as shown in Figure 4–3. They also include duct, pipe, cable tray, and conduit types, as well as some annotation types, such as text and dimensions.

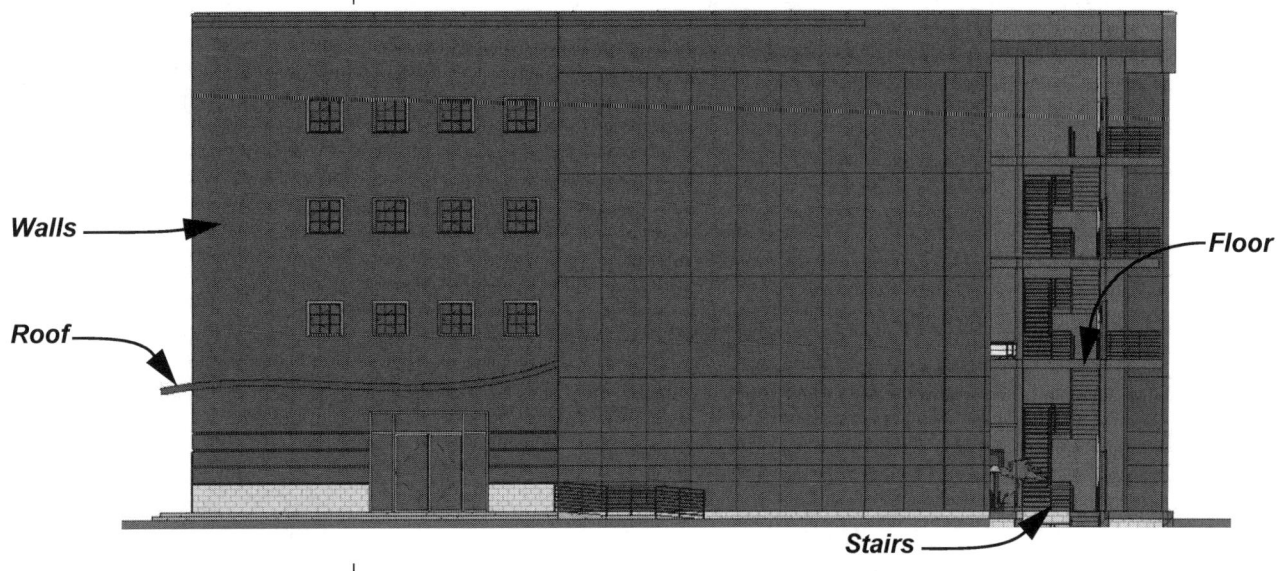

Figure 4–3

- System families are added to the model by starting a specific command from the appropriate tab in the ribbon. These will be further discussed in the *Design Development* section.

- System families cannot be saved out of a project or loaded from a library, but they can be customized by duplicating an existing type and modifying the *Type Parameters*, as shown in Figure 4–4. This can only be done within a project and helps to establish the company standards for the families set up in a template file. System families can be shared by using the **Transfer Project Standards** tool.

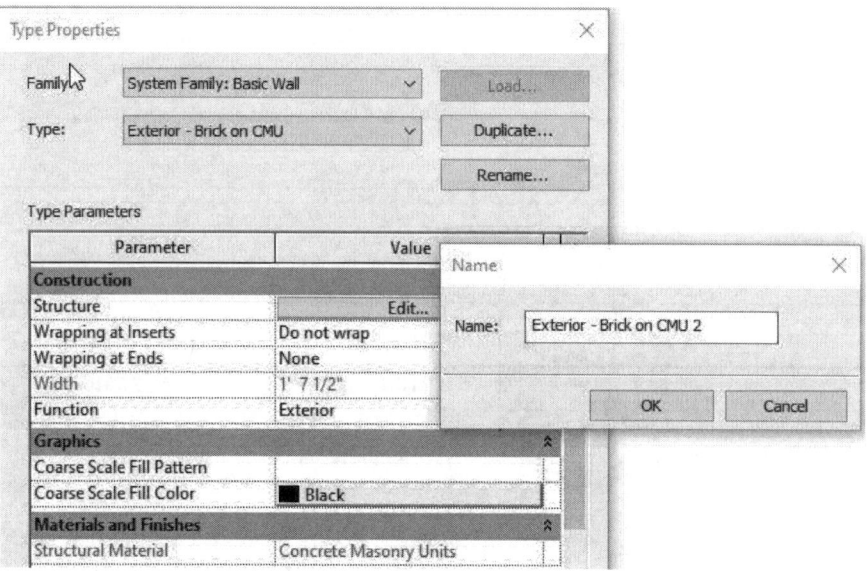

**Figure 4–4**

*For more information on creating component families, refer to the ASCENT guide Autodesk Revit BIM Management: Template and Family Creation.*

**Loadable families** are external component families that are created outside of the project. Frequently used components can be saved to a custom library for future use.

- Loadable families are typically elements that would be purchased, delivered on-site, and installed in a building, such as furniture, plants, windows, doors, and casework, as shown in Figure 4–5.

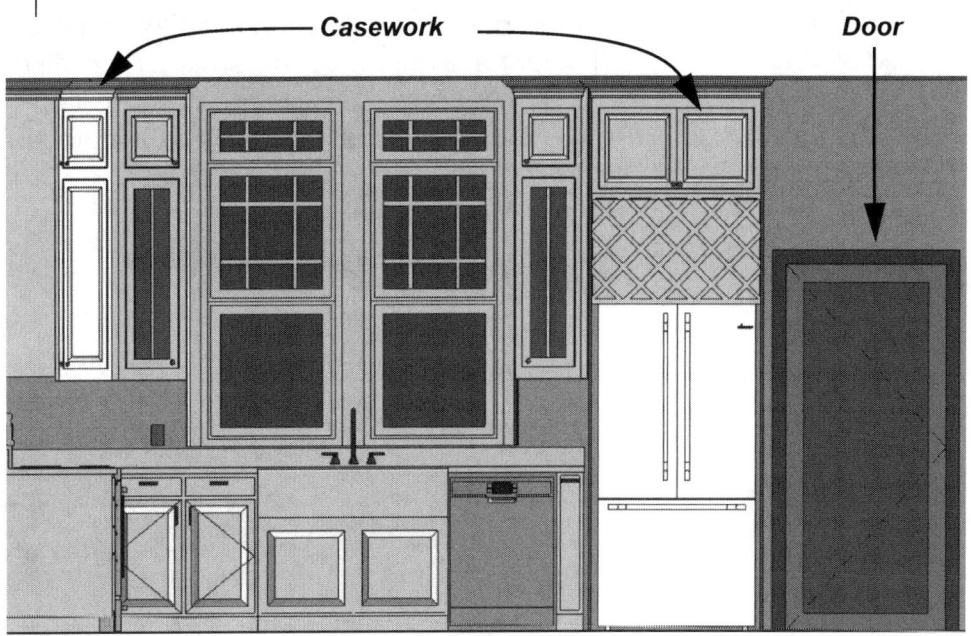

Figure 4–5

- Annotation components are tags (shown in Figure 4–6), symbols, and title blocks. (They will be discussed further in *Adding Tags and Schedules*.)

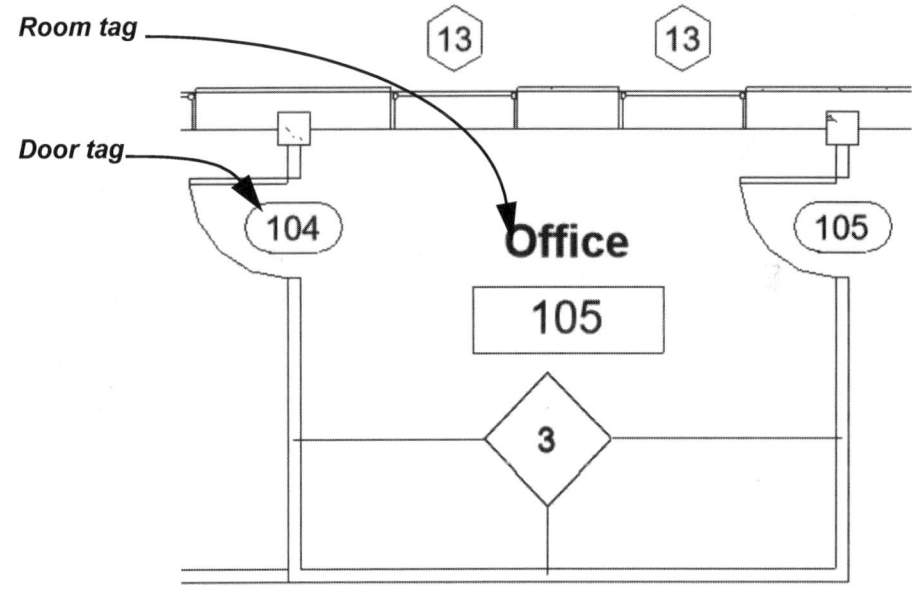

Figure 4–6

**In-place families** are families that are created within a project that are unique to the project and will most likely not be used in another, for example a custom built-in shelf system (as shown in Figure 4–7) that needs to be built to suit.

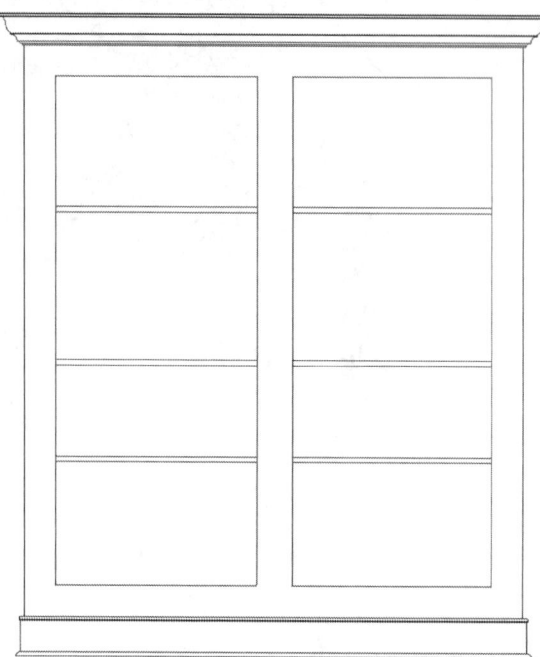

Figure 4–7

## Working with Component Families

To optimize project size and improve performance, by default the Revit project templates are not fully loaded with all available Revit families. However, you can load more families with multi-options from the Revit Library or the Autodesk website. You can also load your company's custom component family or families from other manufacturers that you may have available on your local machine. Some Revit component families have a type catalog associated with them that enables you to select specific types of that family to load. This helps with keeping the file size down.

- You can also check which custom component families your company has and find vendor-specific components. More BIM objects can be found at bimobject.com.

- You can copy a component family to the clipboard in one project and paste it into a different project that is open in the same session of Revit.

- You can load as many components into a project as needed or create your own.

# Revit Families

## Loading Components

- Components are family files with the extension .RFA. For example, a component family named Desk.rfa can contain several types and sizes.

You can load components from the Revit Library or from a custom library before starting the component command, or you can loading after starting the command.

### How To: Load a Component Family

1. In the *Insert* tab>Load from Library panel, click (Load Family).
   - Note: To use the Load Family method, you must install the **Autodesk Revit 2023 Content** in your desired language from the Autodesk website.
2. In the Load Family dialog box, locate the folder that contains the family or families you want to load and select them, as shown in Figure 4–8. To load more than one family at a time, hold <Ctrl> while selecting.

   - If the Load family dialog box does not default to the Revit Library folder, click on **Imperial Library** in the Places panel.

*Go to the Autodesk.com website and search Autodesk Revit 2023 Content.*

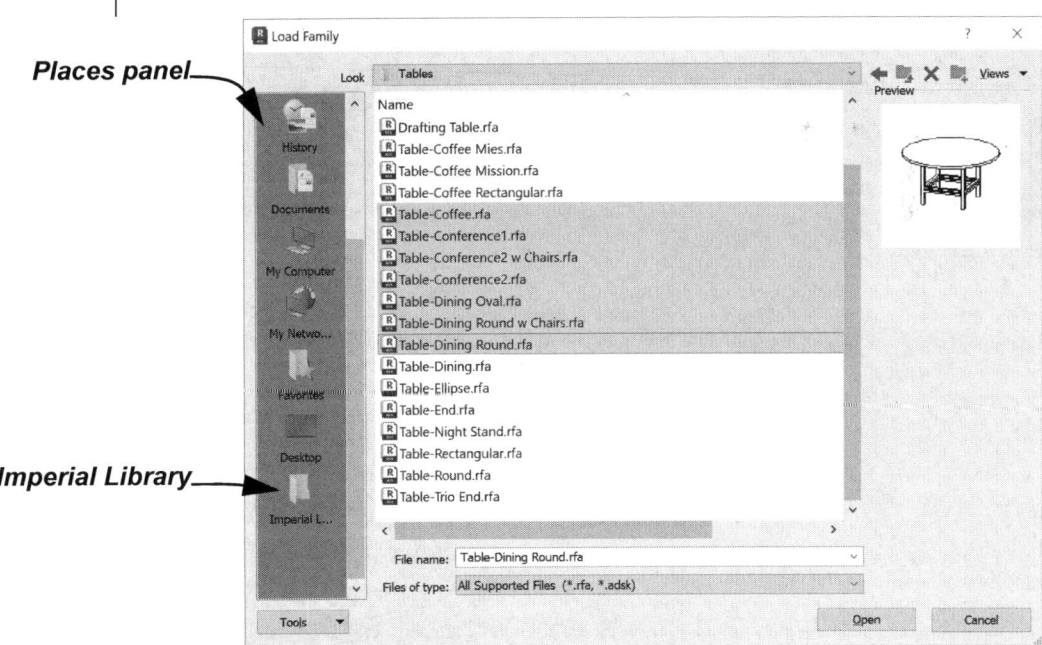

**Figure 4–8**

- The program remembers the last used folder.
3. Click **Open**.

4. For some families, the Specify Types dialog box displays, as shown for a door in Figure 4–9. Select the types you want to include in your project and click **OK**.
   - To select more than one type, hold <Ctrl> as you select.
   - You can use the drop-down lists under the columns to filter the sizes.

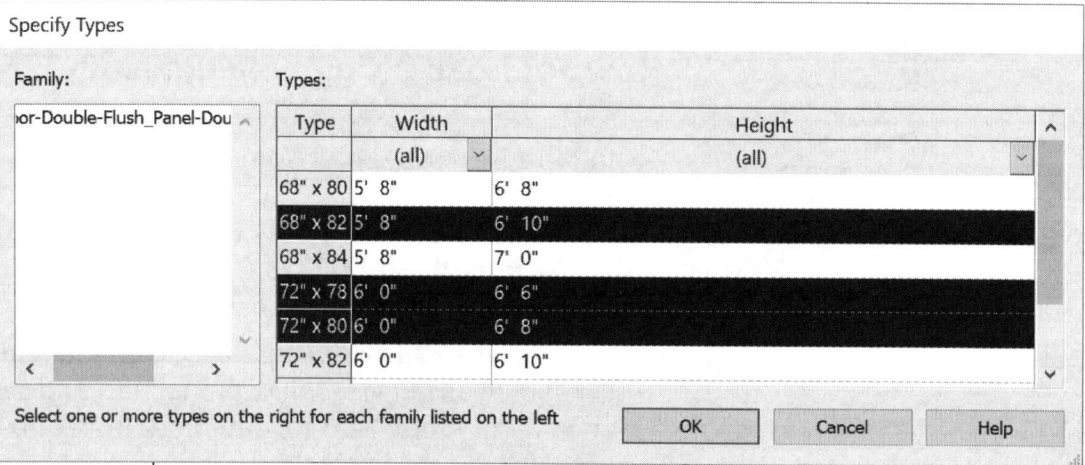

Figure 4–9

5. Once the family (or families) is loaded, in the Type Selector, select the type you want to use, as shown in Figure 4–10.

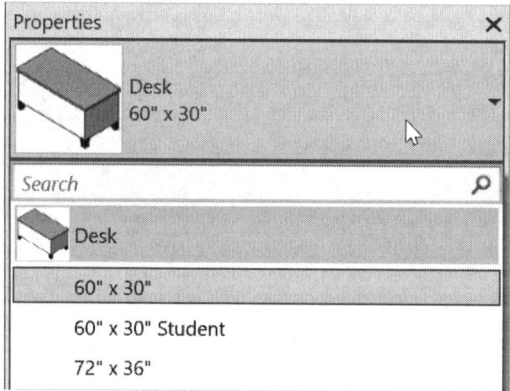

Figure 4–10

### Hint: Using Families with This Learning Content

For the practices in this learning content, all families that are used have been provided with the practice files. This was done to ensure that all users can easily locate and use the required files to successfully complete all practices. In general, it is recommended that you use families from the provided Autodesk Revit Content via downloaded content or the cloud, or from your own custom company library.

# Revit Families

## How To: Use Load Autodesk Family

1. In the *Insert* tab>Load from Library panel, click (Load Autodesk Family).
2. In the Load Autodesk Family dialog box, filter your search by typing in what kind of family you are looking for, or click on a category in the Browse section, as shown in Figure 4–11.

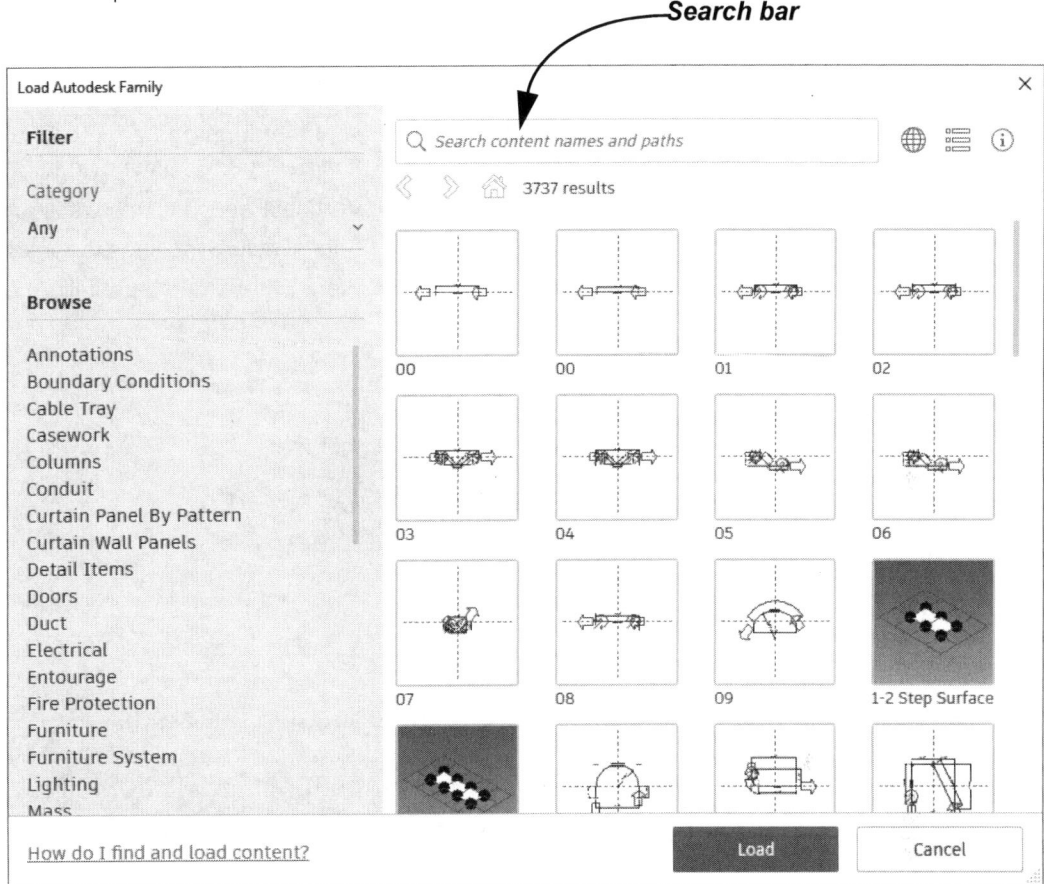

Figure 4–11

3. You can select as many families as needed, then click **Load** to load them into your project.

## Placing Components

When placing components, you have several options available to you, including specifying a placement, utilizing snaps, and using snap overrides.

### How To: Place a Component

1. In the *Architecture* tab>Build panel, click (Place a Component), or type **CM**.
   - If you have not yet loaded your component, in the *Modify | Place Component* tab>Mode panel, click (Load Family) and load your component.

2. In the Type Selector, select the component you want to add to the project.
3. Proceed as follows, based on the type of component used:

| If the component is... | Then... |
| --- | --- |
| Not hosted | Set the *Level* and *Offset* in Properties, as shown in Figure 4–12. |
| Wall hosted | Set the *Elevation* in Properties, as shown in Figure 4–13. |
| Face hosted | Select the appropriate method in the contextual tab> Placement panel, as shown in Figure 4–14.<br>• Vertical Faces include walls and columns.<br>• Faces include ceilings, beams, and roofs.<br>• Work Planes can be set to levels, faces, and named reference planes. |

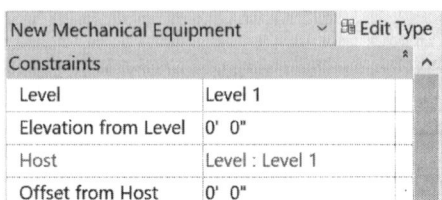

Figure 4–12

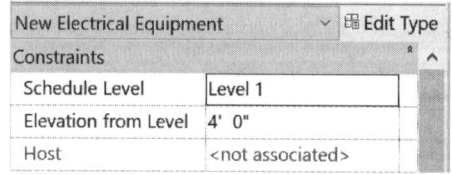

Figure 4–13

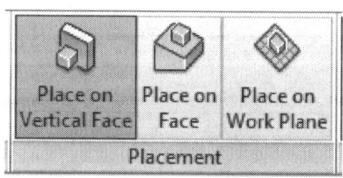

Figure 4–14

4. Place the component in the model.

- Work plane-based families will default to the last work plane option used.

- Many components can be rotated by pressing <Spacebar> when placing them. This will rotate them in 90° increments, unless your cursor is over an angled wall, reference plane, or grid line.

- In the Options Bar, many components will have an option to **Rotate after placement**, as shown in Figure 4–15. This enables you to rotate the element by any degree immediately after placing the family.

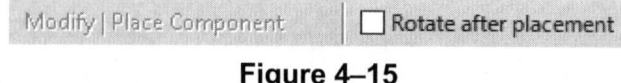

Figure 4–15

- When placing a component, you can use the **Snap Mid Between 2 Points** temporary snap override by selecting it from the right-click menu (as shown on the top in Figure 4–16) or typing **S2**, then selecting two points in the view. The object is placed at the middle of the two selected points, as shown on the bottom in Figure 4–16.

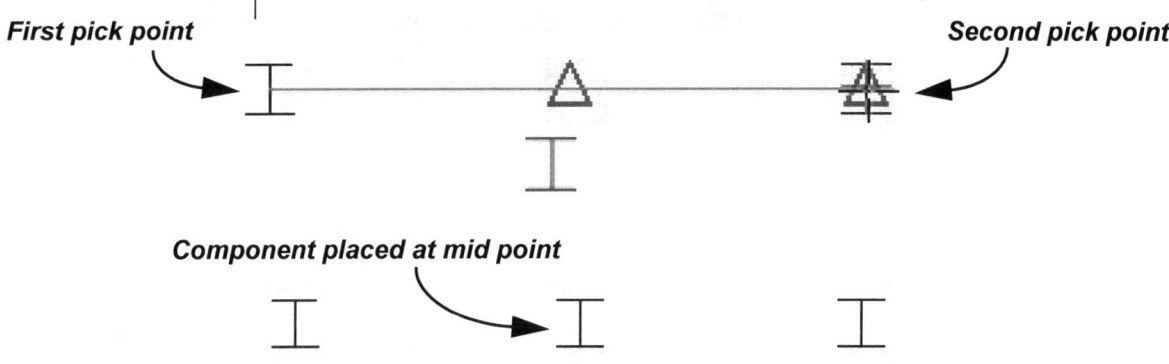

Figure 4–16

*Create Similar* works with all elements.

5. A fast way to add components that match those already in your project is to select one, right-click on it, and select **Create Similar**. This starts the **Component** command with the same type selected.

## 4.2 Modifying Components

Components can be modified when they are selected by changing the type in the Type Selector. For example, you might have placed a task chair in a project (as shown in Figure 4–17), but now you need to change it to an executive chair. With some types, you can use controls to modify the component. You can also select a new host for a component and move components with nearby elements.

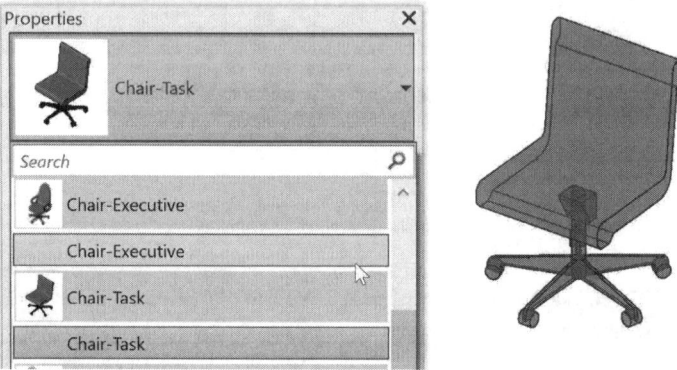

**Figure 4–17**

### How To: Modify a Component

1. Select an element in the model.
2. In the Type Selector, select the family type that you want to change it to.
   - If needed, modify the component's instance or type properties.

### Modify Host Elements

If you need to move a component from the level on which it was inserted, you can change its host. For example, one of the desks in Figure 4–18 is floating above the floor. It was placed on Level 1 when it was inserted, but needs to be located on the floor that is below the level.

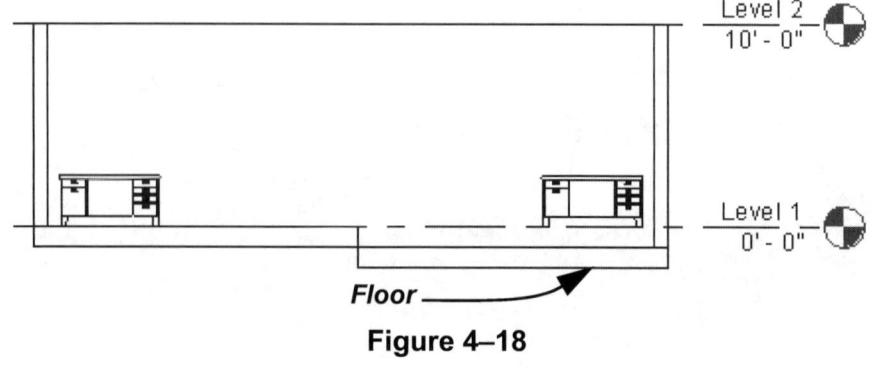

**Figure 4–18**

## How To: Pick a New Host Element

1. Select a component.
2. In the *<component type>* contextual tab>Host panel, click  (Pick New Host).
3. Select the new host (e.g., the floor).

- You can select a floor, surface, or level to be the new host for the components depending on the requirements of the component.

## Moving with Nearby Host Elements

Components have the capacity to move with nearby host elements (such as walls) when they are moved. Select the component and in the Options Bar, select **Moves With Nearby Elements**. The component is automatically assigned to the closest host elements.

For example, a desk near the corner of two walls is linked to those two walls. If you move either wall, the desk moves as well. However, you can still move the desk independently of the walls.

- You cannot specify which elements the component should be linked to; the software determines this automatically. This option only works with host elements (such as walls), not with other components.

# 4.3 Creating Additional Family Types in a Project

As you work within your project, you may find that you need different sizes than what is provided. For example, a table family only has one size, but you need several different sizes, as shown on the left in Figure 4–19. You can also duplicate a family type and have the same family but with different materials. Both loadable and system families can be duplicated to modify the parameters within the instance and type properties. Once you duplicate the existing family type, you can choose it in the Type Selector, as shown on the right in Figure 4–19.

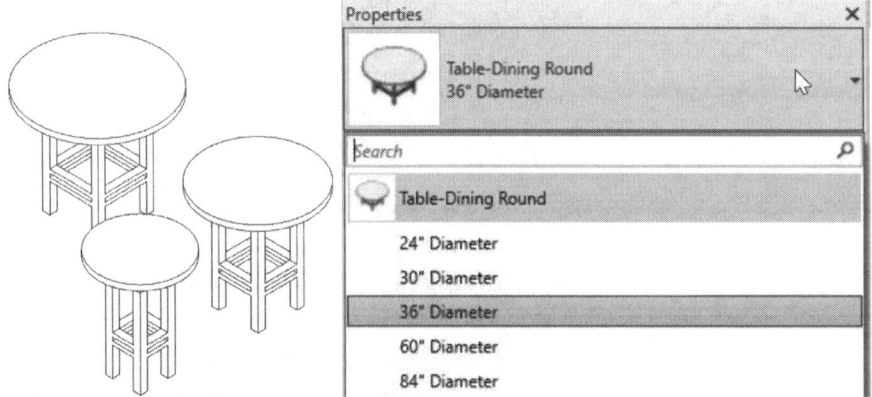

Figure 4–19

- A new family type that is created in a project will only exist in that project.

## How To: Create Additional Family Types

1. Start the **Component** command.
2. In the Type Selector, select the type you want to modify. In Properties, click ▦ (Edit Type) or in the *Modify* tab> Properties panel, click ▦ (Type Properties).
3. In the Type Properties dialog box, click **Duplicate**.
4. Type a new name for the element and click **OK**.
5. In the Type Properties dialog box, change the various parameters to the desired values.
6. Click **OK** to close the dialog box. The new type is now available for use.

# Families with Connectors

Revit's default library comes with loadable lighting, plumbing, and electrical fixtures, as well as equipment that has connectors.

Fixtures are families that are placed using the ▭ (Component) command. Many of the fixture families included with Revit have multiple sizes. The recessed light shown in Figure 4–20 has different sizes and voltages.

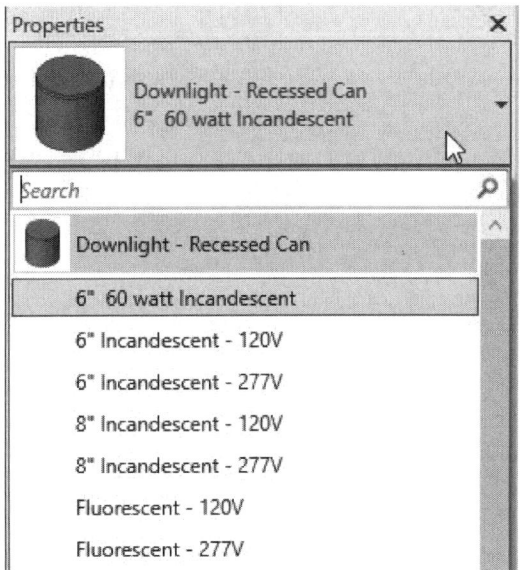

**Figure 4–20**

- Both lighting, plumbing fixtures and equipment have a folder for architectural and MEP. The fixtures that are in the *Architectural* folder are families that do not have connectors, whereas the fixtures in the *MEP* folder are used for the plumbing discipline to connect pipes or electrical wires to calculate plumbing systems and electrical flow.

# Practice 4a  Load Components

## Practice Objective

- Load and add components.

In this practice, you will add furniture to the lobby of the hotel. Figure 4–21 shows a sample furniture arrangement. You will load a component from a custom library and use controls to modify the placement. If you have time, add casework and equipment to the Breakfast and Preparation areas. Finally, you will add footing components to the base of the columns.

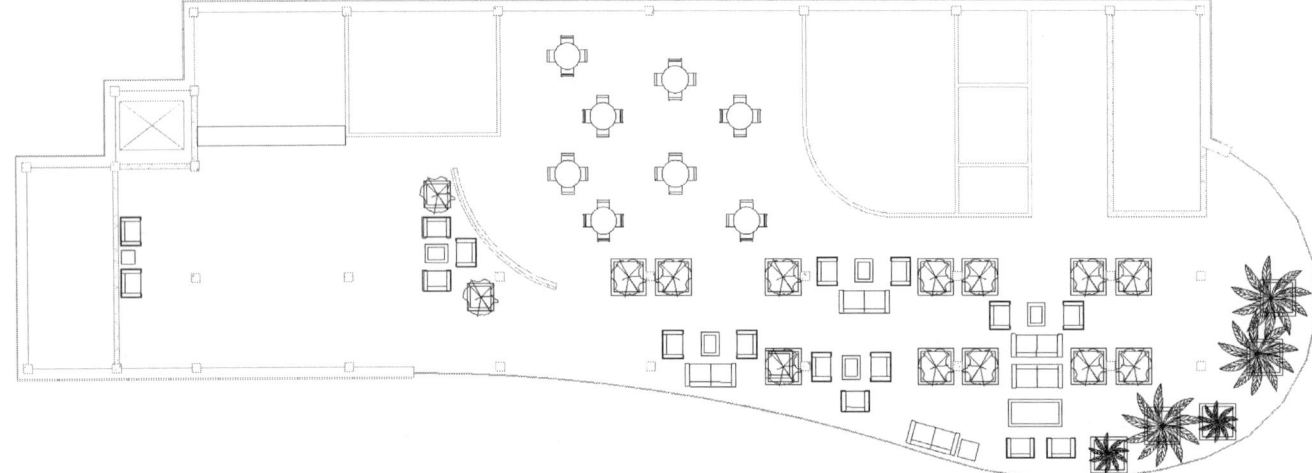

Figure 4–21

### Task 1 - Add furniture to the first floor.

1. Open the project **Hotel-Components.rvt** from the practice files folder.

2. In the Project Browser, duplicate the **Floor 1** view.

3. Rename it to **Floor 1 - Furniture Plan**. The view is now the active view.

4. In the Project Browser, right-click on **Floor 1 - Furniture Plan** and select **Apply Template Properties...**.

5. In the Apply View Template dialog box, in the *Name* section, select **Furniture Plan** (as shown in Figure 4–22) and click **OK**.

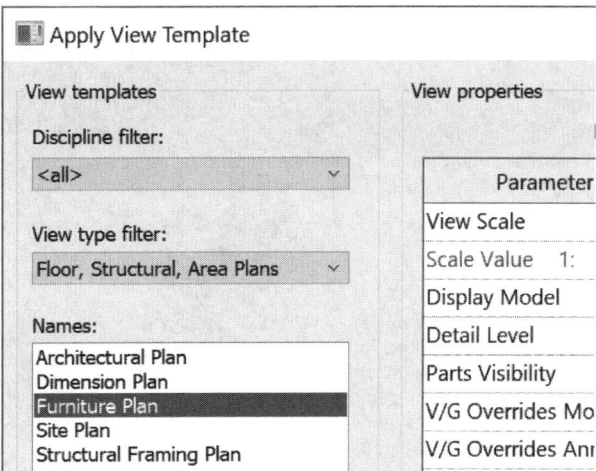

Figure 4–22

6. Type **VV** to open the Visibility/Graphic Overrides dialog box. Click on the *Revit Links* tab and clear the **Hotel-Pool.rvt** option in the *Visibility* column.

7. In the *Architecture* tab>Build panel, expand (Component) and click (Place a Component).

8. In the Type Selector, review the various furniture components that are available for the project. Select **Chair-Corbu** and place it in the lobby area near the curved curtain walls.

    • Use <Spacebar> to rotate the component, as needed.

9. Open the **Floor Plans: Floor 1** view. The chair does not display in this view because the Furniture category (and several others) has been toggled off.

10. Return to the **Floor Plans: Floor 1 - Furniture Plan**.

11. In the *Insert* tab>Load from Library panel, click (Load Autodesk Family).

*You must have an internet connection to use the Load Autodesk Family method. This family is also provided in the practice files Families>Tables folder.*

12. In the Load Autodesk Family dialog box, type **Table-Dining Round w Chairs** in the search field. Select the image of the table and chairs (as shown in Figure 4–23) and click **Load**.

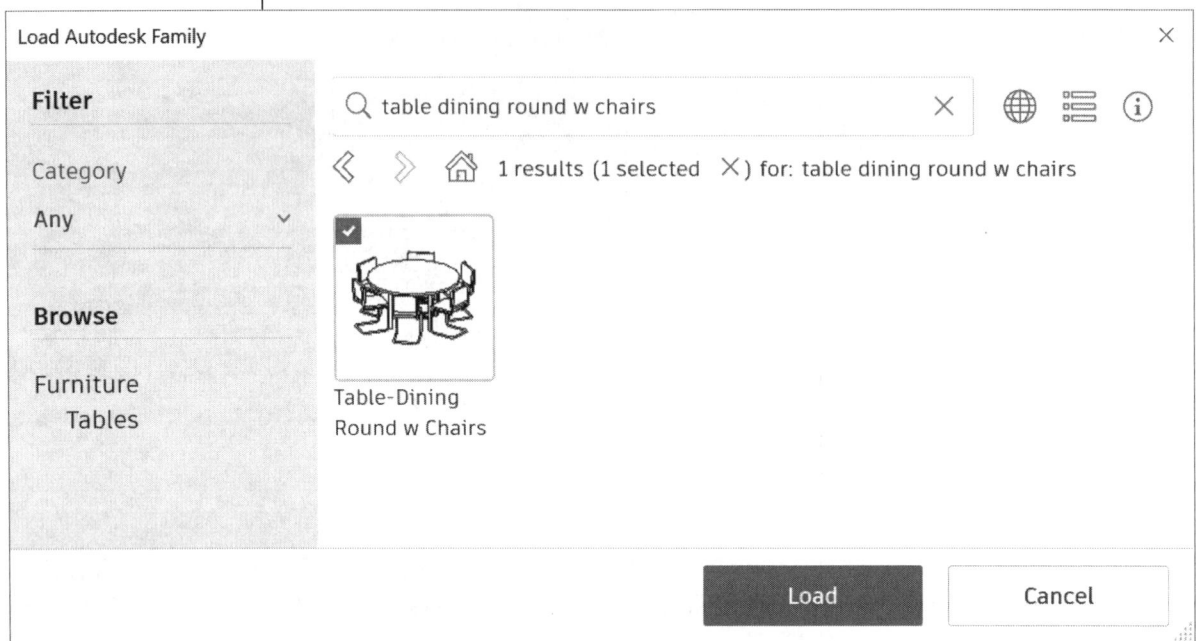

Figure 4–23

13. Start the **Component** command.

14. In the *Modify | Place Component* tab>Mode panel, click (Load Family).

*Use <Shift> or <Ctrl> to select more than one .RFA file*

15. In the Load Family dialog box, navigate to the practice files *Families* folder. Load the following components:
    - *Planting* folder: **Planter.rfa**, **RPC Plant-Tropical.rfa**, and **RPC Tree-Tropical.rfa**
    - *Furniture* folder: **Countertop-Lobby.rfa**
    - *Doors* folder: **Elevator-Door-Center.rfa**
    - *Specialty Equip* folder: **Elevator-Electric.rfa**

16. Place and arrange the components, placing the dining tables in the breakfast area and other elements in the lounge, as shown in Figure 4–24. Place at least one plant in a planter. You can follow the suggested layout or create your own design.

# Revit Families

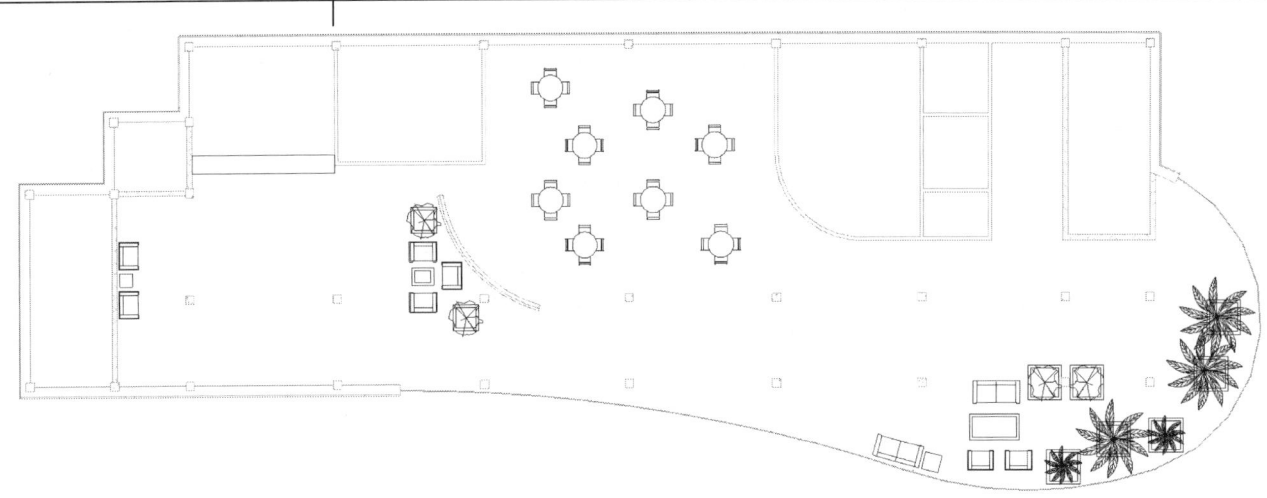

Figure 4–24

17. Save the project.

**Task 2 - Place custom components.**

1. In the *Architecture* tab>Build panel, expand (Component) and click (Place a Component). In the Type Selector, select **Elevator-Electric 2500 lbs** and place it inside the elevator shaft.

2. In the Type Selector, select the **Elevator Door - Center 42" x 84"** and place it in the wall between grids 3B and 3C, as shown in Figure 4–25. Note that the door is also a component.

*The image shows the elevator shaft cropped for better viewing.*

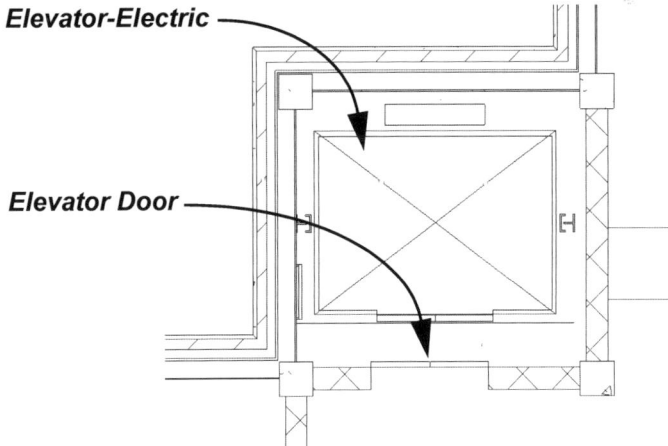

Figure 4–25

3. Select the elevator door component and make sure the flip grips are on the outside of the wall.

4. In the *Modify | Specialty Equipment* tab>Clipboard panel, click (Copy to the Clipboard).

5. In the Clipboard panel, expand (Paste) and click (Aligned to Selected Levels).

6. In the Select Levels dialog box, select **Basement** and **Floor 2** through **Floor 8**, as shown in Figure 4–26. Click **OK**. This copies the door to the rest of the levels.

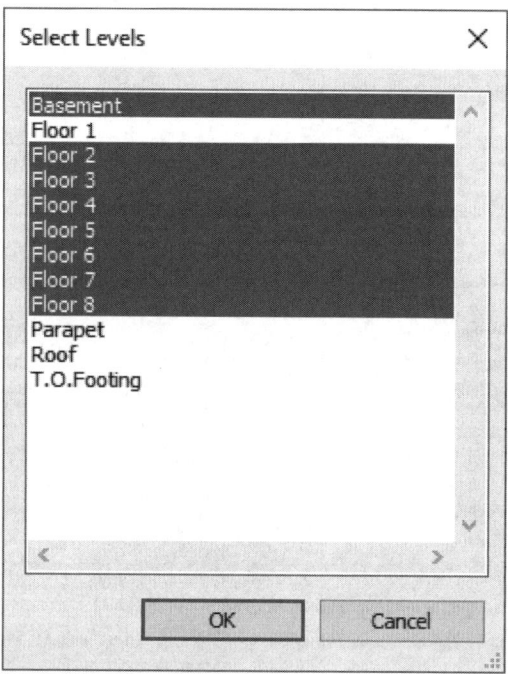

**Figure 4–26**

7. Save and close the project.

# Chapter Review Questions

1. How do you change the family type when inserting a component?

    a. Quick Access Toolbar

    b. Type Selector

    c. Options Bar

    d. Properties Palette

2. If the component you want to use is not available in the current project, where do you go to get the component? (Select all that apply.)

    a. In another project, copy the component to the clipboard and paste it into the current project.

    b. In the current project, use (Insert from File) and select the family from the list in the dialog box.

    c. In the current project, use (Load Family) and select the family from the list in the dialog box.

    d. Search a manufacturer's site for a component and download it.

3. When you use the **Moves with Nearby Elements** option, can you control which elements a component moves with?

    a. Yes, select the element with which you want it to move.

    b. No, it moves with the closest host element.

4. Which of the following commands would you use if you want to move a furniture component to a floor that is lower than the level where it was original placed, as shown in Figure 4–27?

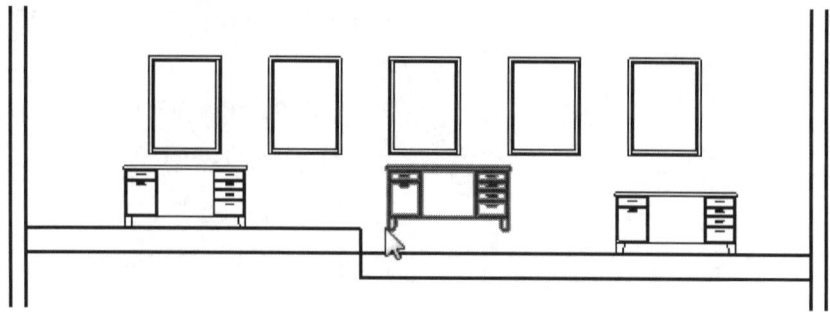

Figure 4–27

a. Use (Level) and add a level at the height of the lower floor.

b. Use (Reference Plane) and draw a plane aligned with the lower floor.

c. Use (Pick New Host) and select the lower floor.

d. Use (Edit Family) and change the work plane in the family so that it matches the height of the lower floor.

# Command Summary

| Button | Command | Location |
|---|---|---|
| | Load Family | • **Ribbon:** *Modify | Place Component* tab>Load panel or *Insert* tab>Load from Library panel |
| | Pick New Host | • **Ribbon:** *Modify | Multi-Select* or *component type* contextual tab>Host panel |
| | Place Component | • **Ribbon:** *Architecture* tab>Build panel> expand Component<br>• **Shortcut:** CM |
| | Place on Face | • **Ribbon**: *Modify | Place Component* tab> Placement panel |
| | Place on Vertical Face | • **Ribbon**: *Modify | Place Component* tab> Placement panel |
| | Place on Work Plane | • **Ribbon**: *Modify | Place Component* tab> Placement panel |
| | Purge Unused | • **Ribbon:** *Manage* tab>Settings panel |

# Chapter 5

# Basic Sketching and Modify Tools

When you start adding general building elements (e.g., walls, floors, and ceilings) to a project, you will use basic sketching, selecting, and modifying tools. Using these tools with drawing aids helps you to place and modify elements to create accurate building models.

## Learning Objectives in This Chapter

- Sketch linear elements such as walls, beams, and pipes.
- Ease the placement of elements by incorporating drawing aids such as alignment lines, temporary dimensions, and snaps.
- Place reference planes as temporary guide lines.
- Use techniques to select and filter groups of elements.
- Modify elements using a contextual tab, Properties, temporary dimensions, and controls.
- Move, copy, rotate, and mirror elements and create array copies in linear and radial patterns.
- Align, trim, and extend elements with the edges of other elements.
- Split linear elements anywhere along their length.
- Offset elements to create duplicates a specific distance away from the original.

# 5.1 Adding General Building Elements

When you start a general building element command, the contextual tab on the ribbon, the Options Bar, and Properties (as shown in Figure 5–1) enable you to modify element-specific features for the new element you are placing in the project. As you are working, several features called *drawing aids* display, as shown in Figure 5–1. They help you to create designs quickly and accurately.

- There will be different drawing aid and Options Bar options depending on which building element command is started.

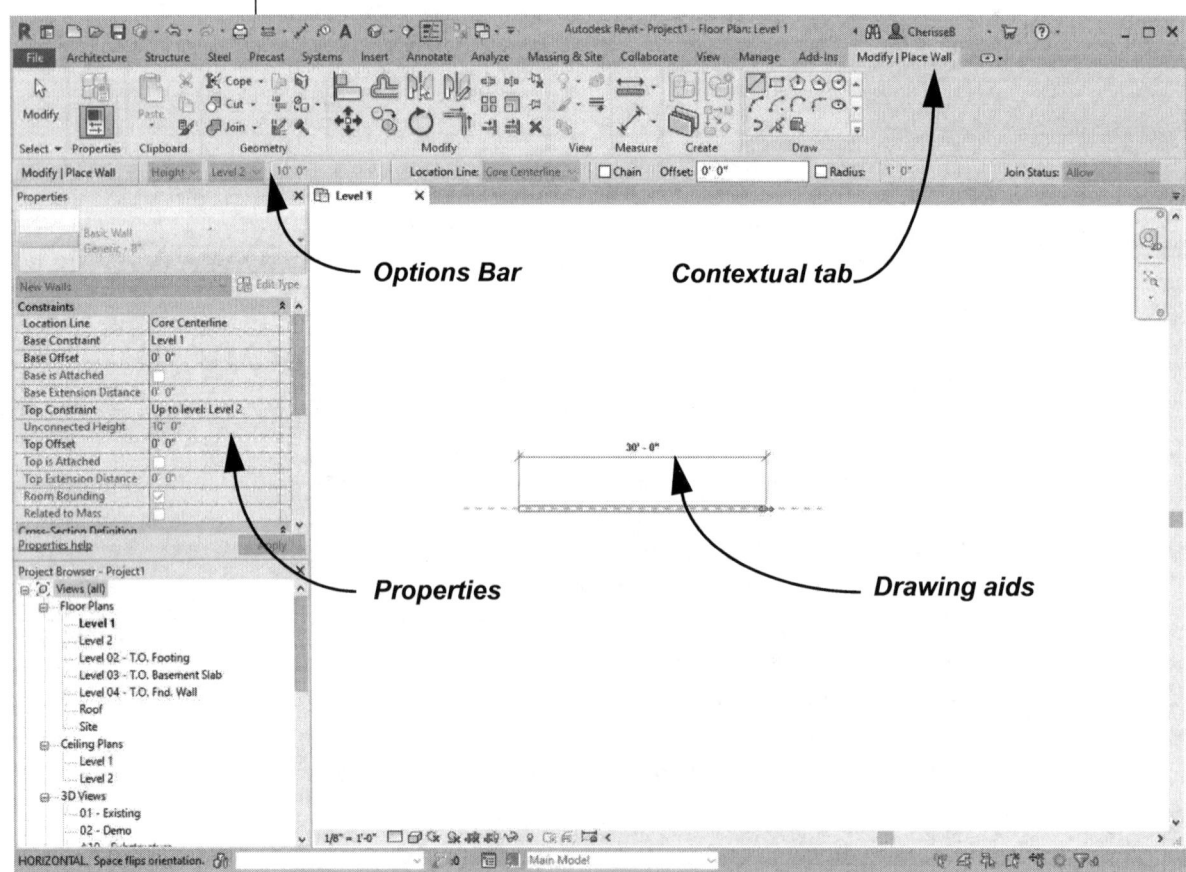

Figure 5–1

- In Revit, you are most frequently creating 3D model elements rather than 2D sketches. These tools work with both 3D and 2D elements in the software.

General building element commands are found on the *Architecture*, *Structure*, and *Systems* tabs and are for elements such as walls, slabs, ducts, etc. You can change the type of these elements using the Type Selector.

# Basic Sketching and Modify Tools

## How To: Start a General Building Element Command

In this How To, a wall has been used as an example, but these steps apply to any general building command in the ribbon.

1. In the *Architecture* tab>Build panel or *Structure* tab>Structure panel, expand ⌷ (Wall) and select ⌷ (Wall: Structural) or ⌷ (Wall: Architectural).
2. In Properties, verify or change the wall type (for example, **Basic Wall: Generic - 8"**) in the Type Selector.
3. Place the wall in the model using the draw tools.

## Draw Tools

*The exact tools vary according to the element being modeled.*

Many elements (such as walls, beams, ducts, pipes, and conduits) are modeled using the tools on the contextual tab in the *Draw* panel. Other elements (such as floors, ceilings, roofs, and slabs) have boundaries that are sketched using many of the same tools. Draw tools are also used when you create details or schematic drawings.

Two methods are available:

- *Draw* the element using a geometric form.
- *Pick* an existing element (such as a line, face, or wall) as the basis for the new element's geometry and position.

## How To: Use Draw Tools

1. Start the command you want to use.
2. In the contextual tab>Draw panel (shown in Figure 5–2), select a drawing tool.

**Figure 5–2**

*You can change from one Draw tool shape to another in the middle of a command.*

3. Depending on the draw tool selected, select points to define the elements or watch the Status Bar, in the lower-left corner, for hints on what to do.
4. Finish the command using one of the standard methods:

   - Click ▷ (Modify).
   - Press <Esc> twice.
   - Start another command.

## Options Bar Draw Options

When you are in drawing mode, several options display in the Options Bar, as shown in Figure 5–3.

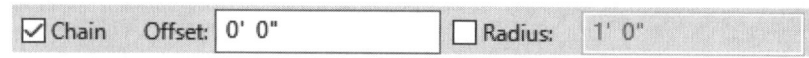

Figure 5–3

*Different options display according to the type of element that is selected or the command that is active.*

- **Chain:** Controls how many segments are created in one process. If this option is not selected, the **Line** and **Arc** tools only create one segment at a time. If it is selected, you can continue adding segments until you press <Esc> or select the command again.

- **Offset:** Enables you to enter values so you can create linear elements at a specified distance from the selected points or element.

- **Radius:** Enables you to enter values when using a radial tool or to add a radius to the corners of linear elements as you sketch them.

## Draw Tools

| | | |
|---|---|---|
| | Line | Draws a straight line defined by the first and last points. If **Chain** is enabled, you can continue selecting end points for multiple segments. |
| | Rectangle | Draws a rectangle defined by two opposing corner points. You can adjust the dimensions after selecting both points. |
| | Inscribed Polygon | Draws a polygon inscribed in a hypothetical circle with the number of sides specified in the Options Bar. |
| | Circumscribed Polygon | Draws a polygon circumscribed around a hypothetical circle with the number of sides specified in the Options Bar. |
| | Circle | Draws a circle defined by a center point and radius. |
| | Start-End-Radius Arc | Draws a curve defined by a start, end, and radius of the arc. The outside dimension shown is the included angle of the arc. The inside dimension is the radius. |
| | Center-ends Arc | Draws a curve defined by a center, radius, and included angle. The selected point of the radius also defines the start point of the arc. |

# Basic Sketching and Modify Tools

| | | |
|---|---|---|
| | **Tangent End Arc** | Draws a curve tangent to another element. Select an end point for the first point, but do not select the intersection of two or more elements. Then, select a second point based on the included angle of the arc. |
| | **Fillet Arc** | Draws a curve defined by two other elements and a radius. Because it is difficult to select the correct radius by clicking, this command automatically moves to edit mode. Select the dimension and then modify the radius of the fillet. |
| | **Spline** | Draws a spline curve based on selected points. The curve does not actually touch the points (sketches, model lines, and detail lines only). |
| | **Ellipse** | Draws an ellipse from a primary and secondary axis (walls, sketches, model lines, and detail lines only). |
| | **Partial Ellipse** | Draws only one side of the ellipse, like an arc. A partial ellipse also has a primary and secondary axis (sketches, model lines, and detail lines only). |

## Pick Tools

| | | |
|---|---|---|
| | **Pick Lines** | Use this option to select existing linear elements in the project. This is useful when you start the project from an imported 2D drawing. |
| | **Pick Face** | Use this option to select the face of a 3D massing element (walls and 3D views only). |
| | **Pick Walls** | Use this option to select an existing wall in the project to be the basis for a new sketch line (floors, ceilings, etc.). |

# Drawing Aids

As soon as you start sketching or placing elements, the following drawing aids display (as shown in Figure 5–4), depending on which tool you are using:

- Alignment line
- Temporary dimensions
- Snaps

These aids are available with most modeling and many modification commands.

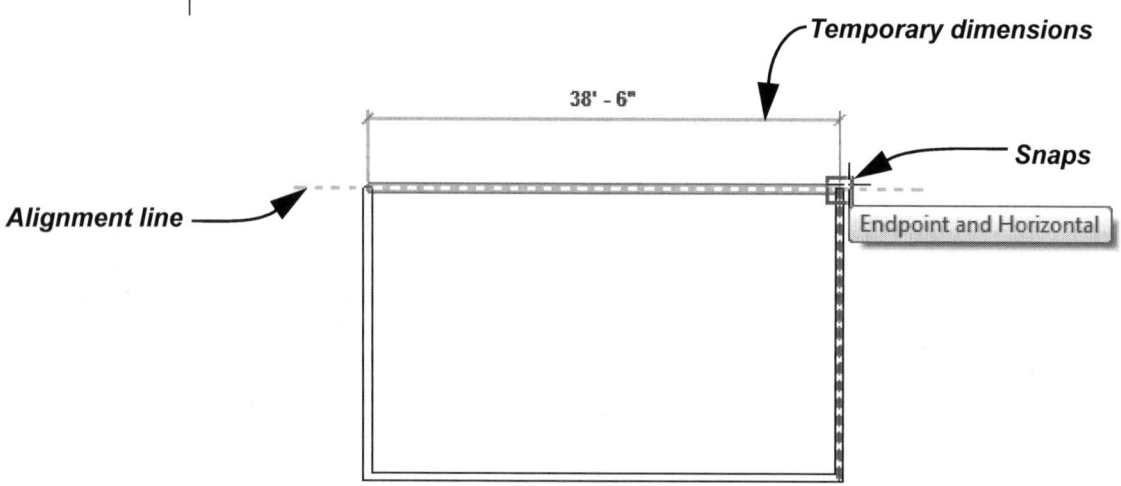

Figure 5–4

**Alignment lines** display as soon as you select your first point. They help keep lines horizontal, vertical, or at a specified angle. They also line up with the implied intersections of walls and other elements.

- Hold <Shift> to force the alignments to be orthogonal (90° angles only).

**Temporary dimensions** display to help place elements at the correct length, angle and location.

- You can type in a value, or move the cursor until you see the dimension you want, or you can place the element and then modify the value as needed.

- The length and angle increments shown vary depending on how far in or out the view is zoomed.

# Basic Sketching and Modify Tools

- For imperial measurements (feet and inches), the software uses a default of feet. For example, when you type **4** and press <Enter>, it assumes 4'-0". For a distance such as 4'-6", you can type any of the following: **4'-6"**, **4'6**, **4-6**, or **4 6** (the numbers separated by a space). To indicate distances less than one foot, type the inch mark (") after the distance, or enter **0**, a space, and then the distance.

- Temporary dimensions disappear as soon as you finish adding elements. If you want to make them permanent, select the dimension symbol ( ⊢⊣ ), as shown in Figure 5–5.

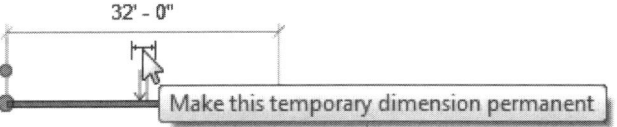

**Figure 5–5**

**Snaps** are key points that help you reference existing elements to exact points when modeling, as shown in Figure 5–6.

**Figure 5–6**

- When you move the cursor over an element, the snap symbol displays. Each snap location type displays with a different symbol.

**Hint: Snap Settings and Overrides**

In the *Manage* tab>Settings panel, click (Snaps) to open the Snaps dialog box, which is shown in Figure 5–7. The Snaps dialog box enables you to set which snap points are active, and set the dimension increments displayed for temporary dimensions (both linear and angular).

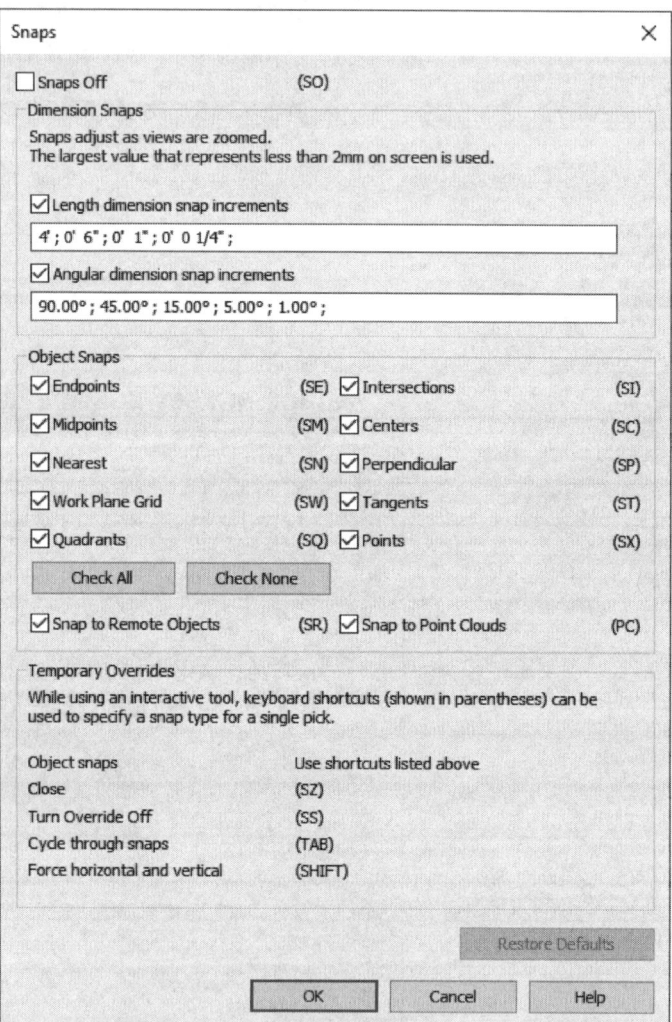

Figure 5–7

- Keyboard shortcuts for each snap can be used to override the automatic snapping. Temporary overrides only affect a single pick, but can be very helpful when there are snaps nearby other than the one you want to use.

# Reference Planes

*Reference planes do not display in 3D views.*

As you develop designs in Revit, there are times when you need lines to help you define certain locations. You can sketch reference planes (displayed as dashed green lines) and snap to them whenever you need to line up elements. For the example shown in Figure 5–8, the lighting fixtures in the reflected ceiling plan are placed using reference planes.

- To insert a reference plane, in the *Architecture, Structure*, or *Systems* tab>Work Plane panel, click (Reference Plane), or type **RP**.

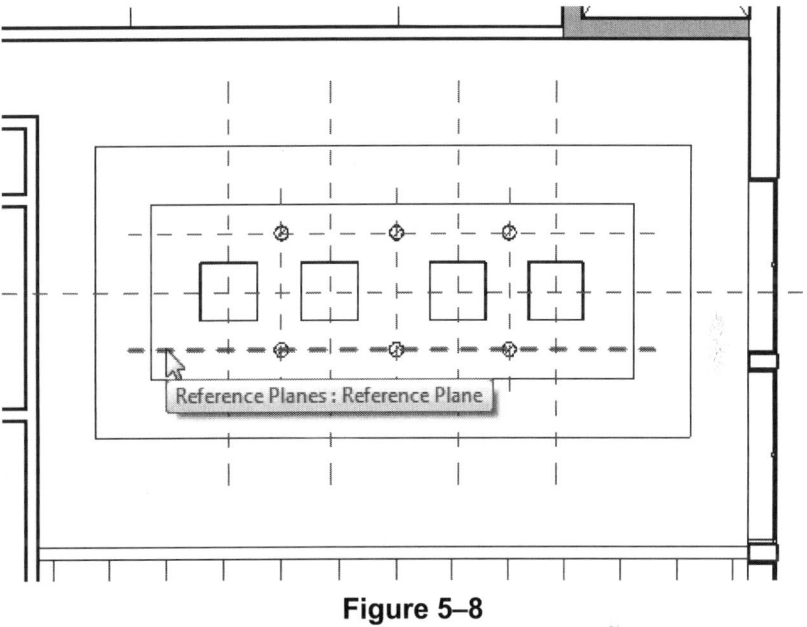

Figure 5–8

- Reference planes display in associated views because they are infinite planes and not just lines.
- You can name reference planes by clicking on **<Click to name>** and typing in the text box, as shown in Figure 5–9.

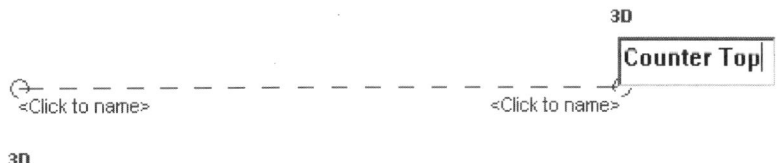

Figure 5–9

- If you sketch a reference plane in sketch mode (used with floors and similar elements), it does not display once the sketch is finished.
- Reference planes can have different line styles if they have been defined in the project. In Properties, select a style from the *Subcategory* list.
- Creating different reference plane subcategories can help visually show different line styles using different lineweights and colors.

# Basic Sketching and Modify Tools

**Hint: Model Line vs. Detail Line**

While most of the elements that you create are representations of actual building elements, there are times you may need to add lines to clarify the design intent. These can be either detail lines, as shown in Figure 5–10, or model lines. Detail lines are also useful as references because they are only reflected in the view in which you sketch them.

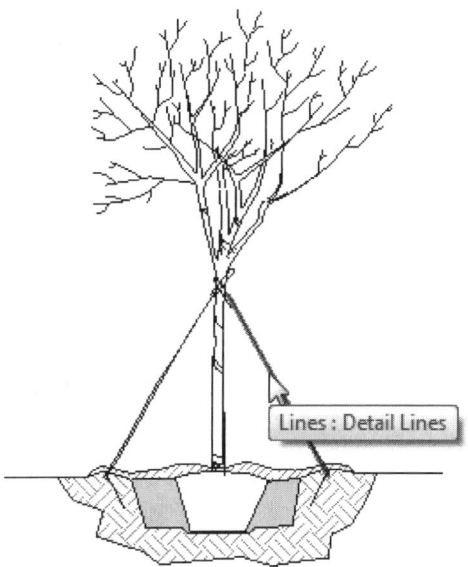

Figure 5–10

- A model line (*Architecture* or *Structure* tab>Model panel> (Model Line)) functions as a 3D element and displays in all views.

- A detail line (*Annotate* tab>Detail panel> (Detail Line)) is strictly a 2D element that only displays in the view in which it is drawn.

- In the *Modify* contextual tab, as shown in Figure 5–11, select a *Line Style* and then the Draw tool that you want to use to draw the model or detail line.

Figure 5–11

## Editing Building Elements

Building design projects typically involve extensive changes to the model. Revit was designed to make such changes quickly and efficiently. You can change an element using the following methods, as shown in Figure 5–12:

- The Type Selector enables you to specify a different type. This is frequently used to change the size and/or style of the elements.

- Properties enables you to modify the information (parameters) associated just with the selected elements. These are referred to as **instance properties**.

- **Type properties** are accessed through Properties by clicking **Edit Type**. They enable you to modify parameters for all of the same element type in the model.

- The contextual tab in the ribbon contains the Modify commands and element-specific tools.

- Temporary dimensions enable you to change the element's dimensions or position.

- Controls enable you to drag, flip, lock, and rotate the element.

- Shape handles enable you to drag elements to modify their height or length.

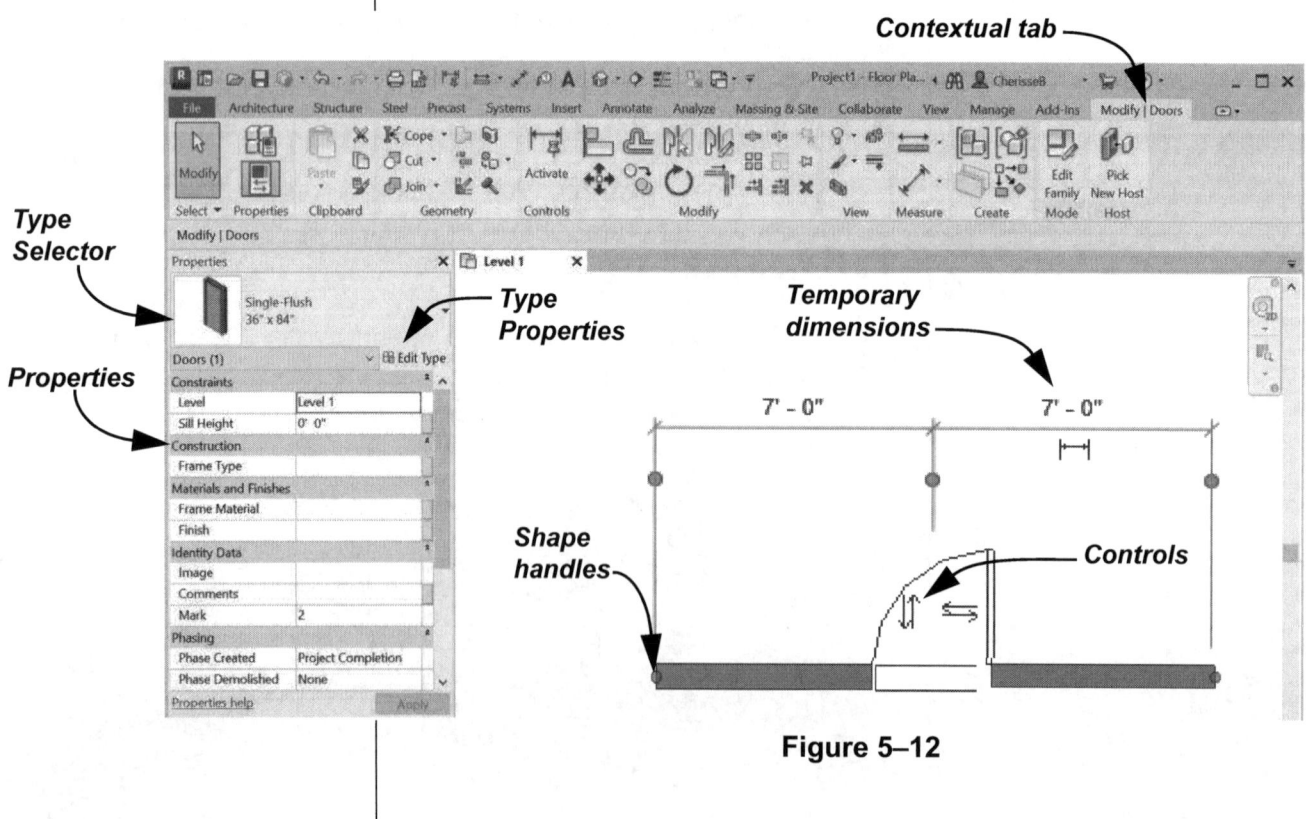

Figure 5–12

# Basic Sketching and Modify Tools

- To delete an element, select it and press <Delete>, right-click and select **Delete**, or in the Modify panel, click ✕ (Delete).

## Working with Controls and Shape Handles

When you select an element, various controls and shape handles display depending on the element and view. For example, in plan view you can use controls to drag the ends of a wall and change its orientation. You can also drag the wall ends in a 3D view and use the arrow shape handles to change the height of the wall, as shown in Figure 5–13.

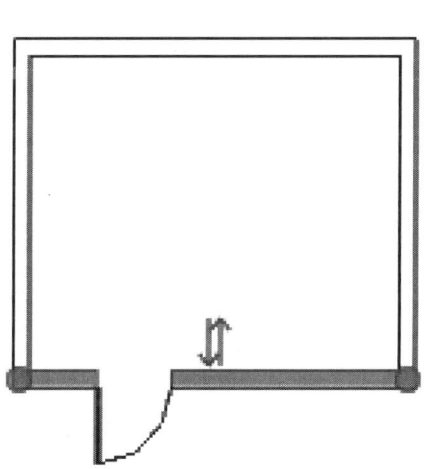
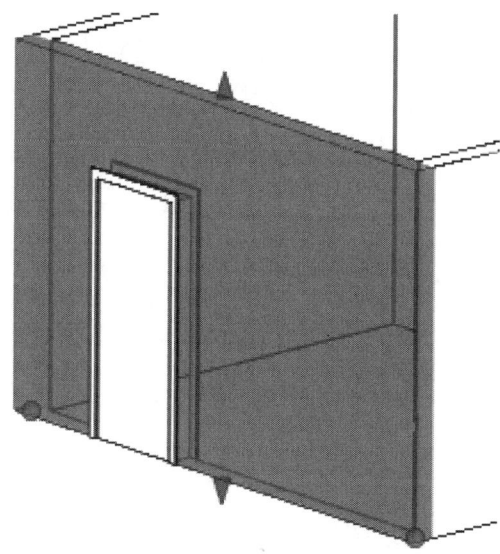

**Figure 5–13**

- If you hover the cursor over the control or shape handle, a tooltip displays showing its function.

## Editing Temporary Dimensions

Temporary dimensions automatically link to the closest wall. To change this, drag the *Witness Line* control, as shown in Figure 5–14, to connect to a new reference. You can also click on the control to toggle between justifications in the wall.

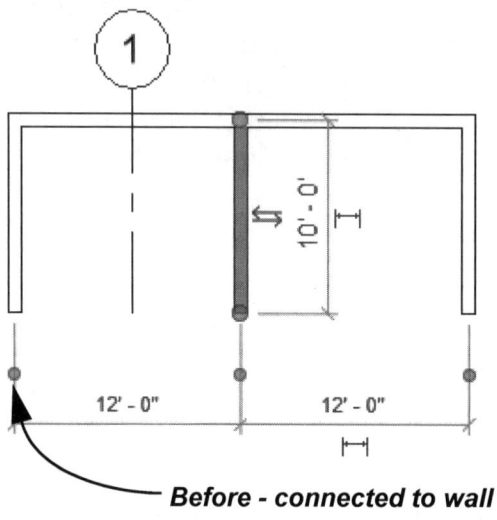

*Before - connected to wall*

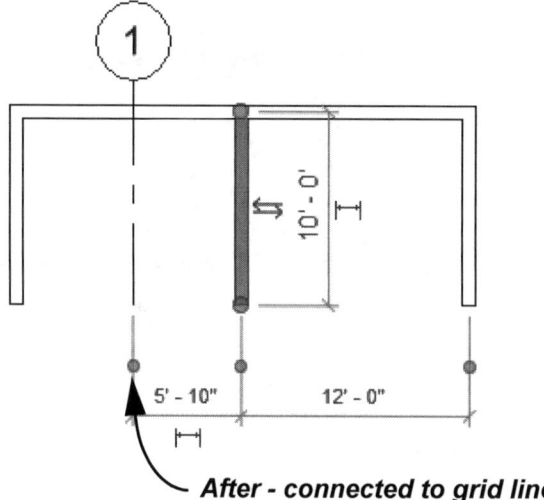

*After - connected to grid line*

**Figure 5–14**

- The new location of a temporary dimension for an element is remembered as long as you are in the same session of the software.

Basic Sketching and Modify Tools

## Selecting Multiple Elements

You can select more than one element at a time using the various methods described below, as well as remove elements from a group of selected elements by filtering out specific categories. When selecting more than one element in a model, you may also see controls like temporary dimensions and pin controls, as shown in Figure 5–15. You have the ability to hide these controls and temporary dimensions if they make viewing the selected elements difficult using the **Activate Controls and Dimensions** option.

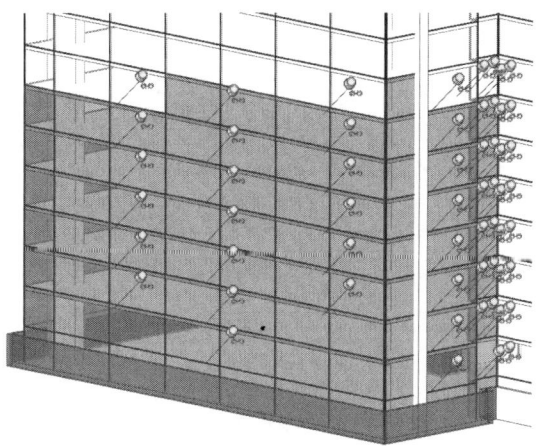

Figure 5–15

### How To: Manually Select Multiple Elements

1. Once you have selected at least one element, hold <Ctrl> and select another item to add it to your selection.
2. To remove an element from a group of selected elements, hold <Shift> and select the element you want removed.
   - If several elements are on or near each other, hover your cursor over an edge and press <Tab> to cycle through them before you click.
   - If there are elements that might be linked to each other, such as walls that are connected, pressing <Tab> selects the chain of elements.

### How To: Select Multiple Elements with a Window Selection

1. Click and drag the cursor to *window* around elements using one of two selection options:
   - Click and drag your cursor from left to right (as shown in Figure 5–16). With this option, you only select the elements completely inside the window.

*You can save selections and use them again. For more information, see A.1 Selection Sets.*

- Click and drag your cursor from right to left (as shown in Figure 5–16). With this option, you select elements that are both inside and crossing the window.

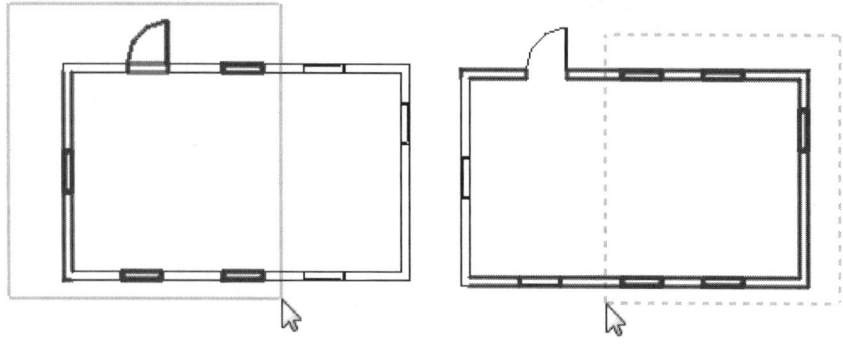

    **Window: left to right**    **Crossing: right to left**

**Figure 5–16**

- If you are accidentally clicking on elements and dragging them out of place when trying to window around elements, you can turn off (Drag Elements on Selection) in the lower-right corner of the Status Bar. When off, the icon will display with a red X.

## How To: Quickly Select a Previous Group of Selected Elements

1. Press <Ctrl>+<Left Arrow> to reselect the previous group of element selection.
    - Alternatively, right-click in the view window with nothing selected and select **Select Previous**.

## How To: Quickly Select All of the Same Element

1. To select all elements of a specific type, right-click on an element.
2. In the menu, select **Select All Instances>Visible in View** or **In Entire Project**, as shown in Figure 5–17. For example, if you select a column of a specific size and use this command, only the columns of the same size are selected.

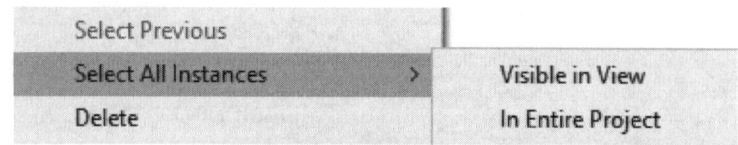

**Figure 5–17**

- Alternatively, select the element in the view and type **SA**. This selects all elements of the same type in the view.

Basic Sketching and Modify Tools

## How To: Use Activate Controls and Dimensions

1. With multiple elements selected in the model, in the *Modify* contextual tab>Controls panel, click (Activate Controls and Dimensions).
   - Alternatively, in the Quick Access Toolbar, click (Activate Controls and Dimensions), or type **AC**.
2. When this option is toggled on, the controls and temporary dimensions are hidden in the view, as shown on the left in Figure 5–18. Toggle (Activate Controls and Dimensions) off to display the controls and dimensions again, as shown on the right.

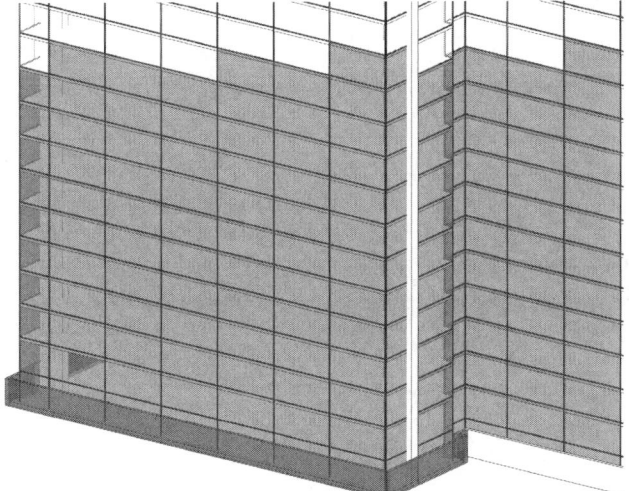
*Activate Controls and Dimensions toggled on*

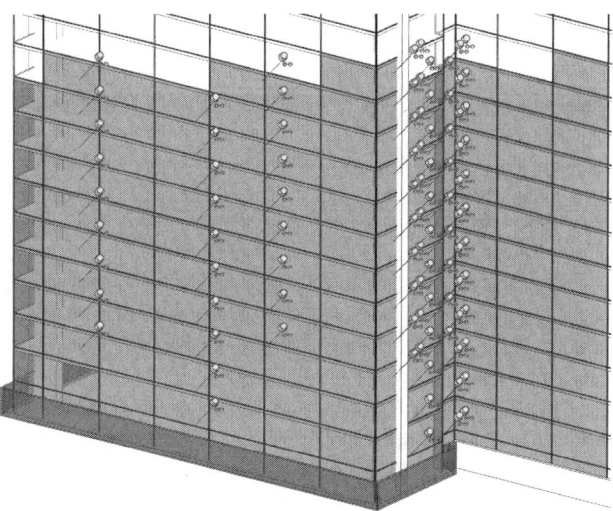
*Activate Controls and Dimensions toggled off*

Figure 5–18

## Measuring Tool

When modifying a model, it is useful to know the distance between elements. This can be done with temporary dimensions or, more frequently, by using the measuring tools found in the Quick Access Toolbar or in the *Modify* tab>Measure panel, as shown in Figure 5–19.

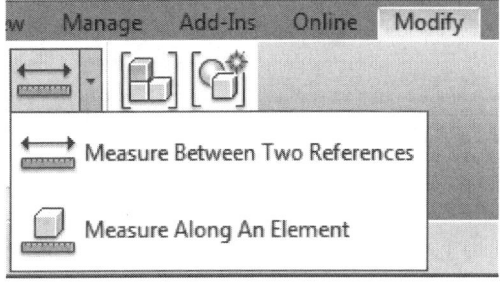

Figure 5–19

-  (Measure Between Two References): Select two elements and the measurement displays. This can be done in both 2D and 3D views.

  - If you select **Chain** in the Options Bar (as shown in Figure 5–20), you can get the total length of multiple measurements.

  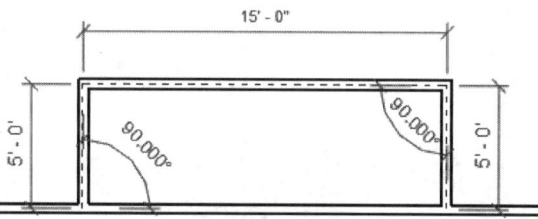
  Figure 5–20

- (Measure Along An Element): Select the edge of a linear element and the total length displays. Use <Tab> to highlight other elements and then click to measure along all of them, as shown in Figure 5–21. This can be done in 2D views only.

  Figure 5–21

- References include any snap point, wall lines, or other parts of elements (such as door center lines).

## Filtering Selection of Multiple Elements

When multiple element categories are selected, the *Multi-Select* contextual tab opens in the ribbon. This gives you access to all of the Modify tools and the **Filter** command. The **Filter** command enables you to specify the types of elements to select. For example, you might only want to select columns, as shown in Figure 5–22.

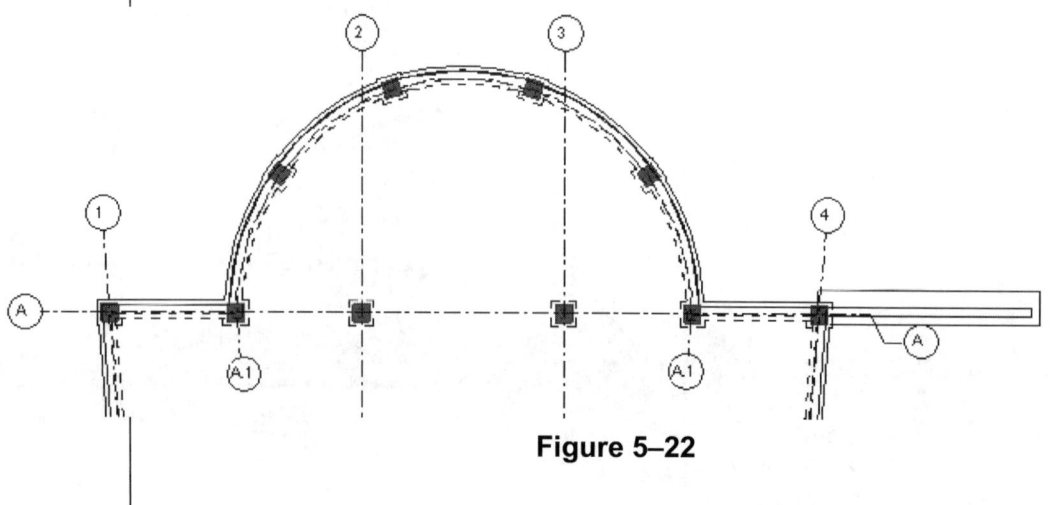
Figure 5–22

# Basic Sketching and Modify Tools

## How To: Filter a Selection of Multiple Elements

1. Select everything in the area with a window selection.
2. In the *Modify | Multi-Select* tab>Selection panel, or in the Status Bar, click  (Filter). The Filter dialog box opens, as shown in Figure 5–23.

*The Filter dialog box displays all types of elements in the original selection.*

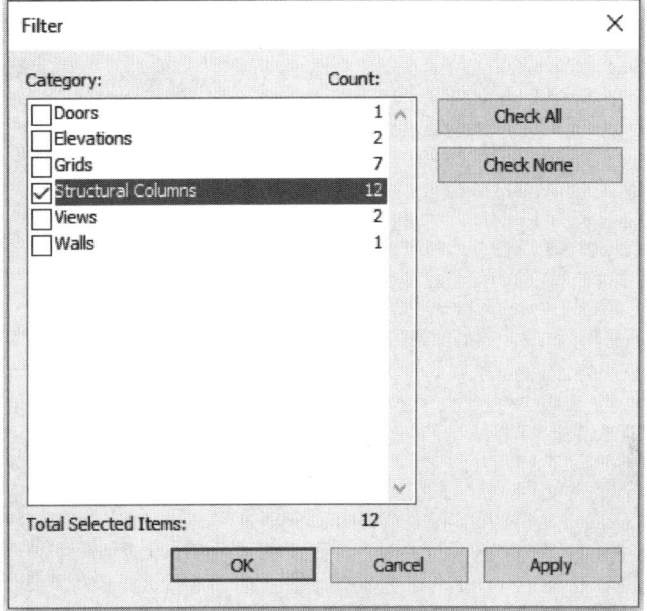

**Figure 5–23**

3. Click **Check None** to clear all of the options or **Check All** to select all of the options. You can also select or clear individual categories as needed.
4. Click **OK**. The selection is now limited to the elements you specified.

- The number of elements selected displays on the right end of the Status Bar and in Properties.

# Practice 5a

# Sketch and Edit Elements

## Practice Objective

- Use sketch tools and drawing aids.

In this practice, you will use the **Wall** command along with sketching tools and drawing aids, such as temporary dimensions and snaps. You will use the **Modify** command and modify the walls using grips, temporary dimensions, the Type Selector, and Properties. You will add a door and modify it using temporary dimensions and controls. The completed model is shown in Figure 5–24.

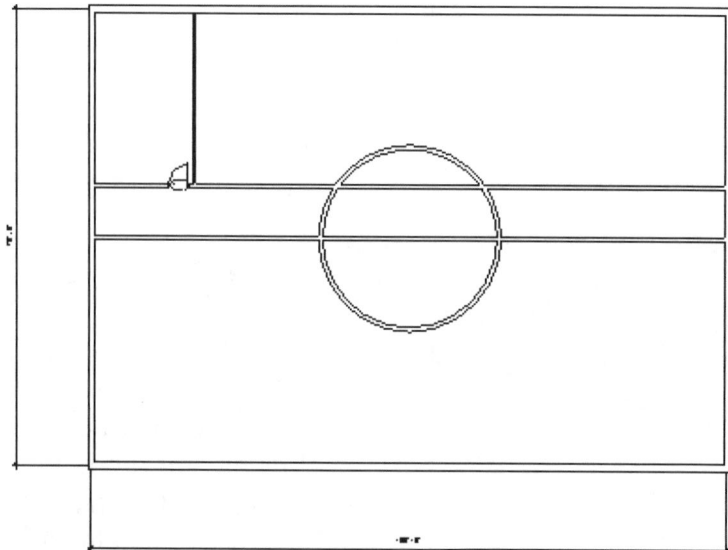

Figure 5–24

- A simple model is used for this exercise so you can practice using the tools before working on the main building model.

### Task 1 - Use sketching tools and temporary dimensions to model and modify walls.

1. In the *File Tab*, click  (New)>  (Project). If you are on the Home screen, in the *MODELS* section, click **New...**.

2. In the New Project dialog box, select **Imperial-Architectural Template** in the Template file drop-down list, and click **OK**.

3. In the Quick Access Toolbar, click  (Save). When prompted, name the project **Starting Project.rvt**.

4. In the *Architecture* tab>Build panel, click (Wall), or type **WA**.

5. In the *Modify | Place Wall* tab>Draw panel, click (Rectangle) and sketch a rectangle approximately **100' x 70'**. Drag your mouse from right to left in a diagonal direction. You do not have to be precise because you can change the dimensions later.

6. Note that the dimensions are temporary. Select the vertical dimension text and type **70'-0"**, as shown in Figure 5–25. Press <Enter>.

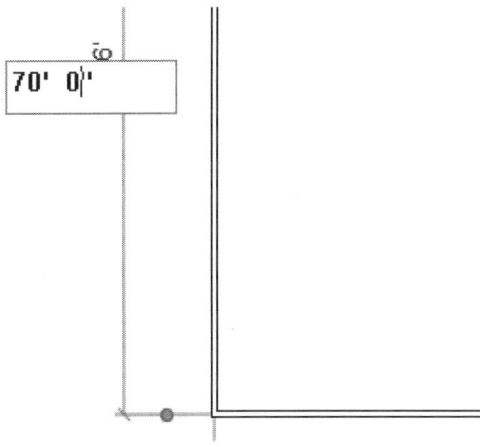

Figure 5–25

7. The dimensions are still displayed as temporary. Click the dimension controls of both the dimensions to make them permanent, as shown in Figure 5–26.

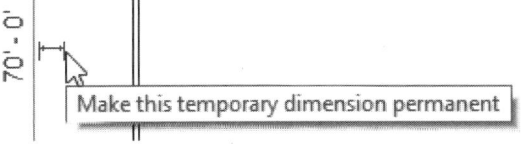

Figure 5–26

8. Click (Modify).

9. Select either vertical wall. The horizontal dimension becomes active (changes to blue). Click the dimension text and type **100'-0"**, as shown in Figure 5–27.

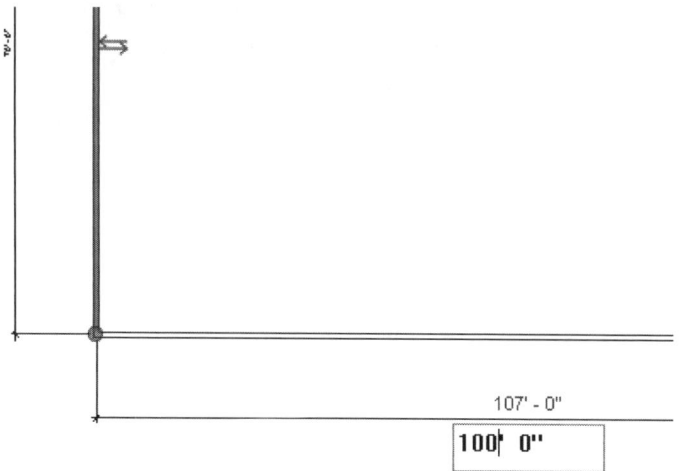

Figure 5–27

10. Click in an empty space in the view to end the selection. You are still in the **Modify** command.

11. In the *Architecture* tab>Build panel, click (Wall). In the Draw panel, verify that (Line) is selected. Sketch a wall horizontally from midpoint to midpoint of the vertical walls.

12. Draw another horizontal wall **8'-0"** above the middle horizontal wall. You can use temporary dimensions to adjust if needed.

13. Draw a vertical wall exactly **16'-0"** from the left wall, as shown in Figure 5–28.

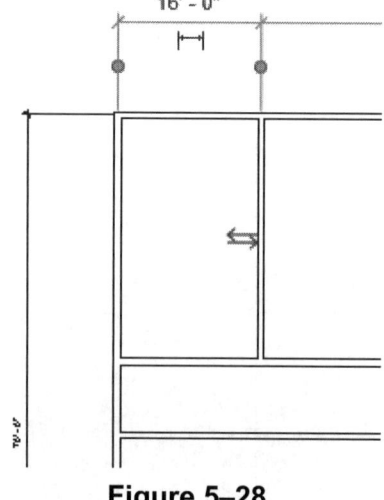

Figure 5–28

Basic Sketching and Modify Tools

14. In the Draw panel, click (Circle) and sketch a **14'-0"** radius circular wall at the midpoint of the lower interior horizontal wall, as shown in Figure 5–29.

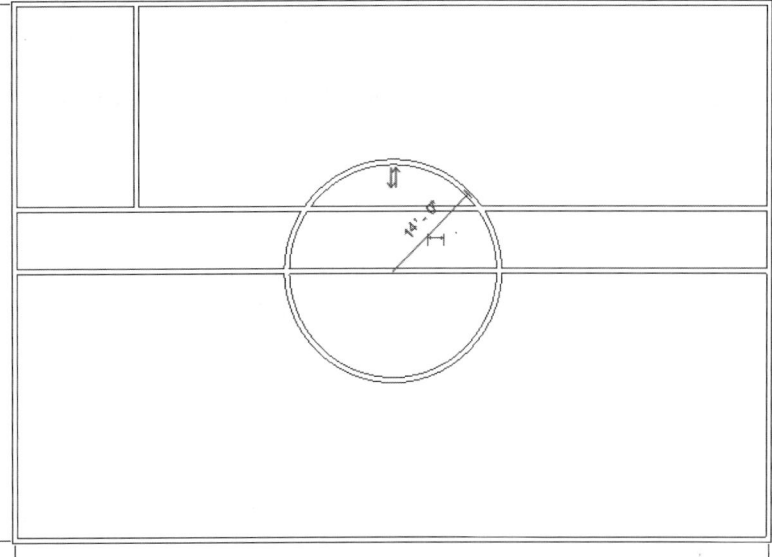

Figure 5–29

15. Click (Modify).

16. Hover the cursor over one of the outside walls, press <Tab> to highlight the chain of outside walls, and click to select the walls.

17. In the Type Selector, select **Basic Wall: Generic - 12"**, as shown in Figure 5–30. The thickness of the outside walls change.

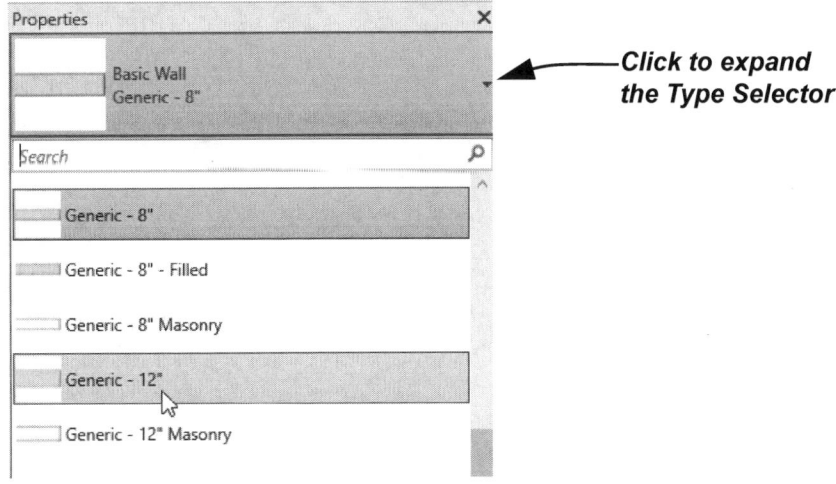

Figure 5–30

18. Click in an empty space in the view to release the selection.

19. Select the vertical interior wall. In the Type Selector, change the wall to one of the small interior partition styles.

20. Click in an empty space in the view to release the selection.

21. Save the project.

### Task 2 - Add and modify a door.

1. Zoom in on the room in the upper-left corner.

2. In the *Architecture* tab>Build panel, click (Door), or type **DR**.

3. In the *Modify | Place Door* tab>Tag panel, click (Tag on Placement).

4. Place a door anywhere along the wall in the hallway.

5. Click (Modify).

6. Select the door. Use temporary dimensions to move it so it is **2'-6"** from the right interior vertical wall. If needed, use controls to flip the door so it swings into the room, as shown in Figure 5–31.

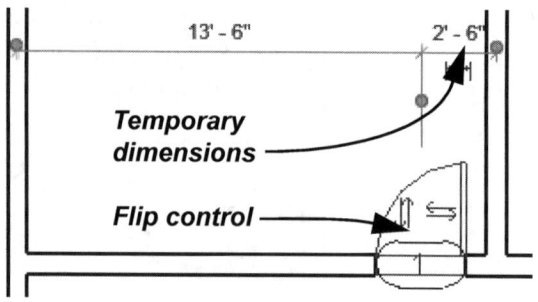

Figure 5–31

7. Type **ZE** to zoom out to the full view.

8. Save and close the project.

# 5.2 Working with Basic Modify Tools

The basic modifying tools, **Move**, **Copy**, **Rotate**, **Mirror**, and **Array**, can be used with individual elements or any selection of elements. They are found in the Modify panel (shown in Figure 5–32), in the *Modify* tab, and in contextual tabs.

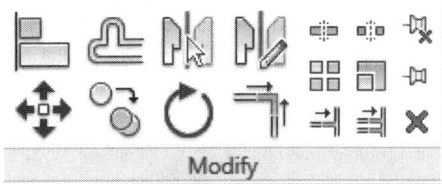

**Figure 5–32**

- For these modify commands, you can either select the elements and start the command, or start the command, select the elements, and press <Enter> to finish the selection and move to the next step in the command.

**Moving and Copying Elements**

The **Move** and **Copy** commands enable you to select the element(s) and move or copy them from one place to another. You can use alignment lines, temporary dimensions, and snaps to help place a second column, as shown in Figure 5–33.

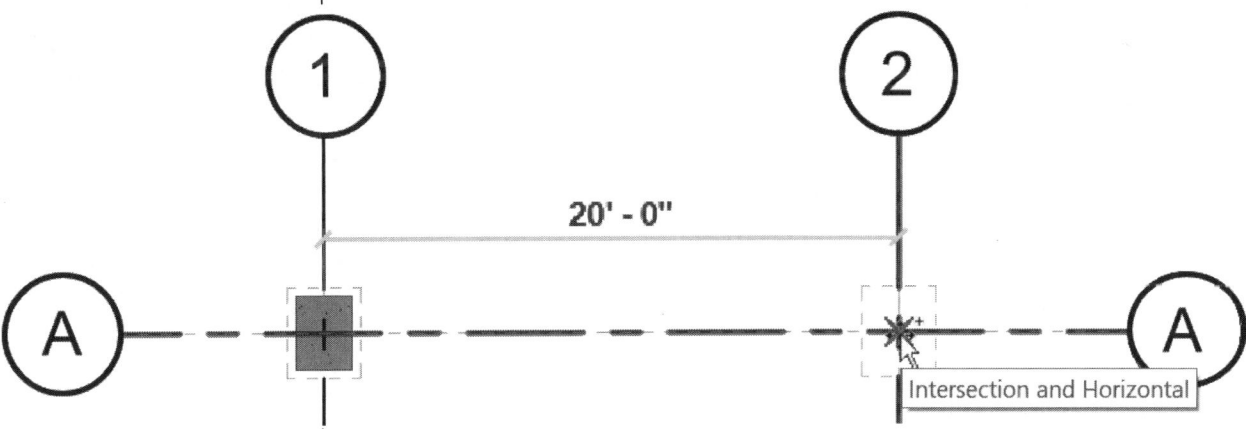

**Figure 5–33**

## How To: Move or Copy Elements

1. Select the elements you want to move or copy.
2. In the Modify panel, click ✥ (Move) or ⟲ (Copy). Alternatively, you can type **MV** for **Move** and **CO** for **Copy**. A boundary box displays around the selected elements.
3. Select a start point on or near the element.
4. Select a second point. Use alignment lines and temporary dimensions to help place the elements.
5. When you are finished, you can start another modify command using the elements that remain selected, or select ▸ (Modify) to end the command.

- You can drag elements to new locations without starting the **Move** command. Holding <Ctrl> and dragging copies the element. This is quick but not very precise.

## Move/Copy Elements Options

The **Move** and **Copy** commands have several options that display in the Options Bar, as shown in Figure 5–34.

☐ Constrain  ☐ Disjoin  ☐ Multiple

**Figure 5–34**

| | |
|---|---|
| **Constrain** | Restricts the movement of the cursor to horizontal or vertical, or along the axis of an item that is at an angle. This keeps you from selecting a point at an angle by mistake. **Constrain** is off by default. |
| **Disjoin** (Move only) | Breaks any connections between the elements being moved and other elements. If **Disjoin** is on, the elements move separately. If it is off, the connected elements also move or stretch. **Disjoin** is off by default. |
| **Multiple** (Copy only) | Enables you to make multiple copies of one selection. |

- These commands only work in the current view, not between views or projects. To copy between views or projects, In the *Modify* tab>Clipboard panel use 🗐 (Copy to Clipboard), ✂ (Cut to the Clipboard), and 📋 (Paste from Clipboard).

# Basic Sketching and Modify Tools

> **Hint: Pinning Elements**
>
> If you do not want elements to be moved, you can pin them in place, as shown in Figure 5–35. Select the elements and in the *Modify* tab, in the Modify panel, click (Pin) or type **PN**. Pinned elements can be copied, but not moved. If you try to delete a pinned element, a warning dialog displays reminding you that you must unpin the element before the command can be started.
>
>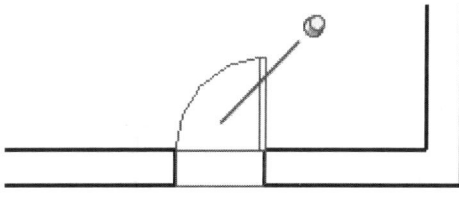
>
> Figure 5–35
>
> Select the element and click (Unpin) or type **UP** to unpin the element.

## Rotating Elements

The **Rotate** command enables you to rotate selected elements around a center point or origin, as shown in Figure 5–36. You can use alignment lines, temporary dimensions, and snaps to help specify the center of rotation and the angle. You can also create copies of the element as it is being rotated.

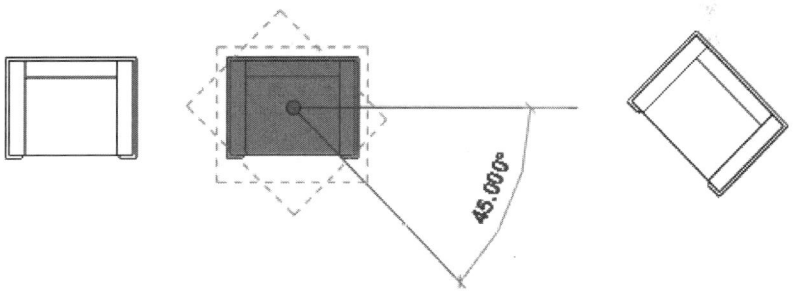

Figure 5–36

### How To: Rotate Elements

1. Select the element(s) you want to rotate.

2. In the Modify panel, click (Rotate), or type **RO**.

3. The center of rotation is automatically set to the center of the element or group of elements, as shown on the left in Figure 5–37. To change the center of rotation, as shown on the right in Figure 5–37, use the following:

- Drag the ⟲ (Center of Rotation) control to a new point.
- In the Options Bar, next to **Center of rotation**, click **Place** and use snaps to move it to a new location.
- Press <Spacebar> to select the center of rotation and click to move it to a new location.

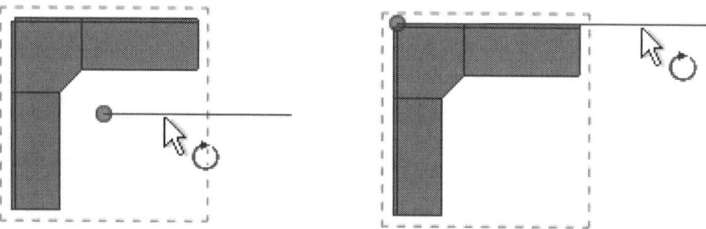

**Figure 5–37**

*To start the **Rotate** command with a prompt to select the center of rotation, select the elements first and type **R3**.*

4. In the Options Bar (shown in Figure 5–38), specify if you want to make a copy (select **Copy**), type an angle in the *Angle* field, and press <Enter>. You can also specify the angle on screen using temporary dimensions.

**Figure 5–38**

5. The rotated element(s) remain highlighted, enabling you to start another command using the same selection, or click ▷ (Modify) to finish.

- The **Disjoin** option breaks any connections between the elements being rotated and other elements. If **Disjoin** is on (selected), the elements rotate separately. If it is off (cleared), the connected elements also move or stretch, as shown in Figure 5–39. Disjoin is toggled off by default.

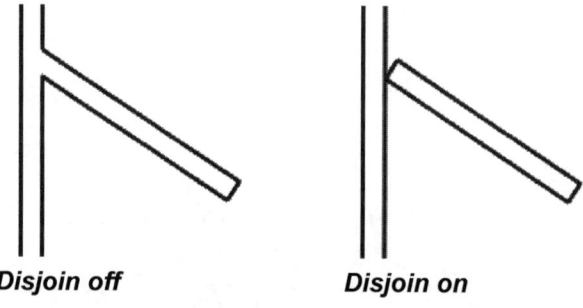

*Disjoin off*     *Disjoin on*

**Figure 5–39**

# Basic Sketching and Modify Tools

## Mirroring Elements

The **Mirror** command enables you to mirror elements about an axis defined by a selected element, as shown in Figure 5–40, or by selected points.

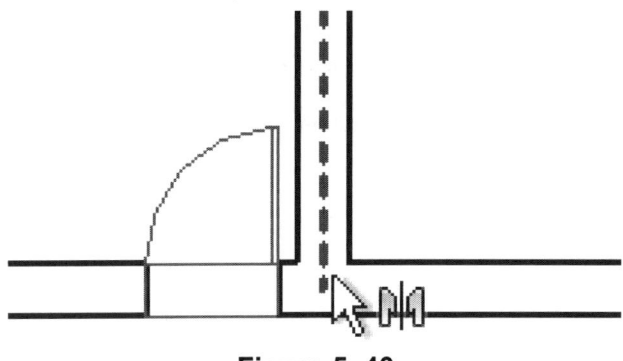

Figure 5–40

### How To: Mirror Elements

1. Select the element(s) to mirror.
2. In the Modify panel, select the method you want to use:

    - Click (Mirror - Pick Axis) or type **MM**. This prompts you to select an element as the **Axis of Reflection** (mirror line).

    - Click (Mirror - Draw Axis) or type **DM**. This prompts you to select two points to define the axis about which the elements mirror.

3. The new mirrored element(s) remain highlighted, enabling you to start another command, or return to **Modify** to finish.

- By default, the original elements that were mirrored remain. To delete the original elements, clear the **Copy** option in the Options Bar.

> **Hint: Scale**
>
> Revit is designed with full-size elements. Therefore, not much should be scaled. For example, scaling a wall increases its length but does not impact the width, which is set by the wall type. However, you can use (Scale) in reference planes, images, and imported files from other programs.

# Creating Linear and Radial Arrays

*A linear array creates a straight line pattern of elements, while a radial array creates a circular pattern around a center point.*

The **Array** command creates multiple copies of selected elements in a linear or radial pattern, as shown in Figure 5–41. For example, you can array a row of columns to create a row of evenly spaced columns on a grid, or array a row of parking spaces. The arrayed elements can be grouped or placed as separate elements.

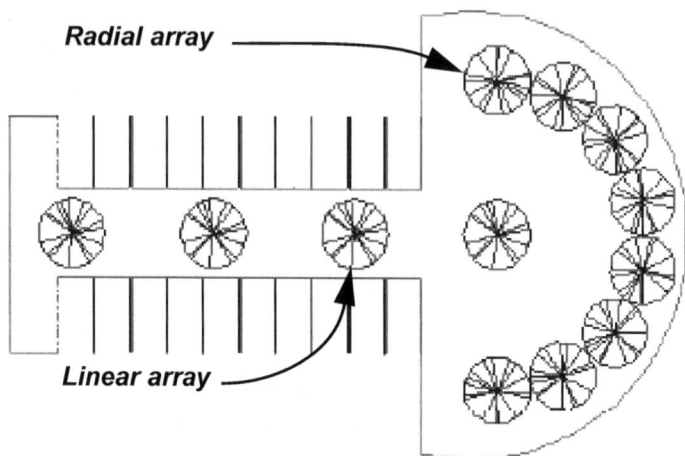

Figure 5–41

## How To: Create a Linear Array

1. Select the element(s) to array.
2. In the Modify panel, click ▦ (Array) or type **AR**.
3. In the Options Bar, click ⇒ (Linear).
4. Specify the other options as needed.
5. Select a start point and an end point to set the spacing and direction of the array. The array is displayed.
6. If **Group and Associate** is selected, you are prompted again for the number of items, as shown in Figure 5–42. Type a new number or click on the screen to finish the command.

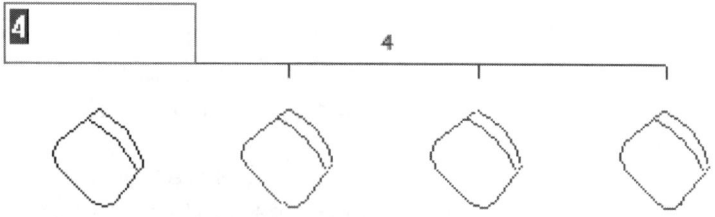

Figure 5–42

- To make a linear array in two directions, you need to array one direction first, select the arrayed elements, and then array them again in the other direction.

# Basic Sketching and Modify Tools

## Array Options

In the Options Bar, set up the **Array** options for **Linear Array** (top of Figure 5–43) or **Radial Array** (bottom of Figure 5–43).

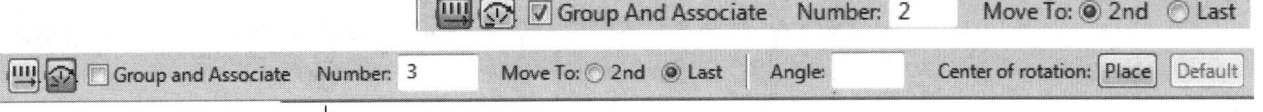

Figure 5–43

| | |
|---|---|
| **Group and Associate** | Creates an array group element out of all arrayed elements. Groups can be selected by selecting any elements in the group. |
| **Number** | Specifies how many instances you want in the array. |
| **Move To:** | **2nd** specifies the distance or angle between the center points of the two elements. **Last** specifies the overall distance or angle of the entire array. |
| **Constrain** | Restricts the direction of the array to only vertical or horizontal (Linear only). |
| **Angle** | Specifies the angle (Radial only). |
| **Center of rotation** | Specifies a location for the origin about which the elements rotate (Radial only). |

## How To: Create a Radial Array

1. Select the element(s) to array.
2. In the Modify panel, click (Array).
3. In the Options Bar, click (Radial).
4. Drag (Center of Rotation) or use **Place** to the move the center of rotation to the appropriate location, as shown in Figure 5–44.

*Remember to set the **Center of Rotation** control first, before specifying the angle.*

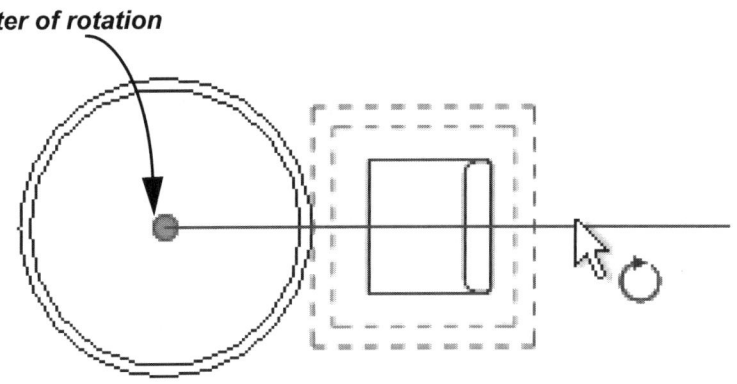

Figure 5–44

5. In the Options Bar, type an angle and press <Enter>, or specify the rotation angle by selecting points on the screen.
6. Specify the other options as needed.

## Modifying Array Groups

When you select an element in an array that has been grouped, you can change the number of instances in the array, as shown in Figure 5–45. For radial arrays, you can also modify the distance to the center.

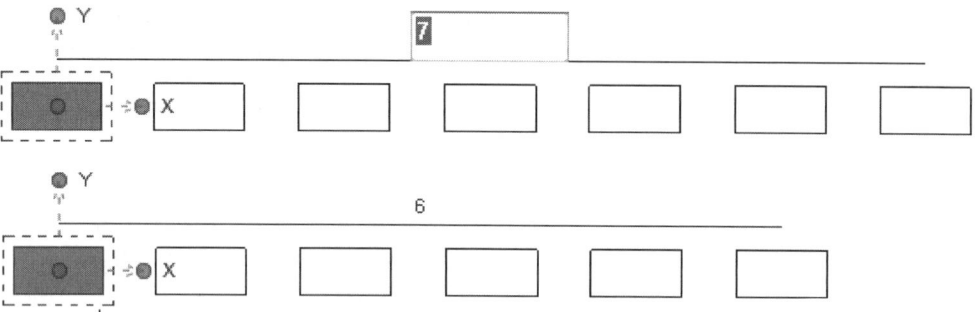

Figure 5–45

- Dashed lines surround the element(s) in a group, and the XY control lets you move the origin point of the group.

If you move one of the elements in the array group, the other elements move in response based on the distance and/or angle, as shown in Figure 5–46.

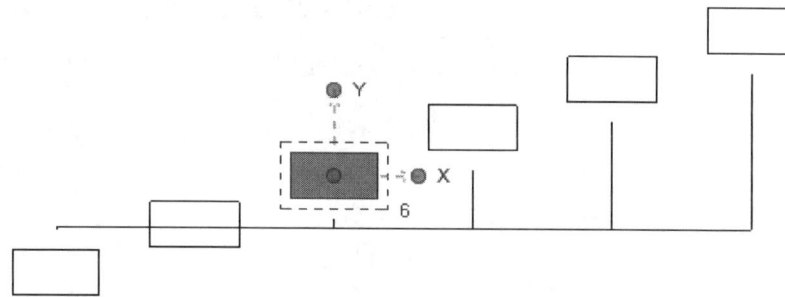

Figure 5–46

- To remove the array constraint on the group, select all of the elements in the array group and, in the *Modify* contextual tab>Group panel, click  (Ungroup).

- If you select an individual element in an array and click  (Ungroup), the element you selected is removed from the array, while the rest of the elements remain in the array group.

- You can use  (Filter) to ensure that you are selecting only **Model Groups**.

Basic Sketching and Modify Tools

# Practice 5b

# Work with Basic Modify Tools

## Practice Objective

- Use basic modify tools such as Move, Copy, Rotate, and Array.

In this practice, you will create a series of offices using the **Copy** and **Mirror** commands. You will then array desks around a circular wall, then rotate and array a pair of columns across the front of a simple building, as shown in Figure 5–47.

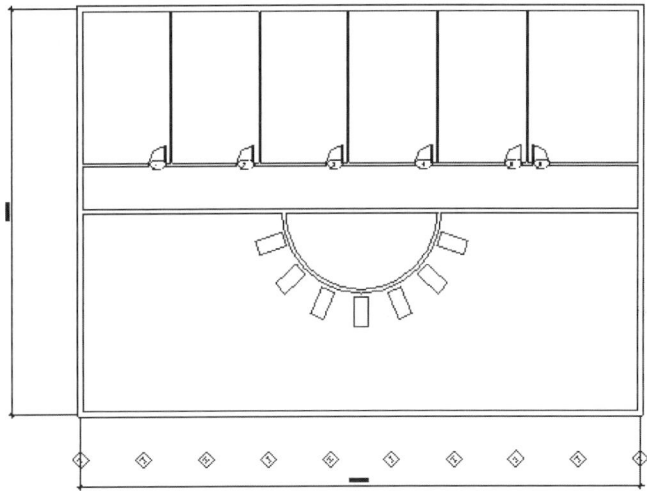

**Figure 5–47**

- A simple model is used for this exercise so you can practice using the tools before working on the main building model.

## Task 1 - Modify walls and doors.

1. Open the project **Simple Building-1.rvt** from the practice files folder.

2. Select the top arc of the circular wall.

3. In the Modify panel, click ✕ (Delete). The walls that the circular wall crossed are automatically cleaned up.

4. Select the vertical interior wall, door, and door tag. Hold <Ctrl> to select more than one element, or use a selection window.

5. In the Modify panel, click (Copy), or type **CO**.

*Remember that you can also press <Delete>, or right-click and select **Delete**.*

© 2022, ASCENT - Center for Technical Knowledge®

5–33

6. In the Options Bar, select **Constrain** and **Multiple** (adding a check mark means the setting is on). The **Constrain** option forces the cursor to move only horizontally or vertically.

7. Select the start point and, using the temporary dimensions, pick the end point **16'-0"** away from the start point, as shown in Figure 5–48. The wall, door, and door tag are copied to the right and the door tag displays **2**.

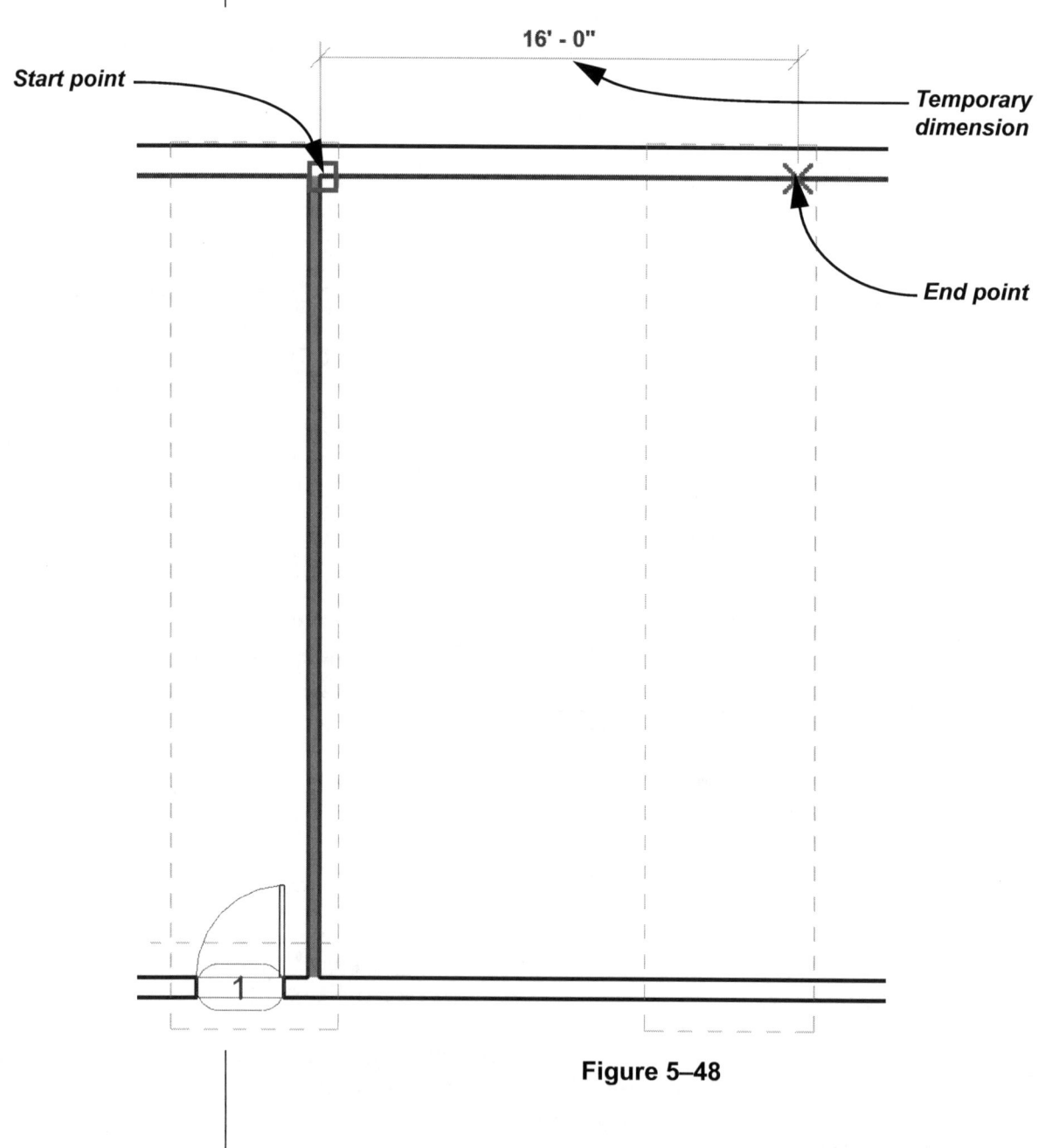

Figure 5–48

# Basic Sketching and Modify Tools

8. The new elements are still selected and you can continue to copy them. Use similar start and end points for the additional copies, or type **16** (16'-0") and press <Enter> to set the distance between each copy. The final layout is shown in Figure 5–49.

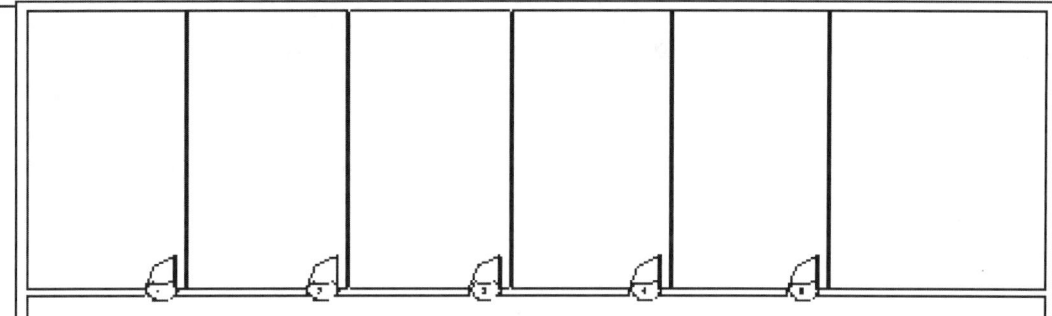

**Figure 5–49**

9. Click ▷ (Modify).

10. Zoom in on the room to the far right.

11. Select door #5 and the associated door tag.

12. In the Modify panel, click ▷|◁ (Mirror - Pick Axis), or type **MM**. In the Options Bar, ensure that **Copy** is selected.

13. Select the vertical wall between the rooms as the mirror axis. An alignment line displays along the center of the wall. Place the new door, as shown in Figure 5–50.

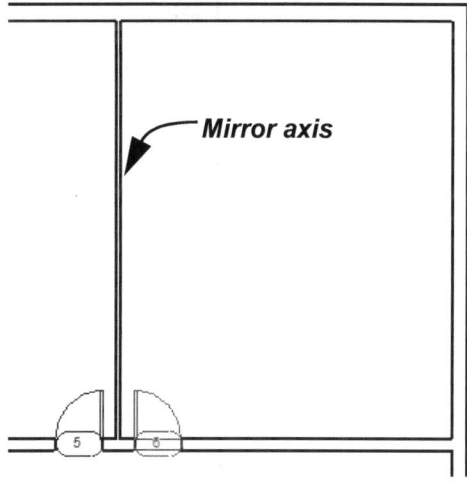

**Figure 5–50**

14. Click in an empty space in the view to release the selection.

15. Save the project.

## Task 2 - Add reference planes and use them to place a component.

1. In the *Architecture* tab>Work plane panel, click (Reference Plane).

2. Draw two reference planes, as shown in Figure 5–51. The vertical one starts at the midpoint of the wall. Place the horizontal plane **20'-0"** from the horizontal wall, or place the reference plane at any distance and then use temporary dimensions to place it more exactly.)

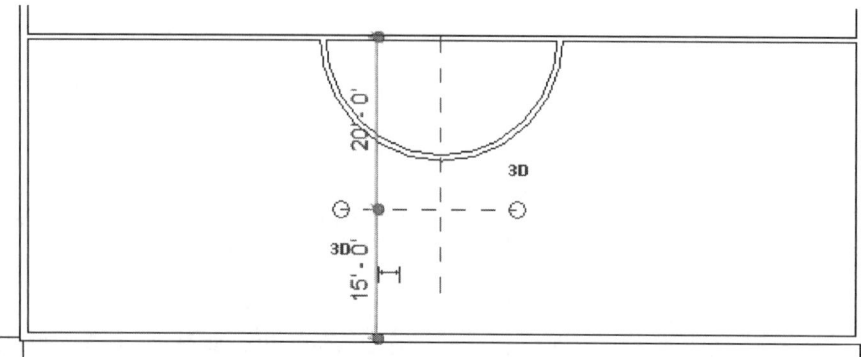

Figure 5–51

3. In the *Architecture* tab>Build panel, click (Component), or type **CM**.

4. In the Properties, in the Type Selector, verify that **Desk: 60" x 30"** is selected, as shown in Figure 5–52.

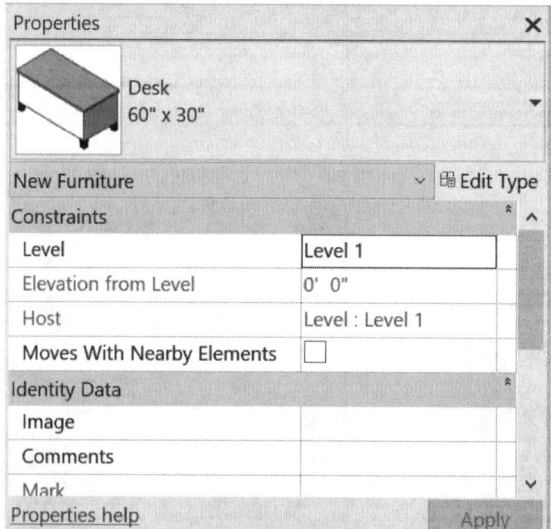

Figure 5–52

5. As you move the cursor, you can see that the desk is horizontal. Press <Spacebar> to rotate the desk 90°.

6. Place the desk at the intersection of the two reference planes, as shown in Figure 5–53. Zoom in as needed to ensure that you are connected to the reference planes, and not to any other alignment lines.

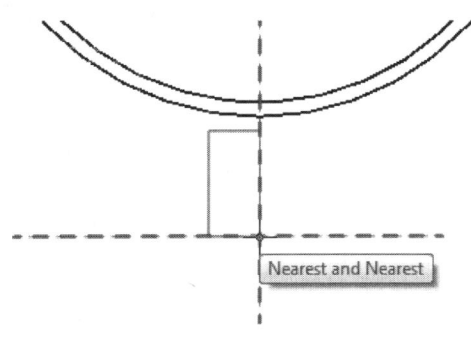

Figure 5–53

7. Click (Modify) and select the desk you just placed.

8. In the Modify panel, click (Move). In the Options Bar, select **Constrain**.

*Type **SM** to snap to Midpoint and **SE** to snap to Endpoint.*

9. Select the start point of the move as the midpoint of the desk and the end point as the vertical reference plane, as shown in Figure 5–54.

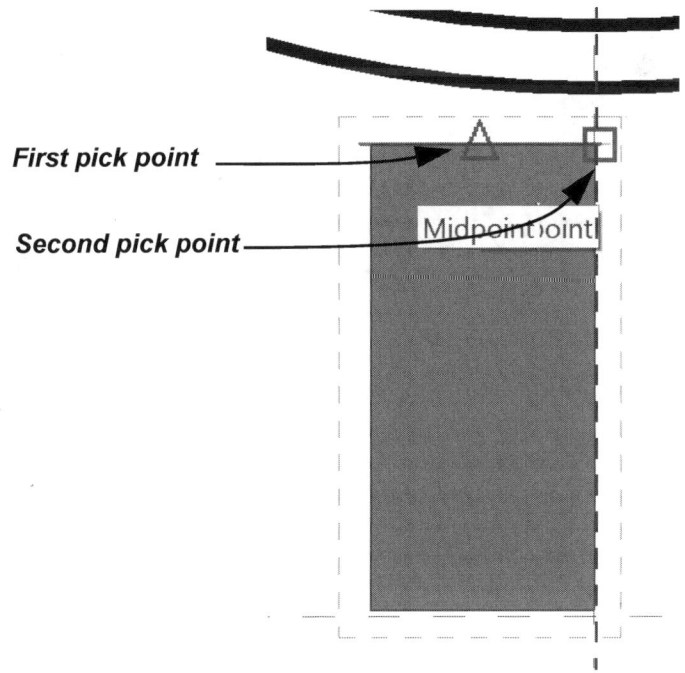

Figure 5–54

10. Save the project.

## Task 3 - Create a radial array.

1. Select the desk.
2. In the Modify panel, click ⬚ (Array), or type **AR**.
3. In the Options Bar, click (Radial). Clear the **Group And Associate** option, set the *Number* field to **15**, and set *Move To:* to **2nd.**
4. Drag the center of rotation from the center of the desk to the midpoint of the wall, as shown in Figure 5–55. Alternatively, you can select **Place** in the Options Bar and snap to the midpoint of the wall.

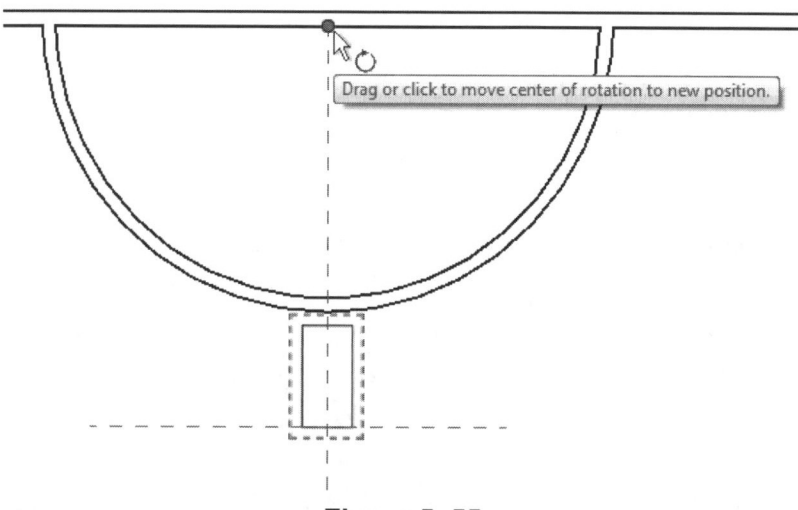

**Figure 5–55**

5. Return to the Options Bar and set the *Angle* to **360**. Press <Enter>. The array displays as shown in Figure 5–56.

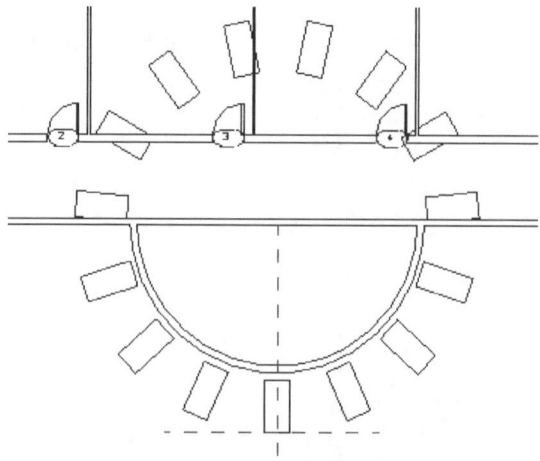

**Figure 5–56**

*Sometimes it is easier to create more elements then you need, and then delete the ones that are not required, as is done in this example.*

# Basic Sketching and Modify Tools

6. Delete all of the desks that are outside of the room.

7. Zoom out to display the entire view.

8. Save the project.

**Task 4 - Place columns in appropriate locations.**

1. Pan and zoom to the lower-left side of the model. Two columns (one architectural and one structural) have been added to the project.

2. Select the square architectural column and drag it over so that it lines up with the wall, as shown in Figure 5–57. Use the temporary dimension to set the distance off the wall to **8'-0"**.

3. Place the structural column at the center of the architectural column, as shown in Figure 5–58, using the **Midpoint** and **Extension** snaps.

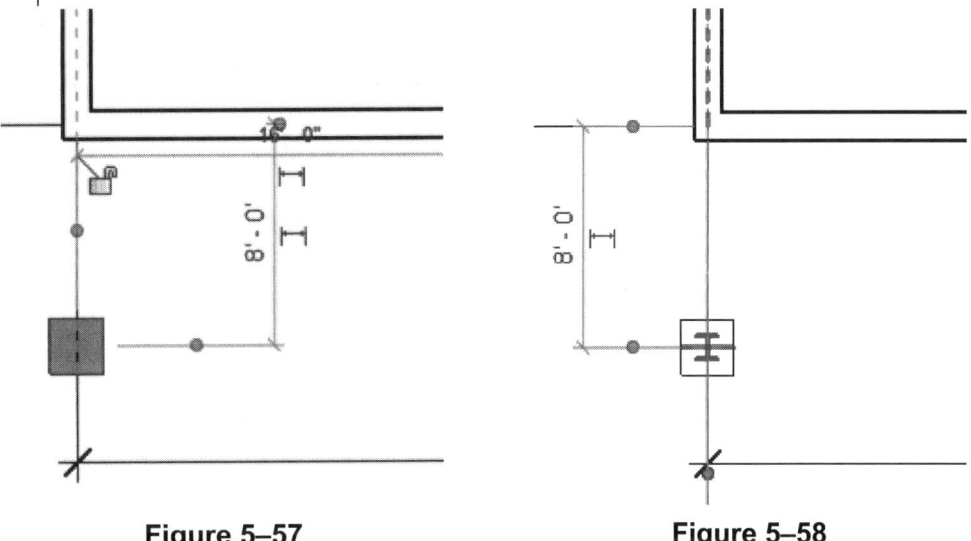

Figure 5–57                     Figure 5–58

4. Save the project.

**Task 5 - Rotate and array the columns.**

1. Click (Modify) and select the two columns.

2. In the *Modify | Multi-Select* tab>Modify panel, click (Rotate), or type **RO**.

3. For the start ray, click horizontally, as shown in Figure 5–59.

4. Move the ray line until you see the temporary dimension **45.00°**, as shown in Figure 5–60.

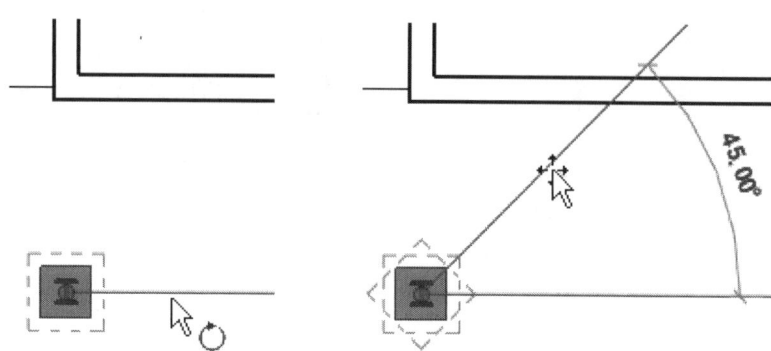

Figure 5–59    Figure 5–60

5. With the two columns still selected, in the *Modify | Multi-Select* tab>Modify panel, click (Array), or type **AR**.

6. In the Options Bar, click (Linear), clear **Group And Associate**, set the *Number* to **10**, and set *Move To:* to **Last**.

7. For the start point, click the midpoint of the columns. For the endpoint of the array, select the **Horizontal and Extension** of the center of the far right wall as shown in Figure 5–61.

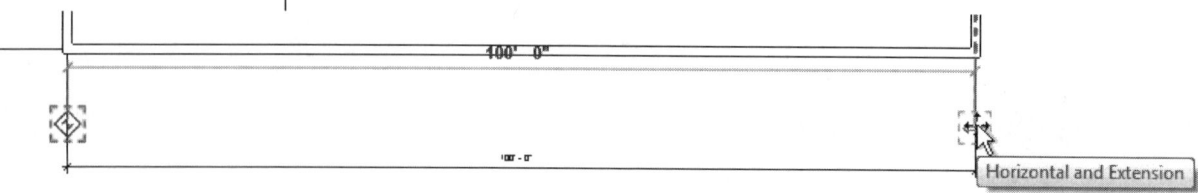

Figure 5–61

8. Zoom out to display the entire building.

9. The columns are arrayed evenly across the front of the building as shown in Figure 5–62.

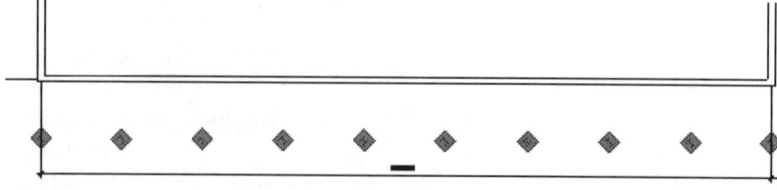

Figure 5–62

10. Save and close the project.

# 5.3 Working with Additional Modify Tools

As you work on a project, some additional tools found on the *Modify* tab>Modify panel, as shown in Figure 5–63, can help you with placing, modifying, and constraining elements. **Align** can be used with a variety of elements, while **Split Element**, **Trim/Extend**, and **Offset** can only be used with linear elements.

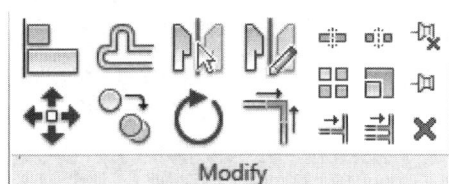

Figure 5–63

## Aligning Elements

The **Align** command enables you to line up one element with another, as shown in Figure 5–64. Most Revit elements can be aligned. For example, you can line up the tops of windows with the top of a door, or line up furniture with a wall.

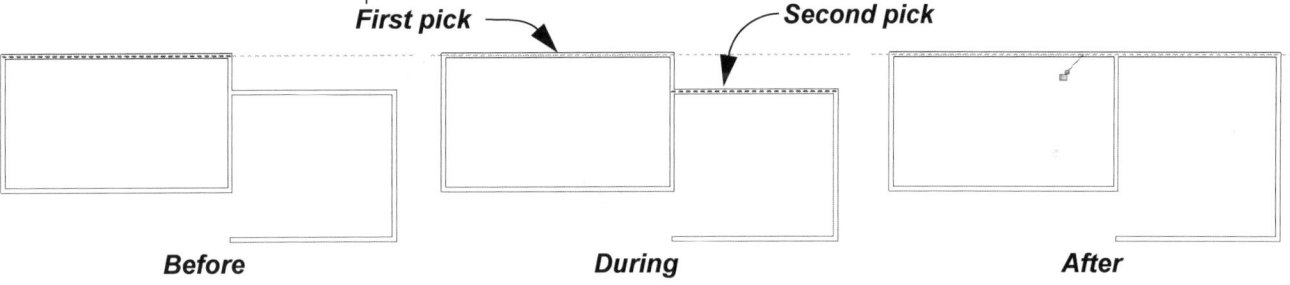

Figure 5–64

- The **Align** command works in all model views, including parallel and perspective 3D views.

### How To: Align Elements

1. In the *Modify* tab>Modify panel, click ▢ (Align), or type **AL**.
2. Select a line or point on the element that is going to remain stationary. For walls, press <Tab> to select the correct wall face.
3. Select a line or point on the element to be aligned. The second element moves into alignment with the first one.

- You can manually lock alignments so that the elements move together if either one is moved.

*Locking elements enlarges the size of the project file, so use this option carefully.*

- Once you have created the alignment, a padlock is displayed. Click on the padlock to lock it, as shown in Figure 5–65.

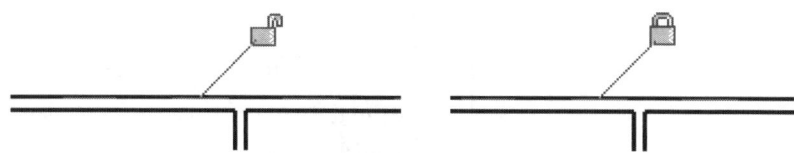

Figure 5–65

## Align Contextual Tab Options

- If you need to align multiple elements, in the *Modify | Align* tab>Align panel, select **Multiple Alignment Prefer:** to select multiple elements to align with the first element. You can also hold <Ctrl> to select multiple elements to align.

- If you want to lock your alignments as you go, in the *Modify | Align* tab>Align panel, you can check the check box for **Lock** to lock any alignments made so you do not need to go back and lock them manually.

- For walls, you can specify if you want the command to prefer **Wall centerlines**, **Wall faces**, **Center of core**, or **Faces of core**, as shown in Figure 5–66. The core refers to the structural members of a wall as opposed to facing materials, such as sheet rock.

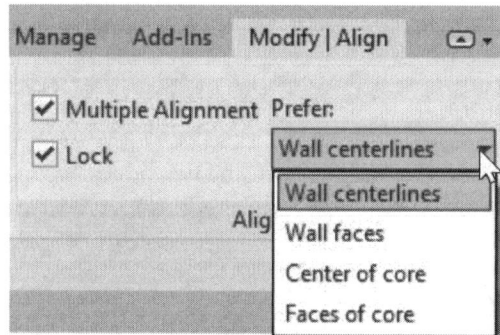

Figure 5–66

# Splitting Linear Elements

The **Split Element** command enables you to break a linear element at a specific point. You can use alignment lines, snaps, and temporary dimensions to help place the split point. After you have split the linear element, you can use other editing commands to modify the two parts, or change the type of one part, as shown with walls in Figure 5–67. You can split walls in plan, elevation, or 3D views.

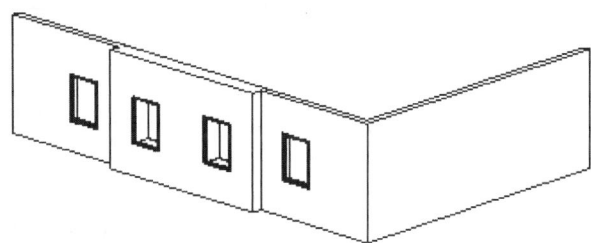

**Figure 5–67**

- The **Split with Gap** command only works when splitting walls.

### How To: Split Linear Elements

1. In the *Modify* tab>Modify panel, click (Split Element), or type **SL**.
2. In the Options Bar, select or clear the **Delete Inner Segment** option.
3. Move the cursor to the point you want to split and select the point.
4. Repeat for any additional split locations.
5. Modify the elements that were split, as needed.

- The **Delete Inner Segment** option is used when you select two split points along a linear element. When the option is selected, the segment between the two split points is automatically removed.

- An additional option, (Split with Gap), splits the linear element at the point you select, as shown in Figure 5–68, but also creates a *Joint Gap* specified in the Options Bar.

*This command is typically used with structural precast walls.*

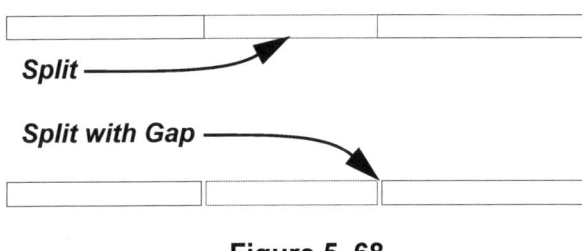

**Figure 5–68**

# Trimming and Extending

There are three trim/extend methods that you can use with linear elements: **Trim/Extend to Corner**, **Trim/Extend Single Element**, and **Trim/Extend Multiple Elements**.

- When selecting elements to trim, click the part of the element that you want to keep. The opposite part of the line is then trimmed.

### How To: Trim/Extend to Corner

1. In the *Modify* tab>Modify panel, click (Trim/Extend to Corner), or type **TR**.
2. Select the first linear element on the side you want to keep.
3. Select the second linear element on the side you want to keep, as shown in Figure 5–69.

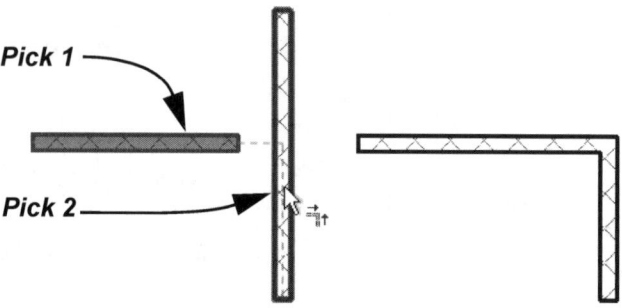

Figure 5–69

### How To: Trim/Extend a Single Element

1. In the *Modify* tab>Modify panel, click (Trim/Extend Single Element).
2. Select the cutting or boundary edge.
3. Select the linear element to be trimmed or extended, as shown in Figure 5–70.

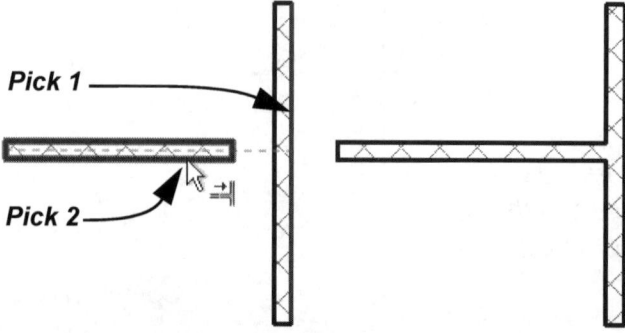

Figure 5–70

## How To: Trim/Extend Multiple Elements

1. In the *Modify* tab>Modify panel, click ⇉ (Trim/Extend Multiple Elements).
2. Select the cutting or boundary edge.
3. Select the linear elements that you want to trim or extend by selecting one at a time, or by using a crossing window, as shown in Figure 5–71. For trimming, select the side you want to keep.

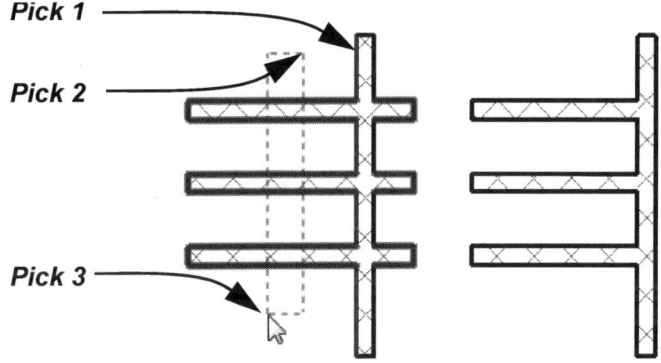

Figure 5–71

- You can click in an empty space in the view to clear the selection and select another cutting edge or boundary.

## Offsetting Elements

The **Offset** command is an easy way of creating parallel copies of linear elements at a specified distance, as shown in Figure 5–72. Walls, beams, braces, and lines are among the elements that can be offset.

Figure 5–72

- If you offset a wall that has a door or window embedded in it, the elements are copied with the offset wall.

The offset distance can be set by typing the distance (**Numerical** method, as shown in Figure 5–73) or by selecting points on the screen (**Graphical** method).

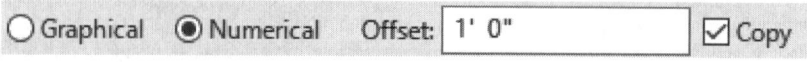

Figure 5–73

### How To: Offset Using the Numerical Method

1. In the *Modify* tab>Modify panel, click (Offset), or type **OF**.
2. In the Options Bar, select the **Numerical** option.
3. In the Options Bar, type the required distance in the *Offset* field.
4. Move the cursor over the element you want to offset. A dashed line previews the offset location. Move the cursor to flip the sides, as needed.
5. Click to create the offset.
6. Repeat Steps 4 and 5 to offset other elements by the same distance, or to change the distance for another offset.

- With the **Numerical** option, you can select multiple connected linear elements for offsetting. Hover the cursor over an element and press <Tab> until the other related elements are highlighted. Select the element to offset all of the elements at the same time.

### How To: Offset Using the Graphical Method

1. In the *Modify* tab>Modify panel, click (Offset), or type **OF**.
2. In the Options Bar, select **Graphical**.
3. Select the linear element to offset.
4. Select two points that define the distance of the offset and which side to apply it. You can type an override in the temporary dimension for the second point.

- Most linear elements connected at a corner automatically trim or extend to meet at the offset distance, as shown in Figure 5–74.

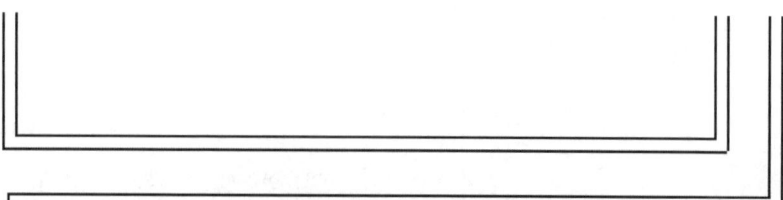

Figure 5–74

*The **Copy** option (which is on by default) makes a copy of the element being offset. If this option is not selected, the **Offset** command moves the element the set offset distance.*

# Practice 5c  Work with Additional Modify Tools

### Practice Objective

- Align, Split, Trim/Extend, and Offset elements.

In this practice, you will split a wall into three parts and delete the middle portion. You will offset walls and then trim or extend them to form new rooms. You will then align the new walls to match existing walls, as shown in Figure 5–75.

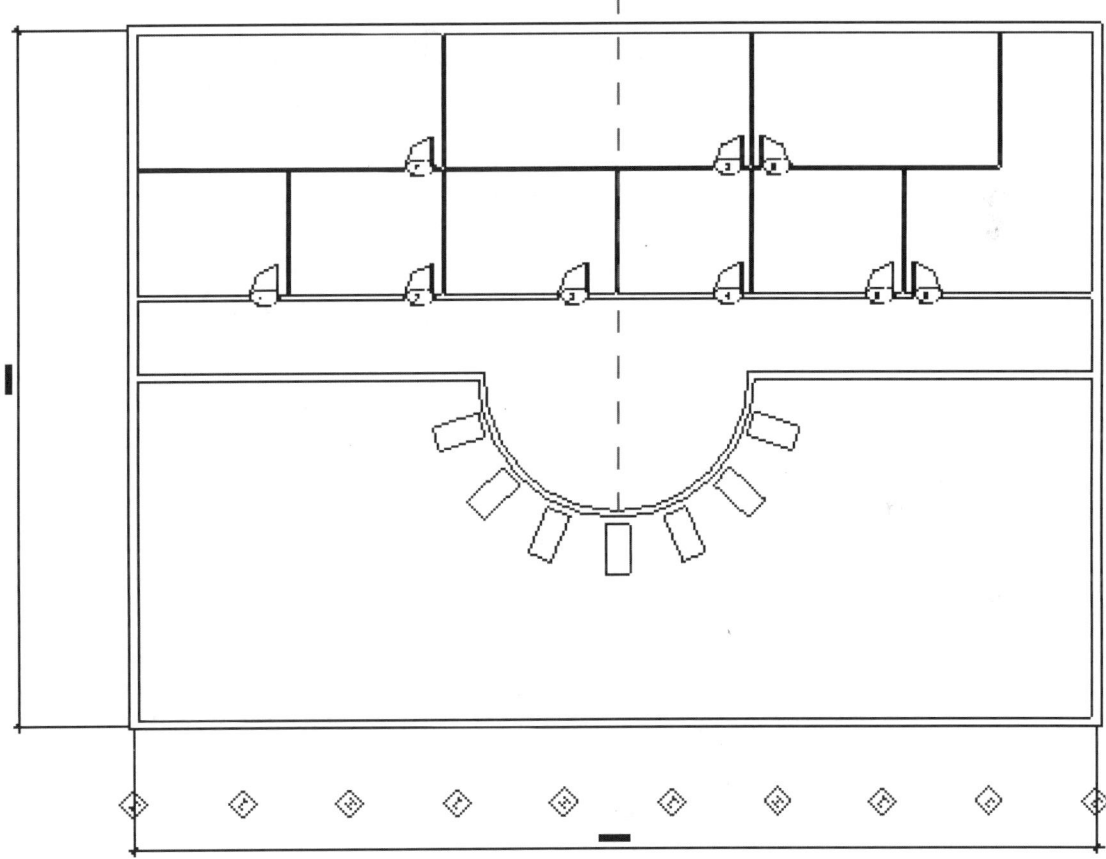

**Figure 5–75**

- A simple model is used for this exercise so you can practice using the tools before working on the main building model.

### Task 1 - Split and remove walls.

1. Open the project **Simple Building-2.rvt** from the practice files folder.

2. In the *Modify* tab>Modify panel, click (Split Element), or type **SL**.

3. In the Options Bar, select **Delete Inner Segment**.

4. Click on the horizontal wall where it intersects with the curved wall at both ends. The wall segment between these points is removed, as shown in Figure 5–76.

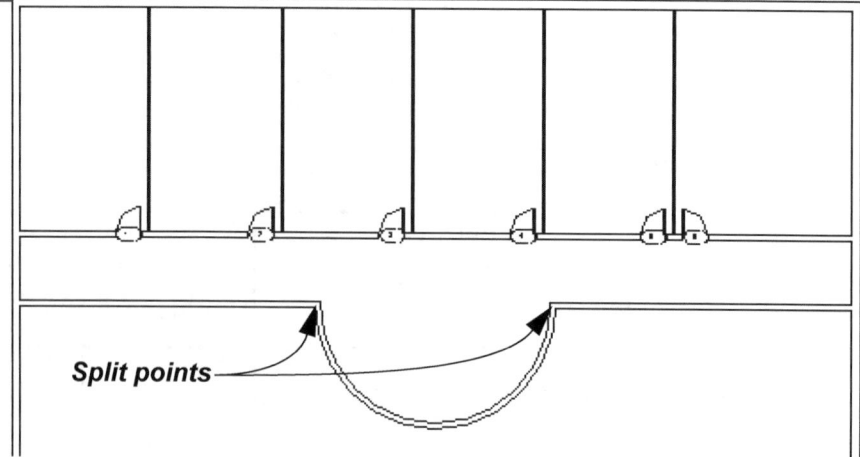

Figure 5–76

5. Click (Modify) to finish.

6. Save the project.

### Task 2 - Offset and trim walls.

1. In the *Modify* tab>Modify panel, click (Offset), or type **OF**.

2. In the Options Bar, set the *Offset* to **14'-0"** and ensure that **Copy** is selected.

3. Select the top horizontal wall while ensuring that the dashed alignment line displays inside the building, as shown in Figure 5–77.

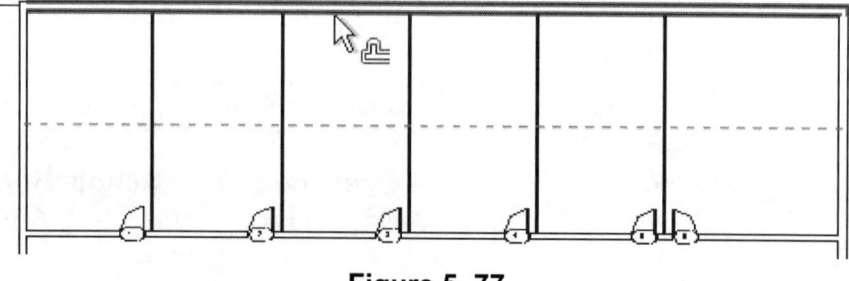

Figure 5–77

4. With **Offset** still active, change the *Offset* to **10'-0"** and offset the last vertical interior wall to the right, as shown in Figure 5–78.

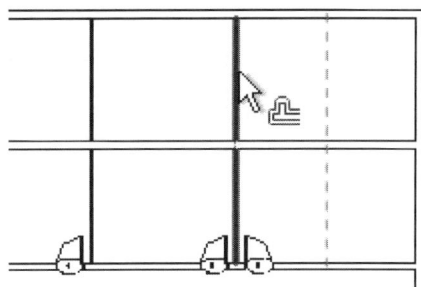

Figure 5–78

5. Click (Modify) and select the new horizontal wall that was created from the exterior wall. Change the wall to **Basic Wall: Interior - 3 1/8" Partition (1-hr)**. The layout of the new walls should display as shown in Figure 5–79.

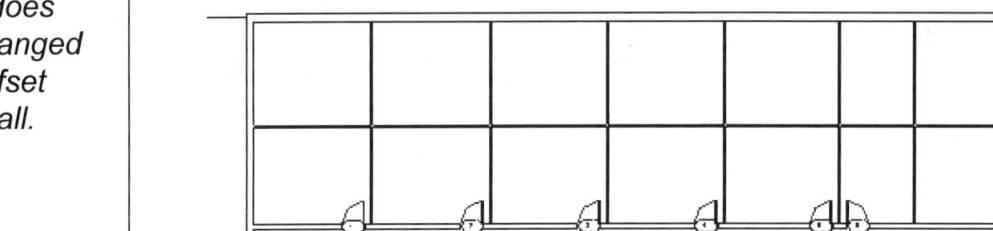

Figure 5–79

*The vertical wall does not need to be changed because it was offset from an interior wall.*

6. In the *Modify* tab>Modify panel, click (Trim/Extend Multiple Elements).

7. Select the new horizontal wall as the element to trim against.

8. Select every other wall *below* the new wall. (Remember, you select the elements that you want to keep.) The walls should display as shown in Figure 5–80.

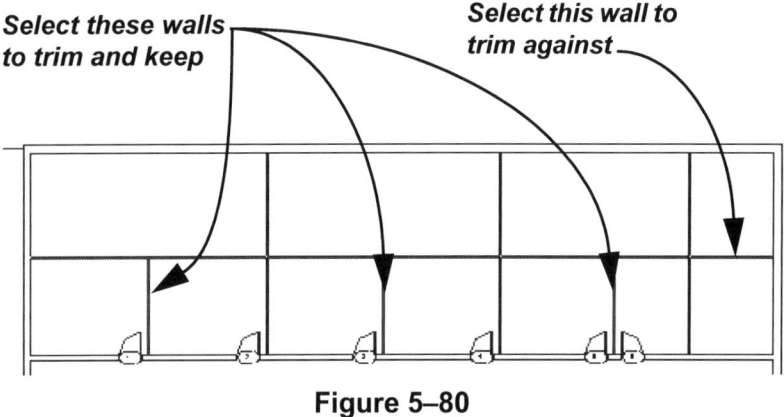

Figure 5–80

9. In the *Modify* tab>Modify panel, click (Trim/Extend to Corner), or type **TR**. Select the two walls to trim, as shown in Figure 5–81.

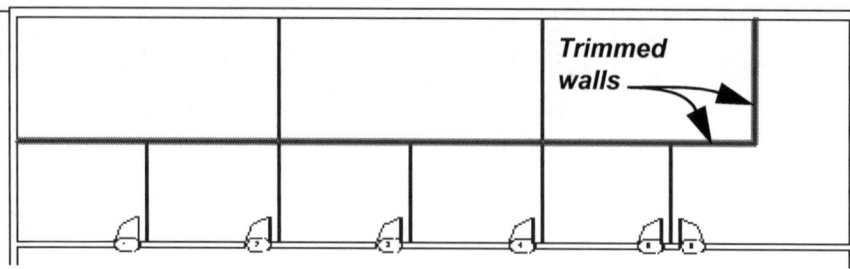

Figure 5–81

10. Add doors into the three new rooms.

11. Save the project.

### Task 3 - Align walls.

1. Select and extend the vertical reference plane. Use the control to drag the top end so it extends beyond the outer wall, as shown in Figure 5–82.

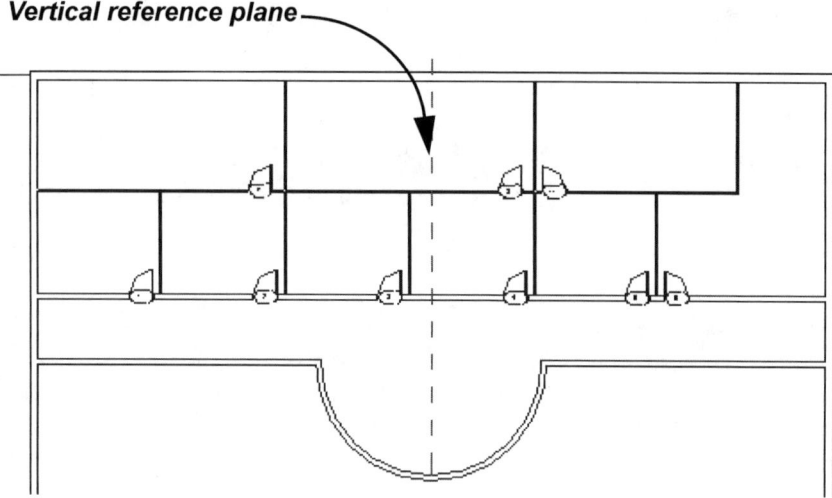

Figure 5–82

2. In the *Modify* tab>Modify panel, click (Align), or type **AL**.

3. Select the reference plane, and then the wall to the left. The wall should line up with the reference plane.

4. Save and close the project.

# Chapter Review Questions

1. What is the purpose of an alignment line?

    a. Displays when the new element you are placing or modeling is aligned with the grid system.

    b. Indicates that the new element you are placing or modeling is aligned with an existing element.

    c. Displays when the new element you are placing or modeling is aligned with a selected tracking point.

    d. Indicates that the new element is aligned with true north rather than project north.

2. When you are modeling (not editing) a linear element, how do you edit the temporary dimension shown in Figure 5–83?

    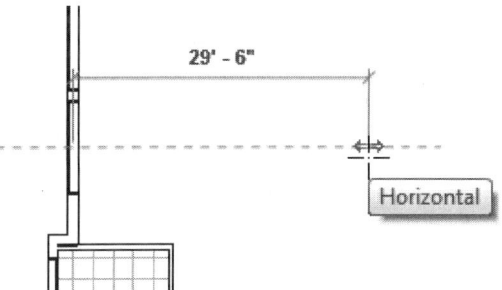

    **Figure 5–83**

    a. Select the temporary dimension and enter a new value.

    b. Type a new value and press <Enter>.

    c. Type a new value in the Distance/Length box in the Options Bar and press <Enter>.

3. How do you select all the doors of various sizes, but no other elements in a view?

    a. In the Project Browser, select the *Door* category.

    b. Select one door, right-click and select **Select All Instances>Visible in View**.

    c. Select all of the elements in the view and use (Filter) to clear the other categories.

    d. Select one door, and click (Select Multiple) in the ribbon.

4. What are the two methods for starting commands such as **Move**, **Copy**, **Rotate**, **Mirror**, and **Array**?

   a. Start the command from the *Modify* tab and select the elements, then start the command.

   b. Start the command from the *Modify* tab and select the elements, then select the command from the Status Bar.

   c. Start the command from the *Modify* tab and select the elements, then right-click and select the command from the list.

5. Where do you change the wall type for a selected wall, as shown in Figure 5–84?

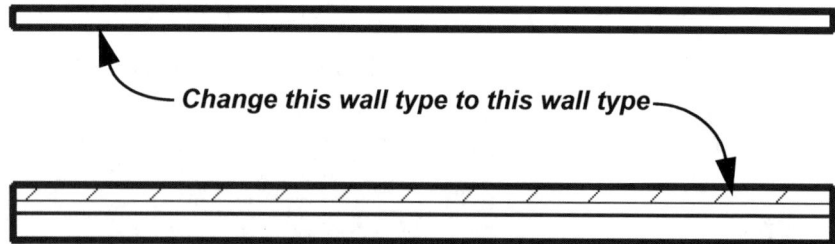

Figure 5–84

   a. In the *Modify | Walls* tab>Properties panel, click (Type Properties) and select a new wall type in the dialog box.

   b. In the Options Bar, click **Change Element Type**.

   c. Select the dynamic control next to the selected wall and select a new type in the drop-down list.

   d. In Properties, select a new type in the Type Selector drop-down list.

6. Both (Rotate) and (Array) with (Radial) have a center of rotation that defaults to the center of the element or group of elements you have selected. How do you move the center of rotation to another point, as shown in Figure 5–85? (Select all that apply.)

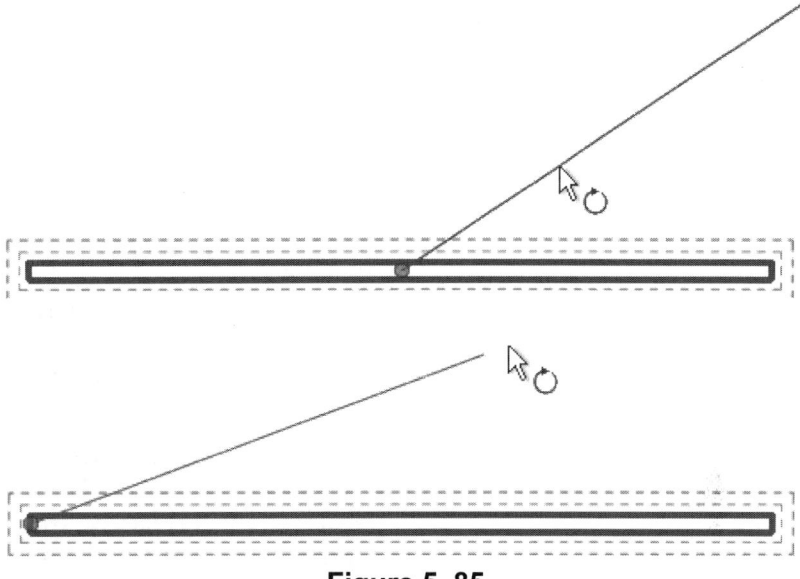

Figure 5–85

   a. Select the center of rotation and drag it to a new location.

   b. In the Options Bar, click **Place** and select the new point.

   c. In the *Modify* tab>Placement panel, click (Center) and select the new point.

   d. Right-click and select **Snap Overrides>Centers** and select the new point.

7. Which command would you use to remove a part or a segment of a wall?

   a. (Split Element)

   b. (Wall Joins)

   c. (Cut Geometry)

   d. (Demolish)

8. Which of the following are ways in which you can create additional parallel walls, as shown in Figure 5–86? (Select all that apply.)

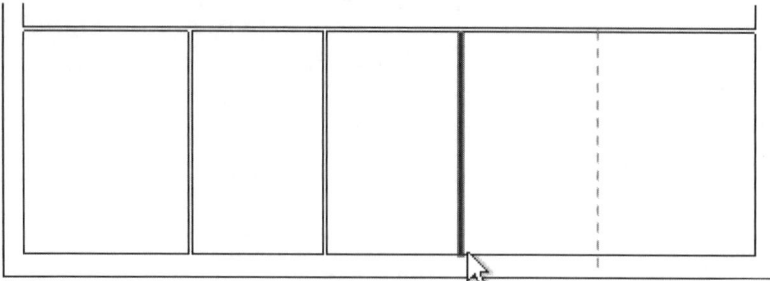

Figure 5–86

a. Use the **Trim/Extend Multiple Elements** tool.

b. Use the **Offset** tool in the *Modify* tab.

c. Select an existing wall, hold <Ctrl> and drag the wall to a new location.

d. Use the **Align** command with an offset.

9. Which command do you use if you want two walls that are not touching to come together, as shown in Figure 5–87?

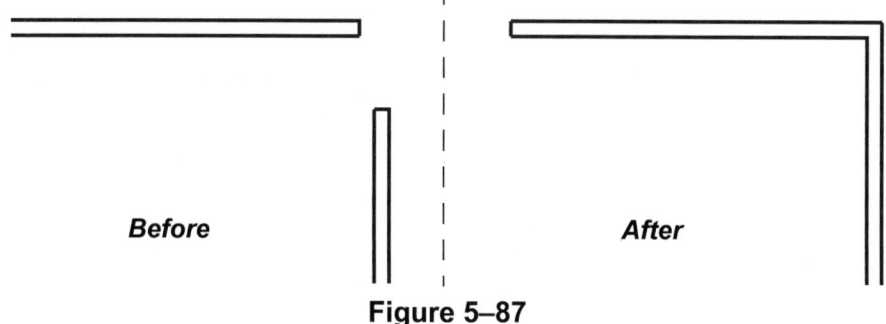

Figure 5–87

a. (Edit Wall Joins)

b. (Trim/Extend to Corner)

c. (Join Geometry)

d. (Edit Profile)

# Command Summary

| Button | Command | Location |
|---|---|---|
| **Draw Tools** | | |
| | Center-ends Arc | • **Ribbon:** *Modify | (various linear elements) tab>Draw panel* |
| | Circle | • **Ribbon:** *Modify | (various linear elements) tab>Draw panel* |
| | Circumscribed Polygon | • **Ribbon:** *Modify | (various linear elements) tab>Draw panel* |
| | Ellipse | • **Ribbon:** *Modify | Place Lines, Place Detail Lines, and various boundary sketches>Draw panel* |
| | Ellipse Arc | • **Ribbon:** *Modify | Place Lines, Place Detail Lines, and various boundary sketches>Draw panel* |
| | Fillet Arc | • **Ribbon:** *Modify | (various linear elements) tab>Draw panel* |
| | Inscribed Polygon | • **Ribbon:** *Modify | (various linear elements) tab>Draw panel* |
| | Line | • **Ribbon:** *Modify | (various linear elements) tab>Draw panel* |
| | Pick Faces | • **Ribbon:** *Modify | Place Wall>Draw panel* |
| | Pick Lines | • **Ribbon:** *Modify | (various linear elements) tab>Draw panel* |
| | Pick Walls | • **Ribbon:** *Modify | (various boundary sketches)>Draw panel* |
| | Rectangle | • **Ribbon:** *Modify | (various linear elements) tab>Draw panel* |
| | Spline | • **Ribbon:** *Modify | Place Lines, Place Detail Lines, and various boundary sketches>Draw panel* |
| | Start-End-Radius Arc | • **Ribbon:** *Modify | (various linear elements) tab>Draw panel* |
| | Tangent End Arc | • **Ribbon:** *Modify | (various linear elements) tab>Draw panel* |
| **Modify Tools** | | |
| | Align | • **Ribbon:** *Modify tab>Modify panel*<br>• **Shortcut:** AL |
| | Array | • **Ribbon:** *Modify tab>Modify panel*<br>• **Shortcut:** AR |
| | Copy | • **Ribbon:** *Modify tab>Modify panel*<br>• **Shortcut:** CO |

| | Copy to Clipboard | • **Ribbon:** *Modify* tab>Clipboard panel<br>• **Shortcut:** <Ctrl>+<C> |
|---|---|---|
| | Delete | • **Ribbon:** *Modify* tab>Modify panel<br>• **Shortcut:** DE |
| | Mirror - Draw Axis | • **Ribbon:** *Modify* tab>Modify panel<br>• **Shortcut:** DM |
| | Mirror - Pick Axis | • **Ribbon:** *Modify* tab>Modify panel<br>• **Shortcut:** MM |
| | Move | • **Ribbon:** *Modify* tab>Modify panel<br>• **Shortcut:** MV |
| | Offset | • **Ribbon:** *Modify* tab>Modify panel<br>• **Shortcut:** OF |
| | Paste | • **Ribbon:** *Modify* tab>Clipboard panel<br>• **Shortcut:** <Ctrl>+<V> |
| | Pin | • **Ribbon:** *Modify* tab>Modify panel<br>• **Shortcut:** PN |
| | Rotate | • **Ribbon:** *Modify* tab>Modify panel<br>• **Shortcut:** RO, R3 |
| | Scale | • **Ribbon:** *Modify* tab>Modify panel<br>• **Shortcut:** RE |
| | Split Element | • **Ribbon:** *Modify* tab>Modify panel<br>• **Shortcut:** SL |
| | Split with Gap | • **Ribbon:** *Modify* tab>Modify panel |
| | Trim/Extend Multiple Elements | • **Ribbon:** *Modify* tab>Modify panel |
| | Trim/Extend Single Element | • **Ribbon:** *Modify* tab>Modify panel |
| | Trim/Extend to Corner | • **Ribbon:** *Modify* tab>Modify panel<br>• **Shortcut:** TR |
| | Unpin | • **Ribbon:** *Modify* tab>Modify panel<br>• **Shortcut:** UP |

**Additional Tools**

| | Aligned Dimension | • **Ribbon:** *Modify* tab>Measure panel<br>• **Quick Access Toolbar** |
|---|---|---|
| | Component | • **Ribbon:** *Architecture/Structure/Systems* tab<br>• **Shortcut:** CM |
| | Detail Line | • **Ribbon:** *Annotate* tab>Detail panel<br>• **Shortcut:** DL |
| | Filter | • **Ribbon:** *Modify | Multi-Select* tab>Filter panel<br>• **Status Bar** |

## Basic Sketching and Modify Tools

|  | Model Line | • **Ribbon:** *Architectural* tab>Model panel<br>• **Shortcut:** LI |
|---|---|---|
|  | Reference Plane | • **Ribbon:** *Architecture/Structure/ Systems* tab>Work Plane panel |

# Design Development

The second section of this guide focuses on teaching you how to use the tools available in Revit® to create the building model.

This section includes the following chapters:

- Chapter 6: Adding Columns
- Chapter 7: Modeling Walls
- Chapter 8: Working with Doors and Windows
- Chapter 9: Working with Curtain Walls
- Chapter 10: Modeling Floors
- Chapter 11: Modeling Ceilings
- Chapter 12: Modeling Roofs
- Chapter 13: Modeling Stairs, Railings, and Ramps

# Chapter 6

# Adding Columns

Revit includes two types of columns: architectural and structural. Architectural columns are placeholders or decorative elements, while structural columns include more precise information relative to strength and load-bearing parameters.

## Learning Objective in This Chapter

- Add columns to the project as the first design consideration.

## 6.1 Adding Columns

Architectural columns (shown on the left in Figure 6–1) are typically placed from the level that you are on up to a specific height. Structural columns (shown on the right in Figure 6–1) are typically placed from the level you are on down to a specific depth.

Architectural columns can only be placed vertically with settings that can be modified in the Options Bar and Properties. They cannot be placed at grid lines or slanted.

Structural columns can be vertical or slanted, placed at grids or at columns, and tagged upon placement. Additionally, you can modify structural column settings in the Options Bar and Properties.

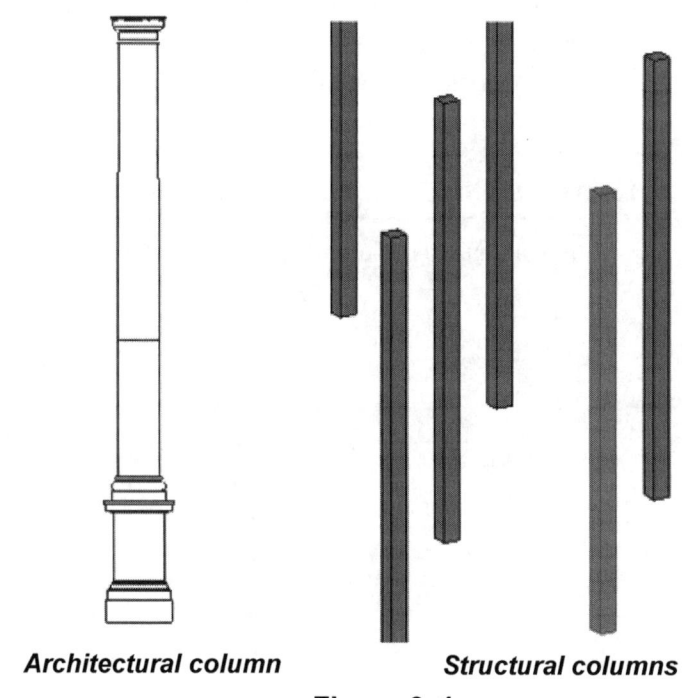

***Architectural column***     ***Structural columns***

**Figure 6–1**

### How To: Add Columns

*Structural Column is always the default.*

1. In the *Architecture* tab>Build panel, expand ▯ (Column) and click either ▯ (Column: Architectural) or ▯ (Structural Column).
2. In the Type Selector, select the column you want to use.

3. In the Options Bar, set the *Height* (or *Depth*) for the column. For the Level/Unconnected drop-down list, you can either select a level (as shown in Figure 6–2) or select **Unconnected** to specify a height.

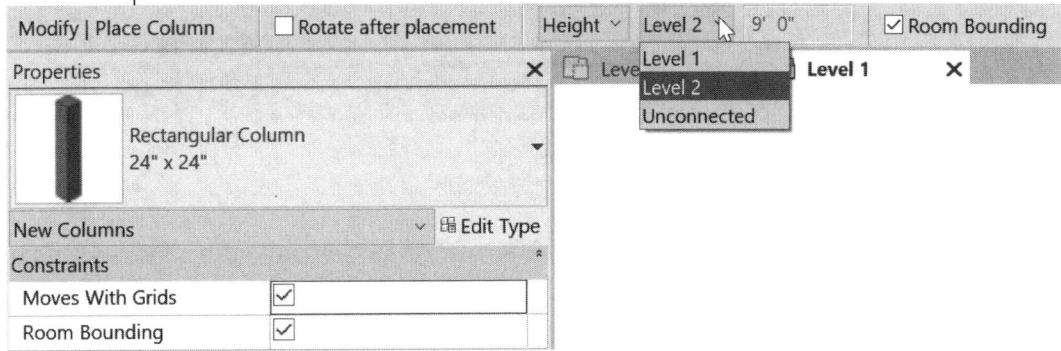

**Figure 6–2**

4. Place the column as required. It snaps to grid lines and walls.
   - Columns can be placed as a free instance unconnected to any grid lines.
   - If you select **Rotate after placement**, you are prompted for a rotation angle after you select the insertion point for the column.
5. Continue placing columns as needed.

- If you are working with structural columns, you have two additional options for placing columns in the *Modify | Place Structural Column* tab>Multiple panel:

  - To place columns at the intersection of grid lines, click (At Grids) and select the grid lines. Columns will only be placed at the intersections of the selected grid lines.
  - To place structural columns wherever you have an architectural column, click (At Columns) and select the architectural columns. The structural columns are placed at the center of the architectural columns, as shown in Figure 6–3.

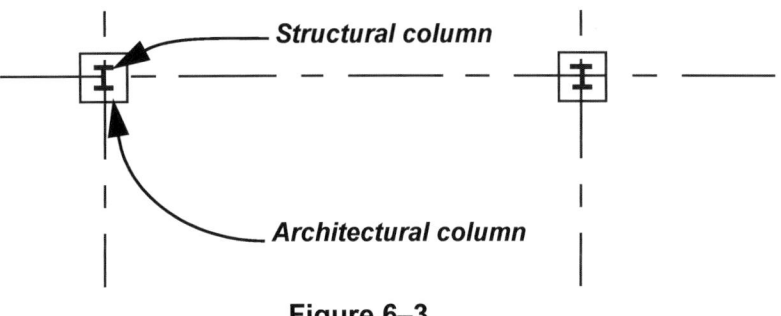

**Figure 6–3**

- An architectural column placed in a wall is automatically cleaned up if the material of the column and wall match. Structural columns remain separate even if they are the same material as the surrounding walls, as shown in Figure 6–4.

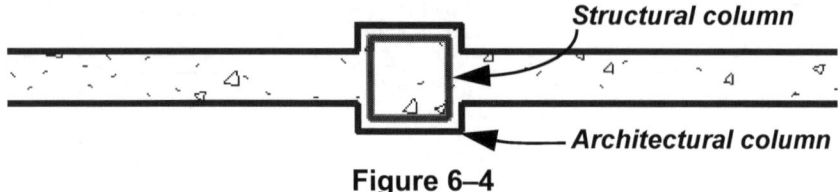

Figure 6–4

- You can select additional column types from the *Columns* (for architectural) or *Structural Columns* folders in the Revit Library, as shown in Figure 6–5.

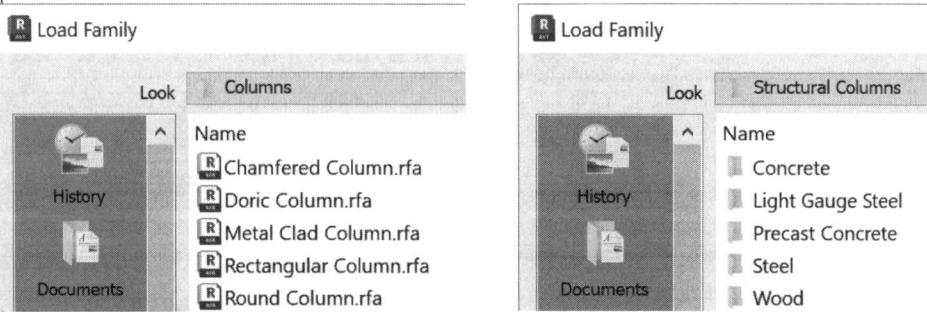

Figure 6–5

- When you open a structural column family, you are prompted to choose from a list of types, as shown in Figure 6–6. Hold <Ctrl> or <Shift> to select more than one and click **OK** to load them.

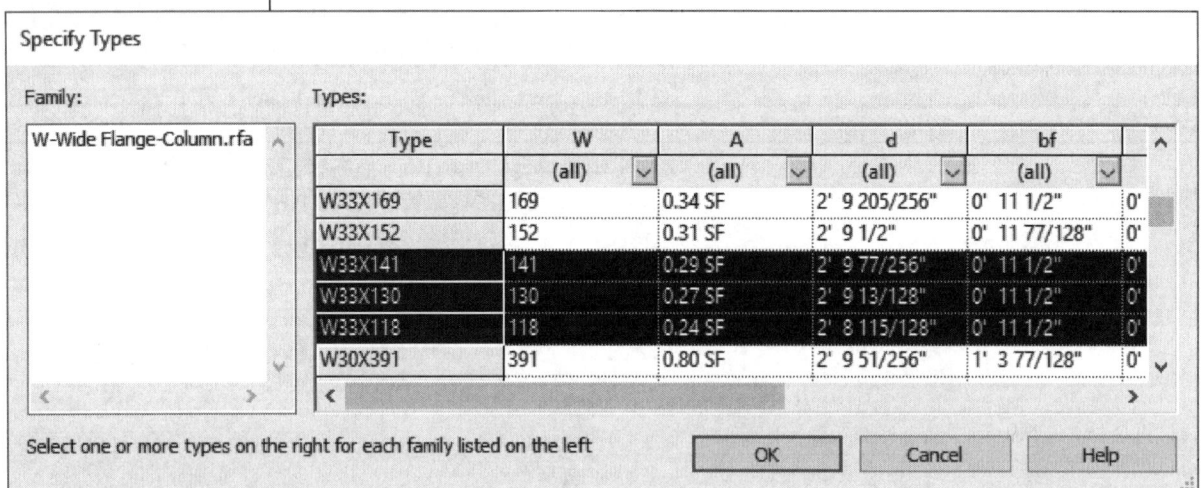

Figure 6–6

## Modifying Columns

*Structural columns have additional parameters.*

When selecting a column, you can modify the constraints within Properties and change the *Base Level* and *Top Level*, as well as the offsets from these levels and several other options, as shown in Figure 6–7. You can also attach columns to other elements so that they move with those elements.

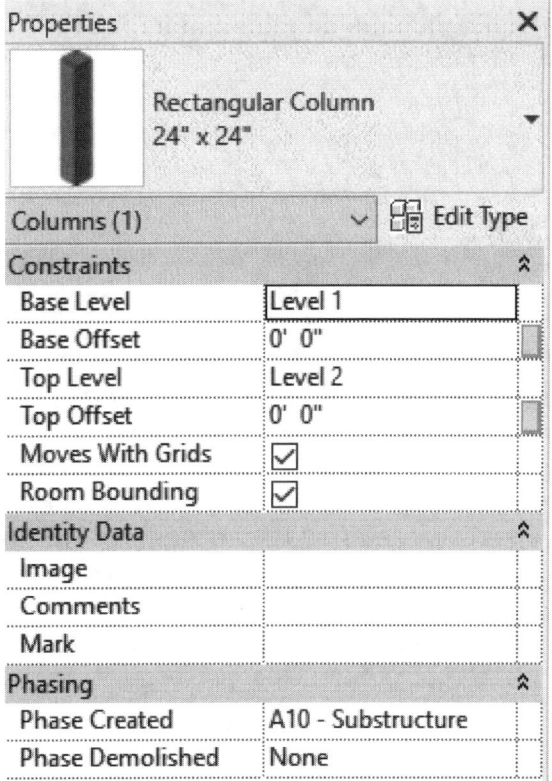

Figure 6–7

- When changing the top and base levels and offsets, you should make these changes in a logical order, as having a zero or negative height column results in an error message.

- Deleting a grid line or wall does not delete the columns placed on them.

- By default, columns placed at grid intersections will move with the grids, although you can still move the columns independently of the grid. Select the column(s) and, in the Options Bar or Properties, select or clear **Move With Grids** to change the method. This toggle is normally on by default, but it is good practice to check its status.

- In the *Modify | Column* tab>Modify Column panel, shown in Figure 6–8, you can attach or detach a column's top and base to floors, ceilings, roofs, reference planes, and structural framing.

Figure 6–8

## How To: Attach Columns to Other Elements

*Attaching columns to other objects associates or constrains certain parameters, such as the height.*

1. Select a column or group of columns.
2. In the *Modify | Structural Columns* tab>Modify Column panel, click (Attach Top/Base).
3. In the Options Bar, set *Attach Column* to **Top** or **Base** and set the *Attachment Style* (as shown in Figure 6–9), *Attachment Justification*, and *Offset From Attachment*.

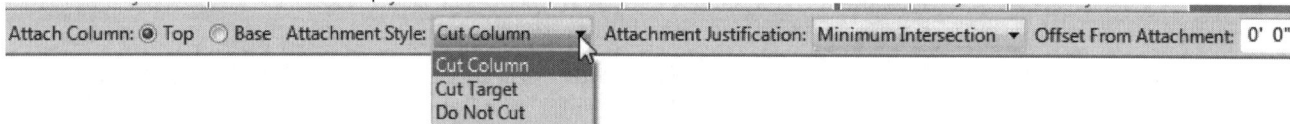

Figure 6–9

4. Select the floor, roof, footing, beam, reference plane, or level to which you want the column(s) attached.

- If you want to detach a column that has been attached, select the column and click (Detach Top/Base).

- You can use the **Attach Top/Base** command to attach structural columns to isolated foundations and footings. If the foundation height changes, the length of the column changes with it.

## 6.2 Adding Isolated Footings

Footings for columns (shown in Figure 6–10) are placed using the **Structural Foundation: Isolated** command. When you select a column, the footing automatically attaches to the bottom of the column. This is true even when the bottom of the column is on a lower level than the view you are working in.

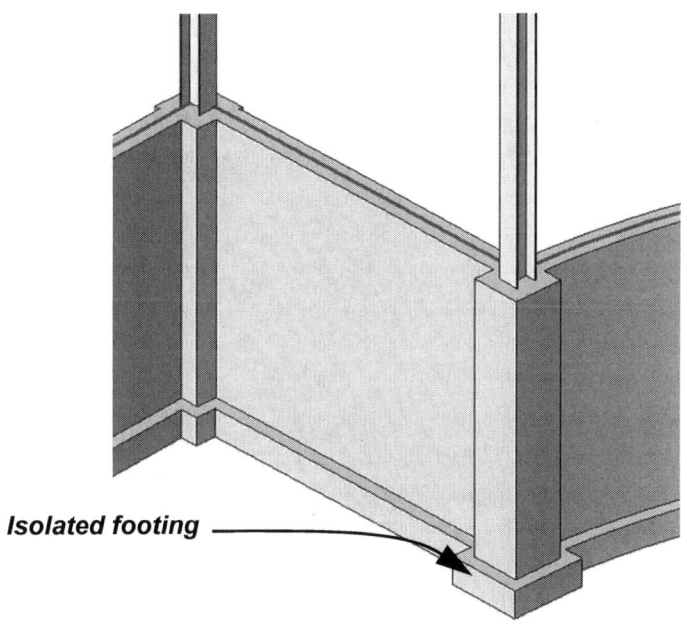

Figure 6–10

### How To: Place an Isolated Footing

1. Open a plan view, such as a **T.O. Footing** structural floor plan.
2. In the *Structure* tab>Foundation panel, click (Isolated) to start the **Structural Foundation: Isolated** command.
3. In the Type Selector, select a footing type.
4. In the view, click to place the individual footing, as shown in Figure 6–11.
   - If needed, press <Spacebar> to rotate the isolated footings after they are placed.

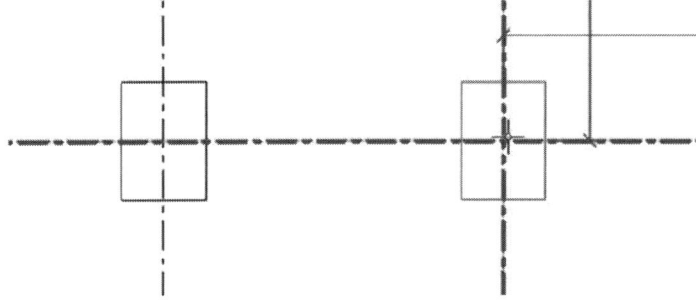

Figure 6–11

- To add more than one footing at a time, in the *Modify | Place Isolated Foundation* tab>Multiple panel, select ⊞ (At Grids) or ▯ (At Columns) and select the grids or columns.
  - If needed, press <Spacebar> to rotate the isolated footings after they are placed.
- If the material of the wall footing and the material of the isolated footing are the same, they automatically join, as shown in Figure 6–12.

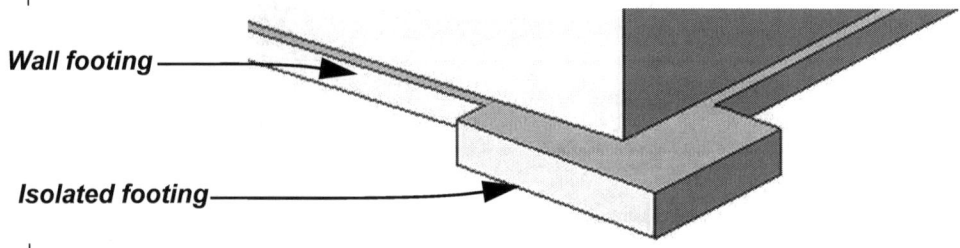

Figure 6–12

### Hint: Foundation Element Properties

Some of the element properties are automatically generated from the location and size of the element in the model and are grayed out, for example *Host*, *Elevation at Top*, and *Elevation at Bottom* as shown in Figure 6–13. These can be used in tags and schedules.

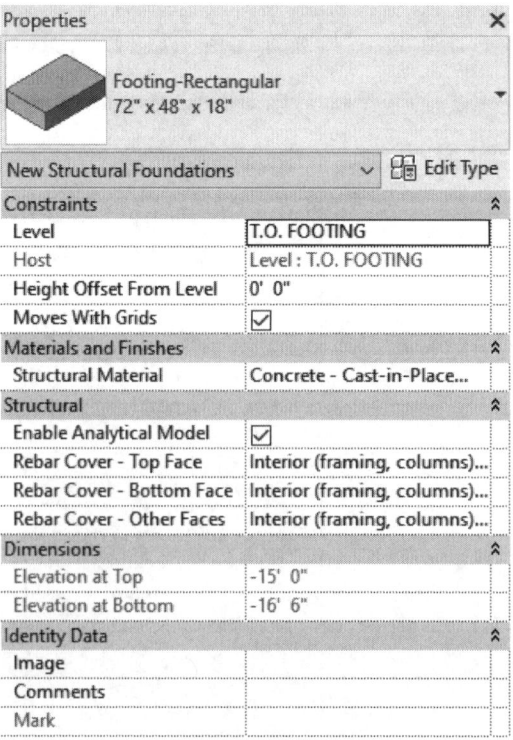

Figure 6–13

# Practice 6a

# Add Columns

### Practice Objective

- Add structural columns.

In this practice, you will add structural columns to grids and modify the height of the columns, as shown in Figure 6–14.

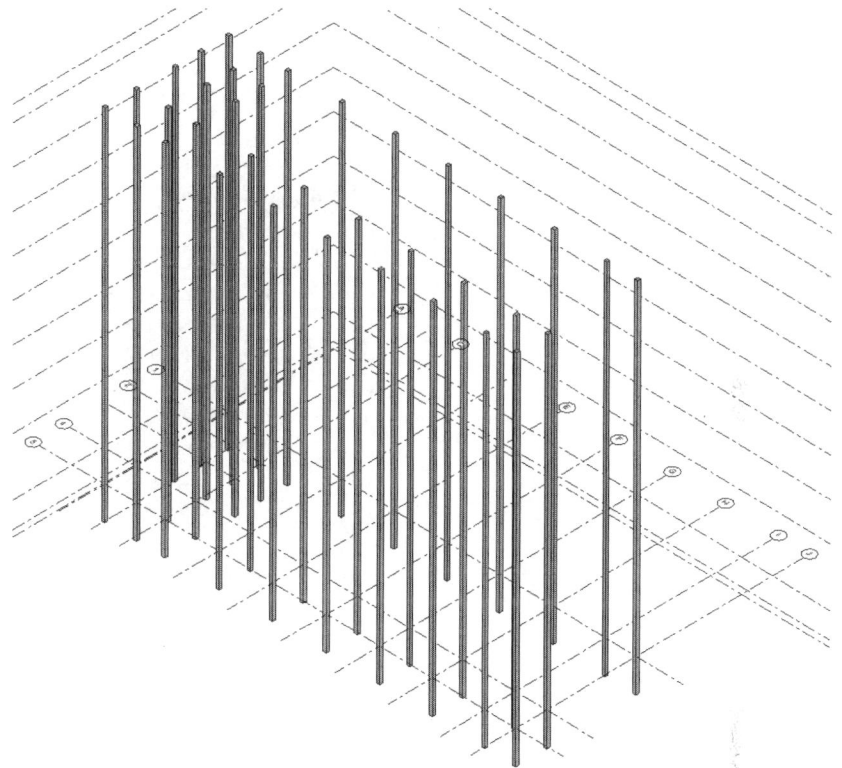

Figure 6–14

- Now that you have practiced the basics in previous exercises using a simple model, you will return to the main building model project to add the columns.

### Task 1 - Add columns.

1. Open the project **Hotel-Columns.rvt** from the practice files folder.

2. Verify you are in the **Floor Plans: Floor 1** view.

3. Open the Visibility/Graphic Overrides by typing **VV**.

4. In the Visibility/Graphic Overrides dialog box, click on the *Imported Categories* tab.

5. In the *Visibility* column, click on the node next to **Hotel-Level-1.dwg** so you can see all the levels, as shown in Figure 6–15.

6. Uncheck **A-ANNO-DIM**, **A-ANNO-TEXT**, and **A-ANNO-SYMB** (as shown in Figure 6–15) and click **OK**. Note that the DWG's annotations are no longer displaying in the view.

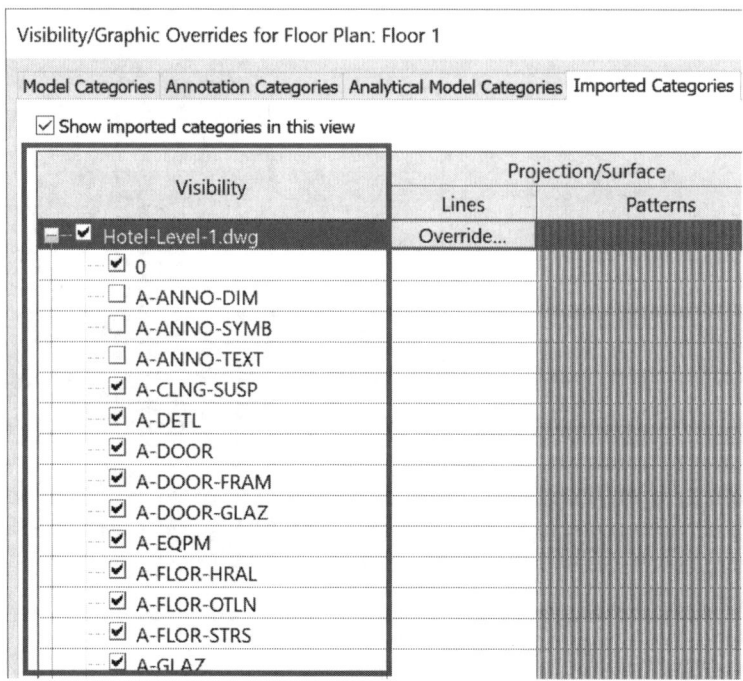

Figure 6–15

7. In the *Architecture* tab>Build panel, click (Structural Column).

8. In the Type Selector, select **Precast-Square Column: 12" x 12"**.

9. In the Options Bar, do the following:

    - Uncheck **Rotate after placement**.
    - Change *Depth* to **Height**.
    - Set the Level/Unconnected drop-down list to **Floor 2**.
    - Check the **Room Bounding** option.

10. In the *Modify | Place Structural Column* tab>Multiple panel, click (At Grids).

# Adding Columns

*Use a crossing window from right to left to select the grids. All other elements are automatically filtered out.*

11. Select all of the horizontal and vertical grid lines in the project using a crossing window (right to left).

12. In the *Modify | Place Structural Column>At Grid Intersection* tab>Multiple panel, click ✓ (Finish).

13. Click ▷ (Modify) to end the command.

14. Delete the columns at locations **A1**, **A2**, **A4**, **B1**, and **B4**. The project displays as shown in Figure 6–16.

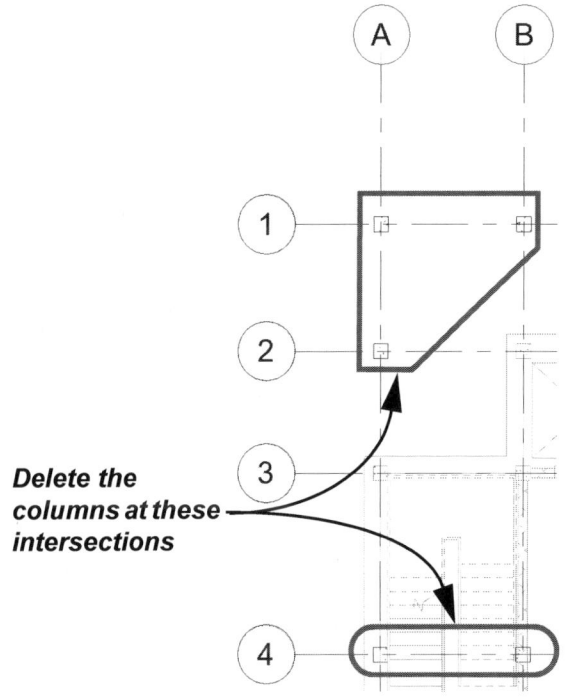

Figure 6–16

15. Save the project.

## Task 2 - Modify the columns.

1. In the Quick Access Toolbar, click 🏠 (Default 3D View).

2. Select the poolhouse and type **VH** to hide it in the view.

3. Note that the columns are only set to the height of Floor 2, as shown in Figure 6–17.

*The DWG linked file does not display in the 3D view because it was only linked into the Floor 1 plan view.*

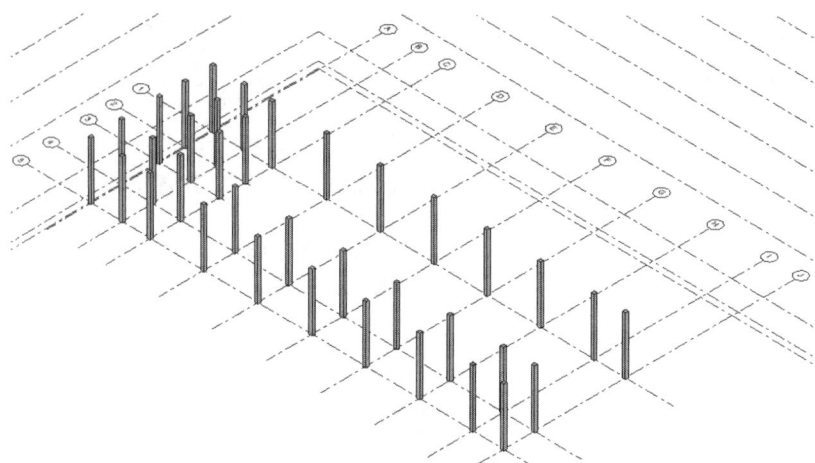

**Figure 6–17**

4. Select all of the columns. You can select one column, then right-click and select **Select All Instances>Visible in View**.

5. In Properties, in the *Constraints* section, change the following:

   - *Base Level* to **T.O. Footing**
   - *Top Level* to **Roof**

6. Click **Apply** or move the cursor into the view window. The columns now extend from the top of the footing to the roof level.

7. Save the project.

### Task 3 - Add column footings.

1. Open the **Floor Plans: T.O. Footing** view and select everything in the view.

2. In the Status Bar (or in the *Modify | Multi-select* tab>Selection panel), click (Filter).

3. In the Filter dialog box, clear **Structural Columns** and click **OK**.

4. In the Status Bar, expand (Temporary Hide/Isolate) and select **Isolate Element**.

5. Click in an empty space in the view to release the selection.

- Everything except the columns should be hidden, as shown in Figure 6–18. It is now easier to identify the locations of the footings.

Figure 6–18

6. In the *Structure* tab>Foundation panel, click (Isolated).

7. A dialog displays that there is no structural foundations family loaded, as shown in Figure 6–19. Click **Yes** to load a foundations family.

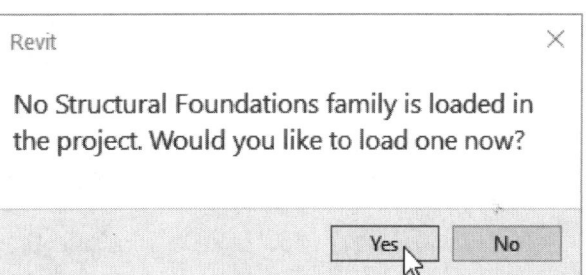

Figure 6–19

8. In the Load Family dialog box, navigate to the practice files *Families>Structural* folder, select **Footing-Rectangular.rfa**, and click **Open**.

9. In the Type Selector, verify **Footing-Rectangular: 72" x 48" x 18"** is selected. Set the *Level* to **T.O. Footing**.

*When hovering your cursor over a column, type **SM** to snap to the midpoint.*

10. Place a footing at each column's midpoint. Once you have placed at least one footing, you can use **Copy** to add the others. Ensure that you are copying from the column midpoint, as shown in Figure 6–20.

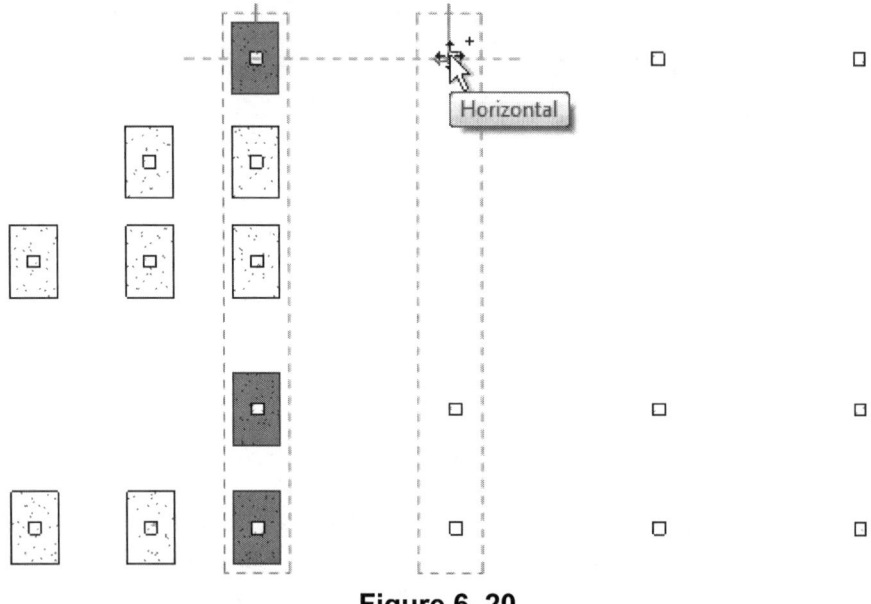

Figure 6–20

11. Click (Modify).

12. In the View Control Bar, click (Temporary Hide/Isolate) and select **Reset Temporary Hide/Isolate**.

13. Save and close the project.

# Chapter Review Questions

1. Where can columns be placed?

    a. Columns can only be placed on grids.

    b. Architectural columns can be placed anywhere, but structural columns can only be placed on grids.

    c. Both types of columns can be placed wherever you want.

    d. Grid-based column types must be placed on the grid, but free-standing column types can be placed anywhere.

2. Architectural columns can be placed At Grids automatically.

    a. True

    b. False

3. In order for architectural columns to move with grids, what needs to be selected when placing the column?

    a. In the ribbon, select **At Grids**.

    b. Set the *Top Constraint* to grids.

    c. Columns always move with grids no matter what type.

    d. In Properties, select **Moves With Grids**.

# Command Summary

| Button | Command | Location |
|---|---|---|
| | At Columns | • **Ribbon:** *Modify | Place Structural Column* tab>Multiple panel |
| | At Grids | • **Ribbon:** *Modify | Place Structural Column* tab>Multiple panel |
| | Column | • **Ribbon:** *Architecture* tab>Build panel |
| | Column> Column: Architectural | • **Ribbon:** *Architecture* tab>Build panel>expand Column |
| | Column> Structural Column | • **Ribbon:** *Architecture* tab>Build panel>expand Column |

# Chapter 7

# Modeling Walls

Walls are the primary elements that define rooms in buildings. Revit® contains a variety of wall types that are available in different widths and materials. You can change the height, length, and type as needed. After you have added walls, you can add room elements to areas defined by the walls.

## Learning Objectives in This Chapter

- Model walls using specific wall types.
- Modify walls by changing the wall type, height, and length.
- Define how walls join at intersections.
- Add wall openings that are not cased or filled with a door or window.
- Add room elements and tags that display the room name and room number.

# 7.1 Modeling Walls

Walls in Revit are more than just two lines on a plan. They are full 3D elements that store detailed information, including height, thickness, and materials. This means they are useful in 2D and 3D views, and also impact material takeoff schedules, as shown in Figure 7–1.

- Walls are system family that are predefined in the Revit template file and cannot be loaded in from an external location or saved out to a external location.

- Walls can be customized to suit your company needs, if necessary.

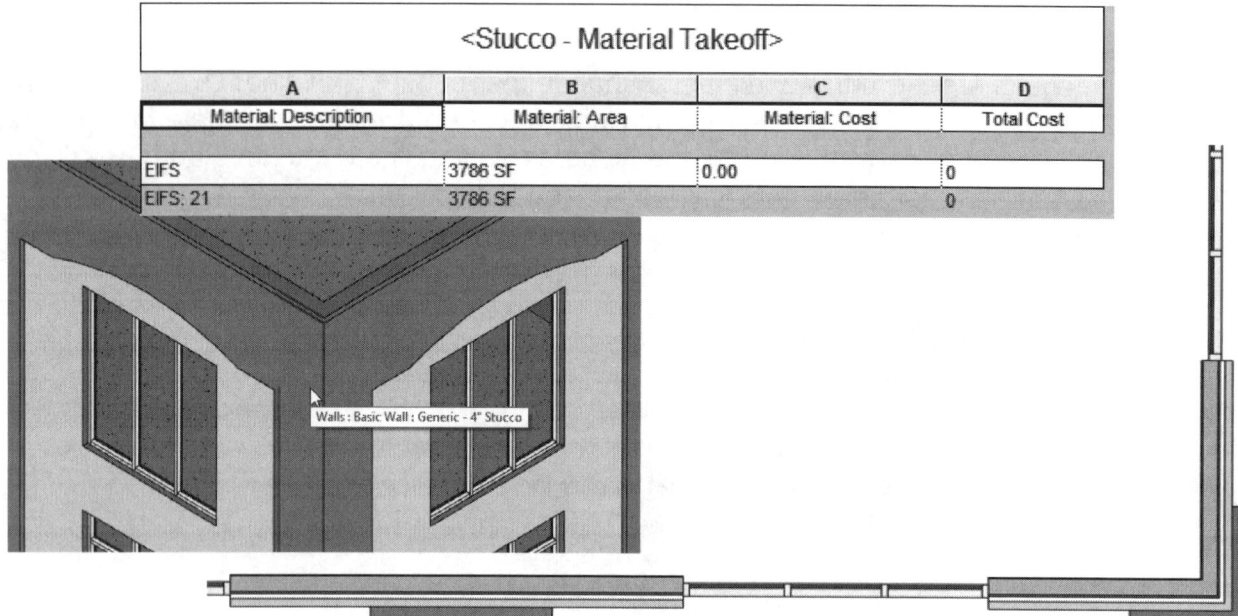

Figure 7–1

There are three broad categories of walls:

- *Basic walls:* Compound walls that contain one or more layers (e.g., blocks, air space, bricks, etc.).

- *Curtain walls:* Non-bearing walls made of glass with mullions.

- *Stacked walls:* Includes one wall type above another wall type, such as a brick wall over a concrete wall.

## Wall Cross-Section

- The *Cross-Section* for the basic wall category can be modified to be **Vertical**, **Slanted**, or **Tapered**, as shown in Figure 7–2.

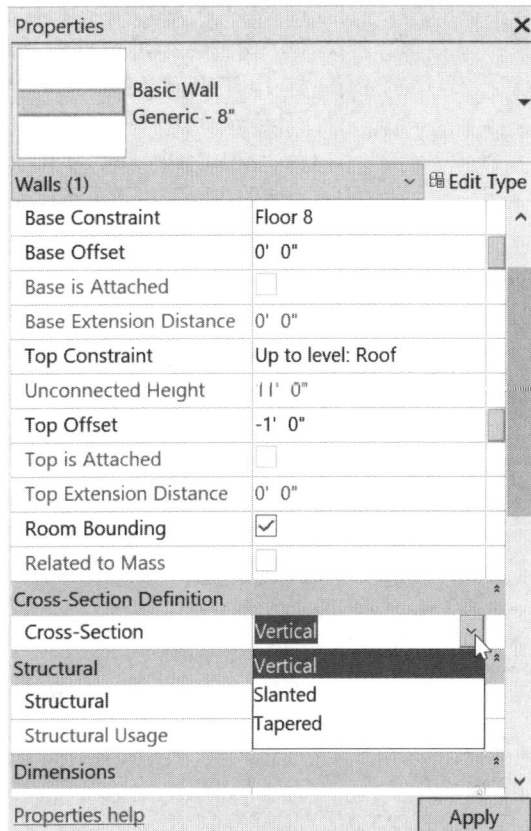

Figure 7–2

### Vertical Wall

All walls are drawn by default as a vertical wall and are at a 0° vertical when comparing it to a slanted wall type.

Note: If you change a wall's cross-section to **Tapered** and adjust the settings for the tapered wall, then you will see only the Tapered wall types displayed in the Type Selector. If you need to draw a vertical or slanted wall after the tapered wall is drawn, you will need to set the cross-section back to **Vertical** or **Slanted** so that you can see all the wall types in the Type Selector.

### Slanted Wall

You can draw a slanted wall type and specify the **Angle From Vertical** degree value in Properties. The slant degree needs to be within -90° to 90°. You can also change a vertically drawn wall to a slanted wall type. If there are any doors, door openings or window added to the wall, you will need to select those objects and, in Properties, specify their *Orientation*. The direction to which the wall has been drawn (right to left or left to right) will determine the direction the angle will go. Figure 7–3 shows that when drawing from left to right the wall slant will go in the negative direction, and drawing from right to left the slant wall goes in the positive direction.

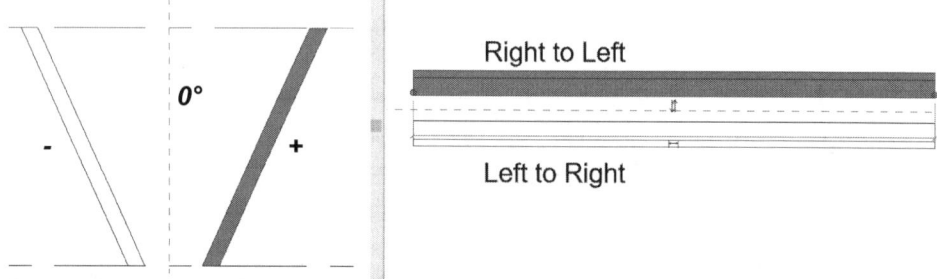

Figure 7–3

- Slanted walls can be modified in a plan, 3D, section, and perspective views.

- You can create a slanted wall with curved, circle, arc, polygon, or elliptical paths.

- If the angle is not going in the correct direction, + or -, you can add a (negative) - symbol in front of the degree value in Properties.

### Tapered Wall

You can create a tapered wall from any wall type except walls with sweeps and reveals. You must first edit the structure of the wall to set the variable thickness for the available wall layers. If not, you are prompted to set this before drawing the wall, as shown in Figure 7–4.

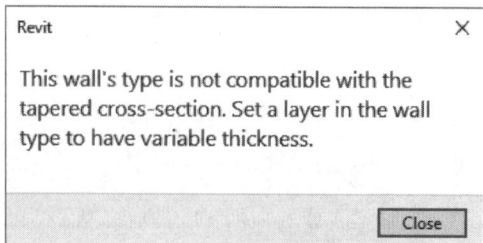

Figure 7–4

# Modeling Walls

- To set the default angles of the tapered wall, in Type Properties, you can set the *Default Exterior* and *Interior Angle*.

- If you have multiple instances of the same tapered wall type, you can select a tapered wall, and in Properties, override the angles by selecting the **Override Type Properties** option and also setting the *Exterior Angle* and *Interior Angle*, as shown in Figure 7–5.

| Cross-Section | Tapered |
|---|---|
| Override Type Properties | ☑ |
| Exterior Angle | 5.00° |
| Interior Angle | 0.00° |

**Figure 7–5**

- Curtain walls and stacked wall types cannot be tapered.

- If doors, door openings, or windows are placed in a tapered wall, you can specify the orientation of the door and wall. See "Modifying Door and Window Properties" on page 8-4.

## Wall Display per View

You can alter the way a wall is displayed in the active view by setting the *Detail Level*, as shown in Figure 7–6. You can also override the visibility settings of all walls in a view by opening the Visibility/Graphic Overrides dialog box and modifying the wall category. To change the way selected walls display in the active view, you would override the setting for graphics in view by element.

- To display the hatching in all walls in the active view where a wall is being cut through, in the View Control Bar, set the *Detail Level* to **Coarse**, **Medium** or **Fine**, as shown in Figure 7–6.

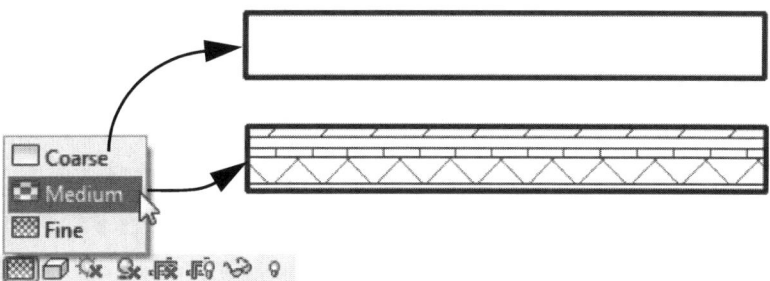

**Figure 7–6**

- To access the Visibility/Graphic Overrides dialog box to change all walls in a view, go to the *View* tab>Graphics panel and click (Visibility/Graphics), or type **VG** or **VV**. You can uncheck **Non-Core Layers** (as shown in Figure 7–7) to only view the core layer in the view. This overrides all walls in the view.

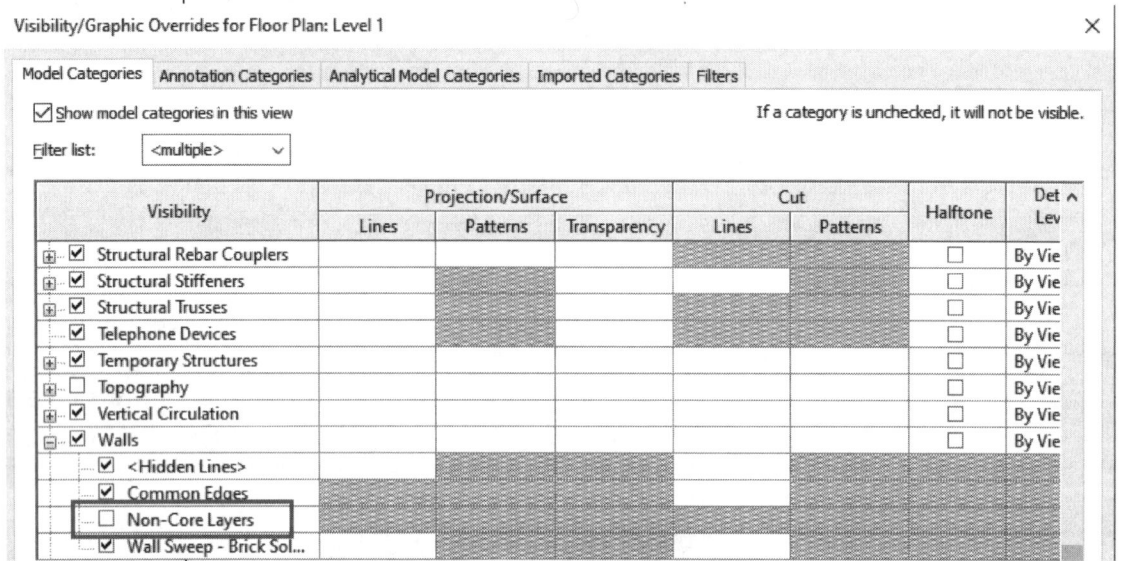

Figure 7–7

- To modify a single or a select few walls in the view, select the walls, right-click, and select **Override Graphics in View >By Element**, as shown in Figure 7–8.

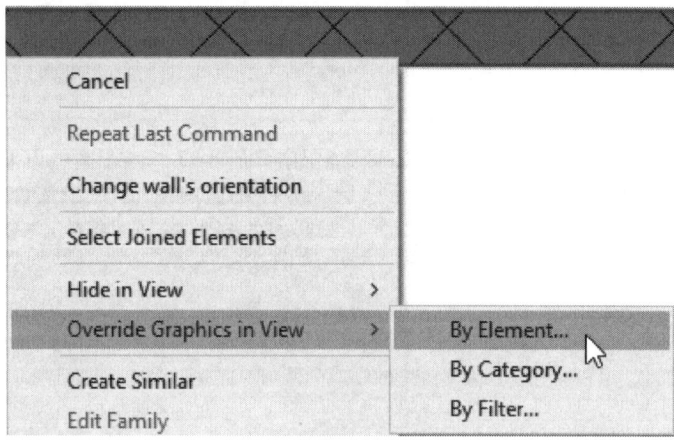

Figure 7–8

## How To: Model a Wall

1. In the *Architecture* tab>Build panel, click (Wall), or type **WA**.
2. In the Type Selector, select a wall type, as shown in Figure 7–9. You can use the search box to quickly find specific types of walls.

Modeling Walls

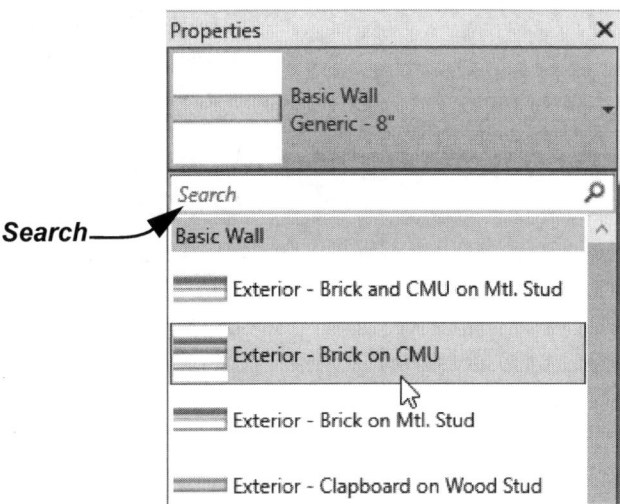

Figure 7–9

3. In Properties, set the *Cross-Section* to **Vertical**, **Slanted**, or **Tapered**, depending on the wall you need to create, as shown in Figure 7–10. Specify the Properties and Type Properties as needed. If this is not set at the beginning of drawing a wall, the last cross-section used will be the default.

- If you set the *Cross-Section* to **Slanted**, you are able to set the *Angle From Vertical* degree, as shown in Figure 7–10.

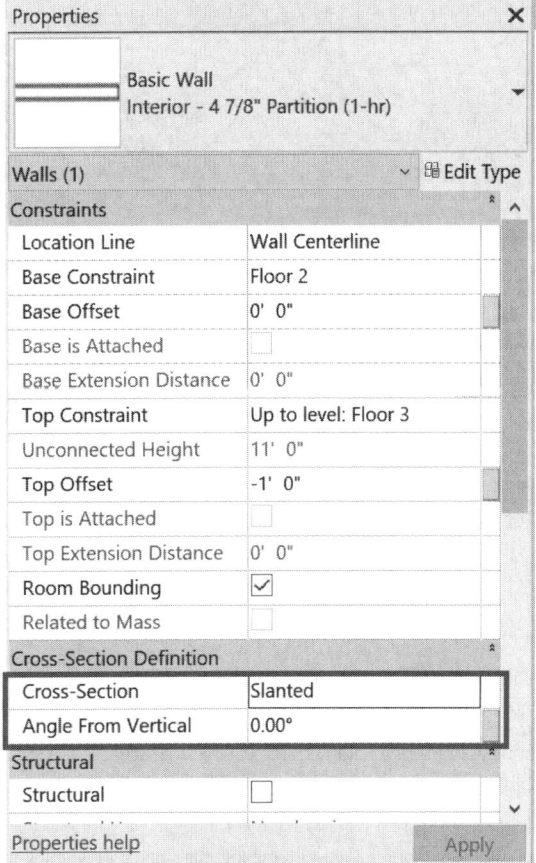

Figure 7–10

- If you set the Cross-Section to **Tapered**, you will get a warning about the wall type. You must first edit the structure of the wall before setting the Cross-Section to **Tapered**.

    - With the wall type selected, click **Edit Type** in Properties.
    - Click **Edit...** next to Structure.
    - In the Edit Assembly dialog box, select the option in the Variable column (as shown in Figure 7–11) for the layer that you want tapered.

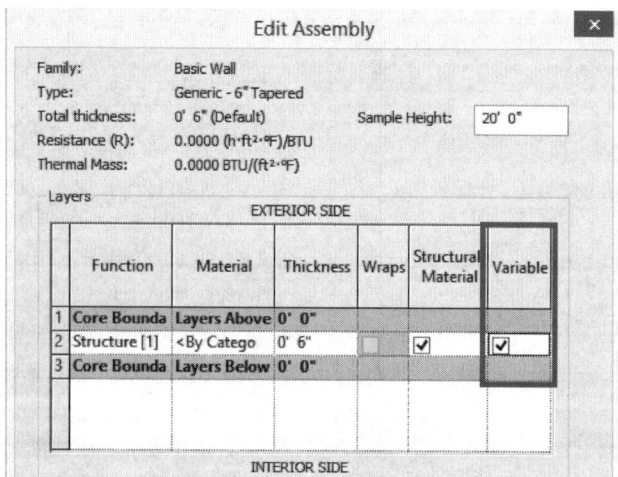

Figure 7–11

- Click **OK**.
- In the Type Properties dialog box, you will now have the ability to set the Cross Section Properties, as shown in Figure 7–12.

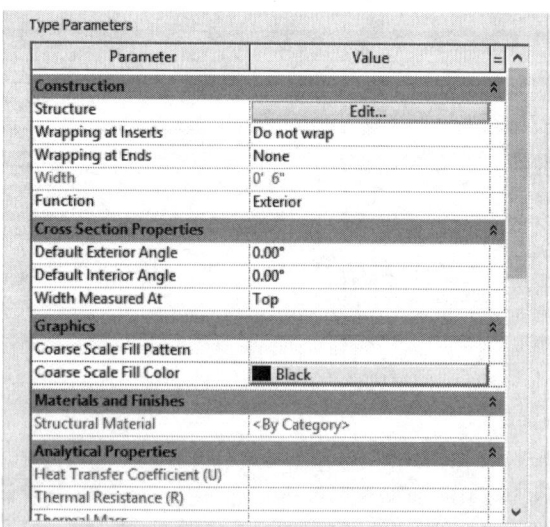

Figure 7–12

# Modeling Walls

4. In the Options Bar, shown in Figure 7–13, specify the following information about the wall before you start modeling:

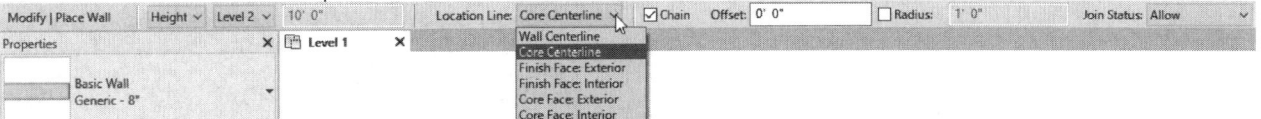

Figure 7–13

- *Height:* Set the height of a wall to either **Unconnected** (with a specified height) or to a level.
- *Location Line:* Set the justification of the wall using the options shown in Figure 7–13, above.
- *Chain:* Enables you to model multiple connected walls.
- *Offset:* Enables you to enter the distance at which a new wall is created from an existing element.
- *Radius:* Adds a curve of a specified radius to connected walls as you model.
- *Join Status:* **Allow** or **Disallow** automatic wall joins.

5. In the *Modify | Place Wall* tab>Draw panel (shown in Figure 7–14), select one of the options to create the wall.

Figure 7–14

- Use alignment lines, temporary dimensions, and snaps to place the walls.
- As you are sketching you can press <Spacebar> to flip the orientation of compound walls.
- When using the *Chain* option, press <Esc> once to finish the string of walls and remain in the **Wall** command or <Esc> twice to get out of the wall command completely. Hint: <Esc> works similarly on other commands.

## 7.2 Modifying Walls

There are several methods of modifying walls. You can change the type of wall using the Type Selector, modify the Properties, use controls and shape handles to modify the length and wall orientation, and use temporary and permanent dimensions to change the location or length of a wall in 2D and 3D views, as shown in Figure 7–15. Additional tools enable you to modify wall joins, edit the profile of a wall, and add wall openings.

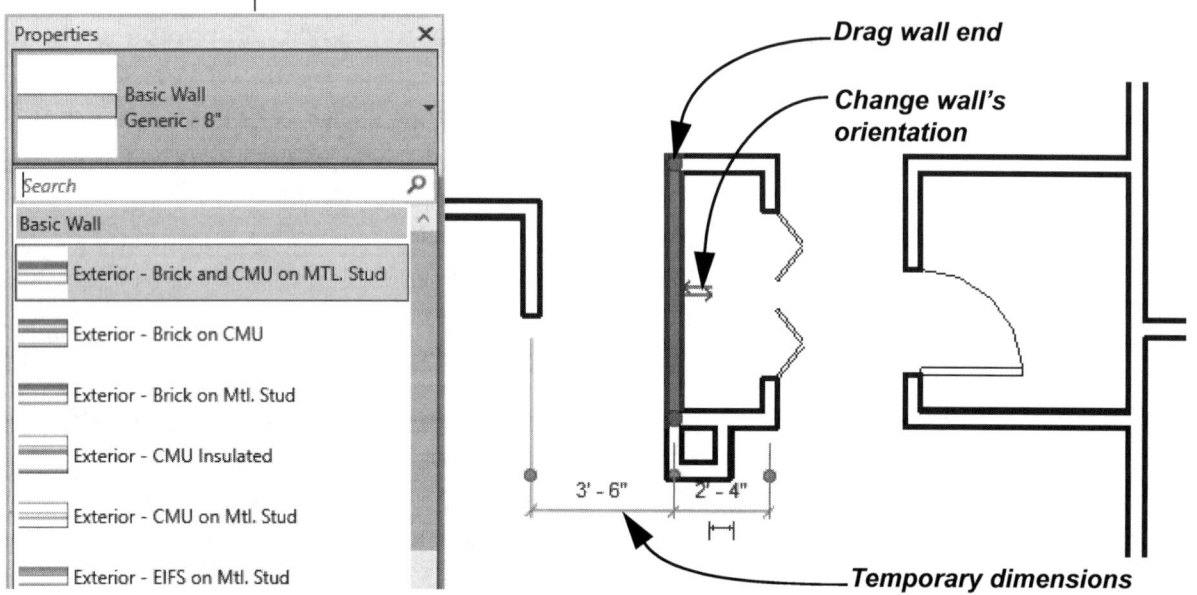

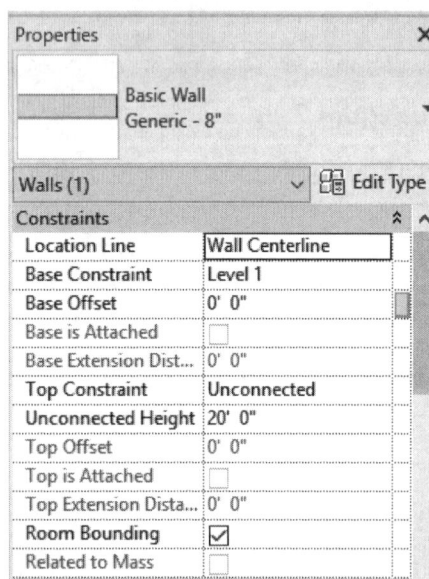

Figure 7–15

## Modifying Slanted and Tapered Wall

Modifying a slanted or tapered wall is similar to modifying a vertical wall type with the exception of modifying the angle.

- When modifying a slanted wall type, you have the ability to modify the Drag Wall Slant grip or modify the temporary dimension in a 3D, section, elevation, or isometric view, as shown in Figure 7–16.

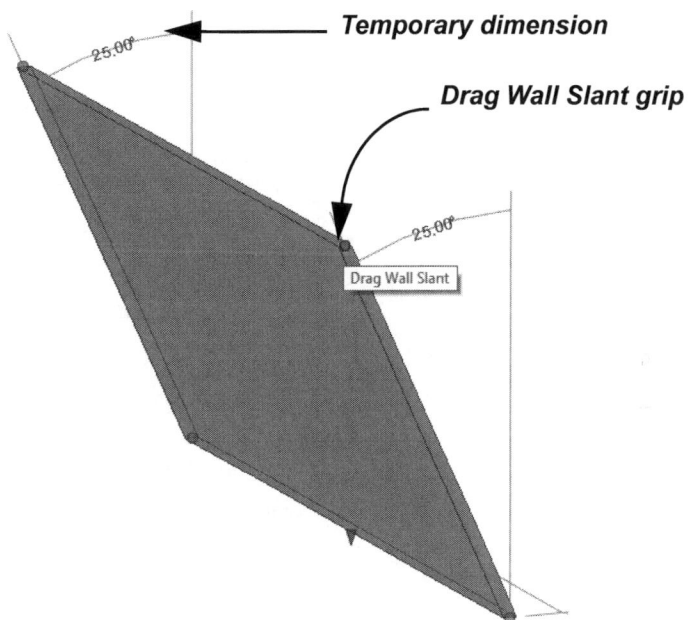

**Figure 7–16**

- When modifying a tapered wall, you have the ability to modify the Drag Wall Exterior Face Slant and Drag Wall Interior Face Slant grips or modify the temporary dimension in a 3D, section, elevation, or isometric view, as shown in Figure 7–17.

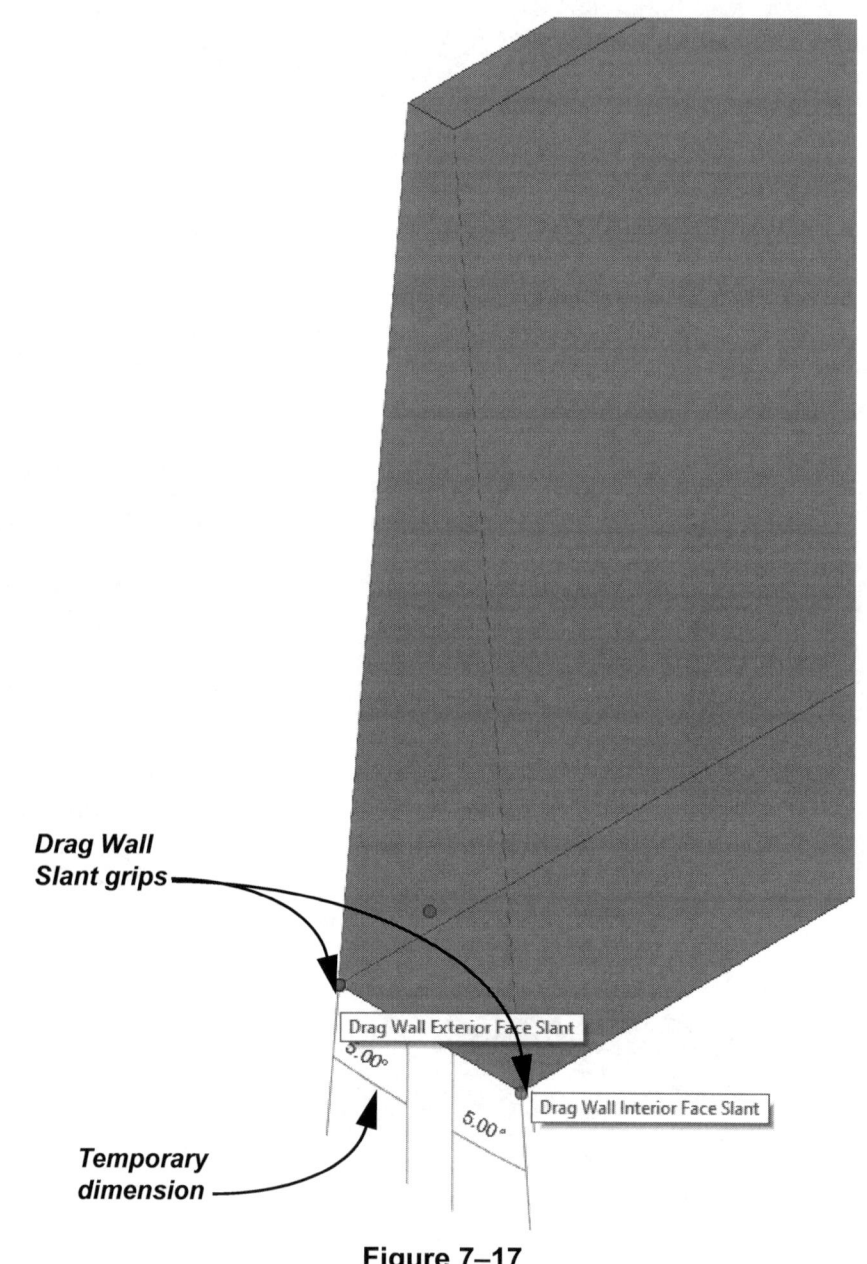

Figure 7–17

# Modeling Walls

- You can set the wall's structural properties as **Non-bearing**, **Bearing**, **Shear**, or **Structural Combined**, as shown in Figure 7–18.

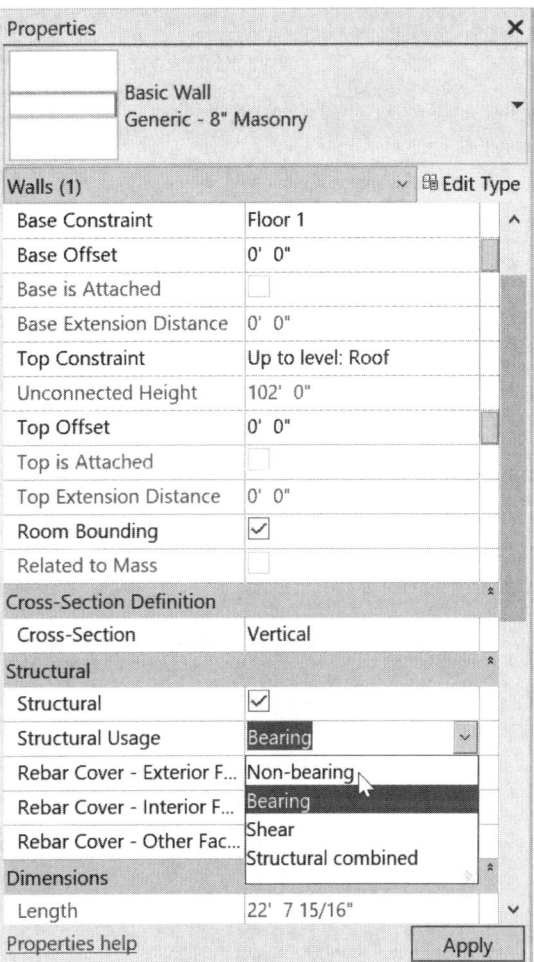

Figure 7–18

## Wall Joins

The software automatically joins walls with common materials when they come together at an intersection, as shown on the left in Figure 7–19. However, there are times when you do not want the walls to clean up, such as when one fire-rated wall butts into another, or when a wall touches a column surround, as shown on the right in Figure 7–19.

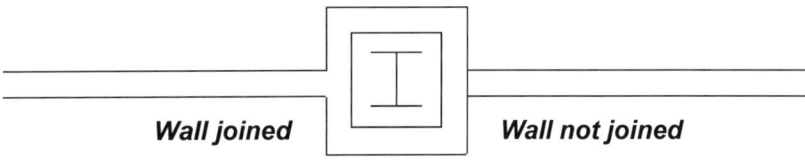

Figure 7–19

- While you are creating walls, change the *Join Status* to **Disallow** in the Options Bar.

- If a wall is already placed, select the wall and right-click on the Drag Wall End control at the end of the wall and select **Disallow Join**, as shown on the left in Figure 7–20. Once the end is not joined, you can drag it to the appropriate location, as shown on the right in Figure 7–20.

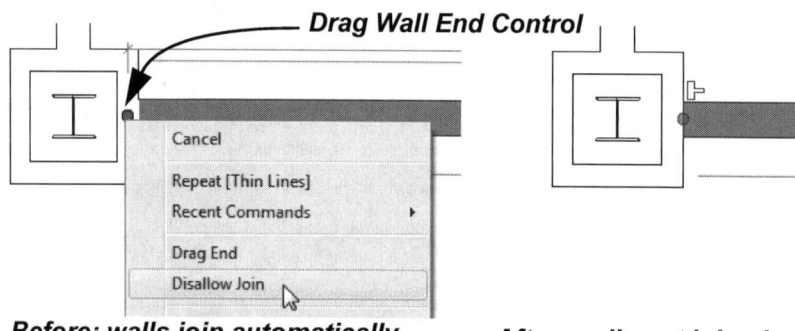

*Before: walls join automatically*     *After: walls not joined*

**Figure 7–20**

- To rejoin the walls, click (Allow Join) or right-click on the end control and select **Allow Join**. Manually drag the wall back to where you want it to touch the target wall.

Modeling Walls

> **Hint: Using Thin Lines**
>
> The software automatically applies line weights to views, as shown for a section on the left in Figure 7–21. If a line weight seems heavy or obscures your work on the elements, toggle off the line weights. In the Quick Access Toolbar or in the *View* tab>Graphics panel, click  (Thin Lines) or type **TL**. The lines display with the same weight, as shown on the right in Figure 7–21.
>
>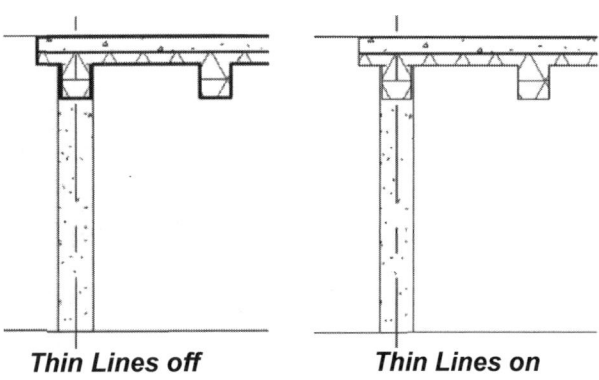
>
> *Thin Lines off*      *Thin Lines on*
>
> **Figure 7–21**
>
> - The **Thin Line** setting is remembered until you change it, even if you shut down and restart the software.

## Editing Wall Profiles

Walls often follow the contours of a site or an angle, such as following a line of stairs, as shown in Figure 7–22. If needed, you can edit the profile of a wall.

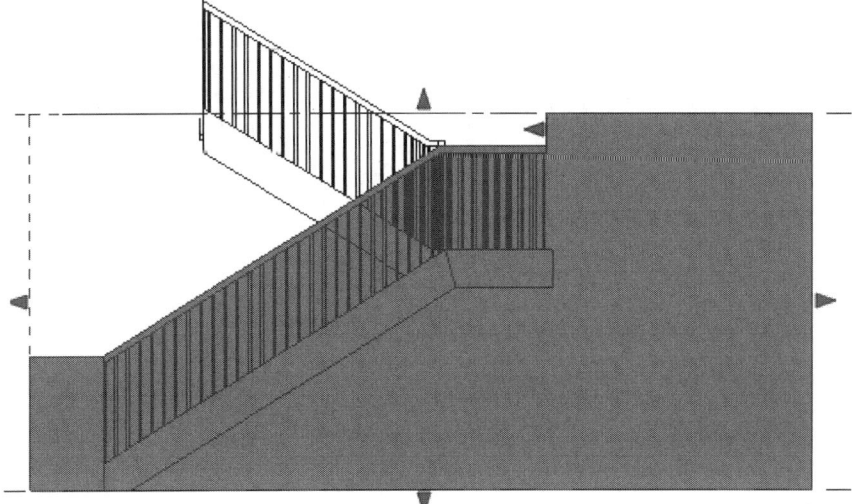

**Figure 7–22**

### How To: Edit the Profile of a Wall

1. Open an elevation or section view in which you can see the face of the wall that you want to edit.
2. Select the wall (by highlighting the wall boundary). You can also double-click on a wall to edit the profile.
   - You cannot edit the profile of a tapered wall.
3. In the *Modify | Walls* tab>Model panel, click (Edit Profile). The wall is outlined in magenta indicating the profile of the wall.
4. In the *Modify | Walls>Edit Profile* tab>Draw panel, use the tools to modify the profile sketch of the wall, as shown on the top in Figure 7–23.
   - The sketch must form a continuous loop. Verify that the lines are clean without any gaps or overlaps. Use any of the tools in the Modify panel to clean up the sketch.
5. Once the profile is complete, click (Finish Edit Mode). The wall now follows the new profile, as shown on the bottom in Figure 7–23.

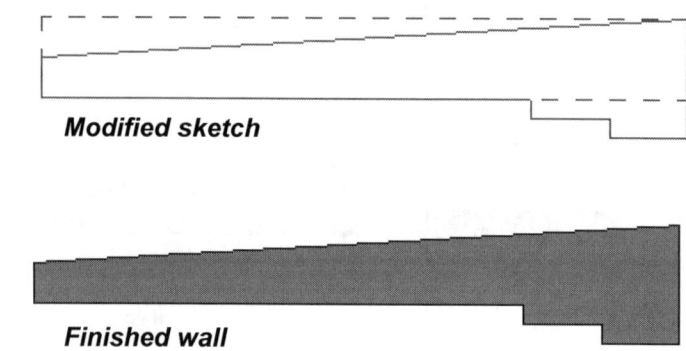

**Modified sketch**

**Finished wall**

**Figure 7–23**

- For more information about editing walls and wall joins, see *A.3 Editing Wall Joins* and *A.4 Wall Sweeps and Reveals*.

# Wall Openings

You can add openings in walls that are not windows or doors by using the **Wall Opening** tool. This creates rectangular openings for both straight and curved walls, as shown in Figure 7–24.

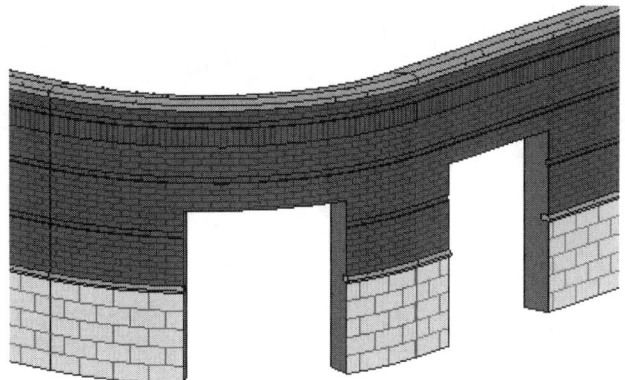

**Figure 7–24**

### How To: Add Wall Openings

1. Open a plan, elevation, section, or 3D view.
2. In the *Architecture* tab>Openings panel, click (Wall Opening).
3. Select the wall.
4. Pick two points on the diagonal to determine the opening size, if in elevation, section, or 3D view. If you are in plan, you need to pick the start and stop points for the wall opening.

- You can use temporary dimensions to size the opening while in the command and both temporary dimensions and shape handles to modify the opening when it is selected, as shown in Figure 7–25.

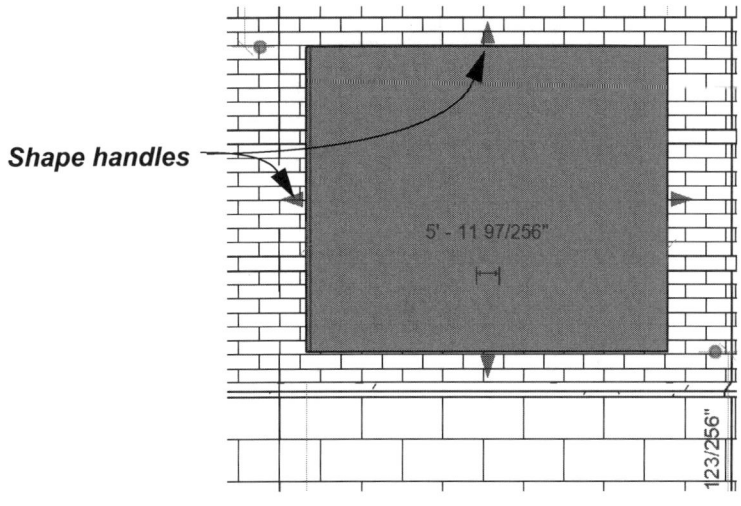

**Figure 7–25**

**Hint: Matching Properties**

You can select an existing wall and use it to assign the wall type and instance properties to other walls by using the **Match Type** command. This command also works with all elements that have types.

1. In the *Modify* tab>Clipboard panel, click  (Match Type) or type **MA**. The cursor changes to an arrow with a clean paintbrush.
2. Select the source element that you want all of the others to match. The paintbrush changes to look as if it has been dipped in black paint as shown in Figure 7–26.

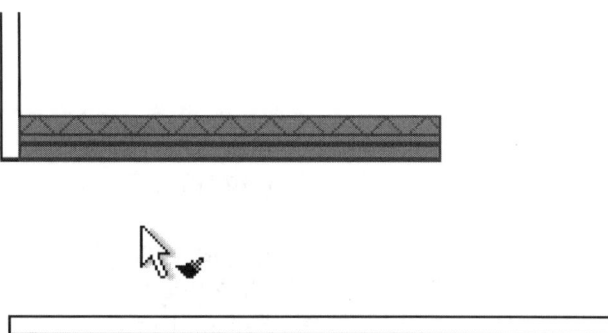

Figure 7–26

3. To select more than one element, in the *Modify | Match Type* tab>Multiple panel, click  (Select Multiple). You can then use windows, crossings, <Ctrl>, and <Shift> to create a selection set of elements to change.

4. Click  (Finish) to apply the type to the selection.

- Click in an empty space in the view to empty the brush so that you can repeat the command with a different element.

- Elements to be matched must be of the same type (e.g., all walls, all doors, etc.).

5. Click  (Modify) to end the command.

# 7.3 Adding Wall Footings

Wall footings for bearing and retaining are hosted by the walls. Once a footing is in place, you can add reinforcement, as shown in Figure 7–27. With the advantages of having a true foundation in place, you can accurately tag and schedule the footings.

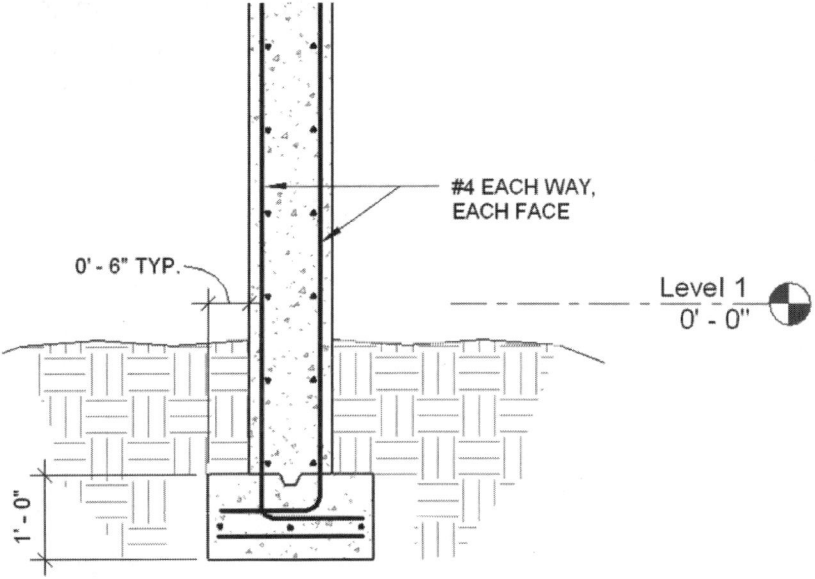

**Figure 7–27**

- You can apply two types of continuous footing systems, as shown in Figure 7–28. You must have walls in your model to add a footing system.
    - **Retaining footings:** A footing with one side offset to accommodate additional lateral loads and reinforcement.
    - **Bearing footings:** A footing with an equal distance on either side of the bearing wall.

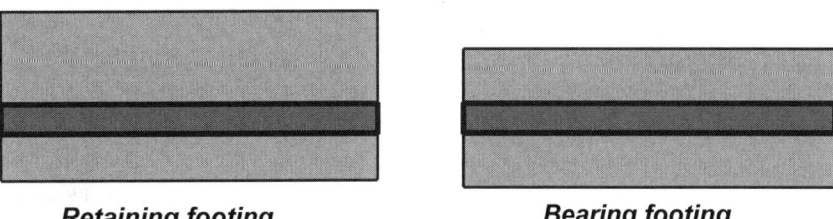

*Retaining footing*        *Bearing footing*

**Figure 7–28**

## How To: Place a Bearing or Retaining Footing

1. Create or use existing walls in a 3D, section, or elevation view.
   - A wall must be in place to add a bearing or retaining footing.
2. Open a foundation plan and set it up so that the walls are displayed and you can select them.
3. In the *Structure* tab>Foundation panel, click (Wall) to start the **Structural Foundations: Wall** command, or type **FT**.
4. In the Type Selector, select a type, as shown in Figure 7–29.

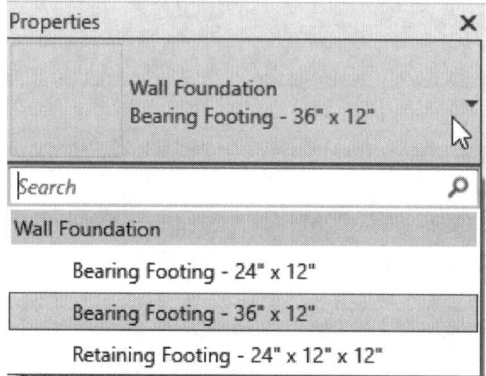

**Figure 7–29**

5. Select a wall. The footing is placed beneath the wall, as shown in Figure 7–30.

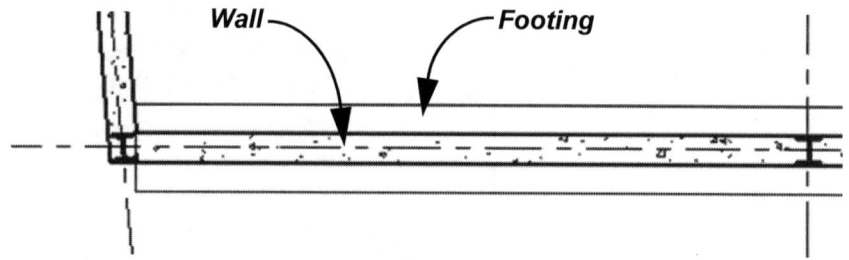

**Figure 7–30**

- To select multiple walls, hover over one wall and then press <Tab> to select all connected walls. Alternatively, in the *Modify | Place Wall Foundation* tab>Multiple panel, click (Select Multiple). Select the walls using any selection method and click (Finish) to place the footings.

Modeling Walls

- You can flip retaining footings using the Flip control, as shown in Figure 7–31.

**Figure 7–31**

## Wall Profiles and Footings

Footings are appended to the bottom of a wall, which means that any change to the base of the host wall influences the footing. This occurs for lateral movement and horizontal movement. For the example shown in Figure 7–32, when the wall profile changes based on a sloped site (as shown on the left), the footing breaks and follows the modified profile (as shown on the right). This is accomplished by editing the profile of the foundation wall.

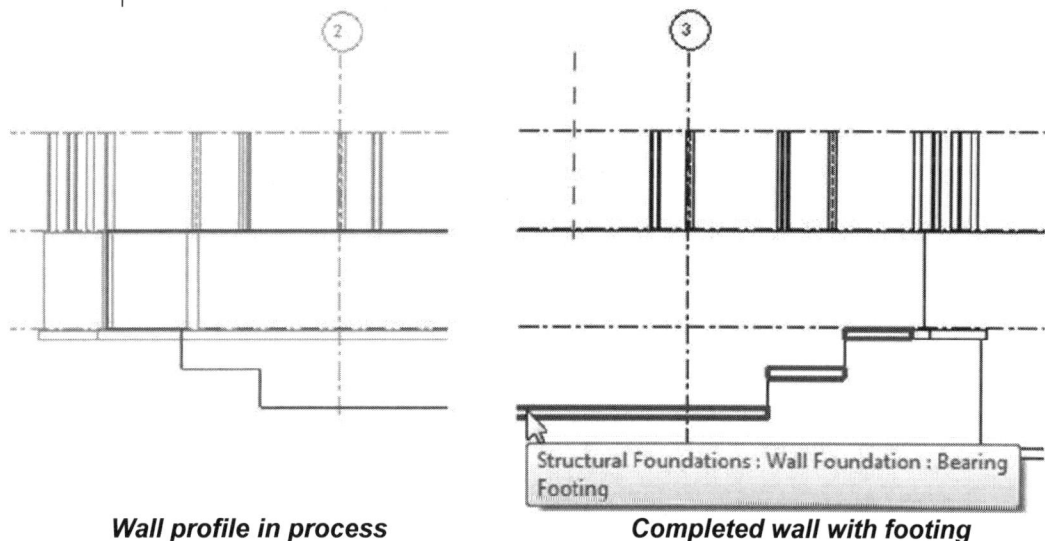

*Wall profile in process*  *Completed wall with footing*

**Figure 7–32**

### How To: Edit the Profile of a Wall

1. Open an elevation or section view in which you can see the face of the wall that you want to edit.
2. Select the wall (by highlighting the wall boundary).
   - Note: You cannot edit a tapered wall's profile.
3. In the *Modify | Walls* tab>Mode panel, click (Edit Profile). The wall is outlined in magenta, indicating the profile of the wall.

4. In the *Modify | Walls>Edit Profile* tab>Draw panel, use the tools to modify the profile sketch of the wall, as shown on the top in Figure 7–33.
5. Once the profile is complete, click ✓ (Finish Edit Mode). The footing now follows the new profile, as shown on the bottom in Figure 7–33.

*The sketch must form a continuous loop. Verify that the lines are clean without any gaps or overlaps. Use any of the tools in the Modify panel to clean up the sketch.*

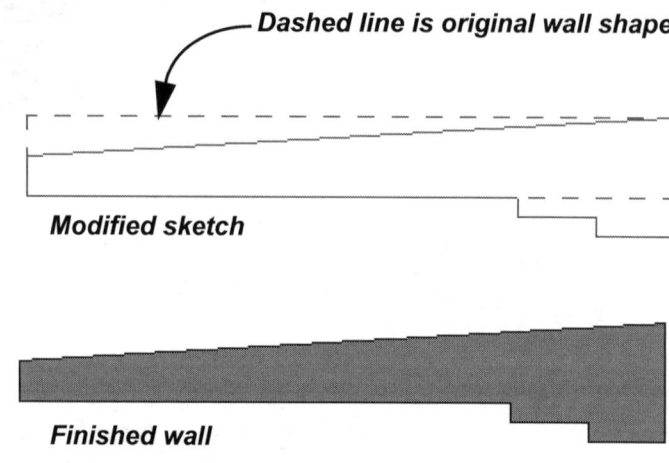

Figure 7–33

- After you adjust the sketch, you can add isolated footings to create the appropriate shape.

## Hint: Materials

When you are creating some types, such a wall footings, one option is to set the *Structural Material*. In Type Properties, in the *Materials and Finishes* section, click in the *Value* column and then click ⬚ (Browse), as shown in Figure 7–34.

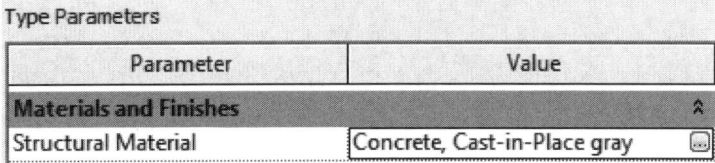

Figure 7–34

In the Material Browser (shown in Figure 7–35), specify the material you want to use and click **OK**.

Figure 7–35

## Practice 7a

# Model the Exterior Shell

**Practice Objectives**

- Add walls by tracing over lines in an imported DWG file.
- Add curtain walls.

In this practice, you will add exterior walls, including a curtain wall, to create the exterior shell of the project. You will use an imported file to help establish the location of the walls. The completed model is shown in Figure 7–36.

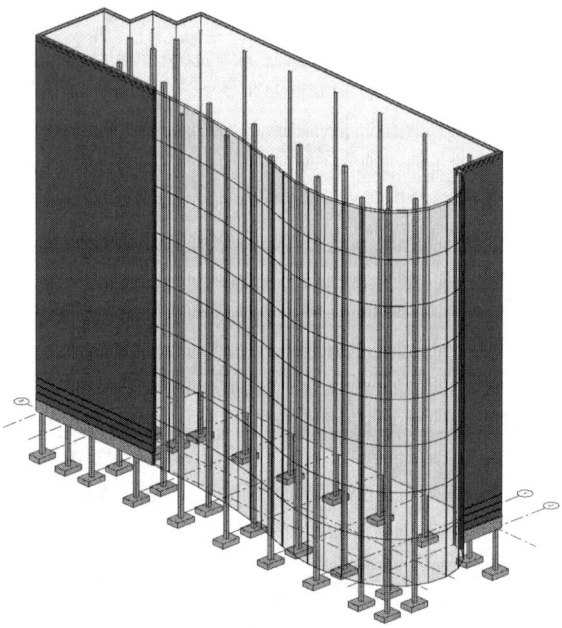

Figure 7–36

### Task 1 - Add walls by picking lines.

1. Open the project **Hotel-WallsExt.rvt** from the practice files folder.

2. Verify that you are in the **Floor Plans: Floor 1** view.

3. In the View Control Bar, set the *Detail Level* to (Medium). Doing so will display wall layers in this current view only.

4. In the *Architecture* tab>Build panel, click (Wall).

5. In the Draw panel, click (Pick Lines).

# Modeling Walls

*Offset on the Options Bar offsets the wall from where you are drawing it and not from a level perspective, like Base and Top Offset do.*

6. In the Type Selector, scroll through the list and select **Basic Wall: Exterior - Brick and CMU on MTL. Stud**.

7. In the Options Bar, set or verify the following options:
   - *Height:* **Parapet**
   - *Location Line:* **Finish Face: Exterior**
   - *Join Status:* **Allow**

8. In Properties, set or verify the following options:
   - *Base Offset:* **0'-0"**
   - *Top Offset:* **0'-0"**
   - *Cross-Section:* **Vertical**

9. Pan and zoom over to the west stairwell. Select one of the exterior walls in the imported DWG file, as shown in Figure 7–37. Ensure that the dashed line displays inside the wall. This wall is a compound wall and you want the brick to display on the outside.

10. At the door openings for the stairwells on either end of the building, do not add walls on one side of the door (labeled in Figure 7–37) because you will modify the walls later.

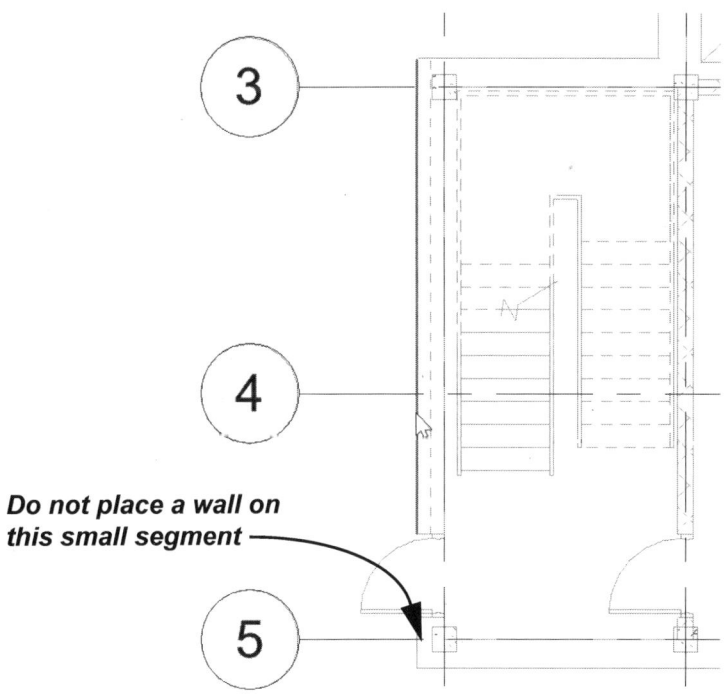

Figure 7–37

11. Continue selecting lines around the exterior of the building. Do not select the curved curtain wall lines.

    - Use ⇄ (Flip) to change the wall's orientation if the brick side of the wall is not on the outside.

12. Click (Modify).

13. Select the wall and use the **Drag Wall End** control, as shown in Figure 7–38, to lengthen the wall across the opening. The walls should clean up automatically.

*You can also use (Trim/Extend to Corner) to clean up the walls.*

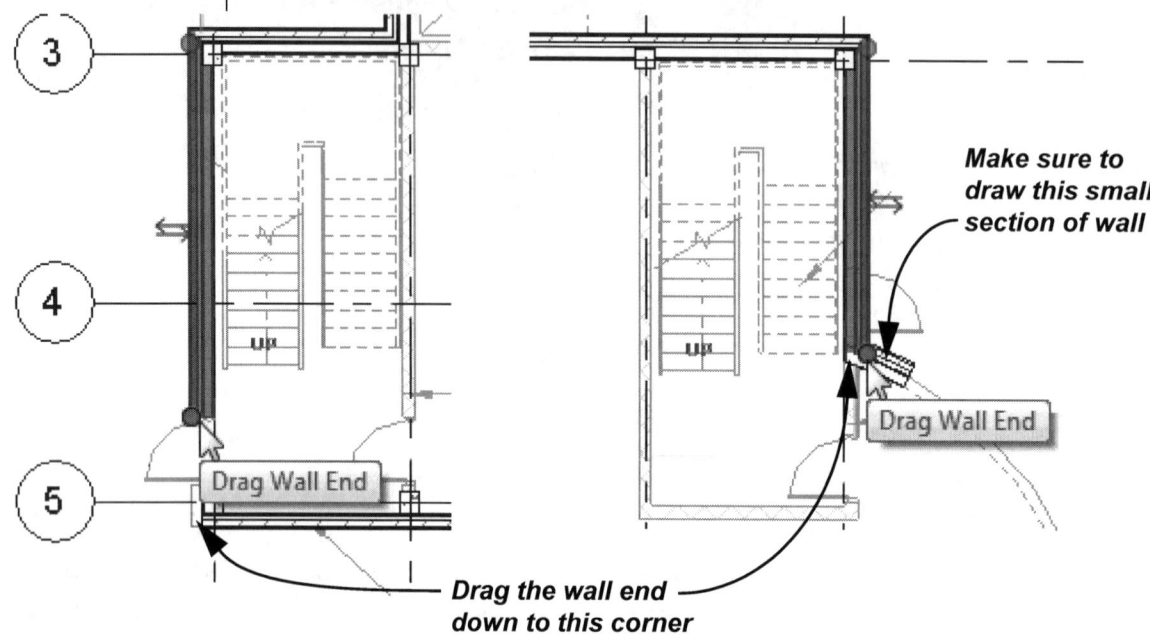

**Figure 7–38**

14. Save the project.

### Task 2 - Add basic curtain walls.

1. In the *Architecture* tab>Build panel, click (Wall).

2. In the Draw panel, click (Pick Lines).

3. Verify that **Height** is selected in the Options Bar.

4. In the Type Selector, scroll down to the Curtain Wall section and select **Curtain Wall: Exterior Glazing**, then verify or set the following properties:

    - *Base Constraint:* **Floor 1**
    - *Base Offset:* **0'-0"**
    - *Top Constraint:* **Up to level: Parapet**
    - *Top Offset:* **0'-0"**
    - *Cross-Section:* **Vertical**

# Modeling Walls

5. Select the curved lines at the southeast end of the building (you will create three curtain walls along this curved wall), as shown in Figure 7–39.

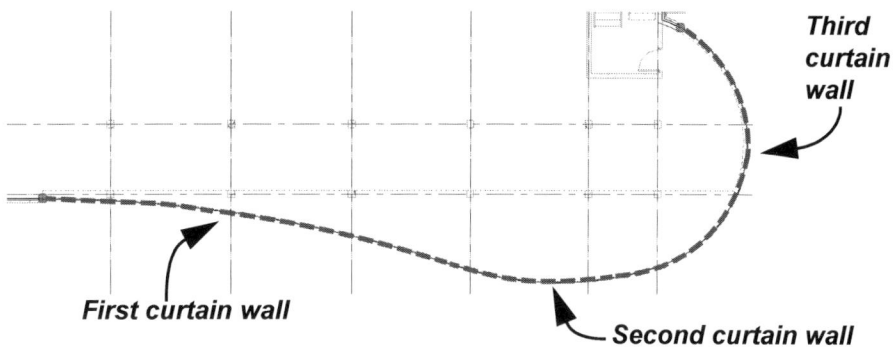

Figure 7–39

6. Click (Modify).

7. In the Quick Access Toolbar, click (3D View). The model displays as shown in Figure 7–40.

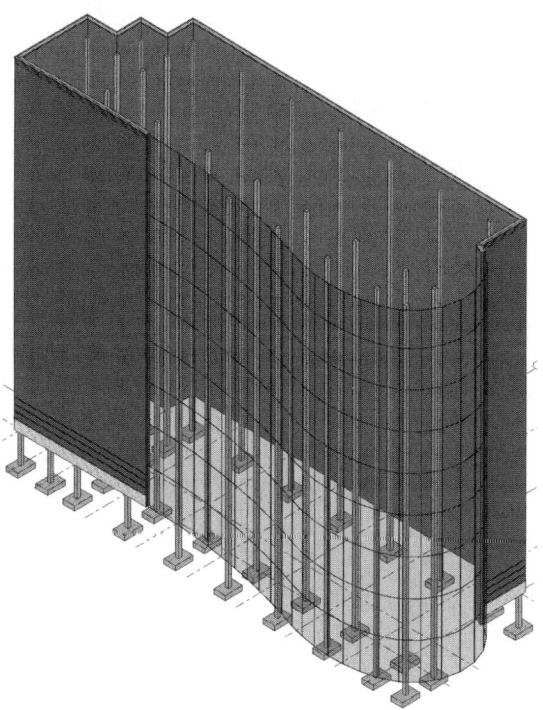

Figure 7–40

8. Save and close the project.

• An additional task to add a parapet to the exterior wall can be found in the *Model Additional Walls* practice.

## Practice 7b  Add Interior Walls

### Practice Objectives

- Model and modify walls.
- Use modify tools, including Align, Offset, Trim/Extend, Copy, and Mirror.

In this practice, you will add interior walls to the first floor plan, as shown in Figure 7–41, and use **Offset**, **Split Element**, **Trim**, and **Align** to help create them.

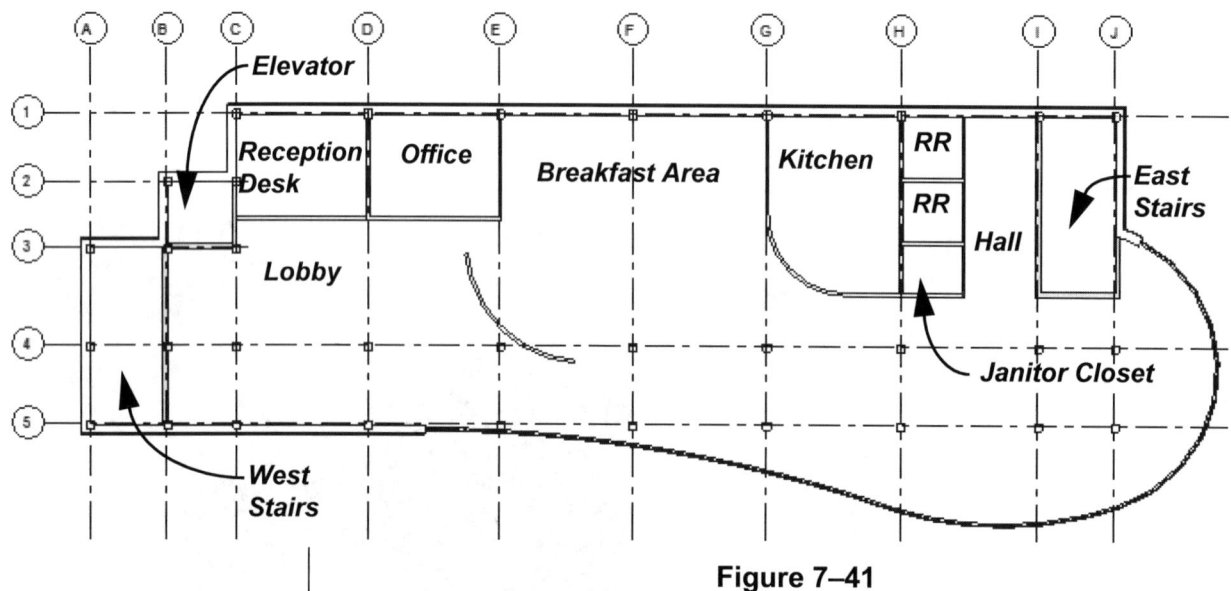

Figure 7–41

### Task 1 - Add and align the stair and elevator walls.

1. Open the project **Hotel-WallsInt.rvt** from the practice files folder.

2. Open the **Floor Plans: Floor 1** view.

3. Zoom in on the stair and elevator area on the west side of the building.

4. In the *Architecture* tab>Build panel, click  (Wall).

Modeling Walls

5. In Properties, set the following:
   - *Wall Type:* **Basic Wall: Generic 8" Masonry**
   - *Location Line:* **Wall Centerline**
   - *Base Constraint:* **Floor 1**
   - *Base Offset:* **0'-0"**
   - *Top Constraint:* **Up to level: Roof**
   - *Top Offset:* **0'-0"**
   - *Cross-Section:* **Vertical**

6. In the Options Bar, uncheck **Chain**. If you leave the **Chain** option on, the wall will snap to other walls rather than the columns.

7. Draw the walls around the stairs and elevator, as shown in Figure 7–42. Draw each wall separately from column to column.
   - If needed, you can use the **Align** command to ensure that the walls are in the right place.

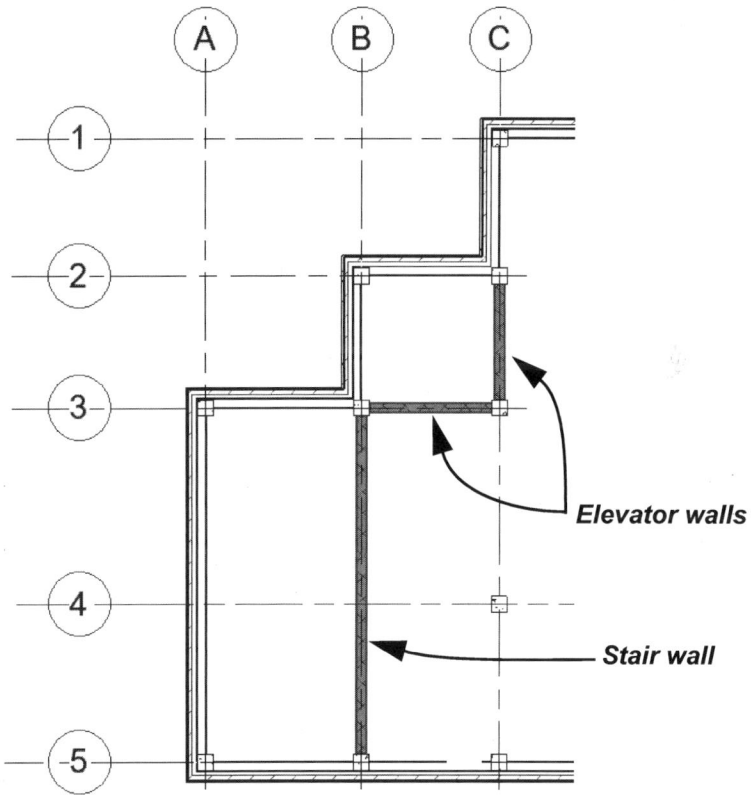

Figure 7–42

8. Click (Modify).

9. To view the walls you just created, select the linked DWG. In the View Control Bar, click (Temporary Hide/Isolate), then select **Hide Element** to hide the DWG.

10. In the View Control Bar, click (Temporary Hide/Isolate) and select **Reset Temporary Hide/Isolate**.

11. Click (Modify).

12. Pan over to the east stairwell. Using the same wall type Options Bar settings, and Properties, add the walls (as shown in Figure 7–43) using the DWG as a guide for placement.

13. To view the walls unobscured, select the DWG and type **VH** to hide it in the view, as shown in Figure 7–43.

*Grid bubbles have been modified in the image for clarity.*

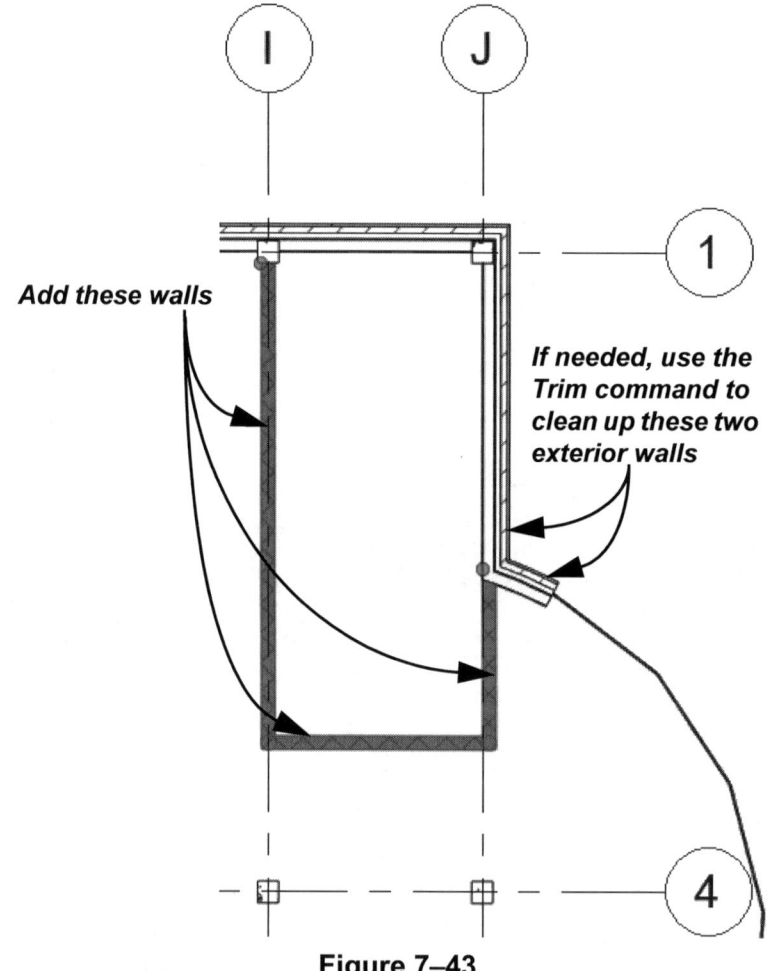

Figure 7–43

14. Zoom out or type **ZA** or **ZF** to display the entire building floor plan.

15. Save the project.

# Modeling Walls

**Task 2 - Add the reception and office walls.**

*Setting the Top Offset to a negative number leaves room for the floor above.*

1. Start the **Wall** command and set the following properties:

   - *Wall type:* **Basic Wall: Interior - 4 7/8" Partition (1-hr)**
   - *Location Line:* **Wall Centerline**
   - Base Constraint: **Floor 1**
   - *Top Constraint:* **Up to level: Floor 2**
   - *Top Offset:* (negative) **-1'-0"**
   - *Cross-Section:* **Vertical**

2. Draw the walls shown in Figure 7–44, starting at the exterior column on grid E, down **13'-0"**, then a middle wall on grid D and the bottom horizontal wall from grid E to C.

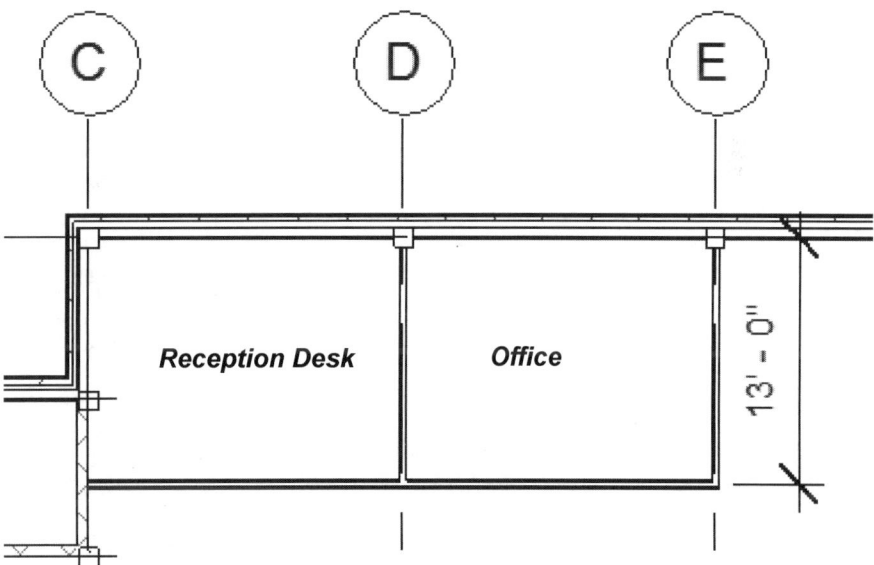

**Figure 7–44**

3. Zoom in to the interior wall connection on grid D and select the bottom horizontal wall.

4. In the *Modify | Wall* tab>Modify panel, click (Split Element).

*Click (Thick Lines) to toggle on and off to display the line thickness.*

5. Click the horizontal wall at the point shown in Figure 7–45.

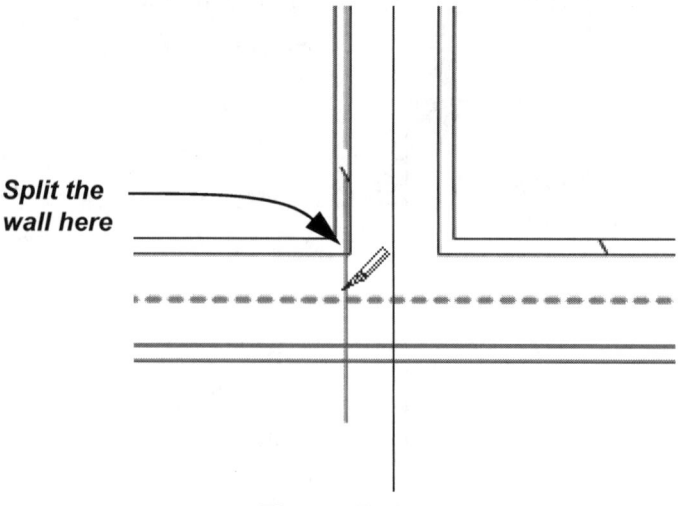

Figure 7–45

6. Click (Modify).

7. Select the left part of the split wall.

8. In Properties, set the following:

    - *Top Constraint:* **Unconnected**
    - *Unconnected Height:* **4'-0"**

- This split wall will now become the base for the reception desk.

9. Click (Modify).

10. In the *Modify* tab>Modify panel, select (Trim/Extend to Corner). Select the right piece of the split wall and then the vertical wall to join them as shown in Figure 7–46.

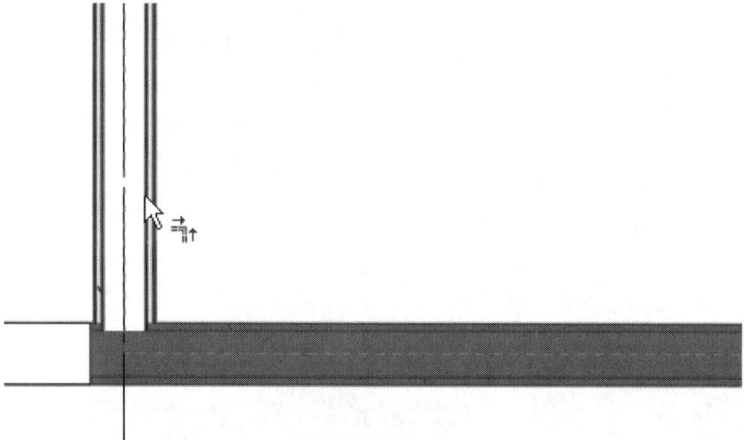

Figure 7–46

Modeling Walls

*In the Quick Access Toolbar, click (Thin Lines) to make the close-up easier to see.*

11. Modify the reception counter wall to butt up against the middle vertical walls. Selecting the split wall on the left, right-click on the wall end control (shown in Figure 7–47), and select **Disallow Join**.

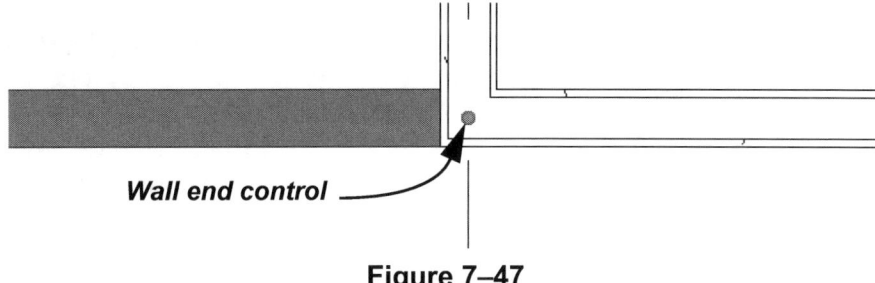

**Figure 7–47**

12. Select the wall end control and drag it so it butts up against the edge of the wall, as shown in Figure 7–48.

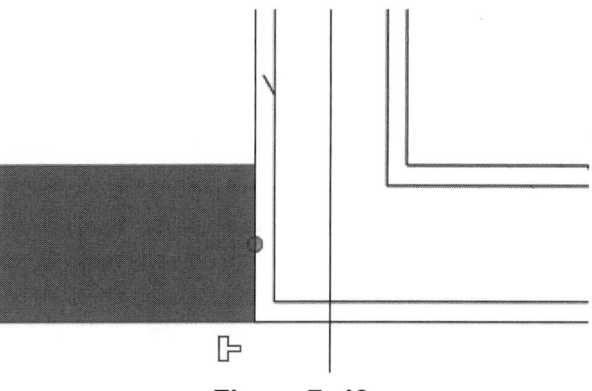

**Figure 7–48**

### Task 3 - Add the reception desk.

1. Zoom in to the grid 2C area (Reception Desk), as shown in Figure 7–49.

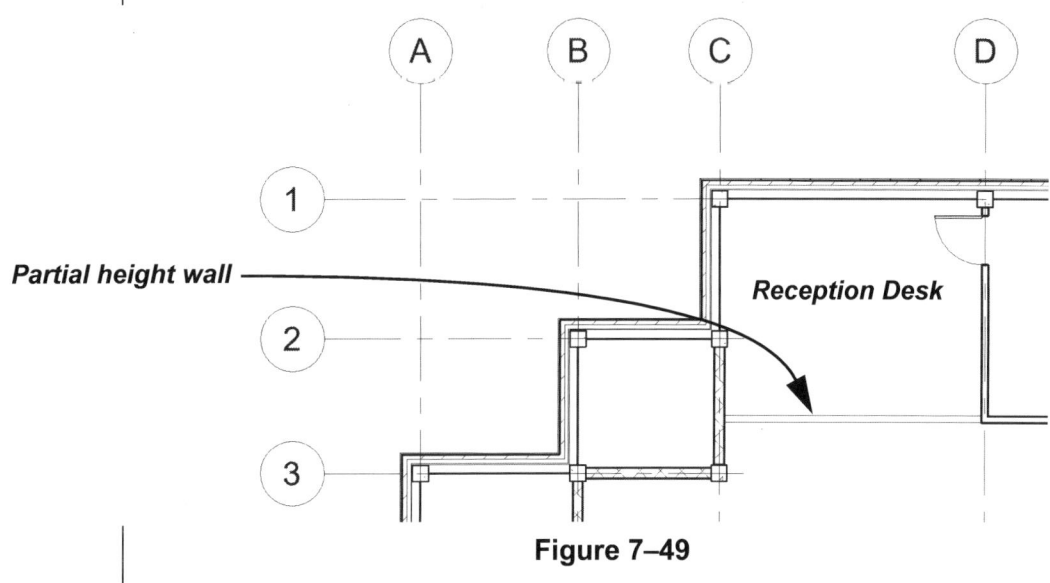

**Figure 7–49**

2. In the *Architecture* tab>Build panel, expand (Component) and click (Place a Component). In the Type Selector, select **Countertop-Lobby 24" Depth**.

3. In Properties, set the *Offset from Host* to **1'-1-5/8"**.

   - You need to set the *Offset from Host* because the countertop family's default height is **3'-0"** above the level. (This Dimensions parameter can be viewed by selecting the countertop and clicking **Edit Type** in Properties.) The partial height wall in the project is **4'-0"** high and the countertop thickness is about **1-1/2"**.

4. Place the countertop component over the partial height wall.

5. Click (Modify).

6. Select the countertop. Move it, if needed, and modify its length using the control grips on each end, as shown in Figure 7–50. Extend it so that it touches the vertical walls on both ends.

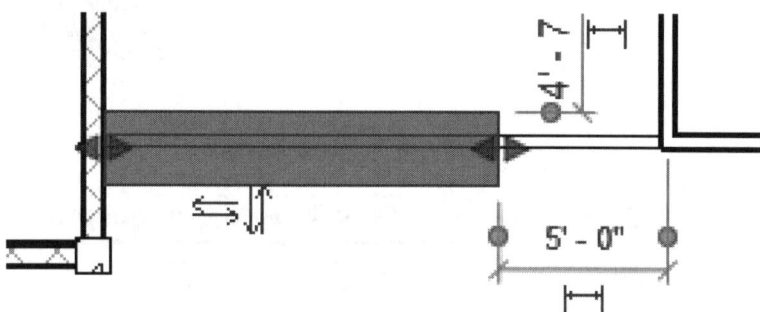

**Figure 7–50**

   - To get a better view of this offset, place a section through the countertop and open the section view. Adjust the crop region, if needed. Remember to unhide the section markers before you draw one.

7. Save the project.

# Modeling Walls

**Task 4 - Add the kitchen walls.**

1. Pan over to the east stairwell.

2. In the *Architecture* tab>Work Plane panel, click (Reference Plane) and draw a reference plane from the exterior face of the stairwell wall over to grid G, as shown in Figure 7–51.

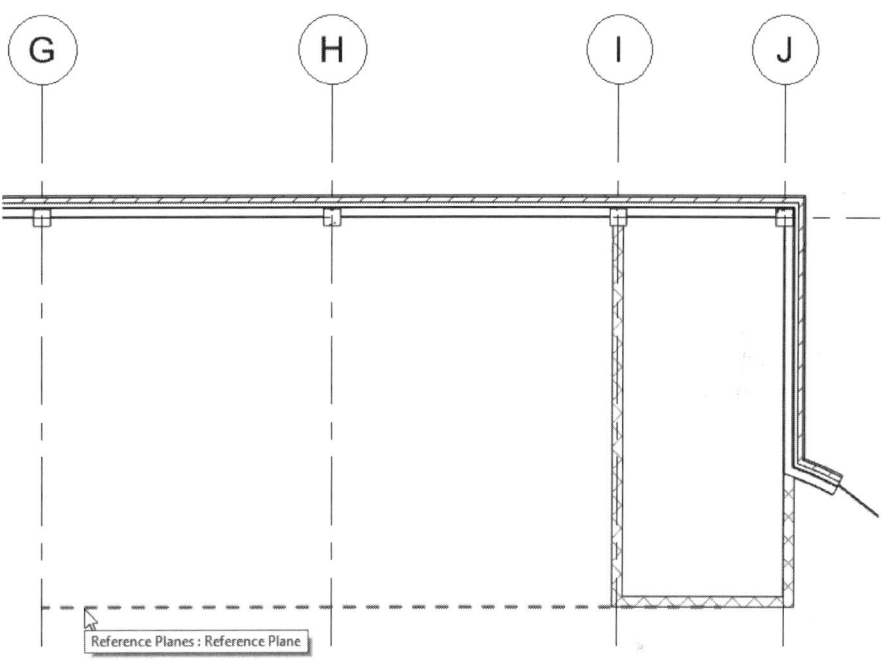

**Figure 7–51**

3. Start the **Wall** command and set the following properties:

    - *Wall type:* **Basic Wall: Interior - 4 7/8" Partition (1-hr)**
    - *Location Line:* **Wall Centerline**
    - Base Constraint: **Floor 1**
    - *Top Constraint:* **Floor 2**
    - *Top Offset:* (negative) **-1'-0"**
    - *Cross-Section:* **Vertical**

4. In the Options Bar, select **Chain**.

5. Draw a wall along grid G down to the reference plane, then over to grid H along the reference plane and up to the exterior wall, as shown in Figure 7–52.

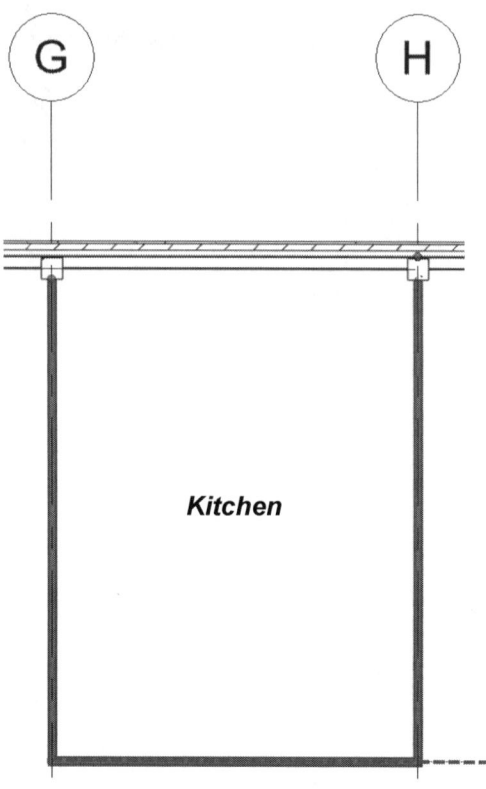

Figure 7–52

6. Click  (Modify).

7. Zoom in on the bottom wall and the horizontal reference plane.

8. In the *Modify* tab>Modify panel, click  (Align).

9. Align the exterior face of the wall (as shown in Figure 7–53) with the reference plane (select the reference plane first, followed by the face of the wall).

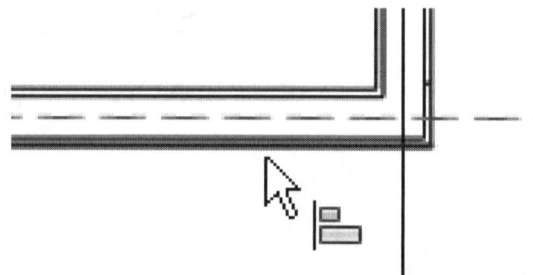

Figure 7–53

# Modeling Walls

10. Click (Modify).

11. Start the **Wall** command. In the *Modify | Place Wall* tab> Draw panel, select (Fillet Arc), and in the Options Bar, select **Radius** and set the *Fillet radius* to **10'-0"**.

12. Select the wall along grid G and the wall along the reference plane to create the arc at the corner, as shown in Figure 7–54.

13. Click (Modify).

## Task 5 - Add the restroom and janitor closet walls.

*Use (Trim/Extend to Corner), (Trim/Extend Single), and (Trim/Extend Multiple) as needed to get the walls in place.*

1. Start the **Wall** command and use the same wall properties as before. In the Options Bar, set the *Offset* to **8'-0"**.

2. Use the (Pick Lines) draw tool and hover over the wall on grid H. When you see the dashed preview line to the right of grid H (as shown in Figure 7–54), click to place the wall.

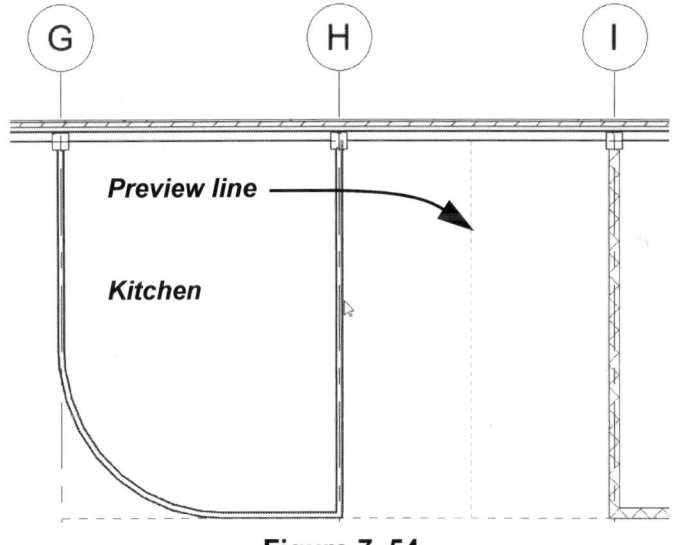

Figure 7–54

3. Start the **Trim** command and trim the lower kitchen wall to the restroom and janitor closet wall, as shown in Figure 7–55.

Figure 7–55

4. Draw a wall **5'-6"** above the bottom wall as shown in Figure 7–56. Use temporary dimensions to get the wall into the correct position. You may need to move the temporary dimension witness lines.

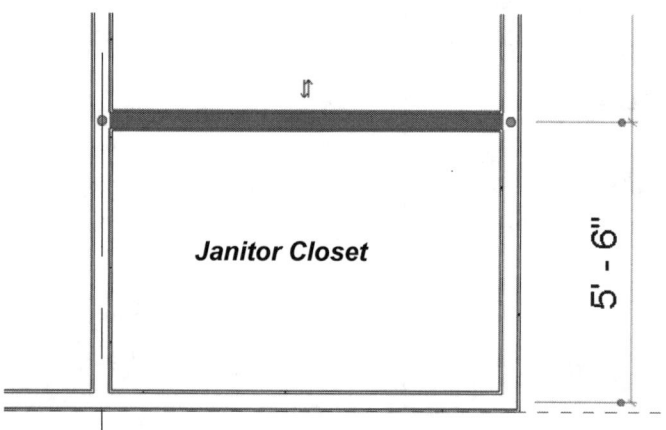

Figure 7–56

5. Select the new wall. In the *Modify |Walls* tab>Modify panel, click  (Offset). In the Options Bar, click **Copy** and set the *Offset* to **8'-8 15/16"**.

Modeling Walls

6. Hover your cursor over the wall (as shown in Figure 7–57), and when you see the dashed preview line above the janitor close wall, click to place the wall.

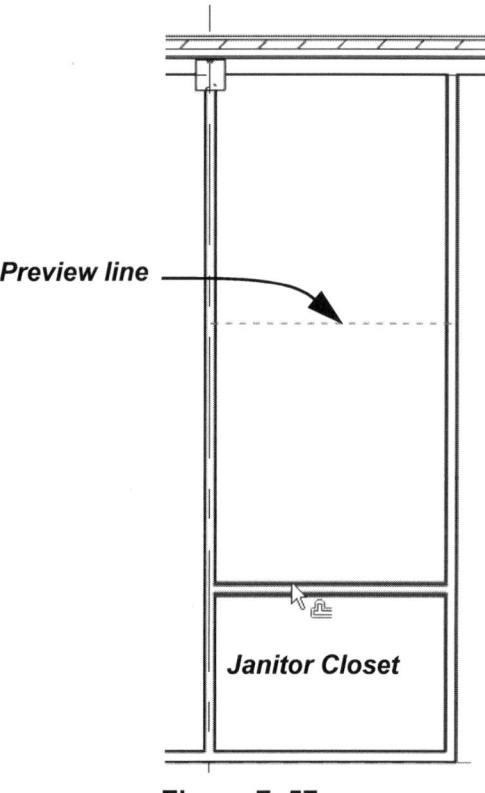

Figure 7–57

*Reference planes will display in all other plan views and can cause confusion for others.*

7. Click  (Modify) and delete the reference plane.

8. Zoom and pan below the reception desk and office area.

You need to create a curved slanted wall to separate the breakfast area from the lobby. The curved walls placement doesn't need to be precise but drawing reference planes will help guide you while drawing the wall.

9. Start the **Reference Plane** command.

10. Starting at grid E and the corner of the office walls, draw reference planes intersecting each other, as shown in Figure 7–58. To quickly offset the reference planes, use  (Pick Lines) and set the *Offset* in the Options Bar to the desired distance. Select the exterior face of the wall and grid E.

- You do not need to draw the dimensions; this is for reference only.

11. Click (Modify).

12. Stretch the reference planes so that they intersect each other as shown in Figure 7–58.

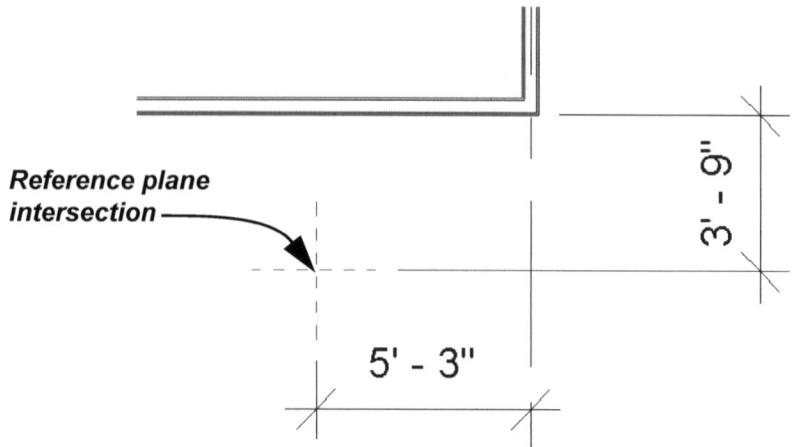

Figure 7–58

13. Start the **Reference Plane** command again.

14. Offset from grid E and grid 4 and draw reference planes intersecting each other, as shown in Figure 7–59.

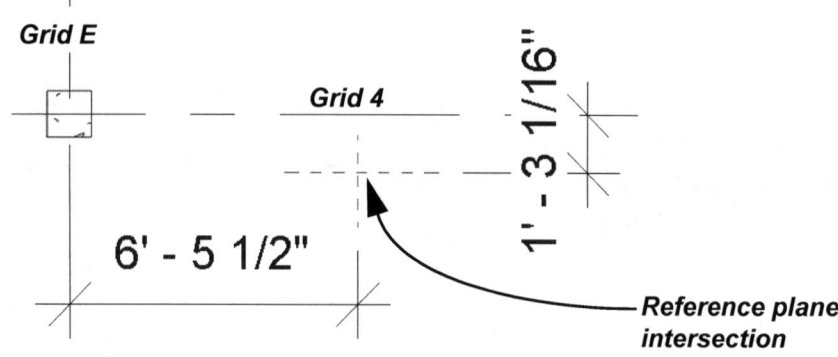

Figure 7–59

15. Start the **Wall** command, select (Start-End-Radius Arc) draw tool, and in Properties, set the following:

- *Wall type:* **Basic Wall: Interior - 4 7/8" Partition (1-hr)**
- *Location Line:* **Wall Centerline**
- *Base Constraint:* **Floor 1**
- *Top Constraint:* **Unconnected**
- *Top Offset:* **8'-0"**
- *Cross-Section:* **Slanted**
- *Angle From Vertical:* **4.00°**

16. In the Options Bar, uncheck **Chain**.

17. Draw the slanted curved wall starting from the top reference lines intersection to the bottom and for the last pick create a slight arc, as shown in Figure 7–60.

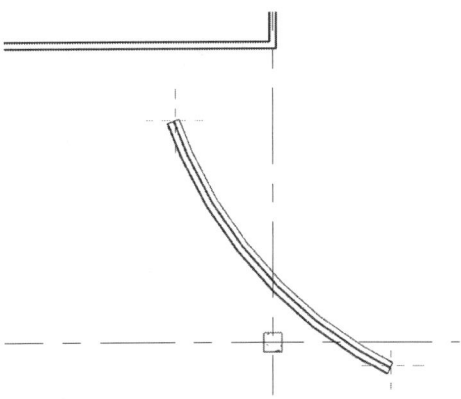

Figure 7–60

18. Delete the reference planes that you created.

19. Zoom out and save and close the project.

*The exact size and location does not matter, but ensure that there is enough room for people to get by on both sides.*

# Practice 7c  Model Additional Walls

### Practice Objective

- Model and modify additional walls.

If time permits, you can add a parapet above the curtain walls (as shown in Figure 7–61), as well as walls to the second floor, basement, and footings.

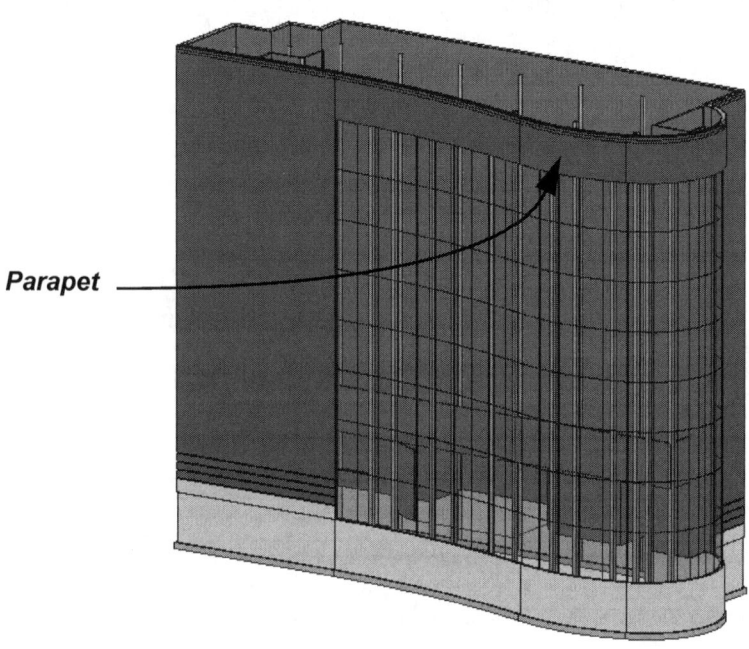

*Parapet*

Figure 7–61

### Task 1 - Add a parapet.

1. Open the project **Hotel-WallsOpt.rvt** from the practice files folder.

2. In the Quick Access Toolbar, click (Default 3D View).

3. From the tabs along the top of the view, click the X next to **Floor 1** to close it.

4. Open the **Floor Plans: Roof** view.

5. Type **WT** to tile the Roof and 3D view, then type **ZA** or **ZF** to zoom both views.

6. In the **Roof** view, select the three curtain walls in the southeast area of the building.

Modeling Walls

7. In Properties, set the *Top Constraint* to **Up to Level: Roof** and the *Top Offset* to (negative) **-6'-0"**. This will give you room to draw the parapet walls.

   - The curtain walls display in halftone because the tops of the curtain walls are now below the Roof level.

8. Select the small curved piece of wall at the northeast corner of the building along column line J. Right-click on the right end point grip and select **Disallow Join,** as shown in Figure 7–62.

*Some walls, when they try to automatically clean up, cause problems. Disallowing a join can resolve the issue.*

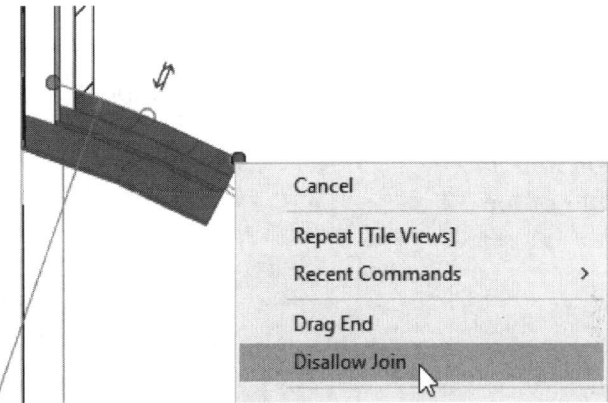

Figure 7–62

9. Pan to the lower southwest of the building and repeat the process again on the other wall (shown in Figure 7–63) that connects to the curtain wall near the intersection of grid D5.

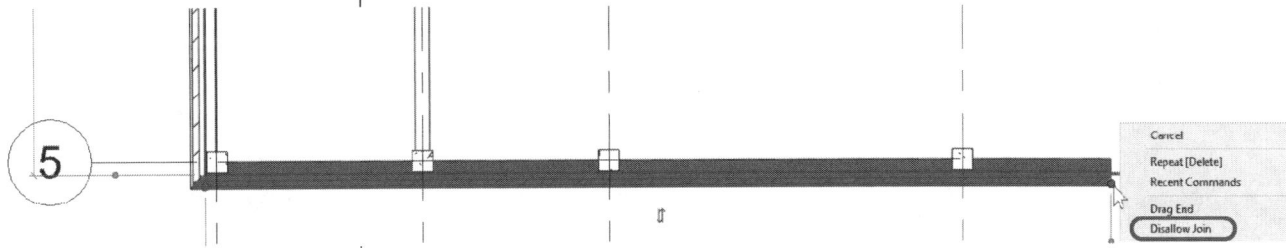

Figure 7–63

10. Zoom back to the southeast corner and start the **Wall** command.

11. In the *Modify | Place Wall* tab>Draw panel, click (Start-End-Radius Arc).

12. In the Type Selector, select **Basic Wall: Exterior - Brick on MTL. Stud - parapet** and set the following properties:

    - *Location Line:* **Wall Centerline**
    - *Base Constraint:* **Roof**
    - *Base Offset:* (negative) **-2'-0"**
    - *Top Constraint:* **Up to level: Parapet**
    - *Top Offset:* **0'-0"**
    - *Cross-Section:* **Vertical**

13. In the Options Bar, verify **Chain** is unchecked.

14. Starting at the exterior wall of the east stairs, the first selection point is at the end of the existing wall. The second selection point is at the intersection of grid J and the curtain wall (not the curtain panel). The third selection point is at the tangent point along the curtain wall, as shown in Figure 7–64.

    - Select the points in the order shown in Figure 7–64. Ensure that you select the endpoints before selecting the tangent point on the arc.

*Ensure that you are selecting the main line of the curtain wall or a curtain wall grid line, and not one of the curtain wall panels.*

*The model's grids I and J end symbols have been turned on in the figure for clarity.*

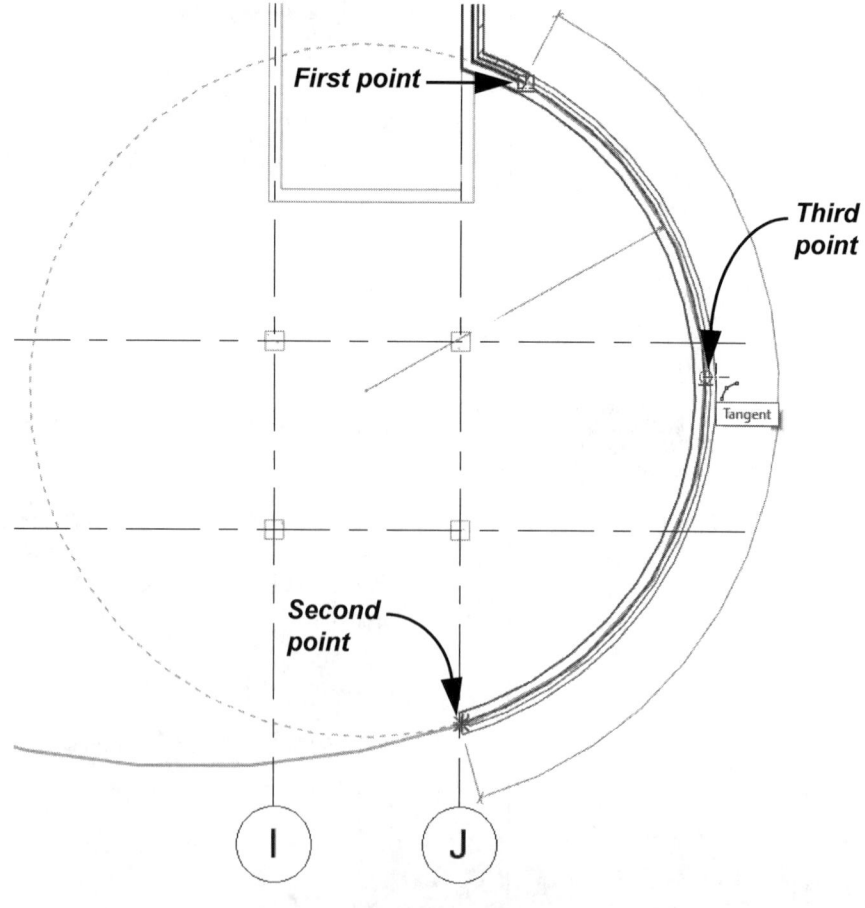

Figure 7–64

15. Still in the **Wall** command, draw another arc wall from grid J to grid H. Then again from grid H to the end of the existing exterior wall, as shown in Figure 7–65.

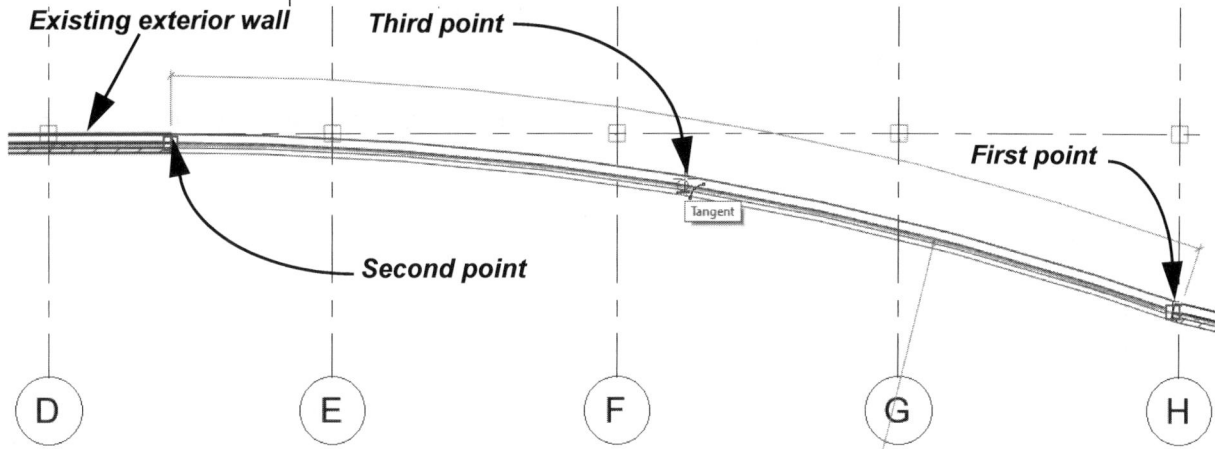

Figure 7–65

- Creating the wall this way solves some issues because the center line of the curtain wall is at a slight offset from the main wall.
- If a warning displays about a wall sweep you can ignore it.

16. Click  (Modify).

17. Type **ZA** to display the full floor plan.

18. Return to the 3D view. The new parapet wall over the curtain wall displays, as shown in Figure 7–66.

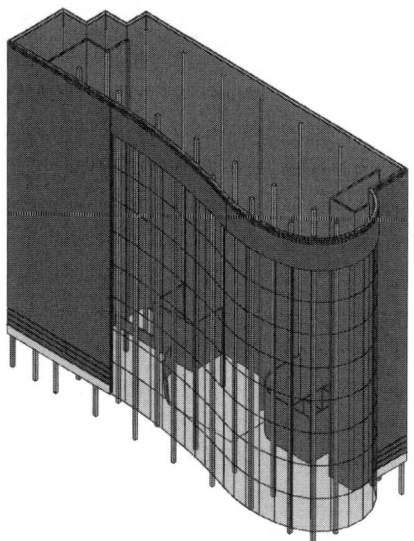

Figure 7–66

19. Type **TW** to set the views back to tile view.

20. Save the project.

### Task 2 - Add Floor 2 walls.

1. Open the **Floor Plans: Floor 2** view. The view displays the walls created in the project and the linked drawing of the second floor.

2. Add walls for the guest rooms, as shown in Figure 7–67, using the following options:

   - *Wall type:* **Interior - 4 7/8" Partition (1-hr)**
   - *Location Line:* **Wall Centerline**
   - *Base Constraint:* **Floor 2**
   - *Top Constraint:* **Floor 3**
   - *Top Offset:* (negative) **-1'-0"**
   - *Cross-Section:* **Vertical**
   - Align the center of the vertical walls to the grids.
   - Ignore all of the door openings.
   - You can use the (Copy) and (Mirror) tools to duplicate the walls once you have modeled one guest room layout.

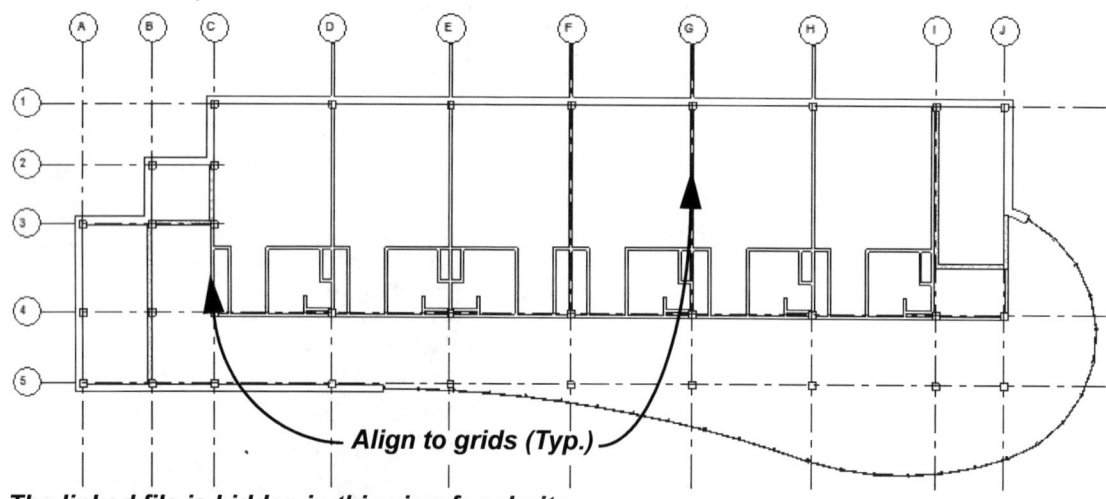

*The linked file is hidden in this view for clarity*

Figure 7–67

3. Save the project.

### Task 3 - Add basement walls.

1. Open the **Floor Plans: T.O. Footing** view.

2. In Properties, in the *Underlay* section, set the *Range: Base Level* to **Floor 1** to see where the walls must be placed.

Modeling Walls

3. In the *Architecture* tab>Build panel, click (Wall).

4. In the Options Bar, uncheck the **Chain** option.

5. In Properties, set the following options:

   - *Wall type:* **Basic Wall: Generic - 12" Masonry**
   - *Location Line:* **Core Centerline**
   - *Base Constraint:* **T.O. Footing**
   - *Base Offset:* **0'-0"**
   - *Top Constraint:* **Up to Level: Floor 1**
   - *Top Offset:* **0'-0"**
   - *Cross-Section:* **Vertical**

*Hover the cursor over a wall and then press <Tab> until the center line displays.*

6. Starting at the west stairwell, draw the interior foundation walls between columns, then the two walls around the east stairwell, as shown in Figure 7–68 (column footings are turned off in image for clarity).

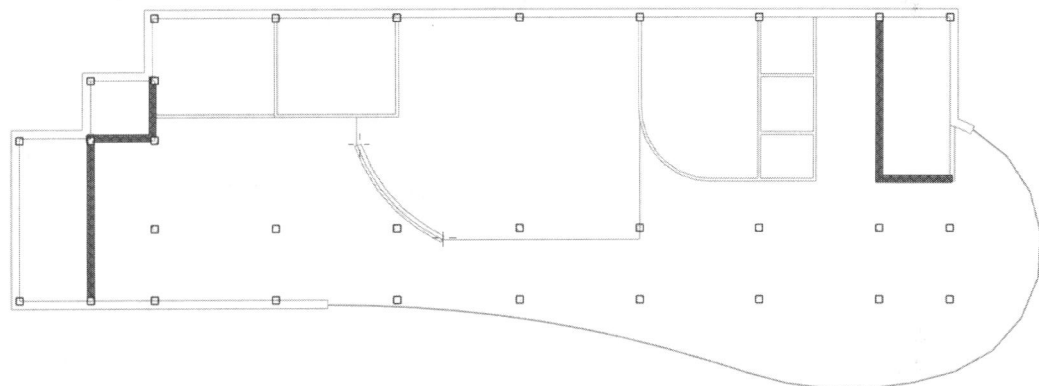

**Figure 7–68**

7. Click (Modify).

8. Zoom out so you can see the entire building.

9. Start the **Wall** command again. The settings should all be the same. Click (Pick Lines) from the draw tools.

10. Hover your cursor over the exterior wall of the west stairwell.

11. Press <Tab> until you see all the walls' centerlines highlight as shown in Figure 7–69. Once the walls are highlighted, click to select them.

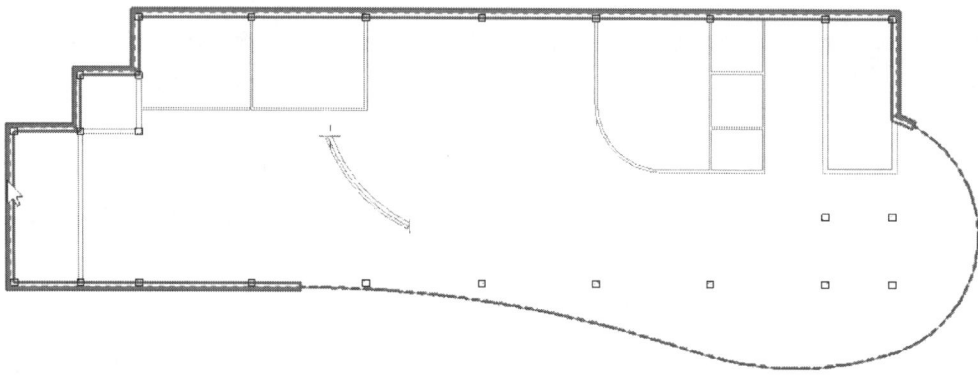

Figure 7–69

- Alternatively, you can use ✏ (Pick Lines) and pick the walls individually.

12. Click ▷ (Modify).

13. Extend the east stairwell's wall to intersect with the stairwell wall, as shown in Figure 7–70.

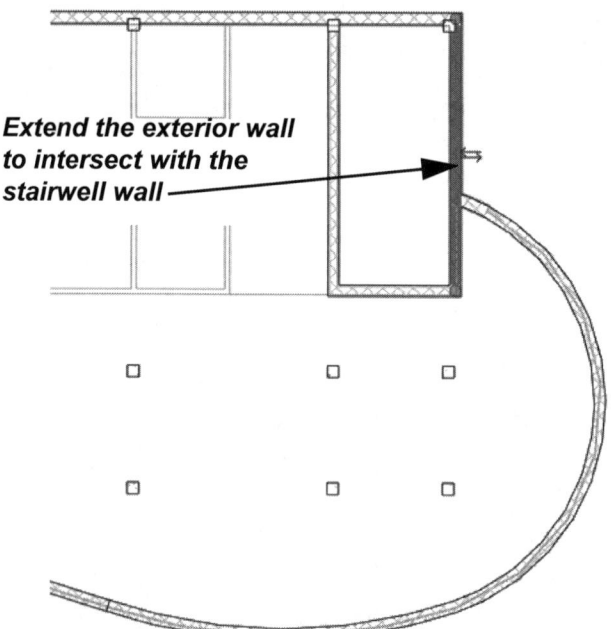

*Extend the exterior wall to intersect with the stairwell wall*

Figure 7–70

- Use **Align** and other modify tools to get them in place if needed.

14. Click (Modify).

15. Save the project.

**Task 4 - Add footings to the basement walls.**

1. Start the **Wall** command and click (Pick Lines) from the draw tools.

2. In Properties, set the following options:

    - *Wall type:* **Basic Wall: Generic - 24" Concrete**
    - *Location Line:* **Core Centerline**
    - *Base Constraint:* **T.O. Footing**
    - *Base Offset:* (negative) **-1'-6"**
    - *Top Constraint:* **Up to Level:T.O. Footing**
    - *Top Offset:* **0'-0"**
    - *Cross-Section:* **Vertical**

*You might need to zoom in and use <Tab> to highlight the core center line.*

3. Select the core center line of all the foundation walls. The wall footings display, as shown in Figure 7–71 (column footings are turned off in image for clarity).

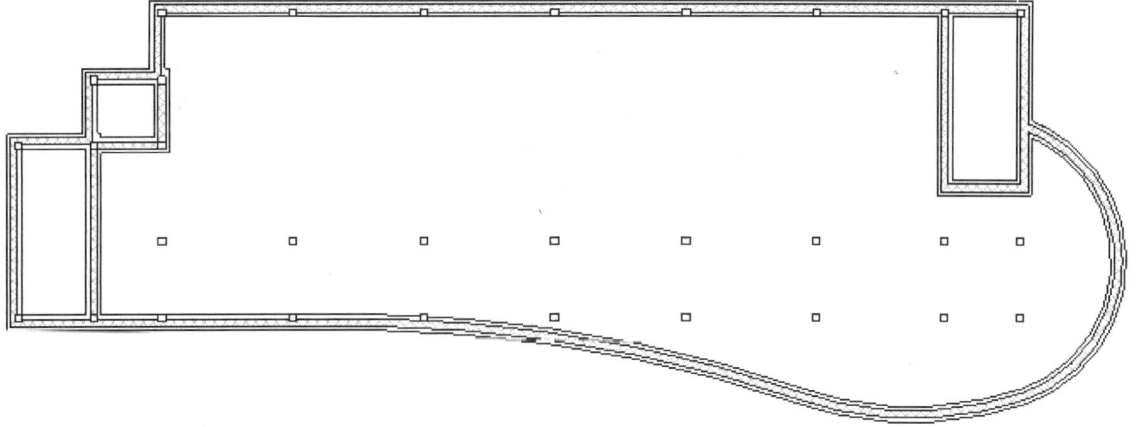

Figure 7–71

4. Open the 3D view and orbit to view the foundation walls and footings.

5. Save and close the project.

# 7.4 Adding Room Elements

Room elements are important for room names and numbers, as well as adding room information to schedules. You can place a room element in any space bounded by walls (as shown in Figure 7–72) or by room separation lines. Room separation lines enable you to divide an open space into more rooms.

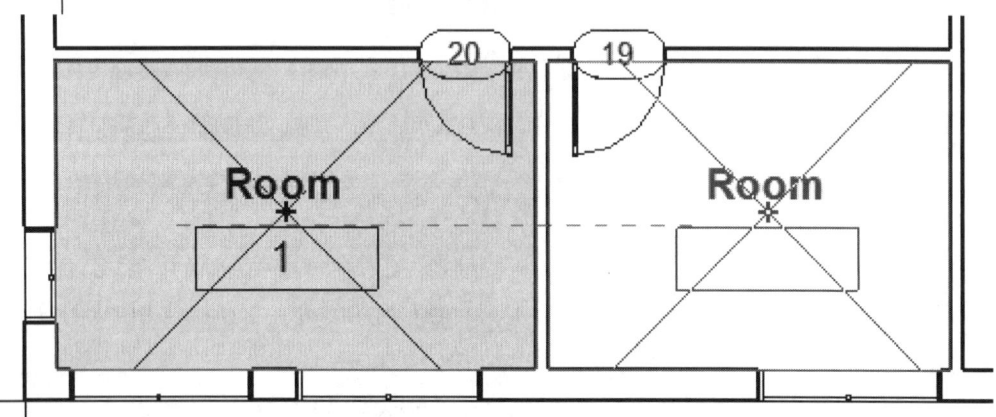

Figure 7–72

### How To: Add Rooms

1. In the *Architecture* tab>Room & Area panel, click (Room) or type **RM**.
2. Move the cursor inside a boundary and click to place a room element. If you have **Tag on Placement** active, it also places the tag at the point you selected.
3. Continue clicking inside boundaries to add other rooms.

- To add multiple rooms at once, in the *Modify | Place Room* tab>Room panel, click (Place Rooms Automatically). Rooms are added in every bounded area that does not already have a room.

- Rooms are inserted with the default name of *Room*. Numbers increment automatically as you place rooms. Select the first room on a floor, change the number as needed, and then add the rest of the room locations.

# Modeling Walls

- To select rooms, hover the cursor near the room tag or move the cursor around slowly until you find the X to highlight the room element, as shown in Figure 7–73.

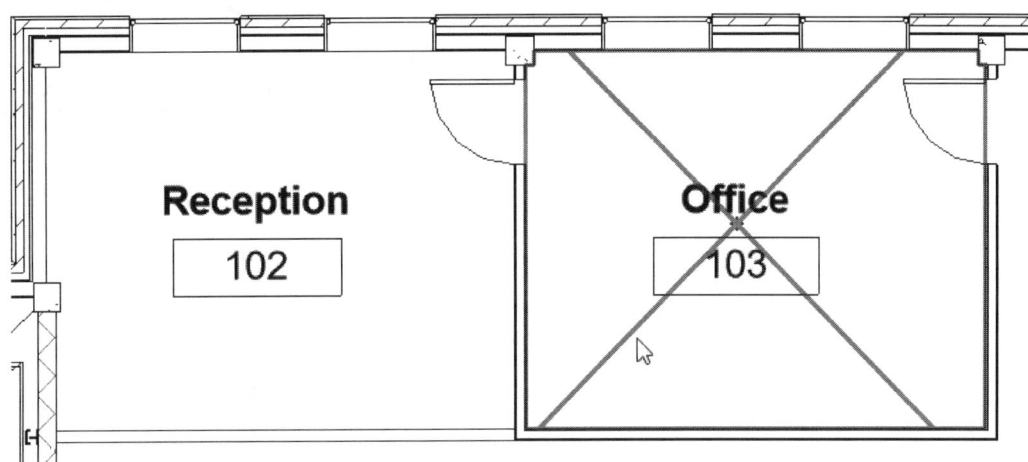

Figure 7–73

- To change the names of several rooms, select the room elements and in Properties, change the *Name* parameter, as shown in Figure 7–74. All the rooms that were selected will update to show the same name.

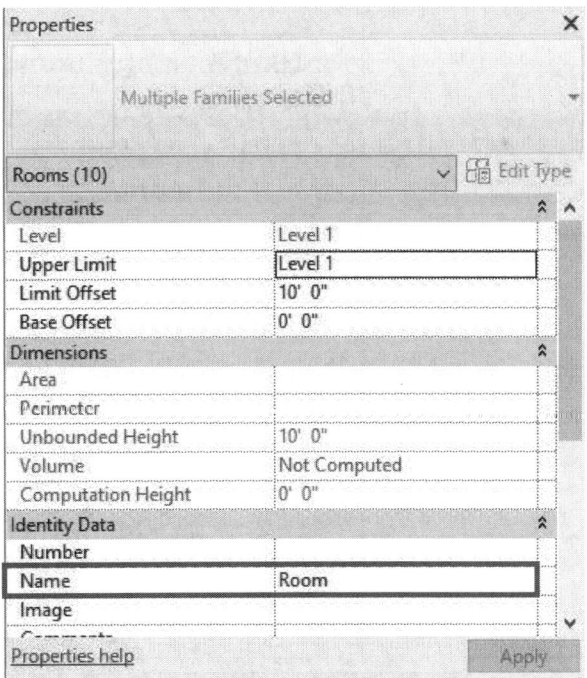

Figure 7–74

- To change the name of one room, select the tag, then select the tag name and type the name of the room.

- You can also click on the room number and type a new number, as shown in Figure 7–75. Any room tags placed thereafter will increment using the last tag's number. Example, if you change a room tag's number to 101, the next tag will be 102, and so on.

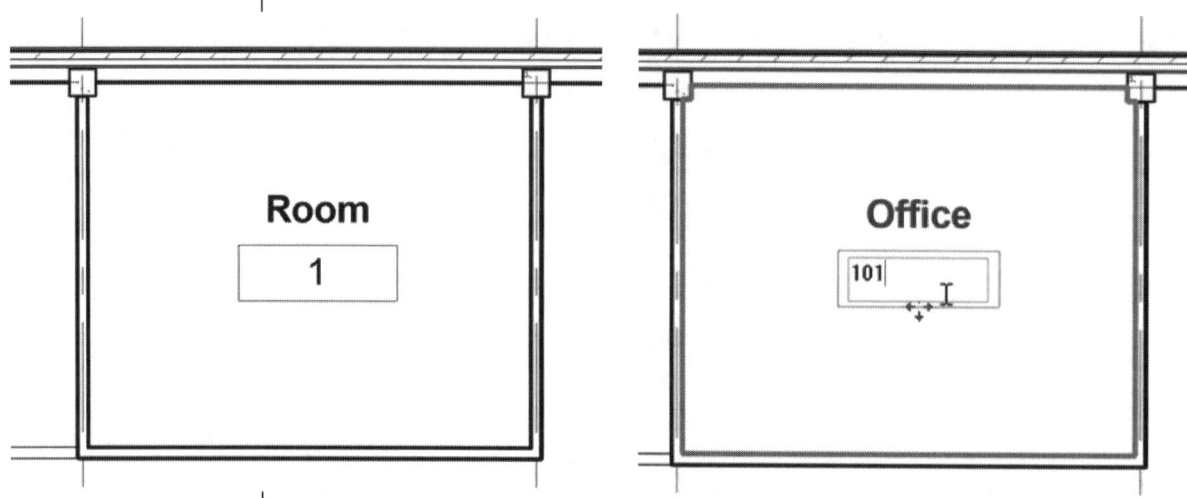

Figure 7–75

- Other information, such as finishes, can also be added in the room properties. This information is made available to schedules.

### Hint: Making Rooms Visible

If rooms are not visible in a view, in the Visibility/Graphic Overrides dialog box, expand **Rooms** and select **Interior Fill** and/or **Reference**, as shown in Figure 7–76.

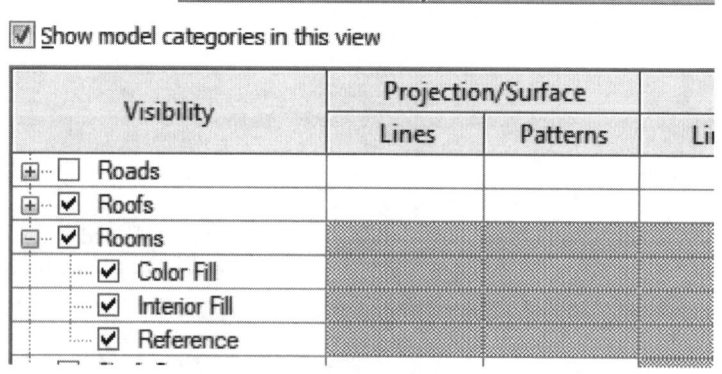

Figure 7–76

- Color Fill is used when a color scheme is applied to a view.

## How To: Add Room Separation Lines

1. In the *Architecture* tab>Room & Area panel, click (Room Separator).
2. Use the Draw tools to place lines that divide the spaces.
3. After creating the room separation lines, use the **Room** command to add the rooms, as shown in Figure 7–77.

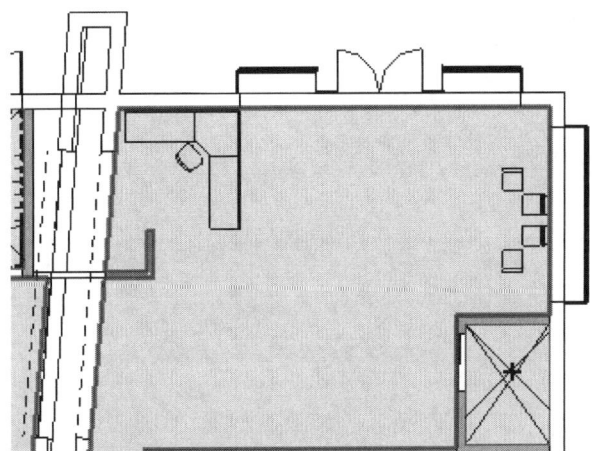
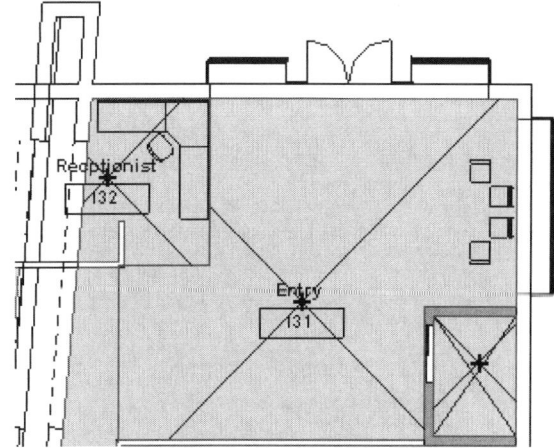

***Before room separation lines***     ***With room separation lines***

**Figure 7–77**

## Practice 7d  Add Room Elements

### Practice Objectives

- Set up a view that displays rooms.
- Add rooms and room separation lines.

In this practice, you will add rooms to the model. You will change the names and numbers of rooms using tags and Properties. You will add room separation lines to break up the larger open areas, as shown in Figure 7–78.

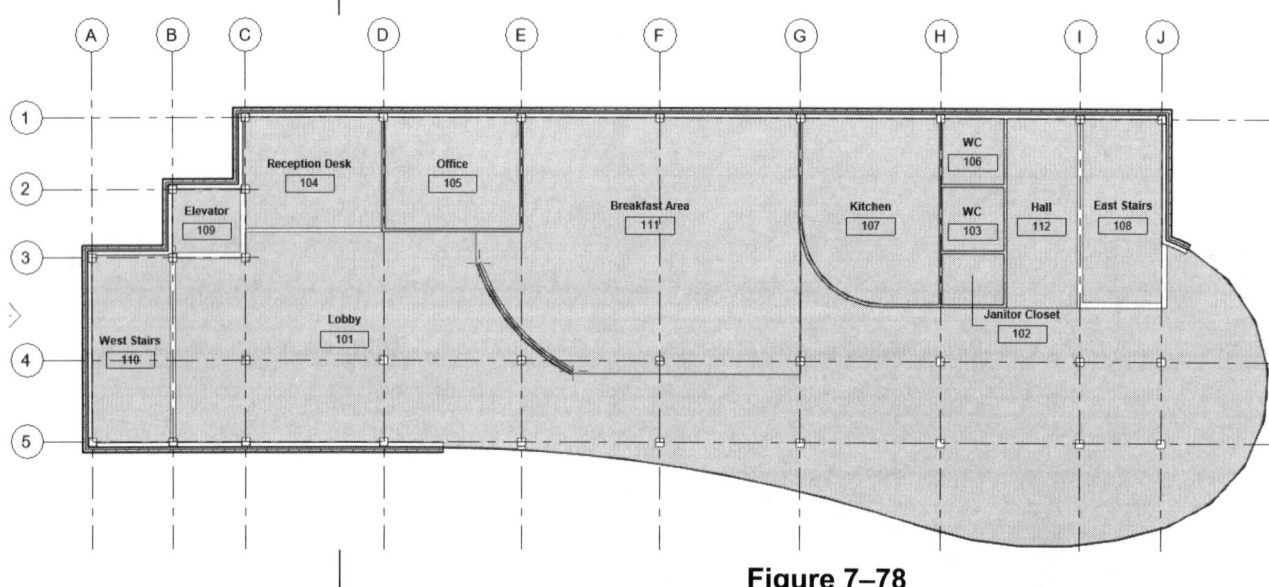

Figure 7–78

### Task 1 - Add rooms and room tags.

1. Open the project **Hotel-Rooms.rvt**.

2. Verify that you are in the **Floor Plans: Floor 1** view.

3. In the *View* tab>Graphics panel, select  (Visibility/Graphics), or type **VV**.

4. Select the *Model Categories* tab.

# Modeling Walls

5. Scroll down the categories list and expand **Rooms**. Select **Interior Fill**, as shown in Figure 7–79, so that you can see the room color as you place rooms.

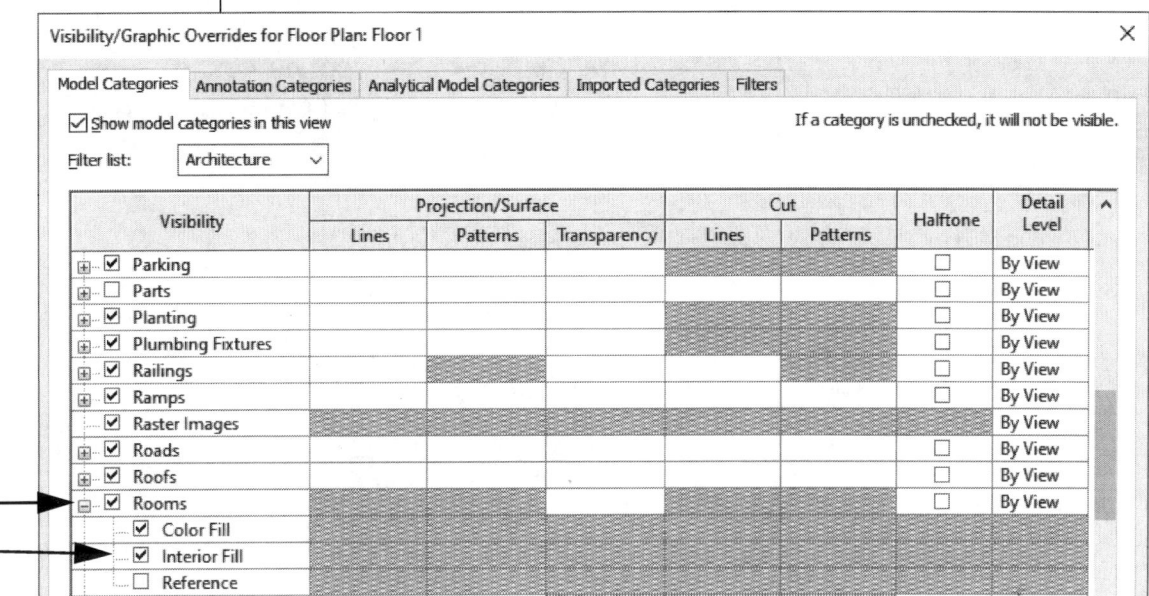

Figure 7–79

6. Click **OK**.

7. In the *Architecture* tab>Room & Area panel, click ⬚ (Room).

8. In the *Modify | Place Room* tab>Tag panel, verify that ⬚ (Tag on Placement) is selected. The icon will be highlighted in blue if tagging is turned on and gray (not highlighted) if it is turned off, as shown in Figure 7–80.

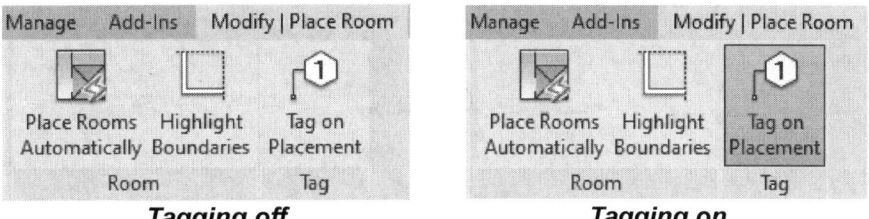

             Tagging off              Tagging on

Figure 7–80

9. Place a room element inside the lobby area (to the left of the curved wall).

10. Click ⬚ (Modify) and zoom in on the room tag.

11. Click on the tag and then click on the room name change the room name to **Lobby** and click on the room number to change it to **101**, as shown in Figure 7–81. Double-click in an empty space in the view to finish the command.

    - Changing this first room number ensures that the rest of the numbers increment correctly.

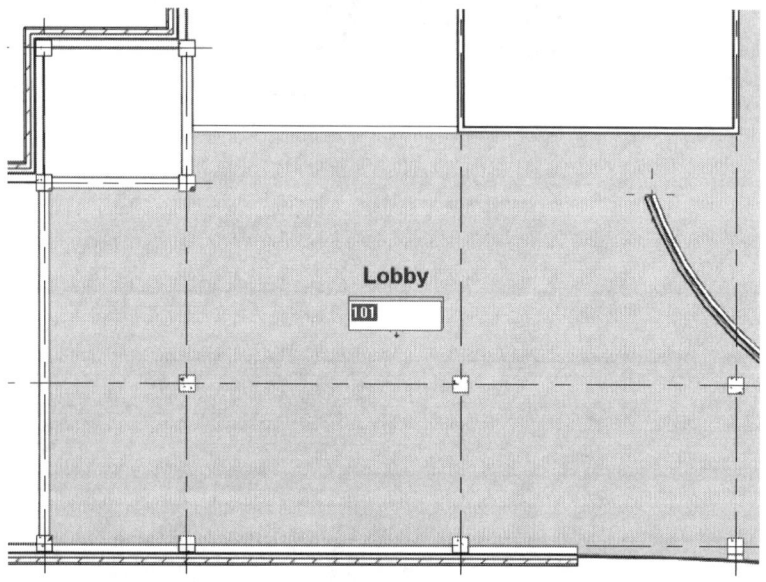

**Figure 7–81**

12. Zoom out and start the **Room** command again.

13. In the *Modify | Place Room* tab>Room panel, click (Place Rooms Automatically). The rest of the rooms are added to the model. Your room numbers might differ from what is shown in the book. You can renumber them after they are all added.

14. Click **Close** in the dialog box, as shown in Figure 7–82.

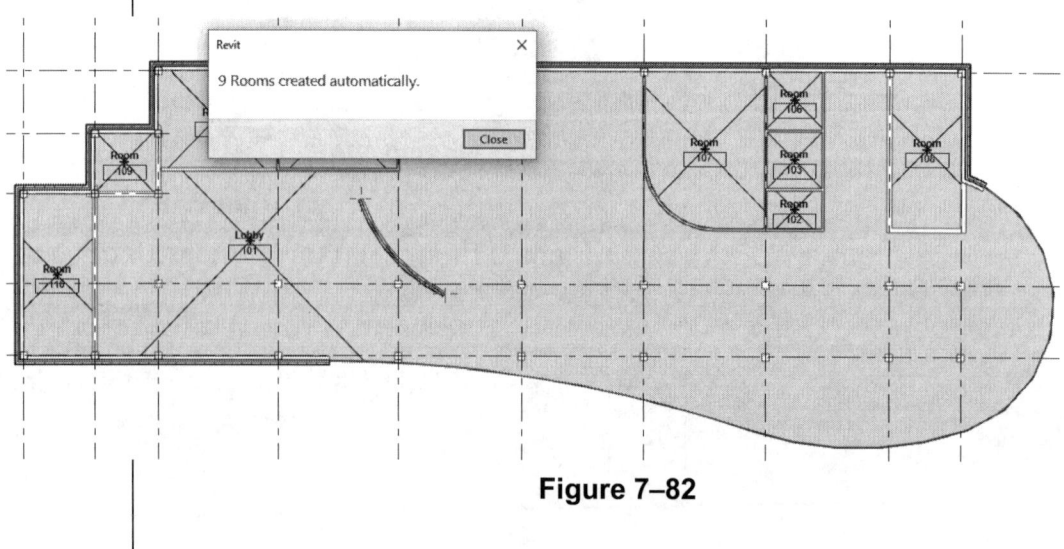

**Figure 7–82**

# Modeling Walls

15. Select the room (the X and not the tag) above the Lobby between grids C and D, as shown in Figure 7–83.

16. In Properties, in the *Identity Data* section, note that the *Number* is automatically incremented. Set the *Name* to **Reception Desk** (as shown in Figure 7–83).

*Your room number might differ from this example.*

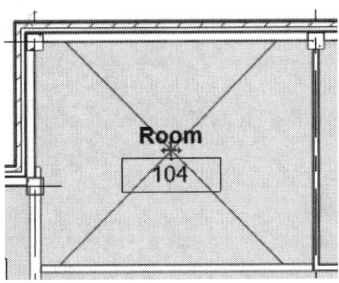

Figure 7–83

17. Click **Apply** or move your cursor into the view window area to see the tag update, as shown in Figure 7–84.

18. Click on the room tag in the room beside the Reception Desk room, and change the name to **Office**, as shown in Figure 7–84.

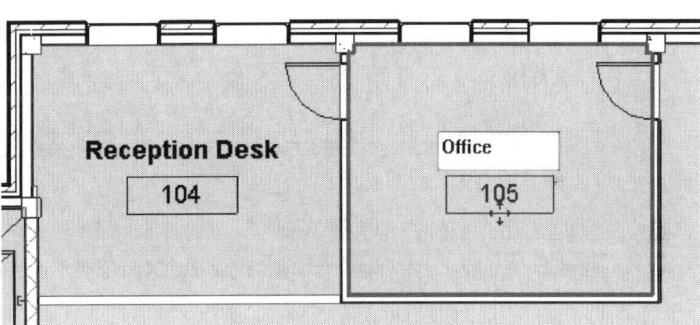

Figure 7–84

19. Rename and renumber the rest of the rooms (shown in Figure 7–85) by selecting the tag and changing the information in the view; alternatively, you can select the room (the X and not the tag) and change the name in Properties.

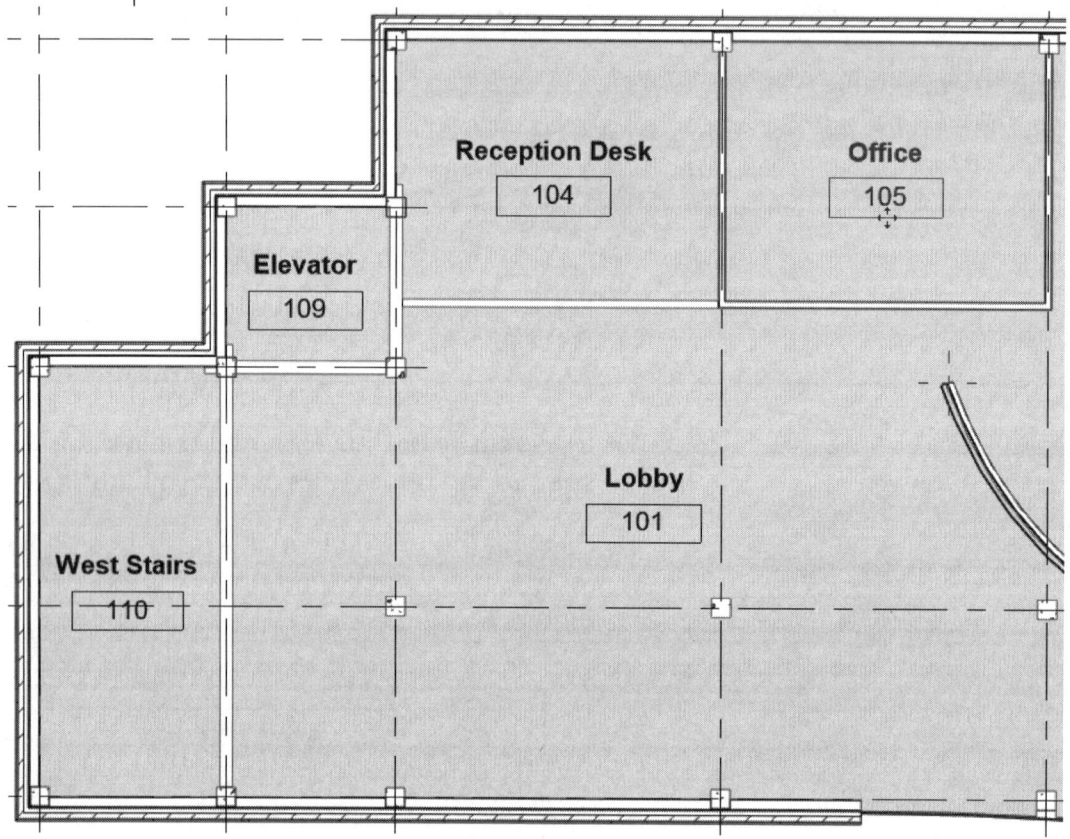

Figure 7–85

20. Pan and zoom over to the east side of the hotel and rename the rooms similar to that shown in Figure 7–86.

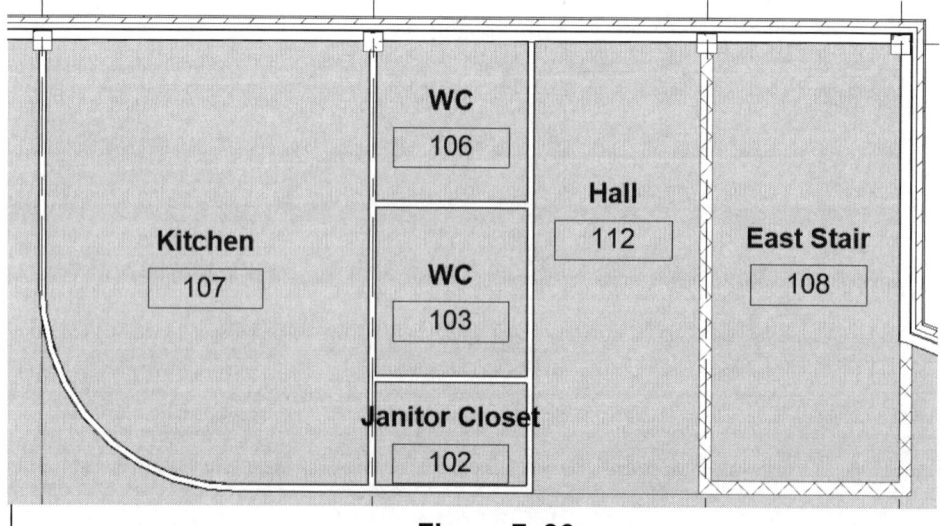

Figure 7–86

21. Note that the janitor closet does not fit inside the room. Select the tag and drag it outside of the room. Note that the room name and number turn to question marks and a warning pops up as shown in Figure 7–87.

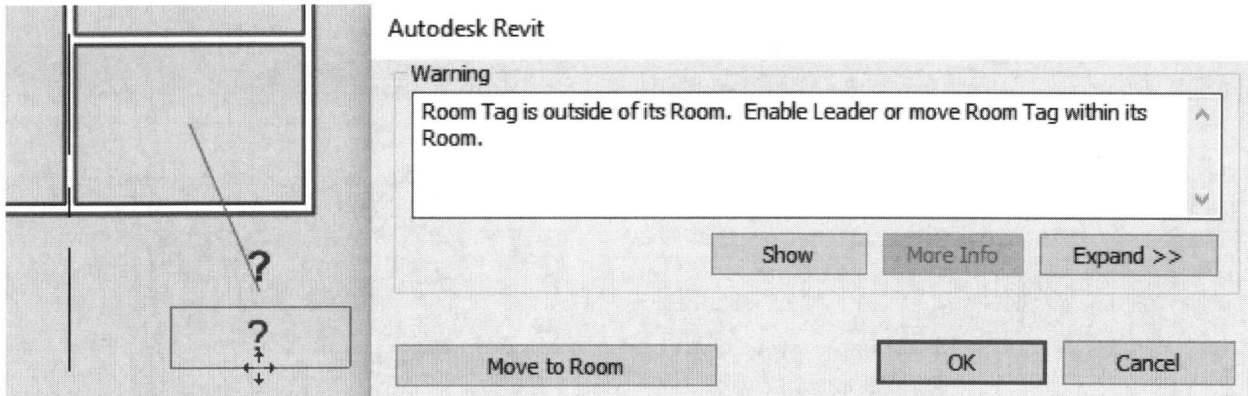

Figure 7–87

22. Read the warning and click **Move to Room**. This puts the tag back into the room.

23. With the tag still selected, in the Options Bar, check **Leader** and drag the tag outside of the room again. Adjust the leader, as needed, using the grips. Figure 7–88 shows the tag now placed outside of the room and the leader indicating which room it belongs to.

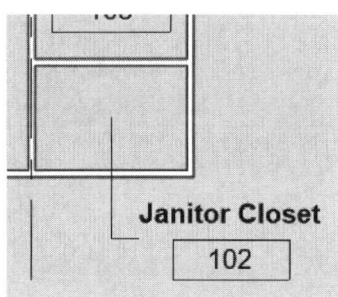

Figure 7–88

24. Save the project.

### Task 2 - Add room separation lines and additional rooms.

In this task, you will separate the breakfast area and hallway from the lobby.

1. In the *Architecture* tab>Room & Area panel, click (Room Separator).

2. Draw room separation lines to separate the breakfast area and hallway from the main lobby, as shown in Figure 7–89.

    - For the breakfast area, draw the separation lines to include the curved slanted wall.

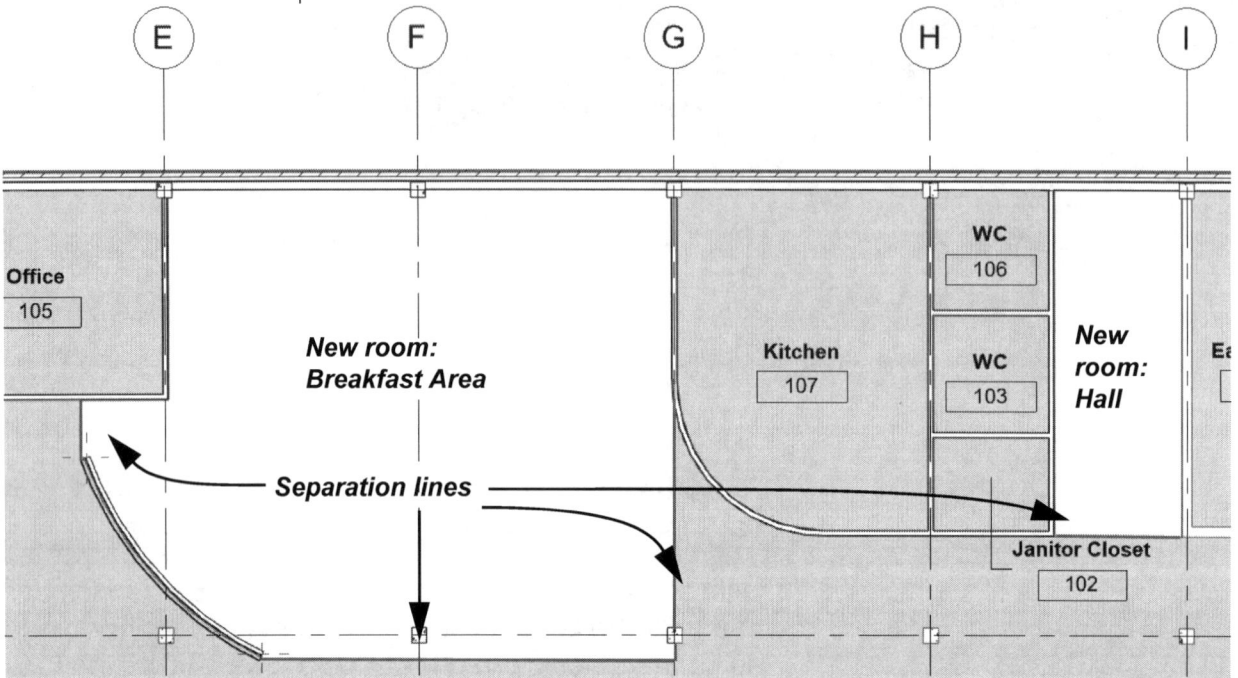

Figure 7–89

3. Start the **Room** command and verify that **Tag on Placement** is on. In Properties, in the *Name* field, type **Breakfast Area**, and then place the room in the location shown in Figure 7–89 above.

4. While still in the **Room** command, in Properties, change the *Name* value to **Hall** and place a room in the hallway shown in Figure 7–89 above.

5. Move tags around, as needed.

6. Type **VV** to open the Visibility/Graphic Overrides dialog box and turn off the **Interior Fill** under *Rooms*.

Modeling Walls

**Task 3 - Add rooms and room tags to Floor 2.**

1. Open **Floor 2** and add rooms and room tags as shown Figure 7–90. Rename the first room **Guest Room** and modify the room number to be **201**.

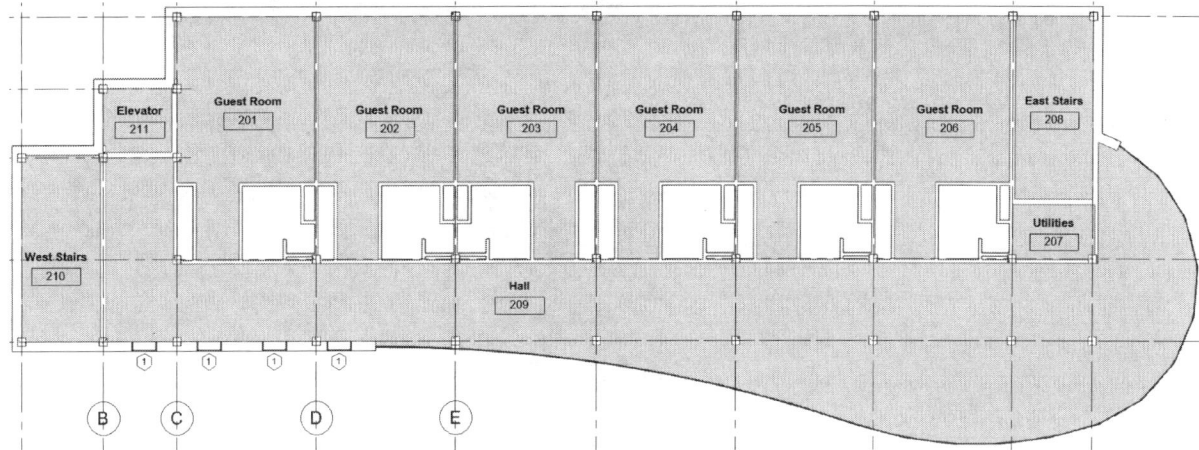

**Figure 7–90**

2. Zoom in to room 201, select the walls for the closet, bathroom, and bathroom closet that are just inside guest room 201.

- Do not select any of the separating walls (as shown in Figure 7–91), such as:

    - The wall that separates the guest rooms from each other
    - The wall that separates the guest room from the hallway
    - The wall that separates the room from the utilities room
    - The walls around the elevator or the walls around the east stairs

3. In Properties, in the *Constraints* section, uncheck **Room Bounding**.

4. Click in an empty space in the view to clear the selection. The entire guest room 201 is now included in the room tag, as shown in Figure 7–91.

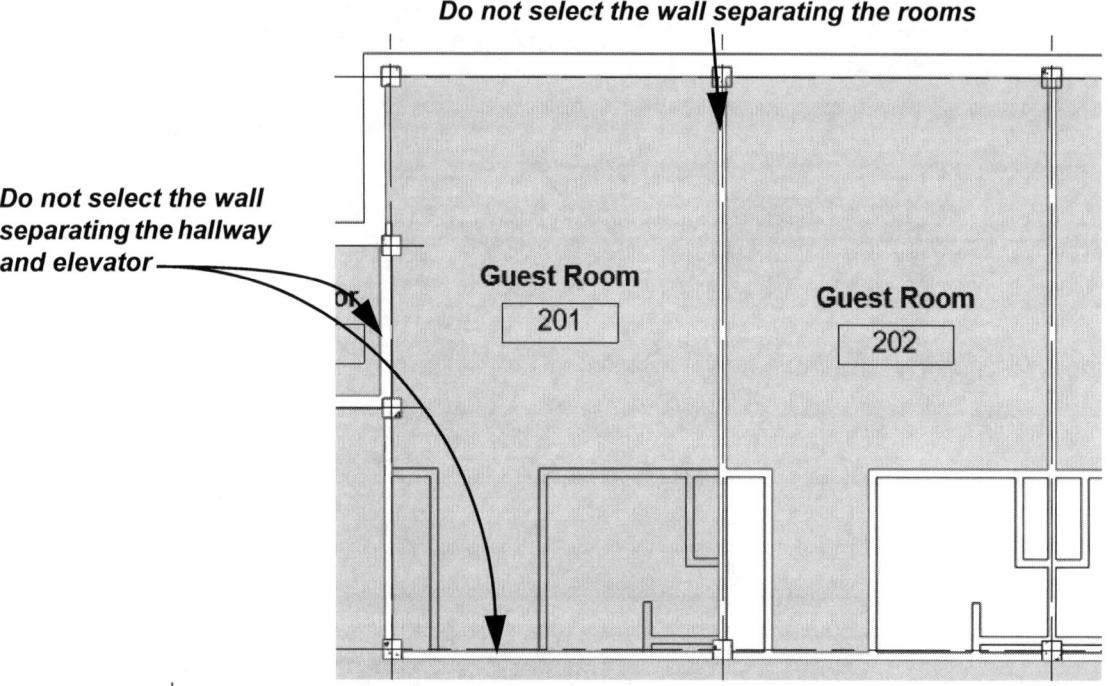

Figure 7–91

5. Save and close the project.

# Chapter Review Questions

1. Where do you specify the height of a wall before you start modeling it?

    a. In the *Modify | Place Wall* tab.

    b. In the Options Bar or Properties.

    c. In the Status Bar.

    d. In the Quick Access Toolbar.

2. Some walls are made from multiple layers of materials, such as brick, block, and drywall, as shown on the bottom in Figure 7–92. If the hatching for these materials is not displayed (as shown at the top in Figure 7–92), how do you change this?

    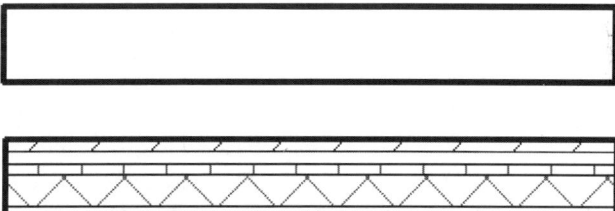

    **Figure 7–92**

    a. Set the *Visual Style* to **Realistic**.

    b. Set the *Detail Level* to **Medium**.

    c. Set the *View Scale* to be higher.

    d. Set the *Phase* to **New**.

3. Which of the following tools enables you to change a wall from one made out of studs and brick to one made out of concrete?

    a. Properties

    b. Change Wall

    c. Type Selector

    d. Edit Wall

4. Match the names for the following controls with the numbers shown in Figure 7–93.

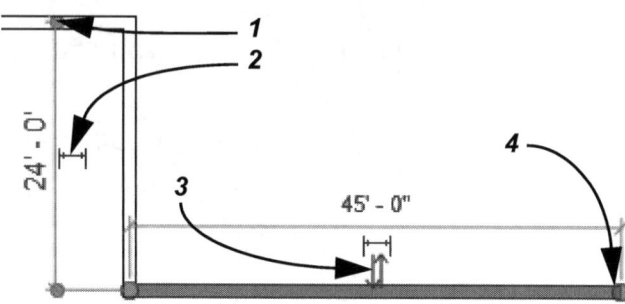

Figure 7–93

| Control | Number |
|---|---|
| Drag wall end | |
| Flip | |
| Move witness line | |
| Make this temporary dimension permanent | |

5. Which of the following are potential differences between the column surround wall and the associated walls, as shown in Figure 7–94? (Select all that apply.)

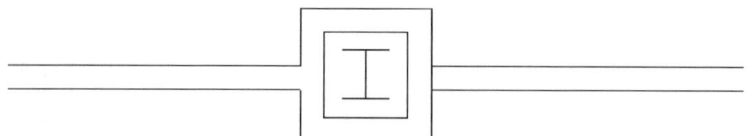

Figure 7–94

a. The column surround and wall on the left are made with the same wall type, while the wall type on the right is a different wall type.

b. The wall on the left has been joined together with the column surround, while the wall on the right was set to **Disallow Join**.

c. The wall on the left was trimmed against the column surround.

d. The wall on the right was extended to the column surround.

6. Which of the following would be true if you changed the top constraint of one wall from an unconnected height to a level?

   a. All walls of that type would also change height.

   b. Only that wall would change height.

   c. You cannot change just one walls height.

7. When you want to add rooms with the same name (as shown in Figure 7–95), you need to modify each one separately.

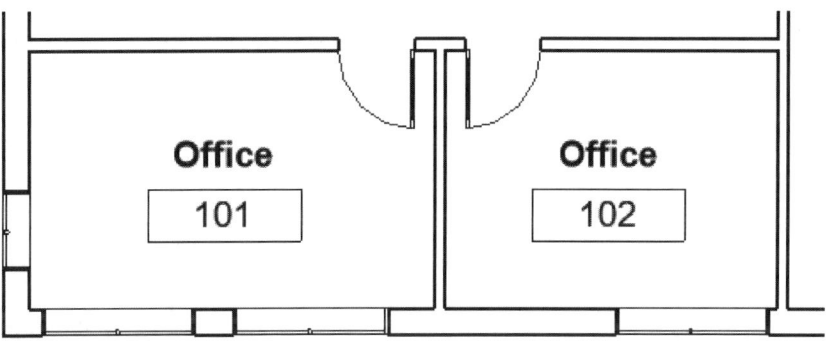

**Figure 7–95**

   a. True

   b. False

# Command Summary

| Button | Command | Location |
|---|---|---|
| | Detail Level: Coarse | • **View Control Bar** |
| | Detail Level: Fine | • **View Control Bar** |
| | Detail Level: Medium | • **View Control Bar** |
| | Edit Profile | • **Ribbon:** (when a wall is selected) *Modify | Walls* tab>Mode panel |
| | Match Type | • **Ribbon:** *Modify* tab>Clipboard panel<br>• **Shortcut:** MA |
| | Properties | • **Ribbon:** *Modify* tab>Properties panel<br>• **Shortcut:** PP |
| N/A | Type Selector | • **Properties palette**<br>• **Ribbon:** *Modify* tab (*Optional*)<br>• **Quick Access Toolbar** (*Optional*) |
| | Wall | • **Ribbon:** *Architecture* tab>Build panel |
| | Wall Opening | • **Ribbon:** *Architecture* tab>Opening panel |
| | Room | • **Ribbon:** *Architecture* tab>Room & Area panel<br>• **Shortcut:** RM |
| | Room Separator | • **Ribbon:** *Architecture* tab>Room & Area panel |

# Chapter 8

# Working with Doors and Windows

Doors and windows are host elements that are placed in walls. There are many different types of doors and windows available in the Revit® libraries, and you can easily create additional sizes of the types that come with the software to meet your design requirements.

## Learning Objectives in This Chapter

- Insert doors and windows in walls.
- Modify door and window locations and properties that can be referenced in schedules.
- Load additional door and window types from the Revit Library.
- Create additional door and window sizes of a selected type.

## 8.1 About Doors and Windows

Doors and windows in Revit are designed to be hosted by walls. You can use temporary dimensions (as shown in Figure 8–1) as well as alignment lines and snaps to help place the openings exactly where you need them in the walls.

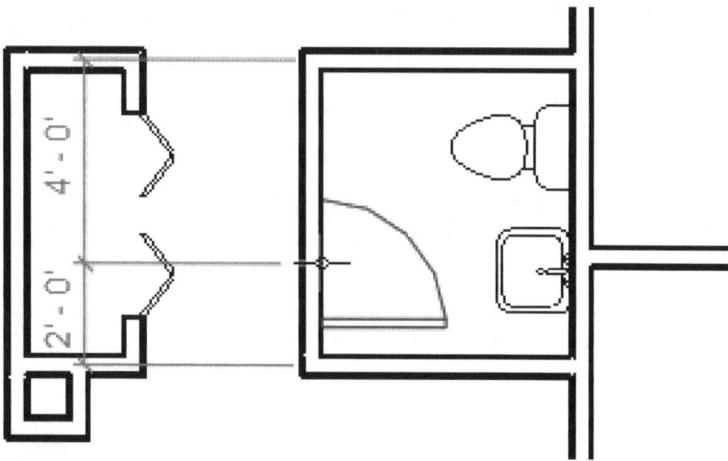

Figure 8–1

- You can add doors and windows in slanted and tapered walls.

### How To: Add a Door or Window

1. In the *Architecture* tab>Build panel, click  (Door) or  (Window). The keyboard shortcuts are **DR** for doors and **WN** for windows.

2. To insert a tag with each door or window, verify that  (Tag on Placement) is toggled on. You can specify the tag options using the Options Bar, as shown in Figure 8–2.

Figure 8–2

3. In the Type Selector, select the type of door or window.
4. Hover over the wall that you want to place the door or window. Use the temporary dimensions and/or other drawing aids to properly locate where you want the door.
   - Press <Spacebar> to change the swing of the door before placing it.
5. Select the wall once you are in the correct location to place the door or window.

6. Continue adding other doors or windows as needed.

- While placing or modifying doors or windows, you can adjust the element using temporary dimensions and the **Flip the instance facing** and **Flip the instance hand** controls to change the swing and hinge locations, as shown in Figure 8–3. With windows, you can flip the interior and exterior using the same technique.

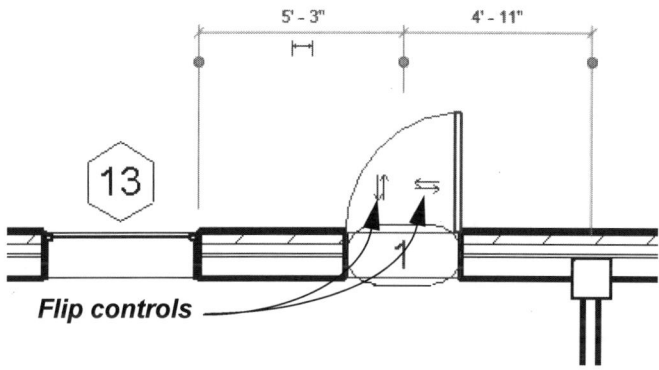

Figure 8–3

- If you are including window tags, select a point close to the outside of the wall when inserting the window so that the tag is placed on the outside.

- To move a door or window tag, select the tag. A control displays, as shown in Figure 8–4, which enables you to drag the tag to a new location.

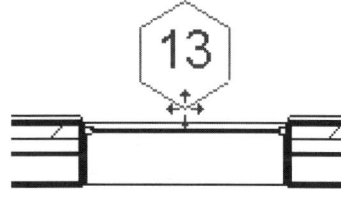

Figure 8–4

## Modifying Door and Window Properties

The door or window types control most of their properties. To change the property information, you change the type in the Type Selector. You can also change Instance Parameters (as shown in Figure 8–5) that impact the specific door or window in the associated schedule. Instance Parameters include things such as the *Swing Angle, Masonry, Drywall Frame*, etc.

*The exact properties vary according to the door or window selected.*

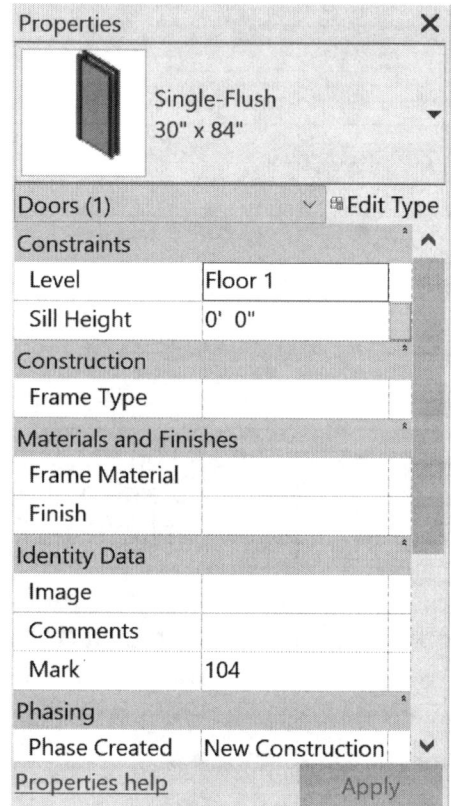

Figure 8–5

If a door or window has been inserted into a slanted wall, you have the option to select the door in the view, and modify the Orientation to either **Vertical** or **Slanted**, as shown in Figure 8–6.

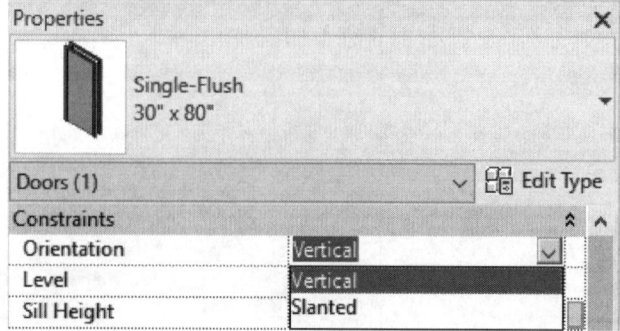

Figure 8–6

# Working with Doors and Windows

If a door or window has been inserted into a tapered wall, you can select the door in the view and set the *Orientation* to **Vertical**, **Slant along exterior**, or **Slant along interior**, as shown in Figure 8–7.

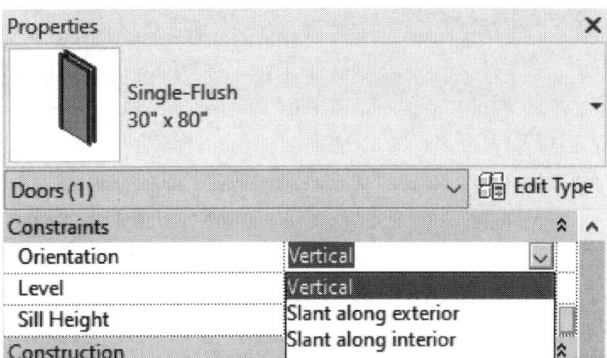

Figure 8–7

### Hint: Copying Elements to Levels

The standard Windows commands ✂ (Cut or <Ctrl>+<X>), 📋 (Copy To Clipboard or <Ctrl>+<C>), and 📋 (Paste From Clipboard or <Ctrl>+<V>) work in Revit just as they do in other Windows-compatible software. They are available in the *Modify* tab>Clipboard panel, but not in the shortcut menu.

In the software, you can also paste elements aligned to various views or levels, as shown in Figure 8–8.

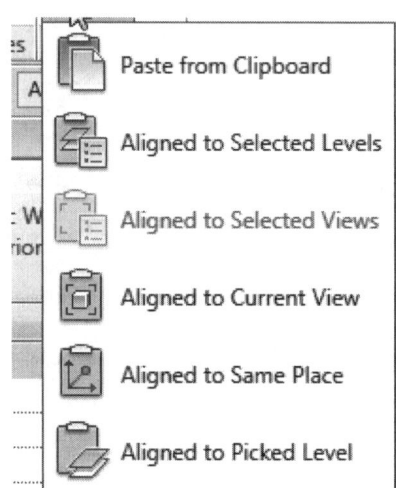

Figure 8–8

- **Aligned to Selected Levels:** Opens a dialog box where you can select the level to which you want to copy. This enables you to copy items on one level and paste them to the same location on another level (e.g., windows in a high-rise building).

- **Aligned to Selected Views:** Copies view-specific elements (such as text or dimensions) into a view that you select in a dialog box. Only the Floor Plan or Reflected Ceiling Plan views are available.

- **Aligned to Current View:** Pastes elements copied in one view to the same location in another view.

- **Aligned to Same Place:** Pastes elements to the same location in the same view.

- **Aligned to Picked Level:** Pastes elements to the level you select in an elevation or section view.

# Working with Doors and Windows

**Hint: Transferring Project Standards**

Some elements (such as wall types) are not accessible from a specific library. However, you can copy them from other projects.

- Transferring project standards does not transfer loadable families like custom families or families from the Revit Library.

1. Open the project from which you want to copy information.
2. Open the project to which you want to copy the information.
3. In the *Manage* tab>Settings panel, click (Transfer Project Standards).
4. In the Select Items To Copy dialog box, select an option in the Copy from drop-down list and then select the settings you want to copy into the current file, as shown in Figure 8–9. Click **OK**.

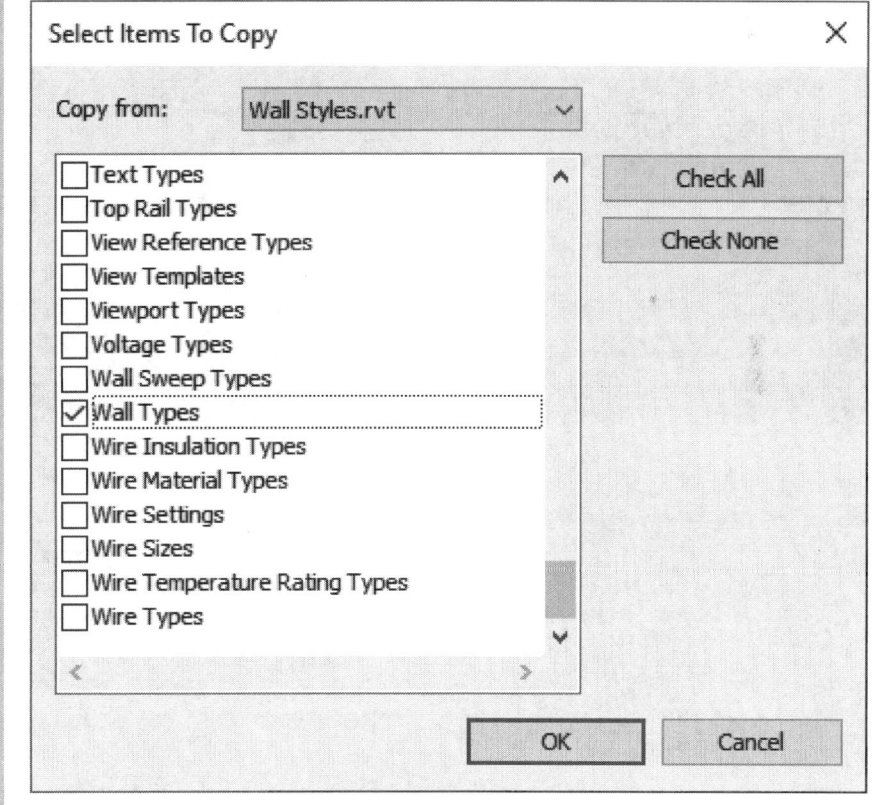

Figure 8–9

5. In the Duplicate Types dialog box, click either **Overwrite** or **New Only** to apply the settings to the current project.

# 8.2 Creating Additional Door and Window Sizes

You can easily add additional sizes to existing families of doors or windows that have been loaded into a project. To do this, you create a new type of the needed size based on an existing type, as shown in Figure 8–10.

*You can specify materials for door and window sub-elements in the Type Properties.*

*The parameters might be different depending on the door or window you selected.*

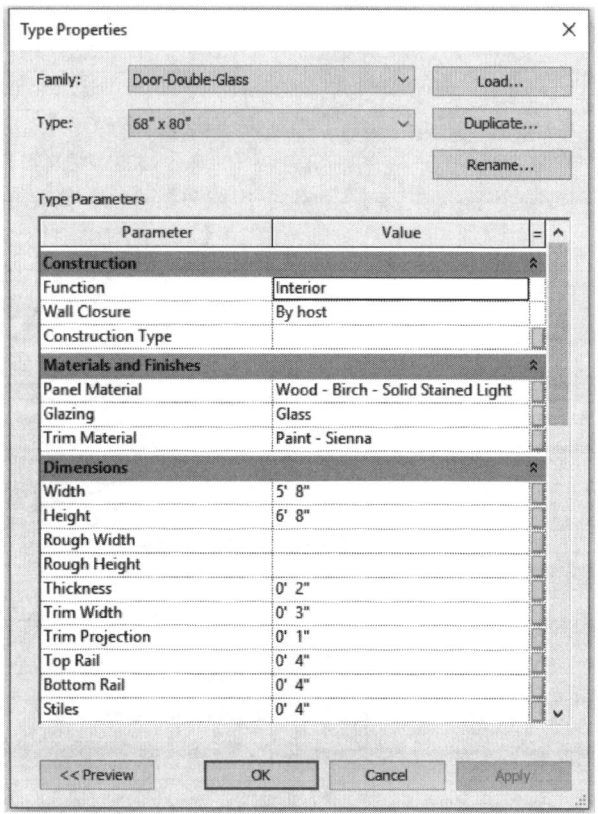

Figure 8–10

## How To: Create Additional Door and Window Sizes

1. Start the **Door** or **Window** command.
2. In the Type Selector, select the type you want to modify. In Properties, click ▦ (Edit Type) or in the *Modify* tab> Properties panel, click ▦ (Type Properties).
3. In the Type Properties dialog box, click **Duplicate**.
4. Type a new name for the element and click **OK**.
5. In the Type Properties dialog box, change the *Height* and *Width* parameters to match the size.
6. Click **OK** to close the dialog box. The new window or door type is now available for use.

# Practice 8a    Adding Doors and Windows

**Practice Objectives**

- Add doors and windows.
- Copy elements to multiple levels.
- Load door types.
- Duplicate and modify a door type.

In this practice, you will add doors and windows to a model, as shown for Floor 1 in Figure 8–11. You will use controls and temporary dimensions to help you place the doors and windows. You will also copy windows to multiple levels. you will load specialty door types used in the guest rooms, create a new door size, and add doors to the second floor

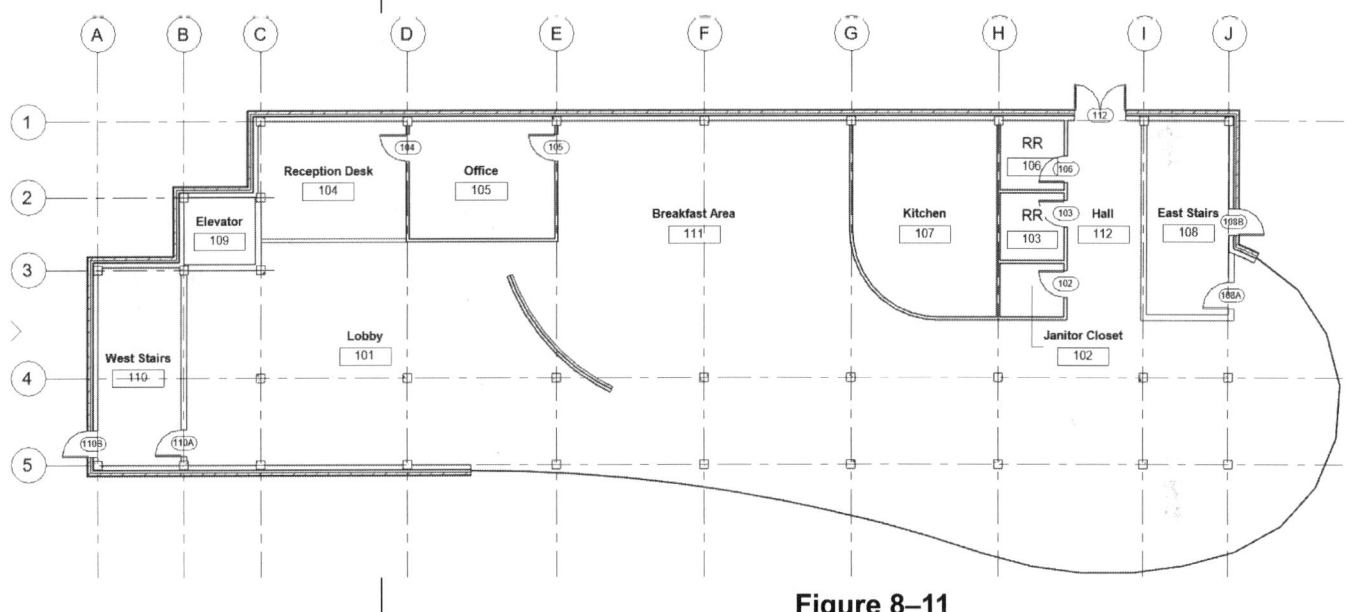

Figure 8–11

## Task 1 - Add doors.

1. Open the project **Hotel-Doors.rvt** from the practice files folder.

2. Open the **Floor Plans: Floor 1** view.

3. Pan and zoom over to the west stairs.

4. In the *Architecture* tab>Build panel, click (Door), or type **DR**.

5. In the Type Selector, select **Door-Single-Panel: 36" x 80"**.

6. In the *Modify | Place Door* tab>Tag panel, verify that (Tag on Placement) is on.

7. Using the linked CAD file as a guide, place the door near the lower corner of the building at grid A5, as shown in Figure 8–12. Use the flip arrows to make it swing in the right direction and use temporary dimensions to place it **3'** from the face of the wall. Click the tag and change the number to **101**.

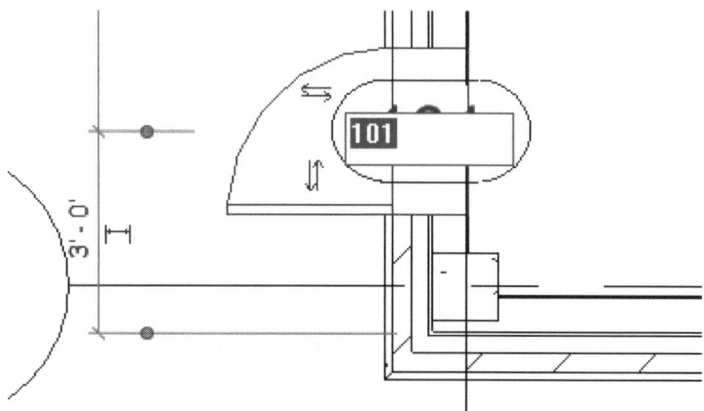

**Figure 8–12**

8. Continue adding single panel doors in the project, similar to the locations shown in Figure 8–13. Use the same door type. The tag number automatically increments.

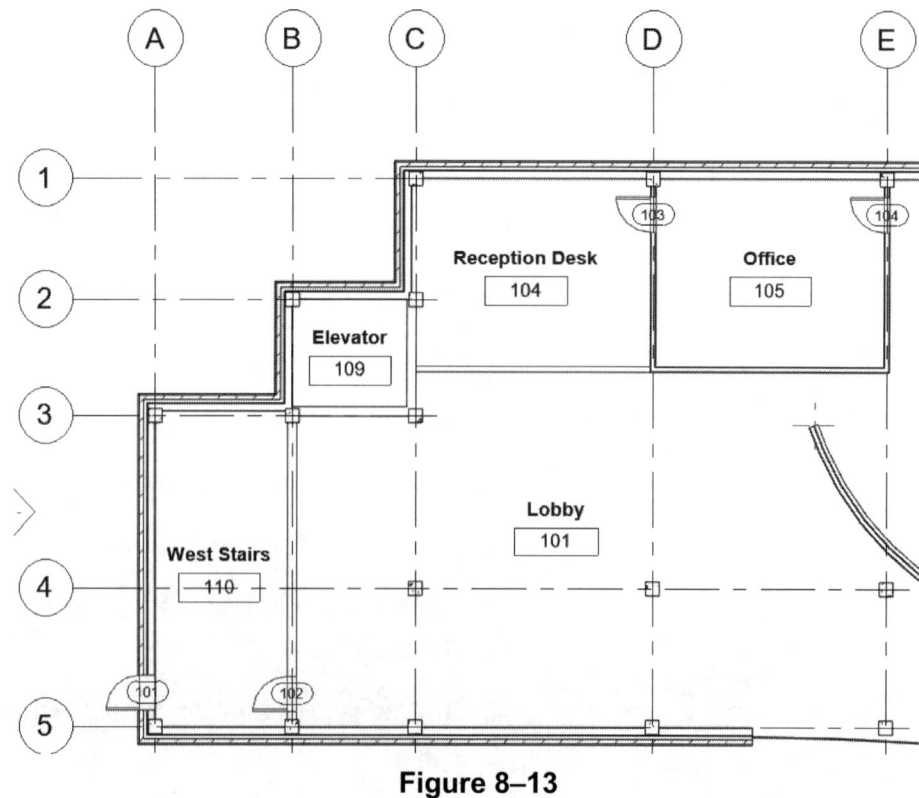

**Figure 8–13**

# Working with Doors and Windows

9. Zoom and pan over to the east stairs and place the **Door-Single-Panel: 36" x 80"** doors in the rooms, as shown in Figure 8–14. (Your numbering may differ from that in the figure below based on the sequence in which you placed the doors.)

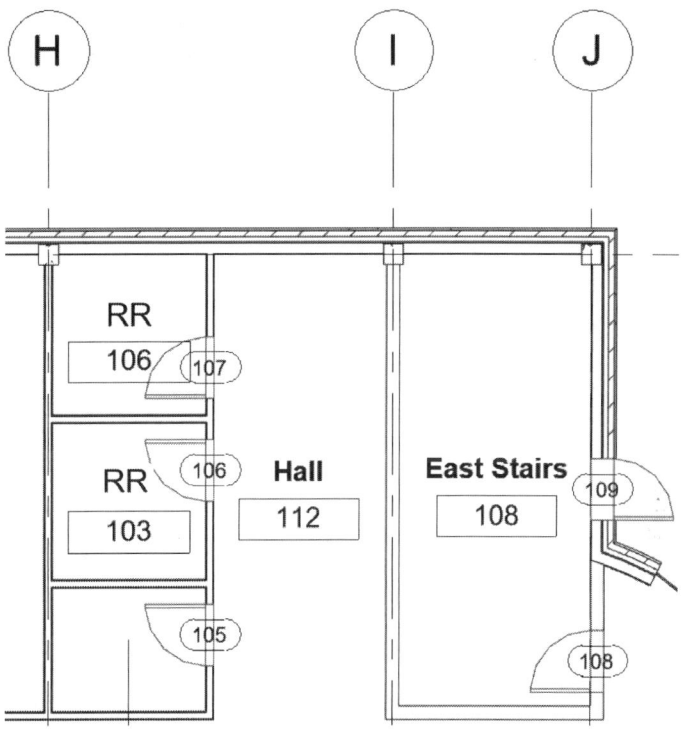

**Figure 8–14**

10. Still in the **Door** command, in the Type Selector, select **Door-Double-Glass: 72" x 84"**.

11. Place the door at the end of the hallway between grids H and I.

12. Zoom out to see the full floor plan.

13. Click ⌃ (Modify).

14. Select the two sets of stairwell doors (the two doors in the west and east stairwells).

    - If you select multiple categories, use ▽ (Filter) to help select only the doors.

15. In the Type Selector, select **Single-Flush Vision: 36" x 84"**.

16. Click in an empty space in the view to clear the selection.

17. (Optional) You can modify the door numbers to match the room numbers similar to the pattern shown in Figure 8–15, or using your office standard if you have one.

    - You may get a warning telling you that elements have duplicate mark values, just ignore it and keep renumbering all the door tags on Floor 1 to match their room number. For the stairwells' two doors, change them to the same number as their stairwell but add an A and B after it.

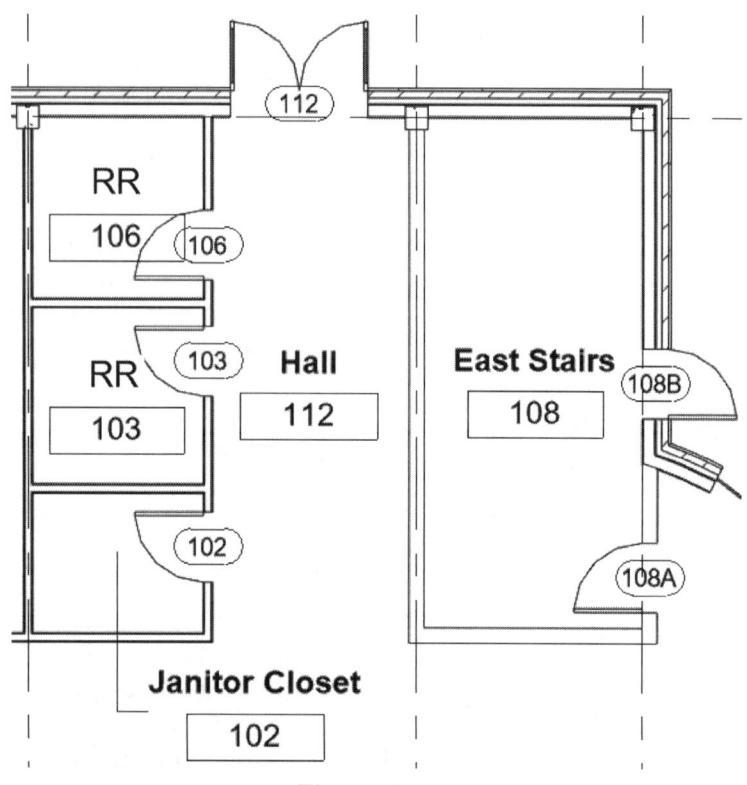

**Figure 8–15**

18. Save the project.

### Task 2 - Load door types.

1. Activate the **Floor Plans: Floor 1** view and zoom in on the kitchen area.

2. In the *Architecture* tab>Build panel, click (Door).

3. In the *Modify | Place Door* tab>Mode panel, click (Load Family).

4. In the Load Family dialog box, navigate to the practice files *Families>Doors* folder and select **Door-Double-Flush_Panel-Double-Acting.rfa**. Click **Open**.

Working with Doors and Windows

5. In the Specify Types dialog box, select **72" x 80"** from the *Type* list, as shown in Figure 8–16, and click **OK**.

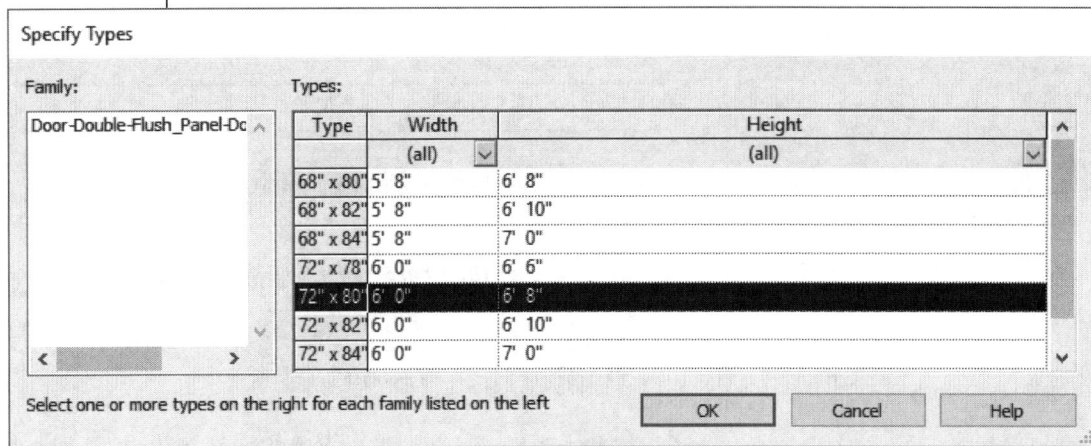

Figure 8–16

6. Start the **Load Family** command again. (Hint: Press <Enter> to repeat the last command.)

7. In the Load Family dialog box, navigate to the practice files *Families>Doors* folder and select **Single-Panel 4.rfa**. Click **Open**.

8. In the Specify Types dialog box, scroll down the *Type* list, select **36" x 80"**, and click **OK**.

9. In the Type Selector, select **Door-Double-Flush_Panel-Double-Acting: 72" x 80"** and place an instance of it in the wall between the kitchen and dining area, as shown in Figure 8–17.

10. If needed, change the door tag to match the kitchen's room number, as shown in Figure 8–17.

*The order the doors are placed will determine the door tag number.*

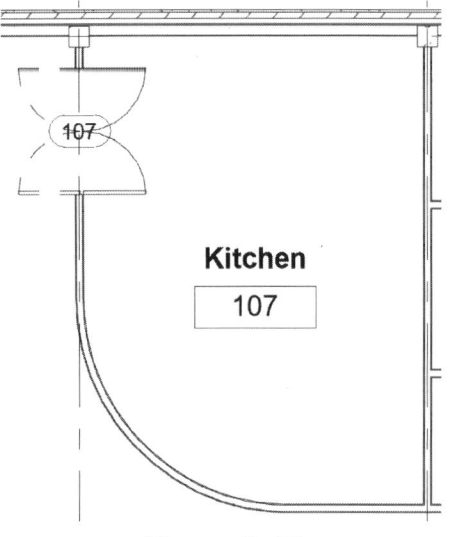

Figure 8–17

11. Click ▸ (Modify).

12. Zoom to the extents of the view and save the project.

### Task 3 - Add doors to Floor 2.

1. Open the **Floor Plans: Floor 2** view.

2. In the *Architecture* tab>Build panel, click  (Door).

3. In the Type Selector, change the door type to **Single-Flush-Vision: 36" x 84"**.

4. Place the first door in the lower left west stairs (as shown in the linked file) and change the tag number to 210 to match the room tag number.

5. Add another door of the same type to the other east stairs at the opposite end of the building and modify the door tag to match the room tag number.

6. Still in the **Door** command, pan over to the first guest room next to the west stairs.

7. In the Type Selector, change the door type to **Single-Panel 4: 36" x 80"** and place a door at the entrance of Guest Room 201. Change the door number to **201**.

*Press <Spacebar> to flip the door swing.*

8. Continue placing doors at the entrance of each guest room and the utilities room, allowing the numbers to increment.

9. Use the same type to add doors to the bathrooms and bathroom closets. This door size is too large for the bathroom closet door but you will modify it later.

10. Continue adding other doors using different door styles (e.g., **Bifold-4 Panel 72" x 84"** for the closets and **Double-Glass 72" x 84"** for the balconies). The rooms should look similar to the layout shown in Figure 8–18, though the numbering might be different.

# Working with Doors and Windows

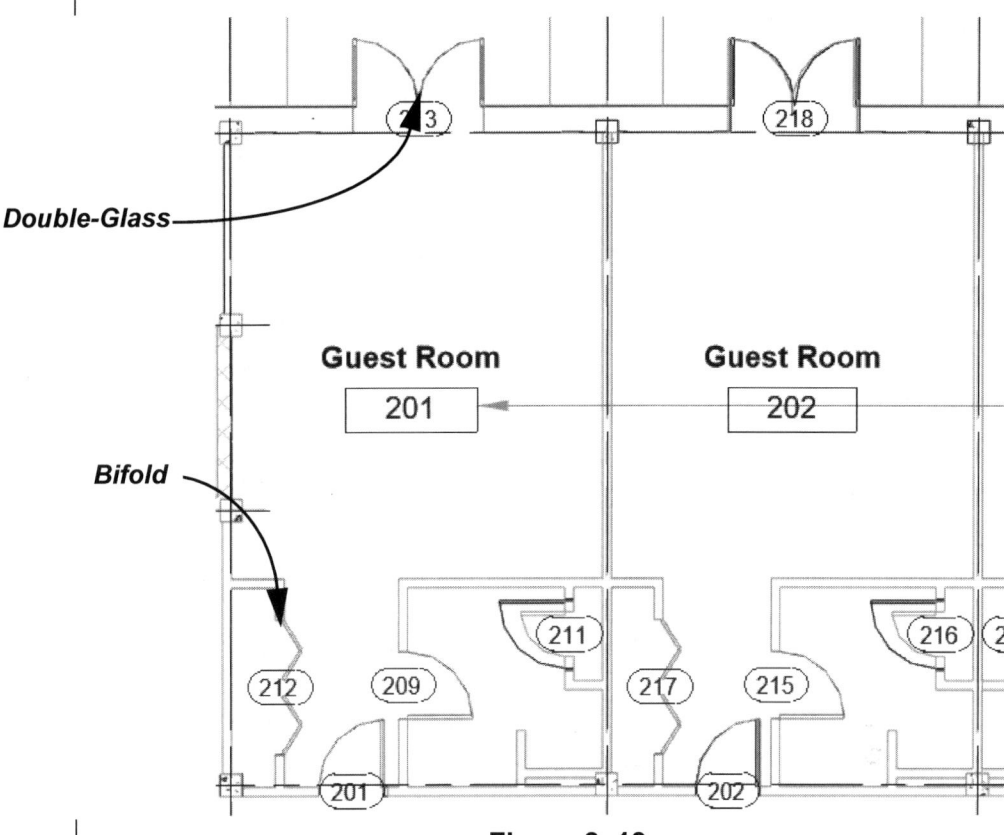

Figure 8–18

11. Click ▷ (Modify).

12. Renumber the doors in the guest rooms based on the room number if you have time (e.g., the doors in room 201 would become 201A, 201B, 201C, and 201D).

13. Save the project.

## Task 4 - Create a new door size.

1. Select one of the bathroom closet doors.

2. In Properties, click ⊞ (Edit Type).

3. In the Type Properties dialog box, change the *Family* to **Single-Panel 4**, as shown in Figure 8–19, and click **Duplicate...**.

Figure 8–19

*Hint: You can type either **2** or **24"**, but you must add the **"** symbol to the value if you are using inches.*

4. In the Name dialog box, type **24" x 80"** and click **OK**.
5. In the *Dimensions* section, change the *Width* value to **2'-0"**.
6. Click **OK** to close the dialog box.
7. Select the bathroom closet doors and change the type to the new door size.

### Task 5 - Add windows to Floor 2.

1. Open the **Floor Plans: Floor 2** view.
2. The linked CAD file is still displayed in this view. Select it and, in Properties, set the *Draw Layer* to **Background**.
3. In the *Architecture* tab>Build panel, click  (Window).
4. In the *Modify | Place Window* tab>Tag panel, verify that  (Tag on Placement) is toggled on.
5. In the Type Selector, select **Casement 3x3 with Trim: 48" x 48"**.
6. Add the window close to the West Stairs and grid B, as shown in Figure 8–20. (For clarity, grid bubbles are turned on in the figure.)
7. Click  (Modify) and select the window. You might need to drag the witness line grip over to the gridline so that it references the grid, as shown in Figure 8–20, rather than a wall.
8. Use temporary dimensions to move the window **5'-0"** from grid line B, as shown in Figure 8–20.

# Working with Doors and Windows

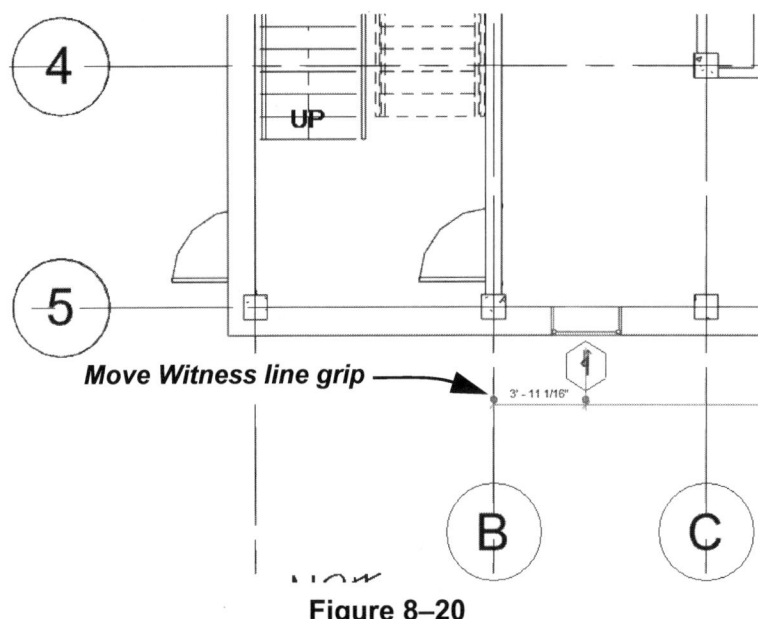

Figure 8–20

9. Click (Modify) and select the window and the window tag.

10. In the *Modify | Windows* tab>Modify panel, click (Copy).

11. In the Options Bar, select **Multiple**.

12. Select a point on the window as the move start point.

*Revit interprets 8 as 8'-0".*

13. Move the cursor to the right and type **8** for the distance. Move the cursor past the new window to the right and type **8** again. Move the cursor over one last time and type **8**, as shown in Figure 8–21. Four evenly spaced windows are created.

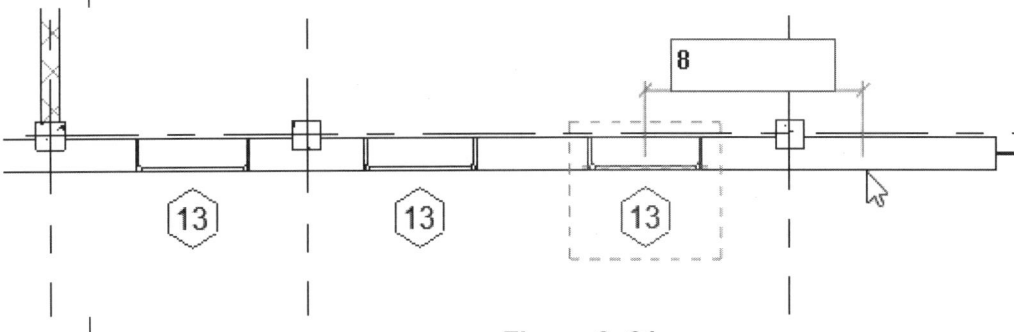

Figure 8–21

14. Click (Modify).

15. Select the linked DWG. In Properties, set the *Draw Layer* to **Foreground**. Zoom in to the group of windows and use the **Align** or **Move** tool to get the windows into the correct position.

16. Click ▸ (Modify).

17. Save the project.

**Task 6 - Copy windows to multiple levels.**

1. Open the 3D view and verify that the front of the building where the windows are located is displayed as shown in Figure 8–22. Change the visual style to **Consistent Colors**, if needed.

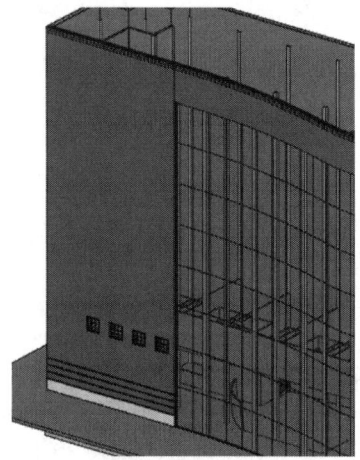

Figure 8–22

2. Select all four windows by holding <Ctrl> and selecting each one.

3. In the *Modify | Windows* tab>Clipboard panel, click ▸ (Copy to Clipboard).

4. In the Clipboard panel, expand ▸ (Paste) and click ▸ (Aligned to Selected Levels).

5. In the Select Levels dialog box, select the floors between and including **Floor 3** and **Floor 8**, as shown in Figure 8–23.

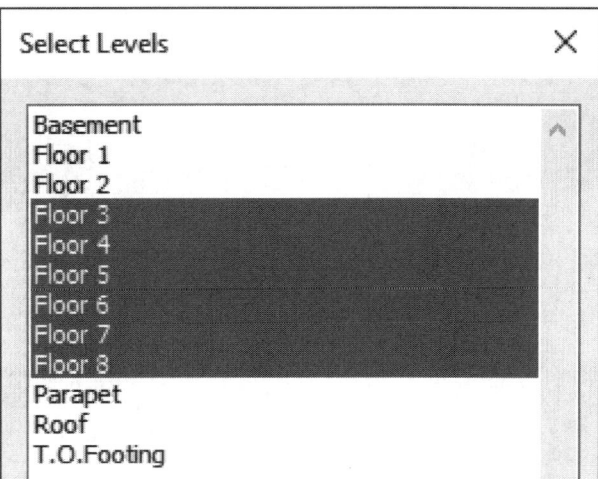

Figure 8–23

6. Click **OK**. The windows are copied up the side of the building, as shown in Figure 8–24.

*Additional doors and windows will be placed using storefront curtain walls in the next chapter.*

Figure 8–24

7. Save and close the project.

# Chapter Review Questions

1. How do you change the swing direction of a door, as shown in Figure 8–25? (Select all that apply.)

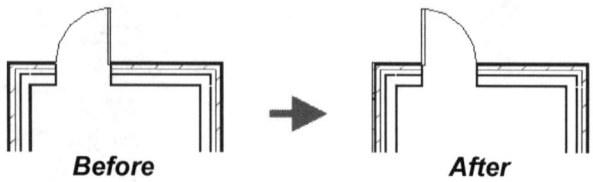

Figure 8–25

   a. When placing the door, press <Spacebar>.
   b. When placing the door, right-click and select **Change Swing**.
   c. Select an existing door and select the flip arrows.
   d. Select an existing door, right-click and select **Change Swing**.

2. How do you add additional window or door families to a project?

   a. Find the window or door family using Windows Explorer, right-click, and select **Import into Revit Project**.
   b. Import them from the Window or Door Catalog.
   c. Load them from the Revit Library.
   d. Use the Window/Door tool to create new families.

3. How do you include a tag with a door or window, as shown in Figure 8–26?

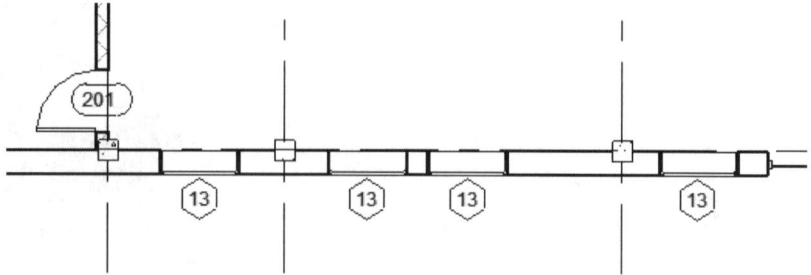

Figure 8–26

   a. Select a door or window family that includes a tag.
   b. Select the Tag box in the Options Bar before placing the door or window.
   c. Tags can only be used after placing the door or window.
   d. Select **Tag on Placement** in the contextual tab.

4. Where are the door and window sizes stored?

    a. In Properties

    b. In Type Properties

    c. In Door/ Window Settings

    d. In the template file

5. How do you create additional door or window sizes, as shown in Figure 8–27?

Figure 8–27

   a. Select the required door or window and use the Size tool to specify a new size.

   b. In Properties, select the required door or window and click **Edit Type**, then select **Duplicate** and modify it.

   c. Find the existing door or window family in the Project Browser, right-click, and select **New Size**.

   d. Select the door or window in the view and edit it using size controls to the needed size.

# Command Summary

| Button | Command | Location |
|---|---|---|
| **Clipboard** | | |
| | Copy to Clipboard | • **Ribbon:** *Modify* tab>Clipboard panel<br>• **Shortcut:** <Ctrl>+<C> |
| | Cut to the Clipboard | • **Ribbon:** *Modify* tab>Clipboard panel<br>• **Shortcut:** <Ctrl>+<X> |
| | Paste - Aligned to Current View | • **Ribbon:** *Modify* tab>Clipboard panel> expand Paste |
| | Paste - Aligned to Same Place | • **Ribbon:** *Modify* tab>Clipboard panel> expand Paste |
| | Paste - Aligned to Selected Levels | • **Ribbon:** *Modify* tab>Clipboard panel> expand Paste |
| | Paste - Aligned to Selected Views | • **Ribbon:** *Modify* tab>Clipboard panel> expand Paste |
| | Paste - Aligned to Picked Level | • **Ribbon:** *Modify* tab>Clipboard panel> expand Paste |
| | Paste from Clipboard | • **Ribbon:** *Modify* tab>Clipboard panel<br>• **Shortcut:** <Ctrl>+<V> |
| **Doors and Windows** | | |
| | Door | • **Ribbon:** *Architecture* tab>Build panel<br>• **Shortcut:** DR |
| | Edit Type/ Type Properties | • **Properties palette:** Edit Type<br>• **Ribbon:** *Modify* tab>Properties panel |
| | Measure | • **Quick Access Toolbar**<br>• **Ribbon:** *Modify* tab>Measure panel |
| | Window | • **Ribbon:** *Architecture* tab>Build panel<br>• **Shortcut:** WN |

# Chapter 9

# Working with Curtain Walls

Curtain walls are often used to create complex windows and storefronts. Curtain walls are created based on a curtain wall type to which additional curtain wall grids and mullions can be added and individual panels swapped out to create the needed pattern.

## Learning Objectives in This Chapter

- Create basic curtain walls and storefronts using curtain wall types.
- Modify the curtain wall grid pattern.
- Switch out curtain wall panels with other panel types, doors, or windows.
- Add mullions to curtain wall grids.

# 9.1 Creating Curtain Walls

Curtain walls are non-bearing walls consisting of panels laid out in a grid pattern. They can encase an entire building like a membrane or, as shown in Figure 9–1, fill a cutout in a standard wall, often called a storefront.

Figure 9–1

- You can create slanted curtain walls but not tapered.

## How To: Create a Curtain Wall

1. In a plan view, model a wall using a curtain wall type.
2. In an elevation or 3D view, add curtain wall grids to the curtain wall.
3. Modify the panels of the curtain wall.
4. Add mullions to separate the panels.

The components of a curtain wall are shown in Figure 9–2.

*Panels can be a specific material (such as glass or stone) or can incorporate doors, windows, or other wall types.*

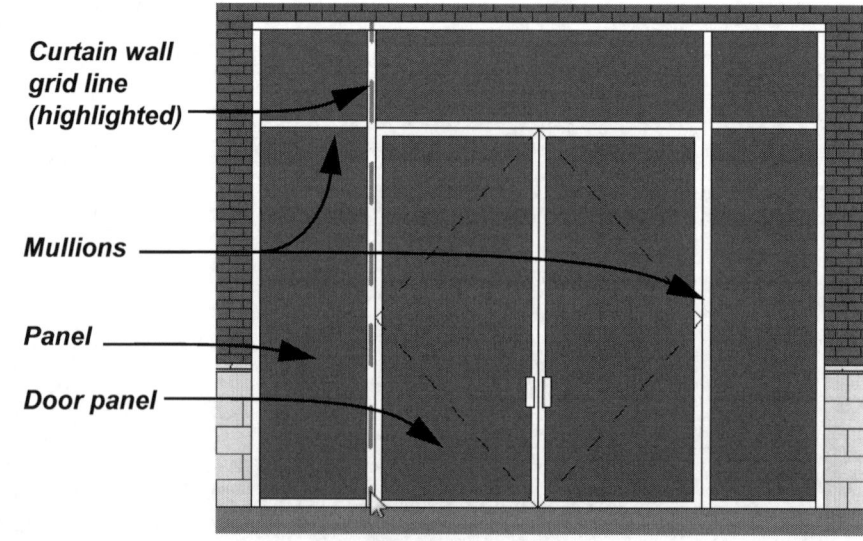

Figure 9–2

- The simplest way to create a curtain wall is to use a curtain wall type with a preset uniform curtain wall grid already applied to it, such as the three types that come with the software, as shown in Figure 9–3.

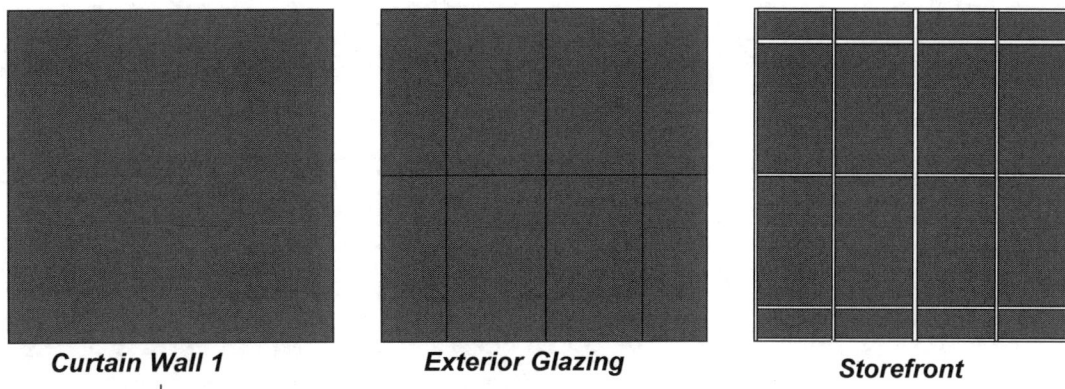

**Curtain Wall 1**  **Exterior Glazing**  **Storefront**

Figure 9–3

- Many curtain walls do not have a uniform pattern of exact distances between curtain wall grids, as shown in Figure 9–4. Therefore, you need to create these designs directly on the curtain wall. You can start with a curtain wall type that has a basic uniform curtain wall grid, if applicable.

Figure 9–4

- For more information on creating curtain wall types, see *A.5 Creating Curtain Wall Types with Automatic Grids*.

Some curtain walls are embedded into other walls, as shown in Figure 9–5. They can also be used to create what looks like a complex set of windows. The **Storefront** curtain wall type is designed to be embedded in another wall.

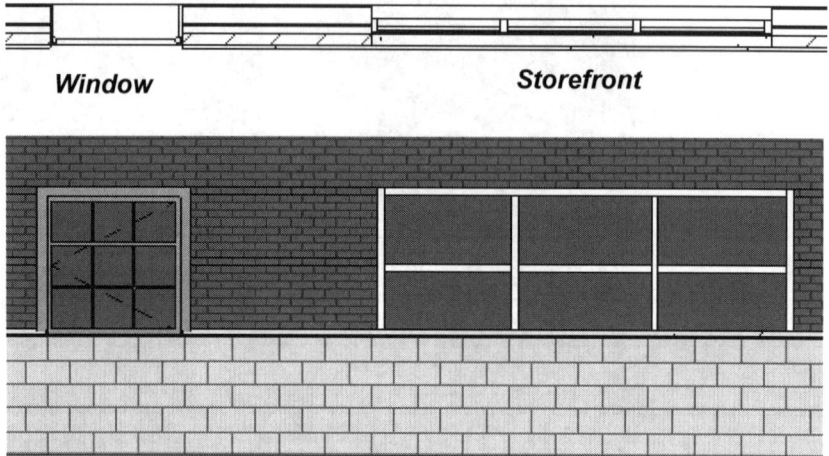

Figure 9–5

## How To: Add a Storefront Wall in an Existing Wall

1. In the *Architecture* tab>Build panel, click  (Wall).
2. In the Type Selector, select **Curtain Wall: Storefront**. In Properties, set the *Base Constraint, Top Constraint*, and *Offsets* as needed. The height can be less than the height of the wall in which you are embedding.
3. Select a point on the existing wall, as shown in Figure 9–6.

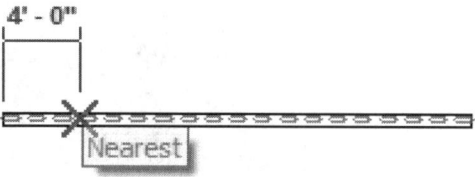

Figure 9–6

4. Select the second point along the wall. (Hint: Press <Tab> to cycle from the default Horizontal and Nearest snap to the dynamic dimension and then type the distance for the embedded curtain wall.) The wall displays, as shown in Figure 9–7.

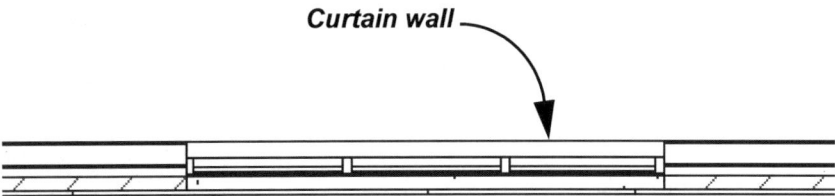

Figure 9–7

5. Open the appropriate elevation view. Select the outside edge of the curtain wall and use the shape handles and dynamic dimensions to modify the size of the storefront, as shown in Figure 9–8.

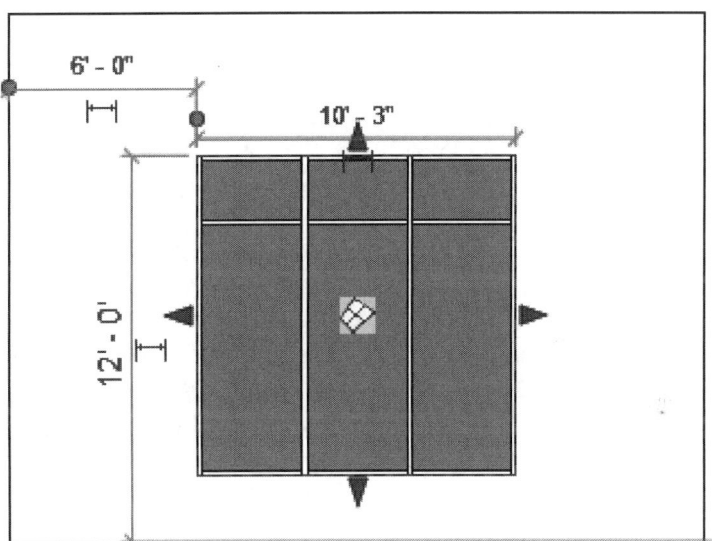

Figure 9–8

# 9.2 Adding Curtain Wall Grids

Once you have a curtain wall in place with at least one panel, you need to separate it into multiple panels for the design. Each curtain wall grid line divides a panel into two or more smaller panels, as shown in Figure 9–9.

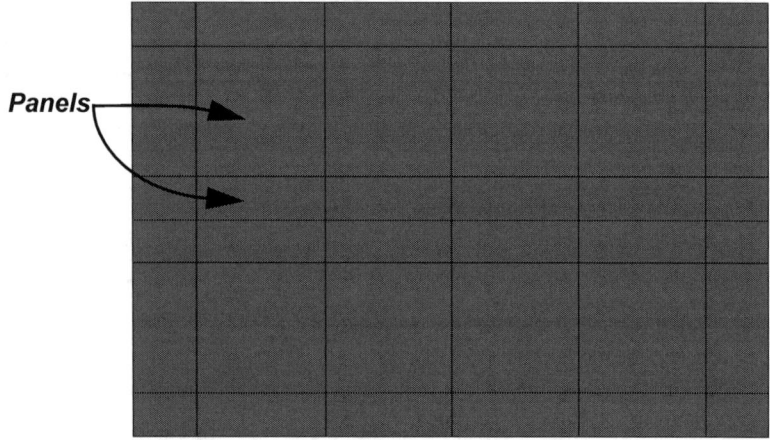

**Figure 9–9**

## How To: Create a Curtain Wall Grid

1. After you have drawn the base curtain wall in a plan view, switch to an elevation or 3D view.
2. In the *Architecture* tab>Build panel, click ⊞ (Curtain Grid).
3. In the *Modify | Place Curtain Grid* tab>Placement panel, select an insertion method, as described below.

| | |
|---|---|
| ╪ (All Segments) | Creates a curtain wall grid line through the entire curtain wall height or width. |
| ╪ (One Segment) | Creates a curtain wall grid line between only the selection point and the next line. The entire curtain wall grid line is established, but only one segment displays. You can add other segments later. |
| ╪ (All Except Picked) | Creates a curtain wall grid line through the entire curtain wall and permits you to go back and remove segments of the curtain wall grid line. The removed segment displays as a dashed line until you add another curtain wall grid line or start another command. |

4. Move the cursor over an edge of the curtain wall or an existing curtain wall grid line. Dynamic dimensions are displayed, as shown in Figure 9–10. The new curtain wall grid line is perpendicular to the edge at the point you select. Click at the required location.

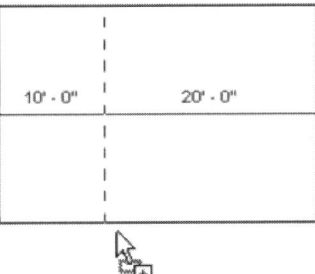 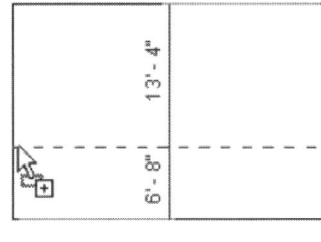

**Figure 9–10**

- Curtain wall grids automatically snap to the midpoint or 1/3 point of the panel. They also snap to levels, column grids, and reference planes.

- You can (Copy) and (Array) curtain wall grid lines. This method can be the fastest way of creating curtain wall grids across the length of a wall.

## Modifying Curtain Wall Grids

Once you have placed the curtain wall grid lines, they might not be exactly where you want them or overlap other lines where you do not want them to overlap. You can modify the location of curtain wall grid lines in the curtain wall and add or remove segments from the lines, as shown in Figure 9–11.

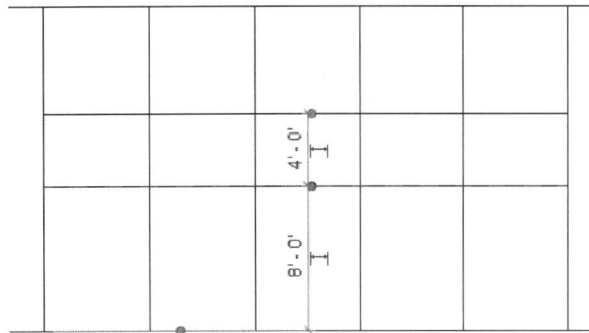

**Figure 9–11**

- To modify the curtain wall grid, you must select a curtain wall grid line, not a wall or the mullion. Hover your cursor over the area and press <Tab> to cycle through elements. Watch the tooltip or Status Bar as you cycle through the elements and click when you see **Curtain Wall Grids : Curtain Wall Grids : Grid Line**, as shown in Figure 9–12.

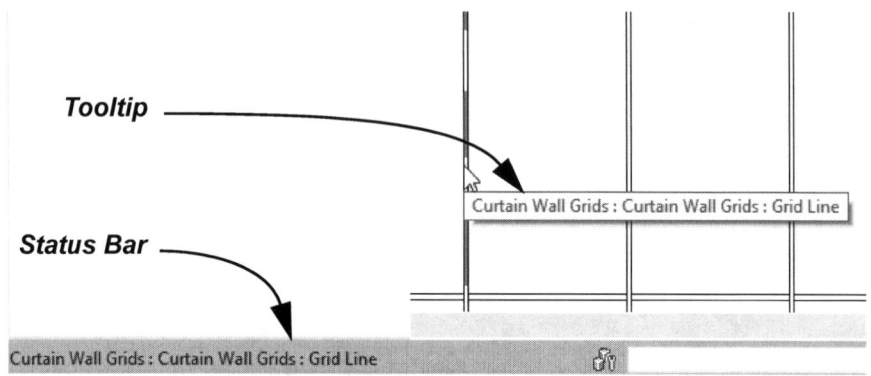

Figure 9–12

- To move a curtain wall grid line, select it and use dynamic dimensions or (Move).

- If you select a curtain wall grid line that was created using the **Curtain Wall** wall style, (Prevent or allow change of element position) is displayed, indicating that the element is constrained to a host element. Click the icon to enable you to move the line.

### How To: Add or Remove Segments of Curtain Wall Grids

1. Select a curtain wall grid line to modify.
2. In the *Modify |Curtain Wall Grids* tab>Curtain Grid panel, click (Add/Remove Segments).
3. Click the part of the curtain wall grid that you want to add or remove. The line displays as dashed when you click to remove a segment, as shown in Figure 9–13. You must select curtain wall grid lines one at a time with this command.

# Working with Curtain Walls

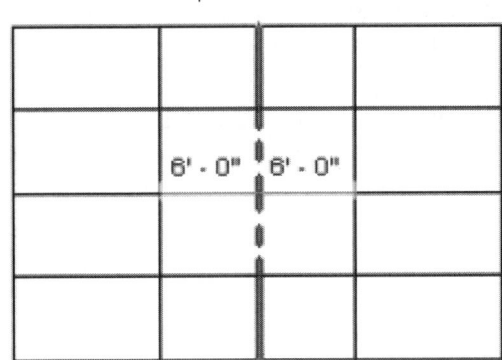
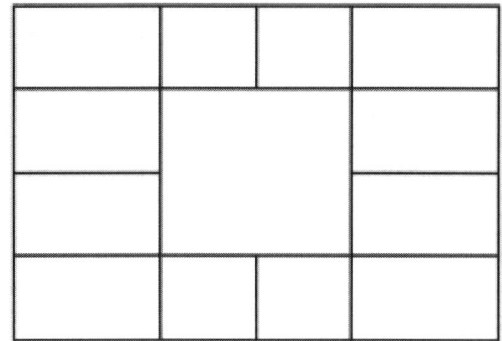

Figure 9–13

4. Click in an empty space in the drawing area to finish the command.

- You can create non-rectangular panels by removing individual curtain wall grid segments.

> **Hint: Aligning and Locking**
>
> When you use the **Align** command, you can also lock the lines together so if one moves, the other does as well. However, locking also causes the software to slow down. Therefore, be careful how much you use the **Lock** option and apply it only when you expect to make a lot of modifications.

## Hide Elements in View

When working in views, there may be some elements or datums that are in the way of your work. To hide such elements, you can select them, then when a selected element turns blue, right-click on that element and the shortcut menu displays. Select **Hide in View**, then select either **Elements** or **Category**, as shown in Figure 9–14.

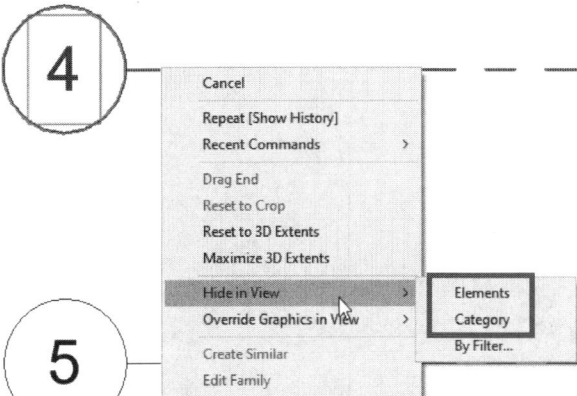

Figure 9–14

© 2022, ASCENT - Center for Technical Knowledge®

- Selecting **Category** will turn everything off in that category (e.g., all the levels and elevation markers).

- Selecting **Elements** will turn off the selected elements (e.g., only the selected level and elevation marker).

# Practice 9a

# Work with Curtain Walls

**Practice Objectives**

- Modify curtain wall properties.
- Add curtain wall grid lines.

In this practice, you will modify a curtain wall using Properties to ensure that the lines match up with other elements. You will also add curtain wall grid lines that follow the pattern of a nearby wall. The finished elevation is shown in Figure 9–15.

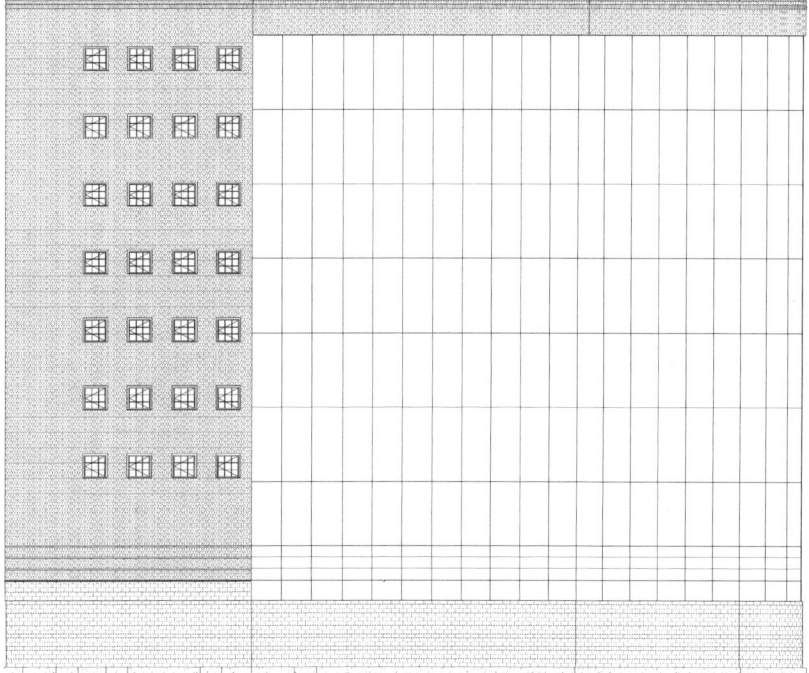

Figure 9–15

### Task 1 - Add curtain wall grid lines.

1. Open the project **Hotel-CrtWall.rvt** from the practice files folder.

2. Verify you are in the **Elevations (Building Elevation):South** view.

3. In order to select the entire curtain wall, verify in the Status Bar that (Select Elements by Face) is toggled on (i.e., there is no red X over the icon).

4. Select the entire curtain wall closest to the exterior brick wall, as shown outlined with dashed lines in Figure 9–16. In Properties, in the *Horizontal Grid* section, change the *Offset* to **6'-0"**. Note that the curtain wall grid lines shift up and are now aligned with the levels.

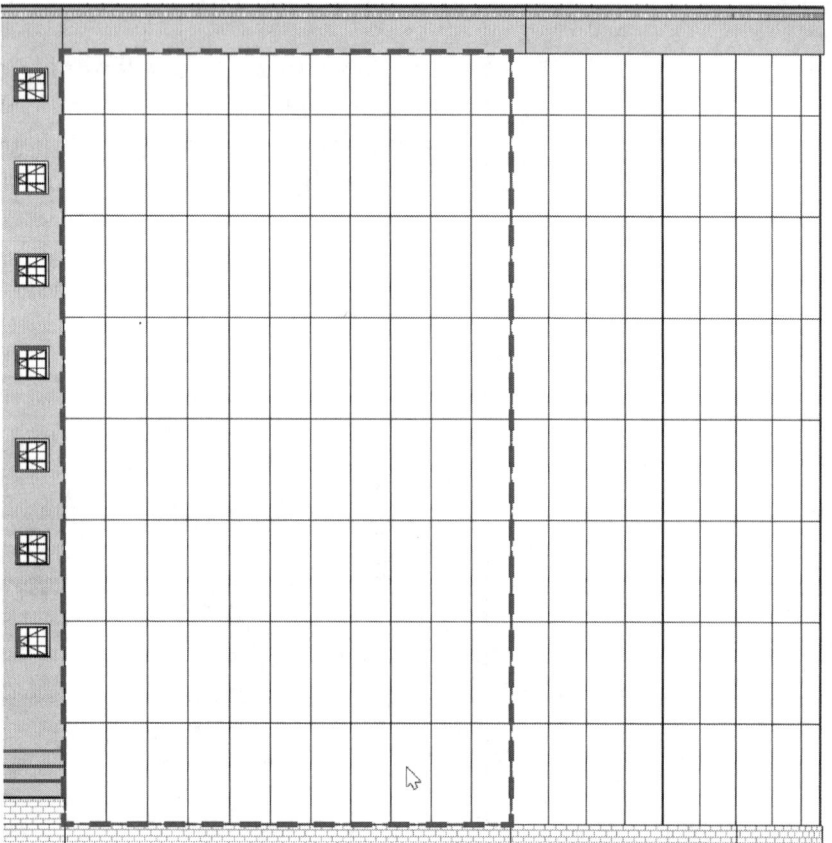

**Figure 9–16**

5. Repeat Step 4 for the second and third curtain walls.

6. Zoom in to the bottom edge of the building and ensure that the brick/CMU and the curtain wall is displayed, as shown in Figure 9–17. Press <Tab> to cycle through the curtain wall elements until you see dashed line shown in Figure 9–17 and click it.

# Working with Curtain Walls

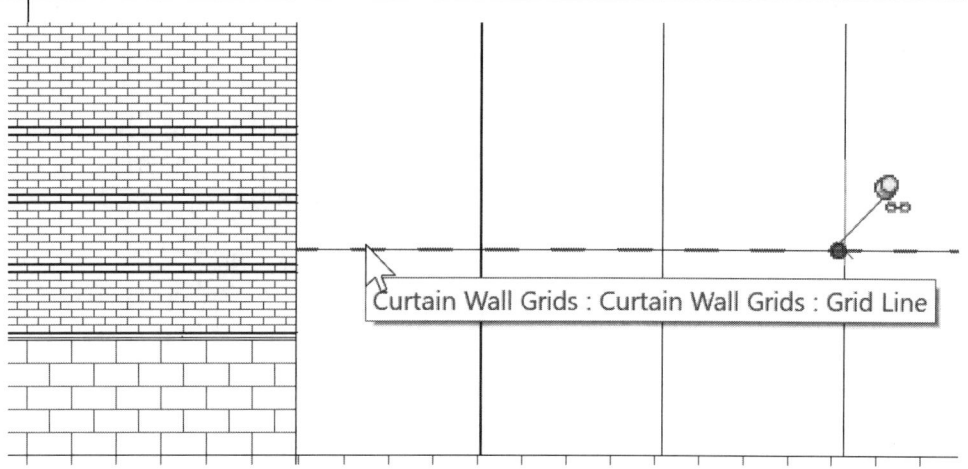

Figure 9–17

7. Along the curtain wall grid line, click ![icon] (Prevent or allow change of element position) or type **UP** to unpin the curtain wall grid line. Alternatively, in the *Modify | Curtain Wall Grids* tab>Modify panel, select ![icon] (Unpin).

8. In the Quick Access toolbar, toggle off ![icon] (Thin Lines). Thin lines on looks like this: ![icon].

9. Start the ![icon] (Align) tool and verify that **Lock** is unchecked in the Align panel. Align the curtain wall grid line so it matches with the top of the CMU sill, as shown in Figure 9–18.

    • Hint: With the **Align** command started, select the top of the CMU as the first pick and then the curtain wall grid as the second pick.

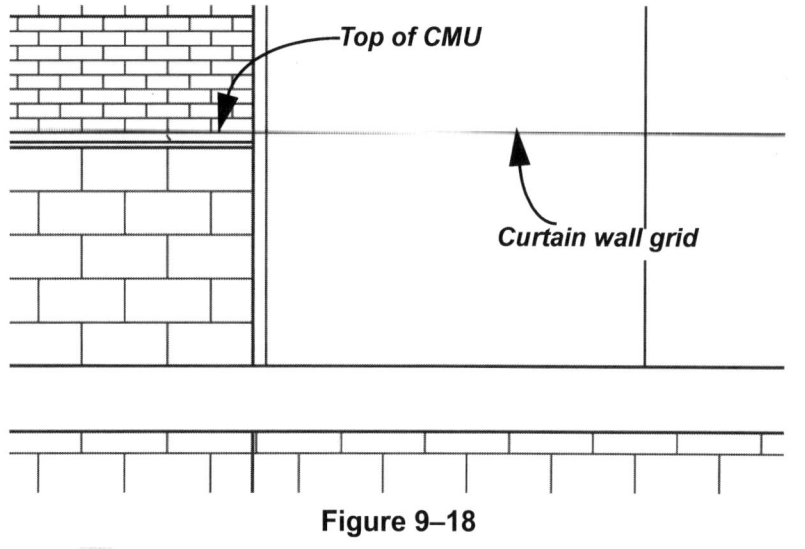

Figure 9–18

10. Click ![icon] (Modify).

11. In the *Architecture* tab>Build panel, click ⊞ (Curtain Grid).

12. Hover your cursor along the edge of the curtain wall and brick. When the curtain wall grid line displays horizontally, as shown in Figure 9–19, click to place the curtain wall grid.

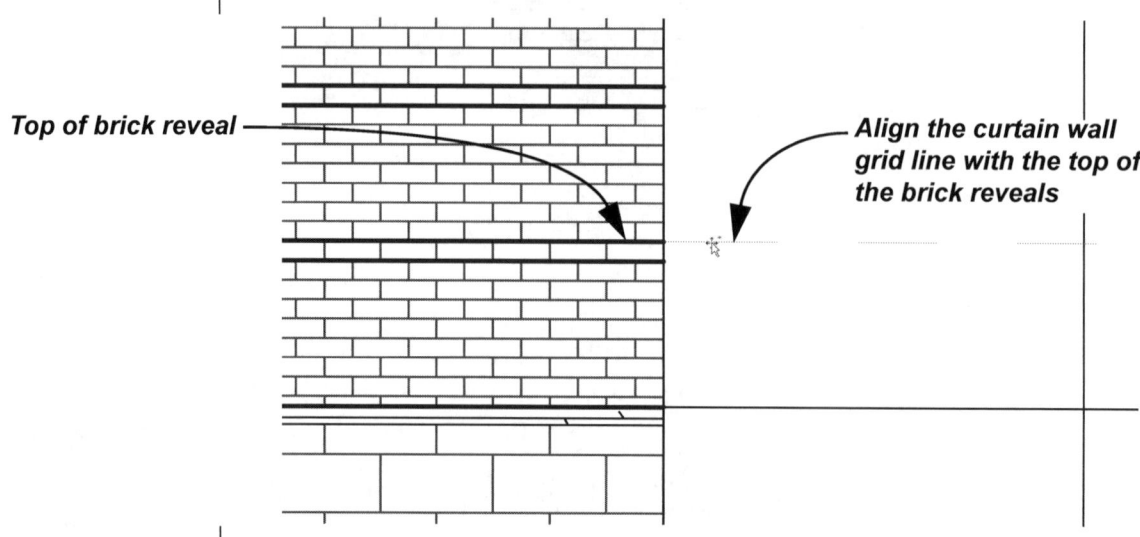

Figure 9–19

13. Click ▷ (Modify).

14. Add two more curtain wall grid lines and align them (if needed) with the top of the reveals in the brick, as shown in Figure 9–20.

*Zoom in until the heavier lines of the brick reveals are displayed.*

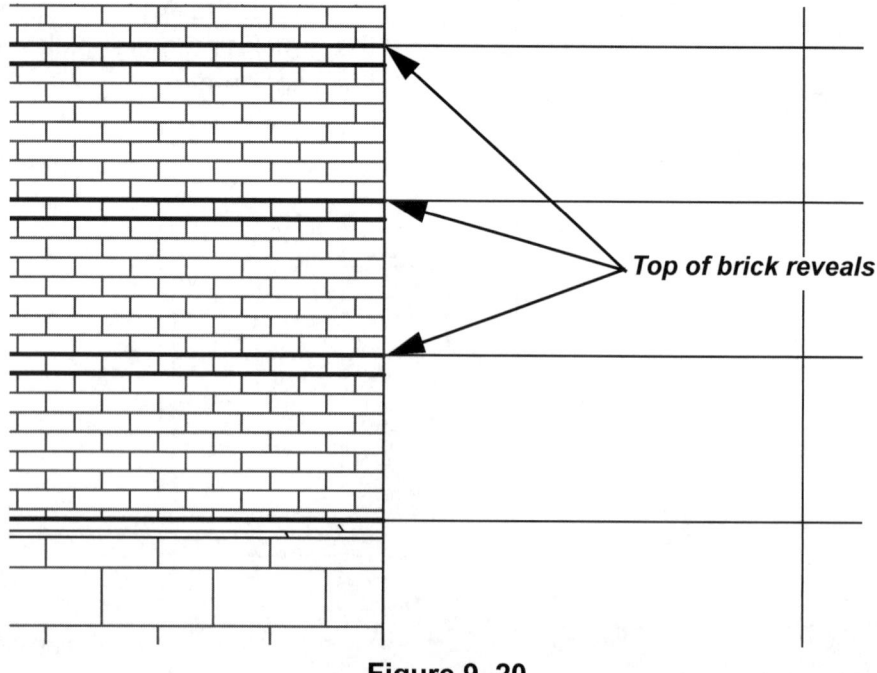

Figure 9–20

# Working with Curtain Walls

15. In the Quick Access toolbar, toggle on  (Thin Lines).

16. Select the four curtain wall grid lines (hold <Ctrl> and select each line individually).

    - Note: Properties will show **Curtain Wall Grids (4)** under the Type Selector.

17. In the *Modify | Curtain Wall Grids* tab>Modify panel, click  (Move).

18. Click one of the curtain wall grid lines for the first selection point and move your cursor down. Type **1 1/4"** and press <Enter>. Ensure that you move the cursor down before entering the move value. This places them correctly for the mullions, that are added later.

19. Click  (Modify).

20. Pan over to the second curtain wall. Note that this curtain wall also needs three curtain wall grid lines and the fourth curtain wall grid line needs to be aligned, as shown in Figure 9–21.

*The curtain wall grid lines that get unpinned need to stay unpinned to maintain their new position.*

21. Select the bottom curtain wall grid line and click  (Prevent or allow change of element position) to unpin the curtain wall grid line, as shown in Figure 9–21.

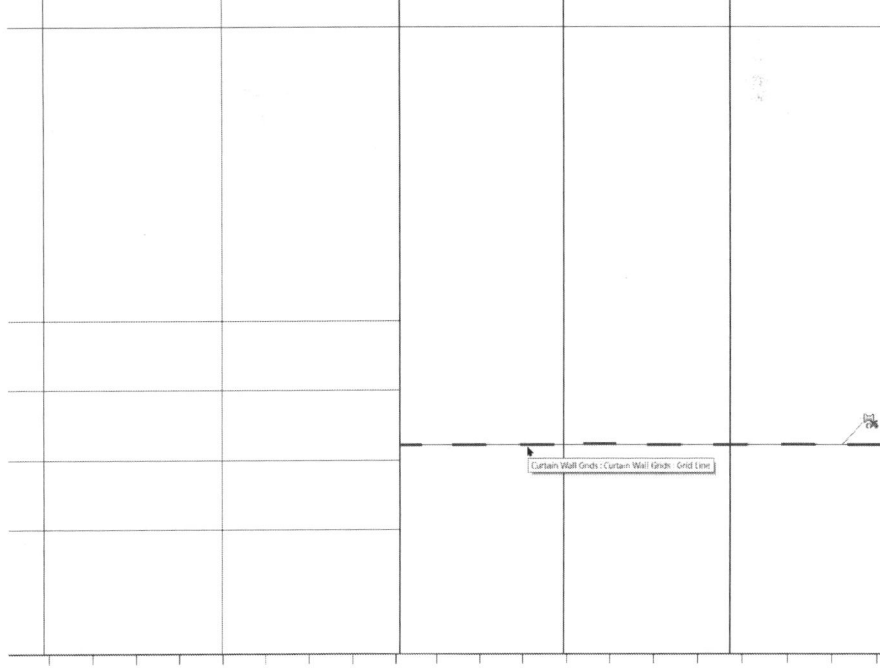

**Figure 9–21**

22. With the curtain wall grid line still selected, in the *Modify | Curtain Wall Grids* tab>Modify panel, click (Align).

23. Align the two curtain wall grid lines by selecting curtain wall grid line on the left first and then the curtain wall grid line on the right.

24. Click (Modify).

25. Note that the third curtain wall's grid line is off, as shown in Figure 9–22. Unpin the grid line and use the **Align** tool to align it as well. Make sure to unpin it before you align it.

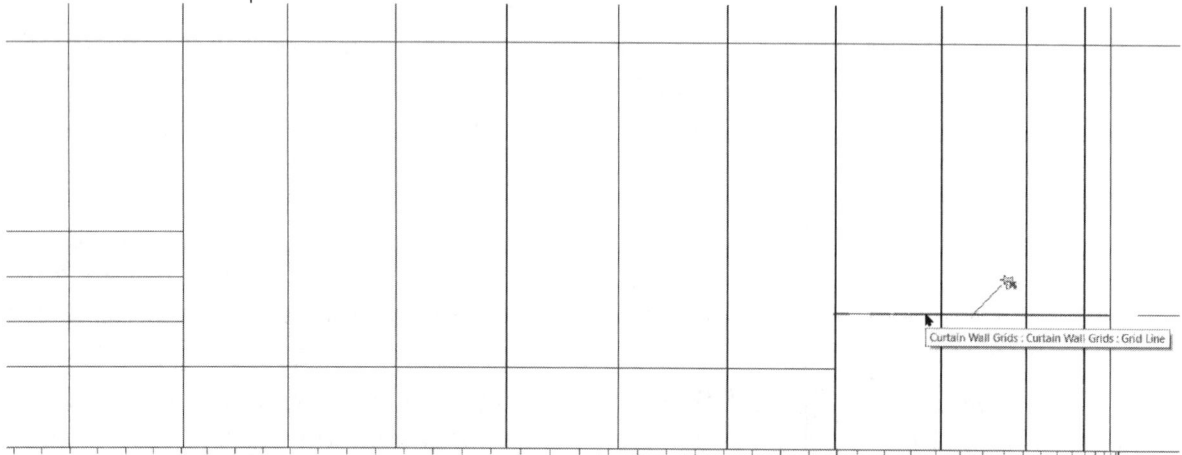

Figure 9–22

26. Click (Modify).

27. Add three horizontal curtain wall grid lines to the two curtain walls to match the first curtain wall, as shown in Figure 9–23 (the three grid lines have been darkened for clarity in the image).

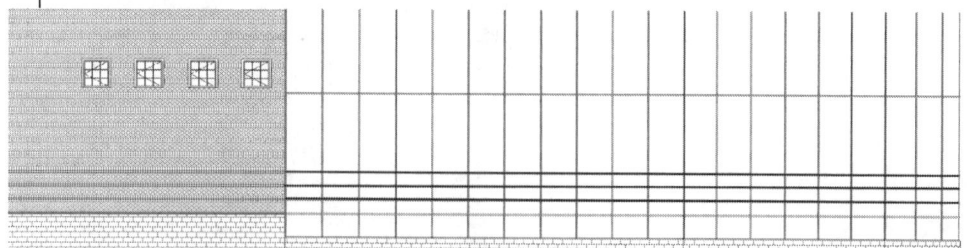

Figure 9–23

28. Zoom out until the entire front of the building is displayed.

29. Save and close the project.

# 9.3 Working with Curtain Wall Panels

The default panel for a curtain wall is typically a glazed panel. As you create the curtain wall grid and refine the wall design, you might want to use other materials for some of the panels, as shown in Figure 9–24. You can select the existing panels and in the Type Selector, select a panel type with the material you want to use.

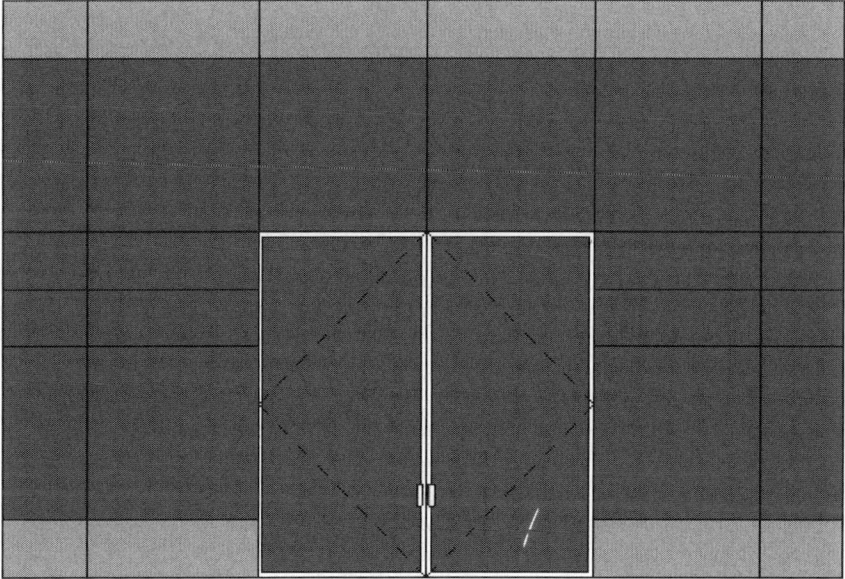

**Figure 9–24**

- Additionally, the panel type controls the thickness and can define a door or window for the panel.

- To select a panel, hover the cursor over its edge, press <Tab> until it highlights, and then click to select it.

- To select all of the panels, select the edge of the curtain wall, right-click, and select **Select Panels on Host.**

- If ⚲ (Prevent or allow change of element position) displays (as shown in Figure 9–25), it indicates that the panel is locked and that changes to the element are not permitted. Click the icon to toggle off the lock and modify the panel.

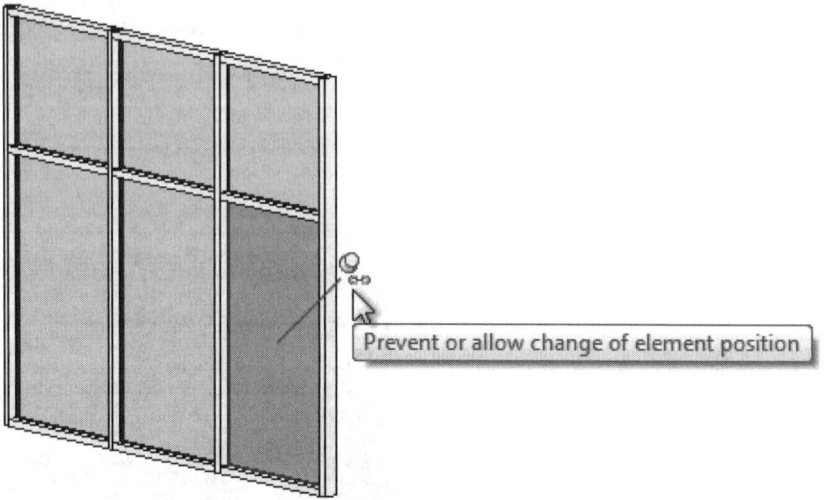

Figure 9–25

- To unpin multiple panels, select them and type **UP** (for **Unpin**).

## Default Panel Types

Three panel types come with the default project template:

| Empty Panel | You cannot delete a panel in a curtain wall, but you can change the panel type to an empty panel. |
|---|---|
| Glazed Panel | A typical panel type with glass as its material. |
| Solid Panel | A panel type using a solid material. You can create variations of this type with other materials. |

- You can use any other wall type (including other curtain wall types) to fill in a panel.

- Door and window panels are available through the Revit Library. Similar to other panel types, door and window panels fill the size of the panel to which they are applied. Adjust the curtain wall grid for the correct sizes, as shown in Figure 9–26.

# Working with Curtain Walls

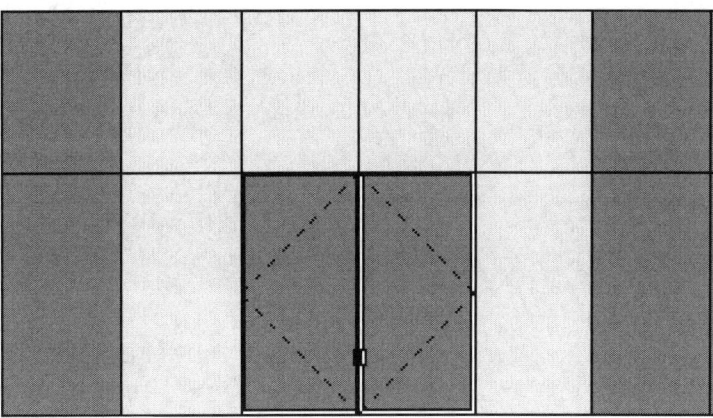

Figure 9–26

### How To: Place Doors and Windows in Curtain Wall Panels

1. Load the door or window type that can be used as a curtain wall panel, such as the **Door-Curtain-Wall-Double-Glass.rfa**.
2. Modify the curtain wall grid layout to ensure that the size of the opening in the curtain wall matches the size of the door you want to use.
3. Select the curtain wall panel.
4. In the Type Selector, select the type that you want to use as the panel.
5. The door or window fills the panel area.

## Creating a Curtain Wall Panel

While you can create curtain wall panels in many complex ways, a basic technique is to specify a material for a flat system panel, as shown in Figure 9–27.

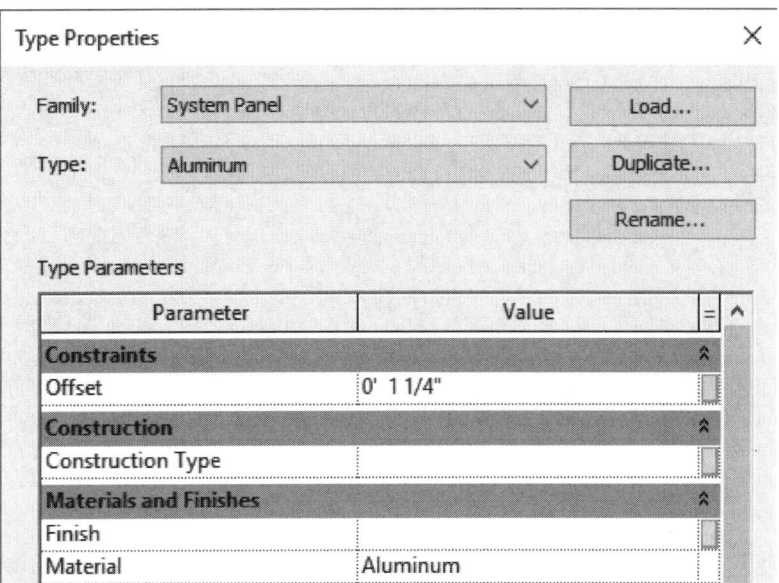

Figure 9–27

## How To: Create a Curtain Wall Panel

1. Select a panel and use <Tab> to select the entire panel (i.e., select a solid panel to create a new solid panel type). If it is pinned, unpin it by clicking  (Prevent or allow change of element position).
2. In Properties, click  (Edit Type), or, in the *Modify | Curtain Panels* tab>Properties panel, click  (Type Properties).
3. In the Type Properties dialog box, click **Duplicate** to create a copy of the existing family type.
4. Give the panel a new name that describes its purpose (e.g., **Brick** or **Aluminum**). The new name automatically includes the family name, such as **System Panel**.
5. Set the *Thickness*, *Offset*, *Material,* and any other parameters as needed. Many materials are available in the Material Browser that opens when you click  (Browse) in the Materials list.
6. Click **OK** to close the dialog box and finish the panel. It is automatically applied to the panel you selected for modification.

- The *Thickness* of the material is centered on the curtain wall grid if you did not specify an *Offset*. If you want the panel to be recessed in the wall, use a negative offset. If you want the panel to stand out from the wall, use a positive offset.

- Materials with patterns, such as the brick shown in Figure 9–28, do not display the pattern when the view is zoomed out far. Zoom in to view the material.

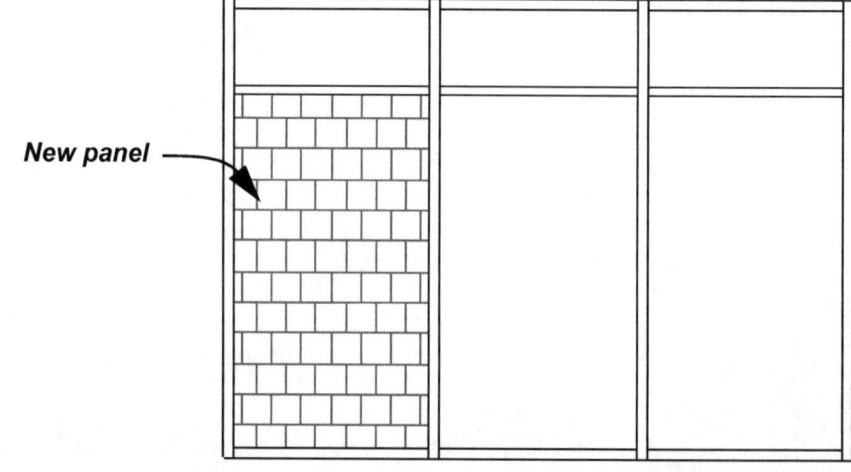

**Figure 9–28**

# 9.4 Attaching Mullions to Curtain Wall Grids

Mullions are the frameworks for curtain wall panels, as shown in Figure 9–29. They can be many sizes, shapes, and materials. Add them as the final step in your curtain wall design after you have placed the curtain wall grid lines.

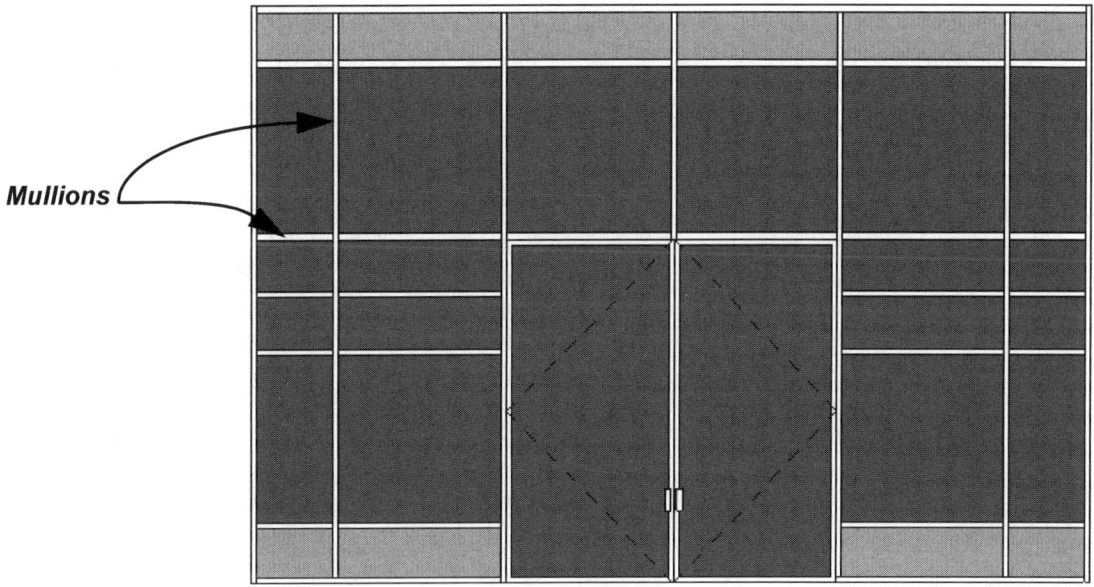

*Mullions*

Figure 9–29

### How To: Add Mullions

1. In the *Architecture* tab>Build panel, click  (Mullion).
2. In the Type Selector, select the mullion style. There are no modifiable properties when you insert a mullion.
3. In the *Modify | Place Mullion* tab>Placement panel, select a *Create Mullion on* method:  (Grid Line),  (Grid Line Segment), or  (All Grid Lines), as shown in Figure 9–30.

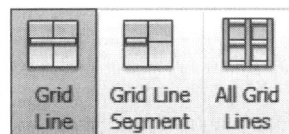

Figure 9–30

*Mullions must be placed individually; they cannot be copied or arrayed.*

4. Select the curtain wall grid line on which you want to place the mullion. If the curtain wall grid line is inside a curtain wall, the mullion is placed on the curtain wall grid's center line. If it is on the edge of the wall, the mullion is placed so that its exterior is flush with the outside of the wall.
   - Hold <Shift> to place a mullion only on the selected segment.
   - Hold <Ctrl> to place the mullion on all empty curtain wall grid segments (i.e., all without mullions).
- Corner mullion types are designed for the intersection of two curtain walls. They adjust to fit the angle of the intersection.

## Modifying Mullions

To quickly select mullions, hover your cursor over a curtain wall or mullion, right-click and select **Select Mullions**. The mullion options include **On Vertical Grid** or **On Horizontal Grid**, **Inner Mullions**, **Border Mullions**, or **Mullions on Host**, as shown in Figure 9–31.

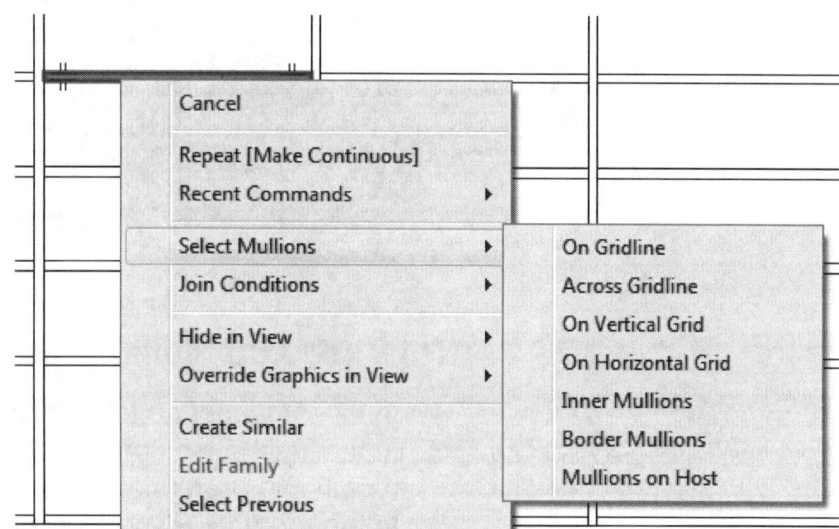

**Figure 9–31**

- Modify mullion styles by changing their type in the Type Selector.

- To move mullions, you need to hover your cursor over the mullion and use <Tab> to select the curtain wall grid, then move the curtain wall grid line and the mullions will move with it.

- If you delete a curtain wall grid line, the mullion is also deleted. However, if you delete a mullion, the curtain wall grid line is not deleted.

- You can change the way mullions intersect. Select the mullion and in the *Modify | Curtain Wall Mullions* tab>Mullion panel, click (Make Continuous) or (Break at Join). Alternatively, select the mullion and click the **Toggle Mullion Join** control, as shown in Figure 9–32.

*Before*  *After*

**Figure 9–32**

# Practice 9b

# Add Mullions and Panels to Curtain Walls

### Practice Objectives

- Add and modify mullions.
- Add a storefront entrance and door panel.

In this practice, you will add and modify mullions along the three curtain walls. You will also create a storefront that includes a door panel as the front entrance of the building. The finished elevation is shown in Figure 9–33.

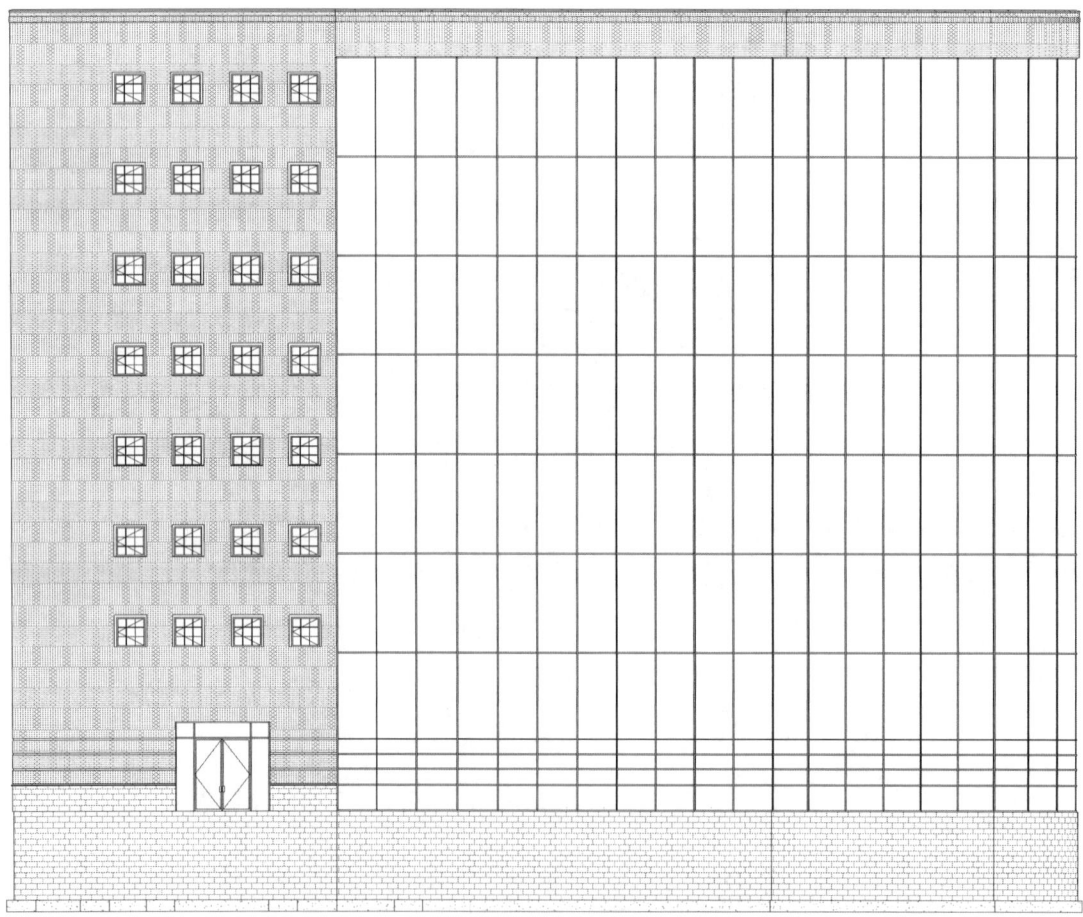

Figure 9–33

### Task 1 - Add and modify mullions.

1. Open the project **Hotel-CrtMullions.rvt** from the practice files folder.

Working with Curtain Walls

2. Verify that you are in the **Elevations (Building Elevations): South** view. Note that the levels have been hidden in the view.

3. Verify in the Status Bar that (Select Elements by Face) is toggled on (i.e., there is no red X over the icon).

4. In the *Architecture* tab>Build panel, click (Mullion).

5. In the *Modify | Place Mullion* tab>Placement panel, click (All Grid Lines).

6. In the Type Selector, select **Rectangular Mullion: 2.5" x 5" rectangular**.

7. Select the first curtain wall. Mullions are placed on all of the curtain wall grid lines. Read and ignore the warning message. Repeat this process for the next two curtain walls.

8. Click (Modify).

**Task 2 - Modify mullions.**

1. Zoom in to where two curtain walls meet. Note that there are two mullions side by side, as shown in Figure 9–34. The second mullion is not needed and should be deleted (it does not matter which of the two mullions is deleted).

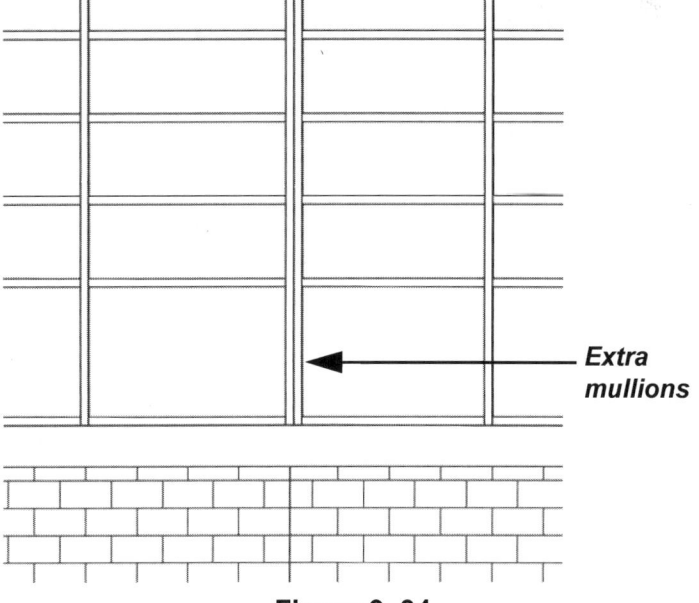

*Extra mullions*

**Figure 9–34**

2. Select one of the mullions. In the View Control Bar, click (Temporary Hide/Isolate) and select **Isolate Category**.

3. Click in an empty space in the view to clear the selection.

4. Select one of the vertical mullion where the two curtain walls meet. Right-click and select **Select Mullions>On Gridline** and then press <Delete>.

5. Zoom and pan over to where the next curtain walls meet and repeat the steps to delete any irrelevant mullions.

6. Zoom out until you can see the bottom of all the curtain walls.

7. Select the entire bottom row of mullions. Draw a selection window (left to right) around the entire bottom row, so only the bottom row is selected, as shown in Figure 9–35.

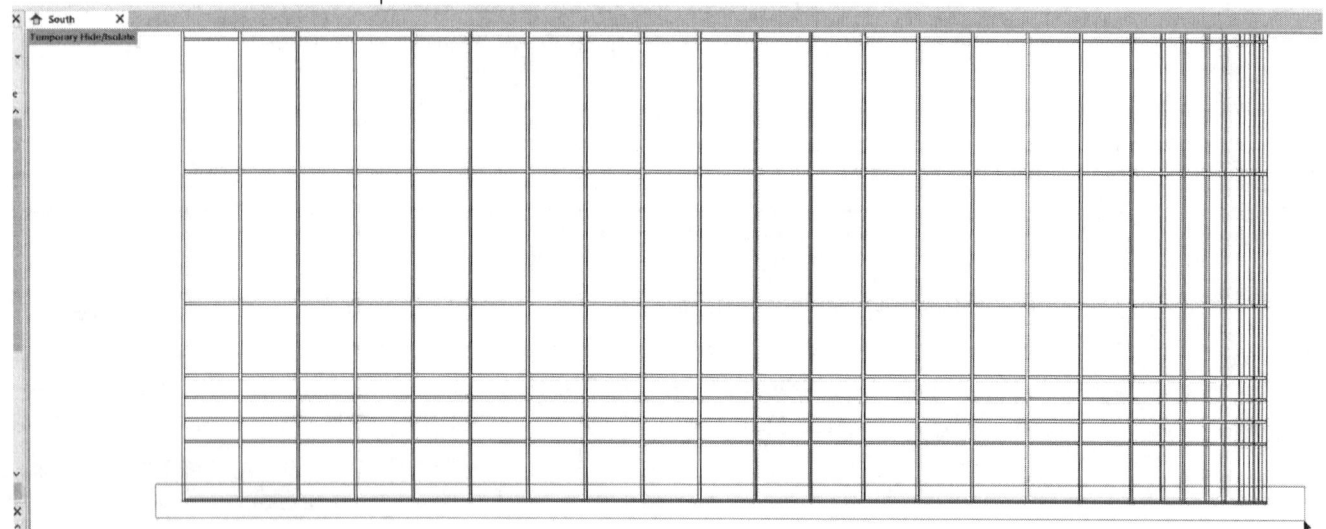

Figure 9–35

8. In the *Modify | Curtain Wall Mullions* tab>Mullion panel, click (Make Continuous). This changes the mullion direction, as shown in Figure 9–36.

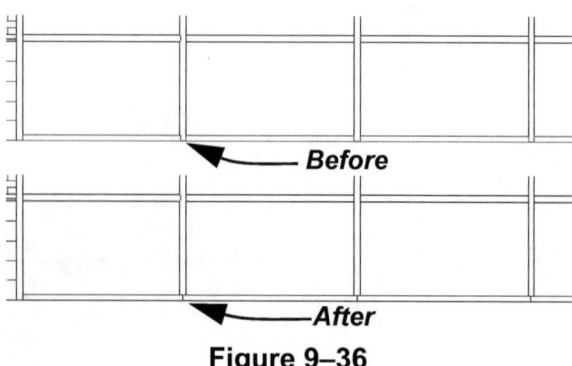

Figure 9–36

9. Zoom and pan along the bottom mullion to where the mullion ignored the **Make Continuous** command. Select the mullion and click the Toggle Mullion Join icon, as shown in Figure 9–37.

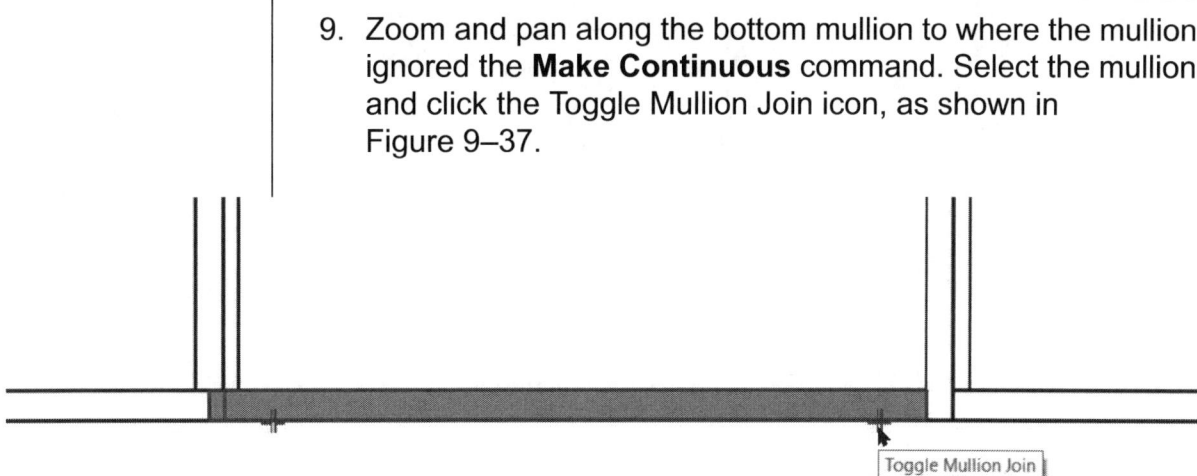

**Figure 9–37**

10. In the View Control Bar, click (Temporary Hide/Isolate) and select **Reset Temporary Hide/Isolate**.

11. Save the project.

### Task 3 - Add the storefront entrance.

1. Open the **Floor Plans: Floor 1** view.

2. Zoom to the lower-left exterior wall along grid 5C. You will add a storefront between grids 5C and 5D.

3. In the *Architecture* tab>Build panel, click (Wall).

4. In the Type Selector, select **Curtain Wall:Storefront**.

5. In Properties, set the following values:

    - *Base Constraint:* **Floor 1**
    - *Base Offset:* **0'-0"**
    - *Top Constraint:* **Up to level: Floor 2**
    - *Top Offset:* (negative) **-6'-0"**

6. Draw the storefront **14'-6"** between grid 5C and 5D, working from right to left. If needed, use temporary dimensions to shift the storefront so the edge is **1'-3"** off of the right column grid line, as shown in Figure 9–38.

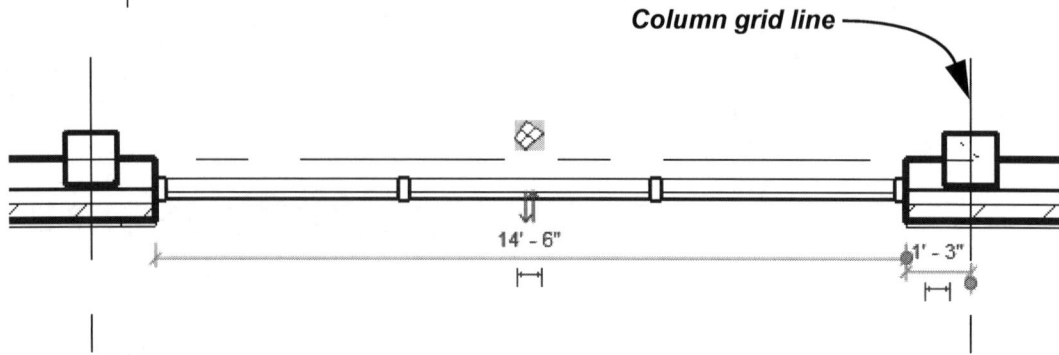

Figure 9–38

7. Click (Modify).

8. Click the *South* tab to activate the view and zoom in on the storefront.

9. In the Quick Access Toolbar, verify that (Activate Controls and Dimensions) is on (it will be highlighted).

10. In the lower-right corner on the Status Bar, click (Drag Elements on Select) so the icon has a red x on it ( ).

11. With nothing selected, use a window selection (left to right) around the storefront to select the panels and mullions.

- Because this curtain wall was created as a preset type, all of the curtain wall grids, mullions, and panels are pinned, as shown in Figure 9–39.

*See "Selecting Multiple Elements" on page 5-15 for more information on window selection.*

12. Type **UP** to unpin the elements, as shown in Figure 9–40.

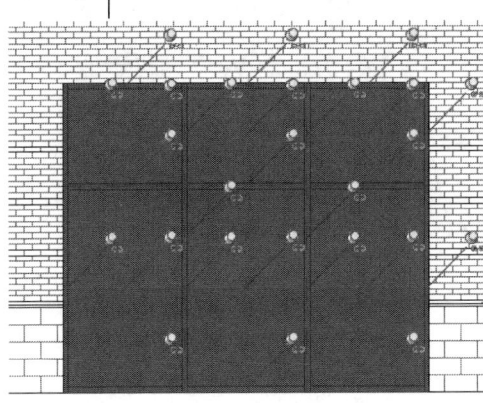

**Figure 9–39**          **Figure 9–40**

13. Click ▸ (Modify).

14. Modify the storefront, as shown in Figure 9–41. Align the horizontal storefront curtain wall grid line with the curtain wall grid line in the main curtain wall.

15. Select the vertical curtain wall grid lines and use temporary dimensions to make the two outer panels **3'-0"**. This will make the center panel **8'-6"**.

    - Ensure that you are selecting curtain wall grid lines as you work and not the mullions. Use <Tab> to cycle through the elements.

*To align: The first pick is the reference or point for alignment. The second pick is what you want to align or move into alignment with the reference.*

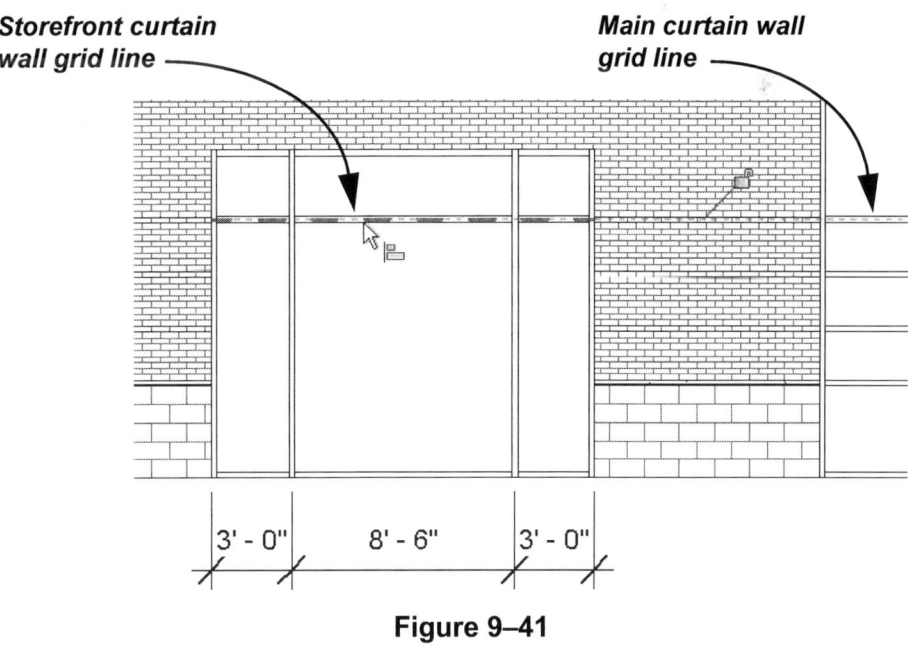

**Figure 9–41**

16. Click ▸ (Modify).

17. Select the three horizontal mullions at the top of the storefront, as shown on the top in Figure 9–42.

18. In the *Modify | Curtain Wall Mullions* tab>Mullion panel, click  (Make Continuous) so that the mullion runs straight across, as shown on the bottom in Figure 9–42.

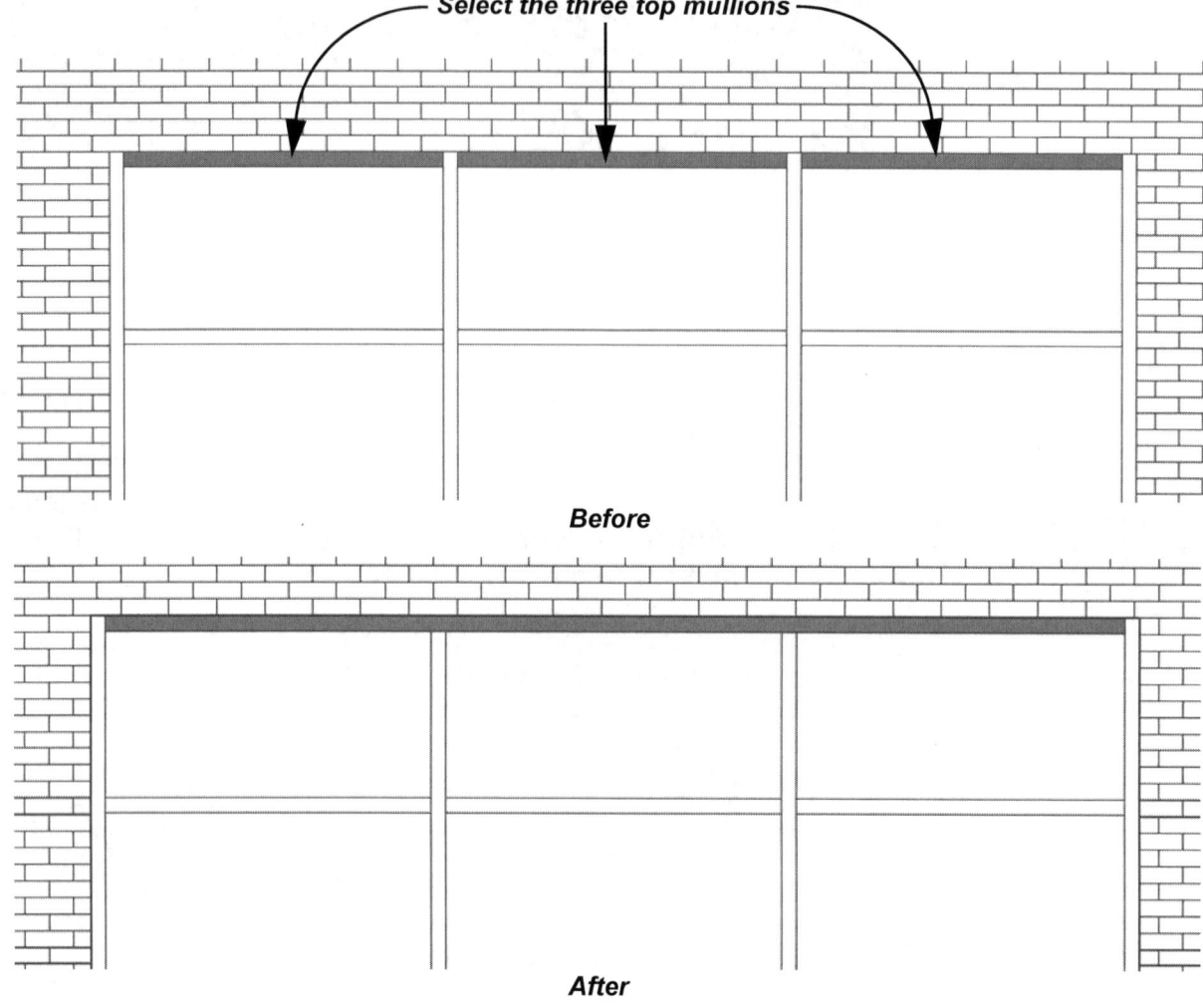

Figure 9–42

19. Click  (Modify).

20. Save the project.

### Task 4 - Add a door in the storefront.

1. In the *Insert* tab>Load from Library panel, click  (Load Family).

2. In the Load Family dialog box, navigate to the practice files *Families>Doors* folder and select the door **Door-Curtain-Wall-Double-Storefront.rfa**, then click **Open**.

3. Select the large panel, as shown in Figure 9–43. Use <Tab> to cycle through the selections and then click to select it.

Figure 9–43

4. In the Type Selector, select **Door-Curtain-Wall-Double-Storefront.** The panel changes to the door.

5. Delete the mullion at the bottom of the door, as shown in Figure 9–44.

*If you cannot delete the mullion, select it and verify that it is unpinned.*

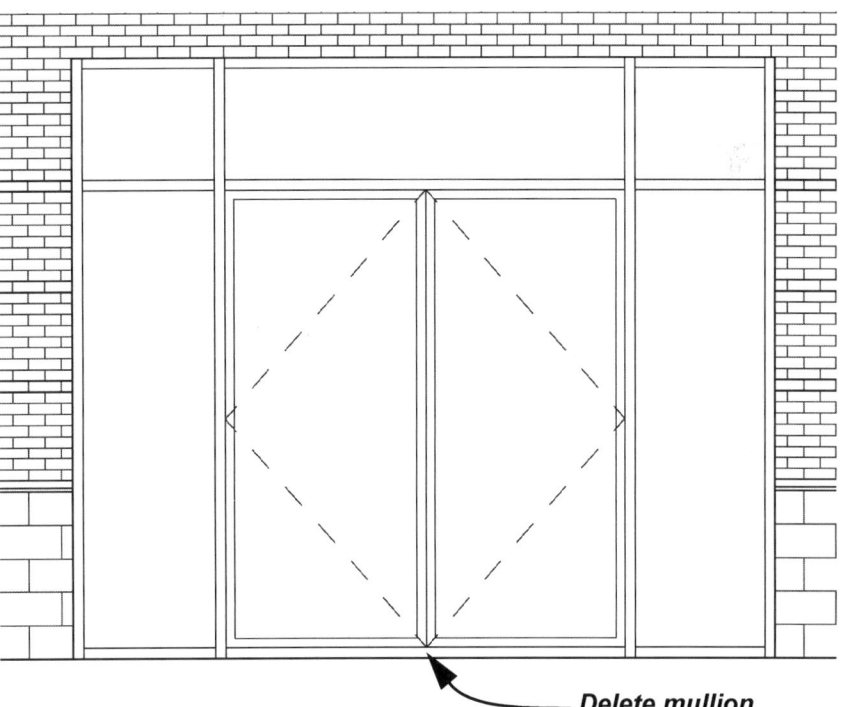

Figure 9–44

6. Change the *Detail Level* to **Fine** to see the door handles.

7. Zoom out until the entire front elevation is displayed.
8. View the project in 3D.
9. Save and close the project.

# Chapter Review Questions

1. Which command do you start with to create a curtain wall?

   a. ▢ (Wall)

   b. ▦ (Curtain Grid)

   c. ▦ (Curtain System)

2. You are placing a curtain wall grid and it keeps snapping to one dimension, such as the TWO-THIRDS OF CURTAIN PANEL shown in Figure 9–45, when you want it to be another. What should you do?

Figure 9–45

   a. Change the snap settings.

   b. Edit the curtain wall type to permit manual curtain wall grid placement.

   c. Use a non-uniform curtain wall type instead of a uniform one.

   d. Place the curtain wall grid anyway, select the temporary dimension, and change it to the required value.

3. How do you select one panel to modify it?

   a. Select the middle of the panel.

   b. Hover your cursor over the edge of the panel and press <Tab> until it is identified.

   c. Select the curtain wall, right-click and select **Panel Select**.

   d. In the Selection Priority drop-down list, select **Curtain Panel**.

4. Once you select a panel, what can you swap it for? (Select all that apply.)

   a. Empty system panel

   b. Storefront door

   c. Blank panel

   d. Wall type

5. How do you change the way in which two mullions intersect, as shown in Figure 9–46? (Select all that apply.)

**Figure 9–46**

   a. Select one of the mullions and press <Tab> until the correct intersection displays.

   b. Select one of the mullions and click **Make Continuous** or **Break at Join** in the contextual tab.

   c. Select one of the mullions and click the **Toggle Mullion Join** control.

   d. Select both mullions and select the **Intersect** box in the Options Bar.

# Command Summary

| Button | Command | Location |
|---|---|---|
| | Add/Remove Segments | • **Ribbon:** *Modify | Curtain Wall Grids* tab> Curtain Grid panel |
| | Curtain Grid | • **Ribbon:** *Architecture* tab>Build panel |
| | Curtain Grid: All Except Picked | • **Ribbon:** *Modify | Place Curtain Grid* tab> Placement panel |
| | Curtain Grid: All Segments | • **Ribbon:** *Modify | Place Curtain Grid* tab> Placement panel |
| | Curtain Grid: One Segment | • **Ribbon:** *Modify | Place Curtain Grid* tab> Placement panel |
| | Mullion | • **Ribbon:** *Architecture* tab>Build panel |
| | Mullion: All Grid Lines | • **Ribbon:** *Modify | Place Mullion* tab> Placement panel |
| | Mullion: Break at Join | • **Ribbon:** *Modify | Curtain Wall Mullions* tab>Mullion panel<br>• **Right-click:** (with mullion selected) Join Conditions>Break at Join |
| | Mullion: Grid Line | • **Ribbon:** *Modify | Place Mullion* tab> Placement panel |
| | Mullion: Grid Line Segment | • **Ribbon:** *Modify | Place Mullion* tab> Placement panel |
| | Mullion: Make Continuous | • **Ribbon:** *Modify | Curtain Wall Mullions* tab>Mullion panel<br>• **Right-click:** (with mullion selected) Join Conditions>Make Continuous |

# Chapter 10

# Modeling Floors

Floors in Revit® can be used as full depth floors or as a thin veneer that shows floor material placed on an underlying floor. You can customize floors by creating slopes for drainage, cutting holes, or shafts that cut through multiple floors.

## Learning Objectives in This Chapter

- Sketch and modify floor boundaries.
- Join geometry between floors and walls for a cleaner visual presentation.
- Add a shaft opening that cuts through multiple floors.
- Slope a floor in one or more directions for drainage.

# 10.1 Modeling Floors

The **Floor** command can generate any flat or sloped surface, such as floors, balconies, decks, and patios, as shown in Figure 10–1. Typically created in a plan view, the floor can be based either on bounding walls or on a sketched outline.

Figure 10–1

- The floor type controls the thickness of a floor.

### How To: Add a Floor

1. In the *Architecture* tab>Build panel, expand  (Floor) and click  (Floor: Architectural) or  (Floor: Structural). You are placed in sketch mode where other elements in the model are grayed out.
2. In the Type Selector, set the type of floor you want to use. In Properties, set any constraints as needed.
3. In the *Modify | Create Floor Boundary* tab>Draw panel, click  (Boundary Line).

    - Click  (Pick Walls) and select the walls, setting either the inside or outside edge. If you have selected a wall, you can click  (Flip) to switch the inside/outside status of the boundary location, as shown in Figure 10–2.

    - Click  (Line) or one of the other Draw tools and sketch the boundary edges.

    - Use the modify tools to align, move, or trim the boundary lines.

*The lines in the sketch must form a closed loop. Use tools in the Modify panel to adjust intersections.*

Modeling Floors

*The span direction is automatically placed on the first sketch line.*

4. Click (Slope Arrow) to define a slope for the entire floor.

5. Click (Span Direction), as shown in Figure 10–2, to modify the direction of the structural elements in the floor.

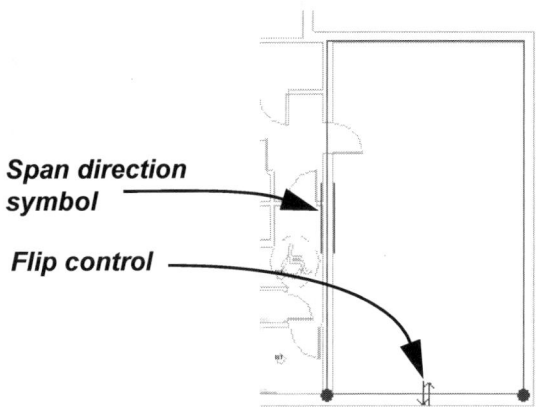

Figure 10–2

6. Click (Finish Edit Mode) to create the floor.

- If you are using (Pick Walls), select the **Extend into wall (to core)** option in the Options Bar if you want the floor to cut into the wall. For example, the floor would cut through the gypsum wall board and the air space but stop at a core layer such as CMU.

- If you select one or more of the boundary sketch lines, you can also set *Cantilevers* for *Concrete* or *Steel*, as shown in Figure 10–3. (You will need to click (Modify) first before selecting a boundary sketch line to get Figure 10–3.)

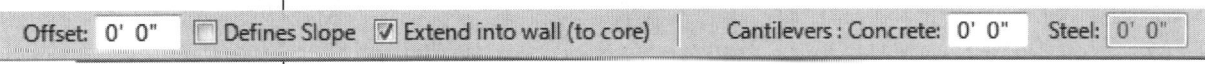

Figure 10–3

- To create an opening inside the floor, create a separate closed loop inside the first one, as shown in Figure 10–4.

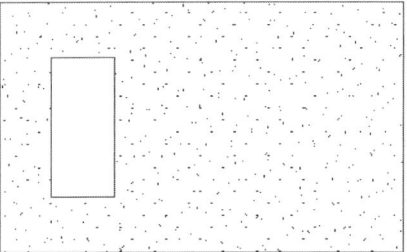

Figure 10–4

> **Hint: Sketched Arcs and Tangent Lock**
>
> If you are adding arcs or ellipses to a sketch that are tangent to other lines, you can lock the geometry in place by clicking on the tangency lock (Toggle Join Tangency), as shown in Figure 10–5.
>
>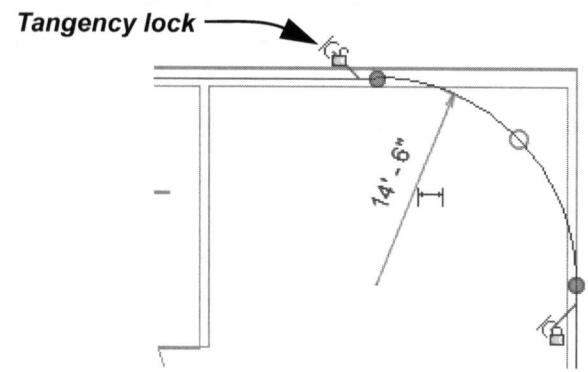
>
> Figure 10–5
>
> - This lock is available whenever you are in sketch mode.

- If you create a floor on an upper level, an alert box displays asking if you want the walls below to be attached to the underside of the floor and its level, as shown in Figure 10–6. If you have a variety of wall heights, it is better to click **Don't attach** and attach the walls separately.

- Another alert box might open as shown in Figure 10–7. You can automatically join the geometry or can do so at a later time.

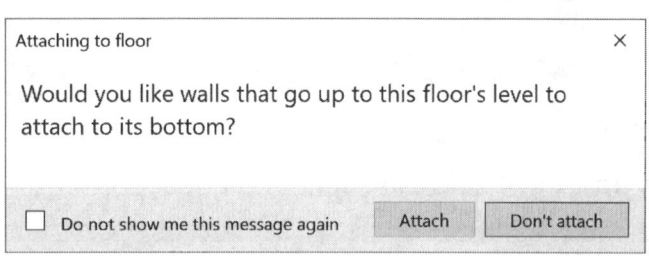

Figure 10–6

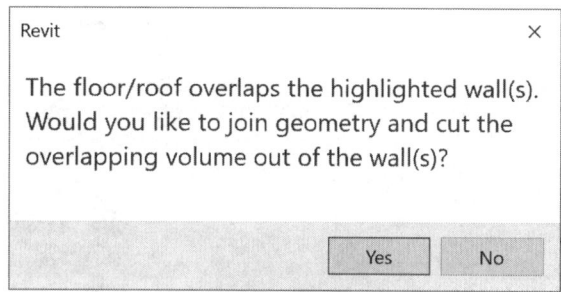

Figure 10–7

- Floors can be placed on top of floors. For example, a structural floor can have a finish floor of tile or carpet placed on top of it, as shown in Figure 10–8. These floors can then be scheduled separately.

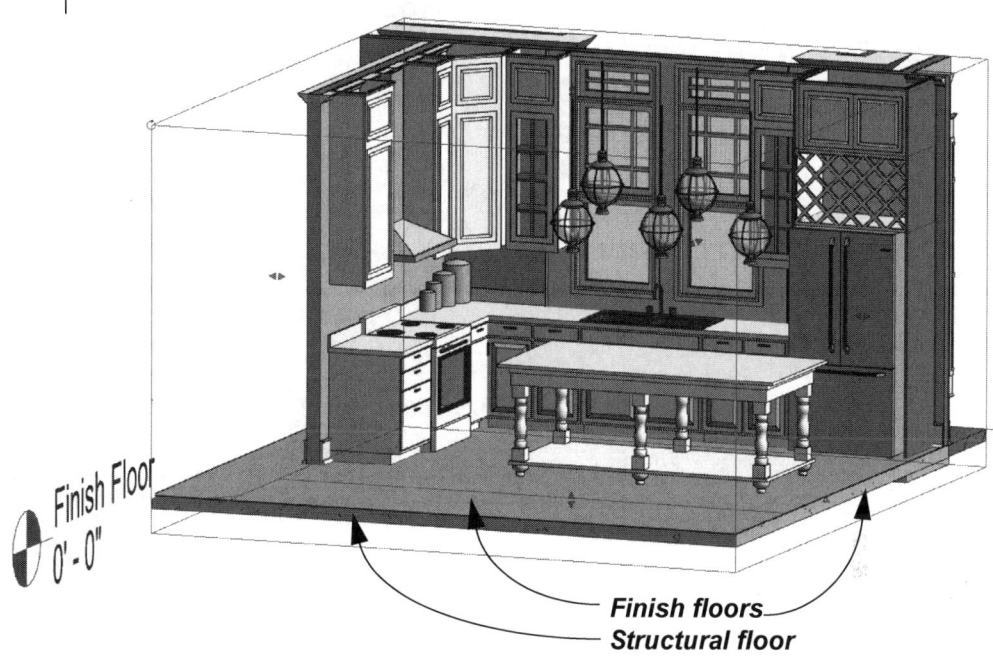

Figure 10–8

## Modifying Floors

You can change a floor to a different type using the Type Selector. In Properties, you can modify parameters including the *Height Offset From Level*, as shown in Figure 10–9. When you have a floor selected, you can also edit the boundaries.

*Many of the parameters in Properties are used in schedules, including Elevation at Top (Bottom) and Elevation at Top (Bottom) Core for multi-layered floors.*

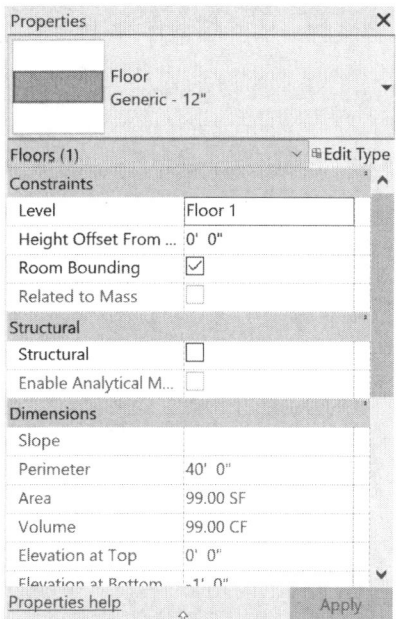

Figure 10–9

### How To: Modify the Floor Sketch

1. Select a floor. You might need to hover your cursor over an element near the floor and press <Tab> until the floor type displays in the Status Bar or in a tooltip, as shown in Figure 10–10.

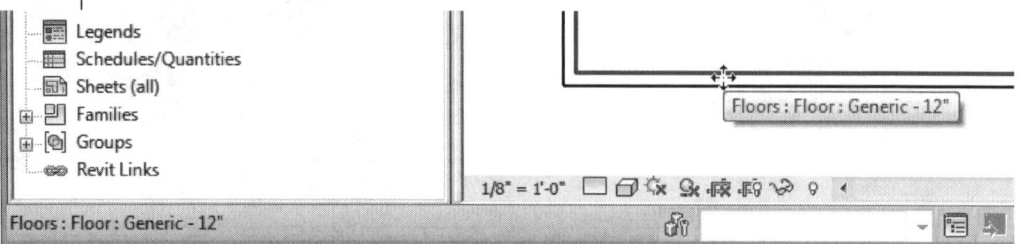

Figure 10–10

2. In the *Modify | Floors* tab>Mode panel, click (Edit Boundary). You are placed into Edit Boundary mode.
3. Modify the sketch lines using the draw tools, controls, and the various modify tools.
4. Click (Finish Edit Mode).

- Select a floor, then double-click on it to be placed directly into Edit Boundary mode.

- Floor sketches can be edited in plan and 3D views, but not in elevations. If you try to edit in an elevation view, you are prompted to select another view in which to edit.

> **Hint: Selecting Floor Faces**
>
> If it is difficult to select the floor edges, toggle on the selection option (Select Elements by Face) from the Status Bar. This will enable you to select the floor face and not just the edges.

## Joining Geometry

**Join Geometry** is a versatile command used to clean up intersections. The elements remain separate, but the intersections are cleaned up. It can be used with many types of elements, including floors, walls, and roofs. In Figure 10–11, the wall on the left and the floor have been joined, but the wall on the right has not been joined with the floor and therefore does not display the lines that define the intersection edges.

*Cutting a section through the objects you want to join helps to display them more clearly.*

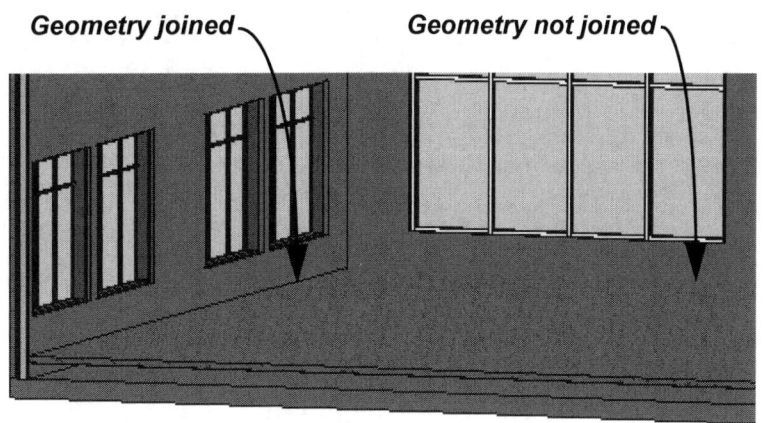

Figure 10–11

## How To: Join Geometry

1. In the *Modify* tab>Geometry panel, expand (Join) and click (Join Geometry).
2. Select the elements to join.

- If you toggle on the **Multiple Join** option in the Options Bar, you can select several elements to join to the first selection.

- To remove the join, expand (Join), click (Unjoin Geometry), and select the elements to unjoin.

### Hint: Selection Sets

If there are elements in the model that you know you will need to select multiple times, you can create a selection set by selecting all the elements in the view and in the contextual tab>Selection panel, select (Save). When you need to select that group of elements again, in the *Manage* tab>Selection panel, click (Load).

For more information on selection sets, see *A.1 Selection Sets*.

# Practice 10a | Model Floors

**Practice Objectives**

- Add floors.
- Copy a floor to multiple levels.

In this practice, you will create and modify floors in the basement, first floor, and second floor of a project. You will then copy the floor on the second floor to other related levels and clean up connections between the floors and wall. The second floor with balconies is shown in Figure 10–12.

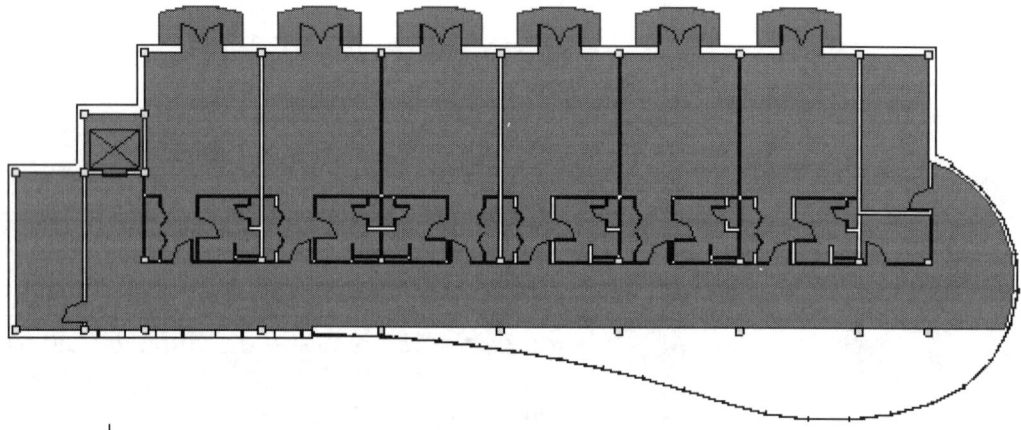

**Figure 10–12**

### Task 1 - Add the basement floor.

*More components have been added to this file and may differ from what you added in the previous practice.*

1. Open the project **Hotel-Floors.rvt** from the practice files folder.

2. Open the **Floor Plans: Basement** view.

3. In the View Control Bar, click (Hide Crop Region).

4. In Properties, in the *Underlay* section, change the *Range: Base Level* to **Floor 2** and *Range: Top Level* to **Unbounded**. This allows you to see the levels above.

5. In the *Architecture* tab>Build panel, click (Floor).

6. In the Type Selector, select **Floor: Concrete-1'-0"**.

7. In the *Modify | Create Floor Boundary* tab>Draw panel, click (Pick Walls) and select the inside face of the exterior foundation walls. Use the Modify tools to ensure that the boundary is a closed loop.

8. Click (Finish Edit Mode).

9. When the alert box about joining geometry opens, click **Yes**. The floor pattern displays as shown in Figure 10–13. (The image has been simplified for clarity.)

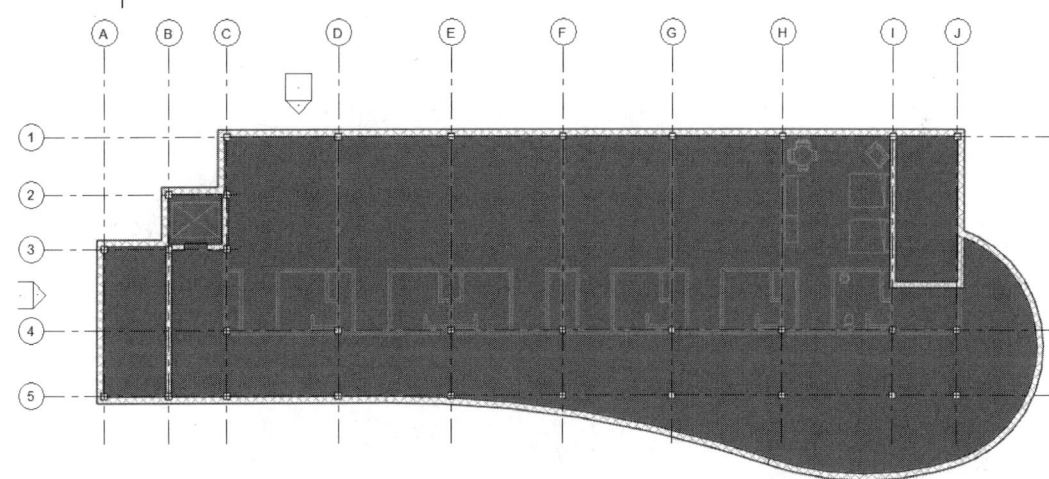

Figure 10–13

10. Click in an empty space in the view to release the floor selection.

11. Start the **Floor** command again.

*Press <Enter> to repeat the last command.*

12. In the Type Selector, select **Floor: Tile**. In Properties, set the *Height Offset From Level* to **1/4"** to match the thickness of the tile.

13. Draw the boundary around the stairwells and hallway, as shown in Figure 10–14.

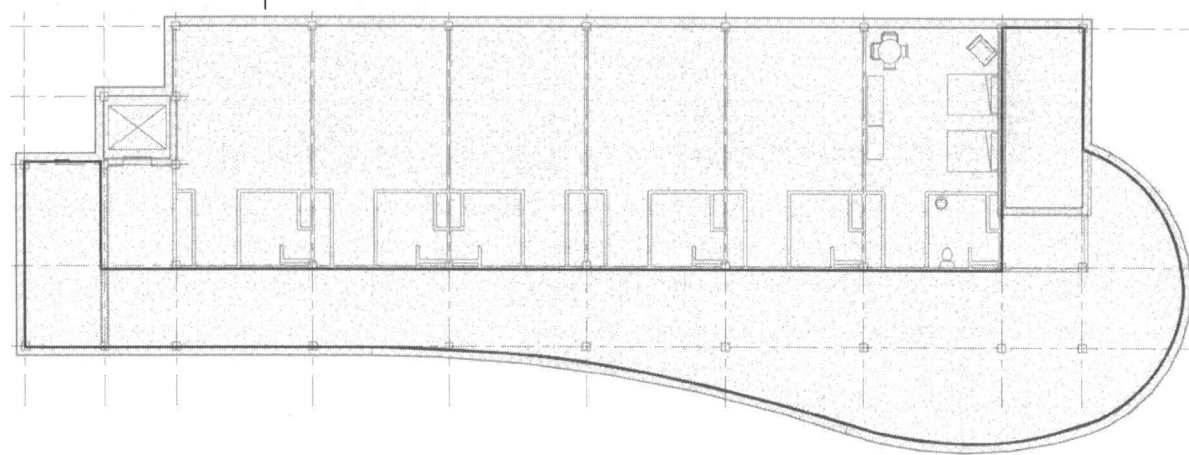

Figure 10–14

14. Click ✓ (Finish Edit Mode).

15. If prompted to join overlapping geometry, click **Yes**.

16. Click in an empty space in the view to release the selection and zoom in to display the different floor coverings, as shown in Figure 10–15.

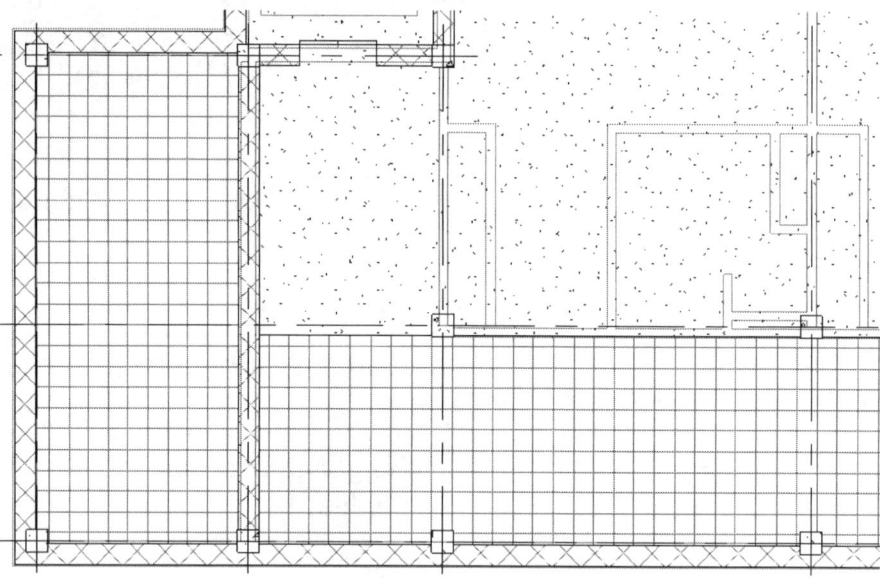

Figure 10–15

17. Zoom in to the west stairs.

18. Double-click on the tile flooring, then select and drag the sketch boundary line so it includes the hall that leads to the elevator, as shown in Figure 10–16.

# Modeling Floors

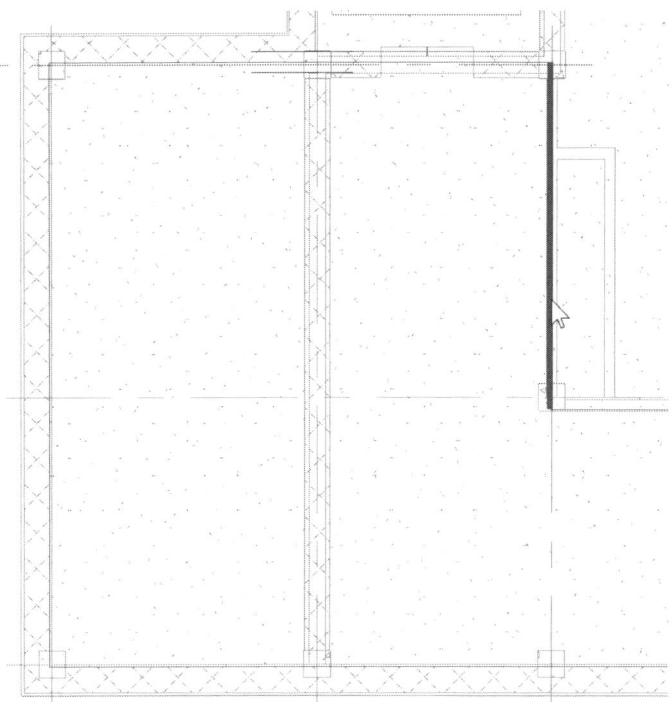

Figure 10–16

19. Click ✓ (Finish Edit Mode).

20. If prompted to join overlapping geometry, click **Yes**.

21. Save the project.

### Task 2 - Add the second floor and balconies.

1. Open the **Floor Plans: Floor 2** view.

2. In the View Control Bar, click 💡 (Reveal Hidden Elements).

3. Select the DWG and in the *Modify | Hotel-Level-2.dwg* tab> Reveal Hidden Elements panel, click (Unhide Category).

4. Select one grid and in the *Modify | Grids* tab>Reveal Hidden Elements panel, click ☒ (Toggle Reveal Hidden Elements Mode).

5. In the View Control Bar, click (Hide Crop Region) to hide the crop region in the view.

6. Select a door tag and room tag, and type **VH** to hide them in the view.

7. In the *Architecture* tab>Build panel, click (Floor). In the Type Selector, select **Floor: Generic - 12"**.

8. In the Options Bar, verify that the *Offset* is **0'-0"** and select **Extend into wall (to core)**.

9. In Properties, set the *Height Offset From Level* to **0'-0"**.

10. Use (Pick Walls) and select the inside of the main exterior walls. Do not select the three curved walls.

11. Change to (Pick Lines) and select the lines of the hallway in the linked CAD (DWG) file, as shown in Figure 10–17.

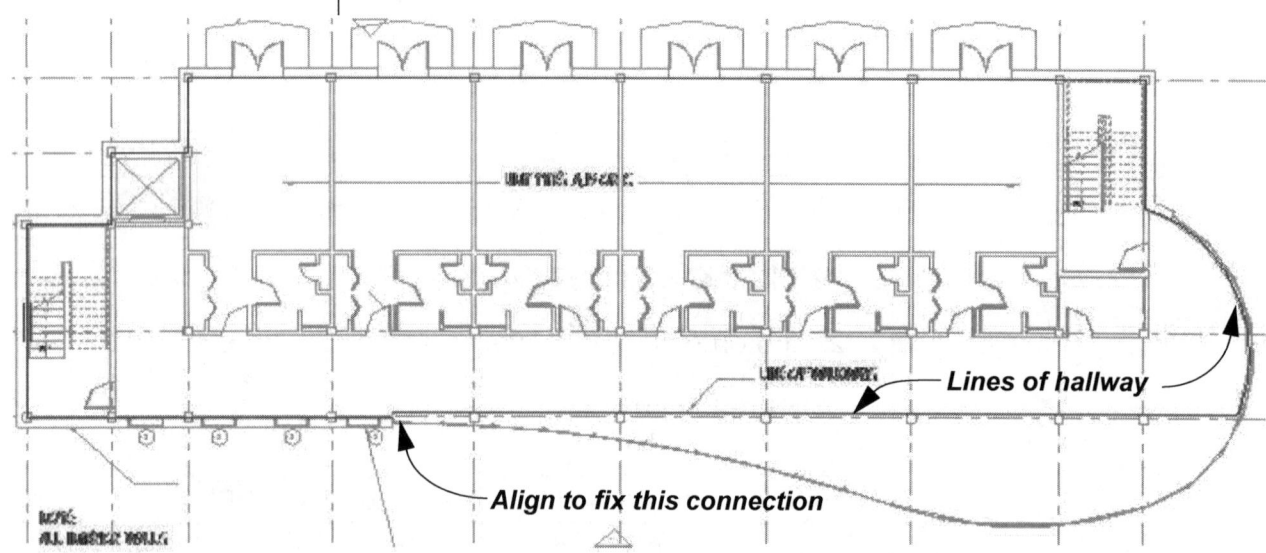

**Figure 10–17**

12. Zoom in and fix the connection at the front wall and hallway. Delete the vertical line. Use the **Align** tool to align the hallway line to the front wall line, as shown in Figure 10–18, and check the other connections.

Modeling Floors

*For accuracy, you need to modify the floor in Revit even though the linked CAD file (DWG) has the floor jogged out.*

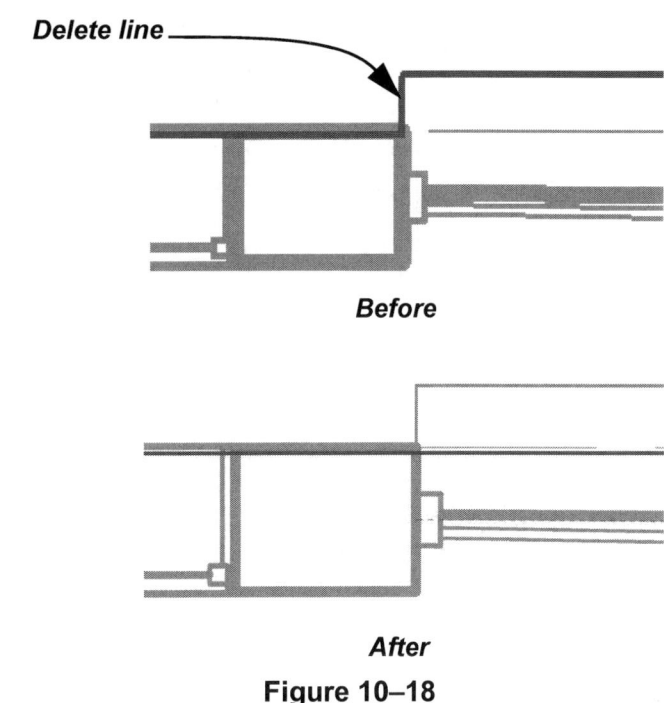

Figure 10–18

13. Click ✓ (Finish Edit Sketch).

- If the alert box displays (as shown in Figure 10–19), click **Don't attach**. You do not want to attach the walls to this floor.
- If the alert box shown in Figure 10–20 displays, click **Yes** to cut overlapping geometry out of the walls.

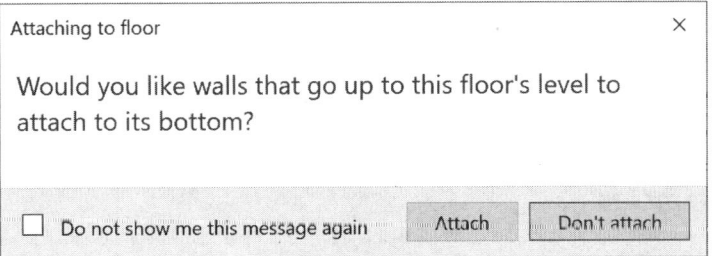

Figure 10–19

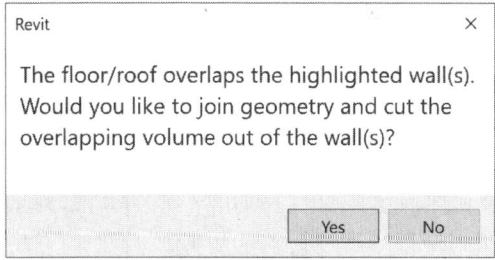

Figure 10–20

14. Click in an empty space in the view to release the floor selection.

15. Pan to the upper-left balcony.

16. In the *Architecture* tab>Build panel, click (Floor) and set the following options:

- In the Type Selector, select **Floor: Generic - 12" Balcony**.
- In Properties, set the *Height Offset From Level* to (negative) **-0'-4"**.

17. Use ✏ (Pick Lines) to create the outline of the balcony, as shown in Figure 10–21. You want the balcony floor to meet the Floor 2 floors.

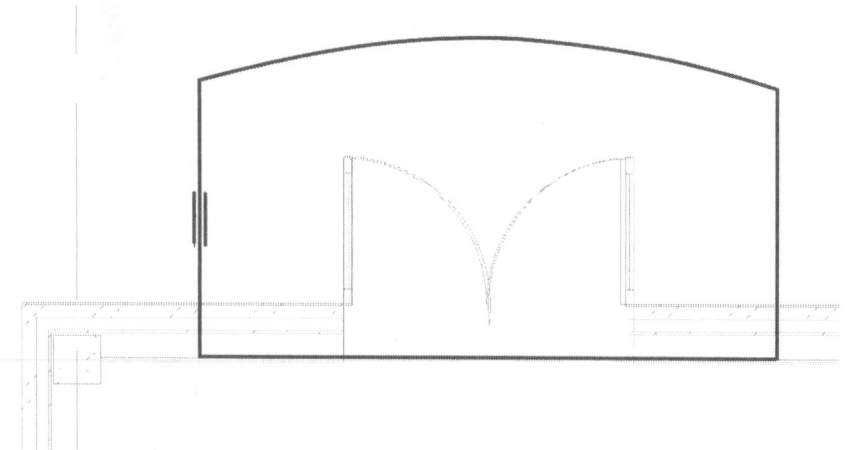

**Figure 10–21**

18. Click ▸ (Modify) and select the balcony elements.

*Use the Trim tool, if needed, to clean up any lines.*

19. Copy the elements to the other balconies.

20. Click ✓ (Finish Edit Sketch).

   - If the alert box displays, click **Don't attach**.
   - Click **Yes** to cut overlapping geometry out of the walls.

21. Click in an empty space in the view to release the floor selection.

22. Select the imported CAD file and type **VH** to hide it in the view.

23. Save the project.

**Task 3 - Copy the floor and balcony floors to the other floors.**

1. Close any open view or projects except for **Floor Plans: Floor 2**. Open the Default 3D view and type **WT** to tile the views.

2. In the **Floor Plans: Floor 2** view, select the new floor and balcony floors.

3. In the *Modify | Multi-Select* tab>Clipboard panel, click 🗐 (Copy to the Clipboard).

4. In the Clipboard panel, expand  (Paste) and click  (Aligned to Selected Levels).

5. In the Select Levels dialog box, select **Floor 3** through **Floor 8**, as shown in Figure 10–22. Click **OK**.

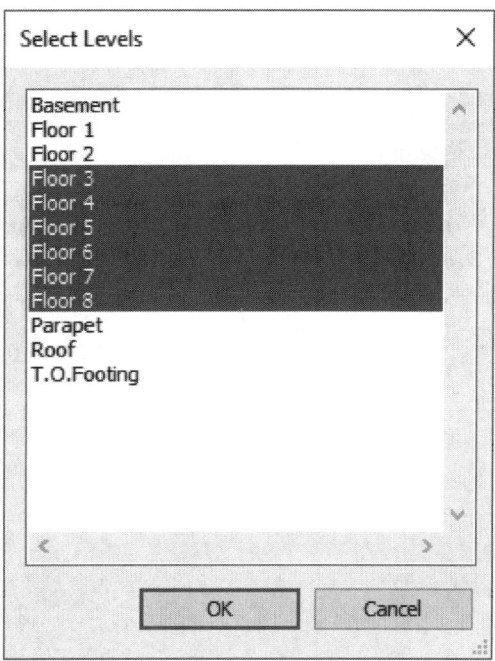

**Figure 10–22**

6. In the 3D view, orbit the view to view the new floors.

7. Save and close the project.

## 10.2 Creating Shaft Openings

Openings can be added to floors (as well as roofs and ceilings) by drawing a closed sketch in an existing floor, roof, or ceiling. When you have elevator shafts or other floor openings that span more than one floor, create a shaft opening and specify the depth to cut through the required levels. Then, place symbolic lines to represent a shaft opening in plan view, as shown in Figure 10–23.

*Note: Shaft openings only cut floors, roofs, and ceilings. They do not cut walls, beams, or other objects. Shafts are their own element so they can be deleted without affecting the host.*

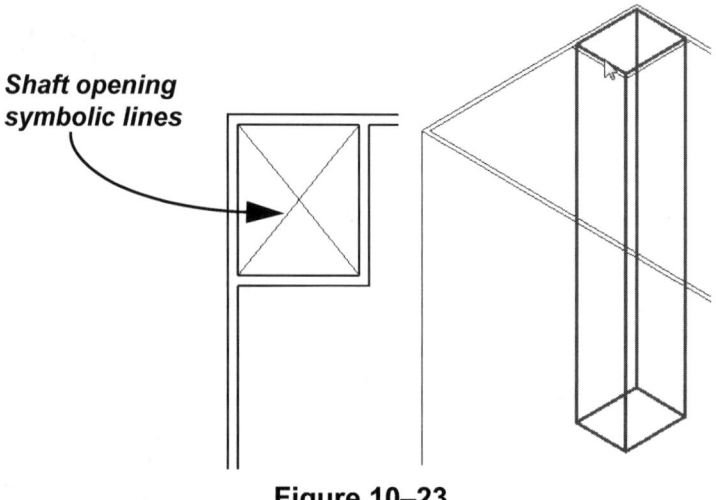

**Figure 10–23**

### How To: Add a Shaft Opening

1. In the *Architecture* tab>Opening panel, click (Shaft).
2. In the *Modify | Create Shaft Opening Sketch* tab>Draw panel, click (Boundary Line) and sketch a line to define the opening.
3. In Properties, set the following:
   - *Base and Top Constraint*
   - *Base and Top Offset* or *Unconnected Height*
4. In the Draw panel, click (Symbolic Line) and add lines that show the opening symbol in plan view.

*Shaft symbolic lines repeat on each level.*

Modeling Floors

# 10.3 Creating Sloped Floors

Floors can have slopes applied to them. To make a floor slope in one direction, you place a *slope arrow* in the sketch of the floor, as shown in Figure 10–24.

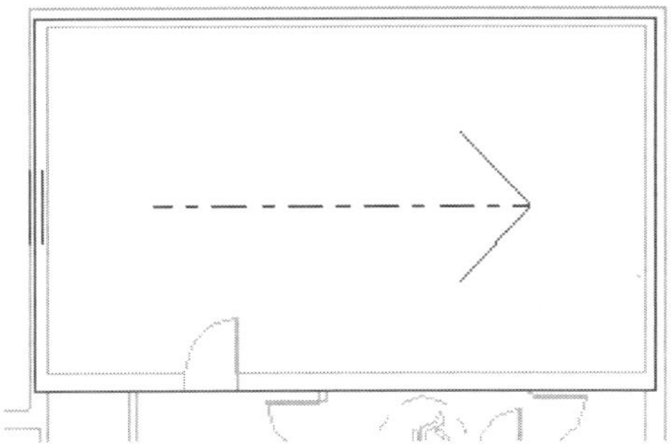

*The slope arrow only displays while sketch mode is active.*

Figure 10–24

- Once the floor is created, you can add multiple drainage points and cause the floor to warp toward them.

- These tools also work with roofs and structural slabs.

## How To: Slope a Floor in One Direction

1. Select the floor you want to slope. In the *Modify | Floors* tab> Mode panel, click (Edit Boundary).
2. In the *Modify | Floors>Edit Boundary* tab>Draw panel, click (Slope Arrow).
3. Select two points to define the arrow. The first point is the tail and the second is the head. The tail and head locations are points at which you can specify heights. The direction of the arrow determines the orientation of the slope.
4. In Properties, you can choose to define the slope arrow by **Height at Tail** or **Slope** by setting the *Specify* value, as shown in Figure 10–25.

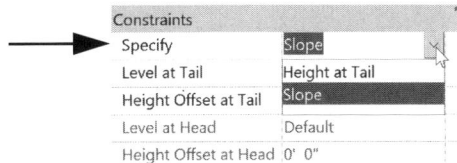

Figure 10–25

- If *Specify* is set to **Height at Tail**, you can modify the *Level at Tail*, *Height Offset at Tail*, *Level at Head,* and *Height Offset at Head*, as shown in Figure 10–26.

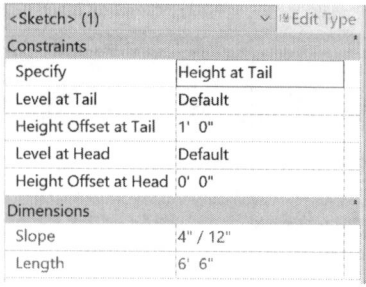

**Figure 10–26**

- If *Specify* is set to **Slope**, you can modify the *Level at Tail*, *Height Offset at Tail,* and *Slope,* as shown in Figure 10–27.

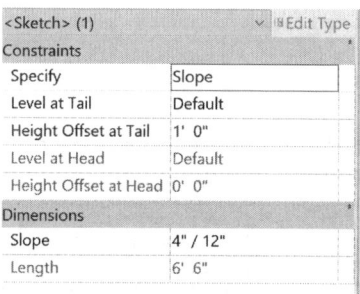

**Figure 10–27**

## Creating Multiple Slopes for Drainage

Restrooms, labs, garages, and other rooms often need to have floors that slope towards drains, as shown in Figure 10–28. In addition, all flat roofs are not actually flat, but also slope towards drains. Several tools provide ways of creating points for the drain locations, as well as creating lines to define how the slope is going to drain.

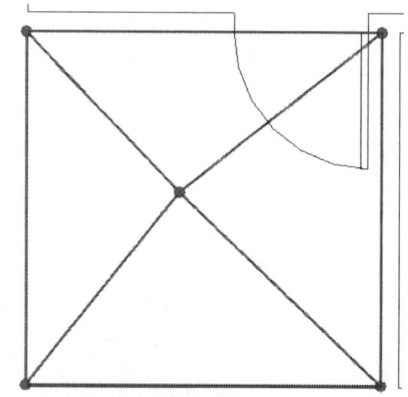

**Figure 10–28**

- These tools work with floors, roofs, and structural floors.

# Modeling Floors

## How To: Create Multiple Slopes for Drainage

1. Select the flat floor, roof, or slab that you want to add a slope to.
2. In the *Modify | Floors* tab>Shape Editing panel (shown in Figure 10–29), select the tools that you want to use to define the slopes.

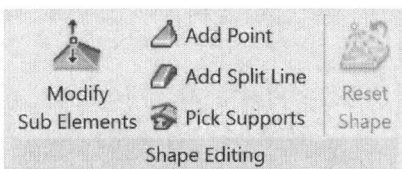

**Figure 10–29**

| | |
|---|---|
|  | **Add Point:** Specify the location of the low or high points on the surface. In the Options Bar, set the *Elevation*.<br><br>• By default, the elevation is relative to the top of the surface. Clear the **Relative** option if you want to use the project elevation.<br><br>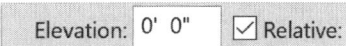<br><br>• ● displays when you place the point. Slope lines are automatically added from the corners of the surface to the point. |
|  | **Add Split Line:** Define smaller areas on the surface when you place more than one drain. Depending on the size of the area you are working with, you might want to create these before you add the drains.<br><br>Select the **Chain** option if you want to add more than one connected segment. |
|  | **Pick Supports:** Select structural beams that define the split lines. |

**Modify Sub-Elements:** Change the elevation of edges and points and change the location of points. You can also move points using shape handles without clicking  (Modify Sub-Elements), as shown in the figure below. Press <Tab> to cycle through the options to reach the element you want to modify.

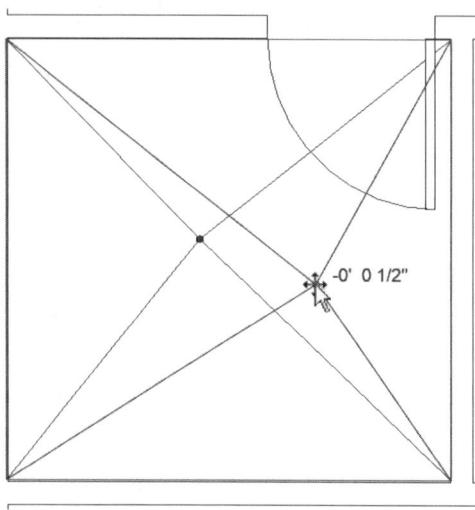

- If you want to remove the slopes from a surface, click (Reset Shape).

- Floors, roofs, and slabs use styles set to a constant thickness (where the entire element slopes) or to a variable thickness (where only the top layer slopes), as shown in Figure 10–30.

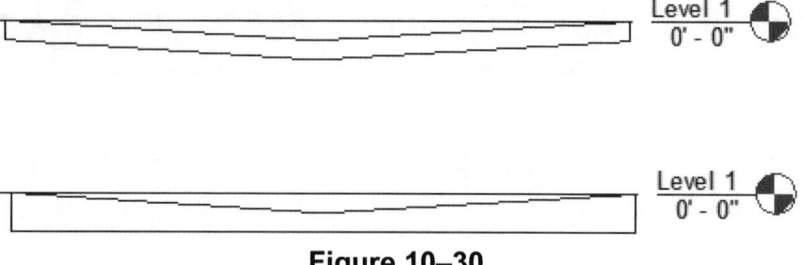

**Figure 10–30**

# Practice 10b

# Create Shaft Openings and Sloped Floors

## Practice Objectives

- Create a shaft opening.
- Slope floors.

In this practice, you will add a shaft opening for the elevator, as shown on the left in Figure 10–31. You will also slope floors for drainage in the restrooms and janitor closet using the Shape Editing tools, as shown on the right in Figure 10–31.

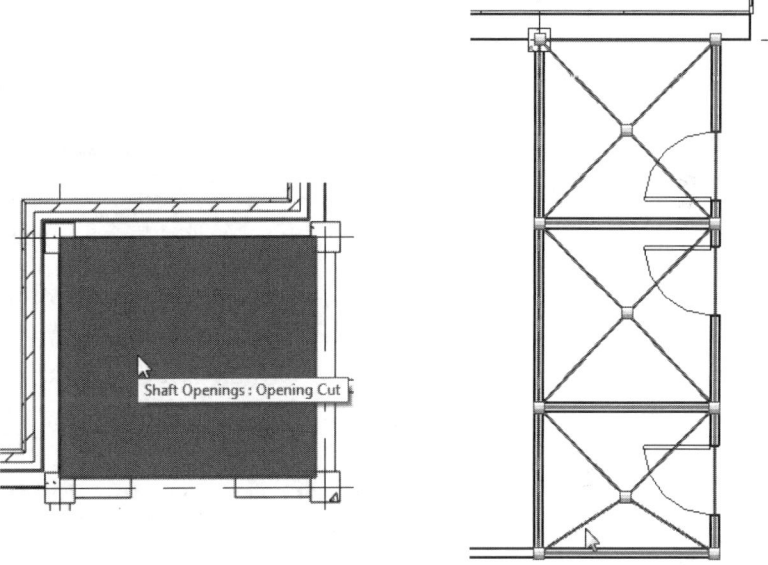

Figure 10–31

### Task 1 - Create a shaft opening.

1. Open the project **Hotel-Slope.rvt** from the practice files folder.

2. Verify you are in the **Floor Plans: Floor 1** view and zoom in to the elevator area.

3. In the *Architecture* tab>Opening panel, click (Shaft).

4. In the *Modify | Create Shaft Opening Sketch* tab>Draw panel, verify that (Boundary Line) is selected.

5. Use  (Pick Walls) to create the boundary, then use  (Trim/Extend to Corner) to ensure that the boundary is closed, as shown in Figure 10–32.

   - Shafts do not cut through structural elements.

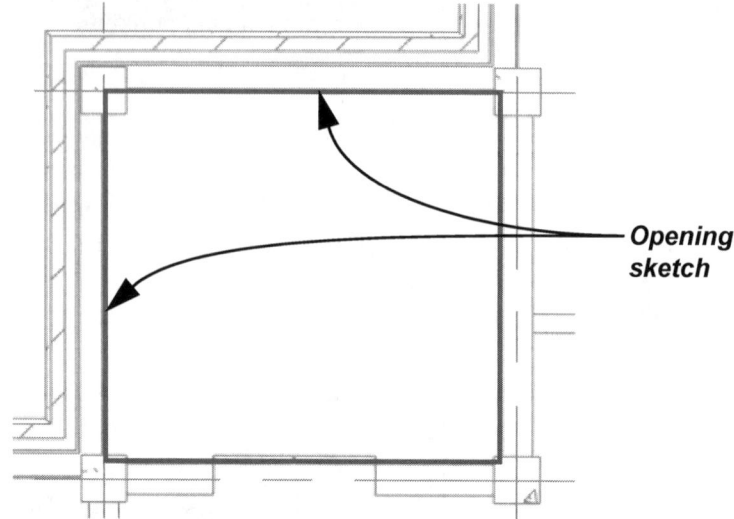

Figure 10–32

6. In Properties, verify that the shaft opening's *Base Constraint* is **Floor 1**. Set the *Base Offset* to (negative) **-1'-0"** and the *Top Constraint* to **Up to Level:Roof**.

7. In the *Modify | Create Shaft Opening Sketch* tab>Draw panel, select  (Symbolic Lines).

8. In the Options Bar, uncheck **Chain**.

9. Draw an X in the shaft opening from corner to corner, as shown in Figure 10–33.

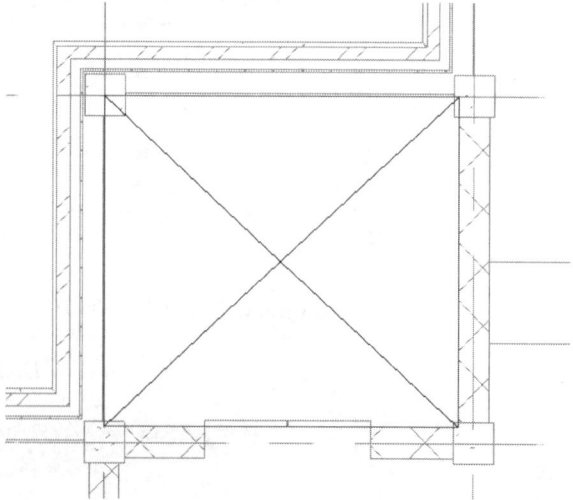

Figure 10–33

10. Click ✓ (Finish Edit Mode).

11. Click (Modify).

12. In the View Control Bar, change the *Visual Style* to (Consistent Colors) to display the opening.

13. Return the *Visual Style* to (Hidden Line).

14. Return to the **Floor Plans: Floor 1** view.

15. Zoom out to display the entire view, if needed.

16. Save the project.

### Task 2 - Slope floors for drainage.

1. Open the **Floor Plans: Floor 1 - Restrooms** view.

2. Expand the size of the crop region so the janitor closet below is also included in the plan.

*Verify **Select Elements by Face** is toggled on.*

3. Click on the face of the floor to select it. Figure 10–34 shows the floor selected.

   • Note: In Properties, you should see **Floor: Generic - 12"** as the selected floor.

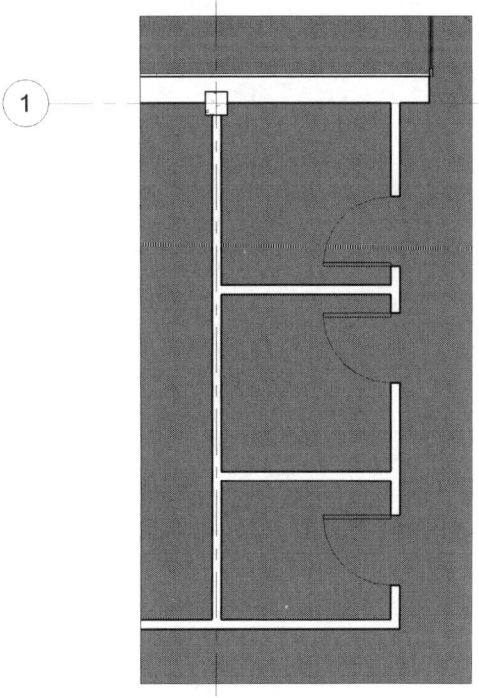

**Figure 10–34**

4. In the *Modify | Floors* tab>Shape Editing panel, click  (Add Split Line).

5. Verify that, in the Options Bar, **Chain** is selected.

6. Draw the outside edges first and then the two internal lines, as shown in Figure 10–35.

    - Because **Chain** is selected, you will have to uncheck **Chain** from the Options Bar, then click  (Add Split Line) to draw the two internal lines.

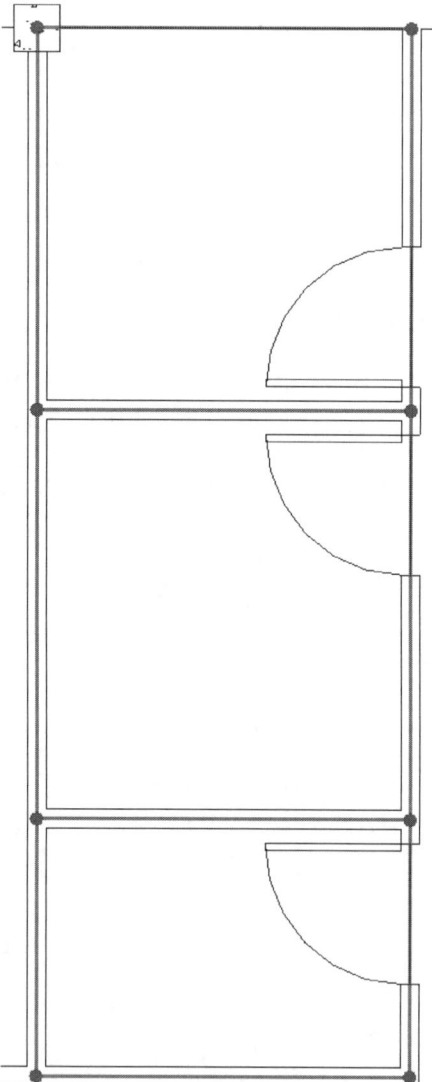

**Figure 10–35**

7. In the Shape Editing panel, click (Add Point). In the Options Bar, set the *Elevation* to (negative) **-1/2"**. Place a point in the center of each room, as shown for one of them in Figure 10–36.

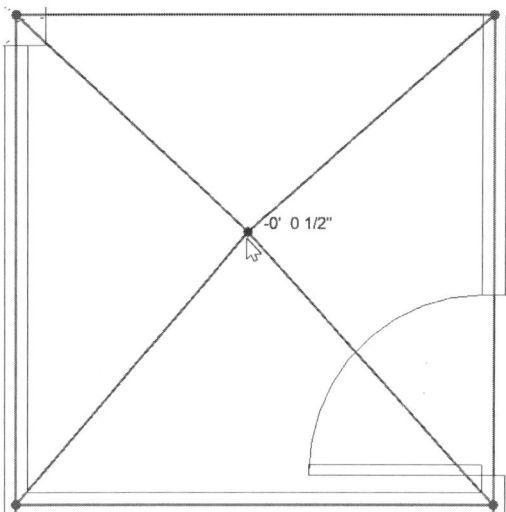

Figure 10–36

8. Click (Modify).

9. Save and close the project.

# Chapter Review Questions

1. When creating a floor, the boundary sketch must be a closed loop to finish the sketch.

    a. True

    b. False

2. How do you change the thickness of a floor, such as those shown in Figure 10–37?

    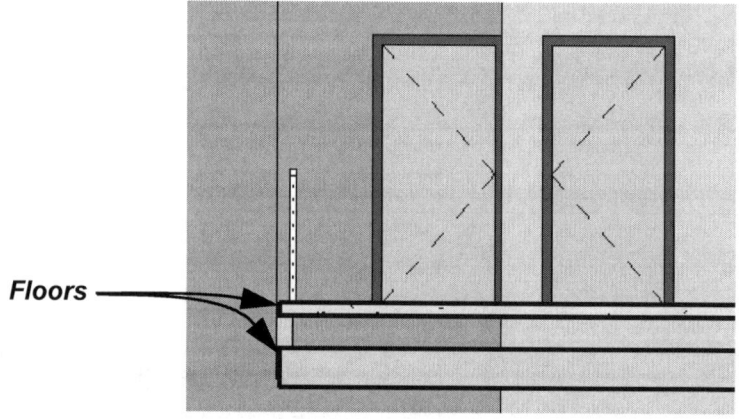

    **Figure 10–37**

    a. In the Type Selector, change the *Floor Type*.

    b. In the Options Bar, change the *Floor Thickness*.

    c. In Properties, change the *Floor Thickness*.

    d. In the contextual ribbon, change the *Offset*.

3. Which of the following Opening commands cuts an opening in multiple floors at the same time?

    a. **By Face**

    b. **Shaft**

    c. **Wall**

    d. **Vertical**

4. When creating a sloped floor, the (Add Points) command places a point where?

    a. The end of the floor where you want the slope to end.

    b. The end of the floor where you want the slope to begin.

    c. The high or low points of a floor.

    d. A point where two slopes converge.

# Command Summary

| Button | Command | Location |
|---|---|---|
| | **Floor: Architectural** | • **Ribbon:** *Architecture* tab>Build panel> expand Floor |
| | **Floor: Structural** | • **Ribbon:** *Architecture* tab>Build panel> expand Floor |
| | **Shaft** | • **Ribbon:** *Architecture* tab>Opening panel |
| **Shape Editing Tools** | | |
| | **Add Point** | • **Ribbon:** *Modify | Floors* tab>Shape Editing panel |
| | **Add Split Line** | • **Ribbon:** *Modify | Floors* tab>Shape Editing panel |
| | **Modify Sub Elements** | • **Ribbon:** *Modify | Floors* tab>Shape Editing panel |
| | **Pick Supports** | • **Ribbon:** *Modify | Floors* tab>Shape Editing panel |
| | **Reset Shape** | • **Ribbon:** *Modify | Floors* tab>Shape Editing panel |

# Chapter 11

# Modeling Ceilings

In Revit®, ceilings are modeled using reflected ceiling plans. You can add ceilings by selecting a room boundary or by sketching ceilings that do not fill an entire room. You can create basic ceilings made of acoustical tile grids, or you can create custom ceilings of different heights with a soffit wall added between. In addition to creating a ceiling, you can also place ceiling fixtures directly onto ceiling elements.

## Learning Objectives in This Chapter

- Add automatic ceilings that fill an entire room boundary and sketched ceilings that are customized to suit a design.
- Modify ceiling boundaries and the grid locations for acoustical tiles to ensure that the tiles fit the room correctly.
- Add ceiling components, including lighting and mechanical fixtures.
- Add soffit walls in the gap between ceilings of different heights.

# 11.1 Modeling Ceilings

Adding ceilings to Revit models is a straightforward process. To place a ceiling, click inside areas that are bounded by walls, and the ceiling is created, as shown in the large room on the right in Figure 11–1. You can also sketch custom ceilings when required. Any fixtures you attach to a ceiling displays in reflected ceiling plans, as well as in sections and 3D views.

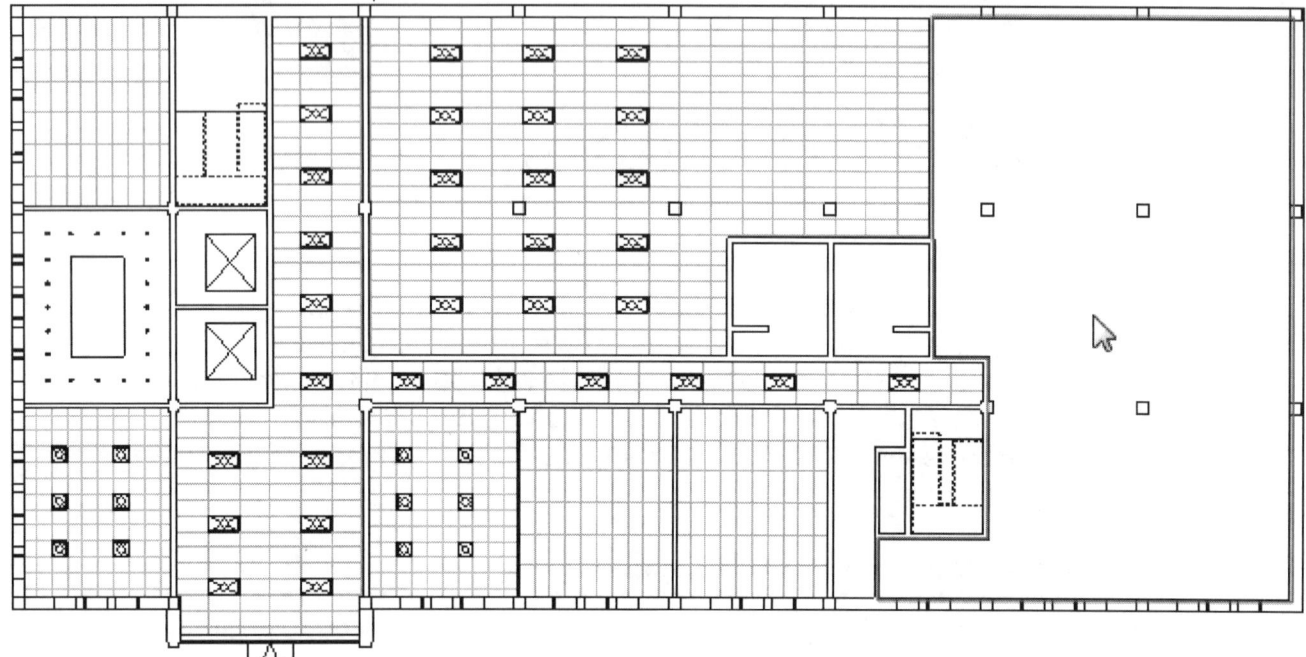

Figure 11–1

- If the walls are lower than what your ceiling properties *Height Offset From Level* is set to, **Automatic Ceiling** will not work and you will see a ⊘ icon. You will have to either lower the ceiling height offset or use the **Sketch Ceiling** tool.

- If multiple ceilings are sketched in a room, you can add a slope to create vaulted or cathedral ceilings.

# Modeling Ceilings

## How To: Create an Automatic Boundary Ceiling

1. Switch to a ceiling plan view.
2. In the *Architecture* tab>Build panel, click (Ceiling).
3. In the Type Selector, select the ceiling type. In Properties, set the *Height Offset From Level*.
4. In the *Modify | Place Ceiling* tab>Ceiling panel, verify that (Automatic Ceiling) is selected. Click inside a room to create a ceiling, as shown in Figure 11–2.

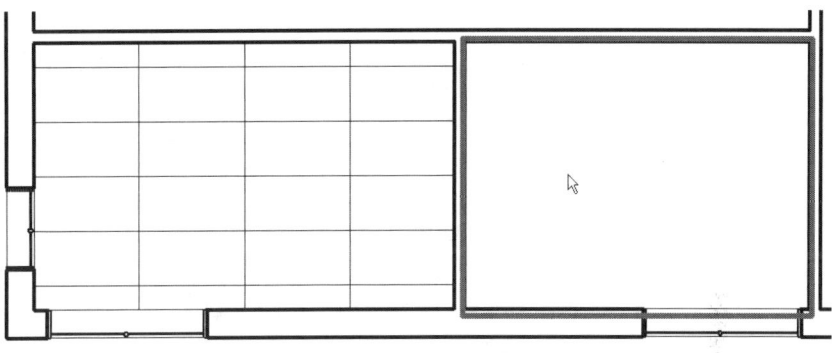

**Figure 11–2**

5. Continue adding ceilings to other rooms, as needed, or click (Modify) to end the command.

> **Hint: Room Bounding Status**
>
> Elements such as walls, floors, ceilings, and roofs have a *Room Bounding* property set in Properties. In most cases, this is toggled on by default as these elements typically define areas and volumes.
>
> The **Automatic Ceiling** tool uses this property to identify walls that set the outline of a ceiling. If you toggle off this property for a wall (such as a partial height wall), the **Automatic Ceiling** tool ignores the wall.
>
> Ceilings can also be used as a room bounding for volume calculations.

- To modify a ceiling boundary, select a ceiling and either:
    - in the *Modify | Ceilings* tab>Mode panel, click (Edit Boundary), or
    - double-click on the ceiling to enter Edit Boundary mode.

## Sketching Ceilings

To add a ceiling to part of a room, as shown in Figure 11–3, or to have two different ceiling types at separate levels, you need to sketch a ceiling.

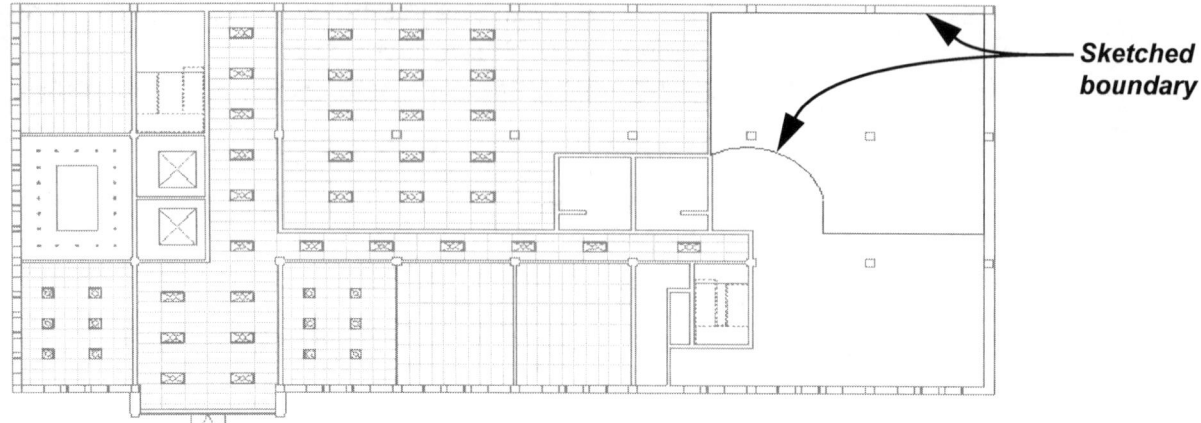

Figure 11–3

### How To: Sketch a Ceiling

1. In the *Architecture* tab>Build panel, click (Ceiling).
2. In the *Modify | Place Ceiling* tab>Ceiling panel, click (Sketch Ceiling).
3. In the Draw panel, click (Line) or (Pick Walls) and define a closed loop for the ceiling boundary, similar to sketching a floor boundary.

- To create a sloped ceiling, in the *Modify | Ceilings>Edit Boundary* tab>Draw panel, click (Slope Arrow) and draw the arrow in the direction you want the slope. Set the Properties for **Height at Tail** or **Slope**, as shown in Figure 11–4.

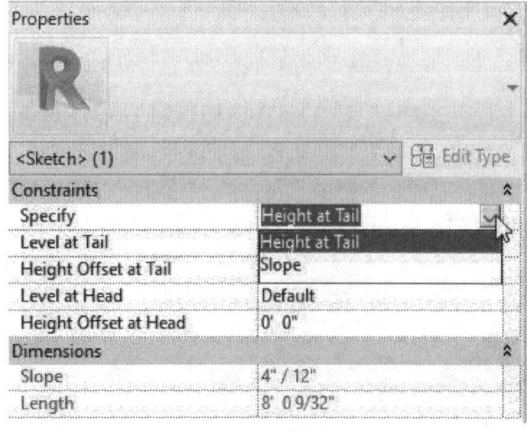 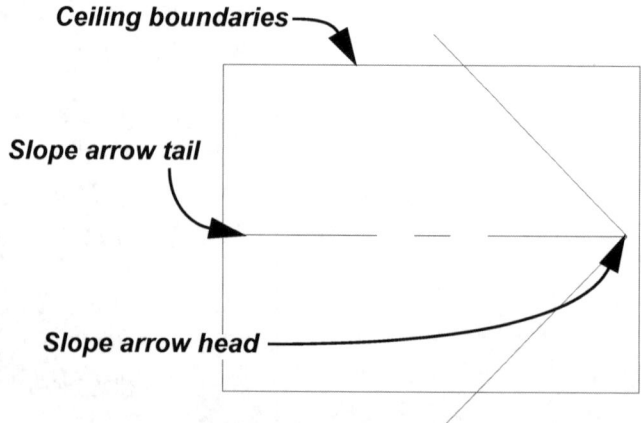

Figure 11–4

# Modeling Ceilings

4. Click ✓ (Finish Edit Mode) to create the ceiling.

- To include a hole in a ceiling, include the hole as part of the sketch. The hole must be a closed loop completely inside the ceiling boundary.

- In the *Architecture* tab>Opening panel, you can also use  (Opening By Face),  (Shaft Opening), or  (Vertical Opening) to cut a hole in a ceiling that is separate from the sketch.

## Modifying Ceiling Grids

*To change a rectangular ceiling tile pattern from horizontal to vertical, select a ceiling grid line and rotate it 90°.*

When using acoustical tile ceiling types, you can reposition the ceiling grid locations by moving or rotating the grid lines, as shown in Figure 11–5.

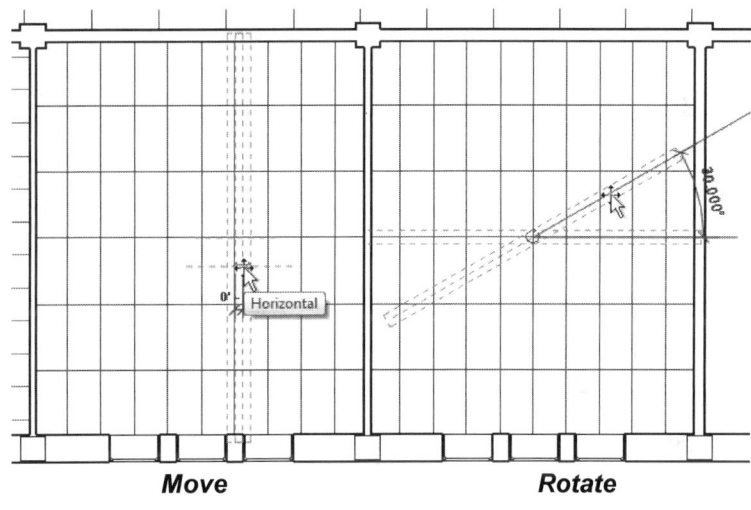

*Move*          *Rotate*

**Figure 11–5**

### How To: Move a Ceiling Grid

1. Select a ceiling grid line in the ceiling that you want to modify.

2. In the *Modify | Ceilings* tab>Modify panel, click  (Move).
   - In order for the **Move** command to work when selecting only an individual ceiling grid line, you must verify that **Disjoin** is turned off. If it is not, select the entire ceiling, and in the Options Bar, clear the **Disjoin** checkbox.

3. Move the cursor to one side and type a distance, typically an increment of the ceiling grid size.

## How To: Rotate a Ceiling Grid

1. Select a ceiling grid line in the ceiling that you want to modify.
2. In the *Modify | Ceilings* tab>Modify panel, click ⟳ (Rotate).
3. In the Options Bar, type an *Angle* or use ⟲ (Rotate) to visually select the angle.

# 11.2 Adding Ceiling Fixtures

Several groups of components are commonly used with ceilings, such as:

- Lighting fixtures (shown in Figure 11–6)

- Mechanical equipment (for registers and diffusers)

- Specialty equipment (such as exit signs or sprinklers)

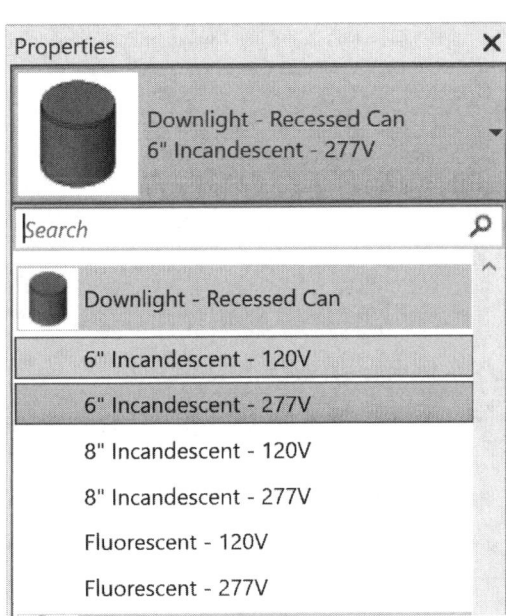

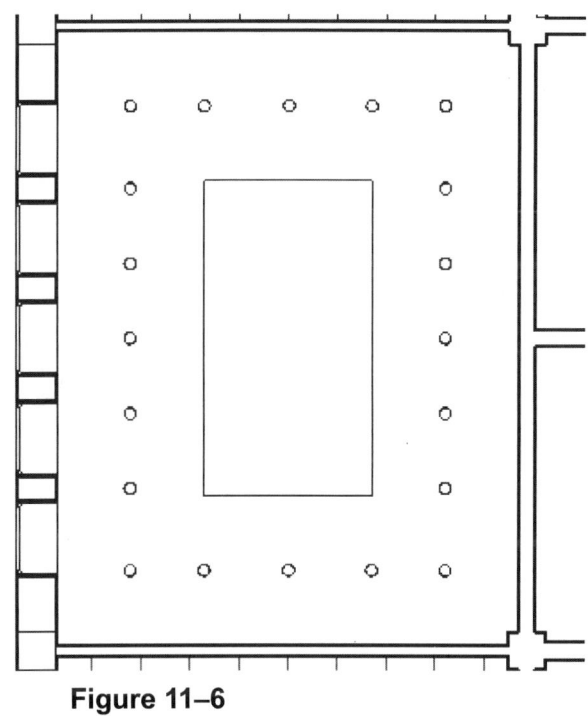

**Figure 11–6**

*After placing a component, press <Spacebar> to rotate it in 90° increments.*

- Use (Component) to place ceiling fixtures in the ceiling view.

- The Revit Library contains a variety of light fixtures and mechanical ceiling fixtures.

- Many light fixtures include types that specify the voltage of the lamp, as shown in Figure 11–6.

- Some light fixtures are wall-based, instead of ceiling-based, and need to be placed on a wall in a floor plan view. These include items such as sconces.

- When you delete a ceiling, the associated components (such as light fixtures) are also deleted.

- Components come in based on their center point and respond to the nearby walls, not to the ceiling grid. Place an instance of the component and use **Move** or **Align** to get it to the correct location on the ceiling grid, then use **Copy** to place additional instances on the ceiling grid.

- Some light fixtures can display the light source, as shown in the section in Figure 11–7. To display the light source, in the Visibility/Graphic Overrides dialog box, on the *Model Categories* tab, expand **Lighting Fixtures** and select **Light Source,** as shown on the left in Figure 11–7.

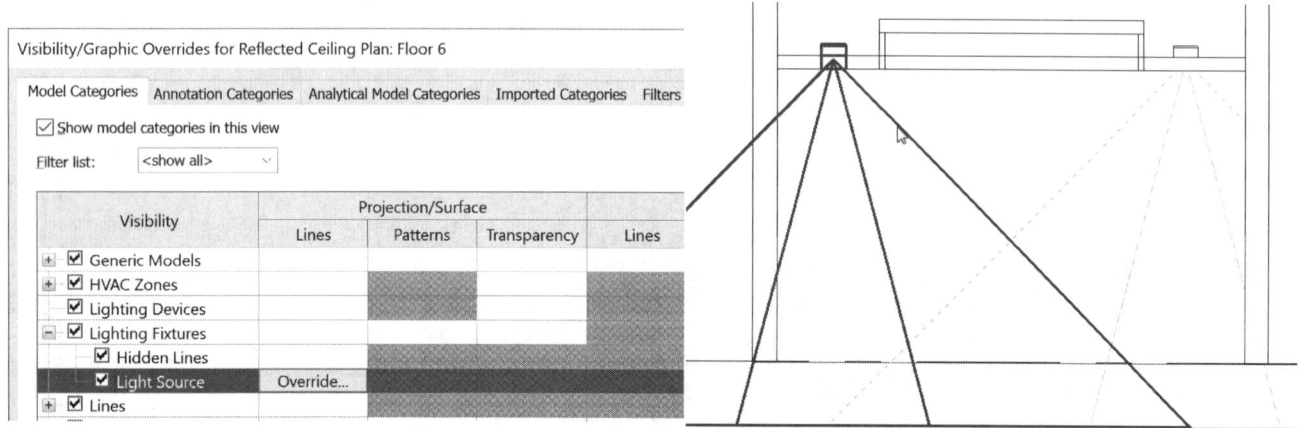

Figure 11–7

- The light sources display their true strength in renderings.

# Modeling Ceilings

**Hint: Placing Components in Rooms Without a Ceiling**

If you need to place components in a room that does not have a ceiling, you can create a reference plane at the height where you want them and place work plane-based families on it. You can also place work plane-based components on the underside of a floor.

1. In a section or elevation view, sketch a reference plane at the required height.
2. Click on the *<Click to name>* field, type a name, and press <Enter>.
3. Open the ceiling plan where you want to work.
4. Start the **Component** command and select a work plane-based component.
5. In the *Modify | Place Component* tab>Placement panel, click (Place on Work Plane), as shown in Figure 11–8.

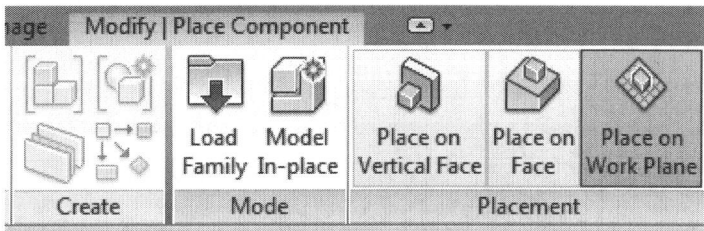

Figure 11–8

6. In the Options Bar, specify the named reference plane from the Placement Plane drop-down list, as shown in Figure 11–9.

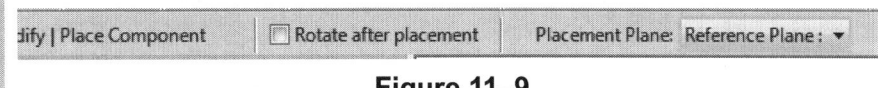

Figure 11–9

7. Place the component.

- These options are only available if you have selected a work plane-based or face-based component.

# Practice 11a

# Model Ceilings and Add Ceiling Fixtures

## Practice Objectives

- Create automatic ceilings with ceiling grids.
- Add ceiling components.

In this practice, while working in a reflected ceiling plan, you will add acoustical tile ceilings to several support spaces. You will then add light fixtures and air terminals, as shown in Figure 11–10.

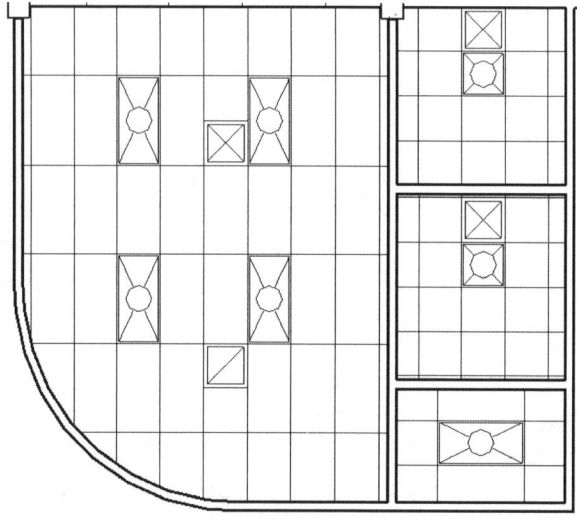

**Figure 11–10**

### Task 1 - Create ceilings with ceiling grids.

1. Open the project **Hotel-Ceilings.rvt** from the practice files folder.

2. Open the **Ceiling Plans: Floor 1** view.

    - To clarify the view, you might want to hide the grids, elevations, and section marker categories. A quick way to do this is to select one of each element and then type **VH**.

3. Pan and zoom in to the kitchen and restrooms area.

4. In the *Architecture* tab>Build panel, click  (Ceiling).

5. In the Type Selector, verify that **Compound Ceiling: 2' x 4' ACT System** is selected.

# Modeling Ceilings

6. In Properties, set the *Height Offset From Level* to **9'-0"**.

7. Click inside the kitchen, in each of the two restrooms (as shown in Figure 11–11), and in the janitor closet to add a ceiling to all four rooms.

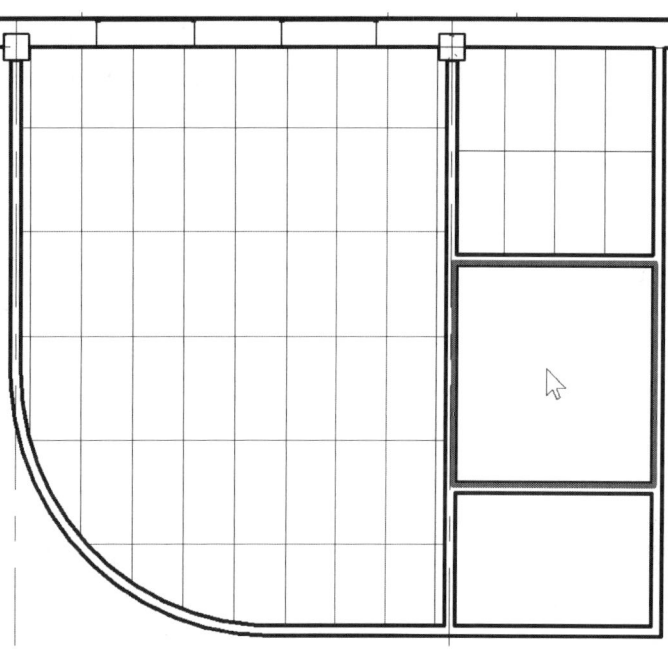

**Figure 11–11**

*Hold <Ctrl> to select more than one element.*

8. Click (Modify).

9. Select a ceiling grid line in the two restrooms.

10. In the Type Selector, select **Compound Ceiling: 2' x 2' ACT System**. In Properties, set the *Height Offset From Level* to **10'-0"**.

11. Save the project.

## Task 2 - Add and modify ceiling-hosted components.

1. In the *Architecture* tab>Build panel, click (Component).

2. In the *Modify | Place Component* tab>Mode panel, click (Load Family) and load the following components from the practice files *Families>Lighting* folder:

    - **Troffer Light 2x2 Parabolic.rfa**
    - **Troffer Light 2x4 Parabolic.rfa**

3. Place one **Troffer Light 2x2** in each of the restrooms, as shown in Figure 11–12. Accuracy is not necessary as you will fix the placement in the next steps.

   - Note that when you are not hovering over a ceiling, your cursor changes from the light fixture to the cannot place icon ( 🚫 ), indicating that you cannot place the element in the area your cursor is currently in as the light fixture belongs to a ceiling-based family.

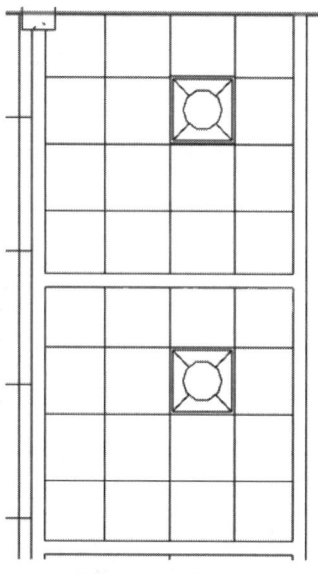

**Figure 11–12**

4. Click (Modify).

5. Zoom in to the top restroom.

6. In the *Modify* tab>Modify panel, click (Align).

7. In the *Modify | Align* tab>Align panel, check the checkbox for **Lock**.

8. Select the ceiling grid first and then the light fixture second, as shown in Figure 11–13. Do this to both horizontal and vertical grid lines.

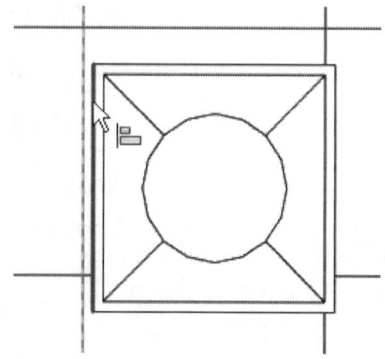

**Figure 11–13**

9. Repeat the alignment in the second restroom.

10. Click (Modify).

11. In the top restroom, select a ceiling grid line.

12. In the *Modify | Ceilings* tab>Modify panel, click (Move).

13. In the Options Bar, verify that **Constrain** is unchecked.

14. Move the grids either vertically or horizontally so that the light fixture is approximately in the center of the room, as shown in Figure 11–14.

    - Hint: After you have moved the ceiling grid, you can use your arrow keys to move the ceiling up or down. Use **Align** to align the two ceiling grids vertically.

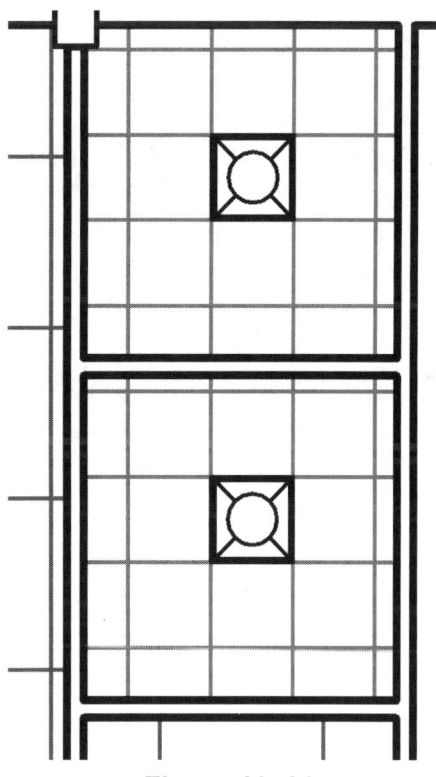

Figure 11–14

15. Click (Modify).

16. Pan and zoom out so you can see the kitchen and the janitor closet.

17. Start the **Component** command again.

18. In the Type Selector, select **Troffer Light 2x4 Parabolic** and place four lights in the kitchen and another one in the janitor closet, as shown in Figure 11–15.

19. Click  (Modify).

20. Select any light fixtures that need to be rotated and press <Spacebar> to rotate the lights 90° so they match the ceiling grid shown in Figure 11–15.

21. Click  (Modify).

22. Use the **Align** and **Move** commands, as well as the arrow keys, to position the lights and ceiling grids as shown in Figure 11–15.

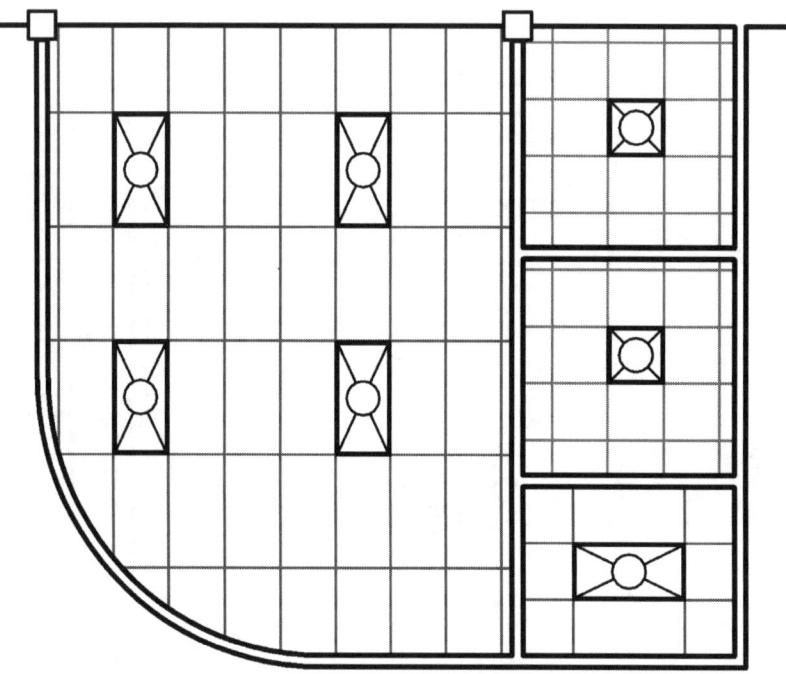

**Figure 11–15**

23. Click  (Modify).

24. Start the **Component** command again.

25. In the *Modify | Place Component* tab>Mode panel, click  (Load Family) and load the following components from the practice files *Families>Air Terminals* folder:

- **Square Return Register.rfa**
- **Square Supply Diffuser.rfa**

26. In the Type Selector, select the supply or return diffuser.

27. Place a supply diffuser in each room (excluding the janitor closet) and a return diffuser in the kitchen, as shown in Figure 11–16.

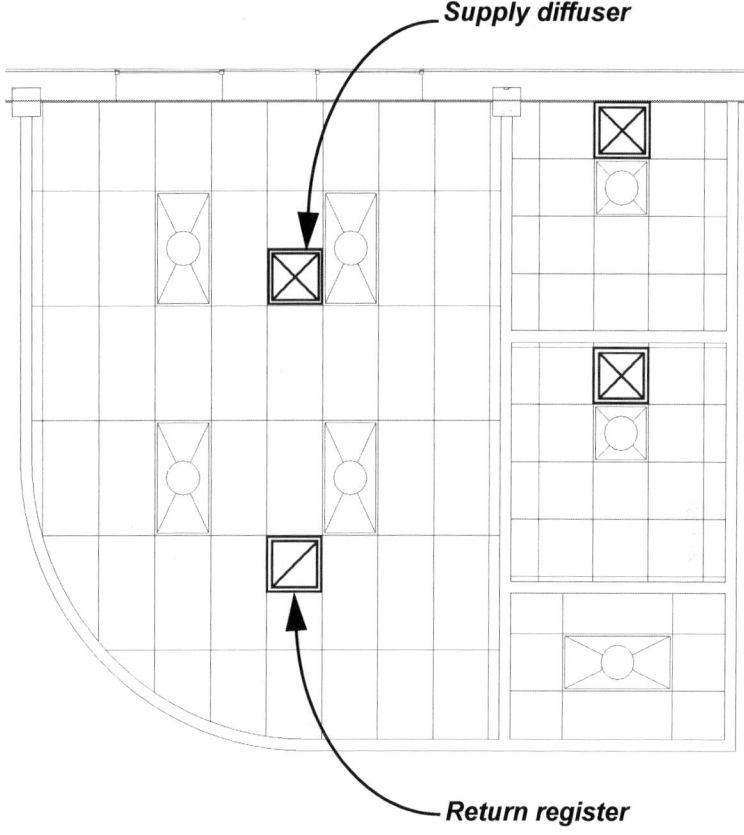

**Figure 11–16**

28. Save and close the project.

## 11.3 Creating Ceiling Soffits

Ceiling soffits are parts of a ceiling that have been lowered, as shown in Figure 11–17, or that connect two ceilings of different heights. Creating a ceiling soffit takes two steps. First, you create a ceiling, and then you model walls using a soffit wall type.

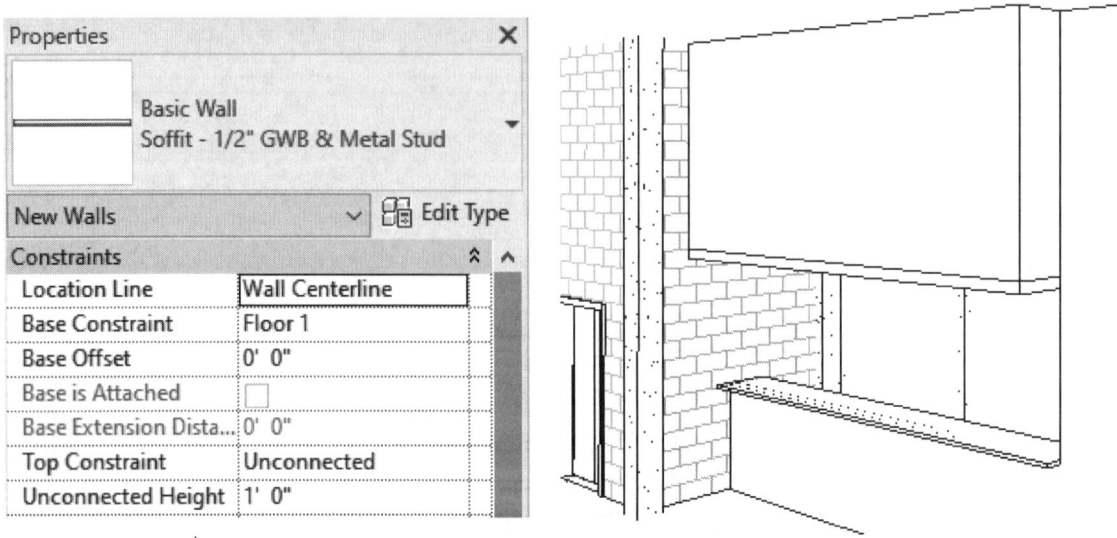

Figure 11–17

### How To: Create a Ceiling with a Soffit

1. Open a ceiling plan.
2. In the *Architecture* tab>Build panel, click (Ceiling).
3. In the Type Selector, select the ceiling type. In Properties, set the *Height Offset From Level*.
4. In the *Modify | Place Ceiling* tab>Ceiling panel, click (Sketch Ceiling).
5. Draw the ceiling outline, such as the example shown in Figure 11–18.

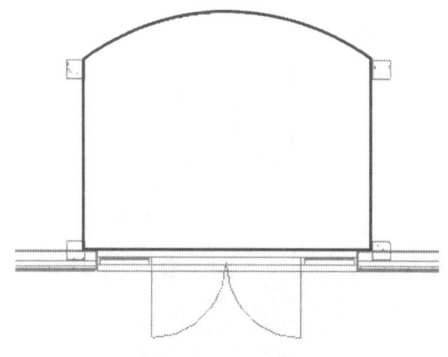

Figure 11–18

# Modeling Ceilings

6. Click ✓ (Finish Edit Mode).
7. In the *Architecture* tab>Build panel, click (Wall) to create the soffit wall.
8. In the Type Selector, select a soffit wall type. In Properties, set the *Base Offset* from the floor and set the *Top Constraint/Unconnected Height* as required to establish the height of the soffit.
   - Sometimes it is easier to set the height of the soffit walls by extending or trimming elements in a section view.
9. In the *Modify | Place Wall* tab>Draw panel, click

   (Pick Lines). Select the edges of the ceiling to create the walls, as shown in Figure 11–19.

*If the wall is on the outside of the ceiling, flip it using the Flip control and create the rest of the walls using the opposite **Location Line** option.*

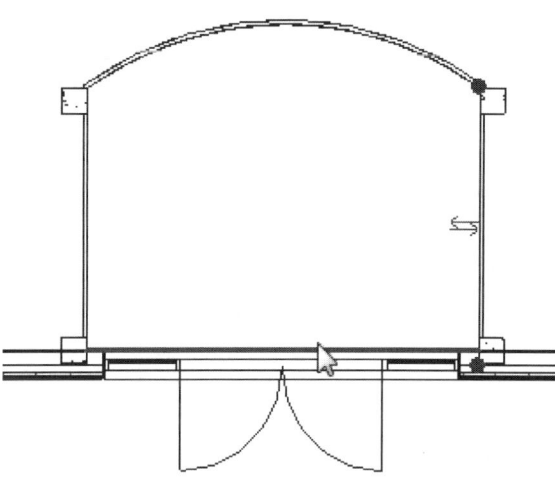

**Figure 11–19**

10. Display the ceiling in a 3D or section view to verify that it is displayed correctly.

---

**Hint: Joining Geometry**

When you are working with elements that are next to each other, they might need additional modification so that they display as expected. For example, one way to fix connections between walls and ceilings is to join the geometry.

In the *Modify* tab>Geometry panel, click (Join Geometry) and then select the elements to join.

---

# Practice 11b  Create Ceiling Soffits

### Practice Objective

- Create ceiling soffits.

In this practice, you will sketch a ceiling, add fixtures, and create a soffit wall in the hallway, as shown in Figure 11–20. Optionally, you will also add a recessed ceiling and soffit to the breakfast area.

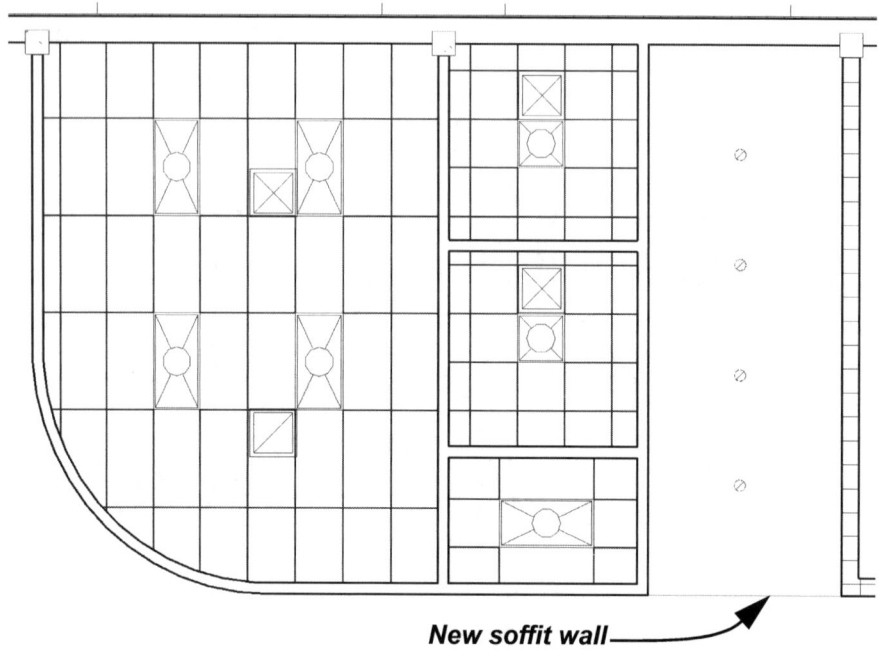

Figure 11–20

### Task 1 - Sketch a ceiling.

1. Open the project **Hotel-CeilingSoffits.rvt** from the practice files folder.

2. Verify that you are in the **Ceiling Plans: Floor 1** view and zoom in on the hallway by the restrooms.

3. In the *Architecture* tab>Build panel, click  (Ceiling).

4. In the *Modify | Place Ceiling* tab>Ceiling panel, click  (Sketch Ceiling).

5. In the Type Selector, select **Compound Ceiling: GWB on Mtl.Stud**, and in Properties, set the *Height Offset From Level* to **10'-0"**.

6. Sketch the outline of the ceiling (as shown in Figure 11–21) in the hallway.

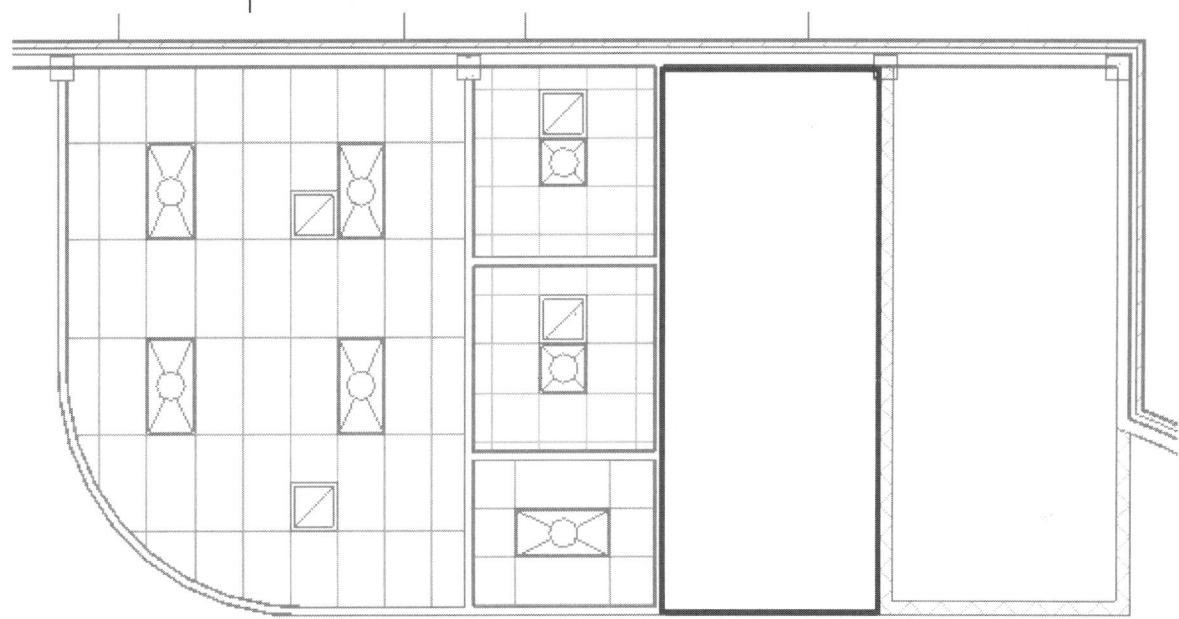

**Figure 11–21**

7. Click (Finish Edit Mode).

8. In the *Architecture* tab>Build panel, click (Component).

9. In the Type Selector, select **Downlight - Recessed Can: 6" Incandescent**.

10. Add four lights down the hallway.

    - Because the lights are being placed on the ceiling, their elevation from level is automatically set to the appropriate height.
    - Use reference planes, detail lines, dimensions set to equal, or the **Array** command to space them equally in the hallway, as shown in Figure 11–22.

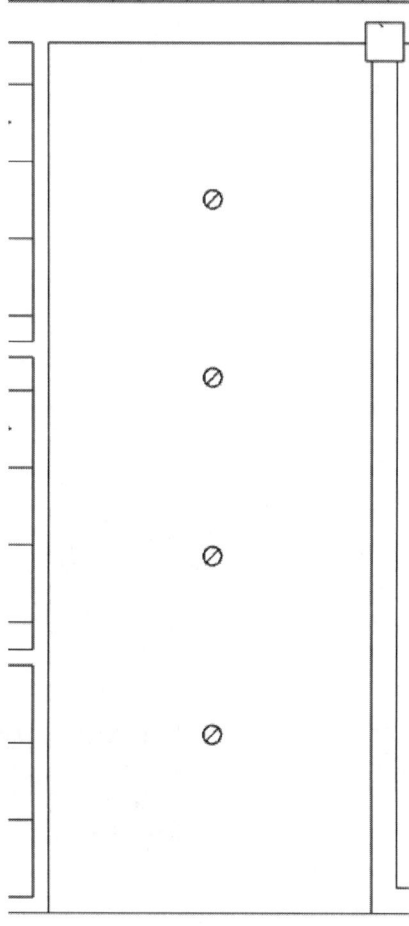

Figure 11–22

11. Save the project.

## Task 2 - Add a ceiling soffit.

1. Open the **Sections (Wall Section): Lobby Hall - Ceiling soffit** view and zoom in on the hallway area between levels Floor 1 and Floor 2 and Grid H and I, as shown in Figure 11–23.

# Modeling Ceilings

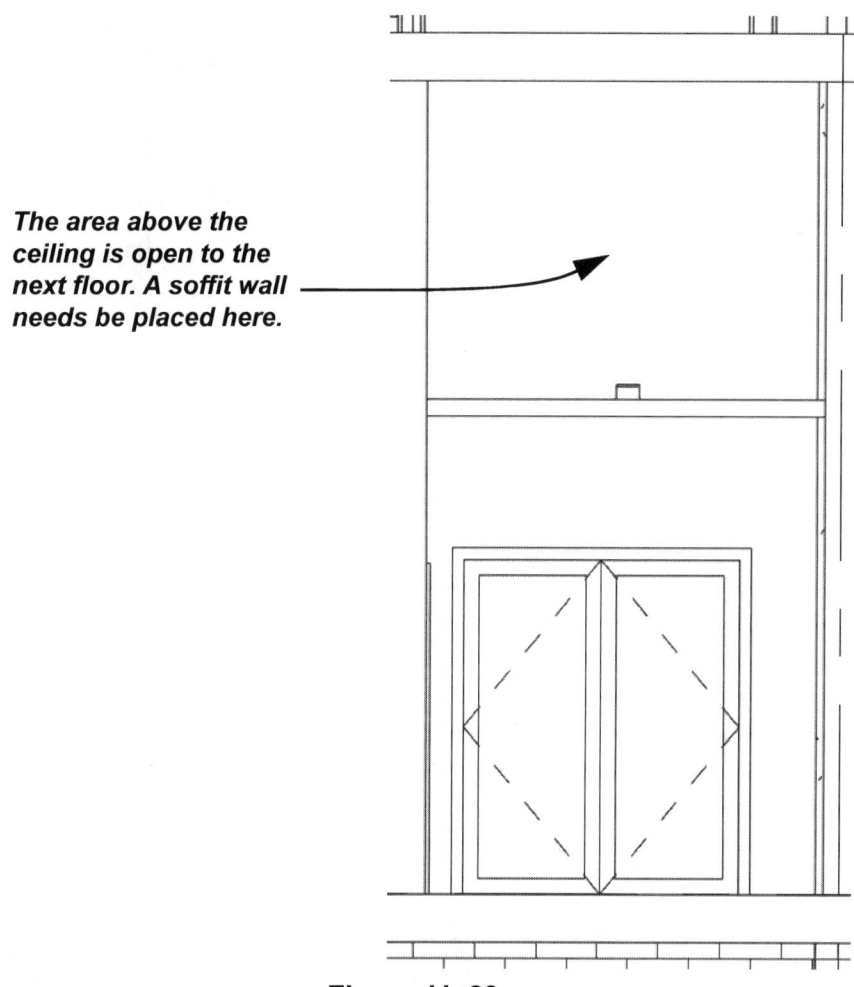

*The area above the ceiling is open to the next floor. A soffit wall needs be placed here.*

Figure 11–23

2. Return to the **Ceiling Plans: Floor 1** view and zoom in to the hallway next to the restrooms.

3. In the *Architecture* tab>Build panel, click (Wall). In the Type Selector, select **Basic Wall: Soffit 1/2" GWB & Metal Stud**.

4. In Properties, set the following:

    - *Location Line:* **Finish Face: Interior**
    - Base Constraint: **Floor 1**
    - *Base Offset:* **10'-0"**
    - *Top Constraint:* **Up to level: Floor 2**
    - *Top Offset:* (negative) **-1'-0"**

5. Draw the wall across the face of the ceiling (from left to right), as shown in Figure 11–24.

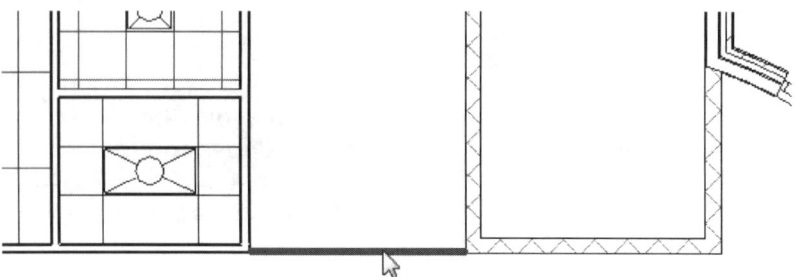

**Figure 11–24**

6. Activate the **Sections (Wall Section): Lobby Hall - Ceiling soffit** view.

7. In the *Modify* tab>Geometry panel, click (Join Geometry).

8. Select the soffit wall above the ceiling and then select the ceiling, as shown on the left in Figure 11–25.

9. Select the ceiling again, and then the wall to the left. The elements clean up, as shown on the right in Figure 11–25.

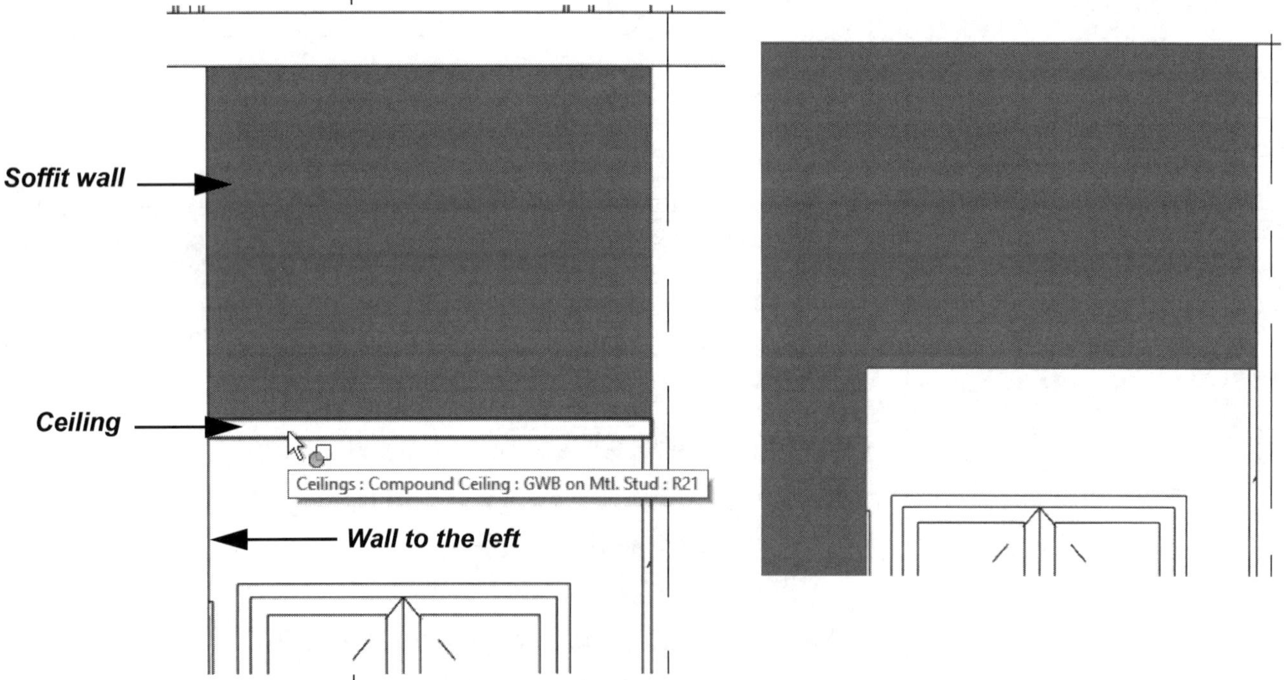

*Soffit wall*

*Ceiling*

Ceilings : Compound Ceiling : GWB on Mtl. Stud : R21

*Wall to the left*

**Figure 11–25**

10. Save and close the project.

# Chapter Review Questions

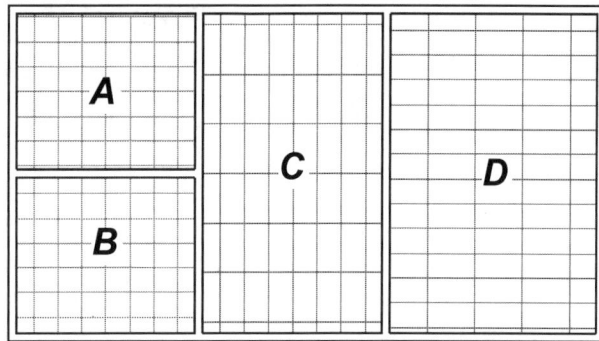

**Figure 11–26**

1. For the rooms labeled A and B in Figure 11–26, which command do you use to change the position of the ceiling grid?

    a. (Align)

    b. (Move)

    c. (Rotate)

    d. (Copy)

2. For the rooms labeled C and D in Figure 11–26, which command do you use to change the direction of the ceiling grids?

    a. (Align)

    b. (Move)

    c. (Rotate)

    d. (Copy)

3. Which of the following component types can be hosted by ceiling elements? (Select all that apply.)

   a. Mechanical diffusers and returns
   b. Lighting fixtures
   c. Curtain wall grids
   d. Columns

4. Which of the following commands would you use to create a ceiling with a soffit around the edges? (Select all that apply.)

   a.  (Automatic Ceiling)
   b.  (Sketch Ceiling)
   c.  (Wall)
   d.  (Component)

5. Which of the following commands can you use to get a light fixture fitted exactly in a ceiling grid, as shown in Figure 11–27? (Select all that apply.)

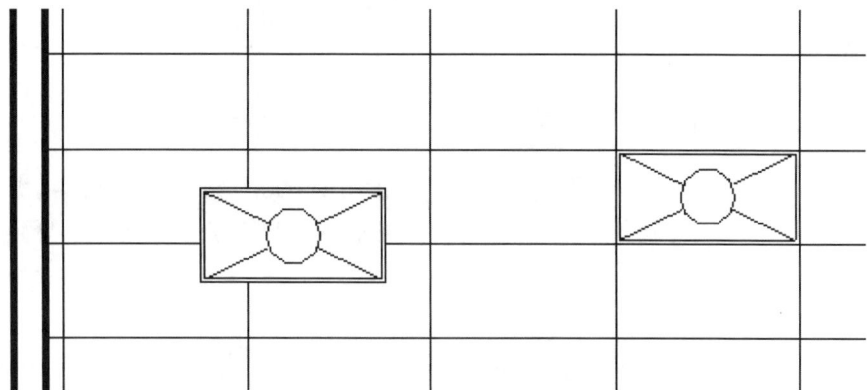

Figure 11–27

   a.  (Trim/Extend to Corner)
   b.  (Align)
   c.  (Join)
   d.  (Move)

# Command Summary

| Button | Command | Location |
|---|---|---|
| | **Automatic Ceiling** | • **Ribbon:** *Modify | Place Ceiling* tab>Ceiling panel |
| | **Ceiling** | • **Ribbon:** *Architecture* tab>Build panel |
| | **Join** | • **Ribbon**: *Modify* tab>Geometry panel |
| | **Place a Component** | • **Ribbon:** *Architecture* tab>Build panel |
| | **Sketch Ceiling** | • **Ribbon:** *Modify | Place Ceiling* tab>Ceiling panel |

# Chapter 12

# Modeling Roofs

You can create simple or very complex roofs in Revit® using two different methods. The Footprint method enables you to create roofs using a process that is similar to that for creating a floor. You can also use the Extrusion method, which is based on a profile that controls the shape of the roof.

## Learning Objectives in This Chapter

- Sketch roofs using the Footprint method for flat, shed, gable, or hip roofs.
- Set work planes to help you create extruded roof profiles.
- Sketch a profile for the roof that can then be extruded.

# 12.1 Modeling Roofs

Revit provides two main ways of creating roofs:

- **Footprint:** Created in a floor plan view by defining the area to be covered.

- **Extrusion:** Created in an elevation or section by defining a profile sketch or using a reference plane drawn in a view to set the work plane.

The footprint method can generate most common roof types, including flat, shed, gable, and hip roofs. The extrusion method is required for an odd-shaped roof, a roof with two slopes on the same face, or a curved roof, as shown in Figure 12–1.

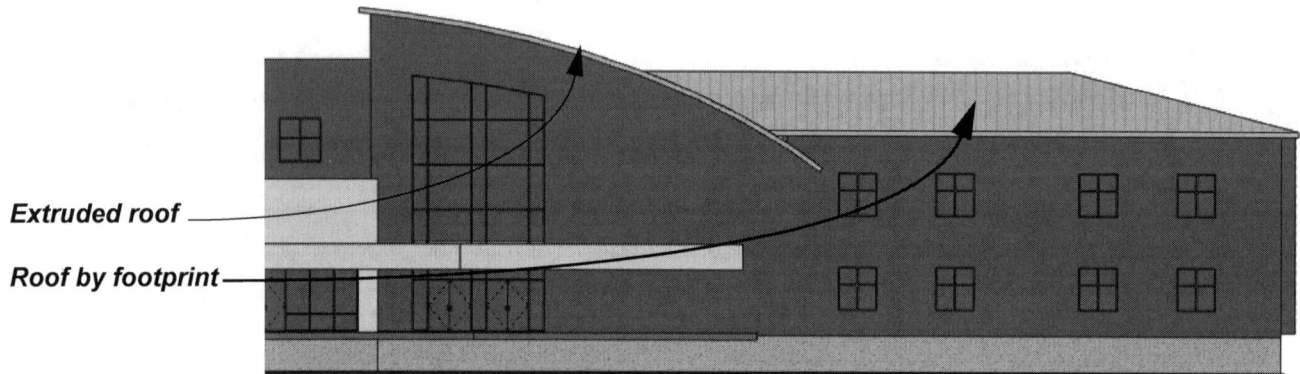

**Figure 12–1**

- Other roof options, found in the Roof drop-down list, include Roof by Face, Roof Soffit, Fascia, and Gutter. **Roof by Face** can be used with massing elements to create irregular shapes. **Roof Soffit** connects the edge of the roof to the wall with a flat footprint. **Fascia** places a profile, whether flat or built-up board, on the outside edge of the roof and can be used for friezes. **Gutter** adds a gutter on the edge of the roof, but does not include downspouts.

For more information on gutters, soffits, and fascias, see *A.3 Editing Wall Joins*.

Modeling Roofs

To create a flat roof or any basic single-sloped roofs (hip, shed, or gable), start with a plan view and define a sketch or "footprint" around the area that you want the roof to cover, as shown in Figure 12–2.

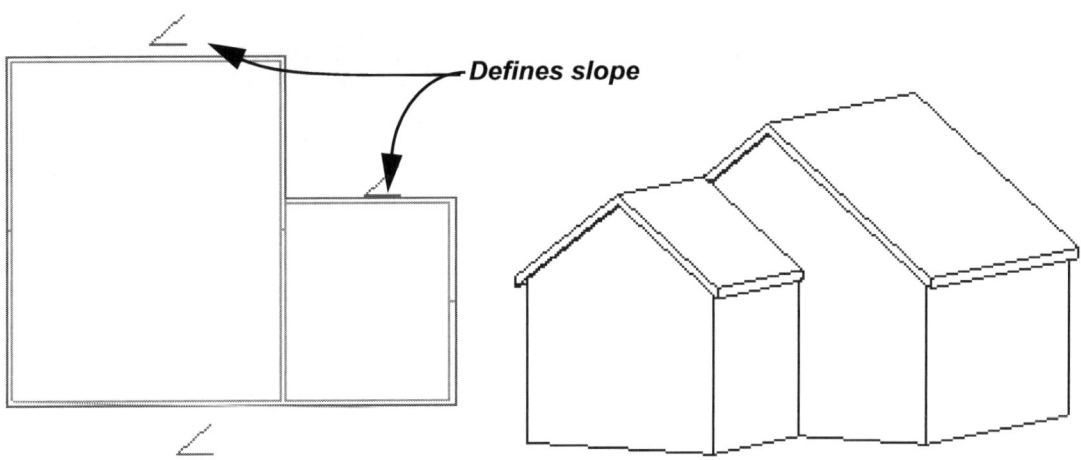

**Figure 12–2**

You control the type of roof by specifying which edge(s) define the slope:

- No edges sloped = flat roof

- One edge sloped = shed roof

- Two opposing edges sloped = gable roof

- All edges sloped = hip roof

## How To: Add a Roof by Footprint

1. Open a plan view at the roof level of the building.

2. In the *Architecture* tab>Build panel, expand  (Roof) and click  (Roof by Footprint).

3. In the Options Bar (shown in Figure 12–3), you can set the following options:
   - **Defines slope:** This checkbox toggles the slope-defining property of the sketch line on and off. When selected (on), the sketch line you create will display an adjacent angle symbol and a value specifying the slope. You can change the slope by editing this value. When not selected (off), the perimeter line you sketch will not define a slope. Note that lines representing gable ends do not define a slope.
   - **Overhang:** When picking walls to define the perimeter, this value lets you specify how far the roof extends beyond the face of the wall.
   - **Extend to wall core:** When selected, the overhang dimension is measured from the roof edge to the exterior core of the wall. When not selected, the overhang is measured from the exterior finish face of the wall.

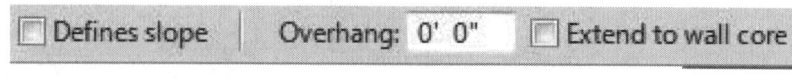

**Figure 12–3**

4. In the *Modify | Create Roof Footprint* tab>Draw panel, click (Pick Walls) or (Line) or any other draw tool to create the roof footprint. You can include arcs in the sketch.
   - The lines must form a closed boundary with no overlapping lines.
   - Use commands such as (Trim), to modify the lines as needed.

5. Select and modify each segment of the sketch as needed using the Options Bar, Properties, or controls, as shown in Figure 12–4. Alternatively, you can modify Properties and the Options Bar settings as you sketch the roof.

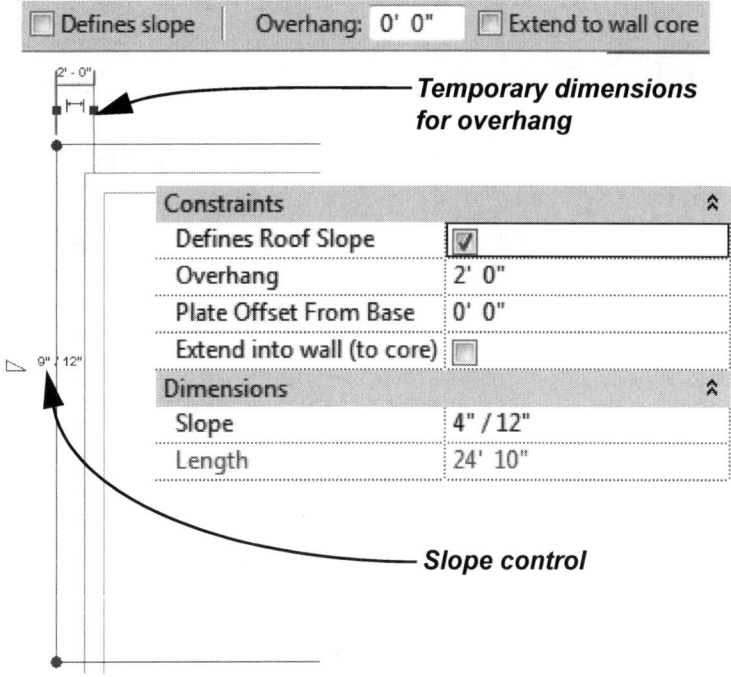

Figure 12–4

6. Click ✓ (Finish Edit Mode).
7. An alert box might open, as shown in Figure 12–5. You can attach the highlighted walls to the roof now or later.

- You have the option to check the box for **Do not show me this message again**. Revit will remember your last selection and do this for every instance this occurs.

Figure 12–5

8. The roof is still selected and, in Properties, you can set the properties for the entire roof. These include roof type, *Base Offset From Level*, *Rafter Cut*, and *Cutoff Level*.

To edit a roof sketch, either:

- double-click on the edge of the roof, or

- with the roof selected, click (Edit Footprint).

For information on dormer roofs, see *A.7 Creating Dormers*.

## Modify the Footprint of a Roof

Once your roof is created, you can modify it by selecting the roof and changing its parameters in Properties. You can also modify the roof footprint sketch or extruded profile of a roof.

### Roof by Footprint Properties

| | |
|---|---|
| **Base Level** | Sets the level for the roof. |
| **Base Offset From Level** | Sets the height of the roof above or below the level where it is being sketched (allows for raised heel truss designs). |
| **Cutoff Level** | Specifies the level at which the roof should be cut off. Typically, another roof will be created to fill the hole created by cutting off the first roof. This property and the *Cutoff Offset* apply to the first roof, not the second roof. |
| **Cutoff Offset** | Specifies the height of the cutoff above or below the level specified by the *Cutoff Level*. |
| **Rafter Cut** | Defines the rafter cut on an eave by selecting from a drop-down list:<br>• **Plumb Cut:** Cuts the roof fascia at a 90° vertical.<br>• **Two Cut - Plumb:** Cuts the roof fascia 90° vertically and horizontally at the *Fascia Depth*.<br>• **Two Cut - Square:** Cuts the roof fascia at 90° relative to the face of the roof and horizontally at the *Fascia Depth*. |
| **Fascia Depth** | Sets the length of the lines defining the fascia. Does not affect the size of additionally applied fascia profiles. |
| **Rafter or Truss** | Select either **Rafter** or **Truss** for the roof construction method to control how the roof sits on the walls. If **Rafter** is selected, the *Plate Offset From Base* is measured from the inside of the wall. If **Truss** is selected, the *Plate Offset From Base* is measured from the outside of the wall, as shown in Figure 12–6. |

Figure 12–6

| **Maximum Ridge Height** | A read-only value that displays the maximum height of the top of the roof above the base level of the building. |
|---|---|
| **Slope** | Controls the value of the slope-defining line. |

## How To: Modify the Footprint of a Roof

1. To edit a roof sketch, double-click on the edge of the roof. Alternatively, with the roof selected, in the *Modify | Roofs* tab> Mode panel, click (Edit Footprint).
2. In the *Modify | Roofs* tab>Mode panel, use the tools to edit the roof's sketch lines.
3. To finish editing the roof, click (Finish Edit Mode).

## Setting Up a Roof Plan View

When creating a roof, add a level with a floor plan view where the bottom of the roof should be located. If there are roofs at different heights, create a level for each location.

Most plan views are typically cut at **3'-0" to 4'-0"** above the bottom of the level, as shown in Figure 12–7. However, this does not work with pitched roofs, whose structures can reach **20'-0"** high or more. To change the height of the area shown in the roof plan, change the *View Range*.

 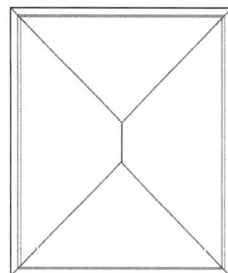

*View Range Cut Plane @ 4'-0"*   *View Range Cut Plane @ 30'-0"*

**Figure 12–7**

## Practice 12a  Create Roofs by Footprint

**Practice Objectives**

- Create flat and sloped roofs using Roof by Footprint.
- Create a roof plan view.

In this practice, you will create a flat roof on the main part of the hotel, and flat and sloped roofs over the poolhouse, as shown in Figure 12–8. The pool curtain wall, soffit, and parapet walls have been added to this practice file.

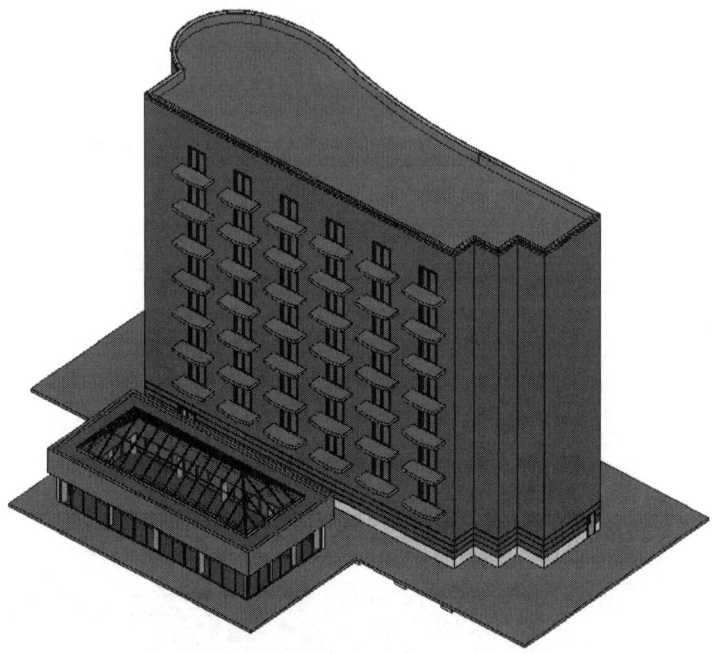

Figure 12–8

- Parapet walls have been added to the poolhouse.

### Task 1 - Create a flat roof.

1. Open **Hotel-RoofFP.rvt** from the practice files folder.

2. Verify that you are in the **Floor Plans: Roof** view, and in Properties, set the *Underlay>Range: Base Level* to **None**.

3. Hide the grid lines and section and elevation markers.

4. Open up the 3D view and type **WT** to tile the views. Type **ZA** to zoom all, if needed.

# Modeling Roofs

5. In the *Architecture* tab>Build panel, expand  (Roof) and click  (Roof by Footprint).

6. In the Options Bar, verify that the **Defines slope** option is cleared and there is no overhang.

7. In the *Modify | Create Roof Footprint* tab>Draw panel, click  (Pick Walls) and select the inside of the walls around the building, as shown in Figure 12–9.

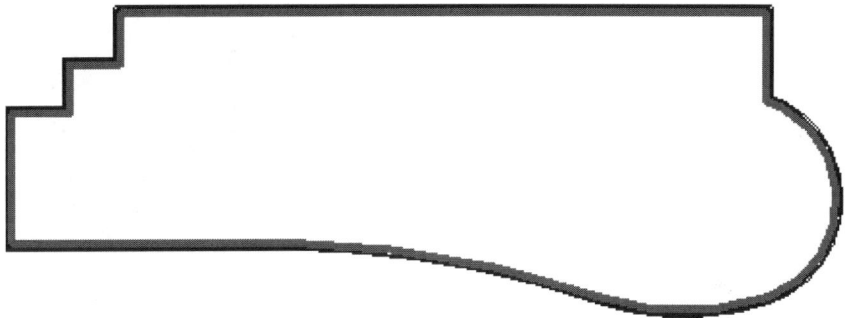

**Figure 12–9**

8. In the Type Selector, select **Basic Roof: Steel Truss - Insulation on Metal Deck - EPDM**.

9. Click  (Finish Edit Mode). The roof is still selected.

10. Click in an empty space in the view to clear the selection.

11. View the building in 3D to display the roof applied below the parapet wall.

12. Close the Roof view so the 3D view is the only one active.

13. Save the project.

*Hold <Shift> and the mouse wheel to orbit in 3D view.*

### Task 2 - Create a poolhouse roof plan view.

1. Orbit the 3D view until the poolhouse at the back of the building displays. Several features are in place, including the parapet walls, as shown in Figure 12–10.

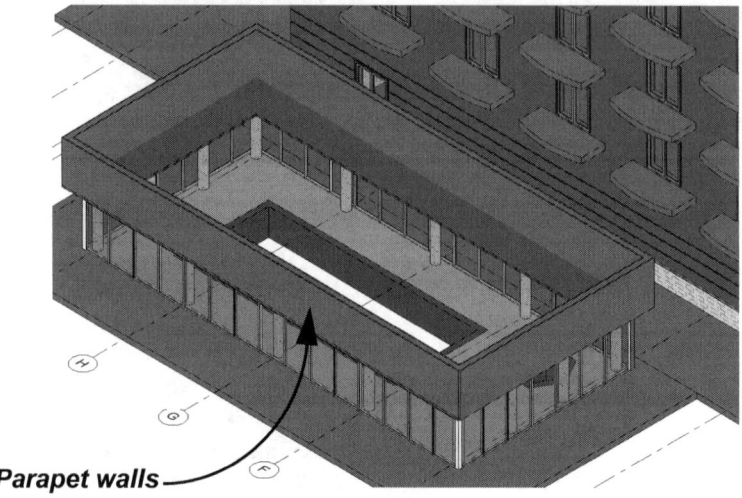

**Figure 12–10**

2. Select the four poolhouse parapet walls. Hold down <Ctrl> to select more than one element.

3. In the *Modify | Multi-Select* tab>View panel, click (Selection Box).

4. Click in an empty space in the view to clear the selection.

5. The parapet walls are within a section box, as shown in Figure 12–11.

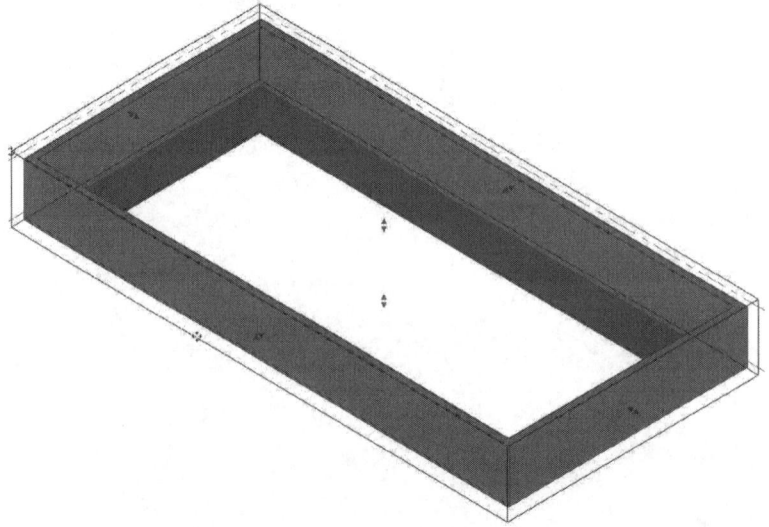

**Figure 12–11**

# Modeling Roofs

6. Use the control grips to stretch the section box to show the entire poolhouse. Make sure to stretch the top control grip up so you can see the roof that will be created.

7. With the section box still selected, right-click on it and select **Hide in View>By Element**.

8. In the Project Browser, rename the {3D} view to **3D - Poolhouse**.

9. Duplicate a copy of the **Floor Plans: Floor 1 - Poolhouse** view, rename it as **Roof - Poolhouse**, and verify that it is open.

10. Change the *Scale* to **1/4" = 1'-0"**.

11. Open the View Range dialog box (type **VR**), as shown in Figure 12–12, and set the following:

    *Primary Range:*
    - *Top*: **Floor 4**, *Offset:* **7'-6"**
    - *Cut plane*, *Offset:* **40'-0"**
    - *Bottom*: **Unlimited**

    *View Depth:*
    - *Level*: **Unlimited**

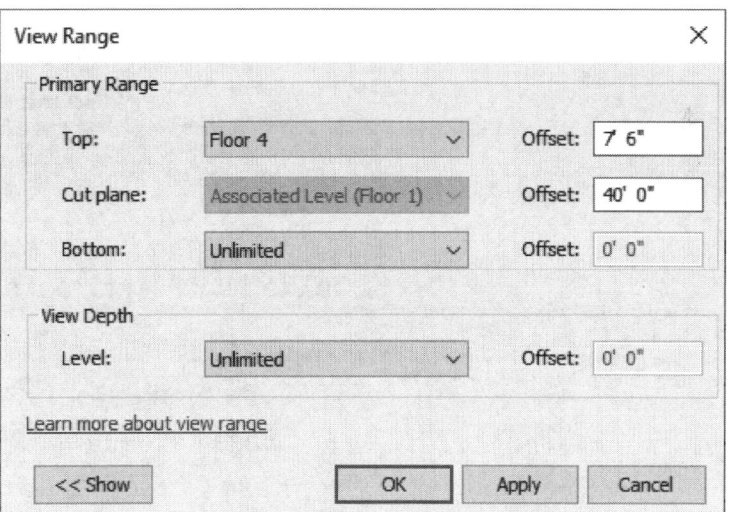

Figure 12–12

12. Click **Apply** and **OK**.

13. Close any other views except for **3D - Poolhouse** and **Roof - Poolhouse**.

14. Type **WT** to tile the two views.

15. Save the project.

### Task 3 - Create roofs on the poolhouse.

1. While in the **Roof - Poolhouse** view, in the *Architecture* tab>Build panel, click  (Roof). The software remembers the most recently used command of **Roof by Footprint**.

2. In the Options Bar, verify that the **Defines slope** option is unchecked and there is no overhang. Do not set the roof type (it will be done later).

3. In the *Modify | Create Roof Footprint* tab>Draw panel, click  (Pick Walls) and select the inside of the parapet walls, as shown in Figure 12–13.

4. Use  (Pick Lines) and select the soffit opening, as shown in Figure 12–13. This creates a flat roof with an opening in it.

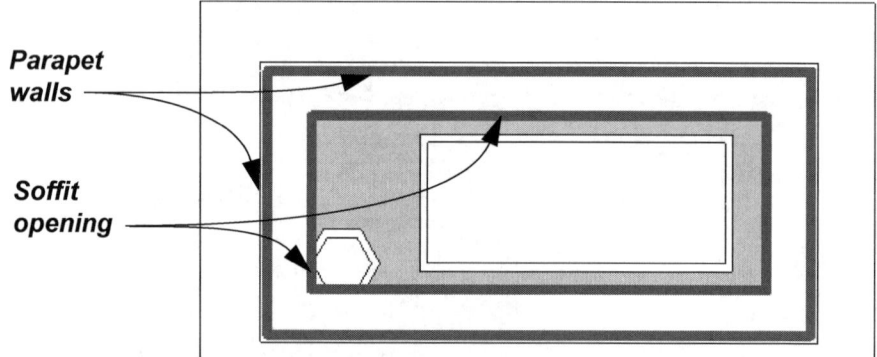

**Figure 12–13**

5. Click  (Finish Edit Mode). If prompted, click **Don't attach** in the Attaching to roof dialog box.

6. With the roof still selected, in Properties, set the following:
   - *Type:* **Basic Roof: Generic - 12"**
   - *Base Level:* **Floor 2**
   - *Base Offset From Level:* (negative) **-2'-0"**

# Modeling Roofs

7. The roof is now in the correct location, as shown in Figure 12–14.

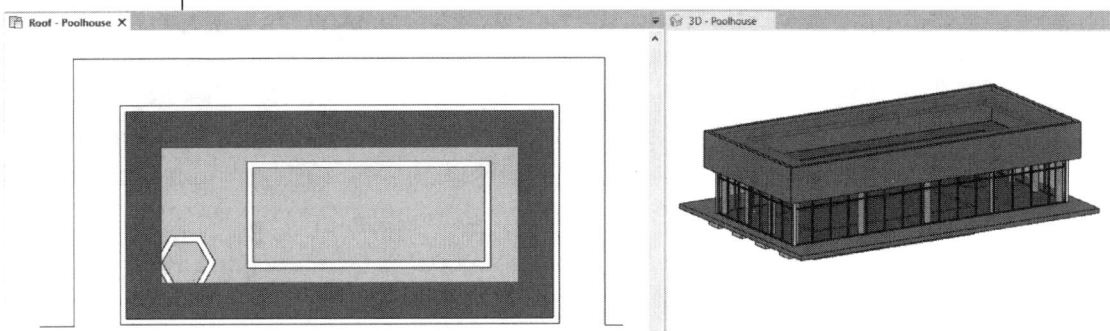

**Figure 12–14**

8. Click in the view to release the roof.

9. Start the **Wall** command.

10. In the Draw panel, select (Pick Lines).

11. In Properties, set the following:
    - *Wall Type:* **Basic Wall: Exterior - EIFS on Mtl.Stud**
    - *Location Line:* **Finish Face: Interior**
    - *Base Constraint:* **Floor 2**
    - *Base Offset:* (negative) **-1'-0"**
    - *Top Constraint:* **Unconnected**
    - *Unconnected Height:* **1'-0"**

12. Draw a short wall around the soffit opening (as shown on the left in Figure 12–15), making sure that the dashed lines are on the inside of the soffit opening (as shown on the right in Figure 12–15).

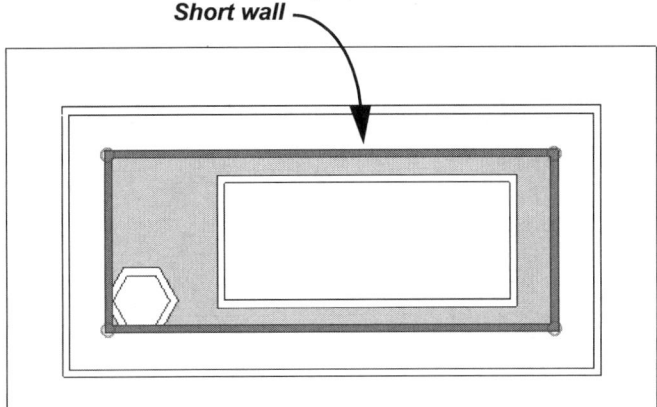
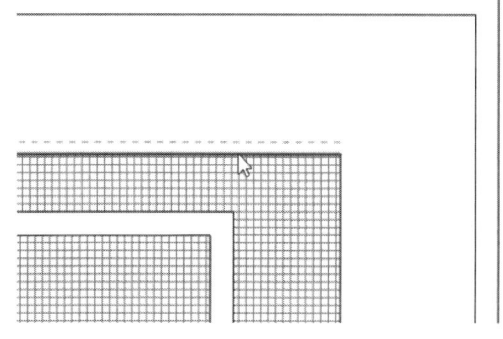

**Figure 12–15**

13. Click (Modify).

14. Start the  (Roof by Footprint) command.

15. In the Draw panel, select  (Pick Walls).

16. In the Options Bar, check the checkbox for **Defines slope**. Verify there is no overhang and that **extend to wall core** is unchecked.

17. In the Type Selector, select **Sloped Glazing: Sloped Glazing Pool Roof** and set the following properties:

    - *Base Level:* **Floor 2**
    - *Base Offset from level:* **0'-0"**
    - *Justification for Grid 1*: **Center**

18. Select the outside of the new walls you just created, as shown in Figure 12–16.

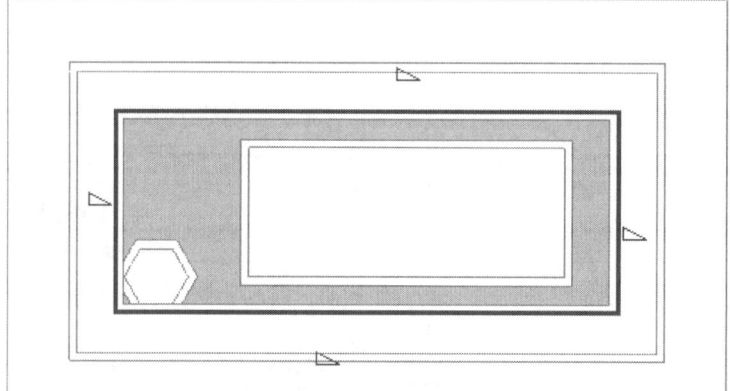

**Figure 12–16**

19. Click  (Finish Edit Mode). If the message dialog box displays, click **Don't attach** to not attach any walls to the roof.

    - If a warning message displays, read and close the warning dialog box.

The new roof displays, as shown in Figure 12–17.

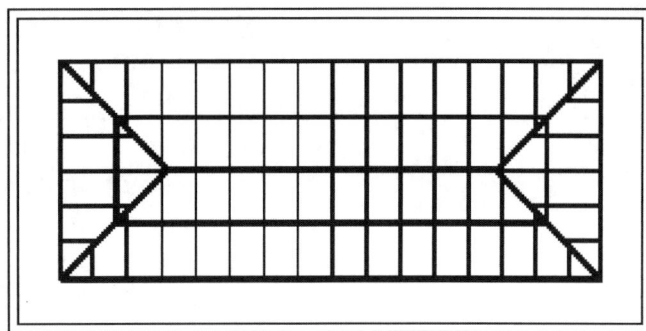

**Figure 12–17**

20. In the Quick Access Toolbar, click (Default 3D view) to open up a default 3D view. Orbit the view to see the poolhouse.

21. Save and close the project.

# 12.2 Creating Roofs by Extrusion

Extruded roofs enable you to create complex roof forms, such as the curved roof shown in Figure 12–18. Extruded roofs are based on a sketch of the roof profile in an elevation or section view and do not need to be a closed sketch. The profile is extruded between a start and end point. From there you can modify the roof by adding openings or joining it to other roofs.

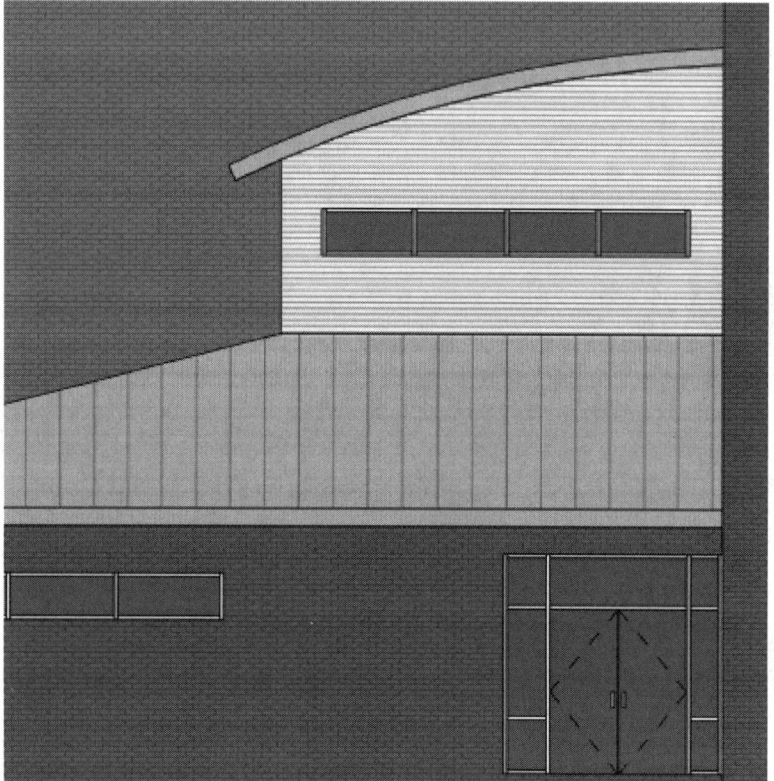

Figure 12–18

## Establishing Work Planes

When creating a roof by extrusion, you are prompted to specify a work plane. A work plane is the surface you sketch on or extrude from.

- In a plan view, the work plane is automatically parallel to the level.

- In an elevation or 3D view, you need to specify the work plane before you start sketching.

To see the active work plane, in the *Architecture* tab>Work Plane panel, click  (Show Work Plane).

Alternatively, you can click  (Viewer). This opens the Workplane Viewer, a separate window showing the current work plane, as shown in Figure 12–19.

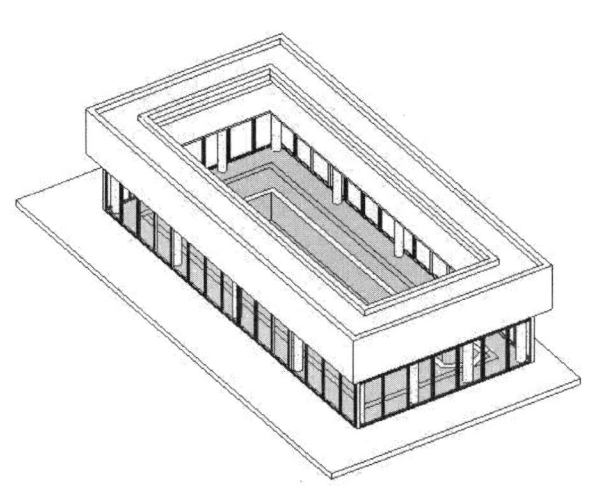
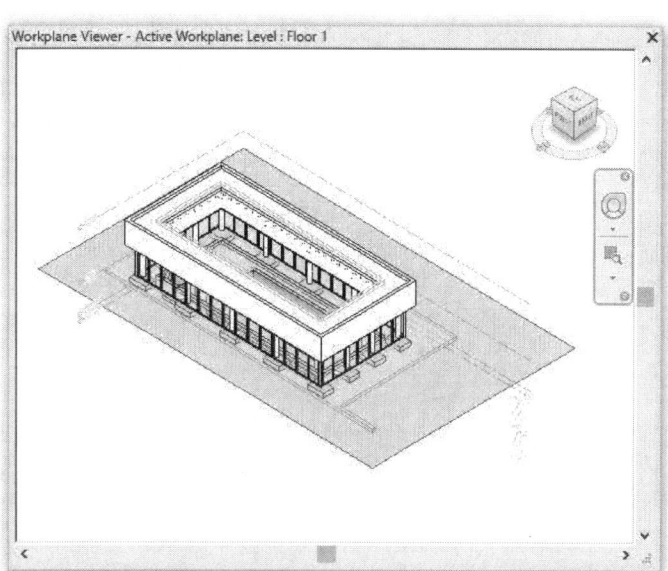

**Figure 12–19**

- Named reference planes can be used to specify a work plane that would otherwise not be displayed in a view. This is especially helpful when creating extruded roofs.

- You can set the work plane by selecting **Set Work Plane**, which opens the Work Plane dialog box with additional options, or **Pick a Plane**, which enables you to select a linear or horizontal plane in the view.

### How To: Pick a Plane

1. In the *Architecture* tab>Work Plane panel, expand  (Set) and select  (Pick a Plane), or type **PK**.
2. Select a work plane in the view.

### How To: Set the Work Plane

1. Start a command that requires a work plane, or in the *Architecture* tab>Work Plane panel, click  (Set).

2. In the Work Plane dialog box, select one of the options.
   - **Name:** Select an existing level, grid, or named reference plane, as shown in Figure 12–20, and click **OK**.

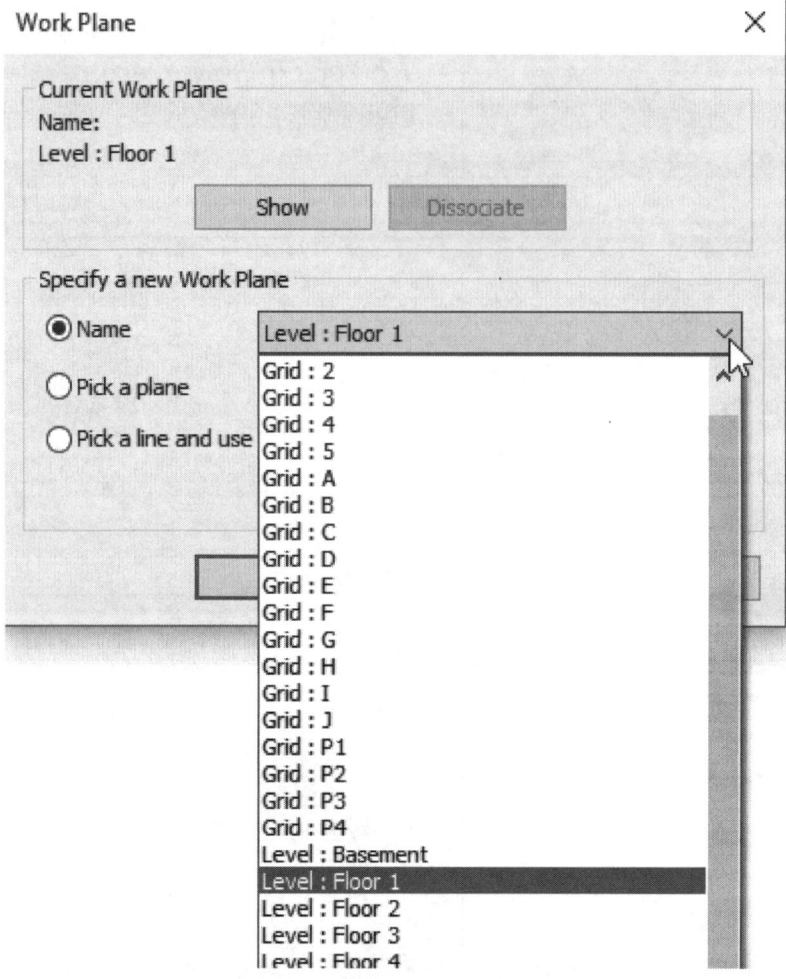

Figure 12–20

- **Pick a plane:** Click **OK** and select a plane in the view, such as a wall face. Ensure that the entire plane is highlighted before you select it.
- **Pick a line and use the work plane it was sketched in:** Click **OK** and select a model line such as a room separation line.

- If you are in a view in which the sketch cannot be created, the Go To View dialog box opens, as shown in Figure 12–21. Select one of the views and click **Open View**.

Modeling Roofs

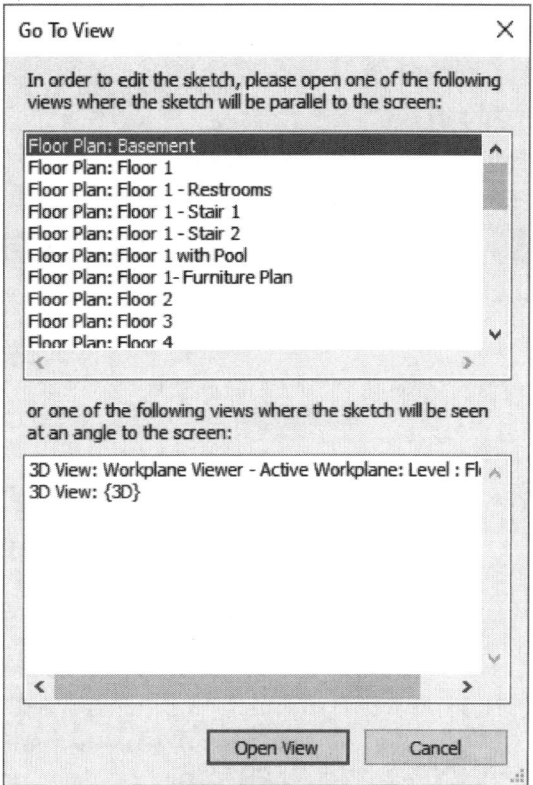

Figure 12–21

## How To: Create an Extruded Roof

1. Open an elevation or a section view.

2. In the *Architecture* tab>Build panel, expand  (Roof) and click  (Roof by Extrusion).
3. In the Work Plane dialog box, select the work plane on which you want to sketch the roof profile and click **OK.**
4. In the Roof Reference Level and Offset dialog box, specify the base *Level* and *Offset* (if any), as shown in Figure 12–22.

*By default, this level is set to the highest one in the project. The offset creates a reference plane at that distance.*

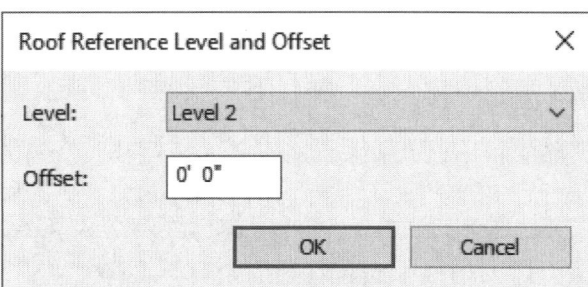

Figure 12–22

- Use reference planes to help you create the roof profile. Reference planes created in sketch mode do not display once the roof is finished.

5. Use the Draw tools to create the profile, as shown in Figure 12–23. Sketch only the shape of the roof in profile, not the thickness.

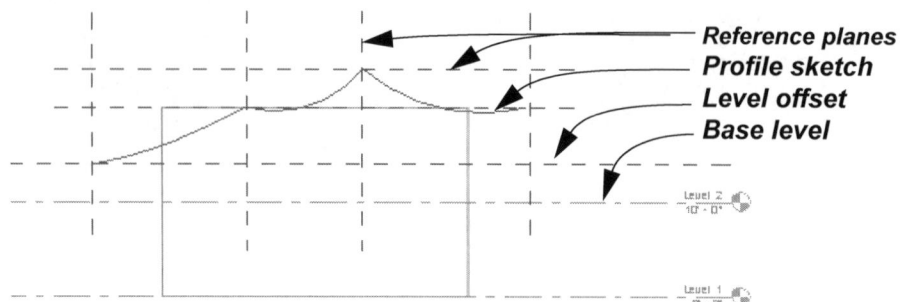

Figure 12–23

6. In Properties, set the *Extrusion Start* and *End*.
   - The direction in which the roof profile extrudes is known as the extrusion direction. The extrusion of a roof can extend in either direction along a line perpendicular to the plane in which the profile is created. To adjust the extrusion distance, click the **Roof Properties** button to display the Instance Properties dialog box and then use the *Extrusion Start* and *Extrusion End* values to adjust the length of the extrusion. You can extend the extrusion towards or away from the view.
   - Extrusion directions that are up or towards the view are positive, and extrusion directions that are down or away from the view are negative.

7. Click (Finish Edit Mode).
8. In the Type Selector, select the roof type.
   - The thickness, which is determined by the roof type, is added below the profile sketch line.

9. View the roof in 3D and make any other needed modifications. For example, you can use the controls on the ends of the roof to extend the overhang (as shown in Figure 12–24), as well as modify the roof using temporary dimensions and Properties.

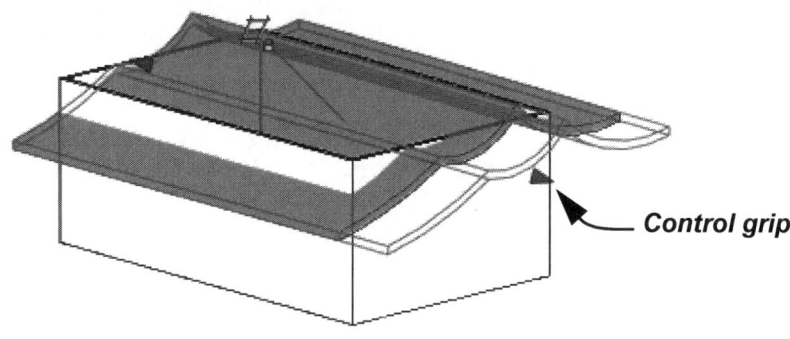

Figure 12–24

10. Attach the walls to the roof.

## Modify Extruded Roof

You can make changes to the roof's profile in one of the following ways:

- Double-click on the edge of the roof.
- Select the roof. In the *Modify | Roofs* tab>Mode panel, click (Edit Profile).

### Roof by Extrusion Properties

| | |
|---|---|
| **Extrusion Start** | Sets the extrusion start point for the roof. |
| **Extrusion End** | Sets the extrusion end point for the roof. |
| **Reference Level** | Specifies the reference level for the roof. |
| **Level Offset** | Specifies the offset from the reference level for the roof. |
| **Rafter Cut** | Defines the rafter cut on an eave by selecting from a drop-down list:<br>• **Plumb Cut:** Cuts the roof fascia at a 90° vertical.<br>• **Two Cut - Plumb:** Cuts the roof fascia 90° vertically and horizontally at the *Fascia Depth*.<br>• **Two Cut - Square**: Cuts the roof fascia at 90° relative to the face of the roof and horizontally at the *Fascia Depth*. |

### How To: Modify the Plan View of an Extruded Roof

1. Open a plan view where the entire roof displays.
2. Select the roof.
3. In the *Modify | Roofs* tab>Opening panel, click (Vertical).
4. In the *Modify | Create Extrusion Roof Profile* tab>Draw panel, use the tools to create a closed boundary. The boundary can be entirely inside the roof or touching the roof boundaries.
5. Click (Finish Edit Mode). The extruded view now has a cutout, as shown in Figure 12–25.

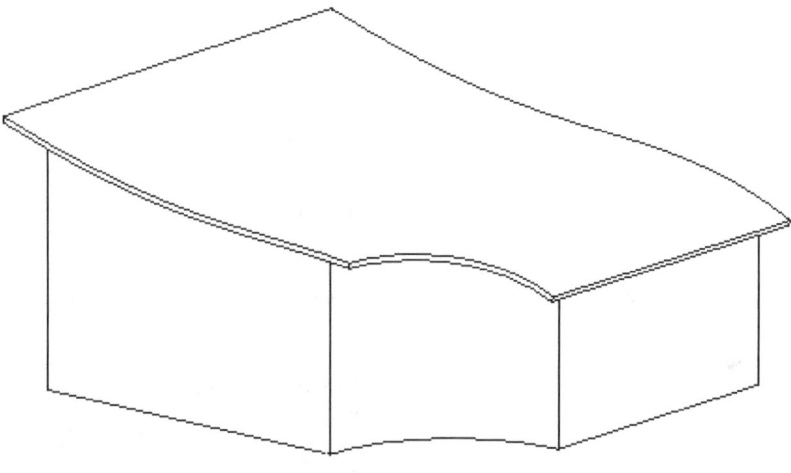

**Figure 12–25**

## Joining Roofs

When you want to join a roof to another roof, or a wall face that is taller than the roof, you can use the **Join/Unjoin Roof** command, as shown in Figure 12–26.

*Before joining roofs*

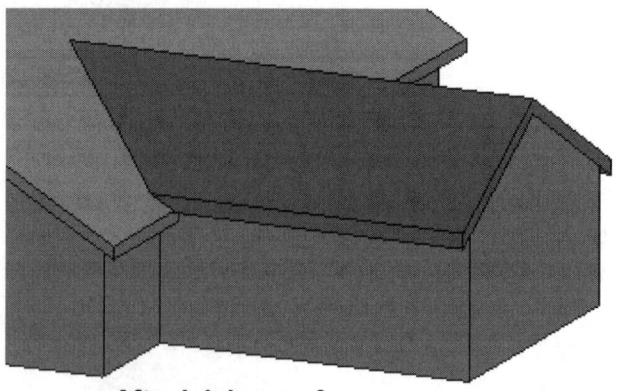
*After joining roofs*

**Figure 12–26**

Modeling Roofs

### How To: Use Join/Unjoin Roof

1. In the *Modify* tab>Geometry panel, click (Join/Unjoin Roof).
2. Select one of the roof edges.
3. Select the other roof or the wall.

> **Hint: Join Geometry**
>
> Where roofs overlap walls or other roofs, use **Join Geometry** to clean up the intersections. The elements remain separate, but the intersections are cleaned up, as shown in Figure 12–27.
>
>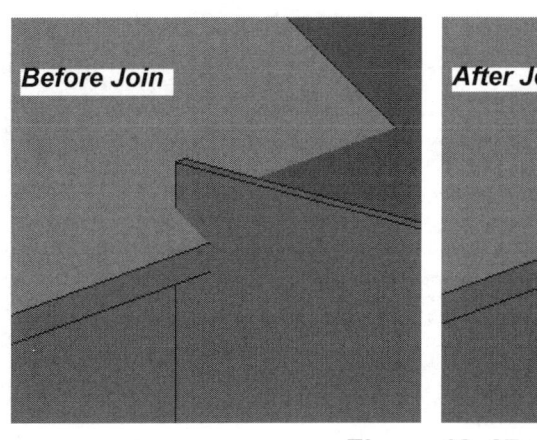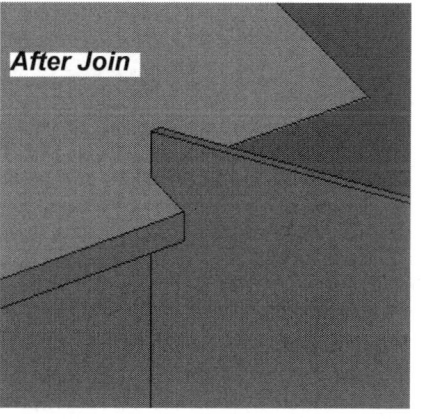
>
> Figure 12–27

## Attaching Walls to Roofs

Attaching walls to the roof extends the walls up to the roof, as shown in Figure 12–28. You attach walls while you are still in the Roof command, or you can use the **Attach Top/Base** commands later in the design process.

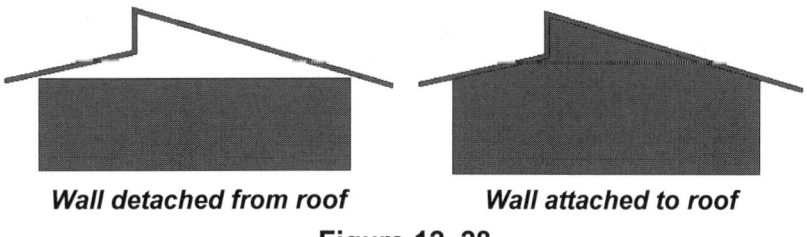

Figure 12–28

- **Attach Top/Base** can also be used with walls that are against sloping floors or topographic site features.

## How To: Attach Walls to Roofs

1. Select the wall or walls that you want to attach to the roof.

2. In the *Modify | Walls* tab>Modify Wall panel, click  (Attach Top/Base). Verify that *Attach Wall* is set to **Top**, as shown in Figure 12–29.

**Figure 12–29**

3. Select the roof. The walls are trimmed or extended to the roof line.

4. Note: Walls will typically need to be attached to the roof in order to match the elevation profile of the roof element. If the walls you previously created extend above the roof, Revit will ask you if you want to attach the highlighted walls to the roof. If you say **Yes**, the profile of the walls will be changed to follow the slope of the roof. If the walls end below the roof, you can select the walls and then attach them to the roof.

*For information on dormer roofs, see A.7 Creating Dormers.*

## Practice 12b

# Create Roofs by Extrusion

**Practice Objectives**

- Create an extruded roof.
- Modify the plan profile of a roof.

In this practice, you will create a curved extruded roof to cover the main entrance of the building and modify its plan profile to cover the side entrance, as shown in Figure 12–30.

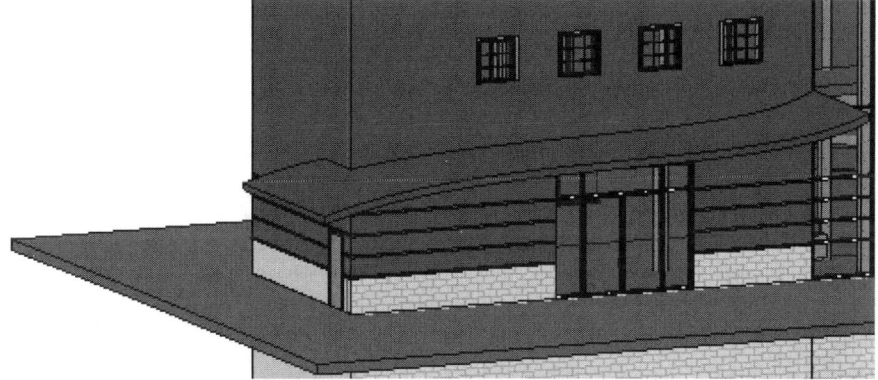

Figure 12–30

### Task 1 - Create a roof by extrusion.

1. Open **Hotel-RoofExtrd.rvt** from the practice files folder.

2. Verify that you are in the **Elevations (Building Elevation): South** view.

3. Zoom in on the area around the front entrance.

4. In the *Architecture* tab>Build panel, expand (Roof) and click (Roof by Extrusion).

5. In the Work Plane dialog box, verify that **Pick a plane** is selected and click **OK**.

6. Select the front face of the exterior brick wall.

7. In the Roof Reference Level and Offset dialog box, set the *Level* to **Floor 2** and *Offset* to **0'-0"**, then click **OK**. A reference plane is set at this level and the model is grayed out.

*The example was created using* ✏ *(Spline).*

8. Sketch the profile of a roof similar to the one shown in Figure 12–31. It should extend beyond the building to the left but finish at the end of the brick wall on the right and no higher than the reference plane.

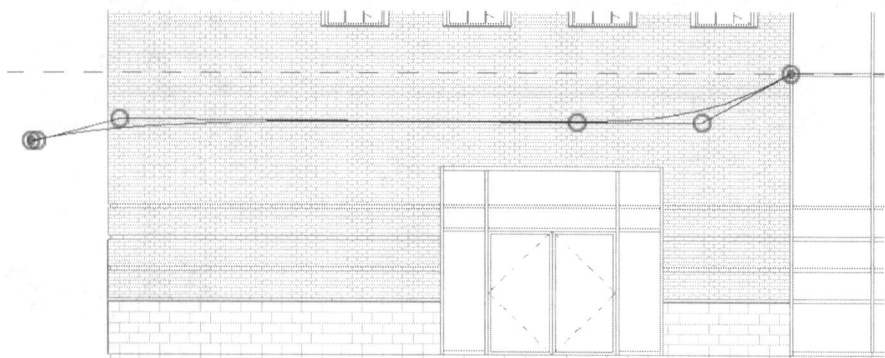

**Figure 12–31**

9. Click ▹ (Modify).

10. In the Type Selector, select **Basic Roof: Generic - 9"**.

11. In Properties, set the *Extrusion End* to (negative) **-6'-0"**. This sets the roof inside the wall.

12. Click ✓ (Finish Edit Mode).

13. View the new roof in 3D. It is mostly inside the building at this point.

14. Save the project.

**Task 2 - Modify the extruded roof.**

1. Open the **Floor Plans: Site** view. This view displays the entire building in plan including all of the roofs.

2. Select the Entrance roof and using controls, move the roof outward so that the length is **20'-0"**, as shown in Figure 12–32.

   • In Properties, the *Extrusion Start* should be **14'-0"** and the *Extrusion End* should be (negative) **-6'-0"**.

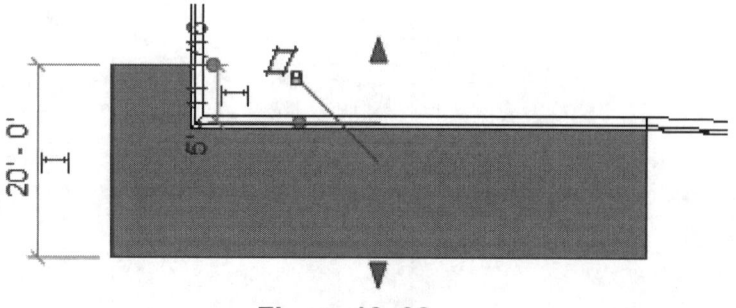

**Figure 12–32**

3. In the *Modify | Roofs* tab>Opening panel, click (Vertical).

4. Create a rectangular cutout of the roof for the portion that passes through the building, as shown in Figure 12–33.

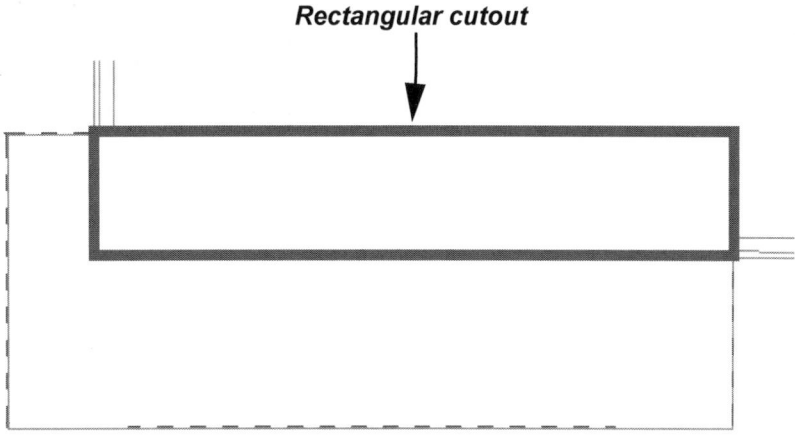

**Figure 12–33**

5. Click (Finish Edit Mode).

6. View the modified roof in 3D. It now wraps around the side of the building to cover the side entrance, as shown in Figure 12–34.

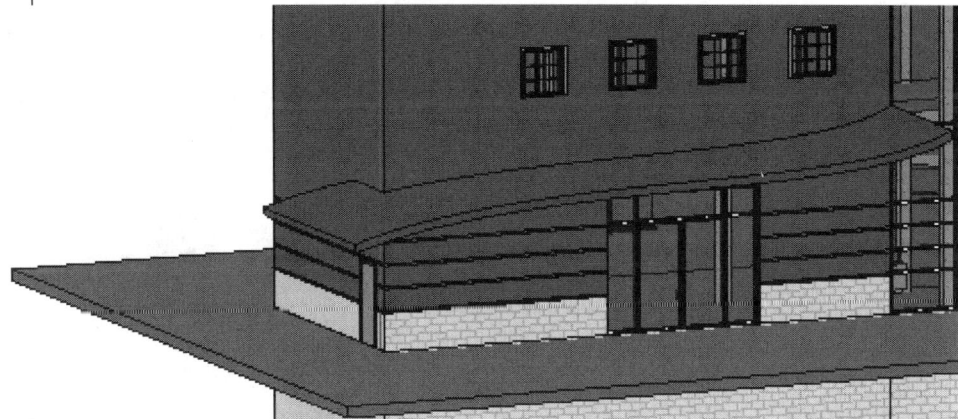

**Figure 12–34**

7. Save and close the project.

# Chapter Review Questions

1. How would you create a roof sloping in one direction only?

    a. By extrusion and rotate the roof to the correct angle.

    b. By footprint and specify the slope along one side.

    c. By extrusion and use the Slope Arrow to define the overall slope of the roof.

    d. By footprint and use the **Shape Editing** tools to create the slope.

2. To create a flat roof, which of the following commands would you use to sketch the boundary of the roof and to set its thickness?

    a. **Roof by Footprint** with the thickness set by the roof type.

    b. **Roof by Extrusion** with the thickness extruded from the sketch.

3. Which of the following methods makes a wall touch the underside of a roof?

    a. Select the wall and use **Attach Top/Base**.

    b. Select the roof and use **Attach Top/Base**.

    c. Select the wall and edit the profile.

    d. Select the roof and use **By Face**.

4. Which roof type and view should you use to create a curved roof, as shown in Figure 12–35?

    **Figure 12–35**

    a. Roof by Footprint, plan view

    b. Roof by Footprint, elevation or section view

    c. Roof by Extrusion, plan view

    d. Roof by Extrusion, elevation or section view

5. A work plane can be assigned using a named reference plane.

   a. True

   b. False

## Command Summary

| Button | Command | Location |
|---|---|---|
| | Attach Top/Base | • **Ribbon:** *Modify | Walls* tab>Modify Wall panel |
| | Join Geometry | • **Ribbon:** *Modify* tab>Geometry panel, expand Join |
| | Join/Unjoin Roof | • **Ribbon:** *Modify* tab>Geometry panel |
| | Reference Plane | • **Ribbon:** *Architecture* tab>Work Plane panel |
| | Roof by Extrusion | • **Ribbon:** *Architecture* tab>Build panel, expand Roof |
| | Roof by Footprint | • **Ribbon:** *Architecture* tab>Build panel, expand Roof |
| | Set Work Plane | • **Ribbon:** *Architecture* tab>Work Plane panel |
| | Show Work Plane | • **Ribbon:** *Architecture* tab>Work Plane panel |
| | Unjoin Geometry | • **Ribbon:** *Modify* tab>Geometry panel, expand Join |
| | Vertical (Opening) | • **Ribbon:** *Modify | Roofs* tab>Opening panel |
| | Viewer | • **Ribbon:** *Architecture* tab>Work Plane panel |

# Chapter 13

# Modeling Stairs, Railings, and Ramps

When modeling in Revit®, you can easily create basic stairs in straight, u-shaped, and multi-landing configurations. To create more complex shapes, you can convert runs and landings to sketches. Ramps can also be created by specifying runs and landings. Railings can be added automatically with the Stair and Ramp commands, or you can sketch railings on stairs and add them to balconies and decks.

## Learning Objectives in This Chapter

- Create and modify component-based stairs made of runs, landings, supports, and railings.
- Convert runs and landings to sketches.
- Add and modify railings that are connected to stairs, as well as free-standing railings for balconies.
- Create ramps to make your design accessible.

# 13.1 Creating Component Stairs

As with other Revit elements, stairs are *smart* parametric elements. With just a few clicks, you can create stairs of varying heights and designs, complete with railings. Stairs can be created by assembling stair components (as shown in Figure 13–1), or by sketching a custom layout.

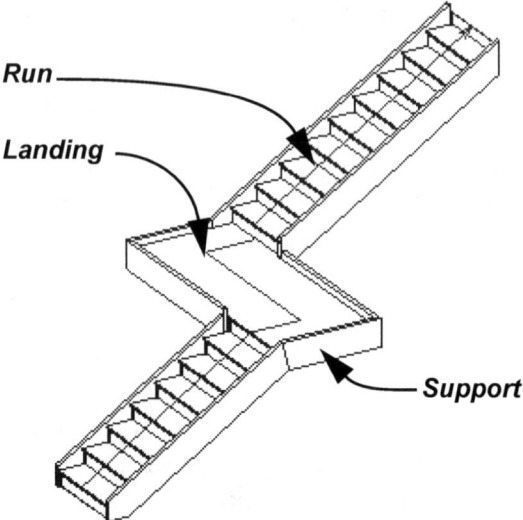

**Figure 13–1**

When creating component-based stairs, there are three parts of a stair that can be assembled, as shown in Figure 13–1:

- **Runs:** The actual stair tread and riser elements. These include straight runs which can be combined for multi-landing stairs, spiral stairs, and L-shaped and U-shaped winders.

- **Landings:** The platform between runs. These are typically created automatically and then modified if needed.

- **Supports:** The stringer or carriage that structurally holds the stair elements. These can be created automatically or you can pick the edges where you want the different types to go. These can be placed on either side of the stairs or in the center of the stairs.

- Railings are typically added in the **Stair** command. They display after you complete the stair.

- You can select and edit each of the components while you are in stair edit mode, or after the stair has been created.

Modeling Stairs, Railings, and Ramps

- Each component of the stair is independent but also has a relationship to the other components. For example, if steps are removed from one run they are added to connected runs to maintain the overall height, as shown in Figure 13–2.

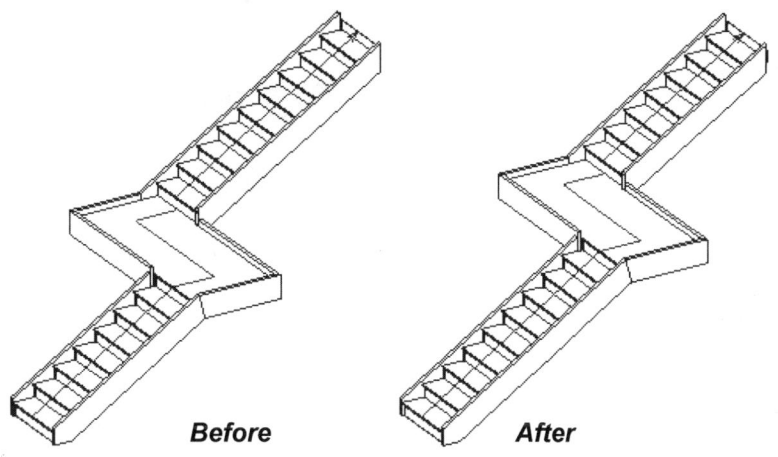

**Before**    **After**

**Figure 13–2**

## Creating Runs

To create a component stair, you must first place the run elements. There are six different options available in the Components panel, as shown in Figure 13–3 and described as follows:

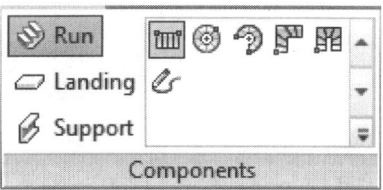

**Figure 13–3**

*Component stairs can include a mix of the different types of runs.*

| | | |
|---|---|---|
| ▥ | **Straight** | Draws a straight run by selecting the start and end points of the run. |
| ⊚ | **Full-Step Spiral** | Draws a spiral run based on a start point and radius. |
| ⤺ | **Center-Ends Spiral** | Draws a spiral run based on a center point, start point, and end point. |
| ⌐ | **L-Shape Winder** | Draws an L-shaped winder based on the lower end. |
| ⊞ | **U-Shape Winder** | Draws a U-shaped winder based on the lower end. |
| ✎ | **Create Sketch** | Opens additional tools where you can sketch stair boundary and risers individually. |

> **Hint: Stairs and Views**
>
> When creating stairs you can work in either plan or 3D views. It can help to have the plan view and a 3D view open and tiled side by side. Only open the views in which you want to work and type **WT** to tile the views.

### How To: Create a Component-Based Stair

1. In the *Architecture* tab>Circulation panel, click  (Stair).
2. In the Type Selector, select the stair type, as shown in Figure 13–4.
3. In Properties (shown in Figure 13–5), set the *Base Level*, *Top Level*, and any other information that is needed.

*The stair type can impact all of the other settings. Therefore, it is important to select it first.*

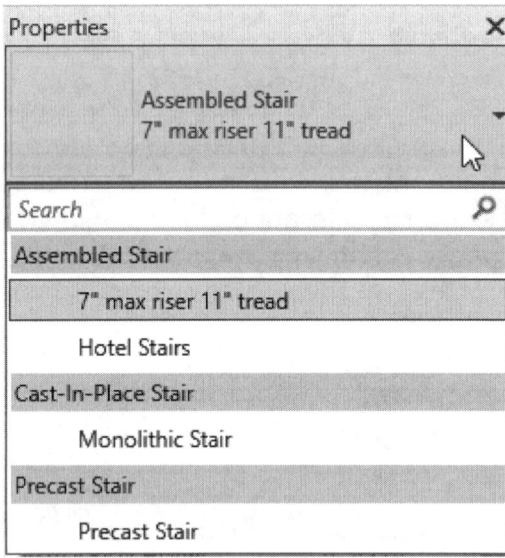

**Figure 13–4**

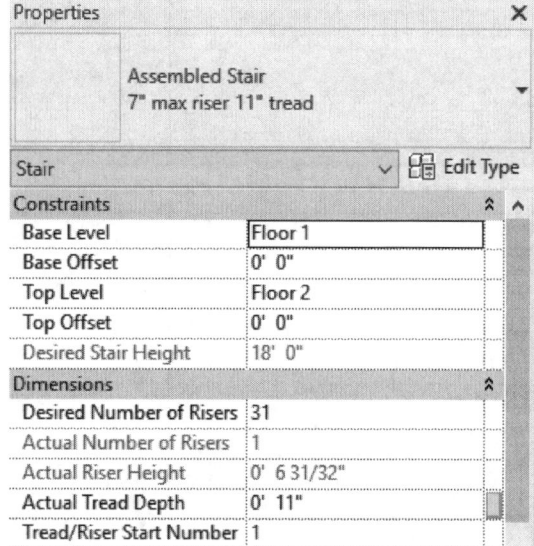

**Figure 13–5**

4. In the *Modify | Create Stairs* tab>Tools panel, click  (Railing), select a railing type in the Railings dialog box (as shown in Figure 13–6), and specify whether the *Position* is on the **Treads** or **Stringer**. Click **OK**.

*Railings can also be added and modified after the stair has been placed.*

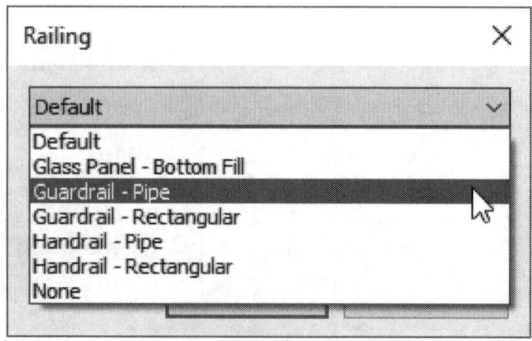

**Figure 13–6**

# Modeling Stairs, Railings, and Ramps

5. In the *Modify | Create Stair* tab>Components panel, click  (Run) and then click  (Straight).
6. In the Options Bar (shown in Figure 13–7), specify the following options:
   - *Location Line:* Select **Exterior Support: Left**, **Run: Left**, **Run: Center**, **Run: Right**, or **Exterior Support: Right**.
   - *Offset:* Specify a distance from the *Location Line*. This is typically used if you are following an existing wall but do not need to have the stairs directly against them.
   - *Actual Run Width:* Specify the width of the stair run (not including the supports).
   - *Automatic Landing:* Creates landings between stair runs (recommended).

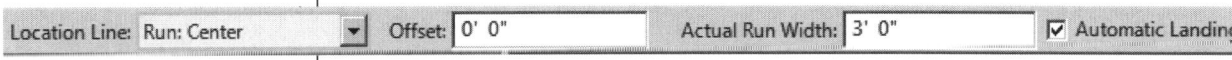

**Figure 13–7**

7. Click on the screen to select a start point for the run. A box displays, indicating the stair orientation and the number of risers created and remaining, as shown in Figure 13–8.

> *If you are creating a complex stair pattern, sketch reference planes in the **Stairs** command to help you select the start and end points of each run.*

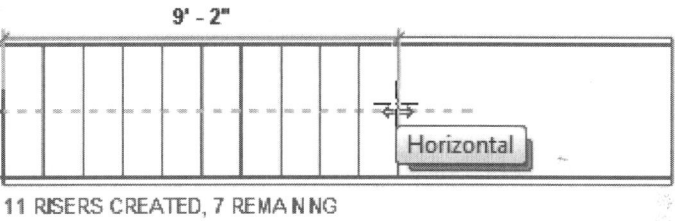

**Figure 13–8**

- For straight stairs of a single run, select a second point anywhere outside the box to create the run.
- For multi-landing or u-shaped stairs, select a second point inside the box for the length of the first run, move the cursor in the direction of the turn, then select a start point and an end point for the next run.
- If the stair is going in the wrong direction, click  (Flip) in the *Modify | Create Stair* tab>Tools panel.

8. Click  (Finish Edit Mode) to create the stairs, complete with railings.

## Creating Other Types of Runs

While most stairs are created using straight runs, there are times when you need to create specialty runs, such as spirals and winders or when you need to sketch a stair such as that shown in Figure 13–9.

Figure 13–9

### How To: Create a Full-Step Spiral Run

1. Start the **Stair** command and set up the properties as needed.
2. In the Components panel, click  (Full-Step Spiral).
3. Select the center point of the spiral.
4. Select (or type) the radius of the spiral. The run is created, as shown in Figure 13–10.

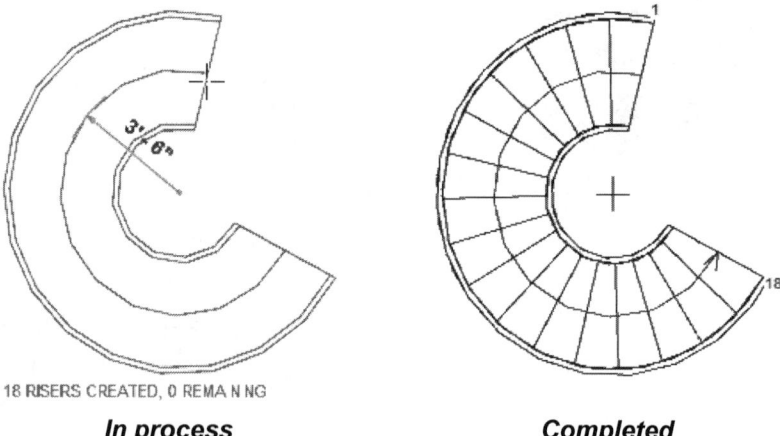

*In process*  *Completed*

Figure 13–10

Modeling Stairs, Railings, and Ramps

## How To: Create a Center-Ends Spiral Run

1. Start the **Stair** command and set up the properties as needed.
2. In the Components panel, click (Center-Ends Spiral).
3. Select the center of the spiral.
4. Select (or type) the radius of the spiral, as shown on the left in Figure 13–11.
5. Drag the cursor to display the number of risers, as shown on the right in Figure 13–11.

*You can create spiral stairs with landings with this option.*

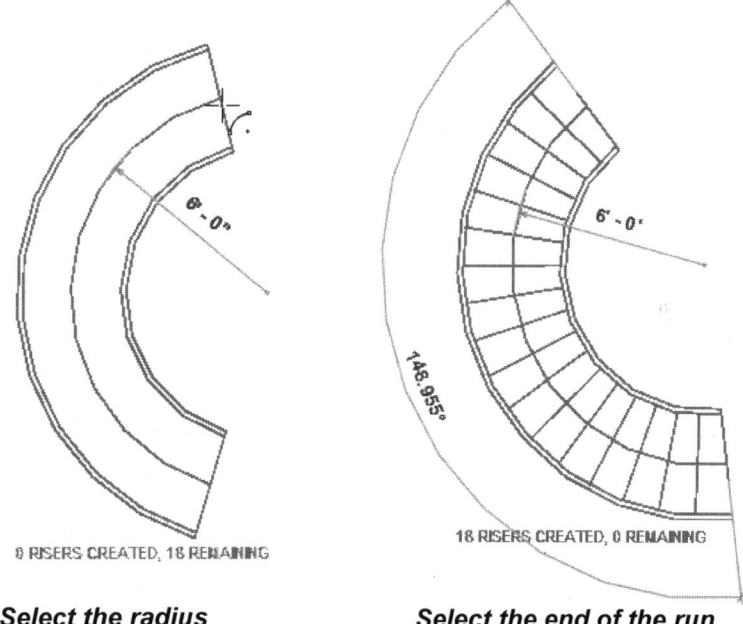

Select the radius                 Select the end of the run

**Figure 13–11**

## How To: Create Winder-Based Stairs

1. Start the **Stair** command and set up the properties as needed.

2. In the Components panel, click (L-Shape Winder) or (U-Shape Winder).

3. Click a start point to place the overall stair.

4. Select the stair and use the arrow controls to modify the length, as shown in Figure 13–12.

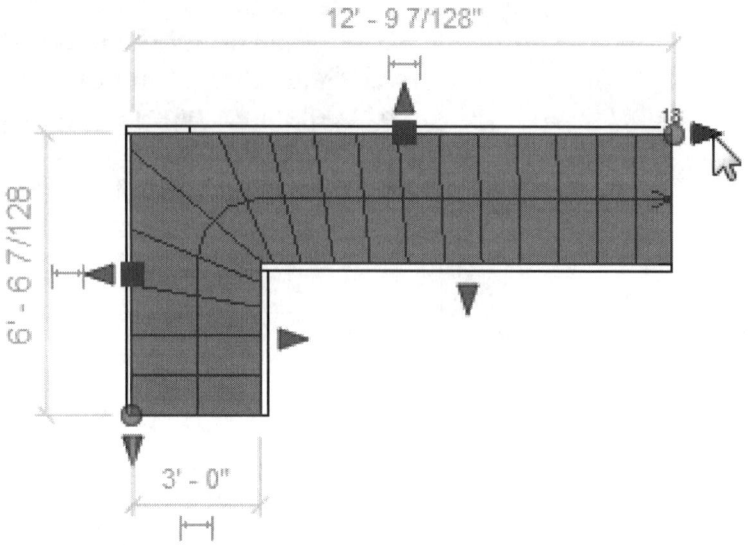

Figure 13–12

## How To: Sketch a Stair

1. Start the **Stair** command and set up the properties as needed.
   - In many cases, a custom stair is shorter and should be set using a base and top offset from the same level, as shown in Figure 13–13. By default, a stair height is from level to level.

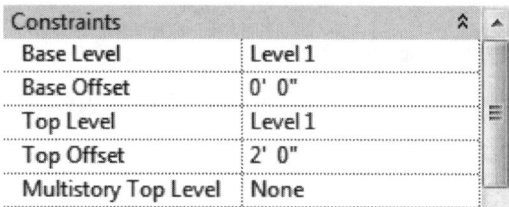

Figure 13–13

2. In the *Modify | Create Stair* tab>Components panel, click (Run) and then click (Sketch).

*Change the level offsets before starting to sketch the stair.*

Modeling Stairs, Railings, and Ramps

3. In the *Modify | Create Stair>Sketch Run* tab, use  (Boundary),  (Riser), and  (Stair Path) to draw the parts of the stair, as shown in Figure 13–14.

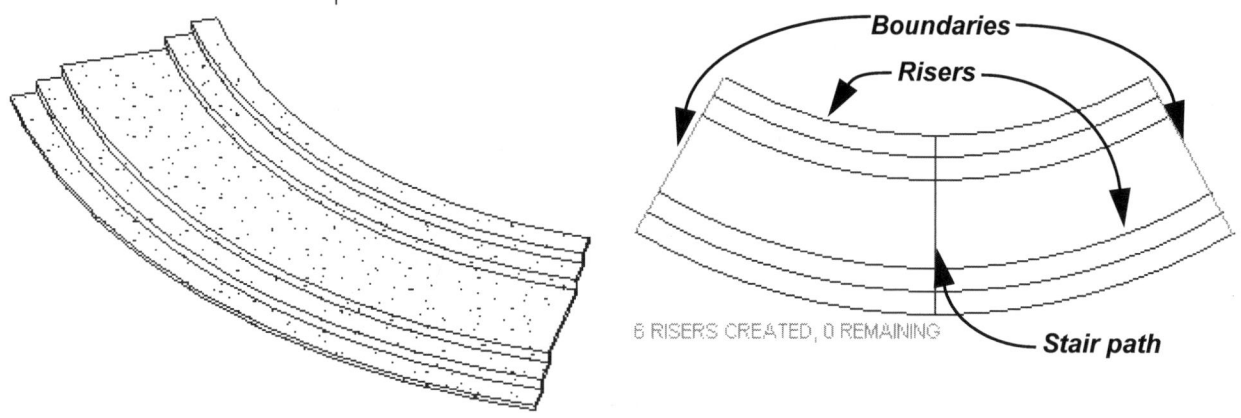

Figure 13–14

4. Click  (Finish Edit Mode).
5. If you want to add a landing, you can sketch one.
6. Click  (Finish Edit Mode) to complete the final assembly.

### Creating Landings

Landings are typically created automatically between any breaks in runs. Once finishing the stair, you can easily modify the landings to create custom designs. There are two additional options to create landings, as shown in Figure 13–15:

- **Pick Two Runs:** Places the landing at the correct height between the runs.

- **Create Sketch:** Enables you to sketch the shape of the landing, but you must place it at the correct height.

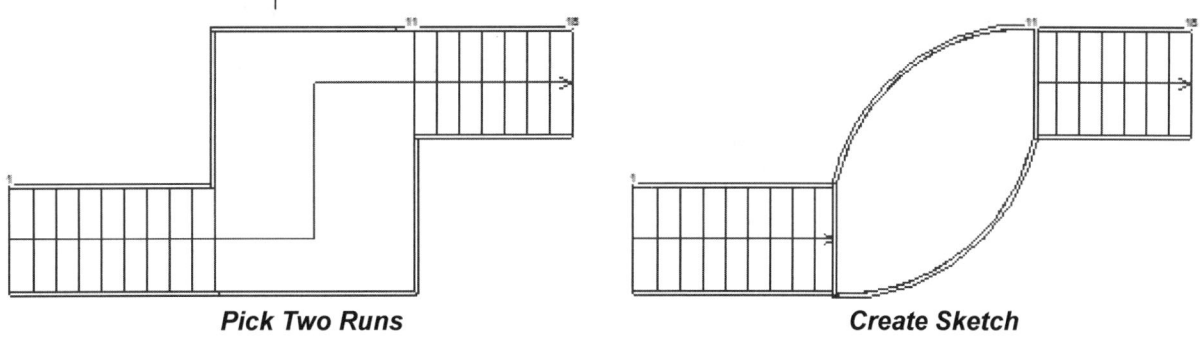

*Pick Two Runs*      *Create Sketch*

Figure 13–15

- You can connect runs with a landing as long as the start level and end level of the runs are at the same height.

## Adding Supports

Stair supports are included in the stair type if needed. However, you might want to delete them and add them later. Note that this only works if the stair type has supports that are specified in the Type Properties.

### How To: Add Stair Support Components

1. If there are no supports, double-click on the stair and in the *Modify | Create Stair* tab>Components panel, click  (Support) and then click  (Pick Edges).
2. Select the edge on which you want to place the support. Hover your cursor over the first support and press <Tab> if you have more than one connected edge on which you want to place the supports.
3. Finish the stair as needed.

> **Hint: Troubleshooting**
>
> When working with stairs and other elements, Warnings (such as the one shown in Figure 13–16) display when something is wrong, but you can keep on working. In many cases, you can close the dialog box and fix the issue or wait and do it later.
>
>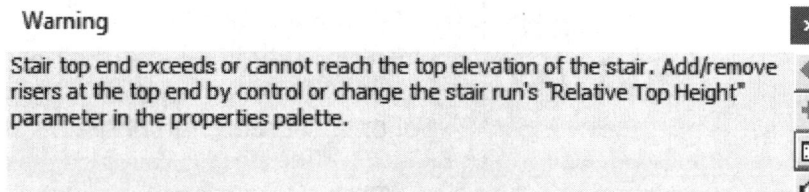
>
> **Figure 13–16**
>
> Sometimes Errors display where you must take action. These force you to stop and fix the situation.
>
> When you select an element that has a related warning,  (Show Related Warnings) displays in the ribbon. When selected, it opens a dialog box in which you can review the warning(s) related to the selected element. You can also display a list of all of the warnings in the project by clicking  (Review Warnings) in the *Manage* tab>Inquiry panel.

# Practice 13a | Create Component Stairs

## Practice Objectives

- Create a component stair.
- Model a custom sketch stair.

In this practice, you will create U-shaped stairs in each of the stairwells, as shown in Figure 13–17. You will also create a sketched stair at the entrance to the building.

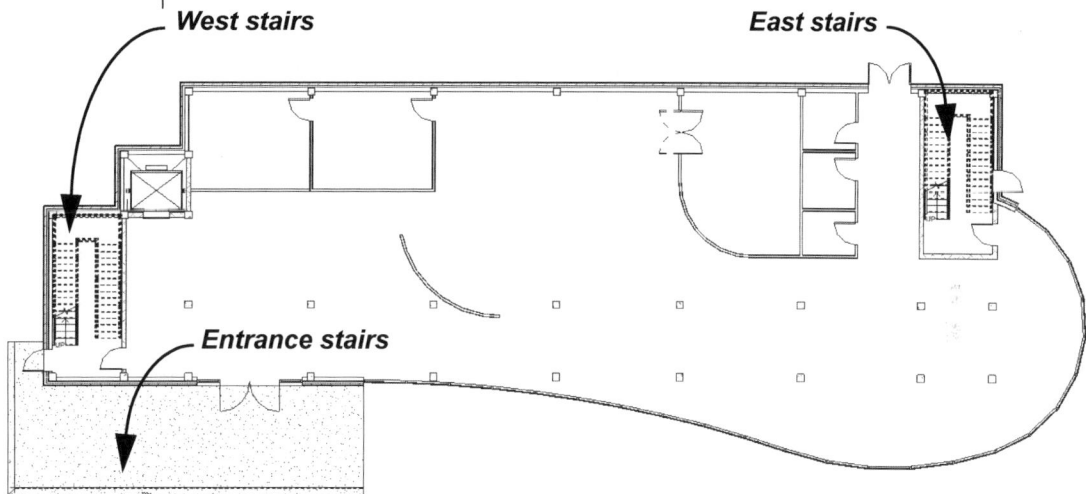

Figure 13–17

### Task 1 - Create Stair 1 on the first floor.

1. Open the project **Hotel-Stairs.rvt** from the practice files folder.

2. Open the **Floor Plans**: **Floor 1 - Stairs-West** view. This is a callout view from the main floor plan.

3. Hide the grid lines, sections, and turn off the crop region.

4. Close any other project or view that is open.

5. Open the **3D - West Stairs** view. Orbit the view as needed to see the stairs. The walls have been set to transparent so you can see the stairs.

6. Tile the view by typing **WT** and then **ZA** to zoom all.

7. Click on the **Floor 1 - Stairs-West** tab to make it the active view.

8. In the *Architecture* tab>Circulation panel, click (Stair).

9. In Properties, set or verify the following properties:

    - *Stair Type:* **Assembled Stair: Hotel Stairs**
    - *Base Level:* **Floor 1**
    - *Base Offset:* **0'-0"**
    - *Top Level:* **Floor 2**
    - *Top Offset:* **0'-0"**

    Note the *Desired Number of Risers* is **31**.

10. In the *Modify | Create Stair* tab>Tools panel, click
    (Railing). In the Railings dialog box, select **Hotel Stair Guardrail**, as shown in Figure 13–18. Verify that the *Position* is set to **Treads** and click **OK**.

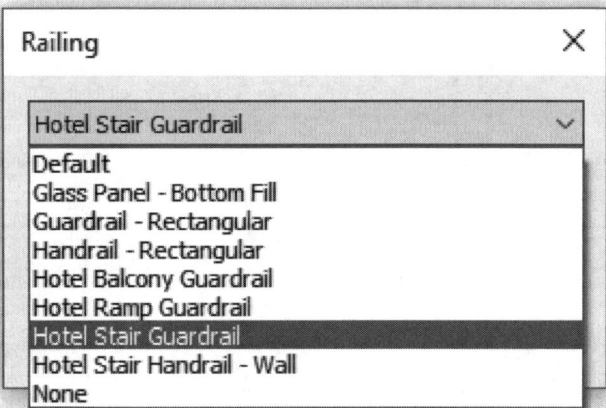

**Figure 13–18**

11. In the *Modify | Create Stair* tab>Work Plane panel, click
    (Reference Plane). Draw a horizontal reference plane **4'-0"** from the interior side of the top wall of the stairwell. Copy or offset another reference plane from the new reference plane **13'-9"** to indicate the start of the run, as shown in Figure 13–19.

*Use Pick Lines and set the Offset in the Options Bar.*

# Modeling Stairs, Railings, and Ramps

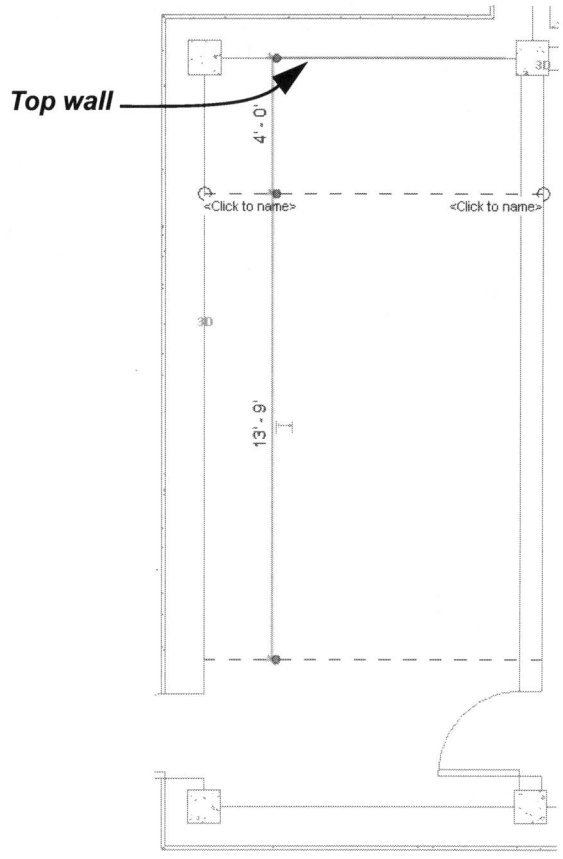

Figure 13–19

12. Click ▸ (Modify).

13. In the *Modify | Create Stair* tab>Components panel, click ▸ (Run).

14. In the Options Bar, set the *Location Line* to **Run: Left**, the *Offset* to **0'-0"**, and the *Actual Run Width* to **3'-8"**, and check the checkbox for **Automatic Landing**.

15. Pick the start point of the first run on the interior side of the exterior wall, as shown in Figure 13–20. Pick the second point near the reference plane and the interior side of the exterior wall.

16. Move your cursor to the opposite side of the stairwell to start the second run.

17. Pick the start point for the second run at the intersection of the wall and reference plane, as shown in Figure 13–20. Pick the second point past the completed number of stairs.

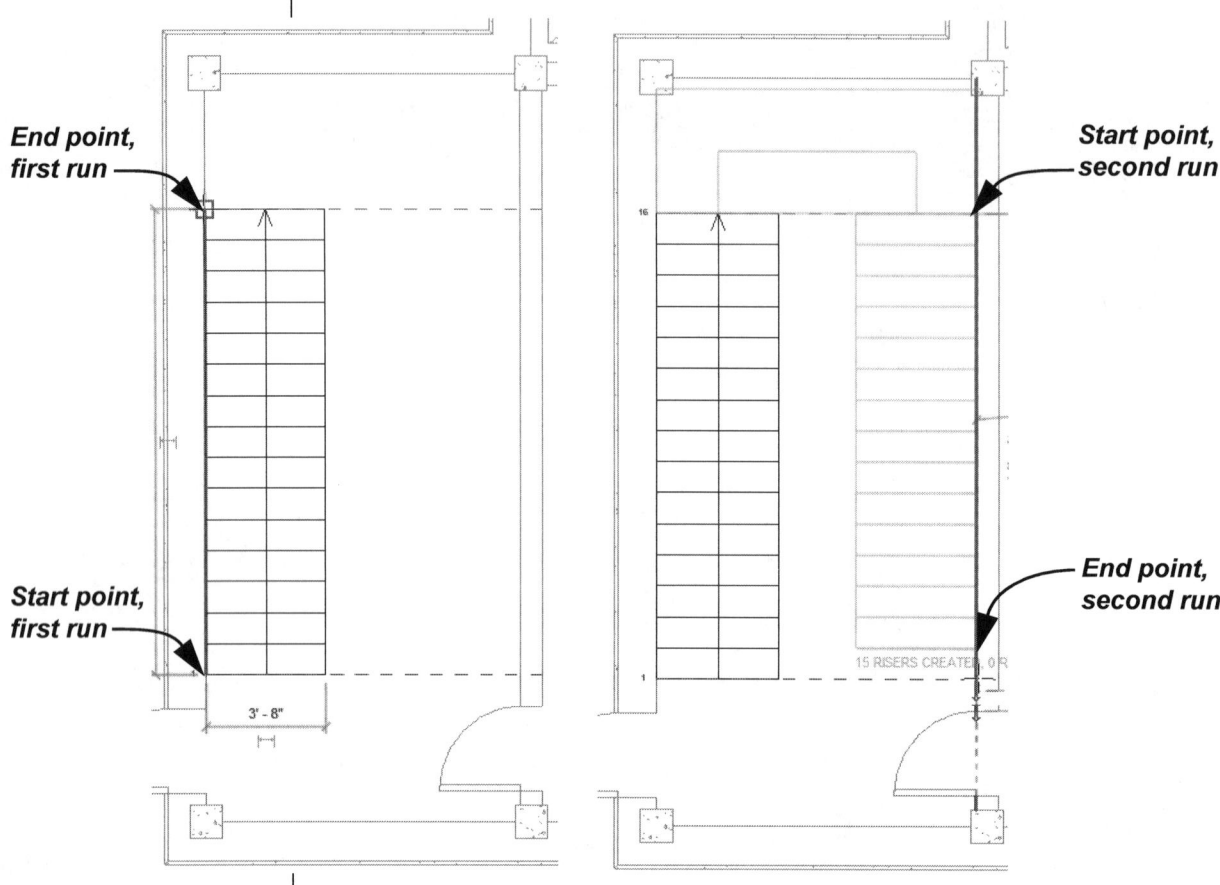

**Figure 13–20**

18. Click ✓ (Finish Edit Mode). The stairs display.

19. Type **TW** to tab the views.

20. Save the project.

### Task 2 - Create the east stairs on the first floor.

1. Open the **Floor Plans**: **Floor 1 - Stairs-East** view and type **ZA** to zoom all.

2. Repeat the process outlined above to create a stair in this stairwell, using the same stair and railing type and the same Options Bar settings and Properties.

3. Save the project.

Modeling Stairs, Railings, and Ramps

### Task 3 - Sketch entrance stairs.

1. Open the **Floor Plans: Floor 1** view.

2. Hide the grid lines, sections, and tags by selecting one of each and typing **VH**.

3. In Properties, set the *Underlay>Range: Base Level* to **Floor 1**. This displays the outline of the entrance roof that you will use to create custom stairs.

4. In the *Architecture* tab>Circulation panel, click (Stair).

5. In the Type Selector, select **Cast-In-Place Stair: Monolithic Stair - Hotel**.

6. In Properties, set or verify the following:
   - *Base Level:* **Floor 1**
   - *Base Offset:* (negative) **-1'-0"**
   - *Top Level:* **Floor 1**
   - *Top Offset:* **0'-0"**
   - *Desired Number of Risers:* **2**

7. In the *Modify | Create Stairs Sketch* tab>Tools panel, click (Railing). In the Railing dialog box, select **None** and click **OK**.

8. In the Components panel, click (Run), then click (Create Sketch).

*The sketch lines in the following figures have been widened for emphasis.*

9. In the Draw panel, click (Boundary), then click (Pick Lines). Select the ends of the roof outline that are labeled "Boundary lines" in Figure 13–21. (Note: The sketch lines in the following images have been widened for emphasis.)

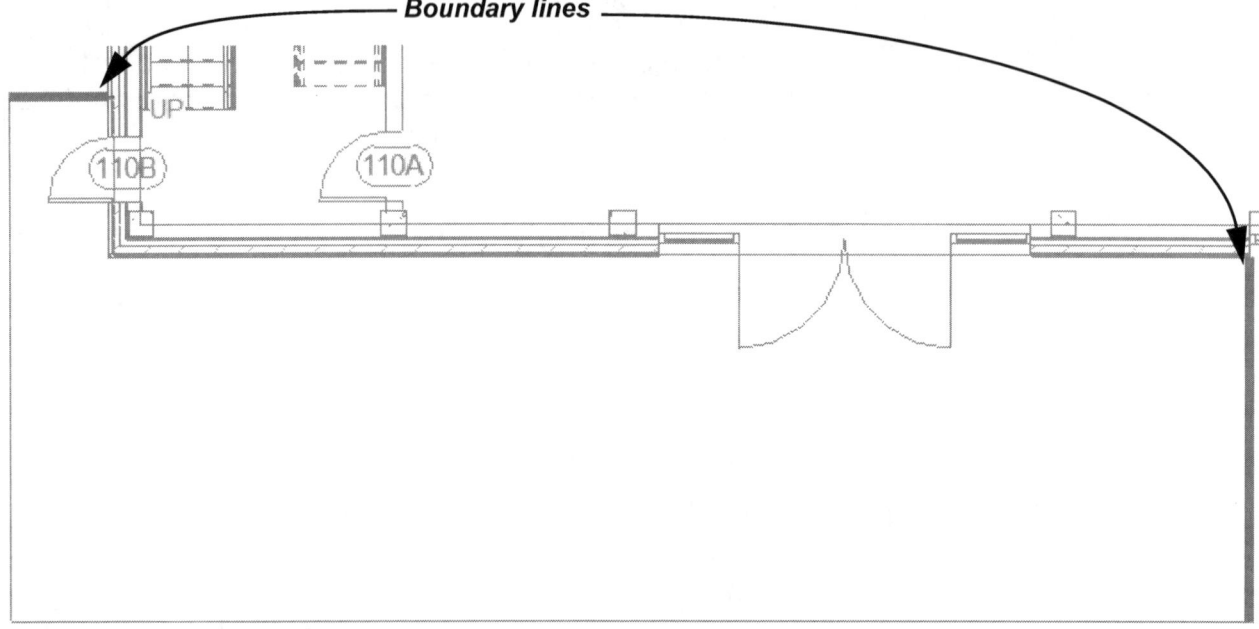

Figure 13–21

10. Click (Riser). Use (Pick Lines) to select the other sides of the roof outline (labeled "First set of riser lines" in Figure 13–22).

Modeling Stairs, Railings, and Ramps

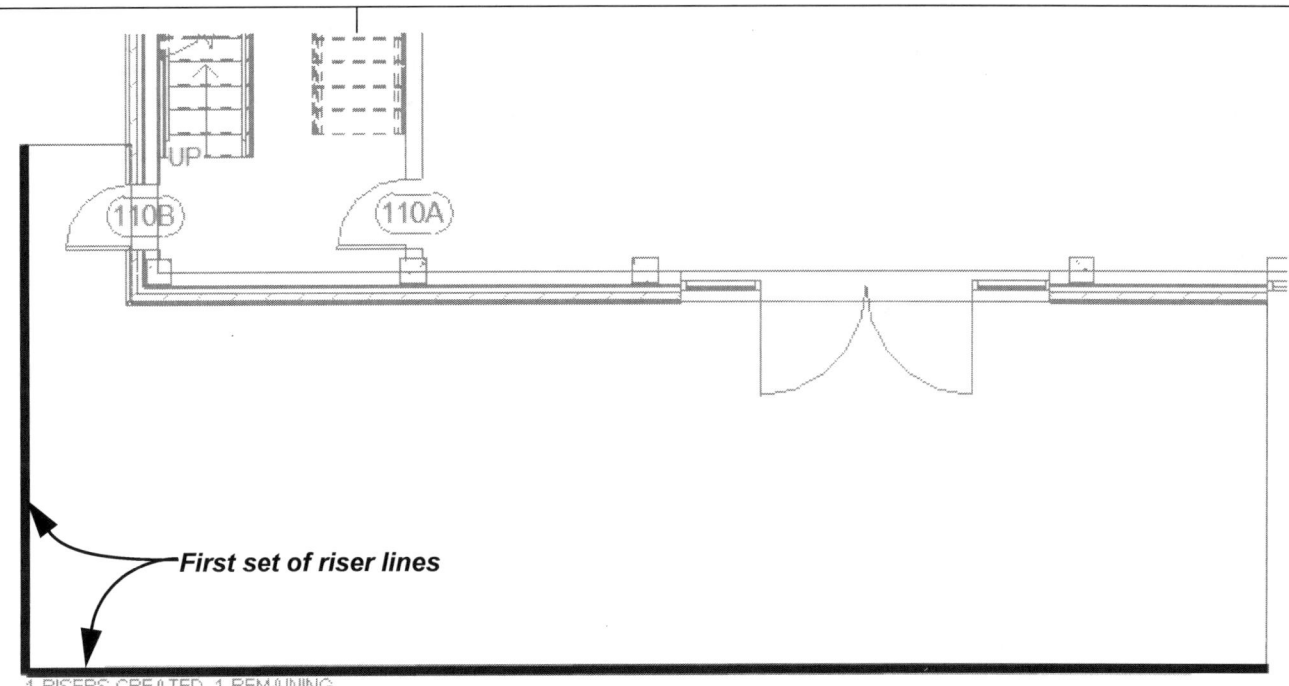

Figure 13–22

11. With (Riser) still selected, click (Pick Lines). In the Options Bar, set the *Offset* to **1'-0"**. Offset another set of risers outside the outline, as shown in Figure 13–23.

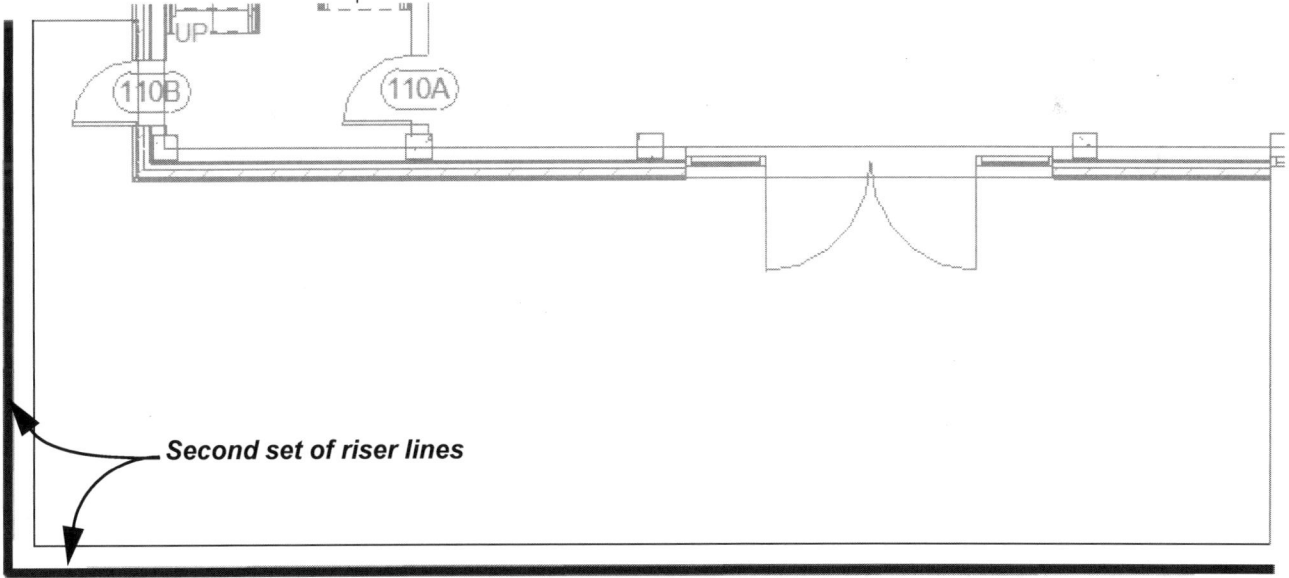

Figure 13–23

12. Click (Modify).

13. Use ⬒ (Trim/Extend to Corner) to clean up the intersections of the boundary lines and outside risers, as shown in Figure 13–24.

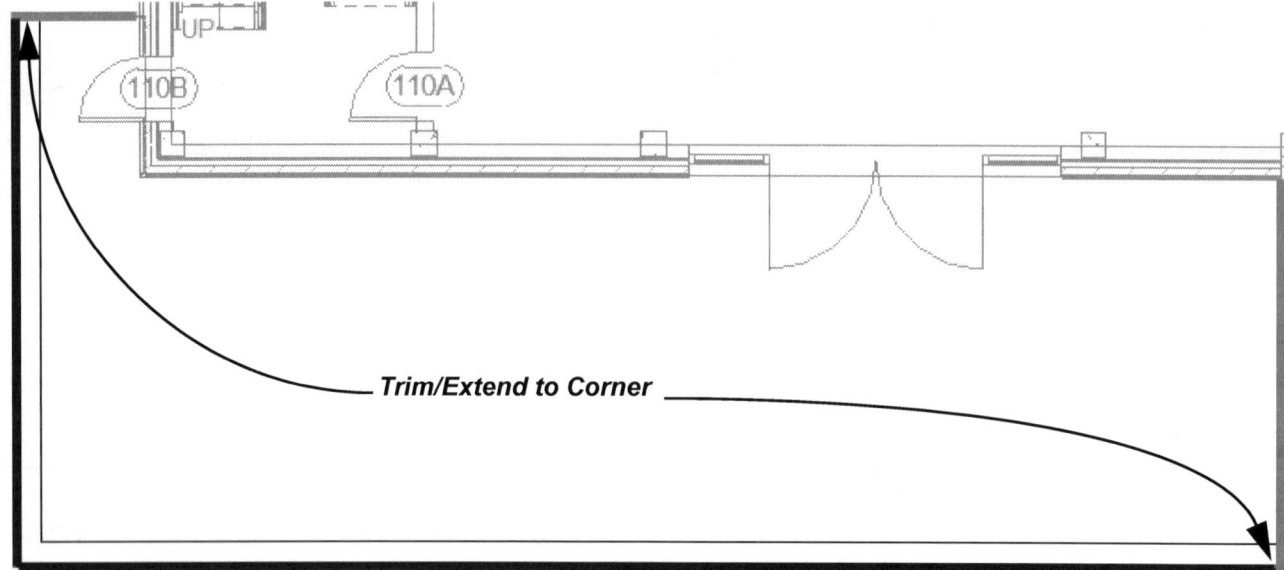

**Figure 13–24**

14. Click ✔ (Finish Edit Mode) to complete the stair portion of the assembly.

15. In the *Modify | Create Stair* tab>Tools panel, click ⬚ (Flip). This will flip the risers to the correct direction.

16. In the *Modify | Create Stair* tab>Components panel, click ▭ (Landing) and then ✐ (Create Sketch).

17. Use **Pick Lines** to create the boundary for the landing, as shown in Figure 13–25.

   - If needed, use ⬒ (Trim/Extend to Corner) to clean up all the intersections of the boundary lines.

# Modeling Stairs, Railings, and Ramps

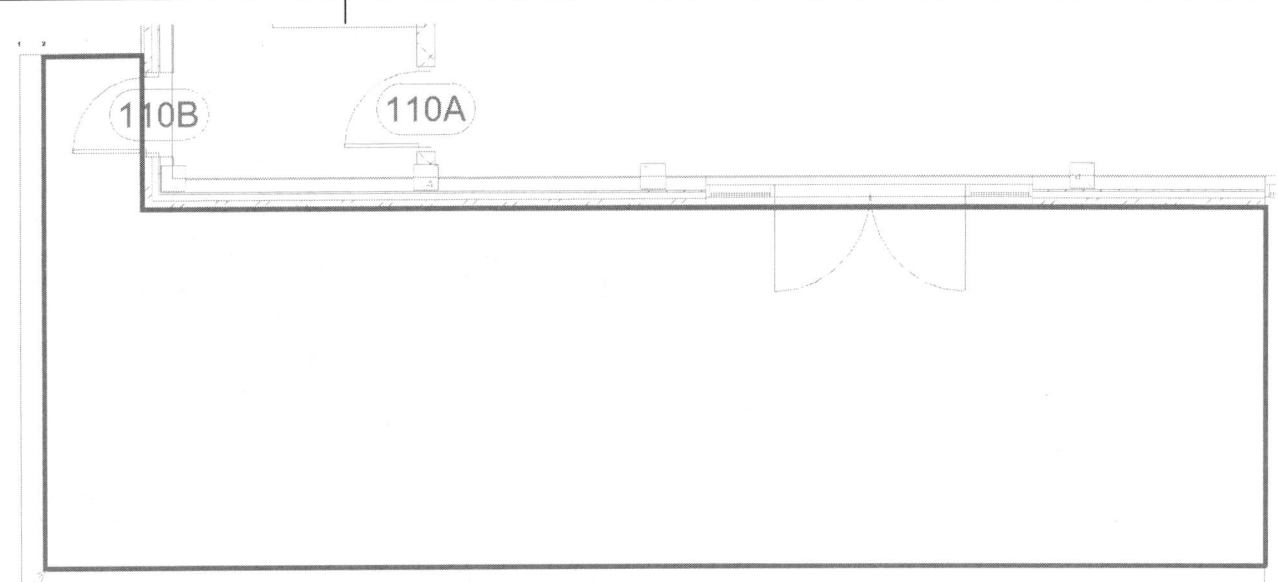

**Figure 13–25**

18. Click ✓ (Finish Edit Mode) twice to create the full stair assembly.

    - Ignore any warnings that display.

19. Select the **DN** tag on the stairs, as shown in Figure 13–26.

**Figure 13–26**

20. In Properties, uncheck *Show Up Text* and *Show Down Text*, as shown in Figure 13–27.

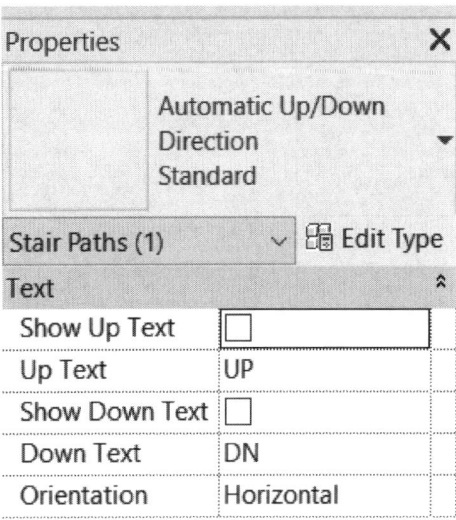

**Figure 13–27**

21. In Properties, set the *Underlay>Range: Base Level* to **None**.

22. View the stairs in 3D, as shown in Figure 13–28.

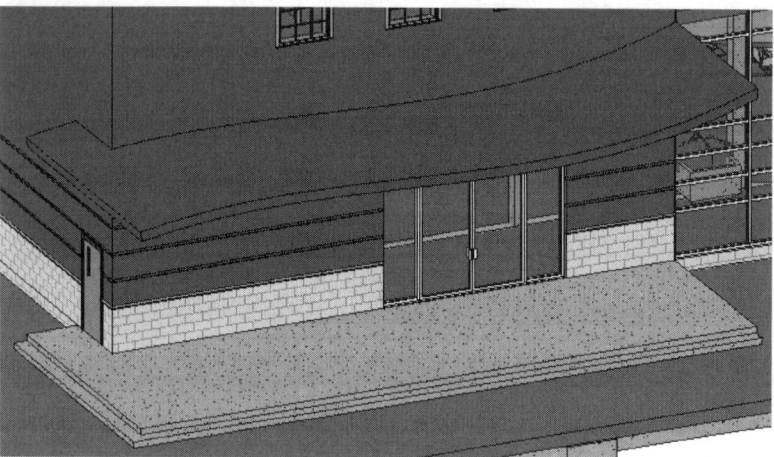

**Figure 13–28**

23. Save and close the project.

# 13.2 Modifying Component Stairs

Stairs can be modified in a variety of ways. For example, in Figure 13–29, a straight stair with a landing has been modified to make one run wider than the other and the landing wider than both runs, creating a balcony. The landing has been further customized by sketching a curved feature.

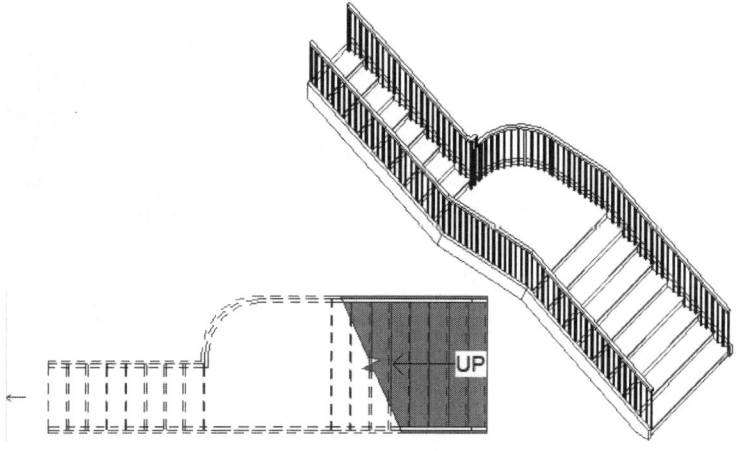

**Figure 13–29**

- Modifying stair components can be done when you first create the stair or later when you edit a stair.

- When working with a finished stair, you can change the type and properties, as well as flip the stair direction, as shown in Figure 13–30. You can select a stair run and use temporary dimensions to modify the length and width, as shown in Figure 13–31.

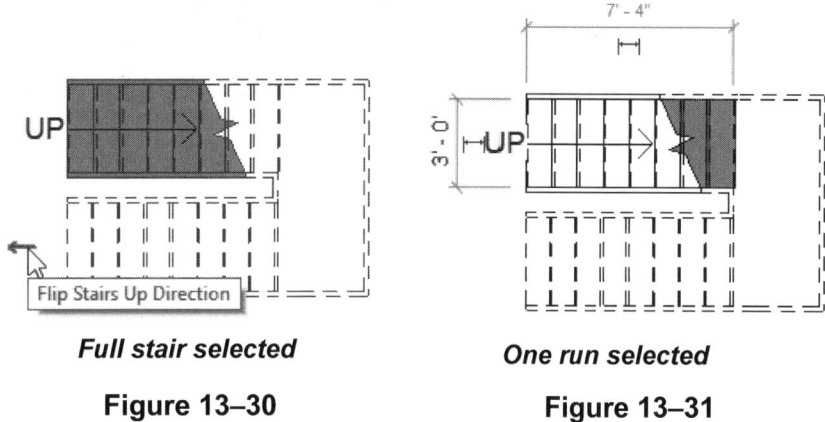

*Full stair selected*      *One run selected*

**Figure 13–30**          **Figure 13–31**

- To select a stair run, hover your cursor over the stair and press <Tab> to cycle through until the one you want highlights.

## Editing Individual Stair Components

Within stair edit mode, you can make more significant modifications to individual components using temporary dimensions and shape handles, as shown in Figure 13–32. Numerous snaps and alignment lines are also available as you modify the components.

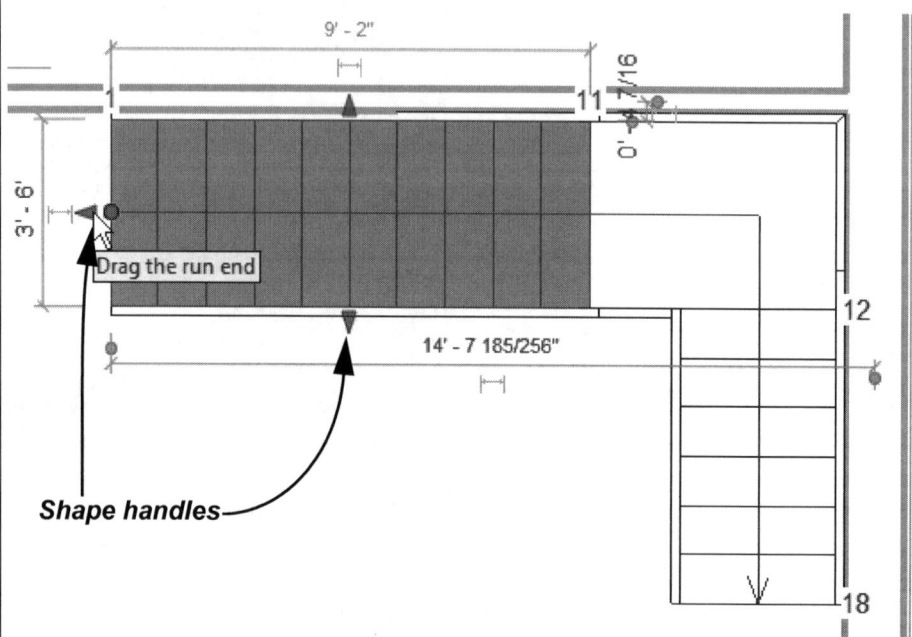

**Figure 13–32**

- To edit stairs, double-click on the stairs or, in the *Modify | Stairs* tab>Edit panel, click  (Edit Stairs).

  - The arrow shape handle at the end of a run lengthens or shortens the run and modifies the other run so that the overall number of steps stays consistent and retains the start and end level.
  - The circle shape handle at the end of a run lengthens or shortens the run, does not modify any other runs, but changes the start and end level.
  - The arrow shape handle on the sides of the runs or landings can be used to modify the width.
  - You can use temporary dimensions for the run width and connections to other elements, but not for run lengths. Use the shape handles instead.
  - When you have finished modifying the stair, click  (Finish Edit Mode).

Modeling Stairs, Railings, and Ramps

## Converting Components to Sketches

To customize a run or landing with more options, convert it into a sketch and modify the outline of the sketch, as shown for a curved landing in Figure 13–33.

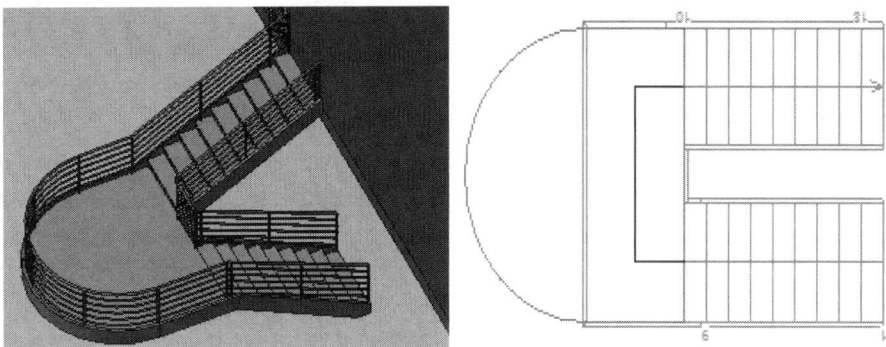

Figure 13–33

### How To: Turn a Stair Component into a Sketch

1. Select a stair.
2. In the *Modify | Stairs* tab>Edit panel, click  (Edit Stairs).
3. Select the run or landing that you want to customize.
4. In the Tools panel, click  (Convert to sketch-based). Doing so turns the component into a custom sketched element.
5. In the Tools panel, click  (Edit Sketch).
6. Use the options in the *Modify | Create Stair>Sketch Landing (or Run)* tab>Draw panel to modify the boundary, riser, or stair path, as needed. The boundary of a landing is shown in Figure 13–34.

*Editing an existing landing is the easiest way to create a custom landing.*

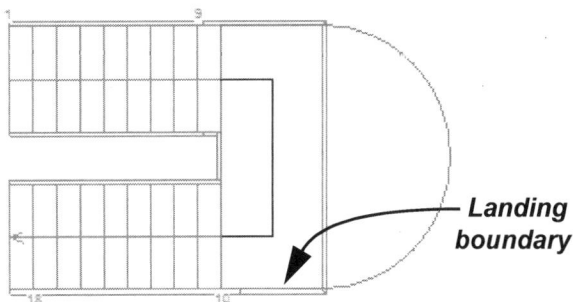

Figure 13–34

7. Click  (Finish Edit Mode) to complete the sketch. Click again to return to the stair.

## Multistory Stairs

Once you have created a component stair that runs from one level to another, you can expand that stair to extend to multiple stories. You can select which levels the multistory stairs extend to and skip levels as needed, as shown in Figure 13–35.

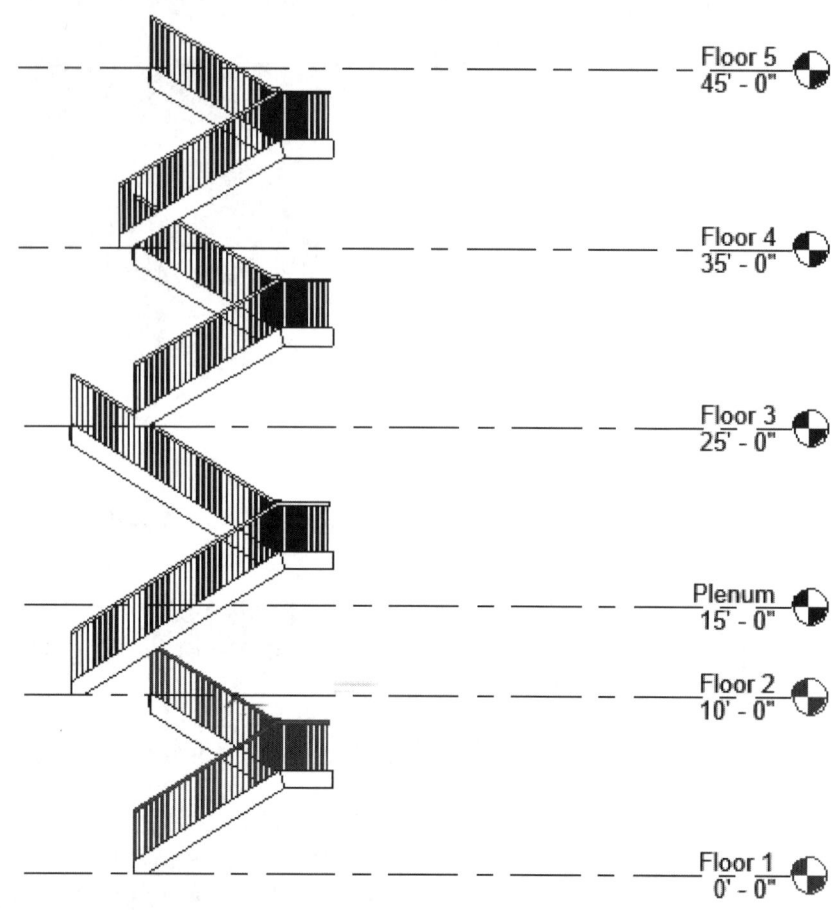

**Figure 13–35**

### How To: Create Multistory Stairs

1. Open an elevation or section view where the base stairs and levels are displayed.
2. Select the stair that you want to turn into a multistory stair.
3. In the *Modify | Stairs* tab>Multistory Stairs panel, click  (Select Levels).
4. In the *Modify | Multistory Stairs* tab>Multistory Stairs panel, click  (Connect Levels).
5. Select the levels you want to connect. Hold <Ctrl> to select multiple levels.
    - If you need to remove any levels, click  (Disconnect Levels) and select the levels you want to remove.
6. Click  (Finish Edit Mode).

*You can also create multistory stairs while you are in the **Create Stair** command.*

# Modeling Stairs, Railings, and Ramps

- If you are not in an elevation or section view when you start the **Multistory Stair** command, the Go To View dialog box displays, enabling you to select and open a view by clicking **Open View**.

- To edit multistory stairs, ensure that you are selecting the full multistory stair element, as shown in Figure 13–36. Press <Tab> to cycle through the various components of the stairs as needed.

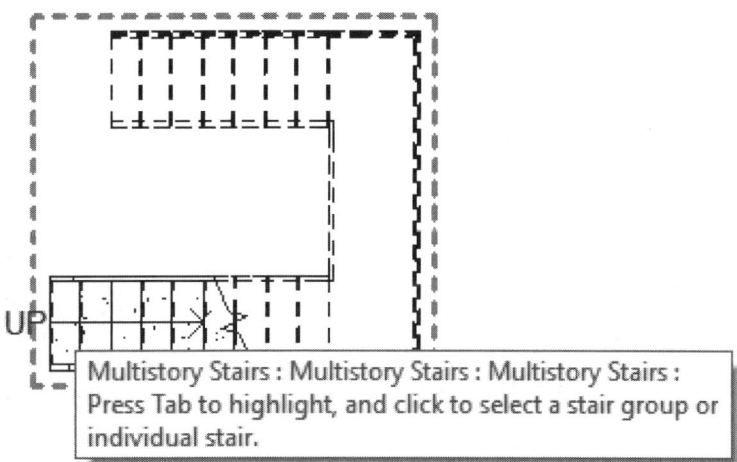

Figure 13–36

- If you change the height of a level, the stair components in the multistory stair are updated to match the new distance.

- If you change the type of a railing after a multistory stair has been placed, any runs of the same height (i.e., grouped together) are also updated. Runs of different heights would need to be modified separately.

## Practice 13b

# Modify Component Stairs

**Practice Objectives**

- Expand a set of stairs to multistory stairs.
- Cut out floors where stairs penetrate them.
- Create shafts.

In this practice, you will modify stairs and turn them into multistory stairs, as shown in Figure 13–37. You will also modify the floors for stair openings and add shafts to create openings for the upper floors.

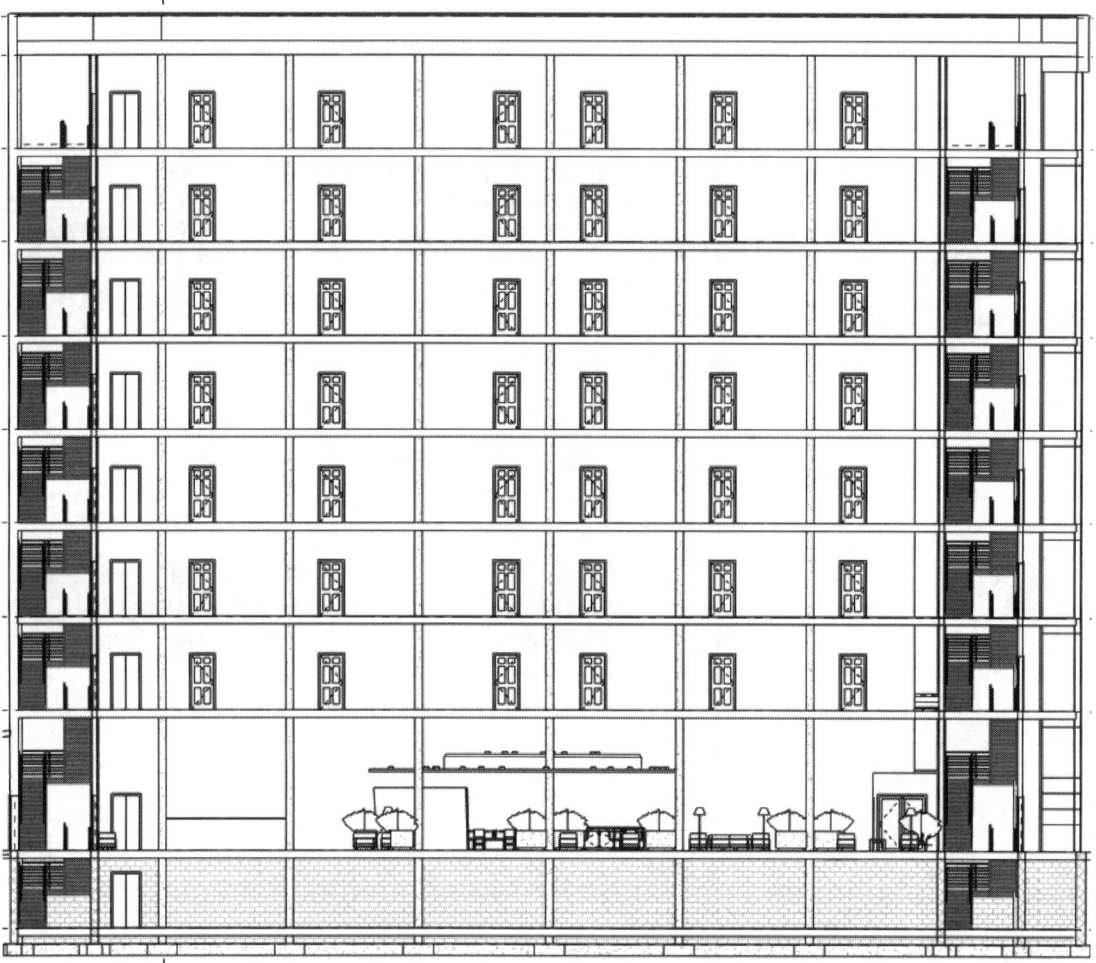

**Figure 13–37**

**Task 1 - Create multistory stairs.**

1. Open the project **Hotel-StairsModify.rvt** from the practice files folder.

2. Open the **Sections (Building Section): E/W Building Section** view. You will see the west stairs.

3. Select the assembled stair shown in Figure 13–38.

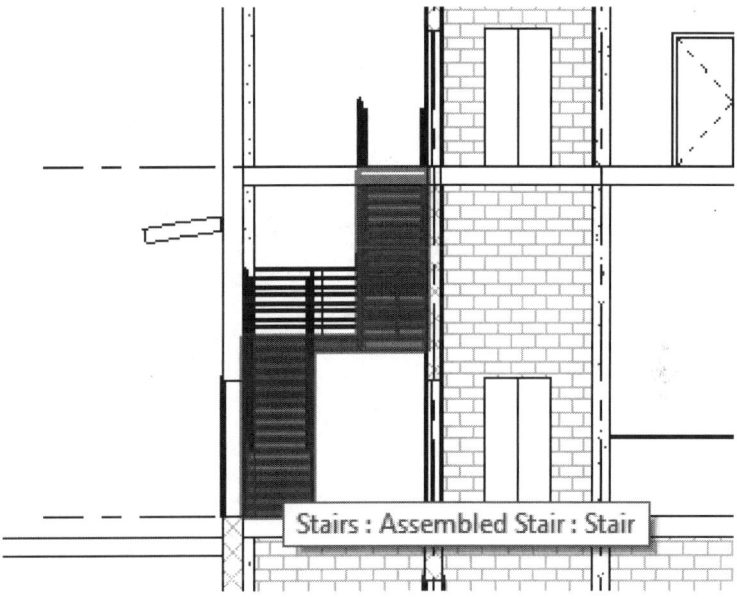

Figure 13–38

4. In the *Modify | Stairs* tab>Multistory Stairs panel, click  (Select Levels). In the Multistory Stairs panel, verify that  (Connect Levels) is selected.

5. Hold <Ctrl> and select the level lines for **Floor 3** to **Floor 8**. (Do not select the **Roof** or **Parapet** levels.)

6. Click ✓ (Finish Edit Mode). The stairs are added between the rest of the floors, as shown in Figure 13–39.

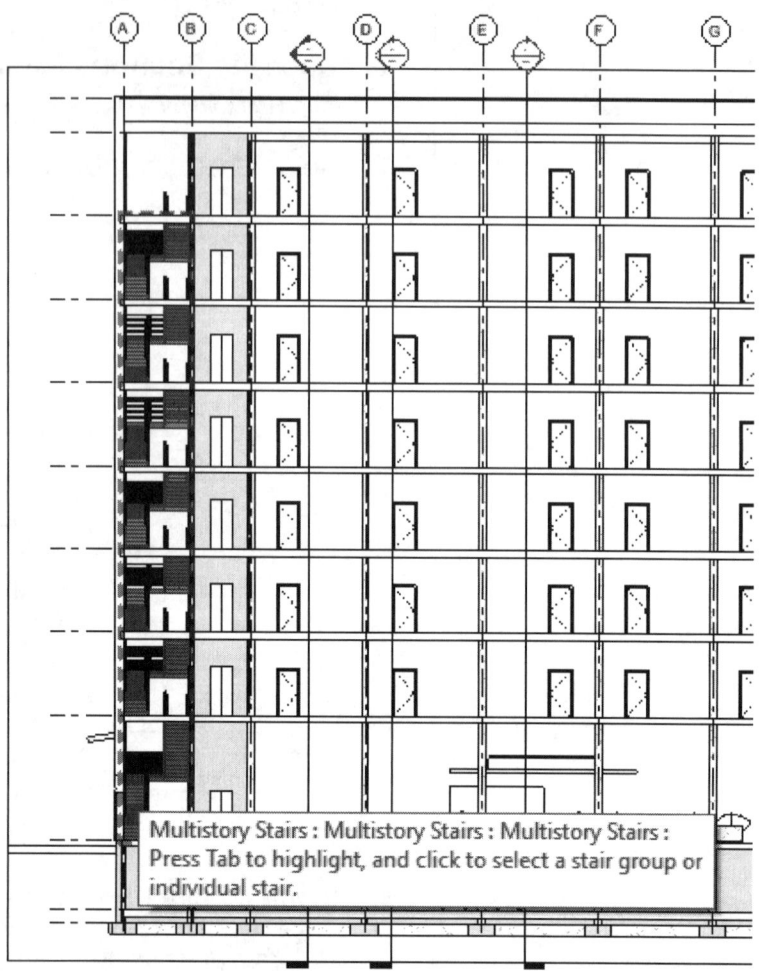

Figure 13–39

7. With the new multistory stairs still selected, in the *Modify | Multistory Stairs* tab>Multistory Stairs panel, click (Connect/Disconnect Levels).

8. Click (Connect Levels) and select the **Basement** level line, then click ✓ (Finish Edit Mode). The stairs to the basement are added.

   - If needed to see the stairs on all of the floors, set the *Visual Style* to (Consistent Colors).

9. Save the project.

# Modeling Stairs, Railings, and Ramps

You need to do this to the east stairs, but they are not visible in the building section view so you will need to modify the section in plan view.

10. Return to the **Floor 1** view.

11. Select the E/W Building Section line (do not select on the section marker head).

12. Pan over to the east stairs area.

13. In the *Modify | Views* tab>Section panel, click (Split Segment).

14. Split the section close to the stairs; you will then click inside the east stairwell to place the split section, as shown in Figure 13–40.

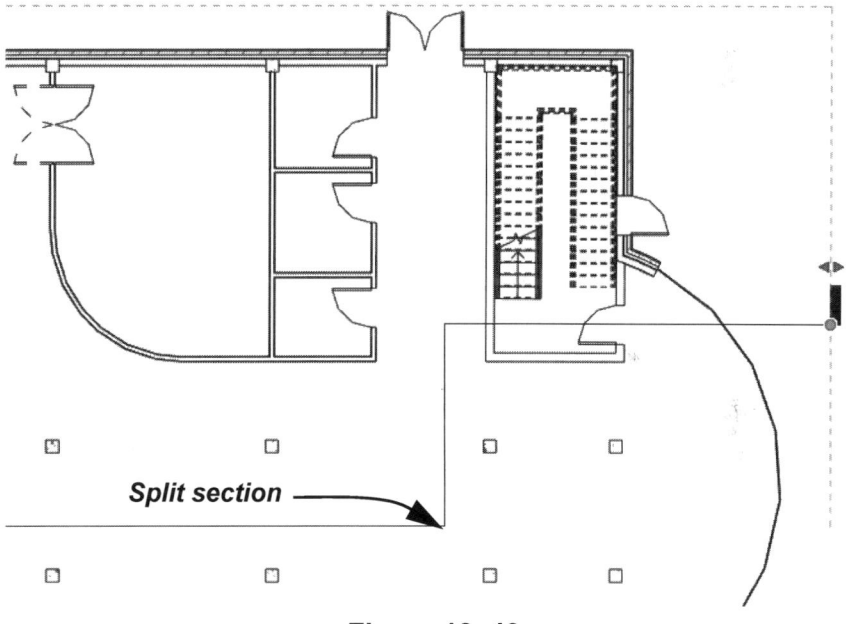

Figure 13–40

15. Click (Modify).

16. Activate the **E/W Building Section**. You are now able to see the east stairs. Repeat the process of turning the east stairs into a multistory stair and adding stairs to the basement.

17. Save the project.

**Task 2 - Modify the second floor stair openings.**

1. Open the **Floor Plans: Floor 2** view.

2. Select the floor.

   *If needed, toggle on (Select Elements by Face).*

3. In the *Modify | Floors* tab>Mode panel, click (Edit Boundary).

4. Zoom in to the west stairs.

5. Modify the floor boundary line so that it creates an opening for the west stairs, as shown in Figure 13–41.

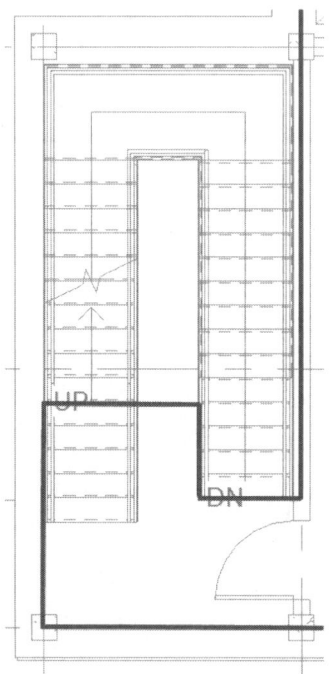

**Figure 13–41**

6. Pan over to the east stairwell and modify the floor boundary there as well, as shown in Figure 13–42.

Modeling Stairs, Railings, and Ramps

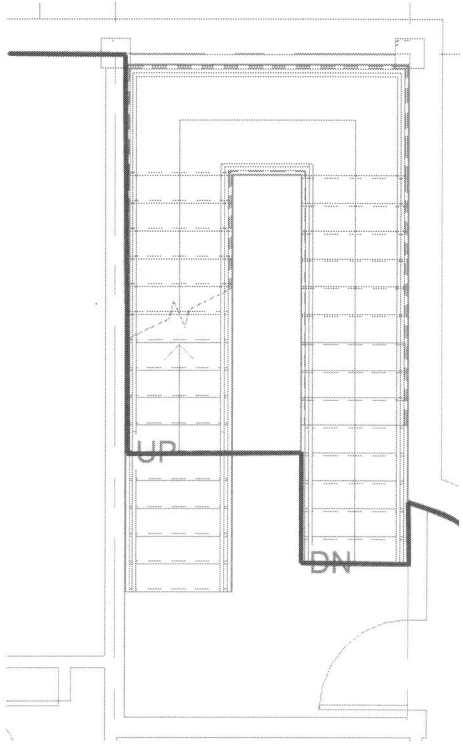

**Figure 13–42**

7. Use (Trim/Extend to Corner) to clean up the intersections of the boundary lines.

8. Click (Finish Edit Mode).

   - If prompted, select **Don't Attach** in the Attaching to floor dialog box. For the following prompt, select **Yes** to overlap the highlighted floor.

9. Zoom out to display the entire second floor, as shown in Figure 13–43.

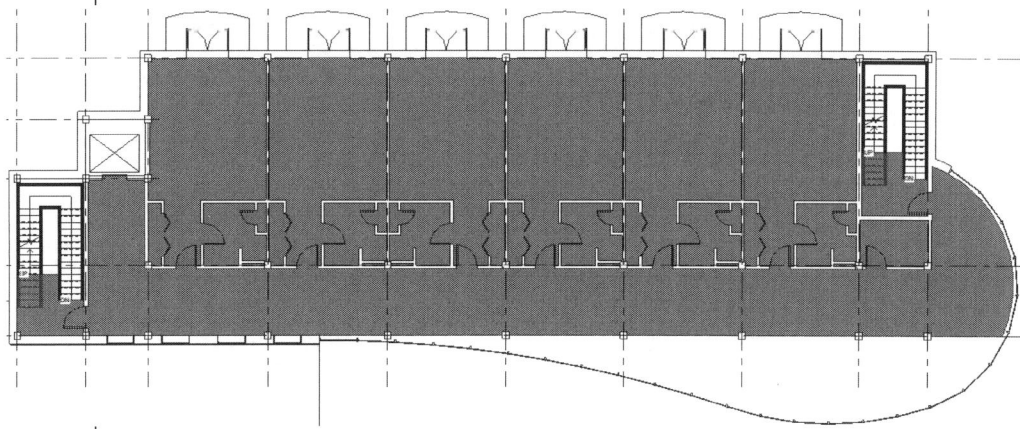

**Figure 13–43**

10. Save the project.

### Task 3 - Add shafts in the stairwells.

1. Open the **Floor Plans: Floor 3** view.

2. In Properties, verify that the *Underlay>Range: Base Level* is set to **None**.

3. In the *Architecture* tab>Opening panel, click (Shaft).

4. Draw the sketch of the shaft similar to that shown in Figure 13–44.

*You can use a shaft here because the openings are the same on all of the floors.*

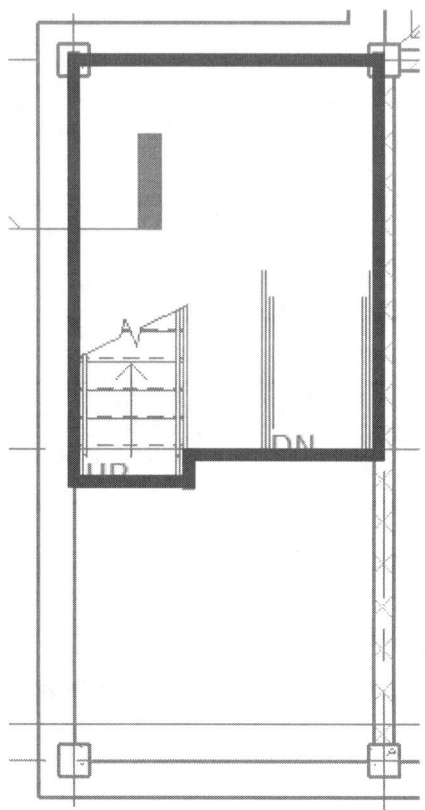

**Figure 13–44**

5. In Properties, set the *Base Constraint* to **Floor 3** with a *Base Offset* of (negative) **-1'-0"** and the *Top Constraint* to **Up to level: Floor 8**.

6. Click (Finish Edit Mode) to create the shaft.

7. Repeat the process on the east stairwell, as shown in Figure 13–45.

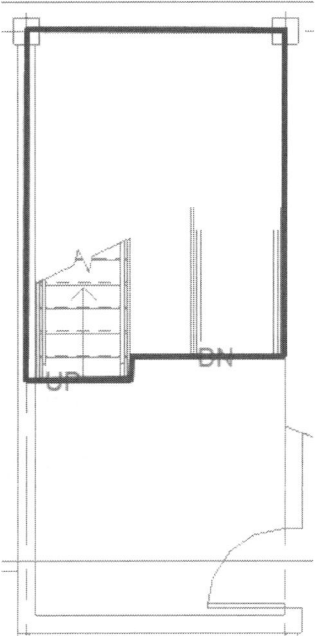

Figure 13–45

8. Go to the **3D View of West Stairs** view, adjust the section box, and inspect the results. Modify the floor boundaries if needed.

9. If time permits, create another shaft on Floor 1 that goes down to the basement to accommodate both sets of stairs.

10. Save and close the project.

# 13.3 Working with Railings

Railings are automatically created with stairs, but you can modify or delete them independently of the stair element. You can also add railings separately from the stairs for other locations, as shown in Figure 13–46.

*Hosts for sketched railings include floors, slabs, slab edges, the top of walls, and roofs. You can also add railings to topographic surfaces.*

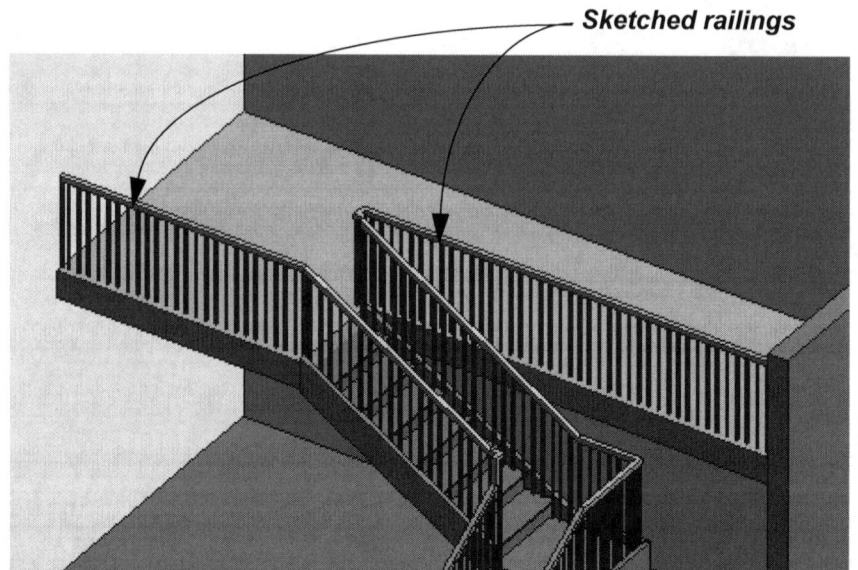

Figure 13–46

- You can add railings to existing stairs and ramps if they were not included when they were created.

## How To: Add Railings by Sketching

1. Open a plan or 3D view.
2. In the *Architecture* tab>Circulation panel, expand  (Railing) and click  (Sketch Path).
3. In the Type Selector, specify the railing type.
4. In the *Modify | Create Railing Path* tab>Tools panel, click  (Pick New Host) and select the element that you want the railing to associate to, such as a stair, floor, or top of a wall.
   - If you are working in a 3D or section view, you can select **Preview** in the *Modify | Create Railing Path* tab>Options panel and the railing displays while you are still in edit mode. This only works if you have selected a host.

- If the host is sloped, the railing will follow the slope, as shown in Figure 13–47. The sketch displays at the host's level.

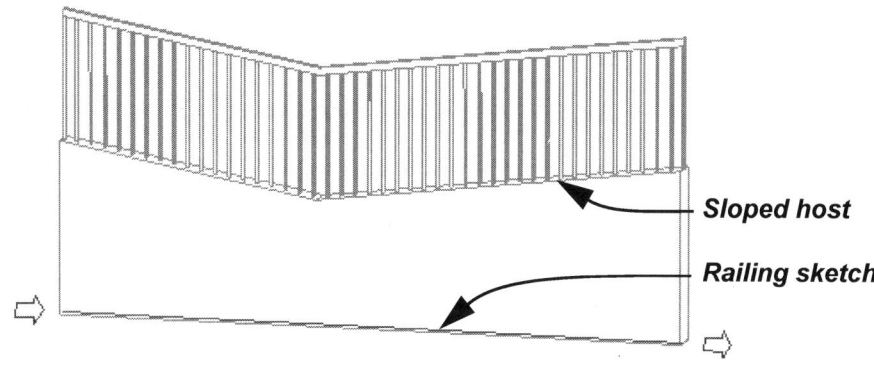

**Figure 13–47**

5. Use the Draw tools to sketch the lines that define the railings.
6. Click ✓ (Finish Edit Mode) to create the railing.

- The railing must be a single connected sketch. If it is not, you are prompted with a warning, such as that shown in Figure 13–48.

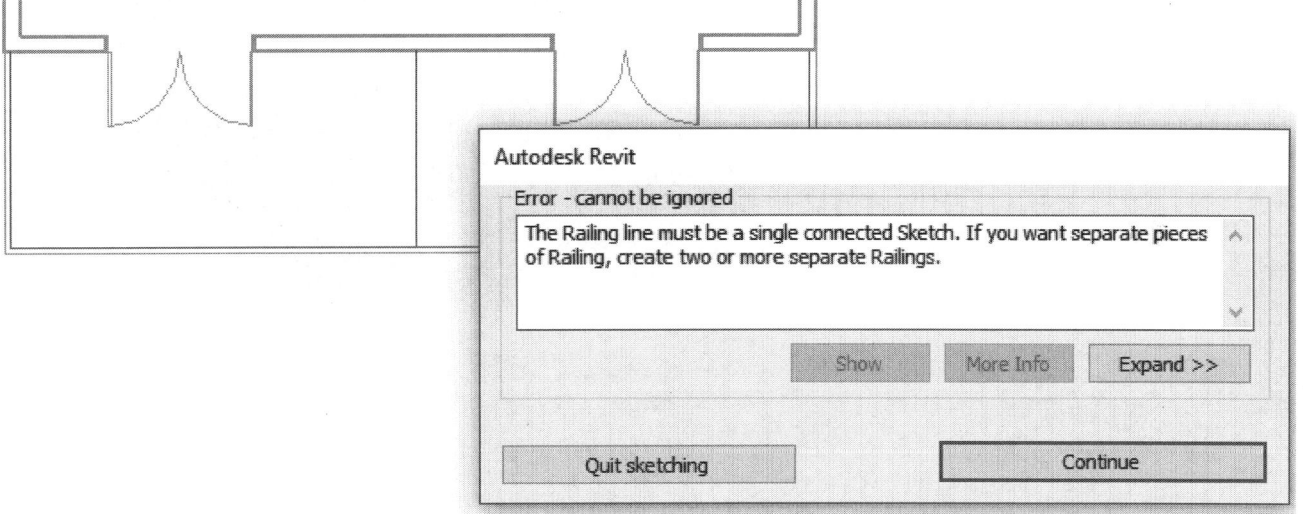

**Figure 13–48**

### How To: Add Railings by Place on Stair/Ramp

1. In the *Architecture* tab>Circulation panel, expand (Railing) and click (Place on Stair/Ramp).
2. In the *Modify | Create Railing Place on Stair/Ramp* tab>Position panel, click (Treads) or (Stringer).
3. Select the stair or ramp where you want to add the railings.

- (Place on Stair/Ramp) only works if there are no railings on the stair. If you want to add an additional railing (e.g., down the middle of a wide stair), you need to sketch the railing.

## Modifying Railings

Modifying railings can be as simple as changing their type, as shown in Figure 13–49. You can also edit the path of a railing.

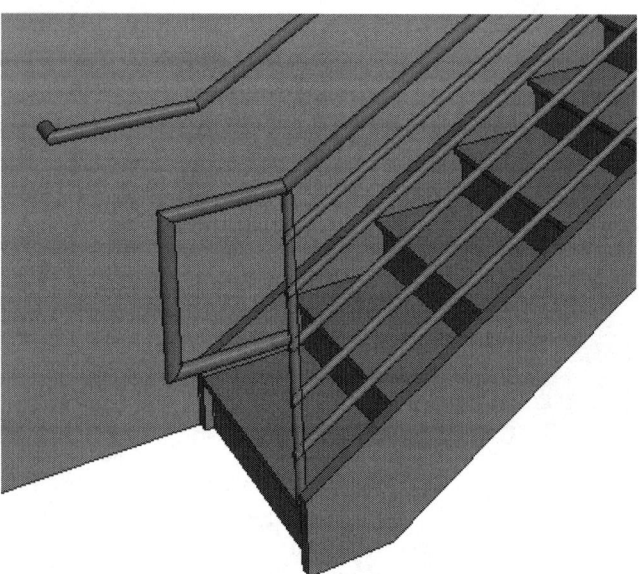

**Figure 13–49**

- You can delete railings separately from stairs or ramps. However, deleting a stair or ramp automatically deletes related railings.

# Modeling Stairs, Railings, and Ramps

- You can use the ⊹ (Split Element) command on railings. Doing so results in separate railings, as shown in Figure 13–50.

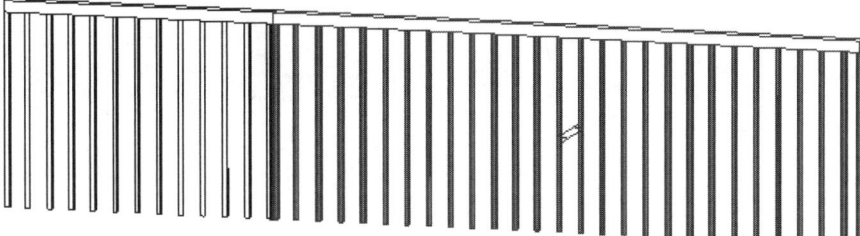

**Figure 13–50**

## Editing the Path of a Railing

To edit the path of a railing, double-click on the railing, or select the railing and in the *Modify | Railings* tab>Mode panel, click ✎ (Edit Path). This places you in edit mode, in which you can modify the individual lines that define the railing, as shown in Figure 13–51. You can create additional lines, but they must be connected to the existing lines.

*Unlike many other elements in edit mode, railings do not have to be in a closed loop.*

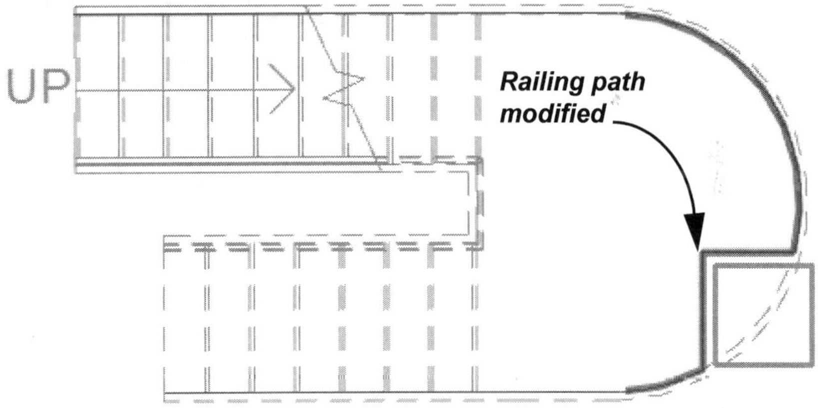

**Figure 13–51**

# Practice 13c  Work with Railings

### Practice Objectives

- Modify railings and handrails.
- Add stand-alone railings.

In this practice, you will modify the railings in the stairwells by changing the railings against the wall to a new type. You will add stand-alone railings to connect the railing for Level 8 to the stairwell wall. You will also add railings to the interior balconies (as shown in Figure 13–52) and to the exterior balconies.

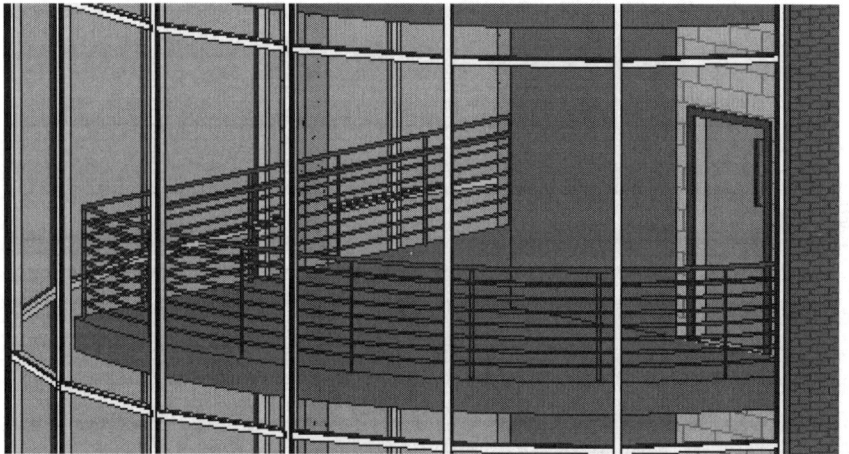

**Figure 13–52**

### Task 1 - Modify the railing type.

1. Open the project **Hotel-Railings.rvt** from the practice files folder. Verify that you are in the **Floor Plans: Floor 1 - Stairs-West** view.

2. Create a camera view looking from the door into the stairwell to display the new stairs and railings, as shown in Figure 13–53.

*In the Quick Access Toolbar>Default 3D view drop-down list, select ▣ (Camera).*

# Modeling Stairs, Railings, and Ramps

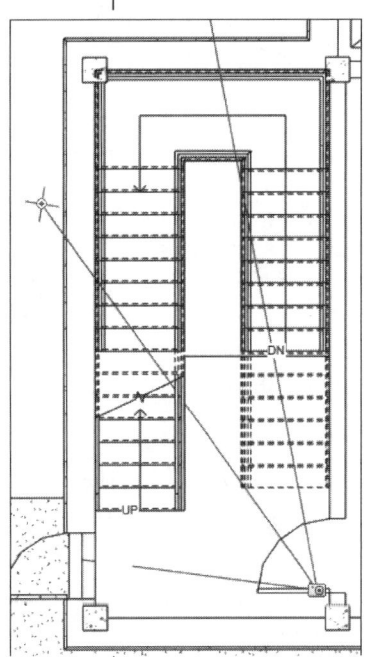

**Figure 13–53**

3. In the Project Browser, in *3D Views*, right-click on the new 3D view and rename it as **CAM - Floor 1 West Stairs**.

4. In the camera view, modify the crop region controls as needed to show the first run of the stair, and set the *Visual Style* to (Shaded).

5. Select the railing that is against the wall and in the Type Selector, select **Railing: Hotel Stair Handrail-Wall**. The railing type changes, as shown in Figure 13–54.

*Press <Ctrl>+<Tab> to move between the **3D Camera** view and the **Floor Plan** view or use the view tabs at the top of the window.*

**Figure 13–54**

6. With the handrail still selected, in Properties set the *Offset from Path* to **0**. This prevents the handrail from sitting too far off the wall.

7. Open the **Floor Plans: Floor 2** view.

8. Zoom in on the west stairwell and select the outside railing.

9. In the Type Selector, change the type to **Railing: Hotel Stair Handrail-Wall**. In Properties, set the *Offset from Path* to **0**.

10. Repeat this on the east stairs.

11. Save the project.

**Task 2 - Modify the existing railing and connect a new railing.**

1. Open the **Floor Plan: Floor 8** view and zoom in to the west stairwell. Close any other open views.

2. Create a camera view looking into the stairwell. Rename the new 3D view **CAM - Floor 8 West Stairs**.

3. Tile the **Floor 8** and **CAM - Floor 8 West Stairs** views.

4. Select the railing that is against the wall. In the Type Selector, select **Railing: Hotel Stair Handrail-Wall**. In Properties, change the *Offset from Path* to **0'-0"**.

5. If needed, select the stairs label **DN**, click on the control (as shown in Figure 13–55), and drag it out of the way.

Figure 13–55

6. Select the inside railing, as shown in Figure 13–56.

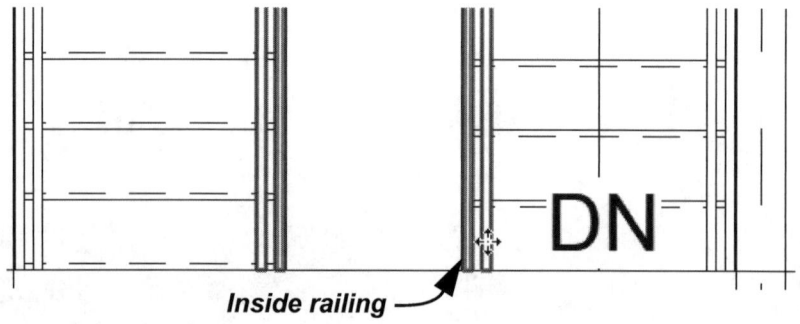

Figure 13–56

7. In the *Modify | Railing* tab>Mode panel, click (Edit Path), or double-click on the railing.

8. In the *Modify | Railings>Sketch Path* tab>Options panel, select **Preview**. This allows you to see the changes as you make them in the camera view.

9. In the *Modify | Create Railing Path* tab>Work Plane panel, click (Ref Plane).

10. Draw a reference plane **4"** from the edge of the floor, as shown in Figure 13–57.
    - Hint: Use the **Pick Lines** draw tool, set the Options Bar *Offset* to **4"**, and hover your cursor over the edge of the floor.

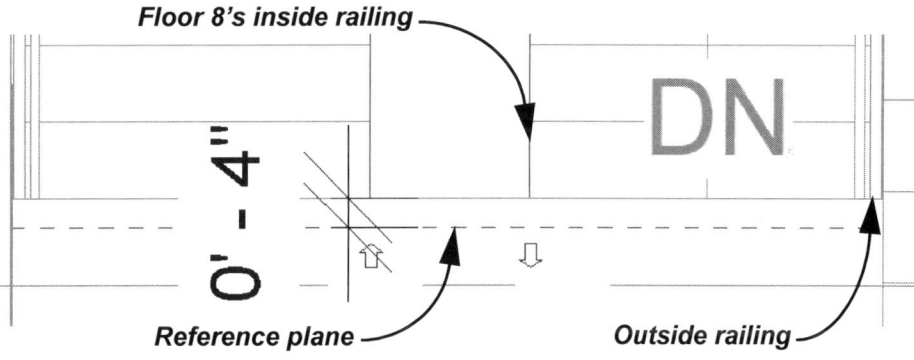

Figure 13–57

11. Click (Modify).

12. Drag the end of the inside railing on the down stairs only to meet the reference plane, as shown in Figure 13–58. (Dimension in figure is for reference only.)

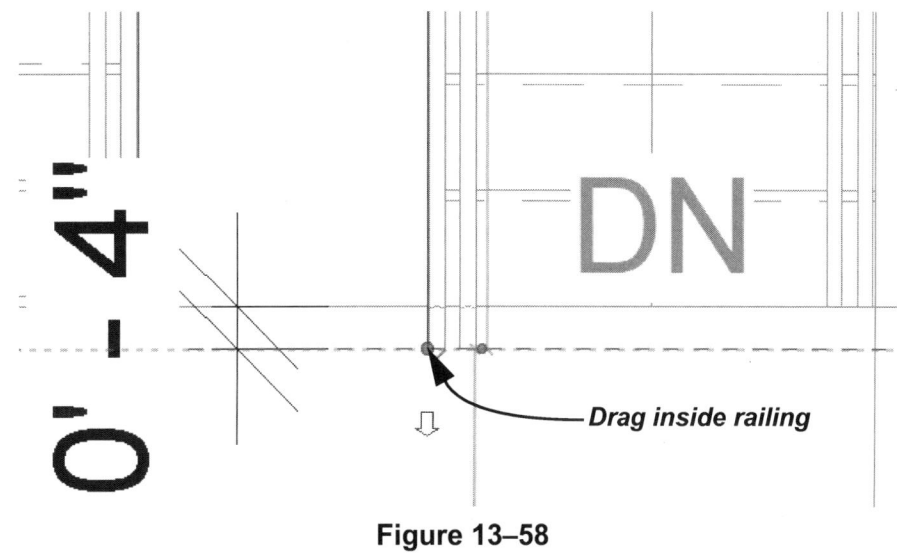

Figure 13–58

13. Click ✓ (Finish Edit Mode).

- Pan and zoom so you can see the exterior wall of the stairwell and the inside railing. You will need to add a railing from the wall, connecting to the stair railing.

14. In the *Architecture* tab>Circulation panel, click (Railing) and select (Sketch Path). Verify that the railing type is the **Hotel Stair Guardrail**.

15. In the Options Bar, select **Chain**.

16. In Properties, set the *Base Offset* to **0'-0"**.

17. Draw a reference plane **6"** from the edge of the floor and another one midpoint of the inside railing, as shown in Figure 13–59.

    - **Hint**: Type **SM** to force a snap to the midpoint of the end of the railing.

*(Dimension in the image is for reference only.)*

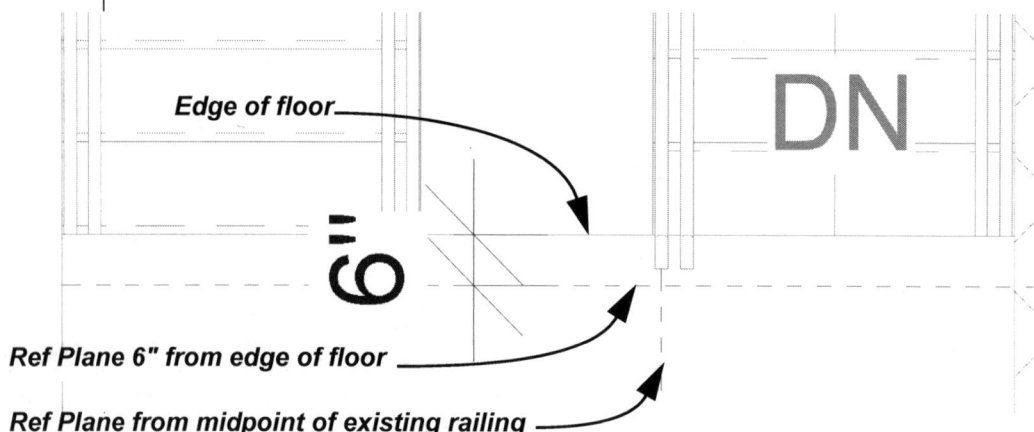

Figure 13–59

18. Click (Modify).

19. Sketch the railing path from the midpoint of the inside railing to the reference plane and then over to the wall, as shown in Figure 13–60.

# Modeling Stairs, Railings, and Ramps

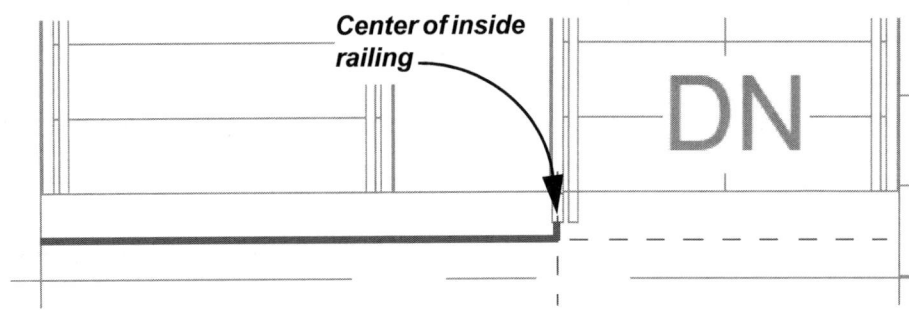

Figure 13–60

20. Click ✓ (Finish Edit Mode).

21. Click ▷ (Modify).

22. In the **CAM - Floor 8 West Stairs** view, review the new railing, as shown in Figure 13–61.

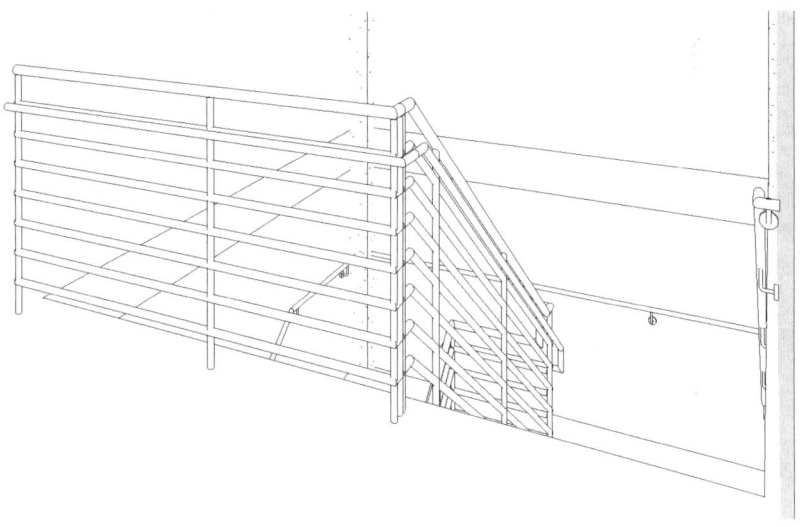

Figure 13–61

23. Type **TW** to tab the views.

24. Save the project.

*If needed, select the new railing and click on the Flip Railing Direction control so the guardrail and handrails match.*

### Task 3 - Add stand-alone railings.

1. Open the **Floor Plans: Floor 2** view and pan and zoom over to the hallway and interior balcony.

2. In the *Architecture* tab>Circulation panel, expand ▤ (Railing) and click ▤ (Sketch Path).

3. In the Type Selector, select **Railing: Hotel Interior Balcony Guardrail**.

4. In the *Modify | Create Railing Path* tab>Draw panel, select  (Pick Lines).

5. In the Options Bar, set the *Offset* to **11"**.

6. Select the edge of the balcony floor, as shown in Figure 13–62. Make sure that the preview dashed line is on the inside of the building.

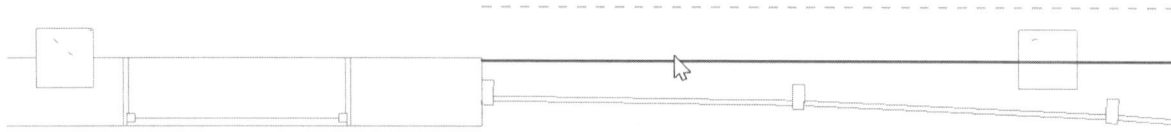

Figure 13–62

7. Add a railing that returns back to the wall, **11"** from the edge of the brick exterior wall, as shown in Figure 13–63. (Dimension in the figure is for reference only.)

   - Hint: When adding railings, remember to leave enough clearance between the wall and railing for the railing mount hardware.

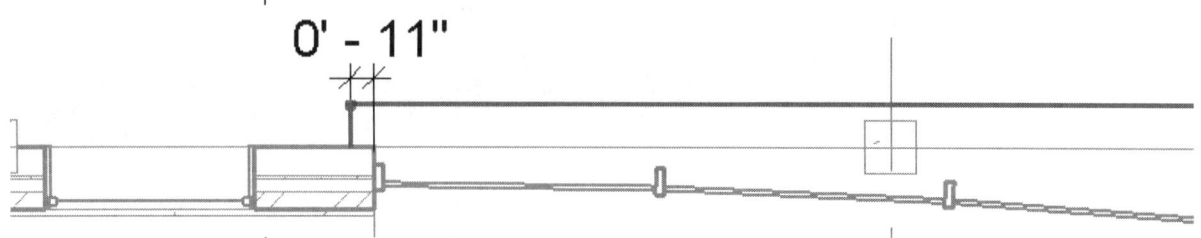

Figure 13–63

8. Continue adding railing with an **11"** offset until you get to the east stairwell (include the curved section), as shown in Figure 13–64.

Modeling Stairs, Railings, and Ramps

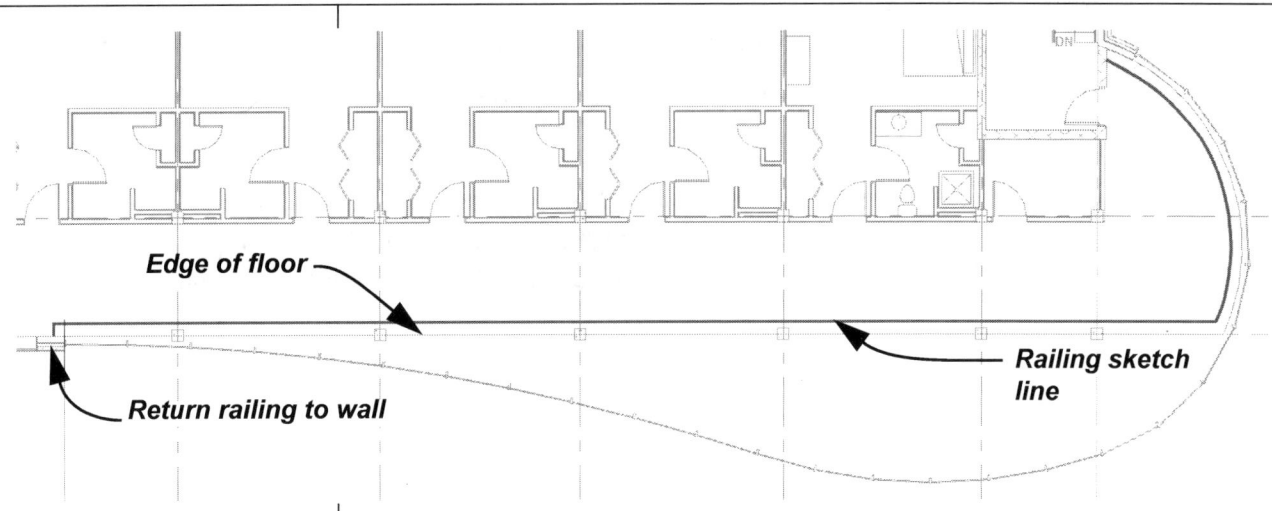

Figure 13-64

9. Click ✓ (Finish Edit Mode).

10. Zoom in on one of the outdoor balconies on the back of the building.

11. Start the **Railing** command again. In the Type Selector, select **Railing: Hotel Exterior Balcony Guardrail**.

12. In Properties, set the *Base Offset* to (negative) **-4"**.

13. In the Options Bar, set the *Offset* to **3"** and select the inside of the balcony floor edge to add railings to the balcony, as shown in the sketch in Figure 13–65. Just draw railings on one balcony.

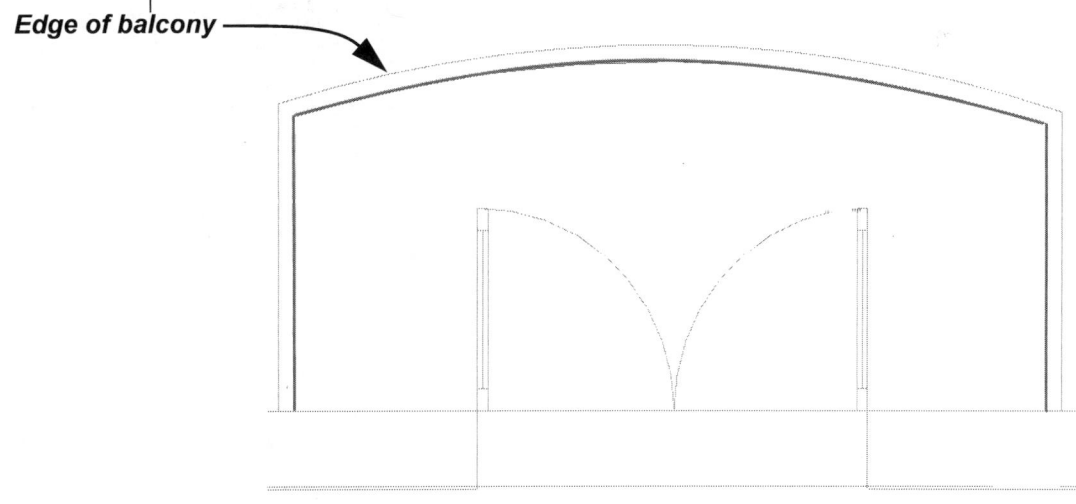

Figure 13-65

14. Click ✓ (Finish Edit Mode).

15. Copy the completed railing to the other balconies on **Floor 2**.

16. Select all the railings both inside and out and copy them to the other floors.

    - Hint: Select one exterior balcony railing, right-click, and select **Select All Instances>Visible in View**, then press <Ctrl> to select the hallway railing as well.

17. In the *Modify | Railings* tab>Clipboard panel, select (Copy to Clipboard).

18. In the Clipboard panel, expand (Paste) and select (Aligned to Selected Levels).

19. In the Select Levels dialog box, select **Floor 3**, then press and hold <Ctrl> and continue selecting each floor up to **Floor 8**.

20. Click **OK**.

21. Open an exterior 3D view and verify the placement of all the railings, as shown in Figure 13–66.

**Figure 13–66**

22. Save and close the project.

## 13.4 Creating Ramps

The process of creating ramps is similar to that of creating stairs with runs and automatic landings. You can also sketch a boundary with risers at the start and end of each slope. Ramps are most often used for short vertical distances, as shown in Figure 13–67, as they require a lot of space for their runs.

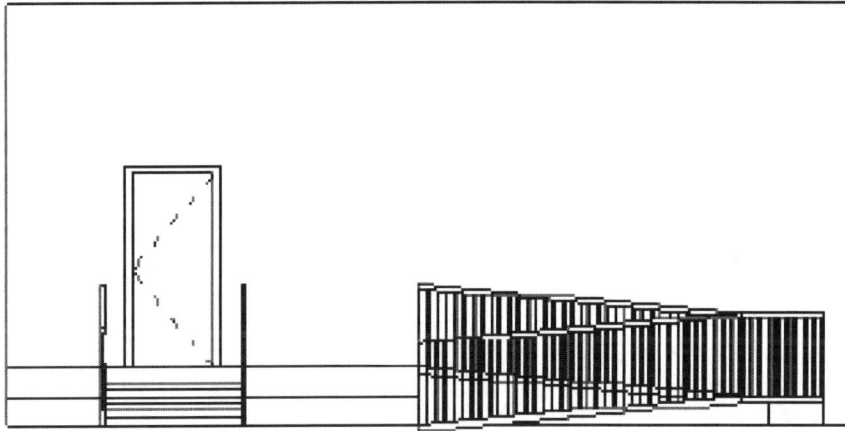

Figure 13–67

After a ramp has been created, you can add a spot slop annotation. A spot slop can be added to a ramp in elevation, 3D, plan, and section views.

- For more information on annotations, see *Chapter 15: Working with Annotations*.

### How To: Create a Ramp Using Runs

1. In the *Architecture* tab>Circulation panel, click (Ramp).
2. In the Type Selector, select the ramp type.
3. In the *Modify | Create Ramp Sketch* tab>Tools panel, click (Railing) and select a railing type in the Railing Types dialog box. Click **OK**.

4. In Properties, specify the *Constraints,* especially *Base Level* and *Top Level* and their offsets (as shown in Figure 13–68), and other properties. The *Width* of the ramp is set in the *Dimensions* section.

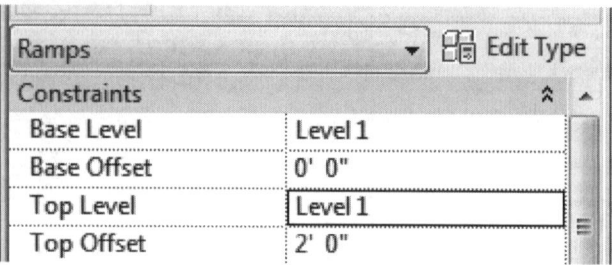

Figure 13–68

5. Draw reference planes to specify the locations of the run start and end points before creating the ramp. The run is based on the centerline of the ramp.

6. In the Draw panel, click (Run) and select a start point for the run. A preview box displays the ramp's orientation and length. Click (Line) or (Center-ends Arc) to switch between linear and curved runs.

- Landings are automatically created between runs, as shown in Figure 13–69.

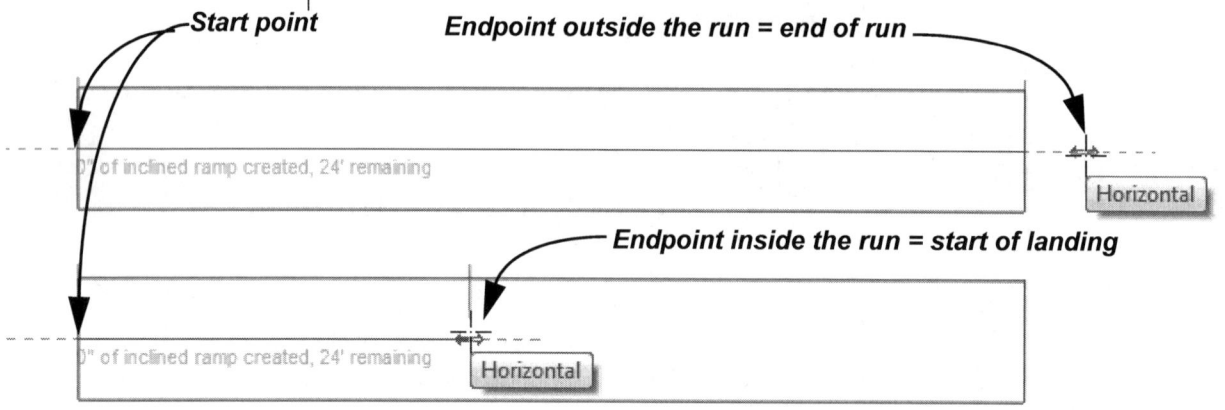

Figure 13–69

7. Click (Finish Edit Mode). The ramp (including railings) is created.

# How To: Sketch a Ramp Using Boundary and Riser

1. Click  (Ramp) and set up the ramp type and properties.
2. In the *Modify | Create Ramp Sketch* tab>Draw panel, click  (Boundary).
3. Use the draw tools to outline the sides (not the ends) of the ramp, as shown by the green lines in Figure 13–70.
4. In the *Modify | Create Ramp Sketch* tab>Draw panel, click  (Riser).
5. Use the draw tools to specify the ends of the slope of each ramp, as shown by the black lines in Figure 13–70.

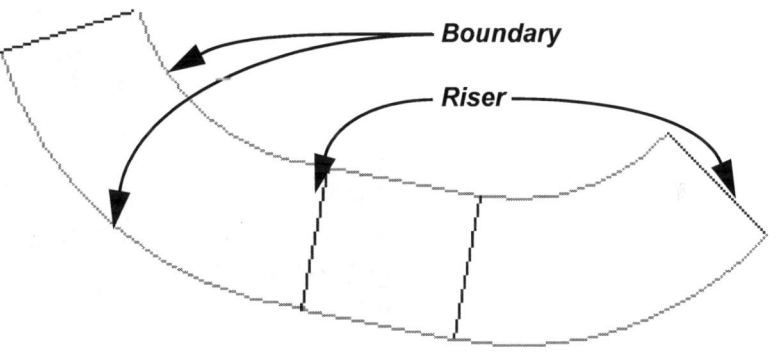

**Figure 13–70**

6. Click  (Finish Edit Mode).

# Practice 13d  Create Ramps

**Practice Objectives**

- Add a ramp.
- Modify ramp railings.

In this practice, you will create a ramp with railings and then modify placement of the railings, as shown in Figure 13–71.

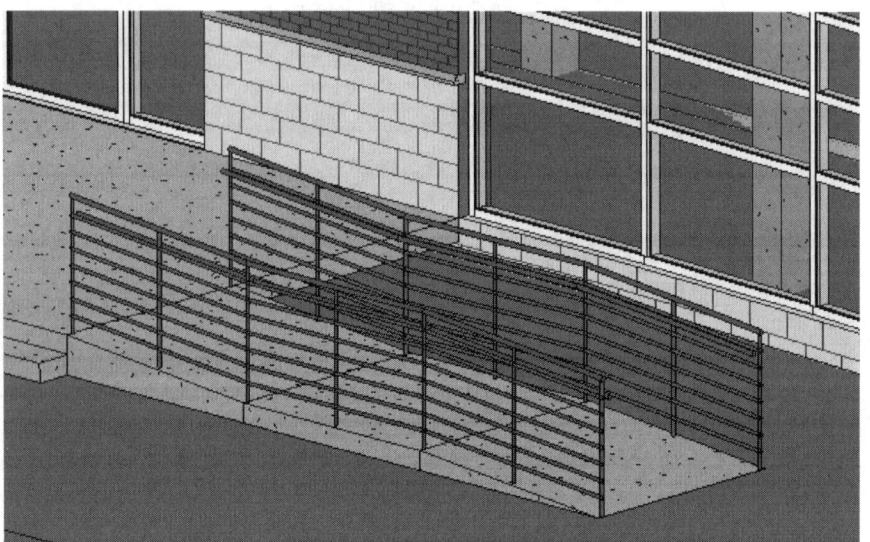

Figure 13–71

**Task 1 - Adding a ramp.**

1. Open the project **Hotel-Ramp.rvt** from the practice files folder.
2. Verify that you are in the **Floor Plans: Floor 1** view.
3. In the *Architecture* tab>Circulation panel, click (Ramp).
4. In the Type Selector, select **Ramp: Hotel Ramp**.
5. In Properties, set the following:
    - *Base Level:* **Floor 1**
    - *Base Offset*: (negative) **-1'-0"**
    - *Top Level*: **Floor 1**
    - *Top Offset*: **0'-0"**
    - *Width*: **6'-0"**

# Modeling Stairs, Railings, and Ramps

6. In the *Modify | Create Ramp Sketch* tab>Tools panel, click  (Railing), select the railing type **Hotel Ramp Guardrail**, and click **OK**.

7. In the Work Plane panel, click  (Reference Plane).

8. Draw the reference planes shown in Figure 13–72.

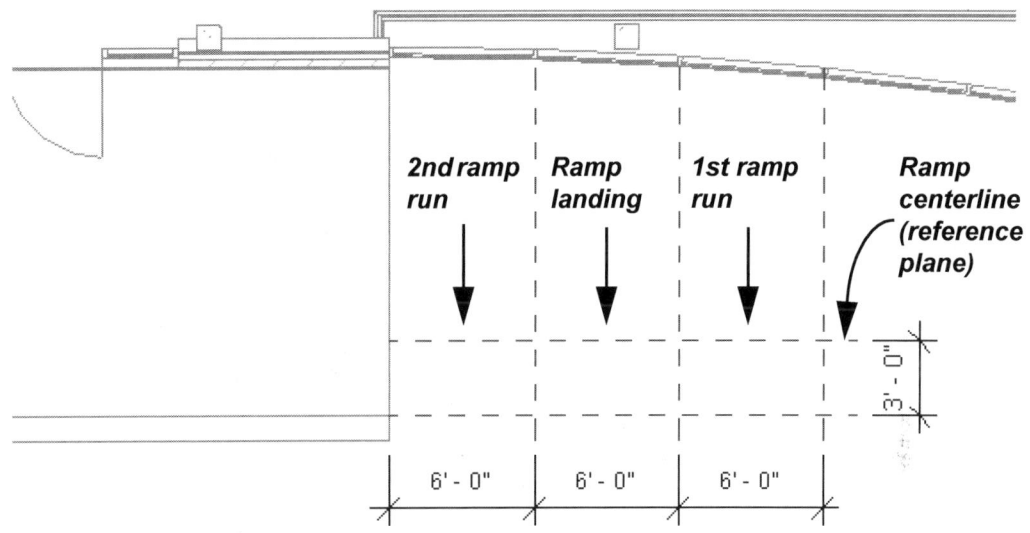

**Figure 13–72**

9. Click  (Modify) to return to the *Modify | Create Ramp Sketch* tab in the ribbon.

10. In the Draw panel, click  (Run).

11. Starting from the rightmost reference plane, pick the reference plane intersection as the start point. Move the cursor to the left and pick the next intersection as the second point, as shown in Figure 13–73.

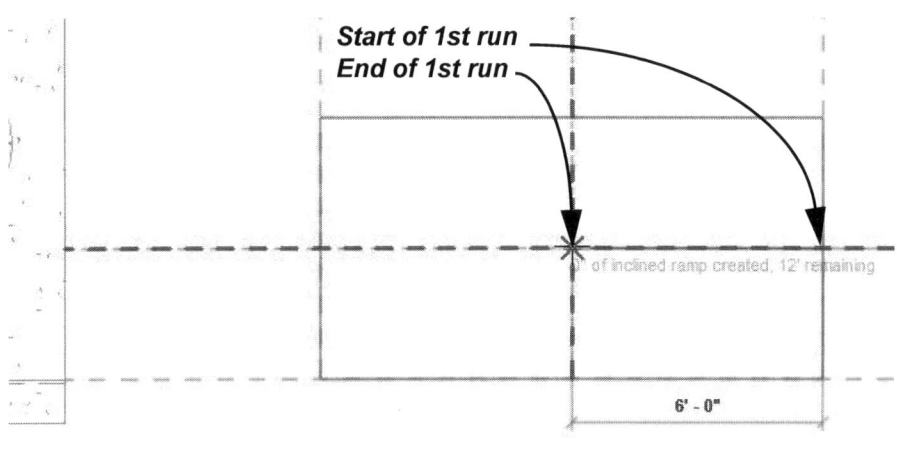

**Figure 13–73**

12. Still in the **Ramp** command, pick the next intersection to start the second run and then the last point at the entrance stairs, as shown in Figure 13–74.

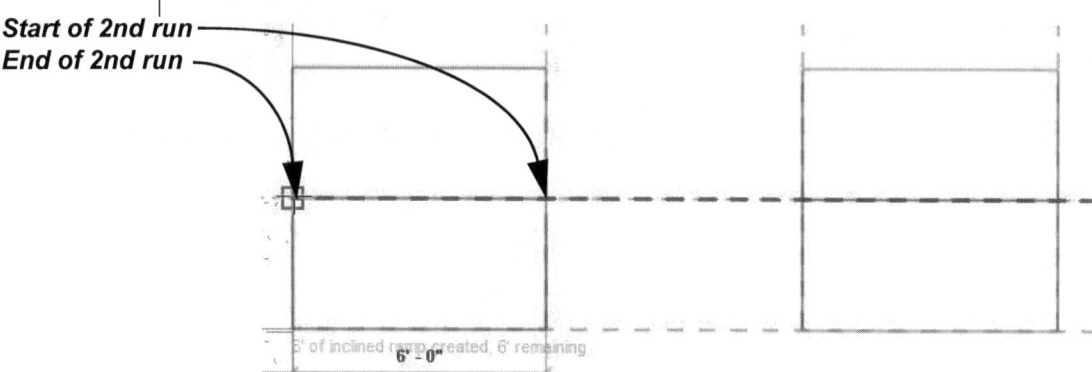

Figure 13–74

13. Click ✓ (Finish Edit Mode).

### Task 2 - Modify ramp railings.

In this task, the railings need to be moved so that they are fixed on the ramp.

1. Select both of the railings and in Properties, change the *Offset from Path* to (negative) **-2"**.

2. Open the 3D view and check that the ramp displays, as shown in Figure 13–75.

3. Zoom in to the railings. Note that they are sitting on the edge of the ramp (as shown in Figure 13–75) and need to be moved inward.

Figure 13–75

4. Save and close the project.

# Chapter Review Questions

1. Which of the following is NOT a stair component?

    a. Runs

    b. Landings

    c. Treads

    d. Supports

2. How do you modify a stair so that it is wider at the bottom than at the top, as shown in Figure 13–76?

    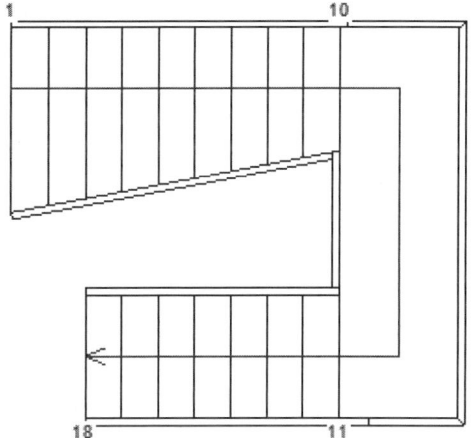

    Figure 13–76

    a. Use the grips located at each corner of the stair and drag them to a new location.

    b. Convert the run to a sketch and modify the boundary and riser lines.

    c. Use <Tab> to cycle through components so that you only select the tread that you want to modify.

    d. Explode the stair into components, and then use grips to modify the stair width.

3. When do you need to use the (Railing) command? (Select all that apply.)

    a. When you want an extra railing in the middle of very wide stairs.

    b. When you create a stair or ramp.

    c. When you create railings that are not attached to stairs or ramps.

    d. When you use the **Stair by Sketch** command.

4. To create a stair that covers multiple floors (as shown in Figure 13–77), what needs to be done after you create the stair?

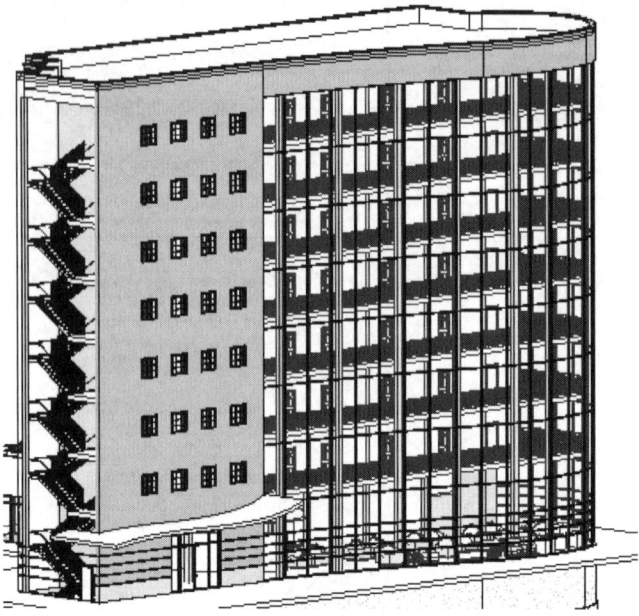

Figure 13–77

a. In Properties, select the **Multistory Top Level** from the drop-down list of levels.

b. Also select a stair created at the top level of the floors, right-click, and select **Multistory Stair**.

c. Copy the new stair to the clipboard, use **Paste Aligned to Selected Levels**, and specify the levels where you want the stairs.

d. Select the stairs, select **Connect Levels** in the ribbon, and then select the levels where you want stairs.

5. Which of the following elements is most helpful in specifying the start and end runs of ramps?

a. Walls

b. Stairs

c. Sketch lines

d. Reference planes

# Command Summary

| Button | Command | Location |
|---|---|---|
| **Stairs and Ramps** | | |
| | Convert to sketch-based | • **Ribbon:** *Modify | Create Stair* tab> Tools panel |
| | Connect Levels | • **Ribbon:** *Modify | Stairs* tab>Multistory Stairs panel |
| | Edit Sketch | • **Ribbon:** *Modify | Create Stair* tab> Tools panel |
| | Edit Stairs | • **Ribbon:** *Modify | Stairs* tab>Edit panel |
| | Flip | • **Ribbon:** *Modify | Create Stair* tab> Tools panel |
| | Landing (Stair) | • **Ribbon:** *Modify | Create Stair* tab> Components panel |
| | Run (Stair) | • **Ribbon:** *Modify | Create Stair* tab> Components panel |
| | Stair | • **Ribbon:** *Architecture* tab>Circulation panel |
| | Support (Stair) | • **Ribbon:** *Modify | Create Stair* tab> Components panel |
| | Ramp | • **Ribbon:** *Architecture* tab>Circulation panel |
| **Railings** | | |
| | Edit Path (Railings) | • **Ribbon:** *Modify | Railings* tab>Mode panel |
| | Railing | • **Ribbon:** *Modify | Create Stair (Create Stairs Sketch) (Create Ramp)* tab> Tools panel |
| | Railing>Place on Stair/Ramp | • **Ribbon:** *Architecture* tab>Circulation panel, expand Railing |
| | Railing>Sketch Path | • **Ribbon:** *Architecture* tab>Circulation panel, expand Railing |
| | Pick New Host | • **Ribbon:** *Modify | Create Railing Path (Railings)* tab>Tools Panel |

# Construction Documentation

The third section of this guide continues to teach the Autodesk® Revit® tools, focusing on tools that help you to create accurate construction documents for a design.

This section includes the following chapters:

- Chapter 14: Creating Construction Documents
- Chapter 15: Working with Annotations
- Chapter 16: Adding Tags and Schedules
- Chapter 17: Creating Details

# Chapter 14

# Creating Construction Documents

The accurate creation of construction documents in Revit® ensures that the design is correctly communicated to downstream users. Construction documents are created primarily in special views call sheets. Knowing how to select title blocks, assign title block information, place views, and print the sheets are essential steps in the construction documentation process.

## Learning Objectives in This Chapter

- Add sheets with title blocks and views of a project.
- Enter the title block information for individual sheets and for an entire project.
- Place and organize views on sheets.
- Print sheets using the default Print dialog box.

## 14.1 Setting Up Sheets

While you are modeling a project, the foundations of the working drawings are already in progress. Any view (such as a floor plan, section, callout, or schedule) can be placed on a sheet, as shown in Figure 14–1.

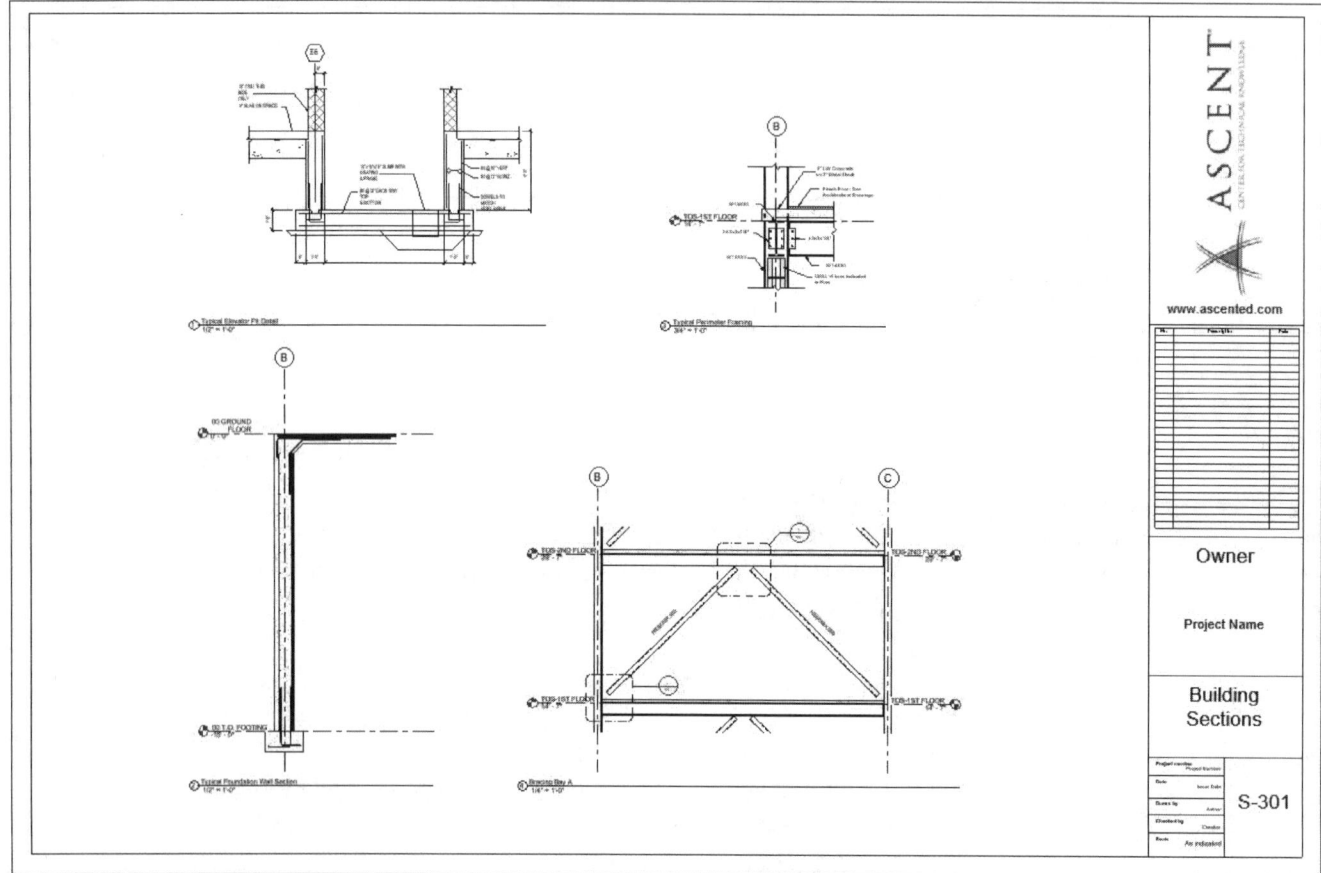

**Figure 14–1**

- Company templates can be created with standard sheets using the company (or project) title block and related views already placed on the sheet.

- The sheet size is based on the selected title block family.

- Sheets are listed in the *Sheets* area in the Project Browser.

- Most information on sheets is included in the views. You can add general notes and other non-model elements directly to the sheet, though it is better to add them using drafting views or legends, as these can be placed on multiple sheets.

# Creating Construction Documents

## How To: Set Up Sheets

1. In the Project Browser, right-click on the *Sheets* area header and select **New Sheet...**, or in the *View* tab>Sheet Composition panel, click (Sheet).
2. In the New Sheet dialog box, select a title block from the list, as shown in Figure 14–2. Alternatively, if there is a list of placeholder sheets, select one or more from the list.

*Click **Load...** to load a sheet from the Revit Library.*

*Hold <Ctrl> to select multiple placeholder sheets.*

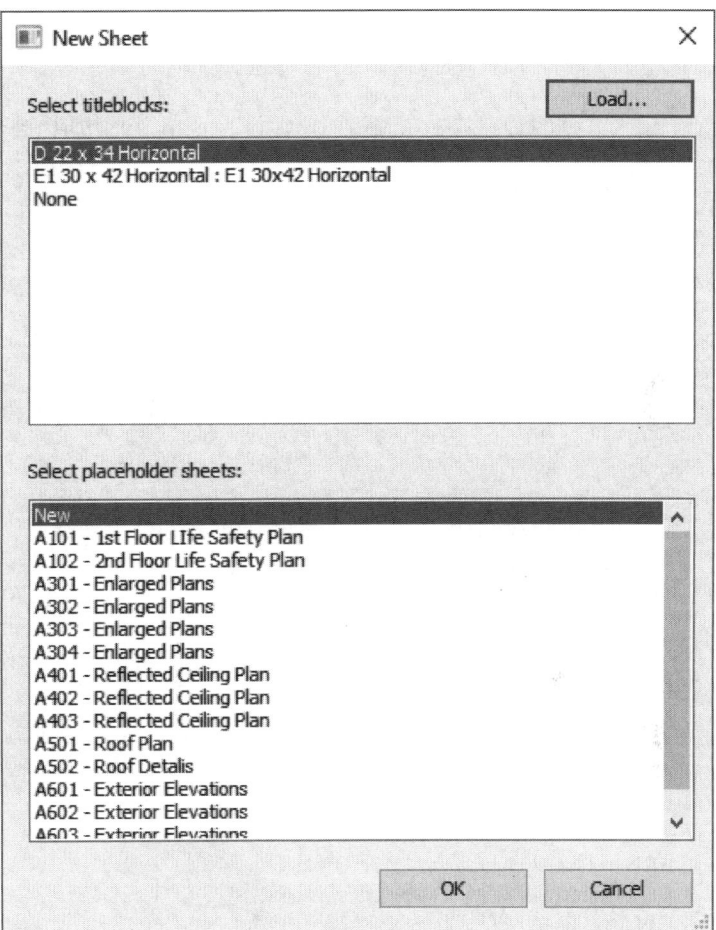

Figure 14–2

3. Click **OK**. A new sheet is created using the selected title block.
4. Fill out the information in the title block as needed.
5. Add views to the sheet.

- When you create sheets, the next sheet is incremented numerically.

- Double-click on the sheet name to change the name and number in the Sheet Title dialog box.

- When you change the *Sheet Name* and/or *Number* in the title block, it automatically changes the name and number of the sheet in the Project Browser.

- The plot stamp on the side of the sheet automatically updates according to the current date and time. The format of the display uses the regional settings of your computer.

- The Scale is automatically entered when a view is inserted onto a sheet. If a sheet has multiple views with different scales, the scale displays **As Indicated.**

## Sheet (Title Block) Properties

Each new sheet includes a title block. You can change the title block information in Properties, as shown in , or by selecting any blue label you want to edit (Sheet Name, Sheet Number, Drawn by, etc.), as shown in Figure 14–3.

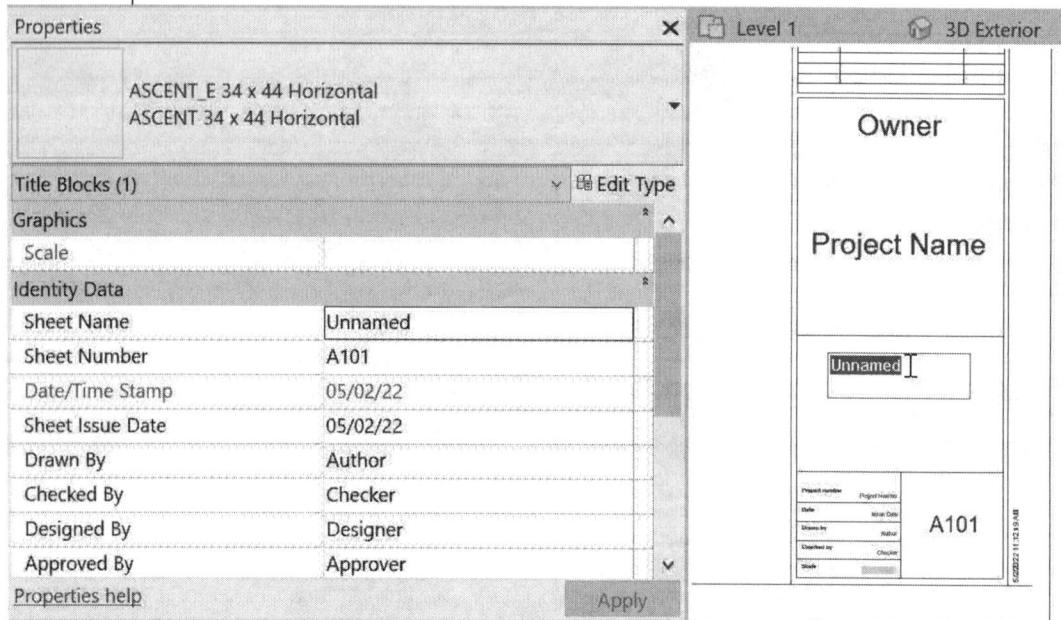

**Figure 14–3**

Properties that apply to all sheets can be entered in the Project Information dialog box (as shown in Figure 14–4). In the *Manage* tab>Settings panel, click (Project Information).

# Creating Construction Documents

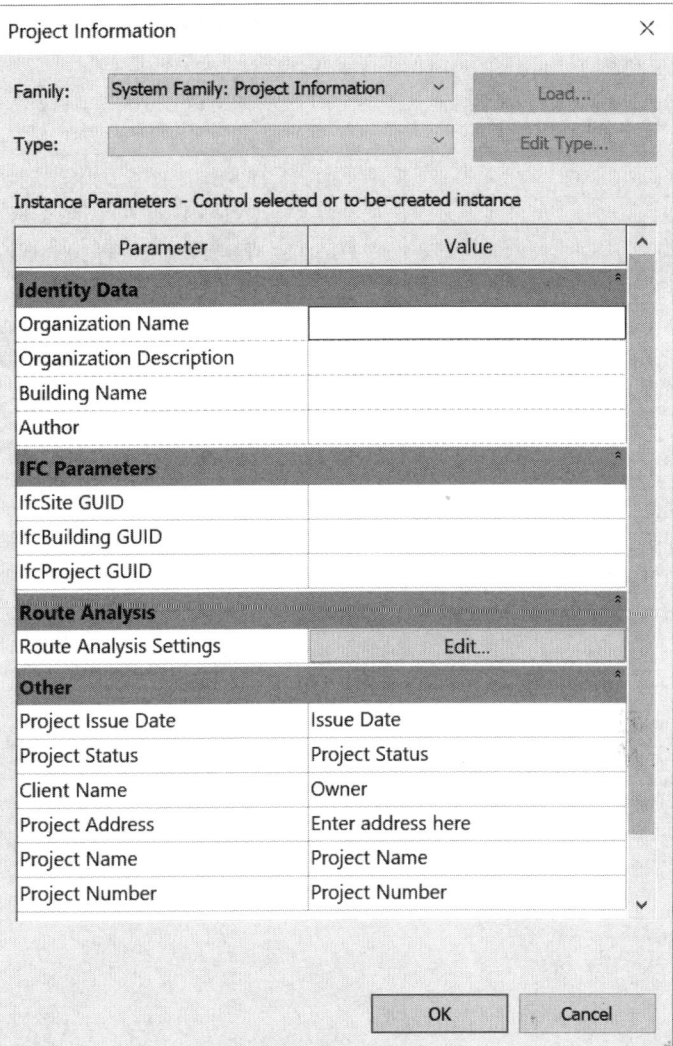

Figure 14–4

## 14.2 Placing and Modifying Views on Sheets

The process of adding views to a sheet is simple. Drag and drop a view from the Project Browser onto the sheet, as shown in Figure 14–5. The new view on the sheet is displayed at the scale specified in the original view. The view title displays the name, number, and scale of the view. Once the view has been placed on a sheet, the icon next to the view name in the Project Browser is filled in.

**Figure 14–5**

### How To: Place Views on Sheets

1. Set up the view as you want it to display on the sheet, including the scale and visibility of elements.
2. Create or open the sheet where you want to place the view.
3. Select the view in the Project Browser, and drag and drop it onto the sheet.
4. The center of the view is attached to the cursor. Click to place it on the sheet.

### Placing Views on Sheets

- Views can only be placed on a sheet once. However, you can duplicate the view and place that copy on a sheet.

- Views on a sheet are associative. They automatically update to reflect changes to the project.

- Each view on a sheet is listed under the sheet name in the Project Browser, as shown in Figure 14–6.

*Alignment lines from existing views display to help you place additional views.*

# Creating Construction Documents

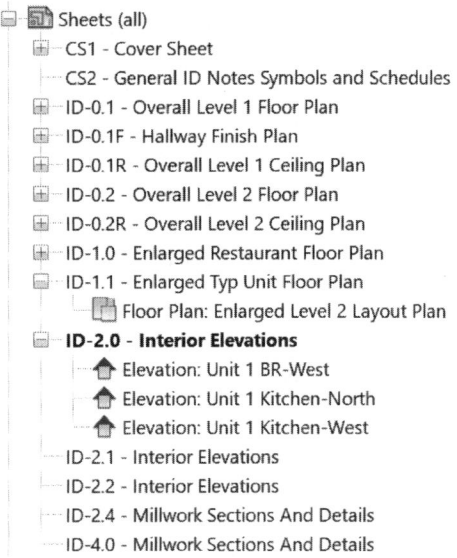

Figure 14–6

- You can also use two other methods to place views on sheets:

    - In the Project Browser, right-click on the sheet name and select **Add View...**.

    - In the *View* tab>Sheet Composition panel, click (Place View).

    Then, in the Views dialog box (shown in Figure 14–7), select the view you want to use and click **Add View to Sheet.**

*This method lists only those views which have not yet been placed on a sheet.*

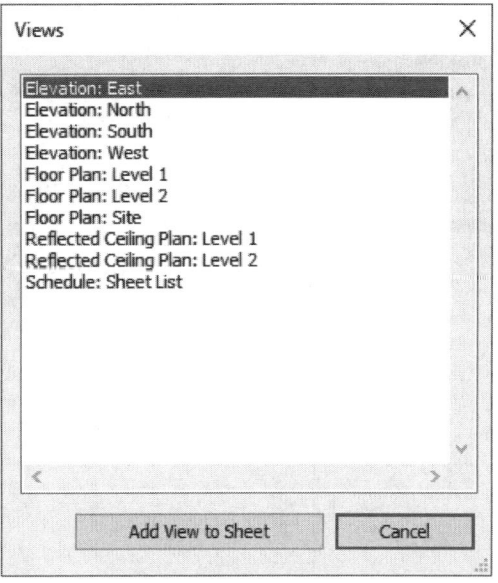

Figure 14–7

- To remove a view from a sheet, select it and press <Delete>. Alternatively, in the Project Browser, expand the individual sheet information to show the views, right-click on the view name, and select **Remove From Sheet**.

# 14.3 Duplicating Sheets and Swapping Views

You can reduce the time it takes to create new sheets, as well as modify the views that are placed on a sheet.

- When swapping views, you cannot select a view that is already placed on a sheet. You will need to first remove the view from its sheet and then swap the view.

- Duplicating a sheet will add a suffix of *Copy 1* after the sheet name, as shown in Figure 14–8. It will also automatically generate with the next available sheet title number, like A1.7 as shown in Figure 14–8.

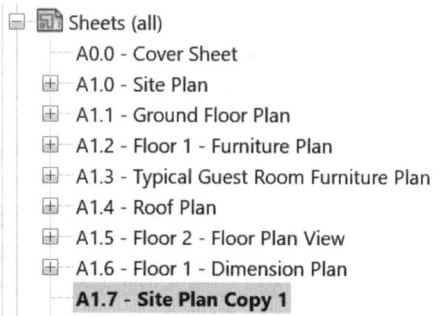

**Figure 14–8**

- If you duplicate a sheet that has views on it, you are prompted to specify how you would like to duplicate the views.

### How To: Swap a View on a Sheet

1. From the Project Browser>*Sheets* node, open the sheet view.
2. Select the view that is on the sheet.
3. In the *Modify | Viewports* tab>Positioning & View panel, expand the views, as shown in Figure 14–9, and select from the list.
   - Views already on sheets will have suffixes at the end of their names with the sheet number.

# Creating Construction Documents

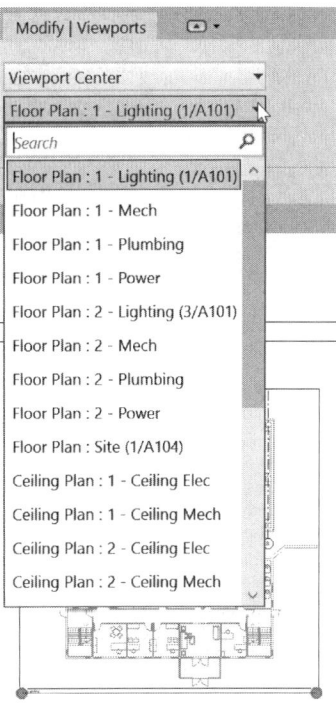

Figure 14–9

- Alternatively, with the viewport selected, in Properties, in the *Identity Data* section, change the *View* on the sheet by expanding the parameter's drop-down list and selecting a different view, as shown in Figure 14–10.

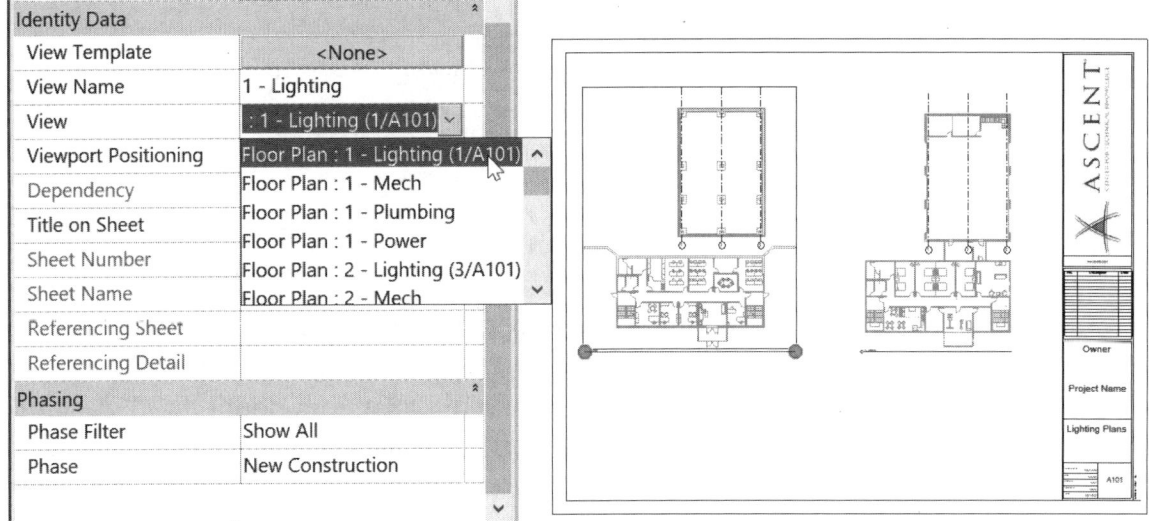

Figure 14–10

- Before you modify views placed on the sheet, you can duplicate sheets to make the process quicker.

## How To: Duplicate Sheets

1. In the Project Browser>*Sheets* node, right-click on a sheet and select **Duplicate Sheet**.
2. Select one of the following options:
   - **Duplicate Empty Sheet:** Creates a new sheet with the same titleblock and project information.
     - No model or annotation elements on the sheet are duplicated.
   - **Duplicate with Sheet Detailing:** Creates a new sheet with the same titleblock, project information, and any legends, keynotes, schedules, and annotations.
   - **Duplicate with Views:** Before a sheet gets created, you are prompted to specify how you would like the views on the sheet to be duplicated, as shown in Figure 14–11.

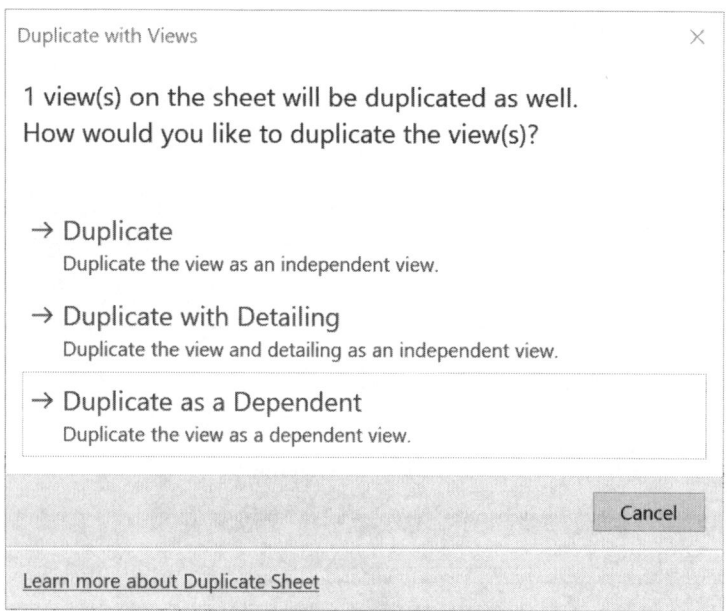

Figure 14–11

- In the Duplicate with Views dialog box, select **Duplicate**, **Duplicate with Detailing**, or **Duplicate as a Dependent**.
  - If you are duplicating a sheet that has drafting views and want to duplicate the view with the model and annotation elements, you need to use the **Duplicate with Detailing** option.

*To review duplicating view types, refer to Chapter 3: Working with Views.*

# 14.4 Modifying Views and View Titles

After you have the desired views on a sheet, you can modify their locations and titles. You can use some of the modify tools, like Move and Rotate, as well as the arrow keys.

- You cannot use any tools that utilize the copy feature, like Copy, Mirror, and Offset.

### How To: Move a View on a Sheet

1. Open a sheet view.
2. Select and drag a view to another location on the sheet. When selecting the view, the view title moves with the view.

### How To: Modify the Viewport's View Title

1. Open a sheet view.
2. Select only the view title and drag it to the new location.

- To modify the length of the line under the title name, select the viewport and drag the controls, as shown in Figure 14–12.

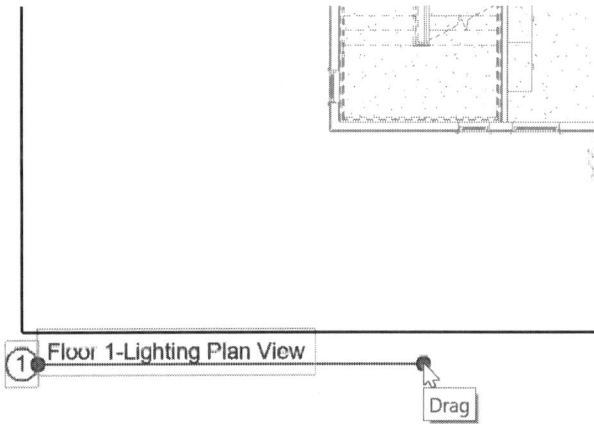

**Figure 14–12**

- To change the title of a view on a sheet without changing its name in the Project Browser, select either the viewport or the view title, then in Properties, in the *Identity Data* section, type a new title for the *Title on Sheet* parameter, as shown in Figure 14–13.

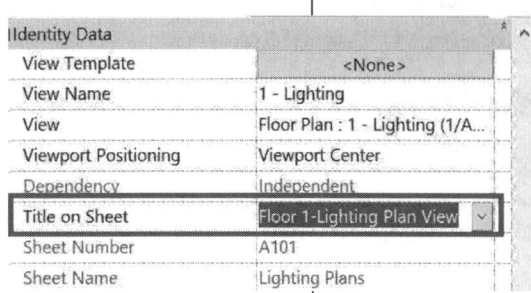
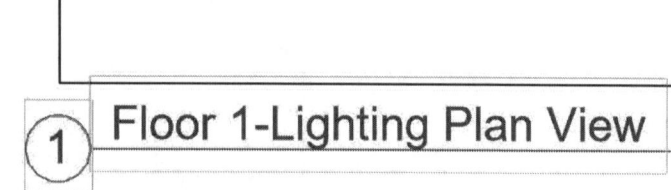

Figure 14–13

## Rotating Views

- When creating a vertical sheet, you can rotate the view on the sheet by 90°. Select the view on the sheet and set the direction of rotation in the **Rotation on Sheet** drop-down list in the Options Bar, as shown in Figure 14–14.

Figure 14–14

## Working Inside Views

To make small changes to a view while working on a sheet:

- Double-click *inside* the view to activate it.
- Double-click *outside* the view to deactivate it.

Only elements in the viewport are available for modification. The rest of the sheet is grayed out, as shown in Figure 14–15.

- Use this method only for small changes. Significant changes should be made directly in the view.

*For more information about rotating the project or individual views to angles other than 90°, refer to the ASCENT guide Autodesk Revit: Site Planning and Design.*

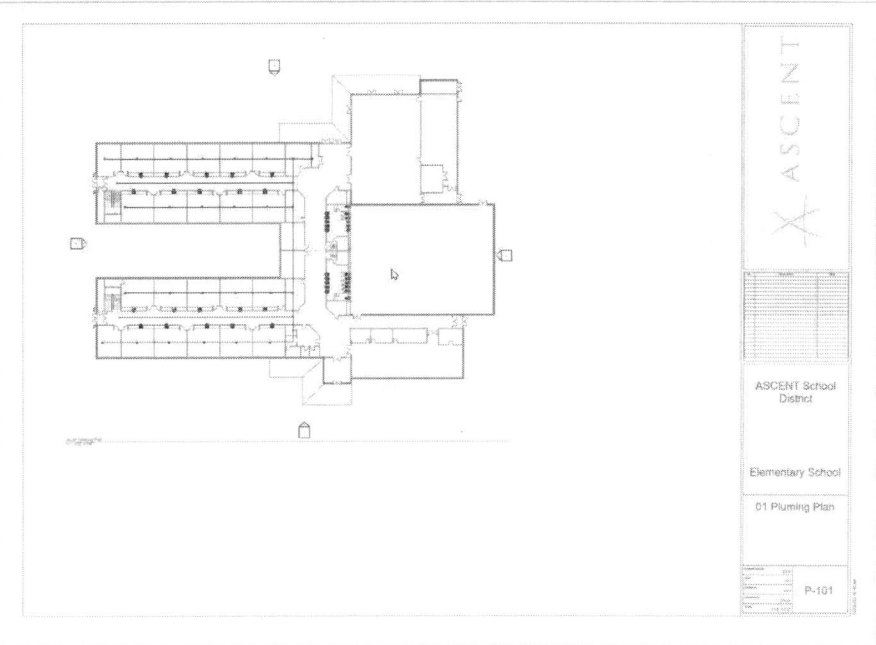

**Figure 14–15**

- You can activate and deactivate views by selecting the viewport, right-clicking, and selecting from the menu, or by using the tools found in the *Modify | Viewports* or *Views* tab>Sheet Composition panel.

- Changes you make to elements when a view is activated also display in the original view.

- If you are unsure which sheet a view is on, right-click on the view in the Project Browser and select **Open Sheet**. This is not available for schedules and legends, which can be placed on more than one sheet.

## Resizing Views on Sheets

*If the extents of the view change dramatically based on a scale change or a crop region, it is easier to delete the view on the sheet and drag it over again.*

Each view displays the extents of the model or the elements contained in the crop region. If the view does not fit on a sheet (as shown in Figure 14–16), you might need to crop the view or move the elevation markers closer to the building.

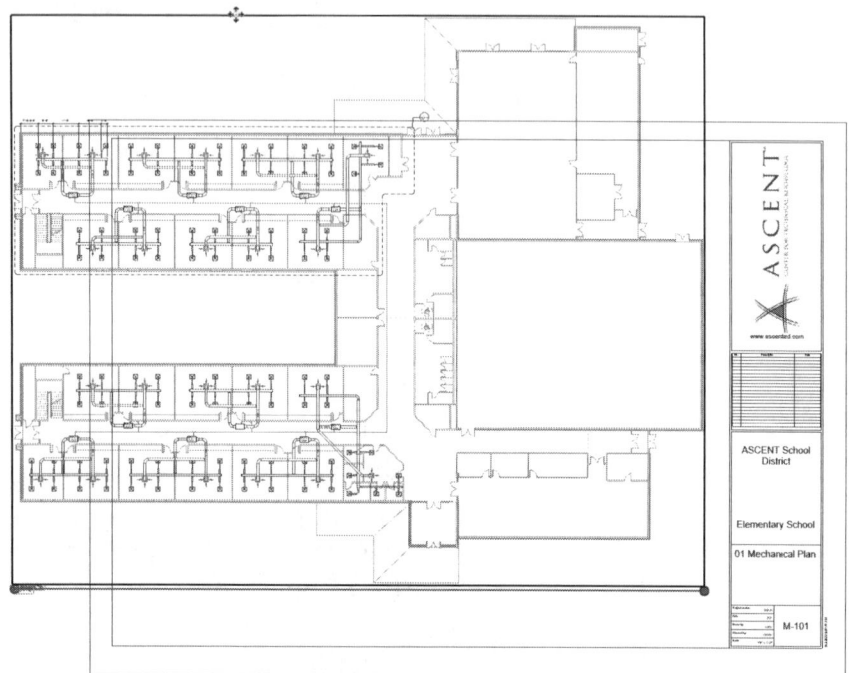

Figure 14–16

- For information about laying out views on sheets using guide grids, see *B.1 Working with Guide Grids on Sheets*.

- For information about working with revisions in views and on sheets, see *B.2 Revision Tracking*.

# Practice 14a | Set Up Sheets

## Practice Objectives

- Set up project properties.
- Create sheets individually.
- Modify views to prepare them to be placed on sheets.
- Place views on sheets.

In this practice, you will complete the project information, create new sheets and then add views to the sheets, such as the building elevations shown in Figure 14–17. You will also fill in title block information and import an image for the cover sheet. Complete as many sheets as you have time for.

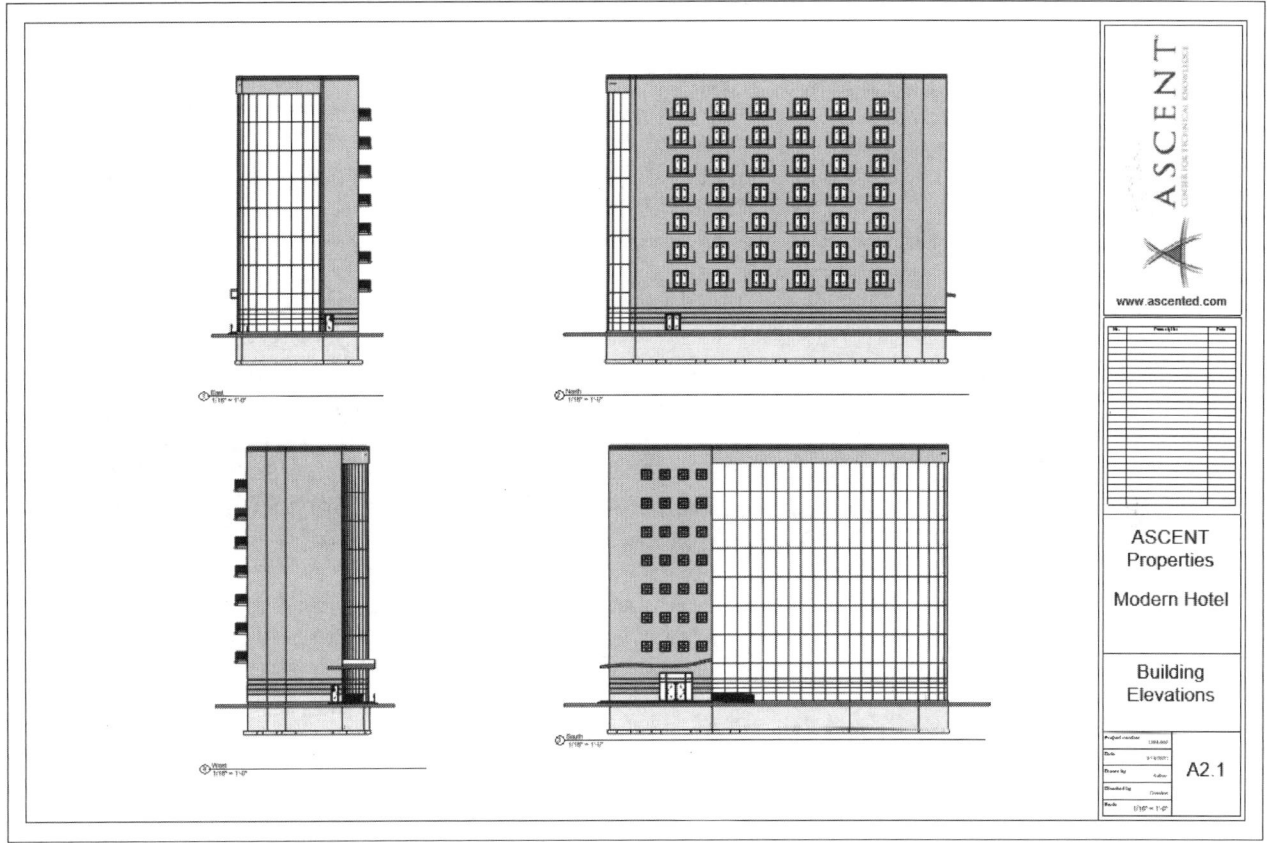

Figure 14–17

### Task 1 - Complete the project information.

1. Open the project **Hotel-Sheets.rvt** from the practice files folder.

2. In the *Manage* tab>Settings panel, click  (Project Information).

*These properties are used across the entire sheet set and do not need to be entered on each sheet.*

3. In the Project Information dialog box, in the *Other* section, set the following parameters:

   - *Project Issue Date:* Enter a date
   - *Project Status:* **Design Development**
   - *Client Name:* **ASCENT Properties**
   - *Project Address:* Click **Edit...** and enter your address
   - *Project Name:* **Modern Hotel**
   - *Project Number:* **1234-567**

4. Click **OK**.

5. Save the project.

**Task 2 - Create a cover sheet and floor plan sheets.**

1. In the *View* tab>Sheet Composition panel, click (Sheet).

2. In the New Sheet dialog box, select the **ASCENT_22 x 34 Horizontal** title block.

3. Click **OK**.

4. Zoom in on the lower-right corner of the title block. The project properties filled out earlier are automatically added to the sheet (e.g., Project Number, Project Status, etc.).

5. Continue filling out the title block by changed *Unnamed* to **Cover Sheet** and the *Sheet Number* to **A0.0**, as shown in Figure 14–18.

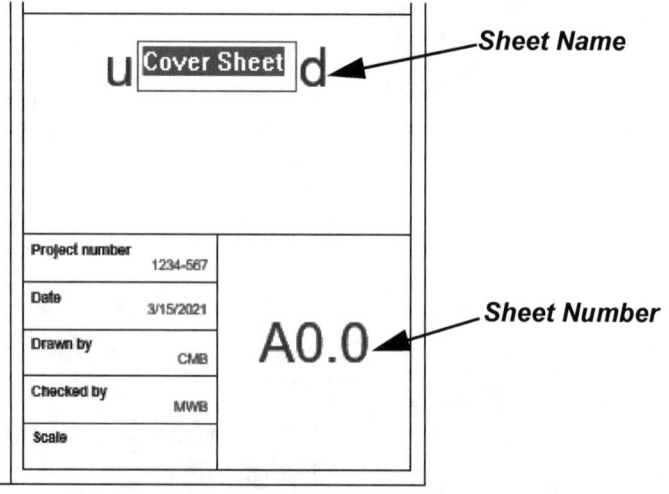

Figure 14–18

6. Zoom back out to display the whole sheet.

Creating Construction Documents

7. In the Project Browser, note that the two items you manually changed on the sheet's title block are shown as your sheet name and sheet number.

8. In the *Insert* tab>Import panel, click (Import Image).

9. In the Import Image dialog box, navigate to the practice files *Images* folder and select **Exterior Front Perspective.jpg** or **Exterior Front Perspective 2.jpg**.

10. Click **Open**.

11. Your cursor will have an X shape (indicating the size of your image), as shown in Figure 14–19. Click to place the image on the sheet.

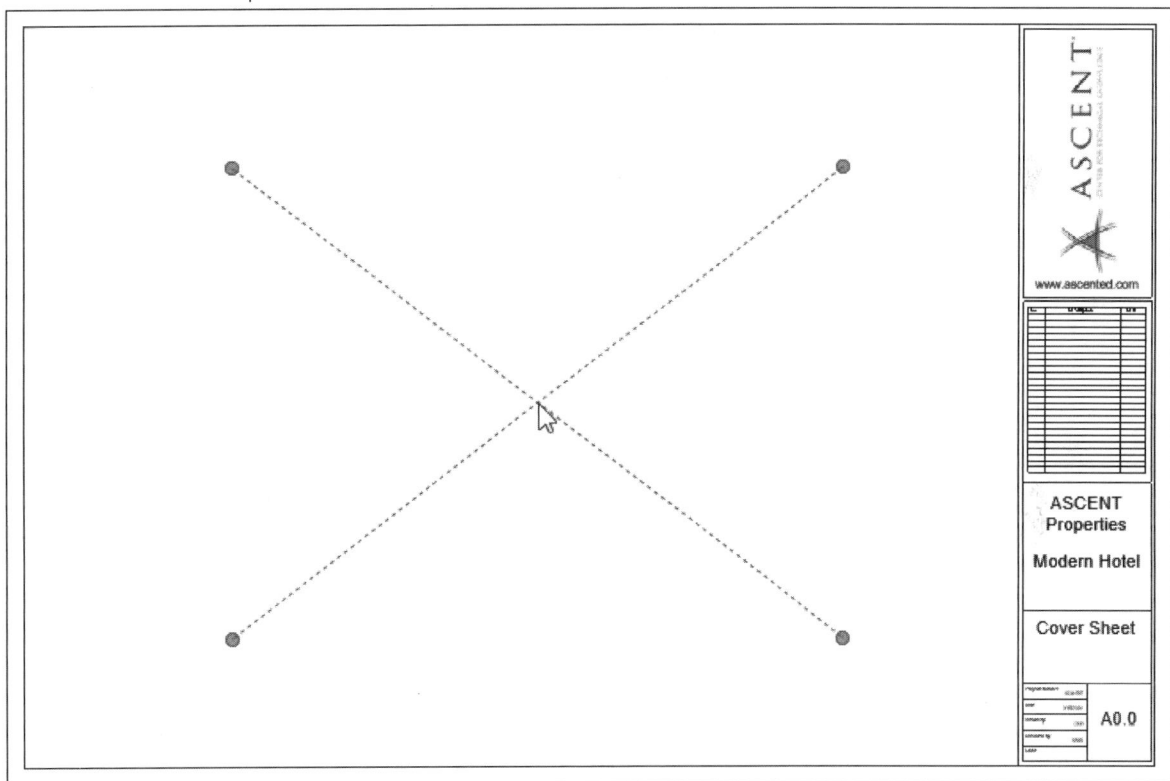

Figure 14–19

12. Click (Modify).

13. Use the grips to adjust the size of the image to make room for notes.

14. Create a new sheet. In the Project Browser, right-click on the **Sheets (All)** node and select **New Sheet...**.

15. In the New Sheet dialog box, select the **ASCENT_22 x 34 Horizontal** title block.

16. In the Project Browser, right-click on the new sheet **A0.1 - Unnamed** and select **Rename...**.

17. In the Sheet Title dialog box, set the *Number* to **A9.1** and the *Name* to **Poolhouse Perspective View**.

18. Click **OK**. The sheet updates with the information.

19. From the Project Browser, drag and drop the **3D - Poolhouse** view onto the sheet, as shown in Figure 14–20.

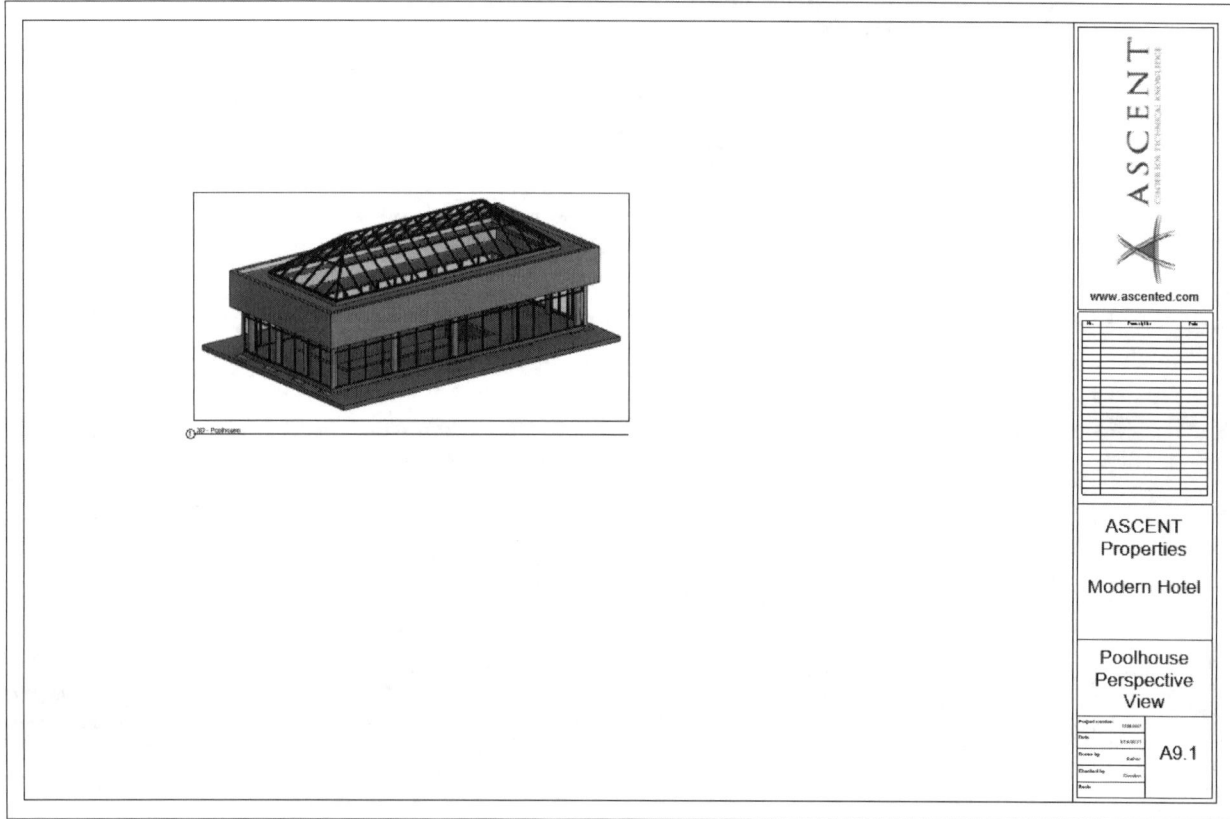

**Figure 14–20**

20. Select the edge of the viewport. In the Type Selector, select **Viewport: NoTitle**.

21. Double-click inside the viewport; the title block grays out and you can modify the actual view.

22. In Properties, in the *Extents* section, clear the check from **Crop Region Visible**. (This could also be done in the View Control Bar.)

23. Double-click outside the viewport to return to the sheet.

24. In the Project Browser, right-click on the **Sheets (all)** node and select **New Sheet**.

25. Using the ASCENT title block, create the following new sheets:

| Sheet Number and Name | View Name |
|---|---|
| A1.1: Ground Floor Plan | Floor 1 |
| A1.2: Floor 1- Furniture Plan | Floor 1 - Furniture Plan |
| A1.3: Upper Floor Plan (Typical) | Typical Guest Room Floor Plan |
| A1.4: Roof Plan | Roof |
| LS1.1: Floor 1 - Life Safety Plan | Floor 1 -Life Safety Plan |
| LS1.2: Floor 2 - Life Safety Plan | Floor 2 - Life Safety Plan |
| A2.1: Building Elevations | North<br>East<br>South<br>West |
| A2.2: Building Sections | E/W Building Section<br>N/S Building Section |
| A2.3: Poolhouse Building Elevations | Pool-North<br>Pool-East<br>Pool-South<br>Pool-West |

26. Save the project.

### Task 3 - Set up and add views to sheets.

1. Duplicate (no detailing) the **Floor Plans: Floor 1** and **Floor 2** views and name them **Floor 1 - Life Safety Plan** and **Floor 2 - Life Safety Plan**.

2. Open the new views and do the following:

    - Hide all elements except the actual building elements.
    - Toggle on the crop region and ensure that it is tight up against the building.
    - Toggle the crop region off.
    - In just the **Floor 2 - Life Safety Plan** view, open the Visibility/Graphic Overrides dialog box and turn off the roof from the *Model Category* tab.

3. Open the sheet **LS1.1 - Floor 1 - Life Safety Plan**.

*The crop region defines the extent of the view on the sheet.*

4. In the Project Browser, right-click on that sheet and select **Add View...**.

5. In the Views dialog box, scroll down and select **Floor Plan: Floor 1 - Life Safety Plan**, as shown in Figure 14–21. Click **Add View to Sheet** and place the view on the sheet.

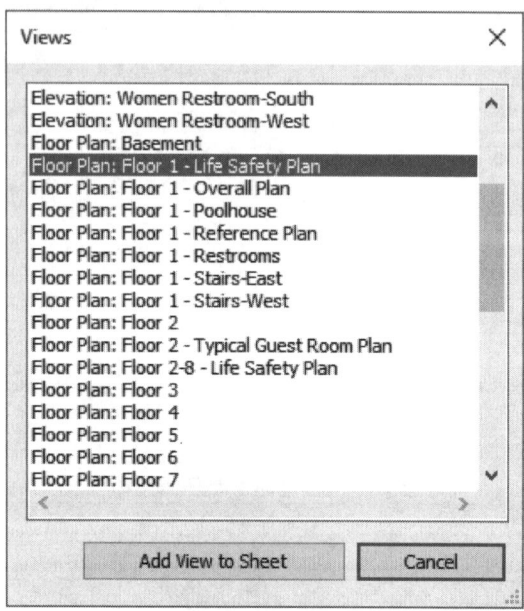

Figure 14–21

6. Repeat the process for the sheet **Floor 2 - Life Safety Plan**.

  - The **Floor 1 - Life Safety Plan** is no longer available in the list because it has already been added to a sheet.

7. Repeat the process of adding views to sheets using the views you have available. For example, modify and add elevations Pool-East and Pool-North and place them on the A2.3 sheet.

  - Modify crop regions and hide unnecessary elements in the views. Toggle off crop regions after you have modified them.

- Use alignment lines to help place multiple views on one sheet, as shown in Figure 14–22.

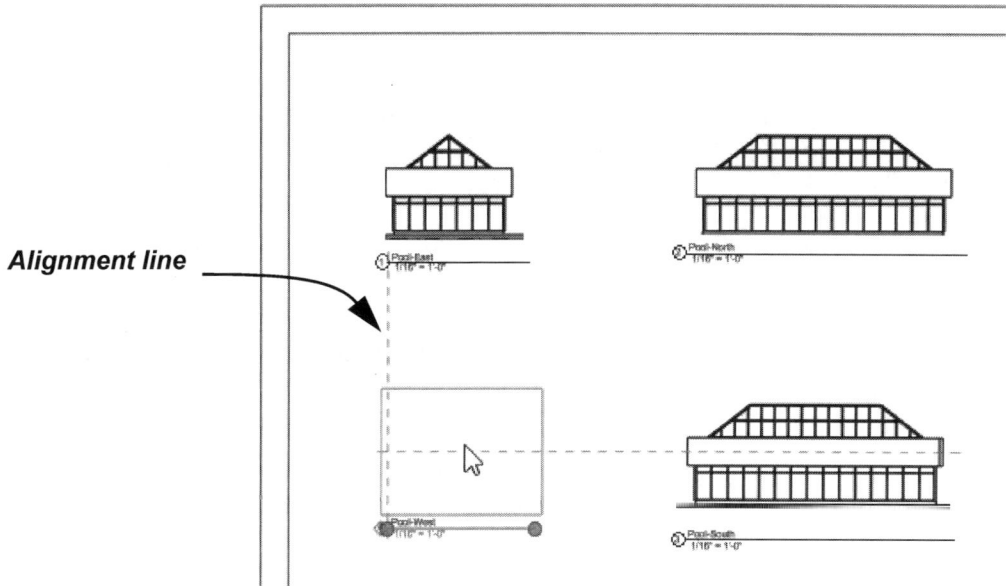

**Figure 14–22**

- Change the view title, if needed, to more accurately describe what is on the sheet.
- To make minor changes to a view once it is on a sheet, double-click inside the viewport to activate the view. To return to the sheet, double-click outside the viewport to deactivate the view.

8. Once you have added section or elevation views to sheets, switch back to the **Floor Plans: Floor 1** view. Zoom in on one of the markers. Note that it has now been automatically assigned a detail and sheet number, as shown in Figure 14–23.

*Your numbers might not exactly match the numbers in the example.*

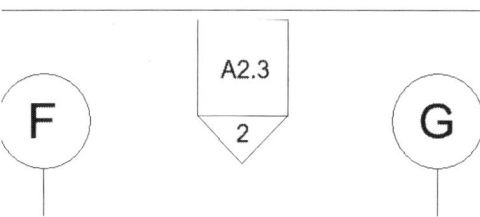

**Figure 14–23**

9. Save and close the project.

## 14.5 Printing Sheets

With the **Print** command, you can print individual sheets or a list of selected sheets. You can also print an individual view or a portion of a view for check prints or presentations. To open the Print dialog box (shown in Figure 14–24), in the *File* tab, click (Print), or press <Ctrl>+<P>.

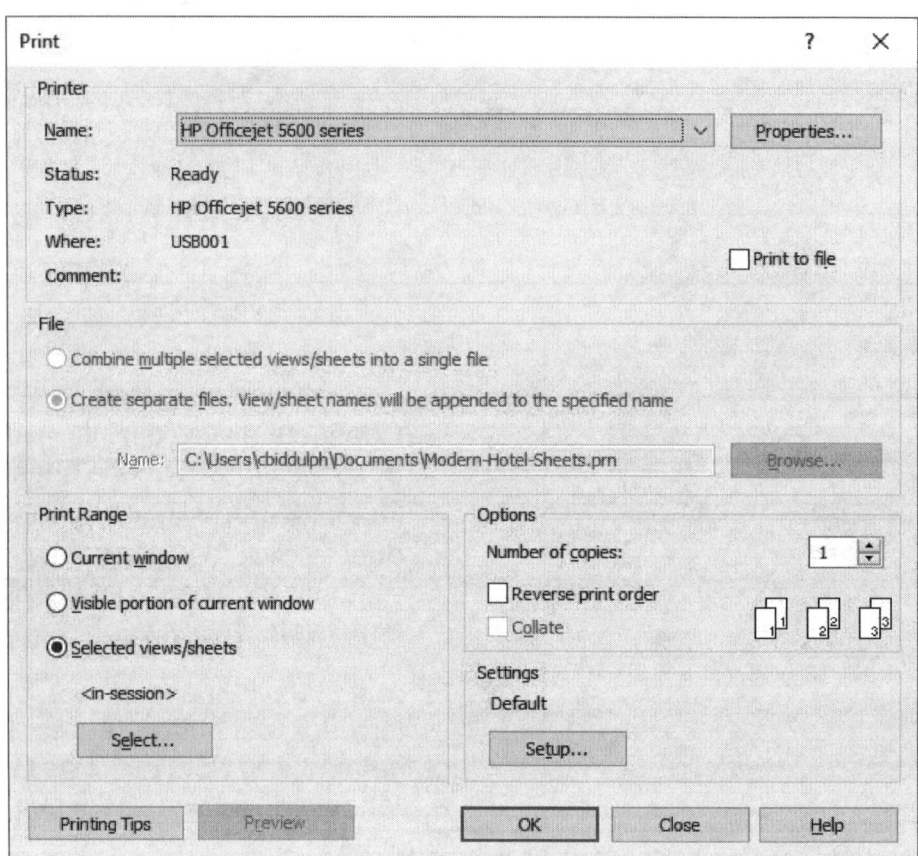

Figure 14–24

### Printing Options

The Print dialog box is divided into the following areas: *Printer, File, Print Range, Options*, and *Settings*. Modify them as needed to produce the plot you want.

- **Printing Tips**: Opens Autodesk WikiHelp online, in which you can find help with troubleshooting printing issues.

- **Preview**: Opens a preview of the print output so that you can see what is going to be printed.

# Creating Construction Documents

## Printer

Select from the list of available printers, as shown in Figure 14–25. Click **Properties...** to adjust the properties of the selected printer. The options vary according to the printer. Select the **Print to file** option to print to a file rather than directly to a printer. You can create .PLT or .PRN files.

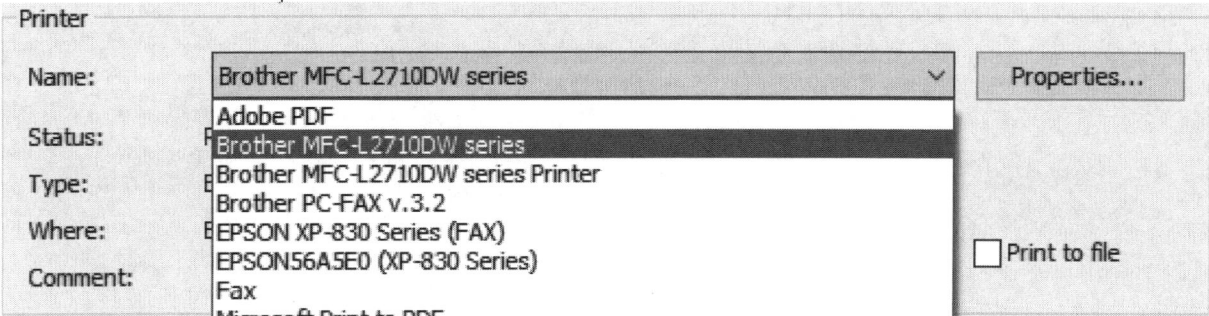

Figure 14–25

- You must have a PDF print driver installed on your system to print to PDF, or you can export views and sheets to PDF.

## File

The *File* area is only available if the **Print to file** option has been selected in the *Printer* area or if you are printing to an electronic-only type of printer. You can create one file or multiple files depending on the type of printer you are using, as shown in Figure 14–26. Click **Browse...** to select the file location and name.

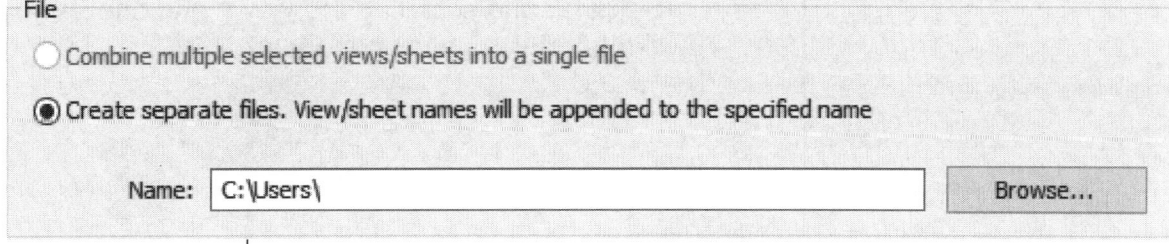

Figure 14–26

## Print Range

The *Print Range* area enables you to print individual views/sheets or sets of views/sheets, as shown in Figure 14–27.

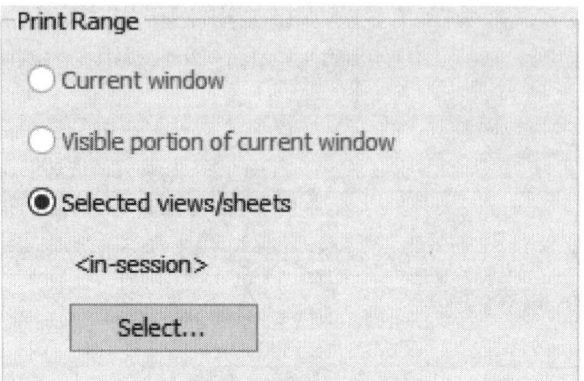

Figure 14–27

- **Current window:** Prints the entire current sheet or view you have open.

- **Visible portion of current window:** Prints only what is displayed in the current sheet or view.

- **Selected views/sheets:** Prints multiple views or sheets. Click **Select...** to open the View/Sheet Set dialog box to choose what to include in the print set. You can save these sets by name so that you can more easily print the same group again.

  - By choosing the **Selected views/sheets** print range, you can modify which views and sheets are printed by clicking **Select...** and selecting the views and sheets you would like to print, as shown in Figure 14–28.

# Creating Construction Documents

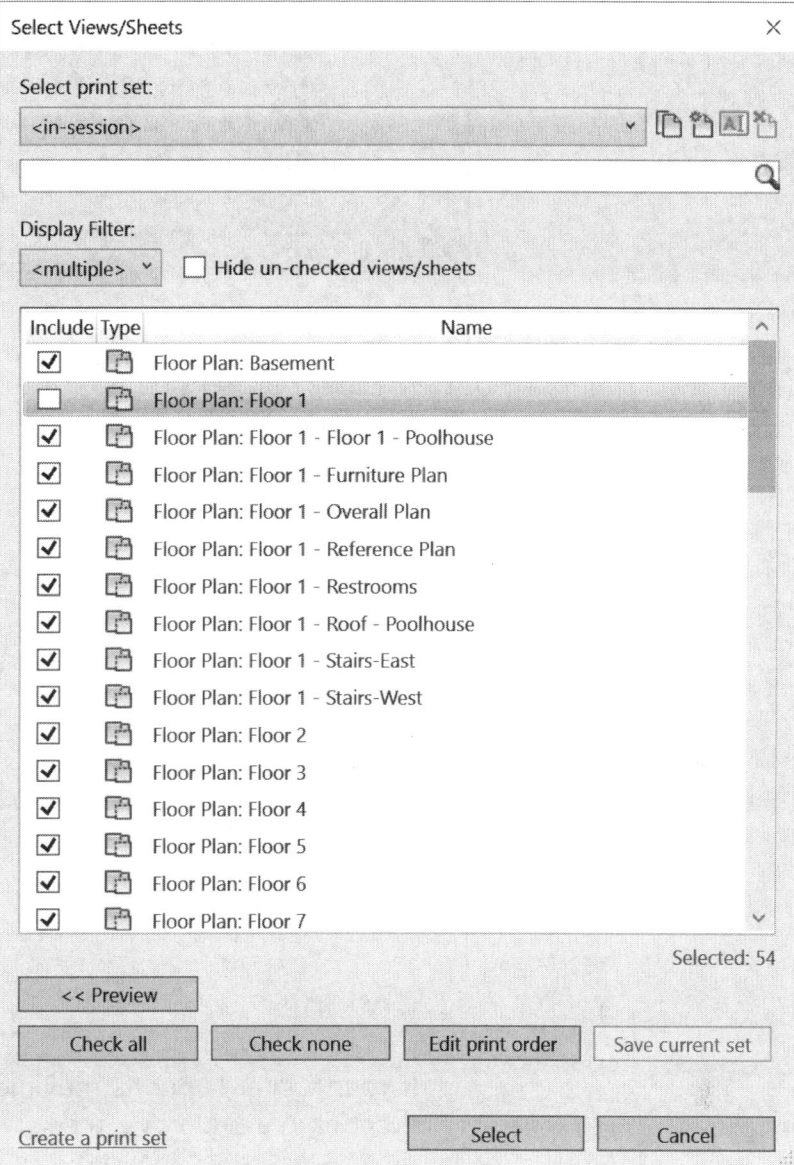

Figure 14–28

- You can edit the selected views and sheets by **Browser organization**, **Sheet Number (Ascending)**, or **Manual order**. If you select **Manual order**, you can drag the views and sheets to put them in a custom order, as shown in Figure 14–29.

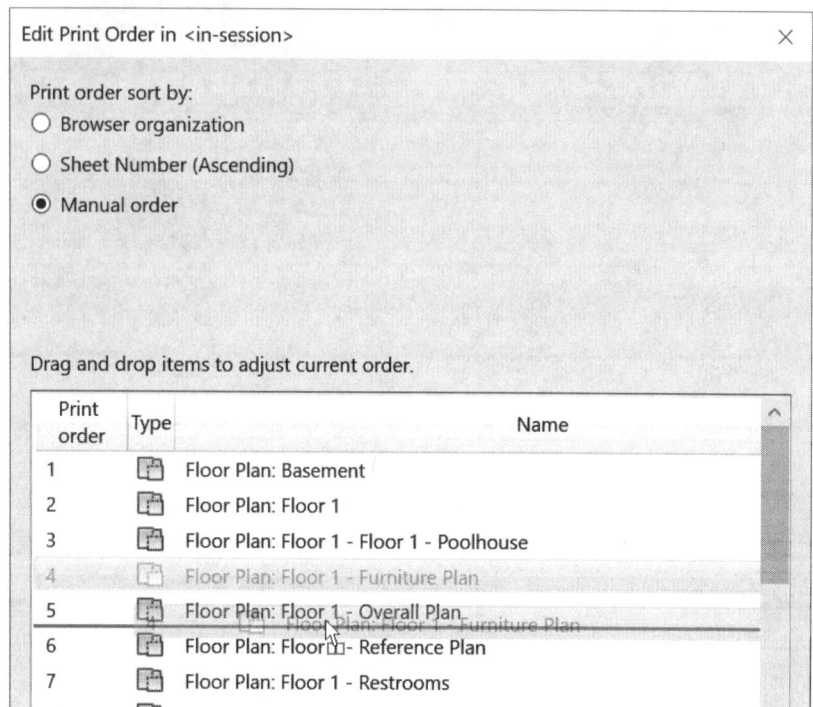

Figure 14–29

## Options

If your printer supports multiple copies, you can specify the number in the *Options* area, as shown in Figure 14–30. You can also reverse the print order or collate your prints. These options are also available in the printer properties.

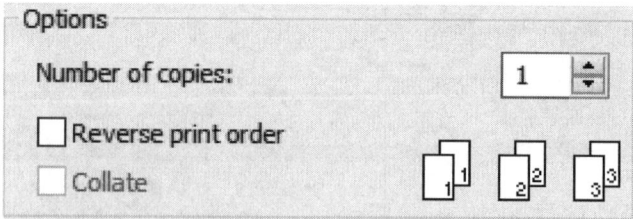

Figure 14–30

# Creating Construction Documents

## Settings

Click **Setup...** to open the Print Setup dialog box, as shown in Figure 14–31. Here, you can specify the *Orientation* and *Zoom* settings, among others. You can also save these settings by name.

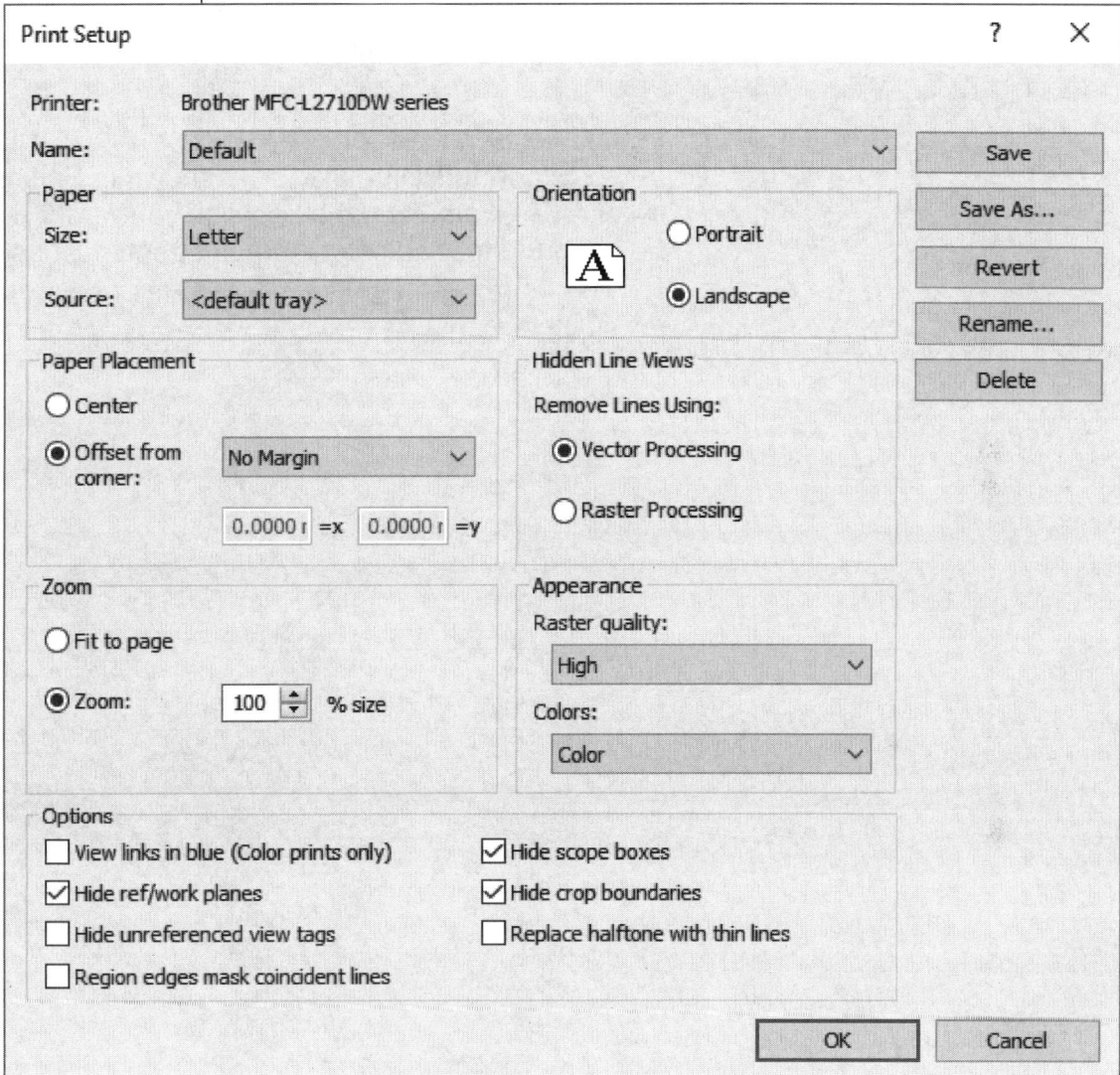

Figure 14–31

- In the *Options* area, specify the types of elements you want to print or not print. Unless specified, all of the elements in a view or sheet print.

- Sheets should always be printed at **Zoom** set to **100%** size unless you are creating a quick markup set that does not need to be exact.

## Export Views and Sheets to PDF

If you do not have a PDF driver to utilize in the Print dialog box, you can export your views or sheets to PDF. If you set the *Export Range* to **Selected views/sheets**, you have the ability to edit the print order of the views/sheets by **Browser organization**, **Sheet Number (Ascending)**, or **Manual order**.

### How To: Export Views and Sheets to PDF

1. In the File menu, select (Export)> (PDF).
2. In the Export to PDF dialog box (shown in Figure 14–32), enter a *File Name* and the *Location* you would like the PDF to be exported to, and select the other settings, as needed.
   - The PDF Export settings are similar to those found in the Revit Print dialog box.

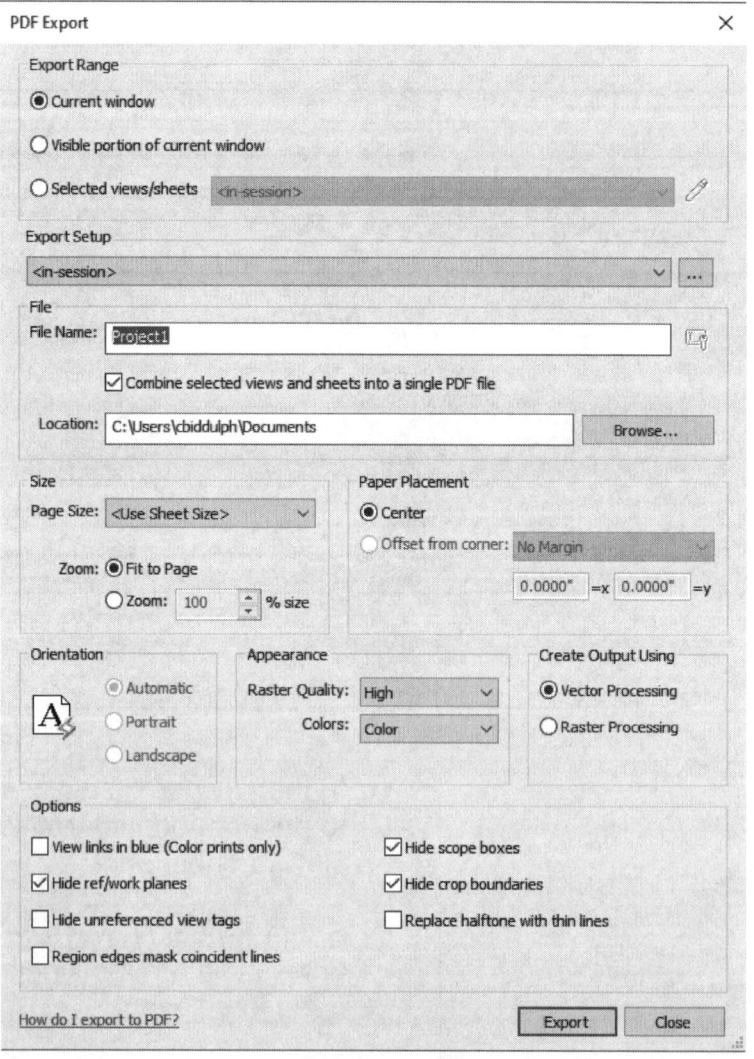

Figure 14–32

3. Click **Export**.

# Chapter Review Questions

1. How do you specify the size of a sheet?
   a. In the Sheet Properties, specify the **Sheet Size**.
   b. In the Options Bar, specify the **Sheet Size**.
   c. In the New Sheet dialog box, select a title block to control the Sheet Size.
   d. In the Sheet view, right-click and select **Sheet Size**.

2. How is the title block information filled in, as shown in Figure 14–33? (Select all that apply.)

Figure 14–33

   a. Select the title block and select the label that you want to change.
   b. Select the title block and modify it in Properties.
   c. Right-click on the sheet in the Project Browser and select **Information**.
   d. Some of the information is filled in automatically from the Project Information.

3. On how many sheets can a floor plan view be placed?
   a. 1
   b. 2-5
   c. 6+
   d. As many as you want

4. Which of the following is the best method to use if the size of a view is too large for a sheet, as shown in Figure 14–34?

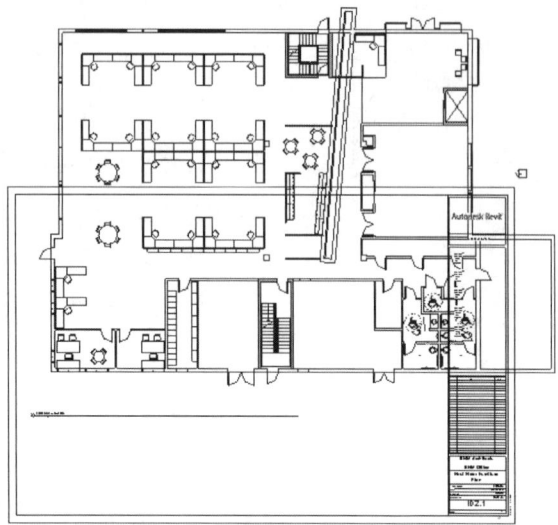

Figure 14–34

   a. Delete the view, change the scale, and place the view back on the sheet.

   b. Change the scale of the sheet.

5. How do you set up a view on a sheet that only displays part of a floor plan, as shown in Figure 14–35?

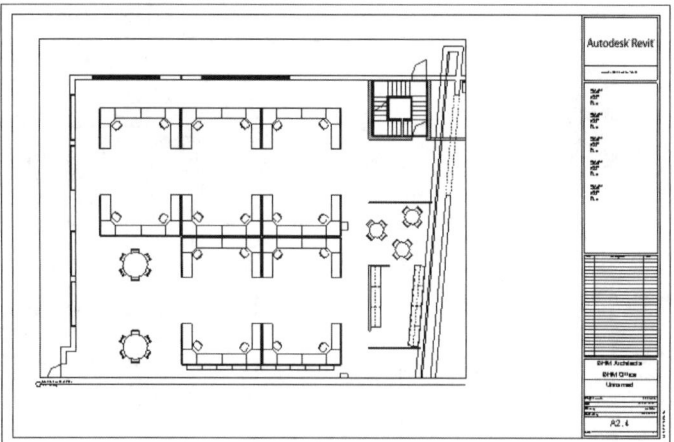

Figure 14–35

   a. Drag and drop the view to the sheet and use the crop region to modify it.

   b. Activate the view and rescale it.

   c. Create a callout view displaying the part that you want to use and place the callout view on the sheet.

   d. Open the view in the Project Browser and change the View Scale.

6. You can only export sheets to PDF.
    a. True
    b. False

# Command Summary

| Button | Command | Location |
|---|---|---|
| | Activate View | • **Ribbon:** (*select the view*) *Modify \| Viewports* tab>Viewport panel<br>• **Double-click:** *(in viewport)*<br>• **Right-click:** (*on view*) Activate View |
| | Deactivate View | • **Ribbon:** *View* tab>Sheet Composition panel, expand Viewports<br>• **Double-click:** *(on sheet)*<br>• **Right-click:** (*on view*) Deactivate View |
| | PDF | • **File tab>Export** |
| | Place View | • **Ribbon:** *View* tab>Sheet Composition panel |
| | Print | • **File tab** |
| | Sheet | • **Ribbon:** *View* tab>Sheet Composition panel |

# Chapter 15

# Working with Annotations

When you create construction documents, annotations are essential for showing the design intent. Annotations such as dimensions and text can be added to views at any time during the creation of a project. Detail lines and symbols can also be added to views as you create the working drawing sheets, while legends can be created to provide a place to document any symbols that are used in a project.

## Learning Objectives in This Chapter

- Add dimensions to the model as a part of the working drawings.
- Add text to a view and use leaders to create notes pointing to a specific part of the model.
- Create text types using different fonts and sizes to suit your company standards.
- Draw detail lines to further enhance the documentation view.
- Add view-specific annotation symbols for added clarity.
- Create legend views and populate them with symbols of elements in the project.

# 15.1 Working with Dimensions

You can create permanent dimensions using aligned, linear, angular, radial, diameter, and arc length dimensions. These can be individual or a string of dimensions, as shown in Figure 15–1. With aligned dimensions, you can also dimension entire walls with openings, grid lines, and/or intersecting walls.

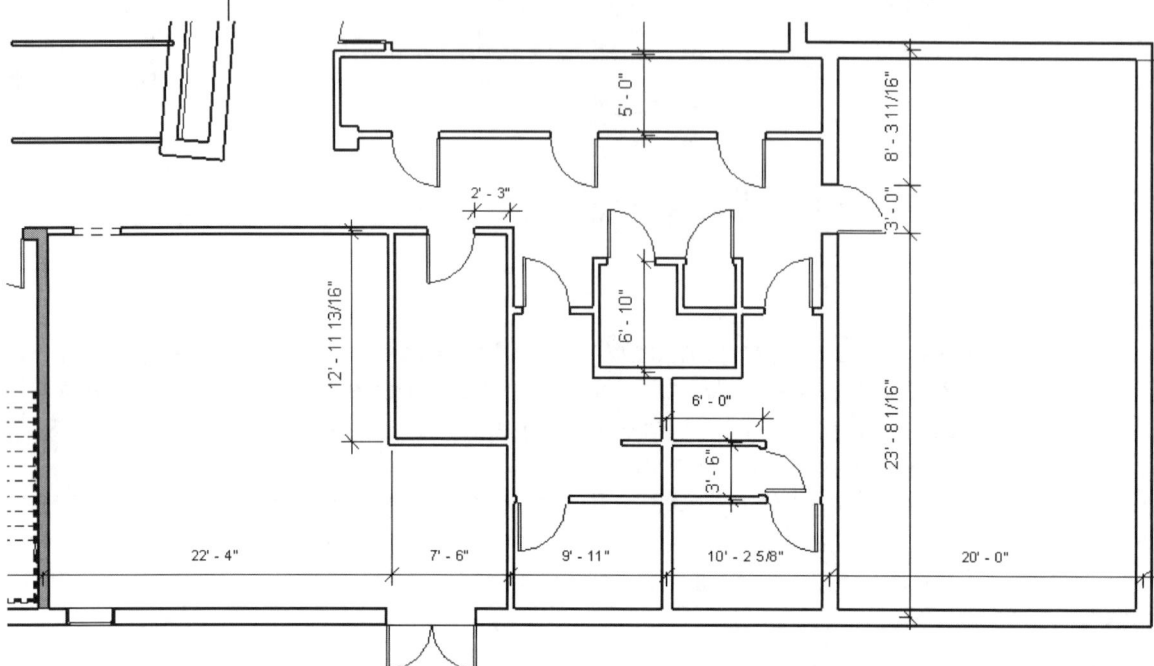

**Figure 15–1**

- Dimensions referencing model elements must be added to the model in a view. You can dimension on sheets, but only to items added directly on the sheets.

- Dimensions are available in the *Annotate* tab>Dimension panel (shown in Figure 15–2) and in the *Modify* tab>Measure panel.

*(Aligned) is also located in the Quick Access Toolbar.*

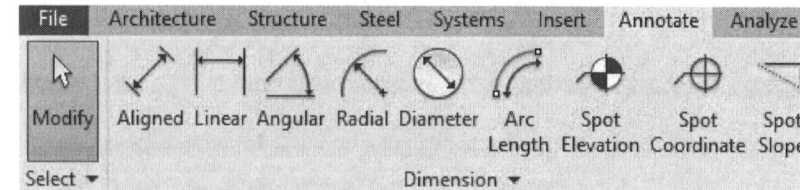

**Figure 15–2**

- Dimensions can be added to isometric 3D views whether they are locked or not. Proceed with caution when selecting the items to dimension. You can set the work plane or use <Tab> to cycle through elements.

# Working with Annotations

- Ensure that the witness lines and text orientation is snapping to and extending in the correct direction as intended.

## How To: Add Aligned Dimensions with Options

1. Start the ✎ (Aligned) command or type **DI**.
2. In the Type Selector, select a dimension style.
3. In the Options Bar, select the location line of the wall to dimension from, as shown in Figure 15–3.
   - This option can be changed as you add dimensions.

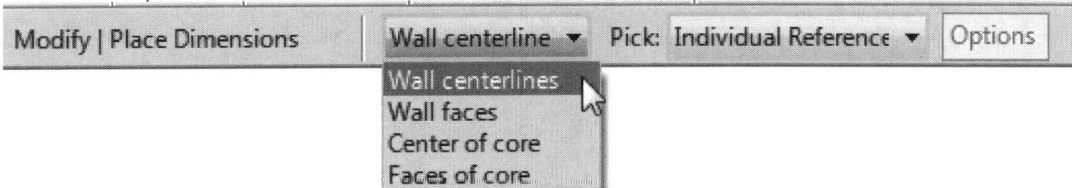

**Figure 15–3**

4. In the Options Bar, select your preference from the *Pick* drop-down list:
   - **Individual References:** Select the elements in order (as shown in Figure 15–4) and then click in an empty space in the view to position the dimension string.

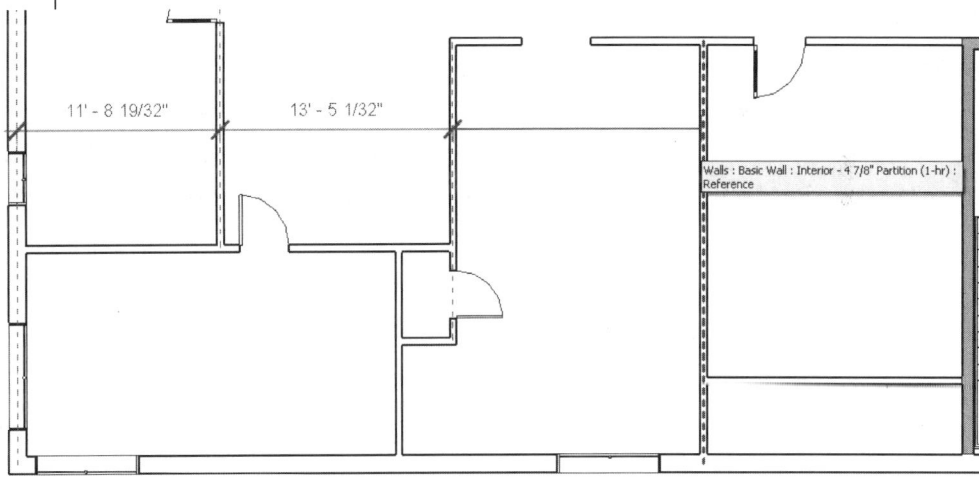

**Figure 15–4**

- **Entire Walls:** Select the wall you want to dimension and then click the cursor to position the dimension string, as shown in Figure 15–5.

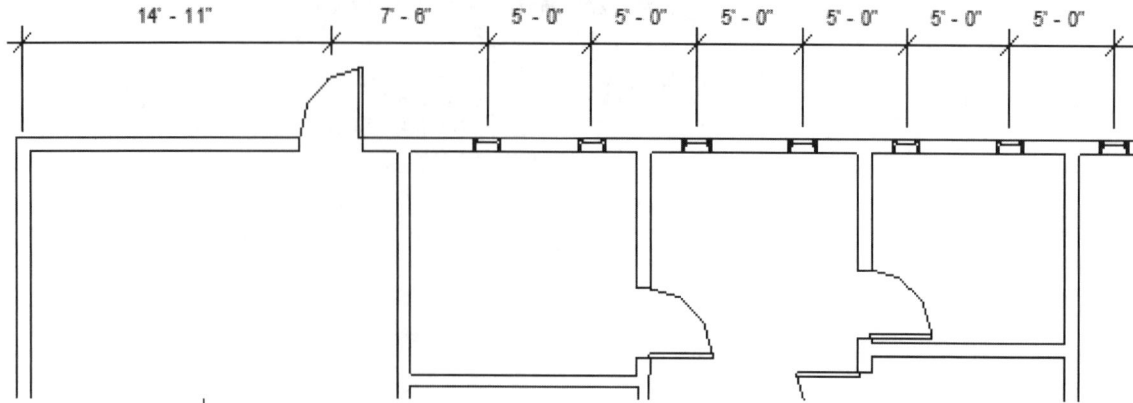

Figure 15–5

- When dimensioning entire walls, you can specify how you want *Openings*, *Intersecting Walls*, and *Intersecting Grids* to be treated by the dimension string. In the Options Bar, click **Options**. In the Auto Dimension Options dialog box (shown in Figure 15–6), select the references you want to have automatically dimensioned.

*If the **Entire Wall** option is selected without additional options, it places an overall wall dimension.*

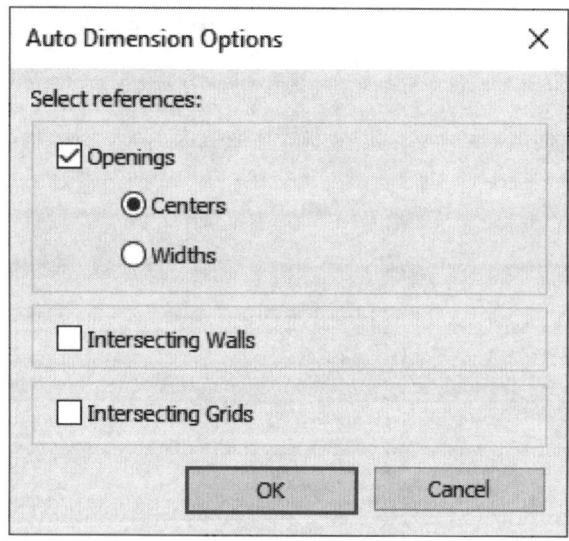

Figure 15–6

## How To: Add Other Types of Dimensions

*The dimension methods are also accessible in the Modify | Place Dimensions tab> Dimension panel when any of the dimension commands is active.*

1. In the *Annotate* tab>Dimension panel, select a dimension method.

| | | |
|---|---|---|
| | **Aligned** | Most commonly used dimension type. Select individual elements or entire walls to dimension. |
| | **Linear** | Used when you need to specify certain points on elements. |

# Working with Annotations

|  | Angular | Used to dimension the angle between two elements. |
|---|---|---|
|  | Radial | Used to dimension the radius of circular elements. |
|  | Diameter | Used to dimension the diameter of circular elements. |
|  | Arc Length | Used to dimension the length of the arc of circular elements. |

2. In the Type Selector, select the dimension type.
3. Follow the prompts for the selected method.

## Modifying Dimensions

When you move elements that are dimensioned (e.g., a wall), the dimensions automatically update. You can also modify dimensions by selecting a dimension or dimension string and making changes. Figure 15–7 shows the various parts of dimensions that aid in modifying.

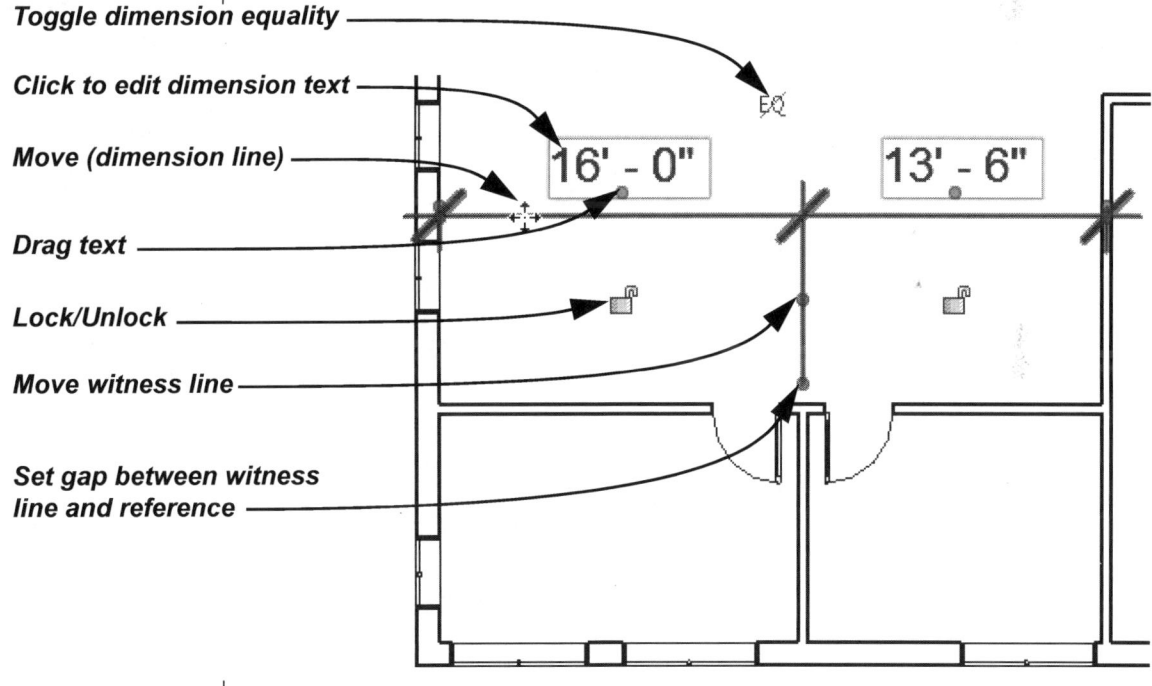

**Figure 15–7**

- To move the dimension text, select the **Drag text** control under the text and drag it to a new location. It automatically creates a leader from the dimension line if you drag it away. The style of the leader (arc or line) depends on the dimension style.

- To move the dimension line (the line parallel to the element being dimensioned), simply drag the line to a new location, or select the dimension and drag the (Drag to new position) control.

- To change the gap between the witness line and the element being dimensioned, drag the control at the end of the witness line.

- To move the witness line (the line perpendicular to the element being dimensioned) to a different element or face of a wall, use the **Move Witness Line** control in the middle of the witness line. While moving the witness line, you can hover your cursor over a element or component and press <Tab> repeatedly to cycle through the various options. You can also drag this control to move the witness line to a different element, or right-click on the control and select **Move Witness Line**.

### Adding and Deleting Dimensions in a String

- To add a witness line to a string of dimensions, select the dimension and, in the *Modify | Dimensions* tab>Witness Lines panel, click (Edit Witness Lines). Select the element(s) you want to add to the dimension. Click in an empty space in the view to finish.

- To delete a witness line, drag the **Move Witness Line** control to a nearby witness line's element. Alternatively, you can hover the cursor over the control, right-click, and select **Delete Witness Line**.

- To delete one dimension in a string and break the string into two separate dimensions, select the string, hover your cursor over the dimension that you want to delete, and press <Tab>. When it highlights (as shown on top in Figure 15–8), pick it and press <Delete>. The selected dimension is deleted and the dimension string is separated into two elements, as shown on the bottom in Figure 15–8.

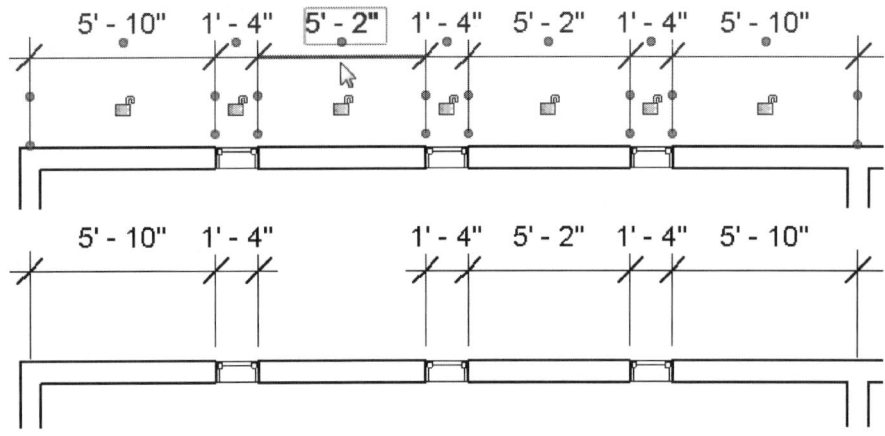

Figure 15–8

## Modifying the Dimension Text

Because Revit is parametric, changing the dimension text without changing the elements dimensioned would cause problems throughout the project. These issues could cause problems beyond the model if you use the project model to estimate materials or work with other disciplines.

You can append the existing dimension text with prefixes and suffixes (as shown in Figure 15–9), or create a dimension style that has a prefix or suffix preset in the Type Properties. This can help you in renovation projects.

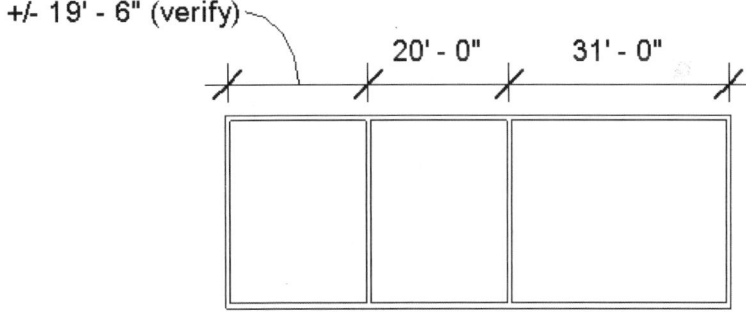

Figure 15–9

Double-click on the dimension text to open the Dimension Text dialog box, as shown in Figure 15–10, and make modifications as needed.

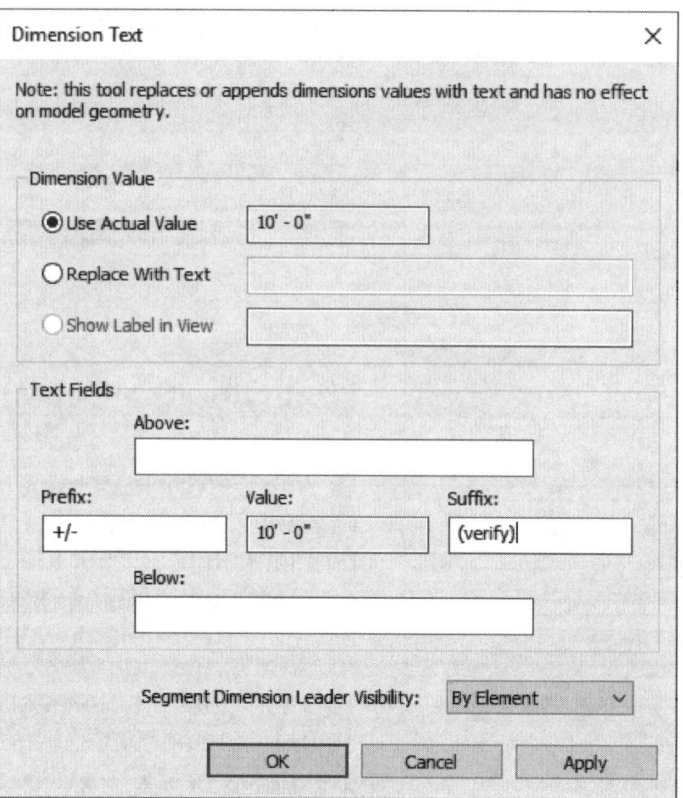

Figure 15–10

# Working with Annotations

### Hint: Multiple Dimension Options

If you are creating details that show one element with multiple dimension values, as shown in Figure 15–11, you can easily modify the dimension text.

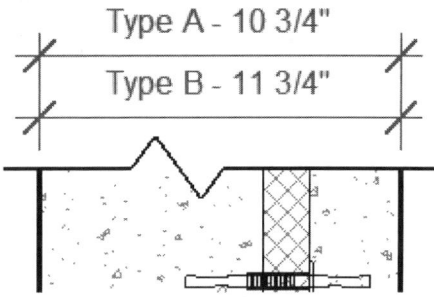

Figure 15–11

Select the dimension and then the dimension text. The Dimension Text dialog box opens. You can replace the text, as shown in Figure 15–12, or add text fields above or below, as well as a prefix or suffix.

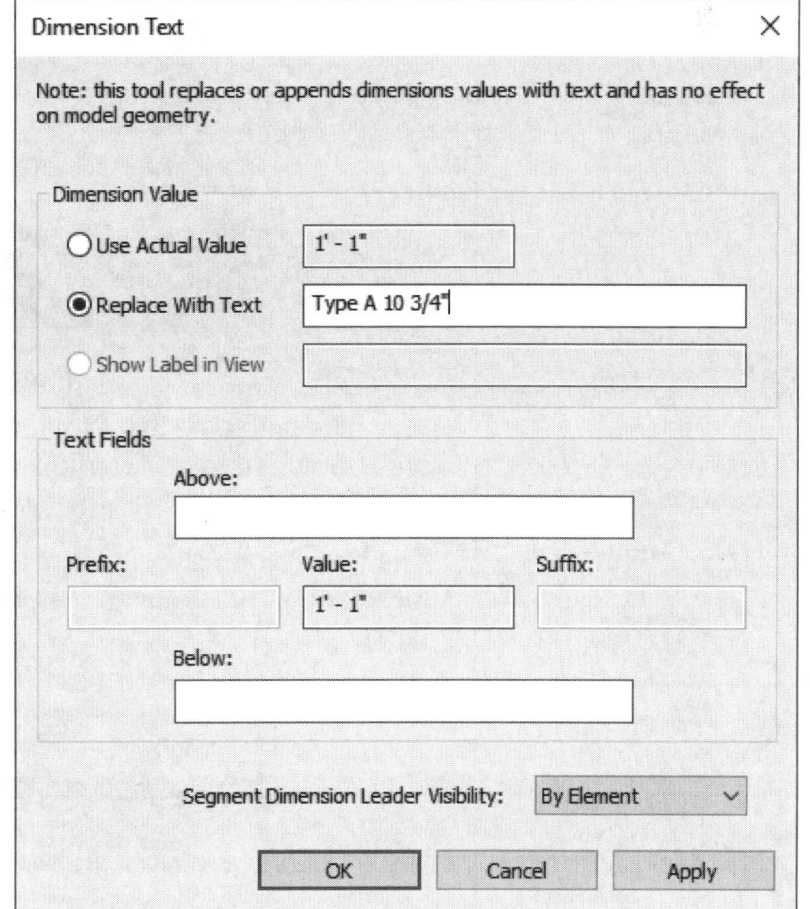

Figure 15–12

- This also works with Equality Text Labels.

If you find that you are always modifying dimensions manually, you can create a type-driven dimension style by duplicating the dimension style and specifying a set prefix and suffix within the type parameters, as shown in Figure 15–13.

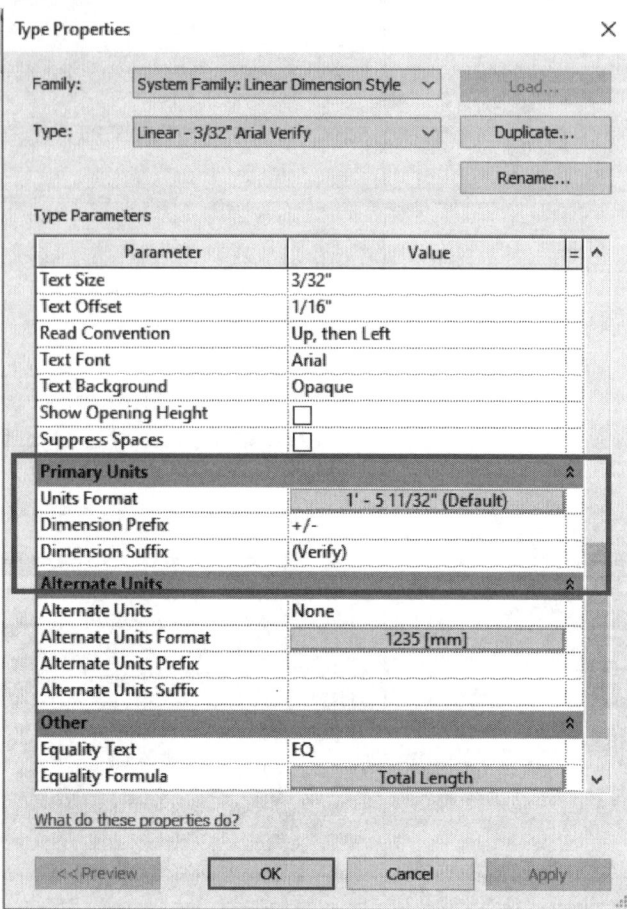

Figure 15–13

This eliminates the need to manually modify the dimension every time you need to add a prefix or suffix.

## Setting Constraints

The three types of constraints that work with dimensions are locks and equal settings, as shown in Figure 15–14, as well as labels.

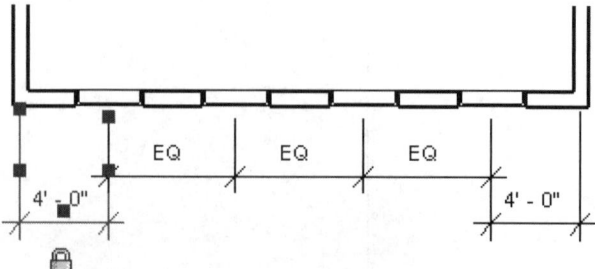

Figure 15–14

# Working with Annotations

## Locking Dimensions

When you lock a dimension, the value is set and you cannot make a change between it and the referenced elements. If it is unlocked, you can move it and change its value.

Note that when you use this and move an element, any elements that are locked to the dimension also move.

## Setting Dimensions Equal

For a string of dimensions, select the **EQ** symbol to constrain the elements to be at an equal distance apart. This actually moves the elements that are dimensioned.

- The equality text display can be changed in Properties, as shown in Figure 15–15. The style for each of the display types is set in the dimension type.

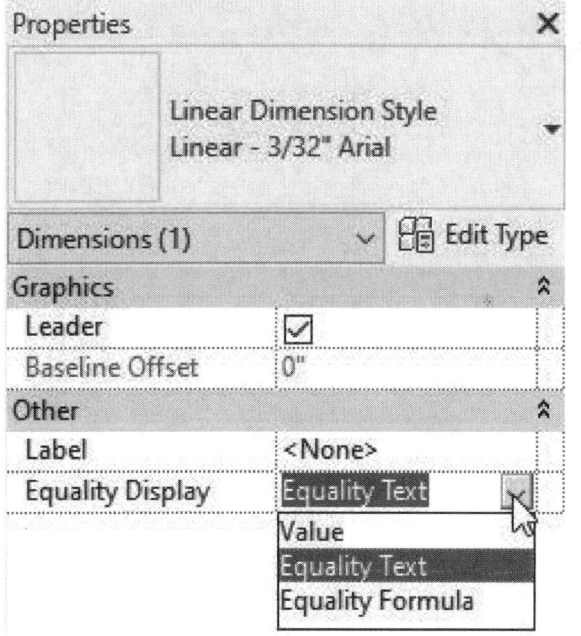

**Figure 15–15**

## Labeling Dimensions

If you have a distance that needs to be repeated multiple times, such as the *Wall to Window* label shown in Figure 15–16, or one where you want to use a formula based on another dimension, you can create and apply a global parameter, also called a label, to the dimension.

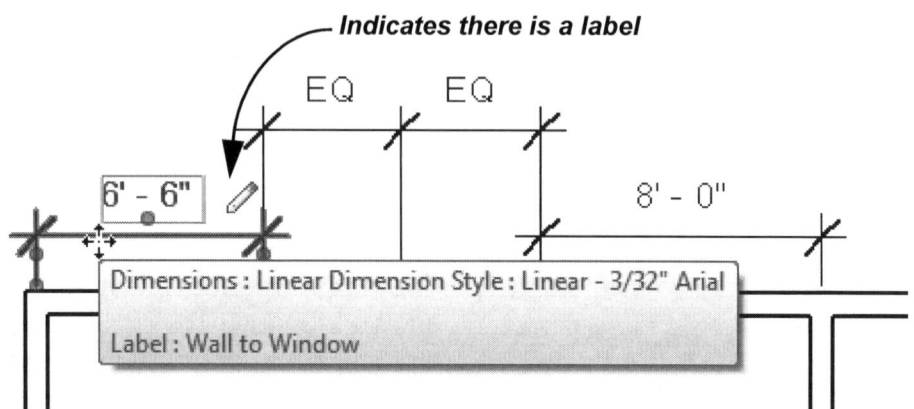

Figure 15–16

- To apply an existing label to a dimension, select the dimension and in the *Modify | Dimensions* tab>Label Dimension panel, select the label in the drop-down list, as shown in Figure 15–17.

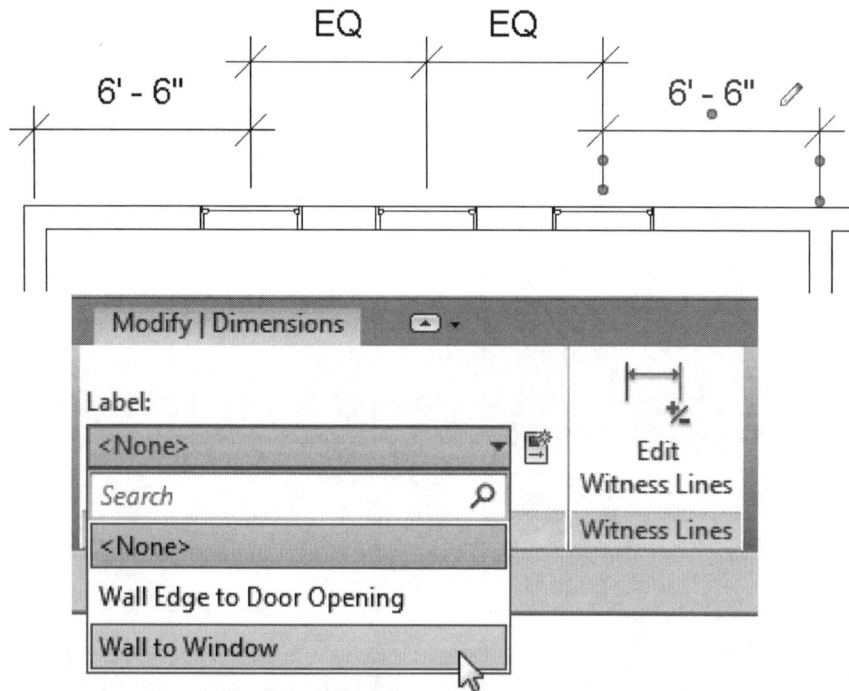

Figure 15–17

## How To: Create a Label

1. Select a dimension.
2. In the *Modify | Dimensions* tab>Label Dimension panel, click ▧ (Create Parameter)
3. In the Global Parameter Properties dialog box, type in a *Name*, as shown in Figure 15–18, and click **OK**.

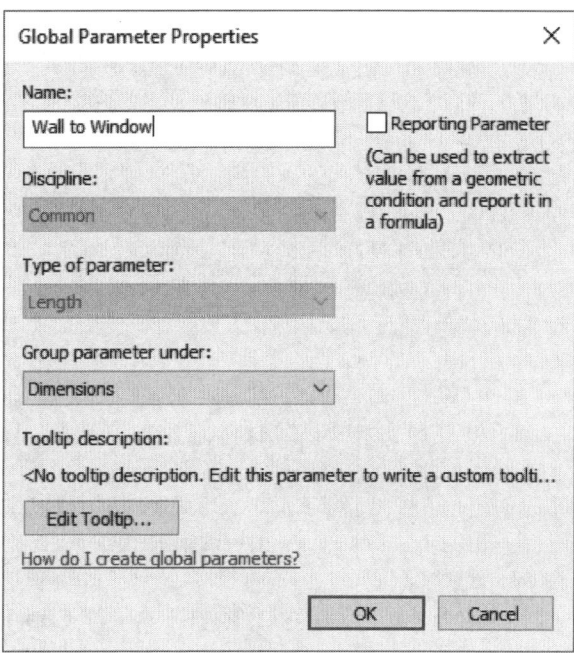

Figure 15–18

4. The label is applied to the dimension.

## How To: Edit the Label Information

1. Select a labeled dimension.
2. Click ✎ (Global Parameters), as shown in Figure 15–19.

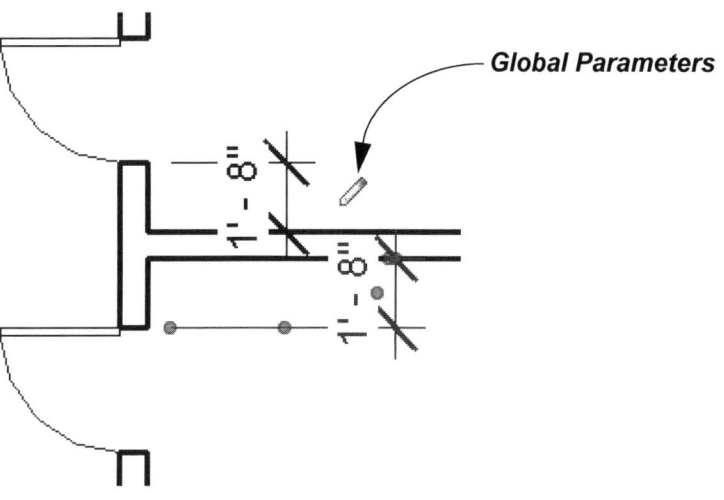

Figure 15–19

3. In the Global Parameters dialog box, in the *Value* column, type the new distance, as shown in Figure 15–20.

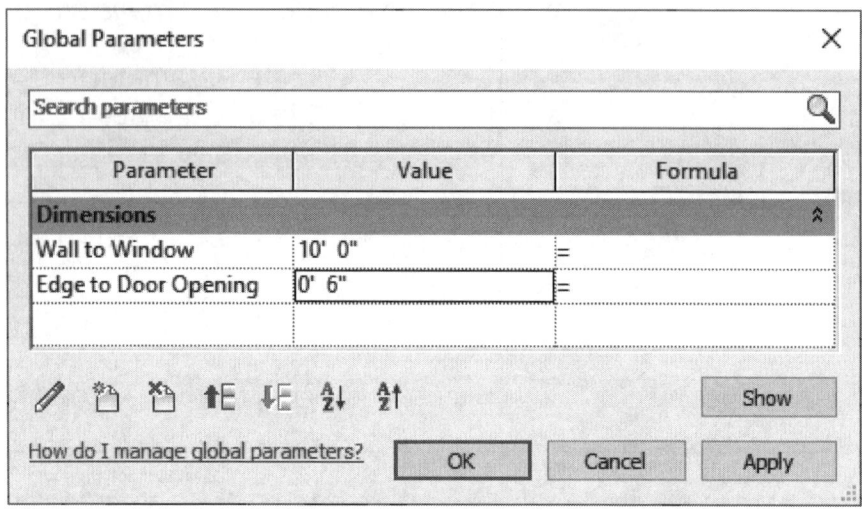

Figure 15–20

4. Click **OK**. The selected dimension and any other dimensions using the same label are updated.

- You can also edit, create, and delete global parameters in this dialog box.

## Working with Constraints

To find out which elements have constraints applied to them, in the View Control Bar, click (Reveal Constraints). Constraints display as shown in Figure 15–21.

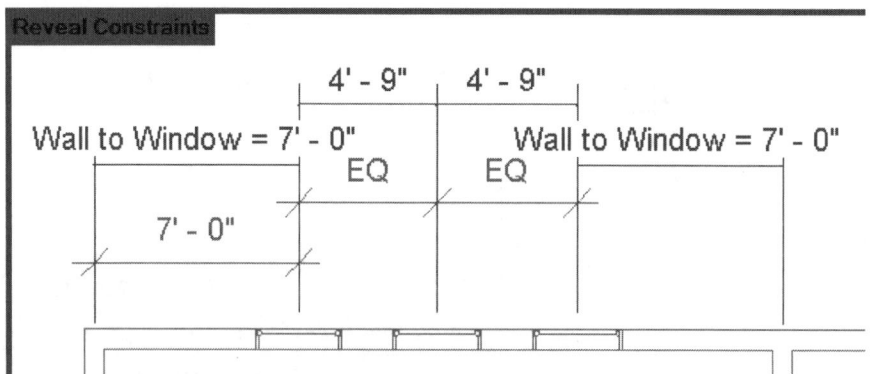

Figure 15–21

# Working with Annotations

- If you try to move the element beyond the appropriate constraints, a warning dialog box displays, as shown in Figure 15–22.

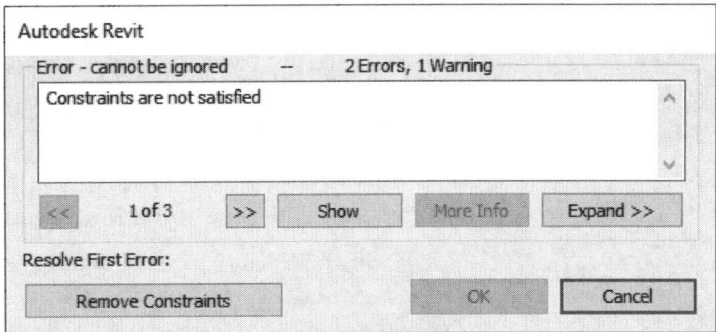

Figure 15–22

- If you delete dimensions that are constrained, a warning dialog box displays, as shown in Figure 15–23. Click **OK** to retain the constraint or click **Unconstrain** to remove the constraint.

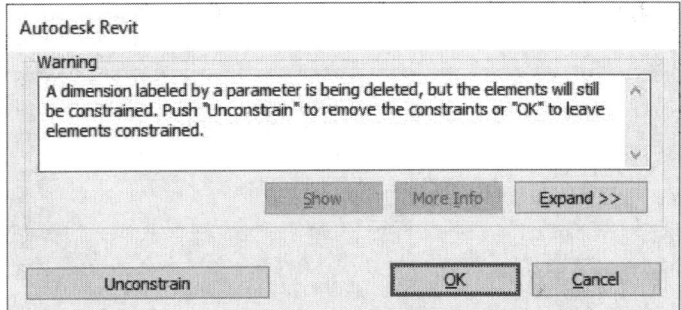

Figure 15–23

## Spot Slope on Ramps

You can add a spot slope to a straight or curved ramp. They can be added in a plan (as shown in Figure 15–24), section, elevation, or 3D view.

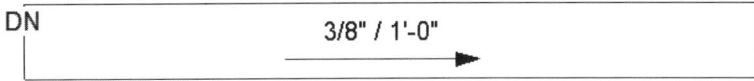

Figure 15–24

### How To: Add a Spot Slope

1. Zoom in to a ramp in the model.
2. In the *Annotate* tab>Dimensions panel, click ◹ (Spot Slope).
3. Click on the ramp surface to place the spot slope.

## Practice 15a

# Work with Dimensions

### Practice Objectives

- Add a string of dimensions.
- Dimension using the **Entire Walls** option.
- Edit the witness lines of dimensions.

In this practice, you will add dimensions using several different methods to a floor plan view, as shown in Figure 15–25. You will also modify the dimensions so that they show what you are expecting. Note that some additional elements, including storefront curtain walls and windows, have been added at the back of the building.

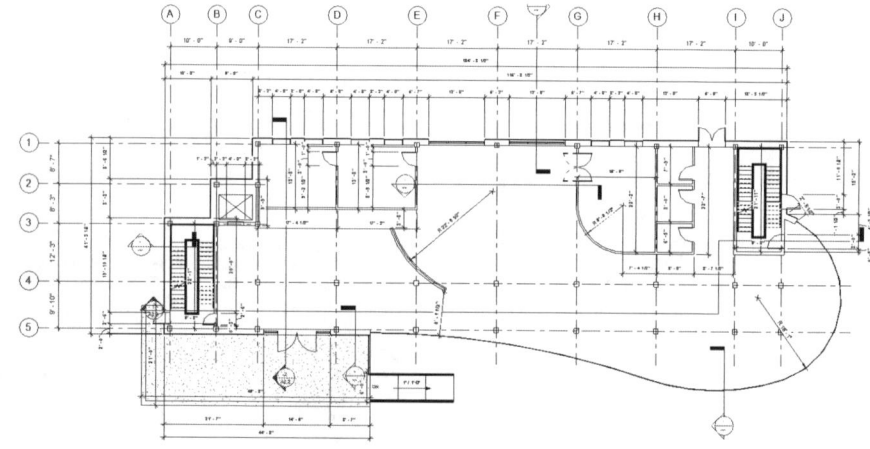

Figure 15–25

### Task 1 - Add dimensions to the column grid.

1. Open the project **Hotel-Dimensions.rvt** from the practice files folder.

2. In the Project Browser, duplicate the **Floor Plans: Floor 1** view (without detailing so that the door and window tags do not display).

3. Rename the new view to **Floor 1 - Dimension Plan**.

*Even though you have a view template for a dimension plan, you will not use it in this exercise so you can practice modifying the view.*

4. Turn on the crop region. In Properties, in the *Extents* section, check **Annotation Crop** and adjust the crop region in the view to only display the hotel and not the poolhouse. Adjust the outer annotation crop region so that the elevation markers are not displayed, as shown in Figure 15–26.

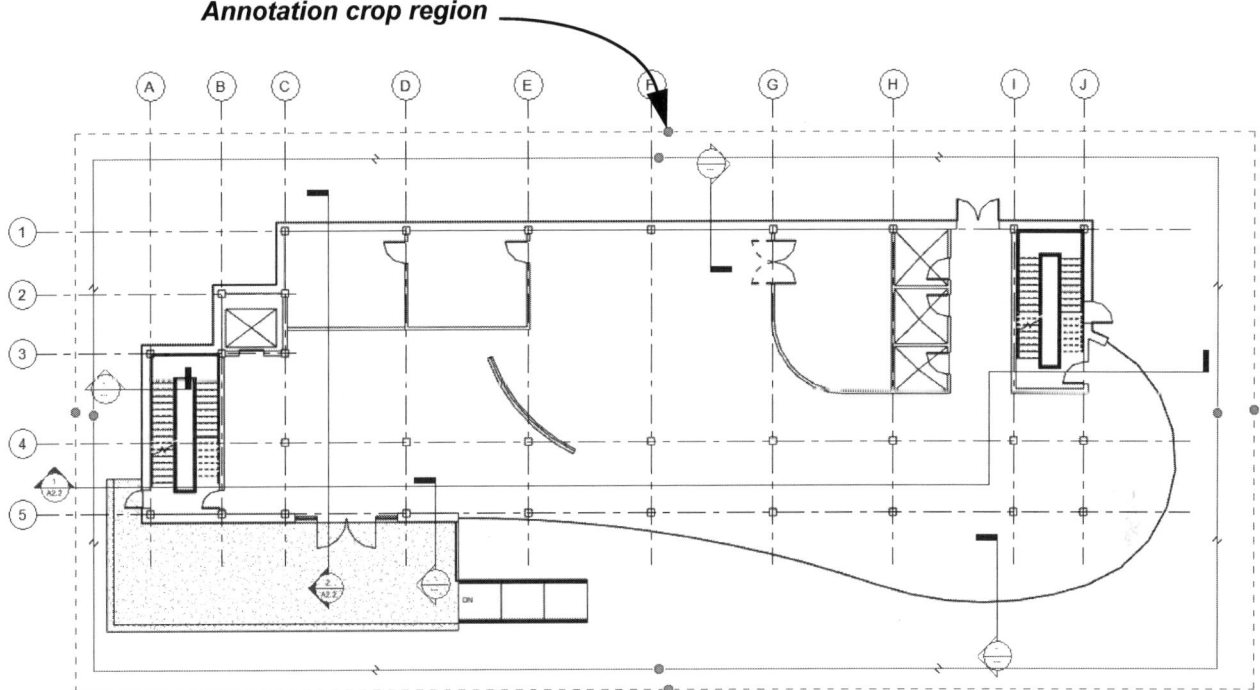

Figure 15–26

5. In Properties, uncheck **Annotation Crop**, and from the View Control Bar, hide the crop region. This needs to be done so you can dimension outside of the crop region area.

6. Open the Visibility/Graphic Overrides dialog box and turn on **Grids** from the *Annotation Categories* tab.

7. Move the location of the grid bubbles so that there is enough room for dimensioning.

8. In the Quick Access Toolbar, click (Aligned).

9. Dimension the column grid lines in each direction, as shown in Figure 15–27.

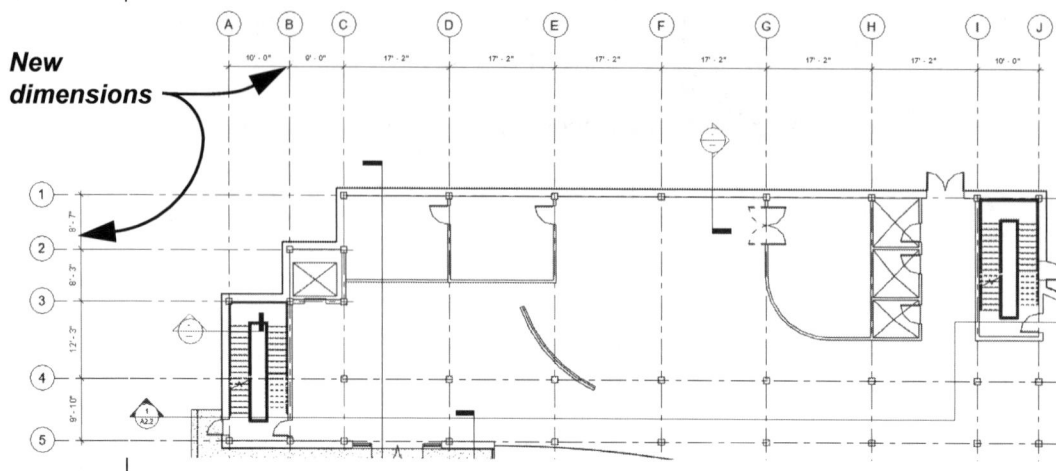

Figure 15–27

10. Click (Modify).

11. Save the project.

**Task 2 - Dimension the exterior and interior walls.**

1. Click (Aligned) to start the **Dimension** command again.

2. In the Options Bar, select **Wall faces** and set *Pick* to **Entire Walls**.

3. Click the **Options** button.

4. Check **Openings** and set the *Openings* to **Widths**, as shown in Figure 15–28. Click **OK**.

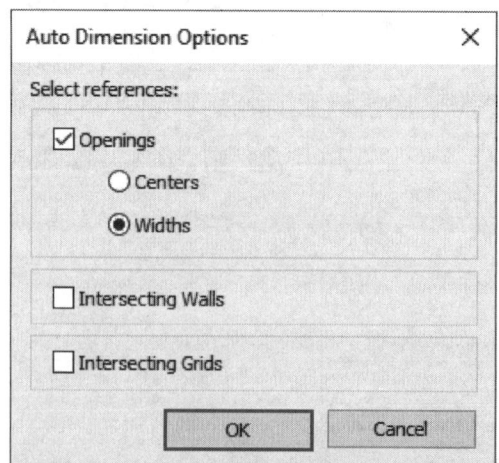

Figure 15–28

5. Select the back wall and place the dimension above it.

6. Zoom in on the upper-left corner of the building. Use the **Move Witness Line** control to relocate the line from the end of the wall (as shown in Figure 15–29) to grid line C, which passes through the column.

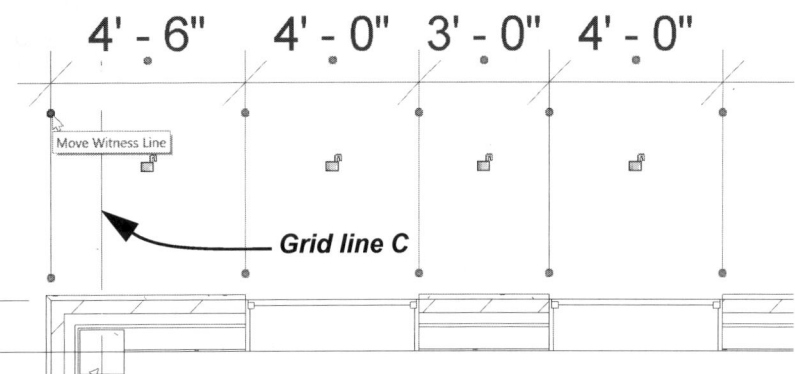

**Figure 15–29**

7. Click (Modify).

8. On the same wall, pan over to the curtain walls between grid lines E, F, and G, where the storefront openings are displayed. These were not dimensioned automatically.

9. Select the wall dimension line. In the *Modify | Dimensions* tab>Witness Lines panel, click (Edit Witness Lines).

10. Select the outside edges of each side of the storefront openings to add the witness lines and then click in an empty space in the view to apply the changes. The modified dimension string displays, as shown in Figure 15–30.

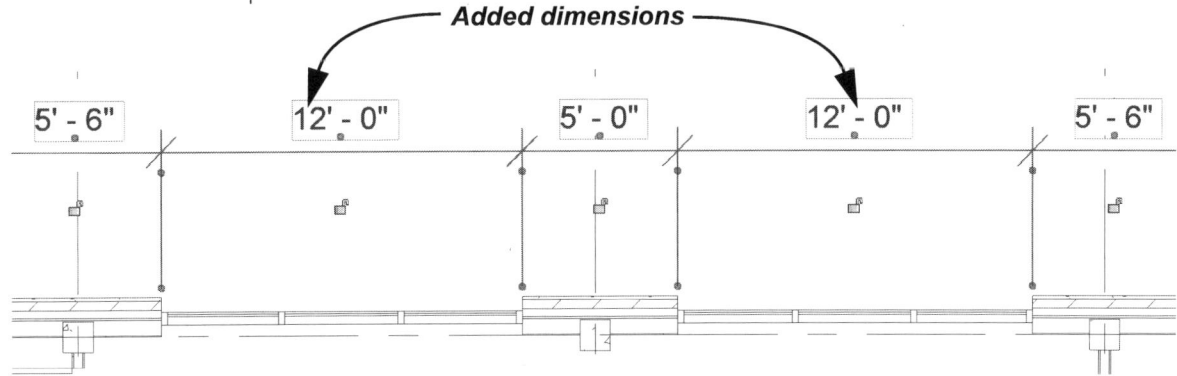

**Figure 15–30**

11. Move the section markers as well as the dimension line to keep the dimensions clear. You might also want to move the dimension text away from the grid lines.

*Use <Tab> to select different faces of a wall to dimension to.*

12. Pan over to the west side of the building.

13. Start the **Aligned Dimension** command and select **Entire Walls** in the Options Bar.

14. Click on the three walls to create a continuous string of dimensions.

15. Note that at grid 3, there are dimensions at the exterior core face and interior core face of the walls, as shown in Figure 15–31.

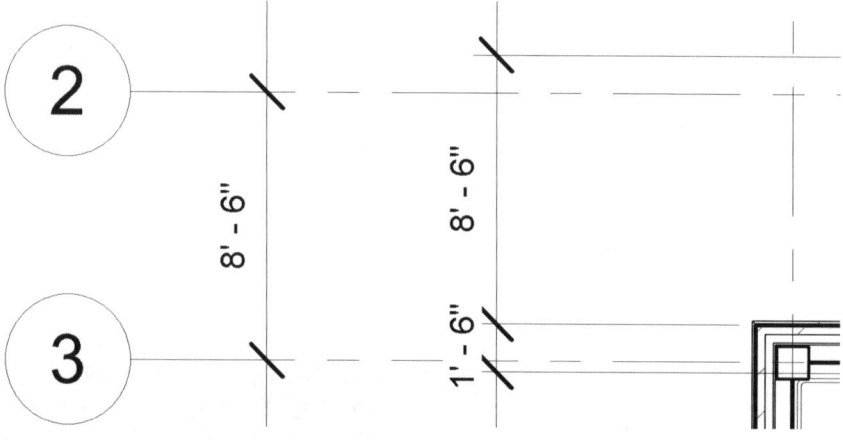

**Figure 15–31**

16. Select the dimension string, right-click on the interior core face witness line grip, and select **Delete Witness Line**, as shown in Figure 15–32.

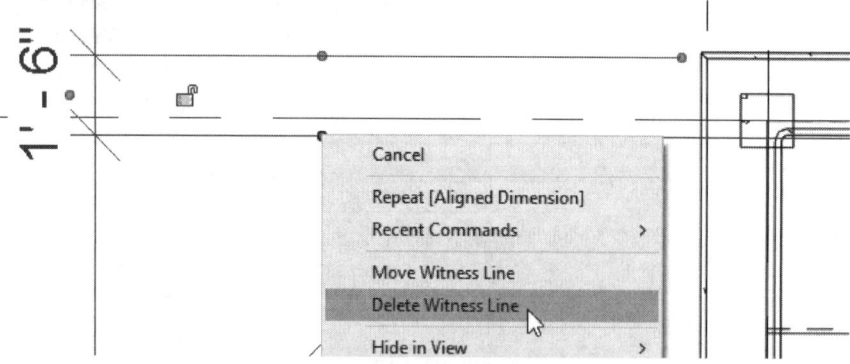

**Figure 15–32**

17. Pan down the same dimension string and note that the two dimensions are too close to each other and the bottom dimension is at the exterior core instead of the center of the column.

18. Modify the end dimension's witness line to be on the center of the column and not the exterior core.

19. Select the dimension string and select the dimension's drag text grip (as shown in Figure 15–33). Drag it outside of the dimension's string, and a leader will display.

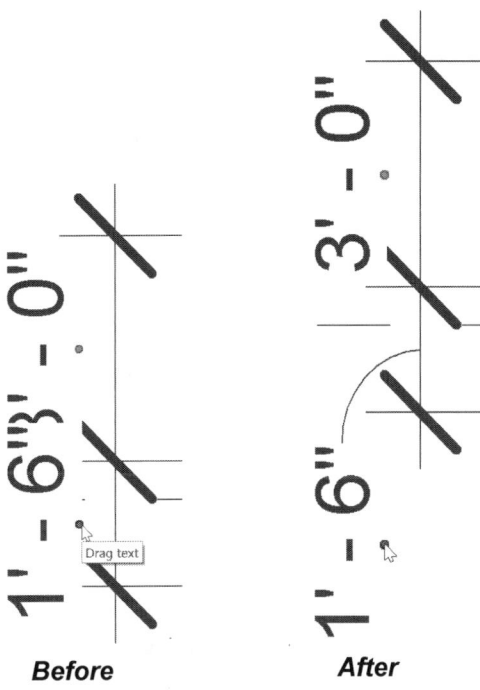

**Before**    **After**

**Figure 15–33**

20. Use the various dimensioning commands and methods to dimension the interior spaces, as shown in Figure 15–34. (Hint: Do not forget to change from **Pick: Entire Walls** to **Pick: Individual References**.) The dimensions might not be exactly as shown in Figure 15–34.

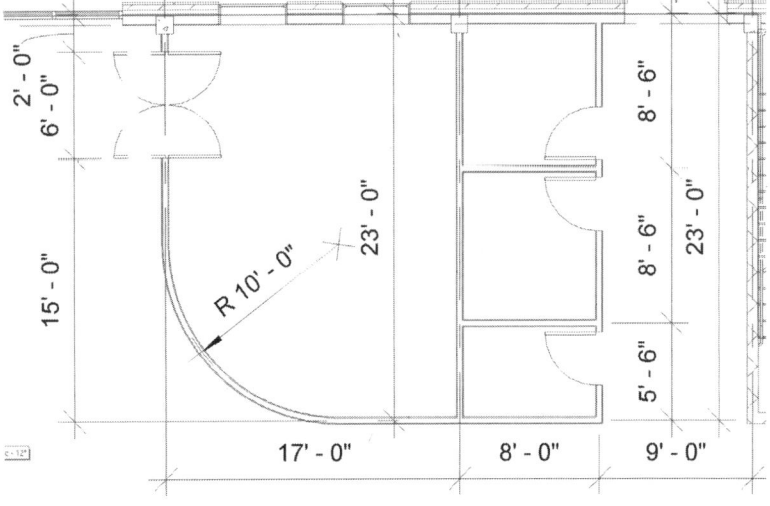

**Figure 15–34**

21. Pan over to the ramp at the south end of the building.

22. In the *Annotate* tab>Dimensions panel, click (Spot Slope).

23. Click on the ramp's surface to place the spot slope.

24. Save the project.

### Task 3 - Dimension the typical guest room.

1. Open the **Floor Plans: Typical Guest Room - Dimension Plan** view. Make adjustments to the crop region as needed.

2. Start the **Dimension** command.

3. In Properties, click **Edit Type....**

4. Duplicate the **Linear Dimension Style: Linear - 3/32" Arial** dimension style and call it **Linear - 3/32" Arial (TYP)**.

5. In the *Primary Units* section, type **(TYP)** next to *Dimensions Suffix* and click **OK**.

6. Dimension the guest room closet as shown in Figure 15–35.

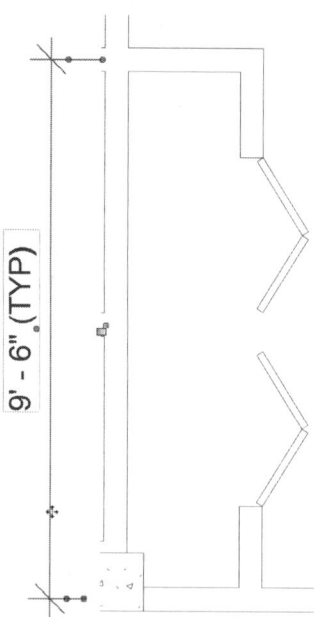

Figure 15–35

7. If time permits, dimension the rest of the typical guest room.

8. Save and close the project.

## 15.2 Working with Text

The **Text** command enables you to add notes to views or sheets, such as the detail shown in Figure 15–36. The same command is used to create text with or without leaders.

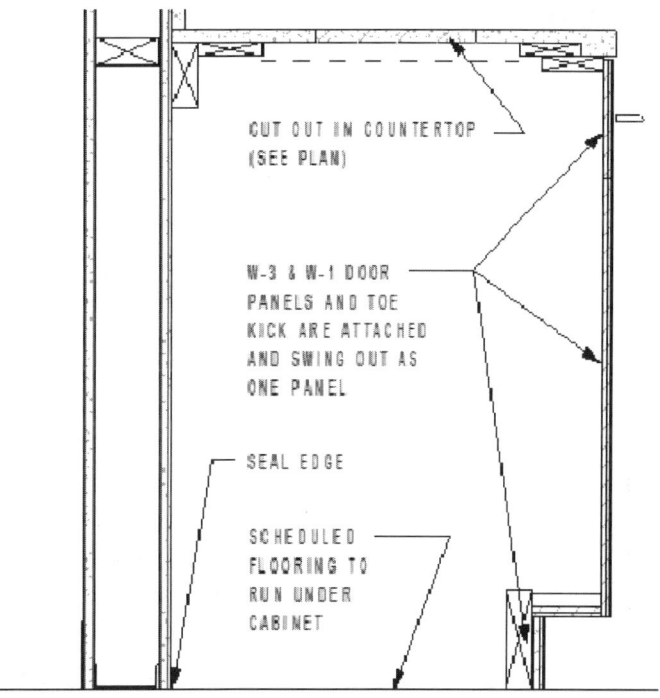

**Figure 15–36**

The text height is automatically set by the text type in conjunction with the scale of the view (as shown in Figure 15–37, using the same size text type at two different scales). Text types display at the specified height, both in the views and on the sheet.

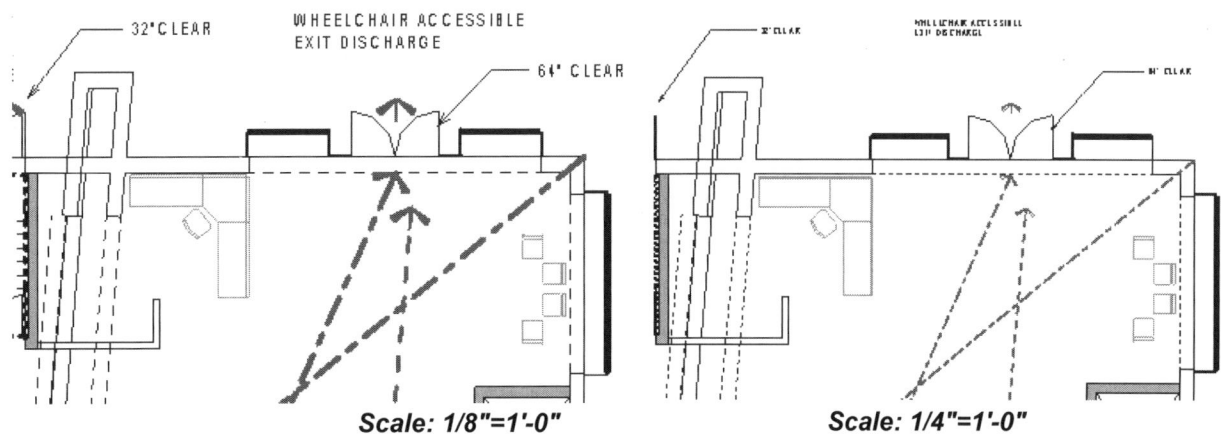

**Figure 15–37**

## How To: Add Text

1. In the Quick Access Toolbar or *Annotate* tab>Text panel, click **A** (Text).
2. In the Type Selector, set the text type.
3. In the *Modify | Place Text* tab>Leader panel, select the method you want to use: **A** (No Leader), **←A** (One Segment), **⌐A** (Two Segments), or **⌐A** (Curved).
4. In the Alignment panel, set the overall justification for the text and leader, as shown in Figure 15–38.

*The text type sets the font and height of the text.*

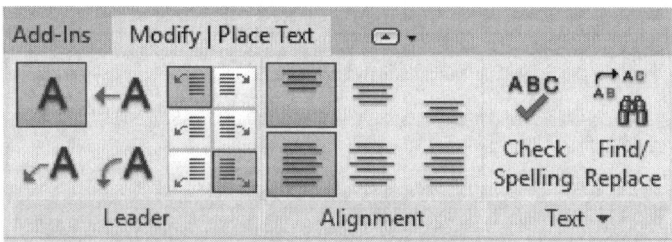

**Figure 15–38**

5. Select the location for the leader and text.
   - If **No leader** is selected, select the start point for the text and begin typing.
   - If using a leader, the first point places the arrow and you then select points for the leader. The text starts at the last leader point.
   - To set a word wrapping distance, click and drag the circle grip controls to set the start and end points of the text.
6. Type the needed text. In the *Edit Text* tab, specify additional options for the font and paragraph, as shown in Figure 15–39.

*Use alignment lines to help you align the text with other text elements.*

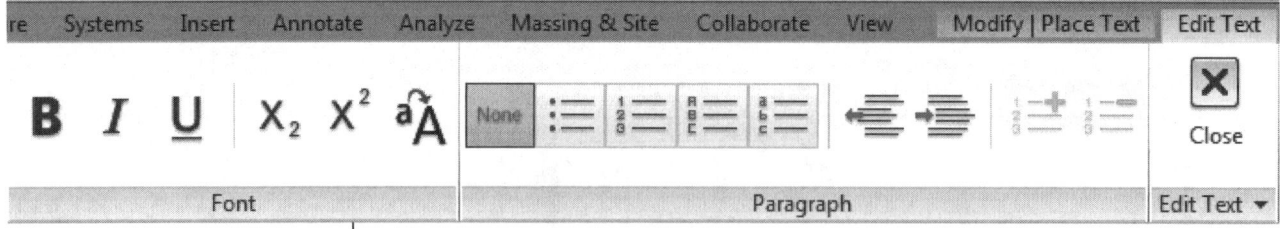

**Figure 15–39**

7. In the *Edit Text* tab>Edit Text panel, click **X** (Close) or click outside the text box to complete the text element.
   - Pressing <Enter> after a line of text starts a new line of text in the same text window.

## How To: Add Text Symbols

1. Start the **Text** command and click to place the text.
2. As you are typing text and need to insert a symbol, right-click and select **Symbols** from the shortcut menu. Select from the list of commonly used symbols, as shown in Figure 15–40.

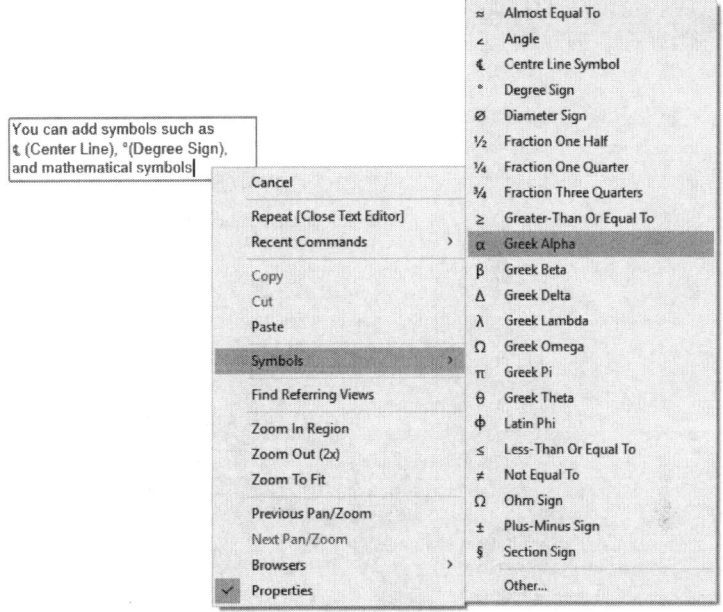

Figure 15–40

3. If the symbol you need is not listed, click **Other**.
4. In the Character Map dialog box, click on a symbol and click **Select**, as shown in Figure 15–41.

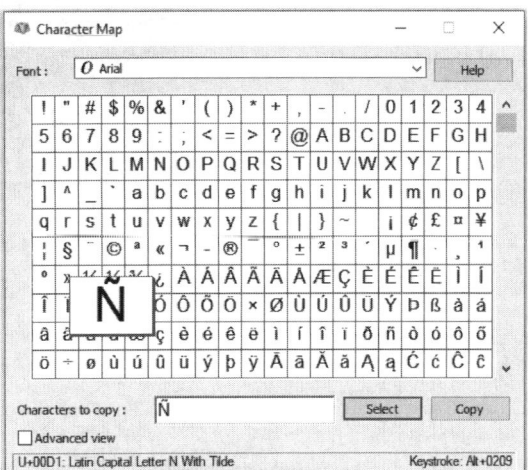

Figure 15–41

5. Click **Copy** to copy the character to the clipboard and paste it into the text box.

- The font in the Character Map should match the font used by the text type. You do not want to use a different font for symbols.

## Editing Text

Editing text notes takes place at two levels:

- Modifying the text note, which includes the **Leader** and **Paragraph** styles.

- Editing the text, which includes changes to individual letters, words, and paragraphs in the text note.

### Modifying the Text Note

Click once on the text note to modify the text box and leaders using controls, as shown in Figure 15–42, or using the tools in the *Modify | Text Notes* tab.

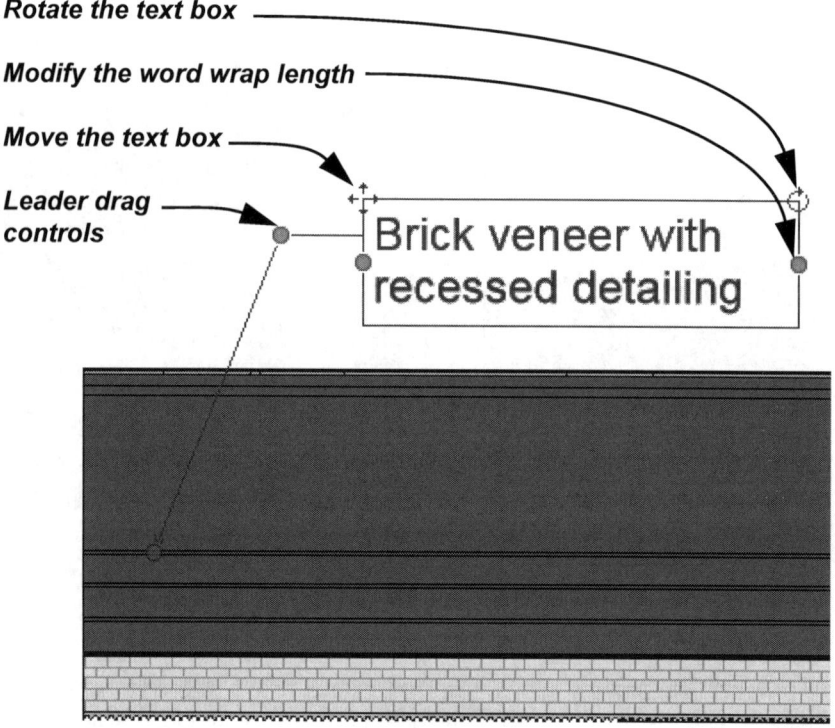

Figure 15–42

## How To: Add a Leader to Text Notes

1. Select the text note.
2. In the *Modify | Text Notes* tab>Leader panel, select the direction and justification for the new leader, as shown in Figure 15–43.
3. The leader is applied, as shown in Figure 15–44. Use the drag controls to place the arrow as needed.

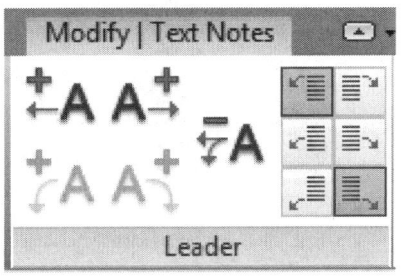

Figure 15–43

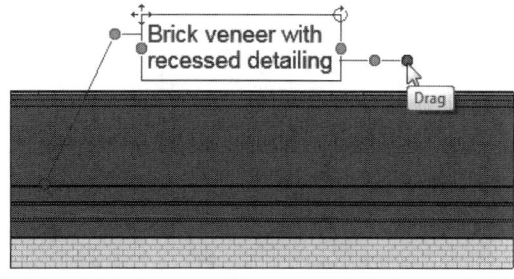

Figure 15–44

- You can remove leaders by clicking ⊼A (Remove Last Leader).

## Editing the Text

The *Edit Text* tab enables you to make various customizations. These include modifying the font of selected words as well as creating bulleted and numbered lists, as shown in Figure 15–45.

<u>General Notes</u>
1. Notify designer of intention to start construction at least 10 days prior to start of site work.
2. Installer shall provide the following:
    - 24-hour notice of start of construction
    - Inspection of bottom of bed or covering required by state inspector
    - All environmental management inspection sheets must be emailed to designer's office within 24 hours of inspection.

Figure 15–45

- You can **Cut**, **Copy**, and **Paste** text using the clipboard. For example, you can copy text from a document and then paste it into the text editor in Revit.

- To help you see the text better as you are modifying it, in the *Edit Text* tab, expand the Edit Text panel, and select one or both of the options, as shown in Figure 15–46.

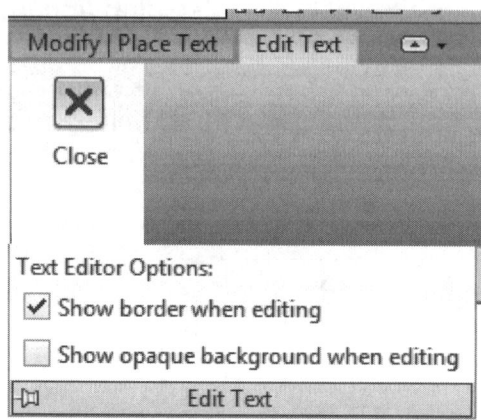

**Figure 15–46**

## How To: Modify the Font

1. Select individual letters or words.
2. Click on the font modification you want to include:

| **B** (Bold) | $X_2$ (Subscript) |
|---|---|
| *I* (Italic) | $X^2$ (Superscript) |
| U (Underline) | ªA (All Caps) |

- When pasting text from a document outside of Revit, font modifications (e.g, Bold, Italic, etc.) are retained.

## How To: Create Lists

1. In Edit Text mode, place the cursor in the line where you want to add to a list.
2. In the *Edit Text* tab>Paragraph panel, click the type of list you want to create:

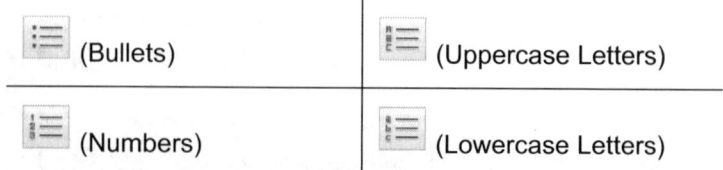

3. As you type, press <Enter> and the next line in the list is incremented.

# Working with Annotations

*The indent distance is set up by the text type Tab Size.*

4. To include sub-lists, at the beginning of the next line, click ▼≡ (Increase Indent) or press <Tab>. This indents the line and applies the next level of lists, as shown in Figure 15–47.

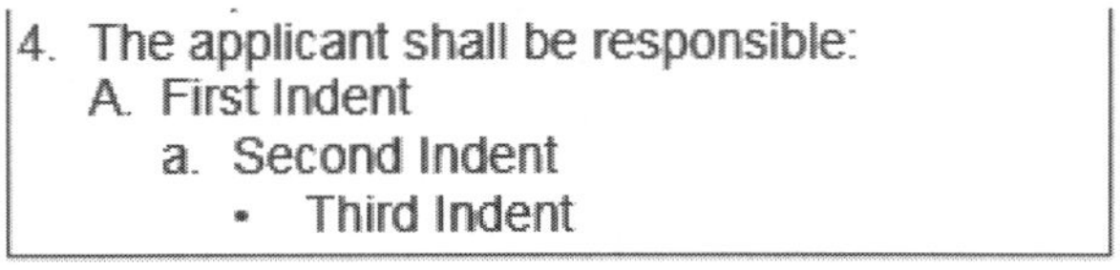

```
4. The applicant shall be responsible:
   A. First Indent
      a. Second Indent
         • Third Indent
```

**Figure 15–47**

- You can change the type of list after you have applied the first increment. For example, you might want to use a list of bullets instead of letters, as shown in Figure 15–48.

5. Click ▲≡ (Decrease Indent) or press <Shift>+<Tab> to return to the previous list style.

- Press <Shift>+<Enter> to create a blank line in a numbered list.

- To create columns or other separate text boxes that build on a numbering system (as shown in Figure 15–48), create the second text box and list, then place the cursor on one of the lines and in the Paragraph panel, click ≡↑ (Increment List Value) until the list matches the next number in the sequence.

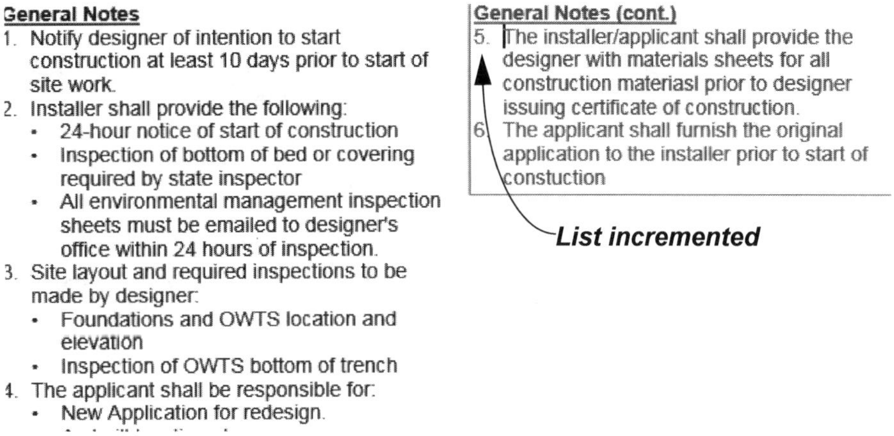

```
General Notes
1. Notify designer of intention to start
   construction at least 10 days prior to start of
   site work.
2. Installer shall provide the following:
   • 24-hour notice of start of construction
   • Inspection of bottom of bed or covering
     required by state inspector
   • All environmental management inspection
     sheets must be emailed to designer's
     office within 24 hours of inspection.
3. Site layout and required inspections to be
   made by designer:
   • Foundations and OWTS location and
     elevation
   • Inspection of OWTS bottom of trench
4. The applicant shall be responsible for:
   • New Application for redesign.

General Notes (cont.)
5. The installer/applicant shall provide the
   designer with materials sheets for all
   construction materiasl prior to designer
   issuing certificate of construction.
6. The applicant shall furnish the original
   application to the installer prior to start of
   constuction
```

— **List incremented**

**Figure 15–48**

6. Click ≡↓ (Decrement List Value) to move back a number.

> **Hint: Model Text**
>
> Model text is different from annotation text. It is designed to create full-size text on the model itself. For example, you would use model text to create a sign on a door, as shown in Figure 15–49. One model text type is included with the default template. You can create other types as needed.
>
>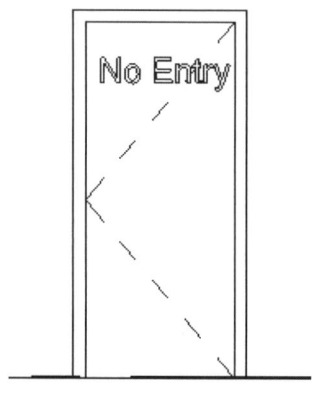
>
> **Figure 15–49**
>
> - Model text can be viewed in all views.
> - Model text is added from the *Architecture* tab>Model panel by clicking  (Model Text).

## Spell Checking

The Check Spelling dialog box displays any misspelled words in context and provides several options for changing them, as shown in Figure 15–50.

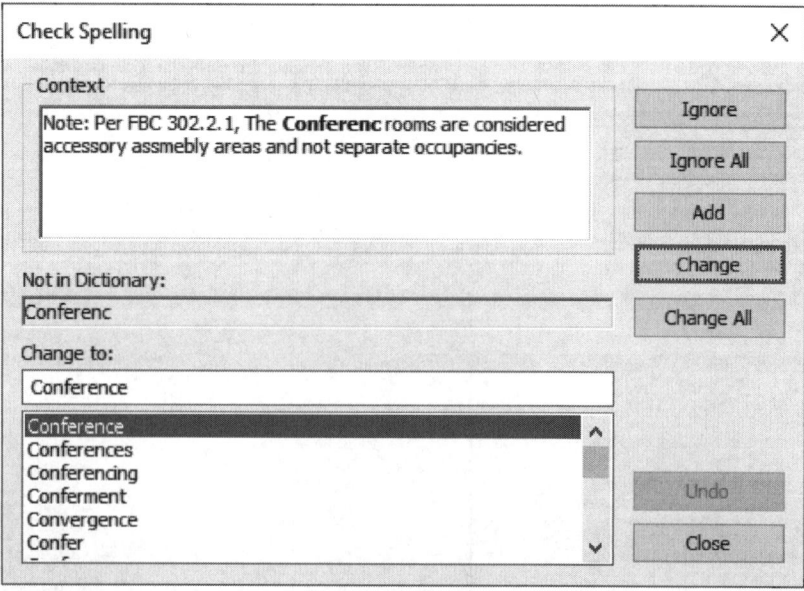

**Figure 15–50**

- Revit does not have active spell checking. It will only spell check when the command is activated.

- To spell check all text in a view, in the *Annotate* tab>Text panel, click ABC✓ (Spelling), or press <F7>. As with other spell checkers, you can **Ignore**, **Add**, or **Change** the word.

- You can also check the spelling in selected text. With text selected, in the *Modify | Text Notes* tab>Tools panel, click ABC✓ (Check Spelling).

## Creating Text Types

If you need new text types with a different text size or font (such as for a title or hand-lettering), you can create new ones, as shown in Figure 15–51. It is recommended that you create these in a project template so they are available in future projects.

<u>General Notes</u>

1. This project consists of furnishing and installing...

**Figure 15–51**

- You can copy and paste text types from one project to another or use **Transfer Project Standards**.

### How To: Create Text Types

1. In the *Annotate* tab>Text panel, click ⌐ (Text Types).
2. In the Type Properties dialog box, click **Duplicate**.
3. In the Name dialog box, type a new name and click **OK**.

4. Modify the text parameters, as needed. The parameters are shown in Figure 15–52.

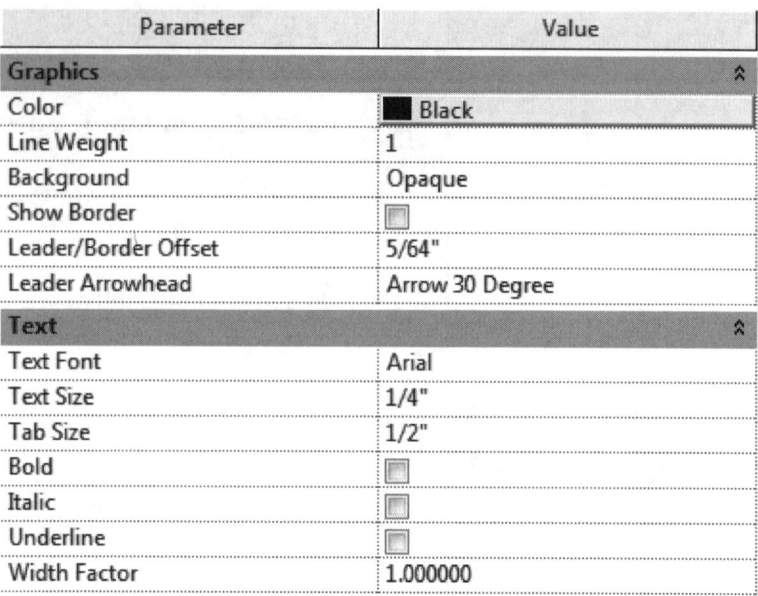

Figure 15–52

- The *Background* parameter can be set to **Opaque** or **Transparent**. An opaque background includes a masking region that hides lines or elements behind the text.

- In the *Text* area, the *Width Factor* parameter controls the width of the lettering, but does not affect the height. A width factor greater than **1** spreads the text out and a width factor less than **1** compresses it.

- The *Show Border* parameter, when selected, includes a rectangle around the text.

5. Click **OK** to close the Type Properties dialog box.

# Practice 15b | Work with Text

### Practice Objectives

- Create text types.
- Add text with and without leaders to a view.
- Add a numbered and bulleted list to a sheet.

In this practice, you will add text with and without leaders to a view. You will also add a text note with numbered and bulleted list on a site plan sheet, as shown in Figure 15–53.

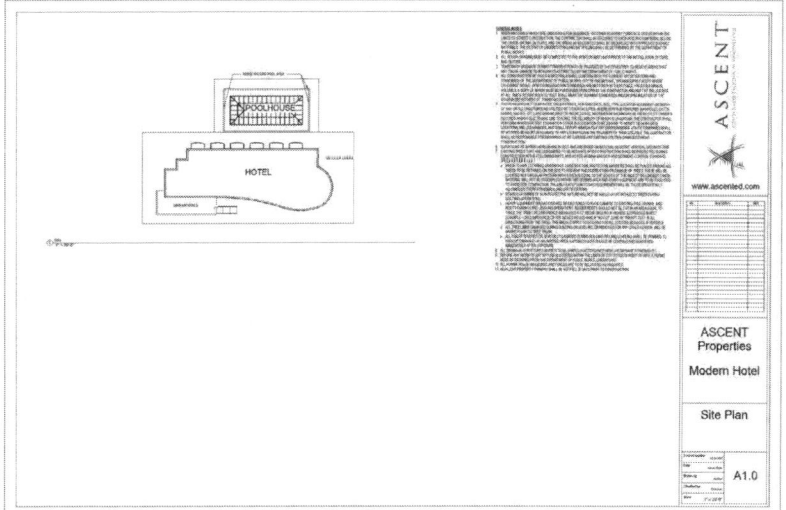

**Figure 15–53**

### Task 1 - Create text types.

1. Open the project **Hotel-Text.rvt** from the practice files folder.

2. In the *Annotate* tab>Text panel, click **A** (Text).

3. In Properties, click (Edit Type).

4. In the Type Properties dialog box, duplicate an existing text type and create new text types using the properties outlined below.

|  | 1/8" Arial | 1/8" Arial Narrow | 1/8" Arial Narrow Italic |
| --- | --- | --- | --- |
| Text Font | Arial | Arial Narrow | Arial |
| Text Size | 1/8" | 1/8" | 1/8" |
| Tab Size | 1/4" | 1/4" | 1/4" |
| Width Factor | 1.0 | 0.9 | .09 |
| Italic | No | No | Yes |

5. Click **OK**.
6. Save the project.

**Task 2 - Add text to a view.**

1. Open the **Floor Plans: Site** view.
2. In the *Annotate* tab>Text panel, click ![A] (Text).
3. In the Type Selector, select **Text: 1/4" Arial**.
4. Add titles for the hotel and poolhouse, as shown in Figure 15–54.
5. Change to **1/8" Arial Narrow** and add text for the other notes shown in Figure 15–54.

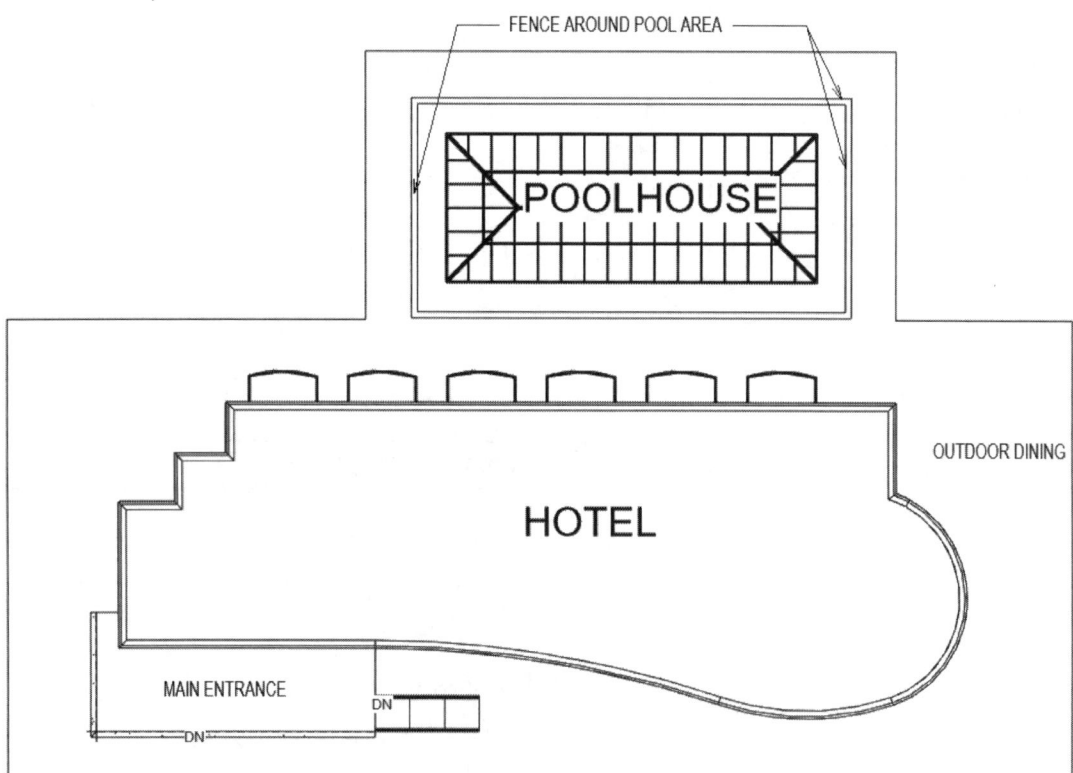

Figure 15–54

- To add the leaders to the fence around the pool text, select the text and in the *Modify | Text Notes* tab>Leader panel, click ![icon] (Add Left Side Straight Leader) and ![icon] (Add Right Side Straight Leader). Then, modify using the Drag controls as needed.

6. Save the project.

### Task 3 - Create a general note.

Note: In this task, you are placing the text directly on the sheet. Check your office standards, as using a Legend view for general notes might be preferred.

1. In the Project Browser, right-click on sheet **A0.0 Cover Sheet** and select **Duplicate Sheet>Duplicate Empty Sheet**. This creates a copy of the cover sheet with the titleblock and no views on it.

2. Rename the sheet **A1.0 - Site Plan**.

3. Add the **Floor Plans: Site** view to the sheet, as shown in Figure 15–55. The added text displays at the correct size for the sheet.

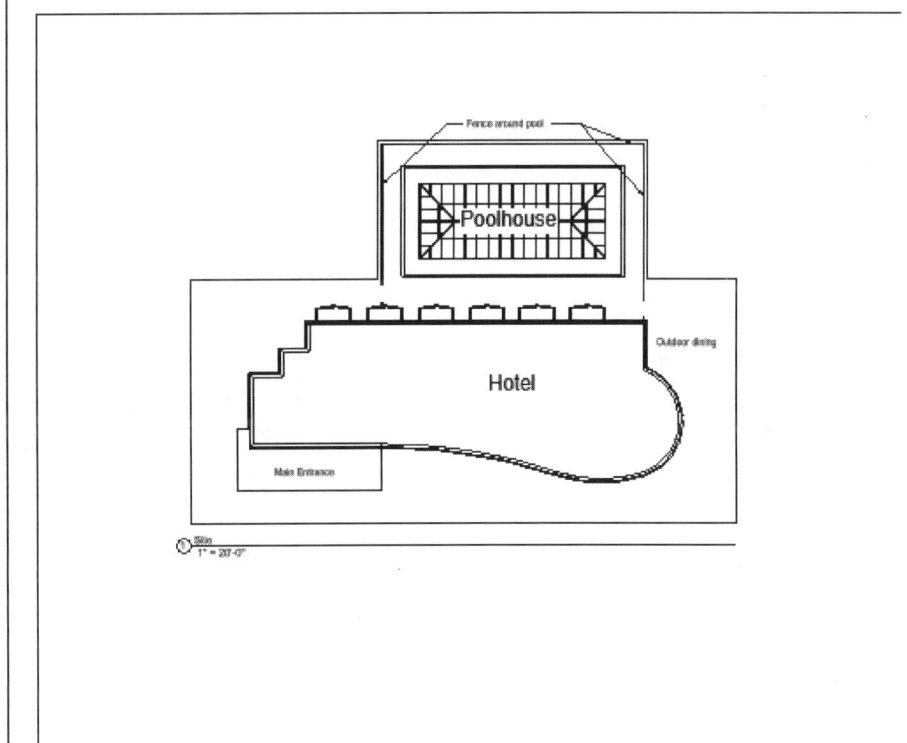

**Figure 15–55**

4. In a text editor (such as Word or Notepad), navigate to the practice files *Documents* folder and open either **General Notes.docx** or **General Notes.txt**.

The rest of the steps below are referencing the text copied from the General Notes.txt file.

5. Copy the entire contents of the file to the clipboard.

6. In Revit, start the **Text** command.

7. Verify that no leader is selected, set the text type to **1/8" Arial Narrow**, and draw a text box similar to the one shown in Figure 15–56.

**Figure 15–56**

8. In the Edit Text dialog box>Clipboard panel, click  (Paste).

9. Remain in Edit Text mode and zoom in on the text box. Note that there are numbered and lettered lists in the text, but the formatting is not quite correct.

10. Select all of the text and, in the *Edit Text* tab>Paragraph panel, click  (List: Numbers).

11. The paragraphs are recognized and numbered but some of the existing numbers are still there, as shown in Figure 15–57. You will need to delete the numbers that were copied in. If you copied the text from the Word doc, you will only see duplicate numbers on 8-11.

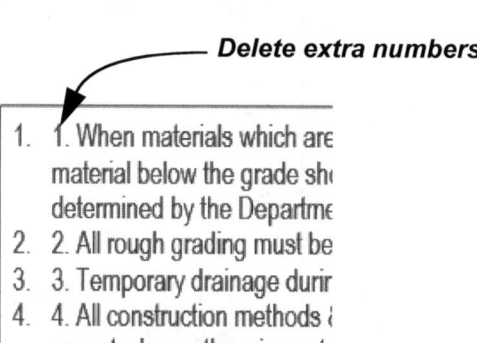

**Figure 15–57**

# Working with Annotations

12. Select the lettered paragraphs that are shown highlighted in Figure 15–58. In the *Edit Text* tab>Paragraph panel, click ▦ (Increase Indent). If you copied the text from the Word doc, the characters do not change.

**Figure 15–58**

13. This changes them to uppercase letters. In the *Edit Text* tab> Paragraph panel, click ▤ (List: Lowercase letters). This changes that list to a lettered list.

14. Zoom in and remove the additional characters, as shown in Figure 15–59.

**Figure 15–59**

15. At the beginning of the list, add the text **General Notes**. Make it bold and underlined, as shown in Figure 15–60.

<u>**General Notes**</u>
1. When materials which are unsuitable for subgrade, or other roadway purposes, occur within the limits of street construction, the contractor shall be required to excavate such material below the grade shown on plans, and the areas so excavated shall be backfilled with approved suitable materials. The extent of undercutting and backfilling shall be determined by the Department of Public Works.
2. All rough grading must be completed to the right-of-way limits prior to the installation of curb and gutter.
3. Temporary drainage during construction to be provided by the Developer to relieve areas that may cause damage to roadways as directed by the Department of Public Works
4. All construction methods & materials shall conform with the current specifications and standards of the Department of Public Works, City of Chesapeake, Virginia (DPW) except where otherwise noted. DPW's construction standards are set forth in their Public Facilities Manual, Volume II. A copy of which must be purchased from DPW by the Contractor and kept at the job site at all times. References to VDOT shall mean the current standards and/or specification of the Virginia Department of Transportation.

**Figure 15–60**

16. Click outside the text box and use the controls if needed to relocate or resize the text note.

17. Zoom out to see the full sheet.

18. Save and close the project.

# 15.3 Adding Detail Lines and Symbols

While annotating views for construction documents, you might need to add detail lines and symbols to clarify the design intent or show information, such as the life safety plan exit information, as shown in Figure 15–61.

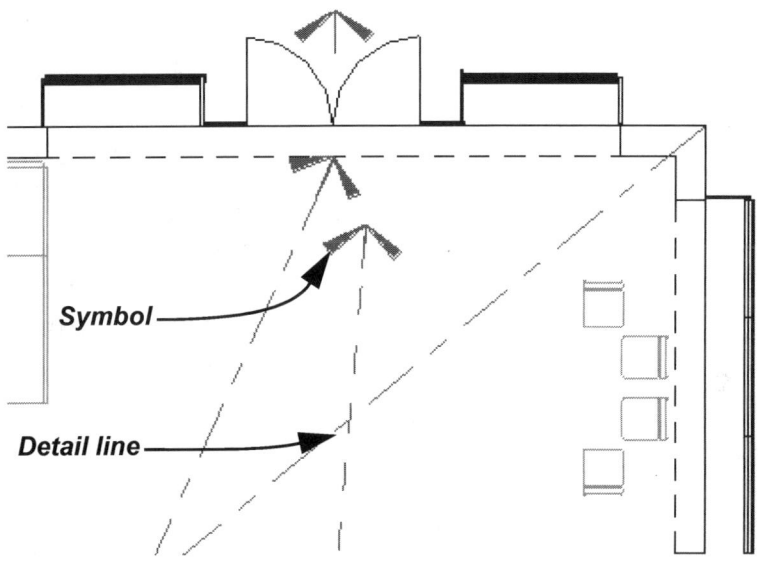

**Figure 15–61**

- Detail lines and symbols are view-specific, which means that they only display in the view in which they were created.

## How To: Draw a Detail Line

1. In the *Annotation* tab>Detail panel, click (Detail Line).
2. In the *Modify | Place Detail Lines* tab>Line Style panel, select the type of line you want to use, as shown in Figure 15–62.

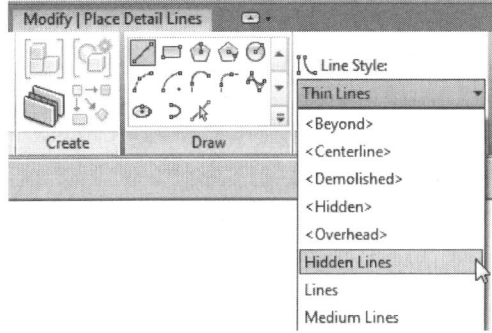

**Figure 15–62**

3. Use the tools in the Draw panel to create the detail line.

# Using Symbols

*Symbols are 2D elements that only display in one view, while components can be in 3D and display in many views.*

Many of the annotations used in working drawings are frequently repeated. Several of them have been saved as symbols in Revit, such as the North Arrow, Center Line, and Graphic Scale annotations shown in Figure 15–63.

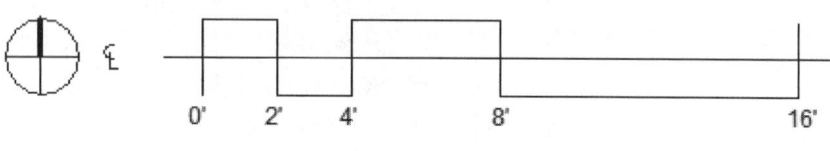

**Figure 15–63**

- You can also create or load custom annotation symbols.

## How To: Place a Symbol

1. In the *Annotate* tab>Symbol panel, click ⊕ (Symbol).
2. In the Type Selector, select the symbol you want to use.
3. In the Options Bar (shown in Figure 15–64), set the *Number of Leaders* and select **Rotate after placement** if you want to rotate the symbol as you insert it.

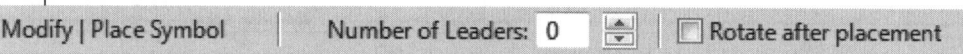

**Figure 15–64**

4. Place the symbol in the view. Rotate it if you selected the **Rotate after placement** option. If you specified leaders, use the controls to move them into place.

- In the *Annotate* tab>Symbol panel, click ▥ (Stair Path) to label the slope direction and walk line of a stair, as shown in Figure 15–65.

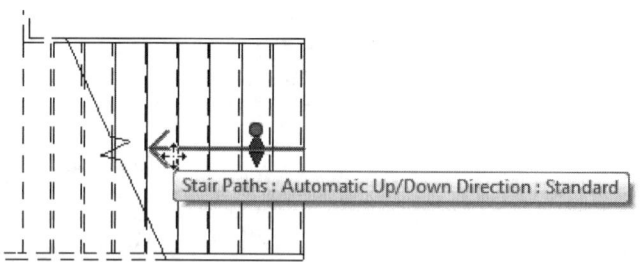

**Figure 15–65**

- For information about adding tags to dependent views, see *B.4 Annotating Dependent Views*.

# Practice 15c | Add Detail Lines and Symbols

## Practice Objectives

- Add detail lines.
- Add symbols.

In this practice, you will modify a site plan by adding detail lines to lay out the utilities. You will also add symbols for a power pole and north arrow, as shown in Figure 15–66.

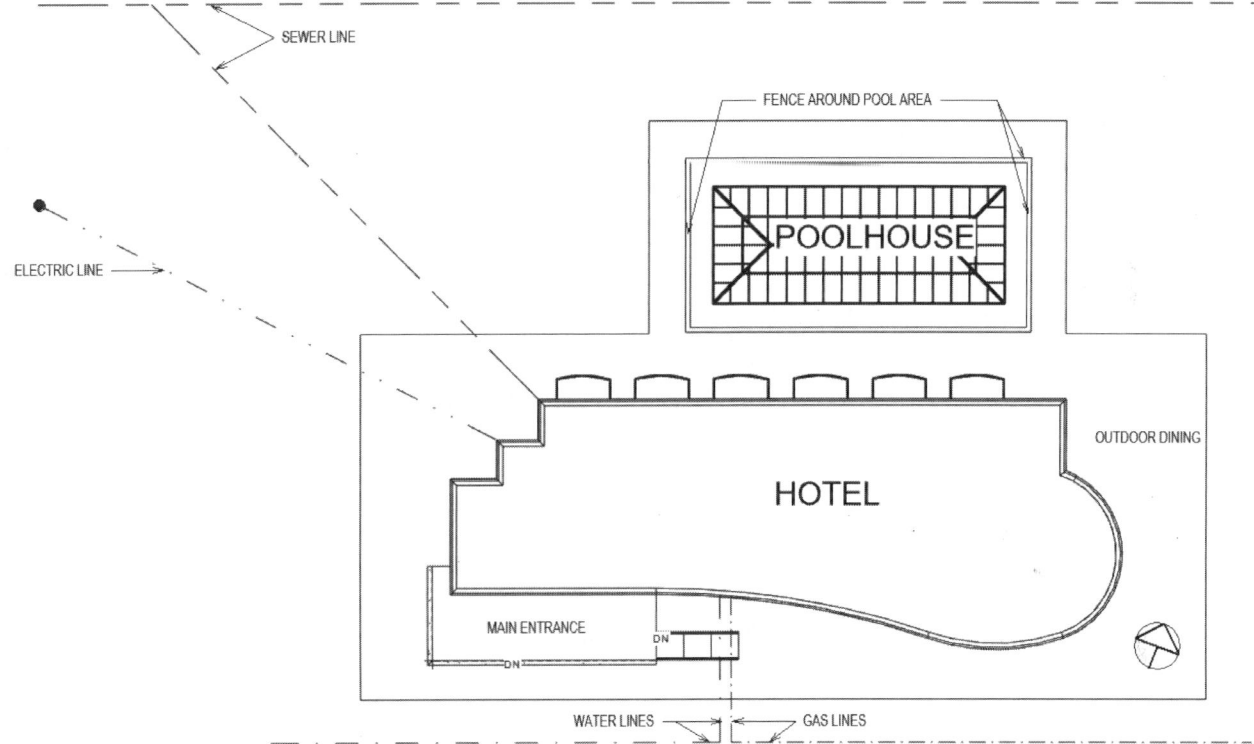

Figure 15–66

### Task 1 - Create a utilities plan using detail lines.

1. Open the project **Hotel-Symbols.rvt** from the practice files folder.

2. Open the **Floor Plans: Site** view.

3. In the *Annotate* tab>Detail panel, click (Detail Line).

4. In the *Modify | Place Detail Lines* tab>Line Style panel, set the *Line Style:* to **Sewer Line**.

5. In the Options Bar, clear the **Chain** option.

6. Draw a diagonal line from the corner of the building, as shown in Figure 15–67.

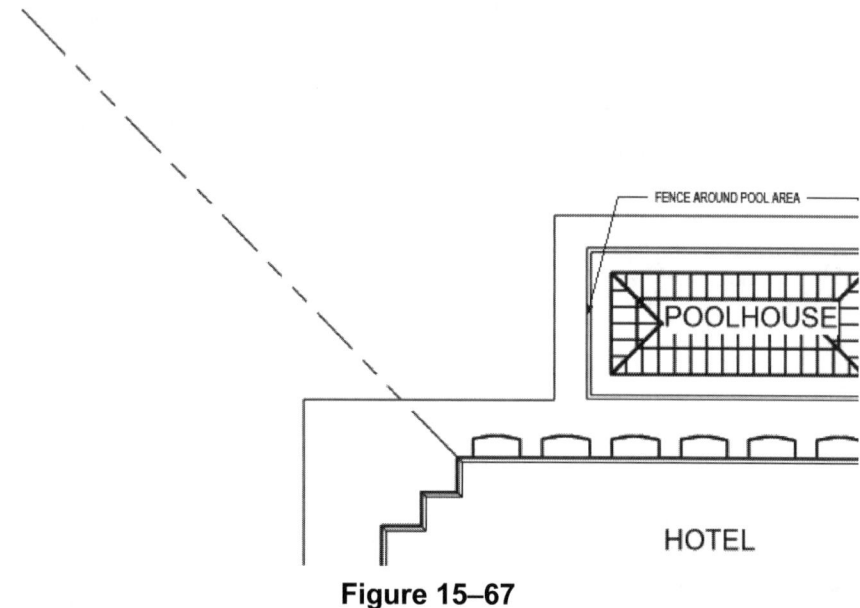

**Figure 15–67**

7. In the *Annotate* tab>Detail panel, click (Detail Line).

8. In the *Modify | Place Detail Lines* tab>Line Style panel, set the *Line Style:* to **Sewer Line**.

9. Select the **Pick Lines** tool from the Draw panel.

10. In the Options Bar, set the *Offset* to **25'**.

11. Hover your cursor over the edge of the floor above the poolhouse (as shown in Figure 15–68) and click when you see the dashed alignment line above the poolhouse area.

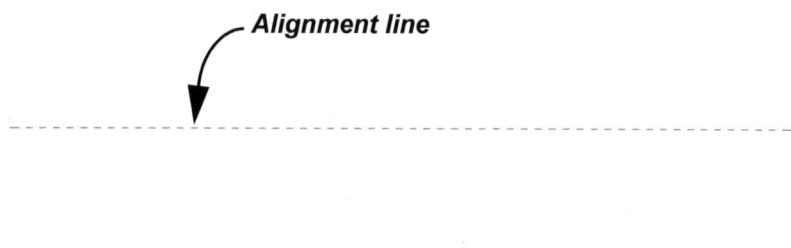

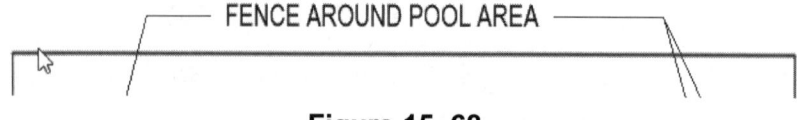

**Figure 15–68**

12. Press <Esc> once. Select the sewer line and stretch it out so that it intersects with the diagonal sewer line, as shown in Figure 15–69.

13. Change the *Line Style* and add **Electric Lines, Water Lines,** and **Gas Lines**, as shown in Figure 15–69.

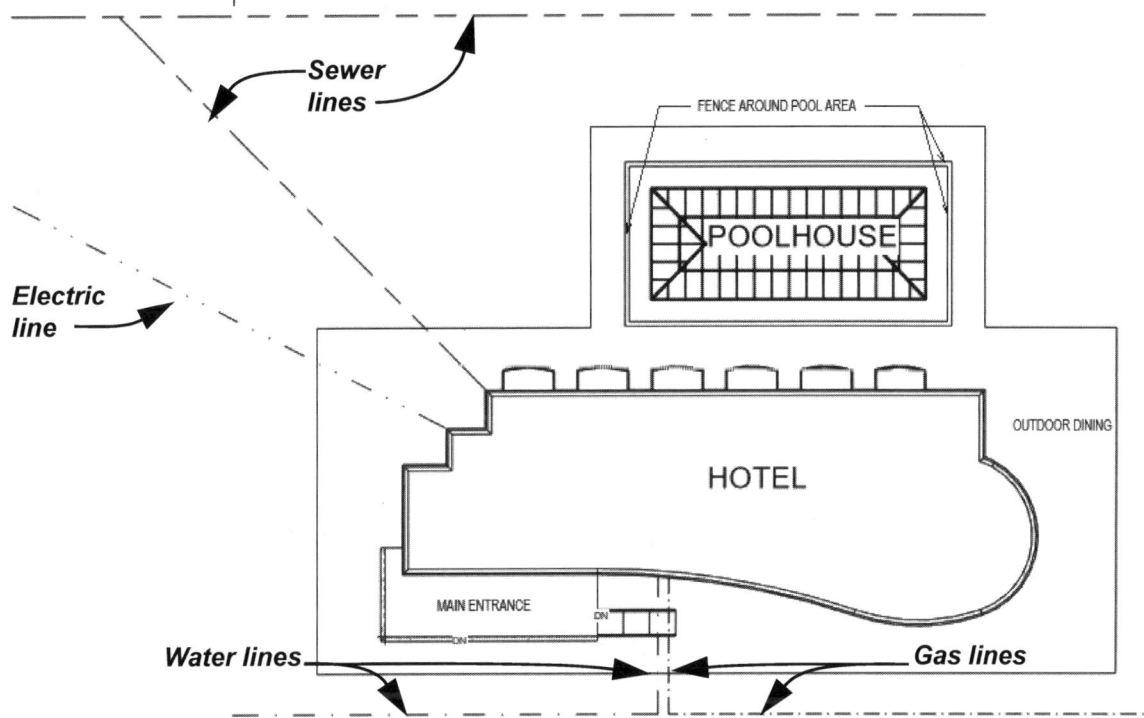

**Figure 15–69**

14. Add text to label them as needed.

15. Save the project.

### Task 2 - Add symbols.

1. In the *Annotate* tab>Symbol panel, click (Symbol).

2. In the *Modify | Place Symbol* tab>Mode panel, click (Load Family).

3. In the Load Family dialog box, navigate to your practice files *Families>Annotation* folder. Select **Power Pole Symbol.rfa** and click **Open**.

4. Add a power pole at the end of the electric line, as shown in Figure 15–70.

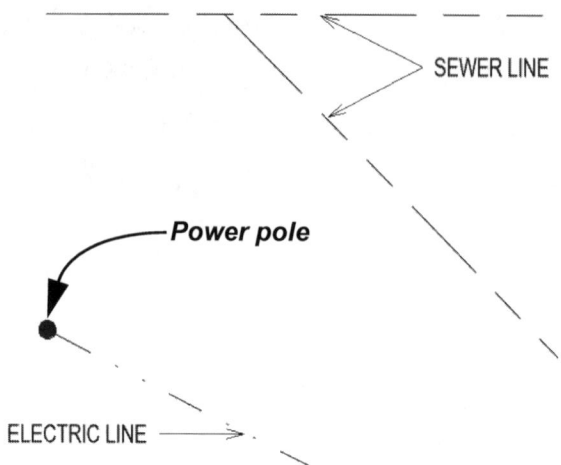

Figure 15–70

5. While still in the **Symbol** command, in the Type Selector, select **North Arrow 1** and place a north arrow to the lower-right side of the hotel.

6. Press <Esc> twice.

7. Select the north arrow and rotate it 20°, as shown in Figure 15–71.

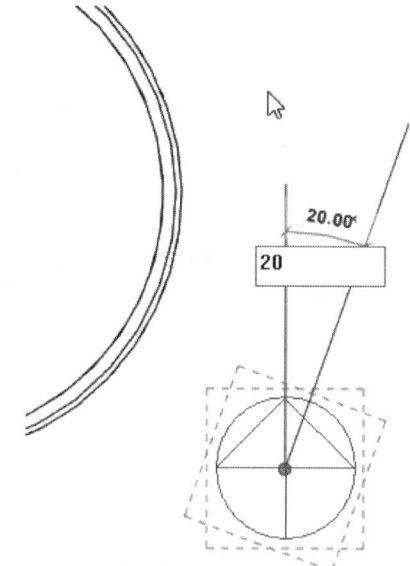

Figure 15–71

8. Open sheet **A1.0 - Site Plan**. Select the viewport and, in Properties, change the view scale to **1/16"=1'-0"**. Move the view and view title as needed.

9. Save and close the project.

Working with Annotations

## 15.4 Creating Legends

A legend is a separate view that can be placed on multiple sheets. Legends can be used to hold installation notes that need to be placed on a sheet with each floor plan, key plans, or any 2D items that need to be repeated. You can also create and list the annotations, line styles, and symbols that are used in your project, and provide explanatory notes next to the symbol, as shown in Figure 15–72. Additionally, legends can provide a list of materials or elevations of window types used in the project.

*The elements in this figure are inserted using the **Symbol** command rather that the **Legend Component** or **Detail Component** commands.*

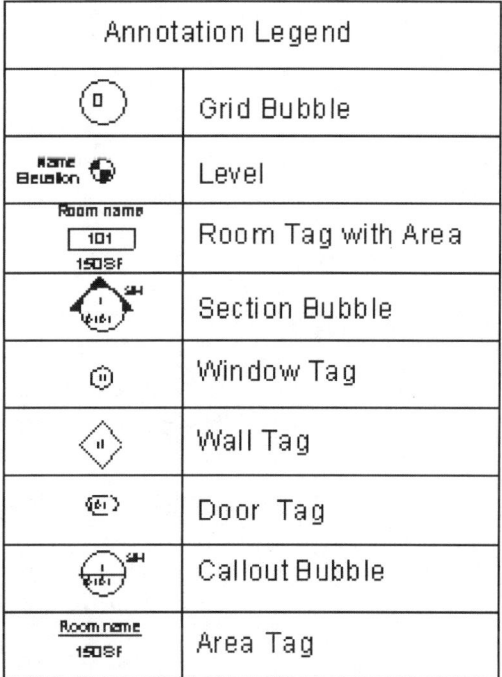

Figure 15–72

- You use  (Detail Line) and  (Text) to create the table and explanatory notes. Once you have a legend view, you can use commands, such as  (Legend Component),  (Detail Component), and  (Symbol), to place elements in the view.

- Unlike other views, legend views can be attached to more than one sheet.

- You can set a legend's scale in the View Control Bar.

- Elements in legends can be dimensioned.

## How To: Create a Legend

1. In the *View* tab>Create panel, expand  (Legends) and click  (Legend), or in the Project Browser, right-click on the *Legends* area title and select **Legend**.
2. In the New Legend View dialog box, enter a name and select a scale for the legend, as shown in Figure 15–73, then click **OK**.

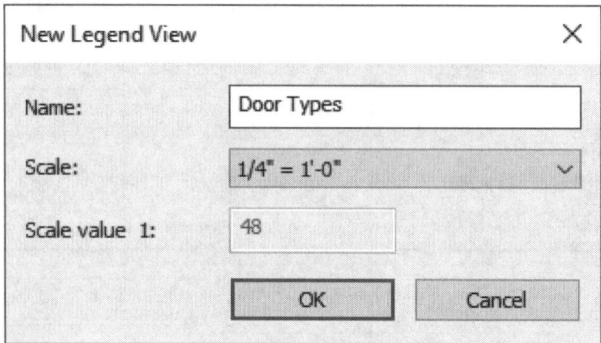

Figure 15–73

3. Place the components in the view first, and then sketch the outline of the table when you know the sizes. Use the **Reference Plane** command to line up the components.

## How To: Use Legend Components

1. In the *Annotate* tab>Detail panel, expand  (Component) and click  (Legend Component).
2. In the Options Bar, select the *Family* type that you want to use, as shown in Figure 15–74.

    - This list contains all of the elements in the project that can be used in a legend. For example, you might want to display the elevation of all door types used in the project.

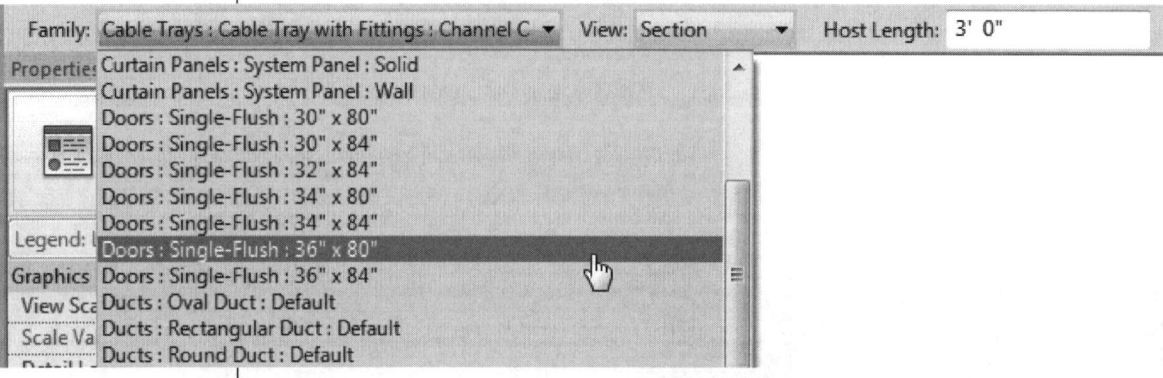

Figure 15–74

3. Select the *View* of the element that you want to use. For example, you might want to display the section of the floors or roofs, and the front elevation of the doors (as shown in Figure 15–75) and windows.

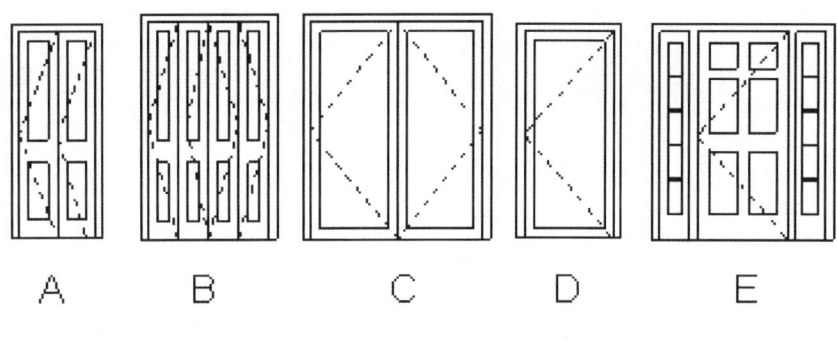

**Figure 15–75**

4. For section elements (such as walls, floors, and roofs), type a distance for the *Host Length*.

- Elements that are full size, such as planting components or doors, come in at their full size.

- Legends are views that can be placed on multiple sheets. You can use **Copy to the Clipboard** and **Paste** to copy legends from sheet to sheet.

# Practice 15d  Create Legends

## Practice Objective

- Create legends using legend components and text.

In this practice, you will create door and window legends (as shown in Figure 15–76) by creating legend views, adding legend components, and labeling the door and window types with text.

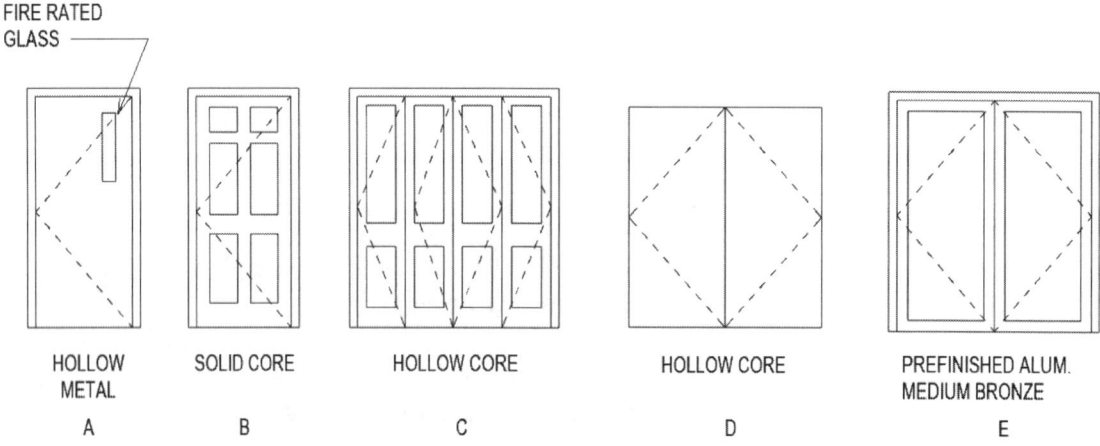

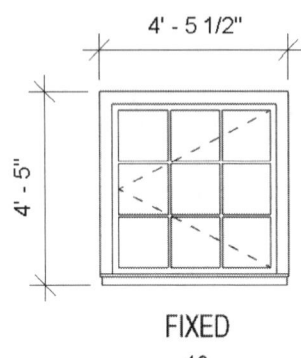

Figure 15–76

1. Open the project **Hotel-Legends.rvt** from the practice files folder.

2. In the *View* tab>Create panel, expand (Legends) and click (Legend) to create a new legend view.

# Working with Annotations

3. Name it **Window Elevations** and set the *Scale* to **1/4"=1'-0"**.

4. In the *Annotate* tab>Detail panel, expand (Component) and click (Legend Component).

5. In the Options Bar, set *Family* to **Windows: Casement 3 x 3 with Trim: 48" x 48"** and *View* to **Elevation: Front**. Place the component in the view. The window displays.

6. Click (Modify).

7. In the *Annotate* tab>Text panel, click (Text).

8. In the Type Selector, select **Text: 3/32" Arial**. Add **Fixed** and the window number **13** under the window.

9. Add dimensions and the note shown in Figure 15–77.

   - If needed, use the **Door and Window Notes.txt** or **Door and Window Notes.docx** found in the practice files *Documents* folder to quickly add the text notes.

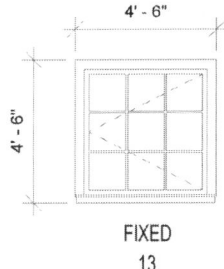

NOTE: WINDOWS SHALL BE PREFINISHED ALUMINUM MEDIUM BRONZE.

**Figure 15–77**

10. Create another legend view. Name it **Door Elevations** and set the *Scale* to **1/4"=1'-0"**.

11. In the legend view, click (Legend Component) and add the elevations of the doors used in the project.

12. Label the doors as shown in Figure 15–78.

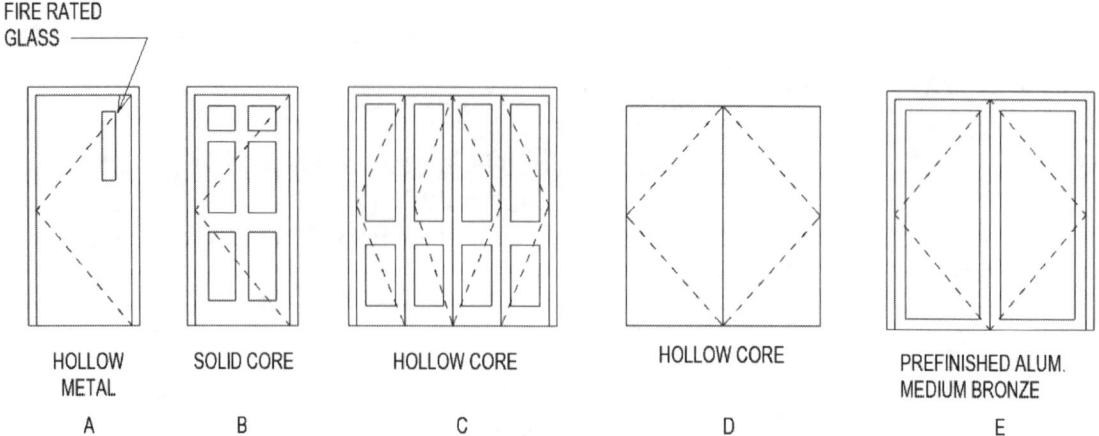

NOTE:
1. REFER TO MANUAL SECTION 09300 FOR LOCKING SYSTEM HARDWARE SETS.
2. REFER TO PROJECT MANUAL SECTION 09200 (2.2 INTERIOR WOOD PANEL DOORS) FOR GUEST SUITE ENTRANCE DOOR SPECIFICATIONS.

**Figure 15–78**

13. Save and close the project.

# Chapter Review Questions

1. When a wall is moved (as shown in Figure 15–79), how do you update the dimension?

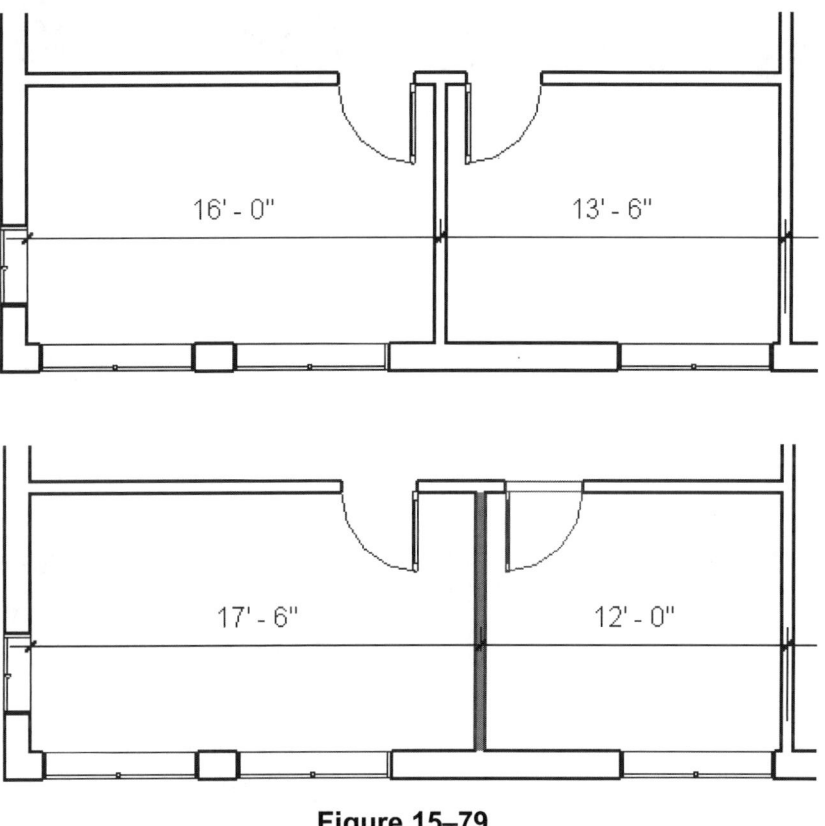

**Figure 15–79**

   a. Edit the dimension and move it over.
   b. Select the dimension and then click **Update** in the Options Bar.
   c. The dimension automatically updates.
   d. Delete the existing dimension and add a new one.

2. How do you create new text styles?

   a. Using the **Text Styles** command.
   b. Duplicate an existing type.
   c. They must be included in a template.
   d. Using the **Format Styles** command.

3. When you edit text, how many leaders can be added using the leader tools shown in Figure 15–80?

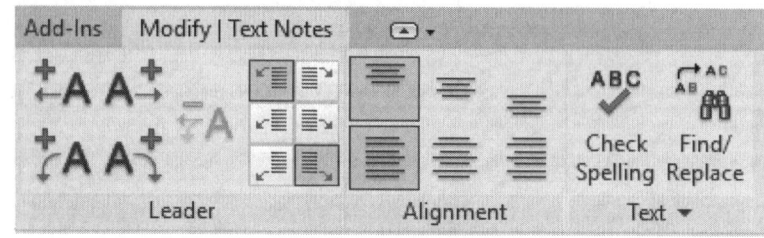

Figure 15–80

   a. One

   b. One on each end of the text

   c. As many as you want at each end of the text

4. Detail lines created in one view also display in the related view.

   a. True

   b. False

5. Which of the following describes the difference between a symbol and a component?

   a. Symbols are 3D and only display in one view. Components are 2D and display in many views.

   b. Symbols are 2D and only display in one view. Components are 3D and display in many views.

   c. Symbols are 2D and display in many views. Components are 3D and only display in one view.

   d. Symbols are 3D and display in many views. Components are 2D and only display in one view.

6. When creating a legend, which of the following elements cannot be added?

   a. Legend components

   b. Tags

   c. Rooms

   d. Symbols

# Command Summary

| Button | Command | Location |
|---|---|---|
| | **Dimensions and Text** | |
| | Aligned (Dimension) | • **Ribbon:** *Annotate* tab>Dimension panel or *Modify* tab>Measure panel, expanded drop-down list<br>• **Quick Access Toolbar**<br>• **Shortcut:** DI |
| | Angular (Dimension) | • **Ribbon:** *Annotate* tab>Dimension panel or *Modify* tab>Measure panel, expanded drop-down list |
| | Arc Length (Dimension) | • **Ribbon:** *Annotate* tab>Dimension panel or *Modify* tab>Measure panel, expanded drop-down list |
| | Diameter (Dimension) | • **Ribbon:** *Annotate* tab>Dimension panel or *Modify* tab>Measure panel, expanded drop-down list |
| | Linear (Dimension) | • **Ribbon:** *Annotate* tab>Dimension panel or *Modify* tab>Measure panel, expanded drop-down list |
| | Radial (Dimension) | • **Ribbon:** *Annotate* tab>Dimension panel or *Modify* tab>Measure panel, expanded drop-down list |
| | Text | • **Ribbon:** *Annotate* tab>Text panel<br>• **Shortcut:** TX |
| | **Detail Lines and Symbols** | |
| | Detail Line | • **Ribbon:** *Annotate* tab>Detail panel<br>• **Shortcut:** DL |
| | Stair Path | • **Ribbon:** *Annotate* tab>Symbol panel |
| | Symbol | • **Ribbon:** *Annotate* tab>Symbol panel |
| | **Legends** | |
| | Legend (View) | • **Ribbon:** *View* tab>Create panel, expand Legends |
| | Legend Component | • **Ribbon:** *Annotate* tab>Detail panel, expand Component |

# Chapter 16

# Adding Tags and Schedules

Adding tags to your views helps you to identify elements such as doors, windows, or walls in the model. Tags are 2D annotation families with labels that extract information about the elements being tagged from its properties. Tags are typically added when you insert an element, but can also be added at any point of the design process. The information captured in the elements in a project is used to populate schedules, which can be added to sheets to complete the construction documents.

## Learning Objectives in This Chapter

- Add tags to elements in 2D and 3D views to prepare the views to be placed on sheets.
- Load tags that are required for projects.
- Modify schedule content including the instance and type properties of related elements.
- Add schedules to sheets as part of the construction documents.

# 16.1 Adding Tags

Tags identify elements that are listed in schedules. Door and window tags are inserted automatically if you use the **Tag on Placement** option when inserting the door or window or other elements. You can also add them later to specific views as needed. Many other types of tags are available in Revit, such as wall tags and furniture tags, as shown in Figure 16–1.

*Additional tags are stored in the Revit Library in the Annotations folder.*

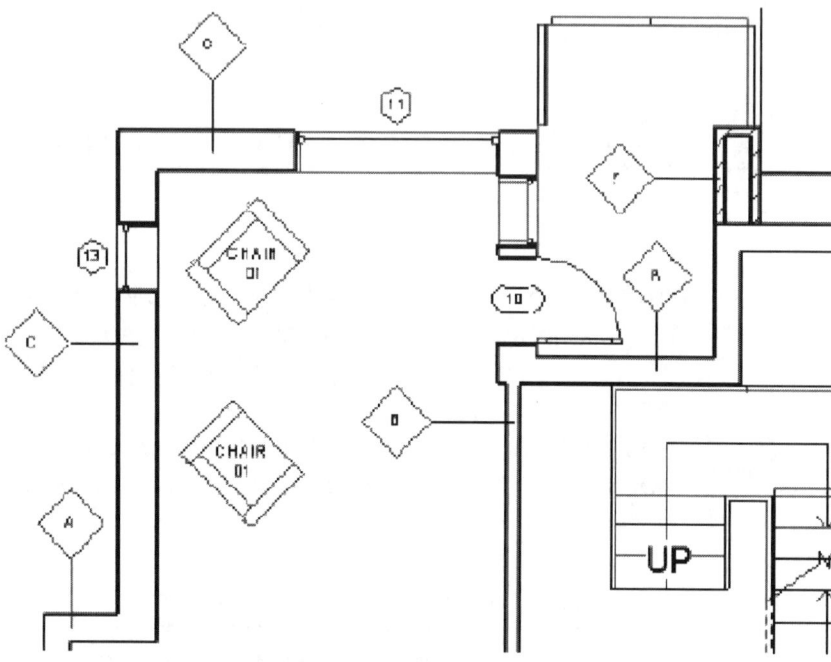

Figure 16–1

- The **Tag by Category** command works for most elements, except for a few that have separate commands.

- Tags can be letters, numbers, or a combination of the two.

You can place three types of tags, as follows:

- (Tag by Category): Tags according to the category of the element. It places door tags on doors and wall tags on walls.

- (Multi-Category Tag): Tags elements belonging to multiple categories. The tags display information from parameters that they have in common.

- (Material Tag): Tags that display the type of material. They are typically used in detailing.

## How To: Add Tags

1. In the *Annotate* tab>Tag panel, click ⬡ (Tag by Category), ⬡ (Multi-Category Tag), or ⬡ (Material Tag) depending on the type of tag you want to place.

2. In the Options Bar, set the options as needed, as shown in Figure 16–2.

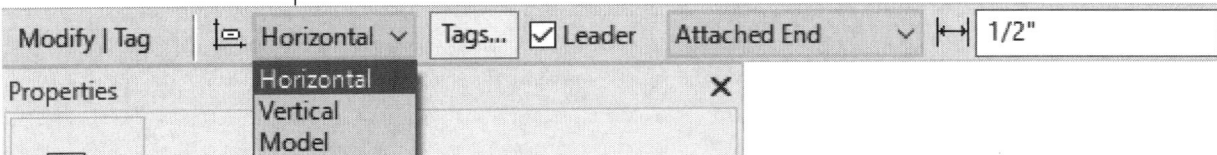

Figure 16–2

3. Select the element you want to tag. If a tag for the selected element is not loaded, you are prompted to load it from the Revit Library.

## Tag Options

- In the Options Bar, you can set tag options for leaders and tag orientation, as shown in Figure 16–3. You can also press <Spacebar> to toggle the rotation while placing or modifying the tag.

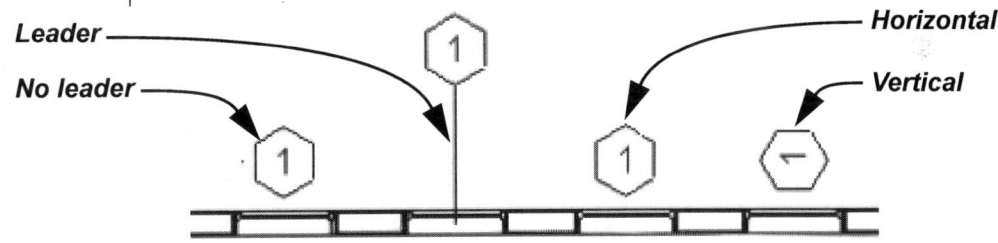

Figure 16–3

- Tag orientation can be set to the following:

  - **Horizontal:** Stays horizontal (0°) to the element it is tagging.
  - **Vertical:** Forces the tag to stay vertical (90°) to the element it is tagging no matter what.
  - **Model:** Rotates freely from the element, similar to room tags.

- Leaders can have an **Attached End** or a **Free End**, as shown in Figure 16–4. The attached end must be connected to the element being tagged. A free end has an additional drag control where the leader touches the element.

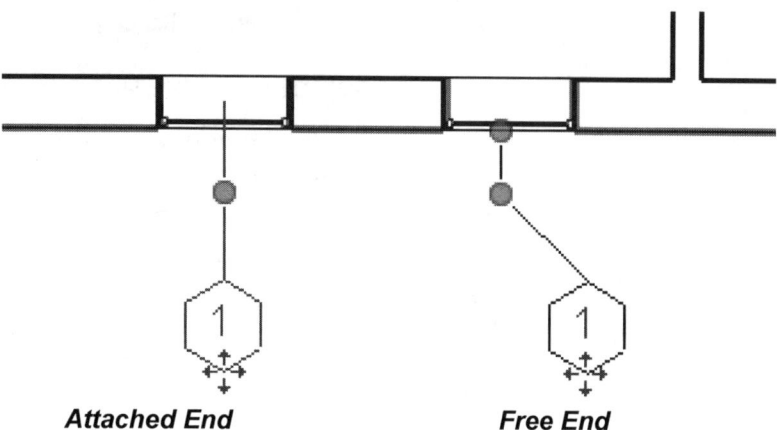

Figure 16–4

- If you change between **Attached End** and **Free End**, the tag does not move and the leader does not change location.

- The **Length** option specifies the length of the leader in plotting units. It is grayed out if **Leader** is not selected or if a **Free End** leader is defined.

- If a tag is not loaded, a warning box opens, as shown in Figure 16–5. Click **Yes** to open the Load Family dialog box in which you can select the appropriate tag.

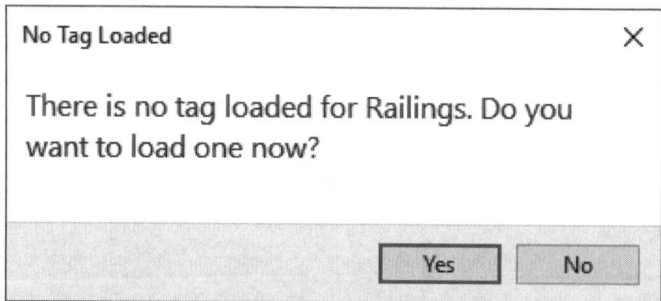

Figure 16–5

- Tags can be pinned to stay in place if you move the element that is tagged. This is primarily used when tags have leaders, as shown in Figure 16–6.

# Adding Tags and Schedules

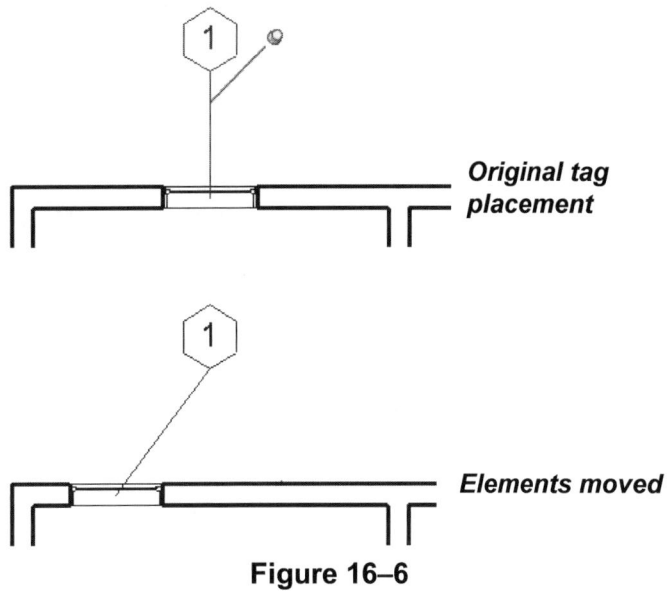

Figure 16–6

## Multi-Leader Tags

If you have elements that need to be tagged that are in close proximity to one another, you can tag one element and then select other similar elements. This adds more leader lines from the elements to the tag, as shown with the windows in Figure 16–7. When selecting the tag, in Properties you can see how many host elements it is tagging (as shown in Figure 16–7).

You cannot select elements that are of different categories, like windows and doors. You can only select similar elements to tag, like all windows or all doors.

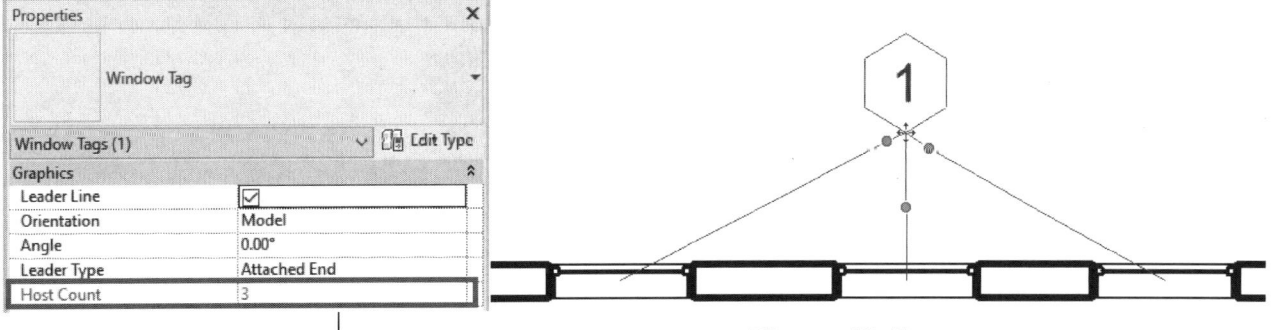

Figure 16–7

You can modify how the leaders are displayed when using the multi-leader tags. You can adjust how they will display in the view by showing all leaders, hiding select leaders, or hiding all leaders.

| | |
|---|---|
| (Show All Leaders) | This turns on all leaders of any tag that is selected that used Multi-Leader tagging. |
| (Hide All Leaders) | This turns off all leaders of any tag that is selected that used Multi-Leader tagging. |
| (Show One Leader) | This turns off all leaders except for one leader of any tag that is selected that used Multi-Leader tagging. |
| (Select Leaders to Show) | This puts you into edit mode and enables you to select specific leaders to show or hide. When finished, you need to click (Finish). |
| (Merge Leaders) | Select to turn this feature on. This will merge all the leader line elbows to one location on the main leader line. You will not have the ability to adjust the leader lines individually. To get the leader line elbows back, select the **Merge Leaders** icon. |

### How To: Add a Multi-Leader Tag

1. Start the **Tag by Category** command.
2. Set the Options Bar settings.
3. Tag one element in the model.
4. Verify **Add/Remove Host** is on, as shown in Figure 16–8.

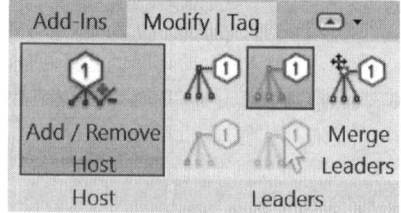

**Figure 16–8**

5. Select the other similar elements to add to the tag.

# Adding Tags and Schedules

- Alternatively, if you have a tag already placed in the model and you want to add elements to the tag, select the tag, and in the contextual tab, click  (Add/Remove Host), then select the other elements.

6. Set the leaders options as needed.
7. A leader line will be added for each element you select.

## How To: Remove Elements from a Multi-Leader Tag

1. To remove an element from the tag, select the tag and in the ribbon, select  (Add/Remove Host).
2. Select the element in the model. The leader line is removed.

## Room Tags

If tags were not added to a room when they were created or you wish to add room tags to another view, you must to use a specific command. In the *Architecture* tab>Room & Area panel, click  (Tag Room).

- Alternatively, in the *Annotate* tab>Tag panel, click  (Room Tag), or type **RT**.
- You can change the name or number by clicking on the tag text to edit it, as shown in Figure 16–9.

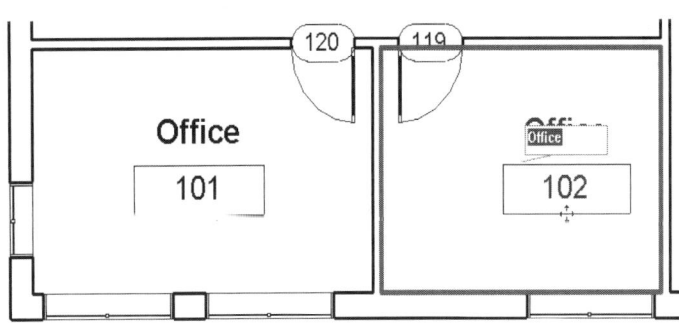

Figure 16–9

*To tag only some elements, select them before starting this command. In the Tag All Not Tagged dialog box, select **Only selected objects in current view**.*

## How To: Add Multiple Tags

1. In the *Annotate* tab>Tag panel, click (Tag All).
2. In the Tag All Not Tagged dialog box (shown in Figure 16–10), select the checkbox beside one or more categories to tag. Selecting the checkbox beside the *Category* title selects all of the tags.

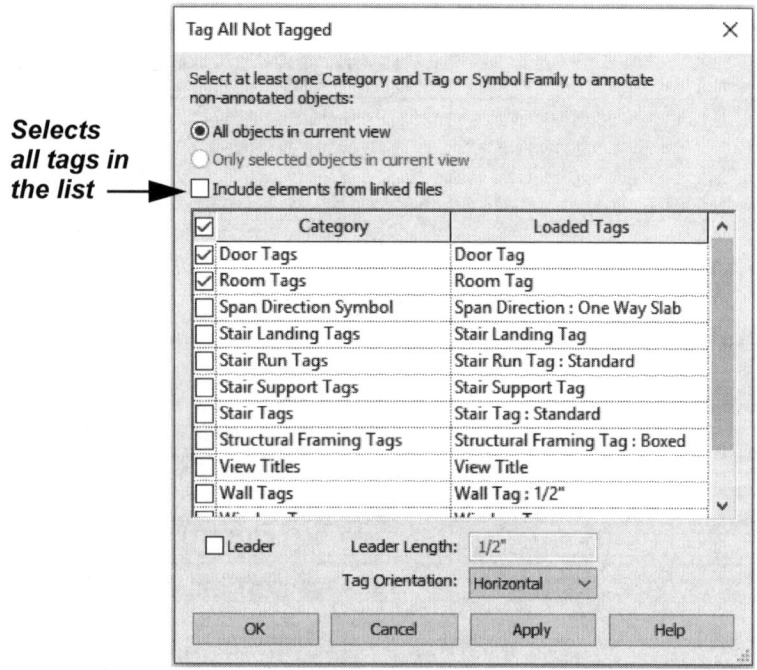

*Selects all tags in the list*

**Figure 16–10**

3. Set the *Leader* and *Tag Orientation* as needed.
4. Click **Apply** to apply the tags and stay in the dialog box. Click **OK** to apply the tags and close the dialog box.

- When you select a tag, the properties of that tag display. To display the properties of the tagged element, in the *Modify* contextual tab>Host panel, click (Select Host).

- Rooms can be tagged using **Tag All Not Tagged**.

# Adding Tags and Schedules

## How To: Load Tags

1. In the *Annotate* tab, expand the Tag panel and click (Loaded Tags And Symbols) or, when a Tag command is active, in the Options Bar, click **Tags...**.
2. In the Loaded Tags And Symbols dialog box (shown in Figure 16–11), click **Load Family...**.

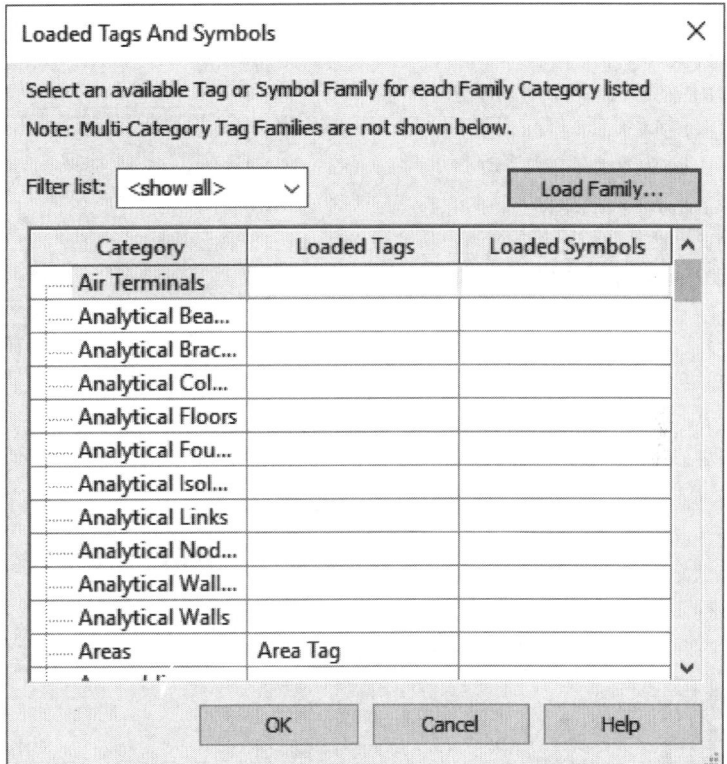

Figure 16–11

3. In the Load Family dialog box, navigate to the appropriate *Annotations* folder, select the tag(s) needed, and click **Open**.
4. The tag is added to the category in the dialog box. Click **OK**.

## Instance vs. Type Based Tags

Doors are tagged in a numbered sequence, with each instance of the door having a separate tag number. Other elements (such as windows and walls) are tagged by type, as shown in Figure 16–12. Changing the information in one tag changes all instances of that element.

*An additional window tag (**Window Tag-Number.rfa**) is stored in the Annotations> Architectural folder in the Revit Library. It tags windows using sequential numbers.*

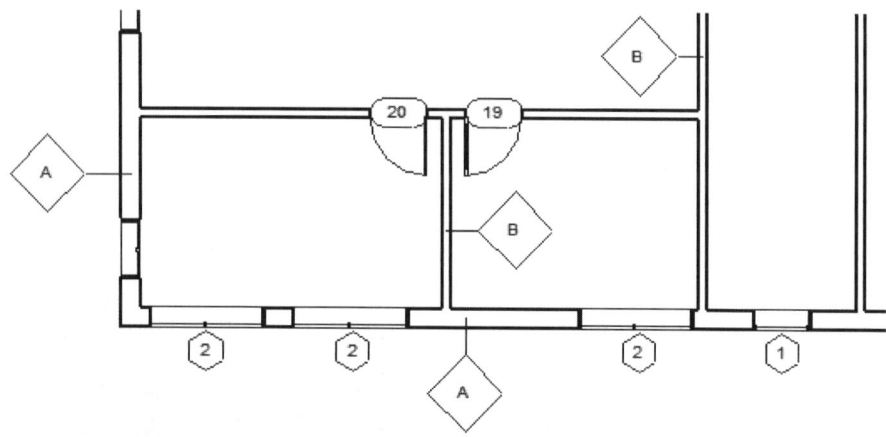

Figure 16–12

- To modify the number of an instance tag (such as a door or room), slowly click twice directly on the number in the tag and modify it, or you can modify the *Mark* property, as shown in Figure 16–13. Only that one door instance updates.

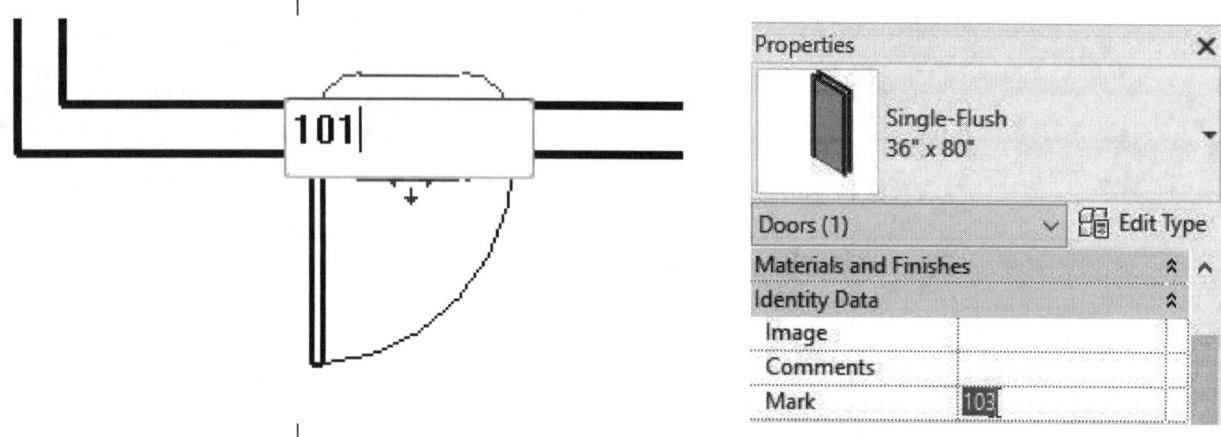

Figure 16–13

# Adding Tags and Schedules

- To modify the number of a type tag, you can slowly click twice directly on the number in the tag and modify it. Alternatively, you can select the element and in the *Modify* contextual tab> Host panel, click (Select Host), then in Properties, click (Edit Type). In the Type Properties dialog box, in the *Identity Data* section, modify the *Type Mark*, as shown in Figure 16–14. All instances of this element then update.

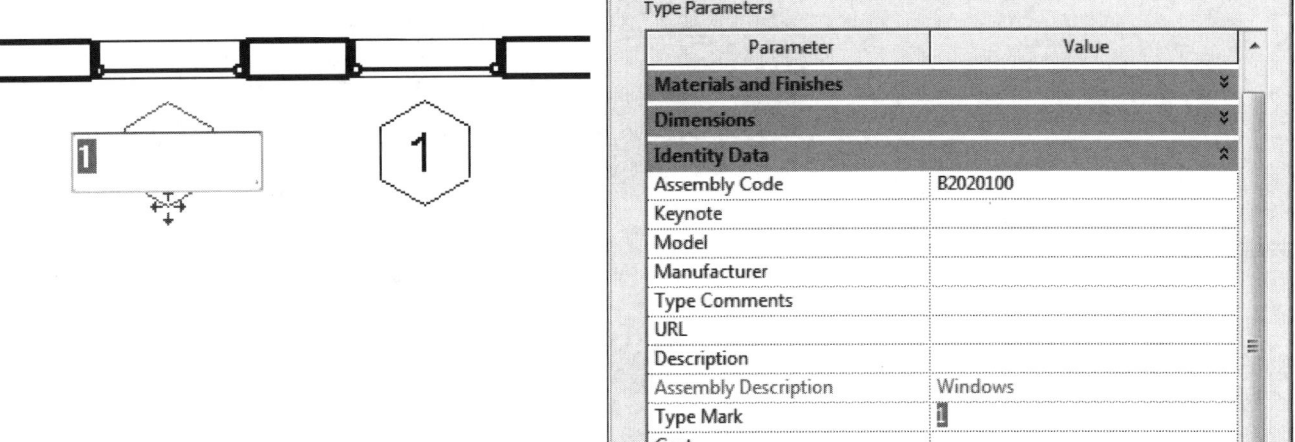

Figure 16–14

- When you change a type tag, an alert box opens to warn you that changing a type parameter affects other elements, as shown in Figure 16–15. If you want this tag to modify all other elements of this type, click **Yes**.

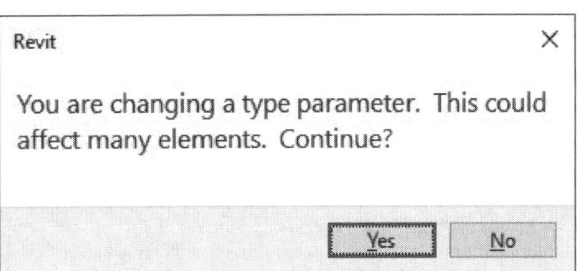

Figure 16–15

- If a tag displays with a question mark, it means that no information has been assigned to that parameter yet.

## Tagging in 3D Views

You can add tags to isometric 3D views, as shown in Figure 16–16, as long as the views are locked first.

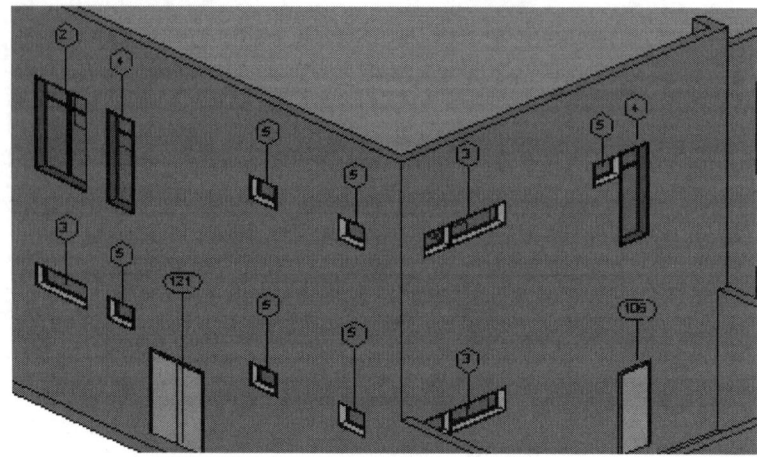

**Figure 16–16**

- You must lock a 3D view in order to place tags.

- You cannot tag in a perspective view, as these are views created with the camera tool.

### How To: Lock a 3D View

1. Open a 3D view and set it up as you want it to display.

2. In the View Control Bar, click (Unlocked 3D View), then click (Save Orientation and Lock View).

- If you are using the default 3D view and it has not been saved, you are prompted to name and save the view first.

- You can modify the orientation of the view by clicking (Locked 3D View), then clicking (Unlock View). This also removes any tags you have applied.

- To return to the previous locked view, click (Unlocked 3D View), then click (Restore Orientation and Lock View).

# Adding Tags and Schedules

### Hint: Stair and Railing Tags

**Tag by Category** can be used to tag the overall stair, stair runs, landings, and railings, as shown in Figure 16–17. An additional type of tag, **Stair Tread/Riser Number**, creates a sequence of numbers for each tread or riser.

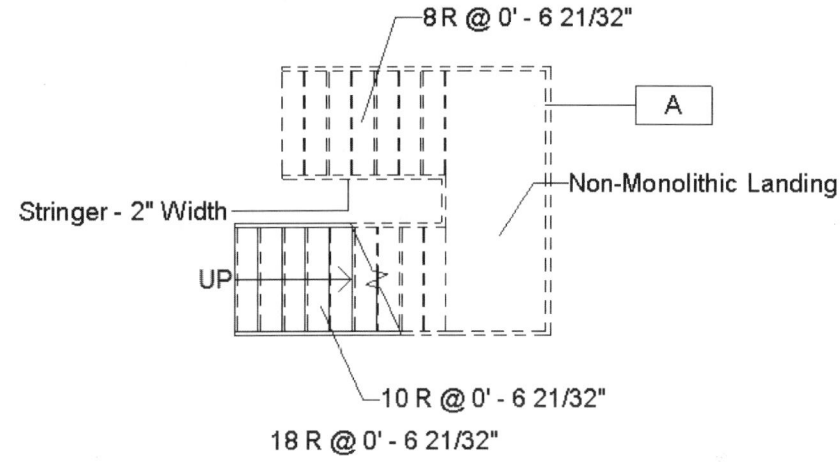

**Figure 16–17**

## How To: Add Tread/Riser Number Tags to Stairs

1. Open a plan, elevation, or section view.
2. In the *Annotate* tab>Tag panel, click (Stair Tread/Riser Number).
3. In Properties, set up the *Tag Type*, *Display Rule*, and other parameters. These remain active for the project.
4. Select a reference line of a stair to place the numbers, as shown in Figure 16–18.

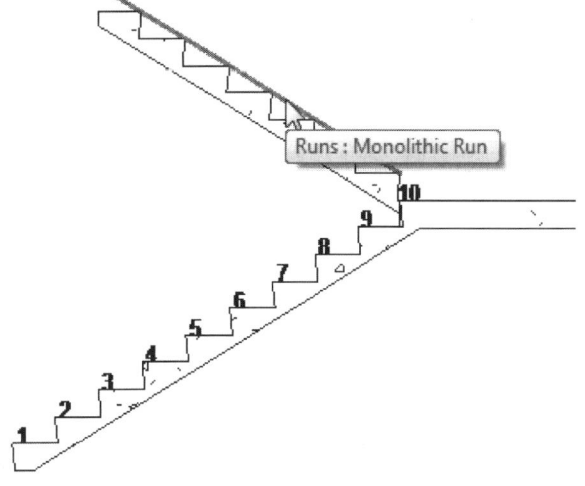

**Figure 16–18**

5. Continue selecting runs as needed.

# Practice 16a  Add Tags

### Practice Objectives

- Add tags to a model.
- Use the Tag All Not Tagged dialog box.
- Set the Type Mark parameter for tags.
- Add room tags.

In this practice, you will add wall tags in a floor plan, as shown in Figure 16–19, and modify the Type Mark numbers for the walls. You will also tag all of the walls using the Tag All Not Tagged dialog box and tag the room elements in a separate view.

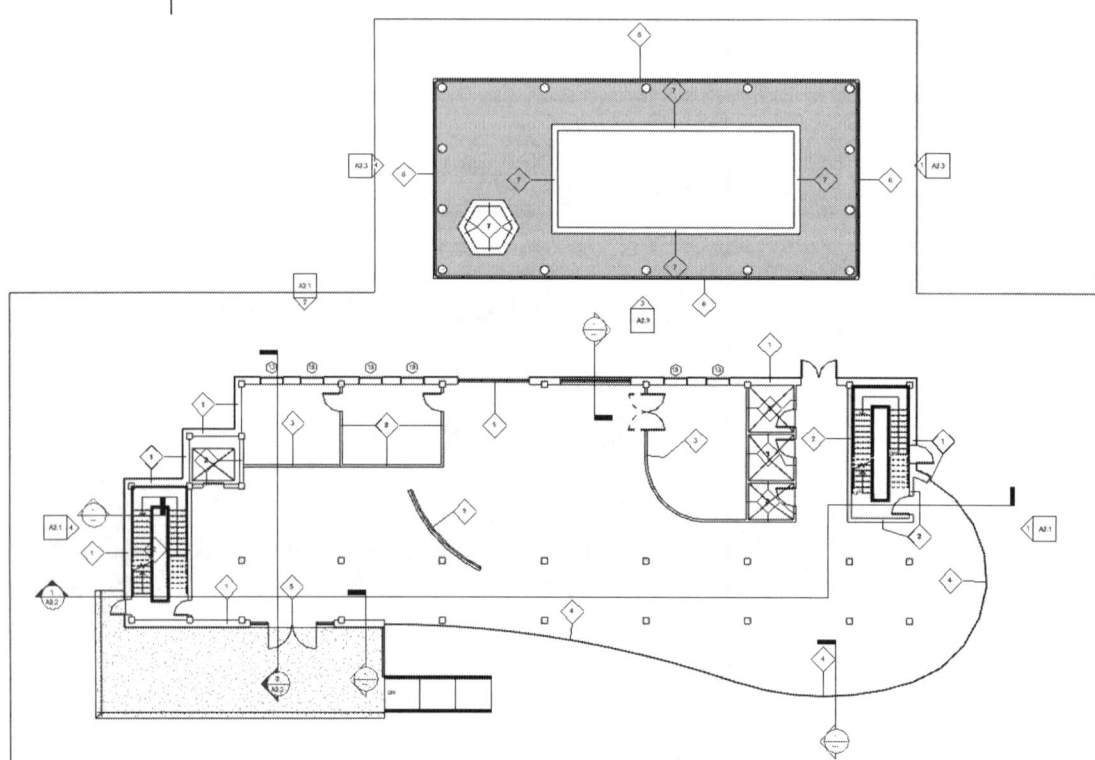

Figure 16–19

### Task 1 - Add tags to a floor plan.

1. Open the project **Hotel-Tags.rvt** from the practice files folder.

2. Open the **Floor Plans: Floor 1** view, zoom in to the elevator and the west stairs area.

3. In the *Annotate* tab>Tag panel, click (Tag by Category). In the Options Bar, select **Leader** and verify that **Attached End** is selected.

4. Select the exterior wall, as shown in Figure 16–20.

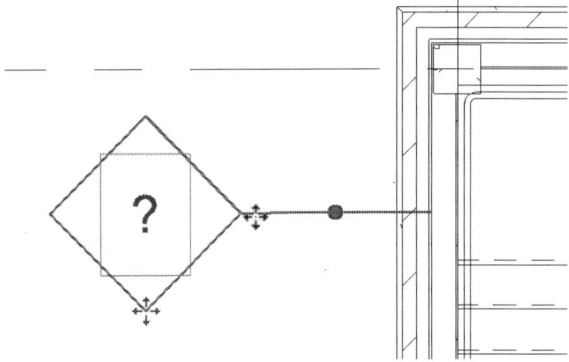

Figure 16–20

5. The tag comes in with a question mark because the wall does not have a *Type Mark* set yet. Click on the **?** in the tag, change the tag number to **1**, and press <Enter>.

6. When alerted that you are changing a type parameter, click **Yes** to continue.

7. You are still in the **Tag** command. Add a tag to the exterior wall above the stairs. This time, the tag number 1 comes in automatically as it is the same wall type as the first one, as shown in Figure 16–21.

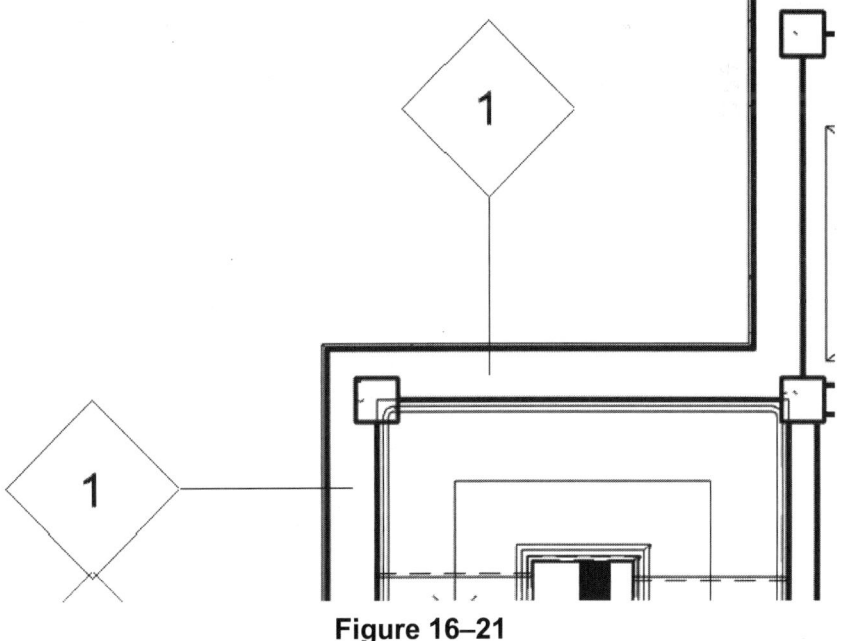

Figure 16–21

8. Click ▷ (Modify).

9. Select the wall dividing the stairs from the lobby.

10. In Properties, click (Edit Type).

11. In the Type Properties dialog box, in *Identity Data* section, set *Type Mark* to **2**, as shown in Figure 16–22. Click **OK**.

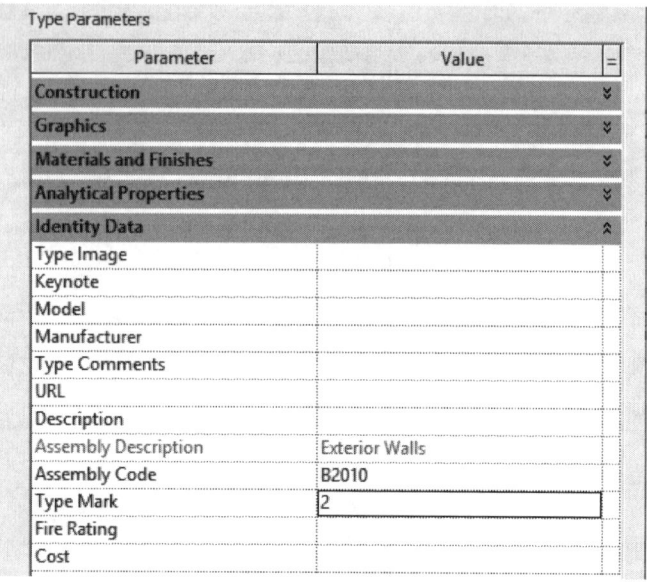

Figure 16–22

12. Select one of the interior partitions and set the *Type Mark* to **3**.

13. Click (Modify).

14. Select the wall tag that is above the stairs.

15. In the *Modify | Walls* tab>Host panel, click (Add/Remove Host). Verify **Show All Leaders** is selected and **Merge Leaders** is off, as shown in Figure 16–23.

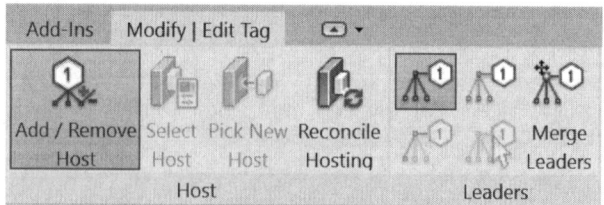

Figure 16–23

16. Select the wall that is to the right of the tag. A leader is added, as shown in Figure 16–24.

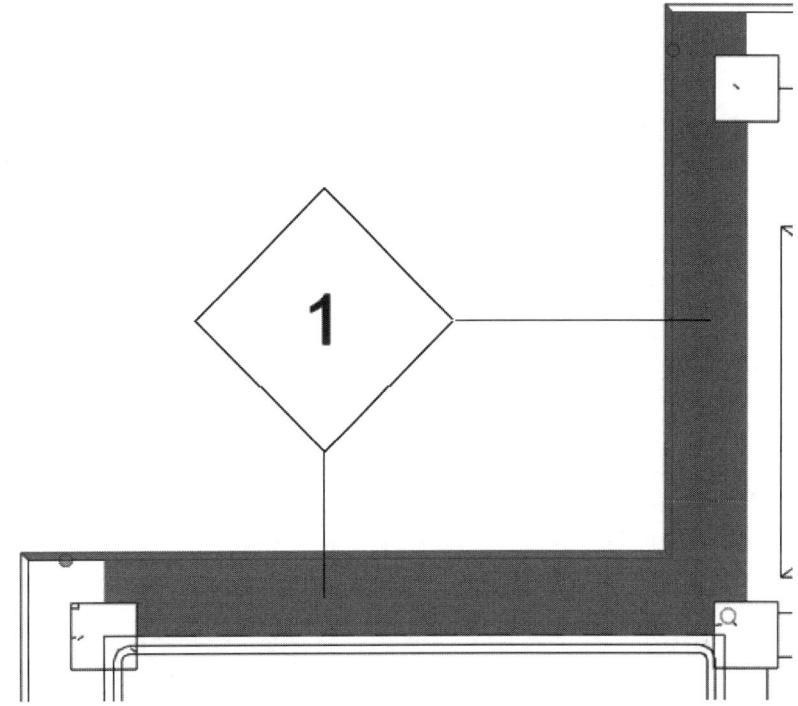

**Figure 16–24**

17. Click (Modify).

18. Start the (Tag By Category) command and continue tagging the walls, using the **Add/Remove Host** tool as needed.

    - Note that when tagging a partition wall type, the Type Mark displays as set in the Type Properties. If you select two different walls, the tag will display *Varies* because there are two different wall types.

19. Save the project.

## Task 2 - Add room tags.

1. Open the **Floor Plans: Floor 1 - Furniture Plan** view.

2. In the Status Bar, click (Select Element by Face). The icon should have a red X ( ) when it is off.

3. Hover the cursor over the open area inside the front entrance until you see the room element, as shown in Figure 16–25. The room elements do not display in this view but are available.

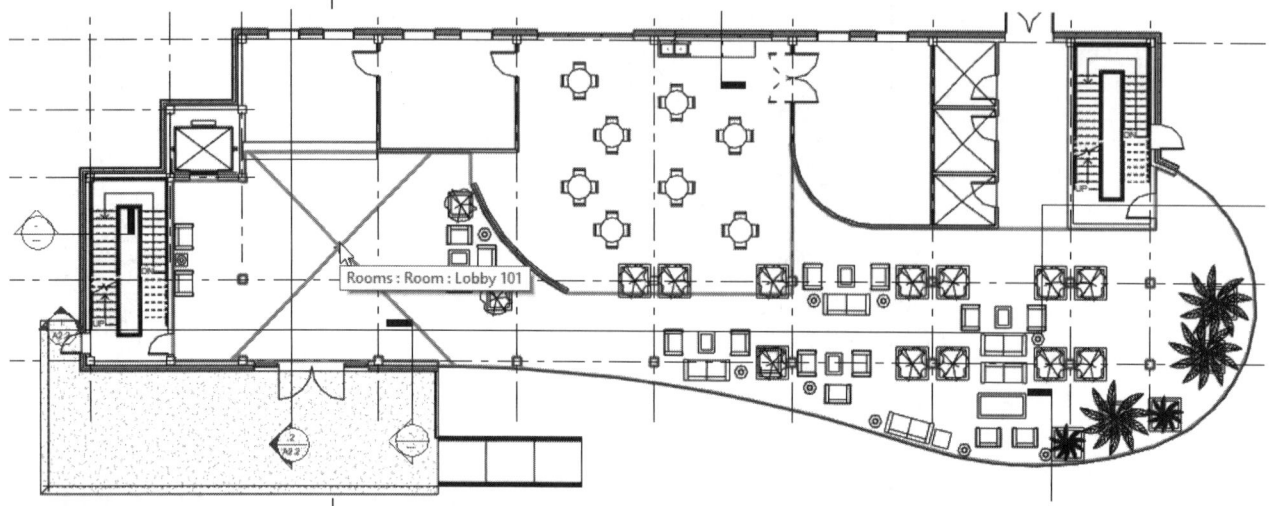

**Figure 16–25**

4. In the *Annotate* tab>Tag panel, click (Tag by Category). Note that you cannot tag rooms using Tag by Category.

5. Click (Modify).

6. In the *Annotate* tab>Tag panel, click (Room Tag). The room elements display. Place tags in one or two rooms, as shown in Figure 16–26.

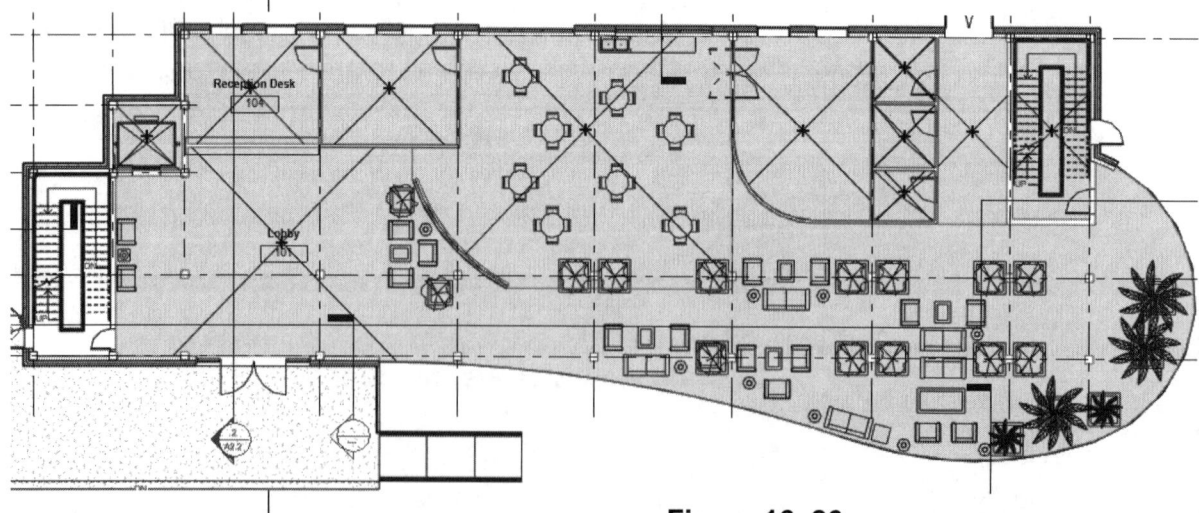

**Figure 16–26**

7. Click (Modify).

8. In the *Annotate* tab>Tag panel, click (Tag All).

# Adding Tags and Schedules

9. In the Tag All Not Tagged dialog box, select **Room Tags: Room Tag** and click **OK**. Room tags are added to all of the rooms in the view.

10. Zoom in on the west stairs and move the tag outside the wall. It is no longer connected to the room element, as shown in Figure 16–27.

11. Read the warning information and click **OK** to close the dialog box.

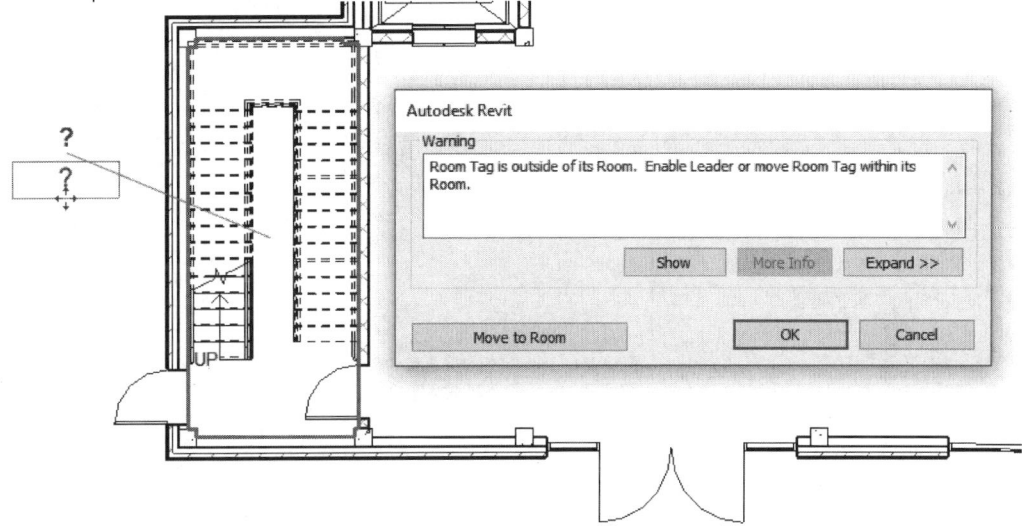

**Figure 16–27**

12. The tag is still selected. In the Options Bar, select **Leader**. The room tag is now connected to the room element and displays the information, as shown in Figure 16–28.

*Your room numbering may be different from that in the figure shown here.*

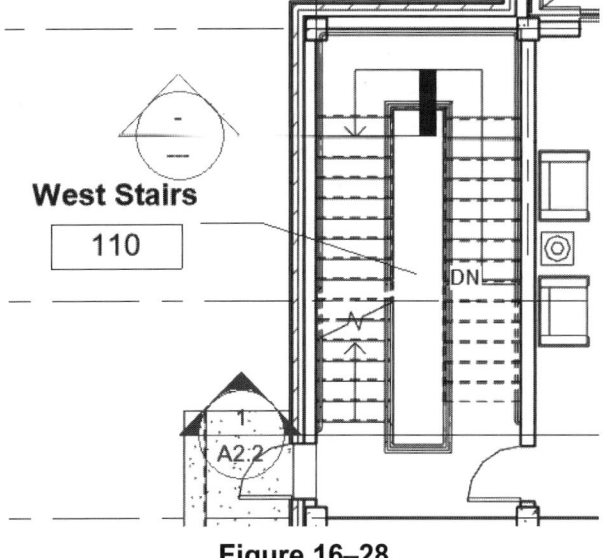

**Figure 16–28**

13. Save and close the project.

## 16.2 Working with Schedules

Schedules extract information from a project and display it in table form. Each schedule is stored as a separate view and can be placed on sheets, as shown in Figure 16–29. Any changes you make to the project elements that affect the schedules are automatically updated in both views and sheets.

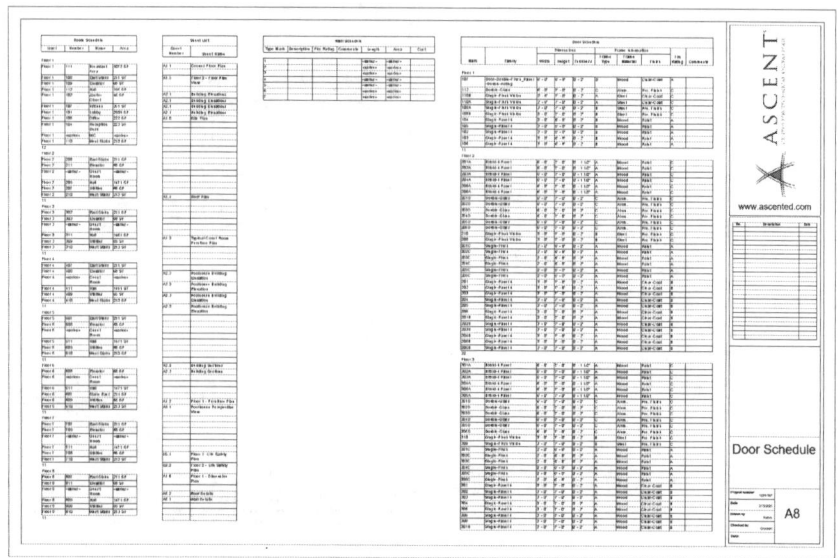

Figure 16–29

The architectural template (**Default.rte**) does not include any schedules, whereas the **DefaultGBRENU.rte** does include schedules. The **Construction-Default.rte**, **Residential-Default.rte**, and **Commercial-Default.rte** template files do include useful schedules.

### Work with Schedules

- In the Project Browser, expand the **Schedules/Quantities** node, as shown in Figure 16–30, and double-click on the schedule you want to open.

Figure 16–30

- Schedules are automatically filled out with the information stored in the instance and type parameters of related elements that are added to the model. Fill out additional information either in the schedule or in Properties.

# Adding Tags and Schedules

- In the *Modify Schedule/Quantities* tab>Appearance panel, you can select (Freeze Header) to keep the header row visible while you scroll through the schedule.

- When selecting on a schedule's row, it will highlight in blue.

- You can drag and drop the schedule onto a sheet.

- You can zoom in to read small text in schedule views. Hold down <Ctrl> and scroll using the mouse wheel or press <Ctrl>+<+> to zoom in or <Ctrl>+<-> to zoom out.

## How To: Create a Schedule

1. In the *View* tab>Create panel, expand (Schedules) and click (Schedule/Quantities), or in the Project Browser, right-click on the **Schedules/Quantities** node and select **New Schedule/Quantities**.
2. In the New Schedule dialog box, select the type of schedule you want to create (e.g., Doors) from the *Category* list, as shown in Figure 16–31.

*In the Filter list drop-down list, you can specify the discipline(s) to show only the categories that you want to display.*

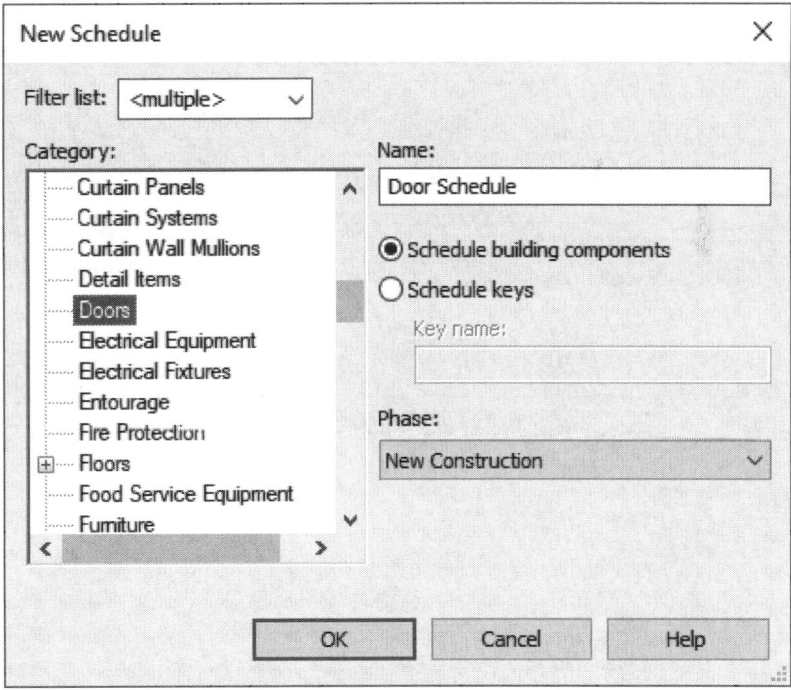

Figure 16–31

3. Revit assigns a name for the schedule. You can also type a new *Name* if the default does not suit.
4. Select **Schedule building components**.
5. Specify the *Phase*, as needed.
6. Click **OK**.

7. Fill out the information in the Schedule Properties dialog box. This includes the information in the *Fields*, *Filter*, *Sorting/Grouping*, *Formatting*, and *Appearance* tabs.
8. Once you have entered the schedule properties, click **OK**. A schedule view is created, displaying a report of the information configured in the schedule.

- Other elements that can be scheduled include model groups and Revit links.

## Schedule Properties – Fields Tab

In the *Fields* tab, you can select from a list of available fields and organize them in the order in which you want them to display in the schedule, as shown in Figure 16–32. You can also sort the available fields by *Parameter Type* (such as Project Parameters), *Discipline*, or *Value Type*.

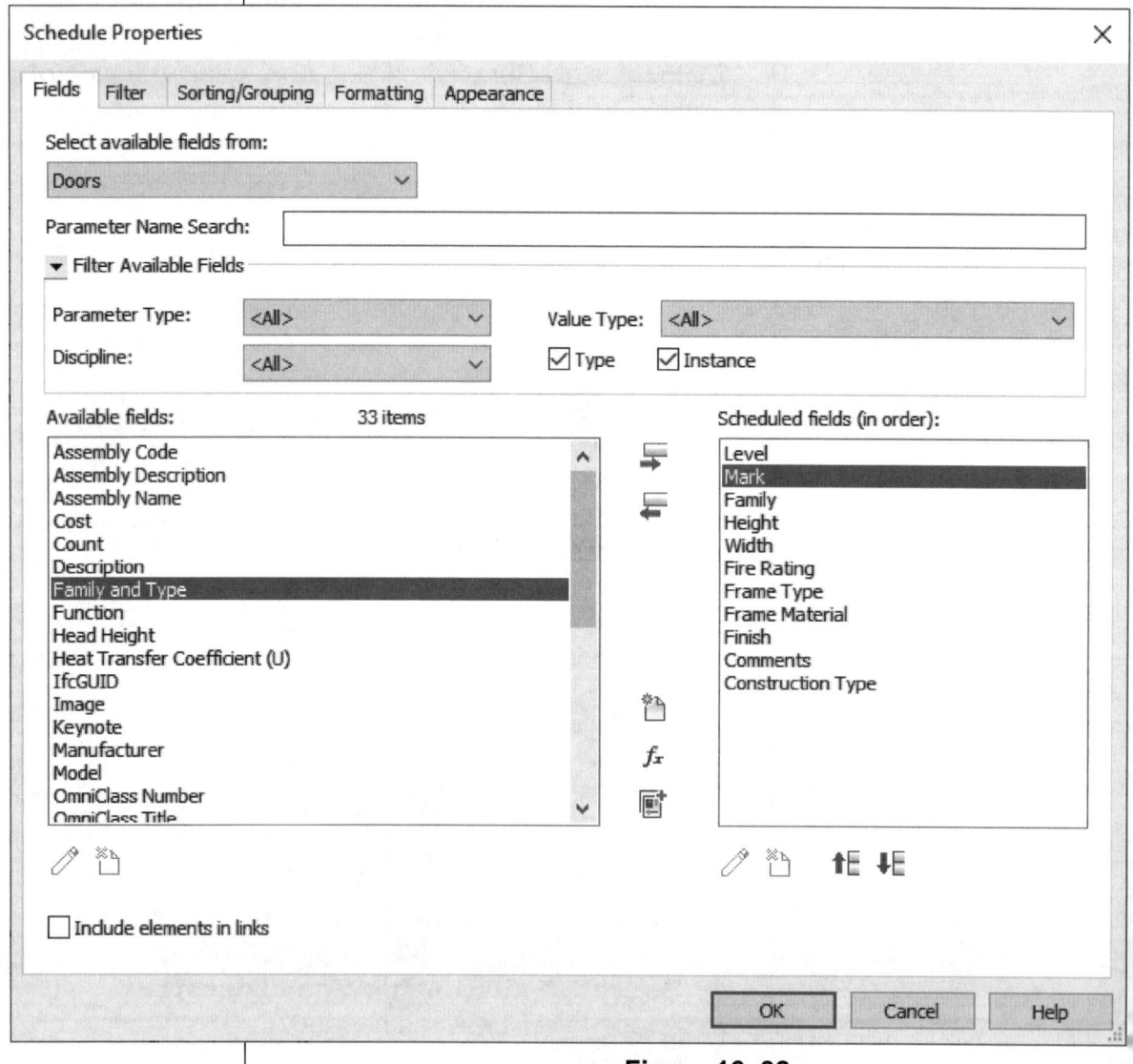

**Figure 16–32**

# Adding Tags and Schedules

## How To: Fill Out the Fields Tab

1. In the *Available fields* area, select one or more fields you want to add to the schedule and click ![icon] (Add parameter(s)). The field(s) are placed in the *Scheduled fields (in order)* area.
2. Continue adding fields, as required.

- Click ![icon] (Remove parameter(s)) to move a field from the *Scheduled fields* area back to the *Available fields* area.

- Use ![icon] (Move parameter up) and ![icon] (Move parameter down) to change the order of the scheduled fields.

*You can also double-click on a field to move it from the Available fields area to the Scheduled fields area, and double-click on a field to remove it from the Scheduled fields area.*

## Other Fields Tab Options

| | |
|---|---|
| **Select available fields from** | Enables you to select additional category fields for the specified schedule. The available list of fields depends on the original category of the schedule. Typically, they include room information. |
| **Include elements in links** | Includes elements that are in files linked to the current project, so that their elements can be included in the schedule. |
| (New parameter) | Adds a new field according to your specification. New fields can be placed by instance or by type. |
| $f_x$ (Add Calculated parameter) | Enables you to create a field that uses a formula based on other fields. |
| (Combine parameters) | Enables you to combine two or more parameters in one column. You can put any fields together even if they are used in another column. |
| (Edit parameter) | Enables you to edit custom fields. This is grayed out if you select a standard field. |
| (Delete parameter) | Deletes the selected custom fields. This is grayed out if you select a standard field. |

## Schedule Properties – Filter Tab

In the *Filter* tab, you can set up filters so that only elements meeting specific criteria are included in the schedule. For example, you might only want to show information for one level, as shown in Figure 16–33. You can create filters for up to eight values. All values must be satisfied for the elements to display.

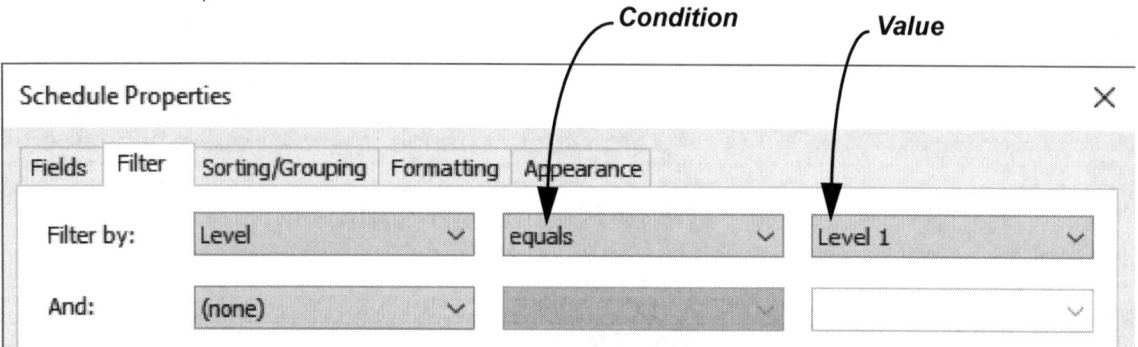

Figure 16–33

- The parameter you want to use as a filter must be included in the schedule. You can hide the parameter once you have completed the schedule, if needed.

| Filter by | |
|---|---|
| Field/ Parameter | Specifies the field/parameter to filter. Not all fields/parameters are available to be used to filter. |
| Condition | Specifies the condition that must be met. This includes options such as **equal**, **not equal**, **greater than**, and **less than**. |
| Value | Specifies the value of the element to be filtered. You can select from a drop-down list of appropriate values. For example, if you set *Filter by* to **Level**, it displays the list of levels in the project. |

## Schedule Properties – Sorting/Grouping Tab

In the *Sorting/Grouping* tab, you can set how you want the information to be sorted, as shown in Figure 16–34. For example, you can sort by **Mark** (number) and then **Type**.

# Adding Tags and Schedules

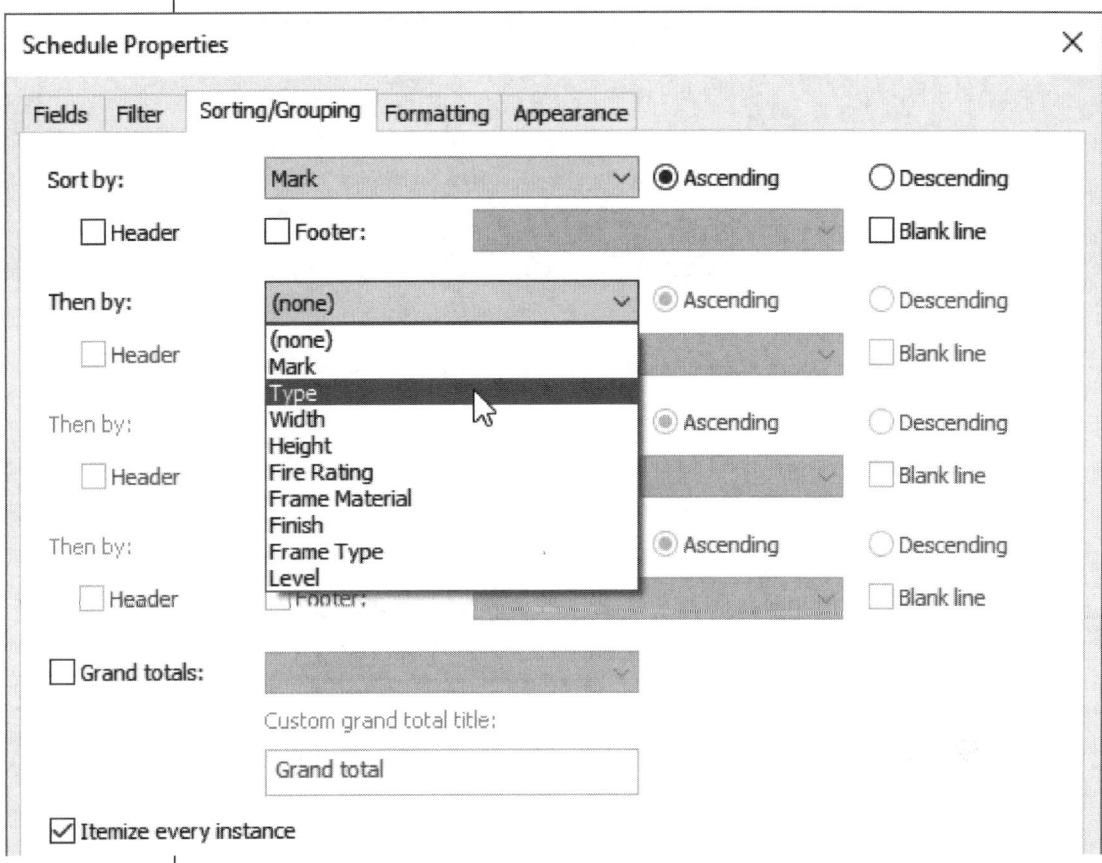

Figure 16–34

| | |
|---|---|
| **Sort by** | Enables you to select the field(s) you want to sort by. You can select up to four levels of sorting. |
| **Ascending/ Descending** | Sorts fields in **Ascending** or **Descending** order based on an alphanumeric system. |
| **Header/ Footer** | Enables you to group similar information and separate it by a **Header** with a title and/or a **Footer** with quantity information. |
| **Blank line** | Adds a blank line between groups. |
| **Grand totals** | Selects which totals to display for the entire schedule. You can specify a name to display in the schedule for the grand total. |
| **Itemize every instance** | If selected, displays each instance of the element in the schedule. If not selected, displays only one instance of each type based on the sorting/grouping categories, as shown in Figure 16–35. |

| <Window Schedule> | | | | | | |
|---|---|---|---|---|---|---|
| A | B | C | D | E | F | G |
| Type | Count | Height | Width | Manufacturer | Model | Comments |
| 36 x 36 | 6 | 3' 0" | 3' - 0" | Anderson | FX3636 | |
| 36" x 48" | 7 | 4' - 0" | 3' - 0" | Anderson | FX3648 | |
| Grand total: 13 | | | | | | |

Figure 16–35

## Schedule Properties – Formatting Tab

In the *Formatting* tab, you can control how the headers of each field display, as shown in Figure 16–36. The *Multiple values indication* options enable you to control how fields with multiple values display.

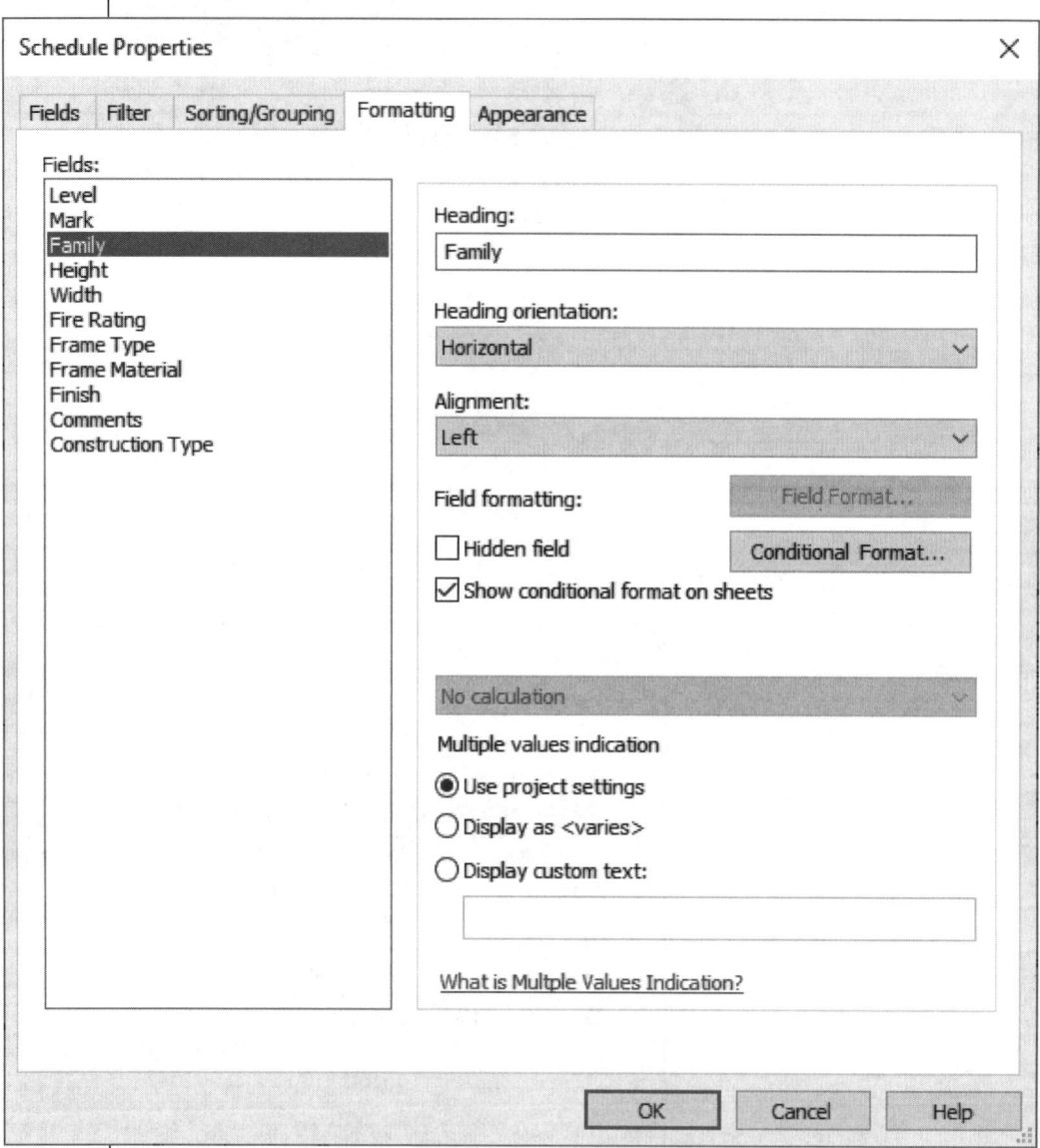

Figure 16–36

| | |
|---|---|
| **Fields** | Enables you to select the field for which you want to modify the formatting. |
| **Heading** | Enables you to change the heading of the field if you want it to be different from the field name. For example, you might want to replace **Mark** (a generic name) with the more specific **Door Number** in a door schedule. |

| | |
|---|---|
| **Heading orientation** | Enables you to set the heading on sheets to **Horizontal** or **Vertical**. This does not impact the schedule view. |
| **Alignment** | Aligns the text in rows under the heading to be **Left**, **Right**, or **Center** justified. |
| **Field Format...** | Sets the units format for numerical fields, e.g., length, area, HVAC air flow, pipe flow, etc. By default, this is set to use the project settings. |
| **Conditional Format...** | Sets up the schedule to display visual feedback based on the conditions listed. |
| **Hidden field** | Enables you to hide a field. For example, you might want to use a field for sorting purposes, but not have it display in the schedule. You can also modify this option in the schedule view later. |
| **Show conditional format on sheets** | Select if you want the color code set up in the Conditional Format dialog box to display on sheets. |
| **Calculation options** | Select the type of calculation you want to use.<br>• **No Calculation:** All values in a field are calculated separately.<br>• **Calculate totals:** All values in a field are added together. This enables a field to calculate and display in the Grand Totals or Footers.<br>• **Calculate minimum:** Only the smallest amount displays.<br>• **Calculate maximum:** Only the largest amount displays.<br>• **Calculate minimum and maximum:** Both the smallest and largest amounts display.<br>Minimum and maximum calculations only show when **Itemize every instance** is unchecked in the *Sorting/Grouping* tab. |
| **Multiple values indication** | When a schedule is not set to itemize every instance, select how the value will display. |

> **Hint: Hiding Columns**
>
> If you want to use the field to filter or sort, but do not want it to display in the schedule, select **Hidden field**. Alternatively, once the schedule is completed, select the column header, right-click on it, and select **Hide Columns**.

## Schedule Properties – Appearance Tab

In the *Appearance* tab, you can set the text style and grid options for a schedule, as shown in Figure 16–37.

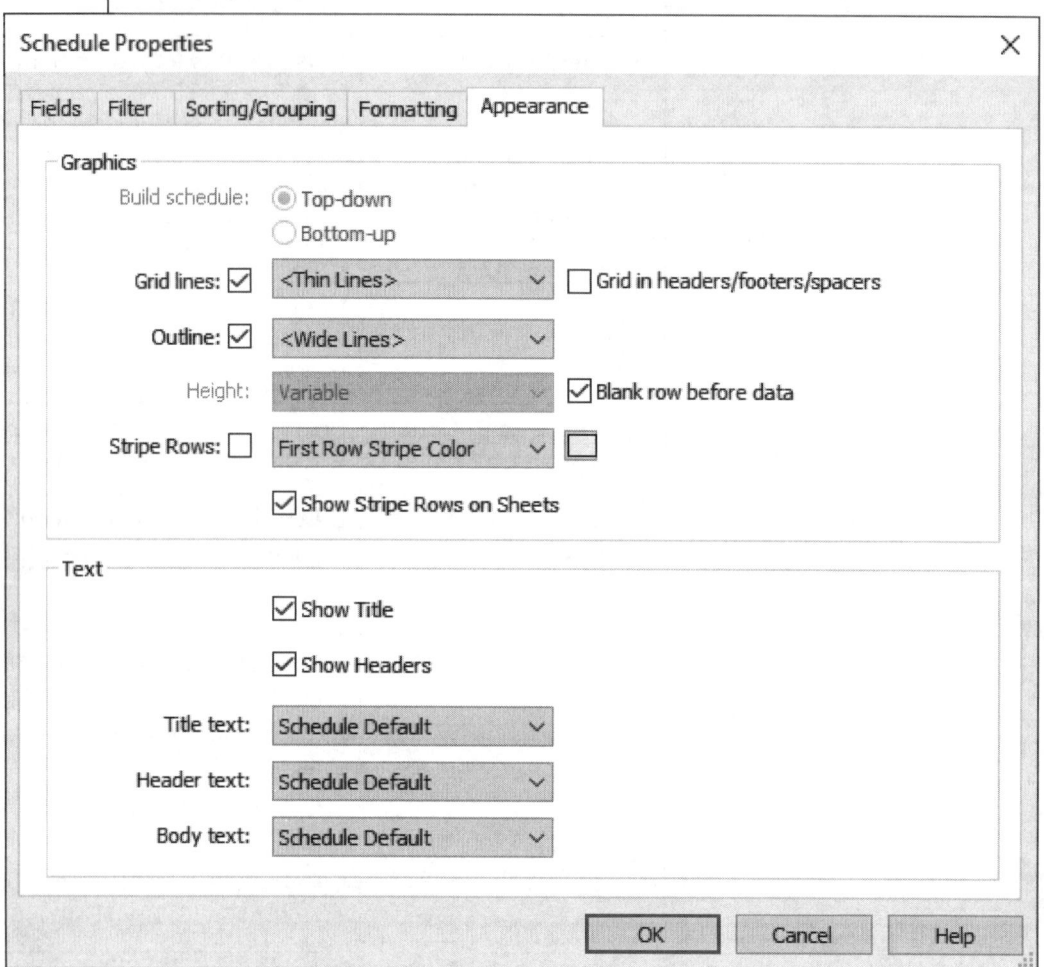

Figure 16–37

| | |
|---|---|
| **Grid lines** | Displays lines between each instance listed and around the outside of the schedule. Select the style of lines from the drop-down list; this controls all lines for the schedule, unless modified. |
| **Grid in headers/footers/spacers** | Extends the vertical grid lines between the columns. |
| **Outline** | Specify a different line type for the outline of the schedule. |
| **Blank row before data** | Select this option if you want a blank row to be displayed before the data begins in the schedule. |
| **Stripe Rows** | Select this option if you want to highlight alternating rows within the schedule to help differentiate the rows in large schedules. |

| | |
|---|---|
| **Show Title/Show Headers** | Select these options to include the text in the schedule. |
| **Title text/Header text/Body text** | Select the text style for the title, header, and body text. |

## Schedule View Properties

Schedule views have properties, including the *View Template, View Name, Phases*, and methods of returning to the Schedule Properties dialog box (as shown in Figure 16–38). In the *Other* section, click the button next to the tab name that you want to open in the Schedule Properties dialog box. In the dialog box, you can switch from tab to tab and make any required changes to the overall schedule.

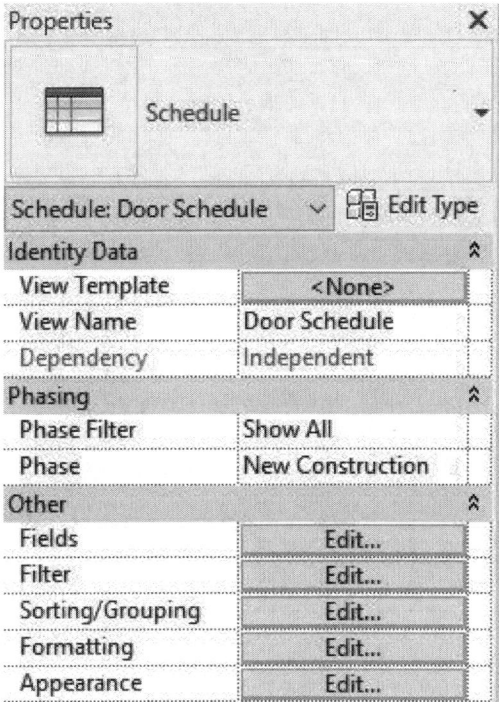

**Figure 16–38**

Just like other views, schedules can have view templates applied. When you specify a view template directly in the view, none of the schedule properties can be modified, as shown in Figure 16–39.

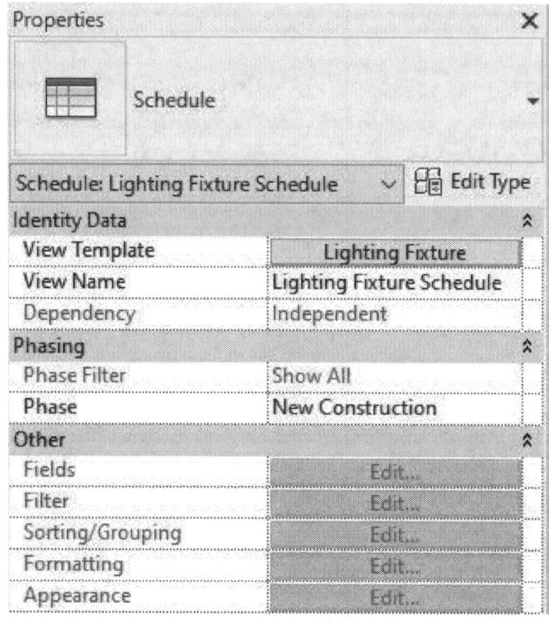

**Figure 16–39**

- Schedule view templates are type-specific. If you apply one to a different type of element, only the *Appearance* information is applied.

- If you apply a schedule view template to a schedule of the same type, it overrides everything in the existing schedule, including the fields.

- If you have a complicated schedule, you might want to create a view template for it to avoid losing that organization.

- To create schedule view templates, you need to create at least one from an existing view, then you can modify it and duplicate it in the View Templates dialog box.

# Filtering Elements from Schedules

When you create schedules based on a category, you might need to filter out some of the element types in that category. For example, in Revit, doors (and windows) in curtain walls are automatically added to a door schedule, as shown at the top in Figure 16–40, but are typically estimated as part of the curtain wall rather than as a separate door. To remove them from the schedule, as shown at the bottom in Figure 16–40, assign a parameter that identifies them and then use that parameter to filter them out of the schedule.

| | | | | | | Door Schedule- 1st |
|---|---|---|---|---|---|---|
| | | Door Size | | Frame | | |
| Door Type | Width | Height | Thickness | Frame Type | Frame Material | Head Detail |
| | 8' - 3 1/2" | 9' - 4 1/4" | | | | |
| | 3' - 0" | 7' - 0" | 0' - 2" | A | Aluminum | |
| | 3' - 0" | 7' - 0" | 0' - 2" | B | Aluminum | |
| | 3' - 0" | 6' - 8" | 0' - 2" | C | Aluminum | |

**Curtain wall doors displayed**

| | | | | | | Door Schedule- 1st |
|---|---|---|---|---|---|---|
| | | Door Size | | Frame | | |
| Door Type | Width | Height | Thickness | Frame Type | Frame Material | Head Detail |
| | 3' - 0" | 7' - 0" | 0' - 2" | A | Aluminum | |
| | 3' - 0" | 7' - 0" | 0' - 2" | B | Aluminum | |
| | 3' - 0" | 6' - 8" | 0' - 2" | C | Aluminum | |
| | 3' - 0" | 6' - 8" | 0' - 2" | C | Aluminum | |

**Curtain wall doors filtered out**

**Figure 16–40**

- This type of filtering can be used for any schedule in any discipline.

## How To: Filter Elements in a Schedule

1. Select an element (such as a door used in curtain walls) and modify the Type Parameters. Add a value to one of the parameters that you are not otherwise using in your schedule. For example, you could set *Construction Type* to **CW**, as shown Figure 16–41.

*Create a type specifically for this if you are using one that is also used elsewhere.*

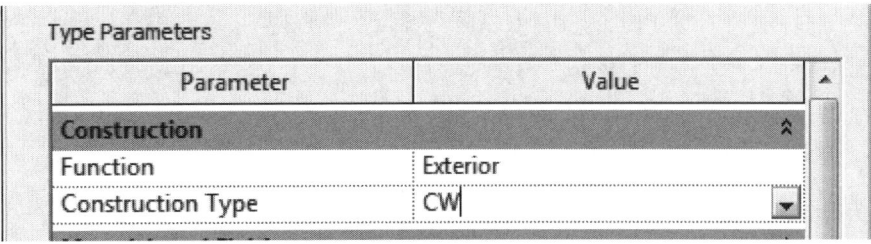

**Figure 16–41**

2. Create a schedule and include the field for the parameter you used (such as *Construction Type* in the above example).
3. Modify the *Filter* of the schedule so that the parameter does not equal the specified value. In the example shown in Figure 16–42, the filter is set so **Construction Type** > **does not equal** > **CW**. Any types that match this filter are excluded from the schedule.

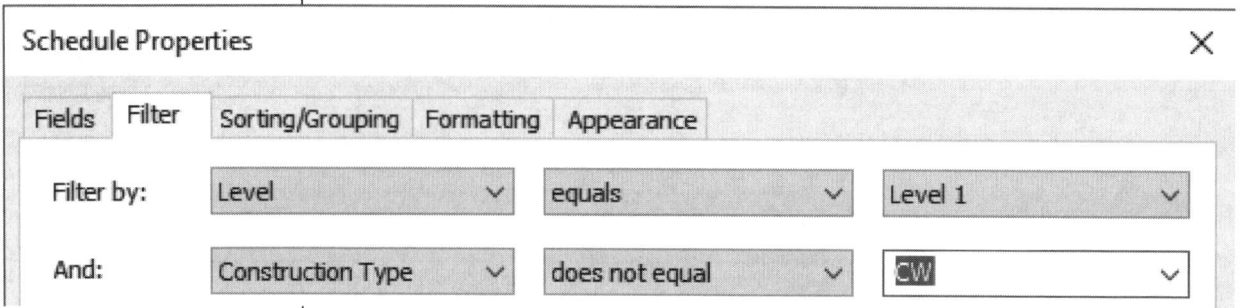

Figure 16–42

*Hiding a parameter/field in a schedule enables you to use it as a filter, but not have it visible in the schedule.*

4. In the final schedule, the elements display with the specified value. Right-click on the column header for the parameter you used to filter the schedule and select **Hide Columns**, as shown in Figure 16–43. It is just used as a filter and does not need to be part of the final schedule.

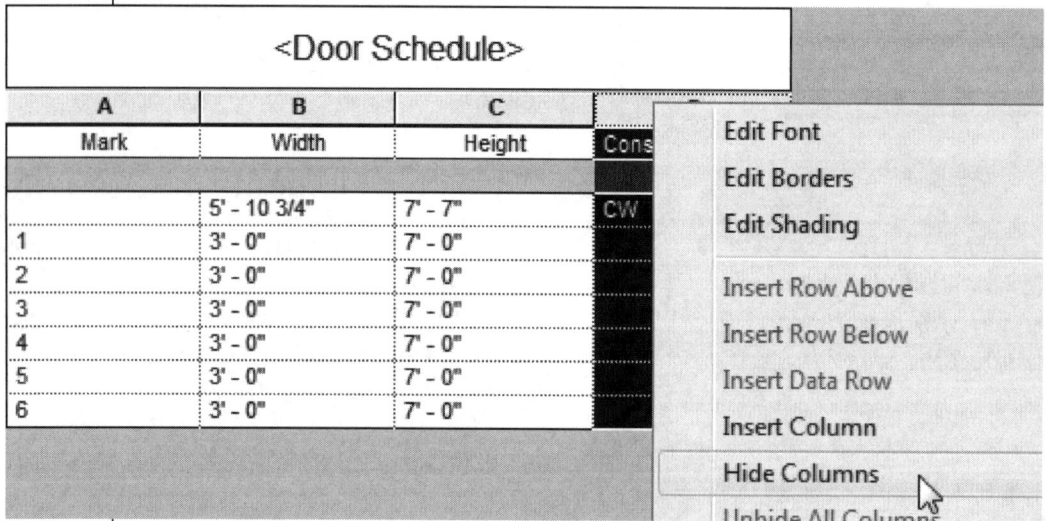

Figure 16–43

# Modifying Schedules

Information in schedules is bi-directional:

- Make changes to elements and the schedule automatically updates.

- Make changes to information in the schedule cells and the elements automatically update.

### How To: Modify Schedule Cells

1. Open the schedule view.
2. Select the cell you want to change. Some cells have drop-down lists, as shown in Figure 16–44. Others have edit fields.

*If you change a type property in the schedule, it applies to all elements of that type. If you change an instance property, it only applies to that one element.*

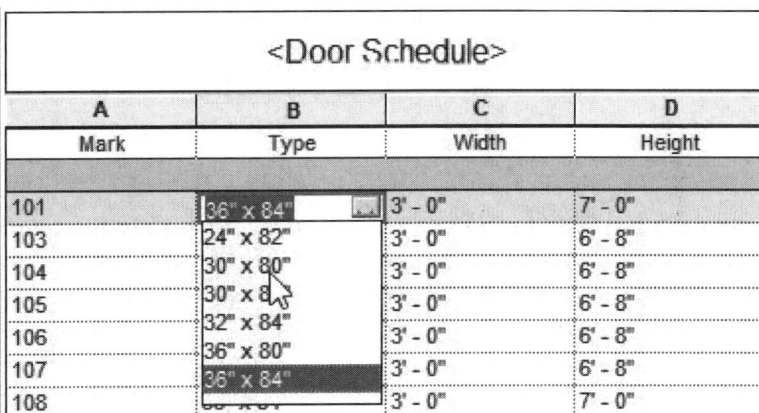

Figure 16–44

3. Add the new information. The change is reflected in the schedule, on the sheet, and in the elements of the project.

- If you change a type property, an alert box opens, as shown in Figure 16–45.

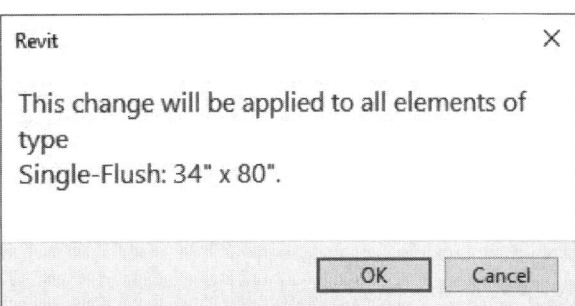

Figure 16–45

- When you select an element in a schedule, in the *Modify Schedule/Quantities* tab>Element panel, you can click

  (Highlight in Model). This opens a close-up view of the element with the Show Element(s) in View dialog box, as shown in Figure 16–46. Click **Show** to display more views of the element. Click **Close** to finish the command.

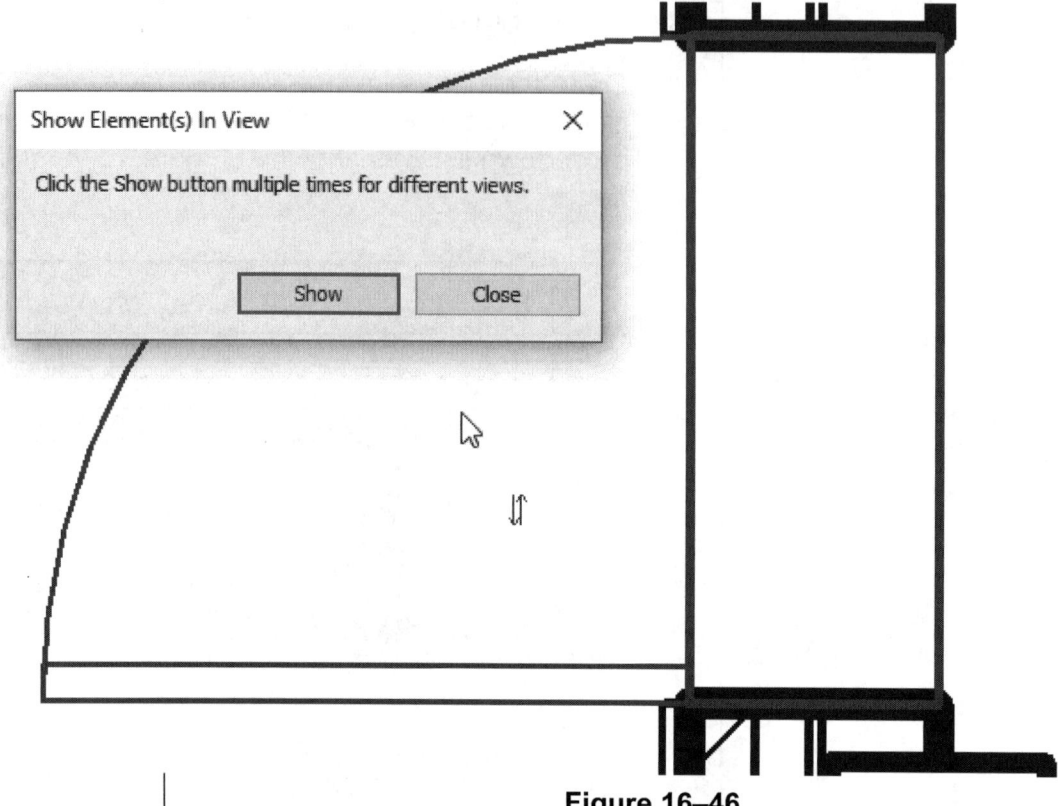

Figure 16–46

### Hint: Customizing Schedules

Schedules are typically included in project templates, which are set up by the BIM manager or other advanced users. They can be complex to create as there are many options.

- For information about creating basic schedules, see *B.5 Creating Building Component Schedules*.

- For information on using schedule data outside of Revit, see *B.6 Importing and Exporting Schedules*.

- For more information about creating schedules, refer to the ASCENT guide *Autodesk Revit: BIM Management: Template and Family Creation*.

# Adding Tags and Schedules

## Modifying a Schedule on a Sheet

Once you have placed a schedule on a sheet, you can manipulate it to fit the information into the available space. Select the schedule to display the controls that enable you to modify it, as shown in Figure 16–47.

- The blue triangles modify the width of each column.

- The break mark splits the schedule into two parts.

- In a split schedule, you can use the arrows in the upper-left corner to move that portion of the schedule table. The control at the bottom of the first table changes the length of the table and impacts any connected splits.

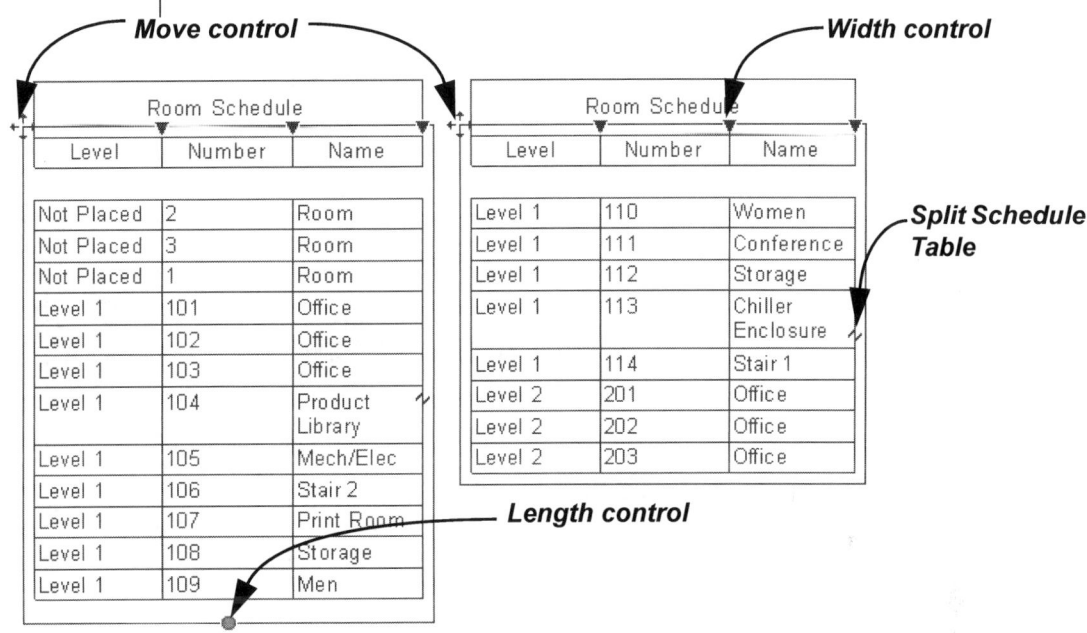

Figure 16–47

- To unsplit a schedule, drag the Move control from the side of the schedule that you want to unsplit back to the original column.

## Split a Schedule Across Multiple Sheets

When a schedule becomes too long, you need to be able to split it and place it on multiple sheets. You can split a schedule evenly or by setting a custom height. When a schedule has been split, you can expand **Schedules/Quantities (all)** in the Project Browser and see the segments of the schedule, as shown in Figure 16–48.

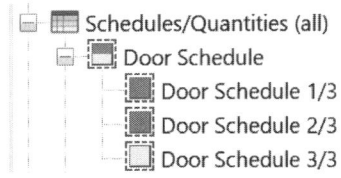

Figure 16–48

If the split is not what you wanted, you can delete the segmented schedules from the Project Browser. Do not delete the main schedule.

## How To: Split a Schedule and Place It on Multiple Sheets

1. Make additional sheets if needed. In a schedule view, in the *Modify Schedule/Quantities* tab>Split panel, click (Split & Place).
2. In the Split Schedule and Place on Sheets dialog box, select the sheets that you want to distribute the split schedule to, as shown in Figure 16–49.

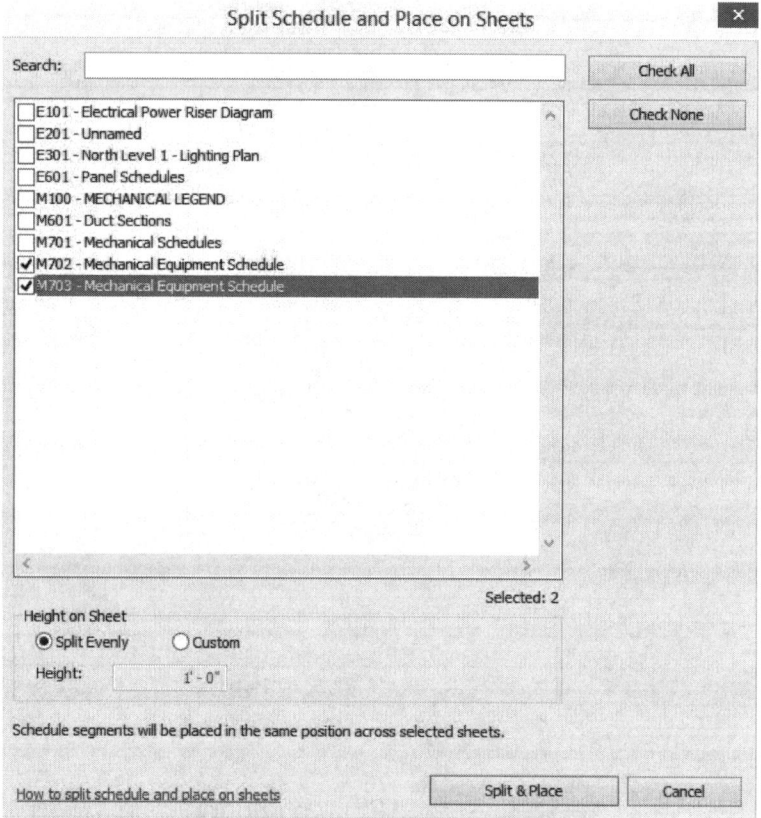

**Figure 16–49**

3. In the *Height on Sheet* section, select **Split Evenly** or **Custom**. If custom is selected, specify a *Height*.
4. Click **Split & Place**.
5. The first sheet selected in the list opens and the first segment of the split schedule is attached to your cursor. Place it on the sheet.
6. If you had selected multiple sheets in the Split Schedule and Place on Sheets dialog box, the rest of the segment schedule will automatically be placed exactly where you had initially placed the first segment of the schedule.

## Adding Tags and Schedules

7. Open each sheet and use the control grips to adjust the columns and stretch the schedule to fit the sheet, as needed.

### How To: Remove Split Schedules

1. In the Project Browser, expand the schedule.
2. Select the segmented schedules and press <Delete>, or right-click and select **Delete**.

## Filter by Sheet

If you place your schedule on a sheet that has a view on it, you can filter the schedule to only display the elements that are in that viewport. In Figure 16–50, the door schedule is only showing Floor 1 doors because the sheet contains the Floor 1 - Plan view and the **Filter by sheet** option has been selected.

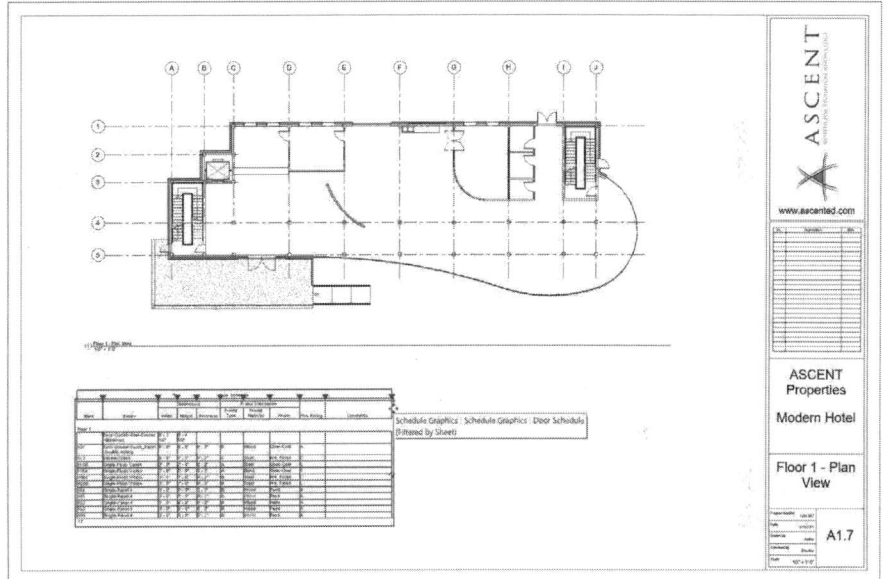

**Figure 16–50**

- If a view is changed or modified, the schedule and the same sheet will update accordingly.

- Schedules that are split across multiple sheets cannot use the Filter by Sheet option.

- Panel and revision schedules cannot use the Filter by Sheet option.

## How To: Filter a Schedule by Sheets

1. Open a schedule view.
2. In Properties, click **Edit...** next to *Filter*.
3. In the Schedule Properties dialog box, check the checkbox for **Filter by sheet**, as shown in Figure 16–51.

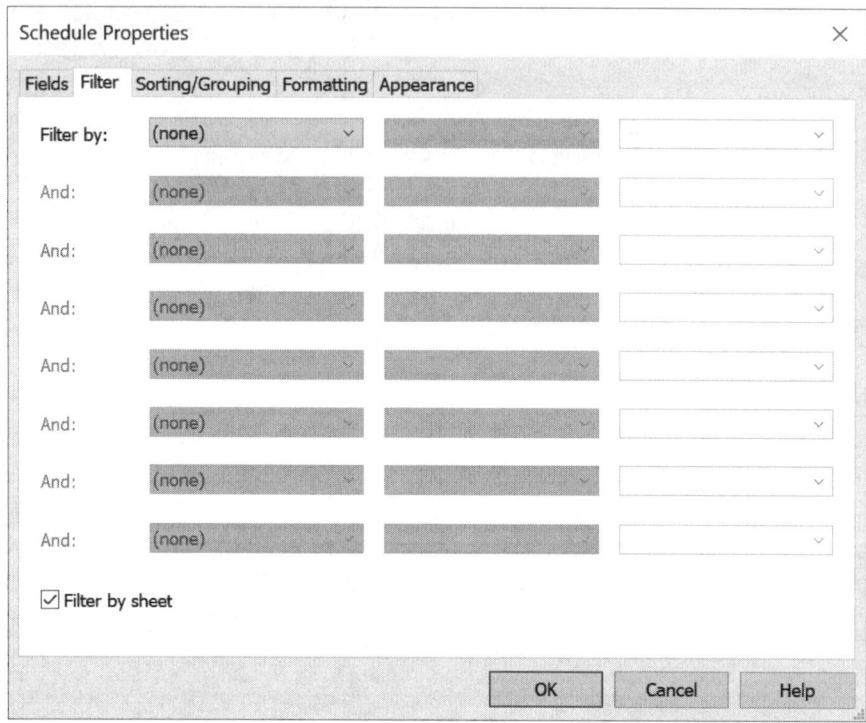

Figure 16–51

4. Click **OK**.
   - You cannot use this feature if you have split the schedule.

# Practice 16b | Work with Schedules

### Practice Objectives

- Update schedule information.
- Add a schedule to a sheet.

In this practice, you will add information to a door schedule and to elements that are connected to the schedule. You will then place the schedule on a sheet, as shown in Figure 16–52.

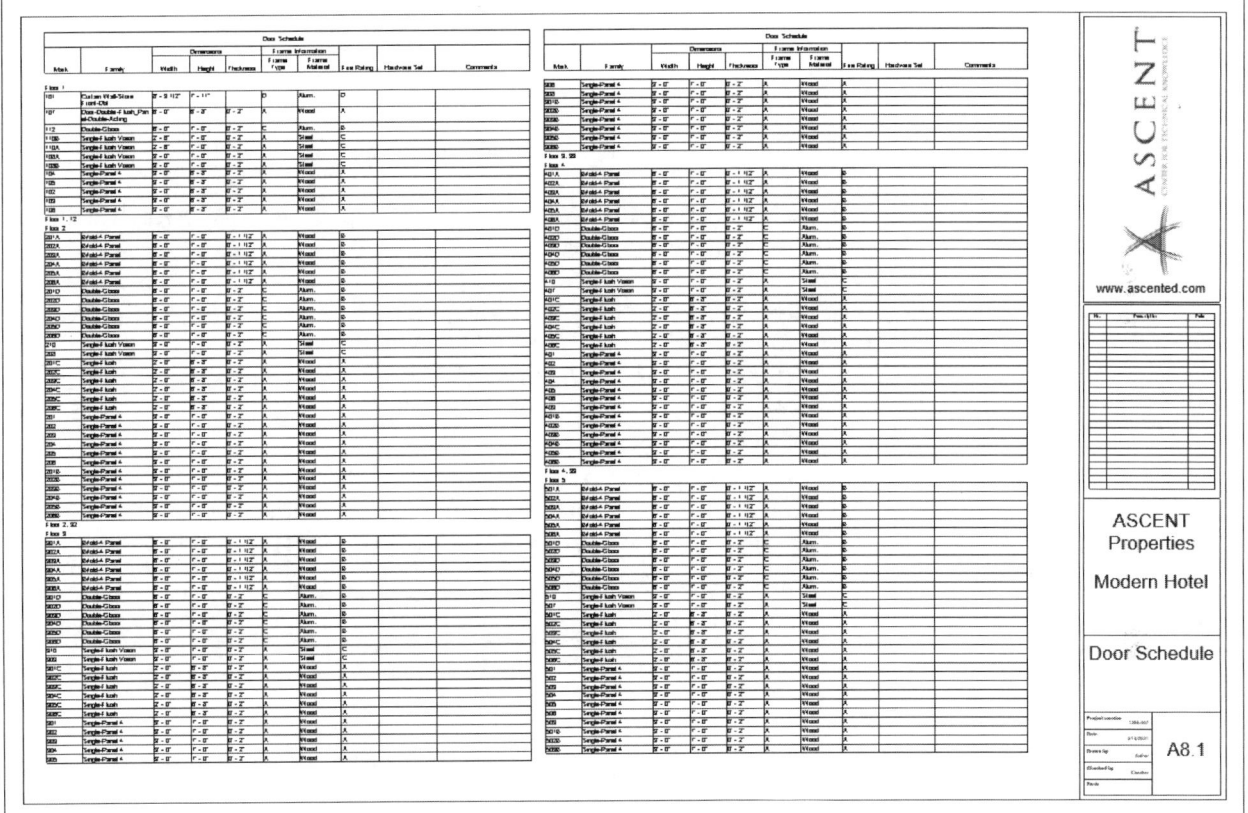

Figure 16–52

### Task 1 - Fill in schedules.

1. Open the project **Hotel-Schedule.rvt** from the practice files folder.

2. Verify that you are in the **Floor Plans: Floor 1** view.

3. In the Project Browser, expand *Schedules/Quantities*. Four schedules have been added to this project.

4. Double-click on **Door Schedule** to open it. The existing doors in the project are already populated with some of the basic information included with the door, as shown in Figure 16–53.

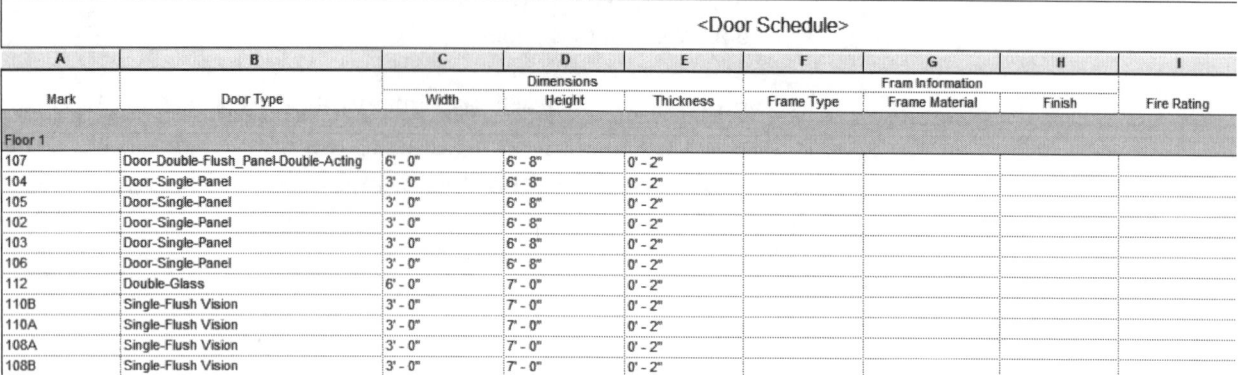

Figure 16–53

5. Close any other views that are open so the Door Schedule is the only view open.

6. In the *Mark* column, select **105**.

7. In the *Modify Schedules/Quantities* tab>Element panel, click  (Highlight in Model).

8. Because there are no other views open in this project, a dialog displays, as shown in Figure 16–54. Click **OK** to continue.

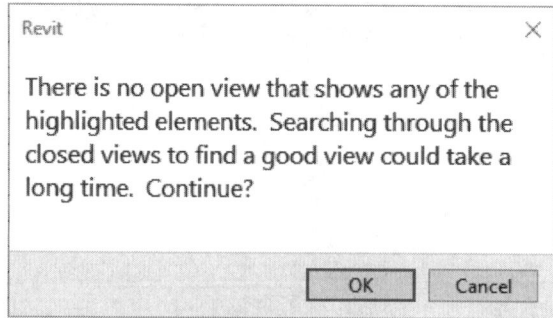

Figure 16–54

9. In the Show Element(s) In View dialog box, click **Show** until you see a plan view of the door, as shown in Figure 16–55. Then, click **Close**.

Note: The door that is found may or may not have a tag like the one shown in Figure 16–55.

# Adding Tags and Schedules

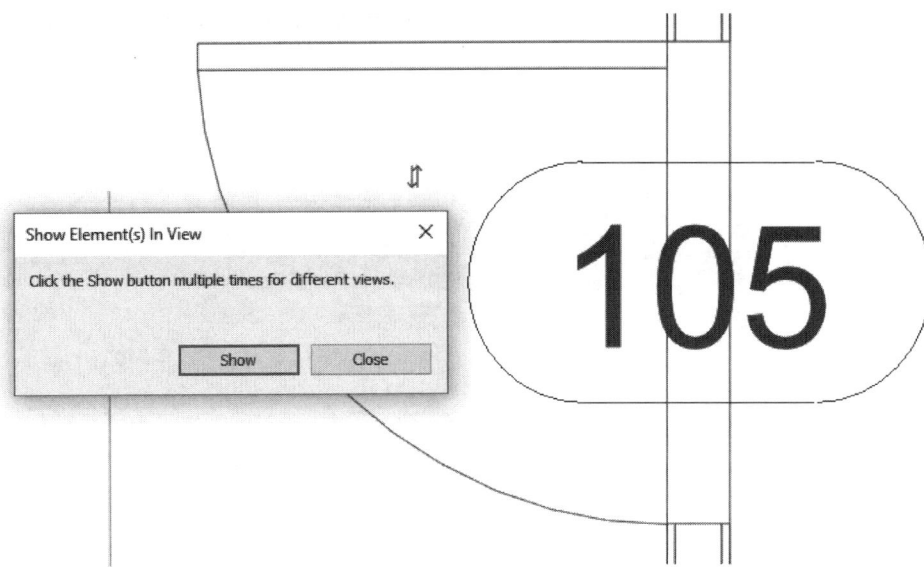

**Figure 16–55**

10. The door is still selected and you are in a plan view. In Properties, set the following:

    - *Frame Type:* **B**
    - *Frame Material:* **Wood**
    - *Finish:* **Coated**

11. Click ▦ (Edit Type).

12. In the Type Properties dialog box, in the *Identity Data* section, set the *Fire Rating* to **A**.

13. Click **OK** to finish.

14. Click ▷ (Modify).

15. Click on the *Door Schedule* tab to open the view.

16. Note that the *Frame Type* and *Frame Material* display for one door and the matching exterior doors also have a fire rating.

    Note: The *Frame Type* and *Frame Material* did not populate on similar door types because the information you changed was in the element property, whereas the *Fire Rating* change was the element's type property so it changes for all similar door types.

17. Use the drop-down list and change the options for the matching doors, as shown in Figure 16–56.

| 107 | Door-Double-Flush_Panel-Double-Acting | 6' - 0" | 6' - 8" | 0' - 2" | | | |
|---|---|---|---|---|---|---|---|
| 104 | Door-Single-Panel | 3' - 0" | 6' - 8" | 0' - 2" | B | Wood | Coated | A |
| 105 | Door-Single-Panel | 3' - 0" | 6' - 8" | 0' - 2" | B | Wood | Coated | A |
| 102 | Door-Single-Panel | 3' - 0" | 6' - 8" | 0' - 2" | B | Wood | Coated | A |
| 103 | Door-Single-Panel | 3' - 0" | 6' - 8" | 0' - 2" | B | Wood | Coated | A |
| 106 | Door-Single-Panel | 3' - 0" | 6' - 8" | 0' - 2" | B | | Coated | A |
| 112 | Double-Glass | 6' - 0" | 7' - 0" | 0' - 2" | | Wood | | |
| 110B | Single-Flush Vision | 3' - 0" | 7' - 0" | 0' - 2" | | | | |
| 110A | Single-Flush Vision | 3' - 0" | 7' - 0" | 0' - 2" | | | | |
| 108A | Single-Flush Vision | 3' - 0" | 7' - 0" | 0' - 2" | | | | |
| 108B | Single-Flush Vision | 3' - 0" | 7' - 0" | 0' - 2" | | | | |

Figure 16–56

18. In the Door Schedule view, specify the *Fire Rating* for some other doors in the schedule. When you change the fire rating, you are prompted to change all elements of that type. Click **OK**.

19. Open the **Floor Plans: Floor 1** view and zoom.

20. Select the door to the east stairs, then right-click and select **Select All Instances>In Entire Project**.

21. Look at the Status Bar beside (Filter) and note that more doors have been selected than are in the current view.

*No visual changes to the door display because these are just text properties.*

22. In Properties, set the *Construction and Materials* and *Finishes* parameters as follows:
    - *Frame Type:* **A**
    - *Frame Material:* **Steel**
    - *Finish:* **Clear-coat**

23. Move the cursor into the view and click in an empty space in the view to clear the selection.

24. Switch back to the schedule view to see the additions.

25. Set the *Fire Rating* for the Single-Flush Vision doors to **C**.

26. Click **OK** to apply the change to all elements, as shown in Figure 16–57.

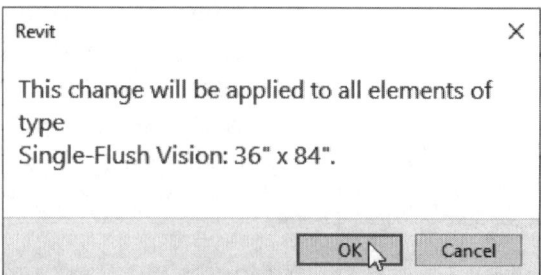

Figure 16–57

27. Save the project.

# Adding Tags and Schedules

## Task 2 - Add schedules to a sheet.

1. In the Project Browser, create three sheets using the title block **ASCENT_22X 34 Horizontal** with the name and sheet number of **A8.1 - Door Schedule**. Name the other two door schedules with a sequential sheet number.

2. Activate the door schedule view.

3. In the *Modify Schedule/Quantities* tab>Split panel, click (Split & Place).

4. In the Split Schedule and Place on Sheets dialog box, select the three door schedule sheets, as shown in Figure 16–58.

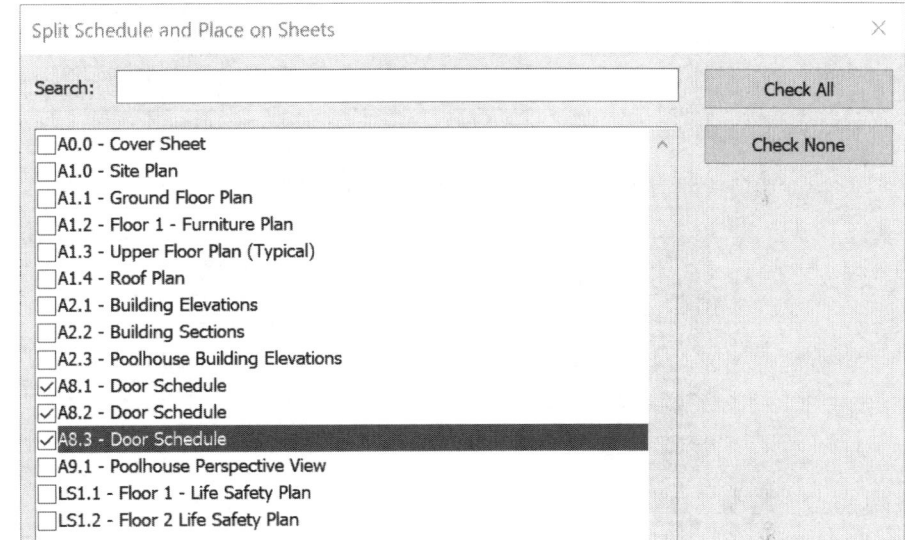

Figure 16–58

5. Click **Split & Place**.

6. The **Sheet A8.1 - Door Schedule** automatically opens and the first segment of the split schedule is attached to your cursor.

7. Place the door schedule in the upper-left corner of the sheet.

8. From the Project Browser, open sheet **A8.2** and **A8.3**. Note that the other segment of the split schedule has automatically been added to the sheets.

9. The schedule will be too long. Activate the **A8.1 - Door Schedule** view, select the schedule, and click ✤ (Split Schedule Table), as shown in Figure 16–59.

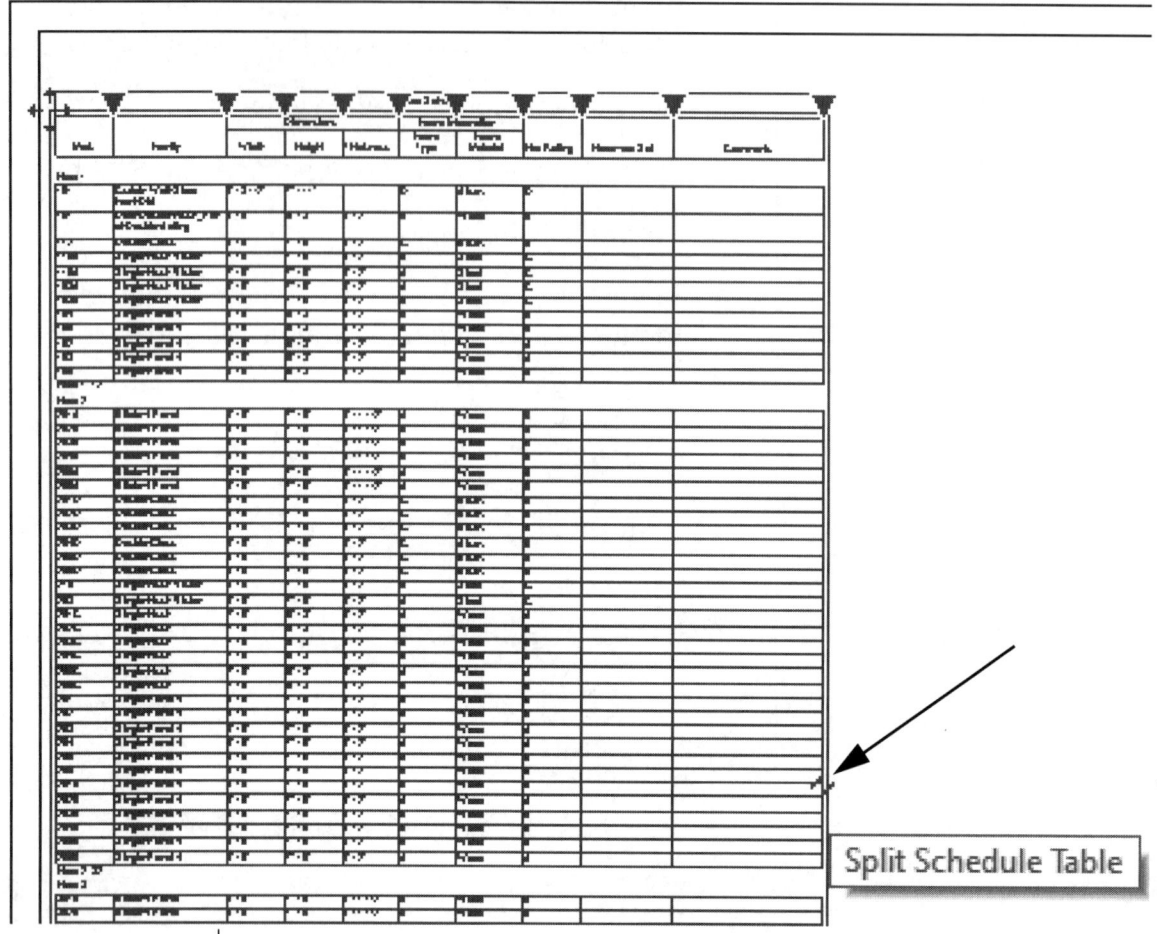

Figure 16–59

10. Select the individual schedules on the sheet and use the control grips at the bottom of the schedule to stretch it to fit the sheet, as shown in Figure 16–60.

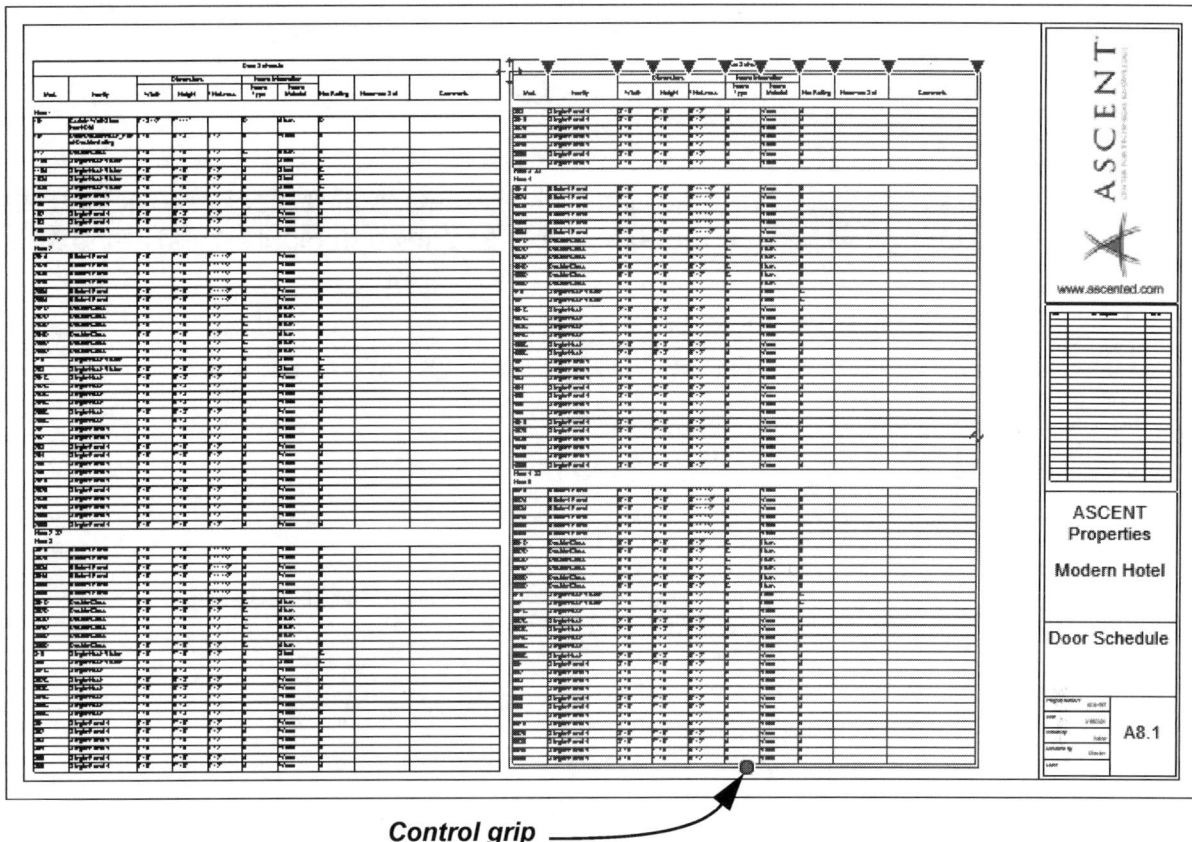

*Control grip*

**Figure 16–60**

11. Zoom in and use the arrows at the top to modify the width of the columns so that the titles display correctly.

12. Click in an empty space in the view to clear the selection.

    - You may find that you will not need the third sheet. You can right-click on the third sheet in the Project Browser and select **Delete** to remove it.

13. Switch back to the **Floor Plans: Floor 1** view and select the double-swing door at the kitchen.

14. In the Type Selector, change the size to **72" x 82"**. In Properties, add a *Frame Type*, *Frame Material*, and *Finish*.

15. Return to the sheet **A8.1 - Schedules**. The information is automatically populated.

16. Open the Room Schedule.

17. Note that for the RR, both the room number and area show as **<varies>**. This means that on Floor 1, there are multiple restroom's with varying room numbers and square footage.

18. Open sheet **A1.2 Floor 1 - Furniture Plan**.

19. Drag and drop the **Room Schedule** onto the sheet. Note that the schedule is showing all levels.

20. Activate the Room Schedule view. In Properties, click **Edit...** next to *Filter*.

21. In the Schedule Properties dialog box, check the **Filter by sheet** checkbox, as shown in Figure 16–61, and click **OK**.

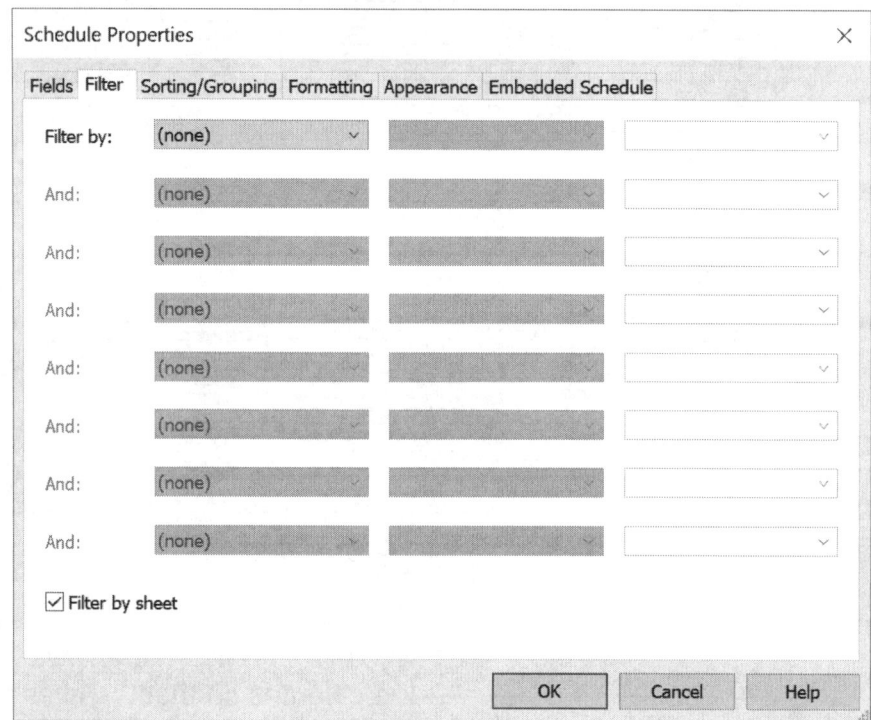

Figure 16–61

22. Activate the **A1.2 Floor 1 - Furniture Plan** sheet and note that the room schedule only shows the rooms that are in the viewport.

23. To see the schedule's ability to change depending on which viewports are placed on the sheet, drag and drop the **Floor 2** view onto the sheet. (This view does not fit on the sheet.)

    - Note that the room schedule will automatically update with Floor 2's room information.

24. Delete the Floor 2 viewport, and note that the schedule updates to just show Floor 1's rooms.

25. Save and close the project.

# Chapter Review Questions

1. You can tag in a 3D view, but you first have to do what to the view?

    a. You cannot tag in 3D view.

    b. Rename the view.

    c. Lock the view.

    d. Unlock the view.

2. Which of the following elements cannot be tagged using **Tag by Category**?

    a. Rooms

    b. Floors

    c. Walls

    d. Doors

3. What happens when you delete a door in a Revit model?

    a. You must delete the door on the sheet.

    b. You must delete the door from the schedule.

    c. The door is removed from the model, but not from the schedule.

    d. The door is removed from the model and the schedule.

4. In a schedule, if you change type information (such as a Type Mark), all instances of that type update with the new information.

    a. True

    b. False

## Command Summary

| Button | Command | Location |
|---|---|---|
| | Material Tag | • **Ribbon:** *Annotate* tab>Tag panel |
| | Multi-Category | • **Ribbon:** *Annotate* tab>Tag panel |
| | Stair Tread/ Riser Number | • **Ribbon:** *Annotate* tab>Tag panel |
| | Tag All Not Tagged | • **Ribbon:** *Annotate* tab>Tag panel |
| | Tag by Category | • **Ribbon:** *Annotate* tab>Tag panel<br>• **Shortcut:** TG |
| | Tag Room (Room Tag) | • **Ribbon:** *Architecture* tab>Room & Area panel<br>• **Ribbon:** *Annotate* tab>Tag panel<br>• **Shortcut:** RT |

# Chapter 17

# Creating Details

Creating details is a critical part of the design process, as it is the step where you specify the exact information that is required to build a construction project. The elements that you can add to a model include detail components, detail lines, text, tags, symbols, and filled regions. Details can be created from views in the model, but you can also add 2D details in separate views.

## Learning Objectives in This Chapter

- Create drafting views where you can add 2D details.
- Add detail components that show the typical elements in a detail.
- Annotate details using detail lines, text, tags, symbols, and patterns that define materials.

## 17.1 Setting Up Detail Views

*Details are created either in 2D drafting views or in callouts from plan, elevation, or section views.*

Most of the work you do in Revit is exclusively with *smart* elements that interconnect and work together in the model. However, the software does not automatically display how elements should be built to fit together. For this, you need to create detail drawings, as shown in Figure 17–1.

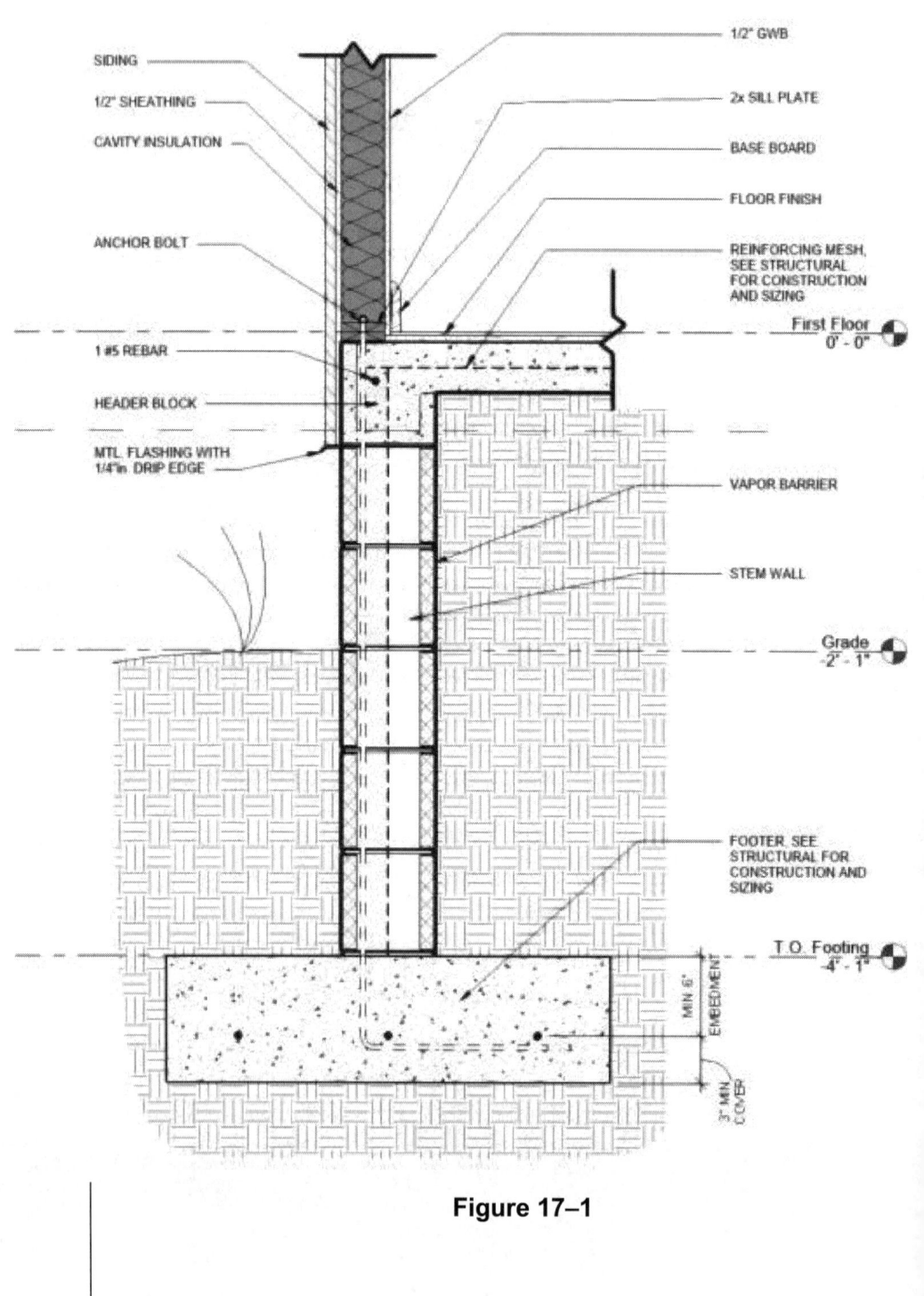

Figure 17–1

## How To: Create a Drafting View

1. In the *View* tab>Create panel, click (Drafting View).
2. In the New Drafting View dialog box, enter a *Name* and set a *Scale*, as shown in Figure 17–2.

*Drafting views are listed in their own section in the Project Browser.*

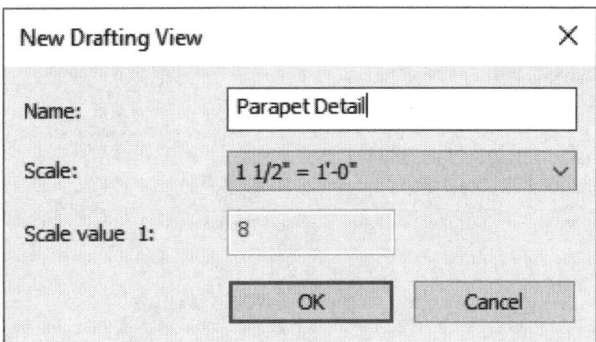

Figure 17–2

3. Click **OK**. A blank view is created with space in which you can sketch the detail.

## How To: Create a Detail View from Model Elements

1. Start the **Section** or **Callout** command.
2. In the Type Selector, select the **Detail View: Detail** type.
   - The marker indicates that it is a detail, as shown for a section in Figure 17–3.

*Callouts also have a Detail View Type that can be used in the same way.*

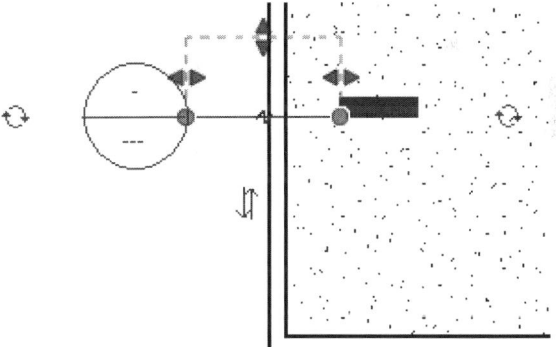

Figure 17–3

3. Place the section or a callout of the area you want to use for the detail.
4. Open the new detail.

- Change the detail level to see more or less of the element materials.

- Use the **Detail Line** tool to sketch on top of or add to the building elements.

- Because you are working with smart elements, a detail of the model is a true representation. When the building elements change, the detail changes as well, as shown in Figure 17–4.

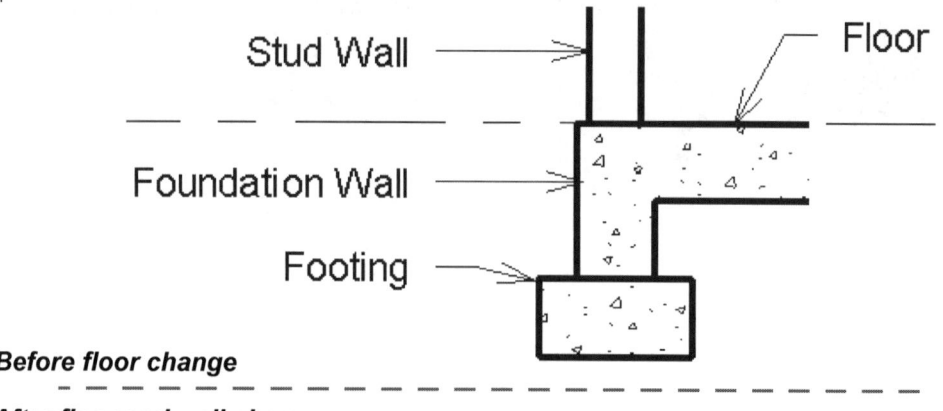

*Before floor change*

*After floor and wall change*

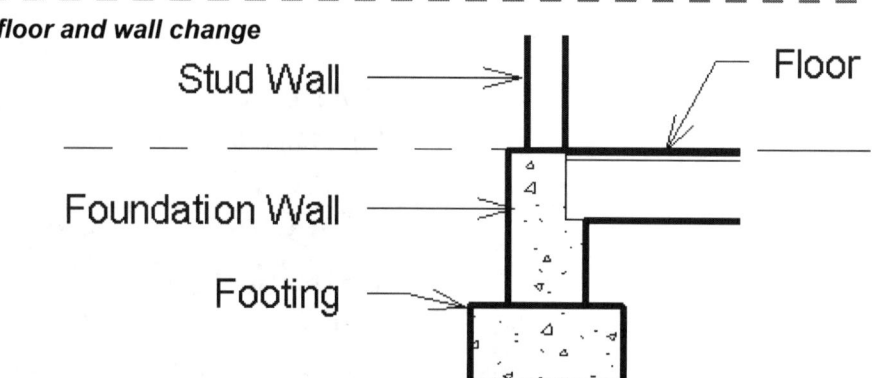

**Figure 17–4**

- You can create detail elements on top of the model and then toggle the model off so that it does not show in the detail view. In Properties, in the *Graphics* section, change *Display Model* to **Do not display**. You can also set the model to **Halftone**, as shown in Figure 17–5.

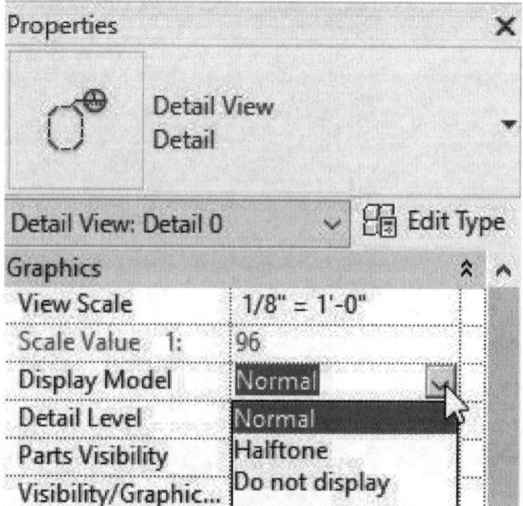

**Figure 17–5**

# Referencing a Drafting View

Once you have created a drafting view, you can reference it in another view (such as a callout, elevation, or section view), as shown in Figure 17–6. For example, in a section view, you might want to reference an existing roof detail. You can reference drafting views, sections, elevations, and callouts.

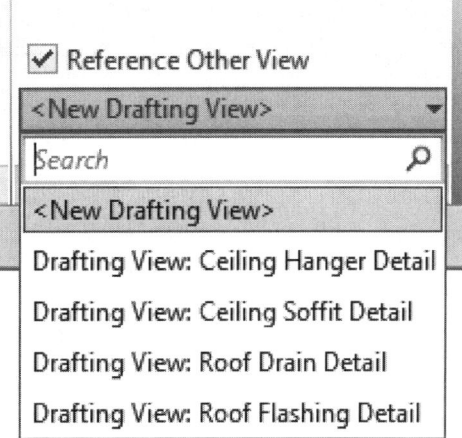

Figure 17–6

- You can use the search feature to limit the information displayed.

### How To: Reference a Drafting View

1. Open the view in which you want to place the reference.
2. Start the **Section**, **Callout**, or **Elevation** command.
3. In the *Modify* contextual tab>Reference panel, select **Reference Other View**.
4. In the drop-down list, select **<New Drafting View>** or an existing drafting view.
5. Place the view marker.
6. When you place the associated drafting view on a sheet, the marker in this view updates with the appropriate information.

- If you select **<New Drafting View>** from the drop-down list, a new view is created in the *Drafting Views (Detail)* area in the Project Browser. You can rename it as needed. The new view does not include any model elements.

- When you create a detail based on a section, elevation, or callout, you do not need to link it to a drafting view.

- You can change a referenced view to a different view. Select the view marker and in the ribbon, select the new view from the list.

## Saving Drafting Views

To create a library of standard details, save the non-model specific drafting views to your server. They can then be imported into a project and modified to suit. They are saved as .RVT files.

Drafting views can be saved in two ways:

- Save an individual drafting view to a new file.
- Save all of the drafting views as a group in one new file.

### How To: Save One Drafting View to a File

1. In the Project Browser, right-click on the drafting view you want to save and select **Save to New File…**, as shown in Figure 17–7.

**Figure 17–7**

2. In the Save As dialog box, specify a name and location for the file and click **Save**.

### How To: Save a Group of Drafting Views to a File

1. In the *File* tab, expand  (Save As), expand  (Library), and then click  (View).
2. In the Save Views dialog box, in the *Views:* area, expand the list and select **Show drafting views only**.
3. Select the drafting views that you want to save, as shown in Figure 17–8.

*You can save sheets, drafting views, model views (floor plans), schedules, and reports.*

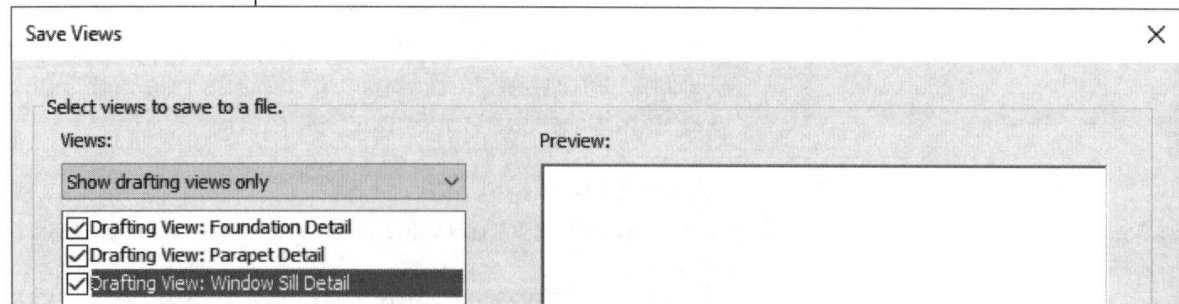

**Figure 17–8**

4. Click **OK**.
5. In the Save As dialog box, specify a name and location for the file and click **Save**.

# Creating Details

## How To: Use a Saved Drafting View in Another Project

1. Open the project to which you want to add the drafting view.
2. In the *Insert* tab>Load from Library panel, expand (Insert from File) and click (Insert Views from File).
3. In the Open dialog box, select the project in which you saved the detail and click **Open**.
4. In the Insert Views dialog box, limit the types of views to **Show drafting views only**, as shown in Figure 17–9.

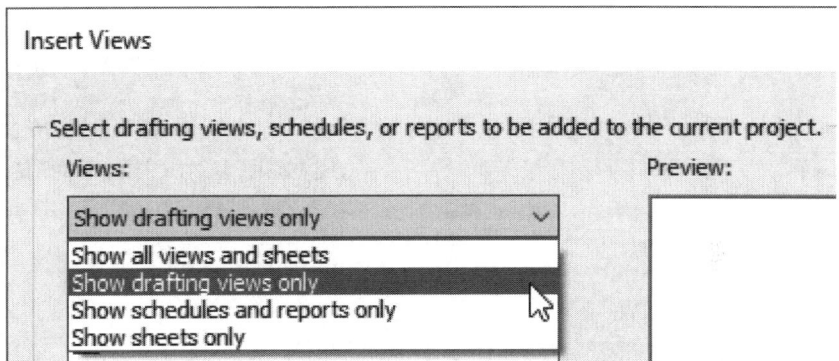

Figure 17–9

5. Select the view(s) that you want to insert and click **OK**.

> **Hint: Importing Details from Other CAD Software**
>
> You might already have a set of standard details created in a different CAD program, such as the AutoCAD® software. You can reuse the details in Revit by importing them into a temporary project. Once you have imported the detail, it helps to clean it up and save it as a view before bringing it into your active project.
>
> 1. In a new project, create a drafting view and make it active.
> 2. In the *Insert* tab>Import panel, click  (Import CAD).
> 3. In the Import CAD dialog box, select the file to import. Most of the default values are what you need. You might want to change the *Layer/Level colors* to **Black and White**.
> 4. Click **Open**.
>
> - If you want to modify the detail, select the imported data. In the *Modify | [filename]* tab>Import Instance panel, expand  (Explode) and click  (Partial Explode) or  (Full Explode). Click  (Delete Layers) before you explode the detail. A full explode greatly increases the file size.
>
> - Modify the detail using tools in the Modify panel. Change all the text and line styles to Revit-specific elements.

# 17.2 Adding Detail Components

Revit elements, such as the casework section shown in Figure 17–10, typically require additional information to ensure that they are constructed correctly. To create details such as the one shown in Figure 17–11, you add detail components, detail lines, and various annotation elements.

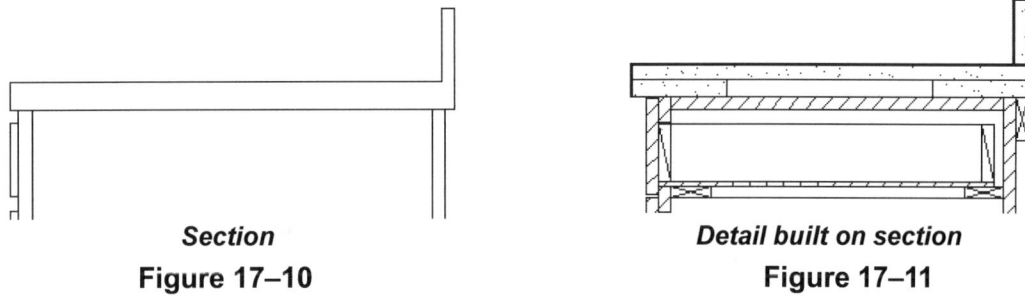

*Section*
**Figure 17–10**

*Detail built on section*
**Figure 17–11**

- Detail elements are not directly connected to the model, even if model elements display in the view.

- If you want to draw detail lines in 3D, use the **Model Line** tool. Detail Line is grayed out when you are in a 3D view or perspective view.

## Detail Components

Detail components are families made of 2D and annotation elements. Over 500 detail components organized by CSI format are found in the *Detail Items* folder of the Revit Library, as shown in Figure 17–12.

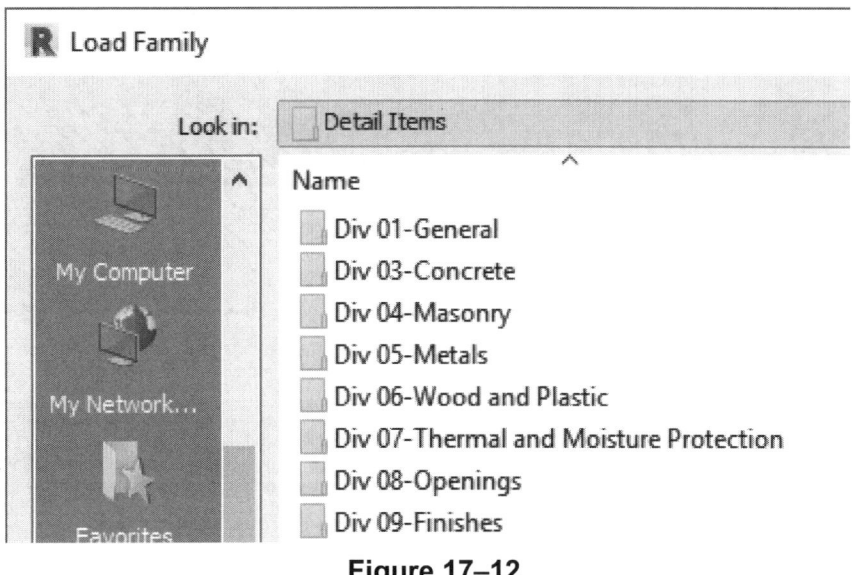

**Figure 17–12**

## How To: Add a Detail Component

1. In the *Annotate* tab>Detail panel, expand (Component) and click (Detail Component).
2. In the Type Selector, select the detail component type. You can load additional types from the Revit Library.
3. Many detail components can be rotated as you insert them by pressing <Spacebar>. Alternatively, select **Rotate after placement** in the Options Bar, as shown in Figure 17–13.

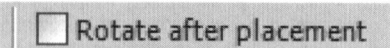

**Figure 17–13**

4. Place the component in the view.

## Adding Break Lines

The Break Line is a detail component found in the *Detail Items\ Div 01-General* folder. It consists of a rectangular area (shown highlighted in Figure 17–14) that is used to block out elements behind it. You can modify the size of the area that is covered and change the size of the cut line using the controls.

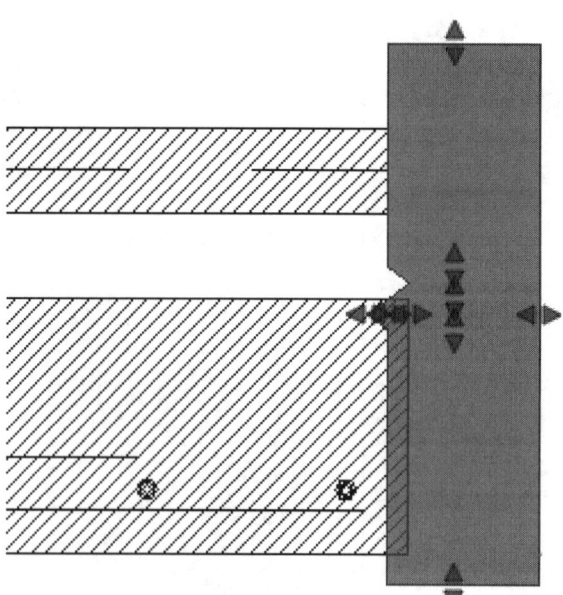

**Figure 17–14**

# Creating Details

> **Hint: Working with the Draw Order of Details**
>
> When you select detail elements in a view, you can change the draw order of the elements in the *Modify | Detail Items* tab> Arrange panel. You can bring elements in front of other elements or place them behind elements, as shown in Figure 17–15.
>
>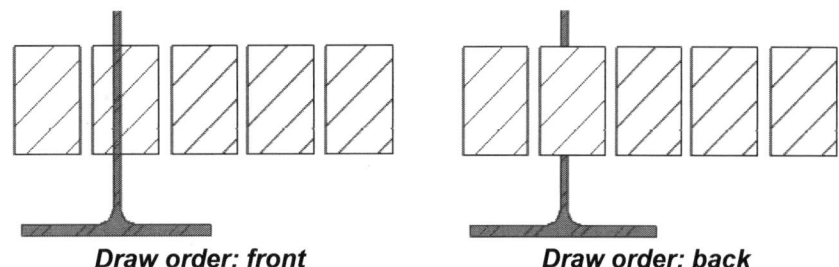
> **Figure 17–15**
>
> - **(Bring to Front):** Places element in front of all other elements.
>
> - **(Send to Back):** Places element behind all other elements.
>
> - **(Bring Forward):** Moves element one step to the front.
>
> - **(Send Backward):** Moves element one step to the back.
>
> - You can select multiple detail elements and change the draw order of all of them in one step. They keep the relative order of the original selection.

## Repeating Details

Instead of having to insert a component multiple times (such as brick or concrete block), you can use (Repeating Detail Component) and create a string of components, as shown in Figure 17–16.

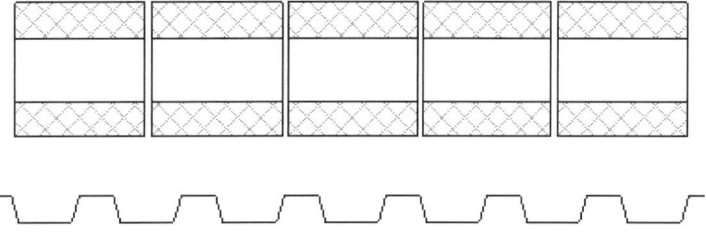
**Figure 17–16**

## How To: Insert a Repeating Detail Component

1. In the *Annotate* tab>Detail panel, expand (Component) and click (Repeating Detail Component).
2. In the Type Selector, select the detail you want to use.
3. In the Draw panel, click (Line) or (Pick Lines).
4. In the Options Bar, type a value for the *Offset*, if needed.
5. The components repeat to fit the length of the sketched or selected line, as shown in Figure 17–17. You can lock the components to the line.

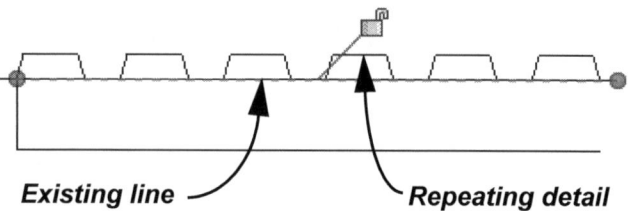

*Existing line* — *Repeating detail*

**Figure 17–17**

- For information on customizing repeating details, see *B.7 Creating a Repeating Detail*.

### Hint: (Insulation)

Adding batt insulation is similar to adding a repeating detail component, but instead of a series of bricks or other elements, it creates the linear batting pattern shown in Figure 17–18.

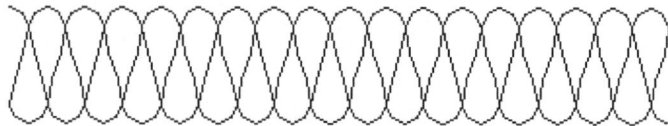

**Figure 17–18**

Before you place the insulation in the view, specify the *Width* and other options in the Options Bar, as shown in Figure 17–19.

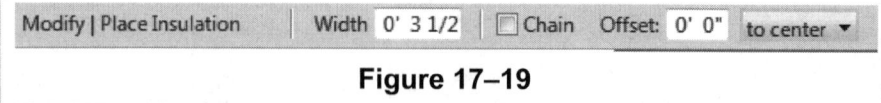

**Figure 17–19**

## 17.3 Annotating Details

After you have added components and sketched detail lines, you need to add annotations to the detail view. You can place text notes and dimensions, as shown in Figure 17–20, as well as symbols and tags. Filled regions are used to add hatching.

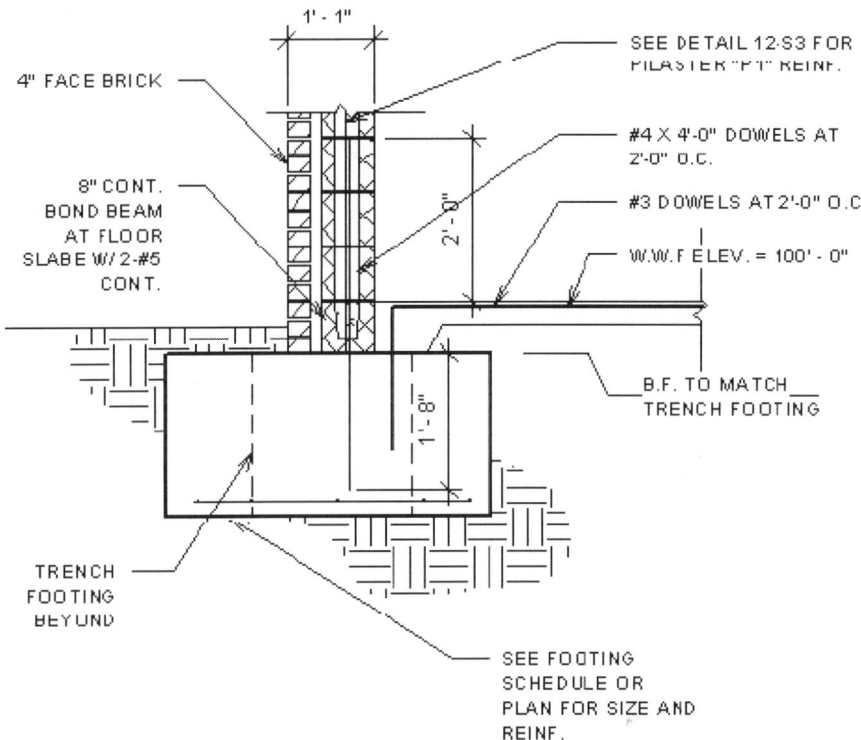

Figure 17–20

**Creating Filled Regions**

Many elements include material information that displays in plan and section views, while other elements need more details to be added. For example, the concrete wall shown in Figure 17–21 includes material information, while the earth to the left of the wall needs to be added using the **Filled Region** command.

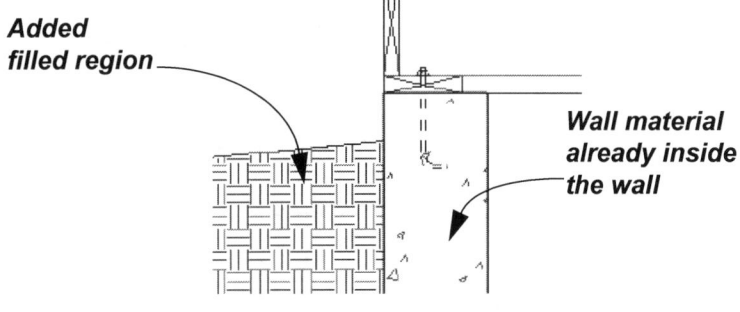

Figure 17–21

The patterns used in details are *drafting patterns*. They are scaled to the view scale and update if you modify it. You can also add full-size *model patterns*, such as a Flemish Bond brick pattern, to the surface of some elements.

### How To: Add a Filled Region

1. In the *Annotate* tab>Detail panel, expand (Region) and click (Filled Region).
2. Create a closed boundary using the Draw tools.
3. In the Line Style panel, select the line style for the outside edge of the boundary. If you do not want the boundary to display, select the **<Invisible lines>** style.
4. In the Type Selector, select the fill type, as shown in Figure 17–22.

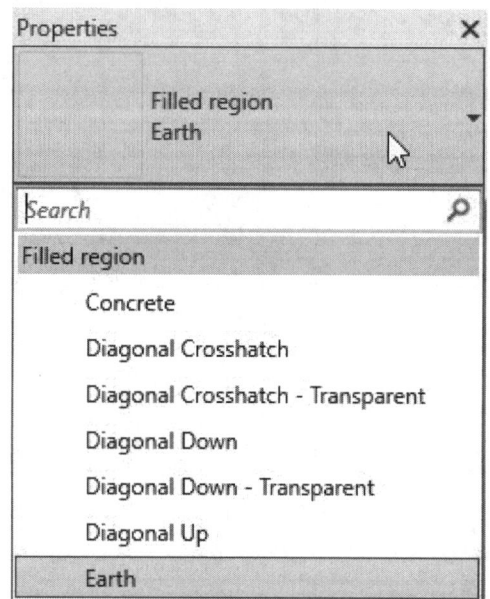

Figure 17–22

5. Click (Finish Edit Mode).

- You can modify a region by changing the fill type in the Type Selector or by editing the sketch.

- Double-click on the edge of the filled region to edit the sketch.

  If you have the Selection option set to (Select elements by face), you can select the pattern.

# Hint: Creating a Filled Region Pattern Type

You can create a custom pattern by duplicating and editing an existing pattern type.

1. Select an existing region or create a boundary.
2. In Properties, click 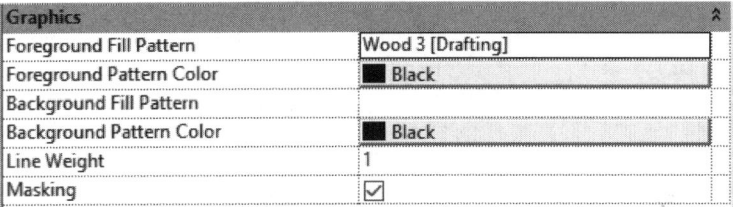 (Edit Type).
3. In the Type Properties dialog box, click **Duplicate** and name the new pattern.
4. Select the *Foreground/Background Fill Pattern* and *Color* and specify the *Line Weight* and *Masking*, as shown in Figure 17–23.

| Graphics | |
|---|---|
| Foreground Fill Pattern | Wood 3 [Drafting] |
| Foreground Pattern Color | Black |
| Background Fill Pattern | |
| Background Pattern Color | Black |
| Line Weight | 1 |
| Masking | ☑ |

Figure 17–23

5. Click **OK**.

- You can select from two types of fill patterns: **Drafting** (as shown in Figure 17–24) and **Model**. Drafting fill patterns scale to the view scale factor. Model fill patterns display full scale on the model.

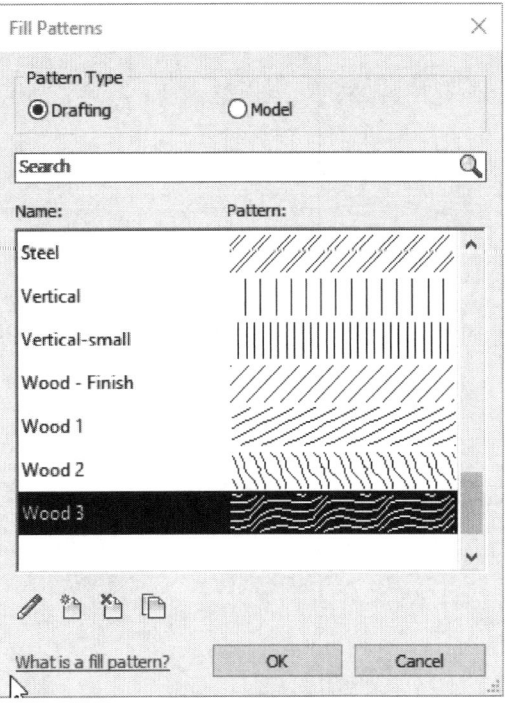

Figure 17–24

# Adding Detail Tags

Besides adding text to a detail, you can tag detail components using 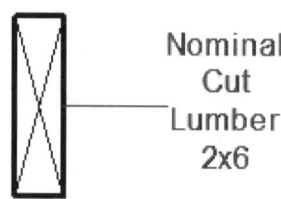 (Tag By Category). The tag name is set in the Type Parameters for that component, as shown in Figure 17–25. This means that if you have more than one copy of the component in your project, you do not have to rename it each time you place its tag.

*The **Detail Item Tag.rfa** tag is located in the Annotations folder in the Revit Library.*

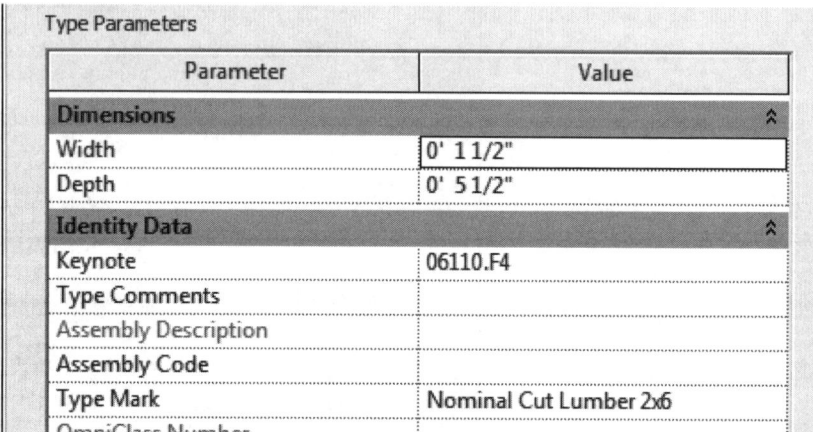

**Figure 17–25**

- For more information on annotating using keynotes see *B.8 Keynoting and Keynote Legends*.

# Practice 17a

# Create a Detail Based on a Section Callout

## Practice Objectives

- Create a detail based on a section.
- Add filled regions, detail components, and annotations.

In this practice, you will create a detail based on a callout of a wall section. You will add repeating detail components, break lines, and detail lines, and add annotations to complete the detail, as shown in Figure 17–26.

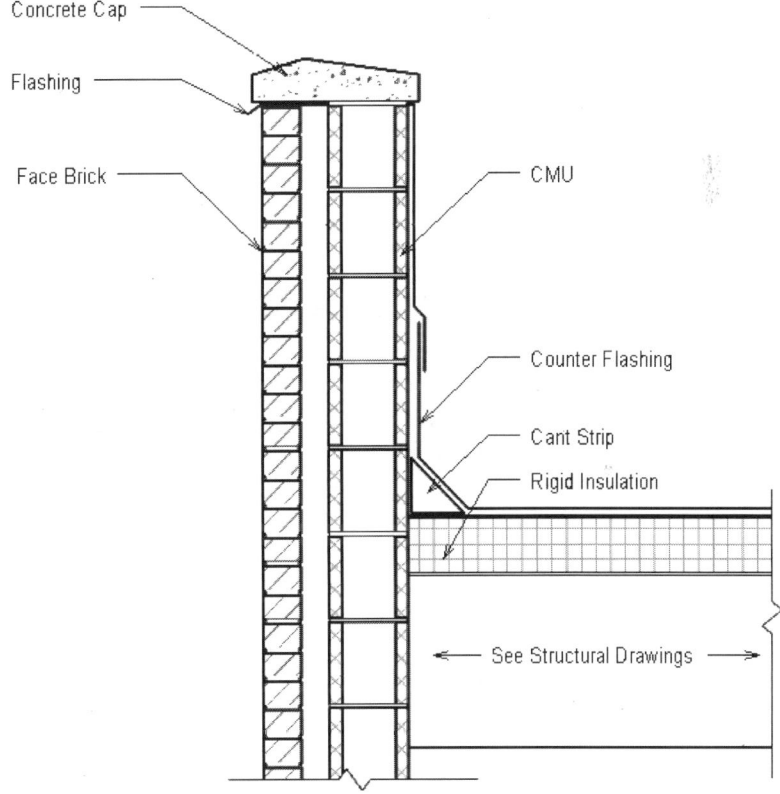

**Figure 17–26**

### Task 1 - Create a callout of a wall section.

1. Open the file **Hotel-Detailing.rvt** from the practice files folder.

2. Open the **Floor Plans: Floor 1** view.

3. Double-click on the wall section head shown in Figure 17–27. This guarantees that you open the correct section.

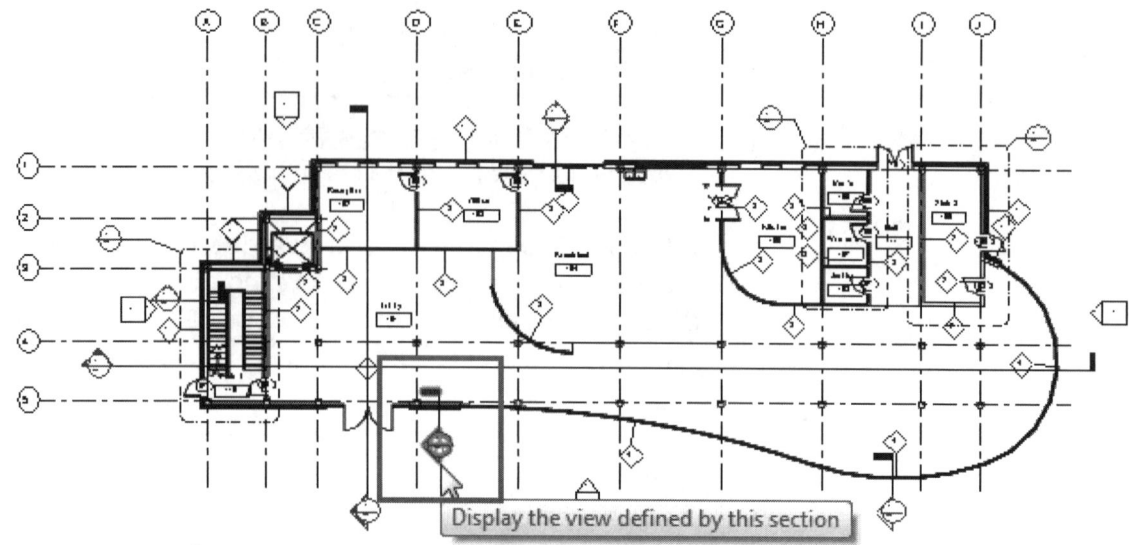

Figure 17–27

4. Zoom in to the top of the wall showing the parapet and the roof.

5. In the *View* tab>Create panel, click (Callout).

6. In the Type Selector, select **Detail View: Detail**.

7. Create a callout as shown in Figure 17–28.

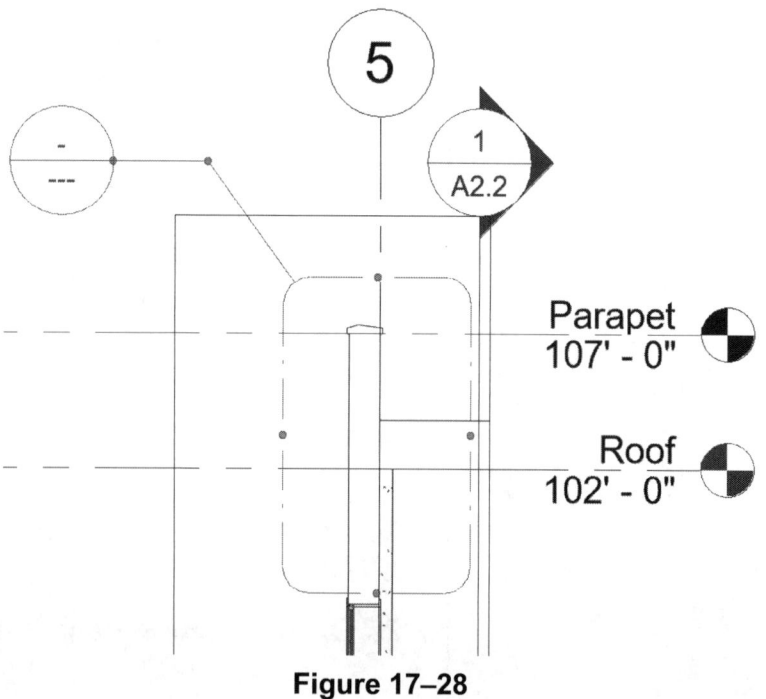

Figure 17–28

8. Click in an empty space in the view to clear the selection.

9. Double-click on the callout bubble to open the callout view.

10. In the View Control Bar, set the following parameters:
    - *Scale*: **1"=1'-0"**
    - *Detail Level*: (Fine)

11. Hide the levels, grids, and section markers (if displayed).

12. Toggle off the crop region.

13. Select the wall, right-click, and select **Override Graphics in View>By Element**.

14. In the View Specific Element Graphics dialog box, expand *Cut Patterns* and for the **Foreground**, uncheck **Visible**, as shown in Figure 17–29. Click **OK**.

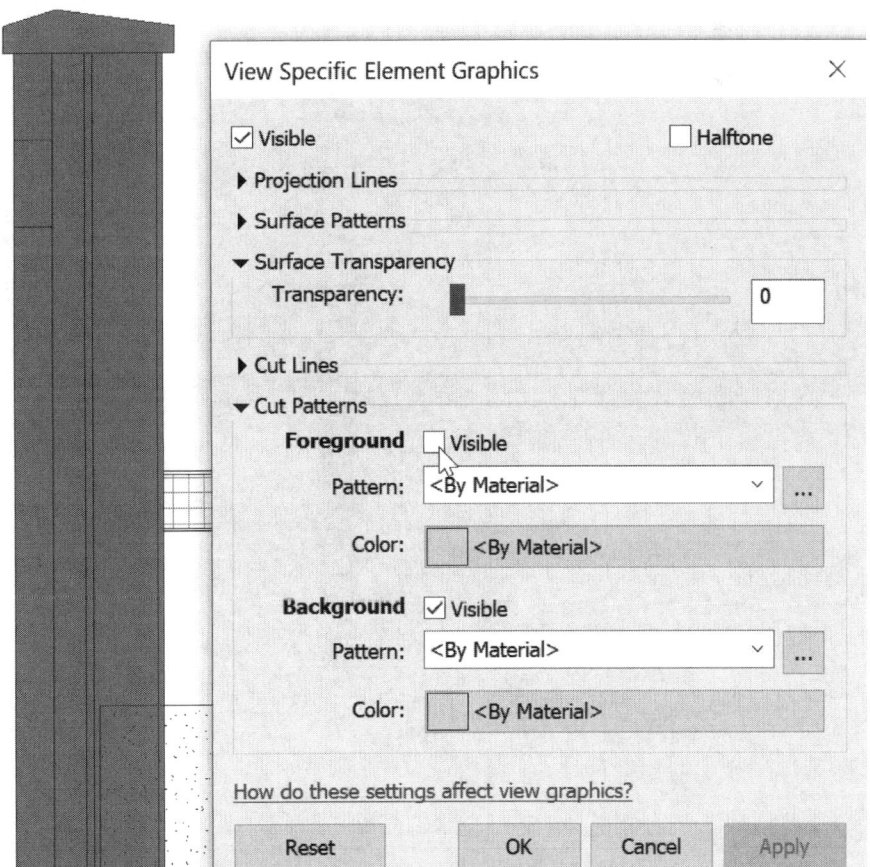

**Figure 17–29**

15. In the Project Browser, in the *Detail Views (Detail)* node, rename the view to **Parapet Detail**.

16. Save the project.

## Task 2 - Add repeating detail components and break lines.

1. In the *Annotate* tab>Detail panel, expand (Component) and click (Repeating Detail Component).

2. In the Type Selector, set the type to **Repeating Detail: Brick**.

3. Draw the brick line from top to bottom, starting at the bottom of the parapet cap, as shown in Figure 17–30.

*Drawing from the top down ensures that "mortar" is between the cap and the brick. This is how the detail elements were created.*

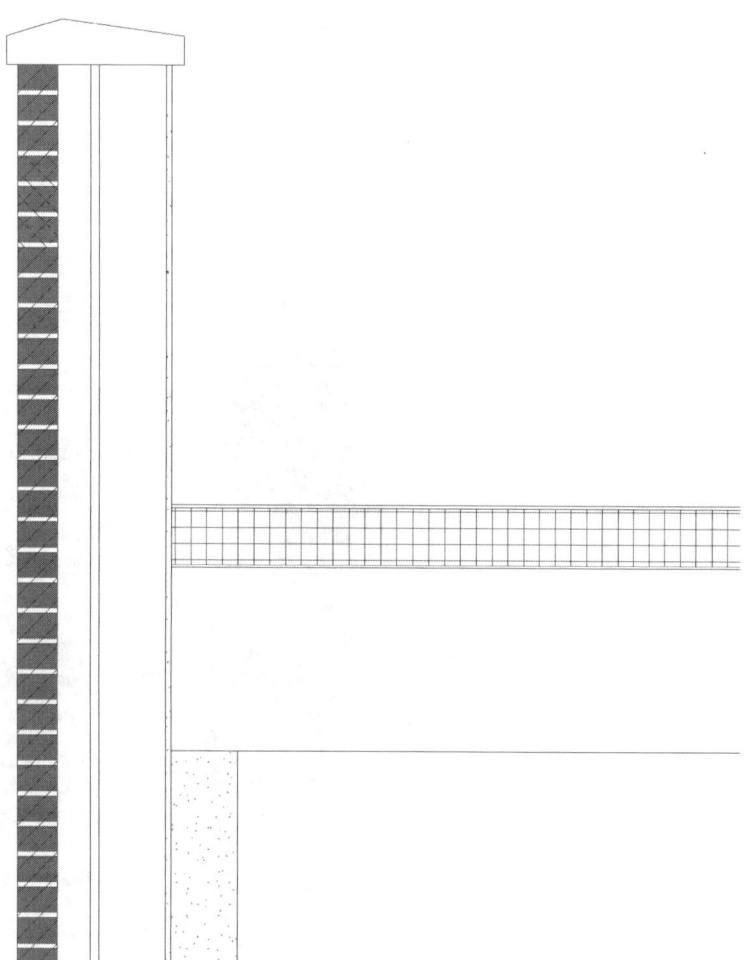

Figure 17–30

4. Click (Modify).

# Creating Details

5. Start the repeating component again. In the Type Selector, select **Repeating Detail: CMU**. Draw down the other side of the wall, as shown in Figure 17–31.

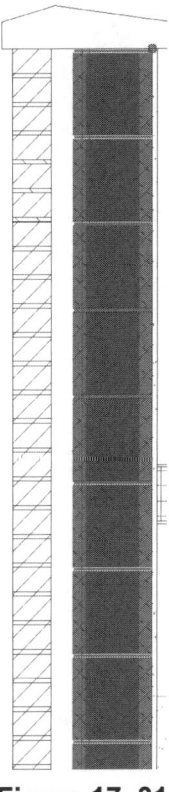

Figure 17–31

*Revit lists the last tool you used at the top of the drop-down list.*

6. In the *Annotate* tab>Detail panel, expand (Repeating Detail Component) and click (Detail Component).

7. In the *Modify | Place Detail Component* tab>Mode panel, click (Load Family).

8. In the Load Family dialog box, navigate to the practice files *Families>Details* folder, select **Break Line.rfa**, and click **Open**.

9. Add break lines to the bottom and right side of the detail. Press <Spacebar> to rotate the break line as needed, and use the controls to modify the size and depth, as shown in Figure 17–32.

   - If you added the break line going in the wrong direction, select the break line in the view and press <Spacebar> until it is rotated correctly.

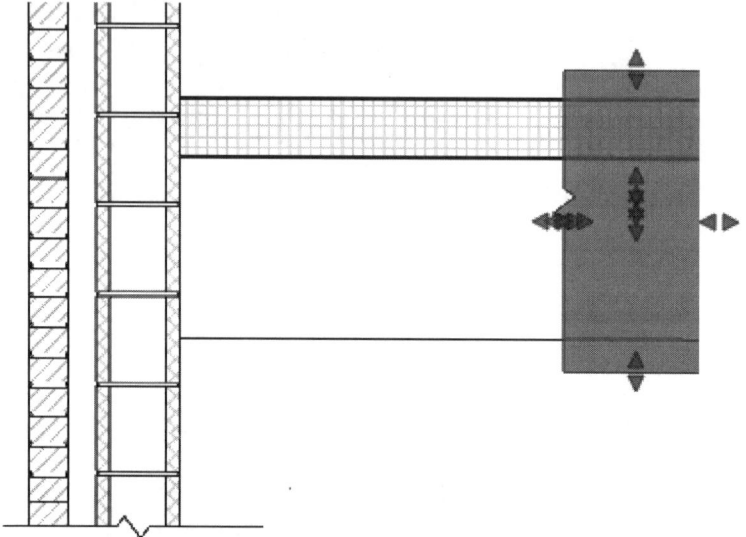

Figure 17–32

10. Save the project.

**Task 3 - Draw flashing using detail lines.**

1. In the *Annotate* tab>Detail panel, click (Detail Line).

2. In the *Modify | Place Detail Lines* tab>Line Style panel, verify that **Wide Lines** is selected, and in the Options Bar, verify that **Chain** is selected.

3. Draw flashing similar to that shown in Figure 17–33. (The lines in image are bold for clarity.)

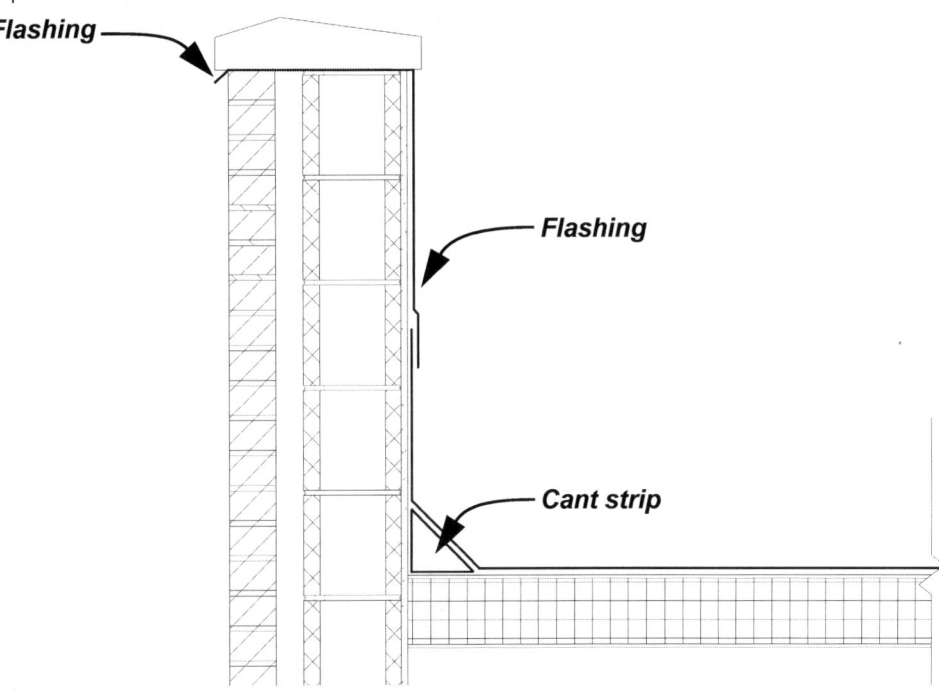

**Figure 17–33**

4. Using the **Detail Line** tool, add a cant strip under the flashing.

5. Save the project

**Task 4 - Add a filled region.**

1. Zoom in to the top of the parapet cap.

2. In the *Annotation* tab>Detail panel, expand (Region) and select (Filled Region).

3. In the Draw panel, select **Pick Lines**.

4. In the Type Selector, select **Concrete**, then trace the parapet cap.

5. Click ✓ (Finish Edit Mode). The parapet cap now shows its concrete detail, as shown in Figure 17–34.

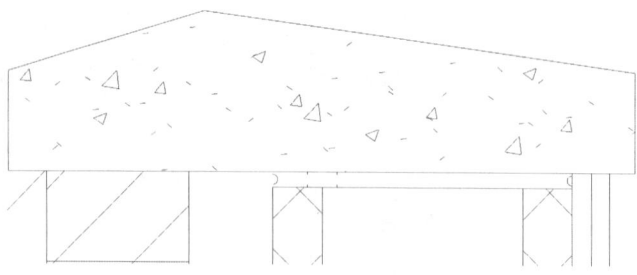

**Figure 17–34**

6. Save the project.

### Task 5 - Annotate the detail.

1. In the Quick Access Toolbar or in the *Annotate* tab>Text panel, click **A** (Text).

2. In the *Modify | Place Text* tab>Format panel, select ↙A (Two-Segments).

3. Add the text and leaders shown in Figure 17–35. Use alignments to place the leader points and text.

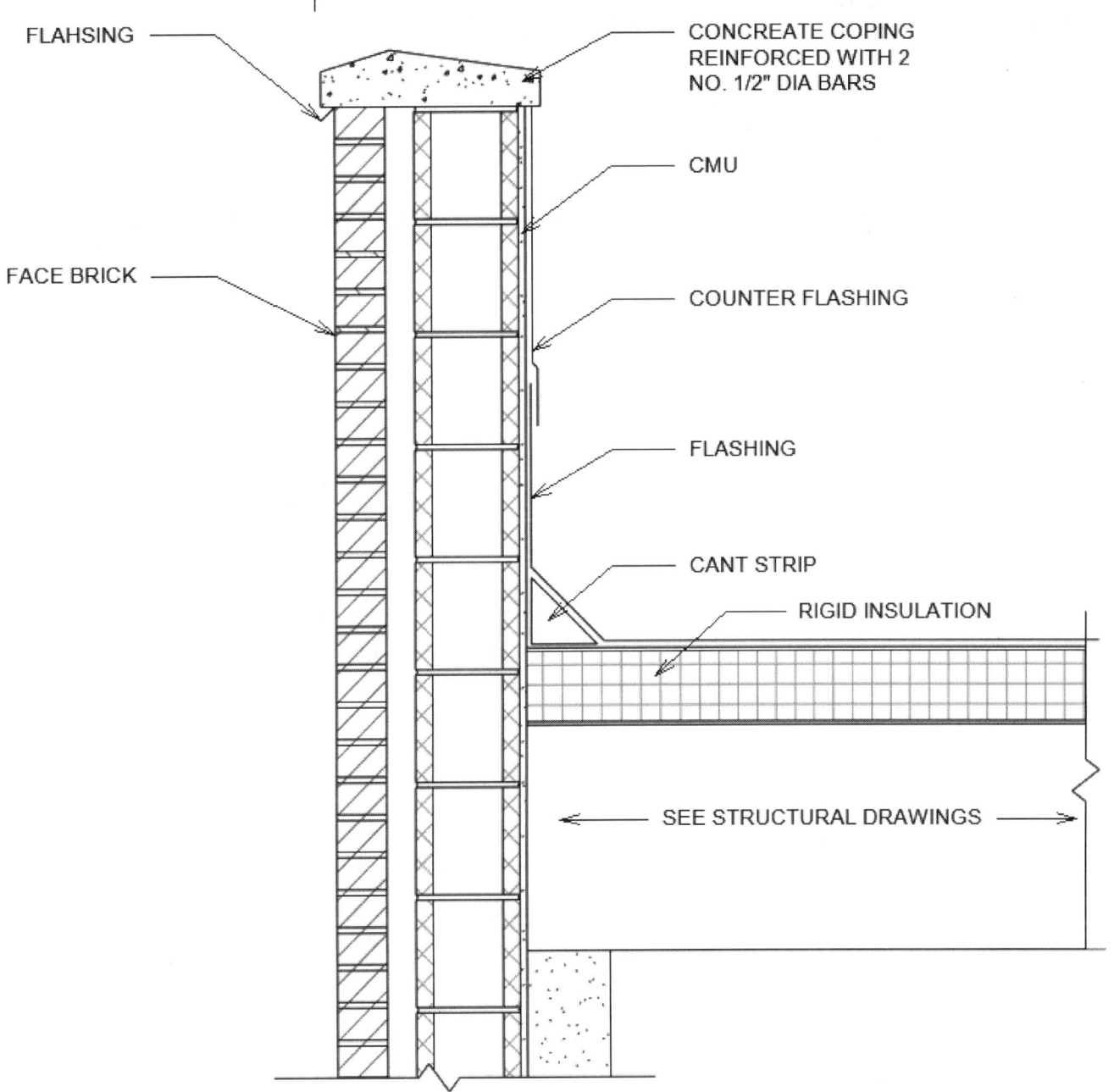

**Figure 17–35**

4. Save and keep the project opened.

At this point, you have a hybrid between detail items and model items. You can continue to add detail items to replace the roofing. You can also add structural elements if you have time.

# Practice 17b  Create a Detail in a Drafting View

## Practice Objective

- Create and annotate details.

In this practice, you will create a footing detail in a drafting view. You will add detail components, lines, and annotations, as well as filled regions. You will place the view on a sheet (as shown in Figure 17–36), and place a callout in another view that references this view.

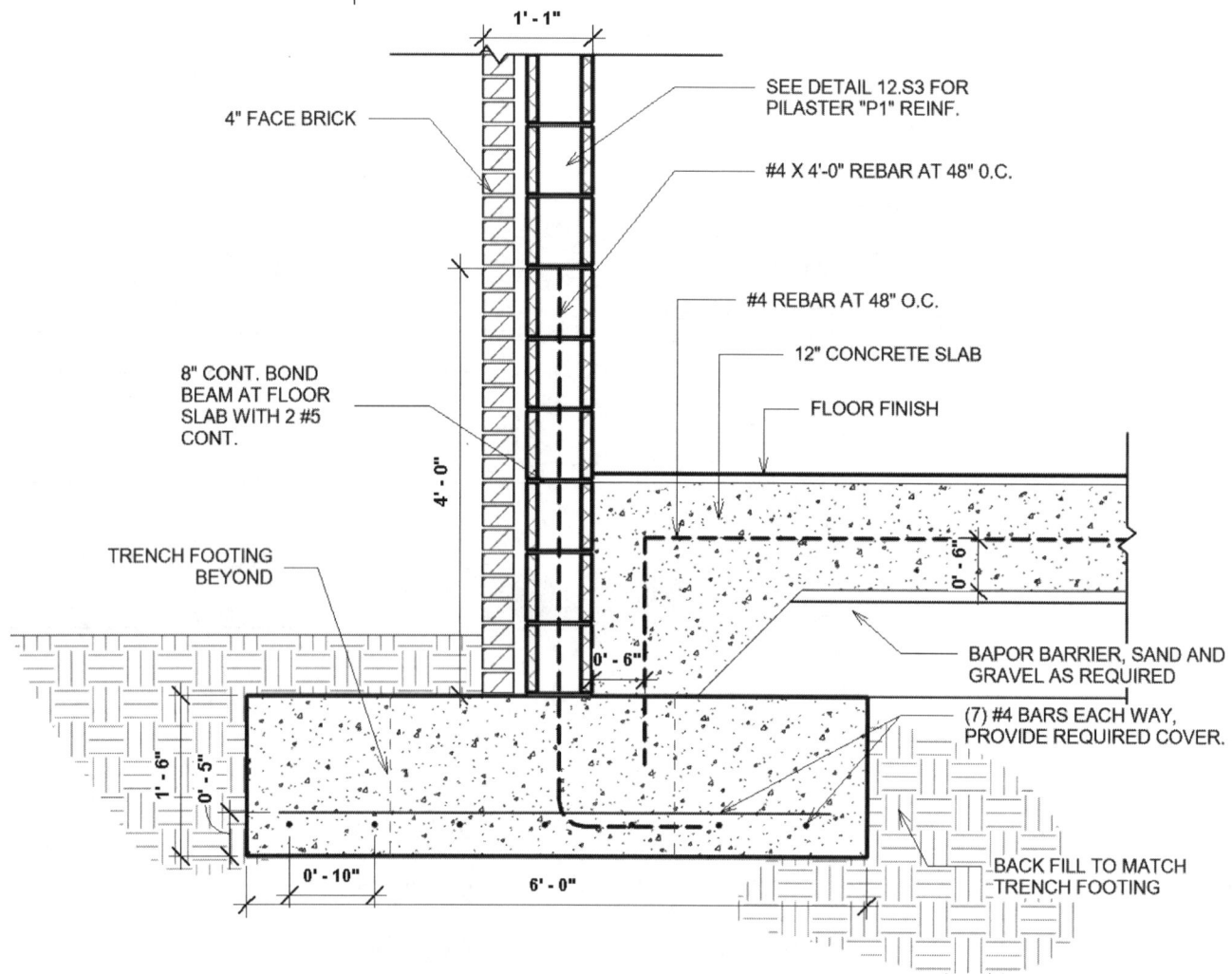

**Figure 17–36**

- This practice is designed with minimal direction so that you can apply what you have learned.

## Task 1 - Create a detail.

1. Continue working in **Hotel-Detailing.rvt**.

2. In the *View* tab>Create panel, select (Drafting View). Create a drafting view named **Footing Detail** at a scale of **3/4"=1'-0"**.

3. Use detail lines and detail components to add the footing, walls, floor, and rebar, as shown in Figure 17–36.

    - Use **Line Styles** to show the different weight and patterns (such as **Wide Line** and **Hidden Line**).

4. Add dimensions and text notes, as shown in Figure 17–36.

## Task 2 - Add filled regions.

1. In the *Annotate* tab>Detail panel, expand (Region) and click (Filled Region).

2. In the *Modify | Create Filled Region Boundary* tab>Line Style panel, select the Line Style **Medium Lines.**

3. Using the draw tools, sketch a boundary around the floor slab, as shown in Figure 17–37.

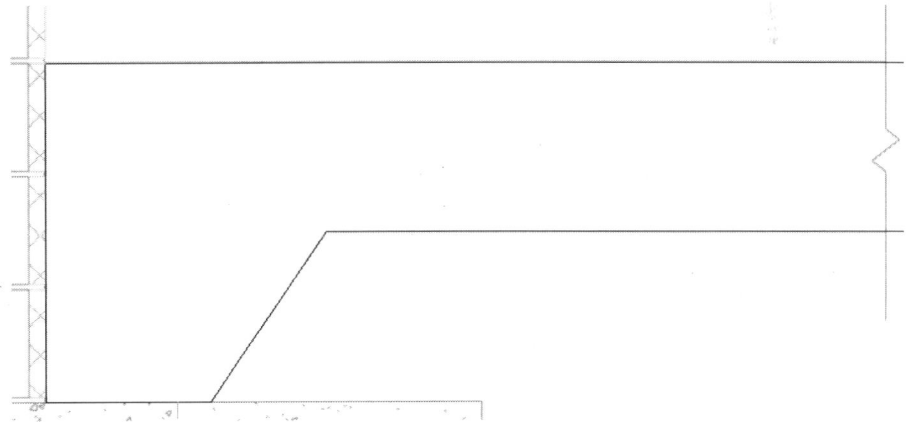

Figure 17–37

4. In the Type Selector, select **Filled region: Concrete**.

5. Click (Finish).

6. Add a filled region to the footing using the same **Concrete** pattern.

7. Create the curved filled regions shown in Figure 17–38, using the Line Style **<Invisible lines>** to sketch the boundary. Set the Filled Region type to **Earth**.

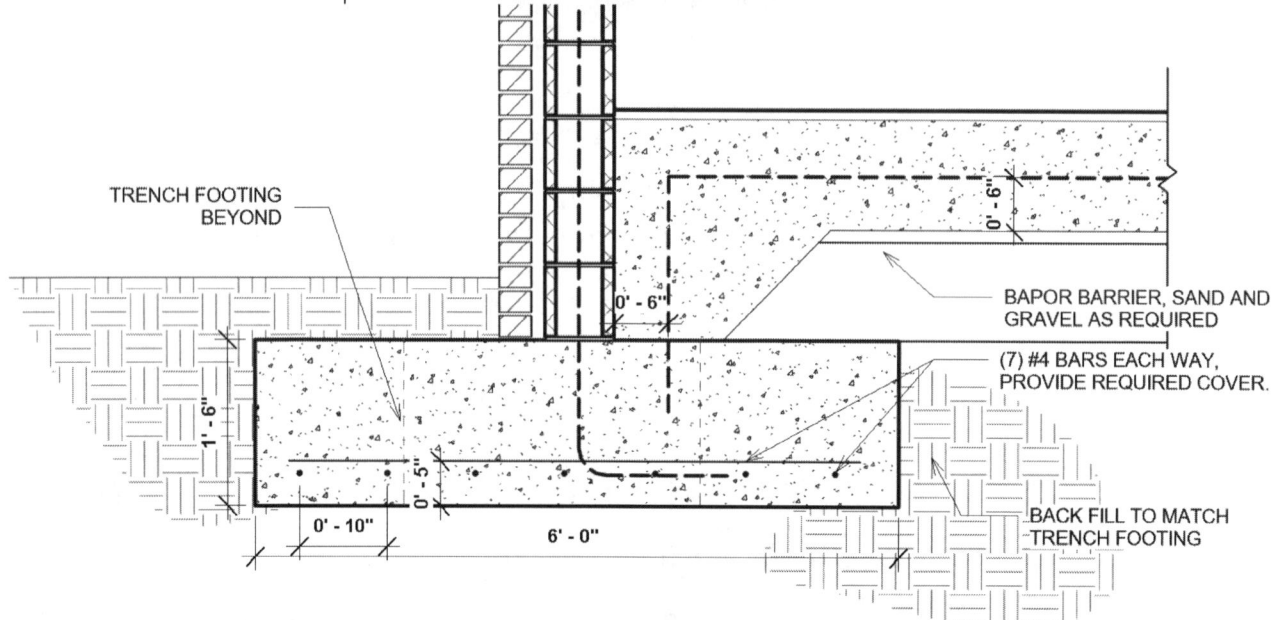

Figure 17–38

- The curved lines are made with splines.

8. The patterns might cover over some elements. Select the filled region and in the *Modify | Detail Items* tab>Arrange panel, click (Send to Back).

9. Make any necessary adjustments to the annotation locations.

10. Save the project.

### Task 3 - Add the detail to a sheet and connect it to a detail callout.

1. Create a new sheet named **A5.1 - Wall Detail** and drag and drop the footing detail to this sheet.

2. Open the **Sections (Wall Section): Section 2** view.

3. Start the **Callout** command and select the **Detail View: Detail** type.

4. In the *Modify | Callout* tab>Reference panel, select **Reference Other View** and in the drop-down list, select **Drafting View: Footing Detail**, as shown in Figure 17–39.

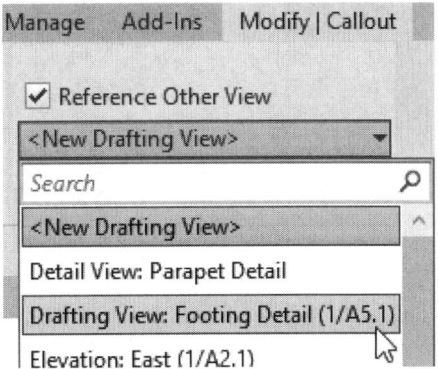

Figure 17–39

5. Draw the callout around the footing area. The correct detail is referenced, as shown in Figure 17–40.

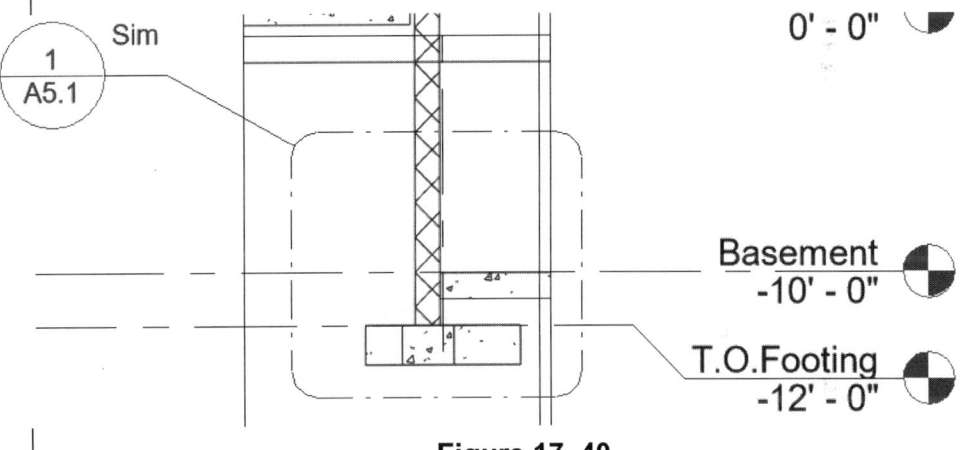

Figure 17–40

6. Save and close the project.

# Chapter Review Questions

1. Which of the following are ways in which you can create a detail? (Select all that apply.)

    a. Make a callout of a section and sketch over it.

    b. Draw all of the elements from scratch.

    c. Import a CAD detail and modify or sketch over it.

    d. Insert an existing drafting view from another file.

2. In which type of view (access shown in Figure 17–41) can you NOT add detail lines?

    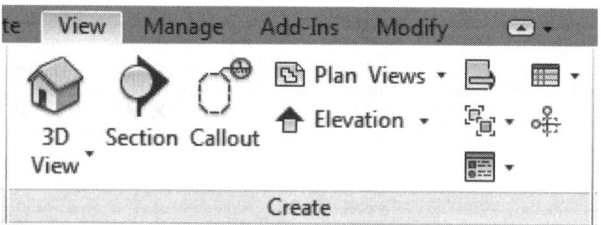

    **Figure 17–41**

    a. Plans

    b. Elevations

    c. 3D views

    d. Legends

3. How are detail components different from building components?

    a. There is no difference.

    b. Detail components are made of 2D lines and annotation only.

    c. Detail components are made of building elements, but only display in detail views.

    d. Detail components are made of 2D and 3D elements.

4. What is a true statement about detail lines?

    a. Always the same width.

    b. Vary in width according to the view.

    c. Display in all views associated with the detail.

    d. Display only in the view in which they were created.

5. Which command do you use to add a pattern (such as concrete or earth, as shown in Figure 17–42) to part of a detail?

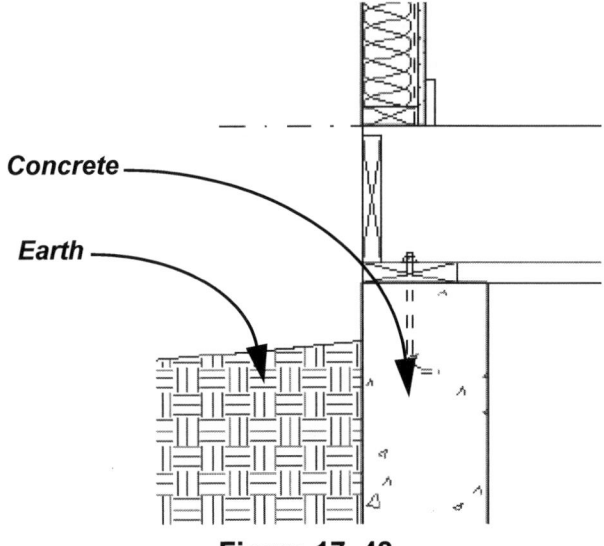

Figure 17–42

    a. Region

    b. Filled Region

    c. Masking Region

    d. Pattern Region

# Command Summary

| Button | Command | Location |
|---|---|---|
| **CAD Import Tools** | | |
| | Delete Layers | • **Ribbon:** *Modify | <imported filename>* tab>Import Instance panel |
| | Full Explode | • **Ribbon:** *Modify | <imported filename>* tab>Import Instance panel, expand Explode |
| | Import CAD | • **Ribbon:** *Insert* tab>Import panel |
| | Partial Explode | • **Ribbon:** *Modify | <imported filename>* tab>Import Instance panel, expand Explode |
| **Detail Tools** | | |
| | Detail Component | • **Ribbon:** *Annotate* tab>Detail panel, expand Component |
| | Detail Line | • **Ribbon:** *Annotate* tab>Detail panel |
| | Insulation | • **Ribbon:** *Annotate* tab>Detail panel |
| | Filled Region | • **Ribbon:** *Annotate* tab>Detail panel |
| | Repeating Detail Component | • **Ribbon:** *Annotate* tab>Detail panel, expand Component |
| **View Tools** | | |
| | Bring Forward | • **Ribbon:** *Modify | Detail Items* tab>Arrange panel |
| | Bring to Front | • **Ribbon:** *Modify | Detail Items* tab>Arrange panel |
| | Drafting View | • **Ribbon:** *View* tab>Create panel |
| | Insert from File: Insert Views from File | • **Ribbon:** *Insert* tab>Load from Library panel, expand Insert from File |
| | Send Backward | • **Ribbon:** *Modify | Detail Items* tab>Arrange panel |
| | Send to Back | • **Ribbon:** *Modify | Detail Items* tab>Arrange panel |

# Appendix A

# Additional Tools for Design Development

There are many other tools available in Revit® that you can use when creating and working in models. This appendix provides details about several tools and commands that are related to those covered in the Design Development section of this guide.

## Learning Objectives in This Appendix

- Save and use selection sets of multiple building elements.
- Purge unused component elements to increase the processing speed of the model.
- Edit wall joins.
- Add wall sweeps and reveals.
- Create a curtain wall type with an equally spaced grid pattern.
- Create roof fascias, soffits, and gutters.
- Add dormers to roofs.
- Clarify views using Split Face, Paint, Linework, and Cut Profiles.
- Understand worksharing and working with workset-related files.

# A.1 Selection Sets

When multiple elements types are selected, you can save the selection set so that it can be reused. For example, a structural column and an architectural column need to move together. Instead of picking each element, create a selection set that you can quickly access, as shown in Figure A–1. You can also edit selection sets to add or remove elements from the set.

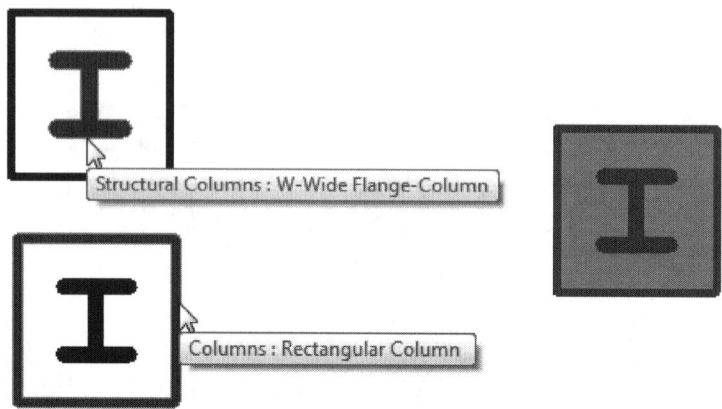

**Figure A–1**

- Selection sets are a filter of specific elements rather than types of elements.

## How To: Save Selection Sets

1. Select the elements that you want to include in the selection set.
2. In the *Modify | Multi-Select* tab>Selection panel, click (Save).
3. In the Save Selection dialog box, type a name for the set, as shown in Figure A–2, and click **OK**.

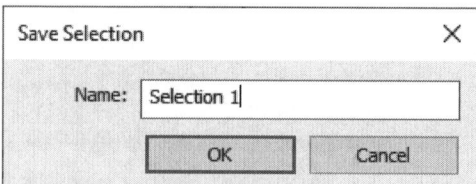

**Figure A–2**

# Additional Tools for Design Development

## How To: Retrieve Selection Sets

1. Select any other elements you might want to use. In the *Modify | Multi-Select* tab>Selection panel, click (Load). Alternatively, without any other selection, in the *Manage* tab>Selection panel, click (Load).
2. In the Retrieve Filters dialog box (shown in Figure A–3), select the set that you want to use and click **OK**.

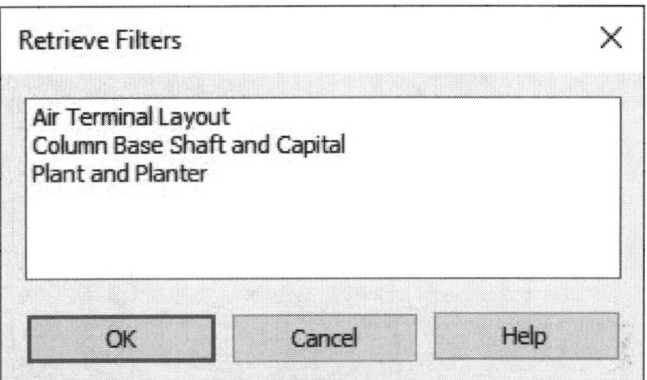

**Figure A–3**

3. The elements are selected, and you can continue to select other elements or use the selection.

## How To: Edit Selection Sets

1. If elements are selected, in the *Modify | Multi-Select* tab>Selection panel, click (Edit). Alternatively, without any selection, in the *Manage* tab>Selection panel, click (Edit).

2. In the Edit Filters dialog box (shown in Figure A–4), in the **Selection Filters** node, select the set that you want to edit and click **Edit...**.

*Rule-based Filters are not selection sets but apply to categories of elements, such as the Interior filter shown in Figure A–4.*

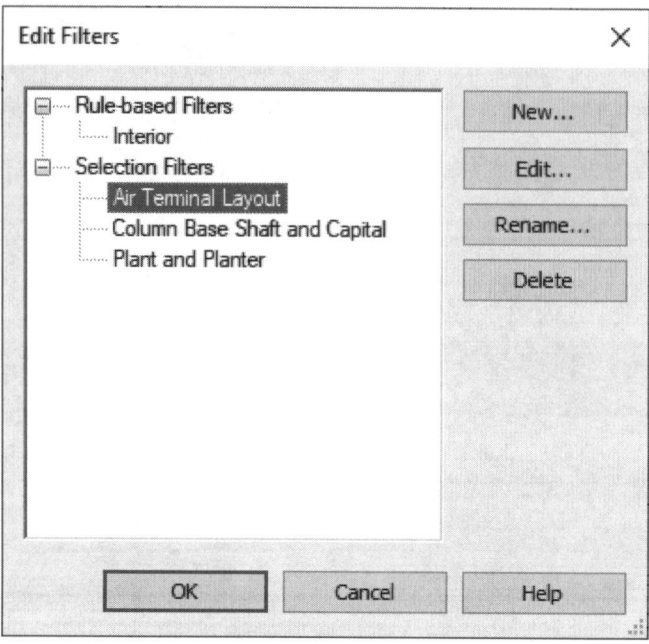

Figure A–4

- If you want to modify the name of the filter, click **Rename...**.

3. The selection set elements remain black while the rest of the elements are grayed out. The *Edit Selection Set* contextual tab displays as well, as shown in Figure A–5.

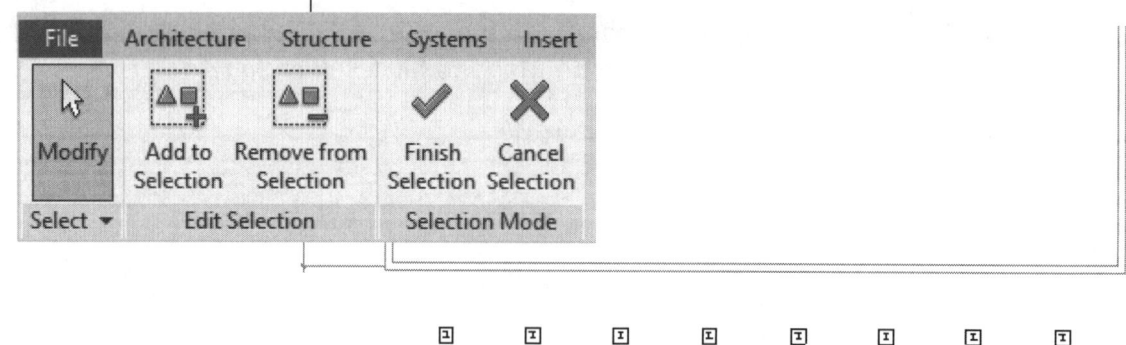

Figure A–5

4. Use (Add to Selection) to select additional elements for the set and (Remove from Selection) to delete elements from the set.

5. When you have finished editing, click (Finish Selection).
6. In the Filters dialog box, click **OK** to finish.

# A.2 Purging Unused Elements

To reduce file size and remove unused elements from a project, including individual component types, you can purge the project, as shown in Figure A–6.

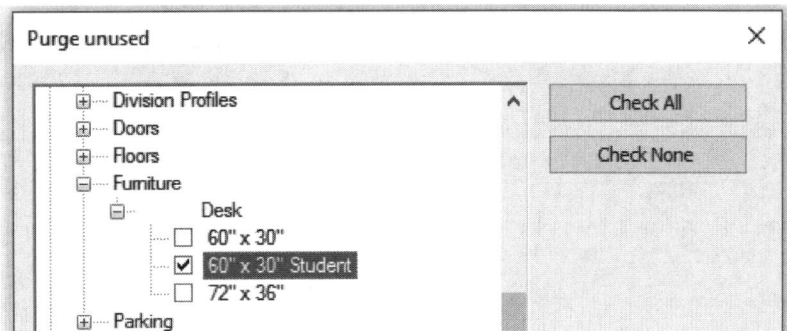

**Figure A–6**

- Some elements are nested in other elements and it might require several rounds of purging the project to remove them.

## How To: Purge Unused Elements

1. In the *Manage* tab>Settings panel, click  (Purge Unused).
2. In the Purge unused dialog box, click **Check None** and select the elements you want to purge.
3. Click **OK**.

- Purging unused components helps simplify the list of families loaded in a project.

## A.3 Editing Wall Joins

Use **Edit Wall Joins** to modify the configuration of the intersections, as shown in Figure A–7. Do not use this command if you have complex wall joins; instead, modify the length of the wall in relation to the adjoining walls.

Figure A–7

### How To: Modify the Configuration of a Wall Join

1. In the *Modify* tab>Geometry panel, click ![icon] (Wall Joins).
2. Click on the wall join that you want to edit. There is a square box around the join. Hold <Ctrl> to select multiple joins.
3. In the Options Bar, the configuration options display, as shown in Figure A–8. Select the required option.

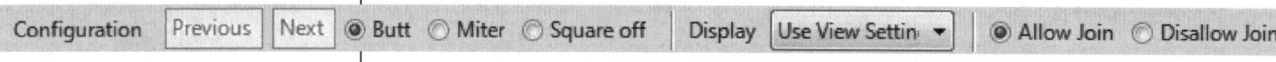

Figure A–8

- Select from three configurations: **Butt**, **Miter**, and **Square off**, as shown in Figure A–9.

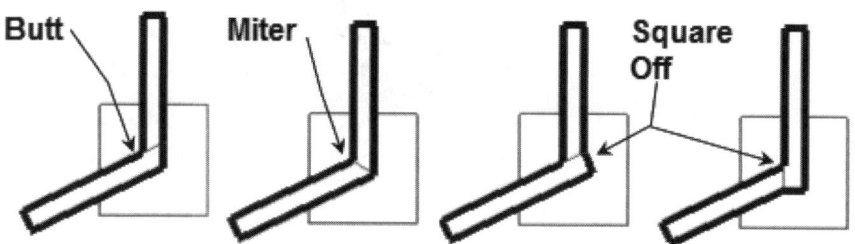

Figure A–9

- Click **Previous** and **Next** to toggle the butt or squared-off corner configurations through the various intersection options.
- **Allow Join** automatically cleans up the join while **Disallow Join** breaks the connection.

4. The **Wall Joins** command remains active until you select another command.

# Additional Tools for Design Development

## How To: Modify Display Options of Wall Joins

1. In the *Modify* tab>Geometry panel, click (Wall Joins).
2. Click on the wall join that you want to edit.
   - To modify multiple joins at the same time, draw a window around several wall intersections (as shown in Figure A–10), or hold <Ctrl> and pick additional intersections. A square box displays around each join.

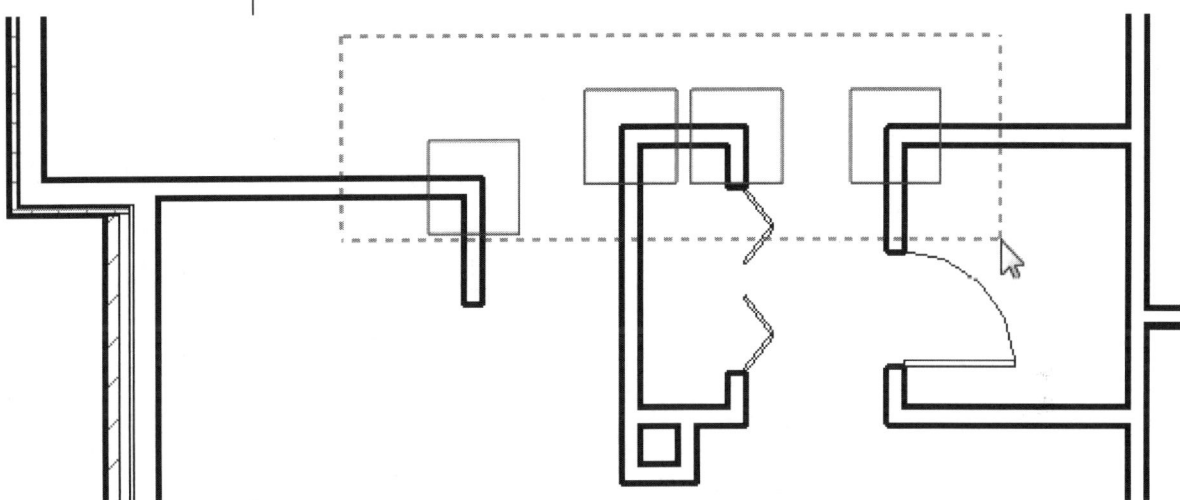

**Figure A–10**

- The *Display* controls whether or not wall joins are displayed. The options are **Use View Settings** (set up in View Properties), **Clean Join**, and **Don't Clean Join**, as shown in Figure A–11.

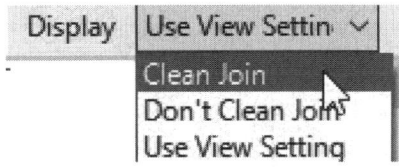

**Figure A–11**

3. If you select the end of a wall that is not joined to another wall, you can change the option to **Allow Join** in the Options Bar, as shown in Figure A–12. Reselect the wall join to make the configurations available.

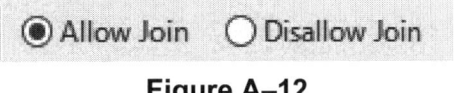

**Figure A–12**

# A.4 Wall Sweeps and Reveals

Revit includes a series of commands that enable you to modify walls, roofs, and floors by sweeping a profile along an element. For example, you can quickly add a gutter along the full length of a roof, or a curb at the edge of a floor used as a balcony, as shown in Figure A–13. The element modified by the sweep is called the host. Therefore, all of these operations are known as host sweeps.

*The process of creating reveals, gutters, and floor slab edges is similar.*

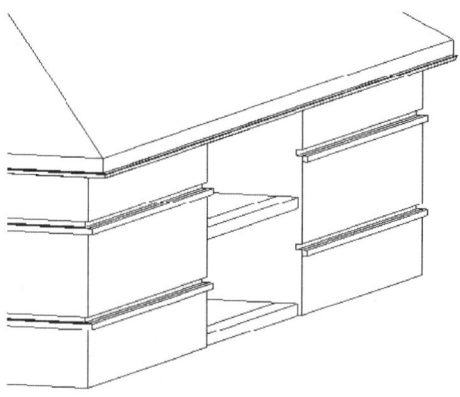

Figure A–13

- The software comes with a few standard profiles for the sweeps. You can also create your own custom profiles.

- Open a 3D view if you are working with walls. You can be in a plan or elevation view for working with roof and floor sweeps.

- There are specific commands to create wall sweeps and reveals, roof fascias and gutters, and floor slab edges. These are located by expanding the associated command in the *Architecture* tab>Build panel, as shown in Figure A–14. For walls and floors, they are also located in the *Structure* tab> Structure panel.

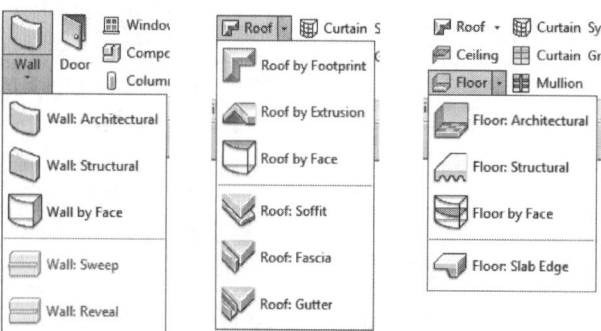

Figure A–14

- Wall sweeps and wall reveals can only be applied in elevation, section, or 3D views.

# Additional Tools for Design Development

## How To: Set Up Sweep Profiles

1. In the *Insert* tab>Load from Library panel, click (Load Family).
2. In the Load Family dialog box, select the profile you want to use (in the *Profiles* folder) or select a custom profile.
3. Start the related host sweep command. For example, if you are working with a gutter, click (Roof: Gutter), or if you are working with a wall reveal, click (Wall: Reveal).
4. In Properties, select a sweep type and click (Edit Type).
5. In the Type Properties dialog box, click **Duplicate...**.
6. Enter a new name for the type.
7. In the Type Properties dialog box, under *Construction*, select the *Profile*. You can also apply *Constraints* (for wall reveals and wall sweeps), *Materials and Finishes*, and *Identity Data*, as shown in Figure A–15.

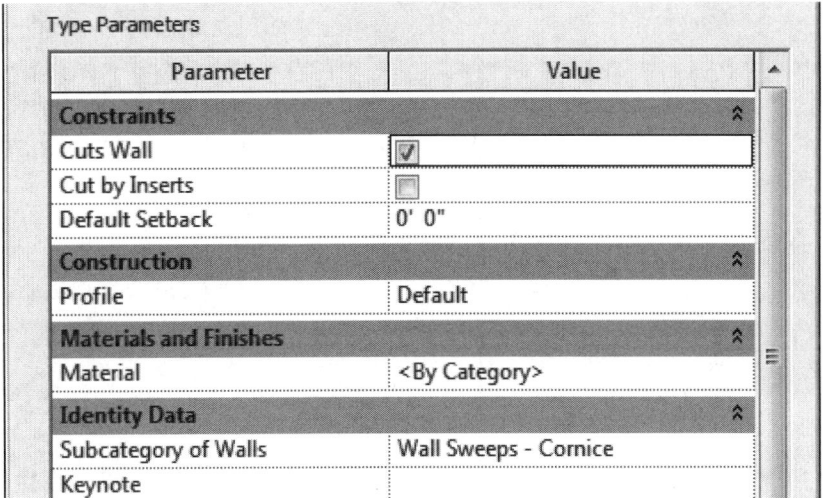

Figure A–15

- Click **OK** to close the dialog box. The new type is set to be current.

## Constraints

Constraints give you more control over how the sweep works.

| | |
|---|---|
| **Cuts Wall** | If selected, cuts the geometry out of the host wall where it overlaps. Toggling this off might increase the performance if the project contains a large amount of sweeps. |
| **Cut by Inserts** | If selected, when doors or windows are inserted into a wall with a wall sweep, the insert cuts the sweep. |
| **Default Setback** | Specify the distance that the sweep is set back from interacting wall inserts. |

### How To: Use the Wall Sweep Command

1. Open an elevation or 3D view.
2. In the *Architecture* tab>Build panel, expand  (Wall) and click  (Wall Sweep).
3. In Properties, select a wall sweep type.
   - The wall sweep type should be set up before you start the command. If you do not have it loaded, you can stay in the command, go to the *Insert* tab>Load from Library panel, and click  (Load Family). In the Load Family dialog box, select the profile you want to use (in the *Profiles* folder) or select a custom profile.
4. In the *Modify | Place Wall Sweep* tab>Placement panel, click either  (Horizontal) or  (Vertical). (This is only for walls.)
5. Move the cursor over the element where you want to add the sweep and click to place it.
6. If you are doing horizontal sweeps, continue selecting elements. The sweep is placed at the same height as the first element.

- To change sweep styles or the height, in the Placement panel, click  (Restart Wall Sweep), or return to the **Modify** command to finish.

*To specify a precise location for the sweep element, select it after you have created it and modify the dimensions as needed.*

# A.5 Creating Curtain Wall Types with Automatic Grids

If you have a curtain wall with a fixed distance or a fixed number of grids in the vertical or horizontal direction, you can create a curtain wall type containing this information, as shown in Figure A–16. The automatic grid lines can also be set to an angle.

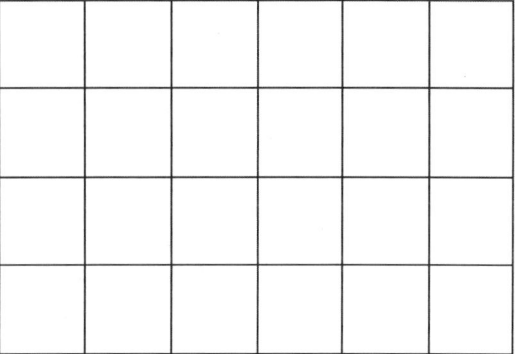

**Figure A–16**

## How To: Create a Curtain Wall with Automatic Grids

1. In the *Architecture* tab>Build panel, click (Wall).
2. In the Type Selector, select a curtain wall similar to the one you want to create.
3. In Properties, click (Edit Type).
4. In the Type Properties dialog box, click **Duplicate...** to create a copy of the existing family type.
5. In the Name dialog box, give the curtain wall a name that describes its purpose, as shown in Figure A–17.
6. The new name automatically includes the family name, such as **Curtain Wall**. Therefore, you do not have to include the family name.

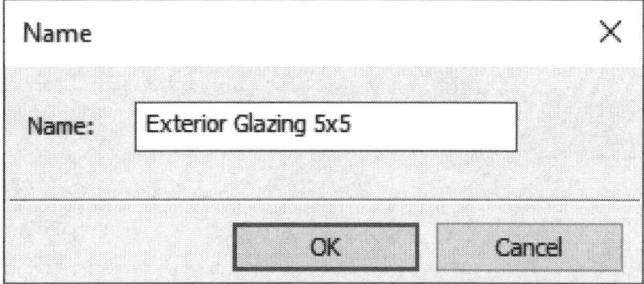

**Figure A–17**

*Type parameters apply to all instances of that type inserted into Revit. This is true for all families (e.g., walls, doors, windows, etc.). Changing a type parameter changes all instances of that type in the project.*

7. In the Type Properties dialog box, enter information for the *Construction*, *Vertical* and *Horizontal Grid Pattern*, and *Vertical* and *Horizontal Mullions* parameters, as shown in Figure A–18.

| Parameter | Value |
|---|---|
| **Construction** | |
| Function | Exterior |
| Automatically Embed | ☐ |
| Curtain Panel | None |
| Join Condition | Not Defined |
| **Graphics** | |
| Display in Hidden Views | Edges Hidden by Other Members |
| **Vertical Grid Pattern** | |
| Layout | Fixed Distance |
| Spacing | 5' 0" |
| Adjust for Mullion Size | ☑ |
| **Horizontal Grid Pattern** | |
| Layout | Fixed Distance |
| Spacing | 5' 0" |
| Adjust for Mullion Size | ☑ |
| **Vertical Mullions** | |
| Interior Type | None |
| Border 1 Type | None |
| Border 2 Type | None |

**Figure A–18**

- Enable the *Automatically Embed* parameter if you want to use the curtain wall as a storefront.
- Set the *Curtain Panel* to the primary type you plan to use. You can modify the panels once they are in the project.
- The Grid Patterns can be set to the following:

| | |
|---|---|
| **Fixed Distance** | Grids are placed a specified distance apart. Specify the size in the **Spacing** option. |
| **Fixed Number** | Grids are divided across a wall based on a specified number. The *Number* of grid lines is specified in the Instance Parameters. |
| **Maximum Spacing** | Grids are spaced evenly with the greatest distance between them specified in the **Spacing** option. |
| **None** | No grids are specified. |

- The **Adjust for Mullion Size** parameter ensures that panels inserted between grid lines are equal in size. This is very important if you use a different size of mullion on the borders from the ones on the interior separations.

# Additional Tools for Design Development

- Mullions can be specified in the Type Parameters for Interior and Border mullions. The vertical **Border 1** type is applied to the left of the curtain wall and **Border 2** is applied to the right. The horizontal **Border 1** type is at the bottom and **Border 2** is at the top.
- You can pre-apply the mullions to the grid in the type or add them later. If you are planning to use the curtain wall type as a base to create a more complex curtain wall, do not add mullions in the type because doing so makes it difficult to select the grid lines to modify them.

8. Click **OK** to close the Type Properties dialog box.
9. In Properties, set the values for *Vertical Grid* and *Horizontal Grid* sections, as shown in Figure A–19.

*The options in Properties are instance parameters applied to the selected instance of the type inserted into Revit.*

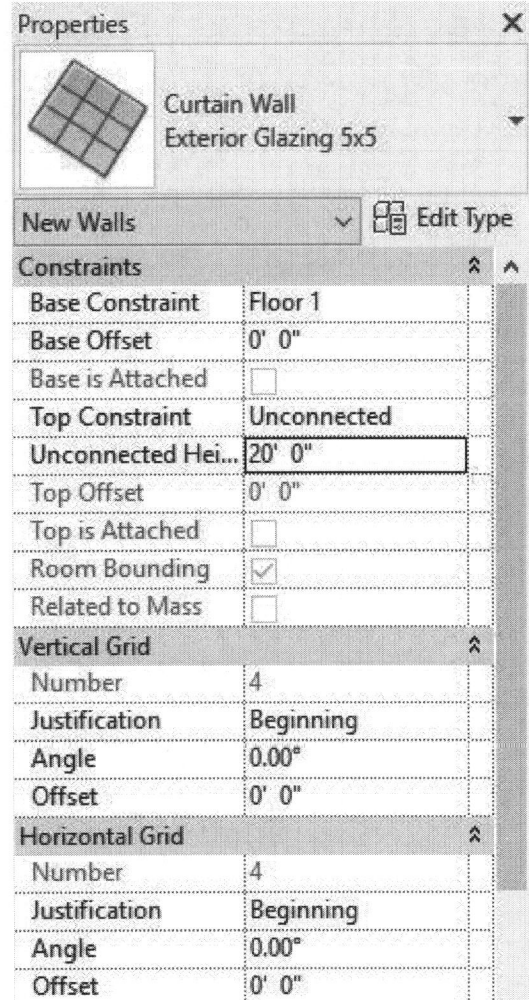

Figure A–19

# A.6 Creating Fascias, Soffits, and Gutters

Revit provides specific tools for adding fascias, soffits, and gutters to your model, as shown in Figure A–20.

Figure A–20

## Fascias

You can add fascia boards to the edge of a roof as one continuous piece or as individual segments. You can also use the **Fascia** tool to create fascia-bands, frieze boards, and bird boxes.

### How To: Apply a Fascia

1. In the *Architecture* tab>Build panel, expand (Roof) and click (Roof: Fascia).
2. Select the desired fascia profile from the Type Selector. (Note that you will need to load the profile from the *Profile>Roofs* folder in the Revit Library using the **Load Family** tool on the *Insert* tab before starting the command.)
3. Highlight the edges of roofs, soffits, other fascias, or model lines and click to place the fascia.
4. Click (Modify) or press <Esc>.

# Additional Tools for Design Development

- As you click edges, Revit treats them as one continuous fascia. If the fascia segments meet at corners, they miter. To start another fascia, in the ribbon, click **Restart Fascia** and then click on a new edge. This creates a different fascia, which does not miter with other existing fascias even if they meet at the corners.

- **Hint:** Offset the fascia from the edge of the roof by setting the *Vertical Profile Offset* in Properties to the thickness of the roof deck finish, then use the Flip control to flip the profile so that it will cut into the roof. Use the **Join Geometry** command to cut the profile from the roof in order to create a drip edge with the deck and finish.

## Soffits

There are many different styles of soffits, so the method you use can vary widely. However, in general, the soffit is created as a roof object and is bounded by a closed loop. You can then use the **Join Geometry** tool to join the soffit and the roof, as shown in Figure A–21. Depending on the construction of the roof and soffit, you may also need to add trim to close spaces at the ends of soffits.

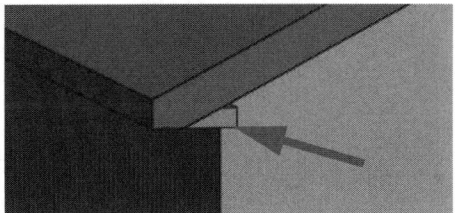

**Figure A–21**

### How To: Add a Soffit

1. In the *Architecture* tab>Build panel, expand ▫ (Roof) and select ▽ (Roof: Soffit).
2. Select the desired soffit type from the Type Selector.
3. In the *Modify | Create Roof Soffit Boundary* tab>Draw panel, select a Draw tool to draw the soffit's boundary.
4. Click ✓ (Finish Edit Mode).

## Gutters

You can add gutters to the edges of roofs, soffits, and fascias, as shown in Figure A–22. You can also add gutters to model lines.

Figure A–22

### How To: Add a Roof Gutter

1. In the *Architecture* tab>Build panel, expand  (Roof) and click  (Roof: Gutter).
2. Select the desired gutter profile from the Type Selector. (Note that you will need to load the profile from the *Profile>Roofs* folder in the Revit Library using the **Load Family** tool on the *Insert* tab before starting the command.)
3. Highlight the edges of roofs, soffits, fascias, or model lines and click to place the gutter.
4. Click  (Modify).

- As you click edges, Revit treats this as one continuous gutter. To start a new gutter, click **Restart Gutter** and click on a new edge.

- After creating a gutter, you can use other tools to resize it, flip the gutter, add or remove segments, and change the horizontal and vertical offsets.

Additional Tools for Design Development

# A.7 Creating Dormers

You can add two types of dormers to a project. One type of dormer cuts through the roof, as shown in Figure A–23. This type has walls supporting a separate roof. You create the supporting walls and dormer roof, and then cut a hole in the main roof.

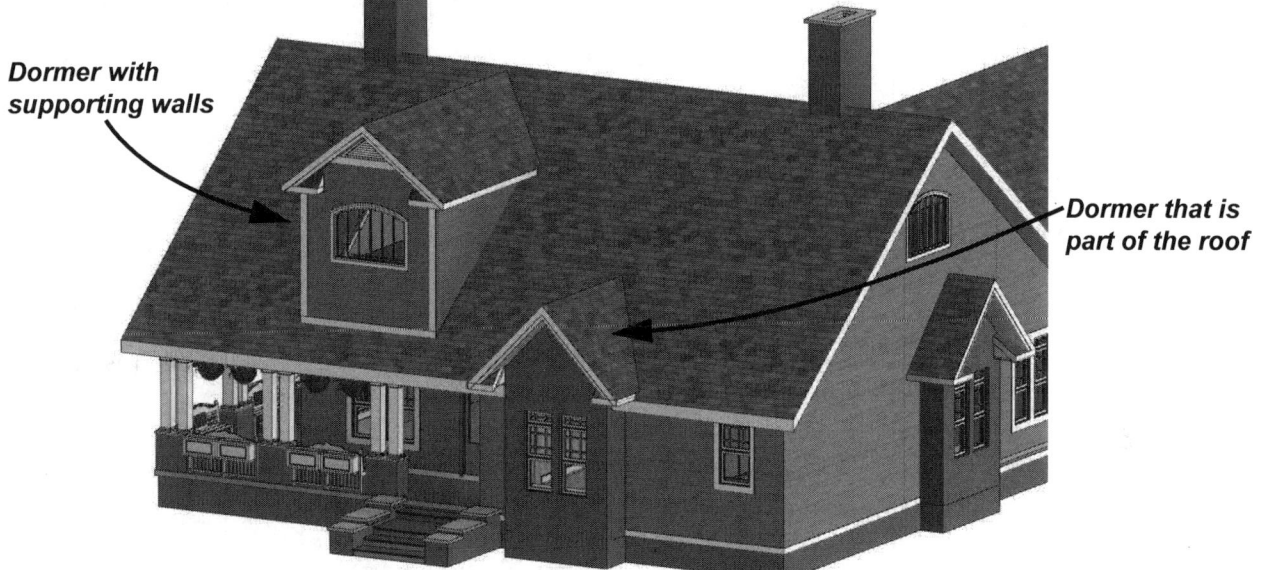

Figure A–23

The other type of dormer is part of the roof, as shown in Figure A–23. This is created by sketching the roof, modifying it, and adding slope arrows to define the additional peak.

- The dormer must be added to a plane that defines a slope.

## How To: Add a Dormer with Supporting Walls to a Roof

1. Draw the main roof. When it is placed correctly, create a secondary dormer roof and supporting walls, as shown in Figure A–24.

Figure A–24

2. Move the new dormer (walls and roof) into position.
3. In the *Modify* tab>Geometry panel, use  (Join Geometry and  (Join/Unjoin Roof) to connect the dormer walls/roof to the existing roof.
4. In the *Architecture* tab>Opening panel, click  (Dormer).
5. In a roof plan view, select the main roof (the one to be cut).
6. In the *Modify | Edit Sketch* tab>Pick panel, click  (Pick Roof/Wall Edges) and select the opening to be cut.

- The dormer opening sketch does not need to be closed.

- Clean up the roofs and roof edges, as needed, using tools such as **Join**, **Attach Top/Base**, etc.

## How To: Add A Dormer Using Slope Arrows to a Roof

1. Draw a roof. When it is placed, select the roof. In the *Modify | Roofs* tab>Mode panel, click  (Edit Footprint) to edit the roof sketch.
2. In the *Modify | Roofs>Edit Footprint* tab>Modify panel, click  (Split Element) to split the edge of the roof between the two points where you want the dormer to be located. Do not delete the inner segment. You can use dynamic dimensions to help locate the points to split.
3. In the Selection panel, click  (Modify) and select the new segment between the split points. In the Options Bar, clear the **Defines slope** option for this segment.
4. In the Draw panel, click  (Slope Arrow).
5. Draw a slope arrow from one end of the segment to the midpoint, then sketch a second slope arrow from the other end to the midpoint, as shown in Figure A–25.

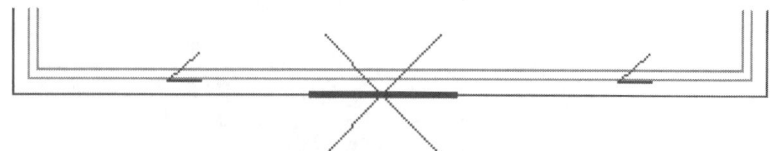

**Figure A–25**

6. Select the slope arrows. In Properties, specify the *Height at the Tail* or *Slope* and type the required properties.

7. In the Mode panel, click ✓ (Finish Edit Mode).
8. View the roof in a 3D view to verify the results, as shown in Figure A–26.

**Figure A–26**

# A.8 Enhancing Views

When you start detailing views (such as elevations and sections), several tools can help clarify what you are trying to show. **Split Face** divides an elevation face into smaller separate faces. You can then use **Paint** to apply different materials to the faces, as shown in Figure A–27. **Linework** enables you to change the lineweight or line style of lines in a view to emphasize various components. In plan views and sections, you can use **Cut Profile** to enhance the views.

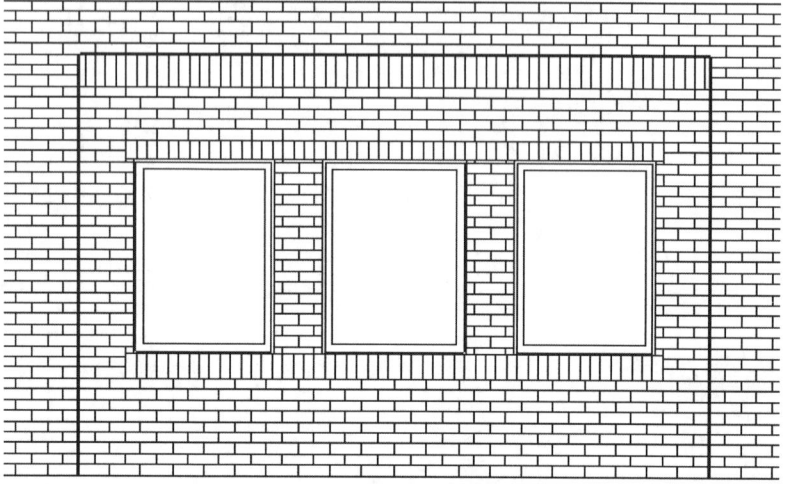

Figure A–27

- The changes made with **Split Face** and **Paint** are displayed in elevation and 3D views.

- Changes made using **Linework** are view-specific, applying only in the view in which they are made.

- Additional options for modifying the look of a view are found in the Graphic Display Options dialog box (in the View Control Bar, expand **Visual Styles** and select **Graphic Display Options....**). These include *Sketchy Lines* and *Depth Cueing* as well as other options for setting up views for rendering.

# Splitting Faces

You can split a face into separate surfaces so you can apply different materials to each part. A sketch defines the split, which must be a closed shape completely inside the face, or an open shape that touches the face edges, as shown in Figure A–28. Windows are cut out of faces automatically.

Figure A–28

- Before you start working with split faces, ensure that the walls are mitered. By default, the walls are butted to each other. This creates a problem when you select faces.

## How To: Create a Split Face

1. Switch to an elevation view (a 3D view works as well).
2. In the *Modify* tab>Geometry panel, click (Split Face).
3. Select the edge of the face that you want to modify. Use <Tab> as needed to toggle through the available faces.
4. In the *Modify | Split Face>Create Boundary* tab>Draw panel, use the sketch tools to create a sketch as required to define the split.
5. Click (Finish Edit Mode).

- To save time, use a wall style that includes the primary material you want to use on the split face. For example, if you are working with brick, set the wall to a type that has a brick face. This way, you can work with the brick courses when you are creating the split face.

*If you have (Select elements by face) toggled on, you can click directly on the face.*

- When using a material such as brick, you can snap to the pattern and even lock the split lines to the pattern, as shown in Figure A–29.

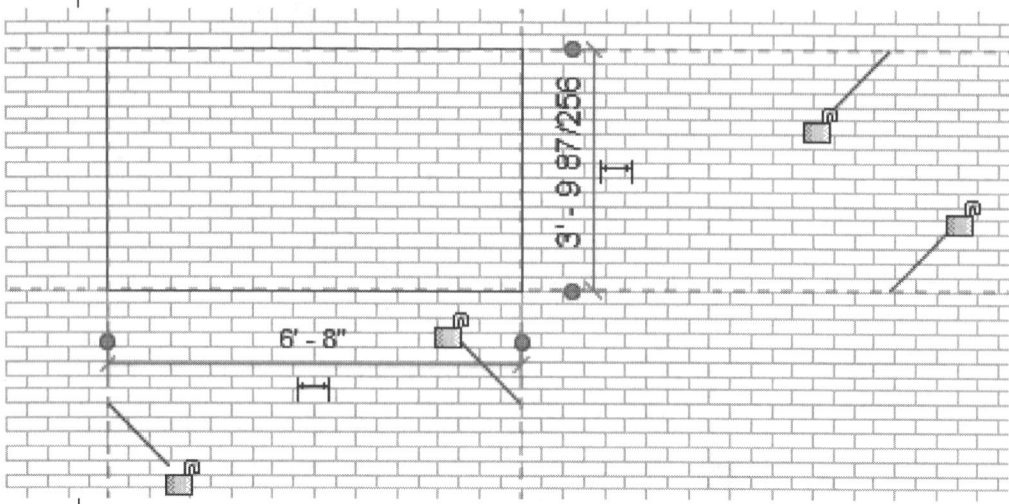

Figure A–29

You can double-click on the edge of the split face lines to switch to Edit Boundary mode. If you double-click on the face with ![icon] (Select elements by face) toggled on, it switches to Edit Profile mode, which impacts the entire wall, not just the split face boundary.

**Applying Materials**

Once you have a face split into sections, you can apply different materials to each part. For example, you might want a soldier course under each window on a brick wall. You would first create the split face and then apply the new material using **Paint**, as shown in Figure A–30.

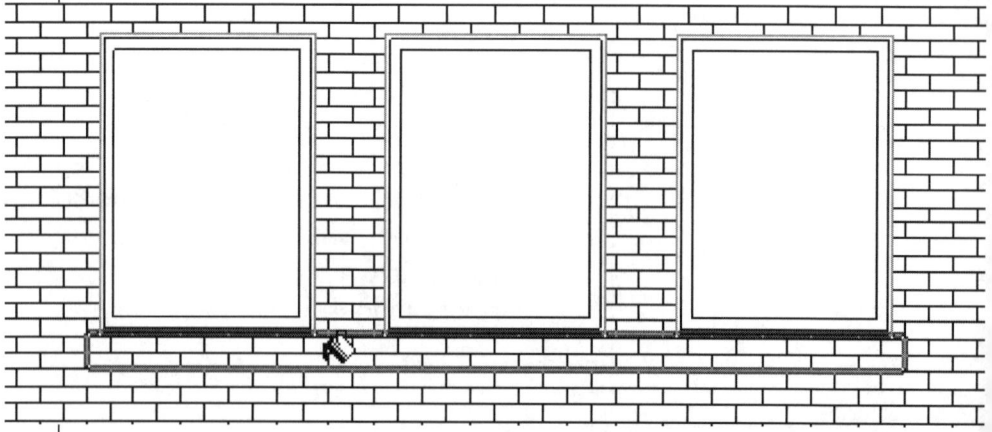

Figure A–30

## How To: Apply Material with Paint

1. In the *Modify* tab>Geometry panel, click (Paint), or type **PT**.
2. In the Material Browser, select a material. You can run a search or filter the list using specific types of materials, as shown in Figure A–31.

*The browser remains open as you are applying the paint.*

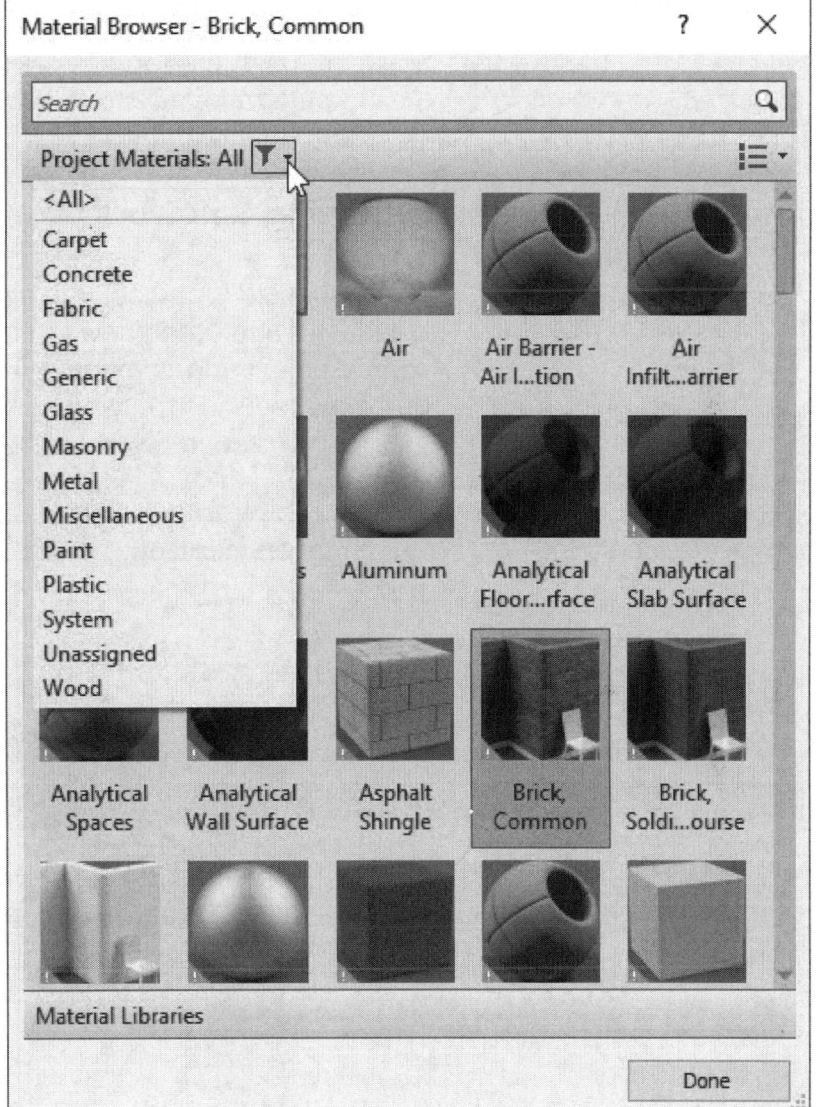

Figure A–31

3. Move the cursor over the face you want to paint. It should highlight. Click on the face to apply the material.
4. Continue selecting materials and painting other faces as needed.
5. In the Material Browser, click **Done** to finish the command.

- Some material patterns display as shaded when you zoom out. Zoom in to display the pattern. Other material patterns only display when you are in the (Realistic) visual style.

- To change the material applied to a face, in the *Modify* tab> Geometry panel, expand (Paint) and click (Remove Paint). Select the face(s) from which you want to remove the material.

- If you paint the top of a wall, you can modify the location of the pattern using **Move**, **Rotate**, and **Align**, as well as by dragging the pattern.

## Adjusting Linework

To emphasize a particular line or change the look of a line in elevations and other views, modify the lines with the **Linework** command. Changes made to lines with the **Linework** command are view-specific, applying only to the view in which you make them, as shown in Figure A–32.

- The **Linework** command can be used on project edges of model elements, cut edges of model elements, edges in imported CAD files, and edges in linked Revit models.

Figure A–32

Additional Tools for Design Development

### How To: Adjust Linework

1. In the *Modify* tab>View panel, click ▱ (Linework), or type **LW**.
2. In the *Modify | Linework* tab>Line Style panel, select the line style you want to use from the list.
3. Move the cursor and highlight the line you want to change. You can use <Tab> to toggle through the lines as needed.
4. Click on the line to change it to the new line style.
5. Click on other lines as needed or return to the **Modify** command to finish.

- If the line is too long or short, you can modify the length using the controls at the end of the line.

## Editing Plan and Section Profiles

In plan and section details, you might need to modify portions of the cut to show the specific intersection of two faces, as shown in Figure A–33. This can be done using **Cut Profile**. The cut profile changes the shape of the elements at their cut plane, but does not modify their 3D information. The cut is only displayed in the view in which it is sketched.

*If you are working on a compound face (such as a wall with several layers of information), change the Detail Level to **Medium** or **Fine** to display the fill patterns.*

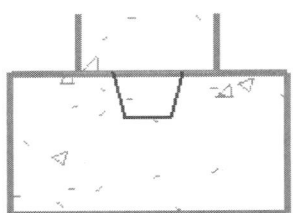 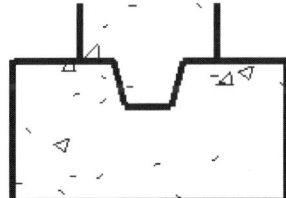

Figure A–33

- You can modify the cut of walls, floors, and roofs.

### How To: Use Cut Profile

1. In the *View* tab>Graphics panel, click ▨ (Cut Profile).
2. In the Options Bar, select to edit the **Face** or the **Boundary between faces**, as shown in Figure A–34.

Figure A–34

3. Select the face or boundary that you want to edit.

4. In the *Modify | Create Cut Profile Sketch* tab>Draw panel, use the sketch tools to sketch a new profile, as shown in Figure A–35.

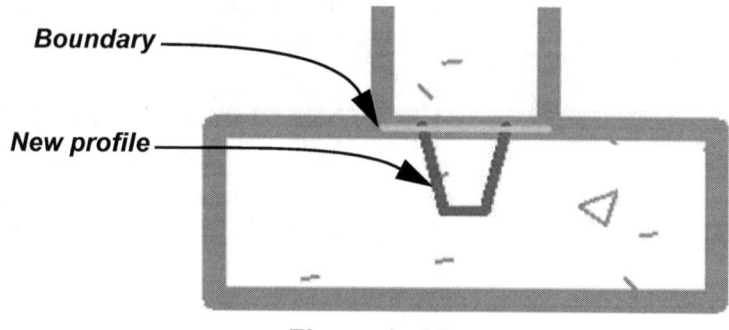

Figure A–35

5. Click ✓ (Finish Edit Mode).

- If a warning box opens, verify that the lines start and end on the same boundary line and that they do not make a closed loop or cross over each other.

# A.9 Introduction to Revit Worksharing

When a project becomes too big for one person, it needs to be subdivided so that a team of people working on the same network can work on it. Since Revit projects include the entire building model in one file, the file needs to be separated into logical components, as shown in Figure A–36, without losing the connection to the whole. This process is called *worksharing* and the main components are worksets.

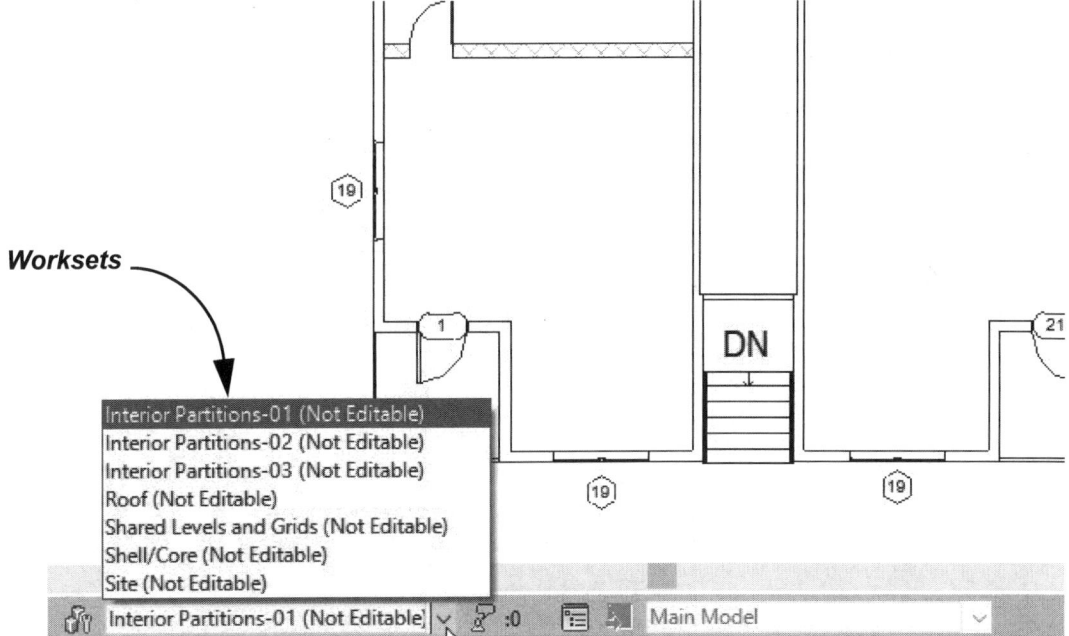

Figure A–36

Revit worksharing gives multiple team members connected on the same network the ability to co-author a single project model (one .RVT file). The appropriate team member creates a central model with multiple worksets (such as element interiors, building shell, and site) that are used by the project team members. Team members open and work in a local copy of the model that is linked back to the central model through saving and synchronizing. For more information about establishing and using worksets, refer to the ASCENT guide *Autodesk Revit: Collaboration Tools*.

A workshared project consists of one central model (also known as a central file) and individual models for each user known as local files, as shown in Figure A–37. Each team member will work in their local file and use a function called *synchronizing with central* to send and receive updates with the central model.

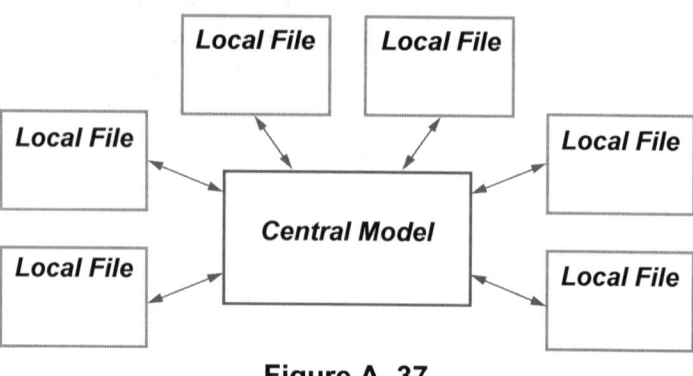

**Figure A–37**

- The **central model** is created by the BIM manager, project manager, or project lead and is stored on a server or in the cloud, enabling multiple users to access it.

- A **local file** is a copy of the central model that is stored on your computer.

- All local files are saved back to the central model, and updates to the central model are sent out to the local files. This way, all changes remain in one file, while the project, model, views, and sheets are automatically updated.

## Worksharing Definitions

**Worksharing:** This is a functionality that, when enabled, allows multiple members of the team to access a project stored in one centralized location, which gives multiple users the ability to work on the same project simultaneously.

**Workshared file:** This is a project that has worksets enabled. If the project has no worksets enabled, it is called a *non-workshared file*.

**Workset:** This is a collection of elements that are related geometrically, parametrically, or by location within an overall project that are subdivided so they can be worked on while isolated from the rest of the model. When worksharing is enabled, worksets are automatically activated and the *Workset1* and *Shared Grids and Levels* worksets are added to the project by default.

# Additional Tools for Design Development

**Central model:** Also called the central file, this is the main project file that is stored on a local network that all users can access. Using a central model is called *file-based worksharing*. The central model stores workset and element information in the project and is the file to which everyone saves and synchronizes their changes. The central model updates all the local files with the latest model information. This file should not be edited directly.

**Local file:** This is a copy of the central model that is saved to your local computer. This is the file that you modify and work in. As you work, you save the file locally and synchronize it with the central model.

**Element borrowing:** This refers to the process of modifying items in the project that are not part of the workset you have checked out. This either happens automatically (if no one else has checked out a workset) or specifically, when you request to have control of the elements (if someone else has a workset checked out).

**Active workset:** The workset that displays in the Status Bar is the active workset. Any new elements that are added will be placed on this workset. As you work, you will change the active workset accordingly.

**Relinquish:** This releases or returns a checked-out workset so that others can work on the elements within that workset. If you do not release or relinquish your checked-out worksets, other users will get a warning that they cannot edit the workset until you relinquish it, and they are given the option to request to borrow the workset. **Relinquish All Mine** allows you to relinquish worksets without synchronizing to the central model.

**Reload Latest:** This updates your local file without you needing to synchronize with the central model.

## General Process of Using Worksets

1. Wait for the appropriate team member to enable worksharing, set up worksets, and create the central model.
2. Create a local file from the central model.
3. Work in your local file and select the worksets that you need to work on by verifying the active workset.
   - Work in your local model by adding, deleting, and modifying elements.
   - You may need to request to borrow elements in worksets that are currently checked out by other team members.

4. Save the local file as frequently as you would save any other project.
5. Synchronize the local file with the central model several times a day or as required by company policy or project status.
   - This reloads any changes from the central model to your local file and vice versa.
   - If the option to **Save Local File before and after synchronizing with central** is checked, your local file will be saved, but it is always recommended to save the local file yourself every time you synchronize to the central model.

## Opening Workset-Related Files

When you open a workset-related file, it creates a new local file on your computer. Do not work in the main central model.

### How To: Create a Local File

1. In the *File* tab or Quick Access Toolbar, click  (Open).
2. In the Open dialog box, navigate to the central model server location and select the central model. Do not work in this file. Select **Create New Local**, as shown in Figure A–38, and click **Open**.

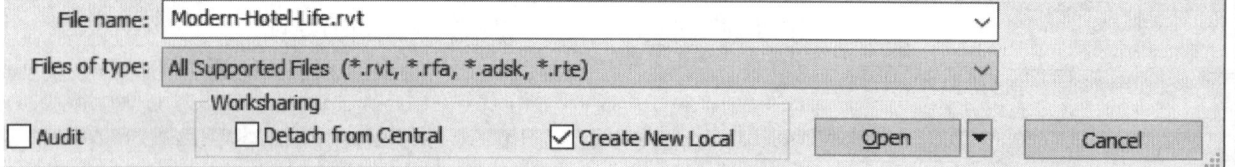

**Figure A–38**

3. A copy of the project is created. It will have the same name as the central model with your Autodesk Revit username added to the end.

# Additional Tools for Design Development

- If you are working with a recently used central model, it may display on the Home screen with the icon shown in Figure A–39. Clicking this file automatically creates a local copy of the model. The first time you use this option, a warning displays, as shown in Figure A–40.

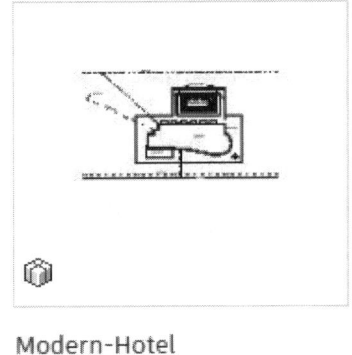

Figure A–39

Figure A–40

4. You can save the file using the default name, or use ![icon] (Save As) and name the file according to your office's standard. It should include *Local* in the name to indicate that it is saved on your local computer, or that you are the only one working with that version of the file.

- Delete any old local files to ensure that you are working on the latest version.

## How To: Work in a Workshared Project

1. Open your local file.
2. In the Status Bar, expand the Active Workset drop-down list and select a workset, as shown in Figure A–41. By setting the active workset, other people can work in the project but cannot edit elements that you add to the workset.

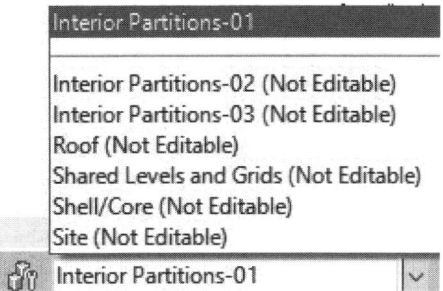

Figure A–41

3. Work on the project as needed.

## Saving a Workshared Project

When you are working on a workshared project, you need to save the project locally and centrally.

- Save the local file frequently (every 15-30 minutes). In the Quick Access Toolbar, click 💾 (Save) to save the local file just as you would any other project.

- Synchronize the local file with the central model periodically (every hour or two) or after you have made major changes to the project.

> **Hint: Set Up Notifications to Save and Synchronize**
>
> You can set up reminders to save and synchronize files to the central model in the Options dialog box, on the *General* tab, as shown in Figure A–42.

**Figure A–42**

### Synchronizing to the Central Model

There are two methods for synchronizing to the central model. In the Quick Access Toolbar or *Collaborate* tab>Synchronize panel, expand (Synchronize with Central) and click (Synchronize Now) or (Synchronize and Modify Settings). The last-used command is active if you click the top-level icon.

- **Synchronize Now:** Updates the central model and then the local file with any changes to the central model since the last synchronization without prompting you for any settings. It automatically relinquishes elements borrowed from any workset but retains worksets used by the current user.

- **Synchronize and Modify Settings:** Opens the Synchronize with Central dialog box, shown in Figure A–43, so you can set the options for relinquishing worksets and elements, add comments, and specify to save the file locally before and after synchronization.

# Additional Tools for Design Development

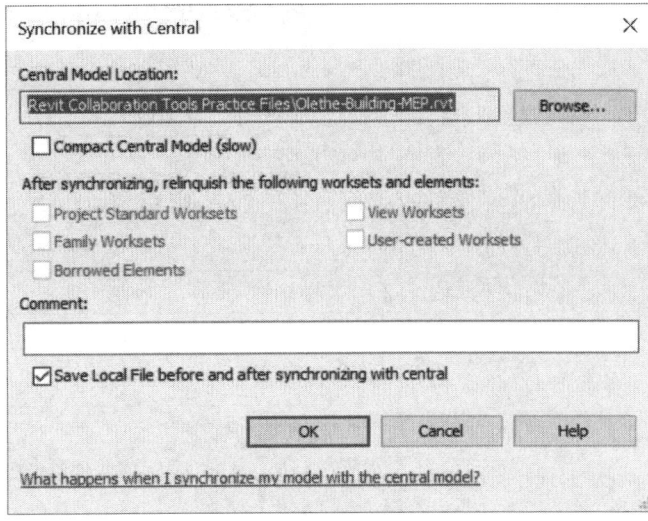

Figure A–43

- Always keep **Save Local File before and after synchronizing with central** checked to ensure your local copy is up to date with the latest changes from the central model.

- When you close a local file without saving to the central model, you are prompted to do so, as shown in Figure A–44.

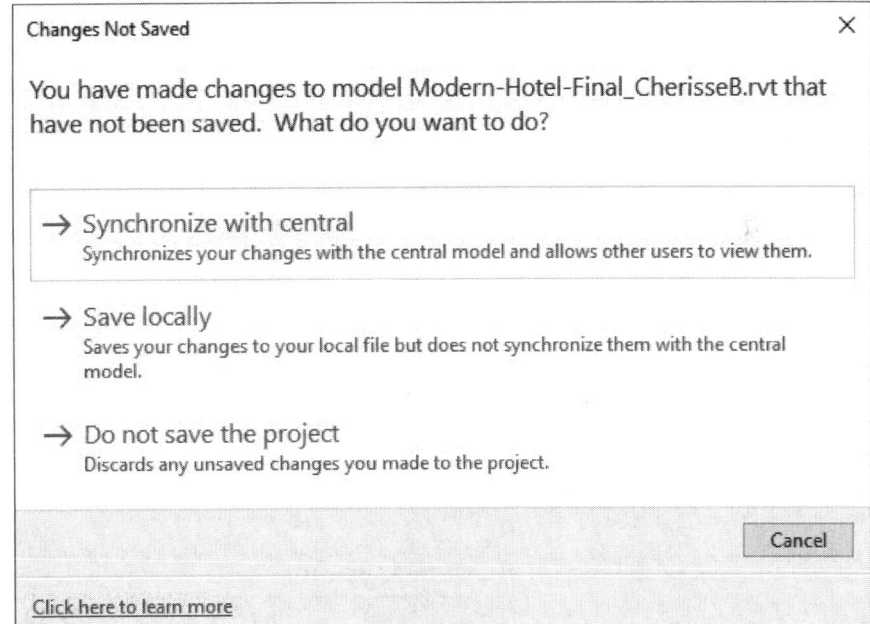

Figure A–44

- The maximum number of backups for workset-enabled files is set to 20 by default.

- Note: Workshared files do not have the same backup files as non-workshared files.

# Command Summary

| Button | Command | Location |
|---|---|---|
| **Curtain Walls** | | |
| | Edit Type | • **Properties** (with a Curtain Wall type selected) |
| **Dormers** | | |
| | Dormer | • **Ribbon:** *Architecture* tab>Opening panel |
| **Selection Sets** | | |
| | Edit Selection | • **Ribbon:** *Modify | Multi-Select* tab>Selection panel |
| | Load Selection | • **Ribbon:** *Modify | Multi-Select* tab>Selection panel |
| | Save Selection | • **Ribbon:** *Modify | Multi-Select* tab>Selection panel |
| | Add to Selection | • **Ribbon:** *Edit Selection Set* tab>Edit Selection panel |
| | Remove from Selection | • **Ribbon:** *Edit Selection Set* tab>Edit Selection panel |
| **Sweeps and Reveals** | | |
| | Floor: Slab Edge | • **Ribbon:** *Architecture* tab>Build panel or *Structure* tab>Structure panel, expand Floor |
| | Roof: Fascia | • **Ribbon:** *Architecture* tab>Build panel, expand Roof |
| | Roof: Gutter | • **Ribbon:** *Architecture* tab>Build panel, expand Roof |
| | Wall: Reveal | • **Ribbon:** *Architecture* tab>Build panel or *Structure* tab>Structure panel, expand Wall |
| | Wall: Sweep | • **Ribbon:** *Architecture* tab>Build panel or *Structure* tab>Structure panel, expand Wall |
| **Worksharing** | | |
| | Save | • **Quick Access Toolbar**<br>• **File tab:** Save<br>• **Shortcut:** <Ctrl>+<S> |
| | Synchronize and Modify Settings | • **Quick Access Toolbar**<br>• **Ribbon:** *Collaborate* tab>Synchronize panel, expand Synchronize with Central |

| | | | |
|---|---|---|---|
| | ![icon] | Synchronize Now | • **Quick Access Toolbar**<br>• **Ribbon:** *Collaborate* tab>Synchronize panel, expand Synchronize with Central |
| **Views** | | | |
| | ![icon] | Cut Profile | • **Ribbon:** *View* tab>Graphics panel |
| | ![icon] | Insert Views from File | • **Ribbon:** *Insert* tab>Load from Library panel, expand Insert from File |
| | ![icon] | Join Geometry | • **Ribbon:** *Modify* tab>Geometry panel, expand Join |
| | ![icon] | Line Styles | • **Ribbon:** *Manage* tab>Settings panel, expand Additional Settings |
| | ![icon] | Linework | • **Ribbon:** *Modify* tab>View panel<br>• **Shortcut:** LW |
| | ![icon] | Paint | • **Ribbon:** *Modify* tab>Geometry panel |
| | ![icon] | Pick New Host | • **Ribbon:** *Modify | varies* tab>Host panel |
| | ![icon] | Split Face | • **Ribbon:** *Modify* tab>Geometry panel |
| | ![icon] | Unjoin Geometry | • **Ribbon:** *Modify* tab>Geometry panel, expand Join |
| | ![icon] | Wall Joins | • **Ribbon:** *Modify* tab>Geometry panel |

# Appendix B

# Additional Tools for Construction Documents

There are many other tools available in Revit® that you can use when creating construction documents. This appendix provides details about several tools and commands that are related to those covered in the Construction Documentation section of this guide.

## Learning Objectives in This Appendix

- Use guide grids to help place views on sheets.
- Add revision clouds, tags, and information.
- Use Path of Travel to analyze travel distances between points in the model.
- Annotate dependent views with matchlines and view references.
- Import and export schedules.
- Create basic building component schedules.
- Create repeating detail types.
- Place keynotes in a detail and add keynote legends that describe the full content of the keynotes.

# B.1 Working with Guide Grids on Sheets

*When moving a view to a guide grid, only orthogonal datum elements (levels and grids) and reference planes snap to the guide grid.*

You can use a guide grid to help you place views on a sheet, as shown in Figure B–1. Guide grids can be set up per sheet. You can also create different types with various grid spacings.

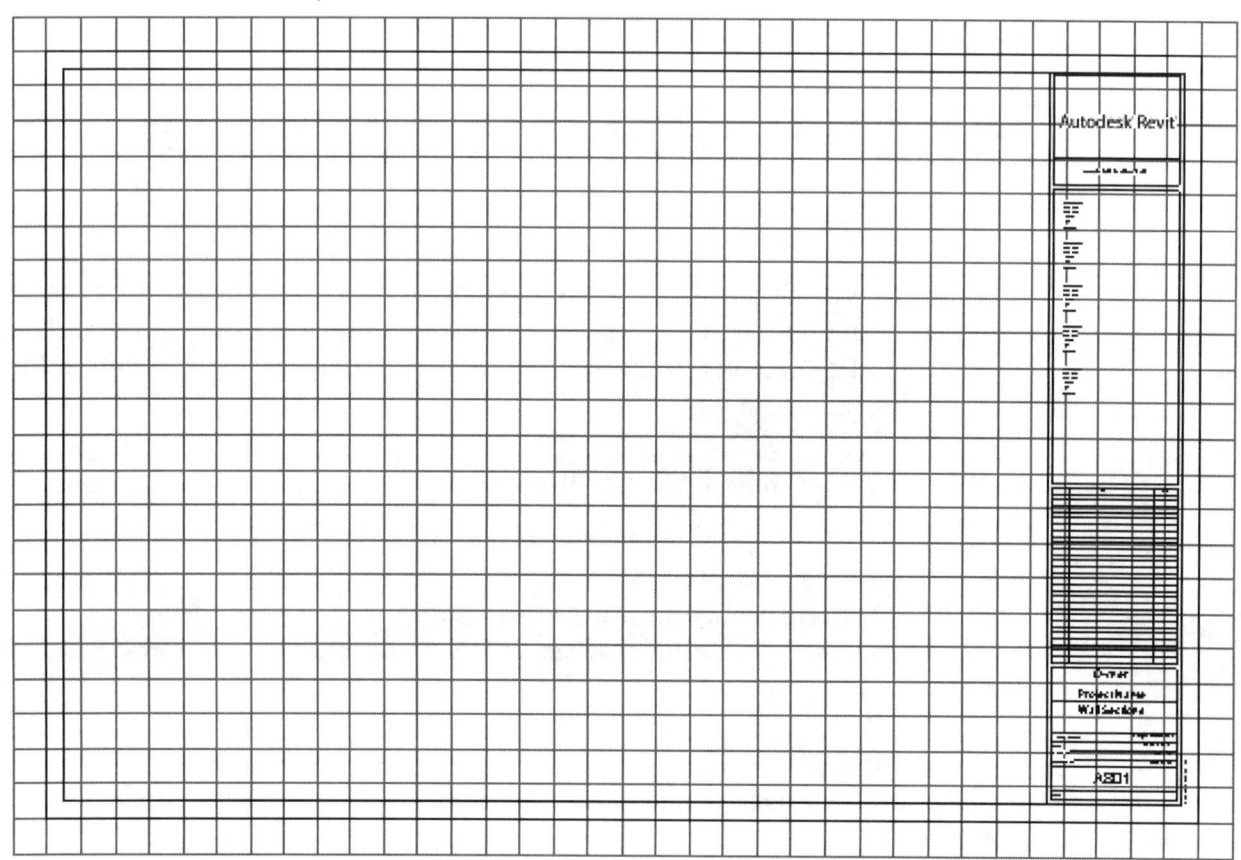

Figure B–1

- You can move guide grids and resize them using controls.

### How To: Add a Guide Grid

1. When a sheet is open, in the *View* tab>Sheet Composition panel, click ▦ (Guide Grid).

Additional Tools for Construction Documents

2. In the Assign Guide Grid dialog box, select from existing guide grids (as shown in Figure B–2), or create a new one and give it a name.

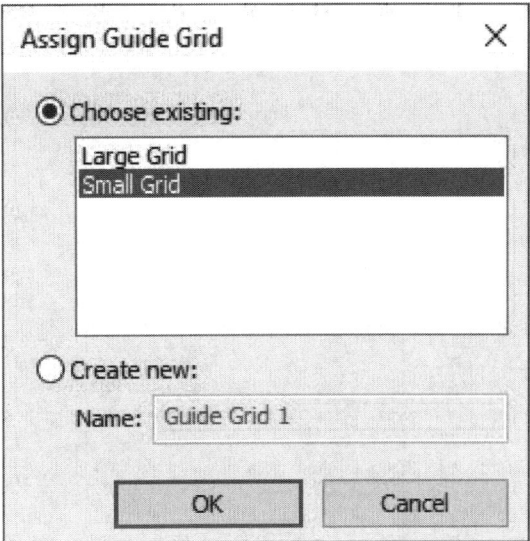

Figure B–2

3. The guide grid displays using the specified sizing.

## How To: Modify Guide Grid Sizing

1. If you create a new guide grid you need to update it to the correct size in Properties. Select the edge of the guide grid.
2. In Properties, set the *Guide Spacing*, as shown in Figure B–3.

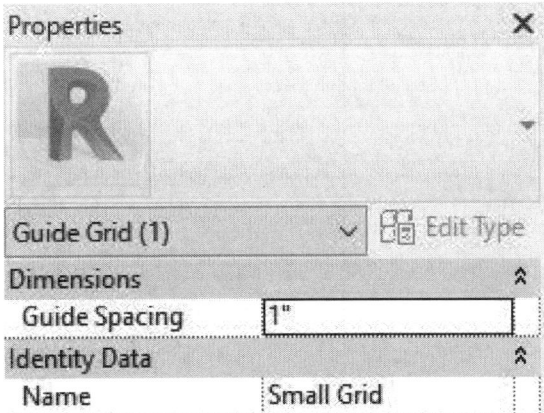

Figure B–3

# B.2 Revision Tracking

When a set of working drawings has been put into production, you need to show where changes are made. Typically, these are shown on sheets using revision clouds and tags along with a revision schedule in the title block, as shown in Figure B–4. The revision information is set up in the Sheet Issues/Revisions dialog box.

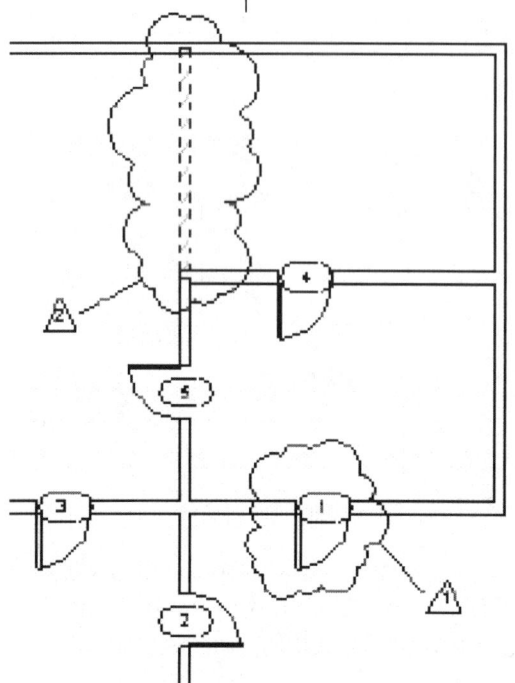

**Figure B–4**

- More than one revision cloud can be associated with a revision number.

- The title blocks that come with Revit already have a revision schedule inserted into the title area. It is recommended that you also add a revision schedule to your company title block.

- You have the ability to create multiple revision numbering sequences and you can use Transfer Project Standards to transfer these custom revision settings and revision numbering sequences to other projects. (For more information on Transfer Project Standards, see "Transferring Project Standards" on page 8-7.)

# Additional Tools for Construction Documents

## How To: Add Revision Information to the Project

1. In the *View* tab>Sheet Composition panel, click (Sheet Issues/Revisions).
2. In the Sheet Issues/Revisions dialog box, set the type of *Numbering* you want to use.
3. Click **Add** to add a new revision.
4. Specify the *Date* and *Description* for the revision, as shown in Figure B–5.

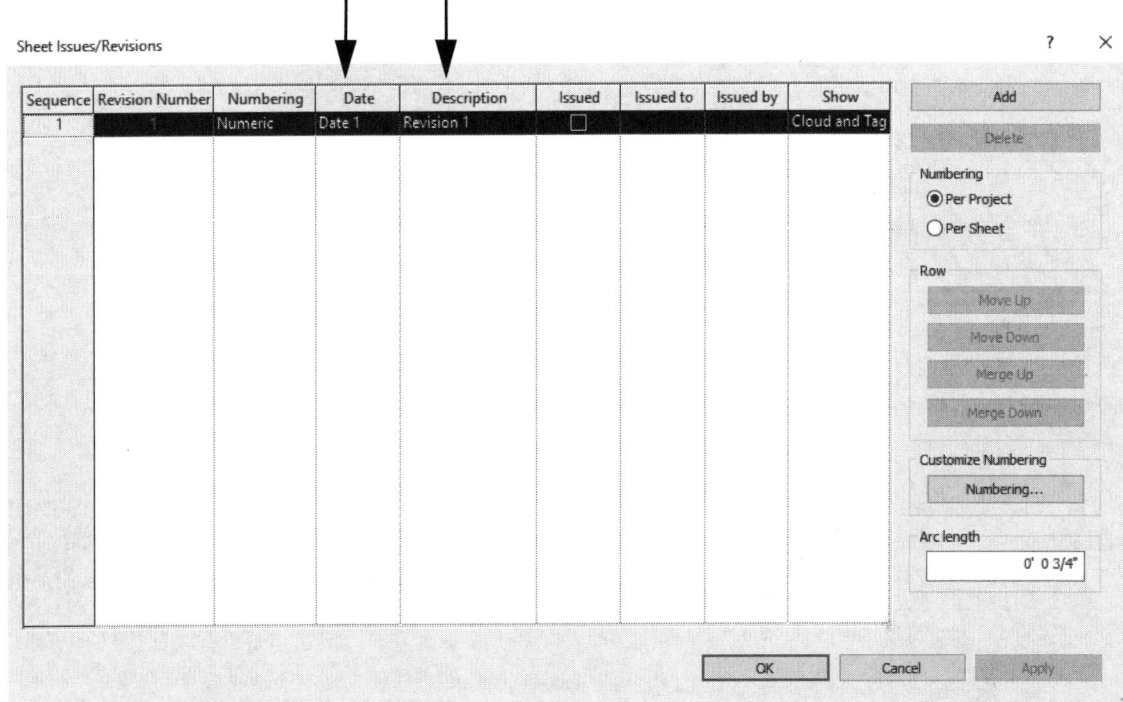

**Figure B–5**

- Do not modify the *Issued*, *Issued by*, or *Issued to* columns. You should wait to issue revisions until you are ready to print the sheets.

5. Click **OK** when you have finished adding revisions.

- To remove a revision, select its *Sequence* number and click **Delete**.

## Revision Options

- *Numbering:* Specify **Per Project** (the numbering sequence is used throughout the project) or **Per Sheet** (the number sequence is per sheet).

- *Row*: To reorganize the revisions, select a row and click **Move Up** and **Move Down**, or use **Merge Up** and **Merge Down** to combine the revisions into one.

- *Customize Numbering:* Click **Numbering...** to bring up the Numbering dialog box (shown in Figure B–6). You can edit the Alphanumeric or Numeric sequences or create custom sequences.

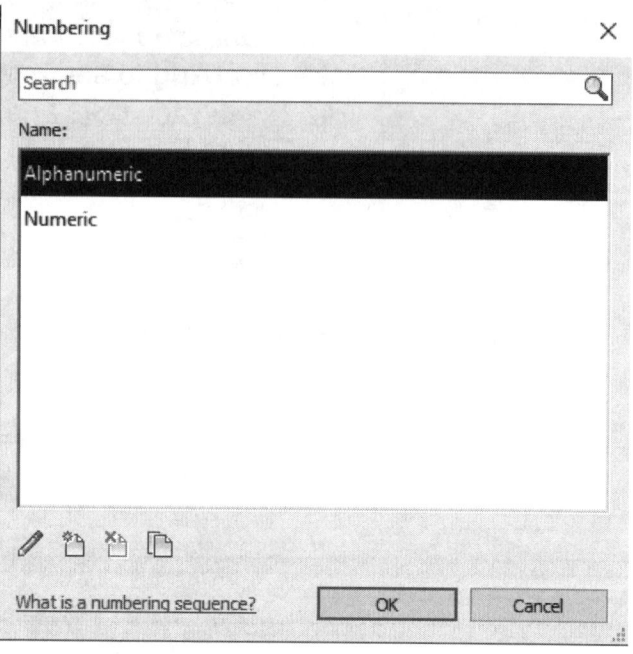

Figure B–6

- You can specify whether to create a new numbering sequence based off of Numeric or Alphanumeric as well as any prefix or suffix, as shown for the New Numbering Sequence dialog box in Figure B–7.

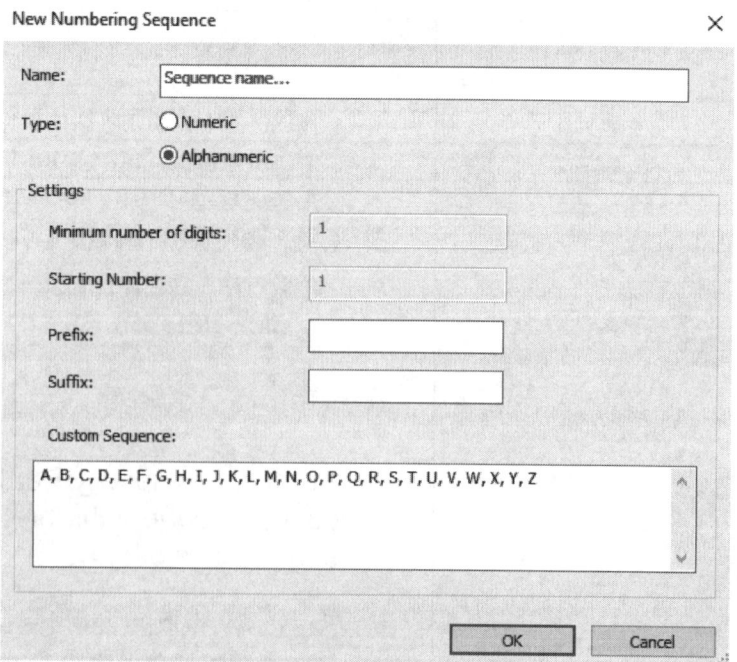

Figure B–7

# Additional Tools for Construction Documents

- *Arc length:* Specify the length of the arcs that form the revision cloud. It is an annotation element and is scaled according to the view scale.

## How To: Add Revision Clouds and Tags

1. In the *Annotate* tab>Detail panel, click (Revision Cloud).
2. In the *Modify | Create Revision Cloud Sketch* tab>Draw panel, use the draw tools to create the cloud.
3. In Properties, select which *Revision* type to use, as shown in Figure B–8.

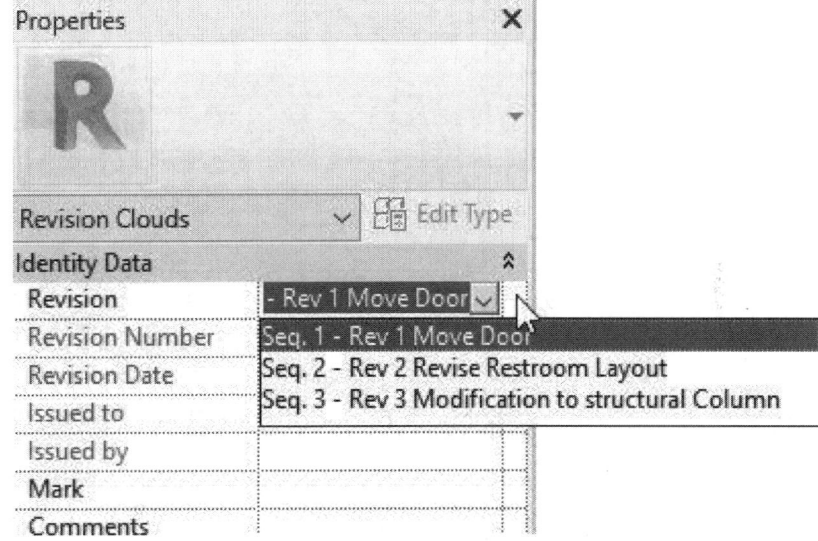

**Figure B–8**

4. Click (Finish Edit Mode).

- To modify a revision cloud, select a revision cloud, then in the Options Bar or Properties, expand the Revision drop-down list and select the revision, as shown in Figure B–9.

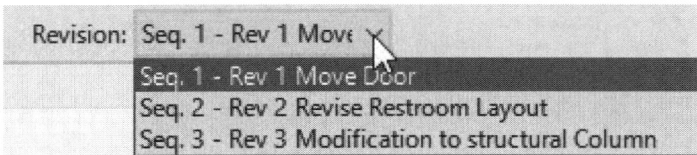

**Figure B–9**

5. In the *Annotate* tab>Tag panel, click (Tag By Category).

*If the revision table has not be set up, you can do this at a later date.*

6. Select the revision cloud to tag. A tooltip containing the revision number and revision from the cloud properties displays when you hover the cursor over the revision cloud, as shown in Figure B–10.

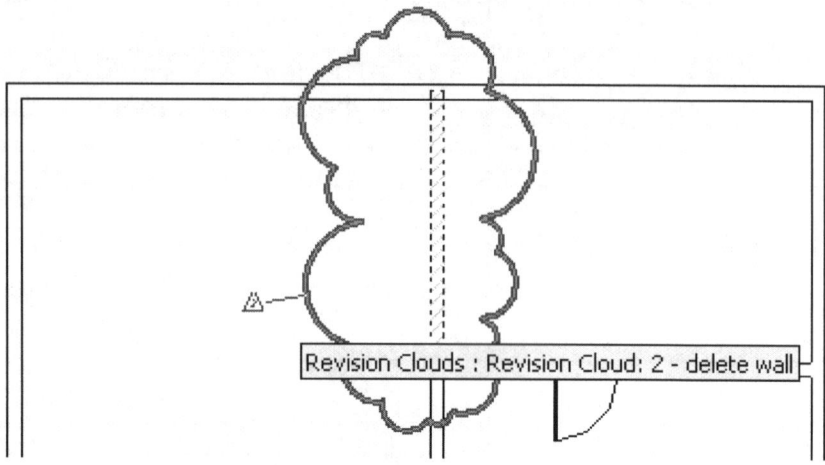

**Figure B–10**

- If the revision cloud tag is not loaded, load **Revision Tag.rfa** from the *Annotations* folder in the Revit Library.

- The *Revision Number* and *Date* are automatically assigned according to the specifications in the revision table.

- Double-click on the edge of revision cloud to switch to Edit Sketch mode and modify the size or location of the revision cloud arcs.

- You can create an open cloud (e.g., as a tree line), as shown in Figure B–11.

**Figure B–11**

# Issuing Revisions

When you have completed the revisions and are ready to submit new documents to the field, you should first lock the revision for the record. This is called issuing the revision. An issued revision is noted in the tooltip of a revision cloud, as shown in Figure B–12.

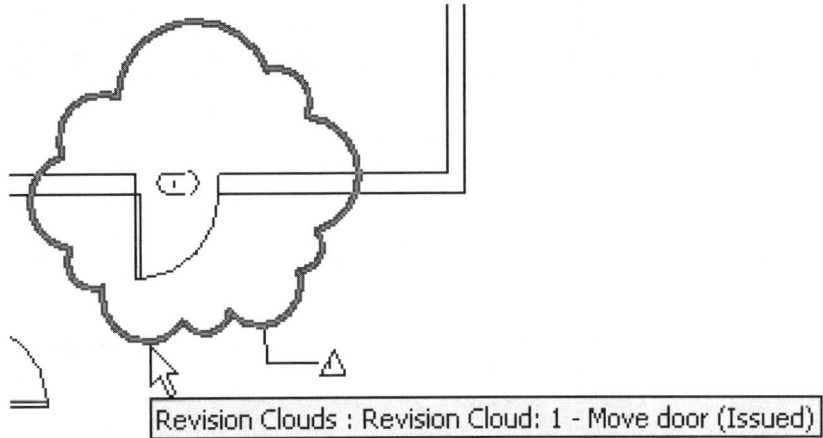

Figure B–12

## How To: Issue Revisions

1. In the *View* tab>Sheet Composition panel, click  (Sheet Issues/Revisions).
2. In the Sheet Issues/Revisions dialog box, in the row for the revision that you are issuing, type a name in the *Issued to* and *Issued by* fields, as needed.
3. In the same row, select **Issued**.
4. Continue issuing any other revisions, as needed.
5. Click **OK** to finish.

- Once **Issued** is selected, you cannot modify that revision in the Revisions dialog box or by moving the revision cloud(s). The tooltip on the cloud(s) note that it is **Issued**.

- You can unlock the revision by clearing the **Issued** option. Unlocking enables you to modify the revision after it has been locked.

# B.3 Path of Travel and Route Analysis

A typical part of a building design includes life safety diagrams that point out how people get out of a building. Codes frequently require specific distances to exits, so it is important to be able to record that information in the building model. The **Path of Travel** tool analyzes these distances between two points specified in plans, as shown in Figure B–13. You can add or remove waypoints, reveal obstacles, and update a path if geometry in the model changes.

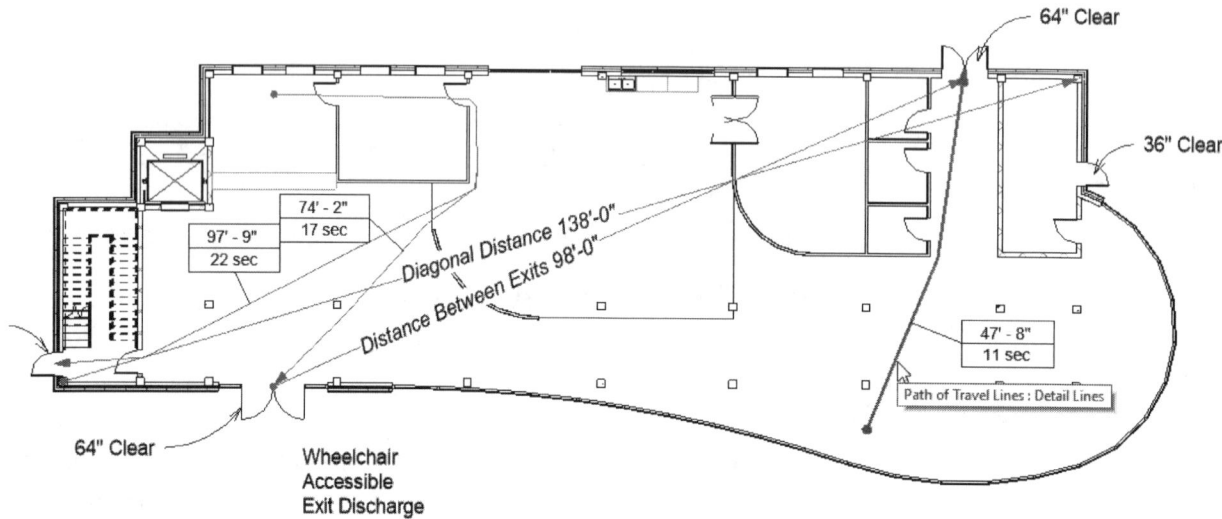

**Figure B–13**

- After a path has been created, you can select the path and select (Add Waypoint) or (Delete Waypoint) as needed.

- You can turn on (Reveal Obstacles).

- Path of travel lines can be tagged and the information can be included in schedules.

- You can modify the start and end points of a path of travel using grips to reposition it.

- If any geometry in the model is modified, you can select (Update) to update the path of travel line.

# Additional Tools for Construction Documents

## How To: Use Path of Travel Lines

1. In the *Analyze* tab>Route Analysis panel, click (Reveal Obstacles) if you need to see what obstacles are in the view.
2. In the *Analyze* tab>Route Analysis panel, click (Path of Travel).
3. In the *Modify | Place Path of Travel* tab>Tag panel, click (Tag on Placement) if you want to add a tag.
    - Load the Path of Travel tag from the Revit Library in the *Annotations* folder.
4. In the *Modify | Place Path of Travel* tab>Line Style panel, select the line style from the drop-down list.
5. Select the start point for the line of travel.
6. Select the end point for the line of travel.
7. Depending on the Route Analysis settings, the route is calculated.
8. Use (Update) as needed if there are any changes in the model's geometry.

## Route Analysis Settings

You can specify categories of elements that impact the analysis and placement of travel lines. For example, in Figure B–14, only the door category is ignored in calculating the route, while, in Figure B–15, all categories are ignored, so you can calculate the distances between exits and the building diagonal.

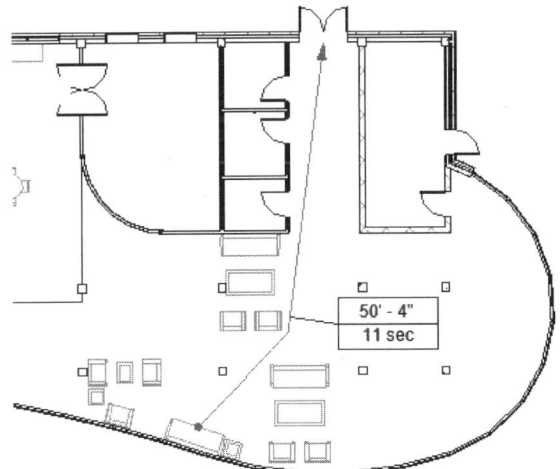

**Figure B–14**

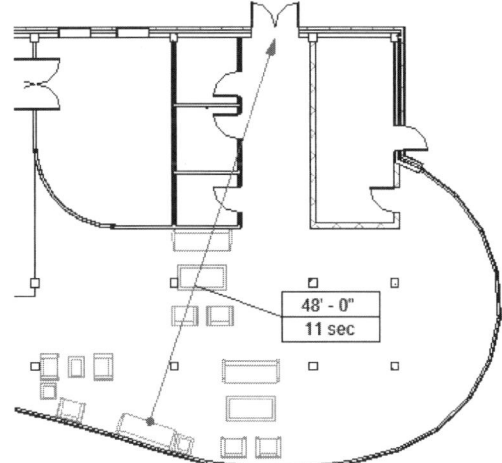

**Figure B–15**

- In the *Analyze* tab>Route Analysis panel title, click (Route Analysis Settings). In the Route Analysis Settings dialog box (shown in Figure B–16), select the model categories you want to include or exclude.

**Figure B–16**

# B.4 Annotating Dependent Views

The **Duplicate as a Dependent** command creates a copy of the view and links it to the selected view. Changes made to the original view are also made in the dependent view and vice-versa. Use dependent views when the building model is so large you need to split the building up on separate sheets, as shown in Figure B–17.

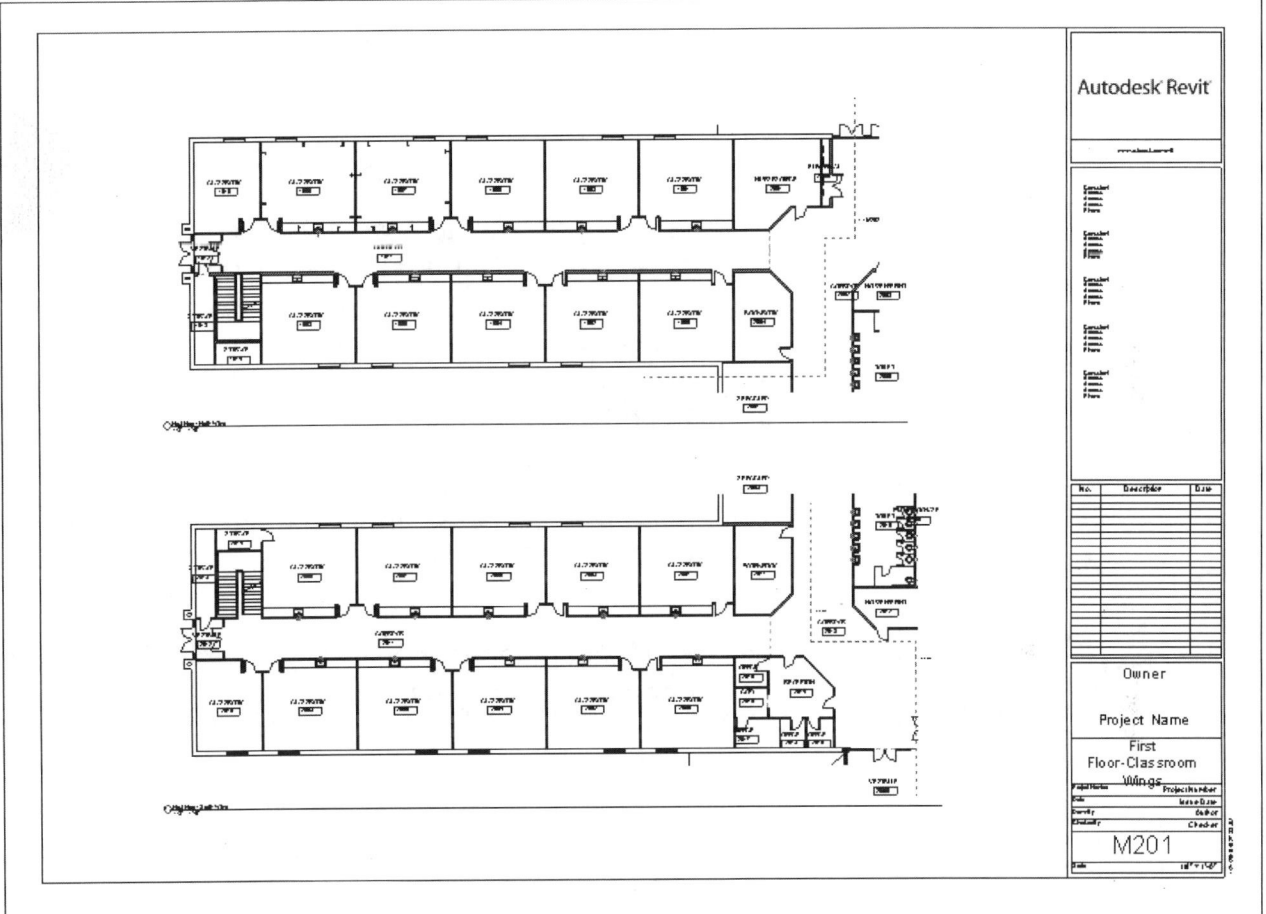

Figure B–17

- Using one overall view with several dependent views makes it easier to see changes, such as to the scale or detail level.

- Dependent views display in the Project Browser under the top-level view, as shown in Figure B–18.

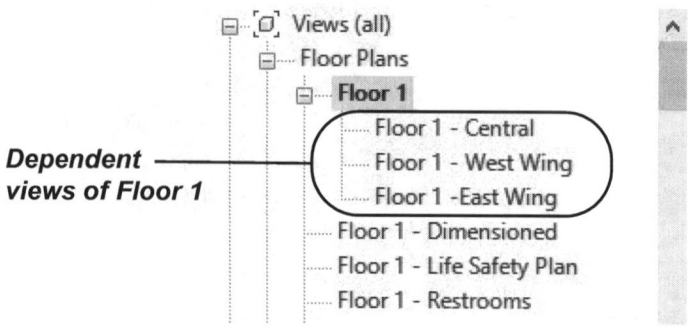

Figure B–18

### How To: Duplicate Dependent Views

1. Select the view you want to use as the top-level view.
2. Right-click and select **Duplicate View>Duplicate as a Dependent**.
3. Rename the dependent views as needed.
4. Modify the crop region of the dependent view to show the specified portion of the model.

- If you want to separate a dependent view from the original view, right-click on the dependent view and select **Convert to independent view**.

## Annotating Views

To clarify and annotate dependent views, use **Matchlines** and **View References**, as shown in Figure B–19.

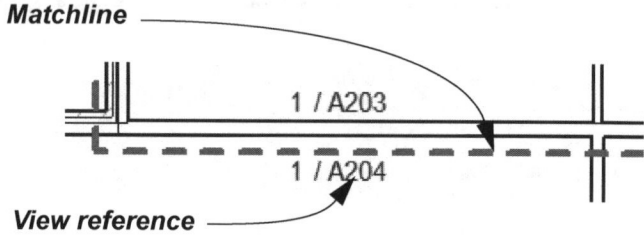

Figure B–19

- Sketch matchlines in the primary view to specify where dependent views separate. They display in all related views and extend through all levels of the project by default.

- View references are special tags that display the sheet location of the dependent views.

# Additional Tools for Construction Documents

## How To: Add Matchlines

1. In the *View* tab>Sheet Composition panel, click (Matchline).
2. In the Draw panel, click (Line) and sketch the location of the matchline.
3. In the Matchline panel, click (Finish Edit Mode) when you are finished.

- To modify an existing matchline, select it and click (Edit Sketch) in the *Modify | Matchline* tab>Mode panel.

- To modify the color and line type of Matchlines, in the *Manage* tab>Settings panel, click (Object Styles). In the Object Styles dialog box that opens, in the *Annotation Objects* tab, you can make changes to Matchline properties.

## How To: Add View References

1. In the *View* tab>Sheet Composition panel or *Annotate* tab> Tag panel, click (View Reference).
2. In the *Modify | View Reference* tab>View Reference panel, search for or specify the *View Type* and *Target View*, as shown in Figure B–20.

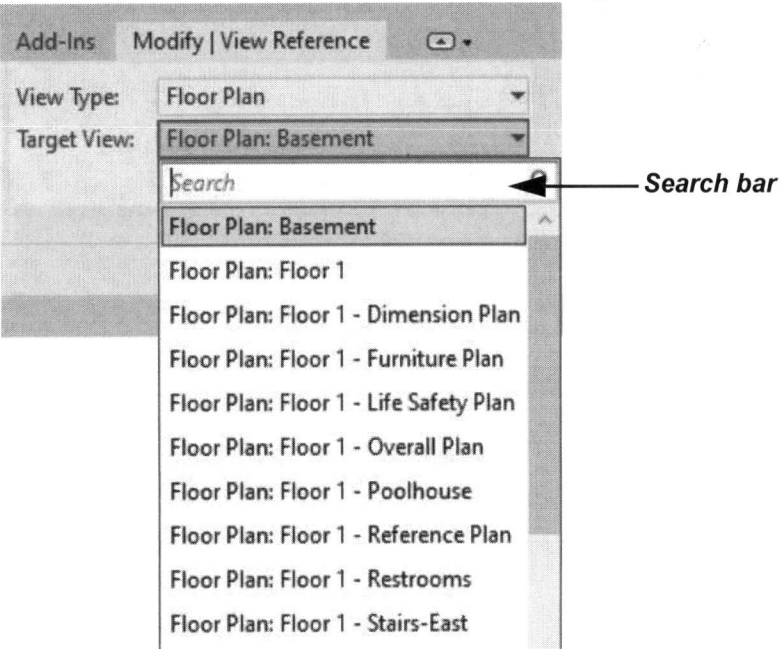

**Figure B–20**

3. Place the tag on the side of the matchline that corresponds to the target view.
4. Click  (Modify) to clear the selection.
5. Repeat the process and place the tag on the other side of the matchline.
6. The tags display as empty dashes until the views are placed onto sheets. They then update to include the detail and sheet number, as shown in Figure B–21.

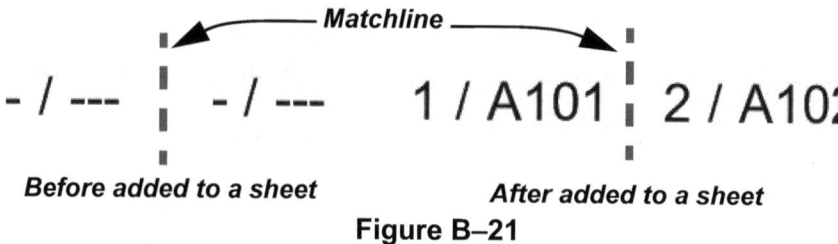

*Before added to a sheet*     *After added to a sheet*

**Figure B–21**

- Double-click on the view reference to open the associated view.

- If only a label named **REF** displays when you place a view reference, it means you need to load and update the tag. The **View Reference.rfa** tag is located in the *Annotations* folder in the Revit Library. Once you have the tag loaded, in the Type Selector, select one of the view references and, in Properties, click  (Edit Type). Select **View Reference** in the drop-down list, as shown in Figure B–22, and click **OK** to close the dialog box. The new tag displays.

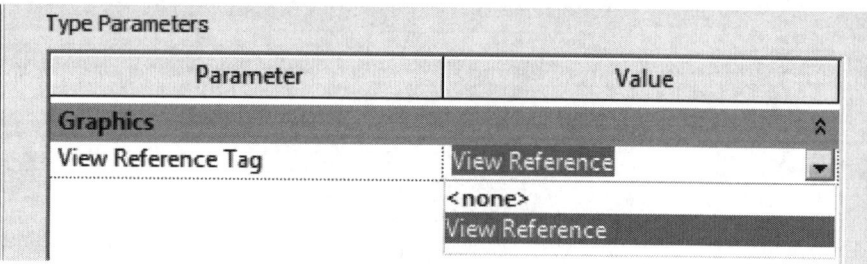

**Figure B–22**

# B.5 Creating Building Component Schedules

A building component schedule is a table view of the type and instance parameters of a specific element. You can specify the parameters (fields) you want to include in the schedule. All of the parameters found in the type of element you are scheduling are available to use. For example, a door schedule (as shown in Figure B–23) can include instance parameters that are automatically filled in (such as the **Height** and **Width**) and type parameters that might need to have the information assigned in the schedule or element type (such as the **Fire Rating** and **Frame**).

## &lt;Door Schedule&gt;

| A | B | C | D | E | F | G | H |
|---|---|---|---|---|---|---|---|
|  | Dimensions | | | Frame Information | | | Fire |
| Mark | Width | Height | Thickness | Frame Type | Frame Material | Finish | Rating |
|  | 8' - 3 1/2" | 9' - 4 1/4" | | | | | |
| 101 | 3' - 0" | 7' - 0" | 0' - 2" | A | Steel | Brushed | A |
| 102 | 3' - 0" | 7' - 0" | 0' - 2" | A | Steel | Brushed | A |
| 103 | 3' - 0" | 6' - 8" | 0' - 2" |  | Wood | Painted | B |
| 104 | 3' - 0" | 6' - 8" | 0' - 2" |  | Wood | Painted | B |
| 105 | 3' - 0" | 6' - 8" | 0' - 2" | B | Wood | Painted | B |
| 106 | 3' - 0" | 6' - 8" | 0' - 2" | B | Wood | Painted | B |
| 107 | 3' - 0" | 6' - 8" | 0' - 2" | B | Wood | Painted | B |
| 108 | 3' - 0" | 7' - 0" | 0' - 2" |  | Wood | Painted | A |
| 109 | 3' - 0" | 7' - 0" | 0' - 2" |  | Wood | Painted | A |
| 110 | 6' - 0" | 7' - 0" | 0' - 2" |  | Wood | Painted |  |
| 111 | 6' - 0" | 6' - 10" | 0' - 2" | C | Aluminum | Brushed |  |

**Figure B–23**

## How To: Create a Building Component Schedule

1. In the *View* tab>Create panel, expand (Schedules) and click (Schedule/Quantities), or in the Project Browser, right-click on the **Schedule/Quantities** node and select **New Schedule/Quantities**.
2. In the New Schedule dialog box, select the type of schedule you want to create from the *Category* list, as shown in Figure B–24.

*In the Filter list drop-down list, you can specify the discipline(s) to show only the categories that you want to display.*

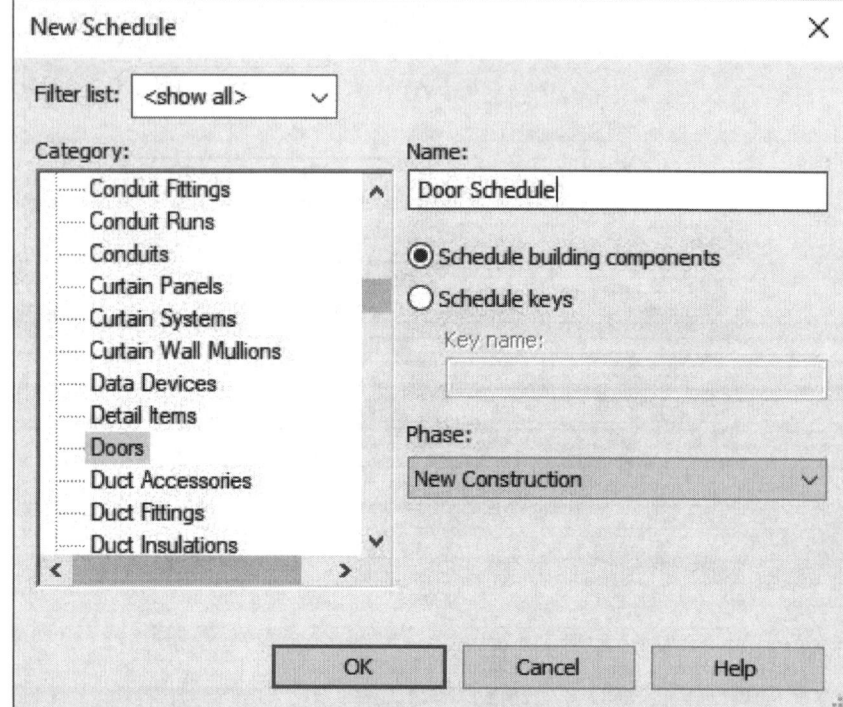

Figure B–24

3. Type a new *Name*, if the default does not suit.
4. Select **Schedule building components.**
5. Specify the *Phase* as needed.
6. Click **OK**.
7. Fill out the information in the Schedule Properties dialog box. This includes the information in the *Fields*, *Filter*, *Sorting/Grouping*, *Formatting*, and *Appearance* tabs.
8. Once you have entering the schedule properties, click **OK**. A schedule report is created in its own view.

# Additional Tools for Construction Documents

## Schedule Properties – Embedded Schedule Tab

With select schedules such as spaces, rooms, duct systems, piping systems, and electrical circuits, you will have the ability to add an embedded schedule. For example, in a room schedule, you can embed a furniture schedule because the furniture elements are aware of the room elements. In these cases, there will be an *Embedded Schedule* tab in the Schedule Properties dialog box, as shown in Figure B–25.

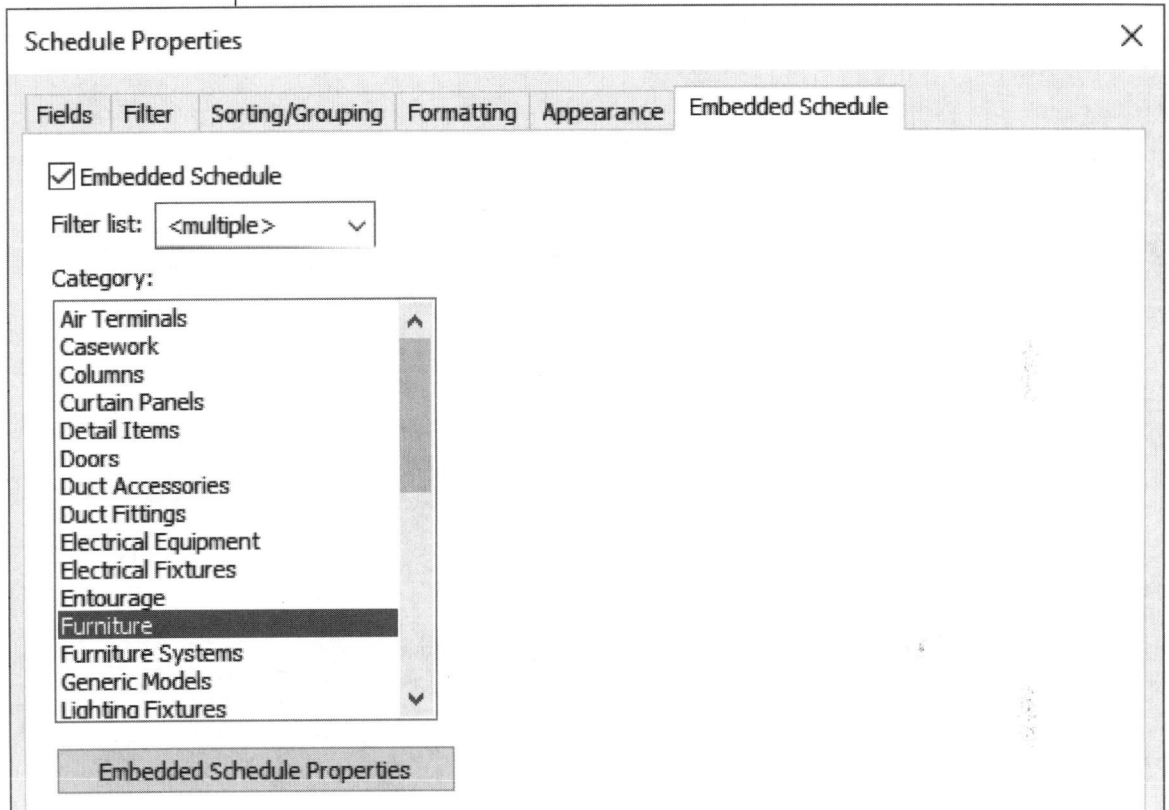

Figure B–25

| | |
|---|---|
| **Embedded Schedule** | Select this to turn on this feature and add an embedded schedule to the existing schedule. |
| **Filter List** | Sort the available categories by discipline. |
| **Category** | Select the category that you want to create the embedded schedule from. |
| **Embedded Schedule Properties** | When clicking on the Embedded Schedule Properties button a new Schedule Properties dialog box opens where you can specify the Fields, Filter, Sorting/Grouping and Formatting for the embedded schedule. |

# B.6 Importing and Exporting Schedules

Schedules are views and can be copied into your project from other projects. Only the formatting information is copied; the information about individually scheduled items is not included. That information is automatically added by the project the schedule is copied into. You can also export the schedule information to be used in spreadsheets.

## How To: Import Schedules

1. In the *Insert* tab>Load from Library panel, expand  (Insert from File) and click  (Insert Views from File).
2. In the Open dialog box, locate the project file containing the schedule you want to use.
3. Select the schedules you want to import, as shown in Figure B–26.

*If the referenced project contains many types of views, change Views: to **Show schedules and reports only**.*

Figure B–26

4. Click **OK**.

## Additional Tools for Construction Documents

### How To: Export Schedule Information

1. Switch to the schedule view that you want to export.
2. In the *File* tab, click ▸ (Export)> ▸ (Reports)> ▸ (Schedule).
3. Select a location and name for the text file in the Export Schedule dialog box and click **Save**.
4. In the Export Schedule dialog box, set the options in the *Schedule appearance* and *Output options* areas that best suit your spreadsheet software, as shown in Figure B–27.

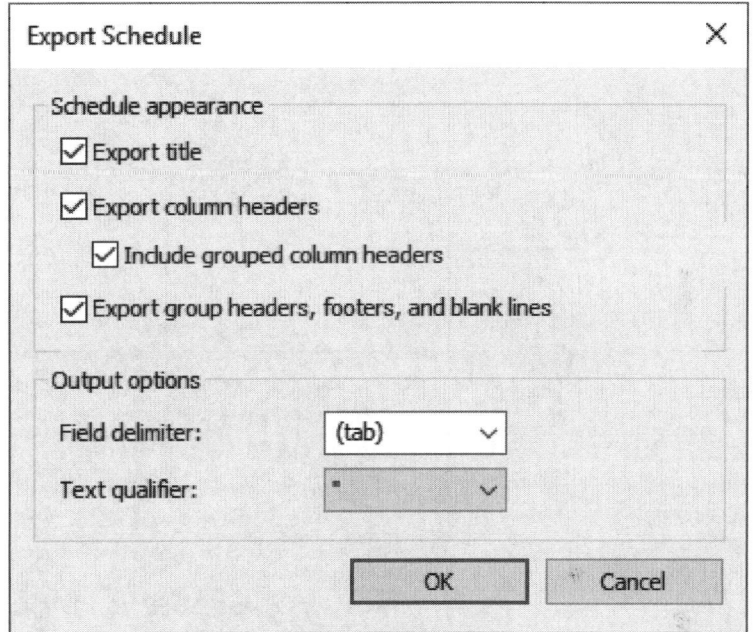

Figure B–27

5. Click **OK**. A new text file is created that you can open in a spreadsheet, as shown in Figure B–28.

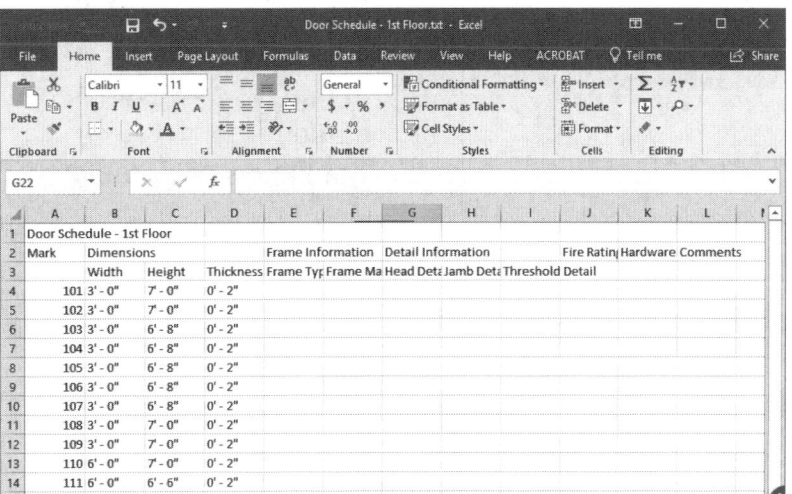

Figure B–28

# B.7 Creating a Repeating Detail

Repeating detail components are very useful when working on complex details, such as those that include a brick wall. You can also create a repeating detail using any detail component, such as the glass block shown in Figure B–29.

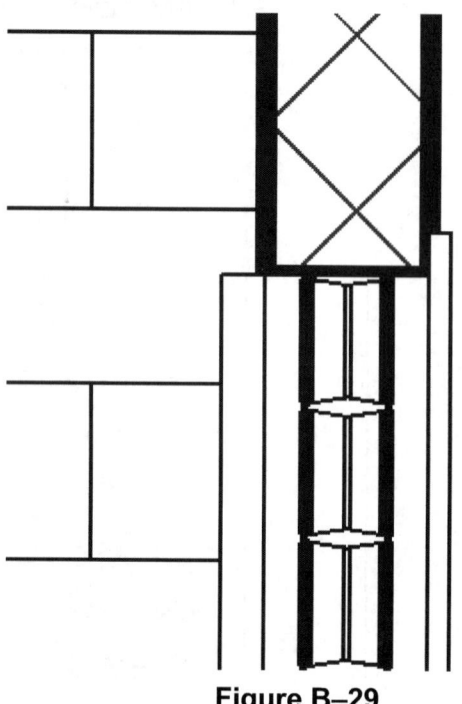

**Figure B–29**

## How To: Create a Repeating Detail

1. Load the detail component you want to use.
2. In the *Annotate* tab>Detail panel, expand  (Component) and click  (Repeating Detail Component).
3. In Properties, click  (Edit Type).
4. In the Type Properties dialog box, click **Duplicate...**. Enter a name.
5. Set the *Detail* parameter. This is the component name.

6. Fill out the rest of the parameters, as shown in Figure B–30.

Figure B–30

7. Set the *Layout* to **Fill Available Space**, **Fixed Distance**, **Fixed Number**, or **Maximum Spacing**. Select **Inside** if you want all components to be within the specified distance or line. Leaving this option clear causes the first component to start before the first point.
8. Set the *Spacing* between components if you are using **Fixed Distance** or **Maximum Spacing**.
9. Set the *Detail Rotation* as needed, and close the dialog box.

# B.8 Keynoting and Keynote Legends

Keynotes are a special kind of tag that apply specific numbers to various elements in a detail. They can be used on all model and detail elements, as well as materials. Using keynotes requires less room on a view than standard text notes, as shown in Figure B–31. The full explanation of the note is shown in a corresponding *keynote legend* placed elsewhere in the sheet or sheet set.

*By default, Revit uses the CSI master format system of keynote designations.*

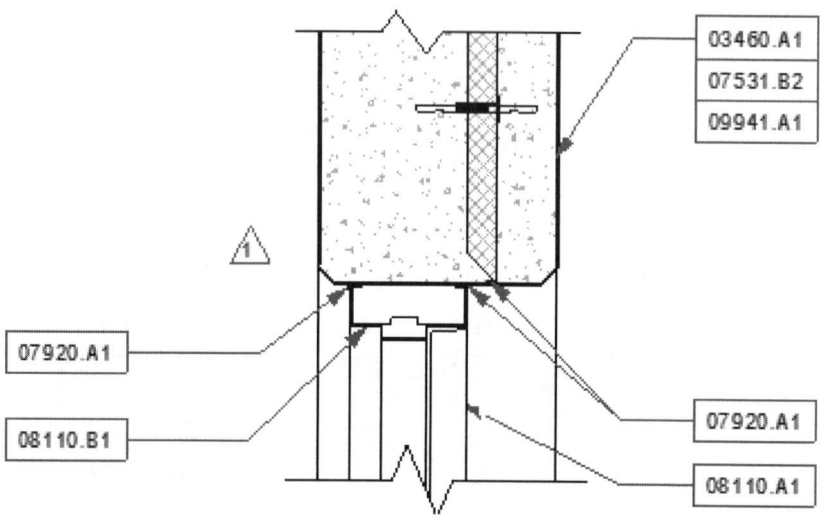

**Figure B–31**

- Keynote tags are found in the Revit Library in the *Annotations* folder and should be loaded into a project before you can apply them.

There are three types of keynote tags:

- **Element:** Used to tag elements, such as a door, wall, or detail components.

- **Material:** Used for the material assigned to a component or applied onto a surface.

- **User:** A keynote that must first be developed in a keynote table.

# Additional Tools for Construction Documents

## How To: Place a Keynote

1. In the *Annotate* tab>Tag panel, expand (Keynote) and click (Element Keynote), (Material Keynote), or (User Keynote).
2. Move the cursor over the element you want to keynote and select it.
3. If an element has keynote information assigned to it, the keynote is automatically applied. If it is not assigned, the Keynotes dialog box opens, as shown in Figure B–32.

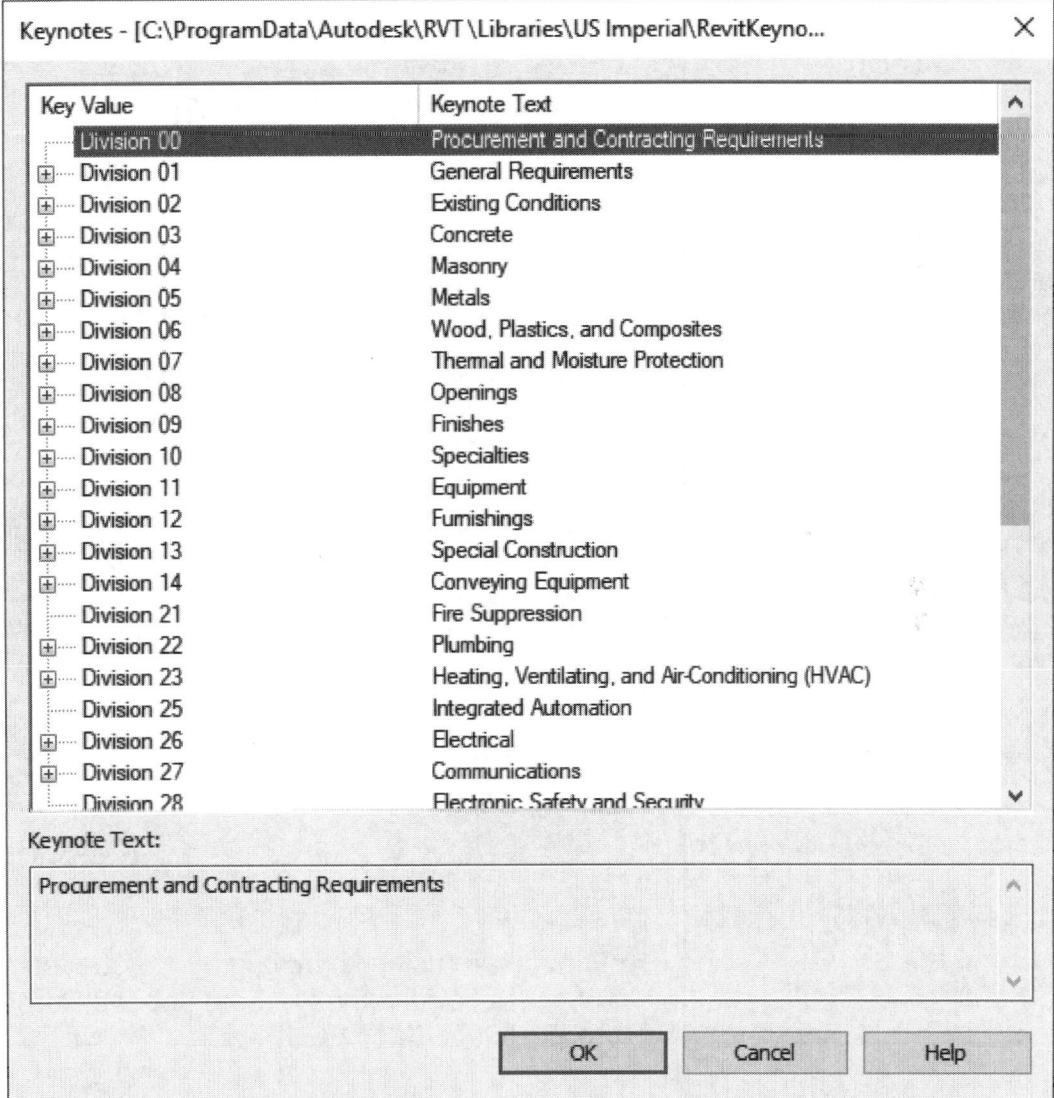

Figure B–32

4. Select the keynote you need from the list of divisions and click **OK**.

- The options for keynotes are the same as for other tags, including orientation and leaders, as shown in Figure B–33.

**Figure B–33**

*The keynote remembers the leader settings from the last time it was used.*

### Hint: Setting the Keynote Numbering Method

Keynotes can be listed by the full keynote number or by sheet, as shown in Figure B–34. Only one method can be used at a time in a project, but you can change between the two methods at any time in the project.

1. In the *Annotate* tab>Tag panel, expand (Keynote) and click (Keynoting Settings).

**Figure B–34**

2. In the Keynoting Settings dialog box, specify the *Keynote Table* information and the *Numbering Method*, as shown in Figure B–35.

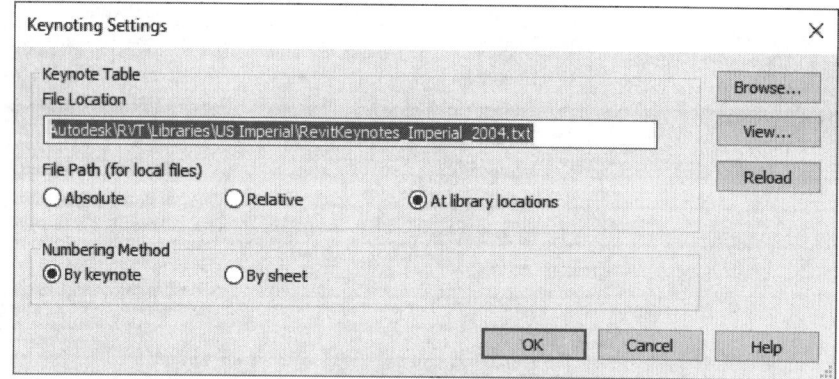

**Figure B–35**

- If you are using keynoting by sheet, create the Keynote Legend, and in the Keynote Legend Properties in the *Filter* tab, select **Filter by Sheet**.

Additional Tools for Construction Documents

- Keynotes are stored in a keynote table (a text file), as shown in Figure B–36. Any updates made to the keynote table are reflected in the project after it is closed and then re-opened.

```
RevitKeynotes_Imperial - Notepad
File  Edit  Format  View  Help
01000    Division 01 - General Requirements
02000    Division 02 - Sitework
03000    Division 03 - Concrete
04000    Division 04 - Masonry
05000    Division 05 - Metals
06000    Division 06 - Wood and Plastics
07000    Division 07 - Thermal and Moisture
08000    Division 08 - Doors and windows
09000    Division 09 - Finishes
10000    Division 10 - Specialties
11000    Division 11 - Equipment
12000    Division 12 - Furnishings
13000    Division 13 - Special Construction
14000    Division 14 - Conveying
```

Figure B–36

## Keynote Legends

*A keynote legend is different from a standard legend.*

A keynote legend is a table containing the information stored in the keynote that is placed on a sheet, as shown in Figure B–37. In Revit, it is created in a similar way to schedules.

| \<Keynote Legend\> | |
|---|---|
| **A** | **B** |
| Key Value | Keynote Text |
| 03 53 00 | Concrete Topping |
| 04 05 19 | Masonry Anchorage and Reinforcing |
| 05 31 00.A1 | 1.5 MR 16 Composite Metal Deck |
| 07 40 00.C2 | 3" x 4" Downspout |

Figure B–37

### How To: Create a Keynote Legend

1. In the *View* tab>Create panel, expand (Legends) and click (Keynote Legend).
2. Type a name in the New Keynote Legend dialog box and click **OK**.

3. The Keynote Legend Properties dialog box typically only displays two scheduled fields, which are already set up for you, as shown in Figure B–38.

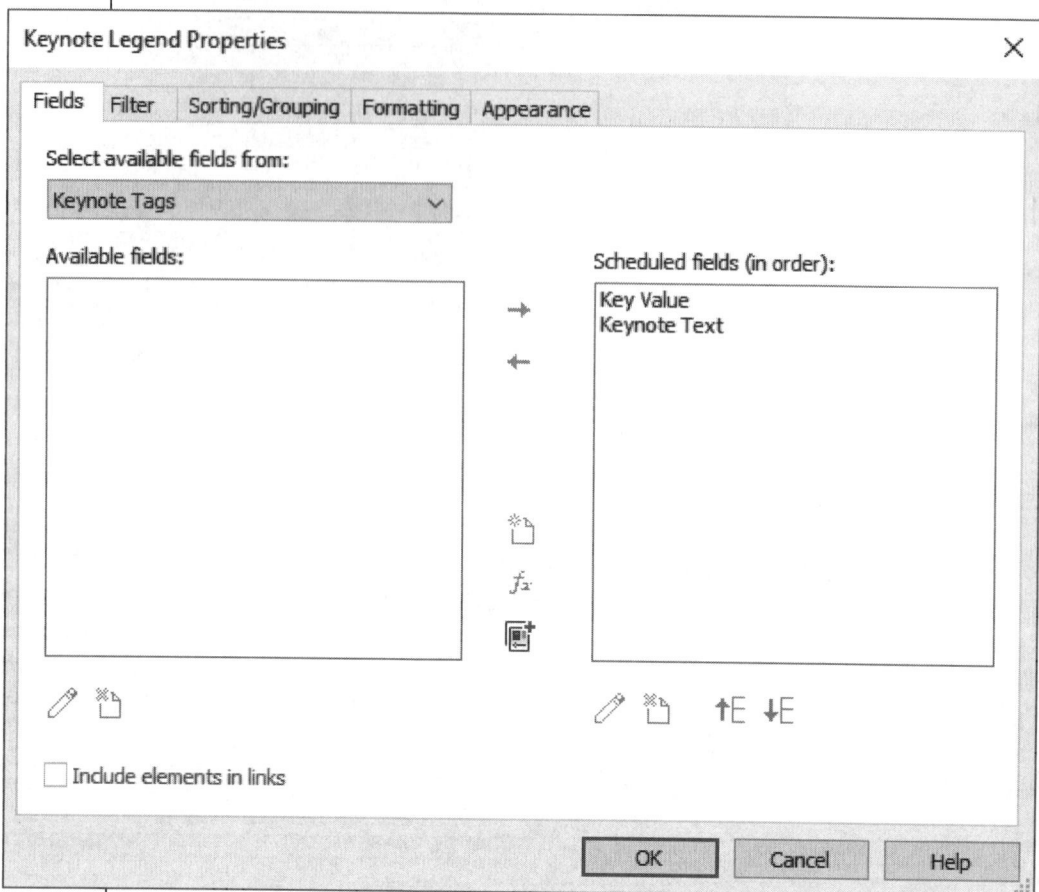

Figure B–38

4. In the other tabs, set up the format of the table as needed.
5. Click **OK** to create the keynote legend.
6. When you are ready to place a keynote legend, drag it from the Project Browser onto the sheet. You can manipulate it in the same way, similar to modifying other schedules.

- As you add keynotes to the project, they are added to the keynote legend.

# Command Summary

| Button | Command | Location |
|---|---|---|
| **Analysis** | | |
| | Path of Travel | • **Ribbon:** *Analyze* tab>Route Analysis panel |
| **Annotations** | | |
| | Matchline | • **Ribbon:** *View* tab>Sheet Composition panel |
| | View Reference | • **Ribbon:** *View* tab>Sheet Composition panel or *Annotate* tab>Tag panel |
| **Details** | | |
| | Edit Type | • **Properties** (with a Repeating Detail element selected) |
| **Revisions** | | |
| | Revision Cloud | • **Ribbon:** *Annotate* tab>Detail panel |
| | Sheet Issues/ Revisions | • **Ribbon:** *Manage* tab>Settings panel, expand Additional Settings |
| **Schedules** | | |
| | Insert Views from File | • **Ribbon:** *Insert* tab, expand **Insert from File** |
| n/a | Schedule (Export) | • **File tab:** expand Export>Reports>Schedule |
| | Schedule/ Quantities | • **Ribbon:** *View* tab>Create panel, expand Schedules<br>• **Project Browser:** right-click on Schedule/Quantities node>New Schedule/Quantities... |

# Index

## #

2022.1 Enhancement
    Automatic locking for Align **5-42**
    Duplicate sheet **14-8**
    Find in Project Browser **1-22**
    Load multiple families from Load Autodesk Family dialog box **4-9**
    Snap mid-point between two points **4-11**

2023 Enhancement
    Activate Controls with multiple element selection **5-15**
    Control Print Order **14-26**
    Customize Multi-Leader tag leader lines **16-6**
    Filter by Sheet for Schedules **16-37**
    Link FormIt Files **2-4**
    Link/Import CAD Files to Reference Plane **2-4**
    Link/Import OBJ and STL files **2-4**
    Measure in 3D views **5-18**
    PDF icon on the Quick Access Toolbar **1-9**
    Project Browser icons for views on sheets **1-20**
    Saved placement setting for work plane-based families **4-10**
    Search/filter View Reference list **B-15**
    Set the work plane quickly **12-17**
    Set wall structure to Non-Bearing **7-13**
    Swap views on a sheet **14-8**

3D Views
    Default **1-34**
    Isometric **1-34**
    Locking **16-12**

## A

Align command **5-41**
Alignment Lines **5-6**
Array
    Linear **5-30**
    Modifying Groups **5-32**
    Radial **5-31**
Attaching to roof **12-5**

## B

Bearing Footings **7-20**
BIM
    Building Information Modeling **1-2**
    Construction Documents **1-5**
    Workflow **1-3**
Break Lines **17-10**

## C

Callout command **3-22**
Callout Views
    Modifying **3-25**
    Rectangular **3-22**
    Sketched **3-23**
Camera **1-34**, **1-35**
Ceilings
    Components **11-7**
    Create **11-3**
    Grids **11-2**
    Sketch **11-4**
    Soffits **11-16**
Clipboard
    Copy to **5-26**, **8-6**
    Cut to **5-26**, **8-6**
Close Inactive Views **1-13**
Columns **6-2**
    Architectural **6-2**
    At Columns **6-3**
    at Grids **6-3**
    Creating **6-2**
    Modifying **6-5**
    Move with Grids **6-5**
    Structural **6-2**
Components
    Adding **4-6**
    Modifying **4-12**
Contextual Tabs **5-12**
Controls **5-12**
Copy **5-26**
    To Clipboard **5-26**, **8-6**

Create
  Building Component Schedules **B-17**
  Ceilings **11-3**
  Curtain Grids **9-6**
  Curtain Wall Panels **9-19**
  Floor Slab Edges **A-8**
  Floors **10-2**
  Gutters **A-8**
  Local Files **A-30**
  Multi-Segment Grid **2-39**
  Ramps **13-47**
  Repeating Details **B-22**
  Schedule/Quantities **B-18**
  Sweep Profiles **A-9**
  Text Types **15-31**
  Wall Reveals **A-8**
  Wall Sweep **A-10**
Curtain Grids
  Add/Remove Segments **9-8**
  Automatic **A-11**
  Create **9-6**
  Curtain Walls **9-6**
  Modifying **9-7**
Curtain Wall **9-2**
  Adding Mullions **9-21**
  Grids **9-6**
Curtain Wall Panels **9-17**
  Create **9-19**
Cut Profile command **A-25**
Cut to Clipboard **5-26**, **8-6**

# D

Datum Elements **1-5**
Default 3D View command **1-34**
Delete **5-13**
Dependent Views **B-14**
Depth Clipping **3-28**
Detail Components **17-9**
  Repeating **17-12**
Detail Lines **15-39**
Details
  Annotating **17-13**
  Import **17-8**
  Tagging **17-16**
Dimensions
  Aligned **15-4**
  Angular **15-5**
  Arc Length **15-5**
  Constraints **15-10**
  Diameter **15-5**
  Feet and inches **5-7**
  Labeling **15-12**
  Linear **15-4**
  Modifying **15-5**
  Radial **15-5**
Doors **8-2**
  Creating Sizes **4-14**, **8-8**

Drafting Views
  Creating **17-3**
  Referencing **17-5**
  Saving **17-6**
Drag Elements on Selection **1-25**
Draw Order **17-11**
Draw Tools **5-3**
Drawing Aids **5-6**
Duplicate
  As Dependent **3-6**
  Detailing **3-5**
Duplicate views **3-5**

# E

Edit Crop **3-24**
Edit Type **4-14**, **8-8**
Edit Wall Joins command **A-6**
Elements
  Datum **1-5**
  Model **1-4**
  View-specific **1-5**
Elevations **3-35**
  Modifying **3-37**
Export Schedules **B-21**

# F

Families
  Create Types **4-14**
  Files (.rfa) **1-27**
Far Clipping **3-28**
File Tab **1-17**
File Types **1-27**
Filled Regions **17-14**
Filter **5-18**
Floor Slab Edges **A-8**
Floors
  Create **10-2**
  Modify **10-5**
  Shape Editing **10-19**
  Slope Arrows **10-17**
Footings
  Bearing **7-20**
  Retaining **7-19**
Foundation Wall **7-20**
Freeze Schedule Headers **16-21**

# G

Geometry
  Join **10-7**
  Unjoin **10-7**
Global Parameters **15-13**
Grids
  Modifying **2-41**
  Multi-Segment **2-39**
Gutters **A-8**

## H

Hide
    Categories **3-13**
Hide Elements **3-13**
Hide in View **3-13**

## I

Import
    Details **17-8**
    Hide Layers **2-19**
    Image Files **2-8**
    Raster Images **2-8**
    Schedules **B-20**
Import CAD command **2-5**
Import Trimble SketchUp files **2-4**
Improved graphics in Realistic views **1-39**
InfoCenter **1-9**
Insert Views from File command **B-20**
Instance Properties **1-18**
Insulation **17-12**
Interface **1-7**
Isolated Footings
    Placing **6-7**
Isometric Views **1-34**

## J

Join Geometry **10-7**

## K

Keynotes **B-24**
    Legends **B-27**
    Placing **B-25**

## L

Legend **15-45**
    Components **15-46**
    Create **15-46**
Levels
    Create **2-26**
    Modify **2-28**
Light Source **11-8**
Linework command **A-25**
Link
    Raster Images **2-8**
Link CAD command **2-5**
Link PDF and Raster images **2-3**
Link Revit command **2-13**
Loaded Tags And Symbols command **16-9**
Local Files
    Create **A-30**
Lock 3D Views **16-12**

## M

Match Type **7-18**
Matchlines **B-15**
Materials **A-22**
Mirror - Draw Axis **5-29**

Mirror - Pick Axis **5-29**
Model Elements **1-4**
Model Text **15-30**
Modify command **1-16**
Modify start and end points for path of travel **B-10**
Move **5-26**
Mullions **9-21**
    Modify **9-22**
Multi-Segment Grid **2-39**
Multistory Stairs **13-24**

## N

Navigation Bar **1-16**
New Project **2-2**

## O

Offset **5-46**
Open **1-28**
Options Bar **1-14**
or **B-15**
Orient to a Direction **3-43**
Orient to a Plane **3-43**
Orient to View **3-42**
Overriding Graphics **3-14**

## P

Paint command **A-23**
Pan **1-31**
Paste
    Aligned to Current View **8-6**
    Aligned to Picked Level **8-6**
    Aligned to Same Place **8-6**
    Aligned to Selected Levels **8-6**
    Aligned to Selected Views **8-6**
    From Clipboard **5-26**, **8-6**
Path of Travel **B-10**
Path of Travel Waypoints **B-10**
Perspective Views **1-34**
Pick New Host command **4-13**
Pick Tools **5-5**
Pin **5-27**
Pinned Elements **5-27**
Plan Regions **3-26**, **3-27**
Plan Views **2-30**
Print command **14-22**
Project Browser **1-20**
Propagating Datum Extents **2-43**
Properties **5-12**
Purge Unused **A-5**

## Q

Quick Access Toolbar **1-9**

## R

Railings
- Add by Selecting a Host **13-36**
- Add by Sketching **13-34**
- Edit Path **13-37**
- Modify **13-34**
- Tags **16-13**

Ramps **13-47**

Raster Images
- Import and Link **2-8**

Reference Plane command **5-9**
Reference Planes **5-9**
Reflected Ceiling Plan Views **2-30**
Rename Views **1-34**
Repeating Detail Component **17-12**
Repeating Details **B-22**
Reports **1-4**
Reset Crop **3-24**
Retaining footings **7-19**
Reveal Hidden Elements **3-17**

Revisions
- Issuing **B-9**
- Tracking **A-27**, **B-4**

Ribbon **1-14**
Riser Numbers **16-13**

Roofs
- Attach Walls **12-24**
- By Extrusion **12-19**
- By Footprint **12-3**
- Dormers **A-18**
- Joining **12-22**
- Modifying Plan Views **12-22**
- Roof Plan View **12-7**
- Slope Arrow **A-18**

Rooms
- Adding **7-50**
- Bounding Status **11-3**
- Separation Lines **7-53**
- Tags **16-7**

Rotate **5-27**
Route Analysis **B-10**

## S

Saving **1-29**
Scale **5-29**
Schedule/Quantities Command **16-21**
Schedule/Quantities command **B-18**
Schedules **16-20**
- Building Component Schedule **B-17**
- Export **B-21**
- Import **B-20**
- Modifying Cells **16-33**
- Properties
  - Appearance Tab **B-19**
  - Fields Tab **B-19**
- Sheets **16-35**

Sections **3-36**
- Add Jog **3-40**
- Modifying **3-37**

Select
- Drag elements **1-25**
- Elements **5-15**
- Links **1-24**
- Pinned elements **1-24**
- Select elements by face **1-25**
- Underlay elements **1-24**

Selection Box **3-41**, **12-10**
Selection Sets **A-2**
Shaft Openings **10-16**
Shape Editing **10-19**
Shape Handles **5-12**

Sheets
- Add **14-3**
- Guide Grids **B-2**
- Placing Views **14-6**

Shortcut Keys **1-15**
Shortcut Menus **1-12**, **1-26**
Size Crop **3-26**
Slanted Walls **7-3**
Slope Arrow **A-18**

Snaps **5-7**
- Settings and Overrides **5-8**

Soffits **11-16**
Spelling **15-30**

Split
- Split Element **5-43**
- Split Face command **A-21**
- Split with Gap command **5-43**

Stairs
- Adding Supports **13-10**
- Assembled Stairs **13-2**
- Convert Component to Sketches **13-23**
- Modify Assembled Stairs **13-21**
- Multistory **13-24**
- Riser Numbers **16-13**
- Runs **13-3**
  - Center-Ends Spiral **13-7**
  - Full-Step Spiral **13-6**
  - Winder **13-7**
- Tags **16-13**
- Tread Numbers **16-13**

Status Bar **1-24**

Structural Columns
- Attach Top/Base **6-6**

Structural Foundation
- Isolated **6-7**
- Wall **7-20**

Sweep Profiles **A-8**
- Create **A-9**

Switch Windows **1-12**
Symbols **15-40**

## T

Tab Views **1-13**
Tags
    3D Views **16-12**
    Adding **16-3**
    Adding Multiple **16-8**
    By Category **16-2**
    Instance vs. Type **16-10**
    Loading **16-9**
    Material **16-2**
    Multi-Category **16-2**
    Railings **16-13**
    Riser Numbers **16-13**
    Room **16-7**
    Stairs **16-13**
    Tag All **16-8**
    Tag All Not Tagged **16-8**
    Tag on Placement **8-2**
    Tread Numbers **16-13**
Tangent Lock **10-4**
Tapered Walls **7-3**
Template Files (.RTE) **1-27**
Temporary Dimensions **5-6**, **5-12**
    Editing **5-14**
Text
    Adding **15-24**
    Create Types **15-31**
    Model **15-30**
    Symbols **15-25**
Thin Lines **7-15**
Tile Views **1-13**
Tooltips **1-15**
Transfer Project Standards **8-7**
Tread Numbers **16-13**
Trim/Extend
    Multiple Elements **5-45**
    Single Element **5-44**
    To Corner **5-44**
Type Properties **1-18**
    Doors and Windows **4-14**, **8-8**
Type Selector **1-19**, **5-12**

## U

Unhide
    Category **3-17**
    Element **3-17**
Unjoin Geometry **10-7**

## V

View Control Bar **1-23**
View Range **3-11**
View References **B-15**
ViewCube **1-37**
Views **1-4**
    Camera **1-33**
    Default 3D View **1-33**
    Dependant **B-14**
    Duplicate View **3-6**
    Duplication Types **3-5**
    Insert from File **B-20**
    Plan Region **3-27**
    Renaming **1-34**
    Roof Plan **12-7**
    Underlay **3-10**
View-Specific Elements **1-5**
Visibility/Graphics Overrides **3-15**
    Halftone **2-15**
Visual Styles **1-39**

## W

Walls **7-2**
    Attach Roofs **12-24**
    Edit Profile **7-16**, **7-21**
    Foundation **7-20**
    Modeling **7-6**
    Modifying **7-10**
    Opening **7-17**
    Reveals **A-8**
    Wall Sweep command **A-10**
Windows **8-2**
    Creating Sizes **4-14**, **8-8**
Work Planes **12-17**
    Workplane Viewer **12-17**
Worksets
    Saving Files **A-32**

## Z

Zoom **1-31**